ARC
LIBRARY

D1506092

Europe Since 1945
An Encyclopedia

Europe Since 1945
An Encyclopedia

Volume II
K–Z

Bernard A. Cook
Loyola University New Orleans
Editor

Garland Publishing, Inc.
New York & London
2001

Published in 2001 by
Garland Publishing, Inc.
29 West 35th Street
New York, NY 10001

Garland is an imprint of the Taylor & Francis Group

Production Editors:	Jeanne Shu, Andrew Bailis
Copyeditor:	Edward Cone
Project Management/Composition:	Impressions Book and Journal Services, Madison, Wisconsin
Editorial Assistant:	Dan Yacavone
Director of Development:	Richard Steins
Publishing Director, Reference:	Sylvia K. Miller

10 9 8 7 6 5 4 3 2 1

ISBN: 0-8153-4057-5 (vol. I)
ISBN: 0-8153-4058-3 (vol.II)
ISBN: 0-8153-1336-5 (set)

Library of Congress Cataloging in Publication Data

Cataloging in Publication data available at the Library of Congress

Printed on acid-free, 250-year-life paper
Manufactured in the United States of America

Contents

Europe Since 1945
An Encyclopedia

Kadannikov, Vladimir V. (1941–)

Principle architect of Russian economic policy from January 1996–March 1997. Vladimir Kadannikov was appointed deputy prime minister by President Boris Yeltsin to replace free-market advocate Anatoly B. Chubais. Chubais was forced out by Yeltsin in the aftermath of the strong Communist showing in the December 1995 parliamentary election. Yeltsin sought to distance himself from unpopular economic measures in an effort to shore up his chances in the June 1996 presidential election.

Kadannikov, a supporter of government protection for Russian industry, worked his way up from engineer to head of Avtovaz, Russia's largest producer of automobiles, based in Togliatti. The notoriously inefficient Avtovaz, which employed 100,000 workers, experienced severe economic difficulties. There was little demand for its automobiles abroad and the internal market was weakened by the availability of Western models for those with money and the prohibitive cost of automobiles for most Russians, who were growing poorer. Kadannikov has been denigrated as a Soviet-style manager, more supportive of restricting foreign competition than of introducing restructuring. His colleague Oleg N. Soskovets, first deputy prime minister, had already attacked the introduction of Western-style market reforms as inappropriate and mistaken.

Kadannikov's appointment further signaled a shift by Yeltsin to appease the many Russians disaffected by the effects of economic shock therapy. However, as governmental debt rose dramatically and the Russian standard of living continued to decline, Yeltsin in March 1997 ousted Kadannikov and reappointed Chubais first deputy prime minister and minister of finance. Kadannikov returned to Avtovaz as director.

BIBLIOGRAPHY

Alierta, Mariano, "Russia's Financial Collapse," *National Security Report,* August 1999. Reserve Officers' Association Web Site ⟨http://www.roa.org/nsr/0899nsr1.html⟩

Bernard Cook

SEE ALSO Chubais, Anatoly

Kádár, János (1912–89)

Hungarian Communist politician, leader of Hungary under various titles from 1956 to 1988. János Kádár had little formal education. He joined a labor union and the illegal Communist movement in his teens, and served a prison term from 1933 to 1935. He emerged as the leader of the illegal underground Hungarian Communists Party in 1943. In the postwar years he was pushed into the background by Communist leaders who had returned from the Soviet Union (Mátyás Rákosi, Ernö Gerö, Mihály Farkas), where they had waited out World War II, but he was minister of the interior from 1948 to 1950 and played a dubious role in the show trial and execution of prominent Communist leader László Rajk in 1949. Kádár was arrested in 1951 and the next year given a life sentence for "crimes" committed against the Communist Party. He was released in 1954 and started to rise in the party hierarchy. On October 25, 1956, he succeeded Ernö Gerö as secretary-general of the Hungarian Workers' Party (MDP), as the Communist Party had been named since 1948, and joined the government formed by Imre Nagy during the revolution of that year. However, Kádár ultimately turned against it, left Budapest, and invited the Soviets to "restore socialism" and put an end to the "counterrevolution." He returned to Hungary with the invading Soviet troops and was installed by the Soviet leadership as the de facto leader of Hungary. He named the Communist Party the Hungarian Socialist Workers' Party (MSZMP) in late October 1956 and hundreds of revolutionaries, including Imre Nagy, Pál Maleter, Miklos Gimes, and others were executed. At the same time, he moved cautiously against the Stalinist wing of the party and managed to expel its most prominent discredited members. From 1961 to 1965 Kádár was prime minister as well as secretary-general of the party; thereafter he kept only the latter title until 1988. He introduced cautious economic reforms in 1968 in which some elements of the market economy were tolerated. His leadership proved to be the most liberal among the hard-line policies of the other Eastern European Communist regimes in the 1970s and 1980s. He was elected Party president, a figurehead position, in 1988. He lived to see the reburial of the martyrs of 1956 in June 1989 and died a broken man a few weeks later.

Kádár spent all his life in the Communist movement. His career was cut short by the Stalinist leaders in the early 1950s, but he came back as one of the leaders of the reform wing within the Communist Party. His popularity dimmed when he betrayed the Revolution of 1956, but he lived down his bad reputation in the ensuing years and bought the tacit support of the people by introducing a series of mild reforms in the 1960s, which created a system that became known as "goulash communism." He became increasingly conservative in his views in the 1980s. When he showed signs of mental instability in 1988, he was relieved of the party leadership and died just before his life work, the Communist regime, collapsed in autumn 1989.

BIBLIOGRAPHY

Felkay, Andrew. *Hungary and the USSR, 1956–1988: Kadar's Political Leadership.* New York: Greenwood Press, 1989.

Kadar, Janos. *Selected Speeches and Interviews.* New York: Pergamon, 1985.

Shawcross, William. *Crime and Compromise: Janos Kadar and the Politics of Hungary since Revolution.* London: Weidenfeld & Nicolson, 1974.

Sugar, Peter F., Peter Hanak, and Tibor Frank, eds. *A History of Hungary.* Bloomington: Indiana University Press, 1990.

Tamás Magyarics

SEE ALSO Gerö, Ernö; Nagy, Imre; Rákosi, Mátyás

Kadaré, Ismail (1936–)

Foremost contemporary Albanian writer. Ismail Kadaré was born in Gjirokastër in 1936. His unusual talents attracted world attention in 1970 with the French translation of his first novel, *General of the Dead Army* (1963), a macabre tale of a foreign army officer's quest to exhume the bones of his nation's war dead.

Kadaré erupted out of the barren years of Albania's "Cultural Revolution" (1965–69) with *The Citadel* (1970), describing a fifteenth-century Turkish siege where the Albanian "Trojans" emerge victorious, and with *Chronicle in Stone* (1971), a magical evocation of Gjirokastër during World War II. The magnificent *Great Winter* (first version 1973), based on the 1961 rift with the USSR, contains a portrait of Enver Hoxha that the dictator was said to have dearly loved, but in 1975 the manuscripts of *Niche of Shame,* where the severed head of rebellious eighteenth-century Albanian warlord Ali Pasha journeys to Istanbul, and the poem *Red Pashas* earned Kadaré a period of internal exile.

Again permitted to write by the regime, which desired to manipulate his international fame, Kadaré wrote several novellas—*The Three-Arched Bridge* (1978), *Doruntina* (1980), and *Broken April* (1980), all three based on Albanian history and myth—but a renewal of the harassment that stalked him even after Hoxha's death in 1985 finally led to his defection to France in October 1990.

Kadaré, resolute in creating real rather than "official" literature, chafed against the government's decreed policy of socialist realism. He drew deeply on the motifs of Albanian folk poetry, which he described as rivaling ancient Greek literature, to construct a haunting world of duality where truth oscillates between darkness and light, hideousness and beauty, precision and ambiguity, the living and the dead, and the apparent stability of established order (usually tyrannical) being weakened and overwhelmed by the dark forces of disorder.

Other works by Kadaré include *Palace of Dreams* (1981), *The Concert* (1988), *Aeschylus* (1980), and *The Weight of the Cross* (1991).

BIBLIOGRAPHY

Faye, Eric. *Ismail Kadaré: Prométhée porte-feu.* Paris: J. Corti, 1991.

Mitchell, Anne Marie. *Un Rhapsode albanais, Ismail Kadaré.* Marseilles: Le Temps Parallèle, 1990.

Kirk West

KAL 007 Incident

In the early morning of September 1, 1983, Soviet aircraft shot down a civilian plane, Korean Airlines (KAL) flight 007, killing all 269 passengers and crew on board. The Boeing 747 had wandered deep inside Soviet airspace, some four hundred miles off its intended course from Anchorage, Alaska, to Seoul, South Korea. The incident touched off a barrage of recriminations between the United States and the USSR. Cold War tensions, steadily on the rise since President Ronald Reagan's assumption of office in 1981, peaked following KAL 007's destruction and remained high until the advent of Soviet leader Mikhail Gorbachev in 1985.

The greatest question surrounding the tragedy of KAL 007 concerns how it could have veered so far off course. Though analysts were (and still are) handicapped by a lack of sources, several have attempted to piece together the available data to form a coherent evaluation of the tragedy. Some have found it hard to believe that the aircraft could have drifted over Soviet territory by accident. For example, Oxford political fellow R. W. Johnson suggested that the pilot was engaged in a clandestine espionage scheme designed to test new Soviet radar defenses, which went tragically wrong. Johnson cannot fathom how an experienced pilot could have failed to detect an error in course, or how the other crew members, the aircraft's computers, and ground control facilities also failed to note, or report, anything amiss. Given that the periodic checking of one's course is the most basic of civil airline regulations, Johnson concludes that the flight must have been part of an elaborate conspiracy hatched within the American intelligence community.

Such theories might be more convincing were history not replete with examples of catastrophes entirely attributable to gross human error. Airline disasters in particular often stem from a confluence of mistakes, and course deviations of great magnitude are not rare. So argues journalist Seymour Hersh, who discounts Johnson's work as error-filled, politically motivated, and wholly unconvincing. Seeing little or no reason for a civilian plane to be sent on a mission of dubious military value, he instead attributes the disaster to pilot error and bad luck. Hersh's thesis depends somewhat on "insider information" obtained from within the intelligence community itself. Yet any conspiracy would have required the connivance of several people, from many different countries. By now, someone would likely have come forward.

Both those who advocate and those who discount conspiracy theories admit that the Reagan administration exploited the incident, ignoring or hiding pertinent details to score a propaganda victory against the USSR. The incident also seemed to demonstrate considerable incompetence within the Soviet military. Not only did they fail to react to an "intruder" until well after it had passed over several important military installations, but they also failed to discern the difference between a military spy plane and a civilian jumbo jet.

BIBLIOGRAPHY

Johnson, R. W. *Shootdown: The Verdict on KAL 007.* New York: Doubleday, 1985.

Hersh, Seymour. *The Target Is Destroyed: What Really Happened to Flight 007.* London: Faber and Faber, 1986.

Jeff Roberts

Kaliningrad Oblast

Region of Russia formed in 1945 from the northern half of East Prussia. This former German area, which was ceded to the Soviet Union at the Potsdam Conference of July 1945, consists of 5,830 square miles (15,100 sq km), centered on the city of Kaliningrad (formerly Königsberg). The oblast, which is wedged between Poland and Lithuania, faces the Baltic Sea. It is now separated from Russia by 600 miles (967 km) of Lithuanian and Belarusan territory. Near the end of World War II, region's German inhabitants fled, perished in the fierce fighting that lasted until April 1945, or were deported. Königsberg, besieged by Soviet forces for two months, was 90 percent destroyed. The rebuilt city, renamed Kaliningrad in 1946, is connected to the Baltic by a 20 mile (32 km) channel, and in 1991 had 412,000 residents. The population of the entire region was approximately 900,000. Russian immigrants and their offspring, mainly from the central regions of Russia, constituted nearly 77 percent of this number. The remainder were principally Belarusans and Ukranians.

The ice-free port of Kaliningrad, or more properly, nearby Baltiysk (Pillau), served as the Soviet Union's principal naval base on the Baltic. Until early 1991 the entire oblast was run as a military area, and most foreigners and nonresident Soviet citizens were refused entry. Since the collapse of the Soviet Union, there has been uncertainty concerning the future of the region. Ardent Lithuanian nationalists have attempted to advance a claim to it as "Lithuania Minor." Some ethnic Russians have expressed concern that German investments might prepare the way for re-Germanization of the area. Germans from the former Soviet Union have been seeking in Kaliningrad an alternative to the post-Soviet independent states of Central Asia. The official count of ethnic German inhabitants in 1994 was 5,000, but others estimate that the number is closer to 20,000. On the other hand, some of Kaliningrad's Baltic neighbors regard the region with its 200,000 Russian troops as a Russian aircraft carrier in their midst.

In 1991 Russia declared the province a "free economic zone." In 1993 a conflict arose between Kaliningrad officials and the federal Russian government over a new law on customs and tariffs. Tax incentives earlier provided by the Russian government and free transit agreements with Lithuania and Belarus had contributed to the increased entry and exit of goods and the establishment of numerous joint economic ventures in the region. The economic and political future of the area will in all probability depend, as it has since 1945, on decisions made in Moscow.

BIBLIOGRAPHY

Peitsch, Helmut. *Wir kommen aus Königsberg.* Ostfriesland, Germany: Rautenberg, 1980.

Schulz-Semrau, Elisabeth. *Drei Kastanien aus Königsberg: Tagebuch einer Reise in das heutige Kaliningrad.* Halle, Germany: Mitteldeutscher Verlag, 1990.

Bernard Cook

Kania, Stanisław (1927–)

First secretary of the Central Committee of the Polish United Workers (Communist) Party, 1980–81.

Stanisław Kania graduated from the Institute of Economy at Social Sciences College of the Central Committee of the Communist Party. Along his path to a party career he was a member of the Young Struggle Union (1945–48) and a presiding official of its successor, the Union of Polish Youth (1952–56). Kania was the head of the Department of Agriculture in the Party's Provincial Committee in Warsaw from 1950 to 1960, secretary of the Provincial Committee from 1960 to 1968, vice member of the Central Committee from 1964 to 1968, member of the Central Committee from 1968 to 1986, head of the Administrative Department of the Central Committee in charge of police, security, and military affairs from 1975 to 1981, and secretary of the Central Committee responsible for political police and relations with the church from 1971 to 1981. Having been dismissed from the post of first secretary at the fourth plenary assembly on October 17, 1981, because of his inability to control the independent labor union, Solidarity, he was nominated as a member of the government's State Council (1982). He retired from that post in 1985.

Kania had always supported those in power, but after the seventh party congress, as first secretary, he tried to be more independent. He promoted broad agreement in society and supported social and systemic change within the context of strict obedience to the law. Impressed by the support of workers for the Solidarity labor union, he favored cooperation with the movement. He advocated economic reforms in which the basic unit would be the local worker-managed enterprise. He also supported changes in agriculture. Kania opposed military intervention in Poland by the Red Army and other armies of the Warsaw Pact to crush Solidarity. To the opposition he was the one who launched the slogan of "Renewal" in September 1980, hoping to bridge the schism between the party and the Polish workers, to his party comrades, however, Kania turned out to be unreliable hedger, whose efforts to work with Solidarity threatened to undermine the Party.

BIBLIOGRAPHY

Andrzej, Albert. *Najnowsza historia Polski 1918–1980.* London: Puls Press, 1991.

Kania, Stanisław. *Zatrzymać konfrontacje.* Warsaw: BGW, 1991.

Krzysztof Janiszewski

Kantor, Tadeusz (1915–90)

Polish director and painter, founder of Cricot 2 Theatre in Kraków. Tadeusz Kantor graduated from the Kraków Academy of Fine Arts in 1939. From 1942 to 1944, under the German occupation, Kantor operated his Independent Theater, which gave performances in private apartments in his hometown. Kantor concentrated on painting first, but he soon began searching for his own theatrical forms by working in set design for professional and amateur productions. Unable to carry out his idea of autonomous theater elsewhere, Kantor founded Cricot 2 in 1955, returning to the tradition of the Cricot Theater founded by Kraków artists and writers in 1933. The first play performed by Cricot 2 was Witkacy's *Mątwa* (*Cattlefish*) in 1956. Stanisław Ignacy Witkiewicz inspired Kantor while he prepared his next plays, among them the 1976 *Umarła klasa* (*The Dead Class*), also based on motifs drawn from Witold Gombrowicz and Bruno Schulz. This play was filmed by Andrzej Wajda.

Kantor's most famous productions include *Wielopole/Wielopole* (1980), *Niech szczezną artyści* (*Let Artists Vanish,* 1985), *Nigdy tu już nie powrócę* (*I Will Never Come Back Here,* 1988), and *Dziś są moje urodziny* (*Today Is My Birthday,* 1991). Some of his plays were partly prepared abroad, and performances in the series The Theatre of Death received theatrical awards in the United States.

Kantor created a unique, nonreproducible theater connected with modern transformations in both theater and painting. In his continual experiments he searched for the form of an autonomous theater, independent from literature, using visual and sound techniques: painting, movement, music, and, particularly important, rhythm. One would not find the traditional stage elements—actors, decorations, dialogue—in Kantor's theater. His spectacles were often defined as the theater of artistic staging. Actors, often nonprofessionals, were totally subordinated to the director, who usually appeared on stage as an artist-demiurge. The basic topics of his performances were death, vanishing, memory, and fundamental events in central European history. Each stage in his theatrical evolution was accompanied by a manifesto expressing his new conceptions.

BIBLIOGRAPHY

Kantor, Tadeusz. *A Journey Through Other Spaces: Essays and Manifestos, 1944–1990.* Berkeley: University of California Press, 1993.

———. *Le Théâtre de la mort.* Ed. by Denis Bablet. Lausanne: L'Age d'homme, 1977.

———. *Wielopole/Wielopole: An Exercise in Theatre.* London: M. Boyars/Rizzoli International Publications, 1990.

Klosowicz, Jan. *Tadeusz Kantor: Teatr.* Warsaw: PIW, 1991.

Pleśniarowicz, Krysztof. *The Dead Memory Machine: Tadeusz Kantor's Theatre of Death.* Kraków: Cricoteka, 1994.

Maria Kalinowska

Karadžić, Radovan (1945–)

Bosnian Serb leader and president of the self-styled Republic of Srpska. Radovan Karadžić, poet, musician, and psychiatrist, was the public spokesman for the Serb military forces that waged war in Bosnia mainly against non-Serb civilians.

Born in 1945 in the republic of Montenegro, Karadžić moved to Sarajevo in the 1950s. Imprisoned in the 1980s for what he claims were political offenses and others have alleged was fraud, he rose to prominence after elections in Bosnia at the end of 1990 in which his Serbian Democratic Party (SDA) came in second with around 30 percent of the vote. The SDA was included in a coalition government headed by the chairman of the state presidency, Alija Izetbegović, a Muslim. But from the outset Karadžić expressed support for the Greater Serbia project being pursued by Yugoslav leader Slobodan Milošević, and that, more than any other factor, led to the breakup of Yugoslavia in 1991. Lacking commitment to Sarajevo's multicultural traditions, Karadžić demanded that the state media and government departments be divided on an ethnic basis, and ultimately called for the partition of Sarajevo itself.

In November 1991 the SDA organized a referendum in areas with a Serbian majority. The result was overwhelming support for staying in a Yugoslav or Serb state. A rival Serb parliament had already been established in Pale, near Sarajevo, and the Bosnian territorial militia had been disarmed by the Yugoslav army and its weapons distributed among the paramilitary formations of the SDA. In 1992 Karadžić claimed that international recognition of the independence of Bosnia-Hercegovina by outside powers had caused the war in Bosnia, but there is substantial evidence that a Serb assault had been planned as far back as 1991. U.S. Secretary of State James Baker actually warned the U.N. Security Council in September of that year about the aggression "beginning to take shape in Bosnia."

On April 7, 1992, Karadžić and his supporters completed their withdrawal from a multiethnic Bosnia by declaring an independent Republika Srpska. The Bosnian government's attempt to remain aloof from the Yugoslav war that erupted in June 1991 as the Serbian Yugoslav forces attempted to prevent the secession of Slovenia and Croatia proved unsuccessful as the epicenter of the conflict moved to Bosnia in April 1992. Karadžić's forces launched their assault on Sarajevo and began driving out Muslims from large areas of the republic. The systematic expulsion, ill-treatment, detention, and murder of one ethnic group by elements of another shocked the world. In 1994 Karadžić was arraigned for war crimes by the tribunal set up by the United Nations under Judge Richard Goldstone to investigate mass killings in Bosnia.

On April 21, 1992, Karadžić told Warren Zimmerman, the last U.S. ambassador to Yugoslavia, "Today [Serbs] cannot live with other nations. They must have their own separate existence. They are a warrior race and they can trust only themselves to take by force what is their due."

By mid-1994 the United Nations estimated that nine out of every ten Muslims and Croats living in territory controlled by Karadžić had been driven out or killed. Despite perpetrating brutalities not witnessed in Europe since 1945, Karadžić became a highly visible figure on the European political stage. He regularly attended peace negotiations in Geneva, received top Western emissaries, and was interviewed frequently on television, where his good command of English and genial manner put a gloss on the atrocities of the brigands and gunmen who answered to him.

Karadžić's star began to wane in 1993 when dissension broke out between the Pale Serbs and Belgrade about whether to accept several U.N. peace plans brokered by Lord David Owen, the British diplomat who served as the European Union's chief mediator for the Bosnian crisis, Cyril Vance, the U.S. diplomat and U.N. mediator, and Thorvald Stoltenberg, the Norwegian diplomat who served as the special representative of the U.N. secretary general in the former Yugoslavia and later became co-chair, with Owen, of the international conference on the former Yugoslavia. The Bosnian Serbs proved obdurate even though they would be awarded 51 percent of the territory. Although he was anxious to be rid of Western economic sanctions, President Slobodan Milošević of Yugoslavia found it difficult to rein in his wayward clients in Pale. After the collapse of the U.N. peace plans, the Belgrade media launched a propaganda offensive against Karadžić accusing him of numerous improprieties. By 1994 he and his military commander, General Ratko Mladić, were at odds and the much-vaunted Serb unity started to crumble. The ability of Karadžić's family to escape the rigors of war earned him the enmity of poorly paid soldiers trapped in a spiraling war. The collapse of the Serb-inhabited Krajina region of Croatia in August 1995 and the massive NATO bombardment of Bosnian Serb positions in September of that year were huge reverses for Karadžić. He was forced by Milošević to accept the November 1995 Dayton peace accords, which the Serbian president negotiated and signed in the name of the Bosnian Serbs.

After Dayton there were increasing denunciations by Bosnian Serbs of the war and Karadžić's political leadership. An opposition Bosnian Serb leader, Miodrag Zivanović of the Liberal Party, said that "our main goal now is to take these war criminals, like Karadžić, and put them on trial. The Bosnian Serbs must punish those who carried out these crimes; otherwise, in the eyes of the world, we will bear the guilt for the atrocities they committed in our name." This disparagement was mirrored by a broader disenchantment among the Serbs of Bosnia. The Dayton agreement prohibited Karadžić, who had been indicted for war crimes, from running for reelection, and the loss of the Serb-controlled suburbs of Sarajevo was viewed by his followers around the city as a betrayal. Many Bosnian Serbs seemed anxious to relegate all blame for the war with its atrocities and hardships on Karadžić and Mladić. In the opinion of many they objected not to the goals of Karadžić but his methods and, especially, his failure. He neglected the rest of Serbian-held Bosnia to concentrate on Sarajevo and, in so doing, ultimately provoked the American-led NATO response.

BIBLIOGRAPHY

Glenny, Misha. *The Fall of Yugoslavia.* New York: Penguin, 1993.

Tom Gallagher

SEE ALSO Mladić, Ratko

Karajan, Herbert von (1908–89)

Austrian conductor. Born in 1908 in Salzburg, Herbert (Heribert) Ritter von Karajan became one of the most famous conductors of the twentieth century. At various times he led opera houses (often producing as well as conducting), festivals, and orchestras including the Vienna State Opera, La Scala Milan, the Bayreuth and Salzburg festivals, the Philharmonia, and, most famously, the Berlin Philharmonic. But more than through live performances alone, he made his mark on the world of classical music through his huge discography, which embraced works from the baroque to the contemporary.

Karajan began his conducting career in Ulm and Aachen, but even at twenty had set his sights on Vienna. Immediately after World War II, de-Nazification difficulties and a campaign waged against him by fellow conductor Wilhelm Furtwängler impeded his career, but thereafter it was a generally smooth ascent to the height of power in the world of European culture.

It began in 1945 with Vienna Philharmonic concerts that were auspicious enough, but his rise began in earnest the following year when he signed a contact with Columbia Records and began an association with the Philharmonia Orchestra in London that is still seen as one of the highlights of that illustrious orchestra's history. Even then he was juggling more than one job at a time and simultaneously took charge of the Salzburg Festival, consolidating his position in European music over the next few years. At around that time he developed an interest in flying (technology of all kinds was an obsession) and gained his license in a surprisingly short time at the age of 41. The year 1950 brought Leipzig's Bach bicentenial celebrations and, despite Furtwängler's opposition, Karajan conducted some of the larger choral works. Later that year he took charge of La Scala's German repertoire while conducting at the first postwar Bayreuth Festival and, with the Philharmonia, produced a series of recordings that remain benchmarks. In 1955 he succeeded Furtwängler as principal conductor of the Berlin Philharmonic, an appointment that was confirmed for life the following year. At the same time he became artistic director of the Salzburg Festival and the Vienna State Opera, and the three posts became the bedrock of the rest of his career, although an acrimonious breakdown in his relationship with the Berlin Philharmonic marred his last years. He also became fascinated by the question of how classical music should be presented on film and television and worked increasingly in those media.

Following his death in 1989 there was a reaction against his musical style, coupled with increasing criticism of his "Nazi" past, though, like many others, he joined the party not as a convinced Nazi but in order to pursue his career in a totalitarian society. Certain parts of the repertoire did not suit him. Baroque music was not a strong point (he completely rejected period-style performance), his forays into the avant-garde only showed his lack of interest, and even his Mozart was surprisingly uneven. Yet a huge range of music suited him admirably, from Sibelius' austerity to the lushness of Richard Strauss.

His recordings are popularly conceived as concentrating on the core repertoire; he recorded symphony cycles by Beethoven four times and those by Brahms, Bruckner, Mendelssohn, Schubert and Schumann at least once each. He became a symbol of the Deutsche Grammophon label's classical output and came almost to embody the public's idea of classical music. Karajan's iconically 'conductor-ish' looks encouraged this perception, as did his habit of conducting from memory with eyes closed, as if in a creative trance. However his recorded repertoire was wide though selective, for example one symphony each by Nielsen and Shostakovich and two by Prokofiev. Yet apparently brief acquaintanceships could produce astonishingly insightful work and many of his recordings still stand to be bettered at the beginning of the twenty-first century.

BIBLIOGRAPHY

Osborne, Richard. *Herbert von Karajan: A Life in Music.* Boston: Northeastern University Press, 2000.

Vaughan, Roger. *Herbert von Karajan: A Biographical Portrait.* New York: Norton, 1985.

John Riley

Karamanlis, Konstantinos (1907–98)

Greek politician who dominated his country's political life for over forty years, serving twice as president (1980–85, 1990–95) and prime minister (1955–63, 1974–80). Born into poverty in the Macedonian village of Proti, Konstantinos Karamanlis graduated in law at the University of Athens, going on to be elected MP for his native province of Serres with the right-wing Populist Party at the age of twenty-eight. Reelected the following year in what proved to be the last free election in Greece for over ten years of domestic dictatorship, Axis occupation, and civil war, Karamanlis spent most of the wartime period in Athens and then in exile in the Middle East. After involvement in resistance activities during the war, he regained his parliamentary seat in 1946, going on to hold various key ministerial portfolios in a number of postwar Greek governments. Mainly involved with postwar economic reconstruction, he also organized the repatriation of seven hundred thousand refugees who had fled Greece after its three-year civil war ended in 1949. Following the dissolution of the Populist Party after the war, he joined the Greek Rally Party led by General Alexander Papagos, serving in a number of his governments until the death of his party leader in 1955. As the chosen successor of Papagos, Karamanlis was then appointed premier for the first time. He then founded a new National Radical Union (ERE) to contest and win new parliamentary elections in 1956. Similar electoral victories followed in 1958 and 1961, leading to an unprecedented eight-year term as Greek premier.

Karamanlis's *oktaetia* (eight-year rule) was the most peaceful and productive period in the turbulence and violence of contemporary Greek history. Externally, one of his major achievements was the independence of Cyprus from Great Britain in 1960. Domestically, Karamanlis's government brought about the rapid economic development of Greece, which was seriously considered for membership in the then European Community (now European Union) as early as 1961. On a more negative note, Karamanlis's inability to fully control King Paul and the Greek armed forces led to his resignation in 1963, when new elections resulted in a political impasse with George Papandreou's Center Union Party gaining a clear parliamentary majority. To help resolve this political crisis, Karamanlis left Greece for Paris after a Center Union government led by Papandreou came to power in late 1963. Residing in Paris as an exile until 1974, he was an implacable opponent of the colonels military junta that ruled Greece for seven years after coming to power in a coup in 1967. Following its chaotic demise after a disastrous Greek intervention on Cyprus, Karamanlis was recalled to his native land to lead a new government of national unity in 1974. New elections were held in November 1974, when Karamanlis's newly founded New Democracy Party (ND) won a decisive victory, which was immediately followed by the abolition of the discredited monarchy, who had not opposed the colonels when they seized power in April 1967, after a national referendum.

Karamanlis achieved a second electoral victory in 1977 and a second long term of office as premier, until 1980. Elected president of Greece for the first time in 1980, Karamanlis resigned in March 1985 over differences with the ruling Pan-Hellenic Socialist Movement, but secured an unprecedented second five-year term as president when the ND party was returned to power in 1990.

After retiring from public life to his family home near Athens in 1995, he lived to see his nephew, Kostas Karamanlis, elected as ND leader in 1997. In 1998 Konstantinos Karamanlis died, having accomplished most of what he had set out to do in the domestic political sphere and in relation to the European Union, which Greece finally joined in 1981. Only in relation to Cyprus and Turkey did Karamanlis and other Greek politicians fail to secure a lasting settlement of a Greco-Turkish dispute.

BIBLIOGRAPHY

Karamanlis, Konstantinos. *Konstantinos Karamanles, epilekta keimena.* Athens: Morphotike Hestia, 1995.

Woodhouse, Christopher Montague. *Karamanlis, the Restorer Greek Democracy.* New York: Oxford University Press, 1983.

Marko Milivojevic

SEE ALSO Mitsotakis, Konstantinos

Kardelj, Edvard (1910–79)

Yugoslav politician and political theorist. Edvard Kardelj was born in Ljubljana, Slovenia (then part of Austria-Hungary), on January 27, 1910. The son of a railroad worker, he graduated from Ljubljana Teachers' College, and at the age of sixteen he joined the outlawed Communist Party. He was jailed for trade union activity in 1930 and fled to the Soviet Union in 1934. He returned to Yugoslavia in 1937 and, after the German invasion, helped organize resistance in Slovenia. He was at Yugoslav leader Marshal Tito's side during much of the wartime struggle. He became vice president of Yugoslavia from 1945 to 1953 and foreign minister from 1948 to 1953.

Comparative constitutional development and the self-management by workers of economic entities were two of his principal interests. Kardelj authored the Yugoslav constitution of 1946 and directed the formulation of the constitutions of 1953, 1963, and 1974. He was also the chief theoretician of the self-management model of socialism, in which workers participate in the management of their factories, in contrast to the centralized command model of state socialism practiced in Stalin's USSR. This self-management model served as the basis for Yugoslavia's economic and political system. Along with his fellow vice-presidents Milovan Djilas and Aleksander Ranković, Kardelj was one of the most influential members of the Yugoslav Communist Party. Unlike the other two, he retained Tito's trust and never fell into disgrace, continuing until his death on February 10, 1979, to influence affairs of state and party. Had he not died a year before Tito, he might well have succeeded him.

BIBLIOGRAPHY

Kardelj, Edvard. *Democracy and Socialism.* London: Summerfield, 1978.

Catherine Lutard

SEE ALSO Djilas, Milovan

Karelia

Area most of which is now in Russia bordering Finland. Although there are different geographical definitions of Karelia, "Karelia" has a special place in Finnish national mythology. The cultural traditions and mythological tales and runes collected from northern Karelian villages in the 1830s and 1840s became the basis of Finland's national epic, the *Kalevala.* Demands for unification of the mystical lands of the *Kalevala* became stronger after Finland's independence from the Russian Empire in 1917. A wave of enthusiasm for Greater Finland influenced Finland's foreign policy toward the East until 1944, when the imminent Soviet victory over Germany and Finland dashed any hope the Finnish nationalists had of regaining the territory left under Russian control in 1917.

The interim peace treaty of 1944 between Finland and the USSR, awarded some islands in the Gulf of Finland, Pechenga (Petsamo), and Karelia, to the Soviet Union. The Gulf islands had some military value before and during the war. In Pechenga, a corridor between Norway and the USSR's Kola peninsula, Finland lost access to the Arctic sea, as well as a strategically important nickel mine. The economic loss was considerable and the psychological loss only aggravated it.

The western part of Karelia, consisting mainly of the Karelian Isthmus, where Viipuri (Russian, Vyborg), the capital of Karelia, was located, became part of Finland in the peace treaty of 1323 between Sweden and Novgorod. In that part of Karelia, both linguistic and religious development was connected to Finland (Sweden). The language became a dialect of Finnish, and the Orthodox population was converted first to Catholicism then to Lutheranism. So-called old Karelia, located between Europe's biggest lake, Ladoga, and the Kola peninsula, did not belong to Finland until 1809; even after that, a major part of old Karelia remained outside the autonomous Finnish Grand Duchy within the Russian Empire. Its population spoke Karelian, a Finno-Ugrian language, and the religion was Orthodox.

In 1944 Finland lost about 12 percent of its land area to the Soviet Union. This meant that 420,000 Karelians, 12 percent of Finland's population, were evacuated and had to be resettled throughout Finland, excluding the Swedish-speaking areas. Some 6.9 million acres (2.8 million hectares) of land were redistributed to Karelians and war veterans, 60 percent and 40 percent, respectively. Through the resettlement, which was completed by 1948, more than 94,000 new farms were created.

In spite of linguistic and religious differences, no fundamental problems emerged between Karelians and Finns. Karelians soon learned local Finnish dialects, and only 4 percent of Karelian refugees were Orthodox. In 1993 there were just 53,000 Orthodox, or 1 percent of the population. Karelian has been almost totally lost as a living language; however, in the Russian Republic of Karelia 7 percent of the population still speak it.

Karelians have had remarkable success in Finnish social and political life. Urho Kekkonen, while not Karelian by birth, was elected to parliament from the Vyborg electoral district. Johannes Virolainen became the leading Karelian politician after the Continuation War; he was prime minister from 1964 to 1966, minister in various governments for about two decades, a member of parliament for about four decades, until 1987, and a presidential candidate in the 1982 elections. Martti Ahtisaari, elected president in 1994, was born in Vyborg.

Hope for the return of Karelia were expressed openly until 1955, when the USSR returned Porkkala to Finland. However, the issue became politically taboo, and during the crisis of 1956–61, when Finnish political parties jockeyed for power amid direct diplomatic pressure by the USSR, the permanent loss of Karelia became an accepted fact. In 1962, the Soviets rented to Finland the Saimaa Canal in the Karelian Isthmus between Saimaa Lake and the Gulf of Finland. By 1968 it had been reconstructed by the Finns. According to President Urho Kekkonen's personal documents, the return of Karelia was agreed on between him and Soviet Prime Minister Nikita Khrushchev in 1963–64; Kekkonen perceived this as a factor causing Khrushchev's ouster in 1964.

A revival of Karelianism emerged at the end of the 1970s, when it became popular to reconsider national and ethnic roots. The Karelian language and culture were propagated among young Karelians by voluntary Karelian civic organizations dedicated to keeping up old traditions; furthermore, the University of Joensuu enhanced the study of the Karelian language and culture. In the 1980s, the heretofore closed military area of Soviet Karelia was gradually opened to tourism, and toward the end of the decade Karelia became a popular area for pilgrims returning to their mythical national roots. Finally, the collapse of the Soviet Union provided a solid impetus for "Karelia Back" movements, among which the Karelian League has taken a leading position. Although the Finnish political leadership still avoids the issue and Russian President Boris Yeltsin strictly denies the existence of a Karelian question, its existence is a fact. However, the return of Karelia or, more exactly, the parts of Finland lost to the Soviet Union in the war, is likely to be hindered by two practical considerations: Finland would gain 300,000 Russians, who would require a minority status, and the rebuilding of an infrastructure would involve a substantial investment.

BIBLIOGRAPHY

Eskelinen, Heikki, et al., eds. *Russian Karelia in Search of a New Role.* Joensuu: University of Joensuu, Karelian Institute, 1994.

Friberg, Eino. *The Kalevala.* Keuruu: Otava, 1988.

Kirkinen, Heikki, and Hannes Sihvo. *The Kalevala.* Forssa: Finnish-American Cultural Institute, 1985.

Purmonen, Veikko. *Orthodoxy in Finland.* Kuopio: Orthodox Clergy Association, 1987.

Vilho Harle

SEE ALSO Kekkonen, Urho

Katyn Forest Massacre

The execution by the Soviet Union of Polish officer POWs in early 1940, one of the major stumbling blocks in post–World War II Polish-Soviet relations. By the end of 1940 the London-based Polish government-in-exile had identified more than 15,000 Polish officers, including at least 295 generals and colonels, who remained unaccounted for after having been captured by the Soviets in September 1939 when they invaded and occupied eastern Poland. In February 1943 the German 537th Signal Regiment discovered graves of some of the missing Poles in the Katyn Forest, near Smolensk, in the western USSR. Although the Third Reich was certainly no friend of the Poles, the Germans quickly seized upon the opportunity to drive a wedge between the Soviets and the Western Allies.

On April 13, 1943, the Germans announced the discovery of 4,143 bodies at Katyn, and immediately set up three investigating commissions, including one formed by the Polish Red Cross. Journalists from Sweden and Switzerland were also allowed to examine the grave sites. The bodies were buried in sandy soil, resulting in a mummification effect that left them fairly well preserved.

The physical evidence was overwhelming. Although almost all the officers had been shot at the base of the skull with German-manufactured 7.65mm bullets, the rope used to tie their hands was Soviet-made. The condition of the corpses indicated that spring of 1940 as the most likely time of death, long before the German invasion of June 1941. More than three thousand documents were found on the bodies, not one with a date later than spring 1940. Some of the bodies bore bayonet wounds, clearly made by the characteristic four-sided Soviet bayonet. Finally, young spruce trees were planted on the grave site, and the tree rings showed they were transplanted in 1940.

The commissions reached the conclusion that the Polish officers at Katyn had been systematically executed by the Soviets. The Soviets, in turn, blamed the Germans. When the Soviets recaptured the Smolensk area in the fall of 1943, they set up their own commission to investigate the "circumstances of the shooting of Polish officer prisoners by the German-Fascist invaders in the Katyn Forest." Staffed by individuals completely answerable to Soviet dictator Stalin, that commission issued findings that were predictable even before it convened.

The crisis over Katyn caused a split between the Soviets and the London-based Polish government. Moscow reacted by forming its own Communist-led Polish government-in-exile and prepared it to assume control of postwar Poland. Because the Western Allies at that point in the war placed such a high premium on Soviet cooperation and goodwill, the London Polish government lost the U.S. and British support and went into a decline from which it never recovered.

After the war the Soviets tried to charge the Germans with the Katyn killings at the Nuremberg trials, but the U.S. and British judges dismissed the charges because the case was so weak. In 1951 and 1952 a select committee of the U.S. Congress held hearings on Katyn and unanimously blamed the Soviet Union in its final report. The Soviets, however, staunchly continued to blame the Germans. The postwar Communist government of Poland officially supported the Soviet line, but the vast majority of the Polish people knew the truth.

In 1981 the Solidarity trade union erected a monument to the victims of Katyn, but the Polish government removed it. In March 1985 the government of General Wojciech Jaruzelski erected its own monument on the exact site of the former Solidarity monument. The inscription on the Communist government's monument read "To the Polish soldiers—victims of the Hiterlite facism."

During the Soviet period of glasnost (openness) of the late 1980s, the Soviet regime gradually began to allow Poles to visit the Katyn grave sites. On April 13, 1990, the Soviet government finally admitted responsibility for the killings. On October 14, 1992, the Russian government of Boris Yeltsin released a March 5, 1940, Politburo document that directly implicated the top Soviet leadership. Apparently still nursing a grudge against the Polish army for its defeat of the Soviets in 1920, Stalin had ordered that the Polish officers be subjected to "the supreme punishment—execution by firing squad."

Yet there was more to it than revenge. The murdered Polish officers included many reservists from the Polish elite—professors, teachers, doctors, lawyers, and clergy. They were the natural leaders of Polish society and by Communist definition were all "class enemies." With these men out of the way, figured Stalin, it would be easier later to impose a Polish leadership corps manufactured in Moscow, which is exactly what happened when the Red Army rolled into Poland in 1944.

With the gradual opening of the Soviet archives most of the facts have finally come to light. Between February and June 1940 almost all the officers at the Kozielsk, Starobielsk, and Ostashkov POW camps were systematically murdered by the NKVD (Soviet secret police). Those buried at Katyn came primarily from the Kozielsk camp. Prisoners from the Starobielsk camp were murdered at the Ukrainian city of Kharkov and buried near the village of Piatikhatki. Those from the Ostashkov camp were murdered at Kalinin (now Tver), about ninety miles north of Moscow, and buried at Myednoye. The NKVD later established a resort on the site.

The killings were carried out under the overall direction of Vsevolod Nikolayevich Merkulov, deputy minister of the interior and a member of the Communist Party Central Committee. For his part in the atrocity Merkulov was awarded the Order of Lenin on April 27, 1940.

BIBLIOGRAPHY

Abarinov, Vladimir. *The Murderers of Katyn.* New York: Hippocrene Books, 1993.

Katyn: Documents of Genocide: Documents and Materials from the Soviet Archives Turned over to Poland on October 14, 1992. Warsaw: Institute of Political Studies, Polish Academy of Sciences, 1993.

Paul, Allen. *Katyn: The Untold Story of Stalin's Polish Massacre.* New York: Scribner, 1991.

David T. Zabecki

Kazakhstan

Independent successor state to the Kazakh Soviet Socialist Republic of the former USSR. The Kazakh SSR was the second-largest union republic of the USSR, and the Republic of Kazakhstan is the largest of the new Central Asian states, consisting of 1,049,155 square miles (2,717,300 sq km). It is surrounded by China, Kyrgyzstan, Uzbekistan, the Aral Sea, Turkmenistan, the Caspian Sea, and Russia. Its territory consists primarily of steppe. Its arid central desert was the site of Soviet nuclear tests at Semipalatinsk (Semey) and the Soviet, now Russian, space center at Baykonur. Only 13 percent of Kazakhstan's area is cultivated, but 58 percent is utilized as pastureland. The cultivated land in the southeast is sustained by irrigation from the Syr Darya and Chu Rivers. The area of black soil along the northern frontier was the "virgin lands" quixotically developed by Soviet Premier Nikita Khrushchev. Kazakhstan possesses 1,440 miles (2,320 km) of Caspian Sea coast. The receding Aral Sea, an ecological disaster area, lies between Kazakhstan and Uzbekistan. The freshwater Lake Balkhash (Kazakh, Balqash Köl) lies entirely within the country to the north of Almaty. Kazakhstan has rich oil fields along the Caspian Sea on the Mangyshlak peninsula and between the mouths of the Ural and Emba Rivers. Kazakhstan has reserves of coal, iron, copper, and lead. The population of Kazakhstan is approximately 17 million. Its capital, Almaty (Zazakh, Alma-Ata) has 1.2 million inhabitants. The capital is scheduled to shift to Aqmola (Russian, Tselinograd) in 2000. The official language, Kazakh, is a central Turkish language. It replaced Russian in September 1989. It has been written in the Cyrillic script since 1940. The dominant religion is Islam. Most Kazakhs are Sunni Muslims. The population in 1989 consisted of 39.7 percent Kazakhs, 37.8 percent Russians, 5.8 percent Germans, and 5.4 percent Ukrainians.

The Kazakhs are descended from Mongols and Uzbek Turks who entered the area in the first century B.C. A tribal confederation, the Kazakh Orda was established in the fifteenth century, and divided into smaller nomadic groups in the seventeenth century. In the eighteenth century, in reaction to an invasion of the Oirot Mongols, the three federations or Hordes of Kazakh groups, sought the protection of the Russian tsar. But the Russians behaved as allies not conquerors, deposing the leaders of the Hordes. In 1854 the Russians built the fortified settlement Vernyi, which became Alma-Ata. After the abolition of serfdom in 1861 many Russian and Ukrainian peasants were given land in Kazakhstan as an incentive to move there. There were clashes between the nomadic Kazakhs and the sedentary settlers. Kazakh resentment against these colonists, who encroached on the best pastureland, resulted in a rebellion in 1916, set off by conscription for forced labor. The Russians brutally crushed the rising at the cost of 150,000 Kazakh lives.

Kazakhstan. *Illustration courtesy of Bernard Cook.*

The area was gripped by civil war after the Russian Revolution of 1917. The nationalist movement, Alash Orda, briefly established an independent Kazakhstan. With the victory of the Bolsheviks, the Kyrgyz Autonomous Soviet Socialist Republic of the Russian Federation was set up on August 26, 1920. The Soviets called the Kazakhs "Kyrgyz" to differentiate them from Cossacks. In 1925 the Kyrgyz ASSR became the Kazakh ASSR. In 1932 the Karakalpak region along the southern littoral of the Aral Sea was separated from the Kazakh ASSR and eventually transferred to Uzbekistan. The Kazakh ASSR became a full union republic of the USSR on December 5, 1936.

The Soviets tried in the early 1920s to force the nomadic Kazakhs to settle permanently and take up farming, for which they were unsuited. The resulting famine killed hundreds of thousands of Kazakhs. The Kazakhs also suffered greatly from forced collectivization under Stalin. Many Kazakhs were executed or sent to labor camps. It is estimated that a million perished in the process and hundreds of thousands fled to Xinjiang province in China. The Great Purges of the late 1930s reached the Communist Party in Kazakhstan and its leadership, which was the first secretary, removed and executed. Repression was accompanied by immigration from the Russian, Ukrainian, and Byelorussian republics. By 1939, 98 percent of the republic's rural inhabitants lived on collective farms, but a census the same year indicated that for the first time, Russians, who constituted roughly 40 percent of the population, outnumbered Kazakhs in Khazakstan. During World War II, many victims of forced relocation—Volga Germans, Crimean Tartars, and peoples from the Caucuses—were deposited in Kazakhstan. Thousands of Russian women and their children were also relocated from the war zone to Kazakh cities. Owing to Khrushchev's virgin lands scheme, the development of Soviet nuclear test sites at Semipalatinsk, and the Soviet space center at Baikonur, many ethnic Russians, Ukrainians, and Byelorussians were drawn to Kazakhstan. Despite high Kazakh birth rates, the Russian percentage of its population increased from 19.7 percent in 1926 to 42.7 percent in 1959.

The Kazakh Communist Party (CPK) was established in 1937. It was headed by Zhumabay Shayakhmetov until he was ousted in 1954 for inadequate support of the virgin lands project. His replacement, P. K. Ponomarenko, was a Slav. Ponomarenko's successor was Leonid Brezhnev. Brezhnev named a Kazakh, Dinmukhamed Kunayev, to be his successor. Though corruption was rampant under Kunayev, Kazakhs did enter leadership roles in the republic in unprecedented numbers.

In the 1980s, Soviet President Mikhail Gorbachev's campaign against corruption led to the ouster of Kunayev and his replacement by Gennady Kolbin, an ethnic Russian. The Kazakhs took this as an affront and rioting erupted in Alma-Ata in December 1986. The police killed four and injured two hundred. Kolbin, nevertheless, removed associates of Kunayev who had been accused of corruption and nepotism. In June 1989 Kolbin was moved to Moscow and Nursultan Nazarbayev (1940–), a Kazakh supporter of perestroika (restructuring), who had become chairman of the Kazakhstan Council of Ministers in 1984, became the head of the CPK.

With the advent of glasnost, culture and the environment became paramount issues. Olzhas Suleimenov, the first secretary of the Kazakh Union of Writers, launched a campaign to rehabilitate Kazakh writers Maghjan Jumabaev and Shakerim Qudayberdiev, both executed in Soviet purges. Maghjan, a founder of the anti-Bolshevik Alasj-Orda, had extolled the Turkic heritage of the Kazakhs in his poetry. Qudayberdiev had promoted Kazakh Islamic culture. The cultural campaign decried the fact that of the four million students in Kazakhstan, only one million studied Kazakh. In September 1989 the Kazakh Supreme Soviet (KSS) made Kazakh the official language. While Russian remained the language of interethnic communication, knowledge of both languages became a prerequisite for public office. This led to protests by Russians. Members of the Russian nationalist organization Yedinstvo (Unity) campaigned for the transfer of northern Kazakhstan to Russia. When Russian writer Aleksandr Solzhenitsyn called for similar measures, Kazakhs took to the streets to demonstrate for the integrity of their republic. Nuclear testing became the primary environmental issue. The organization Nevada-Semipalatinsk, founded in 1989 by Kazakh writer Suleimenov, organized large antinuclear demonstrations in Alma-Ata. This campaign was abetted by the explosion in September 1990 of a nuclear fuel factory in Ulba. A large area including the city of Ust-Kamenogorsk was contaminated and as many as 120,000 people were affected. The Soviet government announced that testing at Semipalatinsk would end by 1992.

In September 1989 under Nazarbayev' leadership, reforms were introduced. Multicandidate elections were to be held for a Supreme Soviet (KSS), which would sit permanently like a parliament. Powers of the first secretary of the PCK were shifted to the chairman of the KSS. Nazarbayev was elected to that post in February 1990. When the new KSS was elected on March 25, many candidates were unopposed and many spots were reserved for members of the CPK or its affiliate organizations. The new KSS elected Nazarbayev to the new post of president, and he was confirmed in this office by a popular vote on December 1. He was the only candidate but received the approbation of 98.8 percent of the 87.4 percent who voted.

On October 25 the KSS passed a declaration of sovereignty. The resolution declared Kazakh control over the economy and resources of the republic, but there was strong support for the preservation of an over-all union. Of the 94.1 percent of Kazakhs who voted in the March 1991 referendum on the Soviet Union, 88.2 percent voted to preserve the USSR. On August 19, the first day of the attempted coup against Gorbachev and his reform program by Communists who felt that the Soviet system was threatened, Nazarbayev hesitated, but on August 20 he denounced the coup leaders. He then resigned from the Politburo and the Central Committee of the Communist Party of the USSR. In September the CPK was transformed into the Socialist Party of Kazakhstan (SPK). Despite Nazarbayev's pique at the initiative of the three Slavic leaders—Russian president Boris Yeltsin, Leonid Kravchuk, the leader of Ukraine, and Stanislav Shushkevich, the leader of Belarus—to destroy the USSR through their December 8, 1991, Minsk Agreement, and what he perceived as their arrogant ignoring of himself and the leaders of other republics, Kazakhstan agreed to join the new weak union, the Commonwealth of Independent States (CIS) on December 13, 1991. Kazakhstan was the last republic to declare its independence, becoming the Republic of Kazakhstan on December 16. It signed the CIS accord at Almaty on December 21 and was recognized as a cofounder of the CIS.

Nazarbayev's hesitancy about independence was rooted in his concern about exacerbating ethnic tensions in Kazakhstan, where Russians and Ukrainians together formed a plurality, and his concern over fueling secessionist sentiments in the largely Russian north of the republic. Though large-scale interethnic violence was avoided, there was still tension. In June 1989 riots in the dismal new oil city Noviy Uzen, precipitated by unemployment, inadequate housing, and miserable to nonexistent urban infrastructure, assumed an ethnic character. Five died as Kazakhs attacked Caucasians brought in to work in the oil fields.

Russians living in Kazakhstan demanded that their language be given equal status with Kazakh. But after a year of national debate, when the constitution was approved in January 1993 it repeated the 1989 law that had recognized Kazakh as the state language. Russian was relegated to the status of a language of interethnic communication. The president was again required to be fluent in Kazakh. Though the state was defined as secular and the government was careful to distance itself from Islamic fundamentalism, emigration of Slavs grew apace, fueled by ethnic tensions and incidents. The government discriminated on behalf of ethnic Kazakhs in government employment, education, and housing. Kazakhs dominated public administration, and there were cases of discrimination against non-Kazakhs. Boris Suprunyuk, Cossack leader of the Russian community in northern Kazakhstan, was arrested and sentenced to two years in prison for "inciting interethnic strife." In October 1995 Nicolai Gunkin, leader of the country's southern Cossacks, was arrested and sentenced to nine months in jail for purportedly organizing unapproved rallies and inciting interethnic hatred. Some 300,000 of the country's 958,000 ethnic Germans, with assistance from Germany, left in the early 1990s, and the emigration of Russians was significant as well.

Ethnic Kazakhs also moved into Kazakhstan in large numbers from its newly independent neighbors. In July 1994 the parliament adopted a proposal by Nazarbayev to move the capital from Almaty in the south to Akmola around 2000. The crowded conditions and vulnerability of Almaty to earthquakes were cited, but the move was probably prompted by the desire to assert control over the predominantly Russian-populated north of the country.

In 1992 the former Communists continued to dominate the government and the parliament, or Supreme Kenges. There was a large demonstration in Almaty in June against the continuing domination by the erstwhile Communists. In October the three big opposition parties—the Azat movement, the Republican Party, and the Zheltoksan National Democratic Party—joined together as the Republican Party-Azat (RP-A). After the Supreme Court refused to legalize the CPK, Nazarbayev, who had not officially been a member of any party since the Moscow coup, agreed in 1993 to lead the Union of National Unity of Kazakhstan. This movement, which had a broad spectrum of ethnic groups among its members, became People's Unity Party (PUP).

On March 7, 1994, a new legislature was elected. Its membership was 177, compared with 360 in the old Supreme Kenges. This election was Kazakhstan's first free multiparty election. Seventy-four percent of the voters participated. There were accusations of irregularities, and a number of candidates claimed that their registration for the election was refused. The claim of discrimination was seemingly reinforced by the fact that 75 percent of the candidates who did register were ethnic Kazakhs. Kazakhs held 59 percent of the seats in the new legislature, or Kenges, Russians held 28 percent, and others held 13 percent. The PUP won 33 seats, more than any other party. When these seats were combined with the 42 seats won by individuals on the so-called President's List, and the 59 largely pro-Nazarbayev independents, the president easily controlled the largest bloc in the legislature. The Confederation of Kazakh Trade Unions (CKTU) was the second-largest group, with 11 seats. The People's Congress Party of Kazakhstan (PCPK) had 9 and the SPK 8.

After the CPK was again legalized in March 1994, it formed a new bloc, the Constructive Opposition Bloc, within parliament in alliance with the SPK, PCPK, RP-A, and CKTU. The professed aim of the coalition was to prevent executive dictatorship. Divisions soon surfaced between the new Kenges and the government over economic and social issues. In May 1994, 96 members of the parliament supported a vote of no confidence. In June Nazarbayev reorganized the government. He sought to promote economic reform by streamlining the administration and removing corrupt officials. But the government resigned in October, admitting that it had failed to introduce effective economic reform. Akezhan Kazhegeldin (1952–), an economist who had served as first deputy prime minister in the outgoing government, was appointed prime minister by Nazarbayev.

At the beginning of 1995 the Kenges, citing its adverse social impact, refused to approve the budget. The government supported by Nazarbayev, asserted that the budget was necessary to maintain support from the International Monetary Fund (IMF) and to attract foreign investment. A complicated constitutional crisis emerged. The Constitutional Court in February declared the parliament invalid because of "procedural infringements." The Kenges failed to counter the Constitutional Court by amending the constitution. Parliament stepped down in March and its resignation brought down the government it had approved. Nazarbayev reconstituted the government, however, with hardly any changes. The crisis gave him virtual dictatorial power, and he ruled by decree until new legislative elections. At the end of March he staged a referendum that enabled him to extend his term until December 1, 2000. Ninety-one percent of the electorate participated in the April 29 vote and, according to the government, 95 percent voted for Nazarbayev's extension.

In May the president set up a special council to draft a new constitution under his supervision. When the draft was finished in June, it was submitted to "national debate." The opposition responded with demonstrations against its "undemocratic" character. It was approved, nevertheless, with amendments by 89.1 percent in an August 30 referendum. The Supreme Kenges was replaced by a bicameral legislature. The Senate consisted of forty members elected by district administrative bodies and seven members appointed by the president. The directly elected lower assembly, or Majlis, consisted of sixty-seven members. The president was given the right to veto rulings of a Constitutional Council, which replaced the old Constitutional Court.

Despite procedural violations cited by international observers in the December legislative elections, the new legislature was seated on January 30, 1996. Umar Baygeldiyev, an adviser to Nazarbayev, was appointed chairman of the Senate, and Marat Ospanov, a former deputy speaker of the Supreme Soviet, was elected to chair the Majlis.

Nazarbayev has been a strong supporter of the CIS and further economic integration of the former Soviet republics. In 1994 Kazakhstan joined Uzbekistan and Kyrgyzstan in a special economic area supervised by an interstate council. In 1995 Kazakhstan established a customs union with Belarus and Russia. In March Kyrgyzstan joined the three to form a "community of integrated states." Kazakhstan also contributed troops to the CIS "peacekeeping" effort in Tajikistan, which was having difficulty controlling a guerrilla campaign by its opponents.

When it became independent, Kazakhstan, as a result of inheriting the Soviet nuclear weapons stationed on its territory, became the world's fourth-largest nuclear power. Its arsenal contained 100 SS-18 intercontinental ballistic missiles with approximately 1,400 nuclear warheads, and approximately 40 nuclear-armed bombers. In September 1992, the Kenges ratified the Strategic Arms Reduction Treaty, START-1. The Nuclear Non-Proliferation Treaty was ratified by the Kenges in December 1993. The United States provided Kazakhstan financial and technical assistance for dismantling its nuclear weapons. By the end of April 1995 all the country's nuclear warheads had been transferred to Russia for destruction.

The collapse of the USSR adversely affected Kazakhstan, as well as the other former Soviet republics. Kazakhstan's economy had been completely integrated into that of the USSR. The interruption of materials, goods, and markets constricted all sectors of the Kazakh economy between 1991 and 1994. Yet reform still continued. Kazakhstan was accepted for membership in the IMF and the World Bank in 1992, and it was designated an operations country, or a special recipient of grants and investment by the European Bank for Reconstruction and Development. At the beginning of 1995 an agreement of partnership and cooperation was entered into with the European Union (EU).

By the end of 1994, 60 percent of state enterprises had been privatized. The old command structure in the agricultural sector had broken down during the Gorbachev era. Restrictions on the number of private livestock had been lifted in 1987, and within several years the number of sheep and goats had climbed by 2.5 million and cattle by 1 million. In 1991 plots of land were distributed to 890,000 families. In 1992 Nazarbayev issued a decree on the privatization of agricultural land, but there was popular resistance to a rapid ending of the old system of collectives. The president then allowed a voluntary process. In 1995 the first signs of economic recovery appeared. Increases occurred in the production of gas, metals, petroleum, and chemicals. Inflation, which had mounted to 2,000 percent in 1992, also diminished significantly.

By the year 2000 Kazakhstan's economic future looked promising. It had a developed industrial sector, and its agricultural sector produced a surplus. It supplied most of its own electricity with its own resources. It also had large, mostly untapped mineral, petroleum, and natural gas reserves. This has drawn significant foreign investment. Chevron and the Kazakh government signed an agreement in April 1993 for a forty-year, $20 billion project to develop the oil fields of Tengiz and Korolev on the northeastern coast of the Caspian Sea. The first step of this project was the construction of a new pipeline. In 1994 Kazakhstan received the largest share, 39 percent, of foreign investments in the former USSR and Eastern Europe.

BIBLIOGRAPHY

Batalden, Stephen K., and Sandra L. Batalden. *The Newly Independent States of Eurasia: Handbook of Former Soviet Republics.* Phoenix, Ariz.: Oryx, 1993.

Critchlow, James. "Kazakhstan: The Outlook for Ethnic Relations." *RFE/RL Research Report* 31 (January 31, 1992).
"Kazakhstan," *Europa World Yearbook.* London: Europa Publications, 1997.
Olcott, Martha Brill. "Kazakhstan," in Mohiaddin Mesbahi, ed. *Central Asia and the Caucasus after the Soviet Union.* Gainesville: University Press of Florida, 1994.
———. *The Kazakhs.* Stanford, Calif.: Stanford University Press, 1987.
Shoemaker, M. Wesley. *Russia, Eurasian States and Eastern Europe, 1997.* Harpers Ferry: Stryker-Post, 1998.

Bernard Cook

SEE ALSO European Bank for Reconstruction and Development; Strategic Arms Limitation Talks II (SALT II)

Kazantzakis, Nikos (1885–1957)

Greek novelist. Nikos Kazantzakis, was born on February 18, 1883, in Iraklion, Crete. He attended universities in Greece, France, Germany, and Italy. Though a great traveler, he chose the Greek island of Aegina for his literary work. He brought to his philosophical works, travel literature, drama, and fiction a broad background in law, philosophy, literature, and art.

Kazantzakis at times put aside his writing for public service. As director general in the Social Affairs Ministry of Greece, he saved from starvation 150,000 Greeks expelled from Asia Minor at the end of World War I. He was appointed minister of education for a short while during 1945; and in 1946 he became president of the Greek Socialist Party's Superior Council. But he soon returned to his true vocation, literature. In 1947 and 1948 he served as director of UNESCO's Classics Translations Bureau. Although he spent his last years in Antibes, France, he was elected president of the Greek Society of Men of Letters in 1950.

In the Anglo-Saxon world, he is best known as the author of *Zorba the Greek* (1946). His fame is based on other novels as well, published in numerous languages, most notably *The Last Temptation of Christ* (1955). Kazantzakis wrote memoirs, colorful travel accounts, and an autobiography, *Report to Greco* (1961). His philosophical works include *The Saviors of God: Spiritual Exercises,* and comments and notes on Nietzsche and Bergson. He wrote poetry, tragedies, and epics, including an odyssey in 33,333 lines, *The Odyssey: A Modern Sequel* (1938), which begins where Homer's *Odyssey* ends, and translated *The Divine Comedy, Faustus,* and *Thus Spaoke Zarathustra.* He died on October 26, 1957, in Freiburg, Germany.

BIBLIOGRAPHY

Bien, Peter. *Kazantzakis: Politics of the Spirit.* Princeton, N.J.: Princeton University Press, 1989.
———. *Nikos Kazantzakis.* New York: Columbia University Press, 1972.
Levitt, Morton. *The Cretan Glance: The World and Art of Nikos Kazantzakis.* Columbus: Ohio State University Press, 1980.

David R. Davila Villers

Keane, John Brendan (1928–)

Irish playwright and poet. John B. Keane was born in Listowel in 1928. After working in London from 1951 to 1953, Keane returned to Listowel, where he bought a pub and still lives. With no theatrical experience he began writing plays. His first play, *Sive,* about an arranged marriage, was an immediate success in 1959 and solidly founded his reputation. *Sharon's Grave* followed in 1960 and *The Highest House on the Mountain* in 1961. Further plays include *The Year of the Hiker* (1963), *The Field* (1966), which has since been turned into a film, *Big Maggie* (1969), *Moll* (1972), *The Good Thing* (1975), and *The Buds of Ballybunion* (1978). Keane's plays deal with traditional themes such as rural life and the folk past, but he also successfully deals with themes such as emigration and modernization in Ireland. Keane has also written popular short stories. Best known are his satirical Letters series including, *Letters of a Love-hungry Farmer* (1976) and *Letters of a Country Postman* (1977). Keane has also written poetry including the collection *The Street* (1961).

Keane is one of the central figures of the County Kerry literary scene, and his plays are central to the repertoire of the Abbey Theatre in Dublin. They have been more successful with the public than with critics.

BIBLIOGRAPHY

Kealy, Marie Hubert. *Kerry Playwright: Sense of Place in the Plays of John B. Keane.* London: Associated University Presses, 1993.
Smith, Gus. *John B: the Real Keane.* Cork, Ireland: Mercier Press, 1992.

Michael J. Kennedy

Kebich, Vyachaslau (1936–)

Chairman of the Council of Ministers of the Belarusan Soviet Socialist Republic and subsequently the Republic of Belarus (1990–94), and the republic's most influential politician during those years. Vyachaslau Kebich was born on June 10, 1936, to a Belarusan peasant family in a village near Valozhyn in the Minsk district. After graduating from the Minsk Polytechnic he worked his way up from mechanical engineer to director of the Minsk S.M. Kirov Machine Tool Factory (1973–78), then became director of the S.M. Kirov Machine Tool Production Association (1978–80).

Kebich joined the Communist Party in 1962 and graduated from the Higher Party School. Politics became his main profession in 1980, when he became second secretary of the Minsk city party committee. In 1983 he took charge of the Heavy Industry Department of the party's Central Committee, and became second secretary of the Minsk district party committee. After 1985 Kebich held positions in government, moving from deputy chairman (1985–90) to chairman (1990–91) of the Council of Ministers. From 1992–1994, he was chairman of a committee in Belarus that was formed to deal with the economic dislocations that accompanied the collapse of the USSR. Kebich lost the 1994 presidential elections to Alyaksandr Lukashenka, who promised to develop closer ties to Russia and combat corruption.

BIBLIOGRAPHY

Urban, Michael and Jan Zaprudnik. "Belarus: A Long Road to Nationhood," in Ian Bremmer and Ray Taras, eds., *Nation and Politics in the Soviet Successor States.* Cambridge: Cambridge University Press, 1993, pp. 99–120.

Zaprudnik, Jan. *Belarus: At a Crossroads in History.* Boulder, Col.: Westview Press, 1993.

Karel C. Berkhoff

SEE ALSO Lukashenka, Alyaksandr

Kekkonen, Urho (1900–83)

President of Finland (1956–81). Urho Kaleva Kekkonen, born on September 3, 1900, received a doctorate in law in 1936, and during the same year became a member of parliament and minister of justice; in 1937 he became minister of the interior. Strongly opposed to the peace treaty following the Winter War with the USSR (1939–40), Kekkonen preferred a new war. But during that Continuation War (1941–44), the name given by Finns to their resumption of hostilities with the USSR after Germany invaded it in June 1941, he realized that the Soviet Union would be victorious over the Germans. Therefore he argued that the arch enemies Finland and the Soviet Union become friends. After the war Kekkonen was appointed minister of justice in the government of Juho Paasikivi. In this role, he was responsible for managing the difficult war crimes trials of Finns accused of criminal acts or of blatant collaboration with the Nazis. Kekkonen served as prime minister in five governments from 1950 to 1956.

Urho Kekkonen, president of Finland from 1956 to 1981. *Illustration courtesy Finnish Embassy, Washington, D.C.*

Before 1950 Kekkonen played a dominant role in forming the outlook within the Agrarian Union Party (ML), but he did not have a formal post. Because President Paasikivi was expected to win the 1950 presidential elections, Kekkonen became without competition the ML's candidate. Kekkonen convinced the Agrarian Union to nominate him as its presidential candidate for the 1956 election as early as 1954. In the meeting of the Electoral College, Kekkonen defeated his major rival, K. A. Fagerholm of the Social Democratic Party (SDP), in the third round by the smallest possible margin of electors, 151 to 149. Kekkonen was supported by the ML and the Communist Party (SKDL), as well as by electors from the small Finnish and Swedish People's Parties. Fagerholm was supported by the SDP and the Conservatives (KOK). The real decision was made by the Communists. They divided votes between Kekkonen and Fagerholm during the second round to get them to the third round. This clever maneuver prevented the reelection of Paasikivi, who had been misled by an anti-Kekkonen delegation and had become a candidate once more.

During his first term (1956–61) Kekkonen, a controversial figure from the beginning of his political career, became a symbol of the power struggle in Finnish politics. The Social Democrats thought him responsible for the party split because of his taking the SDP's internal opposition into the government. Furthermore, he was accused of playing the Soviet card against his opponents in domestic politics during the Night Frost Crisis (1958). In 1957 the SDP elected Väinö Tanner, a convicted war criminal, its chairman. Against warnings from Kekkonen's son and friends in the Agrarian Union (ML), the ML decided to form a government with the SDP. Kekkonen appointed Karl Fagerholm of the SPD prime minister. Furthermore, the Communists (SKDL) were excluded from the new government. The result was the "Night Frost" crisis of 1958. The USSR openly expressed its disapproval of the Fagerholm majority government and applied economic sanctions against Finland, cutting off imports from Finland completely. Consequently, Foreign Minister Johannes Virolainen (ML) resigned, and the other Agrarian Union ministers soon followed him. A minority government formed by the Agrarian Union was appointed, and relations between the two countries immediately improved.

In 1961 Kekkonen became the presidential candidate of the ML, with open support from the Communists and the Social Democratic opposition. However, the SDP, KOK, and Finnish and Swedish People's Parties formed a coalition to stop him. A former minister of justice, Olavi Honka, was recruited as the "Honka Coalition" candidate. The USSR did not remain passive. On October 30, 1961, it sent a diplomatic note to the Finnish government referring to the rearmament of West Germany and its increased naval presence in the Baltic Sea. Kekkonen's response was to avoid suggested consultations with the Soviets for a common defense effort against the alleged military threat. He dissolved parliament on November 14 to break up the Honka Coalition by forcing parties to compete against each other in parliamentary elections that were held almost simultaneously with the presidential vote. This was not enough for the Soviet Union; Kekkonen had to meet Soviet Premier Nikita Khrushchev in Novosibirsk on November 22. There the Soviet Union agreed to postpone the consultations. Having become a national hero, Kekkonen was reelected by a clear majority; his direct support rose from 27 percent in 1956, to 44 percent in 1962 and to 62 percent in 1968, and to 82 percent in 1978.

In the 1968 presidential elections two opposition parties, the Conservatives and the center opposition, the Finnish Agrarian Party, (SMP), appointed their own candidates to challenge Kekkonen. However, Kekkonen received 201 electors out of 300. In 1974 he refused to become a candidate, wishing the Eduskunta (parliament) to make a special law extending his presidency. But the required five-sixths' majority was not obtained, and Kekkonen threatened to resign. Consequently, the Eduskunta elected him for a shortened term (1974–78).

In 1978 the SDP, to prevent the Center's Ahti Karjalainen from becoming Kekkonen's successor, made a public move, most likely with advance support from Kekkonen himself, to nominate Kekkonen as their candidate for the 1978 election. Kekkonen accepted the invitation, forcing the other parties to join. There were four minor rival candidates, but Kekkonen collected 260 electors. But it was not generally known that Kekkonen was seriously ill. Gradually, his illness became so serious that he could not take care of his responsibilities. He went on sick leave on September 11, 1981, and had to resign on October 26. Kekkonen lived his last years in total privacy in the official residence, Tamminiemi. He died on August 31, 1983.

Kekkonen's political ideology was clear and simple. Foreign policy, meaning good relations between Finland and the USSR, stood above all else. Otherwise Finland could not survive and find its place in the world. This relationship with the USSR would give Finland sufficient space for its other international activities, especially for the expansion of foreign trade. Indicative of this, the Conference on Cooperation and Security in Europe (CSCE), which Kekkonen hosted in Helsinki and Finland joined, in 1975 became the most important achievement of Kekkonen's international activity.

Toward the late 1980s Kekkonen became the target of various accusations, especially of asking the Soviet Union to send the 1961 note to establish his power in Finland. While a majority of the elite has tried to paint Kekkonen as a villain, others have pointed out that his efforts were the only way to secure Finnish independence and security during the Cold War against a real Soviet danger. The truth is likely to remain somewhere in between.

BIBLIOGRAPHY

Allison, Roy. *Finland's Relations with the Soviet Union 1944–1984.* Oxford: Macmillan, 1985.

Jakobson, Max. *Finnish Neutrality.* New York: Praeger, 1969.
Kekkonen, Urho K. *Neutrality, the Finnish Position.* London: Heinemann, 1973.
Korhonen, Keijo, ed. *Urho Kekkonen: A Statesman for Peace.* Helsinki: Otava, 1975.
Maude, G. *The Finnish Dilemma.* London: Oxford University Press, 1976.
Väyrynen, Raimo. *Conflicts in Finnish and Soviet Relations.* Tampere: University of Tampere, 1972.

Vilho Harle

SEE ALSO Conference on Security and Cooperation in Europe (CSCE); Koivisto, Mauno; Paasikivi, Juho

Kelly, Petra (Karin) (1947–92)

German political activist and cofounder of the Green Party (Die Grünen). Petra Kelly emerged in the 1980s as one of the most visible, charismatic, and energetic figures of the West German antinuclear and environmentalist Greens, and devoted herself to a diverse array of global environmental and human rights causes until her death in 1992.

Born Petra Karin Lehmann in Günzberg on November 29, 1947, Petra adopted the surname of her stepfather, U.S. army officer John E. Kelly. Her family moved to the United States in 1960, and as an undergraduate studying political science at American University in Washington, D.C., she became active in the 1960s antiwar and civil rights movements. She gained practical political experience as a volunteer in the presidential campaigns of both Robert F. Kennedy and Hubert H. Humphrey. Upon completion of her M.A. at the University of Amsterdam in 1971, she served in various administrative capacities in the European Community (now, European Union) in Brussels until 1982. During this time she involved herself in various social causes in West Germany, where she returned in 1971, and in 1978 terminated her six-year membership in the Social Democratic Party to help found the Greens, which she described as an "antiparty party." Elected to the Bundestag (lower house of parliament) in 1983, she advocated implementation of environmentalist policies and opposed the deployment of U.S. nuclear weapons in Germany. Disillusioned with what she regarded as the amateurish and counterproductive tactics of the radical Greens, whose internal squabbles and rivalries resulted in electoral defeat for the Green Party in 1990, she became increasingly withdrawn from political and public life. In October 1992 German police found her body, along with that of her longtime companion, retired Bundeswehr general and Green Party member Gert Bastion, in their home in Bonn. According to the official report Bastion fatally shot Kelly before committing suicide. This explanation has been questioned by many of her followers, who suspect that Kelly and Bastion were murdered by neo-Nazis or agents of some foreign power.

BIBLIOGRAPHY

Kelly, Petra. *Thinking Green! Essays on Environmentalism, Feminism, and Nonviolence.* Foreword by Peter Matthiessen. Berkeley, Calif.: Parallax Press, 1994.
———. *Nonviolence Speaks to Power.* Ed. by Glenn D. Paige and Sarah Gilliatt. Honolulu: Center for Nonviolence Planning Project, Spark M. Matsunaga Institute for Peace, University of Hawaii, 1992.
Kelly, Petra, Gert Bastian, and Pat Aiello, eds. *The Anguish of Tibet.* Berkeley, Calif.: Parallax Press, 1991.
Parkin, Sara. *The Life and Death of Petra Kelly.* London: Pandora, 1994.

Mark P. Gingerich

Kennan, George Frost (1904–)

U.S. Foreign Service officer, head of the first Policy Planning Staff of the State Department (1947–50), ambassador to the Soviet Union (1952), and ambassador to Yugoslavia (1961–63). George Kennan formulated the post–World War II policy of containment that characterized U.S. policy toward the Soviet Union, and has written widely on diplomatic history and current affairs.

Kennan served with the first U.S. Embassy to Moscow from 1933 to 1936 and was reassigned there in 1944. His "long telegram" from Moscow to the State Department in 1946 advocated that the United States resist Soviet expansion in Eastern Europe. This was followed in 1947 by "The Sources of Soviet Conduct," an essay that articulated the policy of containment, published under the pseudonym X in *Foreign Affairs* magazine. Kennan anticipated that the Soviet Union would attempt to discover weak links in the Western alliance. To meet that threat, he recommended "containment of Russian expansive tendencies through . . . the adroit and vigilant application of counterforce at a series of constantly shifting geographical and political points, corresponding to the shifts and maneuvers of Soviet policies." Though Kennan employed military analogies, he viewed containment as primarily a political strategy and thought it essential that the United States reconstruct the economy of Western Europe to be strong enough to resist Soviet incursions. The policy of containment shaped U.S. foreign policy for the next forty years; it was the foundation for many significant political and diplomatic initiatives, such as the Marshall Plan, the Truman Doctrine, and NATO. Mainly in response to the Korean War, containment underwent a process of militarization. This process was consonant with the objectives of National Security Council Paper-68 (NSC-68) and Paul H. Nitze, who in 1949 succeeded Kennan as director of the Policy Planning Staff at the State Department. Nitze built upon the notion of containment but repudiated Kennan's policies by militarizing the policy.

When Kennan took leave of the Foreign Service in 1950, he was offered an appointment with the Institute for Advanced Studies at Princeton. He became a productive scholar, authoring twenty-one books, and an astute commentator. From 1950 to 1963 he moved between the diplomatic and academic worlds, serving as ambassador to the Soviet Union in 1952 and to Yugoslavia in 1960–63. His later writings were marked in part by proposals for breaking the military deadlock into which the Cold War had deteriorated by the early 1950s. This direction was apparent in his recommendations in the mid-1950s for military withdrawal from Europe, and his later disapproval of U.S. military tactics and dependence on first use of nuclear weapons (*The Nuclear Delusion,* 1982). Kennan was painstaking both in his endeavors to understand the Soviet Union and in his disposition to reproach the United States when necessary for the abuse of its power, as he did in *American Diplomacy 1900–1950* (1951).

Kennan's ideas formed and reflected those of the administrations he served. His strategic design of 1947 was as much a justification for, and sometimes a criticism of, what the administration did during the following three years, as it was a stimulus for those actions. Paradoxically, the architect of the organizing principle of postwar U.S. foreign policy became a prominent critic of the strategic considerations embodied in the policy of containment. By encircling the Soviet Union with inimical states, the West may have intensified Soviet resistance. Consequently, militarizing containment could have prolonged the Cold War rather than have brought it to a conclusion.

BIBLIOGRAPHY

The Kennan archive is housed at Princeton University.

Isaacson, Walter, and Evan Thomas. *The Wise Men: Six Friends and the World They Made.* New York: Simon and Schuster, 1986.

Kennan, George. *Memoirs: 1925–1950.* Vol. 1. Boston: Little, Brown, 1967.

———. *Memoirs, 1950–1963.* Vol. 2. Boston: Little, Brown, 1972.

———. *Sketches from a Life.* New York: Pantheon, 1989.

Miscamble, Wilson. *George F. Kennan and the Making of American Foreign Policy: 1947–1950.* Princeton, N.J.: Princeton University Press, 1992.

Stephensan, Anders. *Kennan and the Art of Foreign Policy.* Cambridge, Mass.: Harvard University Press, 1989.

Kenneth Keulman

Kessler, Heinz (1920–)

East German Defense Minister. Heinz Kessler served in the Wehrmacht during the early stages of World War II before deserting to the Red Army in 1941. A cofounder of the National Committee for a Free Germany, he returned to Germany in 1945 as part of a group of German communists headed by Walter Ulbricht, who had laid the foundations for a Communist regime in East Germany. Kessler earned his political spurs in the Free Democratic Youth, a Communist front youth organization, and entered the Socialist Unity (Communist) Party (SED) Central Committee in 1946. During the 1950s and 1960s he advanced rapidly through the ranks of the armed forces, becoming deputy minister of national defense, chief of the Air Force, and chief of staff of the National People's Army. A close ally of Erich Honecker, the East German head of state (1976–89), he was appointed defense minister in 1985 and, one year later, entered the SED Politburo. After the reunification of Germany in October, 1990 he was arraigned on various charges relating to the shooting of East Germans fleeing the German Democratic Republic. On September 17, 1993 he was found guilty of ordering border guards to kill East Germans who attempted to flee across the border to West Germany and was sentenced to seven and one-half years in prison.

BIBLIOGRAPHY

Childs, David. *The GDR, Moscow's German Ally.* Boston: G. Allen & Unwin, 1983.

Mike Dennis

SEE ALSO Honecker, Erich; Wolf, Markus

KGB

An acronym taken from the Russian language designation Komitet Gosudarstvennoi Beznopasnosti, literally the Committee of State Security in the USSR. A government ministry, the KGB was so-named in 1954, the last in several name changes to the Cheka, the secret police established by Vladimir Lenin in 1917 and finally disbanded by Boris Yeltsin in 1991.

The KGB was a large and complex organization that performed a wide variety of duties. Each section was responsible for specific functions intended to ensure the political loyalty of Soviet citizens and promote Soviet goals abroad. Within the USSR, the KGB closely monitored the Soviet populace, suppressed political discontent, and infiltrated the Russian Orthodox Church. The KGB also guarded the USSR's borders and protected party and government leaders. To carry out these missions, the KGB relied on secret informers and surveillance technology and sent dissidents to the Gulag labor camps. The KGB had a large and active foreign intelligence service whose primary goal was to advance Soviet foreign policy goals by gathering secret political, military, and technological information. Additionally, the KGB conducted propaganda and disinformation campaigns against the West, and relied heavily upon the intelligence services of its Eastern European satellites.

The origins of the KGB date back to the founding of the Cheka under the leadership of Felix Dzerzhinsky in 1917. The Cheka was succeeded by the GPU in 1922 and the OGPU in 1923. Numerous name changes followed: NKVD in 1934, NKGB in 1943, MGB (Ministry of State Security) in 1946, MVD (Ministry of Internal Affairs) in 1953, and finally the KGB in 1954. The 1954 change was initiated in part because of the death of Joseph Stalin in March 1953 and the execution of the MVD head, Lavrenty Beria, by the other party leaders later in the year. Beria had been an agent of Stalin's terror and was feared by other leading Communists. Beria, a victim of the power struggle that followed Stalin's death, was removed as head of the MVD in July 1953 and charged with conspiracy. He was executed in December 1953.

Nikita Khrushchev, who became first secretary of the Communist Party, initiated legal reforms and reorganized the security apparatus. The terror ended, and the KGB was charged with security functions. A new legal code replaced the Stalinist laws, but the party leadership did not eliminate all legal loopholes, and it allowed the KGB to circumvent the law in order to combat political dissent.

After the Beria era, the leadership of the KGB passed through four chairmen before finally being consolidated under Yuri Andropov in 1964. Under the leadership of Andropov from 1964 to 1982, the KGB developed a highly sophisticated system of control within the USSR and of espionage abroad. Andropov's rise to power in conjunction with Leonid Brezhnev, the general secretary who replaced Khrushchev in 1964, saw the reinstitution of harsh policies toward political dissidents. Arrests rose markedly from 1965 until 1973, when they temporarily fell as a result of the Soviet pursuit of détente with the United States. Under Andropov, terror was replaced by a plethora of alternative punishments, including arrest, psychiatric commitment, and other forms of coercion. The KGB also censored literature and other media. In addition to formal censorship, the KGB harassed writers and artists. They were expelled from professional organizations and jobs, and prosecuted for their critical views of the state. Many writers responded by self-censorship and only produced works they felt would be deemed acceptable by the state. The KGB also provided the party leadership with information about dissidents and the political opinions of the public. With the installation of Mikhail Gorbachev as general secretary and his introduction of glasnost (openness), the range of the KGB's arbitrary powers was restricted.

Upon coming to power in 1991, Boris Yeltsin formally dissolved the KGB, splitting it into five organizations. Nevertheless, many of its personnel continued to perform functions in Russia and the other successor states of the USSR similar to those that they had performed in the KGB.

BIBLIOGRAPHY

Andrew, Christopher, and Oleg Gordievsky. *KGB: The Inside Story of Its Foreign Operations from Lenin to Gorbachev.* New York: HarperCollins, 1990.

Courson, William R., and Robert T. Crowley. *The New KGB: Engine of Soviet Power.* New York: Morrow, 1985.

Hill, Ronald J. *The Soviet Union: Politics, Economics, and Society from Lenin to Gorbachev.* Boulder, Col: Lynne Rienner, 1985.

Todd Alan Good

SEE ALSO Andropov, Yuri; Beria, Lavrenty

Khasbulatov, Ruslan Imranovich (1942–)

Chairman of the Russian Supreme Soviet (1991–93) and political foe of President Boris Yeltsin. Ruslan Imranovich Khasbulatov was born in Grozny on November 22, most likely in 1942. He studied both at the Kazakhstan State University and the Faculty of Economics of Moscow State University where he received a Ph.D. in economics in 1965. After graduation he was a professor at Moscow State University, where from 1965 to 1967 he was secretary of the Komsomol, the Communist Youth League, committee. From 1979 to 1990 he was an economist at the Plekhanov Institute for the National Economy in Moscow.

In 1990 Khasbulatov was elected to the Russian Supreme Soviet (parliament), and on June 5, 1990, he was elected first deputy chairman. In August of that year, at the time of the attempted coup to oust Mikhail Gorbachev and preserve the Soviet Union, Khasbulatov resigned his membership in the Communist Party and joined Boris Yeltsin at the Russian Supreme Soviet (parliament) building to oppose the coup. He was then elected chairman of the Russian Supreme Soviet. However, he opposed the "shock therapy" of rapid movement toward a market economy and privatization. He advocated retention of price controls, subsidies for collapsing firms, and a comprehensive system of welfare. As the economy deteriorated Vice President Aleksandr Rutskoi joined Khasbulatov, leading parliament in revolt. When Yeltsin declared parliament dissolved, Khasbulatov and Rutskoi with approximately one-hundred deputies and armed supporters occupied the parliament building. When they attempted to seize control of the state television center at Ostanbino, Yeltsin ordered an armed assault on the parliament. Afterward Khasbulatov and Rutskoi, along with many supporters, were arrested. The new Duma elected in December with its heavy Communist and nationalist representation granted Khasbulatov, Rutskoi, and the others an amnesty in February 1994. Though for a time he unsuccessfully participated in efforts to oust his fellow Chechen Dzhokar Dudayev from Chechnya, Khasbulatov ultimately resumed his academic career.

BIBLIOGRAPHY

Suny, Ronald Grigor. *The Soviet Experiment: Russia, the USSR, and the Successor States.* New York: Oxford University Press, 1998.

Bernard Cook

SEE ALSO Rutskoi, Aleksandr

Khrennikov, Tikhon N. (1914–)

Head of the Soviet Composers Union (1951–91). The socialist realism of Tikhon Khrennikov's 1939 opera, *V Buryu* (*Into the Storm*) won him the favor of dictator Joseph Stalin. In a 1948 speech Khrennikov attacked "formalism" and the compositions of eminent composers Dinitri Shostakovich and Sergey Prokofiev. The speech set the tone for artistic repression in the USSR. Though Khrennikov claims that he did not author the speech, he was personally picked by Stalin to carry out his policy of artistic control. He was the gatekeeper of Soviet music and guarded it against the "decadent" influences of jazz, formalism, and atonality. There is some debate concerning his role. In an effort at self-exoneration, Khrennikov in a 1996 interview stated, "Nobody could say no to Stalin," and claimed that he was the moving force behind the 1958 rehabilitation of Shostakovich and Prokoviev. Khrennikov enjoyed popularity in Russia in the 1990s for the traditional music that he composed for the ballet *Napoleon Bonaparte.*

BIBLIOGRAPHY

Khrennikov, Tikhon Nikolaevich. *Tichon Chrennikow, Werkverzeichnis.* Hamburg: H. Sikorski, 1985.

Martynov, Ivan. *Tikhon Nikolaevich Khrennikov.* Moscow: Muzyka, 1987.

Vorontsova, Irina Vladimirovna. *O stile i muzykal'nom iazyke T. N. Khrennikova.* Moscow: Vses. izd-vo "Sov. kompozitor," 1983.

Bernard Cook

Khrushchev, Nikita Sergeevich (1894–1971)

Soviet political leader, first secretary of the Communist Party of the Soviet Union (1953–64), and premier of the USSR (1958–64). In power only a little over a decade, Nikita Khrushchev had an enduring impact on the Soviet Union because of the early post-Stalin reforms he initiated in the 1950s.

Khrushchev was born into a working-class family in Kalinovka, a small town near the border of the Ukraine. Ethnically Russian, he never lost his regional accent or forgot his humble roots. When he was fifteen, his family moved to Yuzovka (Donetsk) in the Ukraine. With only an elementary school education, the young Khrushchev worked in coal mines, among other places. He married early and had two children by his first wife, who died in 1921. In 1924 he married a teacher, Nina Petrovna Kukharchuk, who was also involved in party work. Their marriage was apparently a happy one, and during his years in power, she became an international symbol of the Soviet grandmother.

Khrushchev joined the Communist Party in 1918 and the Red Army in 1919. In the 1920s he worked both in industry and in the party. In the post-Lenin struggles, Khrushchev allied himself the Stalin faction of the Communist Party, especially with Lazar Kaganovich, a closer supporter of Stalin, whom the Soviet leader had placed in charge of overseeing local party administration. In 1929 he moved to Moscow and studied at a special academy for party functionaries. At the academy he became acquainted with prominent politicians and public figures, among them Nadezhda Alleluyeva, Stalin's wife. With her assistance he attracted the attention of Stalin, and in 1935 Khrushchev was appointed first secretary of the Moscow Communist Party, with responsibilities for oversight of the construction of the Moscow subway.

Khrushchev, unlike many other prominent party members, survived the purges of the mid-1930s and was appointed first secretary of the Communist Party of the Ukraine and a candidate member of the Politburo in 1938. He remained in that position through World War II. His role in the Ukraine was controversial. On the one hand, he was sufficiently successful, by Soviet standards, to attract the attention of the Kremlin leadership and was invited to Moscow to oversee agriculture in 1949. However, he is often blamed for the repression of the Ukraine during the late Stalin period.

In Moscow after 1949, Khrushchev, like others on the Politburo, was caught up in the post-Stalin transition. The struggle for the succession began during Stalin's lifetime, and some contenders fell along the way, principally at the will of Stalin. When Stalin died in 1953 Georgy Malenkov was the clear-cut leader to succeed him, with the wily Lavrenty Beria, head of the Ministry of Internal Affairs (secret police) as his strongest rival. Malenkov became premier (chairman of the Council of Ministers). Almost unnoticed at first was the progress of Khrushchev, who was rising in the party, and in fall 1953 was appointed first secretary. Competition between Malenkov and Khrushchev accelerated after Beria was executed in 1953. Khrushchev gathered his principal support from Communist Party officials and the military during this period. On February 8, 1955, Malenkov was forced to step down as premier by Khrushchev, and he was replaced by the more docile Nikolay Bulganin.

Having removed his chief rival, Khrushchev, as first secretary of the Party, had clearly assumed power. During his early years in power he introduced a number of changes into the economy, some of which were successful while others failed. Probably the single most notable development was the de-Stalinization campaign announced in 1956 at a secret session of the Twentieth Party Congress. At the same congress Khrushchev initiated a number of significant changes in foreign policy and in the official ideology. The changes included a redefinition of "peaceful coexistence"—the official Soviet policy toward relations with the West—and a pronouncement that there were many roads to socialism. This announcement was welcomed by the Soviet satellite countries in Eastern Europe, which had been forced until that time to follow the Stalinist path.

In line with Khrushchev's ambiguous and controversial political style, characterized by dramatic flare and a penchant for impetuosity, changes were adopted and articulated in ways that backfired, internally and internationally. For example, the liberalized version of peaceful coexistence with the West was interpreted in the West as a potential threat and a challenge rather than as an invitation to better relations. Many roads to socialism and its corollaries led to several problems for the Soviet Union. In Eastern Europe it prompted further experimentation, especially in Hungary, which used de-Stalinization and the invitation to diversity to attempt to withdraw from the Soviet-dominated Warsaw Pact. The result was the Hungarian Revolution of October 1956, which was bloodily suppressed by the USSR. The USSR under Khrushchev's direction did not normally consult Communist leaders in other Communist states about major changes made by the Soviet party. Perhaps the most serious omission was the failure to consult China and its leader, Mao Tse-tung. Although the Chinese leadership perhaps tacitly welcomed some changes, Khrushchev's promotion of peaceful coexistence and his attack on Stalin's cult of personality were not. Growing differences led to a rift between the two Communist giants that did not heal for decades.

Khrushchev was first among equals among the party Presidium (Politburo) leadership but often faced opposition, particularly from those leaders who remained from the Stalin era, including Malenkov and Vyacheslov Molotov, among others. As early as 1956 and 1957 Khrushchev was attacked by his peers for the poor performance of some of his economic reforms, and he was blamed for the Hungarian Revolution. A showdown occurred in June 1957 when a majority of the Presidium voted to remove him as first secretary. Khrushchev summoned a meeting of the larger party Central Committee, which upheld his position. In the aftermath a number of Presidium officials were removed, including Malenkov, Molotov, and other holdovers from the Stalin era.

In early 1958, Khrushchev chose to assume the premiership himself, while remaining first secretary of the party. He now headed both the party and the government, as Stalin had once done, but he did not have Stalin's power and authority, facing almost continual opposition. For the next six years he maneuvered successfully, initiating a number of new policies and practices. The Khrushchev period was surely more liberal than the Stalin era but the system remained a dictatorship. Intermittent crackdowns, in cultural policy in particular, reminded the nation that the party still maintained tight control. Khrushchev, for example, permitted publication of Aleksandr Solzhenitsyn's *One Day in the Life of Ivan Denisevich,* a novel about life in the Gulag, but forbade publication of renowned poet Boris Pasternak's novel, *Dr. Zhivago,* an epic of life amidst the turmoil of the Russian Revolution and its aftermath.

Khrushchev often played party and government against each other. As part of the political game, he moved officials from post to post and from institution to institution, thereby diminishing the opportunity for ambitious political officials to build a strong political base. Even Leonid Brezhnev, Khrushchev's protégé and designated heir, was moved from a position in the party Secretariat to the chairmanship of the Presidium of the Supreme Soviet (a position equated with the presidency of the USSR, characterized by ceremonial functions rather than power), and later back to the Secretariat. Uncertainty about their positions led some officials to question Khrushchev's leadership.

Reorganization of the economy in 1957 shifted responsibility from the central ministries in Moscow to designated economic regions, which corresponded, more or less, to the provinces headed by Communist Party secretaries. The move, intended to decentralize the economy, had the perhaps unintended consequence of placing the onus for economic failure on the provincial party secretaries. Intended as a move to strengthen the party's oversight of the economy, it tended to make party secretaries more vulnerable.

Throughout his years in power Khrushchev maintained a strong interest in agriculture. With his rural background he considered himself an agricultural specialist and initiated numerous agricultural policies. Most famous was the attempt to expand grain production in Kazakhstan in 1954 in the so-called virgin lands. This well-known experiment was initially successful but later proved to be costly since the soil was subject to wind erosion and to the vagaries of the Central Asian climate. Over the long run the virgin lands were an important source of grain for the USSR, but during the Khrushchev years they produced mixed results. Khrushchev was the first Soviet leader to travel to the United States, and during his 1959 trip he visited American farms, which greatly impressed him. As a result of his consultation with American specialists, he introduced some American practices into Soviet agriculture. Perhaps most famous was his attempt to introduce corn into Russia for human consumption and animal feed. Indeed, his campaign to promote corn earned him the nickname Tovarishch Kukuruza (Comrade Corn). In the last period before his retirement, Khrushchev promoted increased production and use of mineral fertilizers in agriculture and attempted to enhance the chemical industry in a national campaign characterized by slogans and banners.

Other Khrushchev policies ranged from innovative to unrealistic. In the early 1960s he encouraged a team of economists headed by Evsei Liberman to propose reform of the cumbersome socialist economy. These studies led to the reforms initiated in 1965 by Prime Minister Aleksey Kosygin. In foreign policy Khrushchev's record was checkered. Relations with the West improved during the decade he was in power, but progress was like a roller coaster. While the Cuban Missile Crisis of 1962 may have been the most perilous moment in East-West relations, there were also tense moments involving Berlin. Khrushchev's attempts to settle the Berlin question (West Berlin being an island of freedom and an escape route in the midst of Communist East Germany) resulted in threats to turn East Berlin over to East Germany. The erection of the Berlin Wall in 1961, separating East and West Berlin, resulted from the desire of the USSR and its client state, the German Democratic Republic (East Germany), to end the labor power drain from East to West Germany via Berlin. The erection of the Wall reflected Soviet failure to resolve the German issue to its advantage. In contrast, the Test Ban Treaty of 1963, signed by Khrushchev and U.S. President John Kennedy, was a landmark in the struggle to control nuclear power.

In foreign policy perhaps no issue hurt Khrushchev more than the Sino-Soviet split. Beginning with the Twentieth Party Congress the rift mushroomed. At first the two countries criticized each other obliquely. By the early 1960s the Chinese press lost no opportunity to criticize the Khrushchev leadership, and the Soviet press frequently lashed out at the *Maotsetungisti* (Mao Tse-tung-ites, or followers of Mao), whom they regarded as a regressive element in the international Communist movement. Among the Soviet leadership there appears to have been a perception that Khrushchev was responsible for mishandling the Chinese. Khrushchev's successors, in fact, expected to resolve the differences with China easily and were dismayed when the split continued for about two more decades.

Early in the 1960s a movement began among some Presidium members to remove Khrushchev. By 1964 the movement had gained the acquiescence of Leonid Brezhnev, Khrushchev's designated heir. It is not clear which political officials masterminded the removal; in the West it was assumed that party ideologist Mikhail Suslov was the hidden hand. More recent sources suggest that Suslov may have been only minimally involved.

The year 1964 was one of contradictions for the aging Khrushchev. He was feted on his seventieth birthday while machinations accelerated for his removal. Khrushchev continued his work schedule through the summer of 1964. Although Khrushchev was aware of rumors that there was a plot to remove him in late summer 1964, he seemed complacent about the matter and conducted his usual fall tour of agriculture. But on October 13, 1964, Khrushchev was summoned to a Presidium meeting at which the Presidium asked him to step down. A meeting of the Central Committee was hastily summoned to conform this decision and Khrushchev's resignation from all his positions was then requested. Unlike his performance in 1957, Khrushchev accepted the decision of the Presidium and the Central Committee without protest. Later he commented that he had made possible the peaceful removal of a top Soviet leader, something that had never occurred before.

In retirement Khrushchev lived quietly in a modest dacha outside Moscow. He was permitted to retain a Moscow apartment but was discouraged from coming to the city. Cognizant of his popularity, the leadership wanted him out of sight. Khrushchev eventually dictated his memoirs, which were later published in the West. He died in 1971 at the age of seventy-seven. His son Sergei wrote a book about his father, *Khrushchev on Khrushchev* (1990).

Khrushchev's legacy is controversial, and decades after his passing there is still discussion of his long-term influence on the reforms undertaken by Mikhail Gorbachev in the 1980s. The monument to Khrushchev at his grave site expresses his legacy well. It is a modernistic structure of cleverly stacked, contrasting black and white blocks, symbolizing the man of contradictions whom it memorializes.

BIBLIOGRAPHY

Khrushchev, Nikita S. *Khrushchev Remembers.* 2 Vols. Tr. and ed. by Strobe Talbott. Boston: Little Brown, 1970–74.

Khrushchev, Sergei N. *Khrushchev on Khrushchev: An Inside Account of the Man and His Era.* Boston: Little Brown, 1990.

Ploss, Sidney. *Conflict and Decision-Making in Soviet Russia: A Case Study of Agricultural Policy, 1953–1963.* Princeton, N.J.: Princeton University Press, 1965.

Tatu, Michel. *Power in the Kremlin: From Khrushchev to Kosygin.* New York: Viking, 1969.

Thompson, William J. *Khrushchev: A Political Life.* New York: St. Martin's Press, 1997.

Norma C. Noonan

SEE ALSO Berlin Wall; Brezhnev, Leonid; Cuban Missile Crisis; Lieberman, Evsei; Malenkov, Georgy

Kiesinger, Kurt Georg (1904–88)

West German chancellor (1966–69). Kurt Georg Kiesinger, son of a Protestant bookkeeper at a textile factory, was born in Ebingen on April 6, 1904. His mother, a Roman Catholic, died when he was six months old, but his father married another Catholic and Kiesinger was raised in that faith. His university education at Tübingen was financed by an Ebingen factory owner impressed by Kiesinger's poems published in a Stuttgart newspaper. After studying history and philosophy at the University of Tübingen, Kiesinger transferred to the University of Berlin, where he studied law. While at Berlin he was active in a Catholic fraternity and published religious poems.

He joined the National Socialist (Nazi) Party on March 1, 1933, because of his legal career but also out of nationalist sentiments. Kiesinger became disillusioned with Hitler after the Night of the Long Knives (June 30, 1934), the Nazi leader's bloody purge of his own storm troop organization, the SA. He disassociated himself from the party though he retained his membership. He practiced law first in Würzburg then in Berlin but refused to enter public administration and a teaching post at the university because of his unwillingness to join the Nazi lawyers' association. In 1940 he was assigned to the Foreign Office and employed in its radio section. He has been accused of acting as a liaison between the Foreign Office and Nazi Party propagandist Joseph Goebbles. But there are indications that Kiesinger was denounced for downplaying anti-Semitism and that he was accused of "defeatism." He apparently was involved with the opposition after the failed anti-Hitler plot of July 20, 1944.

After eighteen months of internment by American occupation forces at the end of World War II, he was released but was at first classified as a "fellow traveler," until eventually exonerated and allowed to hold public office. He resumed law practice in Tübingen and became the leader of the Christian Democratic Union in Württemberg. He was elected to the first Bundestag (lower house of Parliament) in 1949 and the next year became a member of the Christian Democrats' executive board. He was particularly interested in Western European cooperation. In 1950 he was elected to the judicial committee for the Schuman Plan, which produced the European Coal and Steel Community, the forerunner of the Common Market, and became a member of the consultative assembly for the Council of Europe, the organization formed in 1949 to promote European unity, becoming its vice president in 1955. Kiessinger was also a member of the assembly of the Western European Union, a defensive alliance that preceded the North Atlantic Treat

Organization, and he led the Bundestag debate in favor of German rearmament.

Though he was selected chair of the Christian Democratic Union's parliamentary group in the Bundestag in 1957, he was disappointed when Chancellor Konrad Adenauer did not appoint him to the cabinet. As a result he returned to his home state of Württemberg and became minister president of the Land (State) Württemberg-Baden on December 17, 1958. During his tenure Kiesinger successfully promoted the development of his Land. In 1962–63 he was president of the federal Bundesrat (upper house). When the Christian Democratic Chancellor Ludwig Erhard's coalition with the Free Democratic Party (FDP) collapsed in 1966, Kiesinger with the support of Franz-Josef Strauss, the leader of the Bavarian Christian Social Union, prevailed among the Christian Democratic Union/Christian Social Union (DCU/CSU) parliamentary representatives over Foreign Minister Gerhard Schröder and Ranier Barzel, chair of the Christian Democratic Union's Bundestag group. Kiesinger, who along with Strauss hoped to clip the wings of the rebellious FDP by upping the 5 percent cutoff of the Basic Law (the constitution of the Federal Republic of Germany), which required parties to win 5 percent of the national vote in order to receive representation in the federal parliament (Bundestag), forged a grand coalition with the Social Democrats (SDP). Kiesinger and Willy Brandt, the Social Democratic leader, agreed to a cabinet on November 30, 1966. The CDU/CSU received ten seats and the SPD received nine, one of which was Brandt as vice chancellor and foreign minister. Kiesinger was approved by the Bundestag on December 1, 1966. The new chancellor staked out a course that, while still friendly toward the United States, gave more consideration to France to the delight of Strauss. He also indicated a willingness to modify the Hallstein Doctrine, which prohibited diplomatic relations with any country other than the USSR (which alone recognized the German Democratic Republic), and make new overtures to the East, a foreshadowing of Brandt's *Ostpolitik*. In a January 1967 meeting with French President Charles de Gaulle, the 1963 Franco-German Friendship treaty, which had formalized a new era of friendly relations between Germany and France, was revitalized. Shortly thereafter, steps were taken to establish diplomatic relations with two Soviet bloc countries, Hungary and Romania.

Following the 1969 election, Kiesinger's government gave way to the first Social Democratic chancellorship of the Bonn republic as Brandt formed a collation with the FDP, which had shifted to the left and was unwilling to countenance a coalition with the Christian Democrats as long as Strauss was a power within their ranks. Between them the SPD and the FDP won 48.5 percent of the vote to 46.1 percent for Kiesinger and the Christian Democrats. Kiesinger relinquished leadership of the Christian Democratic Union in 1971 and died in Tübingen on March 9, 1988.

Kiesinger's chancellorship is significant for heralding the beginning of the effort to improve relations with the Communist bloc, and the opportunity it gave Brandt and the SDP to demonstrate not only their ability to participate in a governing coalition but to lead one.

BIBLIOGRAPHY

Nicholls, A. J. *The Bonn Republic: West German Democracy 1945–1990.* London: Longman, 1997.

Bernard Cook

SEE ALSO Brandt, Willy; Erhard, Ludwig

Kieslowski, Krzysztof (1941–96)

Polish film director and screenwriter. Krzysztof Kieslowski, born in Warsaw on June 27, 1941, studied at the Polish National Film School in Lodz. His productions include feature films, TV films and series, documentaries, and short films. He won the attention of international audiences for his 1988–89 *Decalogue,* a TV series of ten short films exploring the Ten Commandments through the prism of contemporary moral problems. *The Double Life of Véronique* and the trilogy *Three Colours* established his reputation. In 1994 Kieslowski was nominated by the American Academy of Motion Pictures for an Oscar as best director for his film *Red.*

His major films are *First Love* (1974), Golden Dragon, International Festival of Short Films, Kraków 1974; *Personnel* (1975), First Prize, Mannheim Festival 1975; *The Scar* (1976); *Camera Buff* (1979), Fipresci Prize, Moscow Festival 1979; *Blind Chance* (1981); *No End* (1985); *A Short Film About Killing* (1988), Special Jury Prize, Cannes 1988; *A Short Film About Love* (1988); *The Double Life of Véronique* (1991); and *Three Colours: Blue, White, Red* (1993–94).

Kieslowski died of heart failure in Warsaw on March 13, 1996.

BIBLIOGRAPHY

Kieslowski, Krzysztof, and Krzysztof Piesiewicz. *Decalogue: The Ten Commandments.* London: Faber and Faber, 1991.

Kieslowski, Krzysztof, and Danusia Stok. *Kieslowski on Kieslowski.* London: Faber and Faber, 1993.

Krzysztof Olechnicki

Kinkel, Klaus (1936–)

German foreign minister (1992–98). Klaus Kinkel was born in Metzingen on December 17, 1936. He studied law at the Universities of Tübingen, Bonn, and Cologne, and received a doctorate in 1964. From 1965 to 1970 he worked in the Ministry of Interior's Office for Civilian Protection in Balingen. From 1970 to 1974 he was assistant to the minister of the interior and head of the ministerial office. From 1974 to 1977 Kinkel managed the administrative staff at the Foreign Office of the Federal Republic (West Germany). From 1979 to 1982 he directed the *bundesmachrichtendienst* (Federal Intelligence Service). From 1982 to 1991 he was undersecretary of the Ministry of Justice. He was appointed minister of justice in 1991, following the victory of the Christian Democrats and the Free Democrats in the 1990 election, which followed German reunification. At that point Kinkel joined the Free Democratic Party (FDP), but he was not a member of the Bundestag (lower house of Parliament). When Free Democrat Hans-Dietrich Genscher resigned as foreign minister in 1992, Kinkel succeeded him. On April 28, the day after Genscher announced that he would resign, the FDP leaders nominated Housing Minister Irmgard Schwätzer as his successor. However, the FDP parliamentary delegation refused to confirm Schwätzer's nomination. They were annoyed at not being consulted and feared that Schwätzer's inexperience in foreign affairs would permit Helmut Kohl, the Christian Democratic chancellor, to dominate foreign affairs. The FDP leaders had wished for Kinkel to remain in charge of the Justice Ministry while constitutional changes regarding immigration policy were being debated. He was succeeded at Justice by Sabine Leutheusser-Schnarrenberger, an FDP lawyer from Bavaria. After some contention between the FDP and the Social Christian Union, who wanted its leader, Finance Minister Theo Waigel, to be appointed vice chancellor, Jürgen Moellemann, FDP minister of Justice, was appointed vice chancellor to succeed Genscher in that post. But in January 1993 following the resignation of Moellemann, Kinkel became vice chancellor, retaining those posts until the Christian-Liberal coalition was defeated in the September 1998 election. On June 11, 1993, Kinkel was formally elected leader of the FDP to replace Otto Lambsdorff.

As foreign minister Kinkel continued the policy of his mentor, Genscher, asserting a unique German voice in foreign affairs. He was outspoken in his blame of Serbia for the conflict in Bosnia and pushed for a European response and solution; when that was not forthcoming, he supported the U.S.-led NATO effort. Kinkel lobbied for a constitutional amendment to permit German forces to participate in peacekeeping missions outside the boundaries of NATO. When Minister of Defense Volker Rüehe and the Christian Democrats wanted to proceed without an enabling amendment, Kinkel, who had constitutional qualms, tested the issue at the Constitutional Court in Karlsruhe with the permission of Kohl. When the court decided not to bar German participation, Kinkel stated that though "politically, I have always wanted this . . . the court used not legal, but political arguments and was more concerned about disappointing our alliance partner [the United States] than about constitutional issues." In pursuit of a new, explicit world role for Germany, Kinkel also called for the admission of Germany and Japan to the U.N. Security Council to reflect better the current world order.

BIBLIOGRAPHY

Kinkel, Klaus. *In der Verantwortung: Hans-Dietrich Genscher zum Siebzigsten.* Berlin: Siedler, 1997.

———. *Schiedsgerichtsbarkeit im Umfeld von Politik, Wirtschaft und Gerichtsbarkeit.* Cologne: C. Heymann, 1992.

Schmidt-Eenboom, Erich. *Der Schattenkrieger: Klaus Kinkel und der BND.* Düsseldorf: ECON, 1995.

Bernard Cook

Kinnock, Neil (1942–)

British Labour Party leader, member of Parliament, and member of the European Commission. Neil Kinnock played a central role in the "modernization" of the Labour Party during the 1980s, leading the party in two general elections in 1987 and 1992. Despite the party's defeat in those elections he is seen as having helped prepare the ground for its later success.

Kinnock entered the House of Commons in 1970 as MP for Bedwelty. In the tradition of radical politicians from south Wales, he was an active and vociferous backbench MP, supporting traditional labor unionist and Labour causes, while opposing Britain's membership in the European Economic Community (now, European Union). He was briefly parliamentary private secretary to the secretary of state for employment in the 1974 Labour government, but maintained his reputation for radical activism. Following the 1979 general election defeat of Labour, Kinnock became the opposition spokesman on education. He was, in addition, a member of the party's National Executive Committee from 1978 onward.

The 1979 defeat led to a prolonged period of reassessment for the Labour Party as social democrats and more radical, socialist factions battled for control of the labor movement. The departure of a small number of well-known MPs to form the Social Democratic Party in 1981 appeared to confirm the strength of the left. However, the general election defeat sustained by the party under the leadership of Michael Foot in 1983 led to Kinnock's becoming leader. His program centered on reestablishing the leadership's control over both the parliamentary and the constituency party. In particular, Kinnock defeated the Militant Tendency organization, a left-wing group, which was strong in some constituencies. Having gained more effective control over the party, Kinnock began "modernizing," or moderating, the party's program, taking account of the apparent rightward shift in British politics in the 1980s.

The party failed to win the 1987 general election but saw a noticeable improvement in its fortunes. After the decline of the Conservative government, it was widely expected that Kinnock and Labour would win the 1992 general election. Yet the Conservatives won a fourth consecutive term. While accusing the press of uniting to defeat Labour, Kinnock accepted responsibility for that defeat and resigned the leadership. His modernizing program was continued by his successors, John Smith and Tony Blair. Kinnock himself became transport commissioner for the European Union in 1995.

Kinnock's central achievement was the revitalization of the Labour Party during the 1980s, enabling it once again to appear as a potential party of government, following the disastrous 1983 election defeat.

BIBLIOGRAPHY

Drower, George. *Neil Kinnock: The Path to Leadership.* London: Weidenfeld and Nicolson, 1984.

Harris, Robert. *The Making of Neil Kinnock.* London, Faber and Faber, 1984.

Jones, Eileen. *Neil Kinnock.* London, Hale, 1994.

Kinnock, Neil. *Thorns and Roses: Neil Kinnock, Speeches, 1983–1991.* London: Hutchinson, 1992.

Stephen M. Cullen

Kiriyenko, Sergey N. (1962–)

Russian prime minister, March 23 to August 23, 1998. Sergey Kiriyenko, son of a Jewish father and Ukrainian mother, was born in Sukhumi in the Abkhazian region of Georgia on July 26, 1962. The family moved to Nizhny Novgorod (at the time, Gorky). He studied shipbuilding at the Gorky Institute of Water Transport Engineering then worked as a foreman in a shipyard. From 1990 to 1992 he was an officer in the local branch of the Komsomol, the Communist youth organization.

He took advantage of the collapse of the USSR and the introduction of a market economy to work as a senior manager for several large concerns. He served as the CEO of the Garantiya Bank, a new private bank in Nizhnii Nougorod, and as president of Norsi-oil, a company also based in that city. He also developed close relations with Boris Nemtsov, the reformist governor of the Nizhny Novgorod region. When Nemtsov was named first deputy prime minister in March 1997, Kiriyenko followed him into the government, first as first deputy of the ministry of energy, then in November as minister of fuel and energy.

Kiriyenko, a supporter of the market economy, was appointed prime minister by Russian President Boris Yeltsin on March 23, 1998, to replace Viktor Chernomyrdin. His departure was as dramatic as his appointment. Yeltsin again changed course. Under great political pressure from the Duma (the Russian Parliament) because of the increasingly disastrous state of the Russian economy, he attempted to make Kiriyenko, the scapegoat. Though the problems clearly predated Kiriyenko, he was nevertheless fired on August 23.

Bernard Cook

Kitovani, Tengiz Kalistratovich (1938–)

Georgian politician. Tengiz Kitovani was born in Tbilisi, Georgia, on June 9, 1938. After graduating from the Tbilisi Arts Academy, Kitovani taught at a boarding school in the town of Tetri-Tskaro, and then became a main painter in an advertising bureau.

His political career began in the early 1990s when he became an adviser to Eduard Shevardnadze, the minister for foreign affairs of the USSR and after 1992 the president of post-Soviet Georgia. For many Georgians it was surprising when Kitovani, an artist known as a member of the so-called creative circles, in 1992 became the commander of the National Guard of the Republic of Georgia, a member of the presidium of the State Council, and deputy prime minister. In May 1992 he was appointed the minister of defense of Georgia.

Nickolaj Sannikov
Valery V. Sokolov

Klarsfeld, Beate (1939–)

Since the late 1960s, Beate Klarsfeld and her husband have worked to bring Nazi war criminals to justice. Beate

Kunzel was born in Berlin on February 13, 1939. A Lutheran, she married Serge Klarsfeld, a French Jew whose father had been exterminated at Auschwitz.

Klarsfeld's first target was Kurt Georg Kiesinger, chancellor of West Germany and a former member of the Nazi Party. In April 1968 she shouted "Nazi, Nazi" at Kiesinger from the visitors' gallery of the Bundestag, and on November 7, 1968, she slapped his face at a Christian Democratic Party meeting.

Klarsfeld and her husband located former Lyon, France, Gestapo Chief Klaus Barbie in Bolivia in 1971, and he was extradited to France in 1983. In 1980, a Cologne court found Kurt Lischka, Herbert Hagen, and Ernst Heinrichsohn, three former SS members identified by the Klarsfelds, guilty of complicity in the deportation of approximately fifty thousand Jews from occupied France.

In 1984, Klarsfeld organized demonstrations in Chile against Walter Rauff, inventor of the mobile gas van used in World War II by the Germans on the eastern front. She traveled to Damascus in 1991 to publicize Syria's harboring of Alois Brunner. Brunner was one of the principal subordinates of Adolf Eichmann, who organized the round-up and transportation of Jews to the death camps in German-occupied Poland. For these efforts Klarsfeld was arrested, briefly imprisoned, and expelled from Chile and Syria, without achieving her primary objectives.

BIBLIOGRAPHY

Hellman Peter. "Nazi-Hunting Is Their Life." *New York Times Magazine.* November 4, 1979, pp. 34–37.

———. "Stalking the Last Nazi." *The New York Times Magazine.* January 13, 1992, pp. 28–33.

Klarsfeld, Beate. *Wherever They May Be.* New York: Vanguard Press, 1975.

Sheldon Spear

Klaus, Václav (1941–)

Czech politician and first prime minister of the independent Czech Republic. Educated at the Prague School of Economics and Cornell University in the United States, Václav Klaus worked at the Czechoslovak Academy of Sciences Economic Institute during the 1960s, but was purged in 1970 after the Prague Spring and the Soviet-led Warsaw Pact invasion of Czechoslovakia in 1968. Employed by the Czechoslovak State Bank in a low-level position from 1970–88, he briefly returned to the Academy's Forecasting Institute before becoming politically active as a founder in November 1989 of Civic Forum, a movement representing all of the democratic forces in Czech Republic of Czechoslovakia. Following the Velvet Revolution at the end of the same year, which ended Communist rule in Czechoslovakia, Klaus became finance minister in the new federal government inaugurated in December 1989. Reappointed to this key position after federal parliamentary elections in June 1990, he vacated his leadership of Civil Forum and became chairman of the conservative Civic Democratic Party (CDP) after the movement from which it emerged split in 1991. In late 1991 he became a deputy federal premier but declined the federal premiership once it became clear that the Czechoslovak state would be dissolved by the end of 1992. In July of that year, therefore, he became premier of the Czech Republic, leading a coalition government dominated by his CDP. He remained in this position after the formal dissolution of Czechoslovakia into the Czech Republic and Slovakia on January 1, 1993. Although this divorce between the two parts of the country was amicable on the whole, Klaus was criticized in some quarters as being overly hasty in his rejection of the former federation. This charge was also leveled against his Slovak counterpart, Vladimir Mečiar. A proponent of hard-line right-wing economic policies and an extremely abrasive politician, Klaus made many enemies and often needlessly alienated people. In particular, he had generally poor relations throughout the 1990s with his former Civic Forum colleague Václav Havel, who served as the president of both Czechoslovakia and then the Czech Republic. Another bitter political adversary was another former friend, Miloš Zeman, leader of the Czech Social Democratic Party (SDP). At the popular level, however, Klaus's political dominance of Czech politics was assured as long as his seemingly successful management of the post-Communist Czech economy continued to yield results in terms of higher living standards. Although an undoubted success when compared with other former Communist economies undergoing transition to the market, the Czech economic miracle of the 1990s was to prove illusory in the longer term. By 1996 the Czech Republic's economic performance began to falter, resulting in a fall in popular support for Klaus's CDP at the time of parliamentary elections in May–June 1996. Although reappointed as premier of a minority coalition government after this poll, Klaus was thereafter a lame duck leader increasingly at odds with his own party and Havel. With the further worsening of the Czech economy in 1996–97, he was subsequently dismissed by Havel but stayed on as a caretaker premier pending new parliamentary elections in 1998.

BIBLIOGRAPHY

Klaus, Vaclav. *Renaissance: the Rebirth of Liberty in the Heart of Europe.* Washington, D.C.: Cato Institute, 1997.

Rothschild, Joseph, and Nancy M. Wingfield. *Return to Diversity: A Political History of East Central Europe since World War II.* 3rd ed. New York: Oxford University, 2000.

Marko Milivojevic

SEE ALSO Havel, Václav

Klestil, Thomas (1932–)

Austrian president. Although not the prototype of a partisan politician, Thomas Klestil is responsible for moderating the steady decline of the Austria's Conservative People's Party (ÖVP) in the beginning of the 1990s and leading it back to its traditional role as the stronghold of Christian social conservative Austria.

Klestil was born in a typical proletarian Viennese district, the youngest of five children. Overcoming the poverty that characterized his childhood became the driving force behind his steady rise in education and politics. He pursued an education in business economics at the University of Vienna, from which he graduated in 1957.

Klestil immediately joined the Department for Economic Coordination of the Austrian Federal Chancellery. That position was followed by three years on the staff of the Austrian Mission to the Organization for Economic Cooperation and Development (OECD) in Paris. His diplomatic career was continued by a four-year post at the Austrian Embassy in Washington, D.C., until 1966. He then moved back to Austria to become the private secretary of Josef Klaus, who had become chancellor of the Conservatives' one-party government.

Klestil returned to diplomacy as the first Austrian consul general in Los Angeles, where he established close ties with former Austrians such as oil tycoon Arthur Spitzer and hotelier George White, as well as political advisers of Ronald Reagan, who was at the time governor of California. These contacts became indispensable during his time as Austrian ambassador to the United States (1982–87).

The mid-1970s saw Klestil charged with organizing the establishment of the Vienna International Center as the third U.N. location, a project that Bruno Kreisky, the Socialist chancellor of Austria from 1970 to 1983, had designed as a political shield for neutral Austria in the Cold War era. As a consequence of his successful completion of that project, Klestil was appointed Austria's permanent representative to the United Nations with ambassadorial rank in 1978.

In 1987 he was recalled to Vienna to become secretary general for foreign affairs. The four-year term of his presidential predecessor, Kurt Waldheim, had left Austria widely isolated in the international arena because of revelations about Waldheim's wartime activities in association with the Nazis, and the ÖVP searching for a candidate when Waldheim declared that he would not run for office again. Erhard Busek, who just had become leader of the ÖVP and was convinced of the capabilities of the eloquent and ambitious diplomat, presented Klestil as a nonpartisan presidential candidate.

In the presidential election of 1992 Klestil received 57 percent of the second-round vote, the highest number of votes ever won by a federal president in an election for a first-term of office. Especially during his first two years of office, he kept his promise and demanded more effective participation of the president in Austria's negotiations for accession to the European Union. At an early stage in developing discussions, he questioned Austria's neutrality status and called for association with NATO.

During his 1998 presidential reelection campaign, Klestil's refusal to participate with other candidates in a TV discussion, earned him criticism for being conceited. Nevertheless, he overwhelmingly won the election in the first ballot with 65 percent. The advantage of incumbency coupled with the fact that the Social Democrats did not field a candidate of their own—because no incumbent president had ever been defeated in Austria and because they wished for a decisive defeat of the right-wing Freedom Party candidate, Jorg Haider—contributed decisively to his electoral success.

BIBLIOGRAPHY

Klestil, Thomas. *Themen meines Lebens: Österreich auf dem Weg ins nächste Jahrtausend.* Graz: Styria, 1997.

Riedl, Joachim. *Thomas Klestil: Macht braucht Kontrolle.* Vienna: Ed. S-Print, 1993.

Stefan Mayer

SEE ALSO Busek, Erhard; Haider, Jörg; Kreisky, Bruno; Waldheim, Kurt

Klima, Viktor (1947–)

Austrian Social Democrat politician, Klima served as chancellor from January 1997 to February 2000. Viktor Klima was born in Vienna in 1947 into a socialist family. He studied business and computer science at the Vienna Technical University and the University of Vienna.

After graduation, Klima worked for the Institute for Automation and Business Consultation before joining the Austrian Mineral Oil Administration (ÖMV), a state-owned oil corporation, in 1969. Klima rose from a staff position in the managing director's office to become the head of the ÖMV personnel office in 1985. Klima joined the ÖMV board of governors in 1990. He also served as chairman of the committee on labor legislation of the Petroleum Industry Federation and the Working Committee on Public Nonprofit-making Enterprises in the federal economics ministry.

Klima has been involved in the Social Democratic Party of Austria (SPÖ) for most of his life. He worked on party campaigns during his youth and officially joined the party in 1966. During his time at university he was involved in several SPÖ youth organizations. In April 1992, Klima entered government service when Chancellor Franz Vranitzky appointed him the federal minister for public industry and transportation. Klima remained in this post until January 1996, when he was named the finance minister in a reshuffled Vranitzky cabinet. After Vranitzky resigned unexpectedly, Klima assumed the chancellorship on January 28, 1997, and governed as head of a red-black (socialist-conservative) coalition with the People's Party.

Klima's hopes of retaining power after the October 1999 parliamentary election were short-lived. Although his SPÖ received the largest share of votes, Klima's coalition partners, the People's Party, did poorly. His attempt to rule as head of minority red-black coalition failed in early February 2000, and Klima refused to form a coalition government with Jörg Haider's nationalist Freedom Party. In turn, President Thomas Klestil announced the formation of a blue-black (nationalist-conservative) coalition between Haider's Freedom Party and the People's Party, with People's Party leader Wolfgang Schüssel as the new Austrian chancellor.

Todd Alan Good

SEE ALSO Haider, Jörg; Vranitzky, Franz

Koestler, Arthur (1905–83)

Novelist, political activist, and social philosopher. A Communist in the 1930s, Koestler became famous after World War II as an anti-Communist who exposed the inner workings of totalitarianism in his influential novel, *Darkness at Noon.*

Born in Budapest and educated in Vienna, Koestler moved to Berlin in 1929, where he worked briefly as a science correspondent. Horrified by fascism and the rise of Hitler, he secretly joined the Communist Party in 1931. After spending a year and a half in the Soviet Union, Koestler settled in Paris, where he spent most of the 1930s working for the Soviet Union's underground propaganda apparatus. When the Spanish Civil War broke out, he traveled to Spain as a newspaper correspondent. Captured by Franco's forces and sentenced to death, he was released only after an extended international campaign spearheaded by the British. His months in a Spanish prison are described in his memoir, *Dialogue with Death* (1937).

In 1938 Koestler resigned from the Communist Party, denouncing in a secret letter the constant fear and ideological cynicism engendered by the vicious cycle of purges and show trials that had ravaged the Communist International since the mid-1930s. Stalinism, Koestler argued, was grounded in the belief that the ends justified any means, and therefore lacked any system of ethics or morality. These convictions led Koestler to publish one of the greatest antiauthoritarian novels of the twentieth century—*Darkness at Noon* (1940). The novel describes the imprisonment and death of an old Bolshevik, Rubashov, a character loosely based on Nikolay Bukharin, one of the original members of Lenin's Politburo who was eventually arrested, tried, and executed by Stalin in 1938. The novel derives much of its power from its psychological portrait of Rubashov, a man who acquiesces in his own destruction by a totalitarian system that demands blind obedience and total conformity.

Darkness at Noon attracted little attention when it was first published in England, where Koestler made his home after 1940. Not until after World War II, with the first stirrings of the Cold War, did the novel became famous as a revelation of the evils of Stalinism. The book, along with a collection of essays entitled *The Yogi and the Commissar* (1945), was hailed by many Europeans and Americans as a demystification of the pernicious wartime view of Stalin as a progressive-minded ally. In the decade after the war Koestler's novels, reportage, autobiographical works, and political and cultural writings established him as one of the world's most influential anti-Communist writers.

After 1955 Koestler declared that his literary-political career was over and turned to the study of the history and philosophy of science. Most notable among his publications in this field are *The Sleepwalkers* (1959), *The Act of Creation* (1964), and *The Ghost in the Machine* (1967). In the 1970s he became preoccupied with extrasensory perception and parapsychology. He committed suicide in 1983.

BIBLIOGRAPHY

Hamilton, Iain. *Koestler: A Biography.* London: Sechler and Warburg, 1982.

Koestler, Arthur. *Arrow in the Blue: An Autobiography.* 2 Vols. New York: Macmillan, 1952–54.

Scammel, Michael. "Arthur Koestler Resigns." *New Republic* (May 4, 1998): 27–33.

Barbara Keys

SEE ALSO Congress for Cultural Freedom

Kohl, Helmut (1930–)

The Federal Republic of Germany's sixth chancellor, known as the "chancellor of unity" for his role in German reunification. Born on April 3, 1930, in Ludwigshafen, Helmut Kohl joined the Christian Democratic Union (CDU) in late 1946. Before becoming chancellor in 1982, Kohl served as minister-president of the state of Rhineland-Pfalz.

After completing his *Abitur* in 1950 Kohl studied law at the University of Frankfurt am Main. His interest in history, however, won out. Kohl transferred to Heidelberg, where he earned a doctorate in 1958 through an analysis of the revival of political parties in Germany after 1945, focusing on events in the Pfalz.

Helmut Kohl, the longest-serving chancellor of the Federal Republic of Germany (1982-1998) and one of the principle architects of German reunification in 1990. *Illustration courtesy of German Information Center.*

Kohl first held political office in 1947 as chair of the junior organization of the CDU, the Young Union, in the Rhineland-Pfalz town of Friesenheim. In 1953 he was appointed to the Executive Council of the Pfalz's CDU and served as chair from 1955 to 1966. In 1957 Kohl led the CDU with 41.7 percent of the vote to the best electoral results it had yet achieved in the working-class-dominated Ludwigshafen region. From 1959 to 1969 Kohl was adviser to the chemical industry in Ludwigshafen, and after winning a seat on the Ludwighafen's city council, chaired the CDU group (*Fraktion*) on the council from 1960 to 1967.

In 1959 Kohl was elected to the state parliament in Rhineland-Pfalz, where he eventually led the CDU caucus. As CDU party chairperson in Rhineland-Pfalz (1966–73), Kohl maneuvered himself into position to become minister-president. After the resignation of Minister-President Peter Altmeier in May 1969, Kohl became the logical successor. Under his leadership the CDU achieved an absolute majority in the March 1971 state elections. As minister-president (1969–76) Kohl pursued a policy of modernizing Rhineland-Pfalz. He reformed the educational system, reduced the size of the state administration and the number of counties, and improved centralized planning within the state. State elections in 1975 confirmed popular support for Kohl's policies with 53.9 percent of the vote going to the CDU.

Paralleling his rise in state politics, Kohl's image as a national leader and alternative to Rainer Barzel, the chairman of the CDU 1971–73, rose. By 1964 Kohl had obtained a seat on the CDU's federal committee (Bundesvorstand) and from 1969–73 served as vice chair of the federal committee of the CDU. In 1969 the CDU and its Bavarian sister party, the Christian Social Union (CSU), moved into the ranks of the political opposition. And in 1972 the CDU suffered its worst showing at the polls since 1949, with only 44.9 percent of the vote. In view of declining electoral support and Barzel's resistance to Chancellor Willy Brandt's popular *Ostpolitik,* Kohl succeeded Barzel as the party's head in June 1973. In 1976, chairing the Bundestag's CDU/CSU caucus and as the CDU/CSU chancellor candidate, Kohl led the party to improved electoral returns on October 3, 1976. The CDU took 48.6 percent of the vote and became the largest party within the Bundestag.

This improvement inspired further internal reforms for the CDU. Assisted by Richard von Weizsäcker, deputy chairman of the CDU/CSU parliamentary caucus (1973–

79) and the vice president of the Bundestag (1979–81), and Kurt Biedenkopf, general secretary of the CDU (1973–87), Kohl helped expand the party's base. As such, the CDU strove to embrace voters within the middle of the political spectrum, including center-left and center-right elements. Three fundamental principles would guide the party: linking productivity with social justice, competition with social solidarity, and individual responsibility with social security. In practical terms, the CDU accepted from the center-left the social welfare state created during the era of social democracy (1969–82), the foreign policy premises of *Ostpolitik,* and the addressing of ecological issues. From the center-right the CDU talked in terms of family and a general Christian morality. These ideas and others were imbedded in the party platform during the party convention in Ludwigshafen in October 1978.

Political currents ebbed, however, toward the center-right, which raised Kohl's political rival and CSU head, Franz-Josef Strauss, into the position of CDU/CSU chancellor candidate in 1980. Division within the CDU/CSU camp and the reservations of many toward Strauss pushed electoral support down to 44.5 percent of the popular vote. However, political polls in 1982 suggested that Kohl's conservative CDU/CSU might have an absolute majority in the Bundestag after the 1983 elections. Presented with the possibility of becoming part of the political opposition, the Free Democratic Party opted to break with their Social Democratic coalition partner and support Kohl as West Germany's new chancellor, thus creating a coalition of the middle. Using the instrument of a constructive vote of no-confidence, Kohl propelled himself forward as Helmut Schmidt's successor and succeeded him as chancellor in October 1982.

Chancellor Kohl led the CDU/CSU into federal elections in 1983, in which the CDU/CSU had its best showing since 1957; the *Wende* (turn) had begun. Kohl's conservative-liberal coalition achieved only limited improvements in the economic situation it inherited. Confronted with a growing budget deficit, spending had to be brought under control. Changes in tax policy and the termination of various government programs failed to stimulate significant economic growth or reduce unemployment. On the other hand, Germany returned to its status as the world's number-one exporting nation. Internationally, Kohl supported European integration, a single European currency, a strong NATO, a German seat on the United Nations Security Council, the placement of Pershing and Cruise missiles in Germany in response to Soviet SS-20s, and continued good relations with France. Public response to the conservative-liberal policies was passively supportive. Voter turnout for the 1987 federal elections was relatively low while support for the CDU/CSU dipped to 44.3 percent. By 1989 polls projected that the CDU/CSU might receive less than 40 percent of the vote in the next round.

Kohl proved his political instincts by seizing the chance for reunification after East Germany's collapse in late 1989. In November 1989 Kohl outlined his Ten Points leading to reunification. As communism fell in East Germany and East Germans voted for reunification in March 1990, Kohl's popularity in West Germany experienced a dramatic turnaround. By May 1990 popular support for Kohl had fallen to roughly 39 percent, versus 50 percent for his challenger, Oskar Lafontaine. Shortly before elections that fall, however, Kohl's popularity rose to 56 percent versus 37 percent for his rival.

Several factors account for the shift—the July 1990 currency reform, the unity treaty, and his opponent's initial rejection of German reunification. In addition, by supporting the Maastricht treaty and combating rising xenophobia, Kohl sought to anchor reunified Germany in a unified Europe. He also acknowledged that a reunified Germany would have to assume greater responsibilities on the international stage. In 1995 Kohl sent German military units, as part of a larger contingent of NATO forces, into Bosnia to assist in implementing the Bosnian peace plan, and became the first German chancellor since World War II to send German military units into a combat situation.

In the September 27, 1998, Bundestag election, Kohl and the Christian Democrats went down to defeat, rejected by voters for a number of reasons. Some had tired of his leadership. Others were disaffected by continuing high levels of unemployment, especially in the east. Others reacted against the long and costly process of integrating the two parts of the country. The Christian Democrats won 28.4 percent of the vote and their Christian Social Union allies garnered 6.7 percent. The Social Democrats, led by Gerhard Schröder, won 40.9 percent and formed a coalition with the Greens, who won 6.7 percent of the vote. Kohl, taking responsibility for the defeat, gave up the chairmanship of the CDU, which he had held since 1973. He recommended Wolfgang Schäuble, who led the CDU-CSU parliamentary group, as his successor. Kohl retained the Bundestag seat that he won in the Rhineland-Palatinate.

BIBLIOGRAPHY

Clay, Clemens. *Helmut Kohl.* Durham, N.C.: Duke University Press, 1996.

Maser, Werner. *Helmut Kohl: Der deutsche Kanzler.* Frankfurt am Main: Ullstein, 1990.

Muenchler, Günter. *Helmut Kohl: Chancellor of German Unity, a Biography.* Bonn: Press and Information Agency of the Federal Government, 1992.

David A. Meier

SEE ALSO Biedenkopf, Kurt; Lafontaine, Oskar; Strauss, Franz Josef

Koivisto, Mauno (1923–)

President of Finland (1982–94). Mauno Henrik Koivisto, born November 25, 1923, was the first socialist president in Finland's history. Before his political career he was deputy director of the Helsinki Workers' Savings Bank (1958–59) and managing director (1959–66).

Although Koivisto was outside the Social Democratic Party (SDP) formal hierarchy, he was carefully prepared for leading political posts. He contributed to the SDP's political planning through different working groups and memoranda and saw that the SDP needed to improve its relations both with Urho Kekkonen, president of Finland, 1956–81, and Finnish Communists. Koivisto entered politics first as minister of finance in Rafael Paasio's government (1966–68) then as prime minister (1968–70). In the latter post he became a potential successor to President Kekkonen. But instead Koivisto left politics except for a stint in 1972 as Minister of Finance, becoming managing director of the Bank of Finland.

In 1979, when Prime Minister Kalevi Sorsa's government resigned, Kekkonen invited Koivisto to become the new prime minister to remove him as a potential successor. In early 1981 Kekkonen sent an open letter to the prime minister setting a deadline by which a bill relating to the taxation of welfare benefits had to be submitted to the Eduskunta (parliament) for decision. Kekkonen insisted that if this was not done the government had to resign. Koivisto consulted with Johannes Virolainen, speaker of the Eduskunta; Koivisto also got the Communists to promise their support in a potential vote confidence. Thus he responded on TV to Kekkonen's demand that his government had the right to continue in office as long as it enjoyed the support of parliament.

This successful challenge to Kekkonen was the final step in making Koivisto the leading figure in Finnish politics. According to a poll, 49 percent selected him as their favorite to succeed to Kekkonen, while the other potential candidates were preferred by just 3 to 8 percent. When Kekkonen went on sick leave, Koivisto's popularity rose to 60. In 1981 Koivisto became acting president, an effective platform for the coming campaign.

In the election Koivisto received 43 percent of the vote and 144 electors out of 300. Because of his exceptionally strong popular support, the Communists (SKDL) announced that they would vote for him in the first round of the electoral college. Consequently, Koivisto was supported by 178 electors (SDP, SKDL, and Rural Party). In the 1988 elections Koivisto received 47.9 percent of the popular vote, necessitating a meeting of the electoral college. But while Koivisto received just 128 electors in the first ballot, he was elected during the second round by the SDP, the SKDL, and the Conservatives.

Koivisto's popularity was rooted in his work at the Bank of Finland, which gave him the basis for realistic assessments of the economic situation and his insistence on fiscal restraint and responsibility in managing the nation's economy. Furthermore, anti-Kekkonen and antipolitical movements perceived Koivisto favorably not as a politician but an outsider. Koivisto was also Finland's best-known self-made man.

In foreign policy Koivisto followed a low profile and avoided dramatic moves. However, Finnish foreign policy changed almost unnoticeably under his leadership. The Soviet Union lost its central position for Finland, and the country found its true place among other Western nations. His major contribution appears in the development of Finnish parliamentarism. He attempted to dismantle excessive presidential power and raise the Eduskunta and the Council of State, especially the prime ministership, to the positions they enjoy in modern parliamentary systems. Koivisto was ready to make fundamental changes and to extend parlamentarism to foreign policy, as well. However, the system has been slow to change and a return to more presidential power occurred after the end of Koivisto's second term in 1994.

BIBLIOGRAPHY

Häikiö, Martti, and Pertti Pesonen. *President Koivisto in Finnish Politics.* Helsinki: Ministry of Foreign Affairs, 1992.

Koivisto, Mauno. *Foreign Policy Standpoints, 1982–92.* Nuffield: Aidan Ellis, U.K. 1992.

Koivisto, Mauno, and Pertti Paasio. *Finland in a Changing Europe: Major Speeches.* Helsinki: Ministry of Foreign Affairs, 1990.

Solem, Erik. *The Nordic Council and Scandinavian Integration.* New York: Praeger, 1977.

Vilho Harle

SEE ALSO Ahtisaari, Martti; Kekkonen, Urho

Kok, Willem (1938–)

Dutch prime minister. Willem Kok, son of a carpenter, was born in Bergambacht on September 29, 1938. He attended the Nijenrode Business School, in Nijenrode. He worked for the Netherlands Federation of Trade Unions (NVV) for twenty years, an experience that provided him not only with a livelihood but also a path to political power. He was appointed secretary of the NVV in 1969 and deputy chairman in 1972. Kok served as chairman of the NVV from 1973 until 1985, when it amalgamated with the Dutch Federation of Catholic Trade Unions. From 1979 until 1982 Kok was simultaneously chairman of the European Trade Union Confederation.

In 1986 Kok launched his political career. Within two months, the moderate, pragmatic Kok had displaced the autocratic and ideological Joop den Uyl as leader of the Labor Party (PvdA). The same year Kok was elected to the lower house of parliament. When the Labor Party joined the Christian Democrats to form a governing coalition in November 1989, Kok became deputy prime minister and finance minister. The sweeping reforms of the welfare system carried out by the government alienated many Labor voters and party stalwarts. Although the PvdA dropped from 49 to 37 seats in the 1994 election, the PvdA was the largest party and Kok was asked to form a government. He succeeded in forming a left-liberal coalition with the party known as the Democrats 66 and the Liberals and was appointed prime minister on August 22, 1994.

BIBLIOGRAPHY

Thompson, Wayne C. *Western Europe 1995.* Harpers Ferry, W.V.: Stryker-Post Publications, 1995.

Bernard Cook

Kolakowski, Leszek (1927–)

Polish philosopher and writer. Leszek Kolakowski, a young Marxist, joined the Communist Party in 1945. He studied philosophy at Lodz University, then taught at Warsaw University, where in 1959 he became chairman of the Faculty of History of Contemporary Philosophy. He also worked in the Polish United Workers (Communist) Party's Institute of Social Sciences from 1953 to 1955, and later in the Institute of Philosophy and Sociology at the Polish Academy of Sciences.

After 1956 Kolakowski became one of the most influential anti-Stalinist activists and reformists. In 1966, as a result of his criticism of the government of Władysław Gomułka he was expelled from the party. In 1968, along with a number of other professors, he was accused of revisionism, antisocialist activity, and supporting student unrest. After his dismissal from Warsaw University, he left Poland and went to McGill University in Montreal; the following year he moved to the University of California at Berkeley. In 1970 he became senior research fellow at All Souls College, Oxford. From 1968 to the early 1980s none of Kolakowski's books were published in Poland; even quoting his works was forbidden.

Kolakowski's studies deal with the history of philosophy: *Positivist Philosophy: From Hume to the Vienna Circle* (1966, trans. 1968), *Husserl and the Search for Certitude* (1975), *Bergson* (1985); the philosophy of culture: *The Presence of Myth* (1972, trans. 1989), *Modernity on Endless Trial* (1990); and the philosophy of religion: *Religion. If there is no God . . . on God, the Devil, Sin and Other Worries of the So-called Philosophy of Religion* (1981), *Metaphysical Horror* (1988), *God Owes Us Nothing: A Brief Remark on Pascal's Religion and on the Spirit of Jansenism* (1994). He also wrote a monumental handbook on the history of Marxism: *Main Currents of Marxism: Its Rise, Growth and Dissolution* (1976–78); and brilliant and humorous philosophical stories: *Tales from the Kingdom of Lailonia* (1963, trans. 1972) and *The Key to Heaven* (1964, trans. 1989).

BIBLIOGRAPHY

Beiner, Ronald. "Thin Ice." *History of the Human Sciences* 5 (1992): 65–70.

Flis, Mariola. *Leszek Kolakowski—teoretyk kultury europejskiej.* (*Leszek Kolakowski—A Theorist of European Culture*). Kraków: Universitas, 1994.

Kloczkowski, Jan Andrzej. *Wiecej niz mit: Leszka Kolakowskiego spory o religie* (*More Than Myth: Leszek Kolakowski's Disputes on Religion*). Kraków: Znak, 1994.

Krzysztóf Olechnicki

Konrad, György (1933–)

Hungarian writer. György Konrad was born on April 2, 1933, in Debrecen, Hungary. He graduated from Eötvös Loránd University in Budapest in 1956, but because of his participation in the Hungarian Revolution of the same year, he could not get a job until 1959. Then he was employed as a social worker and a sociologist. In 1973 he became a freelance writer. His works were not published in Hungary from the early 1970s until 1988 because of his strong criticism of the Communist regime. He taught literature in the United States at Colorado College in 1987–88 and served as president of PEN, an international organization of writers that seeks to promote freedom of expression, in 1990–93. He returned to Hungary in 1989 as Communism was collapsing and joined the Alliance of Free Democrats, an opposition group founded in the Communist era, and is still a leading figure in the party. Konrad taught literature in the United States at Colorado College in 1987–88 and was elected president of PEN in 1990–93. He joined the Alliance of Free Democrats in 1989 and is still a leading member of the party.

Konrad is a prolific writer. His first novel, *The Visitor,* appeared in 1969, and since then he has published some ten novels, volumes of essays, and a study with Ivan Szelanyi, *The Intellectuals' Road to Class Power* (1987). Konrad has promoted liberal values both in his works and in his activities as a politician.

Tamás Magyarics

Konwicki, Tadeusz (1926–)

Polish novelist, screenwriter, and director. Tadeusz Konwicki was born in Nowa Wilekja near Vilnius, in present-day Lithuania. In 1944 and 1945 he fought against the Germans in a partisan unit of the Polish Home Army. Later he left the Vilnius region and studied the Polish language and literature in Kraków. After 1947 he lived in Warsaw. His first novel, *Rojsty,* written in 1948 but, for political reasons, published only in 1956, was a romantic assessment of his partisan experience. From 1950 to 1954 he wrote in the socialist realist style as imposed by Communist-bloc governments. After 1956 he used his own biographic experiences, concentrating on the memories of his Arcadian childhood in the charming Vilnius valley, experiences of partisan warfare, his break with communism, and the sad reality of existence in postwar Poland. He also wrote about the 1863 Polish uprising, seeking in it the roots of Polish national-cultural identity. Konwicki gave symbolic meanings to the well-known social-historical reality he described. He contrasted the alluring past with the landscape of contemporary Warsaw, thus creating a mockingly grotesque vision of Communist reality and a society immersed in lethargy. Konwicki's novels have been translated into many languages. Some of the better known are *Dziura w niebie* (*Hole in Heaven,* 1959), *Sennik wspolczesny* (*A Dreambook for Our Time,* 1963), *Wniebowstapienie* (*Ascension,* 1967), *Zwierzoczlekoupior* (*The Anthropos-Specter-Beast,* 1969), *Kompeks polski* (*The Polish Complex,* 1977), and *Mala apokalipsa* (*A Minor Apocalypse,* 1979). The latter two were originally published by the underground publishing house NOWA. In his quasi memoirs, *Kalendarz i klepsydra* (*Calendar and Hour-glass,* 1976) and *Wschody i zachody ksiezyca* (*Moonrise, Moonset,* 1982), he played literary games with the reader.

In his films Konwicki looked into the inner lives of his protagonists, which are marked by suffering and unrest. He directed the films *Ostatni dzien lata* (*The Last Day of Summer,* 1957), *Zaduszki* (*All Souls' Day,* 1961), *Salto* (*The Somersault,* 1965), and *Jak daleko stad, jak blisko* (*How far from Here, How Near,* 1971).

BIBLIOGRAPHY

Czaplinski, Przemyslaw. *Tadeusz Konwicki.* Poznan: Rebis, 1994.

Lubelski, Tadeusz. *Poetyka powiesci i filmow Tadeusza Konwickiego: na podstawie analizy utworow z lat 1947–1965.* (*Poetics of Taduesz Konwicki's Novels and Films: Analysis of his works, 1947–1965*) Wrocław: Wydawn Uniwersytetu, Wrocławskiego, 1984.

Matuszewski, Ryszard. *Literatura polska 1939–1991.* Warsaw: WSiP, 1992.

Szporer, Michael. "Beyond Aesthetics of Censorship: Tadeusz Konwicki's Ordinary Politicking." *Modern Fiction Studies* 32 no. 1 (1986):89–96.

Wegner, Jacek. *Konwicki.* Warsaw: Agence des Auteurs, 1973.

Jerzy Z. Maciejewski

Korean War and Europe

The war that began on June 25, 1950, with North Korea's invasion of South Korea brought about a major and rapid strengthening of NATO as well as West German rearmament. While these changes in the security system of Western Europe had been under discussion in Washington and the European capitals since the summer of 1949, and might have occurred anyway at a later date, they were nonetheless greatly accelerated by the North Korean attack.

When the Korean War began, Europeans could not be certain that the aggression was not part of a larger plan to expand Communist power around the world. In light of the glaring imbalance between Soviet and Western forces on the European continent, all the Western allies, but especially the United States, quickly became convinced of the need to strengthen European defenses. The alternative might be increased European neutralism in the face of overwhelming Soviet power, especially in a Germany resenting its division. Fewer than three months into the war, therefore, U.S. President Harry Truman asked Congress for $4 billion in foreign military assistance, about 80 percent of which was to go to NATO. At a NATO meeting in September 1950, U.S. Secretary of State Dean Acheson argued for German rearmament while offering new U.S. commitments to the defense of Europe.

Although willing to increase their defense commitment, many Europeans, particularly the French, were adverse to the idea of German rearmament. However, Paris realized that under the circumstances it would not be able to block a decision, nor would antagonizing Washington be in the long-term interest of France or Europe. Therefore, the French government took the initiative and in October 1950 proposed the creation of a European army, the Pleven Plan for a European Defense Community (EDC), of which German forces would be a part.

The next year brought agreement on the EDC, as well as its alignment with separate U.S. plans for the strengthening of NATO, and the treaty was signed in May 1952. Ratification, owing to French second thoughts, eluded the Europeans, but a West German contribution to their defense did not. The alternative, German membership in NATO, was made official in May 1955.

BIBLIOGRAPHY

Havenaar, Ronald. *Van Koude Oorlog naar nieuwe chaos, 1939–1993.* Amsterdam: van Oorschot, 1993.

Leffler, Melvyn P. *A Preponderance of Power: National Security, the Truman Administration, and the Cold War.* Stanford, Calif.: Stanford University Press, 1992.

Williams, William J., ed. *A Revolutionary War: Korea and the Transformation of the Postwar World.* Chicago: Imprint, 1993.

Ruud van Dijk

SEE ALSO European Defense Community; North Atlantic Treaty Organization

Kornai, János (1928–)

Hungarian economist. János Kornai started his career as an editor of the Communist daily *Szabad Nep* in 1947, then worked for the Hungarian Academy of Sciences in various capacities in the late 1950s and early 1960s. After 1964 he was invited as a guest professor to universities in Europe and the United States, and became a full professor at Harvard University. He was elected an associate member of the Hungarian Academy of Sciences in 1976 and became a full member in 1982. Kornai was also elected a member of the American, British, Finnish, and Swedish academies. In 1983 he received the Humboldt Award, an award established in 1953 by West Germany out of gratitude for the Marshall Plan and granted by senior German academies to senior researchers at US universities.

Kornai has written over twenty books and a great number of studies. His major fields of interests are the mathematical planning of investments and economic structures, questions of economic development, the description of the socialist economy, and the problems of the economic transformation in the former socialist countries. His major publications in English include *Growth, Shortage, and Efficiency: A Macrodynamic Model of the Socialist Economy* (1982); *Contradictions and Dilemmas* (1986); *The Road to Free Economy: Shifting from a Socialist System, The Example of Hungary* (1990); and *Overcentralization in Economic Administration: A Historical Analysis Based on Experience in Hungarian Light Industry* (1994).

BIBLIOGRAPHY

Kornai, Janos. *Highway and Byways: Studies on Reform and Post-communist Transition.* Cambridge, Mass.: MIT Press, 1995.

———. *Struggle and Hope: Essays on Stabilization and Reform in a Post-socialist Economy.* Northampton, Mass.: E. Elgar, 1997.

Tamás Magyarics

Korzhakov, Aleksandr (1951–)

Chief of presidential security in Russia (1991–96). Aleksandr Korzhakov was born in Moscow in 1951. He worked as an auto mechanic and fought in the war in Afghanistan. After his military service, he joined the security service division of the KGB (Department 9 of the State Security Committee, or secret police). He earned a correspondence law degree from the All Union Institute of Law. In 1985 he was appointed bodyguard to Boris Yeltsin, when Mikhail Gorbachev named Yeltsin Communist Party boss. When Gorbachev ousted Yeltsin from the Politburo for criticizing his leadership, Korzhakov resigned from the KGB to continue to serve as Yeltsin's bodyguard. Yeltsin promoted him to the rank of major general in 1992 and lieutenant general in 1995. In 1993, Korzhakov, who had become a close adviser to Yeltsin, urged the storming of the Russian parliament building (the White House) to crush the rebellion by Yeltsin's parliamentary opponents led by Ruslan Khasbulatov and Aleksander Rutskoi. Yeltsin then made Korzhakov's four thousand-member security force independent of the ministry of interior and answerable solely to Korzhakov.

Korzhakov was taken to task by critics who accused him of interfering in policy matters and exercising an unhealthy and undue influence over Yeltsin. He was accused of playing an important role in the disastrous decision to invade and pursue military action against the breakaway republic of Chechnya in 1994. Yeltsin, in a campaign move in July 1996, dismissed Korzhakov as chief of the presidential security forces. In addition to his other political baggage, Korzhakov had been accused of corruption and of plotting a coup.

Bernard Cook

SEE ALSO Khasbulatov, Ruslan; Rutskoi, Aleksandr; Yeltsin, Boris;

Kosovo

Kosovo (Serbian, Kosovo i Metohija, or Kosmet; Albanian, Kosovë) is situated in the southern part of Serbia. It borders Albania, Macedonia, and Montenegro. In 1991, within its 4,204 square miles (10,887 sq km) of territory, resided 1,954,747 people, of whom 82.2 percent were Albanian, 11 percent Serbs and Montenegrins, 2.9 percent who identified themselves as Muslims, 2.2 percent Gypsies, .6 percent Turks, .4 percent Croats, .2 percent who identified themselves as Yugoslavs, and .5 other. Kosovo is not home to all the predominantly Muslim Albanians of the former Yugoslavia. Others live in Macedonia and Montenegro. Its capital is Pristina, which had 205,093 inhabitants in 1991.

The exacerbation of national antagonisms between Serbs and Albanians is the most severe problem of regional cleavage confronting the third Yugoslav state. Kosovo poses a thorny problem: it represents the historic center of the Serbian people, while its actual population is more than 80 percent Albanian.

The question of Kosovo has been the subject of many historical arguments designed to establish a claim to the territory by legitimizing one people's historic right to the land. For the Albanians, Kosovo is the land of their ancestors, the Illyrians, who have been there for two millennia. The Serbs insist, owing to the historic role of Kosovo in the collective life of the Serbian people, on the inalienability of Kosovo. On the same basis they contest the right of Albanians to self-determination. Kosovo was the heart of medieval Serbia, the heart of Orthodoxy, and the site of the celebrated battle of Kosovo Polje in 1389, which marked the victory of the Ottomans and destroyed the autonomy of the Serbs. There were massive Serbian emigrations from the region in the seventeenth and eighteenth centuries. As a result of the First Balkan War (1912–13), Kosovo was reattached to Serbia. During the Second World War, with the exception of a part of Metohija that was occupied by Bulgaria, Kosovo was annexed by "Greater Albania." Kosovo was organized as an autonomous province of the Yugoslav Federation. It was one of the poorest regions and profited from federal subsidies. Since 1989 Kosovo, reintegrated into Serbia, has lost the prerogatives from which it profited, and has been subjected to the authoritarian politics of Yugoslav leader Slobodan Milošević. The parliament of Kosovo, meeting secretly, proclaimed Kosovo a republic on September 7, 1990. The Republic of Kosovo, although not recognized by the international community, elected a president, Ibrahim Rugova, in May 1992. The parliament of Kosovo consisted of 140 members elected by a vote that combined proportional and majority representation.

A citizen of Kosovo amidst the ruins of her burned home, destroyed in the fighting in 1999. *Illustration courtesy of AFP/Corbis.*

In the early 1980s the economic dissatisfaction of the Albanians of Kosovo produced a wave of nationalism. Students from the University of Pristina played a leading role in riots of March and April 1981. The university was closed by the Yugoslav government on April 2 and there was an effort by the government to clamp down on expressions of Albanian nationalism. In the 1980s there was little sentiment among Albanian Kosovars for joining Albania, which had a repressive regime and even worse economic conditions than existed in Kosovo.

Beginning in 1987 Milošević made use of the resentment of the Serb minority in the province to bolster his political fortunes. His supporters provoked an incident with the local police that he claimed, demonstrated that the Serbs were being persecuted. In November 1988, Kosovo's Albanian Communist leadership, Azem Vllasi and Kaqusha Jashari, were dismissed and replaced with supporters of Milošević. The dismissals provoked a general strike by Albanians. Antiriot police were sent to Kosovo on February 26, 1989, but the Milošević appointees resigned on March 28. Goaded by Milošević, the Yugoslav presidency decreed a state of emergency in Kosovo. When

Albanians demonstrated against increasingly repressive measures, the federal army was deployed in Kosovo. Vllasi was charged with "counterrevolutionary" activity and was arrested. On March 23 the Kosovo parliament was ringed with tanks, and the autonomous status of the province was ended.

Next the Serbian regime attempted to alter the demographic base of the province. The percentage of the Albanian majority had grown steadily since the end of the Second World War because of the emigration of Serbs and the high birthrate of Albanians. Institutional discrimination against Kosovo Albanians was coupled with efforts to encourage them to emigrate. A 1990 law dismissed all Albanian civil servants and teachers. Unemployment became endemic for the Albanians. Serbs, including refugees from the Krajina region of Croatia after 1995, and Montenegrins were settled in the province and given jobs from which Albanians had been expelled and were offered the Albanians' housing as well.

Members of the independent Albanian labor union, BSPK, were subjected to special persecution. Most were fired and their family members denied social and healthcare benefits. In February 1995, 155 labor union members were tried on various charges including "endangering territorial integrity," and most were sentenced to lengthy periods of imprisonment.

Rugova and the Albanian Democratic League of Kosovo (LDK) urged the Albanians of Kosovo to limit themselves to peaceful protests. However, Kosovo and the plight of its majority was ignored in the Dayton-Paris peace accords. The years 1996 and 1997 witnessed the growth of a Kosovo Liberation Army (KLA), which staged numerous armed attacks on Serbian police and civilians and on Albanians accused of collaborating with the Serbs. In a campaign launched in the latter part of 1997, the KLA overwhelmed a number of police stations and captured weapons. Police patrols and checkpoints were attacked and more than fifty Serbian officials and policemen killed. The activity of the KLA, supported by a growing number of LDK leaders, was countered by a Serbian policy of repression. In two weeks of attacks on Albanian villages in late February and March 1998, seventy Albanians, including women and children, were killed. In fighting near the border with Albania on April 23, 1998, an additional twenty-three Albanians were killed.

At the end of May the Serbian army began a major military assault against villages in the southeast of Kosovo, killing as many as two hundred Kosovo Albanians and driving another ten thousand across the border into neighboring Albania. The Serbian assault intensified in July, and by fall it was estimated that 250,000 Albanian Kosovars had been driven from their homes. Some sought refuge in the mountains, but many fled or were pushed into Albania by attacks by the Serbian military and police on Albanian Kosovar villages and towns. NATO, concerned primarily about the possible spread of the conflict, finally reacted to the killing of civilians and this new episode of ethnic cleansing by threatening air strikes. After prolonged and fruitless negotiations with U.S. special envoy Richard C. Holbrooke, Milošević was finally swayed by a credible threat of NATO bombing. On October 13 he agreed to withdraw his forces, allow NATO verification of this, permit two thousand unarmed civilian monitors in Kosovo, and grant partial autonomy to the province. This proved to be merely a tactical retreat, however. His forces launched a new attack in January 1999 against the KLA and Albanian peasant communities. The atrocities committed by the Serbs were aimed at driving the Albanian population from the province. After futile negotiations at Rambovillet, France, NATO, which had once again thought that the threat of bombing would be enough to prevent Milošević from destabilizing the area and, perhaps, provoking a wider war, was forced, for the sake of its credibility, to act.

BIBLIOGRAPHY

Glenny, Misha. "Bosnia II." *New York Times,* December 9, 1997, A21.

———. *The Fall of Yugoslavia: The Third Balkan War.* New York: Penguin, 1993.

Hall, Brian. *The Impossible Country: A Journey Through the Last Days of Yugoslavia.* New York: Penguin, 1994.

Hedges, Chris, "In New Balkan Tinderbox, Ethnic Albanians Rebel against Serbs." *New York Times,* March 2, 1998.

Malcom, Noel. *Kosovo: A Short History.* New York: New York University Press, 1998.

Catherine Lutard
Bernard Cook

SEE ALSO Rugova, Ibrahim; Vllasi, Azem

Kosovo: Ethnic Cleansing and War

Between July and August 1998 Kosovar Albanian rebels, members of the Kosovo Liberation Army (KLA), seized control of 40 percent of the province of Kosovo before being driven into the mountains by a Serb offensive. In September, after attacks by Serb forces on Albanian Kosovar villages and concomitant atrocities, including the massacre of twenty-two Albanians in one central Kosovar village, the United Nations called for an immediate cease-fire and talks between the Yugoslav government and Kosovar representatives. When Serb attacks continued, NATO authorized air strikes in October 1998. At the last moment, after attack planes were under way, Yugoslav leader Slobodan Milošević agreed in talks with U.S. representative Richard C. Holbrooke to withdraw Yugoslav troops, allow Kosovar refugees to return to their homes, and permit two thousand unarmed OSCE (Organization for Security and Cooperation in Europe) monitors to verify compliance. Nevertheless, violence continued. In December the Yugoslav army killed thirty-six rebels and six Serbs were killed in a café in Pec.

On January 15, 1999, Serbian forces executed forty-five Kosovar Albanians outside Racak, and on January 29, Serbian police killed twenty-four Kosovar Albanians in a raid on a reputed KLA hideout. NATO then demanded that the Yugoslav government participate in peace talks or face NATO bombing. Between February 6 and 17 the first round of talks at Rambouillet, France, produced no agreement. The settlement that the Western Allies demanded called for autonomy for the province, which would continue to remain a constituent part of Serbia, and the occupation of Kosovo by twenty-eight thousand NATO troops, who would enforce the agreement. Neither delegation initially agreed to the terms, but after intense pressure the Kosovar Albanians signed the agreement on March 18.

Milošević not only refused to sign but concentrated increasing numbers of troops in Kosovo in violation of the October agreement. As the death toll of Albanians mounted and ethnic cleansing drove increasing numbers of Kosovar Albanians from their villages into Macedonia, Albania, and Montenegro, Holbrooke made one last futile attempt to persuade Milošević to sign. With this failure OSCE observers were withdrawn on March 20 and NATO air attacks began before dawn on March 24. Milošević, whose popularity had significantly declined in Serbia, was able to parlay his resistance to NATO into massive support, and he used the bombing campaign as an opportunity to ethnically cleanse much of Kosovo by the end of April.

Many NATO leaders and planners had erroneously assumed that a few days of bombing would be sufficient to persuade Milošević to accede to NATO demands. However, the initial stance taken by President Clinton that no U.S. ground troops would be involved in the conflict, and the hesitancy of the United States and the other NATO participants to expose their pilots to Serb anti-aircraft defenses by having them attack Serb positions from low attitudes, undercut the effectiveness of the NATO operation. NATO also apparently underestimated the importance of the "Kosovo issue" to Milošević and the Serbs. He had risen to power on this issue and could not relinquish total control over the province without being forced to do so.

After weeks of bombing, which did nothing to prevent the Serbs from driving 850,000 Albanian Kosovars from the province and 500,000 others into the hills, the allies decided to bring the war home to the Serb civilian population by knocking out Serbia's power grid and the urban water systems. The NATO alliance remained intact despite a rising toll of Serb civilian "collateral" damage and open expressions of Russian opposition to the NATO campaign. The Russian government was deeply concerned that Russia not be ignored in this the greatest post–Cold War crisis in Europe. The destruction of Serbia's infrastructure, the growing cost to Serb ground forces (NATO originally estimated that between 4,000 and 10,000 of the over 40,000 Serb soldiers, interior ministry forces, and police sent into Kosovo had been killed or wounded, though this figure was later revised downward), and the failure of Russian displeasure to undermine NATO resolve persuaded the Serbian regime to accept NATO demands.

Clinton rejected President Yeltsin's proposals for ending the conflict, especially an ending of the bombing campaign before Serbia had acceded to NATO demands to remove Serb forces from the province and that Kosovo be occupied by a force under NATO command. However, he acknowledged Russia's interest in being a major player in the solution of the crisis. Viktor Chernomyrdin, the Russian special envoy to the Balkans, was invited to Washington at the beginning of May. Chernomyrdin suggested that NATO pick the leader of a neutral nation acceptable to Milošević but also trusted by NATO to work with him for a settlement. Milošević and the Russian government accepted the proposal of Martti Ahtisaari, the president of Finland. The German government was particularly sensitive to the Russian concerns and worked to actively involve Russia in the search for a solution, and Russia was invited to discuss the crisis at a meeting of the Group of Seven (G-7) industrial nations. A joint statement was issued. Though vague with regard to particulars, it signaled that Russia and NATO were working together for a solution. Ahtisaari and Chernomyrdin worked out an ultimatum embodying NATO demands to be presented to Milošević: the Serbian forces would have to leave Kosovo; all the Albanian Kosovars would have to be allowed to return; and a NATO commanded force would guarantee their security. Though Russia did not endorse the demands, Chernomyrdin agreed not to offer any argument and not to protest when Ahtisaari informed Milošević that if he rejected the demands NATO conditions would only grow harsher. They met with Milošević on June 2 and 3. When Milošević was informed that there would be no negotiations or alterations, he said that the conditions would have to be approved by the Serbian parliament. He unsuccessfully attempted to have Ahtisaari address the parliament, but the acceptance of the plan by the Serbian parliament on June 2 was apparently used as political cover by Milošević, who then informed Ahtisaari that "we accept your terms."

The Serbian parliament approved the plan by a vote of 136 to 74, with three abstentions and one member who refused to vote. The 74 opponents were largely drawn from the 80 representatives of the deputy premier (and radical nationalist) Vojislav Seselj's Radical Party. Seselj said that he would leave the government the day that NATO troops entered Kosovo but later agreed to stay on. Milošević's Socialist Party repeated Milošević's argument, painting him as someone who defended the independence of Serbia against overwhelming odds. It stated that "this decision brings us the cessation of the criminal bombing, of the killing of the people, and it brings us peace. The role of the United Nations is being affirmed in accordance with the U.N. Charter. Through the unity of the people and through the heroism of our army and our police, we have defended the country from a vastly superior enemy who committed aggression against our country with the goal of annulling our integrity and our sovereignty."

According to the terms, all Serbian forces had to withdraw from Kosovo. Subsequently a very small presence of less than 1,000 would be allowed to protect Serbian cultural monuments and maintain a presence at border crossings. The Kosovar Albanians would all be allowed to return home, even those whose documents had been taken or destroyed by the Serbs. Fifty thousand foreign troops under UN auspices but with an "essential NATO participation" and under NATO command would occupy Kosovo to maintain peace. The KLA would be demilitarized. Kosovo, at first administered by the UN, would receive "substantial and essential autonomy" but remain a de jure part of Serbia. Unlike the Rambouillet document, there would not be a plebiscite in three years to determine the future status of Kosovo.

When representatives of the Serbian military met with NATO military representatives on June 5–7 to receive the NATO schedule for the Serbian withdrawal from Kosovo, the plan ran into difficulties. The Serbs objected to NATO demands. Milošević protested to Ahtisaari that he still stood by the agreement. However, he seemed to attempting to create new difficulties that might divide the NATO alliance and enable Russia through its position on the UN Security Council to gain better terms for Serbia. The Russia meeting with G-7 representatives on June 7 refused to assent to a draft proposal on Kosovo for the UN Security Council. Serbia and Russia seemed to be still attempting to have the UN rather than NATO exercise prime military and administrative responsibility in Kosovo. On June 8, however, the Russians agreed in a meeting with the G-7 in Cologne with the G-7 formulation. The following day the Serbs, who had been delaying, finally agreed to a ten-day phased withdrawal of their soldiers, police, and paramilitaries from Kosovo. On June 10, after confirming that the Serb withdrawal had begun, NATO suspended its bombing campaign. The bombing halt was followed by a resolution of the UN Security Council, by a vote of 14 to 0 with China abstaining, which echoed the agreement hammered out by the G-7 and Russia in Cologne. The UN Security Council approved a NATO-led international force of 50,000 soldiers to supervise the withdrawal of the Serbian forces and the return of the Albanian Kosovar refuges and to enforce peace in the province. Kosovo according to the resolution would be placed under a UN "interim administration" that would guarantee the province "substantial autonomy" and set the stage for free elections.

On June 12 the first NATO troops entered the province, but they were pre-empted by a Russian move ordered by Yeltsin. Some 200 Russian troops from IFOR in Bosnia crossed into Serbia on June 11 in armored personnel carriers and trucks and arrived in Pristina (after the Russians had assured NATO that they would not) the evening before the arrival of the British forces. NATO had sought Russian participation in the international force, but the Russians had been unwilling to subject their forces to NATO command. The Russian move came after negotiations between the Russians and Strobe Talbot, the U.S. deputy secretary of state, broke down on June 10. The Russian deployment apparently came without the knowledge of Igor Ivanov, the Russian foreign minister. The move might merely have been an effort on the part of the Russians to assert their independence and to insist that they not be ignored, or an attempt to establish a Russian zone of occupation that could serve as the basis for a partitioning of Kosovo.

Michael Wines wrote that two conclusions could be "drawn from Russia's abrupt and befuddled deployment of troops"—the one that Yeltsin no longer controls the Russian government, but that power is being asserted by shadowy figures including the military, the other that a befuddled Yeltsin, prey to latter-day Rasputins, is still calling the shots. Igor Ivanov, who was apparently taken off guard by the developments, publicly expressed his displeasure with General Leonid Ivanov, who had led the Russian military delegation in talks with NATO on Russia's role. Foreign Minister Ivanov, who said that Russia was willing to cooperate with NATO but not to be subordinate to it, threatened to make a unilateral deal with the Serbs for a sector of northern Kosovo to be controlled by Russian forces.

Negotiations between the United States and Russia eventually led to an agreement on June 18 that would include approximately 3,600 Russian troops in the Kosovo peace-keeping mission. Some 750 of the Russian troops would be deployed at the Pristina airport, the air operations of which, however, would be run by NATO. The Russians did not receive a separate zone of occupation and were, in actuality, to be under overall NATO command. NATO's unity of command was asserted but Russian ministry of defense personnel would be stationed in the NATO command structure. U.S. Secretary of Defense William Cohen said that "Our agreement recognizes the stake that Russia and NATO share in Europe's future. It shows that the U.S. and Russia can work together on important security issues. As major powers, we share a responsibility to work together for peace and stability, and we have shown that we can meet that responsibility."

On June 20 the last of the organized Serb forces left Kosovo. The entry of the NATO forces into Kosovo was followed by a disorganized flood of returning Kosovar Albanian refugees, despite warnings of land mines and booby traps left by the departing Serbs. There was often reluctance on the part of KLA fighters and units, who assumed the aura of a victorious army, to give up their weapons. NATO forces also had difficulty restraining acts of reprisal by ethnic Albanians against Serbs and their property. Many ethnic Serbs fled with the departing Serbian military; others, terrified by the inability of NATO to guarantee their security, joined the exodus, which mounted to over 50,000 by the end of June.

As the NATO forces and the ethnic Albanian refugees entered Kosovo they found mass grave sites and other evidence of atrocities. NATO estimated that during the conflict approximately 10,000 ethnic Albanians had been murdered by Serbian soldiers, police, and irregulars. Forensic experts followed the NATO military units to gather evidence of war crimes for the United Nations Tribunal on War Crimes in the Former Yugoslavia.

BIBLIOGRAPHY

Erlanger, Steven, "Million Refugees Can Return–West Reacts Cautiously," *New York Times,* June 4, 1999.

Harden, Blane, "Milosevic may lose war, but save face," *Times-Picayune,* June 6, 1999.

Hoffman, David, "Talk breakdown sparks Russia's Kosovo move," *Times-Picayune,* June 13, 1999.

Marshall, Tyler, "U.S., Russia Agree to Cooperate in Kosovo," *Los Angeles Times,* June 19, 1999.

Wines, Michael, "West wonders who's giving the orders in Moscow," *Times-Picayune,* June 13, 1999.

Bernard Cook

Kostava, Merab (1939–89)

Georgian dissident and radical nationalist. Merab Kostava was a leading Soviet dissident and human rights activist. With Zviad Gamsakhurdia he founded the Georgian branch of Helsinki Watch in 1975. They were arrested in 1977. While Kostava served a twelve-year sentence, Gamsakhurdia, after incarceration in a psychiatric ward, was released following a humiliating recantation on Soviet television. Kostava after his release, to the dismay of many dissidents, again began working with Gamsakhurdia. They decided to pursue a radical nationalist course that led to war with Abkhazia and its de-facto separation from Georgia. They organized the demonstration in April 1989 in which twenty demonstrators were killed by Soviet security forces. They were jailed for a short time after the clash but were released owing to public pressure.

It was Gamsakhurdia rather than Kostava, who led Georgia to independence and attempted to impose a unitary state on all its peoples. Kostava was killed in an automobile accident on October 13, 1989.

BIBLIOGRAPHY

Goldenberg, Suzanne. *Pride of Small Nations: The Caucasus and Post-Soviet Disorder.* London: Zed Boobs, 1994.

Bernard Cook

SEE ALSO Gamsakhurdia, Zviad

Kosygin, Alexi Nikolaevich (1904–80)

Chairman of the Council of Ministers (prime minister), 1964–80, and coleader with Leonid Brezhnev, of the USSR during the era of détente. Alexi Kosygin was one of the leaders of the USSR in the era when it was a recognized superpower. He lacked the flamboyant personality of Brezhnev, general secretary of the Communist Party (1964–82), and, therefore, did not share the limelight equally during their years in power.

Kosygin was born into a working-class family on February 2, 1904, in St. Petersburg. At fifteen, he joined the Red Army during the civil war. In the 1920s he was trained to work in the cooperative movement at the Leningrad Technicum, then worked in Siberia as a factory supervisor. Kosygin was a member of the Komsomol, the Communist Youth League, and joined the Communist Party (CPSU) in 1927. From 1930 to 1935 he studied at the Leningrad Textile Institute, becoming a textile engineer. He worked in the textile industry, served as mayor of Leningrad (St. Petersburg), and was appointed commissar (minister) of the textile industry in 1939. At the Eighteenth Party Congress, after Joseph Stalin's bloody purges, Kosygin was elected to the Central Committee of the CPSU. In 1940 he became a deputy chairman of Sovnarkom (Council of Ministers). During World War II Kosygin was in charge of the evacuation of Leningrad when the city was under siege by the German army. From 1943 to 1946 Kosygin served as prime minister of the Russian Republic, the largest republic of the USSR. In 1946 he became a candidate member of the party's Politburo and in 1948 a full member. In the late 1940s he held several positions as part of the postwar reconstruction, becoming minister of the light and food Industries (1949–53). During the renewed purges by Stalin of the Leningrad party organization in the late 1940s, Kosygin's future may have been in jeopardy, but his unassuming manner and his competency in several areas probably saved him from the fate of more aggressive, openly ambitious men. Nonetheless, he was demoted to a candidate member of the reorganized and expanded Presidium (formerly Politburo) in 1952. During the Khrushchev years he served as a deputy prime minister (1953–56, 1957–64). A supporter of Khrushchev, Kosygin was made a candidate member of the Presidium in 1957 and a full member in 1960. He also served briefly as head of Gosplan (1959–1960), the State Planning Committee, which oversaw the centrally planned economy of the USSR. Under Khrushchev Kosygin became first deputy prime minister and was widely assumed to be Khrushchev's choice to succeed him as prime minister.

After Khrushchev was removed from power, Kosygin became chairman of the Council of Ministers, a post he occupied for sixteen years. In the early years, he was part of the collective leadership of the USSR, together with Brezhnev and Nikolay Podgorny, who was president. He was credited with the major economic reforms initiated in 1965, which have informally become known as the Kosygin reforms. Based on research done in the Khrushchev years, the reforms allowed state enterprises to exercise more initiative at the local level. The reforms were never fully implemented nationally. In his early years as prime minister Kosygin was also active in diplomacy and was the Soviet spokesman at the summit with Lyndon Johnson at Glassboro, New Jersey, in 1966. As time passed he was overshadowed by Brezhnev. Beginning with the early 1970s Brezhnev played the leading role in Soviet diplomacy and in establishing the general direction of Soviet internal development.

Although Kosygin was perhaps the most capable Soviet leader in the 1970s, he had less and less power as the 1970s progressed. Brezhnev sought to be prime minister as well as general secretary. Eventually Brezhnev settled for the honorary position of chairman of the Presidium of the Supreme Soviet (president, 1977–81) but used his influence to diminish the role of prime minister. Kosygin retired in poor health on October 23, 1980, and died on December 12 of that year.

His career was remarkable in that few political figures survived the politics of the murderous 1930s and 1940s, and even fewer went on to enjoy great success in the post-Stalin period. Widely regarded as a capable technocrat, Kosygin was not considered a political maneuverer, like Brezhnev or Anostas Mikoyan. The longevity of his career as prime minister may be attributed to his acquiescence to Brezhnev's rise to greater power.

BIBLIOGRAPHY

Breslauer, George W. *Khrushchev and Brezhnev as Leaders.* Boston: George Allen and Unwin, 1982.

Linden, Carl. *Khrushchev and the Soviet Leadership, 1957–1964.* Baltimore: Johns Hopkins University Press, 1966.

Medvedev, Roy. *Khrushchev: A Biography.* New York: Anchor Books, 1984.

Schapiro, Leonard. *The Communist Party of the Soviet Union.* New York: Random House, 1959.

Tatu, Michel. *Power in the Kremlin: From Khrushchev to Kosygin.* New York: Viking, 1969.

Norma Noonan

Kovac, Michal (1936–)

First president of the independent Slovak Republic from January 1993 to March 1998, when Premier Vladimír Mečiar, a long-standing adversary of Kovac, left the office vacant. Educated at the Bratislava School of Economics, Michal Kovac worked as an academic economist and became a top banker. However, because of his support for the reforms of Alexander Dubček, the head of the Communist Party of Czechoslovakia, Kovac was demoted to bank clerk and expelled from the party in 1969 after the suppression of the Prague Spring reforms of 1968. A year after the Velvet Revolution in Czechoslovakia in 1989, Kovac was elected to the Czechoslovak Federal Assembly in 1990, when he also became finance minister of the newly formed Slovak Republic, until he resigned in 1991. Appointed chairman of the Federal Assembly in 1992, when it was clear that Czechoslovakia would soon be dissolved, he became president of the Slovak Republic after the formal dissolution of the former Czechoslovak federation on January 1, 1993. Earlier a deputy leader of the Movement for a Democratic Slovakia (MDS), he resigned this position on becoming the Slovak head of state. During 1993 he repeatedly clashed with Mečiar, leader of his former party and Slovak premier, as well as a former boxer inclined toward political thuggery.

Instrumental in bringing about Mečiar's dismissal from the premiership in March 1994, Kovac was later forced to reappoint him to the same office after new parliamentary elections later the same year. An authoritarian populist with a vindictive streak, Mečiar never forgot this supposed treachery on the part of his former MDS colleague. Concerned about Mečiar's undemocratic excesses and the damage they were inflicting on Slovakia in relation to the European Union (EU), which it aspired to join, and the United States, Kovac then constantly blocked Mečiar, mainly by vetoing key ministerial appointments and contentious pieces of legislation. This feud became particularly bitter when Kovac blocked Mečiar's choice for head of the powerful Slovak Intelligence Service (SIS) in 1994. As a result, Mečiar's MDS government managed to reduce the power of the presidency in April 1995, when Kovac was also charged by Mečiar and the MDS with exceeding his presidential powers, followed by a campaign by the MDS government to remove him from office. So bitter did this dispute become that the SIS allegedly kidnapped Kovac's son on Mečiar's orders in August 1995, when the son was also mysteriously handed over to the Austrian police to face charges of alleged embezzlement, thereby causing endless embarrassment for his father. As welcome to Mečiar as it was repugnant to Kovac, this bizarre affair resulted in a libel action by the Slovak president against his premier in 1996. By then it had become clear that Kovac and Mečiar could not both occupy the Slovak political scene. The end of Kovac's five-year term as president in March 1998 forced him to leave an office that was thereafter left vacant by Mečiar. That development left Mečiar the winner in his feud with Kovac, who was thereafter constantly slandered by the government-controlled media.

BIBLIOGRAPHY

Rothschild, Joseph and Nancy M. Wingfield. *Return to Diversity: A Political History of East Central Europe since World War II.* 3rd ed. New York: Oxford University, 2000.

Marko Milivojevic

SEE ALSO Mečiar, Vladimír

Kovacević, Dušan (1949–)

Yugoslavia's best-known playwright and screenwriter. Dušan Kovacević's play *The Professional* began a long and continuous run in Belgrade in 1989. His *Underground* won the Palme d'Or at Cannes in 1995. Kovacević dared to ridicule the nationalism and triumphalism that accompanied the breakup of Yugoslavia. He has become to many the conscience of the former Yugoslavia, and his films have achieved cult status there. The consistent theme of his work is the insecurity of the individual in the face of the system. "It does not matter," said Kovacević, "what the system is called, what ideology it embraces, the distortion done to the individual, the violence carried out by the system against the individual, is always the same and so is the result."

BIBLIOGRAPHY

Goulding, Daniel. *Liberated Cinema: The Yugoslav Experience.* Bloomington: Indiana U. Press, 1985.

Hedges, Chris. "Scathing 'Conscience' of the Balkans Spares No One." *New York Times,* February 8, 1996, A4.

Horton, Andrew, "Satire and Sympathy: A New Wave of Yugoslavian Filmmakers," *Cineaste,* vol 11, No. 2 (Spring 1982), pp. 18–22.

———. "Yugoslavia: Multi-Faceted Cinema," in William Luhr, ed. *World Cinema since 1945.* New York: Fredrick Ungar, 1987.

Bernard Cook

Kovács, Béla (1908–59)

One of the leading politicians of the right-wing, centrist Smallholders Party in Hungary. Béla Kovács was the general secretary of the Peasant Association from 1941, the undersecretary of state in the Ministry of Interior (1944–45), minister of agriculture (1945–46), general secretary of the Smallholders Party (1945–47), and editor in chief of the party newspaper.

In the party Kovács stood near the center with Prime Minister Ferenc Nagy, and represented the interests of the peasants. Kovács was at first restrained in his criticism of the politics of the Communists and the consequences of their radical land reform. In the summer of 1946, however, he tried to establish the Peasant Union, which he hoped would unite the peasantry and weaken the dominance of the left in the government.

In 1946 the state police, dominated by the Communists, accused Kovács of plotting to establish a new coalition under Hungary's authoritarian head of state Miblós Horthy's last prime minister. In February 1947 he was arrested by the Soviet occupation authorities, taken to the Soviet Union, and sentenced to prison for ten years without a trial.

In 1955 Kovács returned from the Soviet Union but was arrested again once in Hungary. In the Hungarian Revolution of 1956, Kovács was a leader of the reorganized Smallholders and was minister of agriculture and minister of state in the cabinet of Imre Nagy. In 1958 Kovács won a seat in parliament but illness prevented him from occupying it. He died in 1959.

BIBLIOGRAPHY

Balogh, Sándor, and Sándor Jakab. *The History of Hungary after the Second World War.* Budapest: Corvina, 1986.

Fehér, Ferenc and Agnes Heller. *Hungary 1956 Revisited: the Message of a Revolution—a Quarter of a Century After.* Boston: Allen & Unwin, 1983.

Lahav, Yehuda. *Der Weg der Kommunistischen Partei Ungarns zur Macht.* 2 Vols. Munich: R. Trofenik, 1985–86.

Litván, György. *The Hungarian Revolution of 1956: Reform, Revolt and Repression, 1953–1963.* Tr. by János M. Bak and Lyman H. Legters. New York: Longman, 1996.

Nagy, Ferenc. *The Struggle Behind the Iron Curtain.* Tr. by Stephen K. Swift. New York: MacMillan, 1948.

Rothschild, Joseph, and Nancy M. Wingfield. *Return to Diversity: A Political History of East Central Europe since World War II.* 3rd ed. New York: Oxford University, 2000.

Vida, István. *A független kisgazdapárt politikája 1944–1947.* Budapest: Akadémiai kiadó, 1986.

Heino Nyyssönen

SEE ALSO Nagy, Ferenc

Kovalyev, Sergei Adamovithe (1930–)

Russian politician and human rights activist. Sergei Kovalyev was born on March 2, 1930, in the small town of Seredina-Buda in the Sumskaja oblast of Ukraine. He received a Ph.D in biology from Moscow State University. While working as a research assistant at the university, Kovalyev assisted the scientist Andrey Sakharov, leader of anti-Soviet opposition and a prominent dissident, in his protest efforts.

Sergei Kovalyev was one of the organizers of the first human rights group in the USSR, the "Initiative Group for Human Rights," founded in 1969. Kovalyev became an editor of the (underground) bulletin "Chronicle of Current Events" in which cases of human rights violations in the USSR were listed and described. In 1970 the administration of Moscow State University dismissed him from the biological laboratory where he had been working as a research fellow. Four years later he was accused of anti-Soviet agitation and propaganda and was arrested. He was sentenced to seven years in a prison camp and to three years of internal exile. After serving the prison sentence, Kovalyev, having been banished from Moscow, lived in the city of Kalinin (now Tver).

In 1987, during the reforms of Soviet leader Mikhail Gorbachev, Kovalyev was allowed to return Moscow. There he became an active member of the human rights group, the International Foundation for the Survival and Development of Mankind. At that time Kovalyev obtained a job as an engineer at the Institute for Information and Communication of the Russian Academy of Sciences.

In 1990 he was elected deputy of the Supreme Soviet of the Russian Soviet Federated Socialist Republic and chairman of its Human Rights Committee. In 1990 and in 1991 he was a co-chairperson of the Soviet delegation at the Moscow Forum of the Conference on Human Rights, sponsored by the Conference for Security and Cooperation in Europe.

From 1990 to 1994 Kovalyev was the head of the Russian delegation at the Human Rights Committee of the UN in Geneva, Switzerland. During the Russo-Chechen War of 1994–96, Kovalyev volunteered to go to Grozny, the capital of the Chechnya, where he provided information on human rights abuses. He was sharply criticized by leading Russian politicians, especially by Defense Minister Pavel Grachev.

Andrey Alimov
Nickolaj Sannikov
Valeriy V. Sokolov

Kozyrev, Andrey V. (1951–)

Russian foreign minister (1991–96). Andrey Kozyrev, the son of Russian parents, was born in Brussels, Belgium, on March 27, 1951. In 1968–69 he worked as a fitter and assembler at a mechanical plant in Moscow. In 1974 he graduated from the Moscow State Institute of International Relations. From 1974 to 1990 he worked his way through the ranks of the Soviet Foreign Ministry as a reviewer, attaché, first secretary, counselor, and department head of the Administration for International Organizations (UMO). He served for a time as a member of the Soviet delegation to the United Nations and became a protégé and aide to Foreign Minister Edvard Shevardnadze. As head of the UMO, Kozyrev decried the waste of the arms race and called for an end to Soviet subsidies for its client states, stating that the majority of developing nations suffered not from capitalism but from a lack of it.

On October 12, 1990, Kozyrev relinquished his career in the Soviet Foreign Ministry to establish a foreign ministry for the Russian Republic. Kozyrev, who joined the Security Council of President Boris Yeltsin, had competition from Vladimir Lukin, the former deputy Soviet foreign minister for policy planning, who was then chairman of the Foreign Relations Committee of the Russian parliament, and Yuri Voronstov, a former ambassador to Afghanistan, who was a member of Yeltsin's personal staff. However, at the time of the attempted August coup by Communists who wished to prop up the USSR and preserve the dominance of the Communist Party, Kozyrev was sent by Yeltsin to Paris (on August 20) to prepare for the establishment of a government in exile. When Yeltsin successfully rallied mass opposition to the coup Kozyrev returned with his foreign affairs dominance secured. Despite the opposition of Mikhail Gorbachev, who was still president of the USSR until on December 25, 1991, and the last Soviet foreign minister, Boris Pankin, Kozyrev presided over the dismantling of the Soviet foreign ministry and the transfer of sovereignty to the republics of the new Commonwealth of Independent States.

Kozyrev is credited with persuading Russia and Ukraine to avoid unilateral action with regard to the disposition of the Soviet Black Sea fleet. He also negotiated the date for the withdrawal of Russian troops from the Baltic states. Kozyrev was forced to resign on January 5, 1996, in the aftermath of the victory of the Communists and nationalists in the December 1995 parliamentary elections. Kozyrev had been excoriated by nationalists for being too accommodating to the West. Yeltsin appointed in his place veteran Soviet era diplomat Yevgeny Primakov, and Kozyrev withdrew to his seat in the Russian State Duma, where he served on the committee for budget, taxes, banks, and finance.

BIBLIOGRAPHY

Kozyrev, Andrei Vladimirovich. *The Arms Trade: a New Level of Danger.* Moscow: Progress Publishers, 1985.

———. *My i mir v zerkale OON.* Moscow: Mezhdunarodnye Otnosheniia, 1991.

———. *Preobrazhenie.* Moscow: Mezhdunarodnye Otnosheniia, 1995.

Suny, Ronald Grigor. *The Soviet Experiment: Russia, the USSR, and the Successor States.* New York: Oxford University Press, 1998.

Bernard Cook

SEE ALSO Primakov, Yevgeny; Yeltsin, Boris

Krag, Jens Otto (1914–78)

Danish Social Democratic politician and prime minister (1962–68, 1971–72). The son of a shopkeeper, Jens Krag was active in the Social Democratic youth movement. He studied economics at the University of Copenhagen and graduated in 1940. He was employed in the agency for currency control and advanced quickly, becoming head of one of the departments in 1945. Parallel with his civil carrier, he was active as a writer and lecturer in the Social Democratic movement, heading the group that between 1943 and 1945 prepared a new party program. Published in 1945, it strongly influenced the postwar period. Elected to parliament in 1947, Krag retained his seat until 1973. From 1947 to 1950 he was minister for trade, industry, and shipping. His marriage to and divorce shortly afterward from Swedish actress Birgit Tengroth and his somewhat bohemian life coupled with an academic style made him unpopular among some of the Social Democratic rank and file. In 1950 after a change in the government he was not given a ministerial post but accepted a post as adviser at the Danish Embassy in Washington, D.C., from 1950 to 1952. But he returned in 1953 and became minister for economy and labor affairs. He was minister for international trade (1957–58), and minister for foreign affairs (1958–62, 1966–67). He finally became prime minister in 1962, holding the post until 1968 and again from 1971 to 1972.

Krag is remembered for his efforts to gain membership for Denmark in the European Community (EC). He succeeded in this with adoption of the treaty of accession to the EC (later European Union, EU) in the Folketing (parliament) and the subsequent successful referendum of October 2, 1972. The day after the referendum Krag announced the resignation not of the whole government but of himself, using this historical event and personal victory to withdraw from political life. After a short time as university lecturer in international politics and head of the EC delegation in Washington, he dedicated the rest of his life to writing and painting.

BIBLIOGRAPHY

Fitzmaurice, John. *Politics in Denmark.* New York: St. Martin's Press, 1981.

Krag, Jens Otto. *Man har et standpunkt—: taler og artikler 1948–1978.* Copenhagen: Aschehoug, 1997.

———. *Travl tid, god tid.* Copenhagen: Gyldendal, 1974.

Martinov, Niels. *Jens Otto.* Copenhagen: Vindrose, 1986.

Virkner, Helle. *Hils fra mig og kongen.* Copenhagen: Aschehoug, 1994.

Jørn Boye Nielsen

SEE ALSO Jørgensen, Anker

Kravchuk, Leonid Makarovych (1934–)

First president of independent Ukraine. Leonid Makarovych Kravchuk was born on January 10, 1934, in Velykyi Zhytyn, Ukraine. He graduated from Taras Shevchenko Kyiv State University in Kiev in 1958 with a degree in economics and political economy. Kravchuk attended the Central Committee of the Soviet Communist Party Academy of Social Sciences in 1970. From 1958 to 1960 he taught political economy in Cherniv, Ukraine. In 1960 he began working for the Communist Party, initially as a lecturer in political education, then as director of the propaganda and agitation division of the Cherniv Branch Communist Party. Moving up in the ranks, by 1988 he became head of the Ideology Section of the Central Committee of the Communist Party of Ukraine. He was elected a member of parliament in March 1990 for Iampil district. He was a member of the Politburo from June 1990, when he was elected speaker of the Supreme Soviet (Parliament) of Soviet Ukraine. Kravchuk presided over the declaration of independence of Ukraine in parliament on August 24, 1991, and was elected the new state's first president on December 1, 1991, by a comfortable 61 percent majority. He succeeded in consolidating statehood and to a large degree nationhood, carving out an international role for Ukraine and moving it out of Russia's shadow. He also negotiated an agreement with the United States and Russia in January 1994 to destroy all nuclear missiles on Ukrainian territory, transferring the warheads to Russia for destruction. But as the domestic economic crisis that accompanied Ukrainian independence (characterized by massive unemployment and extreme inflation) deepened, Kravchuk's support decreased. He was forced to call an early presidential election in 1994, which he lost by a small margin. He was elected to parliament in the 1994 elections representing Terebovlia district. He served as a member of the Parliamentary Committee on Culture and Religion, and as of 1997 was head of the Parliamentary Committee on Administrative Reform. A member of the Social Democratic Party and its Parliamentary Faction since 1998, Kravchuk was reelected to parliament in the 1998 elections. His publications include *Bitva za Bukovinu* (*The Battle for Bukovina,* 1967), *IE taka derzhava—Ukraïna: materialy z vystupiv, interv'iu, pres-konferentsii, bryfinhiv, vidpovidei na zapytannia* (*Our Goal—A Free Ukraine: Speeches, Interviews, Press conferences, Briefings,* 1992), and *Ostanni dni imperiï . . . pershi roky nadiï* (*Last Days of the Empire . . . First Years of Hope,* 1994).

BIBLIOGRAPHY

Kravchuk, L. M. *Our Goal—a Free Ukraine: Speeches, Interviews, Press-conferences, Briefings.* Kiev: Globus Publishers, 1993.

Lytvyn, Volodymyr. *Ukraina: politika, politiki, vlast': na fone politicheskogo portreta L. Kravchuka.* Kiev: Izdatel'skii dom "Al'ternativy," 1997.

Mykhal'chenko, Mykola Ivanovych. *Belovezh'e, L. Kravchuk, Ukraina, 1991–1995.* Kiev: Ukr Tsentr dukhovnoi kul'tury, 1996.

Schneider, Eberhard. *Drei GUS-Führer: Portraits von Jelzin, Krawtschuk und Schuschkewitsch.* Cologne: Bundesinstitut für Ostwissenschaftliche und Internationale Studien, 1993.

Marta Dyczok

SEE ALSO Kuchma, Leonid Danylovych

Kreisky, Bruno (1911–90)

Austrian chancellor. Along with Willy Brandt of West Germany and Olof Palme of Sweden, Bruno Kreisky was one of the Socialist "wise men" who had an impact on postwar Europe equaled by few other politicians. The three friends were in charge of their respective countries' fate in the 1970s and acted as the principal advocates of some of the crucial issues of the era: East-West détente, nuclear disarmament, North-South dialogue, and full employment.

The remarkable career of Kreisky is representative of the exigencies of central European history in the twentieth century. He was born on January 22, 1911, into a well-to-do family of assimilated Viennese Jewish industrialists during the waning days of the Habsburg monarchy. As a high school student in the 1920s he became a leading figure in the Revolutionary Socialist Youth Movement. After the seizure of power and suppression of the Socialists by the "Austro-Fascists", conservative authoritarians un-

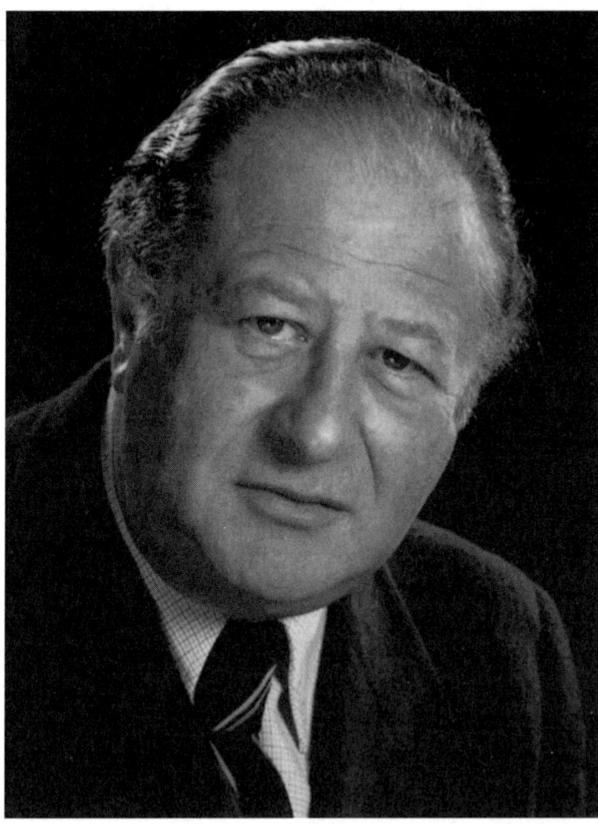

Bruno Kreisky, chancellor of Austria and one of postwar Europe's most influential political leaders. *Illustration courtesy of the Austrian Press and Information Service.*

der Engelbert Dollfuss, in 1934, committed Marxist Kreisky went underground, where he became instrumental in the survival of the youth movement.

After attending a party conference of the Austrian Socialist leadership across the border in Brno, Czechoslovakia, the Schuschnigg regime arrested him in 1935 and jailed him for sixteen months on charges of "high treason." Kreisky shared a cell with "illegal" Austrian Nazis.

On March 14, 1938, the day after Germany's annexation of Austria (*Anschluss*), Kreisky took his final law exams at the University of Vienna. The next day the Nazis arrested him; this time he shared a cell with his former "Austro-Fascist" jailers, including Kurt von Schuschnigg, Dollfuss's successor, who was imprisoned.

In the fall of 1938 Kreisky left Austria and began his wartime exile in Sweden, where his intellectual formation was completed. He began to work as an economic adviser for the Swedish cooperative movement. He also covered the Soviet-Finish Winter War in person as a freelance journalist. In Sweden he became friends with young Socialists like Olof Palme, who instilled in Kreisky his lifelong commitment to the social welfare state and the advantages of neutrality for small nations; in Norway he met exiled young German Socialist Willy Brandt. In 1942 he married Vera Fürth, daughter of a wealthy Austrian-born Swedish industrialist.

After the war Kreisky returned to Austria briefly, only to be recruited personally by President Karl Renner into the foreign service and sent back to Scandinavia to rebuild the Austrian diplomatic missions. After successfully organizing Scandinavian aid for postwar Austria, Kreisky returned to the Ballhausplatz, the seat of the Austrian foreign ministry in Vienna, in 1950. In 1951 the Socialist Party made him political adviser to President Theodor Körner, a politically inexperienced general.

Kreisky's rise to the highest echelons of government began with his appointment as state secretary to the Foreign Office in the government of Julius Raab. After Soviet dictator Joseph Stalin's death in 1953, Kreisky was one of the central actors in the behind-the-scenes bilateral state treaty negotiations with the Kremlin, which culminated in the signing of the treaty in May 1955 and the end of the Austrian occupation by the four wartime allies. He helped define Austria's new international status of "armed neutrality."

In the Raab coalition government formed after the 1959 election, Kreisky was appointed foreign minister, a post in which he served until 1966. He worked tirelessly for East-West détente, presided over the Khrushchev-Kennedy summit in Vienna in 1961, and bargained with Italy to find an acceptable solution for the South Tyrol problem. As a result, autonomous rule was granted to the German speakers of that border territory.

In 1966 the Socialists were decisively defeated at the polls. The victorious conservative People's Party formed their own government and ended twenty years of grand coalition governments with the Socialists. The Socialist Party responded by electing Kreisky chairman the next year. An indefatigable Kreisky revived the Socialist movement in Austria by modernizing the party and making it attractive to people outside the working class. Kreisky coopted the intellectuals and many younger people with his call for modernizing Austrian society. He solicited ideas from a broad spectrum of Austria's "best and brightest" for the new party program that shaped the 1970 electoral campaign.

The Socialist won in 1970 and formed a minority government with Kreisky as chancellor. He called for a new election in 1971, winning an absolute majority and staying in power until 1983, reshaping Austria as no postwar statesman had done before him.

Domestically he pushed his modernizing and democratizing agenda. Ironically, it was a "red" chancellor who rang in the "golden age" of the family in deeply Catholic

Austria. He expanded educational opportunities for poor children and provided better access to higher education with free textbooks and more generous student aid. Major reforms were instituted in the electoral process by granting better protection to small parties, the defense forces were revamped, and state radio and television were modernized. Reforms in the judicial system may have been the most dramatic, with the rewriting of the penal code and family law. Female equality was written into law, divorce law was liberalized, and the outlawing of adultery, homosexuality, and abortion ended. Universities, the media, and the shop floor all were "flooded" with more inclusive democratic practices.

The social welfare state was further expanded, providing Austrians one of the best "social nets" in Europe. Virtually every societal group was included in the social, health, and pension insurance system. Five weeks of vacation was guaranteed to all workers.

Kreisky's economic policy became known as "Austro-Keynesianism." He chose economic instruments to achieve high production and full employment. In the Kreisky era—the recession-ridden 1970s—Austria shoved its way through economic downturns by accepting high budget deficits and an expanded public debt. With an average 2 percent unemployment rate, Kreisky's Austria figured at the low end among the advanced industrial members of the Organization for European Cooperation and Development (OECD) Western European nations viewed Austria's social peace with envy.

The only blemish on Kreisky's record was his courting of former Nazis. He appointed four (one a former SS officer) to his first cabinet.

Kreisky's policies toward the Middle East were more controversial than his forgiving approach to former Nazis. He was the first major Western statesman to argue forcefully that no peace could be constructed without the Palestinians and the radical Arabs. Consequently, he recognized Yassir Arafat's Palestine Liberation Organization and sharply criticized hard-line Israeli governments. As president of the Socialist International (1976–89) Kreisky frequently visited the Near East, promoting political dialogue in the region.

Kreisky kept a tight rein on Austrian foreign affairs while chancellor, consistently pushing the process of Austria's European integration. Under his aegis the European Community and the European Free Trade Association (of which neutral Austria was a member) signed a free-trade agreement in 1972. His relentless advocacy of strengthening East-West détente remained at the center of his bridge-building foreign policy vision. In a period of détente, he argued, the superiority of democracy over communism could be self-evident. Kreisky also was a great champion of the North-South dialogue. As an instigator of the October 1991 Cancun summit, he promoted a "Marshall Plan" of the rich industrial nations for the Third World.

After his retirement from politics in 1983, the Socialist Party honored him as their honorary chairman. Committed to the moral force of traditional Social Democracy, Kreisky also chaired an international commission on employment policies, the Kreisky Commission. The report, issued in 1989, once again drove home his lifelong commitment to Keynesian full-employment policies, particularly in a prosperous world.

Kreisky died on July 27, 1990, in Vienna. No Austrian since Metternich had left a more towering presence in the international arena.

BIBLIOGRAPHY

Bischof, Günter, Anton Pelinka, and Oliver Rathkolb, eds. *The Kreisky Era in Austria.* New Brunswick, N.J.: Transaction, 1994.

Fischer, Heinz. *Die Kreisky Jahre 1967–1983.* Berlin: Locker, 1993.

Kreisky, Bruno. *Zwischen den Zeiten: Erinnerungen aus fünf Jahrzehnten.* Berlin: Siedler, 1986.

———. *Im Strom der Zeit.* Berlin: Siedler, 1988.

———. *Der Mensch im Mittelpunkt: Der Memoiren dritter Teil.* 3 Vols. of memoirs posthumously ed. by Oliver Rathkolb, Johannes Kunz, and Margit Schmidt. Vienna: Dietz, 1996.

Müller, Wolfgang C. "Bruno Kreisky," in Herbert Dachs et al., eds. *Die Politiker: Karrieren und Wirken bedeutender Repräsentanten der Zweiten Republik.* Vienna: Manz, 1995.

Rathkolb, Oliver, and Irene Etzersdorfer, eds. *Der junge Kreisky.* Vienna: Jugend und Volk, 1986.

Secher, H. Pierre. *Bruno Kreisky.* Pittsburg: University of Pittsburg Press, 1993.

Günter Bischof

SEE ALSO Raab, Julius; South Tyrol

Krenz, Egon (1937–)

One of the last Communists to head the government of East Germany. Egon Krenz, son of a tailor, furthered his career, like so many of his contemporaries, through holding office in one of the German Democratic Republic's (GDR) mass organizations, in Krenz's case as first secretary of the Central Council of the Free Democratic Youth (FDJ). His career blossomed under the East German head of state, Erich Honecker's patronage. He entered the Socialist Unity (Communist) Party's (SED) Central Committee in 1971 and the Politburo in 1976. Seven years later he became a full member of the latter body, as well as the Central Committee secretary for youth affairs and security.

A committed Communist functionary, Krenz aroused great antipathy by expressing support for the Chinese leadership during his official visit to Beijing in 1989 in the aftermath of the Tiananmen Square massacre. Increasingly disenchanted with Honecker's sclerotic leadership and the growing influence of Günter Mittag, the director of the East German economy, he cautiously organized a palace revolt against his former mentor, stepping into Honecker's shoes in October 1989 as general secretary of the SED, chairman of the National Defense Council, and chairman of the Council of State. Although Krenz made many concessions, such as the abandonment of the SED's leadership role, he failed to convince East Germans of his democratic credentials. Even his most spectacular action, opening the Berlin Wall on November 9, 1989, failed to save the mortally wounded SED. In 1995, he was charged with manslaughter in connection with shootings along the Berlin Wall. In 1997 he was found guilty and sentenced to six and a half years in prison. On November 9, 1999, an appeals court upheld the manslaughter conviction.

BIBLIOGRAPHY

Jarausch, Konrad H. *The Rush to German Unity.* New York: Oxford University Press, 1994.

Krenz, Egon. *Wenn Mauern fallen. Die friedliche Revolution: Vorgeschichte—Ablauf—Auswirkungen.* Vienna: Paul Neff Verlag, 1990.

Mike Dennis

SEE ALSO Honecker, Erich

Kristensen, Knud (1880–1962)

Danish prime minister (1945–47). Knud Kristensen was born into a farming family in West Jutland and was trained as a farmer. He attended several folk high schools and an agricultural school. He joined the Liberal Party (Venstre) and was elected to parliament in 1920, holding seats between 1920 and 1929, and 1932 and 1949. Kristensen was minister of the interior from 1940 to 1942 and from May until November 1945. He was national president of the Liberal Party from 1941 to 1949 and chairman of its parliamentary group from 1942 to 1945.

Kristensen is remembered for his strong views on a reacquisition of the historical territory of South Schleswig, which was Danish before 1864 but lost in a war with Prussia (Germany). After the First World War a referendum was held in the small municipalities in South Jutland and Schleswig concerning national affiliation. Kristensen's view, shared only by some in the Liberal Party but by most in the Conservative Party, was that the entire territory should be returned to Denmark. But the opposition in parliament, the Social Democratic Party and the Social Liberal Party (Radikale Venstre), wanted a border reflecting the preferences of the people in the area. South Schleswig was populated by a majority of German-speaking people and remained, to the consternation of Kristensen, part of Germany.

In the 1947 election Kristensen campaigned for the reacquisition of land that had historically been Danish and against what he regarded as a Social Democratic planned economy. His party gained seats at the expense of the Conservative Party. The Social Democrats gained a majority and their leader, Has Hedtoft, became prime minister.

Kristensen drifted more and more to the right with regard to the national question and economic issues, and lost influence in the Liberal Party. He resigned from the party's national presidency and his parliamentary seat in 1949. He was a leader of the opposition to modernizing the constitution, which took place in 1953. He left the Liberal Party and founded a new party, the Independent Party (Uafhængige) in 1953, serving as its national president from 1953 to 1956. He left politics in 1956. The Independent Party, in parliament from 1960 to 1966 and from 1973 to 1975, represented national views and opposition to what it saw as a social democratic planned economy.

BIBLIOGRAPHY

Fitzmaurice, John. *Politics in Denmark.* New York: St. Martin's Press, 1981.

Kjersgaard, Erik. *A History of Denmark.* Copenhagen: Royal Danish Ministry of Foreign Affairs, 1974.

Jørn Boye Nielsen

SEE ALSO Hedtoft, Hans

Kristeva, Julia (1941–)

French literary theorist, psychoanalyst, philosopher, and novelist whose writings critically engage a remarkable range of cultural production from linguistics to art, religion, and politics.

Julia Kristeva launched her intellectual career as a linguist amid the swirl of structuralist and poststructuralist theory dominating French thought in the late 1960s. For the next decade and a half she was associated with the odyssey of the avant-garde intellectuals surrounding the journal *Tel Quel,* from their critique of both subject-centered humanism and structuralism, to their fascination with the Chinese Cultural Revolution, and later to their interest in what they regarded as the nonverbal culture of the United States. Her own work focused on the critique of discursive sign systems, specifically psychoanalysis, religion, and ethics, which constitute the identity of the individual in society.

Born in Bulgaria and educated there as a linguist, Kristeva moved to Paris in 1966 to pursue doctoral research that resulted in her important thesis, *La Révolution du langage poétique* (1974; *Revolution in Poetic Language,* 1984). Several articles and two books (*Semeiotike,* 1969; *Le Texte du roman,* 1970) had already appeared by this time, reflecting the influence of her primary mentor, Roland Barthes, and of Mikhail Bakhtin, to whose work Barthes and her compatriot, Tzvetan Todorov, had introduced her. As early as her dissertation, Kristeva's writing reveals interest in psychoanalytic thought, particularly that of Jacques Lacan. Since 1979 she has practiced psychoanalysis in Paris and has taught at the Université de Paris VII, with frequent appointments at Columbia University in New York City. Her major writings from this period include *Pouvoirs de l'horreur* (1980; *Powers of Horror,* 1982), *Histoires d'amour* (1983; *Tales of Love,* 1987), *Au Commencement était l'amour* (1987; *In the Beginning Was Love: Psychoanalysis and Faith,* 1988), *Soleil noir: dépression et mélancolie* (1987; *Black Sun,* 1989), and *Étrangers à nous-mêmes,* (1989; *Strangers to Ourselves,* 1991). She has also written a novel about her intellectual generation, *Les Sammourais* (1990).

The themes that run through these later works—abjection, narcissism, depression, love—reflect Kristeva's turn toward the psychoanalytic without abandoning her earlier emphasis on the instability of meaning in language. She continues to examine critically the major literary and religious texts of the Western tradition as a means of exploring these themes. The human subject she seeks to understand through her explorations lies between essentialist and postmodern views of the self, between the idea of a single fixed identity or human nature and recent efforts to completely dissolve the notion of a self. Kristeva's human subject is a "self-in-process," an always provisional and unfinished becoming of identity and agency within the discursive sign systems of society. She sees the psychoanalytic situation not as mere play of signs and symbols but as a model of the process of the individual's becoming and of dialogue with "otherness." The integrity of the relationship between therapist and patient is the context for her definitions of words like *truth, love,* and *ethics.*

She has given specific attention here to issues of infancy, maternity, and femininity, though her relation to Western feminisms has been somewhat aloof and awkward. Kristeva, self-conscious about her position on the margins, as a woman writing in a male-dominated world and as an exile, has preferred a politics of the individual and of difference to collective struggle, and questioning and subversion to dogma and prescription. The spaces created by interrogation, or what she calls "disquieting thought" and "revolt," allow the individual to return to and transform the self, to open creative possibilities. These are spaces of liberty, free from institutional, political, or religious control. Quite in keeping with the vital and challenging nature of her thought and its willingness to reorder and redefine, Kristeva has referred to these spaces as the sacred.

BIBLIOGRAPHY

Crownfield, David R., ed. *Body/Text in Julia Kristeva: Religion, Women, and Psychoanalysis.* New York: State University of New York Press, 1992.

Moi, Toril, ed. *The Kristeva Reader: Julia Kristeva.* New York: Columbia University Press, 1986.

Oliver, Kelly. *Reading Kristeva: Unraveling the Double-Bind.* Bloomington: Indiana University Press, 1993.

William E. Duvall

Kucan, Milan (1941–)

President of the Republic of Slovenia. Milan Kucan was born on January 11, 1941, in Krizevci, a Slovenian village near the Hungarian border in the Prekmurje region. Kucan was three when his father, a teacher who had become an officer in the wartime resistance, was killed by the Germans.

Kucan received a law degree from the University of Ljubljana in 1964. He became active in the Communist Party and in 1971 helped to prepare the constitutional amendments that provided the legal basis for the decentralization of the Yugoslav Federation. In 1978 he became president of the Slovenian Republican Assembly. From 1982 to 1986 he was one of Slovenia's representatives to the Federal Assembly of Yugoslavia. He returned to Ljubljana and became the president of the League of Communists of Slovenia (LCS). He played a central role in the democratization of the party and the liberalization of

Slovenia. His popularity was rooted in his honest support of reform and decentralization during this period. He resisted the effort of Slobodan Milošević, the president of Serbia, to transform the Yugoslav Federal Republic into a centralized state dominated by Serbs. Following Serbian condemnation of the liberalization and the legalization of non-Communist political parties in Slovenia and a Serbian boycott of Slovenian products, Kucan set the stage for independence when he led the Slovenian delegation out of the Fourteenth Congress of the League of Communists of Yugoslavia (LCY) in January 1990. The League of Communists of Slovenia (LCS) cut its links to the LCY and changed its name to the Party of Democratic Reform (PDR). In Slovenia's first multiparty election since 1945, held in April 1990, Kucan, the candidate of the PDR, was elected president of Slovenia after defeating Lojze Peterle, leader of the Slovenian Christian Democrats, in the second round of voting.

Despite Milošević's machinations, Kucan expressed Slovenia's willingness to remain part of a decentralized federation of sovereign states. After Serbia's refusal to accept the election of the Croatian vice president as president of Yugoslavia, Slovenia declared its independence on June 25, 1991. Kucan led Slovenia through the "weekend war", technically with Yugoslavia but in reality with Serbia, and to internationally recognized independence in January 1992. In 1992 he ran as an independent against seven other candidates in Slovenia's first presidential election since its independence. Of Slovenia's registered voters, 85 percent participated. Kucan won 63.9 percent of the vote in the first round. His closest rival, Christian Democrat Ivan Bizjak, won 21.1 percent. Kucan thus won a five-year, renewable term. However, according to the 1991 constitution, the office had been rendered largely ceremonial.

In 1993, Minister of Defense Janez Jansa, leader of the Social Democratic Party of Slovenia, accused Kucan of protecting former Communist colleagues who were personally profiting from the turmoil of privatization. Subsequently, however, Jansa was forced to defend his own behavior and was dismissed from his ministerial post in March 1994. On November 25, 1997, Kucan was elected to a second five-year term as president. He far outpolled his rival, Janez Podobnik, speaker of parliament. Kucan announced that one of his major goals would be to gain entry for Slovenia into the EU.

BIBLIOGRAPHY

Glenny, Mischa. *The Fall of Yugoslavia: The Third Balkan War.* 3d ed. New York: Penguin, 1996.

Ribicic, Ciril. *Federalizam po mjeri bucucnosti.* Zagreb: Globus, 1989.

Bernard Cook

SEE ALSO Milošević, Slobodan

Kuchma, Leonid Danylovych (1938–)

Second president of Ukraine. Leonid Danylovych Kuchma was born on August 9, 1938, in Chaikyne, Ukraine. He graduated from Dnepropetrovsk State University in 1960 with a degree in mechanical engineering, and subsequently received a PhD. As of 1991 he was a member of the Engineering Academy of Sciences of Ukraine. From 1960 to 1975 Kuchma worked as a technical designer at the Pivdenne Design/Construction Bureau and as technical director of testing at the Baikonur Space Launch Complex. From 1975 to 1982 he was first secretary of the Communist Party in the Pivdenne Design/Construction Bureau. From 1982 to 1986 he was first deputy to the chief designer at Pivdenne, and from 1986 to 1992 director general of the Pivdennyi Mashynobudivelnyi Zavod (Pivden'Mash), the largest nuclear missile factory in the USSR. Kuchma was a member of the Ukrainian Communist Party Central Committee from 1981 to 1991. He was elected to parliament in 1990, representing the Krasnogvardiiskyi district in the Dnepropetrovsk Oblast, and was a member of the State Committee on Defense and National Security. As the USSR collapsed, Ukraine asserted its independence in December 1991. Early in 1992 Kuchma became a member of the Nova Ukraina political group; in October of that year President Leonid Kravchuk appointed him prime minister of Ukraine. In 1993 he resigned on the grounds that parliament blocked his efforts to introduce radical economic reforms. In 1993 he became cofounder of the Interregional Bloc of Reforms political movement and was elected president of the Ukrainian Union of Industrialists and Entrepreneurs. Kuchma ran for president in 1994 on a pro-Russian platform and won by a slim majority in a runoff against incumbent Leonid Kravchuk. Kuchma introduced a policy of radical economic reforms. His foreign policy continued cooperation with both Russia and the West. Under his tenure hyperinflation was brought under control, and Ukraine began receiving financing from the International Monetary Fund (IMF) and the World Bank. In 1998 the economy began showing the first signs of growth since 1990. Kuchma signed a treaty with Russia in 1997 recognizing the inviolability of borders and an accord with NATO on mutual cooperation. Domestically, Kuchma redefined the power structure between parliament and president, and oversaw adoption of the first independent constitution in June 1997. As of 1997 Kuchma served as head of the State Security Council and State Executive Council. His presidential term ended in 1999.

BIBLIOGRAPHY

Lukanov, Iurii. *Tretii prezydent: politychnyi portret Leonida Kuchmy.* Kiev: Taki spravy, 1996.

Marta Dyczok

SEE ALSO Kravchuk, Leonid

Kukan, Eduard (1939–)

Czechoslovak diplomat and Slovak politician. Eduard Kukan was born on December 26, 1939, in Trnovca nad Vahom. He graduated from the Institute of International Affairs in Moscow, and received a doctorate in law from Charles University in Prague in 1964. He joined the Czechoslovak Foreign Ministry and was given his first foreign assignment to the Czechoslovak Embassy in Zambia in 1968. He was the second secretary and the chargé d'affaires at the Czechoslovak Embassy in Uganda from 1977 to 1981. Kukan was assigned to the Czechoslovak Embassy in Washington, D.C., from 1977 to 1981. From 1985 to 1988 he was ambassador to Ethiopia. In 1990 he was appointed ambassador of the Czech and Slovak Federal Republic to the United Nations and remained at the United Nations as the Slovak ambassador after January 1, 1993. He was appointed foreign minister in the government of Jozef Moravcik, formed on March 15, 1994.

BIBLIOGRAPHY

Kirschbaum, Stanislav J. *A History of Slovakia: the Struggle for Survival.* New York: St. Martin's Press, 1995.

Bernard Cook

Kuncze, Gábor (1950–)

A leader of the Alliance of Free Democrats, appointed Hungarian minister of interior in 1994.

Gábor Kuncze studied at an engineering college then at the University of Economic Sciences in Budapest. He held various positions in engineering companies in the 1970s and 1980s. Kuncze joined the Alliance of Free Democrats in 1992 and became a member of the National Committee of the party. He was elected the leader of its parliamentary group in 1993. In 1994 Kuncze became the Free Democrats' candidate for premier, and when that party entered into a coalition with the Socialist Party, the winners of the parliamentary elections, Kuncze became the minister of interior in the new cabinet.

Kuncze represented the orthodox liberal wing of the Alliance of Free Democrats insofar as he supported the radical economic steps to create a full-fledged market economy in Hungary, decentralization of power, and the privatization of companies in almost all fields. As did his party in general, he favored Hungary's joining the European Union and NATO as soon as possible. Hungary joined NATO in 1999. He was chairman of the Free Democrats from 1996 to 1998, when he was succeeded by Bálint Magyar.

Tamás Magyarics

Kundera, Milan (1929–)

Czech novelist, poet, and essayist. Milan Kundera achieved growing international eminence as a novelist and intellectual during the 1970s. His first novel, *The Joke,* was originally published in 1967 in Prague, but he has lived in Paris since 1975, and has become a French citizen.

Born in Brno, Kundera studied philosophy and music in postwar Prague, an intellectual training that informs all his work. A year before the full force of Soviet influence materialized in the country in 1948, Kundera joined the Communist Party, and his first three books of poetry (*Man, the Vast Garden,* 1953; *The Last May,* 1955; *Monology,* 1957) demonstrate his early Marxist commitment.

Turning his back on poetry in 1957, Kundera instead produced a critical inquiry, *The Art of the Novel* (1960); two dramas, *The Owners of the Keys* and *Double Wedding* (1962; French tr. 1968); and three volumes of short stories published under one title, *Laughable Loves* (1963; French tr. 1965; English tr. 1968). Following *The Joke,* Kundera participated keenly in the brief liberalization of public life in 1968 known as the Prague Spring. He secured his reputation as a novelist with *Life Is Elsewhere* (1973), *The Farewell Party* (1976), *The Book of Laughter and Forgetting* (1978), *The Unbearable Lightness of Being* (1984), *Immortality* (1990), *Slowness* (1995), and *Identity* (1997).

Kundera's work might be approached in terms of history, modernity, and literature. Before the age of forty, he saw his homeland ceded to Hitler's Germany in 1938, liberated by the Red Army in 1945, and controlled or occupied by the Soviet Union in 1948 and 1968, respectively. For Kundera, as for Franz Kafka and Jaroslav Hašek, the Czech author of *The Good Soldier Schweik,* history has presented itself as an absurdity.

This experience did not lead to simplistic "anti-Communism," however, and Kundera's work explores classic modernist themes such as the search for self and the meaning of time and memory. Certainly, Kundera believed communism to be an alien way of life, and his work bears loose comparison with that of Orwell, Koestler, and Solzhenitsyn. But he is as likely to be remembered for his intellect, wit, humanity, and eloquence. His antiutopianism is unthinkable without communism, yet the result transcends historical particularity. The self-parodying excess of *The Joke* intersects the political with the personal, so that the self-embroilment of the main character, Ludvik, means that he is finally "condemned to triviality," as is the regime he lives under. This personal tragedy intersects at an even wider level with Kundera's central understanding of modernity as a "terminal paradox," meaning the erasure of rationality just at the moment when rationality fully succeeds, leaving behind a rudderless modernity, driven by irrational "will to power" and itself condemned to "triviality."

Alongside "will to power," Kundera embraces other Nietzschean elements such as a nimble, aphoristic style, the death of God, and the idea of a heroic but tragic existentialism. In *The Unbearable Lightness of Being*, however, he suggests that complete skepticism is actually "unbearable," finding its opposite pole in "heaviness," exemplified by the improbable commitment of Tomáš, a famous Prague surgeon, to the simple, provincial Tereza. By refusing resolution, Kundera intimates the possibility of a middle way between "lightness" and "heaviness."

Kundera is the most widely read central European author of the late twentieth century, and *The Unbearable Lightness of Being* was transformed into a distinguished film. But since eminence does not equate greatness, Kundera's future reputation must remain unclear. *Slowness* and *Identity* have been condemned for their banality and shallow characterization, the fear being that Kundera has himself capitulated to "lightness" with the end of the Cold War. His depiction of women has also come under scrutiny. Better material is to be found in the critical collections *The Art of the Novel* (1986) and *Testaments Betrayed* (1995).

Kundera's greatness lies in the "high modernist" sensibility of his work from the 1970s and 1980s, which relentlessly pits implacable realism against a yearning for durable meaning. Like the music of his beloved Janáček, Bartók, or Stravinsky, Kundera's finest prose is dissonant despite remaining "tonal." Lacking the apodictic quality of philosophy, Kundera sees literature gallantly setting out across a sea of uncertainty with a wisdom of its own. Despite his rejection of religion, he nonetheless bestows a prophetic function upon the novel, which becomes an oracle of modernity shorn of dogma or high priests.

BIBLIOGRAPHY

Aji, Aron, ed. *Milan Kundera and the Art of Fiction: Critical Essays.* New York: Garland. 1992.

Misurella, Fred. *Understanding Milan Kundera: Public Events, Private Affairs.* Columbia: University of South Carolina Press. 1993.

O'Brien, John. *Milan Kundera and Feminism: Dangerous Intersections.* New York: St. Martin's Press. 1995.

Richard Lofthouse

Kuroń, Jacek (1934–)

Polish politician, historian, journalist, and teacher. One of the leaders of the anti-Communist opposition in Poland and minister of labor and social welfare in the governments of Tadeusz Mazowiecki (1989–91) and Hanna Suchocka (1992–93).

Jacek Kuroń was born in Lvov (Polish, Lwów; Ukrainian, L'viv). He came from an intellectual family and received a doctorate in history from the University of Warsaw. He taught in a secondary school and soon afterward began postgraduate studies in pedagogy. Kuroń wrote articles for scouting weeklies from 1957 to 1961. He was the head of the Program Department in the Headquarters of the Association of Polish Scouting in 1960–61, and was co-founder of the so-called Red Scouting, through which he propagated his idea of democratic socialism. When the latter was dissolved, Kuroń was dismissed from all his functions in the scouting organization. He was also a member of the Communist Association of Polish Youth as of 1949. He joined the Polish United Workers (Communist) Party in 1953 but was expelled the same year for his refusal to submit to self-criticism. He joined the party again in 1956 to take an active part in its October 1956 assertion of independence from the dictates of the Kremlin and the development of its own more liberal policy with regard to collectivization, the conditions of workers, and relations with the Roman Catholic Church. The "Open Letter to Party Members," which he wrote with Karol Modzelewski, caused his second expulsion from the party in 1964.

In the 1960s Kuroń and Modzelewski were the leaders of the Young Marxist Revisionists movement. Expelled from the university for his criticism of the Communist establishment, Kuroń was sentenced to three years imprisonment. After his release in 1967 he was again active among students and young intelligentsia. Together with Adam Michnik, a fellow dissident, he became leader of a revisionist movement active in the student rebellion of 1968. Arrested again in March of that year, he spent three more years in prison, during which time he became completely disillusioned with Marxism.

He was a co-writer of "The 59's Letter," a protest against the amendments dealing with the leading role of the party and Poland's allegiance to the Soviet Union, which were added to the Polish constitution in 1975. Together with Antoni Maciarewicz he founded the Committee for Defense of Workers (1976–81) and founded and lectured at the underground Society of Academic Courses (1978–89). A cofounder, member, and adviser of the Solidarity trade union in 1980, he represented a moderate perspective. He was interned on December 13, 1981, and charged with attempting to subvert the political system. Kuroń was the author of "Theses upon Hopeless Plight" (March 1982), a controversial, and soon revised, conception of general uprising against all centers of authority and mass media. Later he argued that violent social rebellions were fruitless and inefficient. Released under amnesty in 1984, he was appointed a member of the Civic Committee by Lech Wałesa, and as such he took part in both the negotiations preceding the Round Table talks and in the meetings themselves, which resulted in the legalization of Solidarity and the free parliamentary elections of June 1989.

Elected to parliament on the Solidarity list in the groundbreaking free election of June 1989, Kuron was elected vice chairman of the Civic Parliamentary Club, which consisted of parliamentarians elected from the Solidarity lists. A member of the Democratic Union, the non-communist political group led by Tadeusz Mazowiecki, and its club in parliament, he withdrew in 1994 and organized the presidential election campaign for Mazowiecki, who was eventually defeated by Lech Wałesa.

BIBLIOGRAPHY

Kuroń, Jacek. *Gwiezdny czas: "Wiary i winy" dalszy ciąg.* London: "Aneks," 1991.

———. *Solidarność: The Missing Link? A New Edition of Poland's Classic Revolutionary Socialist Manifesto, Kuron & Modzelewski's Open Letter to the Party.* London: Bookmarks, 1982.

———. *Wiara i wina: do i od komunizmu.* Wrocław: Wydawnictwo Dolnoslaskie, 1995.

Piotr Skuz
Adam Zdunek

SEE ALSO Mazowiecki, Tadeusz; Wałęsa, Lech

Kwaśniewski, Aleksander (1954–)

President of Poland. A transport economics graduate of the University of Gdansk in 1978, Aleksander Kwaśniewski was also an activist of the Socialist Union of Polish Students, a front organization of the ruling Communist Party. After rising rapidly in the party, he was appointed minister without portfolio from 1985 to 1987, when he had responsibility for youth affairs. Later criticized for his membership in the Communist nomenklatura during the political upheavals of the late 1980s, he was elected leader of the successor to the Communist Party, the Social Democracy of the Republic of Poland (SDRP), at its first congress in January 1990. He was also the later architect of the SDRP's electoral coalition with the All Poland Trade Unions Alliance, known as the Democratic Left Alliance (SLD). First elected to the Sejm (parliament) in 1991, he regained his seat in the 1993 parliamentary elections. From 1993 until his election as president in November 1995, he also presided over the National Assembly's (the Sejm plus the Senate) Constitutional Commission. A young politician with a distinctly modern outlook, he gained the greatest number of votes in the presidential election, securing 51.7 percent of the valid ballot on the second round against the incumbent

Aleksander Kwaśniewski, president of Poland. *Illustration courtesy of the Polish Embassy, Washington, D.C.*

candidate for the presidency, Lech Wałesa. Although denounced as an opportunist neo-Communist by his vociferous opponents on the center-right of Polish politics, Kwaśniewski and his newly resurgent party greatly profited from the divisions among former Solidarity parties at a time when there was a wider move in the region back to the parties of the center-left. Despite his neo-Communist background, Kwaśniewski appointed a government committed to further economic reform and to eventual Polish membership in both the European Union and NATO. These objectives had all but been guaranteed by the third year of his presidency in 1998, and indeed Poland was admitted to NATO in 1999. Barring a major political mishap, Kwaśniewski will remain in office until his current mandate expires in 2000.

BIBLIOGRAPHY

Chroscicka, Agata. *Kwásniewski jestem.* Krakow: Wydawnictwo Amar, 1995.

Kwásniewski, Aleksander. *Kwásniewski: "nie lubie tracic czasul".* Lodz: Hamal Books, 1995.

———. *Wybierzmy przyszlosc: szkice programowe.* Warsaw: Verum, 1995.

Marko Milivojevic

SEE ALSO Wałęsa, Lech

Kyrgyzstan

Independent successor state to the Kyrgyz Soviet Socialist Republic of the former USSR. The Kyrgyz Republic consists of 76,640 square miles (198,500 sq km) of landlocked mountainous territory. It is located on a western spur of the Tien Shan Mountains. Its borders, most of which run, along the crests of mountains, abut Kazakhstan, Uzbekistan, Tajikistan, and China. The country's most noted geographical site is the high mountain lake, Ysyk-Köl. Rich in fish, it is located in the eastern mountains and is bordered by an alpine plateau to the west.

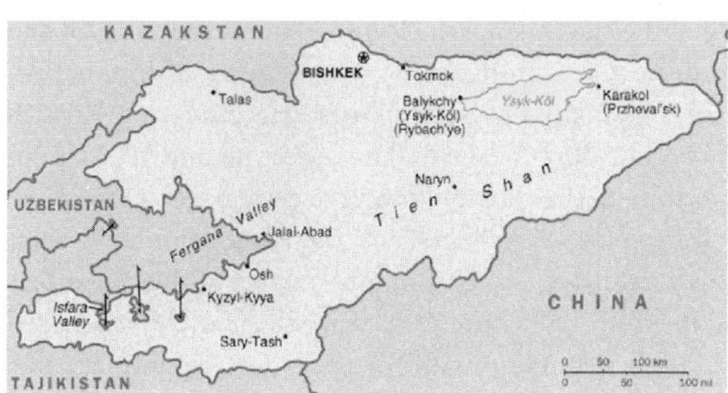

Kyrgystan. *Illustration courtesy of Bernard Cook.*

The country's only lowland regions, constituting a mere 15 percent of its territory, are the Fergana River valley in the southwest and the Chu and Talas River valleys along the border with Uzbekistan in the north. In addition to the country's rivers and Lake Ysyk-Köl, Kyrgyzstan has nearly 3,000 smaller lakes. Kyrgyzstan's population in 1992 was approximately 4,567,000. The principal religion is Islam. Most ethnic Kyrgyz, who constitute 52 percent of the population, as well as some of Kyrgyzstan's Uzbeks, who constitute 12 percent of the population, are Sunni Muslims. In 1989 Kyrgyz, a south Turkic language, replaced Russian as the official language. The Arabic script, used until 1928, was first replaced by the Latin script, and in 1940 by the Cyrillic. In 1993 Latin script was reintroduced. Russians constituted 22 percent of the population in 1992, and another 26 percent are also predominantly non-Kyrgyz speakers. As a practical consequence Russian was declared a joint official language in 1996. The capital, Bishkek, known as Frunze from 1926 to 1991, is located in the Chu River valley and has 631,000 inhabitants.

Kyrgyzstan, along with the Khanate of Korkand, was absorbed by Russia in 1876. The suppression by the Russian government of a widespread Central Asian rebellion against conscription during World War I in 1916, was followed by a large migration of Kyrgyz to China. After the suppression by the Communists of White and local anti-Bolshevik forces, during the Russian Civil War 1918–1920, the basmachi, Kyrgyzstan became part of the Turkestan Autonomous Soviet Socialist Republic. In 1924 the Kara-Kyrgyz Autonomous Oblast was established within the Russian Soviet Federated Socialist Republic. In 1925 the area was renamed Kyrgyz Autonomous Oblast, and in 1926 the Kyrgyz Autonomous Soviet Socialist Republic. On December 5, 1936, it became the Kyrgyz Soviet Socialist Republic of the USSR.

During the 1920s a standard literary language was developed and literacy spread. However, a vital oral tradition preserved Kyrgyz epics and lyric poetry. Two modern Kyrgyz writers have attained prominence. Playwright and novelist Chingiz Aytmatov won the 1963 Lenin Prize for his *Tales of the Mountains and Steppes.* He and Kaltay Muhamedjanov together wrote *The Ascent to Mt. Fuji,* a play dealing with moral compromise during the Stalin era.

Land reform brought about the settlement of many previously nomadic Kyrgyz. Collectivization was resisted by a revival of the Basmachi. During the great purge "national Communists," who advocated a greater administrative role for ethnic Kyrgyz, were suppressed. Ethnic-national tension between Kyrgyz and Russians persisted.

Kyrgyz, along with a million other Central Asians, were drafted during the Second World War. A number deserted to the Germans and others joined the pro-German Turkestan National Committee.

Beginning in the 1930s, there was a large migration of ethnic Russians to the republic. At the time of the 1979 census a million Russians and Ukrainians, nearly a quarter of the republic's population, lived in Kyrgyzstan. The urban centers, especially Frunze (Bishkek) became Russified. Russians dominated the economic and political administration. In Frunze, where Kyrgyz constituted only 20 percent of the population, Slavic students overwhelmingly dominated the student bodies of technical and scientific institutes. For the Kyrgyz of Frunze there was only one Kyrgyz language high school in the 1980s and that was forced to operate three shifts to accommodate demand. In none of the cities of the republic was there a kindergarten in which Kyrgyz was the primary language of instruction.

In 1950 Ishak Razzakov replaced A. Rysmendiev as the first secretary of the Kyrgyz Communist Party (KCP). Razzakov's support for the propagation of Kyrgyz culture was opposed by Russian bureaucrats who controlled life in the republic through their dominance of the administration, and because of his support of glimmers of Kyrgyz national expression he was replaced by Turdakun Usubaliev in 1960. Usubaliev, among his efforts to de-nationalize the Kyrgyz, restricted the publication of Kyrgyz epic poetry. The Kyrgyz claimed that the murder of Sultan Ibraimov, the chairman of the Kyrgyz Council of Ministers, in December 1980 stemmed from his advocacy of greater Kyrgyz autonomy.

The ascendancy of Mikhail Gorbachev resulted in the resignation of Usubaliyev. He was succeeded by Absamat Masaliyev, who, although he attacked the corruption and nepotism of his predecessor, was critical of Gorbachev's policy of glasnost (openness) and further alteration of the Soviet structure.

In 1989 people alienated by the system formed a number of unofficial organizations. The motivation was a severe housing shortage. These groups at first advocated the seizure of unused land and construction of housing on it. However, they rapidly developed broader political aspirations and became the nuclei of a political opposition. They also precipitated ethnic confrontations in the Fergana Valley of the Osh Oblast, where the quest for land and houses for the Kyrgyz came in conflict with the valley's Uzbek majority. Clashes with the Uzbeks, who demanded an autonomous region, resulted in eleven deaths in June 1990. By August at least three hundred and perhaps as many as one thousand people had died in clashes in the Osh region. The border with Uzbekistan was closed and a state of emergency imposed until September 1995.

The February 1990 election for the Kyrgyz Supreme Soviet (KSS), despite glasnost and the developing of an independent political consciousness, Kyrgyz was carried out with a slate of candidates chosen by the Communist Party. In April the KSS elected Masaliyev chairman of the KSS. He expected the KSS to elect him to the new office of president in October. However, his candidacy was undermined by the violence in Osh and the unification of the opposition in the Democratic Movement of Kyrgystan (DMK). As a result the presidency went to Askar Akayev (1944–), a physicist and president of the Kyrgyz Academy of Science, who allied himself with the advocates of political and economic reform. Reformers were appointed to a newly formed State Committee for Economic Reform, and plans were made to transfer state holdings to private ownership.

In December Masaliyev was replaced by Medetkan Sherimkulov as chairman of the KSS, and the KSS voted to change the name of the Kyrgyz SSR to the Republic of Kyrgyzstan; the name of the capital city was changed to its pre-1926 Bishkek. Despite the advance of democracy in Kyrgyzstan, economic realities persuaded 87.7 percent of its voters to preserve a "renewed" USSR in the March 1991 referendum promoted by Gorbachev to demonstrate popular support for the continuation of the USSR.

As a result of his opposition to Akayev's political and economic reforms, Masaliyev resigned as first secretary of the KCP in April 1991. Akayev's plan to end the control of the government and its security forces by the Communist Party raised the ire of the KCP and its new leader, Jumgalbek Amanbayev. At the time of the attempted August coup by conservative Communists against the changes advocated by Gorbachev in Moscow there was also an effort to oust Akayev. The KCP endorsed the coup and the military commander of the district, which encompassed the five Central Asian republics, threatened to send troops into Kyrgyzia. Akayev moved resolutely. He fired the chairman of the Kyrzyz state security (KGB) and ordered forces from the Kyrgyz Ministry of Internal Affairs to guard public buildings. He contacted Russian President Boris Yeltsin and broadcast his and Yeltsin's opposition to the coup on Kyrgyz television. After the failure of the coup, Akayev and Vice President German Kuznetsov repudiated the Communist Party and their membership in it. The entire leadership of the KCP acquiesced and resigned. On August 31 the KSS declared Kyrgyzstan independent. With the KCP dissolved there was no real opposition and Akayev was reelected president in a popular vote on October 12, 1991, in which he was the only candidate. He brought Kyrgyzstan into the new economic community linking eight former Soviet republics which Gorbachev agreed to in October, and the Commonwealth of Independent States (CIS) on December 13. Kyrgyzstan formalized this with ten other new states of the former USSR in the Alma-Ata Declaration of December 21.

Akayev's program of economic and political reform was the most advanced of any of the Central Asian republics. By November 1994, 74 percent of the country's agriculture had been privatized, and the IMF in early 1996 praised its process of economic reform, especially the privatization and restructuring of its industries. Kyrgyzstan, however, is among the poorest of the former Soviet republics. Its per capita gross national product in 1989 of $3,030 exceeded only those of Uzbekistan and Tajikstan. By 1992 the per capita gross national product had sunk to $610, and 70 percent of the population lived in poverty.

Agriculture and forestry employed 43 percent of Kyrgyzstan's workers in 1994. The arable lowlands constitute only 15 percent of the country's territory, and there agriculture depends on irrigation because rainfall amounts to only seven inches a year. The main crops are grain, sugar beets, cotton, and tobacco. Opium poppies, a problematic though profitable crop, are produced in the mountains. Sheep, goats, cattle, and horses are grazed in the land's alpine meadows. Bees, rabbits, and pigs are also tended there. Though self-sufficient in food, Kyrgyzstan must import petroleum and natural gas. In 1994 mining, manufacturing, construction, and power generation together employed 21 percent of the workforce. Approximately 40 percent of this industrial sector had been privatized by 1994, but industrial production, on the other hand, decreased by 25 percent between 1993 and 1994. Between 1985 and 1994 gross domestic production declined by 5.4 percent a year. The worst declines were precipitated by the disruption of markets and supplies that accompanied the collapse of the USSR. The gross domestic product as a whole declined by 5 percent in 1991, 19 percent in 1992, 17 percent in 1993, 26.5 percent in 1994, but only 6.2 percent in 1995. The removal of price controls in 1991 and 1992 resulted in serious inflation, but by 1995 this had been tamed.

Despite economic difficulties and escalating crime Akayev still enjoyed popular support. But opposition in parliament was spearheaded by nationalists and ex-Communists. In mid-1992 the KCP was reorganized under the leadership of Amanbayev. The parliament drew up a new constitution, approved on May 5, 1993, which established a parliamentary government with a prime minister as head of the executive.

Although Akayev unsuccessfully opposed the change of the country's name from the Republic of Kyrgystan to the more ethnically exclusive Kyrgyz Republic, or republic of and for the Kyrgyz the new constitution made Russian the language of interethnic communication. The president wished to preserve social harmony and ease the uncertainty fueling the emigration of Slavs and others from the country. Between 1989 and the middle of 1993, 145,000 Russians and over half the ethnic German population had departed. A blow to Akayev's hope for a more inclusive country and government was delivered in July 1993 when German Kuznetsov, the vice president, a close political ally, declared that because of his feeling of isolation he was leaving for Russia.

In 1993 a series of corruption scandals resulted in the resignation of Kuznetsov's successor Vice President Feliks Kulov and loss of a vote of confidence by Prime Minister Tursunbek Chyngyshev (1942–). The new government was headed by Apas Jumagulov (1934–), the last of the Soviet-era chairmen of the Council of Ministers, and Amanbayev became one of six deputy prime ministers. Akayev, nevertheless, retained popular support. At his initiative a referendum was conducted on January 30, 1994, and he received the endorsement of 96.2 percent of the 95.6 percent of the electorate who participated.

In June 1994, to stem the continuing hemorrhage of Russians, Akayev declared Russian to be the official language in areas where Russians constituted a majority and in "vital areas" of the economy. The application for dual citizenship was to be made simpler, Russians were guaranteed representation in the government, and the date for Kyrgyz to become the fully implemented official state language was delayed.

The clash between reformers and conservatives led to the dissolution of parliament and the government in September 1994. Akayev submitted to a referendum a revised parliamentary setup establishing a two-house legislature. It was overwhelmingly approved by 70 percent of the 87 percent of voters who participated. Elections for the new parliament were held in February 1995, and in April Jumagulov was reappointed prime minister.

Following parliament's rejection of a referendum to extend Akayev's term until 2001, a presidential election was held on December 24, 1995. Akayev won 71.6 percent of the vote; Masaliyev, again head of the KCP, 24.4 percent; and Sherimkulov, 1.7 percent. Akayev immediately called for a referendum to increase his power at the expense of parliament. On February 10, 1996, this was approved by 96.6 percent of the voting electorate. Jumagulov nevertheless was reappointed prime minister. Finally a measure to establish equality for the Russian language was approved by parliament.

Akayev stressed his determination that the Kyrgyz Republic remain a secular state. When Tajik fundamentalist rebels crossed into Kyrgyzstan in January 1993, he strengthened border controls and Kyrgyzstan sent troops to participate in the CIS mission to prevent the infiltration of rebels into Tajikistan from Afghanistan. Kyrgyzstan has advocated close cooperation with the other CIS members. In March 1996 it signed a treaty with Russia, Belarus, and Kazakhstan to establish a customs union and a "community of integrated states."

Kyrgyzstan has a number of assets: a well-educated citizenry, a good infrastructure, a productive agricultural sector, and considerable mineral resources. Kyrgyzstan is one of the principal sources of antimony and mercury. Its Kumtor gold mines are reputed to possess the world's seventh-largest deposits of the precious metal. It also has large coal reserves and lead and zinc. Kyrgyzstan also has ample hydroelectric resources and exports electricity. Its currency, the som, introduced in 1993, is stable and trade has expanded. With time and outside investments the future could be positive.

BIBLIOGRAPHY

Gleason, Gregory, and Alexander J. Motyl, eds. *The Central Asian States: Discovering Independence.* Boulder, Col.: Westview Press, 1997.

Mesbahi, Mohiaddin. *Central Asia and the Caucasus After the Soviet Union: Domestic and International Dynamics.* Gainesville, Fla.: University of Florida Press, 1994.

Olcott, Martha Brill. *Central Asia's New States: Independence, Foreign Policy, and Regional Security.* Washington: United States Institute of Peace, 1996.

Rumer, Boris Z., ed. *Central Asia: the Challenges of Independence.* Armonk, N.Y.: M.E. Sharpe, 1998.

Sagdeev, Roald, and Susan Eisenhower. *Central Asia: Conflict, Resolution, and Change.* Chevy Chase, Md.: CPSS Press, 1995.

Shoemaker, M. Wesley. *Russia, Eurasian States, and Eastern Europe 1995.* Harpers Ferry, W.Va.: Stryker-Post, 1995.

Bernard Cook

L

Lacan, Jacques (1901–80)

French psychoanalyst who revolutionized the theories of Freud. Born into a Parisian middle-class Catholic family in 1901, Jacques Lacan received a doctorate in psychiatry under Gaëtan Gatian de Clérambault in 1932. Greatly influenced by surrealism, Saussurian linguistics, and Alexandre Kojève's lectures on Hegel, Lacan's radical reinterpretation of Freud finally led to his expulsion from the French Psychoanalytic Society in 1953 and prompted him to form the Groupe d'Études et de Recherches Freudiennes. Often identified with the intellectual trend of structuralism and endorsed by Marxist philosopher Louis Althusser, Lacanian psychoanalysis was propelled into the mainstream of French radicalism during the 1960s.

Lacanian psychoanalysis does not aim at the integration of the individual psyche. An antihumanist in philosophical terms, Lacan posits instead a fundamentally divided or split subject striving vainly toward fullness through identifications with objects of desire. Between six and eighteen months, during what Lacan calls "the mirror stage," the infant obtains a sense of selfhood by identifying with his or her mirror image, thus conferring an imaginary sense of corporeal wholeness onto a still immature and uncoordinated body. While this realm of the Imaginary is common to all and mediates the Real, Lacan argues that one must nevertheless make a partial move toward the symbolic order, which coincides with the child's acquisition of language. For Lacan the psychically healthy subject is a split ego that, rather than aggressively projecting its imaginary ideal of wholeness onto others, instead introjects the symbolic/linguistic injunctions of the outside world.

BIBLIOGRAPHY

Grosz, Elizabeth A. *Jacques Lacan: A Feminist Introduction.* New York: Routledge, 1990.

Jay, Martin. *Downcast Eyes: The Denigration of Vision in Twentieth-Century French Thought.* Berkeley: University of California Press, 1994.

Lacan, Jacques. *Écrits: A Selection.* New York: Norton, 1977.

———. *The Four Fundamental Concepts of Psychoanalysis.* New York: Norton, 1978.

———. *The Seminar of Jacques Lacan, Book II: The Ego in Freud's Theory and in the Technique of Psychoanalysis, 1954–1955.* New York: Norton, 1988.

Roudinesco, Elisabeth. *Jacques Lacan & Co.: A History of Psychoanalysis in France, 1925–1985.* Chicago: University of Chicago Press, 1990.

Christopher E. Forth

SEE ALSO Althusser, Louis

Lafontaine, Oskar (1943–)

German Social Democratic politician. Oskar Lafontaine was born in Saarlautern (today Saarlouis) on September 16, 1943. Named after his maternal uncle, killed in action as soldier of the Wehrmacht during World War II, Lafontaine grew up very much under the impact of the war. His father was also killed in the conflict, and Lafontaine and his twin brother were brought up by their mother's eldest sister. From 1953 to 1961 Lafontaine and his brother, studied for the Roman Catholic priesthood, attending a Catholic boarding school in Prüm, near Bitburg.

In school, Oskar Lafontaine came to be feared as a bully, who, although not very tall was known to terrorize those who were physically inferior to him. Early in 1961 he was dismissed from the boarding school but allowed to continue his studies on the outside. The school in Prüm, its teaching styles, and, particularly, some of its teachers, had a decisive influence on young Lafontaine.

He learned Latin and ancient Greek, but his training in French and English was limited. His home room teacher was a former Nazi who agitated in class against the American "occupation" of Bitburg. Oskar, though not the top student of the class, became the teacher's favorite pupil, and he became Oskar's favorite teacher. Oskar seemed to be the perfect student the teacher was looking for: Physically strong, intelligent, domineering to the point of a bully, last not least imbued with an evident and potent strain of sadism—a promising young representative of Germany. Lafontaine not only developed a love for his teacher's main subject, physics, but learned to despise those who were inferior to him. Though his self-confidence increasingly turned into arrogance, Lafontaine was hardly more than a mediocre student. Classified unfit for immediate military service in the West German Bundeswehr (army), Lafontaine studied physics, first in Bonn, then later in Saarbrücken, where he received a diploma in February 1969.

Lafontaine joined the Social Democratic Party (SPD) in 1966 and was elected to the state legislature in 1970. His political career centered from the very beginning on the city of Saarbrücken. In 1974 he was elected deputy mayor of Saarbrücken, and, in 1976, with the help of some maneuvering behind the scenes that left the leading SPD contender out of the race, he became mayor. Lafontaine was one of the few prominent German socialist politicians who had a real Catholic background. He was the youngest mayor of a West German city at that time.

Lafontaine gained fame as the darling of the extreme left in West Germany. In his first book, *Angst vor den Freunden* (Afraid of Friends, 1983), which was widely regarded as a severe criticism of the United States, he stopped just short of demanding a full-blown German departure from NATO. Lafontaine had established contacts with East German Communists in March 1968. Secret meetings with East Germans were held regularly (but were to become known only after the files of the East German secret police became available in 1989). He met Erich Honecker, the leader of East Germany, for the first time in 1982. Between 1982 and 1989, before the downfall of Honecker, no West German politician, except for the leader of the obscure West German Communist Party, met Honecker more often than Lafontaine.

As a result of his rise in the Saar, Lafontaine in 1979 became a member of the SPD's central committee. In the late 1970s, Lafontaine, taking advantage of the developing opposition to the deployment of nuclear weapons in Germany, became a leader of the peace faction against the SPD chancellor Helmut Schmidt. In this role he became the protégé of former chancellor Willy Brandt. In 1982, Lafontaine contributed decisively to the downfall of the Social Democratic government. As the severest critic of NATO's strategy of flexible response, including the option to use nuclear weapons before they had been used by the Soviets, and the chief organizer of the mass demonstrations against it, Lafontaine threatened to split the party, and it was only the demise of Schmidt's government that prevented this. He had publicly said that Schmidt possessed leadership qualities "with which one could also run a concentration camp."

Lafontaine won 49 percent of the Saar vote for his SPD in March 1985 and became the minister president of the state (land). His ultimately conservative responses to the economic and fiscal difficulties of the Saar led the leader of the Saar Free Democrats, Horst Rehberger, to label him as a "brilliantly talented opportunist who had read more Machiavelli than Marx and Engels." He was also referred to as the "Napoleon of the Saar." Infuriated about the press that had publicized his connections to the red light district and his unscrupulous personal gains from several pension funds, Lafontaine turned against what he called "pig-journalism" and promoted legislation in May 1994 considered to be the most drastic infringement of press rights in democratic Germany. The law was only abolished after the CDU won the premiership of the Saar in 1999.

When Brandt stepped down as the leader of the SPD in 1987, the party elected Hans-Jochen Vogel as the new party chairman. Lafontaine, in spite of measures in the Saar that enraged his SPD constituency, was elected first deputy chairman. Following the SPD's defeat in the 1987 election, Lafontaine advanced a radical post-industrial program that would have replaced income taxes with taxes on energy consumption. In contrast to Kohl's enthusiastic espousal of German unification following the collapse of Communism in 1989, Lafontaine's hesitation to embrace the East German Revolution and support reunification even after Germany had already been unified (he prohibited the flying of German flags from private homes in his state on October 3, 1990, the day of reunification) polarized the German people. Though the SPD achieved a significant victory in his own Saar state elections on January 28, 1990, the SPD was eclipsed in the German Democratic Republic on March 18 by the conservative coalition Alliance's call for rapid unification. This failure, notwithstanding, Lafontaine, the next day, was formally nominated by the SPD to lead the party in December 1990 election. Despite having been wounded in an assassination attempt in April, Lafontaine continued his campaign. He futilely opposed, however, the economic union of the two German states concluded in July, in the process led his party to a resounding defeat.

Lafontaine, nevertheless, recovered from that electoral disaster was elected chairman of the SPD in 1995. He played a central role in orchestrating the SPD's electoral victory in September 1998, when Gerhard Schröder was elected the first SPD chancellor in sixteen years. On October 17, Lafontaine was appointed minister of finance in Schröder's cabinet. Under increasing criticism for attempting to interfere with the Eurobank's fiscal policy and after fierce attacks from the British yellow press in particular, his tenure came to an abrupt end on March 11, 1999, when he resigned his ministerial post and simultaneously resigned as chairman of the SPD. Lafontaine's left-oriented economic policy, including the advocacy of higher taxes and wage increases calculated to stimulate demand, had upset financial and industrial interests in Germany had been at odds with Schröder's economic pragmatism.

Schröder, despite the resentment of the party's left wing, was able to win the support of a majority to succeed Lafontaine as party chairman. In the autumn of 1999, Lafontaine accused the chancellor of having renounced traditional socialist values, and his apologetic *Das Herz schlägt links* (The Hearts Beats on the Left Side) became a huge success at the Frankfurt Book Fair.

Amidst a mass of apparatchiks, mediocre teacher-politicians, and party bureaucrats, Lafontaine stood out in modern German politics as a true personality who appealed to and commanded some influence among certain sections of the public. His talents, his rhetorical ability, and, not the least, his impulsive and partly totalitarian traits both attracted and repelled voters.

BIBLIOGRAPHY

Andrews, Edmund L., "German Finance Aide Quits; European Markets Jubilant," *New York Times*, March 12, 1999.

Filmer, Werner, and Heribert Schwan. *Oskar Lafontaine.* Düsseldorf: ECON-Verlag, 1996.

Hermann Joseph Hiery

SEE ALSO Kohl, Helmut; Schmidt, Helmut; Schröder, Gerhard; Vogel, Hans-Jochen

Lahnstein, Anne Enger (1949–)

Norwegian politician. Anne Enger Lahnstein was born in Trøgstad on December 9, 1949. She became a nurse, social worker, and deaconess. She taught nursing at the Norwegian Lutheran Hospital and College from 1975 to 1978. She entered politics as the coordinator of the Campaign Against Abortion on Demand in 1978–79. She headed the secretariat of the Center Party parliamentary group from 1980 to 1985. She was elected to the Storting (parliament) from Akershus county in 1985. She was a member of the Standing Committee on Social Affairs (1985–89), a member of the Standing Committee on Foreign Affairs and the Constitution (1989–93), and secretary to the Foreign Affairs Committee (1993–97). In 1980 Lahnstein became chairman of the Oslo branch of the Center Party, in 1983 deputy chairman of the national Center Party, and in 1991 chairman of the Center Party. From 1989 to 1991 she headed the Center Party parliamentary group. With the formation of the center-right coalition government in 1997 under Kjell Magne Bondevik, Lahnstein became minister for cultural affairs.

Under Lahnstein the Center Party, which draws its strength from the farming community, led a successful campaign in the November 1994 referendum in opposition to Norway's entry into the European Union (EU). The party's anti-EU campaign helped to catapult it into the second-ranking position among Norwegian parties. In the 1993 Storting election it won 32 of the 165 seats, surpassing the 28 seats of the Conservatives, supporters of EU membership, who had formerly held second place. Lahnstein, as befitted her rural constituency, was also highly critical of neoliberal, free-market economic policies. In general the Center Party under her leadership advanced positions that were to the left of the Labor Party, emphasizing the divergence between its position and that of the Conservatives. Her anti-Conservative stance paved the way for the 1997 coalition of Christian Democrats, Liberals, and Center.

BIBLIOGRAPHY

Enger, Trond A. *Anne.* Oslo: Gyldendal, 1994.

"Labour Wins from Feud." *Financial Times* (London), December 18, 1996.

Bernard Cook

Lama, Luciano (1921–96)

Leader of the General Italian Confederation of Labor. As a young socialist, Luciano Lama had used the false name Boris Alberti when he graduated in social sciences at the University of Florence under the Fascist regime with a thesis about peasants in Romagna. He remained a member of the Socialist Party until 1946, when he joined the Italian Communist Party.

His political activities began during the resistance against the German occupation of Italy, when he commanded the eighth Garibaldi partisan brigade. His career in the General Confederation of Italian Labor (Confederazione Generale Italiana del Lavoro, CGIL) Trade Unions began immediately after the war when he was named chief of the Forlì Trade Unions headquarters (the same position Pietro Nenni, who later became head of the Socialist Party, occupied in 1911). In 1947 he was already one of the six vice secretaries of the CGIL led by Giuseppe Di Vittorio. Later, he was appointed chairman of the Chemical Workers Union and of the Mechanical Workers Union (Federazione Italiana Operai Metalmeccanici, Fiom). In 1970 he was elected secretary-general of the CGIL, the most important confederation of labor unions in Italy, counting at that time more than three million workers. By this time he had developed a pragmatic attitude toward union negotiation that led him to advocate an alliance among the major labor unions confederations. In 1972 his commitment led to a Federative Pact signed by the three major unions, the so-called Triplice: the CGIL, the Catholic Italian Confederation of Free Unions (Conferderazione Italiana Sindicati Liberi, CISL) and the Social Democratic and Republican Union of Italian Workers (Unione Italiana Lavoratori, UIL). That would have gained a greater negotiating power for the unions in a period of intense social conflict, when the economic situation of the country was worsening. He also had to face the growth of more radical organizations that attracted workers away from traditional unions and the harsh hostility of new-left political movements. In 1977 the EUR Conference in Rome marked another turning point, a strategic cooperation between the Triplice and the government to implement a policy of wage restraint. In exchange for a policy of public investments devised to bring about higher employment, the labor unions committed themselves not to ask for excessive wage increases in order to curb inflation. It was the beginning of a new model of social relationships. The confederations decided to follow, not the particular interest of a single category of workers but a more general interest that included protection of the unemployed, and to seek a political economy coordinated with the government and with entrepreneurs. Lama thus started the so-called system of *concertatione* (working together), whose main objective was to stop the uncontrolled social conflicts that had swept Italy for many years and that the unions now wanted to bring to an end. *Concertatione* induced government to participate in bargaining not merely as an arbiter but as an active proponent of economic measures to bridge the gaps between parties.

After the death on June 11, 1983, of Enrico Berlinguer, the head of the Italian Communist Party, many expected Lama to succeed him as secretary of the Communist Party, but consistent with his vision that considered the unions autonomous from political parties, he declined to be a candidate. In 1986 he left the chair of the CGIL, becoming an influential member of parliament.

BIBLIOGRAPHY

D'Agostini F. *Il potere del sindacato.* Rome: Riuniti, 1978.

Guarino, M. *Caro Lama.* Viareggio: Laser, 1996.

Pansa, G. *Lama intervista sul mio partito.* Bari: Laterza, 1994.

Riva, M. *Intervista sul sindacato.* Bari: Laterza, 1976.

Turone, S. *Storia del sindacato italiano dal 1943 al crollo del comunismo.* Bari: Laterza, 1992.

Stefania Mazzone

La Malfa, Giorgio (1939–)

Italian Republican politician. Giorgio La Malfa was the son of Ugo La Malfa. He was educated at the universities of Pavia and Cambridge and became the leader of the Italian Republican Party (PRI) in 1987. He led the party into the opposition in April 1991, when he withdrew from the government of Giulio Andriotti. He touted the incorruptible image of the Republicans during the Tangentopoli corruption scandal, but was forced to step down as leader of the PRI on February 26, 1993, when it was announced that he was being investigated in connection with the abuse of party financing.

BIBLIOGRAPHY

"Clean-cut La Malfa Toppled by Corruption Probe." *The Reuter Library Report,* February 25, 1993.

Bernard Cook

La Malfa, Ugo (1916–79)

Ugo La Malfa was born in Palermo on January 13, 1916. He was among the founders of the Party of Action (Partito d'Azione), which he represented in the Committee of National Liberation (Comitato Liberazione Nazionale, CLN). La Malfa was a member of the Constituent Assembly that drafted Italy's constitution in 1946, and is considered one of the founding fathers of the Italian Republic. He joined the Italian Republican Party (Partito Repubblicano Italiano, PRI) in 1946 and served as its political secretary in from 1965 to 1975, then as its president until his death in 1979. La Malfa was elected to parliament as a PRI representative from Bologna. He was elected in 1948 and reelected in 1953, 1958, 1963, 1968, 1972, and 1976. In 1945 he was appointed minister of transportation. In 1950 he became vice premier as well as minister of commerce, and he held that post again in 1951. In 1963 he was minister of the budget. And in 1973, La Malfa served as minister of the treasury. In 1974 he was vice president of the Council of Ministers. On March 21, 1979, La Malfa again became vice president of the council and was appointed minister of the budget, but he died of cerebral thrombosis on March 26.

BIBLIOGRAPHY

Ginsborg, Paul. *A History of Contemporary Italy: Society and Politics, 1943–1988.* New York: Penguin Books, 1990.

"How Little Ugo Delivered Giant Italy Up to the Snake's Jaw." *Economist,* December 16, 1978.

Federiga Bindi Calussi

Lambsdorff, Otto Friedrich (1926–)

West German politician. When Otto Friedrich von der Wenge Count Lambsdorff was born in Aachen on December 20, 1926, the heyday of his family was already over. His father, Herbert Count Lambsdorff worked as a bank employee in Aachen. Otto Friedrich Lambsdorff grew up in Aachen and later in Berlin and Brandenburg/Havel, where he attended school. From the age of fourteen he attended boarding school at an elite school for the Prussian military, the Knight's Academy at the Cathedral in Brandenburg, located on the river Havel. This influenced him strongly. In 1944 he volunteered for military service, which lasted only a short time because a volley from the machine gun of an American aircraft smashed his right thigh, which had to be amputated. He was taken as a prisoner of war by the Americans. After his release in 1945 he followed his parents to Schleswig-Holstein, then moved to Cologne, where he took his *Abitur* examination. From 1947 to 1950 he studied at the universities of Cologne and Bonn and in 1950 took his first state examination in law. In 1952 he received a doctorate under Hans Carl Nipperdey. The topic of his dissertation was "Abandoning the Law of the Reich." In 1955 he passed the second state examination in law, which made him assistant judge. From 1960 onward he worked as a lawyer at the Lower and Superior Court in Düsseldorf. After his studies he completed commercial training in a bank and had a career in the credit business. He became director of an insurance company, Victoria Ruckversicherungs AG, in 1972. In 1953 he married Renate Lepper, with whom he had three children. After their divorce, in 1975 he married Alexandra Quistrop.

On May 1, 1952, he joined the Free Democratic Party (FDP). He became party district chairman in Aachen and became member of the FDP Board of Governors in the *Land* (State) of North Rhine-Westphalia. In 1953 he ran unsuccessfully for a seat in the Bundestag (lower house of parliament). That defeat strengthened his efforts to make a career in the economic sector. In that way he was one of the few party leaders who did not undertake a purely political career, and it was precisely his economic competence that made him indispensable to the FDP. But during his entire business career the rather right-wing Lambsdorff kept in close contact with his party. From 1968 to 1978 he was FDP state treasurer and thereby was in close contact with Walter Scheel and Hans-Dietrich Genscher. As of 1972 he was a member of the Federal Board of Governors of the FDP. From 1978 he was vice chairman of the North Rhine-Westphalia FDP, and from 1980 he was a member of the presidency of the FDP. In 1972 his run for a seat in the Bundestag was successful, and his parliamentary group appointed him economic spokesman. In 1978 he became federal minister of economics. Later he became enmeshed in the "affair on the party donations," which concerned bribery of politicians. As a consequence he had to resign in 1984. In 1987, in the course of the investigations, he was found guilty both of tax evasion and of abetting it. He did not withdraw from politics but held office as federal chairman of the FDP from 1988 to 1993. From 1991 to 1994 he was president of the Liberal International, the organization representing liberal-oriented parties from around the world. At the same time, in 1993 the FDP appointed him honorary chairman, and in April 1995 he became head of the Friedrich-Naumann Foundation, sponsored by the FDP, which distributes German governmental funds for educational and cultural projects.

Apart from his political activity, Lambsdorff holds the Golden Sports Badge for Disabled, and the Action Committee for Social Economy honored him with the Alexander-Rustow medal in 1986. He is second chairman of Deeds instead of Words (TATEN stats WORTE e.V), an initiative for promoting women in business.

BIBLIOGRAPHY

Feyerabend, Joachim. *Die leisen Milliarden: Das Imperium des Friedrich Karl Flick.* Düsseldorf: Econ 1984.

Kilz, Hans Werner. *Flick: Die gekaufte Republik.* Reinbek bei Hamburg: Rowohlt, 1983.

Lambsdorff, Otto Graf. *Aktive Industriepolitik?: Über die Rolle des Staates in der Wirtschaftspolitik: ein Streitgesprach zwischen Otto Graf Lambsdorff und Lothar Späth.* Stuttgart: Verlag Bonn Aktuell, 1987.

Schell, Manfred. *Die Kanzlermacher: erstmals in eigener Sache: Otto Graf Lambsdorff, Hans-Dietrich Genscher, Wolfgang Mischnick.* Mainz: v. Hase & Koehler, 1986.

Schneider, Hans-Roderich. *Otto Graf Lambsdorff.* Bornheim: Zirngibl, 1976.

Ester Trassl

Lampedusa, Giuseppe Tomasi di (1896–1957)

Giuseppe Tomasi, duke of Palma and prince of Lampedusa, was born on December 23, 1896, in Palermo, Sicily. At nineteen he interrupted his studies to take part in the First World War as an artillery lieutenant. He was captured by the Austro-Hungarians and escaped twice. He returned home toward the end of the conflict with shattered nerves. After a slow recovery he resumed studies at the Universities of Genoa and Turin. At the latter, he earned a degree in jurisprudence.

Sponsored by diplomat Pietro Tomasi del la Torretta, the young Lampedusa traveled and lived abroad, particularly in London and Paris. In England, he met Princess Alessandra Wolf-Stomersee, a student of psychoanalysis and the stepdaughter of his patron. He married her in 1932.

Called to arms again, he took part in the Second World War as an artillery captain. After the war, since the Lampedusa Palace had been destroyed in the war, he retired to a house in Palermo. His major work, *Il Gattopardo* (*The Leopard*), was published in 1958 after his death, and was brought to the screen by renowned director Luchino Visconti in 1963. *Il Gattopardo* is a splendid and colorful description of Sicily between the years 1860 and 1883. The story is largely that of the author's family. The Tomasi's coat of arms was a leopard. Prince Salina, the main character of the novel, is as disenchanted as was the author himself. He knows that "for everything to remain the same, everything must change." This adaptive behavior has been called in Italy *gattopardismo* ever since.

Other posthumous pieces by Lampedusa include *Racconti* (1961) and two collections of Literary criticism: *Lezioni su Stendhal* (1971) and *Invito alle lettere francesi del Cinquecento* (1979).

BIBLIOGRAPHY

Fumagalli, Paola. *Il Gattopardo: dal romanzo al film: Tomasi di Lampedusa e Luchino Visconti a confronto.* Florence: Firenze Libri, 1988.

Gilmour, David. *The Last Leopard: A Life of Giuseppe di Lampedusa.* New York: Pantheon, 1991.

David R. Davila Villers

Landsbergis, Vytautas (1932–)

Chair of Sajudis (the Movement for Reconstruction), the Lithuanian reform movement that became an anti-Communist political party, and president of the Lithuanian Supreme Council during the transition to independence (1990–92).

Apart from a period as secretary of the Composers' Union, Vytautas Landsbergis did not participate in politics until the emergence of the reform movement in 1987. Elected to high political office in 1990 and reelected in 1996, arguably his most important contribution was as a defender and symbol of Lithuanian national culture against the Soviet Union and the first president of the post-Soviet independent Lithuania. After the decline of Sajudis, Landsbergis founded and led the Conservative Party, which, with its right-wing allies, won the parliamentary election of 1996.

Landsbergis was born into a family that had made a major contribution to the Lithuanian national "awakening" in the last part of the nineteenth century in philology, lexicography, drama, and journalism. His father, who had fought for Lithuanian independence from the Russian Empire in 1918–20, was a leading architect in independent Lithuania during the interwar period, and served in the short-lived Lithuanian administration under German occupation in 1941. At great personal risk he and his wife sheltered Jewish friends from the Nazis.

Landsbergis, a distinguished musicologist, was a professor at the Vilnius conservatory; he is the greatest authority on Lithuanian composer and artist M. K. Ciurlionis. Landsbergis's championing of Ciurlionis was itself a political act during the Soviet period, when the authorities were hostile to manifestations of cultural nationalism. It illustrates Landsbergis's deepest political commitment to the preservation of Lithuanian national culture in the face of hostility, dilution, or indifference. He is closely associated with the Roman Catholic Church and acknowledges its formative role in Lithuanian history and its capacity to reinforce Lithuanian culture through its ritual and doctrine.

Elected the first leader of Sajudis in November 1988, Landsbergis represented a compromise between the rather cosmopolitan Vilnius intellectuals and the Kaunas nationalists. The emphasis of the former was on reform and reconstruction, whereas the Kaunas group gave priority to the achievement of independence from the USSR. After the emphatic victory of Sajudis in the Supreme Council elections in 1990, the council voted to restore independence and elected Landsbergis its chair, or president. In his two years in office he became the most prominent, though not the most popular, political figure in Lithuania, and represented to the outside world his country's aspirations for independence. In the tense and sometimes violent confrontations with Soviet troops and militia in 1991, Landsbergis showed the courage and conviction of a true leader. He also resisted attempts by Lithuanian nationalists to make citizenship qualifications more rigorous. In order to exclude nonethnic Lithuanians from citizenship. After Lithuania gained its independence in August 1991, he lost popularity and moved increasingly to the right. His allusive and indirect speaking style, the low priority he gave to economic and social questions, his endless foreign travel, and his manifest ambition to become the "Father of the Nation" alienated many of his former supporters. The drastic reduction in living standards as a result of the economic transition and Landsbergis's perceived divisiveness were powerful factors in his declining popularity.

In the parliamentary election of 1992, Sajudis was soundly defeated by the former Communists, who had transformed themselves into the Democratic Labor Party. In February 1993 Algirdas Brazauskas, the former head of the Lithuanian Communist Party, defeated the Sajudis candidate for president. Landsbergis issued dire warnings, largely unfulfilled, about the return of Kremlin influence in Lithuanian politics. As Sajudis broke up, Landsbergis became leader of the newly created Conservative Party, one of a group of right-wing parties that won the 1996 election. Since then he has occupied the position of speaker of parliament, which allows him to pronounce on a range of issues. He has been a strong advocate of Lithuania's membership in the European Union (EU) and NATO.

BIBLIOGRAPHY

Hiden, John, and Patrick Salmon. *The Baltic Nations and Europe: Estonia, Latvia and Lithuania in the Twentieth Century.* Harlow: Longman, 1991.

Lieven, Anatol. *The Baltic Revolution: Estonia, Latvia and Lithuania and the Path to Independence.* New Haven, Conn.: Yale University Press, 1993.

Misiunas, Romuald, and Rein Taagepera. *The Baltic States: Years of Dependence, 1940–1990.* London: Hurst, 1993.

Norgaard, Ole, et al. *The Baltic States after Independence.* Cheltenham, England: Edward Elgar, 1996.

Senn, Alfred Erich. *Lithuania Awakening.* Berkeley: University of California Press, 1990.

Smith, Graham, ed. *The Baltic States: The National Self-Determination of Estonia, Latvia and Lithuania.* Basingstoke, England: Macmillan, 1994.

Thomas Lane

SEE ALSO Brazauskas, Algirdas

La Pira, Giorgio (1904–77)

Giorgio La Pira was born in Pozzallo in the province of Ragusa in 1904. After obtaining certificates in accounting and classical studies on the secondary level, he began law studies at the University of Messina. The years spent in Messina were crucial for his intellectual formation. He moved to Florence, where he concluded his university career and received his degree in 1926. In 1934 he was appointed to the chair of Roman law at the University of Florence. His study of Roman law was combined with reading and reflection on Thomas Aquinas. He became increasingly involved in religious activity, especially care for the poor. He established a number of St. Vincent de Paul associations, charitable organizations of Catholic laypeople, to serve the poor.

His opposition to fascist government was explicit. In 1939–40 he published the small magazine *Principi,* but after a short time it was suppressed by Benito Mussolini's fascist dictatorship. Persecuted by the fascists, he was forced to leave Florence in 1943 but returned in 1944. He was elected as a Christian Democrat deputy to the Constituent Assembly. Reelected to the Chamber of Deputies in the first republican legislature, he took part in government as undersecretary at the Ministry of Employment and Social Insurance, and he was deeply involved with workers in the labor union struggles of postwar Italy.

Although he was not reelected to the Chamber in 1950, La Pira was elected mayor of Florence the same year. He was reelected mayor in 1956 and was returned to parliament in 1958. Once again in Florence, he served as mayor from 1960 to 1964. In 1965 he was elected to the city council.

La Pira's later life was dedicated to the cause of peace. He traveled to Moscow, Hanoi, and the United States, meeting with the likes of John Kennedy, Nikita Khrushchev, Gamal Abdel Nasser, and Charles de Gaulle. He regarded by the prayers of the Sisters of Seclusion, with whom he corresponded (*Lettere alle claustrali*), as an essential component of his work for peace.

In 1976 he accepted the invitation of the Christian Democrats to reenter electoral politics, but he was hampered by ill health. He died in Florence on November 5, 1977.

BIBLIOGRAPHY

Fanfani, A. *Giorgio La Pira: Un profilo e 24 lettere.* Milan: Rusconi, 1977.

La Pira, Gorgio. *L'attesa della povera gente.* (1950). New edition ed. by V. Citterich. Florence: LEF, 1978.

———. *La casa comune: una costituzione per l'uomo.* Ed. by U. De Siervo. Florence: Cultural editrice, 1979.

———. *La nostra vocazione sociale.* Rome: AVE, 1944.
———. *Per una architettura cristiana dello stato.* Florence: LEF, 1954.
———. *Principi.* Florence: LEF, 1975.
Mazzei, F. *Giorgio La Pira: Cose viste e ascoltate.* Florence: LEF, 1980.

Rosanna Marsala

Larsen, Aksel (1897–1972)

Danish politician, founder of the Socialist People's Party in 1959. Aksel Larsen, a foundry worker, was a member of the Communist Party from 1920 to 1958, and served as its chairman and leader from 1932 to 1958. He was a member of the Folketing (parliament) from 1932 to 1972, first for the Communist Party, then from 1960 for the Socialist People's Party.

Larsen, together with underground political leaders from other parties, organized the Danish resistance movement against the German occupation, which began in 1940. He was arrested in 1942, and in 1943 he was sent to German concentration camps, first Sachsenhausen and later Neuengamme. After liberation he served as a minister in the all-party coalition government from May to November 1945. But as a result of the beginning of the Cold War, the popularity that the Communist Party had enjoyed because of its strong participation in the resistance soon waned. The party became more and more isolated. Larsen criticized the Soviet invasion of Hungary in 1956 and was purged as a traitor. He kept his seat in parliament but as an independent. However, he soon became a rallying point for Danish anti-Stalinists. In 1959 with others who wanted a democratic socialist movement, he founded the Socialist People's Party. The party entered parliament in the general election of 1960 with eleven seats and 6.1 percent of the electorate. Larsen served as chairman of the new party organization from 1959 to 1968, and of its parliamentary group from 1960 to 1968. The Communist Party did not survive Larsen's exit and failed to win representation in the Folketing in the 1960 election.

The unassuming Larsen was seen by many as representing the man in the street. He was sent to parliament for forty years with some of the highest votes in the country. His contribution to Danish politics was to create a Nordic-style democratic socialist party to the left of the Social Democratic Party, and to give prominence to day-to-day questions.

BIBLIOGRAPHY

Jacobsen, Kurt. *Aksel Larsen.* Copenhagen: Vindrose, 1993.
Kragh, Jens. *Afrustning og socialisme.* Copenhagen: SP Forlag, 1979.
Larsen, Aksel. *Folkesocialisme.* Copenhagen: SP Forlag, 1977.

Jørn Boye Nielsen

Lasky Melvin J. (1920–)

Editor, writer, and cold warrior. Melvin Lasky was part of a remarkable contingent of intellectual cold warriors formed by *Partisan Review* and the anti-Stalinist Left of prewar New York City. Emerging from New York's City College in 1939, he took graduate courses at Michigan and Columbia Universities and was an assistant editor at the socialist *New Leader* before being inducted in 1943 and serving under General George Patton in World War II as a combat historian. After the war he stayed on in Germany, freelancing for small publications. In 1947 a speech he made in German excoriating Soviet censorship and terrorism in the arts caused an uproar at a conference organized by the Soviets in Berlin. Overnight Lasky became a symbol of artistic freedom throughout Germany, leading him to petition a reluctant General Lucius Clay, U.S. military commander in Berlin, for funds to start an intellectual review to present the West's leading antitotalitarians to a print-starved German audience.

Der Monat (*The Month*), which appeared in October 1948, had an immediate impact, gaining Lasky notice in State Department circles and vaulting him in the front ranks of "fascist/warmongers" in Soviet eyes. Lasky now joined with Michael Josselson of the CIA to organize a response to the Soviet "peace" offensive, an effort by the Soviet-dominated Communist Information Bureau (COMINFORM) to counter the U.S.-sponsored Marshall Plan. This was the Congress for Cultural Freedom, whose founding in Berlin in 1950 brought together dozens of prominent anti-Communists from Europe and America. But so negative were press reports of the orchestrated militancy of the proceedings that the operation was left in disarray. Eventually a more arts-oriented congress was established in Paris, with Josselson in control. Lasky remained in Berlin, nurturing a spirited circle of German editors and writers, and *Der Monat* became a template for other Congress publications.

In 1958 Lasky replaced Irving Kristol on *Encounter,* the congress's greatest asset. Immediately he extended its coverage of Eastern Europe and Africa. *Encounter* became a force in British party politics, while its London offices became something of a salon, where academics, journalists, and public figures from all over the world could meet.

In 1963 Lasky persuaded British press lord Cecil King to become *Encounter*'s patron, a move to uncouple the magazine from its CIA connection. It did not spare Lasky from the storm that engulfed the congress after many of its secrets were exposed in 1967. Amid accusations that he acted for the CIA, Lasky allowed that he had been "insufficiently frank" with his editorial colleagues but insisted he was nobody's agent. Subsequently, an impressive number of *Encounter*'s contributors rallied to his side, and, with King's support, he even weathered a vote of the magazine's trustees to ouste him.

Encounter survived on a diminished basis (it lasted until 1991). Unlike other New York intellectuals, Lasky contributed little to the neoconservatism that took hold after the Vietnam era. He will be remembered as a man of his hour, an editorial impresario of remarkable zest and resourcefulness, whose impact on postwar Germany, East and West, was profound.

BIBLIOGRAPHY

Hegewisch, Helga, ed. *Melvin J. Lasky: Encounter with a Sixtieth Birthday.* London: Encounter, 1980.

Longstaff, S. A. "*Der Monat* and Germany's Intellectual Regeneration, 1947–1950." *History of European Ideas* xx, nos. 1–3 (1994):93–99.

S. A. Longstaff

SEE ALSO Congress for Cultural Freedom

La Torre, Pio (1927–82)

Sicilian Communist leader and opponent of the Mafia. Born in Palermo, Pio La Torre earned a degree in political science at the University of Palermo. He wrote assiduously for *L'Unità, L'Ora, Rinascita,* and *Critica Marxista.*

La Torre joined the Communist Youth Federation in 1945. In 1947 he started his career as an organizer first at the Confederation of Land Workers (Confederterra), then at the Italian Confederation of Labor (CGIL), and finally at the Italian Communist Party. In 1950 he was arrested and kept under preventive custody for eighteen months after organizing peasants to occupy land in the province of Palermo. From 1952 to 1958 he was secretary of the Confederated Work Chamber in Palermo, and in 1959 he became regional secretary of the Sicilian CGIL. In 1960 La Torre became a member of the Central Committee of the Communist Party, and in 1962 he was elected regional secretary of the party in Sicily. In 1969 he was appointed by the Communist Directorate in Rome to take charge of the Agriculture and Southern Sections. At the time of the party's Fifteenth Congress, La Torre was called to take part in the National Secretariat in Rome, but in 1981 he requested to return to Sicily, where he resumed leadership of the Party Regional Secretariat. On April 30, 1982, he was assassinated by the Mafia in a street near the regional political seat of the Communist Party in Palermo.

The role played by La Torre both in politics and in the fight against the Mafia was very important. Abjuring the current moral and intellectual practice of smoothing over differences and avoiding disagreements, he affirmed the necessity of precise ideas and an open and clear political fight against the enemy. He was a persevering and stubborn organizer, because he believed that politics required organized action involving all available forces. For this reason he imparted to several generations of Sicilian Communists a moral lesson on the meaning of political struggle.

His contribution to the fight against the Mafia was remarkable since he tried to follow its evolution and transformation, realizing that a new criminal organization was developing that threatened to destroy not only Sicily's democratic life but Italian democracy itself. La Torre pursued the goal of rescuing both Sicily and the rest of Italy from that mortal enemy.

BIBLIOGRAPHY

Bufalini, Paolo. *Gli anni di Pio La Torre.* Alcamo: Sarograf, 1986.

La Torre, Pio. *Le ragioni di una vita: Scritti di Pio la Torre.* Bari: De Donato, 1982.

Maras, Bruno. *Gli anni di Comiso 1981–1984: Documenti, testimonianze e interventi.* Palermo: Istituto Gramsci Siciliano.

Fabio Marino

Latvia

Successor state to the Latvian Soviet Socialist Republic. The territory of the Latvians was successively overrun by

Latvia. *Illustration courtesy of Bernard Cook*

the Germanic Teutonic Order, Poland, and Sweden, and became part of the Russian Empire in 1721. Latvians, along with Lithuanians, belong to the Baltic language group. Surviving examples of written Latvian date from the sixteenth century, and the first Bible was printed in Latvian in 1689. There was an awakening of Latvian culture in the early nineteenth century when the first newspapers were published in Latvian and a Young Latvia movement fostered the expression of Latvian culture and the development of a Latvian literature. The 1880s witnessed a deliberate policy of Russification, however, as Russia attempted to smother developing peripheral nationalisms. Following the First World War, which left Germany defeated and Russia in revolutionary turmoil, Latvia, along with its neighbors Lithuania and Estonia, experience a brief period of independence. But it was eradicated in 1940, when the Soviet Union formally annexed Latvia.

Latvia is located on the Baltic Sea and is bordered by Estonia, Russia, Belarus, and Lithuania. Its population is 2.7 million, of whom 71 percent live in and around the capital, Riga, a city of 910,000. Latvians, who in 1940 constituted 75 percent of Latvia's population constituted in 1989 only 33 percent of Riga and 51.8 percent of the population of the country as a whole in the late 1990s. Russians, Byelorussians, Ukrainians, and Poles constitute about 48 percent of the nation's population. Some 40 percent of the country 24,900 square miles (64,500 sq km) is cultivated and another 40 percent is forest. Natural resources are sparse, though there is natural gas.

When the Soviet Union occupied Latvia on June 17, 1940, a puppet regime under Augusts Kirchensteins replaced the government of President Karlis Ulmanis. Approximately thirty-three thousand Latvians were deported to Soviet Siberia during the first year of Latvia's Soviet experience. The USSR made a determined effort to suppress the Latvian culture and language. Following the expulsion and defeat of the German at the end of the war 130,000 Latvians fled to the west. Despite, or perhaps because of, an armed resistance movement that lasted into the 1950s, the process of Sovietization was again implemented. Among those who remained there were new deportations. Over 100,000 Latvians were imprisoned or sent to work camps. More were deported to Siberia, forty-three thousand on March 25, 1949, alone. The Communist Party of Latvia (CPL) was led by Janis Kalnerzins and a clique of Latovichi, Russianized Latvians who had spent the 1920s and 1930s in the Soviet Union. Industrialization was promoted and with it the importation of Slavic workers who made Latvia the most "russified" of the three Baltic republics. Before the Soviet occupation, ethnic Latvians had constituted around 75 percent of the population; by 1989 they made up only 51 percent.

Coinciding with a degree of economic decentralization permitted by Moscow in the mid-1950, there was a call within the CPL to nurture cultural and linguistic diversity. Nevertheless, in the late 1950s 2,500 government and CPL bureaucrats were purged for "nationalism." Kalnerzins was ousted as first secretary in 1959. His replacement, Arvids Pelse, was a Moscow loyalist. He and Augustus Voss, first secretary from 1966 to 1984, reversed the limited decentralization and intensified efforts to suppress the Latvian language and culture. Nevertheless, in the 1970s and 1980s there was a decided reaction as groups were organized to promote the revival of Latvian culture. A particularly significant role in raising national consciousness was played by the Environmental Protection Club, established in 1984, and Helsinki-86, a group organized in 1986 to monitor Soviet compliance with the human rights components of the 1975 Helsinki Accords. Despite police repression and the hostility of the new first secretary of the CPL, Boris Pugo, Helsinki-86 took advantage of the new climate proclaimed by Soviet President Mikhail Gorbachev's policy of glasnost (openness) to commemorate significant episodes in Latvian history.

In 1988 Latvia's cultural unions called for Latvian to be made the official republic language. They simultaneously called for the secret protocols of the Soviet-German 1939 agreement, the death knell for independent Latvia, to be published. In October 1988 dissidents outside and within the CPL organized the Popular Front of Latvia (PFL), whose initial objective was Latvian sovereignty within the USSR. This would have provided some local autonomy, especially Latvian language and cultural rights. By the end of the year the PFL, led by the journalist Dainis Ivans, had perhaps 250,000 adherents of whom approximately 85 percent were Latvian.

In September 1988 Pugo was moved to Moscow. Under his replacement, Jan Vigris, the PFL gained a dominant role in the CPL. But with the formation of the Latvian National Independence Movement (LNIM) the call was raised for complete independence. Many of its members also belonged to the LPF, and in May 1989 the leaders of the LPF called for a referendum on independence. In the March 1989 election for the USSR's Congress of People's Deputies, twenty-six of the thirty-four Latvian seats had been won by members of the LPF. In July the Latvian Supreme Soviet (LSS), imitating moves by its counterparts in Lithuania and Estonia, enacted a decree of sovereignty, but for many this was insufficient. Already in June the LPF, prodded by LNIM, had called for independent statehood. On August 23, 1989, in an impressive display of solidarity and an explicit affirmation of their determination to become independent again, millions of Estonians, Latvians, and Lithuanians joined hands in a human chain extending from the Estonian capital, Tallinn, through Riga, to Vilnius, capital of Lithuania.

In January 1990 the LSS ended the CPL's monopoly status. In February it condemned the 1940 absorption of Latvia by the USSR and voted to restore old state symbols. In the March–April elections for the LSS, the PFL won 131 of the 201 seats. The CPL then split into two factions, a hard-line, anti-independence majority led by Alfred Rubiks, and a pro-independence, Independent Communist Party of Latvia, led by Ivars Kezbers. On May 4 the Supreme Soviet, now called the Supreme Council (SC), which chose Ivars Godmanis to head a PFL dominated government, declared the absorption of Latvia by the USSR in 1940 illegal and issued a declaration of Latvian independence to be implemented through a period of staged transition.

Gorbachev responded on May 14. He decreed that the declaration of independence was invalid, but apparently due to international pressure did nothing further until pressed by conservative forces within the Soviet leadership. Tension rose as non-Latvians concerned about their status in an independent Latvia organized demonstrations. Anti-(Latvian) government sentiment was encouraged by the Soviet forces in Latvia, especially OMON, the elite units of the Soviet Ministry of Internal Affairs. In January 1991, Alfreds Rubiks, the leader of the conservative splinter of the CPL, proclaimed a "Committee of Public Salvation" to replace the government of Godmanis. OMON forces took control of the Riga Press House that had been the property of the CPL, and killed five Latvians who attempted to defend the Ministry of Interior from the Soviet-sponsored coup. Altogether twenty Latvians were killed and over one hundred wounded as they manned barricades around government buildings and communication centers. The Latvian administration in response to Soviet violence refused to participate in the March 17, 1990, referendum on a new union treaty for the USSR. Non-Latvians in the republic voted expressing their support for the preservation of the USSR. The Latvians, in their stead, held a referendum on independence on March 3. The turnout was very high and the measure was overwhelmingly approved.

When word arrived on August 19 that a coup was underway in Moscow, despite the presence of Soviet troops and the belief that determined military action was imminent, the Supreme Council met in an emergency session and it declared Latvia completely independent. It also denounced the coup attempt. With the collapse of the coup Godmanis's government took control in Latvia, the CPL was dissolved, and Rubiks was arrested. The USSR State Council bowed to the inevitable on September 6 and accepted Latvian independence. The restored country was admitted to the United Nations shortly afterward.

The issue of citizenship became an immediate ticklish question. The Supreme Council granted full citizenship to the residents and the direct descendants of residents, regardless of ethnicity, of pre–June 17, 1940. Other residents would have to apply for citizenship after appropriate legislation had been approved by a new parliament (Saeima), which would be elected in June 1993. Thus non-Latvians (and their descendants) who had moved to the republic following the Soviet occupation were left in political limbo. Their status and future were uncertain and they would not be allowed to vote in at least the first election of independent Latvia. On July 22, 1994, the Saeima adopted a "Law on Citizenship," which reiterated the June 17, 1940, residency requirement and, thus, in the minds of the legislators established the principle of de jure continuity between the 1918 republic and contemporary Latvia. Perhaps more practically, it was a reaction to the fact that during the Soviet occupation, fewer than 25 percent of non-Latvian residents could speak Latvian, and, according to linguists, Latvian had arrived at the second stage of linguistic extinction. Under the 1994 law permanent residents, regardless of nationality, could apply for citizenship with several exceptions. Excluded were those determined by a court decision to have acted in an unconstitutional fashion against the Latvian state, those who are or were members of foreign security or armed forces, those who engaged in unconstitutional activities as members of specific organizations declared to be hostile to the Republic of Latvia, and those imprisoned for crimes for over a year. Naturalization required five years of residence after May 1990, knowledge of Latvian, and familiarity with the history and constitution of the country, willingness to take an oath of loyalty, a legal income, and renunciation of prior citizenship. Priority was granted to those born in Latvia or who had entered the country as minors. The draft law, submitted to the Council of Europe and the Organization for Security and Cooperation in Europe (OSCE) for evaluation, was criticized for its limited annual quotas. It was therefore rejected by Latvian President Guntis Ulmanis on the advice of the Council of Ministers. The offending quotas were removed in July 1994, after which the law was judged to comply with international norms and Latvia was admitted to the Council of Europe in February 1995. A Latvian National

Human Rights Office, set up in July 1995, was commissioned to investigate individual cases of suspected rights abuse and to investigate activities of state institutions. A Naturalization Board was established and the first applications were accepted on February 1, 1995. Between then and January 1, 1998, of the 120,000 people judged eligible, only 8,810 applied, and of these 7,206 became citizens. On July 22, 1997, the Latvian government decided to promote additional applications by reducing the application fee.

The citizenship issue and the status of Russian military pensioners in Latvia constituted contentious issues between Latvia and Russia. Another problem was the continued presence of one hundred thousand Russian troops on Latvian soil after independence. The United States mediated a schedule for their withdrawal and, following consultations by President Ulmanis in Moscow, the remaining troops were withdrawn ahead of schedule before the end of August 1994. There remained the issue of the border and Latvia's desire to become a full member of NATO. Latvia joined NATO's Partnership for Peace program in 1994. It also claimed 633 square miles 1,640 of territory transferred to Russia during the occupation. However, Latvia gave way and in March 1997 a draft treaty on the border was signed.

The first election for the new parliament took place on June 1993. Latvian Way, a political movement launched in February 1993, won thirty-six of the one hundred seats. The Latvian National Independence Movement (LNIM), which espoused a program of radical nationalism, won fifteen seats; Harmony for Latvia–Revival of the Economy, which advocated a liberal citizenship law, won thirteen; the centrist Latvian Farmers Union (LFU) won twelve; the Equal Rights Movement, led by imprisoned Rubniks (who would be convicted in July of seeking to forcibly overthrow Latvia's state authorities) won seven. The successor to the CPL, the Latvian Socialist Party (LSP), did not win a single seat, nor did the PFL. Godmanis, who had been a founder of Latvian Way, was elected chairman of the Saeima. The constitution of 1992 was restored and Guntis Ulmanis of the LFY, grand nephew of Karlis Ulmanis, one of the founders of independent Latvia in 1918 and its dominant political figure until he was forced out by the Soviets in 1940, was elected president. President Ulmanis appointed Valdis Birkavs, previously a deputy chairman of the Supreme Council and a leader of Latvian Way, prime minister with a coalition composed of Latvian Way and the LFU. In mid-July 1994, however, the LFU withdrew from the cabinet because of its opposition to the government's agricultural policies. In September a new cabinet, again dominated by Latvian Way, was set up under Maris Gailis.

In 1995 the country faced a serious banking crisis, and in May the government closed Banka Baltija, Latvia's largest commercial bank. Though the banking situation stabilized by early 1996, a general election took place on September 30 and October 1 in which Latvian Way was cut back to seventeen seats, while the left-wing Democratic Party Saimnieks (DPS) emerged as the largest party with eighteen seats. A government was formed in late December headed by Andris Skele, a nonparty-member businessman who had served as deputy minister of agriculture. In June Ulmanis was reelected for a three-year term as president. In July the LUP merged with the DPS, strengthening its status as the largest party in the Saeima. Guntars Krasts became prime minister in 1997; he was succeeded by Vilis Kristopans in 1998; and Skele returned in 1999. Skele's center-right People's Party formed a coalition with the centrist Latvia's Way, and the nationalist Fatherland and Freedom. Together they held 62 seats in the 100 seat Saeima. Previous governments had been reluctant to introduce sharp budget cuts and his immediate task was to deal with Latvia's budget deficit that stood at 2.8 percent of the GDP.

On June 17, 1999, Varia Vike-Freiberga was elected president. She was born in Riga on December 1, 1937, but grew up in refugee camps in Germany. She emigrated to Canada where she earned a doctorate and became a professor of psychology at the University of Montreal. She announced that her prime goals were to gain admission for Latvia to NATO and the EU.

Economic reforms were introduced following independence to guide Latvia into a market economy. Industrialization during the foreigners to purchase land and to buy former state enterprises. By 1997 the Saeima approved a balanced budget.

Since Latvian was declared the official language in 1988, all students in the country must study Latvian. Yet during the 1994–95 academic year less than two-thirds of elementary and secondary schooling was conducted in Latvian. There are Russian schools in which the language of instruction is Russian. By 1996–97, 70 percent of primary education was in Latvian, 15 percent in Russian, and 14 percent in both languages. Ethnic schools or at least classes have been established for other ethnic groups such as Poles, Estonians, Lithuanians, and Gypsies.

BIBLIOGRAPHY

Hidden, John, and Patrick Salmon. *The Baltic States and Europe: Estonia, Latvia, and Lithuania in the Twentieth Century.* New York: Longman, 1991.

"Latvia," *Europa World Year Book.* London: Europa Publications, 1997.

"Latvian Woman Is President," *New York Times,* June 18, 1999.

Lieven, Anatol. *The Baltic Revolution: Estonia, Latvia, and Lithuania and the Path to Independence.* New Haven, Conn.: Yale University Press, 1993.

Shoemaker, M. Wesley. *Russia, Eurasian States and Eastern Europe, 1996.* Harpers Ferry: Stryker Post, 1997.

Vipotnik, Maty, "Skele returns to power in Latvia," *Financial Times* (London), July 13, 1999.

Bernard Cook

SEE ALSO Baltic Assembly

Citizenship Issue

The question of who was entitled to Latvian citizenship was a central issue faced by the newly independent state. In Latvia at the restoration of independence in 1991, a significant proportion of the population were migrants from other parts of the former USSR and their children. Latvian nationalists commonly referred to them as "colonists" or "occupiers" and sought to deny them the right to citizenship.

In 1989 the reformist Popular Front of Latvia adopted a more conciliatory approach, promising citizenship to all residents of Latvia who had supported the establishment of independence. This more inclusivist attitude represented a step in the direction of the so-called zero option, guaranteeing citizenship to all residents.

These conflicting approaches to citizenship reflected fundamental differences in historical interpretation. Radical nationalists argued that the Soviet occupations of Latvia in 1940 and 1944 were illegal, and that the Latvian state had continued to exist de jure in the whole of the Soviet period. Consequently, the declaration of independence in 1991 represented a restoration of the pre-1940 Latvian state. It followed that Soviet-era immigrants were agents of the occupying power and therefore had no legal right to remain in Latvia, still less to participate in its politics. Since the ethnic Latvian share of the population was only about 52 percent, the consequences for Latvian identity of giving the vote to ethnic Russians, Belarussians, and Ukrainians would, arguably, have been profoundly damaging.

Opponents of this interpretation argued that the Latvian republic had ceased to exist in 1940 and a new, second republic had been created by the declaration of independence in 1991. All residents of the republic, with a few exceptions, were therefore entitled to citizenship. This approach counterpoised civic nationalism, an "inclusionary conception of community," against ethnic nationalism, which identified the eponymous nation with the state. In 1994 this argument was resolved in favor of a modified restorationism.

This radical nationalist perspective was embodied in the citizenship law passed by the Supreme Council in 1991, which awarded Latvian citizenship to those who had been citizens in 1940, and their descendants. Under these criteria about 80 percent of citizens were ethnic Latvians and about one-third of all non-Latvians gained citizenship. The remaining, mostly Russophone, residents numbered some seven hundred thousand. The conditions under which they could acquire citizenship were to be left to the new parliament elected by citizens under the 1991 act.

Meanwhile, guidelines issued by the Supreme Council in 1991 suggested that residency and language qualifications would figure prominently in new legislation. On the other hand a radical nationalist proposal in 1994, which was rejected by parliament, attempted to prevent former Soviet citizens who settled in Latvia between 1940 and 1992 from acquiring residence permits, without which they could not qualify for citizenship.

The bill that emerged from parliament in the summer of 1994 was returned unsigned by President Ulmanis. Partly as a result of international pressure exerted through organizations such as the Organization for Security and Cooperation in Europe (OSCE) and the Council of Europe, Ulmanis objected to the quota system embodied in the law. This would have restricted the number of naturalizations to a miserly two thousand per year.

International pressure eventually ensured that parliament dropped the quota system, replacing it with a system of naturalization staggered according to age for those noncitizens born in Latvia. This process was due to be completed by the end of the century. For those born outside Latvia, processing of applications would not begin until the year 2000.

Applicants for citizenship had to meet several conditions: residence of at least five years as of May 4, 1990; competence in the Latvian language; the swearing of a loyalty oath to the state; and familiarity with Latvian history, the Latvian constitution, and the Latvian national anthem. Officers of the Soviet security forces and serious criminals were excluded from applying for citizenship.

In 1994 some 61 percent of ethnic Russians residing permanently in Latvia were noncitizens. The 1994 legislation offered a step-by-step approach to the acquisition of citizenship. The gradualism of the 1994 law provided a better chance of improved inter-ethnic relations than a hastily introduced inclusivism that would cause resentment among the majority, or an uncompromising emphasis on "ethnic purity" that would alienate the non-Latvian minorities.

BIBLIOGRAPHY

Citizenship and Language Laws in the Newly Independent States of Europe: Seminar held in Copenhagen, January 9–10, 1993. Copenhagen: Danish Center for Human Rights, 1993.

Norgaard, Ole. *The Baltic States after Independence.* Northampton, Mass.: Edward Elgar, 1999.

Scheinin, Martin, ed. *International Human Rights Norms in the Nordic and Baltic Countries.* Boston: M. Nijhoff Publishers, 1996.

Smith, Inese A. *The Baltic States: Estonia, Latvia, Lithuania.* Santa Barbara, Calif.: Clio, 1993.

Thomas Lane

Political Parties

Pluralistic political activity was renewed in Latvia in the late 1980s after a fifty-five-year interruption. Parliamentary political activity, which occurred between 1920 and 1934, had been halted on May 15, 1934, when Prime Minister Karlis Ulmanis suspended the constitution and disbanded parliament. During World War II Latvia was occupied by the Soviet Union then Nazi Germany, and in 1945, after the war, Latvia was annexed to the USSR. From 1945 to 1990 the only officially sanctioned political party was the Communist Party.

The Communist period in Latvia can be subdivided into the Stalinist era from 1945 to 1953, the rise of national communism during the Khrushchev thaw from 1954 to 1959, and the period of repression of national sentiments up until the "awakening" that began in 1987–88. The repression of national communism had an impact on Latvia's political development in at least two significant ways. First is the influence of these events on the subsequent economic development and the ethnic composition of Latvia. The downfall of proponents of development based on local resources and labor led to the fundamental integration of the Latvian economy into that of the USSR and to large-scale immigration of non-Latvian laborers to Latvia. The second impact was the disillusionment of young Latvians because of the removal of local Communist leaders such as Eduards Berklavs from politics in 1959. Berklavs returned to political life in the late 1980s as one of the founders and leaders of the Latvian National Independence Movement (LNNK). A number of Latvian politicians in the struggle for independence traced the development of their political consciousness to the events of 1959.

The liberalization of the Gorbachev years allowed an awakening of national and democratic political activity in Latvia. Initial activity was characterized by the human rights organization Helsinki '86 and environmental groups such as the Environmental Protection Club, which organized large public demonstrations to commemorate national holidays and to protest against polluting enterprises. The first overtly political pro-independence groups, such as LNNK and the Popular Front, drew many of their activists from these organizations. For the 1990 parliamentary elections to the Supreme Council, two major political groupings were formed: the Popular Front, which was pro-independence, and Equal Rights, which was pro-USSR. The Popular Front won more than 66 percent of the votes of all Latvian residents, and its representatives in the Supreme Council voted on May 4, 1990, to reestablish Latvian independence. An alternative structure, the Citizens Congress, was elected by an electorate limited to those who could prove eligibility for pre-1940 Latvian citizenship.

After Latvia's independence was recognized in 1991, the Popular Front began to fragment owing to the nationality/citizenship question and economic policy. Several political parties whose popularity was well established during Latvia's period of independence after 1917—the Farmers Union and the Social Democratic Workers Party—renewed their activities. The Social Democrats had continued their activities in exile and underground in Latvia during the Soviet years. The 1993 parliamentary elections resulted in a right-of-center majority in the fifth parliament. Some well-known political groups such as the Greens, Social Democrats, Popular Front, and Democratic Labor Party did not achieve the 5 percent necessary to be represented in parliament. The largest share of the vote, 37 percent, was achieved by Latvia's Way, a party recently formed by a combination of Popular Front leaders, including Anatolijs Gorbunovs and Indulis Berzins, and leaders of the Latvian community abroad, such as Gunars Meirovics and Valdis Pavlovskis. The party's platform combined moderate Latvian nationalism with liberal free-market economic policies. The second-largest share of the vote went to LNNK, which espoused a more nationalistic ideology but also supported free-market economic reform. Aleksandrs Kirsteins, who became head of LNNK's faction in parliament, was a strong proponent of radical free-market reforms and rapid integration into Western Europe, and away from Russia, espoused by Mart Laar and his Pro Patria party in Estonia. LNNK subsequently changed its name to Latvia's National Conservative Party, officially transforming itself from a movement to a political party. It became the first party in Latvia led by a woman, Anna Seile, who was elected chair on April 20, 1995. The party formed a coalition with the Greens for the Riga municipal elections in 1994, which it won, and for the parliamentary elections in 1995. The Greens in Latvia, while predominantly concerned with the environment, were right-of-center. The Farmers Union (LZS), which originally formed the ruling coalition with Latvia's Way, supported economic reform and moderate Latvian nationalism but lobbied for agricultural supports for farmers. In preparation for the 1995 parliamentary elections, the Farmers formed a coalition with the right-of-center Christian Democrats and a regional party, the Latgale Democrats. The most right-wing party in parliament was Fatherland and Freedom, whose base was among the supporters of the Citizens Congress. Fatherland opposed the naturalization of post-1940 immigrants and supports affirmative action policies for Latvian citizens within the context of a free-market economy. All these Latvian parties supported Latvian membership in the European Union and the North Atlantic Treaty Organization. The largest left-of-center coalition in the fifth parliament was Harmony for Latvia and Rebirth to the Economy, initially led by former foreign minister Janis Jurkans. The coalition soon split into the Peoples' Harmony Party, led by Jurkans and drawing its support from minority voters, and the Association of Political Economists, which supported a strong state sector in the economy and later joined Latvia's Way in the government. One deputy of the left-coalition joined the Democratic Party-Saimnieks (DPS). DPS, led by Ziedonis Cevers and Alberts Kauls, who held posts in the Communist Youth and the Communist Party, was oriented toward the state sector and the market area formed by the newly independent states of the former Soviet Union. The most left-wing group in the fifth parliament was the Socialist Party, which united with Equal Rights, and whose orientation was toward other former Communist groups in the territory of the former Soviet Union. An interesting phenomenon in the fifth parliament was Joachim Siegerist, chairman of the German Conservatives, who formed the Peoples Movement for Latvia and concentrated his campaigning primarily among pensioners hardest hit by economic reforms, with a message based on virulent anticommunism. Siegerists was elected to parliament as part of LNNK but was expelled from that party in 1993.

BIBLIOGRAPHY

Norgaard, Ole. *The Baltic States after Independence.* Northampton, Mass.: Edward Elgar, 1999.

Smith, Inese A. *The Baltic States: Estonia, Latvia, Lithuania.* Santa Barbara, Calif.: Clio, 1993.

Peteris Zilgalvis

Lauschmann, Bohumil (1903–58)

Czechoslovak Social Democratic politician. Bohumil Lauschmann was minister of industry from 1945 to 1948. He was elected chairman of the Social Democrats in November 1947, replacing the pro-Communist Social Democrat Zdeněk Fierlinger. Lauschmann, joined with Fierlinger however, and remained in the cabinet with Klement Gottwald, the Communist Prime Minister, and the Communists in February 1948. Nevertheless, following the forced amalgamation of the Social Democrats with the Communists, as the Communists consolidated their hold on Czechoslovakia he lost not only his party chairmanship but also his ministerial post. In January 1950 he fled to Germany with his son. There he was kidnapped by Czechoslovak agents and abducted to Czechoslovakia in 1953. He was sentenced to seventeen years in prison, where he died on July 28, 1950. It is suspected that he was murdered.

BIBLIOGRAPHY

Kaplan, Karel. *The Short March. The Communist Takeover in Czechoslovakia 1945–1948.* New York: St. Martin's, 1987.

Bernard Cook

SEE ALSO Fierlinger, Zdeněk

Lawson, Nigel (1932–)

British politician. Nigel Lawson was a Conservative member of Parliament for Blaby (Leicestershire) from 1974 to 1992. He held a number of ministerial posts including financial secretary to the Treasury (1979–81), secretary of state for energy (1981–83), and chancellor of the exchequer (1983–89).

After a career in journalism and broadcasting and brief advisory posts to Prime Minister Alec Douglas-Home (1963–64) and Conservative Party headquarters (1973–74), Lawson entered parliament. He served as opposition whip from 1976 until his appointment as opposition spokesman on treasury and economic affairs (1977). When the Conservatives returned to power in 1979, Lawson became financial secretary to the Treasury. His knowledge of economic issues and commitment to monetarist policies made him an ideal candidate for the secretaryship of the Department of Energy at the time the government was intent on the privatization of industries, cuts in public spending, and the freeing of constraints on consumer credit—the "Lawson boom." Lawson played a key role in the Conservatives' landslide victory in the 1987 election through his short-term managing of the economy.

A serious rift developed between Lawson and Prime Minister Margaret Thatcher over interest rates and membership in the European Exchange Rate Mechanism. As Thatcher began to rely more heavily on her special economic adviser, Alan Walters, rather than her chancellor, Lawson tendered his resignation in October 1989. This marked the beginning of the party split that would result in Thatcher's resignation the following year. In 1991 Lawson announced his decision not to continue in the House of Commons beyond the next general election. In 1992 he entered the House of Lords.

BIBLIOGRAPHY

Keegan, William. *Mr. Lawson's Gamble.* London: Hodder & Stoughton, 1989.

Lawson, Nigel. "The Frontiers of Privatization." Adam Smith Institute, 1988.

———. "Rules vs. Discretion in the Conduct of Economic Policy." University of London, 1990.

———. "Tax Reform." Conservative Political Center, 1988.

———. *The View From No. 11: Memoirs of a Tory Radical.* London: Bantam, 1992.

———. "What Sort of Europe?" Conservative Political Center, 1 1989.

Eileen Groth Lyon

Laxness, Halldór (1902–98)

Icelandic Nobel Prize winner in literature, born as Halldor Gudjonsson, later taking up the name of his birthplace, the farm Laxness, as a pen name. He published his first novel in 1919 and established himself as the leading author of prose literature in Iceland in the 1920s and 1930s. Laxness remained a controversial figure in Icelandic society, however, both for his radical views on politics and his unconventional orthography. The Nobel Prize in 1955 brought him international recognition, and since then he has generally been regarded as the greatest author of twentieth-century Iceland.

Laxness's success has been attributed to his ability to combine Icelandic literary traditions with cosmopolitan influences. He traveled widely throughout his long career, establishing contacts and friendships with colleagues in Europe and the United States. In the early 1920s he converted to Catholicism, but later he renounced religion and became deeply inspired by socialism. His novels are all firmly rooted in Icelandic experience, and his religious or political opinions never dominated his writings.

BIBLIOGRAPHY

Hjalmarsson, Jon R. *History of Iceland: From the Settlement to the Present Day.* Reykjavík: Iceland Review, 1993.

Gudmundur Halfdanarson

Lazar, György (1924–)

Prime minister of Hungary (1975–87). György Lazar replaced reformist-minded Jenö Fock at the head of the cabinet, and during his tenure presided over the gradual decline of the command economy.

Lazar joined the Communist Party early in his career and was entrusted with relatively important positions though he did not have a university degree. Thus, he became vice president of the National Planning Bureau in 1958 and was promoted to head it in 1973. He was minister of labor from 1970 to 1973. He became deputy prime minister in 1973 and prime minister in 1975, a position he held almost until the collapse of Communist rule in Hungary. He was a member of the Party's Central Committee from 1970 to 1988, and of its Political Committee from 1975 to 1988. He functioned as the deputy secretary-general of the party in 1987–88, retiring from political life in 1988.

Lazar was a loyal bureaucrat who showed little originality or initiative. He was always a loyal supporter of the ideologically orthodox and the party's conservative leaders.

BIBLIOGRAPHY

Kis, Janos. *Politics in Hungary: For a Democratic Alternative.* Boulder, Col.: Social Science Monographs, 1989.

Lazar, Gyorgy. *A nep tamogatasaval a szocializmus utjan: valogatott beszedek es cikkek 1971–1983.* Budapest: Kossuth, 1983.

———. *Integralt aramkorok, mikroprocesszorok es mikroszamitogepek muszaki-gazdasagi kerdesei.* Budapest: Kozponti Statisztikai Hivatal, 1979.

Sugar, Peter F., ed. *A History of Hungary.* Bloomington: Indiana University Press, 1994.

Tamás Magyarics

Lazarenko, Pavlo (1953–)

Prime minister of Ukraine (May 1996–June 1997). Pavlo Lazarenko was born on January 23, 1953, in Karpova in the Dnepropetrovsk region of Ukraine. The longtime director of a state farm in the Dnepropetrovsk region, Lazarenko is accused of being one of many Ukrainian officials who used public office to engage in private business deals for self-enrichment. At the time of his appointment Lazarenko declared that he would continue economic reforms and, in particular, speed up privatization. His subsequent actions belied this. Lazarenko is a member of a clique from Dnepropetrovsk formed by the Soviet-era nomenklatura. He was promoted from energy minister to prime minister in May 1996 by President Leonid Kuchma, former manager of the USSR's largest missile factory, also located in Dnepropetrovsk. Natural gas is the most lucrative business in Ukraine, one of the world's largest importers of natural gas. As energy minister Lazarenko assigned to United Energy Systems, which was run by a friend the major trade in natural gas. He has also been accused of being behind the seizure by the state in the fall of 1996 of the control grain shipments, and hence their distribution and sale, a serious blow to development of a market economy in agriculture. Though Kuchma subsequently ordered regional governors to cease the seizures, his order had little effect.

On June 18, 1997, Kuchma, under pressure from Western lenders and donors, removed Lazarenko by decree. Lazarenko, who was the fifth prime minister to be dismissed since Ukrainian independence in, was succeeded by Vasyl Durdynets, who had been first deputy prime minister.

BIBLIOGRAPHY

Koscharsky, Halyna, ed. *Ukraine Today: Perspectives for the Future.* Commack, N.Y.: Nova Science Publishers, 1995.

Kuzio, Taras. *Ukraine under Kuchma: Political Reform, Economic Transformation and Security Policy in Independent Ukraine.* New York: St. Martin's Press, 1997.

Bernard Cook

SEE ALSO Kuchma, Leonid

Lebed, Aleksandr Ivanovich (1950–)

Leading Russian politician, former national security adviser to President Boris Yeltsin, and former commander of the Russian Fourteenth Army, stationed in the Republic of Moldova. Aleksandr Lebed was born in Novocherkassk in the Russian Republic of the former USSR. He graduated in 1967 from secondary school in Novocherkassk, and received degrees from the Ryazan Higher Airborne School in 1973 and the Frunze Military Academy in 1985. From 1973 to 1981 Lebed served as a platoon and company commander at the Ryazan Higher Airborne School.

Lebed served as a battalion commander in Afghanistan in 1981–82 and, after completing a course at the Frunze Academy, was commander of an airborne regiment in 1985–86 and deputy commander and commander of an airborne division from 1986 to 1991. As division commander he took part in military operations in Azerbaijan and Georgia in 1988–90, and as commander of the Tula Airborne Division, Lebed played a crucial role in foiling the August 1991 coup in which Communist conservatives tried to seize power from President Mikhail Gorbachev, although he later contended that he did not take sides in the conflict between President Gorbachev and his opponents.

In June 1992 Lebed was named commander of the Russian Fourteenth Army, the remnant of the former Soviet Fourteenth Army stationed in the Transnistria region of Moldova. Under Lebed's leadership the army intervened to halt fighting between Moldovan forces and Transnistrian separatists in summer 1992, paving the way for the signing of a cease-fire and the deployment of a tripartite, Russian-Moldovan-Transnistrian peacekeeping force in July 1992. Lebed was initially a supporter of the Transnistrians' demands, arguing that the Moldovan government was intent on persecuting ethnic Russians in the republic and unifying the country with Romania. In 1993 he even won a seat in the Transnistrian Supreme Soviet, a post from which he soon resigned. Later, however, serious rifts developed between Lebed and Transnistrian leaders, especially the local president, Igor Smirnov, over Lebed's charges of corruption and arms trafficking by Transnistrian elites. During the October 1993 conflict between Yeltsin and the Duma in Moscow, Lebed refused to take sides, arguing that the army should remain neutral in domestic political conflicts.

In 1994 tensions began to develop between Lebed and his longtime ally Defense Minister Pavel Grachev, with whom he had served at the Ryazan school and in Afghanistan. Lebed was harshly critical of the slow pace of military reform and the dire state of Russian troops stationed outside the Russian Republic. In response, Grachev attempted to remove him in August 1994, but backed down after Yeltsin threw his support behind Lebed.

Lebed's numerous media appearances and his calls for an "iron fist" to combat corruption among Russian politicians and businessmen made him a popular figure in the country. In May 1995 Lebed retired from the military with the rank of lieutenant general and returned to Russia to begin a political career. He developed strong ties with the Communist Party of the Russian Federation, to whose Central Committee he had been elected in June 1990, and with the Congress of Russian Communities (KRO), a nationalist organization headed by Yuri Skokov concerned largely with the plight of ethnic Russian communities outside Russia. Lebed stood as a KRO candidate in the December 1995 parliamentary elections, receiving a seat representing the city of Tula.

In the June 1996 Russian presidential elections Lebed finished in third place in the first round, receiving 14.5 percent of the vote. Eager to secure Lebed's support in the second round, the incumbent Boris Yeltsin appointed Lebed chairman of the Russian Security Council and dismissed Defense Minister Pavel Grachev, who had become Lebed's main rival within the government. Over the following months, however, Lebed's public statements and outspoken criticism of the government caused increasing embarrassment to Yeltsin. Despite Lebed's having brokered a tentative agreement between Russian forces and separatists in the republic of Chechnya in August 1996, Yeltsin dismissed Lebed as security chief in October of that year. He remained a widely popular public figure, a vocal opponent of Yeltsin, and an advocate of strong government to combat corruption and the declining state of Russia's military.

In May 1998 Lebed made a convincing political comeback and positioned himself for the Russian presidential race in 2000. He won a sweeping victory in the runoff election for governor of the Siberian region of Krasnoyarsk, defeating incumbent Valery Zubov, who had been supported by Yeltsin.

BIBLIOGRAPHY

Lambeth, Benjamin S. *The Warrior Who Would Rule Russia.* Santa Monica, Calif.: RAND, 1996.

Lebed, Alexander. *My Life and My Country.* New York: Regnery, 1997.

———. *Spektakl' nazyvalsiia putch.* Tiraspol (Transnistria) Moldova: Rekliz-Eolis, 1993.

———. *Za derzhavu obidno.* Moscow: Moskovskaya Pravda, 1995.

Polushin, Vladimir. *General Lebed': zagadka Rossii.* Moscow: Vneshtorgizdat, 1996.

Charles King

SEE ALSO Chechnya; Transnistrian Moldovan Republic; Yeltsin, Boris

Lem, Stanisław (1921–)

Polish essayist. His works concentrate on the relationship of man to science and technology, and on the future of technical civilization. Stanisław Lem is Poland's eminent science fiction writer. Born on September 12, 1921, in Lvov, after World War II he moved to Kraków. His degree in medicine and vast knowledge in various fields of science allowed Lem to formulate competent interdisciplinary diagnoses about civilization. To present them Lem uses the convention of science fiction and the form of the essay. His philosophy is dominated by his conviction of the fatalistic nature of reality, the transfer of evolutionary mechanisms from the sphere of biology to technology and culture, and the permanence of human nature, which is the last reference point in a world of constant change. His visions of such a world are presented in novels: *Eden* (1959), *Pamiętnik znaleziony w wannie,* 1961), *Solaris* (1961), *Glos Pana* (*His Master's Voice,* 1968), *Fiasko* (1987). After an episode of social realism (*Astronauci,* 1951; *Oblok Magellana,* 1955), Lem utilized several conventions of science fiction: the grotesque (*Dzienniki gwiazdowe,* 1957, full ed. 1994), fantasy (*Cyberiada* [*The Cyberiad,* 1967]), realistic literature of the future (*Opowieści o pilocie Prixe* [*Tales of the Prix, the Pilot,* 1968]), and computer fiction (*Golem XIV,* 1981).

Lem is a master at mixing various literary genres. He convincingly ties knowledge with imagination and language mastery. He was a precursor in dealing with issues of cybernetics (*Dialogi,* 1957; *Summa Technologiae,* 1974). His interest in the theory of literature was expressed in works *Filozofia przypadku* (1968; rev. ed., 1988) and *Fantastyka i futurologia* (1970), as well as numerous essays. As a literary critic Lem is known to verify empirically the ideas and to judge severely the intellectual value of science fiction. He is also the most frequently translated Polish writer.

A film version of *Solaris* was directed by Andrej Tarkovski in 1972.

BIBLIOGRAPHY

Balcerzak, Ewa. *Stanisław Lem.* Warsaw: PIW, 1978.

Bereś, Stanisław. *Rozmowy ze Stanisławem Lemem.* Kraków: Wyd. Literackie, 1987.

Jastrzębski, Jerzy. *Zufall und Ordnung: zum Werk Stanisław Lems.* Frankfurt am Main, 1986.

———, ed. *Lem w oczach krytyki światowej.* Kraków: Wyd. Literackie, 1989.

Stoff, Andrzej. *Powieści fantastyczno-naukowe Stanisława Lema.* Warsaw: PWN, 1983.

———. *Lem i inni.* Bydgoszcz: Wyd. Pomorze, 1990.

Ziegfeld, Richard E. *Stanisław Lem.* New York, 1985.

Andrzej Stoff

Lemass, Sean (1899–1971)

Irish prime minister (1959–66). Sean Lemass is one of the most important figures in post-1945 Irish politics. As prime minister he is widely held to have been the psychological and political regenerative force in postwar Ireland. Lemass was a founding member of Fianna Fáil, the Republican Party, helping to set up the organization at ground level. Before 1932 he was party spokesman on economic affairs. From 1932 to 1948 he was minister for industry and commerce except for the period from 1940 to 1945, when he was minister for supplies with responsibility for provisioning the country throughout World War II, in which Ireland was neutral. Eamon de Valera prime minister of Ireland 1932–48, 1951–4, 1957–9, and president 1959–73 referred to him as "my most brilliant minister," and from the late thirties he was seen by many as prime minister in waiting. Though always appearing deferential to de Valera, he increasingly came to hold power beneath the surface. He became obvious heir apparent after Sean T. O'Ceallaigh was elected to the presidency in 1945.

Lemass was minister for industry and commerce from 1951 to 1954 and from 1957 to 1959. These years saw him jettison his previous belief in economic protectionism in favor of state intervention along Keynesian lines. He became prime minister in 1959, when Ireland was at a low ebb following the unprecedented depression of the 1950s. Lemass imparted a new sense of national direction and proved to be the most dynamic prime minister to date. Unlike de Valera he did not seek uniformity of opinion at cabinet meetings but had a brusque, business-like style of leadership.

Lemass oversaw the dismantling of protectionism and the start of economic planning through the 1959 First Programme for Economic Expansion. His policies led to the economic regeneration of the Irish state. He presided over the most rapid phase of economic growth and material transformation the country had ever seen. His policies gave self-confidence and self-respect to a previously depressed Ireland. He brought in new blood to government such as Charles Haughey, Kevin Boland, Jack Lynch, Neil Blaney, and Brian Lenihan. He took a realistic line on Northern Ireland, for the first time recognizing its existence by holding cross-border talks with Northern Premier Terence O'Neill. It was the first time since the mid-twenties that the prime ministers of North and South had met. His outward-looking policies and cosmopolitan attitude prepared the way for Ireland's admission to the European Economic Community in 1973. He was pragmatic toward neutrality, hinting at Ireland's future membership in the North Atlantic Treaty Organization, and was unreservedly pro-West during the Cold War. He retired abruptly in November 1966 after engineering the succession of Jack Lynch.

Lemass was not the charismatic leader that de Valera had been; rather, he was a tactician behind the mask of a pipe smoking Mr. Plain. Though in recent years the long-run benefit of Lemass's policies has been questioned, their phenomenal short-run impact on the Ireland of the 1960s lives on in popular memory.

BIBLIOGRAPHY

Farrell, Brian. *Chairman or Chief?* Dublin: Gill and Macmillan, 1971.

———. *Sean Lemass.* Dublin: Gill and MacMillan, 1983.

O'Sullivan, Michael. *Sean Lemass.* Dublin: Blackwater, 1994.

Michael J. Kennedy

SEE ALSO De Valera, Eamon; Lynch, Jack

Lenart, Josef (1923–)

Josef Lenart was born in Liptovska Porubka, Czechoslovakia, on April 3, 1923. He joined the Czechoslovak Communist Party in 1943. As pressure mounted in Czechoslovakia after 1960 for liberalization and economic decentralization, President Antonín Novotný in 1963 sacrificed Karol Bacilek, leader of the Slovak branch of the Communist Party, and Premier Viliám Siroky, both of whom had roused the ire of the Slovaks by supporting the centralization espoused by Novotný. Siroky was replaced by Lenart, an apparently more acceptable Slovak, and Bacilek was replaced by Alexander Dubček. These appointments temporarily calmed the situation, and Novotný was reelected president in 1964. Lenart, however, was an opponent of sweeping reform. Unwilling to keep pace with the developing Prague Spring, he was replaced as premier in March 1968 by Oldrich Cernik.

Lenart, despite his ouster as premier, continued to serve as a secretary of the Communist Party. He is one of the conservatives accused of either collaborating with the Soviets to prepare for the invasion of August 1968 or, at least, of rallying to the Soviet cause once the invasion had begun by asserting that the Soviet-led Warsaw Pact invaders had been invited in by party loyalists to thwart a counterrevolution.

Lenart was a member of the party Presidium until he was ousted at the time of the Velvet Revolution in November 1989. He was expelled from the party in February 1990. On August 10, 1995, he was arrested and accused of treason for collaborating with a foreign power—the USSR—at the time of the August 1968 invasion.

BIBLIOGRAPHY

Šimečka, Milan. *The Restoration of Order: The Normalization of Czechoslovakia.* London: Verso, 1984.

Bernard Cook

Lenihan, Brian (1930–95)

Irish politician. Brian Lenihan was one of the brash newcomers brought into Fianna Fáil (Republican party) governments in the 1960s by Sean Lemass, Irish prime minister 1959–66, Lenihan served as a member of the Senate (1957–61), minister for justice (1964–69), minister for education (1968–69), minister for transport and power (1969–73), and minister for foreign affairs (1973). He lost his seat in the Irish Parliament in 1973 but was elected to the European Parliament, where he served until 1977. He was returned to the Dáil for Dublin–South West in 1977. He was minister for forestry and fisheries (1977–79), minister for foreign affairs (1979–81), and minister for agriculture (1982). Lenihan lost this post as a result his alleged attempt to interfere with President Patrick Hillery's power to dissolve the Dáil. In 1987, however, he became deputy prime minister and minister for foreign affairs. He held these positions until 1989 and served as minister for defense from 1989 to 1990. Lenihan was unsuccessful in his bid as the Fianna Fáil presidential candidate in 1990. He died on November 1, 1995.

BIBLIOGRAPHY

Lenihan, Brian. *For the Record.* Dublin: Blackwater Press, 1991.

———. *No Problem.* Dublin, Blackwater Press, 1990.

Michael J. Kennedy

Leone, Giovanni (1908–)

Italian prime minister and president. Giovanni Leone was a lawyer and professor of law and criminal proceedings. He became political secretary of the Christian Democrats of Naples in 1945. On June 2, 1946, he was elected a member of the Constituent Assembly and contributed enormously to the creation of Italy's postwar constitution. He was a member of parliament from 1946 to 1963, and in May 1955 he became president of the Chamber of Deputies, the lower house of the Italian parliament.

He was prime minister from June to November 1963 and again from June to November 1968. In 1967 he was appointed a life member of the Senate by President Giuseppe Saragat, and in 1971 he was elected president of the Italian Republic.

Leone's presidency was tarnished by the Lockheed Scandal. In 1976 it was disclosed that two ministers and the Christian Democratic Party had taken bribes in 1970 from the American company, Lockeed, to buy Hercules air freighters for the Italian air force. The entire Italian political elite was tainted by the scandal. Leone was compromised because of his friendly relations with the brothers Lefebre, who had acted as go-betweens in the transaction.

In the wake of the kidnapping and murder of former prime minister Aldo Moro by the terrorist Red Brigades, and the rejection by the electorate of a referendum on providing government funds to political parties, Leone resigned on June 15, 1978.

BIBLIOGRAPHY

Cederna, Camilla. *Giovanni Leone: La carriera di un presidente.* Milan: Feltrinelli, 1978.

Valentino, Nino. "Giovanni Leone," in *Il Parlamento Italiano: Storia parlamentare e politica dell'Italia 1861–1988.* Milan: Nuova CEI, 1989, Vol. 20, 237–61.

Claudia Franceschini

SEE ALSO Moro, Aldo

Leopold III (1901–83)

King of Belgium 1934–50, whose wartime behavior sparked "the royal question" that threatened to split the country. Leopold III, son of Albert I and Elisabeth of Bavaria, was born in Brussels on November 3, 1901. He served as a private soldier during the final campaign of World War I. On November 26, 1926, he married Astrid of Sweden, and the couple had three children. Astrid was killed in August 1935 in a motoring accident while driving with Leopold. A cult developed around her image that was to haunt Leopold for the rest of his reign. Leopold succeeded his father on February 17, 1934. He favored an independent, "solely Belgian" foreign policy. He withdrew Belgium from its defensive alliance with France and from the Pact of Locarno after German occupation of the Rhineland. The king was determined, however, to resist aggression with help from Britain and France. To support this action he sponsored construction of a fortified defense line facing Germany from Antwerp to Namur.

When the Germans invaded Belgium on May 10, 1940, and defeat seemed certain, the Belgian government fled into exile to carry on the war from France and later from England. Against his ministers' advice on May 25 to form a government-in-exile, Leopold stayed in Belgium to share the fate of his subjects and to assume supreme command of the Belgian army. He capitulated May 26, 1940, and was taken prisoner. The Belgian government criticized the king's decision to surrender and to remain with his troops rather than join the London government.

His refusal to flee and subsequent actions, including his morganatic marriage to commoner Mary Liliane Baels (Princesse de Rethy) in September 1941, a honeymoon in Nazi-occupied Austria, and a November 1940 meeting with Hitler at Berchtesgaden, undermined his credibility with many Belgians. His behavior was perceived as insensitive, even traitorous, and fueled the royal question, which disrupted political life from 1944 to 1950. The controversy surrounding Leopold became one of the most personal and violent public issues in Belgian history, because it touched on the country's weakest element, its unity. The issue had little to do with language, but public opinion rapidly divided along linguistic lines, with the Flemings overwhelmingly supporting the king and the Walloons opposed to his return.

The main complaints against Leopold were the general suspicion that he prematurely surrendered to the Germans in 1940, jeopardizing British and French troops; cooperated with the Germans; and enjoyed unusual benefits for a prisoner of war. There was little evidence of misconduct, but during the war clandestine newspapers in Wallonia, especially those sponsored by the Socialist and Liberal Parties, attacked him virulently. After the war, at the request of the government Leopold remained in exile in Geneva while the question was debated. His brother, Albert, was named regent.

Both the monarch and the government issued White Papers defending their actions. On July 14, 1946, the king officially formed a Commission of Information. The commission issued its final report on March 25, 1947, a defense based on a constitutional interpretation of monarchical power that was at odds with the government's position. It found that Leopold's behavior from May 25, 1940, to June 6, 1944, when the Nazis deported the king to Austria, fell within the king's constitutional authority. It was legitimate only within the frame of constitutional reference defined by Leopold himself, a point challenged by the government and rejected by parliament. The commission claimed that the break between Leopold and his cabinet in 1940, and the resulting consequences of this act, were not constitutional but political in nature, i.e., a dispute over alternative political policies. A two-year stalemate between king and government followed.

On March 12, 1950, a referendum was held to decide whether Leopold should return. Nationally the king was vindicated by a 57.7 percent positive vote. The regional breakdown, however, was significant. Seventy-two percent of Flemings voted in favor but 58 percent of Walloons and 52 percent of the residents of Brussels rejected the king. The referendum, without settling the issue, underscored its divisiveness. Leopold reconsidered his decision to return after the announcement of his imminent return to Belgium provoked mass demonstrations, strikes, and violence in Wallonia. On August 3 Leopold's abdication was submitted to parliament; eight days later, Prince Buadouin, now prince royal, took the oath of office and formally acceded to the throne on July 16, 1951.

Leopold continued to live in Laeken, the traditional home of Belgian kings, with Baudouin until the latter's marriage in 1960. Critics felt that the former king's residence at Laeken gave him too much influence over his son. Leopold III died in Brussels on September 25, 1983.

BIBLIOGRAPHY

Arango, E. Ramon. *Leopold III and the Belgian Royal Question.* Baltimore: Johns Hopkins University Press, 1961.

Cammaerts, Emile. *The Prisoner at Laeken: King Leopold, Legend and Fact.* London: Cresset, 1941.

Keyes, Roger. *Outrageous Fortune.* London: Secker and Warburg, 1984.

Martin J. Manning

SEE ALSO Baudouin

Le Pen, Jean-Marie (1928–)

Longtime president of the far-right French National Front. Jean-Marie Le Pen has led the party since its creation in 1972.

Created in concert with the youthful leaders of the quasi-militaristic Ordre Nouveau, the National Front under Le Pen's leadership has become the dominant French far-right organization. Le Pen's political acumen led the party in 1995 to victory in three medium-sized towns: Toulon, Marignane, and Orange. Vitrolles was added to that list in winter 1997 when those municipal elections were rerun because of electoral fraud in the previous contest. On the national level the front regularly attracts just under 15 percent of the vote. Frequently cited as a candidate for political oblivion similar to the Poujadist phenomenon of the 1950s, the National Front has continued to confound its critics through its slight but inexorable rise in voter support. Much of the party's success has been attributed to the charismatic personality and relentless drive of its first and only president, Le Pen.

Le Pen was born in La Trinité-sur-Mer on June 20, 1928. He studied law at the University of Paris II—Assas.

At the right-wing faculty Le Pen found his niche as a resolutely anti-Marxist student activist. His student activities foreshadowed his political ambitions when he was elected president of the student union. Le Pen abandoned his studies in 1953 when he volunteered to serve in Indochina. Although he had ambitions to be a paratrooper, he spent his time as a journalist with the army's news division.

On his return to Paris and the resumption of his law studies, Le Pen became involved with the youth arm of the burgeoning right-wing Poujadist Protest movement. These contacts brought him to the attention of Pierre Poujade, the leader of the anti-tax protest by small shopkeepers, who was preparing for upcoming legislative elections. Le Pen so impressed Poujade that he invited him to join the ticket and he was elected to the National Assembly in January 1956. At age twenty-seven he was the youngest deputy. Military wanderlust prompted Le Pen to leave the National Assembly in September of the same year to rejoin his regiment in North Africa. The demise of the Poujadist movement did not hinder Le Pen's political ambitions. He was reelected to the National Assembly in November 1958, this time as member of the Centre National des Indépendants et Paysans. Le Pen lost in the next round of National Assembly elections, and his most notable political activity during the 1960s was his stewardship of Jean-Louis Tixier-Vignancour's presidential campaign in 1964.

Although the National Front was chartered in 1972, it remained a marginal political actor until the mid-1980s. Le Pen has described this period of political exile as "the crossing through the desert." Marginal successes in local and by-elections in the early 1980s led to the party's first true national success. Le Pen himself was successful in a local election in Paris in 1983, but it was the success of his number-two man, the late Jean-Pierre Stirbois, that brought the party national attention.

Le Pen's political fortunes as well as those of his party increased dramatically after his February 1993 appearance on the popular television program *L'Heure de vérité* (*The Hour of Truth*). This interview bestowed on Le Pen and the National Front a certain political legitimacy. That combined with his ability to parry the most inflammatory questions helped Le Pen and his cohorts capture 10 percent of the vote for European (EU) parliament in 1994.

Le Pen's public life has been punctuated with episodes that stretch the limits of the law. As a youth he gained a reputation as a barroom brawler. This penchant for physical violence proved costly when in 1958 he lost an eye in an altercation during a political campaign. In 1968 he was fined for disseminating recordings that glorified the German Nazi regime. On a more serious note, he was accused of torturing Algerian prisoners during the Algerian War. And he has been adept at pushing the limits of the acceptable in political speech, in the process solidifying his image as an anti-Semite.

Ironically, Le Pen's most significant electoral accomplishments are linked to losses rather than victories. After failing to gather the necessary sponsorship signatures to place his name on the 1981 presidential ballot, Le Pen rebounded dramatically in 1988. Socialist François Mitterrand's reelection that year was overshadowed by the fact that Le Pen, now the undisputed leader of the French far Right, amassed over four million votes representing 14.4 percent of the total. The presidential elections of 1995 provided Le Pen with another opportunity to exercise his electoral might. In the first round of those elections he garnered just under 15 percent of the vote, the highest yet for a candidate of the far Right.

Since the death of François Duprat in a car bombing in 1974, Le Pen has been the front's dominant political theoretician. Central to his political universe and thus the National Front's is the issue of immigration. Le Pen and his associates have successfully linked France's immigrant population, most notably those from North Africa, to France's seemingly insoluble unemployment problem. With double-digit unemployment figures of the 1980s and 1990s, Le Pen's rhetoric has sown its seeds on the left as well as the right of the French political arena. Politicians from former President Valéry Giscard d'Estaing to former Prime Minister Édith Cresson have parroted Le Pen's anti-immigrant rhetoric. Moreover, Le Pen has used the issue of immigration to exploit the "insecurity" of French citizens, especially in more urban areas. According to the National Front, rising crime rates and increased drug use go hand in hand with the existence of immigrant populations. This xenophobic message coupled with domestic fear of Islamic terrorism have kept Le Pen at the center of the French political stage for more than a decade. He recently broadened the party's political agenda with resurgent themes of French nationalism as he linked the increased integrative efforts inherent in the Maastricht treaty to an attack on French sovereignty.

As Le Pen and the front prepare for the 1998 National Assembly elections there have been increased discussions about whom he will anoint as his chosen successor. Le Pen's ability to remain the undisputed leader of the historically factious French far Right is a significant accomplishment, but his legacy may be in doubt unless a clear successor emerges to inherit the party he has nurtured for nearly three decades.

BIBLIOGRAPHY

DeClair, Edward G. *Politics on the Fringe: The Case of the French National Front.* Durham, N.C.: Duke University Press, 1998.

Simmons, Harvey G. *The French National Front: The Extremist Challenge to Democracy.* Boulder, Colo.: Westview Press, 1996.

Vaughan, Michalina. "The Extreme Right in France: 'Lepenisme' or the Politics of Fear," in *The Far Right in Western and Eastern Europe.* Ed. by Lucian Cheles, Ronnie Ferguson, and Michalina Vaughan, 2d ed. Essex, England: Longman 1995.

Edward G. DeClair

Lettrich, Jozef (1905–69)

Slovak democratic leader. Jozef Lettrich was born in Martin in central Slovakia on June 16, 1905. Lettrich, a member of the Slovak National Council (SNS), planned the Slovak National Uprising, which occurred in the fall of 1944. Following World War II he was elected chairman of the SNS. He headed the Democratic Party (DS) from 1945 until 1948. With Letterich at the helm the DS carried the Slovak vote in the 1946 Czechoslovak parliamentary election. Following the Communist consolidation of power in 1948, Lettrich left Czechoslovakia. He was one of the most prominent Czechoslovak leaders in exile. Lettrich died in New York City in 1969.

BIBLIOGRAPHY

Kaplan, Karel. *The Shoot March: The Communist Takeover in Czechoslovakia.* New York: St. Martin's Press, 1987.

R., P. V. "Jozef Lettrich Remembered." *CTK National News Wire,* June 16, 1995.

Bernard Cook

Levi, Carlo (1902–75)

Italian journalist, physician, painter, and writer. Carlo Levi was born into a Jewish family on November 29, 1902 in Turin. After receiving a medical degree in 1923, he turned his attention to literature and art. He was an active antifascist, and was sentenced to internal exile in a remote village in Lucania in 1935 and 1936. That experience would later give birth to his major book, *Cristo si 'e fermato a Eboli* (*Christ Stopped at Eboli,* 1945). In its highly personal and subjective portrait of poverty and superstition in the south of the country, it is comparable in style to the neorealist films of the postwar era. Also, Levi's presentation of the myth of America as it existed among the peasants of the south can be favorably compared to the treatment of the same topic in the works of such contemporaries as Moravia, Silone, Pavese, and Soldati.

Following his release, Levi fled to France, where he ultimately took part in the resistance against the German occupiers. After the war he worked for a number of Italian newspapers and, in 1963, was elected senator on the Communist ticket. He wrote journalistic pieces based on his wartime experiences, notably *L'orologio* (*The Watch,* 1950); on his views of poverty and the Mafia in Sicily, *Le parole sono pietre* (*Words Are Stones,* 1955); on his travels in Russia, *Il futuro ha un cuore antica* (*The Future Has an Ancient Heart,* 1956) ; and on his visit to the remains of a concentration camp, *Doppia notte dei tigli* (*The Linden Trees,* 1959). He died in Rome on January 4, 1975.

BIBLIOGRAPHY

Baldassaro, Lawrence. *Carlo Levi.* Oxford: Berg, 1996.

De Donato, Giglioa. *Saqqio su Carlo Levi.* Bari, Italy: De Donato Editore, 1974.

Hughes, J. Stuart. *Prisoners of Hope: The Silver Age of the Italian Jews, 1924–1974.* Cambridge, Mass.: Harvard University Press, 1983.

William Roberts

Levinas, Emmanuel (1905–95)

French philosopher, theologian, and Talmudic scholar. Emmanuel Levinas was born in 1905 in Kaunas, then part of Russia, to Russian Jewish parents. He studied in Germany and France. He was drafted into the French army in World War II but was captured by the Germans and subjected to forced labor in a prison camp. After the war, He directed the Israelite Oriental Teachers College in Paris, and in 1961 became a professor at the University of Poitiers.

Levinas is known for his work in the philosophy of religion and his reflections on ethical life. Early in his career he was a follower of the German phenomenologist Edmund Husserl, but after his poison experience, he began to concentrate more on the nature of the relationship between humanity and God. His chief work, *Totality and Infinity* (1961), explores the "face-to-face" relationship among humans and the "face-to-faceless" relationship between humans and the infinite, or God. He contends that we can neither understand nor appreciate the infinite, since it is beyond us, but we can understand its law. The law of the infinite God is to be conceived as a message that calls to us to love and forgive those who are unloving and unforgiving.

Levinas was critical of philosophies of totality, which attempt to explain human and divine life in terms of a structure or system. He objected to the philosophy of indifference in modern atheistic philosophical perspectives, contending that it is not only the sacred texts that reveal God's message, but that within the history of philosophy and literature the divine message can also be found. Levinas's influence has been extensive in the areas of religious studies and Continental philosophy. Some of his most important works on religion are *Difficult Freedom Essays* (1976) and *Beyond the Verse: Talmudic Readings and Lectures* (1982).

BIBLIOGRAPHY

Bernasconi, Robert, and David Wood, eds. *The Provocation of Levinas: Rethinking the Other.* London: Routledge, 1988.

Lescounet, Marie-Anne. *Emmanuel Levinas.* Paris: Flammarion, 1994.

Llewelyn, John. *Emmanuel Levinas: The Genealogy of Ethics.* New York: Routledge, 1995.

Peperzak, Adriaan. *Ethics as First Philosophy: The Significance of Emmanuel Levinas for Philosophy.* New York: Routledge, 1995.

Daniel E. Shannon

Lévi-Strauss, Claude (1908–)

Born in Brussels, Belgium, Claude Lévi-Strauss is the best-known and most influential French social anthropologist. His views have challenged the methods and perspectives of this field and compelled his colleagues to redefine their respective positions. His sophisticated studies of so-called primitive societies tend to encompass the investigation of human nature at its most general level and suggest that the human mind operates according to certain invariant structures.

Lévi-Strauss graduated from the Sorbonne in philosophy but also studied geology, psychoanalysis, and Marxism. This rich background, combined with his structuralist approach and his use of philosophical irony, contributed to the complexity of his thought.

He was a professor of sociology at the University of São Paulo, Brazil, from 1935 to 1939. His trip during this period across central Brazil was the origin of a book, *Tristes Tropiques,* which is both an intellectual autobiography and an investigation of the distance between Western culture and the "savage society."

During World War II Lévi-Strauss joined the prestigious École Libre des Hautes Études in New York City, where some of the most prominent members of the French intelligentsia had taken refuge. His meeting with Roman Jakobson inspired him to use structural linguistics as a scientific model that was particularly well adapted to relate the sensible to the rational.

Lévi-Strauss returned to Paris in 1948, where he was appointed associate curator of the Musée de l'Homme. He became in 1950 director of studies at the École Pratique des Hautes Études. Accepted into the Académie Française in 1973, he has been since 1983 honorary professor at the Collège de France and Doctor Honoris Causa at a great number of universities.

Lévi-Strauss was influenced by Jakobson's and Troubetzkoy's interpretations of Saussure. The former two linguists established the rules of determination, classification, and combination of phonemes. Jakobson demonstrated that the oppositions of phonemes are systematically binary, and that they engender a tertiary model through the presence of graduated or mediating phenomena. This theory of systematically mediated dichotomic relations was reworked by Lévi-Strauss. He reduced anthropological data to binary relations, the elementary cultural units that function through demonstrable models of opposition.

Thus, the *Elementary Structures of Kinship* (1969) attempts to show that behind the diversity of marriage rules there are at play a limited number of combinations, which regulate exchanges and establish alliances between social groups. His largely revised edition of 1967 is an answer to his various critics. *Totemism* and *The Savage Mind,* both published in 1962, deal with the logic of "primitive" cultures. The apparently contradictory ideologies of totemic groups and caste societies are considered as superstructures, from a standpoint that puts historical considerations aside. In fact, for Lévi-Strauss, there is no opposition between archaic and "civilized" societies: both share the two systems of thought, "savage" and scientific, but to varying degrees.

Lévi-Strauss carried on his investigation of such issues in his impressive four-volume *Mythologies.* As in *The Elementary Structures of Kinship,* he investigates the smallest elementary unit, the mytheme, and then moves on to the binary or trinary oppositions. Thus two levels "appear": language, in which mythemes have no meaning, and metalanguage, where they appear as elements of a supermeaning created by their combination. Thus, the signification of the mytheme is not exhausted by language and, indeed, it appears only at the structural level, where mythemes are purely differential signs without any content. Structuralism is the study of the rules and structures of that symbolic function that has no locus. Thus, these universal laws are prior to any given individuals, and although people elaborate myths, those myths can function only in human minds, without the individual being conscious of the ways in which they function.

In *The Raw and the Cooked* Lévi-Strauss demonstrated that it is impossible to understand a particular Bororo myth without taking into account some 187 other myths of about twenty tribes. A myth finds its meaning, therefore, from "the position it occupies in relation with other myths inside a group of transformation."

Lévi-Strauss deals with conceptual and methodological issues at the core of anthropology, so it is not surprising that his work attracts world attention and originates wide discussion because of his challenging conclusions.

BIBLIOGRAPHY

LaPointe, François Y., and Claire C. LaPointe. *Claude Lévi-Strauss and His Critics: An International Bibliography of Criticism (1950–1976). Followed by a Bibliography of the Writings of Claude Lévi-Strauss.* New York: Garland, 1977.

Leach, Claude Edmund. *Lévi-Strauss.* London, Fontana, (1970) 1976.

Ronald Creagh

Liberman, Evsei Grigorevich (1897–1983)

Soviet economic reformer. Evsei Liberman, youngest son of a Jewish forest guard, was born in Slavuta in the Ukraine on October 2, 1897. His older brothers became a lawyer and an economist and his sister became a physician. His family moved to Kiev when he was an infant. Liberman was initially refused entry into a university because of the Jewish quota. After the beginning of World War I, however, because his sister was a military doctor, he was permitted to enter a university. He resumed his studies at the University of Kiev after service with the Russian army on the Romanian front, but again interrupted his studies to fight on behalf of the Russian Revolution of 1917. After graduating from the university in law he moved to Kharkov and served as an economist with the Workers' and Peasants' Inspection. This experience piqued his interest in economics, and he enrolled in the Kharkov Labor Institute. After completing his studies there, Liberman remained at the institute as a researcher and eventually became head of analysis and statistics. He was responsible for the introduction of computers (Powers and Hollerite perforating machines) for planning in Ukrainian factories. A subsequent visit to German factories served as the basis for his theories of production planning. In 1933 he began teaching at the Karkhov Institute for Engineer-Economists and served as a dean there. He was evacuated during the war to head the department of financing industry at the People's Commissariat for Finance in Kirghizia. In 1944 he was appointed to the Research Institute for Finance in Moscow. In 1947 he was appointed to the chair of economics for the engineering industry at the Kharkov Institute. His 1950 *Cost Accounting at an Engineering Works and Economic Management of a Socialist Enterprise* served as the basis for his subsequent economic reform proposals. In 1956 after completing his thesis, "Profitability of Socialist Enterprise," he finally received a doctorate and was appointed professor at the Kharkov Institute.

His idea of using profits on invested capital as the criterion for measuring the success of socialist enterprises eventually attracted the attention of Vasily Nemchinov, the leading Soviet economist. Nemchinov persuaded Soviet Premier Nikita Khrushchev to allow Liberman to publish his article "Plans, Profits, and Bonuses" in *Pravda,* the Communist Party newspaper on September 9, 1962. This article became the foundation of Soviet economic reform known as "Libermanism." Liberman argued that efficiency should be measured on the basis of profit rather than output and that profit would promote efficiency and quality. Liberman recommended that individual concerns be allowed to formulate production plans based on demand and that, as an incentive, profitability be rewarded in wages and salary. Khrushchev was sympathetic and authorized the reform to be tested in two garment factories. Under General Secretary Leonid Brezhnev and Premier Alekseiv Kosygin, who was also an economist, the plan was implemented in a third of the USSR's consumer goods factories. Success was achieved but there was resistance by bureaucrats, who hampered the reforms through control of the allotment of raw materials and control of prices.

In 1963 Liberman began lecturing at Kharkov State University. Though his reform proposals were subsequently adopted with some success by Hungary, because of the opposition of central planners, with whom Brezhnev eventually aligned himself, the reforms were curtailed in the Soviet Union in the early 1970s. The resistance of self-interested administrators to the reforms advocated by Liberman was symptomatic of the resistance to reform that contributed to the demise of the Soviet system.

BIBLIOGRAPHY

Goldman, Marshal I. *USSR in Crisis: the Failure of an Economic System.* New York: W.W. Norton, 1983.

Bernard Cook

Lie, Trygve (1896–1968)

First secretary-general of the United Nations, serving from 1945 to 1953. Trygve Lie was born in Oslo, Norway, in 1896 and studied law at the University of Oslo. Lie was a labor union lawyer who reached maturity during the political and ideological struggles between the world wars. He served as wartime foreign minister of Norway during the government's period of exile from 1941 to 1945. He then continued as foreign minister under the Labor party government of Einar Gerhardsen until accepting the position of secretary-general of the new U.N. organization in New York City in February 1946. As foreign minister Lie learned that foreign relations were not a static set of mechanical rules but a dynamic, fluid process. Although a Westerner at heart, his political initiatives were often interpreted by Western governments as annoying. The Soviets remained supportive of Lie's efforts at bridge building between East and West.

During Lie's tenure at the United Nations, the Cold War began and the world was divided into two ideologically hostile camps. As superpower tensions rose, nuclear war became a possibility. Lie took on the job at the United Nations with great expectations and tried to establish firmly the role of the secretary-general, but he foundered owing to the realities of Cold War politics.

It was clear to Lie that the United Nations was a Western-dominated institution, yet he saw Norway's role (like his own) in the world organization as a contributor to the general improvement of international relations in the long run, rather than as a participant in measures to strengthen its own strategic short-run interests. The key to making the United Nations work, he believed, was consensus among the five permanent members of the Security Council. Lie was dedicated to achieving this consensus, but it was not to be.

Lie invoked powers granted in the U.N. charter and insisted on the right to assume private and especially public political initiatives, even though he had not been invited to so do by member states. He pressed for symbolic and formal respect for his office and its prestige in public affairs. As an activist secretary-general, he often evoked opposition. For instance, his clear support of U.N. intervention in the Korean War in 1950 was met with hostility from the Soviets, who had, up to that time, largely approved of his leadership role. He was also not immune to petty political maneuvering. His spreading of rumors concerning his successor, Dag Hammarskjöld of Sweden, was a case in point. Lie's greatest virtue, however, was his unwavering commitment to the United Nations and its ability to achieve peace.

BIBLIOGRAPHY

Barros, James. *Tryave Lie and the Cold War: The United Nations Secretary General Pursues Peace, 1946–53.* Dekalb: Northern Illinois University Press, 1989.

Lie, Trygve. *In the Cause of Peace: Seven Years with the United Nations.* New York: Macmillan, 1954.

Udgaard, Nils Morten. *Great Power Politics and Norwegian Foreign Policy: A Study of Norway's Foreign Relations, November 1940–February 1948.* Oslo: Universitetsforlaget, 1973.

Bruce Olav Solheim

SEE ALSO Hammarskjöld, Dag; Korean War and Europe

Liechtenstein

Principality of sixty-two square miles (160 sq km) located between Switzerland and Austria, with a population of 31,717. Its capital Vaduz is a town of about 5,000 inhabitants. The Principality of Liechtenstein was incorporated by Napoléon into the Confederation of the Rhine as a sovereign state. This sovereignty was confirmed by the Congress of Vienna in 1815. With the collapse of the Austro-Hungarian Empire in 1918, Liechtenstein oriented itself toward Switzerland. A 1923 customs treaty, which linked Liechtenstein to Switzerland, was subsequently strengthened and is still in force. Liechtenstein escaped German occupation in World War II even though Switzerland chose not to defend it, and it became a refuge for many fleeing Nazi tyranny. On May 2, 1945, soldiers of the First Russian Army of Liberation, which had fought on the side of Nazi Germany, forced their way into the

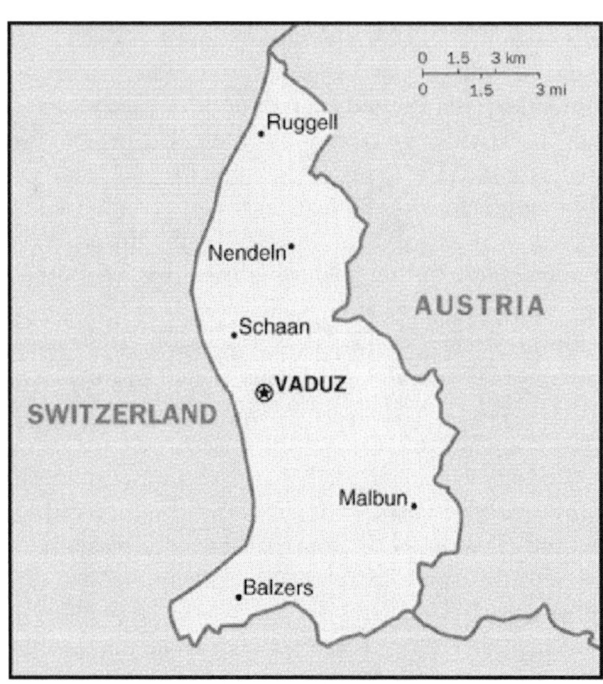

Liechtenstein. *Illustration courtesy of Bernard Cook.*

country. In spite of protests by the Soviet Union, they were interned in a refugee camp until they received permission to emigrate to Argentina.

On October 5, 1921, Liechtenstein became a democratic constitutional monarchy. There is a twenty-five-member parliament (increased from fifteen members in 1988) elected every four years on the basis of proportionality, but the prince retains veto power. In 1984 Johannes Adam (1945–) became regent and formally assumed the role of Prince when his father, Franz Josef II (1906–89), died. The executive branch of the government consists of a five-member Government Council, whose leader is the chief of government. All are chosen by parliament, which also specifies which individual is to serve as chief of government. Though the prince normally avoids involvement in politics, he can introduce legislation and in a crisis can, with the permission of the chief of government, rule by decree. One thousand voters or three communes can also initiate legislation, and a bill passed by parliament may be submitted to popular referendum. Women were not allowed to vote or hold office until 1984. Formerly, women who married noncitizens, lost their citizenship. Until 1986 women were still not allowed to vote in three of the country's eleven communes. However, in April 1986 they received full voting rights. In December 1985 a proposal to add constitutional recognition of the equality between men and women was rejected by a sizable majority in a national referendum, though women constituted approximately 67 percent of the electorate.

The Progressive Citizens Party (FBP) lost its forty-two-year hold on the government in 1970. Since then control of the government has shifted between the FBP and the Fatherland Union (VU). In February 1993 Markus Büchel became chief of the government when the FBP received twelve seats to the eleven won by the VU.

Liechtenstein uses Swiss currency and relies on Switzerland for its border controls and defense. Despite the country's close association with Switzerland, it chose to enter the United Nations in 1990 and voted in a referendum on December 13, 1992, to join the European Economic Area despite the rejection of entry by Swiss voters a week earlier. Liechtenstein is an associate member of the European Union. In 1978 it became a member of the Council of Europe.

Liechtenstein is one of the world's wealthiest nations in terms of its average GNP ($33,510 per capita in 1991). Its economy is primarily geared toward exports, which in 1996 amounted to $77,876 per capita. Citizens of Liechtenstein are covered by a system of compulsory insurance, which includes accident insurance instituted in 1910, old age and survivors' insurance instituted in 1954, and sickness insurance instituted in 1971. Family allowances were established in 1957, unemployment benefits in 1970, and a pension system in 1989.

Since 1962 Liechtenstein has placed strict limits on the entry of foreign, or guest, workers. Nevertheless, guest workers from Switzerland, Germany, and Austria with their dependents constitute approximately 30 percent of the population. Foreigners can become citizens only if they are approved by one of the eleven communal popular assemblies. This rarely happens.

BIBLIOGRAPHY

Kranz, Walter, ed. *The Principality of Liechtenstein: A Documentary Handbook.* Schaan: Lingg, 1973.

Liechtenstein Company Law: The Prevalent Sections from the Personen- und Gesellschaftsrecht. Vaduz: Liechtenstein Verlag, 1992.

Malunat, Bernd M. *Der Kleinststaat im Spannungsfeld von Dependenz und Autonomie: eine Fallstudie über das Fürstentum Liechtenstein.* Frankfurt am Main: P. Lang, 1987.

Raton, Pierre. *Liechtenstein: History and Institutions of the Principality.* Vaduz: Liechtenstein, 1970.

Schlapp, Manfred. *This Is Liechtenstein.* Stuttgart: Seewald, 1980.

Seger, Otto. *A Survey of Liechtenstein History.* Vaduz: Fürstlich Liechtensteinisches Pfadfinderkorps St. Georg, 1984.

Bernard Cook

Ligachev, Yegor (1920–)

Soviet political figure. Yegor Ligachev was born on November 29, 1920, in Dubinkino, a village in the Novosibirsk region of western Siberia. In 1943 he graduated from the Ordzhonikidze Institute for Aircraft Construction in Moscow. He then returned to Novosibirsk and worked as an engineer in an aircraft factory. He joined the Communist Party in 1944 and was active in Komsomol, the Young Communist League. In 1948 he was promoted from district secretary of Komsomol to regional first secretary. He also began a correspondence course from the party's important Central Committee's Higher Party School. When he graduated in 1951 he had already begun his ascent through the party's leadership structure. In 1955 he became vice chairman of the Novosibirsk provincial government, and in 1959 he was appointed regional party committee secretary. In 1981 he went to Moscow as a deputy chief of the Department of Agitation and Propaganda of the Central Committee. In 1966 he became a candidate member of the Central Committee and a deputy member of the Supreme Soviet (legislature), and in 1976 he became a full member of the Central Committee. He had served simultaneously as provincial party leader in Tomsk for eighteen years when Yuri Andropov designated him in 1983 as a candidate for the Politburo of the Communist Party. Andropov wished to invigorate and reform the Soviet leadership and favored Ligachev because of his reputation as a hard worker untainted by corruption. In December 1983 Andropov appointed him to the most select Secretariat, or executive body, of the Central Committee. Ligachev played a central role in Adropov's effort to root out incompetent and corrupt party leaders. After Andropov's death in 1984, the process slowed under his successor, Konstantin Chernenko, but Ligachev blocked the resurgence of Brezhnev-Chernenko cronies. After Mikhail Gorbachev, who had also been singled out for promotion by Andropov at the same time, became general secretary of the party in March 1985, Ligachev was appointed a full member of the Politburo in April, bypassing the customary apprenticeship of nonvoting member. As head of the Departments of Ideology and Personnel, Ligachev became the second-most-important person in the party, spearheading the effort to rid the leadership of the inefficient and corrupt. Ligachev quickly asserted his independence, however, by voicing reservations about the extent of Gorbachev's reforms and the "excesses" of glasnost (openness). On September 30, 1988, Gorbachev ousted Ligachev as director of propaganda and shifted him to the unenviable role of director of agriculture. It is believed that he was not removed earlier by Gorbachev because the general secretary needed Ligachev and the conservatives in his struggle against Boris Yeltsin. Ligachev's popularity among conservatives was confirmed when he was elected to the Soviet parliament in its first free election in March 1989. But the reform forces emerged victorious at the July 1990 party congress. Ligachev was overwhelmingly defeated in the vote for deputy chairman of the party, by his opponent, Vladimir A. Ivashko, who was Gorbachev's choice. On July 13, 1990, emboldened by his victory Gorbachev ousted Ligachev from the Politburo and replaced him with an ally. At that point Ligachev announced his retirement from politics.

BIBLIOGRAPHY

Gwertzman, Bernard, and Michael T. Kaufman, eds. *The Decline and Fall of the Soviet Empire.* New York: Times Books, 1992.

Suny, Ronald Grigor. *The Soviet Experiment.* New York: Oxford University Press, 1998.

Bernard Cook

Liggio, Luciano (1928–93)

Mafia boss who led the Mafia in Corleone, Sicily. Liggio was born in Corleone to a peasant family. At a young age he joined the Mafia and quickly rose through the ranks. Considered especially ruthless, Liggio killed the leading Mafia figure, Michele Navarra, in 1958 for what he called "personal reasons." He then acquired great power and set out to reorganize the Mafia. Within four years of Navarra's murder Liggio became known as one of the most dangerous men in Italy. Though his gang controlled the interior of Sicily, Liggio wanted control of the port city of Palermo. A bloody battle ensued. When his major rival, Gaetano Badalamenti, was serving a jail term, Liggio decided to take over the city. With Salvatore Riina, on whom the fictional Godfather of Mario Piego's novel is based, Liggio killed prosecutor Pietro Scaglione as he was leaving the Palace of Justice to further destabilize the justice system in Palermo and solidify his power base. Although he was arrested and sentenced to jail in 1964 for the murder of Navarra, Liggio was freed on appeal in 1969. In 1970 he was reconvicted but evaded the police until his arrest in 1974, often hiding out in Milan under the assumed name of Antonio Ferrugia. According to Mafia informant Tommaso Buscetta, Liggio wielded a great deal of power even from his jail cell, and his brutality was comparable to that of no one else. Long plagued with health problems, Liggio died of a heart attack in his prison cell in Sardinia at the age of sixty-eight.

BIBLIOGRAPHY

Calvi, Fabrizio. *La vita quotidiana della Mafia dal 1950 ai nostri giorni.* Milan: Biblioteca Universale Rizzoli, 1986.

Nese, Marco. *Nel segno della Mafia: storia di Luciano Liggio.* Milan: Rizzoli, 1975.

Vuillamy, Edward. "Mafia, Inc." *World Press Review* 39 (1992):11.

Wendy A. Pojmann

SEE ALSO Buscetta, Tommaso; Mafia

Lilov, Aleksandur Vasilev (1933–)

Bulgarian party official and scientist, born on August 31, 1933, in Granichak into a poor peasant family. Aleksandur Lilov received a degree in Bulgarian language and literature at Sofia University, received a Ph.D. in the field of Literary and Art Theory in the USSR, and later became correspondent member of the Bulgarian Academy of Sciences.

Lilov started his active public career in 1947, after joining the Communist-oriented Young Workers Union in 1947 and the Bulgarian Communist Party in 1954. He was a leading member of the Dimitrov Young Communist League from 1951 to 1963, and head of the Arts and Culture Department of the party's Central Committee. In 1971 he was elected alternate member, and in 1972 full member of the Central Committee and from 1974 to 1983 (when he was ousted by Todor Zhivkov, the first secretary of the Communist Party), and, again, after 1989, a member of the Politburo of the Central Committee. From 1983 to 1990 he headed the Institute for Contemporary Sciences, and in 1991 became head of the Institute for Strategic Investigations. He was a people's representative (MP) in the Fourth, Sixth, Seventh, and Eight National Assembly (parliament) and a member of the State Council (the council of ministers).

Lilov's political career resumed after Zhivkov's sudden resignation in November 1989, and he became chairman of the party's Supreme Council at its Fourteenth Congress, from January 31 to February 3, 1990. There he proclaimed the party's new ideological orientation toward a "humane and democratic socialism" that was supposed to be achieved through self-reformation from within the party, the only way, in Lilov's view, of overcoming the crisis of confidence toward the party and reestablishing its leading role in the social and political life of the country. Although denouncing the party's authoritarian past and promulgating a decisive break with the former communist regime, Lilov reminded its members of the party's long-term history and positive achievements. Lilov has been frequently named its "chief ideologist" and, after 1989, its main propagator of reforms.

Some of Lilov's more important theoretical works and contributions are *Critique of the Contemporary Bourgeois Aesthetical Principles of Art's Nature* (1971), *Art, Party and the People* (1971), *Imagination and Creativity* (1986), *The Ideological Struggle* (1987), *Europe—To Be or Not to Be* (1988), *Europe—Dialogue and Cooperation* (1988), and *Balkan Security—Political and Military Problems* (1995).

BIBLIOGRAPHY

Crampton, R. J. A. *A Concise History of Bulgaria.* Cambridge, U.K.: Cambridge University Press, 1997.

Lilov, Aleksandur. *Europa vor der Wahl einer neuen Alternative: ein bulgarischer Standpunkt.* Cologne: Bundesinstitut für Ostwissenschaftliche und Internationale Studien, 1989.

———. *Existing Socialism, a Concrete Historic Materialization of Scientific Socialism.* Sofia: Sofia Press, 1979.

———. *The Leninist Idea Content of the Party's April Policy.* Sofia: Sofia Press, 1976.

Stoianov, Ivan. *Nova saga za Lilov, ili, Epitafiia za zhertveni ovni?: opit za politicheska psikhoanaliza na Aleksandur Lilov.* Plovdiv: "Veda Slovena," 1993.

Svetla Baloutzova

SEE ALSO Zhelev, Zheliu; Zhivkov, Todor

Lipponen, Paavo (1941–)

Chairman of the Finnish Social Democratic Party (SDP) (1993–). Paavo Tapio Lipponen was born April 23, 1941, and earned an M.A. in political science. In the March 19, 1995, parliamentary election the SDP, with 28.5 percent of the vote won 63 of the 200 seats. Lipponen formed a government in coalition with the National Coalition Party, the Left-Wing Alliance, and the Green League, and became prime minister in April. Lipponen was elected chairman of the SDP in June 1993, after a crisis in the party leadership. This crisis started when Pertti Paasio, chairman during the 1991 parliamentary elections, had been held responsible for the party defeat. Ulf Sundqvist, a former secretary-general of the party and a minister in

Paavo Lipponen, prime minister of Finland. *Illustration courtesy of the Finish Embassy, Washington, D.C.*

the 1970s, was elected chairman at a special party convention in fall 1991. Sundqvist was expected to become a strong leader but had to resign in February 1992 owing to alleged crimes in his work as managing director of the Workers' Savings Bank. The party congress selected June of 1993 Lipponen.

Lipponen entered politics in the 1960s as a young radical interested in foreign and security politics. From 1967 to 1979 he worked on the party staff as researcher, secretary for international affairs, and chief of the political department. From 1979 to 1982 he was the political secretary of Prime Minister Mauno Koivisto. Lipponen became a member of the Eduskunta (parliament) in 1983, but was not reelected in 1987. After serving as director of the Finnish Institute of International Affairs from 1989 to 1991, Lipponen returned to the parliament in the 1991 elections.

Under Lipponen's leadership the popularity of the SDP grew. After the 1991 parliamentary elections, in which the SDP received 22 percent of the vote, its support started to increase. The party was able to capitalize on antigovernment feelings both in municipal elections (27 percent) and in the 1994 presidential elections.

Lipponen was among the first to demand a change in Finnish foreign policy and membership in the European Union, and is a leading Finnish proponent of European economic and political integration. Lipponen hoped that integration, and consequent ending of public support to Finnish agriculture, would save the welfare state and reduce the high level of unemployment.

BIBLIOGRAPHY

Jutikkala, Eino. *A History of Finland.* 5th rev. ed. Porvoo: W. Soderstrom, 1996.

Vilho Harle

SEE ALSO Aho, Esko; Ahtisaari, Martti

Lithuania

Former Lithuanian Soviet Socialist Republic of the USSR, now an independent republic. The Republic of Lithuania is the southernmost and largest of the three new Baltic states. Its area is 25,200 square miles (65,200 sq km), and its capital is Vilnius. It is on the eastern coast of the Baltic Sea and is bordered by Latvia, Belarus, Poland, and the Russian oblast of Kaliningrad. Its 3,690,000 inhabitants are predominantly Lithuanian. They speak Lithuanian, a Letto-Lithuanian Indo-European language closely related to Latvian. Russians constitute 8.6 percent of the population, Poles 7 percent, and others, including, Tatars, 4.3 percent. The population is predominantly Roman Catholic, but there are Lutherans, Calvinists, and Russian Orthodox. The Tatars are Muslims.

Lithuania. *Illustration courtesy of Bernard Cook.*

The Grand Duchy of Lithuania and Poland were joined together through the Union of Lublin in 1569. In the Third Partition of Poland in 1795 Lithuania was annexed by Russia. Lithuanians rose against the Russians in 1830 and 1863. In an effort to extinguish Lithuanian nationalism, Russian officials pursued a policy of Russification. Publications in Lithuanian were banned. The demise of the Russian Empire in World War I gave Lithuanians the opportunity to assert themselves. An independent Lithuania, headed by Antanas Smetona (1874–1944), was proclaimed on February 16, 1918. Despite Soviet and Polish ambitions to absorb the new state, it survived. Poland did seize the region around Vilnius, however, and Lithuanians were forced to transfer their capital to Kaunas. Independent Lithuania quickly moved in an authoritarian direction. Smetona, leader of the Nationalist Union and Lithuania's first president (1919–20), replaced Peasant Party populist President Kazys Grinius as a result of a coup in December 1926. Smetona, who adopted the title "Leader of the People," ruled as the country's authoritarian president until 1940.

According to the August 23, 1939, Nazi-Soviet Pact Lithuania was to be within the German sphere of influence. A September 23, 1939, agreement transferred the country to the Soviet sphere. Lithuania and the other Baltic states—Latvia and Estonia—were required to sign mutual assistance pacts with the USSR. Though Vilnius was reattached, Lithuanians had little reason to rejoice. In May 1940 the Soviets accused Lithuania of violating the mutual assistance pact and occupied the country. In June its government was replaced with a popular front "people's government" containing Social Democrats and Peasant Populists, as well as Communists. In July, however, all parties other than the Communist Party of Lithuania (CPL) were banned. A People's Seim (parliament) was elected, but only Communists parading as the Working People's League were allowed to run. On July 21 the Siem declared Lithuania a Soviet Socialist Republic and on August 3 it was absorbed by the USSR as a "union republic." During the German occupation (1941–44), 210,000 Lithuanians, 165,000 of them Jews, were murdered by the Nazis and their Lithuanian supporters. The return of the Soviets in 1944 was not welcomed. Lithuanian anti-Communists claim that Lithuanian guerrillas killed 20,000 Soviet troops between 1944 and 1948. However, the CPL imposed its monopoly of power under Antanas Snieckus, who was first secretary from 1940 to 1974. There was a systematic program of "Soviet Russification." The Soviets resumed the deportation of Lithuanians to Siberia and the Central Asian republics of the USSR and by 1949, 150,000 Lithuanians had been removed and replaced by Russians, Belorussians, and Ukranians. Agriculture was collectivized. The Roman Catholic Church was persecuted. In an effort to Russianize the republic all students were taught Russian in school.

During the 1960s and 1970s a dissident movement developed. In May 1972 demonstrators in Kaunas demanded religious and political liberty. Under Soviet President Mikhail Gorbachev's policy of glasnost (openness), public criticism was voiced about the Nazi-Soviet Pact and it was the subject of a demonstration in August 1987. Popular disappointment with the pace of liberalization led to the formation of the Lithuanian Movement for Reconstruction (Sajudis) in June 1988. Its origin stemmed from the recommendation of the Lithuanian Academy of Sciences to form a commission to propose changes to the Lithuanian constitution consonant with the programs of glasnost and perestroika (restructuring) proposed by Gorbachev. The commission composed of party and nonparty intellectuals and professionals became an engine for change. Musicologist Vytautas Landsbergis (1932–) quickly gained a position of leadership within the commission, which was transformed into a movement at a congress in October. Sajudis organized demonstrations against environmental degradation, Russification of Lithuania, and the Nazi-Soviet Pact. Sajudis appealed to the Lithuanian Supreme Soviet (LSS) to declare Lithuanian a state language and to issue a declaration of independence—a principled affirmation rather than a definitive political step. Algirdas Brazauskas (1932–), the new first secretary of the CPL, supported the proposals until he was pressured by Moscow to back down. The LSS, however, complied in November. The CPL attempted to further mollify public opinion by making the February 15 Independence Day a national holiday and by restoring its confiscated property to the Catholic Church.

When Sajudis won the overwhelming majority of seats in the March 1989 election for the All-Union Congress of People's Deputies, the CPL felt compelled to do more to gain the support of the people. In a May 18 declaration of sovereignty the LSS gave precedence to Lithuanian laws over USSR law. A special LSS commission declared that the imposition of Soviet power in 1940 was unconstitutional, and thereafter a million people formed a living chain from Tallinn, Estonia, through Riga, Latvia, to Vilnius on August 23, 1989, the fiftieth anniversary of the Nazi-Soviet Pact. The Communist-dominated LSS continued apace, declaring freedom of religion and legalizing a multiparty system. In December the CPL became the first of the Communist parties of the USSR to divorce itself formally from the Communist Party of the Soviet Union (CPSU).

In the February–March 1990 elections to the LSS Sajudis, despite the transformation of the CPL, won a clear majority. Landsbergis was elected to replace Brazauskas as chairman of the LSS. On March 11 Lithuania became the first union republic of the USSR to declare the official restoration of its independence. The LSS, now renamed the Supreme Council, restored the country's 1940 name, Republic of Lithuania, and declared the constitution of the USSR null in Lithuania. Kazimiera Prunskiene (1943–) of the CPL and previously deputy chairman of the Council of Ministers was appointed prime minister of the restored republic. Differences within the Lithuanian government, specifically over price increases, led to Prunskiene's resignation in January 1991 and her replacement as prime minister by Gediminas Vagnorius (1957–).

A special session of the All-Union Congress of People's Deputies of the USSR condemned the Lithuanian moves as unconstitutional. Soviet troops occupied CPL buildings and newspaper presses in Vilnius. A two-month embargo on fuel was imposed until the Lithuanian government agreed to suspend its declaration of independence for six months during which period formal negotiations would take place between Lithuania and the USSR government. Discussions were initiated but the Soviet government quickly withdrew from them. Landsbergis responded in January 1991 by reactivating the declaration of independence. The Soviet government sent Interior Ministry troops to occupy former property of the CPSU.

Landsbergis called on the people to defend the parliament building and other sites against occupation by Interior Ministry troops. When Soviet troops moved to occupy the broadcast center in Vilnius, thirteen Lithuanians were killed and five hundred injured. Gorbachev claimed that he did not know about the plans for the attack but refused to condemn or repudiate it. The enraged Lithuanians voted in a referendum on independence on February 9. Ninety percent voted for independence and the removal of Soviet troops from Lithuanian territory. The Lithuanian government then refused to participate in the March referendum on the preservation of the USSR organized by Gorbachev in an attempt to demonstrate popular support for the continued existence of a reformed USSR. At the time of the August coup (1991) attempt by conservatives in Moscow to reverse the reforms of Gorbachev and reaffirm the authority of the USSR there were clashes between Soviet forces and Lithuanian self-defense forces and border guards. The Lithuanian Supreme Council, however, met without interference, condemned the coup, and expressed its support for Boris Yeltsin, the president of the Russian Republic, who had rallied opposition against the coup.

With the collapse of the coup, the Supreme Council demanded that all Soviet troops evacuate Lithuania. It also banned the hard-line breakaway Communist Party, which called itself the Lithuanian Communist Party of the CPSU Platform. The CPL, which had transformed itself into the Lithuanian Democratic Labor Party (LDLP), was not outlawed. The Soviet coup brought international recognition of Lithuanian independence. On September 6 the Soviet State Council of the USSR recognized the independence of all three Baltic states. Later in the month they were admitted to the United Nations and the Organization for Security and Cooperation in Europe (OSCE).

Other than the issue of removal of Soviet troops from Lithuanian territory, domestic issues predominated in 1992. Yeltsin agreed to remove the thirty-eight thousand troops as soon as feasible. Withdrawals began in September and were to be completed in 1993. A hitch developed in October, as Yeltsin, responding to nationalist pressure, declared a suspension of the troops repatriation because of the alleged mistreatment of ethnic Russians in the Baltic states. This was a Latvian and Estonian issue. Lithuania allowed all residents in place prior to mid-1990 to apply for citizenship, and by 1993 citizenship had been granted to 90 percent of the country's nonethnic Lithuanian residents. Although Lithuania was included for effect, troop withdrawals from the country did continue on schedule. Another complication arose when Lithuania demanded $166 billion in compensation for damages incurred during the Soviet occupation. But the last Soviet troops left on August 31, 1993, making Lithuania the first of the Baltic republics to be free of Soviet troops.

On the domestic political front there was increasing tension between Sajudis and the left-wing parties, especially the LDPL, led by Brazauskas. A referendum to strengthen the presidency, pushed by Landsbergis, was rejected. Opposition boiled within the Council of Ministers. Eventually the Seimas, as the Supreme Council was now called, voted no confidence in the government in July, and Vagnorius was replaced by Aleksandras Abisala. In the October-November elections for the Seimas, the LDPL scored a convincing win.

The poor showing of Sajudis, which with its alliance partner the Citizens' Charter of Lithuania, won only 30 seats out of 141, was rooted in popular disappointment with economic reform. It was very difficult for Lithuania to reorient its economy from Russia and attract foreign investment. Between 1985 and 1995 per capita GNP declined by 8 percent yearly while population grew at an average rate of 0.5 percent. During the same time Lithuania's gross domestic product (GDP) decreased by 7 percent per annum. GDP decreased by a whopping 30.3 percent in 1993. And while Lithuania was affected by a declining GDP, inflation rose to demoralizing heights. The annual rate of inflation for the period 1991–95 was 242.4 percent. However, in 1991 it reached an astronomical 1,021 percent. Salaries were frozen and workers were paid irregularly. In July 1992, in response to the Russian demand that Lithuanians pay market prices for oil and gas, Lithuania began restricting energy imports. The following winter many buildings were at times without heat.

In an October 25 referendum a preponderant majority approved a new constitution that was then ratified by the Seimas. Until presidential elections scheduled for 1993, the Seimas elected Brazauskas as its chairman and acting head of state. Brazauskas wanted to form a broad national coalition, but Sajudis preferred to play the role of opposition. In December Brazauskas appointed Bronislovas Lubys (1938–) prime minister.

Brazauskas won the February 14, 1993, presidential election. Landsbergis and four other candidates had withdrawn prior to the election, leaving only Stasys Lozoraitis, a long-time émigré in the United States, to oppose Brazauskas. Lozoraitis was regarded by the voters as out-of-touch with the problems of Lithuania, but this soured many in the Lithuanian diaspora, who regarded him as a hero. The new president resigned from the LDLP, and in

March Adolfas Slezevicius (1948–) replaced Lubys as prime minister. In May Landsbergis and former members of Sajudis formed the Conservative Party of Lithuania (CP). The CP became the principal opposition party and Sajudis attempted to find a new role for itself as a popular movement rather than a political organization.

The year 1993 was marred by serious economic distress accompanied by the growth of crime and corruption. The government experienced increasing instability and was dogged by CP accusations of incompetence and demands for a new election. Landsbergis accused LDLP members of the government of personally profiting from the privatization program. The CP gained enough popular support to stage a referendum to terminate privatization, but not enough of the electorate turned out and the referendum was invalidated. Nevertheless, in the March 1995 local elections the CP won 29 percent and its ally, the Christian Democratic Party of Lithuania (CPPL), 17 percent to the 20 percent won by the LDLP.

Gradually market reforms began to have an impact. Through a voucher scheme privatization progressed and by December 1995 almost 85 percent of state holdings had been privatized. The agricultural sector was an important component of the economy and society. In 1995 it employed 28.2 of Lithuanian workers. Also by 1995, 40 percent of arable land was privately farmed. Agricultural output, which had decreased annually by 14.9 percent during the transition from 1992 to 1994, rose by 50.6 percent in 1995. Lithuania's overall GDP grew by 1 percent in 1994 and by 3 percent in 1995. While this was a promising improvement, the economic situation of many individuals was still strained. Despite continuing economic difficulties and scandals, including the failure of a number of commercial banks, the government survived CP-sponsored votes of no confidence.

In December 1995 Lithuanian's two largest commercial banks, which held 23 percent of citizens' deposits, became insolvent. Top officials of both banks were arrested for fraud. When it was disclosed in January 1996 that Slezevicius had withdrawn his deposits two days before the government suspended the operations of the banks a major crisis developed. Slezevicius refused to step down. Romasis Vaitekunas, the minister of interior, was taken to task for his handling of the crisis. Then it was discovered that he too had withdrawn his personal funds before the suspension of the operation of the banks. Brazauskas stepped in and demanded the resignation of Slezevicius. When he refused, Brazauskas appealed to the Seimas. The parliament backed the president by 94 votes to 26. Slezevicius was replaced as prime minister by Laurynas Mindaugas Stankevicius and as leader of the LDLP by Ceslovas Jursenas. To redress the causes of the banking crisis, legislation was passed to regulate banking and foreign banks were allowed to operate in Lithuania.

In the October-November 1996 parliamentary elections the LDLP was cut back to 12 seats, while the CP won 70 and the CDLP 16. The Center Union won 13 and the Social Democrats 12. Landsbergis was elected chairman of the Seimas and a CP-CDLP-Center Union coalition headed by Gediminas Vagnorius replaced the LDLP government. Vagnorius' government was temporarily replaced by that of Irena Degutiene from May 4 to May 18, 1999. On May 18 Rolandas Paksas became prime minister.

On February 25, 1998, Valdas Adamkus succeeded Brazauskas as president. Adamkus was born in Lithuania but fled the soviet reoccupation of the country at the end of the Second World War. He first lived in Germany and then emigrated to the US, where he became a citizen and an administrator for the US Environmental Protection Agency in Chicago. He was supported in the second round of the election in the Seimas by the Social Democrats who said that Adamkus was in favor of an adequate degree of state control over the economy. Adamkus' main challenge is Lithuania's economy that has lagged behind that of Estonia. In 1998 economic conditions for many Lithuanians, especially in the countryside, were worse than they were during the Communist era. Adamkus hopes to gain membership for Lithuania in both NATO and the EU.

Lithuania and Russia have reached agreements on trade and the demarcation of their frontiers. The issue of military transit to and from Russia's Kaliningrad Oblast has caused some friction as has the question of Lithuania's desire to enter NATO. An agreement of friendship was signed with Poland in January 1992 that upholds the existing frontier and guarantees the rights of the countries' respective co-nationals or national minorities. Cooperation and close relations are coordinated with Latvia and Estonia through the Baltic Assembly and the Baltic Council, but there has been disagreement between Lithuania and Latvia over the fixing of their maritime frontier due to the probable existence of oil.

BIBLIOGRAPHY

Gobel, Paul A. "The Baltics: Three States, Three Fates." *Current History* (93) October 1994, 332–36.

Hiden, John, and Patrick Salmon. *The Baltic Nations and Europe: Estonia, Latvia, and Lithuania in the Twentieth Century.* London/New York: Longman, 1991.

"Lithuania," *The Europe World Year Book 1996.* London: Europa Publications, 1996.

Paddock, Richard C., "Lithuania's President-Elect Gives Up U.S. Citizenship," *Los Angeles Times,* February 26, 1998.

Shoemaker, M. Wesley. *Russia, Eurasian States, and Eastern Europe 1995.* Harpers Ferry, W.V.: Stryker-Post, 1995.

Vipotnik, Matej, "Lithuania picks an exile as president," *Financial Times* (London), January 6, 1998.

Bernard Cook

SEE ALSO Brazauskas, Algirdas; Landsbergis, Vytautas

Citizenship Issue

As in the case of Estonia and Latvia, the Lithuanian Supreme Council determined in 1989 that citizenship in an independent Lithuania would automatically be awarded to anyone who had been a citizen in 1940, along with that person's descendants.

However, unlike Estonians and Latvians, Lithuanians also decided to grant citizenship to all permanent residents in the state. By 1991 almost all those who did not qualify for citizenship under the "former citizen" rule had taken up the option as permanent residents. This inclusivist approach reflected the high degree of ethnic homogeneity in Lithuania, where ethnic Lithuanians constituted over 80 percent of the population.

The revision of the law in 1991 established new qualifications for citizenship, including residence in Lithuania for ten years, a legal income, a language test, and an oath of loyalty to the Lithuanian state. Provision was made for exemption from these requirements in a limited number of cases. Vytautas Landsbergis, then president, resisted attempts by nationalist politicians to restrict citizenship in the belief that this would antagonize ethnic minorities and distract attention from more urgent problems.

BIBLIOGRAPHY

Hiden, John, and Patrick Salmon. *The Baltic Nations and Europe: Estonia, Latvia and Lithuania in the Twentieth Century.* Harlow U.K.: Longman, 1991.

Lieven, Anatol. *The Baltic Revolution: Estonia, Latvia and Lithuania and the Path to Independence.* New Haven, Conn.: Yale University Press, 1993.

Misiunas, Romuald, and Rein Taagepera. *The Baltic States: Years of Dependence, 1940–1990.* London: Hurst, 1993.

Norgaard, Ole, et al. *The Baltic States after Independence.* Cheltenham, England: Edward Elgar, 1996.

Senn, Alfred Erich. *Lithuania Awakening.* Berkeley: University of California Press, 1990.

Smith, Graham, ed. *The Baltic States: The National Self-Determination of Estonia, Latvia and Lithuania.* Basingstoke, England: Macmillan, 1994.

Thomas Lane

Political Parties

In 1988 a group of Vilnius intellectuals formed the so-called Initiative Groups for the Perestroika Movement in Lithuania. These groups developed into a nationwide mass movement called Sajudis, (movement). Its first objective was to support perestroika (restructuring) and to develop economic and later political autonomy for Lithuania. Sajudis quickly became a national movement, embracing radicals, who were largely centered in Kaunas, as well as moderates and former Communists. Lithuania's failure to obtain economic autonomy from the Soviet Union radicalized Sajudis, and the division between Kaunas nationalists and Vilnius reformers became more marked.

Sajudis dominated the elections of 1989 and 1990. In March 1989 it won an overwhelming victory in the elections to the Soviet Party Congress in Moscow and repeated this in the 1990 elections for the Lithuanian Supreme Council. The council declared independence on March 11, 1990, and Vytautas Landsbergis was elected as a compromise candidate for speaker.

Unlike his Communist Party colleagues, Arnold Rüutel and Anatolijs Gorbunovs in Estonia and Latvia, respectively, Algirdas Brazauskas was rejected as speaker; the absence of a large Russian minority in Lithuania removed the need to make such a conciliatory political gesture. This gave Brazauskas the opportunity to transform the Communist Party, and to rename it the Lithuanian Democratic Labor Party (LDLP). It promised to go slower on privatization, to sustain market reforms, and to improve relations with Moscow. It won a major victory in the 1992 parliamentary election.

During the same period Sajudis began to fragment under the pressures of governing. In the 1992 election the major battle was between Sajudis and the LDLP, even though seventeen party or faction lists entered the contest, only five of which passed the minimum threshold for obtaining seats. The new Christian Democratic Party and the Social Democrats ran third and fourth, respectively, behind the LDLP and Sajudis. The Union of Poles, which was exempt from the threshold, also returned representatives.

In the aftermath of defeat, what remained of Sajudis converted itself into a new party, Homeland Union, the Conservatives of Lithuania. This became the single-largest party in the local elections of 1995, eclipsing the LDLP. The Christian Democrats increased their share of the vote, remaining in third place; the Social Democrats stagnated; and two parties, the Centre Union and the Peasants' Party, consolidated their position.

BIBLIOGRAPHY

Lieven, Anatol. *The Baltic Revolution: Estonia, Latvia and Lithuania and the Path to Independence.* New Haven, Conn.: Yale University Press, 1993.

Misiunas, Romuald, and Rein Taagepera. *The Baltic States: Years of Dependence, 1940–1990.* London: Hurst, 1993.

Norgaard, Ole, et al. *The Baltic States after Independence.* Cheltenham, England: Edward Elgar, 1996.

Senn, Alfred Erich. *Lithuania Awakening.* Berkeley: University of California Press, 1990.

Smith, Graham, ed. *The Baltic States: The National Self-Determination of Estonia, Latvia and Lithuania.* Basingstoke, England: Macmillan, 1994

Thomas Lane

Longo, Luigi (1900–1980)

Italian Communist leader. Luigi Longo was secretary of the Italian Communist Party (PCI) from 1964 to 1972. Longo, son of a Piedmontese small land-owning peasant, was born at Fubine Monferrato (Alessandria) in 1900. He was one of the founders of the PCI in 1922. An active opponent of fascism, he was jailed after Mussolini came to power. After his release he left Vichy. He participated in the Spanish Civil War, but when he sought refuge in Vichy France after the defeat of the Republic by the forces of Francisco Franco, was jailed by the Vichy administration. After the ouster of Mussolini in 1943, Longo fought as a partisan leader against the German occupation of Italy. He rose through the ranks of the PCI bureaucracy because of his ability as an organizer. Following the death of Palmiro Togliatti in 1964 he was elected to lead the PCI. The Communist Party made steady gains at the polls during his tenure but he opposed a policy of collaboration with the Christian Democrats. The policy of cooperation with the Christian Democrats became the central component of his successor, Enrico Berlinguer's, policy of "Historic Compromise." Longo, however, paved the way to Berlinguer's Eurocommunism, by unequivocally opposing the suppression of the Prague Spring by the USSR. Longo died on October 16, 1980.

BIBLIOGRAPHY

Longo, Luigi. *La nostra parte: scritti scelti, 1921–1980.* Rome: Editori Riuniti, 1984.

Bernard Cook

SEE ALSO Berlinguer, Enrico; Eurocommunism

Loukanov, Andrei Karlov (1938–96)

Bulgarian Communist Party official, diplomat, and businessman. Andrei Loukanov was born on September 26, 1938, in Moscow. He was the son of Karlo Loukanov, a former Politburo member and political émigré in the Soviet Union. He joined the Dimitrov Young Communist League (DKMS) in 1957 and the Bulgarian Communist Party (BCP) in 1966.

Loukanov graduated from Moscow State Institute of International Relations in 1963. He started his career as an official in 1963 and in 1966 became a department head in the Bulgarian Ministry of Foreign Affairs. He became deputy minister of foreign affairs in 1972 and first deputy minister in 1973. From 1969 to 1972 Loukanov worked in the Permanent Mission to the U.N. Office in Geneva and in 1976 became a permanent representative to the Council for Mutual Economic Assistance (CMEA). In 1976 he was elected deputy chairman of the Council of Ministers and in 1986 first deputy chairman, a position he held until 1987. In the period 1976–86 Loukanov also headed the Committee for Economic and Techno-Scientific Cooperation. In 1987 he became Bulgaria's minister of foreign economic relations and from February to November 1990 prime minister. He was elected as a member of the Seventh, Eighth, and Ninth National Assembly (Bulgarian parliament).

Immediately after his election as prime minister, on February 3, 1990, Loukanov announced that he intended to protect the people from extreme hardships resulting from the transition from communism to a market economy. Loukanov suggested cooperation and participation of various social forces in the cabinet-to-be-formed, but his invitation for a coalition met the firm refusal of Bulgaria's anti-Communist opposition. He resigned in November 1990 after a four-day general strike and a two-week long mass demonstration throughout the country. His all-socialist cabinet (with all of its members drawn from the Bulgarian Socialist Party, the new name of the former Communist Party) was followed by a coalition administration headed by Dimitur Popov, a politically independent judge. It included eight socialists, four representatives of the democratic opposition, the Union of Democratic Forces (SDS), and three Agrarians (BZNS).

In 1992, Loukanov was stripped of his MP immunity and arrested on charges of misappropriating significant funds for the benefit of Third World "terrorist countries" in the period from 1986 to 1989. He was freed after a six-month detention because his election to parliament gave him immunity.

After 1990, Loukanov also entered the international business field as chairman of the board of the Russian-

Bulgarian Topenergy company, a position he had to give up in July 1996. On October 2, 1996, he was shot dead at the entrance of his home. Although his murder was publicly condemned by all Bulgarian political forces, the motive for his assassination as well as his murderers have not been discovered.

BIBLIOGRAPHY

Crampton, R. J. A. *A Concise History of Bulgaria.* Cambridge, U.K.: Cambridge University Press, 1997.

Svetla Baloutzova

Lubbers, Ruud (1939–)

Prime minister of the Netherlands (1982–94). Ruud (Rudolphus) Frans Marie Lubbers was born on May 7, 1939, in Rotterdam. He graduated from Erasmus University in Rotterdam in economics and went to work at the family engineering firm, Lubbers Hollandia Kloss, as secretary to the managing board in 1963 and as codirector in 1965. He served as a board member of the Netherlands Christian Employers' Federation. Lubbers was appointed as minister of economic affairs from 1973 to 1977. He was elected to the States-General (parliament) in 1977 and became the parliamentary leader of the Christian Democrats (CDA) a year later. From 1982 until 1994 he served as prime minister. At first he presided over a center-right coalition but as of 1989 the governing coalition was center-left with the Labor Party.

In 1982 Lubbers introduced austerity measures to cut government expenditures. The Netherlands was sorely pressed by a fall in the price of natural gas from its North Sea fields, escalating government expenditures, and the highest unemployment rate in the European Community. Social welfare benefits were cut and the indexing of wages and social benefits was terminated. To jump-start the zero rate of economic growth, business takes were cut and regulations eased. In spite of these austerity measures, Lubbers retained significant voter support because of his determination to deal with pressing problems. In 1991 he became the longest-serving prime minister in the history of the Netherlands. Lubbers, who hoped to succeed Jacques Delors as president of the European Commission, chose not to run for parliament in 1994.

Without his candidacy the CDA suffered a severe setback. Voters were concerned about a renewed rise in unemployment, rising crime rates, and increasing numbers of immigrants. Following the election Lubbers presided over a caretaker government for three months until a new governing coalition could be organized. A left-liberal coalition of Labor Party, was formed with Wim Kok as prime minister.

BIBLIOGRAPHY

Daalder, Hans and Galen A. Irwin, eds. *Politics in the Netherlands: How Much Change?* Totowa, N.J.: F. Cass, 1989.

Bernard Cook

SEE ALSO Kok, Willem

Lübke, Heinrich (1894–1972)

West German president (1959–69). Somewhat ponderous in temperament, Heinrich Lübke began his political career in the Weimar Republic as a Center Party delegate to the Prussian Landtag (parliament). Under the Nazis he was incarcerated twice but was eventually released. During World War II, as would be revealed much later, he worked on projects that employed forced labor drawn from concentration camps.

After the war Lübke joined the Christian Democratic Party (CDU), quickly gaining respect for his dedication, seemingly impeccable integrity, and expertise in agrarian questions. As a moderate conservative he appealed to enough members of Chancellor Konrad Adenauer's coalition to succeed popular Theodor Heuss as president of the Federal Republic in 1959. Reelected to a second term in 1964, Lübke became increasingly controversial because of his unspectacular style of leadership, his occasionally embarrassing speeches and peculiar conduct on foreign visits, and questions about his political past. The improvement of relations with the developing nations stands out as his most noteworthy accomplishment. When evidence surfaced that raised doubts about his personal and political integrity under the Nazis, Lübke decided to resign just before his second term expired and was replaced in office by Gustav Heinemann.

BIBLIOGRAPHY

Bark, Dennis L., and David R. Gress. *A History of West Germany,* 2 Vols. Oxford: Oxford University Press, 1989.

Hermanns, Johannes. *Heinrich Lübke.* Freudenstadt, Germany: Eurobuch, 1966.

Quarta, Hubert-Georg. *Heinrich Lübke: Zeugnisse eines Lebens.* Buxheim, Germany: Berger, 1978.

Eric C. Rust

Lubonja, Fatos (1951–)

Albanian writer and dissident. Fatos Lubonja was the son of Todi Lubonja, a close associate of Albanian dictator Enver Hohxa, and head of the national television until the early 1970s. When his father was arrested for opposing Hohxa's split with the USSR in 1960, Fatos, a physics student at the University of Tirana, was also arrested after his diary, highly critical of Hohxa, was discovered.

As his five-year sentence was ending Lubonja was accused of belonging to a pro-Soviet circle within the prison. He was then sentenced to twenty additional years. After thirteen years at hard labor, Lubonja was moved to solitary confinement. There he wrote on cigarette paper, which was concealed in the spine of a dictionary, a diary and a novel. The novel, *The Last Massacre,* deals with the contradictions of communism under Hohxa.

Freed in 1991 after nineteen years in prison, Lubonja was derided for his independence and critical stance by the government of Albania's president, ex-Communist Sali Berisha, as an "enemy" of the country, whose "dignity" he was accused of assailing. Not only critical of the government, which controlled all the broadcast media, Lubonja derided the national icon, the poet and novelist Ismail Kadare, as a "national Communist." He edits a literary magazine, *Endeavor,* in Tirana.

BIBLIOGRAPHY

Lubonja, Fatos T. *Ne vitin e shtatembedhjete: ditar burgu 1990–1991.* Tirane: Shtepia Botuese "Marin Barleti," 1994.

Perlez, Jane. "A Scoffer at Albania's Old Regime Scolds the New." *New York Times,* October 25, 1996, A4.

Bernard Cook

Luca, Vasile (Luka, László) (1898–1963)

Romanian minister of finance (November 1947–March 1952), vice president of the Council of Ministers, member of the Politburo and secretary of the Central Committee of the Romanian Workers (Communist) Party. A Jew, Vasile Luca (Hungarian, László Luka) was born on June 8, 1898, in Lemnia, then located in Hungary but taken by Romania at the end of World War I. Poorly educated and a locksmith by trade, in the fall of 1918 Luca first joined the National Guard and then the so-called Szeklers' Division. In the fall 1919 he joined the workers' and socialist movements in Brasov, Romania. In 1923 he became president of the Brasov local branch of the Romanian Communist Party (RCP) and in 1924 became regional secretary. At the fourth party congress in 1928, he was elected member of its Central Committee. In 1929 Luca was one of the key organizers and leaders of the Congress of the Unitary Trade Unions in Timisoara, and became involved in a miners' strike in the Jiu Valley, which the Communists attempted to exploit. In 1930 he took sides in the factious fight that took place within RCP, as a supporter of Marcel Pauker, Ana Pauker's husband. Between 1924 and 1939 Luca was arrested and confined several times by the Siguranta (secret police). When the Soviet Union occupied the Romanian regions of Bessarabia and Bukovina in June 1940, Luca was released by the Red Army from the prison of the capital city of Bukovina, Cernauti, where he was serving an eight-month sentence for illegally attempting to cross the border into the USSR.

The ethnically mixed region of Bukovina was absorbed by the Ukrainian Soviet Socialist Republic and Luca became a member of the Ukraine's Supreme Soviet (legislature). In the USSR Luca was instrumental in preparing Romanian wartime prisoners to become Communist propagandists after their return to Romania. In September 1944 Luca himself returned to Romania and became general secretary of the so-called National Democratic Front, which was actually dominated by the RCP. In October 1945 at the national conference of the RCP, he was elected a member of the Politburo and secretary of the Central Committee. In 1952 Gheorghe Gheorghiu-Dej purged Luca along with the two other members of the powerful troika, Ana Pauker and Teohari Georgescu. In August of that year Luca was arrested. A prolonged investigation by the Securitate (secret police) and trial on trumped up charges of treason resulted initially in a death sentence, but later the sentence was commuted to forced labor for life. After eleven years of confinement, Luca died in Romania's Aiud prison on July 27, 1963.

In 1968, during the partial and politically motivated rehabilitations under Nicolae Ceauşescu, a party commission dismissed the bulk of the invented charges brought against Luca by the party and the Securitate. But reasserted the accusation that Luca had adopted a cooperative attitude towards the Siguranta during his prewar imprisonments.

BIBLIOGRAPHY

Deletant, Dennis. *Communist Terror in Romania: Gheorghiu-Dej and the Police State, 1948–1965.* New York: St Martin's Press, 1999.

Georgescu, Vlad. *The Romanians; A History.* Columbus, Ohio: Ohio State University Press, 1991.

Ionescu, Ghita. *Communism in Rumania, 1944–1962.* Westport, Conn.: Greenwood Publishing, 1976.

Adrian Pop

SEE ALSO Gheorghiu-Dej, Gheorghe; Pauker, Ana

Lucinschi, Petru (1940–)

President of the Republic of Moldova, elected in 1996, and former first secretary of the Communist Party of Moldova (CPM). Born in 1940 to an ethnic Moldovan/Romanian family in Radulenii-Vechi village, in Bessarabia. Petru Lucinschi joined the Communist Party of the Soviet Union (CPSU) in 1964. He graduated from Lenin State University in Kishinev, Moldova, and the Higher Party School in Moscow, obtaining a doctorate in philosophical sciences. He made his early career within the ranks of the CPM, first as an instructor with the Central Committee of the Moldovan Communist Youth League (Komsomol), then as first secretary of the Balti (Moldova) Komosomol city party committee and first secretary of the all-Moldovan Komosol organization. From 1971 to 1976 Lucinschi was a secretary on the Central Committee of the CPM, and from 1976 to 1978, first secretary of the Kishinev city party committee. From 1978 to 1986 he worked within the propaganda section of the Central Committee of the CPSU, and from 1986 to 1989 as second secretary of the Communist Party of Tajikistan.

In November 1989 Lucinschi returned to his native Moldova to replace Semion Kuzmich Grossu as first secretary of the CPM. In 1991 Lucinschi left Moldova to become a secretary of the Central Committee of the CPSU and a member of the CPSU Politburo. With the collapse of the Soviet Union later that year, Lucinschi remained in Moscow as Moldova's first ambassador to the Russian Federation. In 1993 he returned to Kishinev and was elected speaker of the Moldovan parliament. In the December 1996 presidential elections Lucinschi received 54 percent of the vote in a second-round victory over the incumbent Mircea Snegur, and was elected to a four-year term as Moldova's second popularly elected president.

BIBLIOGRAPHY

Lucinschi, Petru. *Ostaticii.* Kishinev: Editura Uniunii Scriitorilor, 1993.

Charles King

SEE ALSO Moldova, Republic of; Snegur, Mircea

Lukács, György (1885–1971)

Hungarian philosopher who founded the intellectual tradition of Western, or Hegelian, Marxism. György (Georg) Lukács was born into an assimilated Jewish family in Budapest, the son of a prominent banker. Issuing from the same intellectual milieu as Ernst Bloch and Karl Mannheim, Lukács studied philosophy at the universities of Budapest and Heidelberg. He joined the Hungarian Communist Party in 1918 and fled to Moscow upon the rise of Hitler in the 1930s. Returning to Budapest in 1945, he served in Hungary's Stalinist government until 1956.

Best known for his 1923 work, *History and Class Consciousness,* Lukács conferred intellectual respectability on Marxism by stressing its philosophical, especially Hegelian, elements. Contrary to orthodox proponents of "scientific socialism" and economic reductionism, Lukács conceived of history as a longitudinal process whose ultimate meaning was carried by the proletariat. Drawing on Marx's theory of the "fetishism of commodities," Lukács developed the concept of "reification" to explain capitalism's tendency to reduce relations between people to relations between objects. Though compelled by the Hungarian Communist Party to recant the theses of *History and Class Consciousness* in 1926, Lukács nevertheless inspired a number of Western European intellectuals who sought a version of Marxism that might escape the errors of its Soviet counterpart.

BIBLIOGRAPHY

Gluck, Mary. *Georg Lukács and His Generation, 1900–1918.* Cambridge, Mass.: Harvard University Press, 1985.

Jay, Martin. *Marxism and Totality: The Adventures of a Concept from Lukács to Habermas.* Berkeley: University of California Press, 1984.

Lukács, Georg. *History and Class Consciousness.* Cambridge, Mass.: MIT Press, 1971.

———. *The Theory of the Novel.* Cambridge, Mass.: MIT Press, 1971.

Marcus, Judith, and Zoltán Tarry, eds. *Georg Lukács: Theory, Culture, and Politics.* New Brunswick, N.J.: Transaction, 1989.

Christopher E. Forth

Lukashenka, Alyaksandr (1954–)

First democratically elected president of the Republic of Belarus (1994–). Alyaksandr Lukashenka was born to peasants near the city of Mogilev on August 30, 1954. After graduating from the Mogilev Pedagogical Institute in 1975, he served for two years as a border guard near Brest, while simultaneously teaching Communist politics and ideology. From 1977 to 1978, he was secretary of the city food-commodity administration in Mogilev and instructor on the city's executive committee. He was subsequently director of a regional branch of Znanya (Knowledge), a countrywide educational organization, and served for two years as political officer in a motorized infantry unit. From 1987 until his election as president, Lukashenka was director of a collective farm in his native district of Shklou. Ever since his election to the Supreme Soviet of the Belarusan Soviet Socialist Republic in 1990, the Russophone Belarusan has been a maverick. He opposed the demise of the Soviet Union and gave the only dissenting vote in the Belarusan Supreme Soviet on the formation of the Commonwealth of Independent States. From 1992 to 1994 Lukashenka headed the Supreme Soviet's temporary anticorruption committee, which managed to oust Stanislau Shushkevich as chairman of the parliament.

On June 23, 1994, the populist Lukashenka won a landslide victory in the first presidential elections in the Republic of Belarus. Like his campaign, his policies were erratic. He insisted on a referendum to accompany the parliamentary elections of May 14, 1995. The population endorsed all his suggestions: closer integration with Russia; state status for the Russian language; return of Soviet-style national symbols; and presidential power to dissolve parliament. Lukashenka's policies, however, did not differ significantly from those of former Premier Vyachaslau Kebich, and he was not able to effect a program of economic reform.

On November 24, 1996, a referendum was completed in which 70.5 percent of registered voters approved changes to the constitution, giving the president more control over parliament and the constitutional court, which had attempted to resist Lukashenka's autocratic style, and extending his presidential term to the year 2001. The referendum enabled Lukashenka to remove 89 of the parliament's 199 members. The rump gave him its unanimous support on November 28 and dismissed the impeachment charges that the old parliament had leveled against him for his authoritarian behavior. Lukashenka's new constitutional court was composed of six judges appointed by the president and six elected by parliament. (The old constitutional court had ruled eleven of Lukashenka's decrees unconstitutional.)

Lukashenka exhibited a pro-Russian, anti-Western stance. After becoming president in 1994, he reversed most of the free-market reforms of his predecessor, Stanislav Shushkevich, and resuscitated symbols and practices from the Communist era.

BIBLIOGRAPHY

Markus, Ustina. "Lukasenka's Victory." *Transition* 1, no. 14 (1995):75–78.

Karel C. Berkhoff

SEE ALSO Kebich, Vyachaslau; Shushkevich, Stanislau

Lulchev, Kosta (1892–1965)

Leader of the Bulgarian opposition Social Democratic Party (1945–48). Kosta Lulchev played a central role in organizing the opposition parties during the first years of Communist rule in Bulgaria.

After the invasion of Bulgaria during World War II by the Soviet army on September 8, 1944, the National Front coalition, dominated by the Communist Bulgarian Workers Party (BWPC), established the first postwar government in the country. The ideological conflicts between the left and right wings of the Bulgarian Workers Social Democratic Party (BWSDP), one of the coalition parties, led to its disruption and to the establishment of a new fraction, the BWSDP (Opposition), in September 1945, led by Lulchev, former leader of the BWSDP.

During its short existence the BWSDP (Opposition) collaborated with the Bulgarian Agrarian People's Party (NP), led by Nikola Petkov. Both parties acted in support of the democratic principles and of the decisions made by the Allied conferences of foreign ministers, whose main objective was to implement the guidelines of the Yalta Conference (February 4–11, 1945). Together with Petkov, Lulchev used every opportunity to voice the demand for a truly representative government in Bulgaria that would guarantee the basic freedoms of speech and press, and curb repressive legislation and coercion of opposition groups.

On August 16, 1947, Petkov was sentenced to death on trumped up charges of trying to overthrow the government, and his party was dissolved. In November the BWSDP joined the BWPC, while the BWSDP (Opposition) was practically banned. Meanwhile, Lulchev was charged with counterrevolutionary and anti-Soviet activity, and, along with eight other political leaders, among whom was Peter Dertliev, was sentenced in July 1948 to 15 years imprisonment and the payment of considerable fines. Lulchev died on January 31, 1965.

BIBLIOGRAPHY

Crampton, R. J. *A Concise History of Modern Bulgaria.* Cambridge: Cambridge University Press, 1997.

Issoussov, M. *Politicheskite Partii v Bulgaria: 1944–1948.* Sofia: Naouka i Izkoustvo, 1978.

Oren, Nissan. *Bulgarian Communism: The Road to Power 1934–1944.* New York: Columbia University Press, 1971.

Roumyana Petrova

Luns, Joseph (1911–)

Longtime foreign minister of the Netherlands and NATO secretary-general. Joseph Luns provided stable leadership and high visibility to Dutch postwar foreign policy.

Born to a prominent Catholic family, the young Luns studied law at Leyden and Amsterdam before entering the Dutch foreign service in 1938. He spent the Second World War as a diplomat in Bern, Lisbon, and London for the Dutch government-in-exile. In 1949 Luns was appointed to the Dutch mission at the United Nation and in 1952 became the candidate of the Catholic People's Party (KVP) for foreign minister (a position shared with J. W. Beyen until 1956). Luns, rivaled only by Italy's Giulio Andreotti and Germany's Hans-Dietrich Genscher in durability, served as foreign minister through eight cabinets until 1971. During his tenure Luns acquired a reputation as a staunch Atlanticist and a tepid Europeanist. He fought for Britain's entry into the Common Market. In his first years as foreign minister he was fiercely committed to keeping Dutch New Guinea out of Indonesian hands. Luns's hopes were dashed in 1962, however, when the threat of an Indonesian invasion and U.N. pressure forced the Dutch to abandon their colony.

Luns's pro-American foreign policy and his political conservatism became a political liability in the Netherlands of the late 1960s, and in 1971 he was dropped as foreign minister. Yet no one was considered better suited to head NATO, and in 1972 Luns became the only candidate for the post of secretary-general of the alliance. He advocated the placement of cruise missiles in Europe at the height of the peace movement, when NATO's members, especially the Netherlands, were badly divided over the issue. In 1984 Luns retired from public life.

BIBLIOGRAPHY

Kikkert, I. G. *De wereld volgens Luns.* Utrecht: Het Spectrum, 1992.

Steenhorst, Rene, and Frits Huis. *Joseph Luns: Biografie.* Amsterdam: Teleboek, 1985.

James C. Kennedy

Lutosławski, Witold (1915–94)

Renowned contemporary Polish composer. Witold Lutosławski was deputy chairman of the International Society of Contemporary Music. He taught in music schools in several countries and won the Tribune Internationale des Compositeurs UNESCO (1959, 1964, 1968), Herder Prize (1967), Sonning Prize (1967), Ravel Prize (1971), and Sibelius Prize (1973).

His early works, such as the 1954 *Concerto for Orchestra* were inspired by neoclassicism and folklore. Later he developed an individual style associated with vanguard techniques of world music. His more important works were *Funeral Music* (1958), *Venetian Games,* (1961), *Three Poems of Henri Michaux* (1963), Second Symphony (1967), *Livre pour orchester* (1968), Cello Concerto (1970), and *Seventeen Polish Christmas Songs* (1985).

Lutosławski also wrote for film, radio, and theater.

BIBLIOGRAPHY

Nikoiska, Trina. *Conversations with Lutosławski.* Stockholm: Melos, 1994.

Stucky, Steven. *Lutosławski and His Music.* Cambridge: Cambridge University Press, 1981.

Kinga Nemere-Czachowska

Luxembourg, Grand Duchy of

Constitutional monarchy located among Belgium, France, and Germany. Jean, who became grand duke when his mother, Charlotte, stepped down in 1964, possesses formal executive power. But the constitution of 1868 was amended in 1919 to invest sovereignty in the people. Executive power is actually exercised by the prime minister (president of the government) and the Council of Government (cabinet), all of whose members are required to resign their parliamentary seats upon appointment. The prime minister is appointed by the grand duke but, with the cabinet, is responsible to the Chamber of Deputies (legislature). The Chamber of Deputies consists of sixty members elected every five years through a system of proportional representation.

The Grand Duchy of Luxembourg. *Illustration courtesy of Bernard Cook.*

There are four electoral districts in the country, with each assigned a number of representatives proportional to its population. Citizens, who are sent summaries of parliamentary debates, are required to vote. Each voter casts a number of votes equal to the seats being contested in the district, but the voter can cast more than one vote for an individual candidate.

A twenty-one-member advisory body, the Council of State, is appointed by the grand duke. It must be consulted on proposed legislation. Although it can delay the enactment of laws, the chamber can ultimately prevail. Eleven of the council's members serve as the country's highest administrative court. A separate court system deals with civil, commercial, and criminal cases. Judges are appointed for life by the grand duke, and the system based on the Code Napoléon does not utilize juries.

Six official professional organizations representing agriculture, business, and workers are consulted concerning legislation that affects their members. There is a provision for referendum, but the consultative and deliberative process works so well that it is seldom necessary to utilize the referendum.

Pierre Werner of the Christian Social Party (Parti Chrétien Social, PCS) became prime minister in February 1959. From January 1969 until May 1974 he headed a coalition between his party and the liberal Democratic Party (Parti Démocratique, PD). In the 1974 election the Christian Socials lost the political dominance they had held since 1919. A center-left coalition between the Democrats and the Luxembourgeois Socialist Workers Party (Parti Ouvrier Socialiste Luxembourgeois, POSL) was formed under Gaston Thorn of the Democratic Party. However, following the June 1979 election in which the Christian Socials captured 40 percent of the seats in the Chamber of Deputies, Werner again headed a coalition with Democrats. Austerity measures and unemployment contributed to the growth of the Socialists. Although in June 1984 the Christian Socials won the largest number of seats in the chamber, they lacked a majority. They then formed a new center-left coalition with the Socialists. Jacques Santier replaced Werner, who retired from politics. The center-left coalition continued after the June 1989 election, in which the Christian Socialists won 31.67 percent of the votes and the Socialists 27.23 percent. The two parties were equally represented in the cabinet. That election saw the emergence of three new political groups: the Committee of Action, or 5/6 Party, (Comité d'Action 5/6), which won four seats by advocating improved pensions for private-sector employees, and two Green parties, the Green Alternative and the Green Ecological Initiative, each of which won two seats.

Luxembourg has been in the forefront of the movement toward European integration. A 1956 amendment to its constitution provides for the transfer of executive, legislative, and judicial functions to international bodies. Luxembourg's integrative and cooperative character was embodied in the 1921 Belgium-Luxembourg Economic Union. This union, which became operative in May 1922, abolished custom barriers and made Belgian currency legal tender along with Luxembourgeois currency within the Grand Duchy. Belgium's unilateral devaluation of its franc in 1982 without consulting Luxembourg so angered the Grand Duchy's government that Belgium agreed to take no such unilateral action in the future. In 1948 the Netherlands joined Belgium and Luxembourg to form the Benelux Economic Union. In 1970 the three countries became a single customs area. Luxembourg was a founding member of the 1952 European Coal and Steel Community (ECSC) and in 1957 a founding member of the European Community (EC; European Union, EU, as of 1993). A number of EU offices are situated in Luxembourg: the Secretariat for the European Parliament, the ECSC, Euratom, European Court of Justice, European Audit Court, European Investments Bank, and European Currency Union. The importance of the location of these offices goes beyond prestige. It is estimated that 10 percent of retail sales in the Grand Duchy are made to EU employees or their dependents. In June 1990 through the Schengen Accord, Luxembourg abolished border controls with all of its neighbors. In July 1992 the Chamber of Deputies ratified the Maastricht Treaty on European Union. Constitutional amendments will be required before monetary union and foreigners' voting rights are put into effect. Luxembourg, after a 1948 amendment to its constitution that altered its "perpetually neutral status," was also a founding member of the Western European Union in 1948 and the North Atlantic Treaty Organization in 1949. In March 1987 it signed the Benelux Military Convention, intended to standardize training and equipment for the armed forces of the three member countries. In June 1992, members of its eight hundred-person volunteer army joined the United Nations Protection Force in Croatia.

Secrecy and favorable tax laws have made Luxembourg a major center of international finance. Although the country experienced a trade deficit in 1996, it enjoyed an overall surplus because of its financial sector. In 1991 there were 187 banks in the country and 9,797 holding companies, and 134 reinsurance companies were registered there. The secrecy of Luxembourgeois banking laws was modified in July 1989 to prevent the laundering of drug money by requiring the identification of the holders of accounts.

Luxembourg, the first European country to establish a satellite network, is in the forefront of commercial television in Europe. In 1988 utilizing a European Ariane rocket, it placed its Astra satellite in orbit. Radio-Télé-Luxembourg broadcasts to 500,000,000 viewers. By 1997 it had seven satellites and broadcast 300 television channels.

The gross national product (GNP) of Luxembourg in 1991 was estimated to be $31,080 per capita. By 1995 it had grown to $41,210. Industry contributed 34.9 percent of GNP and accounted for 30.6 percent of employment in 1990. Although iron ore is no longer mined in Luxembourg and the iron and steel industry has declined in importance, that industry, dominated by Aciéries Réunies de Burbach-Esch-Dudelange (ARBED), accounted for 30 percent industrial output in 1990. Though ARBED is partly foreign owned, the state is its major stockholder. It is Europe's fourth-largest steel producer and accounts for approximately 45 percent of Luxembourg's exports in goods, 16 percent of its GDP, and 10 percent of its workforce. An industrial diversification law of 1962 provides state assistance for industrial development. The country's GDP increased annually in real terms by 3.5 percent between 1980 and 1989.

The vast majority of Luxembourg's electricity is produced by hydroelectrical and thermal electrical generation, but the country must import coal and petroleum. The import of petroleum products, however, amounted to only 4 percent of the value of total imports in 1991. These factors plus the disasters of Three Mile Island in the United States and Chernobyl in the Soviet Union totally soured the Luxembourgeoisie on nuclear power. They canceled plans for a plant in their vulnerably small country and withdrew support for a French project in Cattenom just across the border in France.

Changes to the Luxembourgeois constitution in 1948 embodied the right to work, to social security, and to health care. The country developed a comprehensive system of social insurance that covers accidents, health, pensions, and unemployment. This system is administered by semipublic bodies containing representatives of the government, workers, and employers. Family allowances and extended maternity leaves are also provided. Spending on social security and welfare in 1990 amounted to almost half of government expenditures. Twenty percent of the population is over age sixty, the highest percentage of senior citizens in the EU. This places an increasing burden on the country's social system. The constitutional changes of 1948 included recognition of the right to form labor unions. Labor and social peace have been fostered by the automatic indexing of wages and pensions to the rate of inflation.

The population of Luxembourg in 1992 was 389,800, of whom 75,377 resided in the capital, Luxembourg-Ville. Although only 3.3 percent of its population was engaged in agriculture in 1990, the low population density and the absence of large metropolitan areas gives the whole country a pleasantly rural air. In 1992, 114,700 of the Grand Duchy's population was foreign. Guest workers from Portugal, Italy, and Spain, played an essential role in the economic boom of the 1960s and 1970s. These foreign nationals constituted the largest percentage of foreign workers in any EU country in 1992. Half the population of Luxembourg-Ville is foreign and this could well be the case for the country as a whole by 2020. The native Luxembourg population, owing to an extremely low birthrate, is presently declining at the rate of one thousand persons per year. Nonnationals, particularly Italians and Portuguese hold 45 percent of all Luxembourg jobs and 52 percent of industrial jobs. They are particularly prevalent in construction, where they hold 85 percent of the positions, and in the iron and steel industry, where they hold 35 percent. Foreign workers and their families have not been allowed to participate in the political life of the country, though this will change as a result of the Maastricht treaty. It will be difficult for the country to adhere to the desire expressed in its national anthem, "*Mir welle bleiwe wat mir sin*" (We wish to remain what we are).

The spoken language of the country, Letzeburgish—a Moselle-Frankish German dialect—was made the official language in 1985. In the 1990s there was a growing interest in written Letzeburgish. French is used for administrative purposes and German is used in business correspondence and the press. German is also the initial language of instruction. French is begun in the second year of school and becomes the language of instruction in secondary school. Luxembourg national identity is strong, and as all Luxembourgeoisie are trilingual, there is no divisive language issue.

BIBLIOGRAPHY

Christophory, Jul. *Luxembourg,* rev. ed. Santa Barbara, Calif.: Clio Press, 1997.

Clark, Peter. *Luxembourg.* New York: Routledge, 1994.

Eych, F. Gunter. *The Benelux Countries: An Historical Survey.* Princeton, N.J.: Van Nostrand, 1959.

Sheehan, Patricia. *Luxembourg.* New York: M. Cavendish, 1997.

Weil, Gordon L. *The Benelux Nations: The Politics of Small Country Democracies.* New York: Holt, Rinehart & Winston, 1970.

Bernard Cook

SEE ALSO Belgium; Netherlands

Luzhkov, Yuri (1936–)

Mayor of Moscow. Yuri Luzhkov was born in Moscow in 1936. He studied at the Gubkin Institute of Oil, Gas, and Chemical Industries and from 1964 to 1987 worked as a manager in the Ministry of the Chemical Industry.

His political career began in 1977 when he was chosen to serve as a part-time deputy in the Moscow City Soviet. In 1987, at the same time that Boris Yeltsin, the future Russian president, moved from Sverdlovsk to lead the Moscow Communist party, Luzkhov became first deputy chairman of the Moscow executive committee and leader of the Moscow agro-industrial committee. In March 1990, when Gavril Popov became mayor of Moscow, Luzhkov became head of the city executive committee. When Popov was elected mayor in a direct election in 1991, Luzhkov was elected deputy mayor on Popov's reform ticket. Following Popov's resignation in June 1992, Yeltsin, despite a demand from the city council for an election, appointed Luzhkov, who had firmly sided with Yeltsin in opposing the coup against Mikhail Gorbachev in 1991, to succeed him. Though Luzhkov also supported Yeltsin against the Russian parliament in October 1993, he subsequently distanced himself from Yeltsin's numerous governments and their attempts at reform in an effort to separate himself from unpopular measures, demonstrate his independence, and position himself to run for president when Yeltsin's term expired.

Luzhkov, who retained overwhelming support in Moscow, winning 90 percent of the vote in the 1996 city election. His decisive, if authoritarian, leadership, is credited with much of the economic activity and development in post-Communist Moscow. However, he has also been accused of fostering a form of state capitalism through his close ties with businessmen and select banks. During his tenure there has also been a growth in civil disorder and organized crime. Nevertheless, Luzhkov has attacked the looting of public property during the Russian process of "privatization." He has insisted that public property must be sold for sufficiently high prices to provide resources for public endeavors and to encourage the new owners to operate the old public enterprises efficiently in order to recoup their investment.

In August 1999, Luzhkov and Yevgeny Primakov formed a centrist alliance, Fatherland-All Russia, to contest the State Duma elections scheduled for December 19, 1999, and to contest the 2000 presidential election. They had not decided at that time which of them would be the alliance's candidate. Both support a market economy but controlled and regulated by the state, and both have the reputation for being Russian nationalists.

BIBLIOGRAPHY

Hoffman, David, "Primakov, Luzhkov form centrist bloc," *The Times-Picayune* (New Orleans), August 18, 1999.

Klebnikov, Paul, "The slick city boss, or the rough-edged populist general? Who will be the next ruler of Russia?," *Forbes Magazine,* November 16, 1998.

Bernard Cook

Lynch, John (1917–)

Fianna Fáil politician and Irish prime minister (1966–73, 1977–79). John Lynch was born in Cork and was educated at University College, Cork. He qualified as a lawyer, joined the civil service, and was called to the bar in 1945. Lynch entered politics in 1948 as a member of the Dáil for Cork city. In addition to his political career Lynch was renowned as a sportsman in Gaelic games.

Lynch was the first prime minister from the post–civil war generation. He held many government positions, including minister for education (1957), industry and commerce (1959–65), and minister for finance (1965–66). Following Sean Lemass's decision to resign, Lynch became a reluctant leader of Fianna Fáil and prime minister in November 1966. During his first term as prime minister, Lynch did not appear as significant as his ministers but was considered to lack authority. In fact, he saw his cabinet as a team, but he appeared in public as a mediator among its strong ministers.

The period saw cabinet tensions over the outbreak of troubles in Northern Ireland in 1969. Lynch's Northern policy differed from traditional Fianna Fáil policy; under Lynch unity with, and only with, the consent of the North became the party line. The 1970 arms crisis was his most serious test and the most serious crisis to face the state since the end of the Irish civil war era (1922–23). By sacking two of his ministers (Charles Haughey and Neil Blaney) for allegedly seeking to divert funds to buy arms for the Irish Republican Army (IRA), he showed his mettle. By thus reasserting his authority he overcame opposition within his party and strengthened his leadership. He took a firm stand against paramilitaries and terrorists by introducing the Offenses Against the State Amendment Act.

Lynch suffered a slender loss in the 1973 election, but following a brilliant campaign in the 1977 election he brought Fianna Fáil back with an overall majority and an unprecedented 84 of 166 seats. His 1977 administration began a major borrowing program to prime the economy. He remained secure in office until 1979. Internationally he steered Ireland in the immediate wake of its 1973 entry into the European Community (EC, later European Union) and imparted a sense of serenity and security in the troubled 1970s. However, a groundswell of party grassroots opposition developed against him. He resigned his party leadership while serving as president of the EC. Following a leadership contest between Haughey and Lynch's preferred candidate, George Colley, Lynch was replaced by Haughey in November 1979 and retired from active politics.

BIBLIOGRAPHY

O'Mahony, T. P. *Jack Lynch: A Biography.* Dublin: Blackwater Press, 1991.

Michael J. Kennedy

SEE ALSO Haughey, Charles

Lyotard, Jean-François (1924–)

French philosopher and social critic. Jean-François Lyotard is considered by some to be the father of deconstruction, which consists of an interpretation of texts in light of current social conditions, as opposed to what the writer of the text intended. One of the principal leaders of postmodernism, he has had great influential among the French avant-garde. His chief works are *The Postmodern Condition, Libidinal Economy,* and *The Differend.* They develop themes focusing on power, technology, and erotics and how these forces influence and shape contemporary culture. Lyotard is especially concerned with language as a game of social realities and power. His influence has been extensive in sexology, social theory, and contemporary continental philosophy.

BIBLIOGRAPHY

Benjamin, Andrew, ed. *Judging Lyotard.* London: Routledge, 1992.

Bennington, Geoffrey. *Lyotard: Writing the Event.* New York: Columbia University Press, 1988.

Nordquist, Joan. *Jean-François Lyotard: A Bibliography.* Santa Cruz, Calif.: Reference and Research Services, 1991.

Nordquist, Joan, and Bill Readings. *Introducing Lyotard: Art and Politics.* London: Routledge, 1991.

Readings, Bill. *Introducing Lyotard: Art and Politics.* London: Routledge, 1991.

Daniel E. Shannon

MacBride, Sean (1904–87)

Irish politician. Sean MacBride was the son of the actress Maud Gonne MacBride and Major John MacBride, who was executed by the British for his participation in the 1916 Easter Rebellion in Dublin against British rule. Educated in Paris, he was called to the bar in 1937 and in the 1940s was known for his defense of republicans fighting for Irish independence. MacBride had been involved in the 1916 uprising and was an opponent of the 1921 Treaty, which established the Irish Free State in the South but left the counties of the North tied to Great Britain. From 1936 to 1937 he was chief of staff of the Irish Republican Army, which had fought for Irish Independence. After the 1921 treaty, the IRA fought the new Irish government which had accepted the partition of the Island and then fought the British in a campaign of terror designed to force them to leave Ireland. He severed his links with the IRA in the wake of a 1939 bombing campaign in Britain.

MacBride threatened to disrupt the fabric of Irish politics by setting up the republican and radical social-reformist Clann na Poblachta (Republican Family) in 1946. He served as minister for external affairs from 1948 to 1951. A noted anti-Communist, he styled himself in the image of European Christian Democrats. For pragmatic and political reasons he kept Ireland out of NATO in 1949. Although he was minister for external affairs, MacBride played little part in the declaration of the Irish Republic in 1949. He precipitated the collapse of John Costello's coalition government in 1951 by failing to support Noel Browne, minister for health and a member of his own Republican Party, in the Mother and Child Controversy, a church-state conflict over a nonmeans-tested public health service for women and children.

MacBride returned to the bar following the fall in 1957 of the second interparty coalition government which had continued the struggle against British control of Northern Ireland. MacBride precipitated the collapse of the coalition by proposing a motion of no confidence in the government over its handling of the mid-1950s IRA terrorist campaign against the British controlled north border campaign. He began to play an increasing role in international organizations. He was secretary-general of the International Committee of Jurists from 1963 to 1971, chairman of Amnesty International from 1961 to 1974, and U.N. commissioner in Namibia with the rank of assistant secretary-general from 1973 to 1977. In 1976 he received the Nobel Peace Prize, for his work to promote human rights and in 1977 the Lenin Peace Prize from the USSR.

BIBLIOGRAPHY

MacBride, Sean. *A Message to the Irish people.* Cork: Mercier, 1985.

———. *Ireland's Right to Sovereignty.* Dublin: Hyland, 1985.

———. *Crime and Punishment.* Dublin: Ward River Press, 1982.

———. *Many Voices, One World.* London: Kogan Page, 1980.

Michael J. Kennedy

SEE ALSO Browne, Noel

Macedonia

Successor state to the Socialist Republic of Macedonia of the Yugoslav Federal Republic. The name "Macedonia" dates back to the ancient world when a Hellenic empire of that name flourished in the fourth century B.C. The precise reference of the term has changed over time, but during the nineteenth century it came to refer to a broad

Macedonia. *Illustration courtesy of Bernard Cook.*

arc of territory extending clockwise from the river Aliakmon to the Strimion (Struma). Its western extremity is generally taken as marked by Lakes Prespa and Ohrid, and by the Sar Mountains; its northern limit by the Black Mountains and Mt. German; its eastern edge by the Pirin Mountains; and its southern limits by Greece. Macedonia is not understood to include the peninsula of Khalkidiki. At the end of the Balkan Wars (1912–13) the division of most of the remaining European territories of the Ottoman Empire among the victorious Balkan states left Macedonia apportioned among Bulgaria, Greece, and Serbia. The lines along which that division was agreed were broadly confirmed at the end of World War I (1918) and again after World War II (1945). The lines along which the borders were drawn had at the time no consistent geographical or ethnographic basis. The resulting subregions of Macedonia have come to be called "Pirin" Macedonia (Bulgaria), "Aegean" Macedonia (Greece), and "Vardar" Macedonia (Serbia and subsequently Yugoslavia). The formerly Yugoslav portion of Macedonia became the Republic of Macedonia on December 19, 1991, as Yugoslavia disintegrated.

Macedonia is the southernmost of the six republics formerly united in the Socialist Federation of Republics of Yugoslavia. It is bordered to the north by Serbia, to the east by Bulgaria, to the south by Greece, and to the west by Albania. Its area is 9,925 square miles (25,713 sq km), with a population of 1,936,877 (1994 census). The capital city, Skopje, with a population approaching 500,000, is the home of every fourth Macedonian citizen.

Formerly settled largely by Illyrian and Hellenic tribes, the area received many Slav migrants from the end of the seventh century. These Slav peoples are the ancestors of modern ethnic Macedonians, who make up roughly two-thirds of the population of the republic. The Macedonian language is closely related to Bulgarian. There are substantial minorities of Albanians (23 percent), Turks (4 percent) and smaller groups of Roma, Serbs, and others. The majority religion is Orthodox Christianity, but perhaps as many as a quarter of the population identify as Muslims.

During the Ottoman Empire there was no recognition of a Macedonian political or cultural identity. After the Congress of Berlin (1878), however, a small group of intellectuals began to canvass the possibility of an "autonomist" solution to the problem of the future of the region in the event of the breakup of the Ottoman state. There was controversy over the question of whether the Slav population of the region had a separate national identity as "Macedonians" or whether they should be assimilated as Bulgarians. Between 1878 and 1912 Bulgarians, Greeks, and Serbs all contended for control over the Orthodox Church in the region, and competed to open schools that would inculcate an "appropriate" national consciousness. These efforts were supplemented by armed terrorism. The problem was resolved in 1913, at the end of the Second Balkan War, by the division of geographical Macedonia among these three states, each of which adopted energetically assimilationist policies with respect to the Macedonians.

When the "First Yugoslavia" was dissolved by the invasion of the Axis powers in April 1941, the greater part of former Yugoslav Macedonia was handed over to Bulgaria. Taking the approach that it was leading a "national liberation struggle" against the occupier, the Communist Party of Yugoslavia advocated, from 1943, a federal solution to the question of the future shape of a Yugoslav state. The loyalty of all the peoples of the region was sought on the basis that, unlike in the "First Yugoslavia," which had been strongly centralist in its constitution, all nations would have a substantial degree of autonomy within a federation. The victory of the Communists in 1945, and the creation of a "Second Yugoslavia," saw Macedonia recognized as one of its six constituent republics. It was believed that strengthening the position of other nations, such as Montenegrins, Macedonians, and Slovenes, would provide a powerful third force to prevent conflict between Serbs and Croats, which had dominated interwar politics, from getting out of hand. An important stimulus to the growth of a Macedonian national consciousness after 1945 was the formalization of a Macedonian language and its use in education, culture, and mass communication. An autocephalous Macedonian Orthodox Church declared its independence from the Serbian Church in 1967.

The creation of a Macedonian republic and the development of Macedonian cultural autonomy was met with varying degrees of resentment among its neighbors. Bulgarians continued to maintain that Macedonian Slavs were really Bulgarians, and that there was no basis for the recognition either of a separate language or of a state. Greeks feared that fostering a Macedonian state implied that the republic served as a front for continuing Yugoslav territorial ambitions extending to the rest of geographical Macedonia, and especially the port of Salonika. Serbs maintained a title to "South Serbia" on the basis of the fact that Skopje had been the capital of the fourteenth-century Serb Empire of Emperor Stefan Dusan "The Mighty." Albanians feared that in a Macedonian republic their status as a mere national minority would reduce them in effect to second-class citizenship. Consequently, throughout the post-1945 period the existence of a republic within Yugoslavia with the title "Macedonia" was the cause of intermittent friction on all fronts.

For these reasons the disintegration of Yugoslavia in 1991–92 occasioned a good deal of anxiety both within the Balkans and more widely, because it seemed that the breakup of that state would place on the agenda once again the question of the future of Macedonia. There seemed to be a real possibility that cut loose from its secure moorings within Yugoslavia, Macedonia would inevitably become the focus of irredentist ambitions on the part of its neighbors. Of particular concern was the situation of the large Albanian-speaking minority. Many observers anticipated that the collapse of Yugoslavia would result in the secession from Serbia of its own Albanian minority in Kosovo, and that this might trigger a more general challenge to the definition of the borders of Albania that must involve Macedonia. These fears were moderated somewhat by the outcome of the first multiparty elections in December 1990. Although the strongly nationalist Internal Macedonian Revolutionary Organization (IMRO) secured the largest number of seats, the new government was formed by an alliance composed of the former Communists (Party of Democratic Change) and a rather moderate Albanian leadership in the Party of Democratic Prosperity.

As the disintegration of Yugoslavia gathered pace through 1991, the Macedonian government conducted a referendum on September 8. This yielded a 95 percent majority (on a 75 percent turnout) for autonomy and independence "with the right to join an alliance of sovereign states" and kept open the option of the reconstitution of Yugoslavia in a new form. Accordingly, the Sobranie (Macedonian parliament) declared the independence of the republic on September 18. The severance from Yugoslavia passed without difficulty, and the Yugoslav army (JNA) withdrew peaceably from Macedonia in February and March 1992. In recognition of the increasing sensitivity of the area, the United Nations deployed a small monitoring force (UNPREDEP) in the republic in June 1993.

Although Macedonia has managed to remain clear of the violent conflict that engulfed other parts of former Yugoslavia, confounding the early expectations of an uncontrolled conflagration that could embrace the entire Balkan Peninsula, the region still causes anxiety about its future. Macedonia remains vulnerable to destabilization in the event of an intensification of conflict surrounding the Albanian minority elsewhere in former Yugoslavia, especially in Kosovo.

BIBLIOGRAPHY

Ackermann, Alice. *Making Peace Prevail: Preventing Violent Conflict in Macedonia.* Syracuse, N.Y.: Syracuse University Press, 1999.

Kaplan, Robert D. *Balkan Ghosts: A Journey through History.* New York: Vintage, 1994.

Lazarov, Risto. *This Is the Republic of Macedonia.* Skopje, Macedonia: Ministry of Information of the Republic of Macedonia, 1993.

Poulton, Hugh. *Who Are the Macedonians?* Bloomington: Indiana University Press, 1994.

John B. Allcock

SEE ALSO Gligorov, Kiro

Macedonia and Yugoslavia

Yugoslavia was originally formed as the Kingdom of Serbs, Croats, and Slovenes after World War I, a state without ethnic homogeneity. The Serbian national element was the most powerful, and Yugoslavia has always been some version of a Greater Serbia. Vardar Macedonia, the main portion of the geographical district "Macedonia," was annexed to Serbia in 1913, under the name South Serbia. There were two opposing Serbian theories concerning the amalgamation of Macedonia into Serbia. Serbian academic Jovan Cviich asserted that the Slavs in Macedonia were Serbs, not Bulgarians. The other approach was advanced by Serbian diplomat Stoyan Novakovich, who contended that the Bulgarians in Macedonia could not be made into Serbs; therefore they should be transformed into Macedonians.

Following Soviet dictator, Stalin's line of "divide et impera," or dividing larger nations into smaller ones, the organization for the world's communist parties set up by the Soviets, (the Comintern) declared in 1934 that the Macedonians, the Thracians, and the Dobrudjans constituted separate nations distinct from the Bulgarians. Thus the Comintern's decision coincided with Serbian interests. In 1943, at the Second Anti-Fascist Assembly of the People's Liberation (AVNOJ) in Yaitse, within the framework of the reorganization of the state of Yugoslavia into a federal people's republic, six people's republics were established: Slovenia, Croatia, Bosnia and Herzegovina, Montenegro, Serbia, and Macedonia. The Communist leaders, despite the absence of any Macedonian representatives at the assembly, declared the formation of the People's Republic of Macedonia as a part of Yugoslavia. This decision was confirmed on August 2, 1944, in the Prohor Pchinski Monastery, when a separate "Macedonian language" was decreed. The explanation was that such a language was needed in administration. Immediately after this meeting Yugoslav leader Josip Broz Tito established a commission to produce a written Macedonian language. The commission worked under the direct control of the Central Committee of the Yugoslav Communist Party. The language was manipulated in a way that could be characterized as Serbianizing the Bulgarian language, using, of course, as a basis the dialects that were characteristic of the district. All the literature of Macedonian writers, memoirs of Macedonian leaders, and important documents had to be translated from Bulgarian into the newly invented Macedonian.

With the establishment of the Republic of Macedonia, which covered 10.5 percent of the total area of Yugoslavia, the Yugoslav government had three objectives: to strengthen southern Yugoslavia by removing Bulgarian influence; to make Macedonia as a whole, not just the Yugoslav part, a connecting link for the establishment of a federation of Balkan peoples; and to create a Slavic consciousness that would inspire identification with Yugoslavia. Thus the historians of the Yugoslav Republic of Macedonia started declaring that Macedonia as a whole was a Slavic country both in its historical tradition and in its ethnic composition. For this reason, they claimed, it had to be united and form a unified state. The other two parts, Aegean Macedonia and Pirin Macedonia, would have to be restored, i.e., to be united with Yugoslav Macedonia.

The new policy really meant the denationalizing of the Macedonians (or the creation of a new Macedonian identity). After World War II many intellectuals who opposed the denationalizational policy of Yugoslavia were persecuted and sent to prison. The first trials started May 28, 1945. In Skopje alone, eighteen trials were conducted against Bulgarians. Of the 226 accused, 22 were sentences to death, and the others to long years in prison. Similar trials took place elsewhere in Yugoslavia.

In September 1945 a Macedonian organization, the the Democratic Front "Ilinden 1903," sent a lengthy letter to the wartime Allied governments. After cataloguing the sufferings of Bulgarians in Macedonia, it stated that "Without Free Macedonia, there will not be peace in the Balkans." The group was accused by the Tito government of terrorist activities, and its leaders were sentenced by the Yugoslavs to long prison terms. Around the end of 1945 the Internal Macedonian Revolutionary Organization (IMRO) was reorganized and began an illegal struggle. In 1946 IMRO issued a Memorandum to the Great Powers, expressing again the sufferings of the Bulgarian population in Yugoslav Macedonia. The leaders were arrested but were defended by the Communist prime minister of Macedonia, Metody Andonov-Chento. Though a Communist, Chento also felt himself a Bulgarian. He was sentenced to twelve years in prison, and the delegation from the great powers—USSR, United States, France, Great Britain—was not allowed to meet him.

Under the influence of IMRO many pro-Bulgarian organizations arose. Trial after trial followed in Macedonia. From 1944 to 1980 seven hundred political trials were conducted against intellectuals. Hundreds of death sentences were handed down and twenty three thousand individuals disappeared and are presumed to have been murdered. Another 120,000 spent time in prisons and concentration camps. Approximately 180,000 emigrated to Bulgaria, the United States, and other countries. All of this occurred within an area whose population numbered only around two million in 1990.

Even the fall of the Berlin Wall in 1989 did not weaken the resolve of the Serbs to maintain their power in the Socialist Republic of Macedonia. However, on September 8, 1991, a referendum was held in Macedonia that manifested the desire of Macedonians to leave Yugoslavia as the country appeared to be breaking apart. Because Serbia was engaged in other conflicts and also had too much confidence in the pro-Serbian authorities in Vardar Macedonia, a conflict did not arise. In 1992 the Yugoslav army left Macedonia peacefully but carried out many goods, especially armaments and other war materials. Before leaving the country the Serbs disbanded the democratic IMRO-led government, headed by Nikola Kliusev, and replaced it with a pro-Serbian one. But following the victory of IMRO in the 1998 elections, President Kiro Gligorov appointed a new government headed by Liubcho Georgievski.

BIBLIOGRAPHY

Barker, Elisabeth. *Macedonia: Its Place in Balkan Power Politics.* London: Oxford University Press, 1950.

Danforth, Loring M. *The Macedonian Conflict: Ethnic Nationalism in a Transitional World.* Princeton, N.J.: Princeton University Press, 1995.

Gotsev, Dimiter. *The New National-Liberation Struggle in Vardar Macedonia 1944–1991.* Sofia, Bulgaria: Macedonian Scientific Institute, nd.

Kofos, Evangelos. *Nationalism and Communism in Macedonia.* Thessaloníki: Institute for Balkan Studies, 1964.

Nystazopoulou-Pelekidou, Maria. *The "Macedonian Question": A Historical Review.* Corfu, Greece: Ionian University, 1984.

Dimiter Minchev

Macedonia and Greece

Greek governments throughout the post-1945 period have been generally antagonistic to the creation of a Macedonian republic, dating from the support given by Yugoslavia to Greek Communists during the Greek civil war (1944–1949). Before Yugoslav leader Tito's split with Stalin, negotiations were actively underway between Tito and the Bulgarian leader Georgi Dimitrov about creating a Balkan Federation that would have facilitated the reunion of the Vardar and Pirin regions of Macedonia. These events encouraged suspicions that Yugoslav territorial ambitions extended to the incorporation of the whole of geographical Macedonia, including Aegean Macedonia.

In spite of continuing intermittent expressions of antagonism between Greece and Yugoslavia over the issue of Macedonia, fueled by the open anti-Communism of successive Greek governments, the Cold War at least lent an air of stability to the configuration of states in the Balkans, guaranteed by the superpowers. The collapse of Soviet hegemony in the region and the disintegration of the Yugoslav federation leading to the existence of a separate republic of Macedonia stimulated considerable anxiety within Greece.

This anxiety is rooted in part in three aspects of Greek politics. The modern Greek state acquired its boundaries only after 1913. A large proportion of the population of Greek Macedonia are relatively recent arrivals, consisting in substantial measure of the descendants of those ejected from Asia Minor after 1924. The structure of the Greek state has been subjected to repeated challenges of a fundamental nature, during the First and Second World Wars, the Greek Civil War, and the suspension of democracy under the "Colonels' Regime." Placing these facts within the context of the perpetual strain of Greece's relations with Turkey, one can understand that there should be a deep-seated sense of insecurity about a possible absorption of Macedonia by Greece. Greek politicians have been quick to exploit this state of insecurity to their own advantage during the years following the collapse of the Yugoslav federation, as a consequence of which Macedonians faced an intense Greek campaign against the recognition of their state.

Following the declaration of independence of the Republic of Macedonia in January 1992, there was considerable debate about the adoption of a national symbol. The golden lion on a scarlet background favored by many was rejected as possibly provocative to Bulgarian opinion, having heraldic associations with medieval Bulgarian emperors. A deputy in the Macedonian Parliament proposed the use of a sun design found in several historical and archaeological sites in Macedonia, and the sixteen-pointed golden sun on a scarlet background was adopted. The proposal immediately met with a hostile reception in Greece because the best-known instance of this symbol was in an archaeological discovery at Vergina, Greece, not far from Mt. Olympus. Its adoption by the Macedonian republic was seen as implying territorial ambitions to the whole of geographical Macedonia. As Slavs settled in Macedonia only during the seventh century A.D.; it was also taken as claiming an illegitimate connection between the modern Macedonian state and the ancient Macedonian Empire of Alexander.

The use of the sun as the state symbol of Macedonia became one of the primary obstacles to Greek recognition of the republic. Greece imposed a trade embargo against Macedonia when other EU countries and the United States formally recognized Macedonia in February 1994. On September 13, 1995, an agreement was signed in New York City, brokered by U.N. mediator Cyrus Vance, which resulted in the lifting of the Greek trade embargo against Macedonia in return for the abandonment of the use of this symbol. The agreement was ratified by the Macedonian Sobranie (parliament) on October 13, and the offending symbol was replaced by another design, also featuring a sixteen-rayed golden sun on a scarlet background.

In the wake of the EU failure to agree on recognition of the Republic of Macedonia in January 1992 because of persistent objections by Greece, several lines were pursued in the attempt to negotiate a compromise. Since one of the principal obstacles to Greek agreement was use of the name "Macedonia" as the title of the new state, the

United Nations admitted the Macedonian Republic to membership in April 1993 under the provisional title "Former Yugoslav Republic of Macedonia," usually abbreviated FYROM. Consistent use of this title outside of U.N. official documentation is largely limited to Greece and the Federal Republic of Yugoslavia; the great majority of states recognizing the new country have done so under its preferred title, Republic of Macedonia.

BIBLIOGRAPHY

Shea, John. *Macedonia and Greece: the Struggle to Define a New Balkan Nation.* Jefferson, N.C.: McFarland, 1997.

John B. Allcock

Macedonia and Turkey

Macedonia was among the last regions of Europe to be separated from the Ottoman Empire. It was lost to the Ottomans at the end of the Second Balkan War (1913). In spite of strong pressures on its substantial Turkish minority to return to Turkey, both during the time of the "First Yugoslavia" (1919–41) and after the reconstitution of the state in 1945, Yugoslavia retained a significant Turkish-speaking minority, 150,000 in 1921 and 98,000 in 1948. The greater part of these were located in Macedonia, 3.8 percent of its population at the census of 1994. Consequently Turkey has retained an interest in Macedonian matters across the post-1945 period.

As a constitutionally secular state but with a preponderantly Muslim population, Turkey found itself in a difficult situation during the breakup of Yugoslavia, both in relation to the war in Bosnia (1992–95) and also to Macedonia. Turkish political leaders were under considerable pressure from many Islamic states, because of their country's location, military power, and membership in NATO, to engage actively in the search for a solution to the problems of negotiating a post-Yugoslav settlement in the Balkans. Compromised by its ongoing difficulties with Greece, anxious to retain the goodwill and support of the United States, and ambivalent about its prospects for eventual acceptance into the EU, however, the Turkish government of Tansu Çiller vacillated. It hosted a meeting of the Islamic Conference Organization on the Bosnian crisis in 1993 but declined to involve itself in an international academic conference on the same subject in Ankara in 1995.

More significant than any action taken by Turkey has been the specter of such action in the Balkans. A primary factor making for the highly negative Greek response to Macedonian independence was the image of an arc of states friendly to Turkey, each with substantial Turkish or Muslim minorities, stretched across its northern border with Albania, Macedonia, and Bulgaria. Preoccupied with its own internal problems, however, and fundamentally undecided about its foreign policy priorities, Turkey as a factor in relation to Macedonia has remained a matter of potential rather than an actuality.

BIBLIOGRAPHY

Ackermann, Alice. *Making Peace Prevail: Preventing Violent Conflict in Macedonia.* Syracuse, N.Y.: Syracuse University Press, 1999.

John B. Allcock

Macedonia and Bulgaria

Until the World War II Macedonia was populated with a Slav population that called itself Bulgarian and that had conducted bitter struggles against Ottomans, Greeks and Serbs. The Greeks and Serbs wanted to turn this people into Greeks and into Serbs. However, all Macedonian writers and poets wrote in Bulgarian. Until the Balkan Wars of 1912–13 the schools in Macedonia were principally Bulgarian. During World War I thousands of young men deserted from the Serbian and Greek armies and volunteered for service in the Bulgarian army. In 1941 the population was organized by intellectuals into "Bulgarian Campaign Committees," which sought unity with Bulgaria.

Following World War II the Bulgarian Communist Party was compelled by Soviet dictator Stalin to accept the formation of Macedonian, Thracian, and Dobrudjan nations. The idea implied including those nations as separate states in a Balkan Federation. The Bulgarian Communist Party expressed full subordination to the USSR and began repression of Macedonians, who insisted on Bulgarian identity. Many were consigned to concentration camps including one of the best Bulgarian writers, Dimiter Talev, who died in confinement. In the 1947 Bulgarian census everybody born in Macedonia was listed as "Macedonian." The founder of the Bulgarian Communist Party, Georgi Dimitrov, who in 1947 was the head of the party and prime minister, was born in Macedonia, and was said to be proud of being Bulgarian.

Stalin's death in 1953 changed the things somewhat. Bulgarian Communists realized their mistake, but it was too late. Too many people were engaged in the anti-Bulgarian crusade. Nevertheless, little by little, patriotic feelings started to arise among Bulgarians. Even among Bulgarian Communist Party members and leaders there were debates and discussions. Under the control of the party's Central Committee, different institutions were organized to conduct research to challenge the Yugoslav position that the Macedonians were a separate and distinct nationality from the Bulgarians, and the official Soviet political and ideological line. The results of the 1947 census were silently forgotten or explained as the result of pressure by the Soviet Union.

On January 6, 1992, Bulgaria was the first country to recognize the independence of the Republic of Macedonia. This decision contributed to the survival of the Macedonian economy at a time of total economic isolation from Yugoslavia and Greece. Bulgaria refused to consider proposals for the division of Macedonian territory. Nevertheless, owing to pro-Serbian feelings among the top politicians, including the prime minister, Nikola Kljusev, official relations between Bulgaria and Macedonia were not cordial. One issue of contention was the so-called language controversy. There was a question of which language should be used in Bulgarian-Macedonian agreements. Greece and Macedonia had already signed agreements in the English language. When Bulgaria proposed that agreements between Bulgaria and Macedonia be signed in "the official languages of both countries—Macedonian and Bulgarian," the Macedonian government did not like the descriptor "official," which implied that the "Macedonian language" was a political convention rather than a language distinct from Bulgarian.

Elections in Macedonia in 1998 however, gave power to Ljubco Georgievski of the Internal Macedonian Revolutionary Organization (IMRO), which has traditionally been friendly to Bulgaria and relations between the two countries improved.

BIBLIOGRAPHY

Andriotes, Nikolaos P. *The Federative Republic of Skopje and its Language.* Thessaloniki, Greece: Society for Macedonian Studies, 1991.

Kattein, Rudolf. *Das bulgarische und mazedonische Narrativsystem: eine funktionale und kontextabhängige Analyse.* Frankfurt am Main: P. Lang, 1979.

Makedonski Nauchen Institut. *Memorandum of the Macedonian Scientific Institute-Sofia Concerning the Relations between the Republic of Bulgaria and the Republic of Macedonia Regarding the Language Dispute.* Sofia, Bulgaria: Macedonian Scientific Institute, 1997.

Dimiter Minchev

SEE ALSO Crvenkovski, Branko

Macedonia and the European Union

When in December 1991 the European Community set up a commission of inquiry into the question of the recognition of the Yugoslav republics, headed by French jurist Robert Badinter, the Macedonians applied for recognition as an independent state. Badinter recommended recognition without any preconditions. In response to Greek sensitivities on the matter, however, the foreign ministers of the European Community, or European Union (EU) as it was called after 1993, requested that this should depend on certain changes in the Macedonian constitution, in particular making it clear that the Macedonian state had no territorial aspirations with respect to other areas of geographical Macedonia, and affirming that Macedonia would not interfere in the internal affairs of its neighbors. Accordingly, the constitution was amended on January 6, 1992. Even so, Greece continued to resist recognition, and protracted negotiations continued throughout the year. Although the United Nations granted recognition in April 1993 under the provisional title of the "Former Yugoslav Republic of Macedonia," Greek intransigence continued to prevent the development of normal relations between Macedonia and the EU. Not until September 1944, when former Secretary of State Cyrus Vance, then serving as a UN mediator for the conflicts in the former Yugoslavia, negotiated an agreement on behalf of the United Nations was Greece persuaded to end its anti-Macedonian campaign in the EU. According to the agreement, Macedonia would be referred to as the Former Yugoslav Republic of Macedonia.

Previously the EU had not been able to accept the idea that decisions affecting the union might be carried by majority voting. The experience of Greek action against Macedonia was an important factor in moving the union toward abandonment of its former principle of unanimity. As in other aspects of the disintegration of the former Yugoslav federation, the problem of Macedonia highlighted the difficulty experienced by the EU in developing a common foreign policy with respect to issues about which its member states individually had diverse views.

BIBLIOGRAPHY

Shea, John. *Macedonia and Greece: the Struggle to Define a New Balkan Nation.* Jefferson, N.C.: McFarland, 1997.

John B. Allcock

Political Parties

After the collapse of Yugoslavia, the first multiparty elections took place in three rounds on November 9 and 25, and December 9, 1990. These returned the veteran former Communist Kiro Gligorov as president. Twenty-five registered parties contested the poll, and ten of these secured representation, together with three independent candidates, in the 120-seat Sobranie (parliament). A startling feature of these elections was the elimination as an electoral force of the Movement for Pan-Macedonian Action, which had led the drive for multiparty democracy, headed by poet Gane Todorovski. As a movement of urban intellectuals it was brushed aside in the contest for the nationalist vote by the more plebeian Internal Macedonian Revolutionary Organization-Democratic Party for Macedonian National Unity (IMRO-DPMNU).

In August 1991 a coalition was put together, headed by Branko Crvenkovski, that included the former League of Communists, renamed yet again as the Social-Democratic Alliance of Macedonia (SDAM); the main Albanian party, the Party of Democratic Prosperity (PDP); the Liberals (LP); and the Socialists (SPM).

New elections called in 1994 were contested by around sixty parties. These were marred by controversy over the completeness of electoral registers. Organization for Economic Cooperation and Development (OECD) observers described them as "chaotic." Following a poor initial showing in the first round IMRO withdrew, alleging massive electoral fraud by the government coalition. The three-party coalition, the Alliance for Macedonia, gained a secure majority with 95 of the 120 seats (SDAM 58; LP 29; SPM 8). The Liberals, however, withdrew from the coalition in November 1997. Significantly, the Albanian PDP, which had announced a boycott of the Assembly in protest against the trial of ten Albanians on charges of planning armed sedition, returned to the assembly and subsequently joined the governing alliance.

At the end of the 1990s eight principal parties contested for the votes of the Macedonians: the Liberal Party of Macedonia, the Democratic Party, the Social-Democratic Alliance of Macedonia, the Socialist Party of Macedonia, the Internal Macedonian Revolutionary Organization-Democratic Party for Macedonian National Unity, the Party of Democratic Prosperity (Continuity), the Party of Democratic Prosperity (Albanian), and the National Democratic Party.

The Liberal Party of Macedonia (LP) grew out of the Alliance of Reform Forces assembled by Ante Marković on the eve of the disintegration of Yugoslavia, combining with representatives of some minor parties and defectors in July 1993. A great deal of the party's publicity concentrated on economics and the need for liberalization and technical modernization of the economy. Under the leadership of Stojan Andov, the LP secured 29 seats in the assembly in 1994. The LP was a pillar of the ruling coalition—the Alliance for Macedonia—until it withdrew in the wake of the TAT pyramid investment scheme. This scheme took advantage of gullible people unfamiliar with stock markets. They were enticed to purchase shares of a fund that had practically no assets other than what these investors contributed and yet promised high returns. The toleration of this scheme was indicative of wider failings of economic policy on the part of its senior coalition partner, the Social-Democratic Alliance of Macedonia. Its support was concentrated heavily among the urban and educated middle classes.

The Democratic Party (DP), led by Petar Gosev, a former member of the Yugoslav federal presidency, was put together initially as a coalition of four small parties with a commitment to economic reform and moderate nationalism. Created in June 1993, it did not contest the first elections but secured a small representation in the assembly through defections from other groups. In 1994, however, it secured only one seat. The gap between the DP and its major rival, the Liberals, was as much a matter of style as political substance, centered upon Gosev's populist and personal approach.

The Social-Democratic Alliance of Macedonia (SDAM), the former League of Communists of Macedonia (LCM), went through a sequence of attempts to redefine itself to secure its relegitimation. When the League of Communists of Yugoslavia collapsed at its final, extraordinary congress in January 1989, the LCM changed its name to the Party of Democratic Change, and under this title it contested the first open elections in 1990. It performed creditably, winning thirty-one seats, coming in second to IMRO and securing the election of Kiro Gligorov to the presidency. A further reform took place in August 1991, when the current title was adopted. With the fall of the IMRO-led "government of experts" in 1992, the SDAM put together a governing coalition, although at the cost of the secession of Gosev's Democratic Party. The SDAM propounded a moderate and flexible nationalism, and a cautious approach to economic reconstruction, its opponents would say indifference, which led to strain in its relations with its coalition partners. In the second assembly elections of 1994, which it entered as part of the Alliance for Macedonia, it strengthened its position (partly as a consequence of the IMRO boycott), securing fifty-eight seats.

The Socialist Party of Macedonia (SPM) emerged from the former "popular front" organization—the Socialist Alliance of Macedonia—on a platform broadly critical of the former Communists, but wishing to continue within the socialist tradition. It secured four seats in the 1990 elections but was damaged by the secession of Gosev from the SDAM and the setting up of the DPM. The SPM joined with the alliance in the 1994 electoral contest and emerged with eight seats.

Radical Macedonian nationalism was represented by the Internal Macedonian Revolutionary Organization-Democratic Party for Macedonian National Unity (IMRO-DPMNU), which assumed the name of the nineteenth-century Macedonian nationalist organization. But there is no known continuity between the two. It was formed in 1990 from the union between a faction that split from the Movement for Pan-Macedonian Action (MAAK) and an organization of Macedonian émigré workers in Sweden. Its strident nationalism embodied all that Greece feared from an independent Macedonia. Led by Ljupco Georgievski, it gave expression to the dissatisfaction of a wide stratum of the blue-collar and rural population of the republic. Its support declined sharply in the second electoral contest in 1994, from which it withdrew after the first round, alleging widespread irregularity, although it continued as an active and noisy extraparliamentary opposition. The demonstrations that it organized in May 1997 were one of the main causes of the reconstruction of the government. Acrimonious internal disagreements that surfaced in September 1997 brought the party to the verge of schism.

Three parties contested for the vote of Macedonia's Albanian minority. The Party of Democratic Prosperity (PDP) was founded in April 1989 before the disintegration of the Yugoslav federation. It was then one of the few parties to transcend republican boundaries. Yet its formation in Skopje by Nevzet Halili reflected the concentration of its support in Macedonia. It never significantly challenged the Democratic League of Kosovo as the principal voice of Albanians elsewhere in Yugoslavia. In the elections of 1990 it emerged as the undisputed voice of Albanian opinion in the republic. Its moderate nationalism enabled it to participate, originally with five ministerial portfolios, in the coalition government created in July 1992. Relations with the majority Macedonian community were soured by the indictment of several leading Albanian figures on charges of sedition. The party then split in February 1994, with its more radically nationalist wing setting up a rival party. The main PDP is known as the PDP(C) (Continuity), and its secessionist rival the PDP(A) (Albanian). In the elections of November 1994 the PDP continued to command the greater part of Albanian support. It returned to a new governing coalition, although that support has been under constant strain as a consequence of controversies over education policy, access to communications media, and the right to fly the Albanian flag.

The radical nationalist PDP(A), led by Menduh Taçi and Arben Xaferi, broke away from the PDP at its congress in February 1994. In collaboration with the National Democratic Party (NDP), it commanded five seats in the assembly.

The NDP, founded in 1990 by Ilijaz Halili, was the more stridently nationalistic of the two Albanian parties. Based principally in the western Macedonian city of Tetovo, the NDP secured five seats in the assembly elections of November 1994, although two of those defected to the PDP in 1996. Since the split in the PDP its other members cooperated with the PDP(A).

BIBLIOGRAPHY

Profile of The Major Political Parties in Macedonia. Skopje, Macedonia: Macedonian Information Centre, 1994.

John B. Allcock

SEE ALSO Crvenkovski, Branko; Georgievski, Ljupco; Gligorov, Kiro

Economy

Macedonia was the poorest republic of the former Yugoslavia. The per capita income in Macedonia in 1996 was estimated to be $960 and unemployment was approximately 38 percent. The country can meet its own food requirements and has sufficient coal reserves to meet its energy needs. Macedonia depends on imports for all its petroleum and natural gas and most of its machinery and spare parts. Its economy was seriously disrupted by the imposition of international sanctions on Serbia for its part in the wars after the breakup of former Yugoslavia and by an embargo against Macedonia by Greece, which objected to the name and the symbols of the new Macedonian state. Following the lifting of sanctions and the embargo, food, beverages, and tobacco constituted 17 percent of Macedonia's exports; machinery and transport equipment, 13.3 percent; and other manufactured goods, 58 percent. In addition to fuel and chemicals its biggest imports were machinery and manufactured goods. Remittances from Macedonians working in Germany and elsewhere in Western Europe had a positive impact on the economy at the beginning of Macedonian independence, as they did during the later Yugoslav era. Macedonia's isolation, underdevelopment, and potential for political unrest have been deterrents against outside investment. The United States provided $10 million in humanitarian and technical assistance in 1995 and the European Union extended a credit of ECU 21.7 million for investment projects.

BIBLIOGRAPHY

National Development Strategy for Macedonia: Development and Modernization. Skopje, Macedonia: Macedonian Academy of Sciences and Arts/United Nations Dept. of Economic and Social Affairs, 1997.

Oschlies, Wolf. *Makedonien im Sommer 1998: politisch-okonomische Momentaufnahmen im Schatten des Kosovo-Konflikts.* Cologne: Bundesinstitut fur Ostwissenschaftliche und Internationale Studien, 1998.

Useful Information on Investment in Macedonia. Skopje, Macedonia: Institute of Economics, 1995.

Bernard Cook

Albanian Minority

As with all the republics emerging from the former Yugoslav federation, Macedonia has been characterized by its ethnic diversity, only two-thirds of its population being Macedonian Slavs. The largest of its minorities is Albanian, which the census of 1994 recorded as forming around 23 percent of the total. These are primarily located in the communes of Tetovo and Gostivar, both of which have Albanian majorities, but also in Debar, Kicevo, Struga, and Kumanovo, all of which have Albanian minorities of more than 30 percent. The capital, Skopje, also houses a large proportion of Albanians.

The importance of Albanian settlement in Macedonia has grown over the post-1945 period. In 1948 Albanians made up only 11 percent of the republic's population, confined in the main to rural areas. Differential birthrates (Albanians have among the highest rates of natality in Europe) combined with the stronger tendency of Slav Macedonians to emigrate to the cities have resulted in a rapid shift of the proportions of the two groups in the west and north of Macedonia. To a limited extent this pattern has been augmented by immigration from Kosovo and even Albania itself.

In view of the proximity of these areas to the border with the Albanian state and Serbia's Kosovo province, these demographic changes have stimulated concern in Macedonia about the possibility of a bid for secession by its Albanian population. The prevailing poverty of Albania and the climate of ethnic repression that has characterized Kosovo since 1945 have given little incentive to Macedonia's Albanians to contemplate this as an immediate possibility. The prevalence of intercommunal prejudice in Macedonia is reflected perhaps in fact that Macedonians and Albanians have had the lowest rates of intermarriage of all Yugoslavia's ethnic groups. Nevertheless intercommunal relations were always better than in Kosovo and never degenerated into the open disorder that regularly soured Albanian-Serb relations.

The first multiparty elections of December 1990 yielded no clear majority. After a period of unsuccessful experiment with a nonpartisan "government of experts," a coalition was formed around the former Communists—the Party for Democratic Change (subsequently known as the Social-Democratic Alliance of Macedonia, SDAM)—and the larger of the two Albanian parties, the Party of Democratic Prosperity (PDP). This excluded the nationalistic Internal Macedonian Revolutionary Organization-Democratic Party for Macedonian National Unity (IMRO-DPMNU), and gave Albanians a stake in government and the future of the republic. The coalition was heavily criticized by more radical Albanians, however, and in the second elections of 1994 the PDP leadership under Nevzet Halili was challenged by a breakaway faction led by Menduh Taçi. The insurgents have failed to make substantial inroads into the PDP vote but have managed to sustain enough pressure to compel the leadership to distance itself further from the republican government. This was reflected at first in controversy over the conduct of the 1994 census, in which Albanians gained substantial concessions over the conduct of the census. Yet more dramatic, and more difficult to manage has been the struggle over provision of higher education for Albanians.

Within the former Yugoslav federation the University of Pristina emerged as the center for higher education in the Albanian language. Its suppression by the Serbian authorities, and the secession of Macedonia from Yugoslavia, resulted in the loss of any possibility of university-level education in Albanian for young Albanians from Macedonia. Against the resistance of the republican government, plans were mounted to open an Albanian-language university near the western city of Tetovo. This city of approximately 51,000 people is located in the Vardar valley, thirty-five kilometers west of Skopje. With more than 70 percent of its population of Albanian ethnicity—the highest proportion of any municipality in Macedonia—Tetovo has become a kind of informal capital of the predominantly Albanian region, which extends in an arc across western Macedonia from Skopje to Ohrid. It is also the center of the more radically nationalistic wing of Albanian politics, represented by the National Democratic Party. During 1995 an attempt was made to launch an independent Albanian-language university in Tetovo as a consequence of growing impatience on the part of Albanians in the republic with the response of the Macedonian government to their demands for more equal representation of their language in the educational system. At first suppressed with some violence, the new university was subsequently tolerated by the authorities, in spite of their unwillingness to grant the institution legal status.

Tetovo was the focus of concern, both domestic and international, that ethnic tension could draw Macedonia into a wider Balkan conflict should the troubled issue of Albanian political autonomy in Serbia develop into armed conflict. The potential for the further deterioration of intercommunal relations was underlined during 1997 by civil disturbances that erupted around the right to display the Albanian flag on public buildings.

When the Kosovo conflict erupted in 1999, tensions increased in Macedonia between pro-Serb Macedonians and ethnic Albanians. Albanian Kosovar refugees innundated Macedonia during the conflict, and the government was concerned that the refugees not remain in Macedonia and thus increase its Albanian population. After the withdrawal of Serbian forces from Kosovo, the Macedonian government feared that the Albanians would create a Greater Albania and threaten the integrity of Macedonia.

BIBLIOGRAPHY

Glenny, Misha. *The Fall of Yugoslavia: The Third Balkan War.* Second Edition. New York: Penguin, 1997.

John B. Allcock

SEE ALSO Kosovo

Quest for Recognition

As the disintegration of Yugoslavia gathered pace through 1991, the Macedonian government conducted a referendum on September 8. This yielded a 95 percent majority, on a 75 percent turnout, for autonomy and independence, "with the right to join an alliance of sovereign states" keeping open the option of the reconstitution of Yugoslavia in a new form. Accordingly, the Macedonian parliament declared the independence of the republic on September 18. When in December the EU's Badinter Commission canvased the republics of Yugoslavia on the issue of their independence, the Macedonians applied for recognition. Although Robert Badinter recommended recognition without preconditions, in response to Greek sensitivities on the matter, EU foreign ministers requested that this depend on certain changes in the Macedonian constitution. In response, the constitution was amended on January 6, 1992, to the effect that Macedonia had no claims on the territory of other states, and affirmed that it would not interfere in the sovereign rights and internal affairs of other states.

To the surprise of many, the new state was immediately recognized by Bulgaria, although with the paradoxical qualification that recognition of the state did not imply recognition of the language or nation. The Bulgarians still held to their position that the Macedonians were for the most part Bulgarians and that their language was a Bulgarian dialect. Matters were not handled so easily in the case of Greece. Protracted negotiations throughout 1992 failed to mollify the Greeks and the failure of these negotiations brought down the Macedonian government in July. In April 1993 the matter was largely settled when Macedonia agreed to recognition within the United Nations under the provisional title "The Former Yugoslav Republic of Macedonia" (FYROM). General recognition then followed, although the name and the flag still caused offense to the Greeks.

Unfortunately for the Macedonians the UN-imposed economic sanctions against the Yugoslav federation produced acute difficulties. Although the severance from Yugoslavia passed without difficulty, and the Yugoslav Army (JNA) withdrew peaceably from Macedonia in February and March 1992, the only secession from Yugoslavia to be accomplished without violence, the Belgrade government withheld recognition in sympathy with the Greeks. The Yugoslavs relied heavily on Greek support in order to evade international sanctions and reciprocated with support for Greece on the Macedonian question. Consequently, Macedonia was caught in a dilemma, being under pressure to collaborate in the evasion of sanctions to sustain its own economic needs, but in doing so necessarily denying itself the international economic and political support needed for its rehabilitation and development. Desperate attempts were made to explore the possibility of linking Macedonia to the Bulgarian rail network, thereby evading the Serbo-Greek stranglehold.

Anxiety reached its greatest level in the lead-up to the Greek general election of October 10, in which Macedonia was the most pressing issue. The Macedonian economic situation continued to deteriorate, however, when the new Greek government imposed special trade sanctions against Macedonia itself on February 16, 1994. Mesmerized by the need to secure solidarity among member states, the EU was unable to reach agreement on the issue, although loans by the IMF and the World Bank served to ease the pressure on Macedonia.

In September 1994, the UN mediator Cyrus Vance managed to negotiate an agreement between the Macedonians and the Greeks, endorsed by the Sobranie in October, by which the embargo was lifted in return for the withdrawal of the controversial "Sun of Vergina" flag. The situation ameliorated with the general stabilization of the region and the end of sanctions against Yugoslavia after the Dayton Peace Accords in late 1995. The normalization of Macedonia's relations with its neighbors was largely completed with the recognition of Macedonia by the Yugoslav Federation on April 8, 1996. The Greeks, however, are still to be satisfied with respect to the issue of the name.

John B. Allcock

MacEntee, Sean (1899–)

Irish politician. Sean MacEntee was born in Belfast. He was a member of the Irish Volunteers and was imprisoned for his participation in the 1916 Rising. He sat in the first Dáil as a Sinn Fein representative for South Monaghan. He opposed the 1921 Treaty that recognized the Irish Free State in the south but linked the six counties of the north to Great Britain and supported Republicans in the civil war (1922–1923). MacEntee was a founding member of Fianna Fáil in 1926 and served in all Fianna Fáil governments until his retirement in 1965. He held the portfolios of finance (1932–39), industry and commerce (1939–41), local government and health (1941–48), finance again (1951–54), and Health (1957–65). He also held the office of deputy prime minister from 1959 to 1965. He was a noted social and economic conservative in comparison to the progressive Sean Lemass.

BIBLIOGRAPHY

Powell, Frederick W. *The Politics of Irish Social Policy, 1600–1990.* Lewiston, N.Y.: Edwin Mellen Press, 1992.

Michael J. Kennedy

SEE ALSO Lemass, Sean

Macmillan, Harold (1894–1986)

Conservative prime minister of Great Britain from 1957 to 1963. Harold Macmillan was committed to fostering the special relationship between his country and the United States. He joined with the leaders of the United States and the USSR in signing the Nuclear Test-Ban Treaty in 1963.

Educated at Balliol College, Oxford, Macmillan experienced combat during the First World War and became active politically after the war. He held a seat in the House of Commons from 1924 to 1929 and from 1931 to 1964. Ardently opposed to Hitler's expansionist policies, Macmillan joined Winston Churchill's coalition government in 1940 as an assistant to the minister of supply. During the war Macmillan also served as undersecretary of state for the colonies and as British minister attached to the Allied Forces Headquarters, Mediterranean Command. In that capacity Macmillan secured the support of the American and Free-French leadership for British interests and policies. After victory in Europe Macmillan served briefly as secretary of state for air; he lost his position with the defeat of the Conservatives in the July 1945 general elections. Macmillan served in Churchill's second ministry as minister of housing and local government (1951–54) and as minister of defense (1954–55). In Prime Minister Anthony Eden's government Macmillan held the positions of foreign secretary (1955) and chancellor of the exchequer (1955–57). He succeeded Eden as prime minister in 1957 after Eden was forced to resign after the Suez crisis.

When Macmillan assumed the leadership of Great Britain he was confronted by economic, social, and foreign policy problems. He moved to reestablish confidence in the pound by expanding the money supply; the economy responded favorably and employment increased significantly. Socially, he pledged his support to continue the postwar social programs that had been initiated by the Labour governments of Clement Attlee; these measures included national health insurance and expanded old-age pensions. Finally, Macmillan acted to restore cordial relations with the United States. The Suez crisis, which involved a combined British, French, and Israeli military action against Egypt, had resulted in U.S. condemnation of the action and forced the anti-Egyptian coalition to withdraw. Macmillan exercised his personal skills to normalize relations with the United States, which was led by his friend President Dwight Eisenhower. He continued to have a close relationship with President John F. Kennedy, who succeeded Eisenhower in 1961. In 1962 Kennedy and Macmillan signed the Nassau Agreement (1962), in which Britain agreed that the United States would provide nuclear missiles for the British submarine fleet. This agreement was condemned not only by the USSR but also by French President Charles de Gaulle, who insisted that Europeans needed to be free from American influence.

Macmillan failed to gain French support for Britain's entrance into the European Economic Community (EC). His government also failed to recognize the adverse impact of wage and price controls on the economy. With his government under mounting attack and his personal popularity eroding, Macmillan experienced both a substantive victory and a devastating setback in the summer of 1963. The victory was his contribution to the Nuclear Test-Ban Treaty, which had been negotiated with the United States and the USSR. The setback was the fallout from the Profumo affair, in which Macmillan's secretary of state for war was involved in a sordid relationship associated with Soviet espionage. In the fall 1963 Macmillan lost the support of his own party and resigned as prime minister.

Macmillan devoted his remaining years to writing memoirs and history, including *Winds of Change, 1914–1939* (1966), *The Blast of War, 1939–1945* (1967), *Tides of Fortune, 1945–1955* (1969), *Riding the Storm, 1956–*

1959 (1971), *Pointing the Way, 1959–1961* (1972), and *At the End of the Day,* 1961–1963 (1973).

Macmillan successfully repaired the damage to British-American relations caused by the Suez crisis, but his prime ministership was tarnished by the dual economic difficulties of stagnation and inflation, which would plague Great Britain in the 1960s and 1970s, and by the Profumo scandal.

BIBLIOGRAPHY

Fisher, Nigel. *Harold Macmillan, A Biography.* New York: St. Martin's Press, 1982.

Horne, Alistair. *Harold Macmillan.* New York: Viking, 1989.

Lamb, Richard. *The Macmillan Years 1957–1963: The Emerging Truth.* London: J. Murray, 1995.

Turner, John. *Macmillan.* London: Longmans, 1994.

William T. Walker

SEE ALSO Suez Crisis

MacSharry, Ray (1938–)

Irish politician. Ray MacSharry, born in Sligo, was an auctioneer and farmer. He was first elected to the Dáil in 1969. From 1973 to 1975 he served as the Fianna Fáil front bench spokesperson on the Office of Public Works. From 1977 to 1979 he was junior minister of the Department of Finance and the Public Service; minister for agriculture from 1979 to 1981; and deputy prime minister Tanaiste and minister for finance from March to December 1982. He was elected to the European Parliament from Connaught/Ulster, 1984–87. As minister for finance from 1987 to 1989, MacSharry was responsible for cutting public expenditure and reshaping Ireland's ailing national finances. As European Commissioner for Agriculture and Rural Development from 1989 to 1992, MacSharry was responsible for major reform of the Common Agricultural Policy.

Michael J. Kennedy

Mafia

There is no agreement among scholars on the etymology of the word "mafia." It is nevertheless reasonable to assume that "mafia" derives from the Arab *maha fat* (immunity, protection). The word does not appear in formal written form until 1863, when it was used in Palermo, Sicily, in the play *I mafiusi della Vicaria,* by popular writer Giuseppe Rizzotto. This fact is surprising because the Mafia as a phenomenon has an ancient origin. Rather recently it has become customary to use "organized crime" to designate the phenomenon. This is insufficient and in fact quite wrong. "Organized crime" does indeed designate certain criminal phenomena in Italy (Neapolitan Camorra, Calabrian 'Ndrangheta) or similar phenomena in other parts of the world including post-Soviet Russia, but this has little relation to the original and historic Mafia, which is the Sicilian Mafia.

In Sicily the Mafiosi, normally involved in illegal and criminal activity, possess a type of social power flowing from below, from the popular classes, which found protection and complicity from above, from the dominant classes (barons, large property owners, political notables). Not without basis the same mafiosi, regarding themselves as members of a sort of "popular masonry" charged with defending the social order and utilizing every possible arbitrary and violent means, have always defined themselves as "men of honor" (*uomini d'onore*) or "men of respect" (*uomini di rispetto*)—that is, worthy of being respected. The class of *gabelloti,* who stemmed from popular elements able to rent the *latifondi* of the barons, long had such a self-perception in Sicily. In the eighteenth century and the first half of the nineteenth, the *gabelloti* were the principal force of the Mafia. They paid an annual rent to the property owners, thus securing the rent of the owners of the great estates, and they subjected the poor peasants under their domination to a systematic and rapacious exploitation. In this fashion they personally enriched themselves and defended the "social order" by compelling the poor peasants to a desperate obedience through violence and the threat of hunger.

To find out why the land owners conferred so much power on such persons, it is necessary to turn to the particular history of Sicily. The island was officially governed for over eight centuries by foreigners. The foreign authorities, in exchange for revenue and at least formal sovereignty over the island, conceded to dominant indigenous groups a type of feudal power over the land and the people. In conditions of this sort the formation of Sicily into a modern state was rendered impossible, and the local powers did not distinguish between public and private interests. They were pure and simple parasites, and, consequently, had no difficulty in recognizing and accepting the mafiosi (and in the first place the *gabelloti*) as their very special "collaborators" and in a certain sense "colleagues," even if from the popular ranks. The great barons and the mafiosi-*gabelloti* realized their ability together to defend their interests and their privilege against both the state (which represented the foreign dominators) and protests and revolts of the oppressed and the exploited. Together the great barons (with their trappings of nobility) and the mafiosi (with their pursuit of common crime) appropriated the function of representing Sicily and *sicilianità.* The exercise of this function placed them in the position of enjoying great authority and influence over society, and endowed them with a type of leadership over the entire Sicilian people.

Without grasping the possibility of the dominant groups to permeate the society of the island with their thinking and to define and to "defend" its customs, beliefs, and values, it would be difficult to understand how and why the Mafia became such a powerful and rooted phenomenon that efforts undertaken at various times by the state to reduce or eliminate it were so difficult. The mentality of the Mafia, the product or the power of the dominant classes, was fused with a whole society's vision of the world.

The mafiosi were thus accorded the dignity of being the authentic representatives of genuine Sicilian culture and in particular of a society that had always given first importance, among its norms, to respect for tradition and "natural" hierarchies (with primacy to the males), obedience to authority, and the code of silence, and among its goals, social prestige, honorability, riches (called *roba,* or possessions) and the solidarity of the nuclear family in the struggle for life. This culture also characterizes the language that the mafiosi adopted for their organization: family, or *cosche* to indicate the nucleus of their organization; *padrini* to indicate their leaders; *picciotti* (boys) or brothers or cousins, to indicate their initiates.

The Mafia is therefore a systemic phenomenon, a true and proper system of power integrated in a traditional society. As a consequence a political mafiosi class or a class in service to the Mafia developed. This political class has had different versions over the years, but it has always reproduced its original characteristic of diffidence toward and distance from the state. In 1860 it sided with Garibaldi against the Bourbons, thus retaining its power and obtaining major advantages from the unification of Italy. But then the Mafia became disappointed with the politics of the historic Right, which tried to introduce into the island the liberal state without particular regard for the demands of the local powers. Consequently, in 1874 the Mafia contributed to the victory of the Left, which demonstrated its gratitude for the support it had received and was prudent in confronting the interests of the barons and the *gabelloti,* who were allowed to maintain their privilege. In the first years of the twentieth century, when Giovanni Giolitti served as prime minister the power of the Mafia was so great and pervasive to give life to something like a true "Mafia kingdom." After the First World War fascism, unwilling to tolerate that an independent social power was able to survive on the island, struck the Mafia hard with a police operation led by Prefect Cesare Mori. But many important mafiosi avoided punishment by converting to fascism and putting on black shirts. During the fascist years the Mafia camouflaged itself within Mussolini's regime, which only in 1940, during the war, gave the impression, with the "assault on the *latifondi,*" of wishing to reduce the power of the large Sicilian land owners.

After the landing of Anglo-American troops in Sicily in June 1943, the Mafia returned to the open under the leadership of boss Calogero Vizzini di Villalba, and contributed in a decisive manner to the success of the Movement for the Independence of Sicily (Movimento per l'Independenza della Sicilia, MIS), a secessionist movement set up by Andrea Finocchiaro Aprile with the collaboration of the big land owners and numerous bands of bandits, the most famous of which was led by Salvatore Giuliano. To make themselves acceptable to the Allied Military Administration, the separatists and their mafiosi friends declared themselves "democrats" and antifascists. It is also probable that the need to combat communism led the Italian Secret Service and that of the United States to establish contact and operate alliances with the Mafia, which profited from this "legitimization" as a force in the service of the strategic interests of the "free world." Relying on this legitimization, the Mafia ordered Salvatore Giuliano on May 1, 1947, to fire on a peaceful assembly of poor peasants who were celebrating May Day at Portella della Ginestra.

With the establishment of the republican state in Italy after World War II, the mafiosi abandoned separatism and sought to profit thoroughly from its role as an anticommunist force. In pursuit of this strategy the Mafia attempted to eliminate the peasant movement for agrarian reform, killing over fifty unionists. Subsequently it realized the impossibility of opposing agrarian reform, desired not only by Communists and Socialists, but also by Catholics organized as the government of the country presided over by Alcide De Gasperi. Thus in the 1950s the Mafia preferred to abandon its traditional activity in the countryside and concentrated more intensely on *business* in the cities, especially Palermo, profiting first from the *rackets* and then from the beginning of the 1970s from the international business of drug trafficking.

For this new business the Sicilian Mafia strengthened the organic alliances with the U.S. Mafia families, which, through the initiative of boss Lucky Luciano, had been formed in the 1930s into a great international criminal organization called Cosa Nostra. In Sicily the corresponding apex of the "*Cupola*" (dome) was dominated until the

1960s by bosses with a "traditional" outlook such as Gaetano Baldalamente, Stefano Bontate, Giuseppe Di Cristrina, and Tommaso Buscetta. The *Cupola* was able to assert, with the cooperation of the "family" of Michele Greco, called "*il papa,*" its leadership of a ferocious criminal group, the Corleonesi, founded and led by Luciano Liggio with Salvatore Riina, Leoluca Bagarella, Giovanni Brusca, Bernardo Provenzano, Pietro Aglieri, and Catanian Nitto Santapaola. The Corleonesi, imitating the style of American gangsterism, accentuated the criminal character of Cosa Nostra and attempted in the 1980s to deal with the state as an equal. To impose its "law" it assassinated magistrates, police, public officials, contractors, intellectuals, and priests in terrorist attacks executed with military efficiency.

Among the many Mafia terrorist attacks ones that were particularly egregious were carried out against General Carlo Alberto Dalla Chiesa, the anti-Mafia prefect of Palermo appointed by the Spadolini government in 1982; judges Cesare Terranova in 1979, Rocco Chinnici in 1982, Giovani Falcone in 1992, and Paolo Borsellino in 1992; politicians Piersanti Mattarella of the Christian Democrats in 1980 and Pio La Torre from the Communist Party in 1982; contractor Libero Grassi in 1991; and priest Pino Puglisi in 1993.

As a result of its central role in the world of illegal and legal business and offering its electoral support to a number of members of the governing parties (Giovanni Goria, Salvo Lima, Vito Ciancimino, etc.), the Mafia has for many years constituted an important part of the Italian power system and has consolidated an enormous base of economic power (estimated to be over 200 trillion lire, or about $117 billion), which had at its service important economic managers such as the Messina Michele Sindona (for a number of years active in the United States) and the Tuscan Licio Gelli, head of a powerful Masonic lodge that influenced the policies of the government.

Through the Masonic link, the connections between the Mafia and politics became, especially in the 1970s, so continuous and intimate that they reached the summit of the national government. However, a vast anti-Mafia campaign also developed, led by courageous spokesmen of the state and civil society and supported by leaders of the post-counciliar church such as Cardinal Pappalardo of Palermo and Archbishop Bommarito of Catania, as well as the "Arrupe" Center of the Jesuits. This gave birth to a real "revolt on behalf of legality" that supported the authorities engaged in the struggle and opened the way for very public initiatives by the magistrates such as the incrimination of a political figure of the status of Giulio Andreotti (Italian premier 1972–73, 1976–79, and 1989–92), accused of associating with the Mafia. Anti-Mafia campaigns such as the "maxi-trial" of 1986, which imposed heavy sentences on 474 accused members of Cosa Nostra, and movements of cultural and civic rebirth such as the "Palermo spring" initiated in 1985 under the mayor of Palermo, Leoluca Orlando, are especially noteworthy, along with the great inquests launched by magistrates-martyrs Falcone and Borsellino and others, who were aided in their efforts by the mafosi "*pentiti,*" or informers. Among these, Buscetta was especially important, playing a role analogous to that of Joe Valachi at the time of the U.S. Senate investigation headed by Senator Estes Kefauver.

Faced with a violent Mafia terror offensive between 1979 and 1992, the Italian state achieved decisive results, especially after the fall of the Berlin Wall in 1989. With the collapse of Communism, the rationale for the Christian Democratic dominance in Italy also collapsed, and numerous scandals surfaced that ultimately led the Christian Democratic and Socialist Parties to disband. Since these political changes, the Italian state has fought effectively against the Mafia. The Corleone group has been crushed. But the Mafia is reforming and remains an Italian and international problem. The United Nations is very aware of this and has established an "ad hoc" organization, headed by Italian Pino Arlacchi, to combat it.

BIBLIOGRAPHY

Arlacchi, Pino. *La mafia imprenditrice.* Bologna: Il Mulino, 1983.

Lupo, Salvatore. *Storia della mafia dalle origini ai nostri giorni.* Rome: Donzelli, 1993.

Marino, Giuseppe Carlo. *Storia della mafia.* Rome: Newton & Compton, 1998.

Pantaleone, Michele. *Mafia e politica.* Turin: Einaudi, 1962.

Renda, Francesco. *Storia della mafia.* Palermo: Sigma, 1998.

Tranfaglia, Nicola. *Mafia, politica e affari: 1943–91.* Rome: Laterza, 1992.

Giuseppe Carlo Marino
Tr. by B. Cook

SEE ALSO Borsellino, Paolo; Buscetta, Tommaso; Dalla, Chiesa, Carlo Alberto; Falcone, Giovanni; Gelli, Licio; La Torre, Pio; Liggio, Luciano; Sindona, Michele

Major, John (1943–)

Prime minister of Great Britain (1990–97). By profession a banker, John Major was a borough councilor (1968–

John Major, prime minister of Great Britain from 1990 to 1997. *Illustration courtesy of the British Information Service.*

71), Conservative MP (1979–), government whip (1983–85), junior minister (1985–87), chief secretary of the Treasury (1987–89), foreign secretary (1989), and chancellor of the exchequer (1989–90). He was elected Conservative Party leader and became prime minister, following Margaret Thatcher's resignation.

Major's social background was unconventional for a Conservative leader. His father was a small businessman who had once been a circus performer. Major grew up in inner-city London, did not attend a university, worked as a laborer before becoming a junior bank employee, and entered politics through local government. His subsequent career was more orthodox. After quickly rising to management rank in banking, Major became MP for a suburban constituency. He was representative of the Conservatives of lower-middle- and working-class origins who rose to top jobs in Margaret Thatcher's government.

Major won the leadership over more senior Conservatives because he had few enemies and was in the right place at the right time. His amiable personality and knowledge of finance, coupled with political artfulness, attracted Prime Minister Thatcher's benevolent attention and accounted for his rapid promotion to senior cabinet posts. When Thatcher lost her parliamentary party's confidence in 1990, Major was in a solid position to replace her. As Thatcher's protégé, he could count on the loyalty of most of her partisans, but he was also sufficiently detached from Thatcher to be acceptable to her critics. Major defeated two other strong candidates for the leadership, Michael Heseltine and Douglas Hurd, both of whom joined his cabinet. He was the youngest prime minister in almost a century.

Major's first fifteen months as prime minister were successful. He competently handled British engagement in the American-led coalition during the Persian Gulf crisis and war of 1990–91. He also skillfully directed Britain's European Community negotiations at Maastricht, and maintained Conservative unity over the divisive Maastricht treaty (1991). More important politically, the public viewed Major as a welcome change from his abrasive predecessor. He was seen as a consensus builder rather than a confrontationist, and more sympathetic to the disadvantaged. In April 1992, Major won an unprecedented fourth successive parliamentary election victory for the Conservatives, although with a majority much smaller than in the 1987 election. His populist image overcame a heavy Labour Party lead in opinion polls up to election eve.

During the rest of 1992, Major's prime ministership went downhill. Resistance to the Maastricht treaty among a minority of Conservatives who feared loss of British independence grew alarmingly. The government was saved from defeat in a confidence vote on the treaty in December 1992 only with help from the small Liberal Democratic Party. Major was attacked for failing to deal effectively with the consequences of economic recession, particularly rising unemployment and a falling pound. Scandals within the Conservative Party, one involving a close friend of the prime minister, and the royal family, did nothing to improve his government's image. In fewer than two years, Major's poll ratings fell from the highest of any prime minister in a generation to the lowest.

Major experienced further personal and political setbacks during 1993 and 1994, to the point where his survival as prime minister was in doubt. The government was given little credit for the fragile recovery from recession, and distrust of the European Community would not go away. The Maastricht treaty was finally ratified in July 1993, over bitter-end opposition from anti-European Conservatives, only after Major threatened a general election. The memoirs of Lady Thatcher (as she now was), published in 1993, gave her successor barely passing marks, depreciating his personality and intellectual ability. A youthful, attractive Labour Party leader, Tony Blair, elected in 1994, projected a glowing image contrasting with Major's fading one. On the positive side, Major could point to an agreement in 1993 with the Irish Republic over ending violence in Northern Ireland, and, in

1994, to an unconditional cease-fire by the Irish Republican Army and its Protestant paramilitary opponents.

Major was a shrewd political operator, an articulate parliamentary debater, a better-than-average public speaker and media performer, and an efficient executive. His moderately right-of-center political stance was more attractive than Thatcher's doctrinaire neoliberalism. Nevertheless he suffered, no doubt unfairly, from a hostile press, public disenchantment, and, from 1992 onward, bad luck. Among the things telling against Major as a Conservative prime minister were his humble social background, his ordinariness in comparison with Margaret Thatcher, his shaky authority over powerful cabinet colleagues, and Great Britain's obdurate socioeconomic problems in the early 1990s.

BIBLIOGRAPHY

Anderson, Bruce. *John Major: The Making of the Prime Minister.* London: Fourth Estate, 1991.

Ellis, Nesta. *John Major.* London: Futura, 1991.

Jenkin, John, ed. *John Major, Prime Minister.* London: Bloomsbury, 1990.

Junor, Penny. *The Major Enigma.* London: Michael Joseph, 1993.

Pearce, Edward. *The Quiet Rise of John Major.* London: Weidenfeld and Nicolson, 1991.

Don M. Cregier

SEE ALSO Heseltine, Michael; Hurd, Douglas; Thatcher, Margaret

Makarios III (1913–77)

First president of Cyprus. Archbishop Makarios III was born Mikhail Khristodolou Mouskos, son of a poor shepherd, on August 13, 1913, at Pano Panayia, Cyprus. He studied at the University of Athens and at Boston University's School of Theology. He was ordained an Orthodox priest in 1946 and became bishop of Kition (Larnaca) in 1948. He was elevated to the archbishopric of Cyprus in 1950.

As spiritual leader of the Greek community on Cyprus, Makarios became identified with the movement for union with Greece, *enosis.* He opposed not only partition of the island between Greece and Turkey but independence as well. He met with Greek Prime Minister Alexandros Papagos in February 1954 and secured Greek support for *enosis.* In March 1956 Makarios and three other leaders of the independence movement were exiled by the British, who controlled the island. After a year he was allowed to leave the Seychelles but was forbidden to return to Cyprus. Makarios continued his political campaign from Athens.

After the Greek and Turkish governments agreed to independence for the island in February 1959, Makarios returned and ran for president. On December 13, 1959, he was elected the first president of the Republic of Cyprus. As president Makarios worked for the integration of the two national communities on the island. Owing to the opposition of the Turks, Makarios was forced to accept a Turkish Cypriot Provisional Administration, which supervised the affairs of the Turkish community.

Despite the tension between the two communities Makarios was reelected president in 1968 and had no opponent in 1973. However, the die-hard supporters of *enosis* believed that Makarios had betrayed them. There were attempts to assassinate him in 1970 and 1973. In 1973 the three other Cypriot bishops attempted to force him to resign the presidency, but he appealed to a synod convened by the Patriarch of Alexandria and retained his political and ecclesiastical offices.

In July 1974 a segment of the Cypriot National Guard backed by the colonels' regime in Greece launched a coup. Makarios escaped assassination and fled the island. After the defeat of the attempt at *enosis* and occupation of more than a third of the island by the Turks, Makarios returned in December. He worked out an agreement with the leader of the Cypriot Turks, Rauf Denktash, for a bizonal confederation in 1977. The death of Makarios on August 2, 1977, of a heart attack however, resulted in the still-birth of that hopeful compromise.

BIBLIOGRAPHY

Mayes, Stanley. *Makarios: a Biography.* New York: St. Martin's Press, 1981.

Vanezis, P. N. *Makarios: Pragmatism versus Idealism.* London: Abelard-Schuman, 1974.

Bernard Cook

SEE ALSO Cyprus; Ioannides, Demetrios

Malenkov, Georgy Maksimilianovich (1902–88)

Soviet leader and Nikita Khrushchev's chief opponent in the struggle for power after Joseph Stalin's death in 1953. Georgy Malenkov, who rose through the ranks of the Communist Party to become Stalin's heir apparent, lost to Khrushchev in the factional fight for Stalin's throne. Malenkov's policies outlasted his political career, however, as Khrushchev adopted Malenkov's increased attention to consumer needs at the expense of military spending.

Malenkov was born in Orenburg in 1902. He joined the Communist Party in 1920 and rose rapidly as a competent bureaucrat and administrator, showing a talent for picking rising stars with whom to associate himself. His personnel appointments involved him closely in Stalin's purges of former or potential enemies in the late 1930s. Malenkov developed a close association with the calculating Lavrenty Beria, who became the new head of the Ministry of Internal Affairs, the secret police, in 1938.

Malenkov's alliance with Beria served him well. In 1939 he was promoted to the party's Central Committee, and along with Beria purged the USSR's newly occupied western territories seized from Poland, as well as the Baltic states, of all opponents to Soviet rule there. In 1941 he became a candidate member and in 1946 a full member of the party's Politburo. He was also on the State Committee for Defense, which ran the Soviet Union's war effort during World War II.

After the war Malenkov took charge of reparations from the Soviet occupation zone in Germany, confiscating German machinery, raw materials, and whole factories to ship them east. In 1946 he became deputy chair of the Council of Ministers and seemed the leading candidate to succeed Stalin. Malenkov's only rival as Stalin's heir apparent was Leningrad party boss Andrè Zhdanov. Zhdanov died mysteriously in 1948, and Malenkov engineered a massive, bloody purge of Zhdanov's organization in Leningrad. Malenkov's path to power seemed clear, as he and Beria had no serious rivals.

But Stalin preferred having his subordinates plotting against one another to prevent their plotting against him, so he promoted Ukrainian party boss Nikita Khrushchev to the Politburo, where he was placed in charge of agriculture. When Stalin died in March 1953 Beria nominated Malenkov to be both first secretary of the Communist Party and premier, that is, chairman of the Council of Ministers. This move to put the reins of power over party and state in Malenkov's hands proved too much for the rest of Stalin's inner circle, and Malenkov surrendered the job of first secretary to Khrushchev.

With the death of Stalin, Beria and Malenkov began a policy to reduce international tensions. At Stalin's funeral Malenkov announced a peace initiative toward the United States. The Soviet Union moved to help end the Korean War that had erupted in 1950 when Communist North Korea with Soviet encouragement invaded South Korea and restored diplomatic relations with Israel, Greece, and Yugoslavia.

With Stalin gone the collective Soviet leadership saw Beria as the most dangerous threat to their power and safety. Khrushchev convinced Malenkov to abandon his old ally by arguing that their own survival depended on eliminating Beria. Beria contributed to his own fall by promoting moderate, accommodationist policies for East Germany and imposing them on the East German Communist Party. The expectations raised by these partial reforms boiled over into an active revolt in Germany in 1953 crushed by the Soviet military.

This provided the final impetus for the plot against Beria. He was arrested on June 26, 1953, with the help of the Soviet army, which replaced Beria's secret police guards at the Kremlin with army Security personnel, and quickly executed. With Beria gone, the political struggle between Malenkov and Khrushchev for supreme power in the Soviet Union began in earnest. Neither was willing to share power, and each strove to build a coalition sufficiently powerful to defeat the other.

Malenkov tried to win support through a populist domestic policy aimed at boosting production of consumer goods and lowering agricultural taxes, while cutting government expenditures on heavy industry and defense. Though popular with the general public, this alienated key military and industrial constituencies. Khrushchev, on the other hand, argued for the primacy of agricultural development and built ties to the military and to heavy industry. This, combined with Khrushchev's control over the party machinery and support from the Stalinist old guard, assured his victory.

A Central Committee meeting in January 1955 harshly criticized Malenkov's performance in office. Malenkov was forced to confess his errors to a meeting of the Supreme Soviet (parliament) on February 8, 1955, and to resign as premier. He was allowed to remain on the Politburo (renamed the Presidium), though many of his supporters were dismissed from their posts.

Malenkov, a member of the politburo still plotted to eliminate Khrushchev with the cooperation of two others who had been close to Stalin: Lazar Kaganovich, the minister of foreign affairs and Vyacheslav Molotov, supervisor of heavy industry. When Malenkov and his allies made their move on July 18, 1957, they actually achieved a majority in the Presidium against Khrushchev. Khrushchev quickly turned to his allies in the military and the secret police to force a meeting of the party's Central Committee. This group, much larger than the narrow Presidium, was dominated by Khrushchev's supporters. This Central Committee mandate, combined with the support of the military, allowed Khrushchev to turn the tables on what he called the "antiparty group." He expelled Malenkov, Kaganovich, and Molotov from their high-ranking offices.

In Stalin's time, Malenkov would certainly have been shot. Khrushchev eschewed blood purges, however, and merely sent Malenkov into internal exile to manage a power plant in Kazakhstan. Malenkov died in obscurity in 1988.

Malenkov remains an ambiguous figure. His emphasis on consumer goods at the expense of military spending lost him the fight for power against Khrushchev, but Khrushchev adopted exactly those policies, cutting Soviet conventional forces while embarking on a massive program to build housing. Dismissed by many, including Khrushchev, as a mediocrity skilled only at paper shuffling, Malenkov managed to flourish in the internecine world of Stalin's inner circle. Perhaps most impressive, he launched an audacious if unsuccessful attempt to break out of Cold War patterns and reach a negotiated settlement with the West.

BIBLIOGRAPHY

Khrushchev, Nikita. *Khrushchev Remembers.* Boston: Little, Brown, 1970.

Knight, Amy. *Beria: Stalin's First Lieutenant.* Princeton, N.J.: Princeton University Press, 1993.

Malenkov, A. G. (Malenkov's son) *O moem ottse, Georgii Malenkove.* Moscow: MTTs RTekhnoekosS, 1992.

Tompson, William J. *Khrushchev: A Political Life.* London: Macmillan, 1995.

Zubok, Vladislav, and Constantine Pleshakov. *Inside the Kremlin's Cold War.* Cambridge, Mass.: Harvard University Press, 1996.

David Stone

SEE ALSO Beria, Lavrenty; Khrushchev, Nikita

Malle, Louis (1932–95)

French film director. Louis Malle made films both in his native France and in America (where he married actress Candace Bergen). He was born the same year as fellow filmmaker François Truffaut, but was not a major player in the French *Nouvelle Vague* (New Wave), instead tending to go his own way. Although perhaps not a household name in America, his body of work is varied and impressive.

Malle's first notice came as codirector of Jacque Cousteau's *The Silent World* (1956), but *The Lovers* (*Les Amants*) (1958) with Jeanne Moreau, for its time a scandalously erotic tale of an affair between a housewife and a younger man, made Malle internationally famous.

Zazie dans le métro (1960) was a whimsical study of a precocious eleven-year-old girl; it is Malle's film with the most New Wave–like stylistic inventiveness. *Murmur of the Heart* (*Le souffle au cœur*) (1971) is an unsensationalized tale of incest of a sickly fourteen-year-old boy and his mother. Malle followed this with *Lacombe, Lucien* (1974), a haunting story of a young, unskilled French laborer who becomes a German collaborator to gain status during the occupation of World War II.

Malle made *Pretty Baby* (1978) in New Orleans, basing it on a true tale of a photographer obsessed with the prostitutes of that city, especially a child prostitute (played by Brooke Shields). *Atlantic City* (1980), with Burt Lancaster and Susan Sarandon, is a poignant tale of the losers who inevitably exist on the fringes of America's gambling meccas. *My Dinner with André* (1982) is a filmed dinner conversation of two New York intellectuals ruminating on life and art. Audiences were fascinated, outraged, or bored.

With *Au Revoir les enfants* (1988) Malle returned to France and the German occupation. In this bittersweet remembrance, a Jewish boy is sheltered in a benign (for once) Catholic boys' boarding school and becomes friends with a French boy who is fascinated by his otherness. In the end the Jewish boy is found out and carted off by the Gestapo and the school closed.

His final film, *Vanya on 42nd Street* (1994), documents a theatrical production of Chekov's *Uncle Vanya:* the film begins with the actors making their way through the streets of New York to the theater.

In his 1992 *Malle on Malle,* the director summed up his director's journey: "The longer I live, the less I trust ideas, the more I trust emotions."

BIBLIOGRAPHY

French, Philip, ed. *Malle on Malle.* London: Faber and Faber, 1993.

William M. Hammel

Malraux, André (1901–76)

Polymath, antifascist, Gaullist minister, and major French cultural icon. Through his varied writings and his political and intellectual activism André Malraux ensured that for many French people his life became synonymous with France in the twentieth century.

Malraux was fascinated by T. E. Lawrence and once declared that "the difference between Lawrence and me is that he was always sure he would fail whereas I have always believed in the success of my undertakings." Yet Malraux's early undertakings were far from successful. He and his wife, Clara Goldschmidt, were arrested in 1923 in French Indochina for attempting to steal archaeological artifacts. Later, Malraux was in further trouble for printing an anti-French newspaper, *L'Indochine enchaînée,* in the colony. Malraux traveled in China and claimed to have been active in revolutionary politics there. He returned to France and in 1928 his novel *Les Conquérants* was published to much critical acclaim. He remained active, in an individualistic fashion, in left-wing politics, and continued writing. His most famous novel, *La Condition humaine,* was published in 1933, winning the prestigious Prix Goncourt.

With the outbreak of the Spanish Civil War in 1936, Malraux quickly threw himself into organizing aid for the Republican government, forming the famous España squadron. He flew many missions and was twice wounded. He also traveled in the United States on behalf of the Spanish Republic. With the opening of the Second World War in Europe in 1939, Malraux joined a tank regiment and saw action in the battle for France in 1940. During the early years of the German occupation Malraux worked on his writings on art. By 1943, despite his earlier association with communism, he had joined the Gaullist resistance. Following the Liberation he led the Alsace-Lorraine Brigade and was made minister of information in General Charles de Gaulle's first, short-lived government.

In the immediate postwar period Malraux continued to publish on art while remaining active in Gaullist politics. He acted as de Gaulle's propaganda agent in the Rassemblement du Peuple Francais, RPF (Rally of the French People). Many saw the RPF as a quasi-fascist organization, and Malraux's involvement illustrates the complexity of his character, as well as his friendship with de Gaulle. The RPF eventually faded, but Malraux's career as an art critic continued.

The Algerian War brought de Gaulle back to power in 1958 and saw the foundation of the Fifth Republic. Malraux was rewarded with the post of minister of cultural affairs, but the divisions in France caused by the Algerian War cast something of a shadow over Malraux's political reputation. However, he strenuously opposed extremist *pieds noirs,* the French settlers in Algeria who adamantly opposed granting independence to the Algerians, and was the target of an assassination attempt in 1962 by a terrorist organization formed within the French army that struggled against the relinquishing of French power in Algeria.

He traveled widely as minister of cultural affairs and was active in promoting art and cultural activity in France and abroad. After the upheavals in France called the Events of May in 1968, and the referendum of 1969, de Gaulle resigned, followed by Malraux. He continued his activist life until his death in 1976. In 1996 his ashes were placed in the Panthéon memorial in Paris, and his cultural canonization was complete.

BIBLIOGRAPHY

Cate, Curtis. *André Malraux: A Biography.* London: Hutchinson, 1995.

Madsen, Axel. *Malraux: A Biography.* London: William Allen, 1977.

Malraux, André. *Antimemoirs.* London: Hamish Hamilton, 1968.

Suares, Guy. *André Malraux: Past, Present, Future: Conversations with Guy Suares.* London: Thames and Hudson, 1974.

Stephen M. Cullen

Malta

Group of five islands in the central Mediterranean Sea, 58 miles (93 km) south of Sicily, 179 miles (288 km) east of Tunisia, and 180 miles (290 km) north of Libya. The Republic of Malta receives its name from the island of Malta, the largest of three inhabited islands. The island of Malta is approximately 17 miles long and 9 miles wide. It has an area of 95 square miles (246 sq km), and 85 miles of shoreline. The island's two deepwater ports were the root of its strategic significance. The islands of Gozo and Comino are also inhabited. Gozo has an area of 26

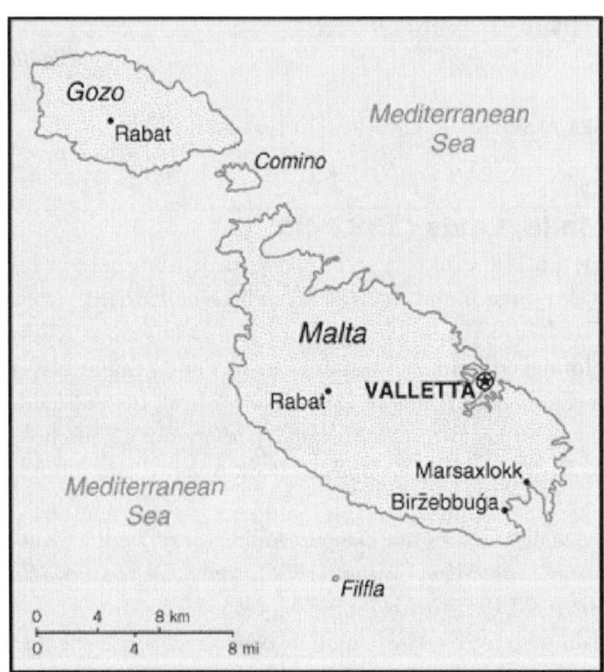

The island nation of Malta, in the Mediterranean. *Illustration courtesy of Bernard Cook.*

square miles (67 sq km) and 27 miles of shoreline. It has roads and villages. Comino is completely rural and has no automobiles. The islands of Comminotto (Kemmunett in Maltese) and Filfla are uninhabited. There is also a small uninhabited islet, St. Paul's. The five islands have a combined area of 122 square miles (316 sq km) and a population of 372,000 in 1996. The capital is Valletta, which has a population of 9,129, but the largest city is Birkirkara, with 21,903 inhabitants.

Malta is among the world's most densely populated countries. In 1976 it had 2,590 persons per square mile (1,000 per sq km). The population, which is now approaching 400,000, has stabilized since the 1950s as a result of a decrease in the birthrate and the government's subsidization of emigration. Though there is full religious freedom, Roman Catholicism is the state religion and 91 percent of the population is Catholic. Maltese and English are the official languages, and many Maltese speak Italian. As a language Maltese is basically of Semitic origin but with a rich superstructure of Romance, especially Siculo-Norman, as well as elements of Spanish, French, and most recently English. It is written in the Roman script, and has had a standard orthography since the 1930s. Maltese literature started to thrive in the nineteenth century and developed further in the twentieth, but there are scattered traces of poetry dating as far back as the fifteenth century. Theories about the origins of the language have included Phoenician, Sicilian Arabic in Norman times, and North African, the closest neighboring country after Italy being Tunisia. The Semitic element in Maltese contains some classical Arabic vocabulary that has ceased to exist in practically all colloquial Arabic dialects today.

The lack of permanent streams and lakes and the islands' very permeable surfaces make the water supply a major concern. A sea-level aquifer has been the traditional source of water, but today desalination plants provide about 70 percent of the water supply. The soil is thin and scarce. By law soil must be moved from construction sites and preserved for agriculture. Organic waste is also used to create new soil. Terrace farming covers much of the countryside, but Malta is dependent on imported food. In 1994 only 2.3 percent of Maltese workers were employed in the agricultural sector. This sector, which also includes fishing, accounted for only 2.8 percent of the gross domestic product (GDP). Manufacturing contributed 23.6 percent of GDP and employed 22.1 percent of Maltese workers. Tourism, which employed 6.4 percent of Maltese workers, was a major source of foreign exchange.

The British first went to Malta in 1801 at the request of the Maltese, with the permission of the Kingdom of Naples, to help them in their uprising against French rule. Naples was the naval power in that area of the Mediterranean and had joined with Britain in the Second Coalition against revolutionary France. The British stayed on and by the Treaty of Paris (1814), Malta was made a crown colony. After abolishing press censorship and recognizing the elective principle in the first half of the nineteenth century, a Maltese nationalist movement led by Fortunato Mizzi strove successfully for representative government, by means of which Maltese elected members in the Council of Government consultative assembly whose members were both elected and appointed by the governor general. In 1887, the nationalists gained a majority of the seats and some executive say. Following clashes over language and taxation policy, representative government was revoked by the British in 1903 and representative government was replaced by the rule of the British governor general. In 1919 social and political unrest resulted in the killing of demonstrators by British troops, but in 1921 Britain gave Malta internal self-government. The first two administrations were Nationalist, who sought independence for Malta and the assertion of its language and culture, the third in 1927–1930 was a Constitutional-Labour "compact," with roots in the dockyard workers union and pro-British segments of the population, that was led by Lord Strickland, a former colonial governor who was partly of Maltese descent. The constitution was suspended by Britain in 1930 during the general election campaign because of strictures imposed on Strickland's Constitutional-Labour coalition by the Catholic episcopacy, with whom relations had become strained. When self-government resumed in 1932, the Nationalists led by Dr. (later Sir) Ugo Mifsud and Dr. Enrico "Nerik" Mizzi swept back to power in a landslide victory, and demanded dominion status for Malta autonomous, self-governing status within the British Empire. Instead, Britain again suppressed the constitution in 1933 in what the Nationalists called a "coup d'état," and the new constitution of 1936 practically reverted to that of 1849. Some confusion resulted from the fact that the Nationalists, especially the Mizzi faction, had always opposed Anglicization in upholding Italian, the language of public life in Malta for centuries. But the advent of fascism in Italy adversely affected the "*italianita*" policy of resistance to assimilation and cultural survival. In 1934 English and Maltese were made the official languages, demoting Italian from its platform in public life, including education. In 1947 under a restored and expanded self-government constitution, with universal suffrage, the Labour Party led by Dr. (later Sir) Paul Boffa won a decisive victory, but two years later Boffa's young and dynamic minister of public works, Dominic Mintoff, split the party when he assailed his leader as being too soft on the British in matters relating to financial aid and full support for and utilization of the dockyard. This brought the Nationalists back to office in 1950, led now by Nerik Mizzi, who had returned from his exile in Uganda after the war. Upon his death he was succeeded by Giorgio "Gorg" Borg Olivier (1911–80), who formed coalitions with Boffa's new Workers Party, but in 1955 the Mintoff-led Maltese Labour Party (MLP) was successful at the polls. Mintoff became prime minister in 1956. In a February referendum 75 percent of those who voted expressed their support for integration with the United Kingdom, a position advocated by the MLP. However, the large majority can be credited to the fact that the Nationalist Party (PN) boycotted the referendum. When the British balked at guaranteeing dockyard employment, Mintoff rejected integration and resigned. As a result the independence movement gained additional support.

By 1962 both parties favored independence. The PN, backed by the Catholic Church, was victorious in the February 1962 elections. Borg Olivier became prime minister and negotiated independence from the British. Malta became an independent member of the British Commonwealth on September 21, 1964. The pro-Western PN sought to diversify Malta's economy and were returned to office in the 1966 elections. In 1964 Malta joined the United Nations, the Council of Europe, and many other international bodies.

After the MLP won the 1971 parliamentary election, Mintoff became prime minister. He pursued a policy of nonalignment, and Malta received technical assistance from Libya. In 1971 his government canceled the 1964 Mutual Defense and Assistance Agreement with the United Kingdom. A 1972 agreement increased British and NATO payments for the use of Maltese military facilities. In March 1979 this ended and the last British forces left the country. Because Malta's economy had become dependent on the British naval docks, this was a serious economic blow.

Over a span of years Malta successfully restructured and diversified its economy. Malta promoted itself as an international financial center, manufacturing for export was encouraged, and tourism was further developed. Internationally Malta looked elsewhere for support. In 1980 Italy guaranteed Malta's neutrality. The USSR followed suit in 1981. Though Malta and Libya temporarily quarreled over their maritime boundary and the potential oil fields under the Mediterranean, the two countries signed a five-year treaty of cooperation in 1984. Libya offered to provide military training for Maltese forces, which numbered fewer than two thousand. More important, it provided Malta with petroleum at preferential rates.

On December 13, 1974, Malta declared itself a republic, but with many cleavages. The left-wing MLP and the conservative PN bitterly opposed each other. The labor unions centered on the docks and drydocks of Valletta were at loggerheads with Malta's middle class. The secularists of the MLP were hostile to the Roman Catholic Church. Traditionally hostile clans were spread across the islands. Towns were divided into rival clubs with different patron saints.

The last governor-general, Sir Anthony Mamo (1909–), became the first president. The MLP was narrowly returned to office in September 1976. In December 1976 Mamo was succeeded by Anton Buttigieg (1912–83), and in February 1982 Buttigieg was succeeded by Malta's first female head of state, Agatha Barbara (1923–), who had previously served as minister of labor. Censu Tabone, an ophthalmologist and former Nationalist minister of labor and foreign affairs, was president from 1989 to 1994, and Ugo Mifsud Bonnici, a lawyer and also a former Nationalist minister, of education and of the interior was president from 1994 to 1999.

Political tension arose during the Mintoff period (1971–84) as a result of cooperation between the MLP and Malta's biggest labor union and because of government regulation of industry and legislation restricting the competence of the courts over the government. The MLP, nevertheless, retained power as a result of the December 1981, election but with a majority of only three seats. The PN, which had actually received a majority with 50.9 percent of the vote, refused to recognize the results, boycotted the legislature, and organized civil disobedience. When PN supporters, protesting the alleged bias of the radio and television, which had been nationalized under Mintoff, boycotted advertising, the legislature made it illegal for citizens to broadcast into Malta from outside the country and temporarily outlawed contact between foreign diplomats and members of the opposition. In February Carmelo Mifsud Bonnici of the MLP threatened to cancel upcoming elections if foreign interests intervened in favor of the opposition.

Malta had entered into an associate agreement with the European Community (EC) in 1970 that gave Malta favorable trade conditions and subsidies from the EC. In contrast to the nonalignment of the MLP, the PN was committed to close relations with the West. In March 1983 the PN ended its boycott of the legislature but walked out almost at once when the government proposed to weaken its links with the EC. President Barbara intervened and Mintoff made concessions. But the truce ended in June, when the government accused the PN of provocations. That month the MLP majority in the legislature also voted to confiscate 75 percent of the property of the Catholic Church to finance free education. At the same time it outlawed tuition-based church schools. In November the government in a provocative move launched a raid on PN headquarters reputedly in search of arms.

In September 1983 the courts voided the antichurch legislation as unconstitutional. But in April 1984 the legislature outlawed the collecting of tuition by any school. The Catholic Archbishop of Malta, Joseph Mercieca, responded by closing all Catholic schools, which educated a third of Malta's children. He kept them closed until the government compromised in November.

Mintoff retired at the end of December and was succeeded as prime minister by Mifsud Bonnici. In April 1985 an agreement between the government and the church guaranteed the independence of the church's schools and made provisions for the introduction over a period of three years of free education in church-run secondary schools. In July 1986 the government agreed to subsidize half the costs of the church schools for two years, but there were still disputes over the degree of government supervision. Bonnici's government also renegotiated agreements with Italy and the EC that had been allowed to lapse under Mintoff.

In the May 1987 election the PN won 50.9 percent of the vote to the MLP's 48.9 percent. A constitutional amendment adopted in January 1987 provided that any party winning over 50 percent of the vote should have a majority in the unicameral legislature or House of Representatives. Therefore the PN was awarded four additional seats. With a majority of one seat the PN ended the MLP's sixteen-year hold on power. Edward Fenech-Adami, head of the PN, became prime minister.

In the February 1992 election the PN, known for its pro-EC stance, increased its majority in the House. Fenech-Adami had announced that his government, though it would continue its nonaligned status and maintain its relationship with Libya, would strengthen its ties to the West and seek full membership in the EC. The EC, which became the EU in 1993, responded favorably and preliminary negotiations on Malta's EU membership began. In April 1995 Malta entered NATO's Partnership for Peace, a less formal relationship offered to countries that are not full members of NATO.

These steps toward integration with Europe, however, were dealt a blow by the October 1996 election. Called in advance by Fenech-Adami to broaden his mandate, the election was won by the MLP with 50.7 percent of the vote. The MLP's victory was partly due to its promise to abolish the value-added tax introduced by the Fenech-Adami government as a prerequisite to EU membership. The MLP, led by Alfred Sant, formed a new government. It called for a "free trade zone" with the EU rather than association or membership and terminated Malta's participation in the Partnership for Peace. In 1998, however, Fenech-Adami was back in power. Malta's application for full EU membership was immediately received and taken up by Brussels. Entry negotiations were approved in December 1999.

BIBLIOGRAPHY

Austin, Dennis. *Malta and the End of Empire.* London: Cass, 1971.

Frendo, Henry, ed. *Maltese Political Development 1798–1964: A Documentary History.* Valletta: Ministry of Education and Human Resources, 1993.

———. *Party Politics in a Fortress Colony: The Maltese Experience,* 2d ed. Valletta: Midsea, 1991.

Frendo, Henry, and Oliver Friggieri, eds. *Malta: Culture and Identity.* Valletta: Ministry for Justice and the Arts, 1994.

Thompson, Wayne C. *Western Europe 1996.* Harpers Ferry, W.Va.: Stryker-Post, 1996.

Henry Frendo
Bernard Cook

SEE ALSO Mintoff, Dom

Maniu, Iuliu (1873–1953)

Leading Romanian politician of the interwar period and prominent figure in the National Peasant Party, arrested and executed by Romanian Communists in 1953. Born in Simleul Silvaniei in the Transylvanian region of Austria-Hungary in 1873, Iuliu Maniu studied law in Vienna and became a lawyer in the Transylvanian city of Blaj and a professor at the Blaj Theological Institute. From 1906 to 1910 he served as a deputy in the Hungarian parliament and became a major spokesperson for the cultural and political rights of ethnic Romanians in Transylvania. During the First World War he served as an officer in the Austro-Hungarian army on the Russian and Italian fronts.

With the disintegration of Austria-Hungary after the war, Maniu became active in the national movement among Transylvania's Romanians. He was a major figure in the Act of Union, which proclaimed Transylvania's union with the Kingdom of Romania on December 1, 1918, and from 1918 to 1920 served as chairman of the National Council of Transylvania, a provisional government that administered Transylvania until its position within Romania was secured by the Treaty of Trianon in 1920.

Maniu was a leading figure in the National Party in Transylvania. Between 1923 and 1926 the party merged with several other political groups and expanded its base from the Transylvanian region to the rest of the enlarged Romanian state, becoming in 1926 the National Peasant Party of Romania (NPP). Maniu was president of the party throughout the interwar years, except for the period from 1933 to 1937.

As NPP leader Maniu served as prime minister in two governments (1928–31, 1932–33). During his first period in office he was instrumental in the return of Prince Carol to Romania to reclaim the throne as Carol II, a move that ultimately proved disastrous for Romania's internal stability and foreign policy. The inconstant and indecisive Carol ruled throughout the turbulent decade of the 1930s, abdicating in favor of his teenage son, Michael, in September 1940. As Europe plunged toward war, Maniu was a strong proponent of closer relations with the Allies and, although Romania had become a supporter of Nazi Germany by autumn 1940, continued to hold secret discussions with Allied representatives. He supported King Michael's coup against wartime authoritarian leader Marshal Ion Antonescu in August 1944.

After the war Maniu once again became an important political figure. His public popularity and his ties with the British and the Americans were major obstacles to the early Soviet domination of Romania. In 1947 Maniu was arrested by the Communist-dominated government, tried on charges of spying for the British and Americans, and sentenced to life imprisonment. He was imprisoned along with other NPP luminaries in the notorious Sighetul Marmatiei prison, where he died from torture and neglect in 1953. After the anti-Communist revolution of December 1989, Maniu's NPP, renamed the National Christian Democratic Peasant Party, was reestablished in 1990 and became one of the most important parties in post-Communist Romania.

BIBLIOGRAPHY

Hitchins, Keith. *Romania, 1866–1947.* Oxford: Clarendon Press, 1994.

Maniu, Iuliu. *Opinii si confruntari politice, 1940–1944.* Bucharest: Editura Dacia, 1994.

Charles King

Mannerheim, C. G. E. (1867–1951)

Finland's regent (1918–19), president (1944–46), and commander in chief (1917–18, 1939–44). Carl Gustaf Emil Mannerheim was born on June 4, 1867. He served in the Russian army from 1887 to 1917 and eventually achieved the rank of lieutenant general.

Following the declaration of Finland's independence on July 20, 1917, and its recognition by the new Bolshevik government in Russia on January 2, 1918, Mannerheim became the commander in chief of the Finnish anti-Bolshevik White Army, and led it to the victory over the Communists in May 1918. In December he was elected Finland's regent. Many expected Mannerheim to become the first president of the country. However, K. J. Ståhlberg, a former Young Finn, or Finnish nationalist, politician and professor of administrative law, won the election in 1919. Consequently, Mannerheim left politics for two decades. From 1931 to 1939 General Mannerheim was chairman of the National Defense Council. He was appointed war marshal in 1933 (and Finland's marshal on June 4, 1942). In the Winter War (1939–40), launched by the USSR to acquire Karelian territory Mannerheim became commander in chief of the Finnish armed forces.

In June 1944, to secure badly needed military assistance from the Germans, President Risto Ryti signed the Ribbentrop Agreement with Nazi Germany, without asking the consent of the Eduskunta (parliament). As soon as Finland halted the Soviet offensive in August 1944, Ryti resigned. The Eduskunta elected Mannerheim president to guarantee the conclusion of an armistice with the Soviet Union on September 1944 and to combine the posts of president and commander in chief for an anticipated war to expel German forces from Lapland in northern Finland (September 1944 to April 1945) and to hopefully somewhat redeem their standing with the USSR.

Mannerheim resigned in 1946 because of illness. Political considerations were also involved. The armistice of 1944 obligated Finland to bring to trial the wartime leaders whom the Soviet Union declared responsible for Finland's involvement in the 1941 Continuation War. Altogether fourteen politicians, were found to have been in violation of Finnish law brought to trial. Ex-president Ryti was sentenced to ten years in prison. The Soviet Union never requested a trial for Mannerheim, but Mannerheim had to relinquish the president's post to J. K. Paasikivi. Mannerheim left Finland for Switzerland after his resignation and never returned.

Mannerheim was, above all his other merits, a professional soldier who became one of the most honored Finnish leaders. Comparable to the prominent military leaders of ancient Greece and Rome, Mannerheim was available when his country needed a strong leader for war. Immediately after he fulfilled his military tasks, Mannerheim, in accord with both Roman and Nordic traditions, bowed out to let the political system elect its leaders for peace. He died in Switzerland on January 28, 1951.

BIBLIOGRAPHY

Lappalainen, Matti. *C. G. E. Mannerheim, the Marshal of Finland.* Helsinki: Recallmed, 1989.

Mannerheim, C. G. E. *The Memoirs of Marshal Mannerheim.* London: Cassell, 1953.

Screen, J. E. O. *Mannerheim.* London: Hurst, 1970.

Warner, Oliver. *Marshal Mannerheim and the Finns.* London: Widenfeld and Nicolson, 1967.

Vilho Harle

Marcel, Gabriel (1889–1973)

French philosopher, Sorbonne professor, dramatist, critic, and musician, was born in Paris in 1889, son of the French ambassador to Sweden who also held administrative posts in the Bibliothèque Nationale and the Musées Nationaux. Gabriel Marcel's broad interests led to prolific productivity in philosophy, drama, and music. Although he preferred to be called a Neo-Socratic because of the ongoing character of his reflections, his contribution to Christian existentialism must be emphasized.

In a special way today, when the recent emphasis on the end of metaphysics puts the very possibility of philosophy into question, Marcel's philosophical reflections can shed light on the philosophical enterprise for the future. His unique brand of existential philosophy has explicitly thematized the mystery of being, turning to lived existence in the break-away from the dominance of the modern Cartesian world view, and leading to the focus and emphasis on the depth of mystery at the heart of human existence, with an essentially religious dimension. The mystery of being in Marcel's philosophy can be related to all his celebrated themes: the contrast between mystery and problem, presence, recollection and second reflection, creative fidelity, participation, charity, hope, and faith.

For Marcel, personal existence as mystery, irreducible to a problem, is not a problem before the individual but one that involves the individual. He cannot abstract himself from the mystery of his own being. He is precisely what (who) is being reflected upon. On this level there is an ontological exigency at the heart of human existence that should prevent the individual from closing himself off into the problematic and the objective. And it is on this level that the "thou" is encountered in presence. If second reflection were to allow itself to begin other than with this realization, i.e., the presence of the other, it would not be possible to get the "other" precisely as person back into reflection. This presence is closely linked to availability or readiness (*disponibilité*) for the other. The unavailable person is not really there for the other, but maintains a certain closedness and distraction toward something else.

With this move in second reflection to existence as mystery, Marcel has turned toward the fullness of existence that eludes first reflection and that is irreducible to it. This concretely situated being, involved and immersed in the concrete situation, cannot be adequately approached in a philosophical reflection that is detached and epistemologically oriented. Thus, in this critique of the primacy of objectivity, Marcel has overcome the primacy of epistemology and, at once, found its source. But what is more important for him is the affirmation that existence is not only given, but it is also giving; that is, existence is the very condition of any thinking whatsoever. Existence as giving encompasses creativity. This giving as creative is the central motif of Marcel's whole philosophy, in the sense that as soon as there is creation, we are in the realm of being. But the converse is equally true in that there is no sense in using the word "being" except where creation, in some form or other, is in view. Marcel says that this insight grew as he concentrated more on the relations among his philosophical thought, his dramatic work, and his musical compositions.

This second reflection is an immediate but blind intuition, which is not mediated by thought or conceptual knowledge, thus reminding us of Kant's Critique of Judgment. However, this intuition can be made the focus of conceptual analysis, which is where reflection begins, but not without a loss of immediacy. This is the place of imaginative presentation at work in positive constructions operating in drama and in narrative. This place in secondary reflection of interpretation and productive imagination at the heart of Marcel's philosophy of mystery makes his thought quite relevant to philosophy for the twenty-first century, in which the interpretation of the role of the imagination, paralleling its various developments during the several decades after the publication of Kant's Critique of Judgment, is so central.

BIBLIOGRAPHY

Cain, Seymour. *Gabriel Marcel's Theory of Religious Experience.* New York: Peter Lang, 1995.

Gallagher, Kenneth. *The Philosophy of Gabriel Marcel.* New York: Fordham University Press, 1975.

Hanley, Katherine R. *Gabriel Marcel's Perspectives on the Broken World: The Broken World followed by Concrete Approaches to Investigating the Ontological Mystery.* Tr. by Katherine R. Hanley. Milwaukee: Marquette University Press, 1998.

Marcel, Gabriel. *Creative Fidelity.* New York: Crossroad, 1982.

———. *The Mystery of Being.* Lanham, Md.: University Press of America, 1984.

Patrick L. Bourgeois

Marchais, Georges (1920–97)

General secretary of the French Communist Party (PCF). In the era of Eurocommunism and the last Soviet leader, Mikhail Gorbachev, Georges Marchais presided over his party's political eclipse. He crafted a shaky alliance with the resurgent Socialist Party but failed to dismantle the PCF's authoritarian internal structure.

From a Norman mining family, Marchais left school at fourteen. A skilled factory aircraft mechanic, he was exempt from military service in 1939. Continuing to work after France's defeat by Nazi Germany in May 1940, he moved to a Messerschmidt plant in Germany in 1943. Although he maintained that this transfer was compulsory, critics later proved that it had been voluntary and dismissed his claim that he escaped from Germany to return to France.

Marchais joined the PCF in 1947 after working as a postwar union organizer. Despite his lack of education and a Resistance record, he became the protégé of party leader Maurice Thorez. A seat on the party's Central Committee in 1956 and an appointment as the influential head of party organization in 1961 followed. When Thorez's successor, Waldeck Rochet, fell ill after 1969, Marchais shared his responsibilities and succeeded him as general secretary in 1972.

Although PCF leaders had engaged in mild criticism of internal Soviet policies, the trials of accussed dissidents, in the late 1940s and the Stalin cult, and initially expressed concern over the 1968 invasion of Czechoslovakia by Soviet-led Warsaw Pact forces, Marchais was known as a harsh critic of the student rebellions in France known as the Events of May 1968 and a pro-Soviet hard-liner. Marchais denounced the radical student leader, Daniel Cohn-Bendit, as a "German anarchist." Nonetheless, Marchais's first major initiative as party leader was to establish an electoral "Common Program" with the Socialist Party (PS) under its first secretary, François Mitterrand. Though dismissing the PS as "fundamentally reformist," Marchais publicly supported Mitterrand's strong 1974 presidential bid. In his speech to the Communist Party's twenty-second congress in 1976, Marchais embraced pluralism and "socialism in French colors" and renounced the goal of a "dictatorship of the proletariat." This "Eurocommunist" line brought little change in the PCF's share of the vote, which remained around 20 percent.

In 1977 the PCF renounced the Common Program, which contributed to the Left's poor electoral showing the next year. The party defended the Soviet invasion of Afghanistan in 1979 and the imposition of martial law in Poland in 1981. Mitterrand's presidential victory in 1981 came without PCF support, and Marchais's first-round candidacy secured only 15 percent of the vote. Four minor cabinet seats in Pierre Mauroy Socialist led government from 1981 to 1984 failed to restore the party's fortunes, with its vote falling to between 7 and 10 percent in the 1986 and 1988 elections, respectively, while the xenopholine National Front won over its voters in working-class neighborhoods. Marchais hung onto power, purging party dissidents and criticizing Mikhail Gorbachev's reforms, but by 1985 only 10 percent of the French polled wanted him "to play an important role in the future," down from 31 percent in 1974. He stepped down as general secretary in 1993 and left his seat on the Central Committee in May 1996, eighteen months before his death.

BIBLIOGRAPHY

Marchais, Georges. *Le Défi démocratique.* Paris: Grasset, 1973.

Robrieux, Philippe. *Histoire intérieure du Parti communiste,* 5 Vols. Paris: Fayard, 1981–85.

Ross, George. *The View from Inside: A French Communist Cell in Crisis.* Berkeley: University of California Press, 1984.

David Longfellow

SEE ALSO Duclos, Jacques; Eurocommunism

Marchuk, Ievhen Kyrylovych (1941–)

Head of Soviet Ukraine's Security Committee during the coup of August 1991; prime minister of Ukraine (1995–96). Ievhen Kyrylovych Marchuk was born on January 28, 1941, in Dolynivka, Ukraine. Marchuk graduated from the Kirovohrad Pedagogical Institute in 1963 with a degree in the Ukrainian and German languages, and he subsequently received a graduate degree in law. Fluent in English and several other European languages, he joined the Kirovohrad branch of KGB the (secret police) in 1963 and moved up in the ranks, becoming by 1990 deputy head of Ukraine's KGB. In March 1991 Marchuk was appointed head of the Ukrainian State Committee of Defense, National Security, and Emergency Situations. In this capacity he played a role in ensuring that violence did not erupt in Ukraine during the Moscow coup of August 1991, launched by conservative Communists in a desperate effort. He was promoted in military rank to general in the newly created Army of Ukraine. In 1994 Marchuk was elected by parliament to head the Security Service of Ukraine (SBU). In 1994 he was appointed presidential representative in Crimea, head of the president's Anti-corruption Committee, and head of the Coordinating Council on Consolidating Borders. In March 1995 Marchuk was named acting prime minister, by President Leonid Kuchma, then prime minister in June 1995. Also in 1995 he won a parliamentary seat for Myrhorod district in a by-election. After being replaced as prime minister by Paolo Lazarenko in October 1996 Marchuk became leader of the Social Democratic parliamentary caucus and an executive member of the Social Democratic Party. He was reelected in the March 1998 parliamentary elections. He served on parliamentary committees for defense and state security, and was chairman of the Committee on Social Issues and Labor. In 1999 Marchuk announced his candidacy for president.

BIBLIOGRAPHY

Koscharsky, Halyna, ed. *Ukraine Today: Perspectives for the Future.* Commack, N.Y.: Nova Science Publishers, 1995.

Kuzio, Taras. *Ukraine under Kuchma: Political Reform, Economic Transformation and Security Policy in Independent Ukraine.* New York: St. Martin's Press, 1997.

Marchuk, Ievhen Kyrylovych. *Vystupy, interv'iu, statti.* Kiev: T-vo "Znannia" Ukrainy, 1997.

Marta Dyczok

SEE ALSO Kuchma, Leonid; Lazarenko, Pavlo

Maritain, Jacques (1882–1973)

French philosopher. Jacques Maritain's intellectual work was developed around the central influence in his life, Roman Catholicism. After nearly committing suicide because of their disillusionment with positivism, Maritain, who had been raised a Protestant, and his wife, Raissa, a Russian Jew, converted to Catholicism in 1906 and later founded the Cercles d'Études Thomistes, a group devoted to the study of Thomas Aquinas and the development of the spiritual life. Maritain produced books on art, spirituality, literature, aesthetics, moral philosophy, ecclesiology, human rights, capitalism, humanism, christology, liturgy, epistemology, education, metaphysics, and the philosophy of science. He was also politically active as the French ambassador to the Vatican and a drafter of the United Nations Declaration on Human Rights. Maritain also was periodically a professor at Princeton University and the Pontifical Institute of Medieval Studies in Toronto, founded by his fellow Thomist the more historically minded Étienne Gilson.

Maritain's masterwork is perhaps the *Degrees of Knowledge,* in which he treats the relationship of scientific knowledge to the philosophy of nature found in Thomas Aquinas. According to Maritain, a more complete knowledge is to be had in the philosophy of nature than in empirical science, but more perfect knowledge still is to be had through theology, which surpasses the knowledge that unaided reason is cable of through the addition of revelation. Also of great significance is Maritain's contribution to moral philosophy. According to Maritain the final end of the human person, as proposed by unaided reason as found in the works of Aristotle, is fundamentally flawed insofar as certain truths known through revelation, such as original sin, are not taken into account. Hence, the role of moral philosophy must always be subordinate to a moral theology based on revelation. Maritain's writings about these subjects in particular sparked intense debate about the relationship of faith to reason and of philosophy to theology. Maritain remained throughout the debate a staunch defender of the belief that Christians could engage in philosophy and that their faith was not a hindrance to this engagement but a help, although in philosophical debate explicit and direct reliance upon revelation is excluded through the nature of the discipline.

BIBLIOGRAPHY

Doering, Bernard E. *Jacques Maritain and the French Catholic Intellectuals.* Notre Dame, Ind.: University of Notre Dame Press, 1983.

Kernan, Julie. *Our Friend Jacques Maritain.* New York: Doubleday, 1975.

McInerny, Ralph. *Art and Prudence: Studies in the Thought of Jacques Maritain.* Notre Dame, Ind.: University of Notre Dame Press, 1988.

Christopher Kaczor

Marković, Ante (1924–)

Last prime minister before the demise of Yugoslavia. Ante Marković, a moderate Croatian politician, was born on November 25, 1924, at Konjić, and studied engineering at the University of Zagreb. He served as secretary of the

League of Communist Youth. For twenty years he was director of Rade Koncar, one of the premier Yugoslav industries. He was president of the Executive Council of Croatia from 1982 to 1986. He was elected president of Croatia in May 1986, and was the last president of the Executive Council of the Yugoslav Federation (1989–91). Pragmatic and known for his liberal ideas, he promoted a market economy and integration into Europe. Dedicated to the idea of Yugoslavia and the founder of a reform party in 1990, he was hostile to separatists of every stripe until the end of his term.

BIBLIOGRAPHY

Glenny, Misha. *The Fall of Yugoslavia: The Third Balkan War.* Second Edition. New York: Penguin, 1997.

Markovic, Ante. *Ekonomisti o krizi: razgovor ekonomista s mandatorom za SIV.* Belgrad: Konzorcijum ekonomskih instituta Jugoslavije, 1989.

Catherine Lutard
(Tr. by B. Cook)

SEE ALSO Tudjman, Franjo

Marković, Mihajlo (1923–)

Mihajlo Marković, a Serb, was one of the principal inspirations behind the Marxist philosophical review *Praxis,* published in Belgrade. In 1975 he was suspended from his professorial functions because of his political opinions and his criticism of Titoism. During the death throes of Yugoslavia, he was a founding member of Sloboban Milošević's Socialist Party of Serbia. Marković became the party's theoretician and vice president. Along with other hard-line nationalists, he was removed from his party post by Milošević in the wake of the November 1995 Dayton Accord. Marković, an ardent proponent of the war in Bosnia, had become critical of Milošević and was attacked by Milošević's wife, Mira Marković, who has a tremendous influence on Milošević, and is regarded by many as the actual power behind the "throne."

At the opening session of the Academy of Sciences of the Republika Srpska on October 11, 1996, Marković stated that the war in Bosnia "had [made] some sense" because it led to the creation of another Serb state, the Republika Srpska, rather than the absorption of the Bosnian Serbs into an integrated Bosnian state with a Bosnian Croat and Bosnian Moslem majority.

BIBLIOGRAPHY

Crocker, David A. *Praxis and Democratic Socialism: the Critical Social Theory of Markovic and Stojanovic.* Brighton, Sussex: Harvester Press, 1983.

Markovic, Mihailo. *The Contemporary Marx: Essays on Humanist Communism.* Nottingham: Spokesman Books, 1974.

———. *Democratic Socialism: Theory and Practice.* New York: St. Martins Press, 1982.

———. *Dialectical Theory of Meaning.* Boston: D. Reidel, 1984.

———. *On the Legal Institutions of Socialist Democracy.* Nottingham: Bertrand Russell Peace Foundation, 1976.

———. *Praxis: Yugoslav Essays in the Philosophy and Methodology of the Social Sciences.* Boston: D. Reidel Pub. Co., 1979.

———. *Yugoslavia: the Rise and Fall of Socialist Humanism: a History of the Praxis Group.* Nottingham: Bertrand Russell Peace Foundation, 1975.

Catherine Lutard
(Tr. by B. Cook)

Marković, Mirjana (1941–)

Wife of Slobodan Milošević and the primary influence on the Serbian leader. Milošević's biographer, Slavoljub Djukić, claimed that Marković "invented" Milošević. Djukić said that she was the most powerful woman in Serbian history, but that "she has been fatal for Serbia."

Marković's mother, who was unmarried at the time of her birth, was secretary of the Belgrade District of Communist Party but was captured and executed in 1942. Marković was raised by an aunt who had been secretary to Tito, the president of Socialist Yugoslavia from its inception. When she was fifteen her father, Draža Marković, a leading Communist, acknowledged her as his daughter. She met Milošević at secondary school in Pozarevac, about forty miles southeast of Belgrade. They married while attending the University of Belgrade. She studied sociology and subsequently taught Marxist theory at the university. Within the university branch of the League of Communists, she worked to rid the university of liberals and impose Marxist orthodoxy. She is credited with prompting and plotting Milošević's rise to power.

BIBLIOGRAPHY

Bennett, Christopher. *Yugoslavia's Bloody Collapse: Causes, Course, and Consequences.* New York: New York University Press, 1995.

Glenny, Misha, and Edin Hanzic, "Serbia's Lady Macdeath." *Australian,* March 30, 1999, 13.

Bernard Cook

Marothy, László (1942–)

Hungarian politician, minister of environmental protection and water management (1987–89).

László Marothy graduated as an agricultural engineer in 1965, but his whole career was in the ranks of the Hungarian Socialist Workers (Communist) Party. He became secretary of the Communist Youth League (KISZ) at his old university in 1965, then worked in various capacities in the Communist Party before being promoted to first secretary of the KISZ in 1973. He held that post until 1980. Marothy worked in the Budapest branch of the party from 1980 to 1984, then became first deputy prime minister. He had a stint as head of the National Planning Office (1986–87) before becoming the minister of environmental protection and water management. Marothy was also a member of the two top decision-making bodies of the Communist Party, the Central Committee and the Political Committee. After the defeat of the Communists in the parliamentary elections in spring 1990, he retired from political life.

Marothy belonged to the younger generation of Hungarian Communists who had some formal education but spent their entire career in various positions in the party. He was the embodiment of the loyal apparatchik, unable to provide meaningful response to the political, social, and economic changes in Hungary in the 1980s and who disappeared from political life after free elections in 1990.

BIBLIOGRAPHY

Kis, Janos. *Politics in Hungary: For a Democratic Alternative.* Boulder, Col.: Social Science Monographs, 1989.

Marothy, László. *A part ifjusagpolitikajanak nehany kerdese: elhangzott 1979. december 12-en.* Budapest: Kossuth, 1980.

Tamás Magyarics

Marshall Plan

The Marshall Plan, proclaimed in a speech by U.S. Secretary of State George Marshall at the Harvard University commencement on June 5, 1947, was the largest and most successful program of foreign assistance ever undertaken by the United States. After World War II, the United States offered $9 billion in economic aid to devastated Europe through the United Nations Relief and Rehabilitation Administration (UNRRA). But UNRRA aid was widely dispersed throughout Eastern and Western Europe according to country-by-country needs, and it was intended only for relief purposes. The harsh European winter of 1946–47 brought home to Washington the failure of such piecemeal aid programs to achieve sustained economic recovery. The withdrawal of the British military presence from the eastern Mediterranean, which led to the proclamation of the Truman Doctrine on March 12, 1947, also signaled the weakness of Western Europe. The failure of the United States at the Moscow Conference in late March and early April 1947 to reach agreement with the USSR on such questions as German reparations forced American leaders to search for a new policy. "The recovery of Europe has been far slower than had been expected," Marshall told a radio audience on April 28, 1947. "The patient is sinking while the doctors deliberate."

Marshall's speech contained the offer of American funding for a cooperative European recovery program. Although there was no plan per se, American officials largely shared the view that an aid program was urgently needed; that there should be a high degree of inter-European cooperation including Germany; and that the program should be developed soon, preferably by the European countries themselves. Marshall even invited the USSR and its satellites in Eastern Europe to participate, arguing that "our policy is directed not against any country or doctrine but against hunger, poverty, desperation, and chaos." But he added that "its purpose should be the revival of a working economy in the world so as to permit the emergence of political and social conditions in which free institutions can exist." Any government willing to assist in the task of recovery would find American cooperation; any seeking to "perpetuate human misery in order to profit therefrom politically" would be opposed. "The whole world's future hangs on a proper judgment, hangs on the realization by the American people of what can best be done, of what must be done."

British Foreign Secretary Ernest Bevin did not even wait for the full text of the Harvard speech before contacting his French counterpart, Georges Bidault, and calling a conference in Paris for all the European countries to consider the proposal. "I grabbed the offer with both hands," Bevin later told the National Press Club in Washington, D.C. Soon after the conference began on June 27, 1947, the USSR walked out of the meeting, refusing to accede to the U.S. demand for disclosure of economic information and claiming that the terms of the plan were incompatible with the Soviet system of central planning. The Soviets, referring disparagingly to the "Marshall Doctrine," also forced their Eastern European allies, Poland and Czechoslovakia, to refuse to participate. Later in the year the Soviet Union created its own trading organization, Comecon, for Eastern Europe. The irony is that if the USSR had chosen to participate, it could have made implementation of the program extremely difficult and decreased significantly the chances of congressional approval of the plan. Nevertheless, the division of Europe, though not unforeseen by the Americans or completely unwanted, was a fallback position, not the primary purpose of the plan.

Fifteen Western European countries—Austria, Belgium, Denmark, France, Greece, Iceland, Ireland, Italy, Luxembourg, the Netherlands, Norway, Portugal, Switzerland, Turkey, and the United Kingdom—remained at the Paris conference and agreed to form the Committee on European Economic Cooperation (CEEC), to prepare a report on European economic capacities and requirements, and to devise a four-year program for economic recovery. At American insistence they included the Western zones of Germany, a critical step in the reintegration of Germany into the international community. The CEEC's four-year program to promote economic recovery aimed at increasing agricultural production to prewar levels and industrial production to even higher levels. It also called for the elimination of the "dollar gap" through an increase in European exports, and for the establishment of an organization to foster economic cooperation. This became the Organization for European Economic Cooperation (OEEC). The final goals were the creation of internal financial stability and a curb on inflation. Though the Europeans estimated their need at some $22 billion in American capital, they heeded American advice to scale back their request to $17 billion before making their formal proposal to Congress in December 1947.

The debate in Congress was bitter, with supporters such as former isolationist Arthur Vandenberg pitted against an opposition led by Senator Robert Taft. Taft attacked the program as a waste of American resources to support the "socialist" governments of Europe. President Truman demonstrated his political skill by insisting that the program be called the "Marshall Plan," asking rhetorically, "Can you imagine its chances for passage in an election year in a Republican Congress if it is named for Truman and not Marshall?" To build support among the public, a group of influential private citizens organized the Committee for the Marshall Plan to Aid European Recovery. President Truman worked to preserve bipartisanship by appointing Paul Hoffmann, a Republican businessman and president of the Studebaker Corporation, to administer the program. Secretary of Commerce Averell Harriman was named as special representative to the participating countries. Public support for the plan increased as American leaders presented it as a way of preventing the Communist takeover of Western Europe. The Communist coup in Czechoslovakia and the murder of foreign minister Jan Masaryk in late February assured congressional action. In April 1948 the European Recovery Program (ERP) was approved in Congress by a more than four-to-one margin. For many Americans the Marshall Plan, along with the Truman Doctrine, had already become part of the containment strategy against the USSR. The two were, as President Truman referred to it, "two halves of the same [containment] walnut." However, American leaders still envisioned containment as primarily a political and economic task, and Congress prohibited Marshall Plan assistance for military supplies. This did not prevent countries with colonies, like France, from indirect use of Marshall Plan assistance to support its war in Indochina.

The Marshall Plan reflected the historical era in which it was born. Stimulated by America's economic performance as the "arsenal of democracy" in World War II, many Americans believed that governmental planning could help steer economic development. Marshall Plan officials assumed that government was part of the solution, not the source of the problem. Many of those active in the program were part of a generation of economists infused with the Keynesian activism that characterized the late 1930s and 1940s. They staffed the offices in Washington, D.C., and various European capitals, dispensing American advice and counsel to their European counterparts.

The Economic Cooperation Administration, the organization that administered the Marshall Plan, did not "control" the Western European economies, though it did exert American influence over the use of the assistance. The aid most often took the form of food and raw materials, which the European governments would sell to their citizens. The money from these sales, called counterpart funds, remained in the local currency and was placed in a special account. These funds were then used for special projects or investments agreed on between the United States and the recipient country. In short, the Americans supplied scarce dollar goods in exchange for a European commitment to invest at home. Countries responded differently, in part reflecting their different political circumstances and needs. Great Britain used the assistance to retire some of its debt, while France channeled funds into the Monnet Plan for the modernization of its infrastructure. The Germans eliminated production bottlenecks within their economy, built housing for workers, and supported the isolated city of Berlin. The bilateral treaty that Germany signed with the United States in December 1949 was the first international treaty signed by its new government under Chancellor Konrad Adenauer, an important symbolic statement of Germany's political recovery. One country in which Marshall Plan assistance had a particularly powerful impact was Austria, whose economic recovery received a vital boost from the American assistance.

Between 1948 and 1951, Congress authorized more than $13 billion for the European Recovery Program. In its initial years of operation Marshall Plan assistance amounted to approximately 10 percent of the annual federal budget, and between 1.0 to 2.0 percent of the national income. In contrast, America of the early 1990s devoted roughly 0.4 percent of its national income to foreign aid. Some 70 percent of the assistance went to the United Kingdom, France, Italy, and Germany. After the outbreak of the Korean War in June 1950, the United States reversed its earlier policy and encouraged the use of Marshall Plan assistance to provide for the rearmament of Western Europe within the NATO alliance. At the end of 1951 this change in emphasis became official as the ECA became the Mutual Security Administration.

Americans tended to overestimate the importance of their aid in the reconstruction of Western Europe. "The Marshall Plan saved Europe," President Truman told a later interviewer, "and that's something I am glad I had some part in helping to accomplish." This overestimation led to frequent calls for Marshall Plans for other parts of the world, such as the Alliance for Progress in Latin America, where the conditions for success were much less favorable. The crucial argument for the role of Marshall Plan assistance was less the sheer magnitude of aid than its key function in overcoming bottlenecks within the economy, and allowing rapid economic growth without imposing undue sacrifices on the Europeans still recovering from World War II. This made political stability under free institutions all the more possible. The plan helped undercut the powerful Communist parties of France and Italy, stabilize the fragile democratic system in the Federal Republic of Germany, and promote Western European cooperation. Western European production rose rapidly, and by 1950 production topped the prewar level by 25 percent. Inflation was largely brought under control, levels of employment increased, and the dollar gap decreased, though not as much as Americans had hoped. Although the goals of some Marshall Plan administrators like Hoffmann, who wanted a European market that looked like the internal market of the United States, were not met, there was a significant restoration of trade and convertibility of currencies, so that French importers could pay for Italian or German goods, and British importers could have the reserves to finance Dutch or Belgian purchases. European cooperation also increased with the creation of such organizations as the European Payments Union and the European Coal and Steel Community, which pooled French, West German, and Benelux coal and steel resources. Later in the 1950s the Europeans would organize their Common Market, which started the movement toward intra-European free trade and common regulation, and is the predecessor to the Maastricht treaty and the European Union. Marshall Plan payments, moreover, rather than draining American resources, as opponents had charged, in various ways supported production at home and encouraged American prosperity. The final legacy of the plan was to further accentuate the division of Europe, breaking the traditional trading patterns between Eastern and Western Europe and binding Western European countries in closer political and economic relationships with the United States.

BIBLIOGRAPHY

Arkes, Hadley. *Bureaucracy, the Marshall Plan and the National Interest.* Princeton, N.J.: Princeton University Press, 1973.

Carew, Anthony. *Labour under the Marshall Plan.* Detroit: Wayne State University Press, 1987.

Fossedal, Gregory A. *Our finest Hour: Will Clayton, the Marshall Plan, and the Triumph of Democracy.* Stanford, Calif.: Hoover Institute Press, 1993.

Gimbel, John. *The Origins of the Marshall Plan.* Stanford, Calif.: Stanford University Press, 1973.

Hogan, Michael J. *The Marshall Plan: America, Britain, and the Reconstruction of Western Europe.* New York, Cambridge University Press, 1987.

Kindleberger, Charles. *Marshall Plan Days.* Boston: Allen & Unwin, 1987.

Maier, Charles S., and Günter Bischof, eds. *The Marshall Plan and Germany.* New York: St. Martin's Press, 1991.

Milward, Alan. *The Reconstruction of Western Europe.* Berkeley: University of California Press, 1984.

Pelling, Henry. *Britain and the Marshall Plan.* New York: St. Martin's Press, 1988.

Pogue, Forrest C. *George C. Marshall: Statesman, 1945–1949.* New York: Viking, 1987.

Thomas Alan Schwartz

SEE ALSO Truman Doctrine

Martens, Wilfried (1936–)

Prime minister and dominant political figure of Belgium in the 1980s. Wilfried Martens was born on April 19, 1936. He attended the University of Leuven and was active there in the Flemish Students' Association. As a Flemish nationalist he painted over signs at the 1958 Brussels World's Fair that were not printed in Dutch as well as French. In 1962 he joined the Flemish Social Christian Party, and by 1972 he had become its chairman. He served as an adviser to various cabinets and offices after 1965.

Martens was elected to parliament in 1974. In 1979 he became prime minister although he had no prior ministerial experience. His first ministry was a fragile coalition of five parties. Except for a brief period in 1981 when a ministry was established under Mark Eyskens, Martens was prime minister until 1992. His tenure was marked by crises between Belgium's French and Flemish communities and their political representatives. Martens was by this time a convinced federalist and worked for cooperation between Belgium's two dominant language communities. His second government was undermined by a combination of disenchantment with his concessions to the language communities and his attempt to reduce government expenditures. In the November 1991 election Martens's center-left coalition suffered a serious reversal but retained a majority. Following a period of weakened government Martens stepped down and was succeeded on March 7, 1992, by Jean-Luc Dehaene.

Martens was a cofounder of the European People's Party in 1976. He was elected its president in 1990, and president of the group of the European People's Party in the European Parliament in 1994. From 1993 to 1996 he was president of the European Union of Christian Democrats.

BIBLIOGRAPHY

Martens, Wilfried. *Europa voorbij Oost en West.* Tielt, Belgium: Lannoo, 1995.

———. *Een gegeven woord.* Tielt, Belgium: Lannoo, 1985.

Ridder, Hugo de. *De strijd om de 16.* Tielt, Belgium: Lannoo, 1993.

———. *Omtrent Wilfried Martens.* Tielt, Belgium: Lannoo, 1991.

Bernard Cook

SEE ALSO Dehaene, Jean-Luc

Masaryk, Jan (1886–1948)

Czechoslovak foreign minister, 1940–48. Jan Garrigue Masaryk, son of Czechoslovak nationalist Thomáš Masaryk and his American wife, Charlotte Garrigue, was born in Prague on September 14, 1886. Masaryk graduated from Prague University and studied at Boston University. While residing in the United States Masaryk worked in an iron foundry and in a motion picture theater as a pianist.

Masaryk served unwillingly in the Austro-Hungarian infantry in World War I. After the war he returned to Prague and joined his father, who was helping to establish an independent state of Czechoslovakia. Masaryk joined the Czechoslovak Foreign Ministry staff. In 1919 he was posted to the United States as chargé d'affairs in Washington, D.C. Two years later he was posted to London, where he served as Edvard Beneš's private secretary. From 1925 to 1938 Masaryk was Czechoslovak ambassador to the United Kingdom. He resigned in protest following the Munich Pact of 1938, which led to the eventual dismemberment of Czechoslovakia. When the Western democracies recognized Beneš's Czechoslovak committee as the Czechoslovak government-in-exile in July 1940, Masaryk was appointed foreign minister. In 1941 Masaryk was appointed deputy prime minister. He advocated postwar federalization of Germany, Italy, the Balkans, Scandinavia, and the other countries of Western Europe. All these units were then to be linked into a Federation of Europe. His wartime radio broadcasts to Czechoslovakia contributed to the solidarity of the Czechoslovak underground. He counseled work slowdowns and inefficiency rather than armed resistance. In April 1944, however, as the Soviet army pushed near the Czechoslovak frontier, Masaryk and Beneš issued a call for armed resistance to the Germans.

Masaryk justified the November 1943 Soviet-Czechoslovak Mutual Assistance Pact saying "Soviet Russia not only is a European power but she will be the most powerful European power when the war is over. In negotiating the treaty we have just signed, we did not sell out to Russia. We know that without Russia's friendship none of her small neighbors can revert to independent national life." In 1944 he announced the intention of post-Czechoslovakia to expel the majority of the Sudeten Germans from its territory and to end any separate German linguistic privileges in the Sudetenland.

Masaryk returned as foreign minister to Czechoslovakia with President Beneš in 1945. Despite his disappointment with the Soviet veto of Czechoslovak participation in the Marshall Plan and his opposition to a Communist-dominated government for his country, Masaryk did not resign when Klement Gottwald, the Czechoslovak prime minister, engineered the Communist takeover in February 1948. Masaryk did not believe that Czechoslovakia could directly oppose the will of the Soviet Union. Two weeks later, however, he was found dead in the courtyard beneath the window of his office in the Foreign Ministry. The Communists asserted that he committed suicide. Some observers, pointing to his distress over the Communist take over, accepted this explanation. Relatives and foreign colleagues have continued to express their belief that he committed suicide. Others asserted that he was thrown to his death by Soviet agents or Czechoslovak Communists. An inquiry after the Velvet Revolution of 1989 came to no definitive conclusion.

BIBLIOGRAPHY

Soukup, Lumir. *Chvile s Janem Masarykem z pameti.* Prague: Charles University, 1994.

Zeman, Z. A. B. *The Masaryks: The Making of Czechoslovakia.* London: I.B. Tauris, 1990.

Bernard Cook

SEE ALSO Beneš, Eduard; Fierlinger, Zdeněk; Gottwald Klement

Maskhadov, Aslan Aliyevich (1951–)

Commander of the Chechen forces during the 1994–1996 war with Russia, elected president of Chechnya, a constituent republic of the Russian Federation located in the northeast Caucasus, on January 27, 1997. Aslan Aliyevich Maskhadov was born in 1951 in Kazakhstan during the forced relocation of the Chechens there from 1944 to 1957 ordered by Stalin, who accused the Chechens of collaborating with the German invaders of the USSR. He joined the Soviet army in 1969 and studied at the Tibilisi Artillery Military Academy and the Kalinin Artillery Academy. He served in the Far Eastern Military District and in Hungary. In January 1990 he commanded an artillery division in Vilnius, Lithuania, and took part in the attack on the Vilnius Television Center.

In 1991, after Dzhokhar Dudayev, the former Soviet Air Force general, who assumed leadership in Chechnya, declared Chechnya sovereign, Maskhadov was appointed head of civil defense and deputy chief of staff. He was appointed chief of the Chechen General Staff after his tenacious defense of Dudayev's presidential headquarters, against the Russians in December 1994 and January 1995. As chief of staff he directed the Chechen military effort during the 1994–96 was with Russia. On August 6, 1996, as the Russians were asserting that they were mopping up Chechen resistance, Maskhadov launched a surprise attack on Grozny, the Chechen capital. With the Russian forces demoralized and poorly led, the Chechens gain control of the city. The desperate situation in which Russian President Boris Yeltsin's government had been placed by this unexpected Chechen victory bolstered the efforts of Aleksandr Lebed, Yeltsin's national security advisor, to negotiate a settlement. Maskhadov and Lebed worked out an agreement, signed on August 31, to end the war and withdraw all Russian forces from Chechen territory but to shelve the question of the status of Chechnya for five years.

On January 27, 1997, Maskhadov was elected president of Chechnya. Though firmly committed to Chechen independence, his moderation in comparison with the other principal candidates appeared to sway many voters. They apparently believed that Maskhadov would be best able to work out a definitive agreement with Russia. His principal rivals were Shamil Basayev, the field commander who had led the daring and successful Chechen raid on Budyonnovsk, Russia in 1995, and Zelimkhan Yabdarbiyev, who became president when Dudayev was killed in April 1996. Basayev received 23.4 percent of the vote and Yabdarbiyev 10.1 percent.

Bernard Cook

Massu, Jacques (1908–)

French army general and leader, with General Raoul Salan, of efforts to keep Algeria part of France. Jacques Massu, who was born on May 5, 1908, in Châlons-sur-Marne, became a professional soldier. He fought with the anti-Vicky Free French forces of General Philippe Leclerc. He distinguished himself as a colonel in fighting in Indochina, as the French fought to hold on to their colony, and, as a general, commanded the elite Tenth Parachute Division during the abortive 1956 Suez invasion.

In January 1957, Governor General Robert Lacoste, faced with a general strike proclaimed in Algiers by the rebel FLN, invested Massu with civil power and ordered him to break the strike at any cost and by any means. Operating with a ruthlessness that included torture of suspects, Massu and his troops won the so-called Battle of Algiers, which lasted until March. Probably the most dramatic episode of the Algerian War, it ended with the paratroopers in command of the city and the casbah, and the FLN terrorist cells broken. This struggle was the subject of the 1966 film *Battle of Algiers,* directed by Gilo Pontecorvo.

On May 13, 1958, when the French army and European Algerians were convinced that France was about to grant Algeria its independence, Massu took the lead in the formation in Algiers of a committee of public safety. He explained in a telegram to French President René Coty that the committee had been formed to "maintain order" and avert bloodshed, and he urged "creation in Paris of a government of public safety, alone capable of preserving Algeria as an integral part of the mother country."

In December 1959, Massu made critical remarks to a journalist regarding President Charles de Gaulle complaining that perhaps the army had made a mistake in bringing him back to power. When these became public de Gaulle immediately recalled Massu to France and chastised him, but eventually gave him command of the army garrison at Metz. Massu remained a loyal Gaullist and refused to lend his support to the January 1960 and April 1961 insurrections in Algiers designed to force de Gaulle's hand to keep Algeria part of France. Massu refused to take any step that might divide the army he loved.

BIBLIOGRAPHY

Horne, Alistair. *A Savage War of Peace: Algeria, 1954–1962.* London: Macmillan, 1977.

Massu, Jacques. *Le Soldat méconnu.* Paris, Mame, 1993.

———. *La vrai Bataille d'Alger.* Paris, Presses pocket, 1974.

Spencer C. Tucker

SEE ALSO Coty, René; De Gaulle, Charles; Salan, Raoul

Masur, Kurt (1927–)

Orchestral conductor who helped avoid bloodshed during the famous 1989 "Monday demonstrations" in Leipzig, where he has been conductor of the Leipzig Gewandhaus Orchestra since 1970. He became music director of the New York Philharmonic in 1991, while maintaining his Leipzig position. His whole musical life had been rooted in the German Democratic Republic (GDR): Masur studied music in Leipzig (1946–48), then worked at the Landestheater in Halle (1948–51), where he accompanied opera singers as they learned their roles; he then moved on to conduct nearly every major orchestra in the GDR (Erfurt, Schwerin, Leipzig, Dresden, Berlin) until being named Gewandhauskapellmeister at Leipzig, where he was also a professor. His work at Leipzig became internationally known and he was soon guest conducting around the world. He also received several honorary doctorates (six in the United States) and international and national prizes. Because of his loyalty first to his art then to his roots and upbringing in the GDR, he had the Gewandhaus renovated—despite the state's chronic lack of funds—using only local GDR labor and materials and made it acoustically one of the best symphony halls in Europe. His prominence in the GDR, where he was something of a national hero, allowed him to help head off violence when protests in favor of human rights and liberalization in the GDR broke out in 1989. To a great extent set the standard for action for other East German public intellectuals, especially those who, like Masur, had strong connections to the state. On October 9, 1989, Masur read a statement by the "Leipzig Six," leaders representing the human rights campaign, a call for open, peaceful dialogue, and it was played in churches, from public loudspeakers, and on Leipzig local radio stations. Many credit Masur's action with heading off violence at that evening's demonstration by tens of thousands of GDR citizens. Over the next several months he organized public meetings in the Gewandhaus and held press conferences and benefit concerts. Hundreds of GDR citizens wrote letters to Masur thanking him for his action and expressing their hopes and fears about the *Wende* (turning point, or the collapse of communism in the DR and the turn toward reunification).

BIBLIOGRAPHY

Schäfer, Ulla, ed. *"Mut und Zuversicht gegeben": Briefe an Kurt Masur, 9. Oktober 1989 bis 18. März 1990.* Frankfurt am Main: Ullstein, 1990.

Zumpe, Karl, ed. *Der Gewandhauskapellmeister Kurt Masur.* Leipzig: Deutscher Verlag für Musik, 1987.

Scott Denham

Mateša, Zlatko (1949–)

Croatian prime minister (1995–). Zlatko Mateša was born in Zagreb on June 17, 1949. He received a law degree from the University of Zagreb after studying for a year in the United Kingdom. In 1978 he served as an assistant judge in the Zagreb municipal court. He then worked in the legal offices of the Yugoslav INA-Trade, rising through the management until in 1990 he became the assistant director general for the administration of INA companies.

In 1992 and 1993 he served as the director of the Agency for Restructuring and Development. In 1993 he was appointed minister without portfolio in the government of Prime Minister Nikica Valentič. In September 1995 he was appointed minister of economics. When the October 1995 elections allowed President Franjo Tudjman to appoint a one-party government he appoint Mateša of his Croatian Democratic Union party prime minister on November 7. He continued to serve as minister of economics.

Bernard Cook

SEE ALSO Tudjman, Franjo

Mattei, Enrico (1906–62)

Italian industrialist and Christian Democrat. During World War II Enrico Mattei was one of the commanders of the Catholic resistance to fascism. In 1945 he was assigned the task of liquidating AGIP, the state petroleum company set up by the Fascist government of Benito Mussolini. Mattei used this as the springboard for the foundation in 1952 of Ente Nazionale Idrocarburi (ENI, National Society for Hydrocarbons). Mattei became president of this new state enterprise for energy. He launched a new political strategy to render Italy more independent in the sphere of energy and, at the same time, to fell the campaign chest of the Christian Democratic Party. To achieve his first goal Mattei adopted an audacious policy toward the oil-producing countries. ENI entered the ranks of the "Seven Sisters" (the biggest oil companies) and gained a leading position in the energy market. Mattei pursued his second goal by establishing a hidden fund drawn from ENI. He thus launched the practice of utilizing state companies as party fiefs, sources of funds for the party, and jobs for party loyalists. Mattei died in 1962 in a mysterious aviation accident. According to some the accident was caused by the Mafia but organized by the oil companies and by the U.S. Central Intelligence Agency, all of whom opposed Mattei's pro-Arab politics.

BIBLIOGRAPHY

Dow, Votaw. *The Six-legged Dog, Mattei and Eni: A Study in Power.* Berkeley: University of California Press, 1964.

Perrone, Nico. *Mattei, il nemico italiano: politica e morte del presidente dell'ENI attraverso i documenti segreti 1945–1962.* Milan: Leonardo, 1989.

Pietra, Italo. *Mattei la pecora nera.* Milan: Sugar, 1987.

Daniele Petrosino

Maurer, Ion Gheorghe (1902–)

Romanian politician and lawyer. Member of the Central Committee of the Romanian Communist Party (RCP, 1945–74), the party Politburo (1960–65), and the Executive Committee of the Permanent Presidium of the Central Committee (1965–74), minister of foreign affairs (1957–58), president of the Presidium of the Grand National Assembly (Romanian parliament, 1958–61), and president of the Council of Ministers (1961–74).

The son of a German father and a French mother, Ion Gheorghe Maurer was born in Bucharest in 1902. After graduating from primary school and military high school in Craiova, he pursued polytechnic university studies, but after one year attending he quit to study law. After graduation he practiced law, first as deputy-judge, then as prosecutor, and eventually as advocate. In the last capacity, he defended many prominent figures of the Romanian Communist movement, including Ana Pauker, Teohari Georgescu, and Ilie Pintilie. In 1936 (or even before that year, according to Maurer) he joined the RCP. Before the start of the Second World War, following Communist tactics of infiltration, he attempted to be elected to parliament on the list of the Liberal Party, headed by historian Gheorghe I. Brătianu, but to no avail.

In 1940 Maurer was ordered by the RCP to become the go-between for the RCP and one of its main leaders, Gheorghe Gheorghiu-Dej, who at that time was confined in the Doftana jail. On August 23, 1944, as the Soviet armies approached Bucharest, King Michael had the Romanian dictator General Ion Antonescu arrested and set up a coalition government that contained one Communist and was headed by Constantu Sánátescu. This new government immediately requested an armistice with the USSR and entered the war on the Allied side. On the eve of the coup d'état, the party gave him another important assignment: to desert from the Romanian army fighting the Germans in order to organize Gheorghiu-Dej's escape from the prison at Targu-Jiu to which he had been moved. His success secured him not only Gheorghiu-Dej's lifelong friendship but a rocketing postwar political career as well. He served as undersecretary with the Ministry of Communications and Public Works (March 6, 1945–November 30, 1946), with the Ministry of National Economy (December 1, 1946–December 29, 1947), and with the Ministry of Industry and Trade (December 30, 1947–April 14, 1948). Maurer gained the enmity of the Soviets for opposing the nomination of Ana Pauker as general secretary of the Romanian Communist Party. Saved from the NKVD's punishment only by his friendship with Gheorghiu-Dej, Maurer reemerged as a key political figure only after the death of Lavrenti Beria the head of the Soviet secret police, in 1953. He became minister of foreign affairs from 1957 to 1958. Later, after the death of Petru Groza, he became the president of the Presidium of the Grand National Assembly (1958–61) and, eventually, the longest tenured head of the government as president of the Council of Ministers in Romania's postwar history, holding that post for thirteen years (1961–74).

After Gheorghiu-Dej's death (1965), to prevent the possibility of Romania's reestablishing a subcurrent relationship with the USSR as had existed during the rule of Stalin, Maurer proposed and obtained Nicolae Ceaușescu's succession as secretary-general of the RCP, though, Gheorghiu-Dej had proposed Maurer himself and, after his refusal, Gheorghe Apostol. Maurer quickly came into conflict with Ceauşescu, however, owing to Ceauşescu's tendency to override Maurer's role as president of the Council of Ministers. Refusing to accept Maurer's resignation but still hoping to get rid of him, on the occasion of a hunting episode in 1972, Ceauşescu apparently staged a car accident in which Maurer was seriously injured. In 1974, Maurer became a pensioner.

BIBLIOGRAPHY

Betea, Lavinia. *Maurer si lumea de ieri: marturii despre stalinizarea Romaniei.* Arad, Romania: Editura "Felix", 1995.

Maurer, Ion Gheorghe. *A 20-a [i.e. douazecea] aniversare a proclamarii republicii: expunere prezentata la sedinta jubiliara a Marii Adunari Nationale a Republicii Socialiste Romania, 29 decembrie 1967.* Bucharest: Editura politica, 1968.

Rothschild, Joseph, and Nancy M. Wingfield. *Return to Diversity: A Political History of East Central Europe since World War II,* 3d ed. New York: Oxford University, 2000.

Wolf, Robert Lee. *The Balkans in Our Time.* New York: W.W. Norton, 1978.

Adrian Pop

SEE ALSO Ceauşescu, Nicolae; Gheorghiu-Dej, Gheorghe

Mauriac, François (1885–1970)

French novelist, poet, biographer, and political essayist, who was awarded the Nobel Prize in literature in 1952. François Mauriac was born into a devout, bourgeois Catholic family in Bordeaux on October 11, 1885.

On completion of his preparatory studies at local schools in Bordeaux, Mauriac entered the École des Chartes in Paris in 1907, with the goal of becoming an archivist. However, a year later he withdrew from school to pursue his literary career. Slowly he established himself as a promising young writer, and in 1922 published the work that made him a literary figure of note, *The Kiss to the Leper.* The years 1922–27 were marked by extraordinary productivity, which culminated in his first masterpiece, *Thérèse Desqueyroux* (1926).

Following a personal spiritual crisis and spiritual conversion to Catholicism, Mauriac published what is considered by most critics his greatest novel, *The Vipers' Tangle* (1932). The inner spiritual conflicts of Mauriac's characters and the role of God's love in their lives led to his designation as a Catholic novelist par excellence. His subsequent novels, especially *A Woman of the Pharisees* (1941) and *The Lamb* (1954), developed similar themes.

Mauriac was militantly antifascist and became one of the greatest writers of the Resistance in France. He was an early supporter of General Charles de Gaulle and in 1964 Mauriac published his biography, *De Gaulle.* Mauriac was admitted to the Académie Française in 1933 and received the Nobel Prize in literature in 1952. He died on September 1, 1970 from the consequences of a fall. Mauriac was hailed at his death and continues to be recognized as one of the greatest French writers of the twentieth century.

BIBLIOGRAPHY

Lacouture, Jean. *Mauriac.* Paris: Seuil, 1970.

O'Connell, David. *François Mauriac Revisited.* New York: Twayne, 1995.

Speaight, Robert. *François Mauriac: A Study of the Writer and the Man.* London: Chatto and Windus, 1970.

Francis J. Murphy

Mauroy, Pierre (1928–)

French politician. Pierre Mauroy was born on July 5, 1928, in Cartignies. From 1950 to 1958 he served as national secretary to the Socialist Youth. He taught in a technical school and was secretary-general of the union of technical college faculty from 1955 to 1959. He then began his rise through the leadership of the Socialist Party (French Section of the Workers' International, SFIO), becoming deputy secretary-general in 1966. He was also a member of the executive committee of the left electoral alliance, the Fédération de la Gauche Démocratique et Socialiste (Federation of the Democratic and Socialist Left) from 1965 to 1968.

When the Socialist Party was reorganized under the leadership of François Mitterrand, Mauroy became its leader in the department of Nord. In 1973 he was elected to the National Assembly and simultaneously mayor of Lille. Following the Socialist electoral victories in 1981 President Mitterrand appointed Mauroy prime minister. Mauroy, a militant socialist, headed a cabinet composed of Socialists and Communists and embarked on an effort to enact a strongly socialist economic program. An ambitious program of nationalization was coupled with expanded social benefits and new taxes on the wealthy. However, economic difficulties followed and Mitterrand replaced Mauroy with technocrat Laurent Fabius in 1984.

From May 1988 to January 1992 Mauroy was first secretary of the Socialist Party. In 1992 he became president of the Socialist International.

BIBLIOGRAPHY

Mauroy, Pierre. *C'est ici le chemin.* Paris: Flammarion, 1982.

———. *Héritiers de l'avenir.* Paris: Stock, 1977.

———. *Parole de Lillois.* Paris: Lieu commun, 1994.

Bernard Cook

Mayhew, Sir Patrick (1929–)

Secretary of state for Northern Ireland (1992–97). Patrick Mayhew was born in 1929. He was the tenth secretary of state for Northern Ireland and, like Peter Brooke who preceded him, had an Anglo-Irish background. Despite this, there were reservations about his becoming secretary of state in the Irish government and among the nationalist community in Northern Ireland. This was because as attorney general from 1987 to 1992 he had made decisions that were resented, including supporting British security agents who had killed three unarmed members of the IRA in Gibraltar. Once he took over as secretary of state, however, opinion of Sir Patrick improved when he decided to press ahead with the talks between Catholic nationalists and pro-British loyalists already underway. He established a good working relationship with Irish Foreign Minister David Andrews and won praise from the nationalist community in 1992 when he banned the loyalist paramilitary organization, the Ulster Defense Association. In 1993 he became embroiled in controversy surrounding newspaper reports that the British government had been in secret contact with the republican movement. He attempted some damage control but in the end had to concede that there was truth to the reports and offered his resignation, which British Prime Minister John Major did not accept. He was replaced by Mo Mowlam in 1997 when Labour came into power.

BIBLIOGRAPHY

Arthur, Paul. *Northern Ireland since 1968,* 2d ed. Oxford: Blackwell Publishers, 1996.

Aughey, Arthur, and Duncan Morrow, eds. *Northern Ireland Politics.* London: Longman, 1996.

Bew, Paul. *Northern Ireland, 1921–1996: Political Forces and Social Classes.* London: Serif, 1996.

Ricki Schoen

Mazowiecki, Tadeusz (1927–)

First postwar Polish premier (August 1989–November 1990) who was not associated with the Communist Party.

Tadeusz Mazowiecki was born on April 18, 1927, in Płock. His family was part of the intelligentsia and he received a degree in law from Warsaw University. In 1947–48 he was chairman of the Academic Publishing Agency in Warsaw. Removed from work by the Communist's because of his Catholic outlook, he began collaboration with PAX, a pro-regime organization of Catholic lay people, and published in *Dziś i Jutro* and the *Słowo Powszechne;* later he became a chief editor of the *Wrocławski Tygodnik Katolicki (WTK)* (Wrocław Catholic Weekly). In 1954, following a conflict with Bolesław Piasecki, leader of the PAX, he was removed from the *WTK.*

In 1956 in Warsaw he coorganized the Catholic Intelligentsia Club (KIK) and served on its board. In 1957–81 he was cofounder and a chief editor of a monthly magazine for young Catholic intelligentsia, the *Więź.* From 1961 to 1971 Mazowiecki was a member of the Sejm (Polish parliament). He was also active in the Znak (the Sign) movement. In outspoken and courageous parliamentary speeches he demanded democratization of public life, just laws, pluralism in education, and autonomy for universities. On behalf of the Znak movement he questioned the government about the repression of opposition to its policies in March 1968. In 1971 he undertook an unsuccessful attempt to create a parliamentary commission to investigate the shooting of protesting workers in Gdansk in December 1970. In 1976 he signed a protest against the change in the constitution recognizing the dominant role of the Communist Party in Polish life. In 1977 he became a secret contact for participants in a hunger strike organized by the Committee for the Defense of Workers (KOR), in St. Martin's church in Warsaw. The same year he organized, within the KIK framework, a session on "Christians and Human Rights," and in 1978 he coorganized the Society for Scholarly Courses to organize lectures and seminars independent of the regime.

In August 1980 he was in the Lenin Shipyard in Gdansk as a representative of intellectuals supporting the striking workers. In the same month he became chairman of the expert committee to the Inter-factory Strike Committee and one of the mediators of the agreement on labor union pluralism. From 1980 he acted as an adviser to the Solidarity (Solidarność) labor union; in 1981 he became chief editor of its weekly, *Solidarność.* When the Polish government attempted to crush Solidarity by imposing martial law, he was put in solitary confinement on December 13, 1981, and was released on December 24, 1982. He cooperated with Lech Wałęsa, the leader of Solidarity, and in 1987 became an adviser to the National Coordination Commission. He was one of the organizers of the Round Table; and in that context he worked as chairman of the team concerned with pluralism in labor unions.

In August 1989 Mazowiecki became the first postwar Polish premier who was not associated with the Communist Party. His government launched a program of economic reforms, the goals of which were privatization, ending inflation, and convertibility of the Polish currency (złoty). After his defeat in presidential elections in November 1990, he resigned as prime minister. In December 1990 he organized a political party, the Democratic Union (UD), and became its first leader. Since April 1994 he has led the Freedom Union (UW) party, created by the fusion of the Democratic Union and the Liberal-Democratic Congress. It advocates pluralism in political life and respect for human freedom. The UW created an opposition shadow government with Mazowiecki as its premier.

In 1992 Mazowiecki served as a special U.N. envoy to former Yugoslavia, investigating human right violations in the wars that accompanied the breakup of the Yugoslav state.

BIBLIOGRAPHY

Ascherson, Neal. *The Polish August: The Self-limiting Revolution.* New York: Viking Press, 1982.

———. *The Struggles for Poland.* New York: Random House, 1988.

Domaranczyk, Zbigniew. *100 dni Mazowieckiego.* Warsaw: Wydawn. Andrzej Bonarski, 1990.

Kuczynski, Waldemar. *Zwierzenia zausznika.* Warsaw: Polska Oficyna Wydawnicza "BGW", 1992.

Mazowiecki, Tadeusz. *Druga twarz Europy.* Warsaw: Biblioteka "Wiezi", 1990.

———. *Raporty Tadeusza Mazowieckiego z bylej Jugoslawii.* Poznan: Agencja Scholar, 1993.

———. *Tadeusz Mazowiecki: polityk trudnych czasow.* Warsaw: United Publishers: Presspublica, 1997.

Marek Jezinski
Pawel Kacprzak

SEE ALSO Balcerowicz, Leszek; Jaruzelski, Wojciech; Wałęsa, Lech

McAleese, Mary (1951–)

President of Ireland. Mary Particia McAleese was born Mary Leneghan in Belfast, Northern Ireland, on June 27, 1951. She attended high school at a Dominican nuns' school on the Falls Road. While attending Queens University in Belfast, where she received a law degree, she lived with her parents until a Protestant attack on their Crumlin Road house in 1974 left them homeless. Her father's pub was also bombed and burned. Following graduation, and after a year's training as a barrister, McAleese became a professor of criminal law at Trinity College, Dublin, succeeding Mary Robinson in that post as she would later succeed her in the presidency. She was professor of criminal law at Trinity (1975–79, 1981–87). She married Martin McAleese, a dentist, in 1976. From 1979 to 1981 she was a television journalist for Radio Telefis Eireann. She has served as director of Northern Ireland Electricity and Channel 4 Television. Since 1987 she has been director of the Institute of Professional Legal studies in Belfast and since 1994 vice chancellor of Queens University in Belfast.

On October 31, 1997, she was elected president of the Republic of Ireland, the first president from Northern Ireland. The election was held to choose a successor to Mary Robinson, the first female president of Ireland. Robinson resigned her post to become U.N. high commissioner for human rights. Robinson supported rights for homosexuals and legalization of divorce and abortion. McAleese, a devout Catholic, though she personally opposed divorce and abortion, said that she would sign any bill passed by parliament to liberalize Ireland's legal prohibition of abortion. The election was unique because four of the five candidates were women.

McAleese was the candidate of Fianna Fáil and the Progressive Democrats, the parties forming the ruling coalition. During the campaign Gerry Adams, head of Sinn Fein, the Catholic republica party that is the political arm of the Irish Republica Army that had been waging a violent campaign to drive the British from Ulster and to unite the north with the rest of Ireland, expressed his party's support for McAleese. McAleese, a nationalist who favored unification of the island, had stated her opposition to IRA violence and expressed hope that she might facilitate understanding between the two contending sides in the North. Nevertheless, she was denounced by Loyalist Ian Paisley's right-wing Democratic Unionist Party as a "bigoted and intolerant nationalist." McAleese was inaugurated on November 11, 1997.

BIBLIOGRAPHY

Clarity, James F. "Hard-Liners Bitterly Attack New Irish Leader." *New York Times,* November 2, 1997.

———. "Ireland Picks Ulster Woman as President." *New York Times,* November 1, 1997.

———. "Woman from Ulster Expected to Win Irish Republic Vote." *New York Times,* October 31, 1997.

Grove, Valerie. "All the President's Mien." *Times,* October 25, 1997.

Kingston, Peter. "Learning Curve: Mary McAleese." *Guardian* (London), October 28, 1997.

Walsh, Dick. "Lurch to the Right Evident in Vote for Traditional Certainties." *Irish Times,* November 1, 1997.

Bernard Cook

McCloy, John Jay (1895–1989)

Preeminent figure in the American foreign policy establishment during the Cold War. Committed to the Atlantic Alliance and Jean Monnet's concept of European integration, McCloy played a central role in shaping American policy toward Europe and especially Germany for almost three decades. Born March 31, 1895, in Philadelphia, McCloy was educated at the Peddie School, Amherst College, and Harvard Law School. He fought with the American Expeditionary Force in World War I, and after the war became a Wall Street lawyer, best known for his success in pursuing the "Black Tom" sabotage case against Germany during the 1930s in which he proved that German agents had set off an explosion at an ammunition factory. During World War II McCloy, as assistant secretary of war, was involved in the controversial decisions to intern Japanese-Americans and not to bomb the German extermination camp at Auschwitz, Poland. Along with Secretary of War Henry Stimson, McCloy helped defeat the Morgenthau Plan to deindustrialize Germany after the war, and helped establish an international tribunal to prosecute German war criminals. After the war McCloy served as president of the World Bank (1947–49) and as high commissioner to Germany (1949–52). McCloy supported the policies of Chancellor Konrad Adenauer, who favored German integration into the Western alliance through such initiatives as the Schuman Plan and the European Defense Community (EDC). McCloy provoked controversy through his leniency toward convicted German war criminals, especially his release of Alfried Krupp. He negotiated the 1952 Paris-Bonn treaties, which linked the restoration of German sovereignty with Germany's participation in the EDC, a European armed force. When France rejected the EDC in August 1954, West Germany entered NATO within a framework similar to the one McCloy had originally established.

Although his position as high commissioner was his most significant public office, McCloy played a continuing role in U.S. foreign policy for the next three decades. His overriding concern was U.S.-European relations, especially the health of the Atlantic Alliance and Germany's secure position within it. He was a frequent conduit between the German and American governments, conducted negotiations with Egypt after the Suez crisis, and served as President John Kennedy's adviser on disarmament. McCloy also played a role in the Cuban Missile Crisis and served on the Warren Commission, which investigated President Kennedy's assassination. In 1966 he served as the U.S. representative to the Trilateral Talks, which adjusted NATO's financial burdens in the aftermath of France's withdrawal from the integrated military command. Although initially supportive of the war in Vietnam, McCloy became more critical as he perceived the war diverting the United States from its main priorities in Europe. A critic of West German Chancellor Willy Brandt's *Ostpolitik,* McCloy continually worried about Germany's commitment to the West. Along with Henry Kissinger and David Rockefeller, he lobbied President Jimmy Carter to allow the deposed Shah of Iran to receive medical treatment in the United States. An unapologetic advocate of a Pax Americana, McCloy never wavered in his belief in America's responsibility for world leadership.

BIBLIOGRAPHY

Bird, Kai. *The Chairman: John J. McCloy.* New York: Simon and Schuster, 1992.

Schwartz, Thomas Alan. *America's Germany: John J. McCloy and the Federal Republic of Germany.* Cambridge, Mass.: Harvard University Press, 1991.

Thomas Alan Schwartz

SEE ALSO European Defense Community; Schuman Plan

McGahern, John (1934–)

Irish novelist and short story writer. John McGahern, raised in County Roscommon, taught at the secondary-school level in Dublin from 1957 to 1964, when his second novel, *The Dark,* was banned by Irish censors, for its explicit sexuality. As an account of the claustrophobia of Irish life dealing with the problems of adolescence and clerical celibacy, it caused McGahern to lose his job and created much controversy about the republic's censorship laws. McGahern moved to London and lectured in Britain and America, but eventually returned to live in County Leitrim.

McGahern is regarded as one of the most existentialist writers today. His novels include *The Barracks* (1963), about the security and sterility of Irish rural life; *The Leavetaking* (1974), which won the Society of Authors Award in 1975; *The Pornographer* (1979), which won the Award of American Irish Foundation in 1985; and *Amongst Women* (1990), which was short-listed for the

1990 Booker prize and won the Irish Times Literary Award in 1990. His short stories include "Nightlines" (1970), "Getting Through" (1978), "High Ground" (1985), and *Collected Short Stories* (1992).

Michael J. Kennedy

McMichael, Gary (1970–)

Ulster Democratic Party (UDP) leader (1994–); UDP councilor for Lisburn Borough (1993–). Gary McMichael was born in Lisburn, Northern Ireland, in 1970. He became involved in community affairs at an early age when he formed a community group in a Lisburn housing estate in 1986. When his father was killed by the IRA in 1987, he became more active on the political scene. By 1993 has was elected councilor to Lisburn Borough Council, and in 1994 he became leader of the UDP after Raymond Smallwoods was murdered. (Smallwoods was one of the principle negotiators bringing about the Loyalist cease-fire in 1994 and was the main political adviser to the Combined Loyalist Military Command [CLMC].) McMichael took over these roles after the murder. He was the first loyalist to share a public platform with Sinn Fein, the Catholic republican party that is the political arm of the Irish Republican Army that had been waging a violent Campaign to drive the British from Ulster and to unite Ireland, when he debated with Mitchell McLaughlin at the Liberal Democrat Conference in Glasgow in 1995. The same month he also met with the leaders of the Rainbow Coalition, who made up the Irish government at the time. While he continued to argue for retaining the union with Britain, he also advocated compromise. He played an important role in the multiparty talks that culminated in the Good Friday Agreement that set the stage for the formation of Protestant-Catholic government in Northern Ireland in 1999. He was part of the successful "Yes" campaign for the agreement in May 1998 when the issue was put before the voters of Northern Ireland in a referendum.

BIBLIOGRAPHY

Arthur, Paul. *Northern Ireland since 1968,* 2d ed. Oxford: Blackwell Publishers, 1996.

Aughey, Arthur, and Duncan Morrow, eds. *Northern Ireland Politics.* London: Longman, 1996.

Ricki Schoen

McQuaid, John Charles (1895–1973)

Roman Catholic archbishop of Dublin and Primate of All Ireland (1940–72). John Charles McQuaid was born in Cootehill, County Cavan. Educated at University College, Dublin, he was ordained a Holy Ghost Priest. He served as dean and then president of Dean of Studies, Blackrock College (1928–39). He was a close friend of Eamon de Valera, prime minister and president of Ireland, and was consulted on the social and religious aspects of the 1937 constitution by de Valera during its drafting. As archbishop McQuaid was interested in educational matters and in the alleviation of poverty. During the Irish economic depression of the 1940s he acted as a mediator in industrial disputes. McQuaid was central in the clerical opposition to the 1951 Mother and Child Scheme to provide aid without a needs test to mothers and children, which brought down the government. McQuaid was a deeply conservative man and was very suspicious of the media. He resigned as primate in 1972 and was replaced by Dermont Ryan.

BIBLIOGRAPHY

Feeney, John. *John Charles McQuaid: The Man and the Mask.* Dublin: Mercier Press, 1974.

O Riordain, John J. *Irish Catholics: Tradition and Transition.* Dublin: Veritas, 1980.

Michael J. Kennedy

SEE ALSO Browne, Noel

McWilliams, Monica (1954–)

Northern Ireland Women's Coalition member (1996–); elected delegate to the multiparty peace talks (1996) between the Northern Irish parties representing the divided Catholic and Protestant communities in an effort to end Sectarian conflict. Monica McWilliams was born in 1954. She is a senior lecturer and course director of women's studies at the University of Ulster. Much of her work concentrated on women's poverty and domestic violence. She also encouraged women to take a more active role in politics. Together with Pearl Sagar, Protestant peace activist from Belfast, she founded the Northern Ireland Women's Coalition in 1996 after John Major, the British prime minister, called an election to the Northern Ireland Assembly. The coalition has no official leader but McWilliams became its best-known face. The coalition, a cross-community group, promotes human rights, inclusion, and equality. McWilliams was involved in bringing about the Good Friday Agreement, and she was part of the "Yes" campaign in the May 1998 referendum that successfully sought the approval of the voters for the agreement.

BIBLIOGRAPHY

Bew, Paul. *The Northern Ireland Peace Process, 1993–1996: A Chronology.* London: Serif, 1996.

Fay, Marie-Therese. *Northern Ireland's Troubles: The Human Costs.* Sterling, Va.: Pluto Press, 1999.

McWilliams, Monica. *Bringing It Out in the Open: Domestic Violence in Northern Ireland: A Study Commissioned by the Department of Health and Social Services (Northern Ireland).* Belfast: HMSO, 1993.

Ricki Schoen

Meade, James Edward (1907–95)

British economist. James Meade was a British government economist from 1940 to 1946 and the Labour government's chief economic consultant in 1946 and 1947. He taught economics at Oxford University and worked as an economist with the League of Nations before World War II. After 1947 he was a professor at the London School of Economics and Cambridge University. Meade, a prolific scholar, was a corecipient with Bertil Ohlin of Sweden of the 1977 Nobel Prize in economics.

An economist of the Keynesian demand-management school, Meade significantly affected wartime and postwar British economic policy. He had major input into wartime budgets and the 1944 White Paper on employment policy. Between 1945 and 1947 Meade frequently clashed with proponents of direct state controls, public ownership, and wealth redistribution, especially Chancellor of the Exchequer Hugh Dalton. Meade's advocacy of restraints on collective bargaining to curtail inflation while maintaining price stability influenced British governments in the 1960s and 1970s. He died on December 22, 1995.

BIBLIOGRAPHY

Meade, James E., and Lionel Charles Robbins. *The Wartime Diaries of Lionel Robbins and James Meade, 1943–45.* New York: St. Martin's Press, 1991.

Solow, R. M. "James Meade at Eighty." *Economic Journal* 97 (1987): 986–88.

Wasson, Tyler, ed. *Nobel Prize Winners.* New York: H.W. Wilson, 1987.

Don M. Cregier

Mečiar, Vladimír (1942–)

Premier of the Slovak Republic (1990–91, 1992–94, 1994–). Although a graduate in law from Comenius University, Bratislava, Vladimír Mečiar became a professional boxer and worked in the Communist youth movement during the 1960s. Accused of supporting the Prague Spring reforms and opposing the Soviet-led Warsaw Pact invasion of Czechoslovakia in 1968, he was expelled from the Communist Party in 1969. After further legal studies while working as a welder in Dubnica, he subsequently worked as a company lawyer until 1989, when the Velvet Revolution in Czechoslovakia propelled him to high political office in Slovakia. After a brief stint as minister of the interior and the environment, he became Slovak premier for the first time after the republican parliamentary elections of June 1990, but then split from the ruling Public Against Violence (PAV), the Slovak equivalent of Civic Forum in the Czech Republic. In March 1991 he founded and thereafter led the Movement for a Democratic Slovakia (MDS), which led to his dismissal from the Slovak premiership by the Slovak National Council (SNC). Following new parliamentary elections in June 1992, when the MDS emerged as the dominant party in the SNC, Mečiar became premier once again, leading a government dominated by his party. By this time it was clear that Czechoslovakia would be dissolved by the end of 1992, not least because Mečiar's strident nationalism had become increasingly irksome to his Czech counterpart, Václav Klaus, who had his own reasons for forcing the pace of a clean break with Slovakia.

Following the formal dissolution of Czechoslovakia on January 1, 1993, Mečiar's authoritarian populism and anti-Hungarian nationalism came to dominate and divide Slovak politics. Unlike Klaus in the Czech Republic, Mečiar sought to avoid radical economic reform in Slovakia. Externally, such policies and Mečiar's marked political thuggery toward his opponents gravely compromised Slovakia's claim to be a democratic state worthy of membership in the European Union (EU). Worst of all for local politics and the country's international standing, Mečiar engaged in a bitter, undignified public feud with President Michal Kovac, a former colleague and cofounder of the MDS.

Following splits with other factions in the divided MDS, Mečiar courted further political controversy by entering into a politically disreputable coalition government in November 1993. In March 1994 Kovac was instrumental in removing Mečiar from power, following a successful opposition no-confidence motion in the SNC. After new parliamentary elections later the same year, Mečiar regained the premiership for an unprecedented third term. Convinced that Kovac had betrayed him in 1994, Mečiar set about strengthening his own position and weakening that of his rival. Among other things, this involved a bitter struggle for control of the powerful Slovak Intelligence Service (SIS) in 1994–95. In April 1995

Mečiar had the SNC reduce the powers of the presidency, a move followed by an all-out government campaign to remove Kovac from office, including an alleged and highly bizarre SIS kidnapping of Kovac's son. Following this strange affair, Kovac instituted legal proceedings against Mečiar for alleged slander in 1996. Two years later, in March 1998, Mečiar won his long feud with Kovac when his rival's five-year presidential mandate expired. Having gotten rid of Kovac, Mečiar than left the office of president vacant, an unconstitutional move suggesting that the Slovak premier was intent on staying in power indefinitely, regardless of future election results in the Slovak Republic.

BIBLIOGRAPHY

Lesko, Marian. *Meciar a meciarizmus: politik bez skrupul, politika bez zabran.* Bratislava: VMV, 1996.

Meciar, Vladimir. *Slovensko, doveruj si.* Bratislava: R-Press, 1998.

Pistanek, Peter. *Skazky o Vladovi: pre malych a velkych.* Bratislava: Filmservice Slovakia, 1995.

Marko Milivojevic

SEE ALSO Kovac, Michal

Mendès-France, Pierre (1907–82)

French politician, and premier (June 1954–February 1955). Born in Paris on January 11, 1907, Pierre Mendès-France was the only son of a moderately prosperous Jewish clothing manufacturer. A brilliant student, he obtained a diploma from the École Libre des Sciences Politiques and the doctor of laws degree from the Faculty of Law. When he was admitted to the law at twenty-one, he was the youngest lawyer in France.

Elected to the Chamber of Deputies (lower house of parliament) as a Radical Socialist in 1932, Mendès-France was the youngest member of the National Assembly. He served as undersecretary for finance in Léon Blum's second government.

In September 1939 Mendès-France became a lieutenant in the French air force. Briefly imprisoned by the wartime Vichy government, he escaped and made his way to London to join the Free French under General Charles de Gaulle. While serving as a captain in a bomber squadron in November 1943, Charles de Gaulle appointed him minister of finance in the new Free French government at Algiers.

As minister for national economy in de Gaulle's provisional government at the end of the war, Mendès-France tried to convince de Gaulle to issue new bank notes and freeze accounts to halt inflation, end the black market, and provide data on profits from collaboration with the Germans. Accompanying this would be an austerity program. Many opposed the plan, including Finance Minister René Pleven. When de Gaulle rejected it, Mendès-France resigned.

Mendès-France later became executive director for France in the International Bank for Reconstruction and Development in Washington, D.C., then French administrator of the International Monetary Fund and French representative to the U.N. Economic and Social Council. Over the next two decades he often found himself in opposition to government policies. Playing a Cassandra-like role in the National Assembly, Mendès-France hammered on the dangers of drift (*immobilisme*) and failure to deal with the French Fourth Republic's many problems. He was critical of France's failure to grant independence to its protectorates of Morocco and Tunisia. He also criticized the war in Indochina, where he said that France had "nothing to win but everything to lose." In May 1954 the French were defeated at the Battle of Dien Bien Phu. The government of Joseph Laniel fell the next month, and Mendès-France became premier.

A nonconformist and independent, Mendès-France pursued the goal of reinvigorating and modernizing the French economy, but he was forced to spend most of his premiership concentrating on foreign affairs.

After Mendès-France assumed the premiership on June 18, he immediately electrified the National Assembly and the world with a proposal to end the war in Indochina within thirty days or resign as premier. The Geneva Conference to end the war was already in session but he won his gamble on the last day of the deadline. With the war terminated, Mendès-France set in motion events that led in 1956 to independence for Morocco and Tunisia. Also controversial was his failure to fight for the European Defense Community (EDC), which was defeated in the Chamber of Deputies while he was premier.

When he attempted to bring about domestic reform, Mendès-France ran into a wall of opposition. He attacked alcoholism and tried to modernize the economy by opening it to free competition. Reviled by many as a Jew, reformer, opponent of the EDC, and "the grave digger of the French Empire," Mendès-France was overthrown by the chamber on February 5, 1955. After his fall the Radical Party split and Mendès-Frances lost his post as party leader.

Although brief, the Mendès-Frances premiership was one of the notable episodes in the history of the Fourth Republic. The failure of the Mendès-France experiment disillusioned many young reformers and helped pave the way for the return to power of Charles de Gaulle in 1958.

Mendès-France remained in the Chamber of Deputies until defeated for reelection in 1958. He served briefly as deputy premier under Guy Mollet in 1956 but resigned over the government's policy in Algeria. He opposed de Gaulle's assumption of power in 1958 and opposed the presidential system of the Fifth Republic. Reelected in 1967, he was defeated the next year in the Gaullist landslide that followed the disturbances of May 1968. He died in Paris on October 18, 1982.

BIBLIOGRAPHY

Fauvet, Jacques. *La quatrième République.* Paris: Fayard, 1959.

Lacouture, Jean. *Pierre Mendès-France.* Tr. by George Holoch. New York: Holmes and Meier, 1984.

MacRae, Duncan, Jr. *Parliament, Parties, and Society in France, 1946–1958.* New York: St. Martin's Press, 1967.

Matthews, Ronald. *The Death of the Fourth Republic.* New York: Praeger, 1954.

Mendès-France, Pierre, and Gabriel Ardant. *Economics and Action.* New York: Columbia University Press, 1955.

Schoenbrun, David. *As France Goes.* New York: Harper and Row, 1957.

Werth, Alexander. *The Strange History of Mendès-France and the Great Struggle over French North Africa.* London: Barrie, 1957.

Spencer C. Tucker

Mercouri, Melina (1925–94)

Greek actress and political figure. Melina Mercouri was born in Athens on October 18, 1925, into a politically active family. Her father was a member of the Greek parliament and a cabinet minister. Her maternal grandfather was mayor of Athens for more than thirty years. After marrying a wealth Greek businessman at seventeen, she entered the Academy of the National Theater. She debuted three years later in Athens in a play by Alexis Solomos. The roles that brought her early notice were as Lavinia in Eugene O'Neill's *Mourning Becomes Electra* and as Blanche DuBois in Tennessee William's *A Streetcar Named Desire.* Her first film role was the title role in Michael Cacoyannis's *Stella* (1954). The role that won her international acclaim was as Ilya in *Never on Sunday* (1960), directed by her second husband, Jules Dassin, the French-American director. The performance merited her the Best Actress Award at the 1960 Cannes Film Festival.

Mercouri's political activism began in response to the military seizure of power in Greece in 1967. Her public opposition to the regime led the colonels to strip her of her Greek citizenship. After the collapse of the regime in 1974, she returned to Greece and joined the Pan-Hellenic Socialist Movement of Andreas Papandreou. Her first run for parliament was unsuccessful, but she was elected in 1977. In 1981 Mercouri was appointed minister of culture in the Socialist government of Papandreou. She promoted great subsidies for the arts but failed to gain the return to Greece of the British-held Elgin Marbles. She held the post until the defeat of the Socialists in 1989, but with their victory in 1993, she was reappointed. Mercouri died in New York on March 6, 1994.

BIBLIOGRAPHY

Mercouri, Melina. *I was Born Greek.* Garden City, N.Y.: Doubleday, 1971.

Bernard Cook

Meri, Lennart (1929–)

First president of Estonia (1992–) after it regained its independence from the Soviet Union in 1991. Lennart Meri was born in Tallinn on March 29, 1929. His father, Georg Meri, a diplomat and writer, had just been appointed ambassador to the United States when the USSR occupied Estonia. While his father was sent to a labor camp by Soviet authorities, Meri, his mother, and brother were exiled to Siberia.

The entire family was allowed to return to the Estonian Soviet Socialist Republic after the war and Meri studied history at the University of Tartu. He wrote books and produced documentary films on the Finno-Ugric people, of whom ethnic Estonians are a part. He and many other historians in the USSR dealt with the distant past rather than the politically sensitive contemporary era in order to be honest historians and still stay out of trouble with Soviet authorities, who did not tolerate critical thinking much less dissidence, but his work is credited with contributing significantly to the maintenance of Estonian identity during the period of Soviet domination. His most widely known book is *Hõbevalge* (*Silverwhite,* 1976), a panorama of Baltic prehistory.

In 1988 Meri established the Estonian Institute, a nongovernmental organization (NGO), to help Estonians study abroad and to establish contacts with the West. The institute's office abroad became proto-embassies, and at the end of August began to officially perform that the function of Estonian embassies.

Meri joined a number of other intellectuals to found the Popular Front and devoted an increasing amount of time to politics. He publicly denounced a Soviet phosphate mining project that threatened a quarter of Estonia with ecological disaster. He also compiled the study *1940 in Estonia: Documents and Materials* (1989), dealing with the Soviet occupation and forced annexation of Estonia, which was distributed in Russian to the Supreme Soviet of the USSR on December 24, 1989.

After the first free elections in Estonia in 1990, Meri was appointed foreign minister. He was directly involved in the reconstitution of the Baltic Council after a fifty-year hiatus. In April 1992 he was appointed ambassador to Finland. That fall he ran for president as the candidate of the Isamaa (Fatherland) nationalist coalition. He came in second, but since no candidate received 50 percent, the election was delegated to the Riigikogu (parliament). There Isamaa had a majority and Meri was elected on October 6, 1992. He was reelected in the popular election on September 20, 1996.

BIBLIOGRAPHY

Lagerspetz, Mikko. *Constructing Post-Communism: A Study in the Estonian Social Problems Discourse.* Annales Universitatis Turkuensis, B: 214. Humaniora, Turku: Turkun Yliopisto, 1996.

Lauristin, Marju, and Peeter Vihalemm, with Karl Erik Rosengren and Lennart Weibull, eds. *Return to the Western World. Cultural and Political Perspectives on the Estonian Post-Communist Transition.* Tarty Universityiet Press, 1997

Liivak, Kroot. *Lennart Meri: Personaalnimestik.* Tallinn: Eesti Rahvusraamatukogu, 1991.

Bernard Cook

Merleau-Ponty, Maurice (1908–61)

French philosopher. Born the son of a Catholic artillery officer in Rochefort-sur-Mer, Maurice Merleau-Ponty attended the prestigious École Normale Supérieure in Paris in 1926 with such intellectual luminaries as Jean-Paul Sartre, Simone de Beauvoir, and Raymond Aron. During the 1930s Merleau-Ponty was introduced to the phenomenology of Edmund Husserl and Martin Heidegger, and attended Alexandre Kojève's lectures on Hegel. An infantry officer during World War II, Merleau-Ponty was active in the Resistance during the German occupation of France. After the Liberation he taught at the University of Lyon, coedited *Les Temps modernes* with Sartre and de Beauvoir, and published his most famous work, *Phenomenology of Perception.* After serving for two years as professor of psychology and pedagogy at the Sorbonne, Merleau-Ponty became in 1952 the youngest man ever to hold the chair of philosophy at the Collège de France. He died unexpectedly of a coronary thrombosis in 1961, leaving behind several unpublished manuscripts that signaled a major revision of his earlier thought.

Though often eclipsed by his more famous colleague Sartre, Merleau-Ponty remains the most philosophically rigorous of the French existentialists. Merleau-Ponty's career is typically divided into two main periods connected by a brief political interlude. In *The Structure of Behavior* (1942) and *Phenomenology of Perception* (1945), the philosopher drew upon Husserlian phenomenology and Gestalt psychology to explore the prereflective experience of being-in-the-world. Here Merleau-Ponty stressed the primacy of perception through the "lived body," a synthetic union of the person with the world. A middle period was devoted largely to questions of history, Marxism, and politics, and culminated in his critique of Sartre's Communist sympathies in *The Adventures of the Dialectic* (1955). Finally, the late discovery of Saussurian linguistics and a renewed interest in psychoanalysis signaled a shift in Merleau-Ponty's thought away from the philosophical humanism that informed his previous works. Several unfinished and posthumously published manuscripts, especially *The Prose of the World, Signs,* and *The Visible and the Invisible,* attest to this change.

BIBLIOGRAPHY

Jay, Martin. *Downcast Eyes: The Denigration of Vision in Twentieth-Century French Thought.* Berkeley: University of California Press, 1993.

Merleau-Ponty, Maurice. *Humanism and Terror.* Boston: Beacon Press, 1969.

———. *Phenomenology of Perception.* London: Routledge, 1992.

Poster, Mark. *Existential Marxism in Postwar France.* Princeton, N.J.: Princeton University Press, 1975.

Schmidt, James. *Maurice Merleau-Ponty: Between Phenomenology and Structuralism.* New York: St. Martin's Press, 1985.

Christopher E. Forth

Mesić, Stipe (1934–)

Croatian politician, last president of the collective presidency of the Federal Republic of Yugoslavia (1991) and president of Croatia (2000–). A lawyer, Stipe Mesić was a member of the League of Communists of Yugoslavia (Communist Party) and a deputy in parliament. His participation in the Croatian nationalist movement in 1971 resulted in a brush with the law and his expulsion from the party. After his rehabilitation he resumed a leading role within Croatia. He was Croatia's representative to the collective presidency as Slobodan Milešović consolidated his power in Serbia. Milošević blocked the scheduled transfer of the federal presidency to Mesić in May 1991. On June 30, 1991, Mesić declared himself president and assumed the post. On October 3, 1991, during Mesić's absence, the Serbs seized control of the presidency. The Slovenes were already boycotting the presidency, and Brenko Kostić from Montenegro was elected with the vote of Montenegro and three votes cast by Serbia, which had ended the autonomous status of Kosovo and Vojvodina. As a result Bosnia and Macedonia withdrew from the presidency.

Mesić, a close associate of Franjo Tudjman, president of Croatia (1990–99), subsequently played an important role in Croatia, where he headed the Independent Democratic Party and was chair of the lower house of parliament. He was elected president of Croatia in February 2000.

BIBLIOGRAPHY

Mesic, Stipe. *Kako je srusena Jugoslavija.* Zagreb: Mislavpress, 1994.

———. *Kako smo srusili Jugoslaviju: politicki memoari posljednjeg predsjednika Predsjednistva SFRJ.* Zagreb: Globus International, 1992.

Catherine Lutard
(Tr. by B. Cook)

SEE ALSO Tudjman, Franjo

Meski, Aleksander (1939–)

Albanian prime minister (1992–97). Aleksander Meski, who received a degree in engineering from the University of Tirana, worked at the Institute for Cultural Monuments and the Institute of Archaeological Excavations as a restorer of medieval sites.

In the March 1992 elections the Democratic Party led by Sali Berisha won 62 percent of the vote. Ramiz Alia, threatened with removal by the new parliament, resigned as president on April 3. The People's Assembly (parliament) then elected Berisha president, and he appointed Meski Prime Minister to head a new government. Meski held the post until March 1997. In May 1996 new elections were held in which the Democratic Party emerged virtually without opposition. It was generally conceded, however, that its victory had been accomplished through intimidation and fraud. The Socialist Party refused to accept the results and boycotted parliament.

In 1997 growing anger seized the country as Albanians expressed their outrage and desperation at the failure of pyramid schemes that wiped out the meager savings of many Albanians and had, at the very least, been tolerated by the government. Berisha had cut back the size of the army after he and his party ousted the Communists in 1992. In Tirana order was maintained by the police supplemented by plainclothesmen and the numerous secret police. But anarchy spread in the countryside. Local police agents were as alienated as civilians, and they often abdicated the maintenance of order to the inadequate efforts of the riot police and secret police. To placate the public, Berisha ousted Meski at the beginning of March. This step still did not save the president's position.

On June 29, 1977, elections were held. The turnout was high. Though international observers said that they were not free or fair, they said that they were "adequate," and for Albania that was an achievement. Voters clearly repudiated Berisha and his misnamed "Democratic" Party. The new government, headed by Socialist Fatos Nano, was sworn in at the end of July and Berisha was forced to resign.

BIBLIOGRAPHY

Done, Kevin. "Albanian Leader Fights to Contain Anarchy." *Financial Times,* March 3, 1997.

Vickers, Miranda and James Pettifer. *Albania: From Anarchy to a Balkan Identity.* New York: New York University Press, 1997.

Vaughan-Whitehead, Daniel. *Albania in Crisis: The Predictable Fall of the Shining Star.* London: Edward Elgar Publishers, 1999.

Bernard Cook

SEE ALSO Berisha, Sali; Nano, Fatos

Miceli, Vito (1916–90)

Career military officer who became head of the Italian military intelligence service. He was later forced to resign from this post after being accused of heading a top secret parallel intelligence apparatus and illegally protecting neofascist extremists involved in coups or terrorist crimes.

Vito Miceli was born in Trapani in 1916. He enrolled in the army's famous Bersaglieri corps at age nineteen, served on Marshal Rodolfo Graziani's headquarters staff in Ethiopia, and was wounded, captured, then imprisoned in British India during World War II. After the war he temporarily became an activist in the neofascist Italian

Social Movement's (Movimento Sociale Italiano, MSI) conservative, pro-Atlantic wing and established the party's Trapani section in 1947. Later, he rose rapidly through army ranks, became commander of the elite Centauro and Ariete armored divisions, took courses at the Italian Higher War College and the NATO Defense College, served as military attaché in Paris and Bonn, and was appointed head of the Army Situation and Operations Intelligence Service (Servizio Informazioni Operazioni e Situazioni-Esercito, SIOS-Esercito) in 1969. Micelli became chief of the Defense Intelligence Service (Servizio Informazioni Difesa, SID) in October 1970. This last appointment coincided with his recruitment into former Italian Social Republic (Repubblica Sociale Italiano, RSI) militiaman Licio Gelli's Propaganda Due (P2) Masonic lodge, an offshoot of the parent Grand Orient lodge, which lay at the epicenter of one of postwar Italy's major scandals.

During this period Miceli began to be implicated in various anticonstitutional activities. While head of SIOS-Esercito he met several times with high-ranking members of Prince Junio Valerio of Borghese's National Front (Fronte Nazionale, FN) organization. His subordinate at SIOS-Esercito, Colonel Fernando Pastore Stocchi, was later appointed commander of the Gladio training base at Cape Alghero, Sardinia. After becoming chief of the SID, a promotion he owed in large part to Gelli's sub rosa backing of his candidacy, he learned of Borghese's projected December 1970 coup in advance. He did not try to impede it, and later protected FN militants being investigated by his own and other security agencies. These militants were subsequently accused by investigating magistrates of having participated in that illegal action. In 1972 Miceli was provided with $800,000 by President Richard Nixon's hand-picked appointee as U.S. ambassador to Italy, Graham Martin. Miceli then distributed this in part to unspecified right-wing groups, ostensibly to fund anti-Communist electoral propaganda campaigns. At that point Miceli had reached the apex of his power and influence.

But the intelligence chief's position worsened dramatically in the second half of 1974. It had become increasingly difficult for him to suppress evidence about the Borghese plotters and to deny that Guido Giannettini, a far-right secret service operative implicated in the neofascist bombing campaign that culminated in the December 1969 Piazza Fontana massacre in Milan, had continued to receive "cover" and financial subsidies from the SID. He was publicly embarrassed by Defense Minister Giulio Andreotti's revelations about the SID-Giannettini connection in July 1974. Three months later Miceli was accused by Padua judge Giovanni Tamburino of heading an illegal organization operating secretly within the bosom of the SID, a "parallel SID," which covertly directed the activities of a mixed civilian-military network, the Rosa dei Venti (Compass Rose), whose aim was to provoke an armed insurrection by means of terrorist provocations. His case was hastily transferred to the more politically docile Rome court, but Miceli's persistent unwillingness to reveal "state secrets" caused Roman magistrate Filippo Fiore to charge him with unlawfully "aiding and abetting" the perpetrators of the Borghese coup. Although Miceli received only a relatively short prison sentence, his intelligence career was destroyed since he had been made the fall guy by his service rivals and political superiors for overseeing various unconstitutional SID operations.

In 1976 he was elected to parliament as an MSI deputy, and thereafter exploited the parliamentary immunity he acquired by informing the judges presiding over the second FN trial about the existence of a parallel organization within the SID that operated outside the service's normal chain of command and engaged in activities other than intelligence gathering. This testimony lent credence to many of Tamburino's earlier charges, and in October 1990 Miceli claimed that these remarks referred to the top secret Gladio stay/behind network in Italy. Nevertheless, the precise nature of the relationship among Gladio, the parallel SID, the Rosa dei Venti, and other clandestine apparatuses remains unclear. In the late 1980s the former general was accused of still other criminal activities, including the withholding of information about Argo 16, a destroyed military cargo plane that had earlier been used to transport "gladiators" to and from their secret Sardinian base, as well as to surreptitiously transfer Palestinian terrorists captured in Ostia to a safe haven in Libya. In December 1990 Miceli died after unsuccessful heart surgery in a Roman clinic, taking his remaining secrets with him to the grave.

BIBLIOGRAPHY

Boatti, Giorgio. *Le spie imperfette: Da Custoza à Beirut.* Milan: Rizzoli, 1987.

Calderoni, Pietro, ed. *Servizi segreti: Tutte le deviazioni.* Naples: Tullio Pironti, 1986.

De Lutiis, Giuseppe. *Storia dei servizi segreti in Italia.* Rome: Rinniti, 1984.

Flamini, Gianni. *Il partito del golpe: Le strategie del terrore e della tensione dal primo centrosinistra organico al sequestro Moro.* 4 Vols. in 6 parts. Ferrara: Bovolenta, 1981–86.

Gatti, Claudio. *Rimanga tra noi: L'America, l'Italia, la "questione comunista": I segreti di 50 anni di storia.* Milan: Leonardo, 1991.

Ilari, Virgilio. *Le Forze armate tra politica e potere. 1943–1976.* Florence: Vallecchi, 1979.

Viviani, Ambrogio. *Servizi segreti italiani, 1815–1985.* Rome: Adnkronos, 1985.

Willan, Philip. *Puppetmasters: The Political Use of Terrorism in Italy.* London: Constable, 1991.

Jeffrey M. Bale

SEE ALSO Gladio

Michael (1921–)

Romanian monarch who reigned from 1927 to 1930 and from 1940 to 1947, when he was forced by the ruling Communist Party to abdicate and go into exile.

Born in Sinaia, Romania, in 1921, Michael (Mihai) was a member of the Hohenzollern-Sigmaringen dynasty, which had ruled Romania since 1866. In July 1927 he assumed the throne at the age of six, under a regency, on the death of his grandfather, King Ferdinand. Michael's father, Carol, had earlier renounced his claim to the throne after a series of sexual scandals. But in June 1930, Carol returned to Bucharest from self-imposed exile in Paris and, aided by local political parties, took the throne as Carol II. Upon Carol II's coronation Michael was given the title of *voievod* (duke) of Alba lulia, and remained largely in the shadow of his inept father. After World War II broke out in Europe, portions of Romania's territory were annexed by the Soviet Union and Hungary. Carol II abdicated in favor of the young Michael in September 1940. The new king's powers were almost immediately curtailed, however, by wartime authoritarian leader Ion Antonescu.

As the tide of war turned against Romania, which had allied itself with Nazi Germany, and a Soviet invasion was imminent, Michael led a peaceful coup against the authoritarian regime on August 23, 1944, arresting Antonescu and switching Romania's allegiance from the Axis to the Allies. After the war the outspoken and popular young king was a major irritant to Romanian Communists and their Soviet supporters. In November 1947, during a trip to London to attend the wedding of Britain's Princess Elizabeth, his second cousin, local Communists formulated plans for his removal. Shortly after Michael's return to Bucharest, Romania was declared a "people's republic" and Michael was forced to sign abdication papers on December 30, 1947. Although the king later refused to acknowledge the legitimacy of his abdication, he and the royal family fled the country. Michael traveled widely in Europe and America over the next several years, working mainly as a pilot. He finally settled in Versoix, Switzerland. In 1948 he married Princess Anne of Bourbon-Parma, with whom he had five daughters (Margareta, Elena, Irina, Sophie, and Maria) but no male heirs.

For nearly fifty years after his abdication Michael was not allowed to return to Romania. Even after the anti-Communist revolution of December 1989, the Romanian government remained wary of Michael, fearing that his continued popularity would lead to the reestablishment of the monarchy. Under the first several post-Communist governments Michael was allowed to return to Romania only once, for a brief visit during Orthodox Easter celebrations in April 1992. However, the victory of pro-democratic opposition parties in the November 1996 presidential and parliamentary elections, especially the strong showing by the National Christian Democratic Peasant Party with its pro-monarchy wing, allowed a warming of relations between the government and the exiled monarch. Michael became an unofficial ambassador for Romania, speaking out in international forums in favor of Romania's entry into the North Atlantic Treaty Organization (NATO) and the European Union (EU).

BIBLIOGRAPHY

Ciobanu, Mircea. *Convorbiri cu Mihai I al României.* Bucharest: Humanitas, 1991.

Hitchens, Keith. *Rumania, 1866–1947.* Oxford: Clarendon Press, 1994.

Ionescu, Ghita. *Communism in Romania, 1944–1962.* Oxford: Oxford University Press, 1964.

Waldeck, R. G. *Athene Palace, Bucharest.* New York: R.M. McBride, 1942.

Charles King

Michnik, Adam (1946–)

Historian, journalist, and Polish dissident. Under the Communist regime, Adam Michnik was frequently imprisoned for his political activities. He was the leader of the Warsaw student movement of 1968 and later an influential figure in opposition circles and in the Solidarity (Solidarność) labor union movement. His writings, especially on the role of the Left and the church in Poland and on a peaceful transition to democracy, were influential all over Eastern Europe. Since 1989 he has been director of the principal Polish newspaper, *Gazeta Wyborcza,* but is no longer directly involved in politics.

Michnik started his dissident activities at secondary school when he organized the Contradiction Seekers Club in 1962. He became nationally known, and a favorite butt of regime propaganda, for his role in the student movement in spring 1968. At that time he was imprisoned for two years for subversive activities. Between 1968 and 1986 he spent ten years in prison. In the 1970s he organized the Flying University, a clandestine circle of scholars, and in the second half of the 1970s he joined the Committee for Workers' Defense (KOR), founded in 1976 by Jacek Kuroń and other opposition figures. In 1980–81, while keeping some degree of autonomy as regards Lech Wałęsa's leadership, he nevertheless was involved in the Solidarity movement as an adviser on the Mazowsze Region Board. From 1982 to 1985 his writings from prison were particularly influential in Solidarity circles. At the same time, however, these writings already contained some criticism of the Union's "new radicals."

In 1989 he took part in the Round Table negotiations between representatives of the regime and of Solidarity concerning the conditions under which Solidarity would be re-legalized after its suppression in 1981, although neither his nor Kuroń's attendance was welcomed by the Communist Party. When Solidarity was legalized in April 1989, Michnik became director of the Solidarity newspaper, *Gazeta Wyborcza.* After the electoral victory of the Solidarity Civic Committees in June 1989, he advocated in a famous article—"Your president, our premier"—the compromise that allowed the creation of the first non-Communist government in the Soviet bloc.

During the presidential campaign of 1990 he strongly criticized Wałęsa's candidacy, and subsequently Solidarity withdrew its logo and its support from *Gazeta Wyborcza.* In the 1990s, Michnik did not involve himself in Poland's domestic political debate and acknowledged that the time for people like himself to engage in politics had come to an end. *Gazeta Wyborcza,* however, retained a broadly liberal orientation.

Ideologically, Michnik, who had always defined himself as part of the Left, shifted from a socialist (he had originally been a member of the Communist Party) to a liberal-democratic orientation. After 1981 he ceased to employ the concept of Right and Left, considering them as unsuitable for the central issues of totalitarianism and civil society.

Michnik's best-known book, *The Church and the Left* (1977), gave a strong impulse to the dialogue between the lay Left, to which he belonged, and the Catholic Church, which contributed to the rise of Solidarity three years later. This book, which contains a severe self-criticism, saw the ground for dialogue not in tactical compromise but in the defense of human values against totalitarianism. After fall of communism Michnik's view of the church became much more critical.

Although often viewed as an idealist, Michnik was aware of the risks of a vain moralism and valued the intellectual who could influence those in power without succumbing to the allurements of power. After 1989 his conception of the role of intellectuals and former dissidents became unwelcome to many of his former allies. As regards the transition from a communist society, Michnik argued against witch hunts and was therefore strenuously attacked by right-wing parties, especially after his meeting within 1991 General Jaruzelski, a meeting that appalled the right wing of Solidarity.

BIBLIOGRAPHY

Michael, John. "The Intellectual in Uncivil Society: Michnik, Poland, and Community." *Telos* 88 (1991): 141–54.

Michnik, Adam. *Letters from Prison and Other Essays.* Berkeley: University of California Press, 1986.

———. *La deuxième Révolution.* Paris: La Découverte, 1990.

———. *The Church and the Left.* Chicago: University of Chicago Press, 1993.

Guglielmo Meardi

SEE ALSO Kuroń, Jacek

Mifsud Bonnici, Carmelo (1933–)

Prime minister of Malta (1985–87). Carmelo Mifsud Bonnici was born in Cospicua on July 17, 1933. After studying at the University of Malta he received a law degree from the University College of London. He was appointed legal counsel to the General Workers' Union in 1969, and he became deputy leader of the Maltese Labour Movement in 1980. He was elected to parliament in 1982 and was appointed minister of labor and social services the same year. In 1983 he became senior deputy prime minister and minister of education. He was chosen leader of the Labor Party in 1984. When Dom Mintoff retired in December 1984, Mifsud Bonnici succeeded him as prime minister. Under Mifsud Bonnici a compromise was reached in the Labour Party's bitter conflict with the Catholic Church over the funding and independence of church schools. From 1985 to 1987, while prime minister, he continued to serve as minister of education. In May 1987 the Nationalist Party narrowly defeated Labor in a parliamentary election, and Mifsud Bonnici was replaced as prime minister by Nationalist Edward Fenech-Adami. But Mifsud Bonnici retained his seat in the Maltese parliament and his role as leader of the Labour Party for some years.

BIBLIOGRAPHY

Frendo, Henry. *Party Politics in a Fortress Colony: The Maltese Experience,* 2d ed. Valletta: Midsea, 1991.

Bernard Cook
Henry Frendo

SEE ALSO Mintoff, Dom

Mifsud Bonnici, Ugo (1932–)

President of Malta. Ugo Mifsud Bonnici was born in Cospicua on November 8, 1932. He received a law degree from the University of Malta in 1955. He was elected to parliament in 1966 as a member of the Nationalist Party. Mifsud Bonnici led the Nationalists during a bitter political struggle with the Labor Party, headed by Prime Minister Dom Mintoff. Mintoff's efforts to assert control over Catholic Church schools in 1983 and 1984 was a particularly divisive issue. Mifsud Bonnici became spokesman on educational issues for the Nationalist Party in 1977. A compromise was reached after Mintoff retired in December 1984 and the office of prime minister was assumed by Labor's Carmelo Mifsud Bonnici. When a slim victory in the May 1987 election enabled the Nationalists to end Labor's sixteen-year reign, Mifsud Bonnici assumed his first ministerial post as minister of education. From 1990 to 1992 he was minister of education and interior, and from 1992 to 1994 minister of education and human resources. He was elected president of Malta by the House of Representatives in April 1994.

BIBLIOGRAPHY

Frendo, Henry. *Party Politics in a Fortress Colony: The Maltese Experience,* 2d ed. Valletta: Midsea, 1991.

Bernard Cook

Miglio, Gianfranco (1918–)

Italian regionalist. Gianfranco Miglio, born in Como, Italy on January 11, 1918, professor of constitutional law at the University of Milan, was the chief ideologist of the Northern League, a political party that advocated autonomy for Lombardy. Miglio called for a complete reorganization of the Italian state into a federal republic modeled on Switzerland or Germany, with a presidential form of government. He was one of the first to popularize the term "Padania" for northern Italy. The archaic linguistic-cultural label has been transformed into a semi-mythical identifier for Northern Italy. Umberto Bossi, the leader of the Northern League, declared an independent Republic of Padania in 1996. Miglio suggested the division of Italy into three regions: *Padania,* the north; *Etruria,* the center; and *Meridione,* the south. Miglio was elected to the Italian Senate in 1996.

BIBLIOGRAPHY

Ferrari, Giorgio. *Gianfranco Miglio: Storia di un giacobino nordista.* Milan: Liber internazionale, 1993.

Miglio, Gianfranco. *Padania, Italia: Lo stato nazionale è soltanto in crisi o non è mai esistito?* Florence: Le lettere, 1997.

———. *Federalismo e secessione: un dialogo.* Milan: Mondadori, 1997.

———. *Io, Bossi e la Lega: Diario segreto dei miei quattro anni sul Carroccio.* Milan: Mondadori, 1994.

Daniele Conversi

SEE ALSO Bossi, Umberto

Mihajlović, Draža (1893–1946)

Leader of the Chetniks, the royalist Serbian forces, in Yugoslavia during World War II. Draža (Dragoljub) Mihajlović was a career officer trained in a French military academy. He was completely faithful to the Serbian monarchy. Mihajlović organized the Chetniks in the middle of May 1941, following the German invasion of Yugoslavia, and placed himself at the service of the royal government-in-exile in London. His objective was to fight the occupying German forces and reestablish the monarchical regime in Yugoslavia after the war. Promoted to general and named minister of war in January 1942, he lost the support of the Allies after the Tehran Conference in November 1943 because he preferred to fight the Communist Partisans organized by Tito, at times even joining the Germans in joint operations against the Partisans. He wanted to preserve his forces for a final contest with Tito after the Germans had been defeated. As a result, British liaison officers sent into Yugoslavia recommended aid to Tito, who was seriously engaging the Germans. Mihajlović was arrested by the Communist government in March 1945 as part of its effort to eliminate the opponents of Tito. Condemned to death by a summary proceeding, Mihajlović was shot on July 17, 1946, for high treason. The monarchists, had their regime survived the war, would have regarded Mihajlović as a defender of Yugoslavia (Serbia) and its monarchy.

BIBLIOGRAPHY

Dedijer, Vladimir. *The War Diaries of Vladimir Dedijer.* Ann Arbor: University of Michigan Press, 1990.

Deroc, Milan. *British Special Operations Explored: Yugoslavia in Turmoil 1941–1943 and the British Response.* New York: Columbia University Press, 1988.

Djilas, Milovan. *Wartime.* New York: Harcourt Brace Jovanovich, 1977.

Milazzo, Matteo J. *The Chetnik Movement and the Yugoslav Resistance.* Baltimore: Johns Hopkins University Press, 1975.

Roberts, Walter R. *Tito, Mihailovic and the Allies, 1941–1945.* New Brunswick, NJ: Rutgers University Press, 1973.

Catherine Lutard
(Tr. by B. Cook)

SEE ALSO Tito

Miklós, Béla (1890–1948)

Prime Minister of Hungary (1944–45). Béla Miklós graduated from the Military Academy in Budapest in 1910 and served on the General Staff during the First World War. He was appointed military attaché to Berlin in 1933 and was stationed in the German capital until 1936. After returning to Hungary, he served in various senior positions in the military, then in 1942 he was appointed senior aide-de-camp to Miklós Horthy, Hungarian Regent, and head of Horthy's military staff. He was appointed commander of the First Hungarian Army on July 1, 1944, during World War II. When the Hungarian Arrow Cross (pro-Nazi) Party took power in mid-October 1944, Miklós crossed the lines with his staff and surrendered to the Red Army. When the Soviets invaded the eastern half of Hungary, a provisional government was formed under the premiership of Miklós in Debrecen on December 22, 1944. He remained the head of government until the first postwar parliamentary election in November 1945, when the Independent Smallholders Party received a 57 percent majority and formed a new government.

Miklós was a soldier throughout his life, and his brief stint in the political life of postwar Hungary was necessitated by the collapse of the wartime regime and the absence of a legitimate new one. His caretaker government functioned under strong Soviet pressure amid the dislocation of the postwar months, and therefore its freedom of action was limited.

BIBLIOGRAPHY

Sinor, Denis. *History of Hungary.* Westport, Conn.: Greenwood Press, 1976.

Sugar, Peter F., Peter Hanak, and Tibor Frank, eds. *A History of Hungary.* Bloomington: Indiana University Press, 1994.

Tamás Magyarics

SEE ALSO Kovács, Béla

Mikołajczyk, Stanisław (1901–66)

Premier of the wartime Polish government-in-exile (1943–44) and leader of the Polish Peasant Party (1945–47). He gained political experience in the Sejm (parliament) during the second Polish Republic. Mikołajczyk was closely associated with Wincenty Witos, head of the Peasant Party and prime minister during the 1920s, and strongly opposed Józef Piłsudski, head of the Polish army who overthrew the government in 1926 and established an authoritarian regime. He was a proponent of the small farmers. From 1933 to 1939 he was deputy chair of the Executive Council of the Peasant Party. He also directed welfare activities in the rural areas of the Wielkopolska region.

In 1939 after the invasion and defeat of Poland by Nazi Germany, General Sikorski nominated Mikołajczyk to be deputy chair of the émigré National Council of the Polish government-in-exile that was first set up in Paris. Owing to Ignace Paderewski's illness, Mikołajczyk in fact directed the work of the council, which moved to the United Kingdom after France's defeat by Germany in 1940. Enjoying Sikorski's trust, Mikołajczyk became his deputy premier and minister of the interior in 1941. After Sikorski's death in July 1943, in an airplane crash, he became premier of the government-in-exile.

As premier Mikołajczyk tried to continue Sikorski's quest for good relations with the USSR. However, he strongly opposed Stalin and Churchill's suggestions of establishing new Polish borders on the Curzon line. Despite many attempts he was not able to prevent the cynical political game that took place behind his back at wartime the conferences of the Big Three at Tehran and Yalta. He did not agree to join the Polish Committee of National Liberation (the Lublin Committee), the government created under the auspices of Moscow in July 1944. Attacked by the opposition in his own government for attempts to reach agreement with Stalin and under constant pressure from Churchill to consent to the new borders, with the USSR, he offered his resignation in November 1944.

In 1945 he attempted again to establish democracy in Poland by consenting to an agreement with the Communists. In June 1945 Mikołajczyk became second deputy premier and minister of agriculture and rural reform in the Provisional Government of National Unity. The Polish Peasant Movement, founded in August 1945 by Mikołajczyk, soon became the largest party in the country, with about one million members. It had a real chance of victory in the upcoming parliamentary elections. The elections, however, were postponed by the Provisional Polish Government of National Unity, the core of which were the Communists from the Lublin Committee, until January 1947 and were then, like the June 1946 referendum on land reform, fraudulent. All the while leading activists of the Peasant Party repressed and persecuted. Faced with inevitable arrest and a political trial, Mikołajczyk decided to leave Poland secretly in October 1947. As a result, his Polish citizenship was revoked by the Communists and restored only posthumously in 1989.

After 1947 Mikołajczyk lived in the United States. Although there he was chairman of the Émigré Polish Peasant Movement and the International Peasant Union, his role among quarreling émigré elites was minimal.

BIBLIOGRAPHY

Mikołajczyk, Stanisław. *The Rape of Poland: Pattern of Soviet Aggression.* Westport, Conn.: Greenwood, 1948; reprint 1972.

Narkiewicz, Olga A. *The Green Flag: Polish Populist Politics (1867–1970).* London: Croom Helm, 1976.

Ryszard Sudziński

SEE ALSO Sikorski, Władysław; Wartime Conferences

Mikoyan, Anastas Ivanovich (1895–1978)

Soviet political leader from the 1920s to the 1970s. A member of the Communist Party's Politburo from 1926 to 1966, Anastas Mikoyan was the consummate survivor. He held numerous positions in the Soviet system, including chairman of the Presidium of the Supreme Soviet (president) and minister of foreign trade.

Mikoyan was born in Sanain, a village in Armenia, on November 25, 1895. As a young man he attended seminary in Armenia, but was never ordained a priest. Mikoyan joined the Bolsheviks in 1915 and participated in the revolutionary movement in Armenia in 1917. He fought in the civil war in the Caucasus from 1917 to 1920, barely escaping death. In 1919 he met with V. I. Lenin, the head of the Soviet government, to discuss the problems facing the Bolsheviks as they attempted to extend their control over the Caucasus. He also worked in the party administration under Serge Kirov, the Leningrad party boss, and Sergo Odzhonikidze during these early years.

In the struggle for power among Soviet leaders after Lenin died, Mikoyan sided with Josef Stalin's faction, and was invited to Moscow in 1926 to serve as commissar (minister) of trade. He also became a candidate member of the Politburo, the apex of Soviet power, remaining a member of this elite body until 1966. Highly successful in the area of foreign trade, he was given a variety of assignments in the domestic economy in the 1930s, and made a full member of the Politburo in 1935.

Mikoyan was one of the few party leaders who survived Stalin's purges of the 1930s. In 1938 he returned to the Ministry of Foreign Trade, became increasingly involved in foreign policy, and was recognized as a leading Soviet negotiator during World War II and afterward.

Mikoyan's political star faded in the last years of the Stalin era and he might have been removed had Stalin stayed in power longer. His career revived after Stalin died in 1953. He supported Nikita Khrushchev during the struggle for succession and was active in the de-Stalinization process. During the Khrushchev era Mikoyan held several high-level positions including chairman of the Presidium of the Supreme Soviet (parliament, 1964–65). He was an influential adviser to Khrushchev for most of this period, often serving as a negotiator in difficult assignments. Mikoyan is credited with persuading Cuban dictator Fidel Castro to give up the missiles that the USSR had placed on the island of Cuba before the Cuban Missile Crisis of 1962.

The durable Mikoyan continued as chairman of the Presidium in the early days of the Brezhnev era, which began in October 1964. He stepped down from the chairmanship in December 1965 and retired from the Politburo in 1966, after a tenure of forty years as a candidate and full member. Unlike most Soviet officials who preceded him, Mikoyan retired in a dignified way, not in disgrace, and lived quietly in retirement until 1978, working on his memoirs and sometimes meeting with small groups.

The most remarkable aspect of Mikoyan's career was its longevity, given the vicissitudes of Soviet politics. His ability to survive was often the subject of humor, such as the quip "no matter who will be first, Mikoyan will be second." His skill as a negotiator and his ability to work with whoever was in power seems to have accounted for his endurance and success.

BIBLIOGRAPHY

Leonard, Wolfgang. *The Kremlin since Stalin.* New York: Oxford University Press, 1962.

Linden, Carl. *Khrushchev and the Soviet Leadership, 1957–1964.* Baltimore: Johns Hopkins University Press, 1966.

Medvedev, Roy. *Khrushchev: A Biography.* New York: Anchor Books, 1984.

Tatu, Michel. *Power in the Kremlin: From Khrushchev to Kosygin.* New York: Viking, 1969.

Norma Noonan

SEE ALSO Cuban Missile Crisis

Milošević, Slobodan (1941–)

Serbian leader, elected president of Serbia in 1990. Slobodan Milošević was born in 1941 in Pozarevać, Yugoslavia. He studied economics at the University of Belgrade and joined the League of Communists of Yugoslavia (LCY) in 1959. He was head of the Belgrade Information Service (1966–69), director general of Tehnogas (1973–78), and president of the Bank of Belgrade (1978–83). In 1984 he became chairman of the Belgrade city committee of the LCY. In September 1987 he became president of the Serbian Central Committee of the LCY. He was a member of the collective presidency of Serbia in 1989–90, and was elected president of Serbia in 1990 and reelected in 1992.

Through a speech in April 1987 at Kosovo Polje, the site of the defeat of the Serbs by the Turks in 1387, that he made his entrée onto the political scene and made a name for himself. He profited from the ethnic tension between Serbs and Albanians in Kosovo in April 1987 to take up the defense of Serbs living there and seize the nationalist banner. He was above all attached to power and was quite pragmatic in his means of achieving and retaining it.

A populist manipulator, Milošević at that time took a strong position: to regain control of the "Serb territories" of Kosovo and Vojvodina amputated by the Constitution of 1974, which transformed them into autonomous provinces of the Yugoslav Federation, and to utilize force, if necessary, to resolve conflicts. Playing on nationalist sentiments about bringing together all the Serbs of disintegrating Yugoslavia into a single state, he built a potent cult of personality for himself. In 1989 he revoked the autonomy of both Kosovo and Vojvodina.

His popularity declined in March 1991 when he ordered the military to repress a demonstration in Belgrade. However, neither the repression of his authoritarian state nor the horrors of war he unleased in Croatia or Bosnia-Herzegovina prevented his reelection in December 1992.

Milošević, regarded by many as primarily responsible for the demise of the Yugoslav state and the ensuing fighting, used the emotional issue of Kosovo to fuel Serbian nationalism. In 1987 he had used nationalism as a force to challenge, oust, and replace his old friend and mentor, Ivan Stambolic, the president of Serbia. Following the overrunning and ethnic cleansing of Krajina by Croatia in 1995, the defeat of the Bosnian Serbs and the imposition of the Dayton Accords, and continuing economic problems and corruption in Serbia, Milošević faced serious opposition at the end of 1996 and the beginning of 1997. His allies were able to have laws passed by the pliable parliament making it illegal to criticize the president or other top officials. Milošević also signed an agreement of cooperation with Bosnian Serb leaders undermining the assertion of his opponents that he had abandoned the Serbs of Bosnia, as he had those of the Krajina. Though he was barred by the constitution from running for the Serbian presidency for a third time when his term expired at the end of 1997, he clung to power by running for president of Yugoslavia, which by then consisted only of Serbia and Montenegro. He then retained power by transforming that position into the dominant position within Serbia.

As president of Yugoslavia he pursued brutal program of repression in Kosovo aimed at destroying the Kosovo Liberation Army and its supporters. When NATO threatened air strikes in October 1998, Milošević at the last moment agreed to withdraw some of his forces and to allow observers from the OSCE to enter the province. When he resumed a policy of repression in early 1999, NATO, finally, backed up its threats with military action on March 24. Milošević used the NATO air campaign in Serbia and Kosovo as an opportunity to engage in brutal and full-scale ethnic cleansing in Kosovo. The initial result of the NATO campaign was to dramatically increase the support of the Serbian people for Milošević.

In view of the blatant atrocities that were carried out by the Serbian forces during the Kosovo conflict, the U.N. International War Crimes Tribunal for the Former Yugoslavia indicted Milošević and four other Serbian leaders for war crimes on May 27, 1999. The arrest warrant issued by the court's chief prosecutor, Louise Arbour, was issued for war crimes dating back to January. Milošević was accused of responsibility for atrocities carried our by Serb forces, including rape and murder, and for ordering the ethnic cleansing of the province. Indicted along with Milošević were Milan Milutinović, the Serbian president, Nikola Sainović, a deputy premier of Serbia and an advisor of Milošević, Vlajko Stojiljković, the Serbian minister of interior, and Dragoljub Ojdanić, head of the Yugoslav army.

BIBLIOGRAPHY

Doder, Dusko. *Milosevic: Portrait of a Tyrant.* New York: Free Press, 1999.

Glenny, Misha. *The Fall of Yugoslavia: The Third Balkan War,* 3d. rev. ed. New York: Penguin, 1996.

Thomas, Robert. *Serbia under Milosevic: Politics in the 1990s.* London: C. Hurst & Co., 1998.

Catherine Lutard
Bernard Cook

SEE ALSO Kosovo: Ethnic Cleansing and War; Marković, Mirjana

Miłosz, Czesław (1911–)

Nobel prize–winning writer, poet, essayist, translator, and professor. Czesław Miłosz was born on June 30, 1911, in Sateiniai (Russia, now Lithuania). In 1931 he cofounded a literary group, Zagary. In 1934 he graduated in law at Vilnius University then went to Paris. He worked in Polish radio in Vilnius and Warsaw from 1936 to 1939. During World War II he participated in the underground literary life of Warsaw. In 1945 he became cultural attaché of the Polish Embassy in Paris and in 1950 its secretary. In February 1950 Miłosz asked for political asylum in Paris and moved to the Literacki. There he published all his books written in the Polish language during his emigration. In 1951–60 he was involved in activities of the Congress for Cultural Freedom, an anti-Communist cultural organization. In 1960 he moved to the United States, where he became lecturer and later professor of Slavic literature at the University of California, Berkeley. In 1981 he was appointed to the Eliot Norton Chair at Harvard University.

Miłosz writes almost exclusively in Polish. In his prose and political writings he discusses issues that the intelligentsia faced under Stalinism; his essays also describe his reflections on literature and its influence on the intellectual development of his generation. His poetry and poetic prose, strongly associated with his birthplace and Polish culture, developed progressively over the years through innovative use of language, surrealism, and fascination with historicism. His work combined biography, religious metaphysics, and politics. Miłosz was greatly influenced by the Bible and the works of Eliot, Weil, Blake, Auden, and Whitman, whom he translated. He has also translated Polish poetry into English.

He was awarded the Nobel Prize in literature in 1980. That same year, after the birth of the Solidarity labor union, Miłosz visited Poland for the first time in thirty years. Between 1977 and 1989, all his books published in the West were also published by Polish underground publishing houses.

His many published books, mainly in Polish and English, include *The Captive Mind* (1953), *The Seizure of Power* (1953), *The Issa Valley* (1981), *Native Realm* (1968), *The History of Polish Literature* (1963), *Land of Ulro* (1984), *Selected Poems* (1980), *The Separate Notebooks* (1984), *Unattainable Earth* (1986), *Beginning with My Streets* (1991), *The Collected Poem 1931–1987* (1988), and *Provinces* (1991).

BIBLIOGRAPHY

Czarnecka, Ewa. *Podrozny swiata: rozmowy z Czesławem Miłoszem.* New York: Bicentennial, 1983.

Davie, Donald. *Czesław Miłosz and the Insufficiency of Lyric.* Knoxville: University of Tennessee Press, 1986.

Lapinski, Zdzisław. *Miedzy polityka a metafizyka: o poezji Czesława Miłosza.* London: Odnowa, 1981.

Volynska-Bogert, Rimma, and Wojciech Zalewski: *Czesław Miłosz: An International Bibliography 1930–1980.* Ann Arbor: University of Michigan Press, 1983.

Mirosław Supruniuk

Mindszenty, József (1892–75)

Roman Catholic primate of Hungary (1945–73). He was born József Pehm on March 29, 1892 in Csehimindszent, near Szombathely, Hungary, later adopted the Hungarian name Mindszenty. In 1973, Pope Paul VI summoned him to resign his title as primate of Hungary. When Mindszenty refused, the Pope declared the position vacant.

Mindszenty was ordained in 1915. After serving in various minor positions in the Catholic Church in Hungary, he was made a prelate in 1937, then the Bishop of Veszprém in 1944. During World War II he was imprisoned by the fascist Arrow Cross party installed by the German Nazis in November 1944 because of his support for the ousted authoritarian conservative Nicholas Horthy. With the defeat of the Nazis he was released from prison. He was made the archbishop of Esztergom by Pope Pius XII in 1945 and a cardinal in 1946. He vigorously opposed the Sovietization of Hungary after the Communists came to power and the confiscation of Catholic schools by the authorities in the late 1940s. He was arrested on December 26, 1948, and put on trial on trumped-up charges. He received a life sentence and was imprisoned. He was set free by revolutionaries on October

31, 1956, during the Hungarian Revolution but four days later, when the Soviets invaded Hungary, he fled to the U.S. legation in Budapest. He lived there until September 1971, when, after protracted talks among Hungary, the United States, and the Vatican, he was allowed to leave the country. He first went to Rome then settled in Austria, where he died in 1975. Mindszenty stood in the way of reconciliation between the Holy See and Hungary. As a result, Pope Paul VI called on him in 1973 to resign as primate. But Mindszenty refused to make concessions to the Communist authorities.

Mindszenty had high moral standards and, in contrast to a number of other clergy in Hungary, was not unwilling to compromise with the Communist regime. He relentlessly fought for the interests of the Catholic Church, but his rigid views at times brought him into conflict with the church as well.

BIBLIOGRAPHY

Kozi-Horvath, József. *Cardinal Mindszenty: Confessor and Martyr of our Time.* Chicester/Chulmleigh, England: Augustine, 1979.

Mindszenty, József. *Memoirs.* London: Weidenfeld and Nicholson, 1974.

Szeplaki, Joseph. *Bibliography of Cardinal Mindszenty.* Youngstown, Ohio: Catholic Hungarians' Sunday, 1977.

Tamás Magyarics

Mintoff, Dom (1916–)

Prime minister of Malta (1955–58, 1971–84). Dom (Dominic) Mintoff, son of a British navy cook and a Maltese mother, was born on August 6, 1916, in Cospicua. Mintoff, after a brief stint in a seminary, earned a degree in architecture and engineering at the University of Malta. Awarded a Rhodes scholarship, he furthered his studies at Oxford University. In England the contrast between British ideals and the experience of imperialism made a lasting impression on him. He worked in Great Britain during World War II from 1941 to 1943 and there met his English wife. He then returned to Malta, where he worked as an architect and engineer in the reconstruction of the war-devastated island.

Mintoff joined the Maltese Labor Party in 1944 and played a central role in its reorganization. In 1945, with the support of dock and shipyard workers, he was elected to the Council of Government, the consultative body under the British governor general, and the Executive Commission, which exercised executive authority under the governor general. Mintoff was elected to the Legislative Assembly, the new legislative body, and served as deputy leader of the Labor Party, deputy prime minister, and minister of works and reconstruction from 1947 to 1949. In 1949 he resigned his posts in a dispute with more moderate party leaders, led by Paul Boffa, who were unwilling to make the kinds of economic demands on Britain that Mintoff and his allies desired. The Labor government fell, but Mintoff gained control of the party and held it until 1984.

In 1955 Mintoff led the party to victory. From 1955 to 1958 he was prime minister and minister of finance. He had championed full integration of Malta into the United Kingdom, but when Britain balked he resigned on April 26, 1958, and demanded complete independence. A bitter struggle also erupted between Mintoff and the Catholic Church and the archbishop of Malta, Michael Gonzi over the future status of the island and the role of the church in its affairs. Mintoff regarded the church as a buttress of the status quo. In 1962 he was temporarily barred from the church's sacraments, and the church openly opposed Labor in the 1962 election, which Giorgio Borg Olivier's Nationalist Party won, regaining office after seven years. Despite his opposition to the politics of the church, Mintoff came to a modus vivendi with it in the late 1960s that improved his political prospects in overwhelmingly Catholic Malta.

When Malta gained independence in 1964, and became a member of the British Commonwealth, Mintoff boycotted the ceremony. In his opinion Malta was still being treated and behaved like a British colony. When in 1971, following the electoral victory of the Labor Party after nine years in opposition, Mintoff again became prime minister, he asserted full independence for Malta, proclaimed it a republic, and charted a nonaligned foreign policy. Mintoff, who simultaneously held the ministry of foreign and commonwealth affairs from 1971 to 1981, and ministry of the interior from 1976 to 1981 and from 1983 to 1984, forced British and NATO forces from the island in March 1979 and developed close relations with Libya until a dispute broke out between the two countries over the potentially petroleum rich sea bottoms between them. He resigned as prime minister in December 1984 after bitter fights with the Nationalist Party, which won the popular vote in 1981, and with the Catholic Church over the status of church schools. Mintoff regarded himself as the champion of the working class against Malta's traditional power structure. Mintoff was succeeded as prime minister and head of the Labor Party by Carmelo Mifsud Bonnici. After Mintoff's resignation, he became special adviser to the prime minister until the Labor Party was displaced by the Nationalists in the May 1987 election.

In 1992, Alfred Sant was elected leader of the Maltese Labour Party. With the victory of the MLP in the 1996 election, Sant became prime minister. Under the leadership of Sant the MLP has shifted away from its previous socialist and sometimes violently confrontationalist stance toward a more liberal economic position and severed its formal ties with the General Workers Union, the powerful Maltese labor union.

BIBLIOGRAPHY

Malta: Church, State, Labour: Documents recording Negotiations between the Vatican Authorities and the Labour Party, 1964–1965. Malta: Malta Labour Party, 1966.

Mangion, Patrick. *The End of an Island Fortress, Malta 1979.* Malta: P. Mangion, 1979.

Bernard Cook
Henry Frendo

Mitchell, George J. (1933–)

Chairman of the Multi-Party Talks in Northern Ireland from June 10, 1996 to April 10, 1998 that laid the groundwork for peace in Ireland. He studied law at Georgetown and was a trial lawyer from 1960 to 1962. When he was appointed attorney general for Maine in 1977, he had been involved in a private law practice for twelve years. In 1979 he was appointed U.S. district judge for Maine, which he remained until he was appointed to the Senate the following year. In 1989 he became Senate majority leader, a position he held until he left the Senate in 1996. Mitchell first became involved in Northern Ireland affairs when he was asked by President Bill Clinton in 1995 to become a special adviser on economic initiatives in Northern Ireland. He then took on the position as chairman of the International Commission on Disarmament in Northern Ireland, set up by the Irish and British governments. This led to his appointment as chairman of the Multi-Party Talks in June 1996 by the Irish and British governments. These talks, culminated in the Good Friday Agreement, which was overwhelmingly accepted on both sides of the Irish border in May 1998.

When in the fall of 1999 it appeared that the agreement would collapse, Mitchell returned to Ireland. He persuaded Sinn Fein, the political arm of the Irish Republican Army, that it must convince its militants to agree to begin decommissioning their weapons after the formation of an all party Northern Ireland government. He also convinced David Trimble, the leader of the Ulster Unionist Party, and the would-be-head of the government of Northern Ireland, that peace required the entry of Sinn Fein into the government.

BIBLIOGRAPHY

Gould, Alberta. *George Mitchell: In Search of Peace.* Farmington, Me.: Heritage Pub., 1996.

Mitchell, George John. *Making Peace.* New York: Random House, 1999.

Ricki Schoen

SEE ALSO Adams, Gerry; Hume, John; Trimble, David

Mitsotakis, Konstantinos (1918–)

Greek politician, leader of the New Democracy Party (ND) in (1987–97) and prime minister (1990–94). A graduate in law from the University of Athens in 1940, Konstantinos Mitsotakis first became active in Greek politics in the Liberal Party in 1946. After 1951 he held several ministerial posts in various governments, mainly in relation to finance and economic issues. In 1965, as minister of finance in the cabinet of the ruling Center Union (CU), he came into conflict with Premier George Papandreou. He went into exile in 1968 following the overthrow of the government by the military, after which he spent six years in Paris. After the restoration of democracy in Greece in 1974, he returned to high office in 1978, when he was appointed finance minister in a government led by veteran politician and ND leader Konstantinos Karamanlis. In 1987 Mitsotakis became party president and successfully stood for election as prime minister in 1990. Was closely allied with Karamanlis. Once in power in 1990 he worked with President Karamanlis to strengthen Greek democracy and to cooperate more closely, after the obstreperous Papandreou regime, with the European Community (EC) it had joined in 1981.

Unfortunately for Mitsotakis, he came to power just as neighboring Yugoslavia descended into civil war in 1991. Extensively criticized by his opponents for formally recognizing the dissolution of the former Yugoslav federation under EC pressure in 1991, he then had to face one of its outcomes—the emergence of an independent Republic of Macedonia (ROM) on Greece's northern border. Widely perceived in Greece as an irredentist entity that threatened the territorial integrity of Greece's own province of Macedonia, the ROM was eventually internationally recognized under the interim name Former Yugoslav Republic of Macedonia (FYROM) in 1993, mainly because of Greek insistence on such a designation in the European Union (EU), as the EC was called and at the United Nations. Yet after November 1993, Greece failed to prevent international recognition of its northern neighbor. This issue fatally split the ruling ND after 1993, when Foreign Minister Antonis Samaras resigned, charging Mitsotakis with incompetence on the Macedonian issue. Greek policy on this problem gravely damaged Greece's standing in the EU during the 1990s, thereby aborting Mitsotakis's hopes of closer relations with Europe's premier grouping after years of difficulties with its members under the Pan-Hellenic Socialist Movement (PASOK) governments of the 1980s. The Macedonian problem also overshadowed all domestic issues. Weakened by constant internal bickering and alleged widespread corruption under its rule, including a major banking scandal on Crete, Mitsotakis's ND Party was defeated by a newly resurgent PASOK in 1994. Later replaced as ND leader by Karamanlis's son Konstantinos "Koslas" Karamanlis, in 1997, Mitsotakis retired from public life, returning to his native Crete.

BIBLIOGRAPHY

Kazakos, Panos, and P. C. Ioakimidis, eds. *Greece and EC Membership Evaluated.* New York: St. Martin's Press, 1994.

Marko Milivojevic

SEE ALSO Karamanlis, Konstantinos

Mittag, Günter (1926–94)

Director of the East German economy (1962–73, 1973–89). Günter Mittag, son of an agricultural laborer, was born near Stettin in 1926. In 1945 he joined the Communist Party, which was renamed the Socialist Unity Party (SED) in 1946, when it absorbed the Social Democratic Party of the Russian zone of occupied Germany. Mittag carved out a career during the late 1940s and early 1950s as an official with the East German railroads and as a full-time labor union functionary. He was appointed candidate member of the SED Central Committee in 1958, then a full member in 1962. He entered the Politburo, the top executive committee of the party in 1962 and achieved full membership status three years later. The main body through which he exercised his influence over economic policy making was that of central committee secretary for economic affairs. This office gave him a high degree of control over many areas of the economy—public finance, planning, basic materials, construction, light industry, metallurgy and machine building. Along with Erich Apel, the chairman of the State Planning Commission, he was one of the leading proponents of the German Democratic Republic's (GDR) modest economic reform program, launched in 1963 as the New Economic System of Planning and Management. Its termination and the ouster in 1971 of its progenitor, Walter Ulbricht, the general secretary of the SED and the GDR head of state led to Mittag's temporary political eclipse. He lost his position as secretary of the Central Committee and was made first deputy chairman of the Council of Ministers (or deputy prime minister). But Mittag's experience and skills proved to be urgently required as the GDR's economy began to flag in the later 1970s, and he was reappointed secretary of the Central Committee. In contrast to his reformist views in the 1960s, the politically ambitious Mittag pushed through a program of tight economic centralization characterized by the formation of large combines and a proliferation of central planning indicators, as well as an overly ambitious attempt to modernize the economy on the basis of new technologies. Though Mittag was regarded by many Western observers as an efficient technocrat, his reputation waned rapidly after 1989, when his dictatorial methods of running the economy and his centralizing zeal were widely regarded as a cause of the chronic condition of the economy. A close ally of Honecker, who relied heavily on Mittag's advice and experience, he shared his patron's political fate when Honecker was ousted as general secretary of the party and head of state in October 1989. Mittag lost his post and was ejected from the SED the following month. Imprisoned in December, Mittag was released because of ill health in summer of 1990.

BIBLIOGRAPHY

Janson, Carl-Heinz. *Totengraber der DDR: wie Günter Mittag den SED-Staat ruinierte.* Düsseldorf: Econ, 1991.

Mittag, Günter. *Um jeden Preis: Im Spannungsfeld zweier Systeme.* Berlin: Aufbau-Verlag, 1991.

Mike Dennis

Mitterrand, François (1916–96)

Socialist president of France (1981–95). François Mitterrand served or held office in the wartime Vichy regime, the provisional government after World War II, and the Fourth and Fifth Republics. He led the revival of the Socialist Party (PS) after 1971, and was an unsuccessful candidate for president in 1965 and 1974, before becoming the first Socialist to win that office in 1981. He was reelected in 1988.

Mitterrand was born in Jarnac (Charente) in October 1916. His large, devout Roman Catholic family had inherited wealth and lived comfortably. From a Catholic

François Mitterrand, president of France, speaking with journalists in April 1988. *Illustration © Reuters/CORBIS.*

secondary school Mitterrand went to the École Libre des Sciences Politiques in Paris, earning a law degree while living in a student house, run by the Catholic Marist religious order, and working for the Society of St. Vincent de Paul, a Catholic charitable organization. His conservative Catholic politics led him briefly into the League of National Volunteers, and his early writings include attacks on the appeasement of Hitler and attacks on ethnic minorities.

Conscripted in 1939 and promoted to sergeant, Mitterrand won the Croix de Guerre before being wounded and captured by the Germans during the fall of France in 1940. He succeeded in his third escape attempt from a POW camp, returned to France in December 1941, and found a job with the Vichy government in a commission aiding returning French POWs. Though he won the Francisque, Vichy's highest civilian decoration, for his work, Mitterrand later denied that he supported Henri Philipps Pétain, the head of State of the Collaborationist Vichy regime, and asserted that Vichy anti-Semitism, in particular, drove him into the Resistance in 1943. Under the nom de guerre "Morland," Mitterrand became the head of a Resistance unit of former POWs, and in that role traveled to Algiers and London for meetings with the Free French under General Charles de Gaulle. At that time he also met and married Danielle Gouze, daughter of Socialist schoolteachers from Burgundy.

Rewarded with a post in the provisional government's Ministry for POWs and Refugees, Mitterrand resigned to lead a federation of former prisoners and deportees. He won a seat from Nièvre in the second constituent assembly running as a member of the Socialist and Democratic Union of the Resistance (UDSR), a small centrist party. He held the seat until 1958 and then again from 1962 to 1981. He also served as mayor of the town of Château-Chinon (Nièvre).

In 1947 Mitterrand became the youngest cabinet member in a century as minister of veterans affairs in the government of Paul Ramadier. He served in eleven subsequent governments, including terms as minister of overseas territories (1950–51), interior (1954–55), and justice (1956–57). After 1953 he headed the UDSR. Despite some acts of principle, such as quitting the government of Joseph Laniel in 1953 to protest its colonial policy, Mitterrand's presence in successive coalition governments and parliamentary maneuvers in the National Assembly (parliament) earned him a reputation for opportunism and Machiavellian cunning. Periodic scandals dogged his career, including charges of leaking defense secrets in 1954 and a still-puzzling incident in 1959 that Mitterrand termed an assassination attempt but critics dubbed a publicity stunt.

His experiences in the Resistance and the provisional government left Mitterrand deeply distrustful of de Gaulle's political goals, and he opposed the dissolution of the Fourth Republic in 1958, a stance that cost him his assembly seat as de Gaulle organized the enduring Fifth Republic. A book he wrote in 1962 criticizing de Gaulle and the direct election of the president after 1962, *Le Coup d'état permanent,* consolidated his position as a leading opposition spokesman. Seeking to unite the anti-Gaullist Left for the December 1965 presidential contest, Mitterrand emerged as its leading candidate and also secured the support of the Communist Party (PCF) on the second ballot.

Although de Gaulle won with 55 percent of the vote, Mitterrand capitalized on his showing to organize a Federation of the Democratic and Socialist Left (FGDS) for the 1967 legislative elections. Socialists (SFIO or French Section of the Workers International as they were called until 1969 when the name was changed simply to the Socialist Party, PS), Radicals, and Mitterrand's newly organized Convention of Republican Institutions (CIR) agreed to choose a single first-round candidate in each constituency, and the Communists and Unified Socialists (PSU) consented to support one leftist candidate on the second ballot. The FGDS won 192 seats in 1967 and reduced the Gaullist majority to 6.

The outbreak of the 1968 student and worker protests, called the Events of May, caught Mitterrand by surprise. He joined the chorus of de Gaulle's critics and declared at a May press conference that he was ready to assume power if the president resigned, words that returned to haunt him when the FGDS disintegrated in the Gaullist legislative landslide in June, losing nearly a hundred seats.

Back in the political wilderness Mitterrand sat out the 1969 presidential contest.

Mitterrand turned to the recently reorganized Socialist Party, merging his CIR with it in 1971 and assuming its leadership, despite his lack of Socialist credentials. The PS and the Communists then negotiated an electoral common program in 1972, and the Left entered the 1973 elections with clear positions on a variety of issues, winning 46 percent of the vote. In Mitterrand's second campaign for the presidency in 1974 he lost to Valéry Giscard-d'Estaing by a single percentage point.

The Socialists' growing dominance of the Left led the PCF to abandon the common program in 1977 and denounce their former allies. The break enhanced Mitterrand's reputation with moderate voters. Attacking Giscard's administration, rising unemployment, and inflation, Mitterrand entered the 1981 presidential campaign with a professional media campaign, whose slogan, "calm force," suggested peaceful change, and 110 specific reform proposals. His victory on May 10 marked the end of twenty-three years of conservative control of the presidency. After naming Pierre Mauroy premier, Mitterrand called a legislative election. The PS won an absolute majority in the new assembly and PCF support was gained by the offer of four minor ministries.

In the next twelve months the Socialists nationalized nine major industrial and financial groups, cut the work week to thirty-nine hours, and extended paid vacations to five weeks. The minimum wage was raised; aid to retirees, single mothers, and the handicapped increased; and one hundred thousand public-sector jobs were created. A decentralization program strengthened regional governments. A Ministry of Women's Rights was created, abortion laws liberalized, and the death penalty abolished. Military spending increased with the creation of a rapid reaction force and modernization of France's nuclear deterrent. French nuclear testing continued.

Increased public spending and Mitterrand's refusal to devalue the franc produced a growing budget deficit and larger trade imbalance while inflation and joblessness rose. Forced to embrace devaluation and an austerity program, the government cut social spending and unemployment assistance after 1982, seeing its popularity plummet and the PCF ministers resign. Socialist losses in local and European Parliamentary elections, and massive protests against a 1984 effort to extend government control over Catholic schools, led Mitterrand to replace Mauroy with Laurent Fabius, who continued the austerity measures.

Foreign policy, which Mitterrand like de Gaulle regarded as a presidential prerogative, saw fewer innovations. France firmly supported European integration, and Mitterrand backed England in the 1982 Falklands War against Argentina and NATO in the Euromissile controversy with the USSR. Relations with the United States under President Ronald Reagan were generally cordial, and a state visit to Israel in 1981 was the first by a French president. Shortly before the 1986 legislative elections Mitterrand was embarrassed by reports that government agents had sabotaged a ship protesting France's Pacific nuclear tests, killing a crewman. Claiming he had not been fully informed, Mitterrand accepted the resignation of his defense minister.

The elections produced a Gaullist majority and Mitterrand named Jacques Chirac, the opposition leader, premier. This unprecedented experiment in "cohabitation," with a president and premier from opposing parties, proved surprisingly popular with French voters and enabled Mitterrand to burnish his image as an international statesman while intervening only selectively in domestic politics. His 1988 reelection campaign against Chirac, vaguely promising a "united France," produced a lopsided victory, 54 to 46 percent. The Socialists failed to win a clear legislative majority then suffered devastating losses in 1993, forcing another period of "cohabitation" with the Gaullists. With few new policies to pursue Mitterrand was criticized for being out of touch with ordinary people and isolated by his office.

Increasingly ill with prostate cancer, Mitterrand focused on diplomacy, the Maastricht treaty, the Channel Tunnel with Great Britain, support for the Gulf War and NATO intervention in Bosnia, and the Parisian monuments he had commissioned—the Bastille Opera, the Louvre reconstruction, the d'Orsay Museum, and the arch of La Défense. The end of his second term brought new controversies about his wartime record and public acknowledgment of a daughter by a longtime mistress. Leaving the presidency in May 1995, Mitterrand died the following January.

Mitterrand's great accomplishment was his revival of the non-Communist Left, which transformed de Gaulle's Fifth Republic into something resembling the Anglo-American two-party system. Though he spent fifty years in public service and wrote a dozen books, Mitterand personally remained an enigma. Politicians and scholars acknowledge his intelligence and ambition but agree on little else.

BIBLIOGRAPHY

Friend, Julius. *The Long Presidency: France in the Mitterrand Years.* Boulder, Colo. Westview Press, 1991.

Laughland, John. *The Death of Politics: France Under Mitterrand.* New York: Viking, 1994.

Mitterrand, François. *The Wheat and the Chaff.* New York: Seaver Books, 1982.
Péan, Pierre. *Une Jeunesse française: François Mitterrand 1934–1947.* Paris: Fayard, 1994.
Ross, George. *The Mitterrand Experiment: Continuity and Change in Modern France.* Oxford: Oxford University Press, 1987.

David Longfellow

SEE ALSO Balladur, Édouard; Bérégovoy, Pierre; Chirac, Jacques; Cresson, Édith; De Gaulle, Charles; Fabius, Laurent; Marchais, Georges; Mauroy, Pierre; Rocard, Michel

Mladenov, Peter Toshev (1936–)

Bulgarian politician, born August 22, 1936, in Toshevtzi. Peter Mladenov graduated from Suvorov School in Sofia and studied at the Moscow State Institute of International Relations. He was an active member of the Dimitrov Young Communist League (DKMS) from 1963 to 1966. He successively occupied the positions of secretary and first secretary of the Vidin District Committee of the DKMS. In 1964 he became a member of the Bulgarian Communist Party (BCP). In March 1966 he chaired the Department of International Relations of the Central Committee of the Dimitrov Young Communist League, and in November 1966 he was elected secretary of the Central Committee of the DKMS. From 1969 to 1971 Mladenov functioned as first secretary of the Vidin District Committee of the BCP. In 1971 he became Bulgaria's minister of foreign affairs, a position he held until the dramatic political changes of November 1989. Since the Tenth congress of the BCP in 1971, Mladenov had been a member of its Central Committee. In 1974 he became an alternate member, and in 1977 a full member, of the Politburo of the Central Committee. Successively he was elected a people's representative (MP) in the Sixth, Seventh, Eighth, and Ninth National Assembly (parliament).

Mladenov's political popularity rose but briefly on November 10, 1989, after he became the new general secretary of the Central Committee (until 1990) and president of the State Council (Council of Ministers), replacing Todor Zhivkov, who unexpectedly resigned. He remained Bulgaria's president until the first post-Communist general elections in July 1990. His former position as minister of foreign affairs was entrusted to Boiko Dimitrov, the son of Georgi Dimitrov, the founder of the Communist state in Bulgaria.

Mladenov's coming to power coincided with the general anti-Communist uproar that swept through Eastern Europe at the end of 1989. From the beginning he pledged to introduce thorough political and economic reforms and to handle extremely grave environmental issues that had led to the first anti-Communist mass demonstration in Sofia several weeks before. His proposal for a coalition government pending elections to the National Assembly, however, was rejected by the Democratic opposition—the Union of Democratic Forces (SDS) and the Bulgarian Agricultural People's Union (BZNS). As a result, an all-socialist (Bulgarian Socialist Party, the Communist Party) cabinet was formed in February 1990 headed by Andrei Loukanov, former minister of foreign economic relations in Zhivkov's government.

Mladenov was forced to resign on July 6, 1990, after an almost monthlong campaign of protests and strikes organized by students against his government. He was accused of having endorsed the use of tanks to crush a spontaneous but peaceful antigovernment demonstration in front of the National Assembly in December 1989. He was replaced as president by Zheluy Zhelev, chairman of the Union of Democratic Forces.

BIBLIOGRAPHY

Crampton, R. J. A. *A Concise History of Bulgaria.* Cambridge, U.K.: Cambridge University Press, 1997.

Svetla Baloutzova

SEE ALSO Zhivkov, Todor

Mladić, Ratko (1943–)

Military leader of the Srpska, the breakaway Serb Republic of Bosnia that was proclaimed on April 7, 1992, who masterminded the campaign resulting in its control of 70 percent of Bosnia in 1992–93. Ratko Mladić was born in eastern Herzegovina in 1943 in a mountainous area that has produced the most intractable nationalists who have emerged from the former Yugoslavia. His father, a Partisan fighter during World War II, was killed when Mladić was two. Mladić spent nearly thirty years in the Yugoslav army (JNA), where he was loyal to the Communist ethos and known for his organizing abilities. When Yugoslavia collapsed in 1991, Mladić was in the key position of chief of staff of the army corps based in Knin, the seat of the Serbian insurgency in Croatia. In April 1992 Mladić was promoted to general. In May, he was appointed military commander of the Bosnian Serbs at Serbian President Slobodan Milošević's special insistence. In previous months Serbia's leader had ensured that the bulk of Serbs from Bosnia serving in the JNA were stationed in Bosnia to ensure that its independence bid failed.

Mladić was the chief strategist in the military campaign by insurgent Serbs to capture all of Bosnia. Given that much of the warfare was targeted against unarmed civilians, he earned a reputation for brutality. Mladić sought to deter Western military intervention by threatening to take the war through a campaign of terrorism to London, Washington and Rome. In 1993–94 his forces shot down NATO planes over Bosnia and kidnapped hundreds of U.N. military personnel. He was instrumental in defeating the Owen-Vance peace plan in 1993 by convincing the Bosnian Serb parliament that it would result in unacceptable territorial losses. In 1994 relations with his political superior, Radovan Karadžić, deteriorated but he still retained close contact with, and autonomy from, President Milošević.

Mladić had already been the subject of an investigation for alleged war crimes by a commission headed by Judge Richard Goldstone when, in July 1995, he directed the slaughter of thousands of unarmed Bosnian men and boys after the fall of the Bosnian city of Srebrenica. The assault on the supposedly U.N. guaranteed safe haven and the subsequent slaughter led in August 1995 to massive aerial assaults by NATO on his military assets and the advantage shifted away from the Bosnian Serbs.

On November 9, 1966, Biljana Plavsić, who was elected president of the Republika Srpska in September 1996, dismissed Mladić, stating that she was also removing General Milan Gvero, Mladić's deputy, and General Manojlo Milovanović, his chief of staff. She said that international opposition to Mladić required his ouster. Mladić was indicted in July 1995 by the International Tribunal at the Hague for atrocities committed against civilians, including the execution of up to eight thousand unarmed Muslims after troops under his command captured the Srebrenica in July 1995. As of December 1999 Mladić is still at large. The NATO forces have, as of yet, been unwilling to provoke the Serbs of Bosnia by arresting the general.

BIBLIOGRAPHY

Glenny, Misha. *The Fall of Yugoslavia: The Third Balkan War,* 3d rev. ed. New York: Penguin Books, 1996.

Malcolm, Noel. *Bosnia: A Short History.* New York: New York University Press, 1994.

Tom Gallagher

SEE ALSO Karadžić, Radovan; Milošević, Slobodan; War Crimes Trial for the Former Yugoslavia

Mlynár, Zdeněk (1930–97)

Czech lawyer, politician, political scientist, writer, and etymologist. Zdeněk Mlynár was born Zedeněk Müller in Vysoke Myto, Czechoslovakia on June 6, 1930. In 1945 he changed his last name to Mlynár. He studied in Moscow at the law school of Lomonosov University between 1950 and 1955. After his graduation he held a position at the Institute of State and Law of the Czechoslovak Academy of Sciences in Prague until 1968. At the end of this period he was head of the institute's department for the general theory of state and law. In 1967 and 1968 he also headed the academy's interdisciplinary research team, which worked out a theoretical scheme for reform of the political system. He had joined the Communist Party in 1946, and in 1964 he was appointed secretary of its Central Committee. In 1968 he became a member and secretary of the Secretariat and later a member of the Presidium of the Central Committee.

Mlynár, one of the liberals in the Czechoslovak Communist Party under First Secretary Alexander Dubček, became a main supporter of the drive for "socialism with a human face" advocated by Dubček that came to be known as the Prague Spring. He was one of the principal authors of the Action Program of 1968, which outlined the aims of the reform movement. After the Soviet-led occupation of Czechoslovakia in August 1968, ended this reform movement, Mlynár returned to his lifelong hobby, etymology. In November 1968 he resigned from all his party positions and in 1970 was expelled from the party. Until January 1977 he worked as an etymologist in the National Museum in Prague. In 1977 he signed Charter 77, a manifesto accusing the Czechoslovak government of violating human rights, was dismissed from his job, and was placed under house arrest. In June 1977 he emigrated to Austria.

In his first years as an exile Mlynár worked as a writer and visiting professor at Austrian, German, British, and U.S. universities. He was active in human rights activities, such as the Helsinki Committee. Beginning in 1979 he headed first a political science project on the Prague Spring that published twenty-six manuscripts, and later a project on the "Crisis in the Soviet System," which published eighteen studies in German, English, and French. As a personal friend of Mikhail Gorbachev Mlynár received media prominence in the West after 1985, when Gorbachev became general secretary of the Communist Party of the USSR.

From 1989 until 1993 he was professor of political science at the University of Innsbruck, Austria. After 1990 he commuted regularly between Austria and Czechoslovakia. He started again to work for the Institute of State and Law at the Academy of Sciences. However, he was disappointed in his hope to restart his political career. For the new generation of Czechs he was a representative of the old guard. And for the numerous supporters of Communism he was a reminder of a past they wanted to forget. During his last years he was active in the Left Bloc, an organization situated ideologically between the Communist Party and the Social Democrats. Until his death on April 15, 1997, in Vienna, Mlynár promoted the idea of socialism with a human face.

Mlynár's book *Nightfrost* is perhaps the internationally best-known work concerning the events leading to the Prague Spring. It has been translated into eleven languages. In it Mlynár describes his own political odyssey with self-criticism as the story of a generation who put its hope in the Communist Party.

BIBLIOGRAPHY

Brus, Wlodzimierz. *"Normalization" Processes in Soviet-dominated Central Europe: Hungary, Czechoslovakia, Poland.* Cologne: Index, 1982.

Mlynár, Zdeněk. *Can Gorbachev Change the Soviet Union?* Boulder, Colo.: Westview, 1990.

———. *Československy pokus o reformu 1968* (*The Czechoslovak Attempt at Reform,* 1968). Cologne: Index, 1975.

———. *Krisen und Krisenbewaltigung im Sowjetblock* (*Crisis and Crisis Management in the Soviet Bloc*). Cologne: Bund, 1983.

———. *Mraz prichazi z Kremlu* (*Frost Comes from the Kremlin*). Cologne: Index, 1975.

———. *Proti srsti* (*Against the Trend*). Prague: Periskop, 1996.

Marta Marková

Mock, Alois (1934–)

Chairman of the Austrian's People's Party (ÖVP) (1979–89) and vice chancellor and minister of foreign affairs (1987–89). Born on June 10, 1934, in Euratsfeld, Alois Mock received a law degree from the University of Vienna. His first government position was as a member of Austria's mission to the Organization for Economic Cooperation and Development (OECD) from 1962 to 1966. In 1966 Mock was appointed private secretary to Chancellor Josef Klaus (1964–70), and in 1968 he was appointed education minister. In 1970 Mock was elected to parliament. As chairman of the ÖVP he served as leader of the opposition from 1979 to 1987.

Before the 1986 election the ÖVP attacked the economic policy of the Socialist Party (SPÖ). Mock, realized however, that the ÖVP would not win a majority in the 1986 parliamentary election. Hoping that his party would win a plurality of the vote, he agreed before the election to form a grand coalition with the SPÖ, but his hopes were misplaced. The SPÖ received the largest number of votes. From 1987 to 1989 Mock, instead of being chancellor in the grand coalition, served as vice chancellor and minister of foreign affairs in a government led by the SPÖ's Franz Vranitzky. In 1989 Mock resigned as chair of the ÖVP and as vice chancellor. He was succeeded in both these posts by Josef Riegler.

BIBLIOGRAPHY

Mock, Alois. *Standpunkte.* Graz: Styria-Verlag, 1982.

John Fink

Modrow, Hans (1928–)

Last Communist prime minister of the German Democratic Republic (GDR). Hans Modrow, born of working-class parents in the area of Pomerania along the Baltic Sea, served in the home guard in 1945 and was subsequently interned in a Soviet prisoner-of-war camp. After joining the Socialist Unity (Communist) Party (SED) in 1949, he climbed the career ladder typical of so many Communist functionaries via a post in the Free Democratic Youth (FDJ) and a period of training at the Komsomol College in Moscow in 1952–53.

Modrow entered the SED Central Committee in 1958, becoming a full member nine years later, and between 1971 and 1973 he headed its Propaganda Department. An efficient first secretary of the SED's Dresden Regional Organization from 1973 onwards, he became increasingly disenchanted during the 1980s, especially after Mikhail Gorbachev's advent to power, in the USSR with the rigidly inflexible policies of Erich Honecker and Günter Mittag, the director of the East German economy. To their intense annoyance he gave out discreet signals that he favored a more flexible system of rule. In fall 1989, reformist-minded Modrow entered into an open dialogue with the opposition Group of Twenty in Dresden.

Appointed chairman of the GDR Council of Ministers shortly after the fall of the Berlin Wall, Modrow earned much respect for his untiring efforts to stave off social and economic chaos in East Germany. However, he failed to achieve his main goal, the establishment of an independent GDR on the basis of a humane socialism in which a reformed SED would play a significant role. In February 1990, he reluctantly acknowledged that German reunification was unavoidable. Although he lost power after the Volkskammer (parliamentary) election in March 1990, he did obtain a seat in the first all-German Bundestag (lower house of Parliament) election in December 1990. He did not seek reelection in 1994 but remained in politics as honorary chairman of the Party of Democratic Socialism (PDS), the new name of the now-liberalized Communist Party. In May 1993, he was found guilty of vote rigging during the Dresden communal elections in May 1989, but the judge did not sentence him to prison.

BIBLIOGRAPHY

Jarausch, Konrad H. *The Rush to German Unity.* New York: Oxford University Press, 1994.

Modrow, Hans. *Aufbruch und Ende.* Hamburg: Konkret Literatur Verlag, 1991.

Mike Dennis

Moldavian Autonomous Soviet Socialist Republic

Small, autonomous republic that existed in western Ukraine, along the border between the Soviet Union and Romania, from 1924 to 1940. The MASSR was set up by the Soviet Union on October 12, 1924, as an attempt to increase Soviet influence across the Dniester River in the Romanian-controlled province of Bessarabia.

Bessarabia, formerly a Russian province, joined Romania at the end of the First World War, but throughout the 1920s and 1930s the Soviet leadership refused to recognize the incorporation of the region into Romania. Soviet propagandists in the MASSR called for the liberation of Bessarabia on the grounds that the region's majority population formed a distinct ethnic group—Moldovans—whose identity was being suppressed by the Romanian authorities. The Soviets portrayed the MASSR as the nucleus of an eventual Soviet Moldavian state.

On June 26, 1940, the Soviet Union forced Romania to cede Bessarabia. Six raions (administrative districts) from the MASSR were then combined with six counties in Bessarabia to form the new Moldavian Soviet Socialist Republic (MSSR), proclaimed on August 14, 1940. Part of the area of the former MASSR became the Transnistria region of the MSSR.

BIBLIOGRAPHY

Heitmann, Klaus. "Rumänische Spache und Literatur in Bessarabien und Transnistrien (die sogenannte moldauische Sprache und Literatur)." *Zeitschrift für romanische Philologie* 81 (1965):102–156.

King, Charles. "The Moldovan ASSR on the Eve of the War: Cultural Policy in 1930s Transnistria." *Romanian Civilization* 4, no. 3 (1995–96):25–52.

Charles King

SEE ALSO Bessarabia; Moldavian Soviet Socialist Republic

Moldavian Soviet Socialist Republic

Second-smallest of the fifteen constituent union republics of the Soviet Union, established on the border with Romania on August 14, 1940. Its name was changed to Republic of Moldova in 1990, and it declared independence from the Soviet Union under that name in 1991.

The Moldavian Soviet Socialist Republic (MSSR) was formed from portions of the Romanian province of Bessarabia, seized by the Soviet Union in June 1940, and portions of the former Moldavian Autonomous Soviet Socialist Republic (MASSR), which had been established inside Soviet Ukraine in 1924. The MSSR remained a source of tension between the Soviet Union and socialist Romania throughout the postwar period, especially after the rise to power of Romanian Communist Party General Secretary Nicolae Ceauşescu in 1965. A local national movement arose in the MSSR in the late 1980s, and the republic seceded from the Soviet Union on August 27, 1991.

During the Soviet period the MSSR was an important agricultural region. In 1990 it accounted for 16 percent of the total Soviet production of bottled wines, 12 percent of brandy, and more than 26 percent of tobacco, even though it accounted for only 0.2 percent of the total territory of the Soviet federation. Several important Soviet party leaders, including Leonid Brezhnev and Konstantin Chernenko, spent part of their careers working in the party and state structures of the MSSR.

BIBLIOGRAPHY

Hill, Ronald J. *Soviet Political Elites: The Case of Tiraspol.* New York: St. Martin's Press, 1997.

Livezeanu, Irina. "Urbanization in a Low Key and Linguistic Change in Soviet Moldavia." *Soviet Studies* 33, nos.: 3–4 (1981):327–51, 573–92.

Vartichan, K. *Moldavskaia Sovetskaia Sotsialisticheskaia Respublika.* Kishinev: Glavnaia Redaktsiia Moldavskoi Sovetskoi Entsiklopedii, 1979.

Charles King

SEE ALSO Grossu, Semion; Moldova, Republic of; Moldavian Autonomous Soviet Socialist Republic

Moldova

Region in southeastern Europe bounded by the Carpathian Mountains to the west, the Dniester River to the north and east, and the Danube River and the Black Sea to the south. The region stretches across present-day eastern Romania, southwestern Ukraine, and the Republic of Moldova. It is also known in English as Moldavia. An independent Principality of Moldavia arose in the mid–fourteenth century and reached its zenith under the powerful lords (*domnii*) Alexander the Good who reigned from 1400 to 1432, and Stephen the Great, who reigned from 1457 to 1504. Owing to the northward expansion of the Ottoman Empire, Moldavia had become by the middle of the sixteenth century a vassal state of the Porte. Moldavia remained an autonomous principality within the Ottoman Empire until 1812. Under the Treaty of Bucharest that year, which ended the Russo-Turkish war of 1806–12, Russian Tsar Alexander I annexed the eastern half of Moldavia, the region located between the Prut and Dniester Rivers known as Bessarabia. Bessarabia became an autonomous region and, later, a province of the Russian Empire. The western half of Moldavia remained under Turkish suzerainty until it merged in 1859 with the Principality of Wallachia to the southwest, forming the United Principalities. The United Principalities remained formally part of the Ottoman Empire until 1878, when they were recognized by the European Great Powers as the fully independent Kingdom of Romania.

Following the Russian Revolution of 1917, a local assembly in Bessarabia voted for union with Romania on April 9, 1918, and the historic Moldavia region was united inside an enlarged greater Romanian state. The Soviets, contended, however, that the union did not express the wishes of the Bessarabian people, and throughout the 1920s and 1930s, Soviet foreign policy focused on retaking Bessarabia from Romanian. In fact, Bessarabia was the only territorial acquisition of Romania after the First World War that was not secured through international treaty. The Molotov-Ribbentrop Pact, signed between Germany and the Soviet Union in August 1939, recognized Bessarabia as part of the Soviet sphere of interest, and on June 26, 1940, the Soviet leadership issued an ultimatum to the Romanian king, Carol II, demanding the cession of Bessarabia. Carol acquiesced and two days later Soviet troops crossed the Dniester into Bessarabia. The region was annexed by the Soviet Union and united with other territories on August 14, 1940, to form the Moldavian Soviet Socialist Republic.

BIBLIOGRAPHY

Cantemir, Dimitrie. *Descrierea Moldovei.* Kishinev: Editura Hyperion, 1992.

Dima, Nicholas. *From Moldavia to Moldova: The Soviet-Romanian Territorial Dispute.* Boulder, Colo.: East European Monographs, 1991.

Hitchins, Keith. *The Romanians, 1774–1866.* Oxford: Clarendon Press, 1996.

Kellogg, Frederick. *The Road to Romanian Independence.* West Lafayette, Ind.: Purdue University Press, 1995.

Nistor, Ion. *Istoria Basarabiei.* Bucharest: Humanitas, 1991.

Seton-Watson, R. W. *A History of the Romanians.* Cambridge: Cambridge University Press, 1934.

Charles King

SEE ALSO Bessarabia; Moldova, Republic of; Moldavian Autonomous Soviet Socialist Republic; Moldavian Soviet Socialist Republic

Moldova, Republic of

State located between Romania and Ukraine that declared its independence from the Soviet Union on August 27, 1991. The Republic of Moldova, generally known as Moldova or Moldavia, is the successor state to the former Moldavian Soviet Socialist Republic (MSSR), one of the fifteen constituent republics of the Soviet Union. Moldova covers an area of 13,012 square miles (33,700 sq km) and, according to the 1989 Soviet census, had a population of 4.3 million, of which 65 percent were ethnic Moldovans (Romanians), 14 percent Ukrainians, 13 percent Russians, 4 percent Gagauz (Orthodox Christian Turks), and 2 percent Bulgarians. The republic is bounded by the Prut River on the west, which forms the border with Romania, and by international boundaries with Ukraine on the north, east and south. Moldova is divided into forty counties and ten municipalities. Major cities include Kishinev (Romanian, Chisinau), the capital, population 665,000, Tirăspol, Bender, Rîbnita, Dubâsari, Bâlti, Soroca, and Ungheni. In 1995 an autonomous region, Gagauz Yeri, was created for the ethnic Gagauz in southern Moldova.

Moldova is divided into two major regions by the Dniester River: the Bessarabia region on the western, or right, bank; and the Transnistria region on the eastern, or left, bank. From the end of the First World War until the establishment of the MSSR in 1940, Bessarabia belonged to Romania, while Transnistria existed within the Moldovan Autonomous Soviet Socialist Republic (MASSR), established inside Soviet Ukraine in 1924. Under the terms of the Molotov-Ribbentrop Pact with Nazi Germany, the Soviet Union presented an ultimatum to Romania in June 1940 demanding the cession of Bessarabia, which, the Soviet leadership contended, Romania had illegally taken from the Russian Empire at the close of the First World War. Soviet troops entered Bessarabia two days later. Bessarabia was carved up, with portions in the north and south given to Ukraine and the remainder

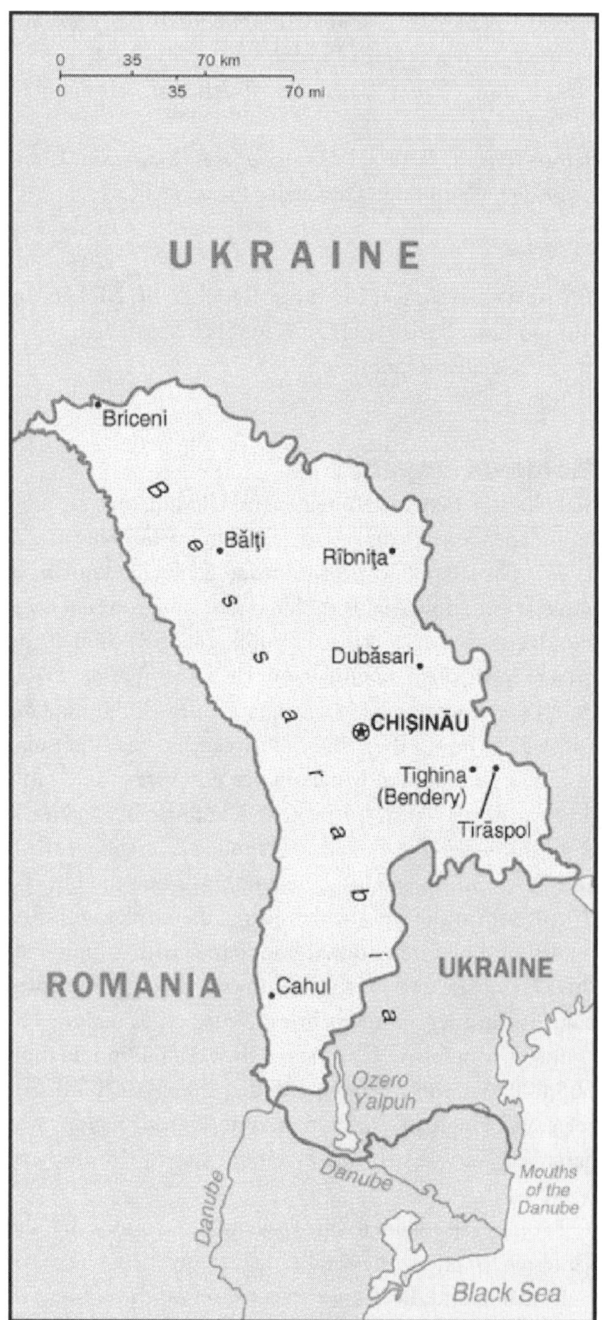

Republic of Moldova. *Illustration courtesy of Bernard Cook.*

joined with part of the MASSR to form the new MSSR. To justify the annexation, Soviet propagandists argued that the majority population in Bessarabia and Transnistria represented a distinct ethnic group, Moldovans, who, while related to Romanians, were nevertheless part of a separate national group. The Romanian government, on the other hand, held that Moldovans were as much a part of the Romanian nation as the inhabitants of any other Romanian region. To underscore the separateness between Romanians and Moldovans the Soviets mandated that the Moldovan language, indistinguishable in its spoken form from Romanian, be written in the Cyrillic alphabet and that the history of Soviet Moldova be rewritten to emphasize the links between Moldovan and Russian culture. Throughout the Soviet period the language issue and other thorny topics such as the famine brought about by the collectivization drive in the late 1940s and the forced deportation of Moldovan villagers to Central Asia were off limits to local researchers.

In the late 1980s, spurred on by Mikhail Gorbachev's reforms, Moldovan intellectuals began to argue for a revision of the official line on the language question. A growing chorus of intellectuals, centered in the local writer's union, called for a recognition that Moldovans and Romanians formed part of a single nation speaking the same language and for the return of written Moldovan to the Latin alphabet. In May 1989 several local groups joined forces to establish the Popular Front of Moldova to press their case for cultural and political reform. Although the Communist Party of Moldova (CPM) initially balked at the proposals, the local Supreme Soviet (parliament), headed by speaker Mircea Snegur, joined the ranks of the reformers. On August 31, 1989, the parliament passed new laws that made Moldovan the official language of the MSSR, mandated a transfer to the Latin alphabet, and implicitly recognized the language's unity with Romanian. Local ethnic minorities and conservative politicians remained opposed to the language reforms. The former feared that the declaration of Moldovan as the sole official language would lead to their forced "Romanianization," while the latter were wary that the language laws would be the first step toward Moldova's secession from the Soviet Union and reunification with Romania. The most conservative elites were located in the Transnistria region, where the local population was largely ethnic Ukrainian and Russian. Transnistrians staged demonstrations in opposition to the language laws and, on September 2, 1990, declared a separate Transnistrian Moldovan Republic. Ethnic Gagauz in southern Moldova had already declared a similar Gagauz Autonomous Republic on August 19, 1990.

Throughout 1990 and 1991 tensions remained high between the central authorities in Kishinev and in the Transnistrian and Gagauz republics, centered in the regional centers of Tirăspol and Comrat. The situation was heightened after Moldova's declaration of independence from the Soviet Union in August 1991. An attempt by Moldovan police forces and its nascent military to take control of Transnistria by force in early 1992 led to the outbreak of intense fighting. Intervention by the Russian

Fourteenth Army, stationed in Transnistria since the Soviet period and headed by Aleksandr Lebed, put a halt to the fighting in June and led to the signing of a cease-fire agreement in July 1992. A zone of separation was created between Moldovans and Transnistrians, and the groundwork was laid for talks on the withdrawal of the Fourteenth Army and the granting of special administrative status to Transnistria. Except for minor clashes in 1990 the situation with the Gagauz did not become significantly violent, and in 1995 the Moldovan government recognized Gagauz claims for local autonomy by creating a special administrative district in southern Moldova.

Much of the energy of Moldovan policymakers in the first years of independence was taken up by dealing with territorial separatism. But by the mid-1990s Moldova began to develop a more assertive foreign policy. Although a member of the Commonwealth of Independent States (CIS), Moldova refused to join in the major economic or military treaties concluded among CIS member. The Moldovan government maintained its neutrality, a position enshrined in the post-Soviet constitution adopted on July 29, 1994, although most politicians were generally enthusiastic about the eastward expansion of the North Atlantic Treaty Organization (NATO). Relations with Romania and Ukraine were particularly important, although questions of identity and historical boundaries were sometimes stumbling blocks to closer relations between Kishinev and Bucharest. Most Moldovans acknowledged that there was no difference between the Romanian and Moldovan languages, but many still insisted that the term "Moldovan" be retained in the constitution to describe the official language. Although many Western observers expected quick reunification of Romania and Moldova after the latter's declaration of independence from the Soviet Union, most Moldovans remained far less enthusiastic about this prospect.

BIBLIOGRAPHY

Crowther, William. "The Politics of Ethno-National Mobilization: Nationalism and Reform in Soviet Moldavia." *Russian Review* (April 1990): 183–202.

Dima, Nicholas. *From Moldavia to Moldova: The Soviet-Romanian Territorial Dispute.* Boulder, Colo.: East European Monographs, 1991.

Dyer, Donald L. *Studies in Moldovan: The History, Culture, Language and Contemporary Politics of the People of Moldova.* Boulder, Colo.: East European Monographs, 1996.

Fedor, Helen, ed. *Belarus and Moldova: Country Studies.* Washington, D.C.: Government Printing Office, 1995.

King, Charles. "Moldovan Identity and the Politics of Pan-Romanianism." *Slavic Review* 53, no. 2 (1994): 346–68.

———. *Post-Soviet Moldova: A Borderland in Transition.* London: Royal Institute of International Affairs, 1995.

Charles King

SEE ALSO Bessarabia; Gagauz; Lucinschi, Petru; Snegur, Mircea; Transnistria Moldovan Republic

Political Parties

Before the abolition of the leading role of the Communist Party of Moldova (CPM) in March 1990, the party system in the Republic of Moldova was the same as that in any other Soviet republic. The CPM, the local branch of the Communist Party of the Soviet Union (CPSU), was established at the time of the annexation of Bessarabia from Romania and held its first congress on February 6–8, 1941. Previously, a local Moldavian party organization had existed within the Moldavian Autonomous Soviet Socialist Republic (MASSR) as the local representative of the Communist Party (Soviet) of Ukraine.

As a potential Romanian irredenta, the MSSR was of particular concern to Soviet policymakers, and several important Soviet party leaders cut their teeth in the Moldavian party organization. Nikita Khrushchev, as a party functionary in Ukraine in the 1920s and later as Ukrainian party first secretary from 1938, had direct experience with the Moldavian regional party committee within the MASSR. Leonid Brezhnev served as first secretary of the CPM from 1950 to 1952. Konstantin Chernenko headed the CPM Central Committee propaganda section from 1948 to 1956 and was a deputy to the MSSR Supreme Soviet from 1955 to 1959.

After 1965, under Nicolae Ceauşescu, Romania became more assertive in its claims to Bessarabia, and the Soviet leadership therefore insisted on stability and security in the MSSR. Whereas the CPM had five first secretaries from 1940 to 1961, the leadership was changed only once, from 1961 to 1989. Ivan Ivanovich Bodiul, first secretary of the CPM from 1961 to 1980, was the last party leader in all the Soviet republics to be replaced by General Secretary Leonid Brezhnev, and Semion Kuzmich Grossu, the first secretary of the CPM from 1980 to 1989, was similarly the last to be replaced by General Secretary Mikhail Gorbachev.

The party system of the Republic of Moldova, the successor state to the MSSR, had its roots in a range of cultural and pro-reform organizations established in the late 1980s. On May 20, 1989, the most important of these groups banded together to form the Popular Front of

Moldova (PFM), a group that represented an informal movement in opposition to the most conservative elements within the CPM. Supported by key reformist members of the CPM and the speaker of the MSSR Supreme Soviet, Mircea Snegur, the PFM staged demonstrations in the Kishinev arguing for far-reaching cultural reforms such as the declaration of Moldovan as the state language and the transition from the Cyrillic to the Latin alphabet, as well as accelerated political and economic reform. On August 31, 1989, the PFM organized a mass demonstration to press its case, and on the same day the Supreme Soviet adopted laws acceding to the group's main demands regarding the Moldovan language. The adoption of the new language laws caused a reaction among ethnic minorities within the MSSR and among more politically conservative groups, who felt that the newfound assertiveness among local political elites would lead to the republic's secession from the Soviet Union. These groups were represented primarily by the Edinstvo (Unity) group, established in 1989 as part of the conservative, all-union Interdvizhenie movement.

After the declaration of independence from the Soviet Union in 1991, the issues of language and culture remained the primary cleavage lines within the Moldovan political elite. The Christian Democratic Popular Front (CDPF) was established in February 1992 as the successor to the PFM; the CDPF continued to call for a Moldovan/Romanian cultural renaissance and the eventual unification of Moldova with Romania. More moderate pro-Romanian groups, whose members had at one time also been members of the PFM, included the Congress of the Intelligentsia (CI, established in 1993) and the Party of Democratic Forces (the successor to the CI, 1996). Both radical and moderate pro-Romanian groups found their main support base among urban ethnic Moldovan/Romanian intellectuals and among certain sectors of the ethnic Moldovan/Romanian peasantry. The powerful Agrarian Democratic Party (ADP, 1991) emerged from the republic's agrarian elite, including former members of the CPM as well as heads of collective farms and other agricultural concerns. The Edinstvo movement yielded its own array of radical and moderate pro-Russian parties, including the Socialist Party (SP, 1992) and the Party of Communists (PC, 1994). Other, smaller groups included the Social Democratic Party, the Gagauz People's Party, and the National Liberal Party. A wave of new parties, each supporting particular presidential candidates, appeared on the eve of the presidential elections of 1996. More parties were formed and new electoral alliances concluded in advance of the 1998 parliamentary elections, only the second parliamentary ballot since Moldova's independence.

Under the 1993 electoral law and the 1994 constitution, elections to the unicameral Moldovan parliament were conducted on the basis of proportional representation, using a party list system with a 4 percent threshold. The parliamentary term is four years.

In the 1994 parliamentary elections the Agrarian Democratic Party led with 43 percent of the vote. The Socialist Party-Edinstvo received 22 percent, but dropped to 7 percent in the local elections the following year. The Bloc of Peasants and Intellectuals composed of the Congress of the Intelligentsia and other moderate pro-Romanian groups received 9 percent, but under the new name, the Alliance of Democratic Forces, increased its percentage to 19.67 percent in the subsequent local elections in the 1995 local elections. The Christian-Democratic Popular Front Bloc won 7.53 percent in the parliamentary election, the Social Democratic Party 3.66 percent. The Party of Communists, which did participate in the 1994 parliamentary election won 15.74 percent in the 1995 local elections.

BIBLIOGRAPHY

King, Charles. "Moldova," in Bogdan Szajkowski, ed. *Political Parties of Eastern Europe, Russia and the Successor States.* London: Longman, 1994, 293–311.

Charles King

SEE ALSO Grossu, Semion; Snegur, Mircea

Mollet, Guy (1905–75)

French Socialist, premier of the Fourth Republic (January 1956–May 1957). A doctrinaire Marxist politician, Guy Mollet was secretary-general of the Socialist Party (SFIO) officially the French Section of the Workers' International from 1946 to 1969, and he was active in the drafting of the constitutions of 1946 and 1958. He participated in several ministries of both the Fourth and Fifth Republics.

After graduating with a degree in English from the University of Lille, Mollet taught English at the college and then at the lycée of Arras. Having joined the SFIO in 1921, he was elected secretary-general of a Socialist teachers' union in 1939. During World War II wounded and imprisoned by the Germans from 1940 to 1941, Mollet escaped and returned to Arras to participate in the Resistance. After the war he was elected mayor of Arras as well as a representative to the Chamber of Deputies (lower house of parliament), and he worked on drafting committees in the two constituent assemblies of 1945 and 1946. During this period he opposed the conciliatory socialism of Léon Blum, and at the SFIO's congress of March 1946, the radical wing elected him secretary-general of the party, a post he held for twenty-three years. An effective organizer, he emphasized party discipline.

As the Cold War progressed Mollet became an outspoken anti-Communist increasingly willing to cooperate with bourgeois parties. After serving as minister of state in the cabinets of Léon Blum, René Pleven, and Henri Queuille, Mollet joined with Pierre Mendès-France to lead the left-center Republican Front in the election of 1956. As premier during 1956–57, he successfully advanced his social agenda of paid vacations and improved old-age pensions, and he also helped inaugurate the European Common Market, which France joined in 1957, improved Franco-German relations, and granted partial autonomy to France's sub-Saharan colonies. Mollet was criticized for the failure of his efforts at compromise in Algeria and for his commitment to the Anglo-French intervention with Israel in Egypt in November 1956. He resigned in May 1957 when parliament refused to raise taxes for social programs and to fight the Algerian rebellion. A supporter of Charles de Gaulle's return to power, Mollet was a member of de Gaulle's cabinet in 1958 and 1959, but after 1962, due to disagreement with de Gaulle's change in the constitution of the Fifth Republic to allow popular election of the president, Mollet broke with de Gaulle, and supported the combined left-wing opposition to de Gaulle. Although he remained a deputy until 1973, his influence waned when the SFIO ceased to be a viable force in the late 1960s.

An activist politician rather than a consistent theorist, Mollet often contradicted his moderate policies with revolutionary declarations, and when faced with a choice between Marxist ideals and patriotism, he usually gave priority to the latter.

BIBLIOGRAPHY

Codding, George, and William Safran. *Ideology and Politics: The Socialist Party of France.* Boulder, Colo.: Westview Press, 1979.

Laurent, Augustin, et al. *Temoignages Guy Mollet, 1905–1975.* Paris: Fondation Guy Mollet, 1977.

Mollet, Guy. *Bilan et perspective socialiste.* Paris: Plon, 1958.

Simmons, Harvey. *French Socialists in Search of a Role, 1956–1967.* Ithaca, N.Y.: Cornell University Press, 1970.

Touchard, Jean. *La Gauche en France depuis 1900.* Paris: Seuil, 1977.

Thomas T. Lewis

SEE ALSO Algerian War; Blum, Léon; Mendès-France, Pierre; Pleven, René; Suez Crisis

Molotov, Vyacheslav Mikhailovich (1890–1986)

Foreign minister of the Soviet Union, (1939–48, 1953–56). Known for negotiating the Nazi-Soviet Pact in 1939, Vyacheslav Molotov was considered second only to Stalin in power within the Soviet Union from 1931 to 1949. He earned the nickname "Stonebottom" for his shrewd diplomacy and adherence to hard-line Stalinist policies in dealing with the USSR's wartime Allies after 1945. The Soviet counter to the U.S. Marshall Plan, the Molotov Plan, a Soviet economic plan for Eastern Europe, bore his name, and Molotov was pivotal in developing the USSR's nuclear program. He played a central role in bringing on the Cold War and in the break with Yugoslavia in 1948. Molotov was a close supporter of Soviet dictator Josef Stalin and defended Stalinism until his death in 1986.

Loyal Molotov was removed from office by Stalin in 1949, and it is believed that Stalin marked him to be a victim of the "Jewish doctors' plot" purge initiated in 1952. Molotov returned to power upon Stalin's death in March 1953; he reclaimed the Foreign Office and the position of chairman of the Council of Ministers, which he had held from 1931 to 1941.

As part of the USSR's new collective leadership, Molotov played a vital role in foreign and domestic politics. Internally, he was moderate, supporting first Georgy Malenkov, Nikolav Bulganin, and Nikita Khrushchev against secret police chief Lovventy Beria in 1953 and then Khrushchev against Malenkov in 1955. In foreign policy, Molotov oversaw the early thaws in the Cold War. He is credited with contributing to the cease-fire in Korea in 1953 and the Geneva Agreement of 1954, which ended the war between France and the Viet Minh in Vietnam.

Because of statements he made during the debate over Yugoslavia that contradicted First Secretary Khrushchev's assertion that socialism already existed in the USSR, Molotov was removed as chairman of the Council of Ministers in 1955. He was also forced to publicly accept responsibility for the 1948 break and acknowledge other doctrinal "errors." In 1956, Molotov was dismissed as foreign minister for resisting Khrushchev's policy of "peaceful coexistence" with the West. He also opposed Khrushchev's internal reforms and was expelled from the

Politburo, the Communist Party's highest organ, as part of the "Anti-Party Group" in 1957.

Molotov continued to be active in Soviet foreign politics however. He served as ambassador to Mongolia from 1957 to 1960 and was then appointed as the Soviet representative to the International Atomic Energy Commission in Vienna, where he served until 1962.

In late 1961, Molotov was denounced as "in the Maoist camp" against the Soviet government. After recalling him in 1962, Khrushchev orchestrated Molotov's expulsion from the party. Though his writings were banned, Molotov continued to oppose reform and to petition for reinstatement in the party. The request was granted by General Secretary Konstantin Chernenko in 1984 and made retroactive to 1962, giving Molotov the longest period of unbroken membership in party history (1906–86). Molotov denied the Anti-Party charges and defended until his death in 1986 the policies he and Stalin enacted in the 1930s and 1940s.

BIBLIOGRAPHY

Bromage, Bernard. *Molotov: The Story of an Era.* London: Peter Owen, 1961.

Chuev, Feliks. *Molotov Remembers.* Paris: YMCA Press, 1980.

Timothy C. Dowling

SEE ALSO Khrushchev, Nikita; Stalin, Josef

Molyneaux, Sir James (1920–)

Ulster Unionist Party (UUP) leader (1979–95); MP for South Antrim (1970–83); MP for Lagan Valley (1983–). James Molyneaux was born in 1920. He has been heavily involved in Ulster Unionist politics since the 1970s. He was elected vice-president of the Ulster Unionist Council, Imperial grand master of the Orange Order and sovereign commonwealth grand master of the Royal Black Institution. He took over as leader of the UUP at a time when it was still trying to recover from the blow it received when Ian Paisley overwhelmingly won a seat for the European Parliament in 1979. When the Anglo-Irish Agreement in which the British and Irish governments agreed to work more closely concerning Northern Ireland was signed in 1985, it was seen as a major blow to Molyneaux and his party because he had always advocated against giving the Irish government any say in the affairs of Northern Ireland. The agreement helped to bring him closer to Paisley and his Democratic Unionist Party. They led the Ulster Says No campaign rejecting any voice in Northern Ireland by the Republic of Ireland together with much vigor. Molyneaux seemed to soften his stance somewhat in 1988 after the Irish prime minister Charles Haughey had offered to talk with the Unionists about the problems of Northern Ireland without any preconditions. Nonetheless, the idea of power sharing was anathema to him, and he argued that no agreement would be possible unless Ireland dropped its claim to the north. He steadfastly opposed to the political contacts and talks between John Hume, the leader of the moderate Catholic Social Democratic Labour Party, and Gerry Adams, the leader of Sinn Fein, the political arm of the militant Irish Republican Army, and said that they had destroyed any chance of holding interparty talks. But by 1994 he was advocating a Northern Ireland assembly, an Ulster representative body that would restore self-rule to the province, that would involve Dublin to a certain extent, i.e., without executive powers. He resigned as party leader in 1995 and was replaced by David Trimble.

BIBLIOGRAPHY

Arthur, Paul. *Northern Ireland since 1968,* 2d ed. Oxford: Blackwell Publishers, 1996.

Aughey, Arthur, and Duncan Morrow, eds. *Northern Ireland Politics.* London: Longman, 1996.

O'Malley, Padraig. *Northern Ireland, 1983–1996: For Every Step Forward.* Boston: John W. McCormack Institute of Public Affairs, 1996.

Ricki Schoen

SEE ALSO Hume, John; Paisley, Ian; Trimble, David

Monaco

Principality of 0.73 square miles (1.5 sq km) on France's Mediterranean coast. Monaco was ceded by Genoa to the Grimaldi family, one of the major Genoese families, in 1297. Absorbed by revolutionary France in 1793, Monaco was restored to the Grimaldi family by the Congress of Vienna in 1814. However, it was placed under the protection of the Kingdom of Sardinia. France resumed control of it in 1848 and in 1861 granted independence to a small segment of the earlier principality. Since 1865 the principality has been tied to France by an economic union. Monaco is associated with the European Union through its customs union with France. In a 1918 treaty with France, Monaco agreed that it would act in conformity with the military, political, and economic interests of its protector. Though France controls its foreign affairs, Monaco has observer status at the United Nations; embassies in Paris, Rome, Bern, and Brussels; and over one hundred consulates. A 1919 treaty stipulated that if

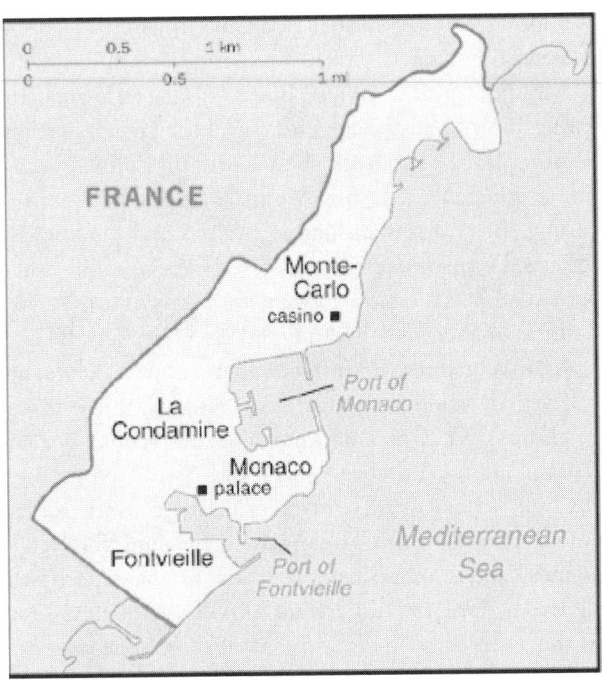

Monaco. *Illustration courtesy of Bernard Cook.*

the ruling Grimaldi died without a male heir, the principality would revert to France. The heir apparent is Albert (1958–).

Monaco was ruled as an absolute monarchy until Albert I granted a constitution in 1911. Louis II was prince from 1922 until 1949, but during World War II the Germans took control of Monaco from November 1942 until it was liberated in 1944 by the Americans. In 1949 the present prince, Ranier III (1923–), inherited his grandfather's position. Ranier married American actress Grace Kelly (1929–82) in 1956. He suspended the old constitution on January 28, 1958, and granted a new one on December 17, 1962, which increased the power of parliament, granted women the right to vote, and abolished the death penalty. Not until 1992 were female citizens allowed to pass on their nationality to their children. The prince appoints a minister of state, who must be a French citizen and is nominated by the French government, to run the government. The prince also appoints three state counselors to assist the minister. The National Council (legislature) consists of eighteen members elected for five-year terms by the 20 percent of Monaco's approximately twenty-nine thousand inhabitants who are citizens. The prince shares the right to initiate legislation. The judicial system is run by the French. Roman Catholicism is the official state religion. Primary schools are run by the church.

Monaco does not tax its citizens, known as Monégasques. Many companies have located their headquarters in Monaco to avoid taxation. Because of pressure from France, all French companies that conducted more than a quarter of their business outside Monaco became subject to French tax laws in 1963. In 1966 after a long struggle with Aristotle Onassis, the Greek shipping magnate, who controlled the holding company Société des Bains de Mer, which owned the Cassino Monte Carlo and most of the hotels, clubs, and beaches of the principality, a law gave the government of Monaco greater control over the company. In 1967, Onassis sold his shares to the government. Monaco's citizens are not allowed to gamble in the casino, which produces about 4 percent of the government's revenue. The principal source of revenue is tourism.

BIBLIOGRAPHY

Bregeon, Jean-Joel. *Les Grimaldi de Monaco.* Paris: Criterion, 1991.

Grinda, Georges. *Les Institutions de la principauté de Monaco: Notions sur l'organisation politique, administrative, économique et sociale,* 2d ed. Monaco: Conseil National, 1975.

Hudson, G. L. *Monaco.* Oxford: ABC-Clio, 1990.

Robert, Jean Baptiste. *Histoire de Monaco.* Paris: Presses Universitaires de France, 1973.

Tur, Jean Jacques L. *Les micro-États européens: Monaco, Saint-Marin, Liechtenstein.* Paris: La Documentation Française, 1975.

Bernard Cook

Monnet, Jean (1888–1979)

French diplomat, technocrat, and advocate of European cooperation. Born at Cognac on November 8, 1888, Jean Monnet, often referred to as Mister Europe (a title he sometimes shared with Belgium's Paul-Henri Spaak), was the guiding force behind the European integration.

Monnet's interest in international affairs began early; from the age of sixteen he traveled abroad to promote his family's brandy. Monnet ultimately became independently wealthy and hence free to pursue other interests. Without the First World War he might never have left the family business. But declared physically unfit for military service, Monnet served France as a member of the French Purchasing Commission in London. He was appalled that as late as 1916 the French and British allies were competing in shipping and commodities, and in the process driving up prices. His ideas led to the creation of the Allied Maritime Transport Committee, with broad powers. Thus an unknown brandy salesman was responsible for the first institutionalized supranational pooling of resources and played a key role in the First World War.

Monnet also played a central role in the League of Nations and became its deputy secretary-general. His actions in helping to rescue Austria from bankruptcy foreshadowed the operation of the International Monetary Fund and the World Bank. As war approached in the 1930s Monnet was convinced that the key to victory would be superiority in armaments. Concerned by his own country's lack of preparedness, Monnet headed a mission to secure arms from the United States. But his effort to purchase aircraft had not borne fruit before the defeat of France in June 1940. At that time Monnet proposed an Anglo-French Union to British Prime Minister Winston Churchill, who then proposed it to the French. The French government rejected the idea.

Monnet turned down an invitation to join Charles de Gaulle's London-based government-in-exile. His vision was always international and in his *Memoirs* Monnet reserved his sharpest barbs for those who, like de Gaulle, insisted on a more narrow, national approach. Monnet sought to appeal to reason rather than national emotion and pride.

Monnet believed that Allied victory depended on British survival of the German onslaught, and this meant arousing the productive capacity of the United States. He went to Washington, this time as a member of the British Purchasing Mission. Monnet had considerable influence on President Franklin Roosevelt, Harry Hopkins, Roosevelt's closest adviser during the war, and even Churchill. The phrase "arsenal of democracy" used by Roosevelt was Monnet's own, and the lend-lease program was in large part his conception. One long-term consequence was that Monnet's distrust of de Gaulle helped shape U.S. policy toward the general.

Some Frenchmen, particularly the Gaullists who later showed a degree of vindictiveness toward Monnet, resented that Monnet's vision led him to work for the Americans and British. They accused him of being an Anglo-Saxon agent.

With the return of peace in 1945, Monnet was placed in charge by de Gaulle of a government committee entrusted with rebuilding the shattered French economy. He worked out a five-year plan that incorporated the views of leaders of government, business, and labor for the management of national resources, and in 1947 he became director of the planning commission. The resultant Monnet Plan was a brilliant success and a model for central economic planning through the democratic process. Without it, U.S. Marshall Plan aid might have been wasted on France.

Monnet's greater services, however, were to Europe. In spring 1950 he approached his friend the French Foreign Minister Robert Schuman about a plan for European economic integration. It was Monnet's conviction that by ending their narrow economic rivalries and pooling resources, European states could have both economic prosperity and peace. Schuman wanted to overcome the basic political differences between France and Germany. If Germany were tied into an international economic fabric, he believed it would no longer be a military threat to its neighbors. What became known as the Schuman Plan resulted in the European Coal and Steel Community (ECSC), which opened markets in these commodities among France, West Germany, Italy, Belgium, the Netherlands, and Luxembourg. A treaty to that effect was signed in April 1951 and went into effect the next year. Monnet served as the first president of its nine-man executive, the High Authority. The ECSC was spectacularly successful and led directly to the European Common Market and the dream of a United States of Europe. In 1955 political expediency led French Premier Pierre Mendès-France to replace Monnet as president of the High Authority of the ECSC. Monnet saw his ideas triumph as he himself was jettisoned.

Fearing a loss of momentum after the failure of the European Defense Community in August 1954, Monnet formed an Action Committee for a United States of Europe. This group of approximately fifty political, business, and labor leaders renewed interest in the European unification movement. In part because of their efforts, foreign ministers of the six ECSC states agreed to work for the expansion of the original common market. This led to the Treaty of Rome in March 1957 that set up the European Economic Community, known as the Common Market, and also Euratom, a cooperative agreement for the peaceful development of atomic energy.

Monnet was always better judged and appreciated outside his own country. In the late 1950s and 1960s French Gaullists sought to marginalize him and his role. Although Monnet was for a long time a prophet almost without honor in France, his humanity, vision, selflessness, determination, and persistence were responsible for France's rapid economic recovery at the end of the Second World War and for the European Common Market. Monnet died at Montfort-l'Amaury on March 16, 1979.

BIBLIOGRAPHY

Brinkley, Douglas. *Jean Monnet: The Path to European Unity.* New York: St. Martin's Press, 1991.

Duchene, Francois. *Jean Monnet: The First Statesman of Interdependence.* New York: Norton, 1994.

Fontaine, Pascal. *Jean Monnet, a Grand Design for Europe.* Luxembourg: Office for Official Publications of the European Communities, 1988.

Giles, Frank. *The Locust Years: The Story of the Fourth French Republic, 1946–1958.* New York: Carroll & Graf, 1994.

Giordano, Renato. *La formazione dell'Europa comunitaria: lettere a Jean Monnet, 1955–1959.* Manduria, Italy: P. Lacaita Editore, 1997.

Monnet, Jean. *Memoirs.* Garden City, N.Y.: Doubleday, 1978.

Spencer C. Tucker

SEE ALSO Marshall Plan; Schuman Plan

Monnet Plan

After World War II, Jean Monnet, a France technocrat and diplomat, was appointed head of the French Commissariat du Plan by General Charles de Gaulle, and in 1947 he organized Le Plan (the Plan), popularly known as the Monnet Plan for modernizing or restructuring France. In 1950 he and Robert Schuman the French foreign minister drafted the Monnet-Schuman Declaration, proposing the twin principles of European integration and equal national status for Germany. These principles were to become the bases for a common market of six member countries in the European Coal and Steel Community (ECSC) and the European Defense Community. From 1952 to 1955 Monnet was president of the ECSC. After the war coal remained in short supply, especially during the grim winter of 1947. Planners assumed that the fuel shortage would continue for many years; few imagined that by the late 1950s there would be a glut of coal and steel in Western Europe. Ecological considerations played little part in the thinking of a generation that equated clear, smoke-free skies with wartime hunger. More important, community and capitalist planner alike continued to regard railroads, coal mines, and steel mills as the commanding heights of the economy. Railwaymen, miners, and steel workers were the working-class elite. Given these assumptions, nothing seemed more reasonable than to build European unity on a foundation of coal and steel.

The main initiative derived from France, from leaders such as Monnet, a brilliant promoter and public relations expert, as well as from technocrats, and from (MRP) the Popular Republican Movement, the French counterpart of Christian Democracy leaders such as Georges Bidault and Schuman, liberal Catholics schooled in the Resistance. After the end of World War II the French reverted to a punitive line toward Germany reminiscent of their policy after World War I. But relations between French and German steel magnates had always been friendly (as evidenced by the International Steel Cartel formed after World War I). Their ties survived wars and occupations. France was moreover less Germanophobe in 1945 than in 1918. By the end of World War II the two countries had shared common experiences of defeat, disgrace, foreign occupation, and striking diminution in national status. As American economic historian John Gillingham has shown, Schuman, and especially Bidault, played a decisive part in persuading French public opinion that traditional hostility toward *les boches* would no longer serve their interests. (The so-called Schuman plan might more aptly have been named the Bidault plan.)

The French came to understand that their country must henceforth cooperate with Germany, and that France could not expect existing controls on German production to continue indefinitely, especially at a time when the Korean War (1950–53) had generated increased demand for steel. French and German heavy industries were interdependent. West Germany, for instance, was by far the most important supplier of coke for French steel mills; France was Germany's largest market for coal exports. From the French standpoint, it was better to negotiate when the West German state was still in semitutelage and before the German Federal Republic was fully admitted into a Western military alliance. The French had everything to gain from an arrangement that would do away with discriminatory German railroad rates, assure access to German coal and steel, secure German goodwill, and thereby guarantee the success of French mobilization plans in case of war with the USSR.

In 1952 the governments of West Germany, France, Italy, and the Benelux countries ratified the treaty establishing the European Coal and Steel Community (ECSC, widely known as the Schuman plan). The treaty served as a customs union for coal, iron, and steel. The pact imposed common tariff rates on coal and steel products from other countries, although this was not put into operation until 1958. It provided for the elimination of measures likely to distort competition—for example, subsidies, double pricing, and discriminatory transport schedules. In addition, it gave to the High Authority, the ECSC's executive organ, the power to fix price limits as well as production and trade quotas during periods of manifest crisis. The High Authority had the right to be consulted on all major investment programs of enterprises within its purview, and it was empowered to issue loans and to contribute to investments it regarded as desirable. The ECSC thus established a single market for the coal, iron, and steel of the six member countries and eliminated, at least in theory, all barriers among the members to competitive trading and all forms of price discrimination, including those in transport. The ECSC derived revenue by levies on enterprises within its sphere of operation. In 1953 the High Authority imposed contributions on coal and steel production—the first European, as opposed to national, tax in history. These funds financed the ECSC's working expenses, built reserves, guaranteed its loans, and financed a readaptation fund providing grants to workers thrown out of employment by the conversion of their enterprises.

Politically the ECSC represented a compromise among Catholics, liberals, and socialists; among capital, labor, and the state. Paul-Henri Spaak, the Belgian foreign minister, chaired the Common Assembly; Massimo Pilotti, a distinguished Italian jurist, presided over the Court of Justice. Monnet took charge of the High Authority, whose remaining members included individuals as different as Léon Daum, French businessman and steel expert; Heinz Potthoff, former steel worker from West Germany; Paul Finet, Belgian former foundry worker who had served as first president of the International Confederation of Free Trade Unions; and Albert Coppé, a Fleming, who had been Belgium's minister of economic affairs. Different in temperament, background and political conviction, they nevertheless cooperated well under Monnet's guidance and quickly acquired the habit of seeing the community's problems as a whole.

The ECSC and European Defense Community had begun the program for integrating Western Europe economically and for rearming West Germany. When the French rejected the EDC, Monnet left public service but took part as a private citizen in negotiations to create the European Economic Community (EEC, or Common Market) and Euratom. In 1955 he started an Action Committee for the United States of Europe and served as its president until 1975. His entire professional life was dedicated to integrating Europe and expanding the Common Market to include Britain.

Monnet, thanks to his personal relationships with the leaders of the Atlantic Alliance, played an important role in the establishment of new relationships among the states of Western Europe and in their recovery from the war. The Monnet-Schuman Declaration guided the functions and development of the European Community, according equal status to all its members and creating transnational organizations such as the ECSC, EEC, Euratom, the European Court of Justice, and the European Parliament—a protean United States of Europe. In 1976 the heads of the nine Common Market governments appropriately named Monnet a "Citizen of Europe."

BIBLIOGRAPHY

Brinkley, Douglas. *Jean Monnet: The Path to European Unity.* New York: St. Martin's Press, 1991.

Duignan, Peter, and L. H. Gann. *The United States and the New Europe, 1945–1993.* Oxford: Basil Blackwell, 1994, p. 5.

Fontaine, Pascal. *Europe, a Fresh Start: the Schuman Declaration, 1950–90.* Luxembourg: Office for Official Publications of the European Communities, 1990.

———. *Jean Monnet, a Grand Design for Europe.* Luxembourg: Office for Official Publications of the European Communities, 1988.

Peter Duignan

SEE ALSO Schuman Plan

Monod, Jacques (1910–76)

French biologist, Nobel laureate, and philosopher. In 1956 Jacques Lucien Monod, with André Lwoff and François Jacob, received the Nobel Prize in medicine for work on the chemistry of protein synthesis in cells. Monod was fascinated by speculative questions about the nature of life and change. His 1970 *Chance and Necessity* advocated a philosophical system based on modern science and argued that the evolutionary process was entirely the result of chance.

Monod studied biology at the University of Paris. His Ph.D. thesis was a study of enzyme adaptation, the field of most of his later research. During World War II he was active in the French Resistance while he continued his research at the Pasteur Institute in Paris. In 1961 Monod and Jacob demonstrated the existence of a messenger ribonucleic acid, and they also showed that DNA is organized into working gene clusters, called operons, that allow cells to adapt to new conditions. In 1971 Monod became director of the Pasteur Institute. He died at Cannes on May 31, 1976.

BIBLIOGRAPHY

Chiari, Joseph. *The Necessity of Being.* New York: Gordian Press, 1973.

Monod, Jacques. *Chance and Necessity: An Essay on the Natural Philosophy of Modern Biology.* Tr. by Austryn Wainhouse. New York: Knopf, 1971.

Thomas T. Lewis

Montale, Eugenio (1896–1981)

Italian poet, editor, translator, and author; winner of the 1975 Nobel Prize in Literature. Eugenio Montale was born in Genoa on the Italian Riviera, which provided the striking physical environmental of his early poems. In 1915 he began studying opera performance, but turned from music to poetry with the death of his maestro in 1916. He served as a soldier from 1917 to 1919, then joined antifascist literary circles after the war. In 1925 Piero Gobetti published Montale's first book of poems, *Ossi di seppia* (*Cuttlefish Bones*), and Montale attached his name to Benedetto Croce's Manifesto of Anti-Fascist Intellectuals. In 1927 Montale moved from Genoa to Florence to work as a copywriter; in 1929 he became director of the Vieusseux Research Library but was dismissed in 1938 because he was not a Fascist Party member. Montale rejected the heroic, romantic aesthetic of Gabriele D'Annunzio; instead, his early poems explore the margins of the environmental and internal, social and personal, historic and timeless, veiled in coded allusions and understatement and therefore associated with hermeticism. Montale edited a literary journal, drawing attention to modernist Italo Svevo, and translated T. S. Eliot, Yeats, Shakespeare, and Melville. His understated non-fascist poetry *La casa dei doganieri e altri versi* (*The Custom Officer's House and Other Verses,* 1932) was also included in *Le occasioni* (*The Occasions,* 1939). In 1943 another antifascist collection was published in Switzerland, *Finisterre.* In 1946, after the war, he began work in Milan at the newspaper *Corriere della Sera* as theater critic and later music critic. His third major collection at age sixty, *La bufera e altro* (*The Storm and Other Things,* 1956) appeared to be his last work. Montale then surprised critics by publishing new poetry in *Satura: 1962–1970* (*Miscellany, 1971*); *Xenia* (*Guest Offerings,* 1966), in memory of his wife Drusilla Tanzi (Mosca), who died in 1963; *Diario del '71 e del '72* (*Diary, 1971, 1973*), and *Quaderno di quattro anni* (*Notebook of Four Years,* 1977). This new work was less lyrical, more satirical and humorous, often addressing ghosts from his past who appear in his dreams and illusions. Throughout his long career Montale emphasized the relationship of poetry with music and prose, the Crocean separation of art and politics, and the importance of quiet humanity.

BIBLIOGRAPHY

Becker, Jared. *Eugenio Montale.* Boston: Twayne Publishers, 1986.

Biasin, Gian-Paolo. *Montale, Debussy, and Modernism.* Princeton, N.J.: Princeton University, c1989.

Cary, Joseph. *Three Modern Italian Poets: Saba, Ungaretti, Montale,* 2d ed. Chicago: University of Chicago Press, 1993.

Mark I. Choate

Montenegro

Constituent republic with Serbia of the Federal Republic of Yugoslavia. When Yugoslavia fell apart in 1991 and 1992, Montenegro was the only republic to agree to maintain its link with the other remaining republic, Serbia. Montenegro's 5,333 square miles (13,812 sq km) are surrounded by twenty-five miles of Adriatic seacoast, site of the small ports of Bar (Antivari) and Ulcinj (Dulcigno), Croatia, Bosnia-Herzegovina, Serbia, and Albania. Its capital, Podgorica, was formerly Titograd. Montenegro's population in 1993 was 626,000. The majority consider themselves Montenegrin but are closely related to the Serbs. They speak Serbo-Croatian, use the Cyrillic alphabet, and are Orthodox. Albanians and Muslims constitute approximately 20 percent of the population. Some 66 percent of Montenegrins in 1992 identified with the concept of *srpstvo,* regarding themselves as inseparably linked ethnically, linguistically, and politically to Serbia. The other 33 percent identified with the concept of *crnogorstvo,* emphasizing that Montenegro had a separate identity from Serbia.

The name Montenegro (from *Crna Gora,* Black Mountain) refers to Mount Lovcen, the historic center of Montenegro, the center of the prolonged resistance of

Montenegro, shown in relation to its domineering neighbor, Serbia. *Illustration courtesy of Bernard Cook.*

Montenegrins against the Turks. Montenegro was absorbed by the Serbian Empire toward the end of the twelfth century but maintained its independence after the Turks defeated the Serbians at the battle of Kosovo in 1389. Montenegrins maintained their independence continually fighting Turks and Albanians. They allied themselves with Russia in 1711, and the independence of Montenegro was confirmed by the Congress of Berlin in 1878, but the king of Montenegro, Nicholas I, was ousted and the country was absorbed by Serbia in 1918.

During World War II, Italy occupied Montenegro in April 1941. The area was contested by the Yugoslav Partisans under Tito until it was liberated toward the end of 1944. Montenegrins constituted many of the most dedicated fighters and leaders of the Yugoslav resistance, and in 1946 Montenegro became one of the six constituent republics of Communist Yugoslavia.

As Yugoslavia disintegrated in 1991 Slobodan Milošević undermined the government of Montenegro, which opposed his policies. He helped Momir Bulatović, a lecturer in economics and chairman of the Communist Party organization at Titograd University, to gain dominance in Montenegro. Bulatović fomented thirty hours of street demonstrations on January 10 and 11, 1989, which led to the resignation of the government and the party leadership of the small republic. Over 120,000 people, angered by an annual inflation rate of 251 percent and 15 percent unemployment, filled the streets of Titograd. The root of the "street" coup, however, lay in anger over the suppression by the Montenegrin government of demonstrations in October 1988 organized by Milošević supporters to protest the alleged mistreatment of Serbs and Montenegrins in Kosovo by the Albanian minority. Bulatović, with the blessing of Milošević, moved into the vacuum to become head of the Montenegrin Communist Party and president of the republic. In March 1992 Montenegrins, led by Bulatovic, voted overwhelmingly in a referendum to remain with Serbia in what was left of the Yugoslav Federation.

Owing to the economic strain brought on by sanctions imposed by Western nations on Serbia, opinion in Montenegro turned against Serbia and Bulatović. Milo Djukanović, the prime minister of Montenegro and a former ally of Milošević, broke with Milošević and agitated for greater Montenegrin independence. Milošević responded by imposing border controls between Serbia and Montenegro, but this only further antagonized many Montenegrins. On October 5, 1997, Djukanović defeated Bulatović in a hard-fought presidential race. In the Montenegrin parliamentary election on May 31, 1998, the Montenegrin Election Commission, a coalition led by Djukanović, won 49.5 percent of the vote. This defeat of Bulatović's Socialist People's Party, which was financed and backed by Milošević, enabled Djukanović to assert Montenegro's opposition to integration with Serbia. Bulatović's Socialists won approximately thirty seats in the seventy-eight-seat parliament, compared with the forty assigned to Djukanović's supporters. The Liberal Alliance, which unambiguously called for secession, won 6 percent.

To influence the election and counter Djukanović, Milošević had his pliable federal parliament appoint Bulatović federal prime minister on May 20. The Montenegrin parliament asserted that it did not recognize the new federal prime minister and would no longer regard laws passed by the parliament in Belgrade as binding. Milošević, then, cut off pension payments and the transfer of federal funds to Montenegro and refused to allow Djukanović to exercise his constitutional role in the federal government. Nevertheless, late in 1998 Djukanović remained in office and asserted that the influence of the Serbian-dominated Yugoslav Federation had been limited to the common currency of Montenegro and Serbia and the army.

BIBLIOGRAPHY

Glenny, Misha. *The Fall of Yugoslavia: The Third Balkan War.* New York: Penguin, 1996.

Hedges, Chris. "Montenegro Chief's Victory Widens Rift with Belgrade." *New York Times,* June 2, 1998.

———. "It's Serb vs. Serb in Montenegro Vote." *New York Times,* May 28, 1998.

Jovanovich, William. *Serbdom.* Tucson, Ariz.: Black Mountain Publishers, 1998.

Judah, Tim. *The Serbs: History, Myth, and the Destruction of Yugoslavia.* New Haven, Conn.: Yale University Press, 1997.

Kamm, Henry. "The Yugoslav Republic That Roared." *New York Times,* January 22, 1989.

O'Connor, Mike. "The Next Trouble Spot in the Balkans: Montenegro." *New York Times,* November 2, 1998.

United States Congress. Commission on Security and Cooperation in Europe. *Presidential Elections in Montenegro.* Washington, DC: CSCE, 1998.

Bernard Cook

Economy

The collapse of Yugoslavia and the eruption of hostilities there in 1991–92 ended the existing trade links among the old federal republics. Montenegro depended on other republics of the federation for food, manufactured goods, and energy. Olives, citrus fruit, grapes, and rice are grown along the coast, which enjoys a Mediterranean climate, and sheep and goats are tended widely in the country. But overall, the Montenegrin agricultural sector is small. The factories of Montenegro depended on other republics for raw materials, parts, and markets. The breakup of the federation resulted in a serious decline in production in Montenegro and its sister republic, Serbia. Output dropped by half in 1992–93, but leveled off in 1994.

As in Serbia, the old Communist bureaucratic apparatus remained intact in Montenegro. Political and military considerations took precedence over economic rationality. Montenegro was also damaged economically by the U.N. imposition of international economic sanctions in 1993. The economic embargo was imposed upon the Federal Republic of Yugoslavia (Serbia and Montenegro) because of its support of the military effort of the Bosnian Serbs against the Bosnian government. It was hoped by the Montenegrians that the lifting of sanctions following Serbia's acceptance of the 1995 Dayton Peace Accords that ended the war in Bosnia would lead to a dramatic improvement of the economy. This did not occur. A new currency was adopted in June 1993 to counter hyperinflation. This move stabilized prices somewhat.

Montenegrin per capita GDP was estimated to be $1,000 in 1994. But the unemployment rate was estimated to be 40 percent.

Bernard Cook

Moravcik, Jozef (1945–)

Slovak prime minister. Jozef Moravcik was born on March 19, 1945, in Ocovej, Czechoslovakia. He studied law at Charles University in Prague and at Comenius University in Bratislava. He served as Czechoslovak foreign minister from July 2, to December 31, 1992. After the country split into the Czech Republic and Slovakia, he served as minister of foreign affairs of the Slovak Republic under Prime Minister Vladimír Mečiar from March 19, 1993, to February 23, 1994. Moravcik had been a member of the Movement for a Democratic Slovakia, but after leaving the government he formed a new party, Democratic Union of Slovakia. He led a coalition of five parties that agreed to form a government after Mečiar received a vote of no confidence on March 11, 1994. The five parties were the Party of the Democratic Left, Democratic Union of Slovakia, Alliance of Democrats of the Slovak Republic, National Democratic Party, and Christian Democratic Movement. On March 15, 1994, Moravcik became prime minister. His government lasted until Mečiar returned to power following the next election on September 30, 1994.

Bernard Cook

Moravia, Alberto (1907–91)

Pseudonym of Italy's best-known postwar author. Born Alberto Pincherle in Rome on November 28, 1907, to Jewish Italian parents, Alberto Moravia first gained critical attention for his novel *Gli indifferenti* (*The Time of Indifference,* 1929), published at his own expense. When the Germans occupied Rome in 1943, following the fall of Mussolini during World War II, Moravia was forced to go into hiding. After the war as his reputation as a writer developed, he quickly became an international celebrity. He published *La romana* (*The Woman of Rome,* 1947), *Racconti romani* (*Roman Tales,* 1954), *La ciociara* (*Two Women,* 1957), *La noia* (*The Empty Canvas,* 1960) and *L'attenzione* (*The Lie,* 1965). A more recent collection of short stories explores contemporary civilization from a feminist viewpoint. These have been collected into three volumes: *Il paradiso* (*Paradise,* 1970); *Un'altra vita* (*Lady Godiva,* 1973); and *Boh* (*Who Knows?* 1976).

Moravia's approach to fiction has been described by critics as resembling American realism rather than the traditional Italian style of verismo, the realist form used by many contemporary Italian writers. He abandoned third-person narrative for the more subjective first-person point of view. He also proposed the writing of "essay-novels," which would be constructed along ideological lines. After the war Moravia had been briefly drawn to Catholicism, but when some of his works were placed on the Roman Catholic Church's Index of prohibited books, he reverted to his earlier skepticism. Moravia also published several travel journals on such diverse areas as Russia, India, Africa, and China.

BIBLIOGRAPHY

Cottrell, Jane E. *Alberto Moravia.* New York: Ungar, 1974.

Heiney, Donald. *Three Italian Novelists.* Ann Arbor: University of Michigan Press, 1968.

Sanguineti, Edoardo. *Alberto Moravia.* Milan: Mursia, 1962.

William Roberts

Moro, Aldo (1916–78)

Prime minister of Italy (1964–68, 1974–76). Aldo Moro played an important role in the democratic reconstruction and political modernization of Italy after World War II. He was the leader of the Christian Democrats (DC) from 1959 to 1964 and president of the DC National Council from 1976 until he was kidnapped and executed by the Red Brigades (Brigate Rosse) on May 19, 1978.

Moro graduated in law from the University of Bari and taught criminal law and philosophy of law. From 1963 until his death he was professor of legal institutions and penal procedure at the faculty of political sciences at the University of Rome.

From the late thirties Moro was active in Catholic university circles and was president of the Italian Catholic University Federation (FUCI) from 1938 to 1942, when he was succeeded by Giulio Andreotti. Moro served as secretary of the Catholic University Movement in 1945 and 1946. He also became chief editor of the journal *Studium*, a position he retained until 1948. From these positions, Moro observed the evolution of the Catholic movement and helped define its role in postfascist Italy. He stressed the moral underpinnings of Catholic involvement in the political, social, and economic life of the country. Above all, he made a contribution to the definition of the functions and limits of the state.

Because of the role he played in the Catholic world, he was invited to be a DC parliamentary candidate. On June 2, 1946, he was elected a member of the Constituent Assembly from the constituency of Bari-Foggia. He was then elected to the committee charged with drafting the text for a new constitution. Moro believed the constitution should define individual and social freedoms and responsibilities and serve as a barrier to authoritarianism.

The constitution came into force on January 1, 1948, and the DC received more than 48 percent of the vote in the election of April 18. Moro was again victorious in the Bari-Foggia constituency as he would be until his death. Moro took part in the government of Alcide De Gasperi (May 1948–January 1950) as undersecretary of the Foreign Ministry. In 1953 Moro was elected president of the DC Parliamentary Group of the Chamber of Deputies. He became minister of justice in the government of Antonio Segni (January 1955–May 1957), then minister of education in the government of Adone Zoli (May 1957–June 1958) and that of Amintore Fanfani (July 1958–January 1959).

The idea of making overtures to the Italian Socialist Party (PSI) advanced by Fanfani led to a crisis among the major DC groups, as some felt that the "opening to the left" was premature. Fanfani was forced to resign as DC national secretary and on March 16, 1959, Moro was chosen to take his place.

At the DC national congress in Florence in October 1959, during which he was confirmed as party leader, Moro spoke of the need to widen the democratic basis of Italian political life. He thought that the DC should guarantee continuity with what had been achieved in the past and, at the same time, support the creation of decentralizing institutions such as the regions, foreseen in the constitution.

At the national congress in January 1962, Moro stressed the importance of Christian values, while reaffirming the importance of political parties as a guarantee of democratic life. Reelected party leader by a clear majority, Moro became prime minister in November 1963 of a center-left government.

On more than one occasion, Moro suggested outlines for a renewal of the Italian political system and for a national modernization process. But his agenda was undermined by disunity within the government and internal and external difficulties. Under Moro's leadership the nationalization of energy was realized; a process of reinvigorating the industrial and agricultural sectors was begun; and, above all, huge interventions were proposed to reestablish economic balance between the well-to-do north and the impoverished south. These interventions were not totally effective, owing to inflation and international currency speculation. The action in favor of the South was obstructed by the resistance of local interests and the corrupt practices of political parties. Only in 1970 were regions created.

After June 1968, first as minister of foreign affairs then once again as prime minister (November 1974–January 1976), Moro worked to make the European Economic Community (EEC) have a positive impact on the European economy by reinforcing European political integration. Moreover, he committed himself to create the necessary guarantees for the development of human rights by signing the 1975 Final Act of the Helsinki Conference on Security and Cooperation in Europe.

In 1968, Moro was among the first to understand the reasons for student demonstrations sweeping Western Europe and the controversial process of the emancipation of the Italian Communist Party (PCI) from the system of Soviet totalitarianism. In a critical phase of Italian democratic life threatened by terrorist groups of left and right, Moro undertook his fifth tenure as prime minister (February–April 1976). The following June he was elected president of the National Council of the Christian Democrats. In this new role, Moro outlined what he thought was an escape route from the crisis through which the country was passing. This entailed the legitimization of the PCI as a group that could participate in a coalition government. Moro's vision was more or less in agreement with the proposed "historical compromises," advocated by PCI leader Enrico Berlinguer. The proposal to solve the contradictions of the "blocked democracy" was opposed by those unwilling to accept the decline of the DC, those opposed to a sharing of power by the two giant parties, and those unwilling to give up their dream of revolution.

After the elections of June 1976, few governments were formed in Italy without the support of the Communists. On February 28, 1978, during the negotiations preceding the formation of Andreotti's fifth ministry, which was apparently going to include the PCI, Moro, in his last speech to the Christian Democrats' parliamentary groups, advocated a united effort to solve the political and cultural crisis the country was going through. On March 16, while en route to parliament to take part in a vote of confidence in the government, Moro was kidnapped by the Red Brigades while his escort was assassinated. His ordeal lasted fifty-five days. During that period Moro asked the parties to enter negotiations with the Red Brigades so he could be reunited with his family. On May 9, Moro's corpse was found in Rome, riddled with bullets. The debate on the circumstances of the kidnapping and its meaning for the subsequent history of Italy is still ongoing.

BIBLIOGRAPHY

Campanini, G. *Aldo Moro: Cultura e impegno politico.* Rome: Studium, 1988.

De Rosa, G. *Da Luigi Sturzo ad Aldo Moro.* Brescia: Morcelliana, 1988.

Moro, A. *Discorsi politici.* Rome: Cinque Lune, 1978.

———. *L'intelligenza degli avvenimenti: Testi 1959–1978.* Ed. by G. L. Mosse. Milan: Garzanti, 1979.

———. *La democrazia cristiana e la cultura cattolica.* Rome: Cinque Lune, 1979.

Scaramozzino, P., ed. *Cultura e politica nell'esperienza di Aldo Moro.* Milan: Giuffre, 1982.

Nicola Antonietti

SEE ALSO Berlinguer, Enrico; Fanfani, Amintore

Mowlam, Marjorie (1949–)

Secretary of state for Northern Ireland (1997–); MP for Redcar (1987–). Marjorie (Mo) Mowlam was born in 1949. She was educated in Britain and the United States, where she obtained a doctorate at the University of Iowa. After returning to Britain she worked as a research assistant to Labour MP Tony Benn and as a lecturer and adult education administrator at Northern College in Barnsley, England. She joined the Labour Party in 1969 and became an MP in 1987. From 1988 to 1990 she was frontbench spokeswoman on Northern Ireland for the Labour Party. In 1994 she was elected as the Shadow Northern Ireland secretary, replacing Kevin McNamara. British Prime Minister Tony Blair appointed her secretary of state for Northern Ireland when his party came to power in a landslide victory in May 1997. Two of her main aims when she first took office were to bring about a restoration of the Irish Republican Army (IRA) cease-fire and to bring Sinn Fein, the political arm of the militant IRA, into the multiparty talks. Both happened within a few months of her becoming secretary of state. The signing in April 1998 of the Good Friday Agreement to form a government of Northern Ireland consisting of the major parties of the Catholic and Protestant communities was seen as a major achievement for her. In October 1999 she was succeeded by Peter Mandelson, who had previously served as secretary of state for the British department of trade and industry and export credits guarantee, and cabinet minister for science and technology under British Prime Minister Tony Blair. Mowlam entered the British cabinet as minister and chancellor of the Duchy of Lancaster.

BIBLIOGRAPHY

Arthur, Paul. *Northern Ireland since 1968,* 2d ed. Oxford: Blackwell Publishers, 1996.

Aughey, Arthur, and Duncan Morrow, eds. *Northern Ireland Politics.* London: Longman, 1996.

Mowlam, Marjorie. *Debate on Disarmament.* London: Routledge & Kegan Paul, 1982.

O'Malley, Padraig. *Northern Ireland, 1983–1996: For Every Step Forward.* Boston: John W. McCormack Institute of Public Affairs, 1996.

Ricki Schoen

Mrożek, Sławomir (1930–)

Polish playwright and satirist. Sławomir Mrożek was born on June 26, 1930, in Borzęcin near Kraków. After 1963 he lived abroad in Italy, France, and Mexico. He gained notice first as a satirist and journalist. His popularity and recognition are due to his rich dramatic creativity. As a playwright Mrożek debuted in 1958 with the play *Policja* (*Police*). His position in Polish and world culture was assured by *Tango* (*The Tango,* 1964), a pessimistic interpretation of political and social tendencies of modernity. In his plays he takes stereotypical thinking to task and unveils the real causes of human behavior in a world dominated by ideology and politics. He often utilizes the contradictory attitudes of a villain and a person of intelligence, the poetics of the parable allowing him to combine experiences of Polish reality with a universal perspective. His more important plays include: *Emigranci* (*Emigrants,* 1974), *Garbus* (*The Hunchback,* 1975), *Krawiec* (*The Tailor;* written 1961, published 1977), *Vatzlav* (staged in 1979), *Ambassador* (*The Ambassador,* 1982), and *Alfa* (1984). Mrożek's prose is characterized by terseness and a parable form that intensified as he departed from satire on modernity toward psychological reflection on man (*Opowiadania,* 1964; *Dwa listy,* 1974; *Małe prozy,* 1990; *Opowiadania,* 1990–93, 1994). Mrożek's satirical drawings share their subject matter with his plays and prose (*Polska w obrazach,* 1957; *Rysunki,* 1990). Besides Tadeusz Różewicz and Witold Gombrowicz, Mrożek is the best-known and most frequently translated and staged Polish playwright.

BIBLIOGRAPHY

Blonski, Jan. "Mrozek i Mrozek," in *Romans z tekstem.* Ed. by Blonski Jan. Kraków: Wydawn Literackie, 1981.

Klossowicz, Jan. *Mrożek.* Warsaw: Agencja Autorska, 1980.

Nyczek, Tadeusz. "Obrona Tradycji," in *Emigranci.* Ed. by Tadeusz Nyczek. London: Aneks, 1988.

Andrzej Stoff

Mulcahy, Richard (1886–1971)

Irish politician, founder of Fine Gael, and its leader from 1944 to 1959. Following involvement in the revolutionary movement from 1916 to 1921, Richard Mulcahy became minister for defense of the Irish Free State from 1922 to 1924, when he resigned. His ruthless policies in defense of state security during the Civil War of 1922–23 were to haunt his postwar political career. From 1927 to 1932 he was minister for local government. Mulcahy in 1933 was a founding member of moderate Fine Gael. In 1944 he succeeded W. T. Cosgrave as party leader and leader of the opposition. The radical republican Clann na Poblachta (Republican Family) would not accept his leadership of the 1948–51 interparty government because of his civil war record, and Mulcahy had to abandon his quest for the prime ministership in favor of the compromise candidate, John A. Costello. In this government Mulcahy held the education portfolio. He held the same portfolio from 1954 to 1957 in the second interparty government. He was succeeded as party leader by James Dillon in 1959 and retired from active politics in 1961.

BIBLIOGRAPHY

Valiulis, Maryann. *Portrait of a Revolutionary.* Dublin: IAP, 1992.

Michael J. Kennedy

Muraviev, Konstantin Vladov (1893–1965)

Bulgarian politician and journalist closely linked after 1918 with the Bulgarian Agrarian Union (BAU). Educated in Istambul (Tsarigrad) and a graduate of the Bulgarian Military Academy in Sofia, Konstantin Vladov Muraviev served as a minister in a number of Bulgarian governments. He was minister of war in the last cabinet of Agrarian leader Aleksandur Stamboliiski, overthrown by a military coup in 1923, and a minister of education in the cabinets of Alexander Malinov and Nikola Mushanov in 1931 and 1932. Following a split in the BAU in 1926, Muraviev became one of the leaders of its right wing, Vrabtcha-1. However, in recent Bulgarian history he remained popular as the last non-Communist prime minister of Bulgaria before the advent of communism. Through his desperate attempts to negotiate armistice with the United Kingdom and the United States, begun by his predecessor, Ivan Bagryanov, Muraviev sought to prevent a Soviet invasion of Bulgaria. In spite of a proclamation of armed neutrality, the severing of diplomatic relations with Nazi Germany, and openness to democratic changes and peace negotiations with the Soviet Union, Muraviev's government was overthrown by a coup d'état on September 9, 1944. The coup was encouraged by an antifascist upheaval in the country and the presence of the Soviet army, which had crossed the Bulgarian border on September 8.

Like many progressive and moderate politicians of the time, Muraviev did not escape the repressions that followed soon afterward. Having been sentenced to life imprisonment by a people's court, he was unexpectedly released in 1955, most probably as someone who was no longer a threat to the firmly established Communist regime.

BIBLIOGRAPHY

Crampton, R. J. *A Short History of Modern Bulgaria.* Cambridge: Cambridge University Press–Open Society Foundation, Bulgaria, 1994.

Lyudmila Iordanova Dicheva

SEE ALSO Georgiev, Kumon

Music

European music during the second half of the twentieth century debated in sound such basic questions such as: freedom versus order and the value of the Western art music tradition vis-à-vis non-Western musics and popular culture—particularly that stemming from the apparent hegemony of the United States. Two composer patriarchs of the early century who led the extension of and rebellion against nineteenth-century romanticism continued to influence the second half-century. Russian-born Igor Stravinsky (1882–71) remained the cosmopolitan icon of Franco-Russian theater music and neoclassicism while seeming to absorb and epitomize all major musical trends. Austrian-born Arnold Schoenberg (1874–1951) led the middle-European Germanic school from romantic chromaticism toward a new compositional system—serialism—a method of arranging all twelve tones of the chromatic scale (corresponding to the black and white keys within an octave on a piano keyboard) in a predetermined series that does not rely on traditional notions of scales or harmony. By idealizing the music of Schoenberg's pupil, Austrian Anton Webern (1883–1945), members of the influential Darmstadt Summer School for New Music that began in 1946 constructed complex, dissonant, and often terse musical structures. The principle of serialism was extended beyond sets of musical pitches to predetermined sequences of duration, intensity, timbre, and texture in Frenchman Olivier Messiaen's (1908–92) Mode de Valeurs et d'Intensités (Quatre Études de Rhythm for the Piano, no 3., 1949). The best known work of this leader of the Darmstadt movement is his Quatuor pour la fin du temps (Quartet for the End of Time), written in 1941 while he was a war prisoner. Evincing a cosmopolitanism that extended to animal and inanimate creation as well as globally to exotic cultures and chronologically back to the Gregorian chant, the complex rhythmic modes and patterns of Messiaen, who had been trained as an organist, obliterate a sense of regular meter to express the sense of timelessness found in the Asian musics that he admired. Birdsong provided further inspiration that complemented his lifelong Roman Catholic mysticism expressed in coloristic organ works such as the Méditations sur la mystère de la Sainte Trinité (1969). Like many composers of the last half century, Messiaen sought a motivation for artistic activity that transcended the music industry, making him religious in a sense not contained within typical denominational dogma.

The music actually employed in the religions that had once been primary forces in European artistic life seemed to oscillate between Pollyannaish attempts at reinvigoration by imitating successful commercial styles on the one hand and nostalgia for a lost world of Christian civilization on the other. The Roman Catholic Second Vatican Council (1964–66), which aimed for the renewal of liturgical life, resulted in the virtual elimination of the artistic patrimony of that church from its ritual without calling forth alternatives that come up to the standard of the entertainment industry that has appropriated the popular imagination. In Europe, outside Bavaria and Ireland, churches are more likely to be filled for concerts than for services.

Two of Messiaen's pupils were Parisian Pierre Boulez (1925–) and German Karlheinz Stockhausen (1928–). Relaxing the rigidity of total serialism, Boulez's *Le Marteau sans Maître* (1954, revised 1957) combined the mathematical formulas of serialism with sensitivity to the use of music as a tool for enhancing a text. Strictly notated passages alternate with others where much of the realization is left to the discretion of the performer. Using a method analogous to contemporary improvisatory trends in drama and experimental films where the choice of options was left to the actors or even the audience, he employed mobile form wherein music is intended to be a process of creation, rather than a faithful report of a printed musical "text." Reminiscent of the Balinese gamelan orchestras that had bemused the French prophet of twentieth-century composition, Claude Debussy (1862–1918), Boulez's music often sounds transparent and appears to float without teleological direction. He is widely known for his advocacy of modern music as author, lecturer, and conductor, including appointments with the BBC Orchestra (1971–74) and the New York Philharmonic (1971–78).

Stockhausen addressed the question of determinacy versus indeterminacy or chance in music that is sometimes termed aleatoric after the Latin *aliae* (dice). He was influenced by American John Cage (1912–93), who insisted that all sonic phenomena, including silence or the recorded quotation of earlier composers, occurring within a given space or time may be considered music. Stockhausen's Klavierstücke XI (1956) allows the performer to choose or omit from among nineteen groups of notes arranged on a single page. He also began to explore electronic music as an entity in itself, as in his Gesang der Jünglinge (1956) (Song of the Youths in the Fiery Furnace), which mingles purely electronic sounds with manipulation of recorded snippets.

During the last quarter of the century composers turned away from theory-based systems that had been taken as a norm during the 1950s and 1960s. Instead, experimentation and eclecticism marked an anarchic postmodern musical scene. Sometimes inspired by percussion instruments that are prominent in African and Asian music, new timbres, often based on a vastly enlarged use of percussion instruments, were employed by composers seeking new effects not restricted to the European concert tradition. Edgard Varèse (1883–1965) created a *Poème électronique* that provided a sonic ambiance coordinated with lighting effects for the Philips pavilion designed by architect Le Corbusier at the 1958 Brussels World's Fair. Coining the term *musique concrète* to denote the sounds producible on any object, he had earlier composed for a massive battery of percussion instruments including sirens and motors. Greek architect-composer of *Metastasis* (1967) Iannis Xenakis (1922–) offered random (stochastic) music as a method for superseding the rigidities of serialism with the mathematical principle of probability. Expansion of the definition of music is evident also in each "Sequenza" of many composed for various instruments or combinations (1958–85) by the Italian Luciano Berio (1925–), who employs multiphonics from instruments previously supposed capable of producing only one note at a time. He also asks singers to produce sounds of the human voice formerly alien to Western music and languages.

Of all the developments in twentieth-century culture, however, the greatest single influence arose from the impact of new technology, whether as medium for combining elements of culture formerly kept separate, as museumlike reproducer for archiving existing performances, or as tool for creating and inspiring new sonic possibilities. Microtones or other sonic phenomena outside traditional musical scales are readily achievable through electronic means. The original synthesizers and spliced-tape compositions of the postwar electronic music labs in Cologne, Paris, and the United States now seem antiquated when compared with the definition and control of all aspects of sound possible in digitized computer programs that can translate notation directly into music via musical instrument digital interface (MIDI) connections or vice versa.

Although some electronic composers may work alone in the studio and publish their music directly onto a recording without the aid of live musicians, others combine all the new techniques in massive works for live performers. Krzystóf Penderecki's (1933–) *Passio et mors Domini Nostri Jesu Christi secundam Lucam* (*Passion and Death of Our Lord Jesus Christ according to Luke,* 1966) uses the grandiloquent resources of a vast chorus, orchestra, and soloists in a way that is both indebted to modernistic dissonant, electronic sound textures and reminiscent of medieval ritual. He is a representative of the Polish Renaissance, an artistic movement in a Soviet satellite where cultural leaders, despite their position on the geographical periphery of Western Europe, usually sought to ally themselves with Western ideas.

His countryman Witold Lutosławski (1913–94) also allowed much indeterminacy to achieve shimmering sonorities and unusual textures in performed music. In Funeral Music in Memory of Béla Bartók (1954–58) he asserted solidarity with a leading composer of the twentieth century who emulated folk and popular music without prostituting his resources to commercial gain or political propaganda in the way that contemporary Soviet Stalinist artistic policy sought to impose on its empire. Music was an activity that Communist regimes found both a useful image builder to support yet elusive to control. Atmosphères by Hungarian György Ligeti (1923–) employs a precise system of notation to achieve a texture as complex as those sought by the more aleatoric methods of his colleagues. Thus one finds that the possibilities for greater freedom for performers balanced possibilities of greater control available to the composer through new notations and electronic media. A frequent urge among the postserial New Music is the creation of works whose performances will be refreshingly different on each occasion. A literal connection with social and cultural concerns is, as usual, more readily evident in musical works with a literary text. Such are the operas of Englishman Benjamin Britten (1913–76), whose opera *Peter Grimes* (1945) typically combines his love of the British tradition of accessible choral singing with a libretto dealing with the plight of a social outsider. Scotland's Thea Musgrave (1928–) wrote *Harriet, The Woman Called "Moses"* (1984) memorializing a hero of the U.S. Civil War era Underground Railroad. Also sympathetic to the plight of those enslaved in the name of Western civilization, Heinz Werner Henze's (1926–) opera *El Cimarron* combines serial techniques with Afro-Cuban textures, improvisation, a police whistle in the large percussion section, and body slapping, with the panting of an out-of-breath fugitive in a collage that combines European, American, and African sounds while also seeking to cross the border between the techniques learned in conservatories and those transmitted through pop artists innocent of such training.

At the new millennium it is apparent that the European art music tradition is evolving within the West as part of a milieu often centered in the United States. Americans such as Roger Sessions (1896–1985), Elliott Carter (1908–), Milton Babbitt (1916–), Conlon Nancarrow (1912–), Harry Partch (1901–76), George Crumb (1929–), John Cage (1912–93), Steve Reich (1936–), Philip Glass (1937–), John Adams (1947–), Samuel Barber (1910–81), Ned Rorem (1923–), Gian-Carlo Menotti (1911–), Joan Tower (1938–), Ellen Taafe Zwilich (1939–), George Rochberg (1918–), and David Del Tredici (1937–), like the ubiquitous Leonard Bernstein (1918–90), are musical citizens of the world. Many Americans envy creative freedom allowed by the public support given to the arts by European governments, while some

Europeans admire the innovations consequent upon the entrepreneurial spirit of American life. American vernacular styles, particularly jazz, have been emulated by European composers both because of their musical richness and as a statement of sympathy with the oppressed. Meanwhile, indigenous styles seem in retreat before the American hegemony. European youth, like young people worldwide, seem taken by American popular culture as epitomized in rock music, which some ethnomusicologists credited with energizing the will to destroy the Berlin Wall in 1989 and consequently bring down the entire Soviet Empire. Other scholars point out that rock concerts were covertly sponsored by Communist governments in Poland and elsewhere to drain restless energies away from political action.

Both European and American music are now themselves components of an anarchic postmodern musical culture that is freely eclectic in exploiting its resources but dominated by global marketing systems of narrowly profit-driven electronic media corporations. Among the intelligentsia "postmodernism" embraces an eclectic, pluralistic aesthetic in which elements of the past are recombined in new ways, world cultures are more closely integrated, and the barriers among popular, folk, and art music whether of the past or the present are dissolved.

BIBLIOGRAPHY

Morgan, Robert P. *Twentieth-Century Music: A History of Musical Style in Modern Europe and America.* New York: Norton, 1991.

———, ed. *Anthology of Twentieth-Century Music.* New York: Norton, 1992.

———, ed. *Modern Times: From World War I to the Present.* Englewood Cliffs, N.J.: Prentice-Hall, 1993.

The New Grove Dictionary of Music and Musicians, 20 Vols. New York: Macmillan, 1980.

Watkins, Glen. *Soundings: Music in the Twentieth Century.* New York, Schirmer, 1988.

Conrad L. Donakowski

Muslims in Europe

Europe has a long history of confrontation and accommodation with Islam and Muslims from the Middle Ages through the second half of the twentieth century, when Muslims gained an increasing, permanent and visible presence in most European countries. Recent events in the Middle East (the Iranian revolution, the "death sentence" pronounced by the Islamic regime in Iran against the novelist Salmon Rushdie for, supposedly, insulting the Prophet Muhammad, the Gulf War, and the civil war in Algeria) and in former Yugoslavia ("ethnic cleansing" of the Muslim population from Serbian- and Croatian-controlled areas of Bosnia-Hercogovina and from Serbian dominated Kosovo) have created a heightened awareness of Muslims as a world community. Many Muslims within and without Europe came to see Islam as a source of identity in a shifting world and as a means to redress perceived injustices. As a result of this Islamic resurgence, there has emerged an influential view of Islam as a threat to the secular values of European society.

The Christian-Muslim confrontation began with the conquest of Spain by Arabs and Berbers at the beginning of the eighth century. It continued during the long Christian reconquest of Iberia, southern Italy, and the Mediterranean islands. The direct Islamic threat ended with the siege of Vienna by the Ottoman Turks in 1683. During the nineteenth century and the first half of the twentieth century, European colonialism in North Africa, the Middle East, and Asia sparked off new clashes between Christians and Muslims.

Apart from military confrontations, there were also religious and cultural reasons for Europe's troublesome relationship with Islam. European identity, revolving around Christendom, was forged in opposition to Islam, the only world religion that came into existence after Christianity and was hence unacceptable as a true religion. Conversely, Muslims encountered in Christendom a major rival and in many respects a similar religious and political power. In spite of this long-term animosity, there were also periods of peaceful Christian-Muslim cohabitation, of intellectual, cultural and commercial exchanges, diplomacy, intermarriage, and conversion.

According to the best estimates, in which "Muslim" is used as a broad cultural notion, in 1990 there were roughly 25 million Muslims in Europe. They can be divided among the following four categories. The first two are a legacy of the Mongol and Ottoman empires: about 11 million in the former European Soviet Union and 7 million in the Balkans. The third and fourth categories, together close to 7 million, are largely the result of post–Second World War immigration of Muslims into Western Europe. The third category is made up of Muslims who arrived as immigrant workers from the 1950s to the 1970s, followed by their wives and children through the 1980s and 1990s. Political and economic refugees from the Middle East, Asia, and Africa constitute the fourth and most recent set of immigrants with a Muslim background.

The vast majority of the first generation of Muslim immigrants came as unskilled workers from overwhelmingly rural areas with little European language and educational skills. The linguistic barrier is not only an impediment to self-improvement but also an obstacle to integration, as is the high concentration of Muslims in the poor housing districts of large cities. Although there are remarkable improvements among, for instance, Pakistani and Turks of the second generation in Britain and the Netherlands, respectively, and a growing number of self-employed in retailing and catering, the level of unemployment among Muslims remains relatively high. This is also due to the recent economic trend of making unskilled industrial labor redundant.

With 2.7 million Muslims France has by far the largest Muslim population in the European Union. They mainly come from the former French colonies in Africa: Algeria, Morocco, Tunisia, Senegal, and Mali. The largest groups are the harkis, Algerians and their children who remained loyal to the French against the Algerian National Liberation Front and who fled to France in 1962, and the beurs, the rapidly growing second- and third-generation Muslims.

In Germany, Turks form the overwhelming majority of Muslims, almost two million in the mid-1990s. They have been very important in the manufacturing industries of the Ruhr region and are concentrated in Düsseldorf, Cologne, Duisburg, and Darmstadt. There are also concentrations in Berlin, Frankfurt, Hamburg, Stuttgart, and smaller towns. There are also a substantial number of Muslim asylum seekers from former Yugoslavia, Iran, Afghanistan, and Pakistan.

The Muslim population of Great Britain was probably one million in 1991, of whom three-quarters are Pakistanis, Bangladeshis, and Indians. The rest mainly comes from the Middle East and former African colonies. The Netherlands and Belgium had approximately 600,000 and 300,000 Muslims in the mid-1990s, dominated by people of Turkish and Moroccan descent. Given its colonial past, the Netherlands also has Indonesian and Surinamese Muslims. In both countries there are relatively large numbers of Muslim refugees from former Yugoslavia, Somalia, Iraq and Afghanistan.

The mostly illegal arrival of Muslims in Spain, Italy, and Portugal, which until recently were countries of emigration, dates back to the mid-1980s. As controls tightened in the north, Europe's south with its extended coastal borderline became an easy entry point. Since the Single Market and the agreement eliminating border controls came into effect within the European Union in 1993, the countries of southern Europe have legalized the presence of substantial numbers of clandestine immigrants and reinforced the vigilance on their borders. Recently, some Muslim groups, partly converts, have appeared in southern Spain claiming to be heirs of medieval Islamic al-Andalus. The Spanish enclaves Ceuta and Melilla in Morocco have large Muslim minorities. The Muslim presence in Scandinavia is relatively small, ranging from 130,000 in Sweden to less than 10,000 in Finland. Switzerland and Austria each counted about 100,000 Muslims, predominantly from Turkey, in the early 1990s.

Before the disintegration of Yugoslavia (1991–92), more than half of the 7 million Balkan Muslims lived in Bosnia-Hercegovina, Kosovo, and Macedonia. One of the consequences of the territorial subdivision of Bosnia-Hercegovina into Muslim, Croatian, and Serbian segments has been the formation in Europe, for the first time since the fall of the Ottoman empire, of a political entity in which Muslims and Islam constitute the dominant political force. There are also small pockets of Turkish and Gypsy Muslims scattered over the territories of former Yugoslavia. In Bulgaria and northeastern Greece there are, respectively, 700,000 and 150,000 ethnic Turks and Pomaks (Islamized Bulgarians). Albania is the only European country, apart from Muslim Bosnia, where Muslims constitute a majority, two-thirds in a population of 3 million. However, most Albanians are secular Muslims for whom Islam is not a vehicle for political and nationalist aspirations. In spite of the often virulent Communist repression of religion, Islam thus survived in several parts of the Balkans.

The position of Muslims in Western Europe differs considerably, not only in terms of origins, but also with respect to the degree of institutionalization of Islam. The 1970s were a decisive phase in Islamic formation in Europe, for three reasons. First, the dramatic decrease in labor immigration following the economic recession of 1973 fueled family formation and reunification. Religious instruction and observation were becoming more important to Muslim immigrants because of their responsibilities of rearing children in non-Islamic environments. Second, Islam became a major international force in the wake of the Islamic revolution in Iran. And third, part of the oil wealth in the Gulf countries was used to fund the construction of mosques and to pay the salaries of imams in Europe. Hundreds of prayer rooms, mosques, and Muslim centers were founded throughout Western Europe. Their numbers rapidly increased to more than 3,500 in 1990. At the same time, governments became more keenly aware of the religious loyalties of their new citizens.

Family formation and reunion have thus raised the issue of education in general and Islamic instruction in particular. Many Muslim parents are reluctant to send their daughters to mixed schools, mainly because participation in gymnastics and swimming lessons involves body exposure that they consider immodest. The wearing of headscarfs by Muslim girls has led to conflicts with school authorities and national governments not only in France, where the state has a strong lay tradition, but also in Britain and Germany. In several countries there have been problems with the official recognition of imams as religious functionaries.

In the Netherlands state policy vis-à-vis Islam has been more accommodating than in France and Germany. The key slogan of the minority policy in the 1980s was "integration but not without preserving cultural identity." The Dutch Supreme Court recognized imams in 1986. Since then several Islamic primary and secondary schools and an Islamic university have been founded. There are Islamic programs on Dutch radio and television and provisions for the ritual slaughter of animals and dietary requirements. Several Muslims have been elected to municipal councils. Marriages across ethnic boundaries remain exceptional. For example, ninety percent of the 300,000 Dutch Turks, many of whom have been naturalized, still marry a person of Turkish descent. An overwhelming majority of Muslims prefers a funeral in their countries of origin.

The situation of Muslims in Germany differs drastically because the German notion of citizenship is based on ethnic descent rather than place of birth (as in France, the Netherlands and Britain). Being excluded from citizenship, Muslims have limited means for influencing German politics.

The widespread wish among Muslims to maintain a separate identity is reflected in the enormous proliferation of Muslim associations and facilities ranging from mosques and schools to public baths and tea and coffee houses. Many Islamic cultural centers, divided along linguistic and ethnic lines, were founded as local branches of organizations and movements in the countries of origin. Some have a pietist orientation, as the religious organization Jama'at al-Tabligh, whereas others are politically inspired, as is for example, the Turkish Milli Görüs movement. Both movements have a substantial following in several European countries. In most of Europe, governments offer financial aid to Muslim organizations, provided that they meet legal criteria such as a democratic committee structure, voting procedures, and regular subscriptions—criteria, however, that are alien to Islam.

Reliable data on religiosity are scarce and scattered. There are indications that only a tiny minority of mostly elderly Muslim men adheres to the obligation of the five daily ritual prayers. In France and some other countries Islam seems to undergo a major transformation. Whereas the older generation of Muslims relies on prayer rooms and mosques as the centers of religious socialization and sociability, young Muslims now express a desire to have their own meeting places by setting up cultural centers that go beyond ethnic divisions and favor a more open environment.

Until the late 1970s there was a widespread belief among European politicians and intellectuals that Muslims would integrate into the wider society and that Islam would become just another religion similar to Protestantism and Catholicism. During the 1980s and 1990s there has been an ongoing public debate about multiculturalism. Religious pluralism, in which Islam figures prominently, occupies a more focal position in the multiculturalist debate in Europe than in Canada, the United States, and Australia. Sweden is the most striking example of a multiculturalist policy in Europe, followed by Great Britain and the Netherlands. France has favored a more assimilationist policy, whereas Germany has implemented a model of differential exclusion.

During the 1990s the ideology and policy of multiculturalism passed through a crisis. With the exception of the domains of food, music, and folklore, the cultural encounter and dialogue of diverse cultural and religious traditions with more or less equal access to political and economic power, turned out to be almost nonexistent. However, this is not to say that personal contacts among young people of different ethnic and religious backgrounds did not develop. In the late 1980s and early 1990s such face-to-face contacts resulted into protest manifestations against racist attacks and anti-immigrant movements, mainly in France, Belgium, and Germany. The tendency of Muslim minorities in Europe to strengthen their internal relations is reinforced by an attitude of avoidance in the majority populations. At the close of the twentieth century minority policies were under reassessment in most countries of the European Union.

BIBLIOGRAPHY

Driessen, Henk, ed. *In het huis van de islam* (In the House of Islam). Nijmegen: Uitgeverij SUN, 1997.

Gerholm, Thomas, and Yngve Georg Lithman, eds. *The New Islamic Presence in Western Europe.* London: Mansell Publishing, 1988.

Lewis, Bernard, and Dominique Schnapper, eds. *Muslims in Europe.* London: Pinter Publishers, 1994.

L'Islam en Europe, special issue of *Archives de Sciences Sociales des Religions* (1995) 40.

Nielsen, Jorgen. *Muslims in Western Europe,* 2d ed. Edinburgh: Edinburgh University Press, 1995.

Peach, Ceri, and Günther Glebe, "Muslim Minorities in Western Europe," *Ethnic and Racial Studies* 18 (1995): 26–46.

Vermeulen, Hans, "Immigration, Integration and the Politics of Culture," *The Netherlands' Journal of the Social Sciences* 35 (1999): 6–23.

Henk Driessen

Mussolini, Alessandra (1963–)

Granddaughter of Italian dictator Benito Mussolini and a leading figure of the neofascist Italian Social Movement and its successor, the National Alliance Party. In early 1992, Alessandra Mussolini won a seat in the Italian Chamber of Deputies as a representative of her native Naples. The following year she ran for mayor of Naples but lost. Despite her loss, Mussolini has continued to be an important political force. She is a controversial figure because of the pride she expresses in her infamous grandfather. Mussolini is the oldest daughter of Benito Mussolini's youngest son. Neapolitan actress Sophia Loren is her aunt. Before running for office Mussolini had a brief acting career in B movies and attended a medical program. Dissatisfied with these pursuits, she campaigned for office using her name, good looks, and connections to advantage.

Mussolini has stressed her desire for a stronger nation. She has called for tighter control of immigration, a reduction in the size of the government, and tougher measures against crime. Though an important woman in politics, Mussolini does not describe herself as a feminist. But she has supported measures to eradicate the obligatory assignment of the paternal surname to children and to grant maternity leave to female members of parliament.

On November 14, 1996, Mussolini resigned from the right-wing National Alliance (AN). She said that her resignation resulted from differences with party leader Gianfranco Fini, who slighted her when he reorganized the party leadership. However, the resignation followed the inclusion of her husband, head of the state railroad's real estate division, in a corruption inquiry concerning the former head of the state railroad. Mussolini, who upset her AN colleagues on the Naples city council by supporting the city's left-wing administration, led by former Communist Antonio Bassolino, continued to hold her seat in parliament as an independent.

BIBLIOGRAPHY

Butturini, Paula. "A Mussolini Heir Revives the Ghost of Fascism." *Boston Globe* 19 (November 14, 1993): 1191.

Harrison, Barbara Grizzuti. "La Mussolini." *Los Angeles Times Magazine* January 24, 1993, 30.

Nardin, Simonetta. "Italian Women Want More Say in Politics." Reuters, March 28, 1996.

Wendy A. Pojmann

Mutual and Balanced Force Reductions

Arms control reduction talks initiated in October 1973 that sought to limit conventional forces in central Europe between the Warsaw Pact and NATO. These negotiations were terminated in February 1989 and replaced by broader talks on Conventional Armed Forces in Europe (CFE) in March 1989.

The participants of these negotiations were the seven Warsaw Pact and twelve NATO allied countries. The MBFR talks were precipitated by the "Mansfield resolutions," introduced into the U.S. Senate by Senator Mike Mansfield, which unilaterally sought to withdraw American ground troops from Europe. The objective of these talks, besides being used by U.S. and NATO leaders to forestall the passage of these resolutions, was to create a stable military balance in the zone surrounding East and West Germany, to limit rising defense costs for both alliances, and to reinforce warming East-West relations. Central obstacles to this agreement dealt with the disparity in size of NATO and Warsaw Pact ground forces, the types of forces to be reduced, how the phasing of reductions would take place, the status of Soviet forces stationed outside central Europe, and verification of draft treaty force limitations.

Most of these obstacles to a MBFR agreement were solved between 1975 and 1978 by means of bilateral concessions; however, a dispute over data concerning the size of Warsaw Pact ground troops stationed in central Europe ensued, and this deadlocked the talks over the next decade. In an attempt to break the impasse, Soviet leader Mikhail Gorbachev introduced proposals in April 1986 that became known as "the Budapest Appeal" and formed the basis of new negotiations that resulted in the CFE treaty in March 1989.

BIBLIOGRAPHY

Dean, Jonathan. *Watershed in Europe: Dismantling the East-West Military Confrontation.* Lexington, Mass.: Lexington Books, 1987.

Hopmann, P. Terrence. "From MBFR to CFE: Negotiating Conventional Arms Control in Europe," in Richard Dean Burns, *Encyclopedia of Arms Control and Disarmament,* Vol. 2. New York: Scribner, 1993.

Keliher, John G. *The Negotiations on Mutual and Balanced Force Reductions: The Search for Arms Control in Central Europe.* New York: Pergamon Press, 1980.

Robert J. Bunker

Myrdal, Gunnar (1898–1987)

Swedish political economist, noted for his study *An American Dilemma: The Negro Problem and Modern Democracy* (1944), which pointed out the problems of race relations in the United States. He had done an earlier study of Sweden's declining population, which he published with his wife, Alva Reimer, in 1934; this led the Carnegie Corporation to invite him to do the survey on the American Negro, which he began in 1938. The book illustrated the great gap between America's ideal of equality and the reality of the negro condition of Black Americans at that time, and pointed to the need for change to lessen the gap between blacks and whites. Myrdal used anthropological, economic, sociological, legal, and political data gathered from diverse sources.

(Karl) Gunnar Myrdal was born in Gustaf, Sweden, and attended the University of Stockholm, where he received both a law degree and a Ph.D. He became a professor of economics at Stockholm University in 1933 and served as a Social Democrat in the Riksdag (upper house of parliament) from 1936 to 1938. During the 1930s he assisted the Swedish government in initiating a national program of state responsibility for welfare for children.

Myrdal returned to parliament in 1944 and served in the cabinets of Per Albin Hansson and Tage Erlander from 1945 to 1947. After 1947 he was executive secretary of the United Nation's Economic Commission in Europe, assisting in the rebuilding of Western Europe at the time of the U.S. Marshall Plan. He resigned his professorship at Stockholm University in 1950 but resumed it again in 1960 as a professor of international economics. His publications include *Monetary Equilibrium* (1939), *An International Economy: Problems and Prospects* (1956), *Value in Social Theory: A Selection of Essays on Methodology* (1958), *Development and Underdevelopment, Rich Lands and Poor: The Road to World Prosperity* (1958), *Beyond the Welfare State* (1960), *Challenge to Affluence* (1963), and *The Challenge of World Poverty* (1970).

Barbara Bennett Peterson

Nagorno-Karabakh

Mountainous region of 1,700 square miles (4,300 sq km) predominantly inhabited by Christian Armenians. The region was turned over to Azerbaijan in July 1921, marking the end of the short-lived Soviet Republic of Armenia, which came into existence after the people living in the area, threatened by Mustafa Kemal's Turkey, accepted the Bolsheviks as protectors. In 1921, Nagorno-Karabakh was handed over to the Muslim Azeris by the Communist regime in Moscow, though its population was 92 percent Armenian and it was separated by only 15 kilometers from the rest of Armenia. It has been argued that this move was out of deference to Turkey, but Josef Stalin, who was commissar for national minorities in the USSR, often deliberately mixed peoples to dilute national cohesiveness and enable Moscow to pit group against group.

The Azerbaijani administration belied the autonomous status of Nagorno-Karabakh. Armenians even in this enclave were discriminated against and their language and cultural expression was restricted. As Armenians left for the cities of Azerbaijan the Armenian majority dropped to 75 percent, or about 150,000 people. In February 1988, when Armenians in Nagorno-Karabakh took advantage of the impending disintegration of the USSR to vote for a transfer of their region to Armenia, the Azeri government responded with a pogrom in the Azerbaijani City of Sumgait. When massive demonstrations were organized by Armenian Nationalists in Yerevan, the Armenian capital, and in Stepanakert, the principal town of Nagorno-Karabakh, the Azeris again responded with anti-Armenian violence. The Nagorno-Karabakh issue certainly involved primordial memories and insecurities; for the Armenians of Nagorno-Karabakh, however, it was also a question of interests. As Armenian speakers they believed they would have no educational or economic future in an independent Azerbaijan. Unable to speak Azeri and a Christian minority in a Muslim state, their interests, they perceived, lay with Armenia, the Commonwealth of Independent States (the weak organization for security and economic cooperation that replaced the USSR in December 1991), and Europe, rather than with Azerbaijan.

Soviet President Mikhail Gorbachev had attempted in January 1989 to defuse the Nagorno-Karabakh issue by replacing Azerbaijan's control of the autonomous republic with direct control from Moscow. He eventually surrendered to Azeri opposition, however, including a rail and road blockade of Armenia, and returned it to Azeri control in November.

Following a referendum on December 10, 1991, Nagorno-Karabakh declared itself independent on January 2, 1992. This tactical move was meant to serve as a way station on the road to reunion with Armenia. In January 1992 Azerbaijan's president, Ayaz Mutalibov, imposed direct presidential rule on Nagorno-Karabakh. The Azeris launched an offensive, surrounding Stepanakert, which they bombarded until May. Armenian self-defense forces, counterattacked in May, seizing the predominantly Azeri town of Shushi and the Lachin Strip, which established road contact with Armenia proper. The Azeris responded with a major offensive in June that overran about half the region. In August they resumed their bombardment of Stepanakert. The Nagorno-Karabakh legislature responded with a declaration of martial law and set up a state defense committee with close ties to Armenian President Levon Ter-Petrossian's government. Karabakh forces, bolstered by support from the Armenian diaspora and undoubtedly from Armenia itself clandestinely, then launched a successful counterdrive that, between October 1992 and September 1993, drove the Azeri military and their foreign mercenaries from all of Nagorno-Karabakh and some additional 2124 square miles (5,500 sq km) of Azerbaijani territory. When the Armenians occupied the

Azeri district of Kelbajar, they were able to open another land bridge to Armenia proper, and they subsequently added to their territory all the intervening land between Kelbajar and Lachin. Some 250,000 to 300,000 Azeri civilians fled as the Armenians advanced and Azerbaijan was gripped by political turmoil.

Armenian success was protested by Iran and Turkey, which sponsored a successful U.N. resolution demanding Armenian evacuation of Azeri territory. The Armenians of Nagorno-Karabakh ignored this and by October extended their control over Azeri territory all the way to the border of Iran. In 1993 the Azeris regained some of their territory, and several temporary cease-fires were arranged in 1994. In May 1994, through the mediation of the Organization for Security and Cooperation in Europe (OSCE) and Russia, a lasting cease-fire was signed by representatives of Armenia, Azerbaijan, and Nagorno-Karabakh. In late July the three parties formalized the agreement. In September Ter-Petrossian met with Azeri President Heydar Aliyev in Moscow. They reached agreement on some provisions of a peace settlement, but Aliyev insisted that a final accord depended on the evacuation of Azeri territory by Armenians. Negotiations continued in 1995, but the principal obstacles were Azeri insistence that the Armenians return the Lachin corridor and their unwillingness to accept the Nagorno-Karabakh representatives as equals. Although the conflict has not been settled and there have been minor clashes, full-scale hostilities have not resumed.

BIBLIOGRAPHY

"Armenia," *The Europa World Year Book 1996,* London: Europea Publications Limited, 1996. 1:408.

Chorbajian, Levon, Patrick Donabedian, and Claude Mutafian. *The Caucasian Knot: The History and Geo-Politics of Nagorno-Karabagh.* London: ZED, 1994.

Goldenberg, Suzanne. *Pride of Small Nations: The Caucasus and Post-Soviet Disorder.* London: Zed Books, 1994.

Bernard Cook

SEE ALSO Ter-Petrossian, Levon

Nagy, Ferenc (1903–79)

Prime minister of Hungary (1946–47). Ferenc Nagy was the general secretary of the Independent Smallholders Party from 1930 to 1945 and party president from 1945 to 1947. He was a member of parliament from 1939 to 1942, and was arrested by the Gestapo in 1944 when the Germans replaced the government of Miklós Horthy with a Hungarian fascist regime. He entered the government as minister of reconstruction in 1945 and became minister of defense in 1946.

Of peasant origins, Nagy began his career demanding radical reforms in the 1930s, calling for secret ballots and increased influence of peasants in the government. His position strengthened when Zoltán Tildy became head of the party in 1941. Nagy supported Tildy's Initiative of cooperation with the Social Democrats, opposed anti-Semitism, and demanded the withdrawal from the war of Hungary, which had joined Nazi Germany in its invasion of the USSR in June 1941.

By the time that Soviet forces began driving the Germans out of Hungary, Nagy had decided to cooperate with the Communists, and he accepted the social program of the provisional government. When Tildy was elected president in February 1946, Nagy became prime minister. His new government sought friendly relations with the Soviet Union, Great Britain, and the United States, against whom Hungary had been allied with Nazi Germany during the war.

In the coalition government the Smallholders, who had won a majority of seats in November 1945, equaled the combined strength of the Communists, Social Democrats, and National Peasants. Tactically Nagy considered a coalition with the communists necessary until a prospective peace treaty would be signed in 1947. Thus the Soviet-backed Communists could put pressure on him simply by leaving the coalition. Nagy accepted Communist demands for the expulsion of a number of MPs from his party as reactionaries, some nationalization, state control over the big banks, and reduction of the state administration.

In 1946 Nagy was satisfied with the accomplishments of the government. However, if he opposed the conservative Horthyist reaction, he also opposed further socialist measures. A crisis developed within the coalition when the Left wanted to go further in the direction of socialism. The Communist-dominated political police utilized allegations that there was a conspiracy to establish a new coalition under Horthy's last prime minister. After the arrest of Smallholders General Secretary Béla Kovács by the Communists in February 1947 for allegedly conspiring against the occupying Soviet military, Nagy, in a desperate if futile effort to assuage the Communists and thus continue his coalition with them, agreed to expel more Smallholders, and the party lost its majority. In May, while Nagy was on vacation in Switzerland the Communist leaders gave him the option of staying abroad or being charged with conspiracy when he returned.

Nagy sought refuge in the United States, where he purchased and ran a dairy farm in Virginia. He held offices in international and emigrant organizations and became one of the leading figures in the campaign against the Communist regime in Hungary during the Cold War. In 1956, in the name of emigrant Hungarians, he formulated a political program and during the Hungarian Revolution of that year tried to establish contacts with the reorganized Smallholders Party. In the 1960s Nagy abandoned politics and lectured at U.S. universities. In 1977, Nagy helped to return the crown of Saint Stephen to Hungary. The crown, the most important Hungarian national symbol, was taken by Hungarian fascists to Austria at the end of World War II, and later seized by the U.S. army and kept in Fort Knox, Kentucky.

Nagy was a tragic figure, who attempted to prevent the total communization of Hungary by working with the Communists. Most historians would assert that his effort was doomed from the start, while some argue that the fate of Hungary was not predetermined from the beginning and that the Communist monopoly there was influenced by the developing Cold War.

BIBLIOGRAPHY

Balogh, Sándor, and Sándor Jakab. *The History of Hungary After the Second World War.* Budapest: Corvina, 1986.

Nagy, Ferenc. *The Struggle Behind the Iron Curtain.* Tr. by Stephen K. Swift. New York: Macmillan, 1948.

Vida, István. "Ferenc Nagy: A Hungarian Agrar-Democrat in the First Half of the Twentieth Century (Sketch of His Portrait)." *Reformists and Radicals in Hungary.* Ed. by Ferenc Glatz. Budapest: MTA Történettudományi Intézet, 1990.

Heino Nyyssönen

SEE ALSO Kovács, Béla; Tildy, Zoltán

Nagy, Imre (1896–1958)

Communist politician and prime minister of Hungary (1953–55, 1956). Imre Nagy fought on the side of the Communists in the Russian Civil War following the Russian Revolution of 1917. In 1921 he returned to Hungary and joined the Social Democratic Party; in 1925 he joined the Hungarian Socialist Workers (Communist) Party. In 1928, Nagy went to Austria, and from there emigrated to the USSR. During World War II he was in charge of the Hungarian broadcasts of Radio Kossuth to Hungary from the USSR.

After World War II Nagy returned to Hungary and became minister of agriculture (1944–45), minister of interior (1945–46), chairman (speaker) of parliament (1947–49), minister of supply (1950–52), minister of harvest gathering (1952), and vice prime minister (1952–53). After Soviet dictator Stalin's death in 1953, Nagy became prime minister.

A program of radical land reform in 1945 was created mainly by Nagy. It gave him popular support among poor peasants and workers. During the Stalinist years Nagy did not completely agree with the policy of other Hungarian Communist leaders but nevertheless held high positions in the party. After Stalin's death the "Hungarian Stalin," Mátyás Rákosi, was forced to relinquish the premiership to Nagy. During the following two years there was a struggle between Nagy and Rákosi's followers, who were entrenched in the administration.

The new prime minister introduced a program to encourage production of consumer goods at the expense of heavy industry, stopped collectivization, and strove for a Hungarian variety of socialism. Heavy industry was allocated approximately 40 percent fewer funds than the previous year. Nagy also supported the release of political prisoners and the rehabilitation of some of the victims of Stalinism. The Patriotic People's Front, mainly a nonparty organization to win for the government broader support among the Hungarian people, was also founded through Nagy's initiative.

The Soviet Union supported these "revisionist" ideas mainly because Rákosi's unpopularity was widely known and Georgy Malenkov threw his support to the reform-minded Nagy. But following Malenkov's dismissal as chairman of the Council of Ministers in February 1955, Nagy was ousted in April and in November expelled from the party.

Following the Twentieth Congress of the Soviet Communist Party, changes in the USSR again had an impact on Hungary. As a result of Premier Nikita Khrushchev's de-Stalinization campaign, Nagy was readmitted to the party on October 13, 1956. Following Soviet concessions to Poland, which allowed the Polish Communist Party to determine its own internal policies, a spontaneous rebellion broke out in Budapest on October 23. The demonstrators demanded the return of Nagy to the leadership, and this took place on the following day. Nagy attempted to restore order by promising to renew his reforms of 1953. By October 28, however, Nagy sensed that a national democratic movement was under way, and two days later he believed that Hungary had passed into a revolutionary situation. On October 30 the single-party system was suppressed and a multiparty government was established. On November 1 Nagy declared Hungary's neutrality and its departure from the Soviet-dominated Warsaw Pact. He also intended to democratize the Communist Party that was renamed the Hungarian Socialist Workers Party.

The USSR, which initially had been willing to accept a degree of Hungarian independence as long as the dominance of the Communist Party was assured, responded to the potential loss of Communism and the Eastern bloc with a massive attack. Nagy called for resistance and there was bitter street fighting in Budapest. On the last day of the fighting Nagy and his closest followers escaped to the Yugoslav Embassy. On November 23 they were apprehended after a false guarantee of personal safety and taken to Romania. In a secret trial, which began in Budapest in February 1958, Nagy was found guilty of treasonously conspiring with "fascists" and the West to overthrow the "People's Democracy," or less euphemistically, the Communist state. He was sentenced to death and hanged on June 16, 1958.

After the execution Nagy was buried inside the prison to avoid demonstrations, and in 1961 his remains were transferred to an unmarked grave in the general cemetery of Budapest. When János Kadar, who succeeded Nagy as head of the Hungarian Communist Party and later served as head of state from 1956 to 1958, was forced to resign his post as party secretary in May 1988, the new party first secretary, Károly Grósz, promised to rebury Nagy privately. However, the reburying of Nagy and his followers on June 16, 1989, was one of the symbolic events marking Hungary's move from the Communist system to democracy. The event was publically billed, a day of reconciliation, and a number of former émigrés were present for it. Nagy was fully rehabilitated in July 1989.

In 1989 the memory of Nagy inspired the reformers against the conservatives in the Communist Party, but the memory of Nagy also provided potent inspiration to opponents of any form of communism.

BIBLIOGRAPHY

Aron, Tóbiás, ed. *In memoriam Nagy Imre: Emlékezés egy miniszterelnökre.* Budapest: Szabad Tér Kiadó, 1989.

Dér, Ferenc, ed. *Nagy Imre egy magyar miniszterelnök élettörténeti kronológia, dokumentumgyűjtemény.* Pécs: Régio, 1993.

Lahav, Yehuda. *Der Weg der Kommunistischen Partei Ungarns zur Macht,* 2 Vols. Munich: R. Trofenik, 1985–86.

Molnár, Miklós, "The Communist Party of Hungary," in *The Communist Parties of Eastern Europe.* Ed. by Stephen Fischer-Galati. New York: Columbia University Press, 1979.

Molnár, Miklós, and László Nagy. *Reformátor vagy forradalmár volt-e Nagy Imre?* Paris: Magyar Füzetek and Highland Lakes Atlanti Kutató és Kiadó Társulat, 1983.

Nagy, Imre. *On Communism: In Defense of the New Course.* Tr. by Hugh Seton-Watson. New York: Praeger, 1957.

Trugly Jr., Edmund, ed. *Nagy, Imre: Politisches Testament.* Munich: Kindler, 1959.

Heino Nyyssönen

SEE ALSO Rákosi, Mátyás

Nano, Fatos (1952–)

Albanian politician. Fatos Thanas Nano was born in Tirana in 1952. Trained as an economist, Nano was an economic adviser to the Central Committee of the Albanian Communist Party (PL). When the Party came under pressure in 1990, as a result of growing student demonstrations, to introduce reforms, it turned to Nano, who had been advising the government since the late 1980's on steps toward general reform and reform of the economy. On December 22, 1990, he was appointed general secretary to the Council of Ministers. In January and February 1991 he served as deputy prime minister. In February Ramiz Alia, president and party first secretary, attempted to respond to growing popular opposition by removing the chairman (prime minister) of the Council of Ministers, Adil Carcani, a hard-liner, and establishing a presidential council until elections in March. Alia appointed Nano prime minister. Though the opposition Democratic Party dominated the urban vote, the Communist Party dominated the countryside. Nano was reappointed prime minister. A general strike and a pitched battle between police and fifty thousand demonstrators in Tirana's Skanberbeg Square on May 29 led to Nano's resignation in the first week of June. He was succeeded by an engineer, Ylli Bufi, who presided over a council equally divided between the PL and the opposition.

Before convening the party's Tenth Congress on June 10, Alia resigned as party head. The party, in an effort to regain support, changed its name to Socialist Party of Albania and chose Nano as its new leader. In July 1993, in a move that Socialists denounced as a political attack by President Sali Berisha and his Democratic Party, Nano's parliamentary immunity was revoked and he was charged with embezzlement of Italian food aid for Albania in 1991. In April 1994 Nano was convicted in a highly politicized trial of misappropriating state funds, dereliction of duty, and falsification of documents and sentenced to prison for twelve years. The Socialists, nevertheless, continued to recognize Nano as their leader.

On December 13, 1994, Nano was released from prison for twenty-four hours to attend the funeral of his mother. Some 2,500 supporters took advantage of the funeral to stage a demonstration on his behalf, but he returned to prison until 1997. Nano gained his freedom and again became prime minister as a result of popular outrage surrounding disastrous pyramid schemes, in which Albanians unfamiliar with the workings of the stock market were encouraged to invest their often meager savings in fraudulent investment plans. The schemes, which Berisha and the government tolerated, collapsed and Albanians who lost their money responded with violence. On March 13, 1997, as chaos gripped the capital, with rioting, looting, and the seizure of weapons, about three hundred prisoners, including Nano and Alia, escaped from the central jail in Tirana. Berisha's government however, attempting to turn the situation to its advantage, stated that the prisoners had been pardoned. Nano immediately called for Berisha to step down or be removed by democratic means.

Elections held on June 29 at which the turnout was high were characterized by international observers as not free or fair but "adequate"—an achievement of sorts for Albania. In the first vote and a July 6 runoff voters rejected Berisha and his misnamed Democratic Party. The new government, headed by Nano, was sworn in at the end of July. It consisted of the Socialist Party, Democratic Alliance, Social Democratic Party, Agrarian Party, Human Rights Party, and one independent.

BIBLIOGRAPHY

"Albania Alters Cabinet, Naming Reformist." *New York Times,* December 24, 1990.

Dinmore, Guy. "Berisha Is Urged to 'Step Aside.' " *Financial Times,* March 18, 1997.

Perlez, Jane. "Bitter Albanians, Facing Anarchy, Arm Themselves." *New York Times,* March 14, 1997.

"Rebuilding Albania." *New York Times,* July 2, 1997.

Bernard Cook

SEE ALSO Alia, Ramiz; Berisha, Sali

Napier, Oliver (1935–)

Northern Irish Alliance Party leader (1972–84). Oliver Napier was born in 1935. He trained as a solicitor and was elected to the Assembly of Northern Ireland (1973–1974) and the Constitutional Convention (1975–76) as the member for East Belfast. He was a cofounder of the Alliance Party but secured a seat for the party in British general elections. He also did not win a seat in the 1979 European Parliament elections. He decided to step down as party leader in 1984 but was honored with a knighthood in 1985. From 1988 to 1992, he was chairman of the Standing Advisory Commission on Human Rights.

BIBLIOGRAPHY

Arthur, Paul. *Northern Ireland since 1968,* 2nd ed. Oxford: Blackwell, 1996.

Aughey, Arthur, and Duncan Morrow, eds. *Northern Ireland Politics.* London: Longman, 1996.

Ricki Schoen

SEE ALSO Alderdice, John; O'Neill, Terrence

Napolitano, Giorgio (1925–)

Italian leftist politician. Giorgio Napolitano was born in Naples on June 29, 1925. He received a law degree from the University of Naples in 1947, joined the Italian Communist Party (PCI) and was elected to parliament in 1953. He served in every parliament until 1996, except for the period 1963–68, when he chose not to stand as a candidate. He was the leader of the PCI parliamentary delegation from 1981 to 1986. During this time he was the foreign affairs spokesman for the PCI. He was a member of the North Atlantic Assembly, an organization of legislators from NATO member countries designed to foster mutual understanding of security, economic, and social issues, from 1984 to 1989. Napolitano served as a member of the Italian parliament's Foreign Affairs Committee from 1987 to 1992, and a member of the European Parliament from June 1989 to June 1992.

Napolitano was a proponent of Eurocommunism, a democratic socialist alternative to Soviet-style communism, and advocated the transformation of the PCI into a Western-style social democratic party. He played a leading role in the transformation of the PCI into the Democratic Party of the Left (PDS) in February 1991. He was speaker of the Chamber of Deputies (lower house of parliament) from June 3, 1992, to April 14, 1994. On March 8, 1995, he was appointed president of a special commission impaneled to reorganize the Italian radio and television sector. Napolitano, though he was not a candidate for the Chamber of Deputies in April 1996, was appointed minister of interior in the government formed by Romano Prodi in May 1996.

BIBLIOGRAPHY

Giorgino, Francesco. *Intervista alla prima Repubblica: Taviani, Napolitano, Amato: scene (e retroscena) da cinquant'anni di politica.* Milan: Mursia, 1994.

Hobsbawm, Eric J. "The Italian Road to Socialism: An Interview." Westport, Conn.: L. Hill, 1977.

Napolitano, Giorgio. *I comunisti nella battaglia delle idee.* Rome: Editori riuniti, 1975.

———. *Dove va la Repubblica: 1992–94, una transizione incompiuta.* Milan: Rizzoli, 1994.

———. *Europa e America dopo l'89: il crollo del comunismo, i problemi della sinistra.* Rome: Laterza, 1992.

———. *Oltre i vecchi confini: il futuro della sinistra e l'Europa.* Milan: Mondadori, 1989.

Bernard Cook

Nationalism and Regionalism

Nationalism, in various forms, was the dominant ideology throughout Europe in the period ending in 1945. Whether expressed in terms of a supposedly "neutral" geography, language and "ethnicity," political loyalty, or the cruder terms of "racial" identification, most Europeans identified themselves, or were identified, in "national" terms. The ideal political unit, and thus the proper goal for humanity, was the nation. Regionalism was viewed, at least by nationalists, as the political expression either of "folkloric" and/or retrograde ambitions or as a form of nascent nationalism that had as yet failed to achieve a concrete state. Regionalism was not a unified movement but a label for two types of political and/or social attitudes that did not necessarily lead to political movements. One was ethnonationalism, which was linked to identification with an ethnically or culturally defined region, either a "nation" that had failed to attain statehood or one that had never realistically sought it. The other consisted of feelings of political and social loyalty toward a subnation-state area that, while perhaps not culturally distinct from adjacent regions, had some claim to historical separateness. While the former was traditionally associated with regionalism, ethnonationalism was to prove the more powerful force in promoting the cause of regions.

"Nation-state" nationalism, whether based on the principles of the French Revolution or the *völkisch* ideals that surrounded the birth of German nationalism and most of the nationalist movements of central and Eastern Europe, was the leading way of seeing oneself as a political being. The very vocabulary of "citizenship" reflected these assumptions. To exist as a political/social person required membership in a national "community" that, in turn, implied the existence of these communities as the natural foci for political and social organization. Proponents of the nation-state ideology had spent much time and effort creating economic and social systems, from railroads to schools and compulsory military service, that would both inculcate a sense of "national" distinctiveness and eradicate all other identities that might challenge that of the nation-state. This applied to transnational ideas such as Christianity or socialism or to "subnational" ideas based on a region or a political identity other than the nation-state. The creation of nation-states depended not just on concrete systems and structures to foster nationalism, and on specific measures to combat opposition to nationalism, but also on an ideology of nationalism and of the "nation" as an "imagined community" in which all had a place. Nationalism was, and is, a powerful tool for creating such communities and setting them apart from all other political entities. To be British, French, German, or Italian was both a positive statement about what one was but also a negative statement about what one was not. The arguments about whether this was "good" or merely divisive, whether "citizens" understood the same thing by the statement or even willingly accepted it, were rarely heard. Nationalism was the dominant ideological paradigm, and its "naturalness" was seldom questioned. The cataclysm of the Second World War brought all these issues into discussion again and allowed long-submerged doubts to come to the surface.

In Western Europe, especially in Germany and to some measure in Italy, nationalism emerged from the Second World War thoroughly discredited. In the United Kingdom, feelings of identification with the nation-state were both high and positive, as was the case in Scandinavia, Ireland, and the Netherlands. In France, Belgium, and Greece the results were more mixed, while in Iberia, untouched directly by the war, the ideology of the nation-state was still officially the only acceptable one. Beneath all of these apparent certainties, however, there was much to question. In central and Eastern Europe nationalism had been invoked by both Left and Right during the war, but was now officially subsumed under a blanket of "socialist universalism." Only in Austria were there any attempts, domestically and internationally, to foster self-conscious feelings of national identification. In most of the Soviet sphere folkloric "nationalism" was still encouraged. The cults of the balalaika and the "Cossack" dance troupe were officially sanctioned, but nationalism itself was both too tainted by the war and too dangerous to Soviet power to have anything other than a shadowy and harassed existence. The activities of the Western powers, especially the United States, to cultivate the most reactionary of nationalisms encouraged these tendencies. In the Eastern bloc only Yugoslavia, alongside efforts to eradicate or at least degrade previously existing nationalisms, made the gallant attempt to both foster a "new" nationalism and a "new" identity, that of being a Yugoslav. The particularly vicious manifestations of divisive nationalism in wartime Yugoslavia, especially in Bosnia and Croatia, led to some initial reprisals against former Croat Ustaši and some "show trials," most noticeably that of Cardinal Alojzíje Stepinac of Zagrel, but on the whole Yugoslavia settled for a path of "nation building" rather than one of repression.

If nationalism was widely brought into question by the events of the war, manifestations of regionalism or ethnonationalism were also somewhat discredited in certain areas. The wartime behavior of some regionalist groups, mainly in Alsace, Brittany, and Flanders, left them open to criticism and, in the first two areas at least, the continuing centralizing Jacobin approach of the French administration augmented the tendency to repress ethnonationalism. In the United Kingdom, though regionalism survived the war in Scotland and Wales, it had no real mass base and was restricted to a small number of adherents. In Italy a turning away from the excesses of fascism strengthened ethnonationalism in some areas, largely in the north and most particularly in the South Tirol and the Val D'Aosta. Outside of these regions movements in favor of regionalism or ethnonationalism barely existed with the exception of Sicily. In Sicily the liberation of the island was assisted by popular support augmented by peasant unrest and the support of elements of organized crime. Though this would lead to some regionalist agitation in the immediate postwar years, the Mafia, once it opted for Italian unity, proved to be the stronger in its contest with the peasantry, and most traces of effective regionalism were suppressed. Despite this victory for centralism, a series of hastily contrived "special regions," with varying and hotly contested economic and political powers, was created in Italy. This gave at least some recognition to regionalism. Finally, in Spain the victory of Franco in the Civil War, which officially concluded in 1939, resulted in the repression of regionalism and ethnonationalism throughout Spain and most particularly in the Basque provinces, Catalonia, and Galicia.

The score card for nationalism and regionalism by the 1950s was in many ways uneven. However, Italy aside, there was one major victory if not for regionalism then at least for decentralization. In Germany the new constitution was an explicitly federalist one with Länder (states) being created that reflected in many respects the pre-unification states. These Länder also had (and have) a great deal of independence with respect to the federal government. A similar structure was created for Austria when the Allied occupation ceased. The situation in Germany reflected the development of a form of regionalism based on a combination of economic and historic factors that lacked explicit cultural or ethnonationalist component. This falling back on civic traditions separate from cultural and/or linguistic factors of difference had deep roots in many areas, most noticeably Bavaria and the former Hanseatic League cities of northern Germany, and was increasingly seen to represent a potential model for many areas of Europe.

The 1960s saw a resurgence of ethnonationalism in many areas alongside a steady growth in respect for regionalism based on noncultural and nonethnic factors. In turn these were accompanied by the beginnings of a weakening of nation-state nationalism and a strengthening of the idea of some form of European unity. The creation of the Nordic Customs Union in 1962, paralleling the creation of the Benelux (Belgium, Netherlands, Luxembourg) Customs Union in 1945, was an indicator of this. The formation of the European Economic Community (EEC) in 1957 was, on the surface, clearly based on the alliance of a group of European nation-states for exclusively economic and pragmatic purposes, despite the aspirations of the idealistic for something more. This was the case despite the exclusion of the United Kingdom, which was already establishing a reputation for itself as the most recalcitrant "European" and the most zealous centralizer in its domestic affairs. Despite this auspicious beginning for nation-state nationalism in the EEC, many of those involved in its creation were strongly influenced by federalist ideas, and its successful working was posited on the surrender of at least some aspects of national sovereignty in the economic sphere. Both these factors were to continue to push the EEC toward being more than merely another venue in which nation-state nationalism could be practiced.

This actual and potential diminution of the powers of some of the nation-states was paralleled by a strengthening in various ethnonationalist movements. In Italy both the South Tirol and the Val D'Aosta experienced growth in electoral strength for ethnonationalist movements, and similar movements were formed or re-formed in Friulia-Venezia Giulia, Sardinia, and other areas. Such was also the case in the Flemish-speaking parts of Belgium. In the United Kingdom, both Plaid Cymru in Wales and the Scottish Nationalist Party (SNP) began to assert some political influence. The general climate of the 1960s also encouraged a growth in regionalist sentiment in France both in traditional centers such as Brittany and in areas where such sentiment was weaker such as Occitania. In particular Corsica became a flashpoint that was only further heightened by the movement of former French colonialists (*pieds noirs*) from Algeria to the island with the progressive collapse of French domination in that African country. In Spain the weakening of the Franco regime allowed some space for the political growth of regionalism in the traditional ethnonationalist areas, particularly the Basque provinces and Catalonia. In most areas this ethnonationalist sentiment was expressed in largely electoral and peaceful terms, but in the South Tirol, Basque regions, and Corsica a more violent approach began to develop. Finally, the creation of the civil rights movement in Northern Ireland and its repression led to a renaissance of violence in that province and to the dismantling of the separate administration created by the United Kingdom in 1921. With the events of 1968 in Europe and their aftermath in the early 1970s, many of the more peripheral ethnonationalist movements declined, but the more resilient, whether violent or not, remained and even gained in strength.

In central and Eastern Europe the death of Stalin in 1953 led to some weakening in the more visible aspects of Soviet hegemony. While the Hungarian Revolution of 1956, which was actively supported by many overtly nationalist political elements, was violently suppressed by the Soviet army, the politics of much of Soviet-dominated Europe included ever greater doses of traditional nationalism alongside continued appeals to "socialist universalism." The Czechoslovak experiment of Alexander Dubček, which was crushed in 1968, proved the clear limits to which the Soviets could be pushed, but the gradual, peaceful incorporation of more nationalist elements continued. Though the New Economic Mechanism introduced in Hungary in 1968 suffered brief reversals in the early 1970s, it remained in force and was emulated in a variety of Soviet-bloc countries, including Bulgaria in 1979. This reassertion of nationalist tendencies in the Soviet bloc encompassed a greater interest in traditional cultural manifestations, including church practices, but had obvious negative features. Most noticeable among these were efforts to "nationalize" minorities and an irridentist stress on the potential realignment of borders. Both these tendencies were to continue, and gain in strength, as of the 1970s.

In the 1970s the four dominant traits identified earlier (the decline of nation-state nationalism; the resilience of certain manifestations of ethnonationalism; the growth of "nonethnic" regionalism; the growing significance of Pan-European organization) continued to strengthen in Western Europe. The entry of the United Kingdom, alongside Denmark and Ireland, into the EEC in 1973 represented, whether acknowledged or not, the acceptance that policies exclusively oriented toward the nation-state were no longer as viable as they had appeared to be and was a recognition of the change that had already taken place and of the changes that were still to come. In the United Kingdom these changes were also reflected in rising pressures for "devolution" in Scotland and Wales. More effective devolution was also implemented in Italy and, with the death of Franco in 1978, the beginnings of a thoroughgoing federalism were being created in Spain. Belgium, too, under pressure from Flemish-speaking political groups, was moving to a devolved, federal form of government. Direct elections to the European Parliament, which began in 1979, added to the recognition of ethnonationalist and regionalist parties and cemented the first stage of building a commonality of objectives between the two principal interest groups who doubted the future of nation-state nationalism.

In central and Eastern Europe, on the other hand, the situation was reversed. The weakening, at least on the surface, of Soviet hegemony led to an increasing adoption of more overtly nationalist, or even chauvinist, tendencies among the governments of the centrally planned economies. This in turn led to measures to actively repress manifestations of loyalties to anything other than the nation-state. Of the "traditional" nonterritorial victims of such strategies, primarily the Jews and the Rom (Gypsies), only the Rom remained in sufficient numbers. Both groups were the subject of official moves to integrate them into the "national" societies. Increasingly the perennial repression of transborder minorities also became a feature of many of these polities, most noticeably those of Albania, Bulgaria, and Romania. Macedonians, Turks, Pomaks (Slavs who had converted to Islam), Germans, and Hungarians were all subject to such pressure. Once again Yugoslavia proved an exception, but with the death of Tito in 1980, it was to begin to join the mainstream with excessive, because long-repressed, vehemence.

The 1980s increased all these tendencies throughout Europe and added new dimensions to the nationalist/regionalist dialog. In France the plan of giving a representative dimension to the regions, which had been instrumental in the fall of President Charles de Gaulle in 1969, was made a reality by President François Mitterrand in 1982. While this "regionalization" of France was undoubtedly ambitious, the regions were given greater power than most of the "special regions" of Italy; their borders were designed along economic and planning lines and only coincidentally reflected an ethnocultural element. The Spanish regions, led by the demographically and economically powerful Catalonia, continued to gain greater internal powers and more independence from the central government in Madrid. This independence was assisted by the importance of the *convergencia,* the Catalan Convergence Party, led by Jordi Pujol, to the maintenance of Spanish governments that lacked a clear majority in parliament. The same situation held true in the Basque provinces, though here the continuing violence of a small group of Basque activists (ETA) and the relative weakness of Basque speakers in the area complicated matters somewhat. Even in the United Kingdom the Scottish Office and the Welsh Office beginning in 1963 assumed more powers within their respective areas. Though "devolution" was fairly decisively rejected in 1979 in both areas, it remained, and remains, an issue that the growing strength of the SNP and Plaid Cymru can only underline.

East of the European Community dramatic changes were taking place that led both to a widely acclaimed "freedom" for Soviet-bloc countries and to a resurgence of intense nationalism and often xenophobia. The loosening of the Soviet grip begun in the 1970s accelerated, especially after the accession of Mikhail Gorbachev in 1985 as general secretary of the Soviet Communist Party. The reforms he introduced in economic and political life were mirrored, and often amplified, in the Soviet satellites. The independent Polish labor union movement, Solidarity (Solidarność), founded in 1980, slowly became the voice of Polish labor and Poland in general. Non-Communist opposition movements came to prominence throughout the Soviet bloc pressing for economic and social reforms and free elections. In 1989 Solidarity came to power in Poland, and the rulers of Bulgaria and Romania were replaced; in the latter, Nicolae Ceauşcescu was executed. The collapse of the Berlin Wall that same year, assisted by the new Hungarian government's unwillingness to restrict the flow of "tourists" from East to West Germany, led directly to the formal reunification of Germany in 1990. Throughout central and Eastern Europe free elections were being held, and the independence of the three Baltic states—Estonia, Latvia, and Lithuania—was recognized by the USSR after the failure of the attempted coup by hardline Communists in August 1991.

If long-suppressed freedoms were now being restored, so too were long-suppressed antipathies and disputes. From Estonia in the north to Macedonia in the south, a chain of border disputes and interethnic tensions was revealed to be alive and well after the placidity of much of the Soviet period. Many countries in this arc had actual or potential claims on the territory or ethnic allegiance of their neighbors; likewise they also had substantial ethnic minorities within their borders who often looked to these selfsame neighbors for support. If the Romanian "revolution" was actually triggered by political action taken by activists among the Hungarian population of Transylvania, it did not result in any long-standing interethnic alliances. Romanian nationalism, intolerant of all minorities but especially of the German, Hungarian, and Rom populations, was soon to be acceptable rhetoric. The violence of the Romanian revolution, alongside the changes in other areas, led to a mass exodus of Germans and Rom, the latter as stateless refugees. Nationalism likewise quickly altered the character of the Velvet Revolution in Czechoslovakia, leading to the official breakup of the state at the beginning of 1993. The Baltic states stressed a nationalist approach in the face of large Russian-speaking minorities. Belarus, Ukraine, and Moldova all grapped with similar questions; (re)establishing a "national identity" is hard when the national community is so fragmented. The most tragic resurgence of nationalism was in the former Yugoslavia, where, with the exception of the establishment of Slovenia, the breakup of the country was associated with violent nationalism, war, and genocide. The war between Croatia and Serbia escalated into a genocidal struggle for control of Bosnia. The historic Serbian province of Kosovo with its majority Albanian population remained in turmoil at the millennium, and the very existence of the Republic of Macedonia was questioned by Greece and at least certain elements in Albania and Bulgaria. Moreover, virulence of nationalistic rhetoric in Greece, right-wing violence in reunited Germany, and the dramatic rise of the Freedom Party led by Jörg Haider in Austria indicated that the countries of the European Union (EU) were themselves not immune from virulent nationalism.

The EU, especially after the Treaty of Maastricht, reflected an increasingly federal unity based on federal or quasi-federal states with a formal place for regions at the European level. Interregional cooperation was becoming the norm throughout the EU, and even the most centralizing of states, the United Kingdom, seemed set to grant even wider autonomies to its constituent nations, though not as yet the independence that the SNP would like. With the exception of the continued violence in Northern Ireland and to some extent in the Basque lands, the path of regionalism seemed smooth. Yet the regions recognized by the EU were largely defined by zones of economic influence rather than ethnoculture. The line between the two is often blurred, as in Scotland and northern Italy, but to the extent that there has been a "triumph of regionalism," it has been the new, economically defined regions rather than the old, ethnically defined ones that led the way. Nation-state nationalism of the more chauvinistic kind could not be discounted in most of the EU but appeared to be increasingly anachronistic. East of the EU this has not been the case, and nationalism there and in the east, even in its most virulent form, seemed still to flourish.

BIBLIOGRAPHY

Anderson, Benedict. *Imagined Communities.* London: Verso, 1983.

Caplan, Richard, and John Feffer, eds. *Europe's New Nationalisms.* Oxford: Oxford University Press, 1996.

Harvie, Christopher. *The Rise of Regional Europe.* London: Routledge, 1994.

Hobsbawm, E. J. *Nations and Nationalism Since 1780.* Cambridge: Cambridge University Press, 1990.

Weber, Eugen. *Peasants into Frenchmen: The Transformation of Rural France.* London: Chatto and Windus, 1979.

Mícál Thompson

SEE ALSO Alsatian Identity; Corsican Nationalism; Friuli-Venezia Giulia; Galicia; Sardinian Autonomism; Sicilian Autonomism; South Tyrol; Valle D'Aosta; Welsh Nationalism

Natta, Alessandro (1918–)

Leader of the Italian Communist Party (PCI). Alessandro Natta was born on January 7, 1918, in Imperia. He attended the Superior Normal School of Pisa. During that period Natta became involved in anti-Fascist activity. Wounded fighting the German during World War II, after Italy's break with Nazi Germany, he was deported to a prison camp in Germany and took part in the officers' resistance movement while a P.O.W.

In 1945 he entered politics, joining the Italian Communist Party. He became municipal Councilor in the city of Imperia from 1946 to 1960 and was elected to the Chamber of Deputies (lower house of parliament) from the district of Genoa-Imperia-La Spezia-Savona in 1948. He was reelected several times. Natta long served as a member of the Chamber of Deputies' Committee on Education. He was appointed to the National Directorate of the PCI and was elected president of the Communist Parliamentary Group. After General Secretary Enrico Berlinguer's death in 1984 Natta was elected general secretary of the PCI and was unanimously confirmed in that office at the Congress of Florence in April 1986.

In 1987, elected deputy from the electoral wards of both Rome-Viterbo-Latina-Frosinone and of Genoa-Imperia-La Spezia-Savona, he opted for the latter. However, the PCI did so poorly in the election that Natta resigned as general secretary in 1988 and was succeeded by Achille Occhetto.

BIBLIOGRAPHY

Chiaromonte, G. *Le scelte della solidarietà democratica: Cronache, ricordi e riflessioni sul triennio 1976–1979.* Rome: Editori Riuniti, 1986.

Gismondi, A. *Alle soglie del potere: Storia e cronaca della solidarietà nazionale.* Milan: SugarCo, 1986.

La Navicella: I Deputati e i Senatori del 10° Parlamento Repubblicano. Città di Castello: INI, 1988.

Lorusso, M. Occhetto: *Il comunismo italiano da Togliatti al PDS.* Florence: Ponte Alle Grazie, 1992.

Natta, Alessandro. *L'altra Resistenza: i militari italiani internati in Germania.* Turin: Einaudi, 1997.

Turi, Paolo. *L'ultimo segretario: vita e carriera di Alessandro Natta.* Padua: CEDAM, 1996.

Fabio Marino

SEE ALSO Berlinguer, Enrico; Occhetto, Achille

Negri, Antonio (1932–)

Professor at the University of Padua, considered one of the ideological fathers of the leftist group Autonomia Operaia (Workers' Autonomy). Antonio Negri is one of the leading Spinoza scholars and one of the most esteemed Italian experts on Marxism. He contributed the doctrinal bases of "*operaismo,*" an ideology affirming the absolute centrality of the working class. Negri asserted that their revolutionary aims have been repressed by labor unions and leftist parties. He was jailed in 1979, accused of being one of the leaders of the Italian leftist terrorism. According to the so-called Calogero proposition, named after the judge who formulated it, Negri participated in the transformation of Autonomia Operaia into an armed gang and was one of those responsible for the Moro kidnapping. Aldo Moro, the prominent Christian Democratic politician, was kidnapped and eventually murdered by the Red Brigades in 1978. Negri was elected to parliament in June 1983 and, thanks to this, was able to leave prison. He then escaped to Paris, where he currently lives and works.

BIBLIOGRAPHY

Bocca, Giorgio. *Il caso 7 aprile: Toni Negri e la grande inquisizione.* Milan: Feltrinelli, 1980.

Palombarini, Giovanni. *7 aprile: il processo e la storia.* Venice: Arsenale cooperativa editrice, 1982.

Daniele Petrosino

SEE ALSO Moro, Aldo

Nemeth, Miklós (1948–)

Prime minister of Hungary (1988–90), in which position Miklós Nemeth played an important role in insuring the peaceful transition from communism to parliamentary democracy.

Nemeth graduated from the University of Economic Sciences in Budapest. He became an assistant professor there and spent a year at Harvard University in 1974–75. He worked for the Hungarian government in the National Planning Bureau, then held various positions in the Hungarian Communist Party in the 1980s. He was appointed prime minister in 1988, and held that position until parliamentary elections in May 1990, when his party, the Socialist Party (the former Communist Party), was defeated. He was elected to parliament in the May 1990 election but resigned in 1991, when he was invited to become one of the deputy directors of the London-based European Bank for Reconstruction and Development.

Nemeth represented a new generation of Communist leaders who had not been compromised either in the Stalinist era (pre-1953) or in the suppression of the Hungarian Revolution of 1956. This new generation rejected the dogmatism of Marxism-Leninism and allowed liberalization in the political, economic, social, and cultural fields. The gradual introduction of reforms under his premiership resulted in a smooth transition from communism to parliamentary democracy, and from a command economy to a market economy in the late 1980s and early 1990s.

BIBLIOGRAPHY

Kis, Janos. *Politics in Hungary: For a Democratic Alternative.* Boulder, Col.: Social Science Monographs, 1989.

Rothschild, Joseph, and Nancy M. Wingfield. *Return to Diversity: A Political History of East Central Europe since World War II.* 3rd ed. New York: Oxford University, 2000.

Sinor, Denis. *History of Hungary.* Westport, Conn.: Greenwood Press, 1976.

Sugar, Peter F., Hanak, Peter, and Tibor Frank, eds. *A History of Hungary.* Bloomington: Indiana University Press, 1994.

Tamás Magyarics

SEE ALSO Antall, József

Nemtsov, Boris Yefimovich (1959–)

Russian politician. Boris Nemtsov was born in Sochi on October 9, 1959. He received a Ph.D. in physics and mathematics from Gorky State University. Nemtsov left science for politics in the wake of the disastrous release of radiation in the 1986 reactor melt-down at Chernobyl, Ukraine. He led the effort to stop the construction of a nuclear reactor near his home town of Nizhny Novgorod (then Gorky). He was elected to the Duma (parliament) in 1990. During the attempted coup by hard-line Communists in August 1991, he agitated among the soldiers not to participate. In September Russian President Boris Yeltsin appointed Nemtsov to be his personal presidential representative to the Nizhny Novgorod region. He was then elected governor by the regional Soviet. In April 1992 he launched one of the first privatizations in Russia by auctioning twenty-two retail stores previously operated by the state. He brought Grigory Yavlinsky in to oversee economic reform in the region. However, Nemtsov took acting prime minister Yegor Gaidar to task for his precipitous removal of price controls in 1992. Gaidar believed that removing the old prices fixed by the state would stimulate production. Given inadequate supply, however, prices soared. When he was unable to persuade Gaidar to provide the region with more currency, he used his position as governor to authorize the issuing of local currency. His relative economic success in the region led to his election as governor in a popular election in December 1995.

On March 17, 1997, Nemtsov was appointed first deputy prime minister of the Russian Federation. In April he was appointed minister of fuel and energy but was removed from that post in November by Prime Minister Viktor Chernomyrdin, who apparently regarded Nemtsov as a rival for the presidency in 2000. Nemtsov, nevertheless, continued as first deputy prime minister and a member of the Russian Security Council. On March 23, 1998, President Yeltsin, in a surprise move, dismissed Chernomyrdin and replaced him with a young bureaucrat, Sergei Kiriyenko. On August 23, 1998, a week after Kiriyenko's government devalued the ruble to avert financial disaster, Yeltsin reappointed Chernomyrdin prime minister, and Nemstov resigned as first deputy prime minister. In September, in the midst of political turmoil as the Duma refused to approve Chernomyrdin, Nemtsov was appointed to the Council for Local and Self-Government Relations, where he oversaw relations between mayors and the central government.

Bernard Cook

SEE ALSO Chernomyrdin, Viktor; Gaidar, Yegor

Nenni, Pietro (1891–1980)

Italian Socialist leader. Pietro Sandro Nenni was born in Faenza on January 9, 1891. He organized a strike against the Italian invasion of Libya in September 1911. However, he supported Italy's entry into World War I in 1915 and collaborated briefly with the pro-war Benito Mussolini, who had been expelled from the Socialist Party for his advocacy of Italian entry into the war. After the war he broke completely with Mussolini and cut his old ties to the Republican Party to join the Italian Socialist Party (PSI) in 1922. He became editor of the party newspaper *Avanti!,* in which he attacked both Mussolini and his Fascist Party, and those Socialists who formed the Italian Communist party and joined the Communist International. Nenni was temporarily detained by the Fascists in 1925 for publishing a booklet denouncing the murder of Socialist leader Giamoco Matteotti by the Fascists. In 1926 the Fascist government closed *Avanti!* and Nenni sought refuge in France. He was an architect of the 1930 amalgamation of the reformist Unitary Socialist Party with his own revolutionary Italian Socialist Party. Confronted with the threat of fascism, he reversed himself on the issue of cooperating with the Communists. He was the co-organizer and leader of the Garibaldi Brigade during the Spanish Civil War. Nenni was arrested by the Gestapo in occupied France in 1940 and sent back to Italy in 1943, where he was interned on the island of Ponza, in the Tyrrhenian Sea south of Rome. Following the ouster of Mussolini in July 1943 by King Victor Emmanuel on the recommendation of the High Council of the Fascist Party, he was released. After the Nazi-Soviet Non-Aggression Pact of 1939, Nenni had been ousted as leader of the Socialist Party for his espousal of cooperation with the Communists, but he reasserted his leadership after the collapse of the Italian Fascist regime. He served as representative of the Socialists on the National Liberation Council and was appointed vice president of the Council of Ministers under Feruccio Parri. He was elected secretary-general of the PSI in 1945. The following year he was elected to the Constituent Assembly and served as vice premier in the coalition government of Alcide De Gasperi. His continued preference for unity with the Communists led to the breakaway of a portion of the PSI, which under the leadership of Giuseppe Saragat formed the Social Democratic Party of Italy (PSDI). This split enabled De Gasperi to oust the PSI and the Communists from the government and form a ministry without them.

Following the repression of the Hungarian Revolution of 1956 by the Soviet Union, Nenni broke with the Communists. He and Amintore Fanfani, the leader of the Christian Democratic Party, laid the groundwork for a political alliance of the PSI and the dominant Christian Democrats, termed the "Opening to the Left." The PSI, though not part of the government, supported the Fanfani ministry of February 1962 to February 1963. Finally, in December 1963 the PSI directly entered the government of Christian Democrat Aldo Moro. Nenni served as vice premier in three cabinets and was foreign minister in 1968–69. The PSDI combined with the PSI between 1966 and 1969. However, the Opening to the Left did not live up to the expectations of Nenni or Moro. A segment of the Socialist Party seceded and formed the Italian Socialist Party of Proletarian Unity, and Socialist strength slipped as the Communists experienced a resurgence. After the PSDI resumed its separate existence and the center-left alliance collapsed in 1969, Nenni resigned as leader of the PSI. He was appointed a senator for life in 1970 and was elected president of the Senate in 1979. He died on January 1, 1980. Nenni's political career was largely a failure. His PSI was eclipsed by the PCI on the left and the Opening on the Left failed to draw working class votes to the Socialists. Morally he can be credited for preserving the independence of the PSI from the PCI, and repudiating the Communists following the Soviet repression of the Hungarian Revolution in 1956.

BIBLIOGRAPHY

De Grand, Alexander. *The Italian Left in the Twentieth Century: A History of the Socialist and Communist Parties.* Bloomington: Indiana University Press, 1989.

Nenni, Pietro. *Gli anni del Centro sinistra.* Milan: SugarCo, 1982.

———. *Intervista sul socalismo italiano.* Bari: Laterza, 1977.

———. *Tempo di Guerra Freddo: Diari 1943–1956.* Milan: SugarCo, 1981.

Tamburrano, Giuseppe. *Pietro Nenni.* Bari: Laterza, 1986.

Bernard Cook

SEE ALSO Fanfani, Amintore; Moro, Aldo

Neofascism in Western Europe

Since its heyday in the 1920s and 1930s, fascism has at best led a marginal existence in Western Europe. This is especially so if one defines fascism in the strict sense of the term and as practiced by both Mussolini and Hitler, namely, as a form of nationalistic, totalitarian, socialist corporatism. In fact, with the passing of time this phenomenon became more irrelevant as those who were involved with its prewar manifestations gradually died out. The only country where fascism has been politically relevant into the 1990s is Italy, where the "neo"-fascist Italian Social Movement (Movimento Sociale Italiano, MSI)

Skinheads in Leipzig, Germany, raise their arms in an all-too-familiar salute. *Illustration courtesy of Reuters/ Bettmann.*

consistently gained about 6 percent of the national vote. But even there the ideological purity of the "Movement" was always in doubt as hard-liners and "moderates" perennially fought for control of the party. After the collapse of the Italian party system in the early 1990s, the MSI reconstituted itself as the National Alliance (Alleanza Nazionale, AN), and it became a partner in the governing coalition after the 1994 election. In 1996 the AN improved on its 1994 result, winning almost 16 percent of the vote, even though the coalition in which it had been involved lost power. However, the AN has been cultivating a much "softer" and more democratic image since then, and it is now perhaps best classified as "conservative-statist." A "rump" MSI also remains.

Germany, the other nation in Europe where fascism once held power, also is home to two parties possibly deserving of the label "neofascist." The National Democratic Party, (Nationaldemokratische Partei Deutschlands, NPD) was founded in 1964 by survivors of the overtly neo-Nazi Socialist Reich Party (Sozialistische Reichspartei, SRP), which had been banned by the Constitutional Court in 1952. The other party, the German People's Union (Deutsche Volksunion, DVU), dates from 1971. Both parties are under extreme pressure to stay within the letter of the law, which requires all parties to adhere to democratic principles lest they be banned. This fact makes it difficult to classify parties unambiguously as nondemocratic or even fascist. Nevertheless, both parties have at times glorified the Nazi era and denied its crimes. Their programs are cast in language that is often very similar to that employed by the Nazis. Both parties have experienced occasional electoral successes, especially at the local level, but observers generally agree that these successes are due as much to protest voting than to the existence of a large, hard-core extremist potential in Germany.

More unambiguously (neo)-fascist are neo-Nazis, skinheads, and similar groups that exist on the very fringes of the German political spectrum and that make no secret of their admiration for National Socialism. Such militants also exist in other Western European countries, including the United Kingdom, which, with the possible exception of two brief periods during the 1950s and 1970s, has experienced little organized extremism since World War II. The German Office for the Protection of the Constitution (Verfassungsschutz) estimates that in 1996 there were approximately 45,000 persons in Germany with a right-wing extremist "potential," of whom 6,000 were classified as violent skinheads and 2,400 as openly neo-Nazi. These groups have the capacity to make a lot of noise, and they occasionally do physical damage as well as engage in violence against persons, but there is absolutely no question that they have no support among the German population. The same is true for most other European countries.

Much more numerous, and thus worrisome, are the various "New Right" parties and organizations that have sprung up in recent years all over Europe. The ideological differences among these groups and classical, as well as neo-, fascism are substantial enough to warrant not considering them fascists, although the neofascist label is often pinned on them by the media and by various advocacy groups. In any case, all these groups explicitly reject any comparison between themselves and fascism. The most successful of these new radical right parties is the French National Front (FN), led by the colorful Jean-Marie Le Pen. Founded in 1972, the FN languished in obscurity for many years only to experience a sudden and dramatic improvement of its fortunes beginning in late 1983. By the late 1990s the FN had established itself, in terms of the popular vote, as the third-largest political party in France, albeit one without any allies and thus virtually no hope of gaining a significant share of parliamentary seats, much less of being involved in government. The FN, however, does have some influence at the regional and local levels. In 1997 the FN won nearly 16 percent of the vote in parliamentary elections, although it won only one seat in the National Assembly. Similar parties have sprung up: the Vlaams Blok and the Front National in Belgium, the Freedom Party in Austria, the Republican Party in Germany, the Northern League in Italy, and even groups in the Scandinavian countries, although the differences among these parties must not be overlooked. Thus, whereas the French National Front operates very close to the border of what is still considered democratic (using the most generous definition of the term possible), the Progress Parties of Denmark and Norway, as well as the New Democracy Party of Sweden, are best understood as Petit bourgeois protest parties.

Yet some key principles unite these new parties of the far right. First, they tend to be oriented toward a free market, although their support for it is justified less in philosophical and more in pragmatic terms: lower taxes, less bureaucracy, and fewer welfare benefits for "undeserving" foreigners and various domestic "freeloaders." Second, they are authoritarian and xenophobic, opposing any notion of a broadly based, multicultural society. Finally, they are populist with their antielitist rhetoric and their exploitation of the economic, social, and cultural anxieties of many Europeans who are faced with increasing crime, lower job security, and an influx of poor immigrants from all corners of the globe. The New Right thus pitches its message not just to a specific social class but to the disgruntled of all classes. Ironically, this puts them into a situation very similar to that of the fascists of the 1920s, who as late comers onto the political scene were confronted by a fully mobilized party system and thus had to develop an appeal that cut across social class divisions. For this reason the New Right has had to be quite opportunistic, and it pursues every opportunity that is deemed useful in furthering its goals. For example, the French National Front has lately abandoned its free-market platform in favor of a protectionist, anti–European Union, anti-American rhetoric when it appeared that such a plank was a vote winner among France's working class. Above all, then, the New Right is a movement of resentment against the status quo and against the political elites who are considered to be responsible for creating it.

BIBLIOGRAPHY

Cheles, Luciano, et al. *Neo-Fascism in Europe.* London: Longman, 1991.

DeClair, Edward. *Politics on the Fringe: The Case of the French National Front.* Durham, N.C.: Duke University Press, 1998.

"Report of the Committee on Inquiry into Racism and Xenophobia." Luxembourg: Office of Official Publications of the European Communities, 1991.

Andreas Sobisch

SEE ALSO Le Pen, Jean-Marie

Netherlands

Constitutional monarchy located on the North Sea with Germany to the east and Belgium to the south. The Netherlands, a small, densely populated country, industrialized significantly after World War II and also greatly expanded its commercial sector. A founding member of NATO and the European Economic Community (now the European Union, EU), it has played a major role in European integration.

Much of the Netherlands was liberated from German occupation only at the very end of World War II, after the intense suffering of the "hunger winter" of 1944–45. In addition to rebuilding the country, the Dutch also attempted to recover the Dutch East Indies (today, Indonesia). Unsuccessful in this, they acknowledged the country's independence in 1949.

Despite concerns about the viability of the economy without its former Southeast Asian colony, the Netherlands not only recovered from the war but rapidly achieved levels of prosperity previously unknown. A cooperative workforce was one important factor. A willingness to work with other countries, first Belgium and Luxembourg (in Benelux) and then also France, Germany, and Italy (in the European Coal and Steel Community [ECSC] and the European Economic Community) was another factor. The economy also drew strength from several large Dutch companies such as Royal Dutch Shell and Philips. Additionally, the Dutch rebuilt Rotterdam, much of which was destroyed by the Germans in World War II, and it became the largest port in the world, and made Schiphol Airport, near Amsterdam, a major hub for air traffic.

Netherlands. *Illustration courtesy of Bernard Cook.*

A flood in the south in 1953, in which about 1,800 people died, was an important setback to economic growth. From these tragic circumstances, however, came a bold plan to protect the south from future storms—the Delta Works. This gigantic engineering project, which opened up previously isolated areas in the province of Zeeland, was completed only in 1986. Another large engineering project, begun in the interwar period, resulted in closing off the Zuider Zee from the North Sea, turning it into a lake, the Ijsselmeer. After the war two large land areas were reclaimed, but a third area near Amsterdam has not been reclaimed and will remain as a recreation area and wildlife refuge.

The Netherlands is a constitutional monarchy. In this century all the monarchs have been female. Wilhelmina reigned from 1890 to 1948, abdicating in favor of her daughter, Juliana. Juliana reigned until 1980, then abdicated in favor of her daughter, Beatrix. There is presently a male heir to the throne, Willem Alexander.

The government is based on a modified parliamentary system. Parliament consists of two houses, the First and Second Chamber. The Second Chamber furnishes the basis for the inevitable coalition government. After an election, the monarch appoints an *informateur,* who determines what kind of coalition government is possible. Then a *formateur,* who may in fact have just served as the *informateur,* actually constructs the government.

For most of the first three decades after the war, cabinets were made up of coalitions based on the five major parties: Labor Party (PvdA), Liberals (VVD, conservative and libertarian), Catholic People's Party (KVP), Anti-Revolutionary Party (ARP, the more conservative Protestant Party), and Christian Historical Union (CHU, a moderate Protestant Party). Governments were either left-center or right-center, depending on whether the Labor Party was involved.

The system placed a premium on accommodation by those at the top. This stood in stark contrast to the sharp division of life in the Netherlands into blocs, or pillars (Dutch, *zuilen*). The educational system, for example, was divided into a public division, a Protestant division, and a Catholic division, all state-supported. Radio and TV programs were produced by associations based on the existence of liberal, socialist, neutral, Catholic, and Protestant blocs. The nation was deeply divided by these blocs, which represented differing world views, but it was united in a determination to make the system work by accommodation at the top.

The system was challenged in the 1960s, first by the Provos, a playful, anarchistic group that called into question the materialism and aggression that appeared to characterize modern life, then by Democrats '66 (D 66). The second challenge was the more influential. D 66 criticized the unrepresentative nature of the government and the clubby way in which the country was governed. At the same time, and as the result of different factors, the blocs began to fray. Since the 1970s this has resulted in a shift in voting support within the five major parties, with Liberals and Labor gaining. The response of the confessional parties was to form an electoral alliance and in 1980 a single party, the Christian Democratic Appeal (CDA). Another result was that the several smaller parties gained a larger share of the vote. D 66, in fact, became a major player in Dutch politics. Overall, Dutch politics have become more competitive, although the system may still be described by the linked concepts of accommodation and blocs.

Major issues for the government and the nation have been the economy, the welfare state, and the environment. In the 1980s and the 1990s the Netherlands faced economic problems with unemployment, low rate of growth, and inflation similar to those experienced by other European nations. The Netherlands has been luckier than most in that it benefited from the enormous natural gas fields discovered on its continental shelf in the North Sea. The weakness of the economy had much to do with questions about the nature of the welfare state. As in other European countries, the Dutch had come to expect the welfare system not simply to maintain itself but constantly to expand. The debate in the 1990s led to the recognition of limits and, in some areas, to trimming.

The environment has always been of great concern to the Dutch, given that a major portion of the country is the product of a constant give and take with the North Sea. As a very densely populated country, particularly in the Randstad concentration (Ring City) in the west, the Netherlands has always looked carefully at environmental issues affecting the quality of life. The major problem continues to be water, in particular, the pollution of water, especially from the intensive agriculture practiced in the country. A National Environmental Policy Plan was developed (1989, updated 1990), but only continuing effort will keep the situation in balance.

Although a small country with only fifteen million inhabitants, the Netherlands plays an important role in a number of areas. Among these are, in addition to the environment, economic cooperation, social services policies and practices, and international aid and development. Many Dutch are exploring what will likely be the future of those who now live in highly urbanized, industrialized countries.

BIBLIOGRAPHY

Bailey, Anthony. *The Light in Holland.* New York: Knopf, 1970.

Daalder, Hans, and Galen A. Irwin, eds. *Politics in the Netherlands: How Much Change?* London: Frank Cass, 1989.

Gladdish, Ken. *Governing from the Center: Politics and Policy Making in the Netherlands.* DeKalb: Northern Illinois University Press, 1991.

Goudsblom, Johan. *Dutch Society.* New York: Randon House, 1967.

Griffiths, Richard T., ed. *The Economy and Politics of the Netherlands since 1945.* The Hague: Nijhoff, 1980.

King, Peter, and Michael White, compilers. *The Netherlands,* Vol. 88 in "World Bibliography Series." Oxford: Clio Press, 1988.

Lijphart, Arend. *The Politics of Accommodation: Pluralism and Democracy in the Netherlands,* rev. 2d ed. Berkeley: University of California Press, 1975.

Shetter, William Z. *The Netherlands in Perspective: The Organization of Society and Environment.* Leiden: Martinus Nijhoff, 1987.

Michael Richards

Decolonization

A traumatic attempt to hold on to the Dutch East Indies (Indonesia) followed by a political accommodation with the supporters of independence in the Dutch West Indies. In their futile attempt to retain the East Indies (1945–49) the Dutch military suffered 5,000 deaths, a higher percentage of its population than U.S. losses in Vietnam, and in its aftermath, the Netherlands was forced to receive 250,000 refugees, a relatively higher number than the French *pieds noirs* who fled Algeria to France after the Algerian War.

Shortly after the Japanese surrender in August 1945 at the end of World War II, nationalist leader Sukarno proclaimed the independent Republic of Indonesia, a move greatly aided by the absence of Dutch or Allied troops in the Indies. The Dutch government, which viewed Sukarno and the Japanese-trained *pemuda* paramilitary as collaborators and terrorists, angrily dismissed the proclamation and mobilized troops to restore "order" in the Indies. The Dutch public, too, proved passionately committed to the restoration of Dutch rule. In the meantime, however, the Dutch were dependent on first the Japanese, then the British to hold the Indies for them, a task that both powers were reluctant to perform. By the time large numbers of Dutch troops arrived in 1947, most of Indonesia was in the hands of the pro-independence Republicans.

Attempts at negotiations went badly, since the Republicans wanted nothing less than complete independence, while the Dutch were, at best, willing to countenance the Republicans only within the larger framework of a Dutch-Indonesian commonwealth. The accords reached between the parties at Linggadjati, Java in 1946 and the Renville Agreement in 1948, were interpreted differently by both sides and had little long-term effect. Instead the Dutch, anxious to restore the colonial economy and to force Republican moderation, launched two "police actions" in 1947 and 1948 against the Republican stronghold of Java. Although initially successful the police actions embroiled the Dutch colonial army in a vicious and brutal guerrilla war with the Republicans that showed few signs of abatement.

In the end, world opinion in general and American pressure in particular put an end to Dutch hopes for colonial restoration. The United Nations issued calls for the end of fighting and installed commissions that, while seeking a solution, generally favored the Indonesians. The U.S. government, committed to an anticolonial policy and favorably impressed with Sukarno's willingness to crush a Communist uprising in 1948, strongly urged the Dutch to relinquish the Indies, lest they forfeit their Marshall Plan aid. In 1949 negotiations for Indonesian sovereignty got underway, and Queen Juliana signed the treaty for the country's independence on December 27, 1949. The Dutch, hoping to limit the power of the Javanese Republicans, had successfully insisted on a decentralized, federal state. However, in 1950 the Indonesian government abrogated this in favor of a unitary state, sidestepping the last Dutch barrier to Republican control of Indonesia.

The conflict between the Netherlands and its former colony did not end, however. Western New Guinea (Irian Jaya) remained under Dutch administration, and Indonesia's claim to it as an integral part of the country were consistently rejected by the Dutch government. By 1962 Sukarno appeared ready to take the island by force, and scores of Indonesian and Dutch servicemen died in the conflict. The threat of a full-scale invasion, along with U.N. and American pressure, at last persuaded the Dutch government to sign a 1962 agreement that would transfer Irian Jaya to the Indonesians in 1963.

In contrast, political developments in the sparsely populated Dutch West Indies were quiescent. In 1973 the Labor-led Dutch government decided to grant Surinam independence. Realized in 1975, independence triggered mass emigration to the Netherlands, in which the majority of Surinamese opted for Dutch citizenship. The Netherlands Antilles, composed of six Caribbean islands, after an initial wave of pro-independence sentiment, chose to remain under Dutch rule. These islands remain the last vestiges of an empire that the Dutch once proudly claimed as evidence of their global importance. Yet if the loss of their colonies caused some emotional distress to the Dutch, economically it had little affect on the Netherlands, the prosperity of which was rooted in its educated population, its natural gas, and its location in and association with the European Community.

BIBLIOGRAPHY

Grimal, Henri. *Decolonization: The British, French, Dutch and Belgian Empires, 1919–1963.* Boulder, Colo.: Westview Press, 1978.

Lijphart, Arend. *The Trauma of Decolonization: The Dutch and New Guinea.* New Haven, Conn.: Yale University Press, 1966.

Mun Cheong Yong. *H. J. van Mook and Indonesian Independence: A Study of his Role in Dutch-Indonesian Relations, 1945–1948.* The Hague: Martinus Nijhoff, 1982.

Reid, A. *The Indonesian National Revolution, 1945–1950.* Westport, Conn.: Greenwood, 1986.

Sadoc-Dahlberg, Betty, ed. *The Dutch Caribbean: Prospects for Democracy.* New York: Gordon and Breach, 1990.

Wesseling, H. L. "Post-Imperial Holland." *Journal of Contemporary History* 15 (1980):125–42.

James C. Kennedy

Political Parties

In 1945 many Dutch political leaders hoped for a political breakthrough in which the prewar dominance of the Christian parties would be replaced by a secular, bipolar party system. But the pro-"breakthrough" Social Democrats, who had reorganized themselves into the more inclusive Labor Party (PvdA) in 1946, failed to force a change in the elections of that year. Instead, the Catholic People's Party (KVP) reemerged in modified form, as did the much smaller Calvinist Anti-Revolutionary Party (ARP) and the broadly Protestant Christian Historical Union (CHU). Despite its failure, the PvdA found a willing partner in the KVP in the construction of the postwar welfare state. These two parties, each representing nearly a third of the electorate, participated in a stable alliance until 1958, in which the Protestant parties, representing nearly 20 percent of the electorate, and the liberal People's Party for Freedom and Democracy (VVD) often took part. During the period of reconstruction after World War II (1945–58), in fact, the Big Five parties achieved a high degree of political consensus.

After 1958 the religious parties adapted a strategy in which they played the VVD and PvdA, sharply divided on economic issues, against each other, thus ensuring their centrist dominance of the political system. Liberal and Labor unwillingness to play the religious parties' game, however, led to the VVD and the PvdA's attempts at political polarization. The Liberals and Labor sought to undermine the Christian Democratic center by forcing it to choose between the VVD and the PvdA. Polarization and demands for political clarity hit the KVP hard, since they coincided with Vatican II and the social emancipation of Dutch Catholics. The KVP's identity as a distinctly Catholic party disintegrated. Between 1967 and 1972 it lost half its electorate, and attempts to salvage the KVP through forming a united Christian Democratic party with the wary Protestants took years to negotiate. The CHU, also in decline, cooperated with the KVP, but the more stable ARP did not want to sacrifice its Calvinist political principles. At the same time, the PvdA was partially co-opted by the party's militant New Left, many of whom opposed cooperation with the centrist Christians. Finding stable coalitions became even more difficult in the 1960s with the proliferation of small parties, which were encouraged by the Dutch system of proportional representation, including the right-wing Farmer's Party, the pragmatic liberal Democrats '66 party (D'66), the Party of Political Radicals (a KVP left-wing offshoot), and Democratic Socialists '70 (a PvdA right-wing offshoot). In 1973 it took a record 163 days to form a cabinet.

In the 1970s this chaotic situation gradually stabilized. The VVD, under the leadership of Hans Wiegel, grew dramatically as it drew support from those opposed to the welfare state. Labor leader Joop den Uyl managed to create a "big tent" PvdA that undermined support for the "small left" parties, including the Radicals and the Communists, whose ever-smaller memberships eventually merged into the Green Left Party in 1986. Most important, Catholics and Protestants succeeded in founding the Christian Democratic Appeal (CDA) in 1977. This halted the decline of the old Christian parties and offered a largely secularized centrist party attractive to voters. This achievement ushered in a long period of CDA domination (1977–94), in which the party, first under Premier Andries van Agt (1977–82), then under Premier Ruud Lubbers (1982–94), alternately opted between the VVD and PvdA as coalition partners, usually preferring the former. Lubbers was extremely successful in maintaining his own popularity and in finessing a series of painful but carefully nuanced budget cuts. In the end, however, the PvdA and the CDA's popularity was severely tested by budget cuts and rising social problems, and in both parties, coherent ideological identity disappeared. When Lubbers retired, his party declined severely, and its PvdA partners also lost heavily. The new coalition of 1994, marked by the premiership of PvdA leader Willem Kok and the substantial gains of the VVD and the pragmatic D'66 was the first cabinet since 1918 not to include any Christian Democrats. The attempt at breakthrough against Christian Democratic dominance, begun in 1945, thus was reached only in the post–Cold War politics of the 1990s.

BIBLIOGRAPHY

Bakvis, Herman. *Catholic Power in the Netherlands.* Kingston, Canada: McGill-Queens University Press, 1981.

Daalder, Hans, and G. A. Irwin, eds. *Politics in the Netherlands: How Much Change?* London: Frank Cass, 1989.

Gladdish, Ken. *Governing from the Centre.* London: Hurst, 1991.

Houska, Joseph J. *Influencing Mass Political Behavior: Elites and Political Subcultures in the Netherlands and Austria.* Berkeley, Calif.: Institute of International Studies, 1985.

Lijphart, Arend. *The Politics of Accommodation: Pluralism and Democracy in the Netherlands,* rev. ed. Berkeley: University of California Press, 1975.

James C. Kennedy

SEE ALSO Kok, Willem; Lubbers, Ruud

Economy

The postwar Dutch economy has generally followed Western European trends, with some significant exceptions. After a few years of reconstruction the Netherlands experienced some two and a half decades of economic growth, with characteristic dependence on international trade. From the early 1970s to the early 1980s growth rates fell and unemployment grew, before a partial improvement of both as of the mid-1980s.

The postwar economic recovery of the Netherlands was slower than that of many of its neighbors. The war in Europe inflicted substantial capital losses, and the decolonization war in Indonesia from 1945 to 1949 drained limited resources, sharpened balance-of-payments deficits, and thus limited trade. Furthermore, currency reform sacrificed efficiency for equitability, and inflationary pressures remained. The Netherlands did not reliberalize trade by lifting import bans until the late 1940s, much later than Belgium, for example. Textiles, shipbuilding, and metalworking went into sharp decline. But a relatively high share of Marshall Plan aid from the United States, starting in 1948, and a 30 percent currency devaluation in 1949 following that of Great Britain, greatly improved the situation.

Meanwhile, the groundwork for a corporatist economy was laid in the 1945 Extraordinary Decree on Labor Relations. A new guided wage policy involved government guidelines and approval of collective labor agreements (CAOs) between labor and business, and strikes in the postwar era have been extraordinarily rare.

In the golden years, from 1950 to 1973, industry and agriculture fared well as the GDP grew at an annual average of 5 percent. Rotterdam's port enhanced the continued growth of the older industries of oil refining, bulk chemicals, basic metals, paper, and food processing, and multinational firms prospered. Many large firms diversified their businesses in the 1960s, and trade grew more rapidly because of the new European Economic Community (EEC, 1957), whose common agricultural policy particularly benefited the Netherlands. Much of the 1960s growth occurred in the service sector.

During this period wage policy passed through three stages. Wages were linked first to the cost of living from 1946 to 1953, and then to productivity. After this system began breaking down in the late 1950s, the whole guided wage system was officially abrogated in 1963. The result was a "wage explosion," and unemployment began to rise from its low below 2 percent.

Although the 1973 oil crisis shocked the Dutch economy, stagflation, which combined unemployment and inflation, had already begun, and the effects of this first oil crisis were less severe in the Netherlands than elsewhere in Western Europe. Dutch inflation was already at 7 percent in the late 1960s, and peaked just three points higher in the mid-1970s. For 1973–79 economic growth rates close to 3 percent outperformed the European average, as did unemployment, hovering around 6 percent.

The second oil crisis, from 1978 to 1979, proved too much for the Dutch economy to sustain, as GDP growth fell to 1.2 percent for 1979–87, well below the European average. The independent Central Bank controlled inflation but at the cost of appreciating the Dutch guilder by some 30 to 40 percent and thus reducing international competitiveness. Furthermore, cheap natural gas resources in the 1960s had led to the increase in industrial energy consumption. The second oil crisis finally forced the government to allow Dutch natural gas prices to rise to world levels, which compounded production cost increases. Expanding environmental legislation further increased costs, and labor unions insisted on maintaining inflation-indexed wage increases. Unemployment approached 12 percent by 1982 as employment dipped dramatically between 1970 and 1984. During the same period, government expenditures, discounting income transfers, rose from 30 percent of GDP to 40 percent, and the budget deficit from 2 to 9 percent.

Although economic performance did not start to improve until the mid-1980s, the institutional groundwork was laid by a new center-right government in 1982. State expenditures were decreased, and some national firms were privatized. Most significantly, the Wassenaar wage agreement reintroduced a system of voluntary wage constraint, in exchange for a reduction of the work week from forty to thirty-eight hours. As a result, Dutch labor costs remained almost level during the next decade, while those in neighboring European countries increased by as much as 37 percent in Germany's case. Unemployment fell from 12 percent in 1984 to 5 percent in the late 1990s. The largest employment gains were in temporary work, and the proportion of part-time workers expanded; as in the 1970s, female labor participation continued to grow. Union influence declined with membership, although CAOs continued their constant postwar growth to include an ever larger portion of the workforce. The GDP growth of 2.54 percent between 1987 and 1994 outpaced the European average; unlike earlier growth fueled by productivity gains, this growth stemmed largely from increased labor inputs.

At the same time, businesses sold off many acquisitions of the 1960s, and shareholders gained greater power in relation to company managers. After a long slump, share prices entered a steady climb, and only in the mid-1980s did real share prices reach and surpass the peak of the early 1960s.

After the deep crisis of the early 1980s the Dutch economy emerged by the 1990s as a frequently cited model of European success.

BIBLIOGRAPHY

Central Bureau voor Statistiek (Central Statistical Bureau). *Jaarcijfers voor Nederlanden.* The Hague: Staatsuitgeverij, 1945–68. *Statistical Yearbook of the Netherlands.* The Hague: Central Bureau of Statistics, 1969–95; Voorburg/Heerlen: Statistics Netherlands, 1996 to present.

Griffiths, Richard T., ed. *The Economy and Politics of the Netherlands since 1945.* The Hague: Martinus Nijhoff, 1980.

Hartog, F. *Nederland en de Euromarkt.* Leiden: H. E. Stenfert Kroese, 1971.

Van Zanden, Jan L. *The Economic History of the Netherlands, 1914–1995.* London: Routledge, 1998.

Jeffrey William Vanke

Labor Movement

The character and strength of Dutch sociopolitical movements must be understood against the background of a strong commercial and mercantile economy, a relatively late shift to an industrial economy, mainly after 1945, and a firm, but also permissive, hold of the bourgeoisie as a ruling class. Bad social conditions in the nineteenth century gave rise to the formation of a socialist movement led by a former Lutheran pastor, Ferdinand Domela Nieuwenhuis. The socialists confronted a religiously prescribed spirit of submission and a political system dominated by three groups: laissez-faire liberals, Calvinists, and, eventually, Roman Catholics. From the position of outsiders, reinforced by an anarchist tradition and an early (1909) but isolated Communist Party, the social democratic mainstream had to "grow into" this political system. In 1917 universal suffrage was introduced, and in July 1939 socialists were accepted into a coalition government as another minority in a country characterized by political minorities. The labor union movement paralleled the Dutch system of political minorities by its division between small and spontaneous syndicalist formations, united by an umbrella organization in 1893; large, organizationally strong, and internationally oriented, "modern" social democratic unions, which espoused class struggle but supported collective agreements, and were united in national organization in 1906; small and moderate Calvinist unions, federated in 1909; small, mainly white-collar liberal unions, linked together in 1912; and Catholics unions, which promoted social harmony and were linked in a central organization in 1925.

The strongest and leading unions were those of the diamond and metalworkers. Civil servants were not allowed to strike following a large railroad strike in 1903. Collective agreements were supported by law in 1927 (extended in 1937), although implementation depended on the relative strength of unions and employers in each industry. Many unions supported the idea that men were breadwinners for their families and women should not be employed outside the home.

The German occupation of the Netherlands (1940–45) during the Second World War brought the free labor union movement to a standstill. A new unity labor union organization, illegally organized by the Communist Party in 1944, became a mass organization between 1945 and 1947. It proclaimed plant-based unions and an anticapitalist class struggle. Communist domination isolated this new center during the Cold War. It played its role during strikes but eventually died at the end of the 1950s.

In 1945 the former labor union federations, in particular the social democrats, Calvinists, and Catholics, were reestablished. They shared a common desire to preserve social stability under capitalism. The three organizations formed a loose council in which each maintained its own identity. This turned social democrats, who favored general unions open to everyone instead of a specific group, into an accepted "pillar" ("pillarisation," *verzuiling,* refers to the social organizations and subcultures of the various political minorities). Their common policy rejected class struggle in favor of a mild corporatism, which included an elaborate social security system. This was furthered by government coalitions of Christian and social democratic parties. The government recognized these labor groups and provided them with official advisory positions. The main concession of the unions was that they would not play an active role at plant level. The government recognized the Foundation of Labor, which had been established in 1945 by the central employers' and workers' organizations (now known as "social partners") to discuss policies on a bipartite basis. The 1950 Industrial Organization Act provided for the establishment of joint committees for industrial sectors with both advisory and regulatory competencies. Unions reorganized themselves by branch instead of by craft. The branch committees, however, were superseded by a tripartite Social and Economic Council, one-third of whose members represented employers, one-third represented workers, and one-third were independent specialists.

The council became the government's main advisory body in social and economic affairs. A related Works Councils Act (1950) was of limited importance and was implemented slowly owing to the political compromise. The government maintained a tight control of wages through its "guided wage policy," which hardly left the unions any room for collective bargaining at enterprise or industry level. It officially discriminated against women by allowing them to be paid less than men. However, under pressure by the European Community (EC), this policy was terminated in 1975. Because of tensions in the labor market, the guided wage policy was gradually dismantled since the end of the 1960s.

During the 1970s, in a process led by the social democratic industrial unions, labor unions became more militant and politicized. Related unions merged into larger ones, and the Catholic and social democratic unions and federations merged into the progressive Federation of Dutch Trade Unions (FNV), with 1.1 million members. The more conservative Christian federation (CNV) with 350,000 members did not join. Catholic unions opposed to the FNV and other white-collar unions joined together in 1972 to establish the liberal Middle and Senior Staff (MHP), with 150,000 members.

Actions and strikes in the 1970s led to a growing public acceptance of the right to strike for civil servants as well as others. In 1986 the right to strike was legally recognized, as long as certain procedures were followed according to the European Social Charter, a document formulated by the Council of Europe, which enunciated the rights of workers and was ratified by the Netherlands in 1980. However, because of the traditional Dutch policy of conflict avoidance, Dutch labor relations remained rather harmonious, even when the 1970s and 1980s witnessed an increase in strikes.

The Works Councils Act was renewed and enlarged in 1979 and 1990. A European Union directive in 1994 authorized creation of councils on a European scale. Safety and health is regulated by the Dutch 1980 Work Conditions Act. In all enterprises with over thirty-five employees, workers' representatives are authorized to discuss social and economic questions of the enterprise. Labor union members are active in these works councils as well. Works councils dealing with other working conditions, such as production quotas, work classifications, and over-time, encouraged by enterprises in the interest of flexibility in collective agreements, have led to tensions with unions claiming the right to negotiate about working conditions in the context of collective agreements. There is policy coordination, however, between unions and works councils.

Since the 1980s women have also been well represented among new union membership. The percentage of women in the FNV rose from 10 in 1975, to 17 in 1988 and to 23 in 1994. Twenty-four percent of the works councils members are women. Among salaried executives the percentage rose from 14 in 1988 to 25 in 1992.

Overall union density dropped from 40 percent in the 1950s and 1960s to 30 percent in the 1980s; it was 28 percent in the early 1990s—one out of every three male workers and one out of every five female workers. This density is lower than in Germany and the United Kingdom (35 percent) and higher than in the United States and Japan (14 and 24 percent, respectively). Notwithstanding this decline, unions are still seen as relevant. But the traditional picture of the working male breadwinner with a family, which in the 1960s was still the general case, does not fit anymore. New types of workers, part-timers, the young, and the unattached, often doing unskilled work, are more important in the labor force, but these are underrepresented in union membership.

BIBLIOGRAPHY

Andeweg, B., and G. A. Irwin. *Dutch Government and Politics.* Houndmills: Macmillan, 1993.

European Trade Union Institute. *The Trade Union Movement in the Netherlands.* Brussels: ETUI, 1992.

Jacobs, A. *Labour Law and Social Security in the Netherlands: An Introduction.* Den Bosch: BookWorld Publications, 1995.

Jansen, E. P. *Labor Law in the Netherlands.* Deventer: Kluwer, 1994.

Kendall, W. *The Labour Movement in Europe.* London: Allan Lane, 1975.

Visser, J. *In Search of Inclusive Unionism: A Comparative Analysis.* Amsterdam: University of Amsterdam Press, 1987.

Windmuller, J. P. *Labor Relations in the Netherlands.* Ithaca, N.Y.: Cornell University Press, 1969.

Woldendorp, J. "Neo-corporatism as a Strategy for Conflict Regulation in the Netherlands (1970–1990)." *Acta Politica* 2 (1995): 121–51.

Bob Reinalda

Social Security

The Dutch social security system compensated for the low wages that were due to the "guided wage policy" of the 1950s and 1960s, which deliberately restrained wage increases in order to promote development and retard inflation. Prewar social security included mainly employee insurance schemes. Postwar Dutch politics and social partners programs expanded this but also followed British economist Sir William Beveridge's idea of a general social welfare program for the whole population. This included providing benefits for retirement (1954, General Old-Age Pensions Act); death (1959, General Widows and Orphans Act); large families (1963, General Family Allowances Act); medical expenses (1968, General Act on Exceptional Medical Expenses); and disability (1976, General Disability Act). New employees insurance schemes provided benefits in case of unemployment (1952, Unemployment Benefits Act; 1965, Unemployment Provisions Act; 1986, Income Support Act for Older and Partially Disabled Unemployed Employees), sickness (1966, Compulsory Health Insurance Act) and workers' disability (1967, Disability Insurance Act). Supplementary nonstate social security arrangements (private retirement accounts) provide self-employed or better-remunerated workers with pension options. Early-retirement benefits are part of collective bargaining agreements. The administration of these various schemes is entrusted to a complex of institutions like the Social Insurance Bank (a tripartite board for the whole population); bipartite industrial-sector boards, which administer plans for employees; municipal social assistance; health insurance funds and companies; and private funds and companies for supplementary pensions.

Following European Community (EC) directives on equal treatment of women and men and Dutch court rulings in the 1980s, the social security system, which discriminated against women, had to be cleansed of direct and indirect discrimination. Public criticism of the entire structure and concerns about the high costs compared with other Organization for Economic Cooperation and Development (OECD) countries, prompted reform attempts of both laws and administrative structures. Social security contributions add up to 36.5 percent of Dutch wages (29.3 percent paid by workers and 7.2 percent by employers), compared with 15.2 percent (7.6 percent and 7.6 percent, respectively) in the United States. The political parties and social partners had not by the millennium reached an overall consensus concerning costs and benefits. Since the early 1990s three laws have attempted to reduce the claims for benefit in case of sickness and disability.

BIBLIOGRAPHY

De Kleine Gids voor de Nederlandse sociale zekerheid. Deventer: Kluwer (annual guide to Dutch social security).

Jacobs, A. *Labour Law and Social Security in the Netherlands: An Introduction.* Den Bosch: Book World Publications, 1995.

Jansen, E. P. *Labor Law in the Netherlands.* Deventer: Kluwer, 1994.

Bob Reinalda

Foundation of Labor

Joint board for compromising labor and social issues. Postwar labor relations in the Netherlands have been characterized by an effort to avoid conflict. In 1945 Dutch labor unions and employers' organizations established a private body for bipartite discussions on socioeconomic policies. The Foundation of Labor (Stichting van de Arbeid) was incorporated by the government in a July 5, 1945, special Decree on Labor Relations. Its goal was the fostering of amicable relations between employers and workers, and promotion of lasting harmonious social relationships by institutional cooperation. The board has contributed to a mild form of corporatism, in which the "social partners" and the government negotiate continuously to reach common consent. It played its main role in the context of the "guided wage policy" of the 1950s and 1960s to work out specific guidelines for raises. Later it helped to preserve the system of labor relations through annual negotiations over wages and related topics. It also advises the government on labor law and social security matters. The role of the Foundation of Labor was threatened by the establishment of the official tripartite Social and Economic Council in 1950, but in practice the existence of the two bodies added to the flexibility of the system, in particular during periods of tension. Even in the current, more decentralized system, the advisory and guiding functions of the Foundation of Labor are valued.

BIBLIOGRAPHY

Bottenburg, M. van. *Aan den Arbeid.* Amsterdam: Bert Bakker, 1995.

Windmuller, J. P. *Labor Relations in the Netherlands.* Ithaca, N.Y.: Cornell University Press, 1969.

Bob Reinalda

Social and Economic Council

Dutch government's main advisory body in social and economic affairs. Fifteen of the forty-five members of the tripartite Social and Economic Council are independent advisers representing the crown, fifteen represent workers, and fifteen represent employers. The council was set up in 1950 under the Industrial Organization Act, which enabled the establishment of joint committees with both advisory and regulatory competency. Although in the 1980s the government decided to discontinue many of its advisory bodies, the council survived and is the most important advisory body. It has functioned in such a way that economic and social legislation, given the availability of government funding, depends on agreements between employers and unions, who also meet in the context of the Foundation of Labor, a board consisting of employer and worker representatives intended to promote harmonious labor relations.

Another tripartite structure was created by the government for the national and regional employment services, which had previously been run by the state, but it was placed under the control of Council in 1990.

BIBLIOGRAPHY

Klamer, A. *Verzuilde dromen: 40 jaar SER.* Amsterdam: Balans, 1990.

Singh, R. *Policy Development: A Study of the Social and Economic Council of the Netherlands.* Rotterdam: Rotterdam University Press, 1972.

Windmuller, J. P. *Labor Relations in the Netherlands.* Ithaca, N.Y.: Cornell University Press, 1969.

Bob Reinalda

Education

The Netherlands has an educational system distinguished by its pluralistic character. The Dutch government, rather than maintaining only public education, grants subsidies to religious and other private schools, regardless of creed.

The result of a long campaign on the part of Dutch Catholics and Protestants, the School Law of 1917 funded all schools large enough to be viable, including those of any religious faith. Parent associations were thus free to found their own schools with state support. In return for financial support, the state has retained the right to largely determine the curricula, and has monitored educational quality through the use of national, standardized examinations. As a consequence of this law, religious (as opposed to public) schools have flourished in Holland; in the 1980s, about two-thirds of all Dutch students went to religious schools, roughly half to Catholic, and half to Protestant institutions. However, many of these schools have lost their religious distinctiveness since the rapid secularization of the 1960s, and the scramble for scarce students in the 1980s and 1990s has further eroded their former character. As the result of immigration, a number of Islamic and Hindu schools also have been set up under the provisions of the School Law.

Since 1945 the Dutch educational system has mushroomed in size, developing into a dense network of diverse educational institutions. In the 1960s and 1970s, much of the system was reorganized; for example, institutions specially aimed at training agricultural laborers and housewives were replaced by new, high-tech vocational schools. More important, with the advent of the welfare state, education at all levels became affordable for everyone. But one of its chief features, a tracking system, remained intact. After seven years of primary school, students are tracked into different secondary schools according to their demonstrated aptitude. Some students are sent to vocational schools (LBOs); others are placed in secondary schools that prepare them for higher professional education (HAVOs and MAVOs). Students from these institutions often go on to postsecondary "intermediate" and "higher" education (MBOs and HBOs) that, while not equal in status to the universities, offer training for more advanced technical and professional positions. Only a select number of secondary students go to a gymnasium or athenaeum (VWOs), which prepares them for university. Students may, upon the successful completion of one school program, advance to higher levels of education; they move down the educational ladder if they fail to pass the necessary exams. Regardless of educational level, however, Dutch students remain free to select from Protestant, Catholic, or public institutions.

At the top of this educational hierarchy are Holland's twelve universities (only six in 1970). Although the number of matriculated students exploded, as was true elsewhere in Europe, during the 1960s (from 40,000 in 1960 to 103,000 in 1970), still fewer than one-tenth of all Dutch students entered the universities. As in many other European countries, Dutch university education, in contrast to that in the United States, was narrow and specialized. Students were given five years to pursue a given subject.

Dutch universities are some of the most democratic in the world; the 1970 University Law, passed to prevent new outbreaks of the student unrest that affected the Netherlands in 1968 as it did France, Germany, and Italy, gave students and junior staff considerable say in academic and, to a lesser extent, administrative affairs.

Since about 1980 structural problems increasingly have beset the Dutch educational system. Employment for both university graduates and for those with a "lower" technical education is hard to find, and this predicament has shown little sign of easing. Because of state budget cuts, Dutch educational institutions have faced increasing shortfalls in their budgets. Student fees, particularly for postsecondary education, have risen substantially in recent years. Consolidation of institutions at all levels has already occurred, and the government of Prime Minister Wim Kok, elected in 1994, planned to further promote this process, despite considerable resistance.

BIBLIOGRAPHY

Aarts, J. F. M. C. *Onderwijs in Nederland,* 4th ed. Groningen: Wolters Noordhoff, 1985.

Daalder, Hans. "The Netherlands: Universities Between the 'New Democracy' and the 'New Management,' " in Hans Daalder and Edward Shils, eds. *Universities, Politicians and Bureaucrats: Europe and America.* Cambridge: Cambridge University Press, 1982.

Dodde, N. L. *Dag, Mammoet! Verleden, heden en toekomst van het Nederlandse schoolsystem.* Louvain: Garant, 1993.

Kallen, Dennis. *The Future of Education in the Netherlands: Comments on the Proposals of the "Contours Memorandum."* Amsterdam: Institute of Education, European Cultural Foundation, 1980.

U.S. Office of Education. *The Educational System of the Netherlands.* Washington: U.S. Office of Education, n.d.

James C. Kennedy

Press

Despite the rise of electronic media, daily newspapers in the Netherlands still have the public's interest; circulation remains stable, although there are signs of saturation. The most important trend is concentration.

After 1945 it took the Dutch press about five years to recover from the effects of World War II. Scarcity of paper and insufficient press capacity impeded the resurgence of the press business. In this period most prewar papers reappeared and papers founded illegally during the war, like *De Waarheid, Het Parool,* and *Trouw,* continued aboveground. Papers that had continued to publish during the war were prohibited. The prewar situation of partial press "pillarization" (segmentation through identification with a particular party, ideology, or religious outlook), in which the press was closely linked to the political parties, continued after the war. Next to these papers, nonetheless, some politically more neutral papers existed, like *Het Nieuws van de Dag* and *De Telegraaf.* In the latter half of the 1960s a tendency toward depillarization arose. Various previously pillarized papers became independent from the corresponding political parties, like socialist papers *Het Parool* and *Het Vrije Volk* and the Catholic *De Volkskrant.* Some smaller, pillar-oriented papers remained but could generally not be sustained. Nowadays no paper other than the *Nederlands Dagblad* is pillarized, although most papers still have a specific editorial political character.

The Dutch press produces magazines, free local papers, newspapers, and regional daily newspapers. There are about eight thousand different magazines in the Netherlands, representing all possible genres. Almost half the ten million magazines that come out every week are television guides, magazines published by television companies. The largest Dutch magazine is *ANWB Kampioen,* a magazine of the Dutch AAA.

The free local papers are financed through advertisements and are delivered to all households in a certain district. Most come out once a week. Newspapers appear at least once a week, five times at the most, in a restricted geographical area on the basis of subscription. They focus on regional news and barely contain any national reports. They usually attain relatively high coverage percentages; 50 percent is not exceptional. However, a negative development has set into motion with regard to total circulation as well as the total amount of titles. Local newspapers are being caught between free local papers and regional dailies, which cover both regional and national news. Daily papers come out every day except Sundays and holidays. A great deal of their editorial content consists of political and other news, mainly national and international. Backgrounds, news analyses, opinion commentaries, and entertainment articles are also offered. Distinctions can be drawn between national and regional dailies and between general and specialized dailies. There are no Sunday papers or papers specifically dealing with sports. Other distinctions concern the journalistic character (popular versus more serious) and political and religious orientation. Tabloids do not exist.

Eight national daily papers can be distinguished: *De Telegraaf* (conservative, circulation 762,400 in 1997), *Algemeen Dagblad* (conservative, 403,310), *de Volkskrant* (progressive, 372,100), *NRC Handelsblad* (liberal/conservative, 275,830), *Trouw* (progressive/Christian, 121,600), *Het Parool* (progressive, 95,520), *Reformatorisch Dagblad* (Christian/conservative, 58,000), and *Nederlands Dagblad* (Christian/conservative, 30,450). *De Telegraaf* and *Algemeen Dagblad* often are labeled popular papers, whereas *NRC Handelsblad, de Volkskrant,* and *Trouw* are often called more serious. This distinction basically refers to the amount of political information versus entertainment. Another, more exact distinction between the two groups concerns readership. The latter group, especially *NRC Handelsblad* and *de Volkskrant,* attract many more readers from higher educational and income groups.

Furthermore, four specialized papers are published: *Het Financieele Dagblad* (42,540), *Agrarisch Dagblad* (22,000), *Cobouw* (18,376), and the *Nederlandse Staatscourant* (14,600). They appear only five times a week. The former three focus, respectively, on financial, agricultural, and construction news; *Nederlandse Staatscourant* is a governmental paper, covering legislative news.

There are forty-eight regional papers, including the so-called *kopbladen* (head papers), papers that bear a different name in a certain part of the distribution area and have their own regional editorials and advertisements. Regional papers are not necessarily smaller than national; twelve papers have a circulation exceeding 100,000. Most regional papers have a general rather than a specific political or religious character. An exception is the *Friesch Dagblad,* which bears a Christian signature.

The greatest part of paper sales is through subscription (90 percent of total circulation in 1997). The amount of subscriptions is still increasing.

The Netherlands is a newspaper-reading nation. The penetration rate amounted to 89 percent of all households in 1997. Part of this figure is accounted for by sharing copies; about 21 percent of the total circulation is shared among several households. Total circulation has been fairly constant in the 1990s, and there are signs of saturation. Also, the penetration rate has been decreasing since the 1980s. To a great extent, demographic factors accounted for this effect. Half the rise in households consists of single households, which traditionally are not prone to subscribe to a paper. The circulation of regional papers slightly exceeds that of national papers, but the difference is declining.

Another important trend is concentration. Since the war, the number of independent papers (national and regional) and publishers has declined. At the beginning of 1997 there were twelve independent publishing groups, as compared to eighty-one in 1946. Five publishing groups, with stakes in both the national and the regional press, dominate the market.

The concern with mergers is the threat to editorial independence and thus overall press diversity. Yet no government antitrust legislation pertains to the press. All regulation is self-imposed; in 1993 publishers agreed that one single publisher would never own more than one-third of the market. The moderate governmental stance is accounted for by the pivotal value of press freedom, as guaranteed in the constitution. Government intervention is limited to financial support for economically weak papers, granted through an independent Press Fund.

BIBLIOGRAPHY

Brants, Kees, and Denis McQuail. "The Netherlands," in Bernt Stubbe Østergaard, ed., Euromedia Research Group. *The Media in Western Europe: The Euromedia Handbook,* 2d ed. London: Sage, 1997, 153–67.

Hemels, Joan. "De Krant Koning? Van Klassiek Massamedium tot Modern Communicatieproduct," in Jo Bardoel and Jan Bierhoff, eds. *Media in Nederland,* 9th ed. Groningen: Wolters-Noordhoff, 1997, 68–84.

———. "Social Contextualization of the Press: The Dutch Case." *European Journal of Communication Research,* 22, no. 3 (1997):317–41; Peter Vasterman. "Lezen naar Leefstijl: De Vlottende Positie van het Tijdschrift in de Beeldcultuur," in Jo Bardoel and Jan Bierhoff, eds. Media in Nederland. Groningen: Wolters-Noordhoff, 1997, 102–20.

Ellen Mastenbroek

Immigrants and Immigration

Dutch policy toward immigrants and immigration has been a slow, incremental process. A distinction can be made between policy toward immigrants (minorities policy) and immigration (aliens policy). The Dutch barely use the word "immigrants"; such individuals are referred to as "allochthonous persons" (those transported from other environments) or "ethnic minorities."

After the Second World War Dutch admission policies were quite restrictive. The Dutch government even promoted emigration. Yet this period witnessed large-scale immigration of Indonesian repatriates, Surinamese, and Antilleans. In the 1960s the Netherlands attracted great numbers of so-called guest workers from Mediterranean countries to ease the labor shortage. Yet the government still did not consider the Netherlands a country of immigration. The postcolonial migrants and especially the guest workers were expected to return home some day. Therefore policies in that period aimed at integration with retention of identity. In reaction to economic recession, admission of guest workers became more restricted in 1968. Foreign workers would need preliminary permission to migrate, to be granted by a Dutch embassy or consulate by means of an "Authorization of Provisional Stay." Since 1973 labor immigration has been permitted in exceptional cases only.

The ambivalence of the Dutch toward immigrants lasted throughout the 1970s. The Netherlands still did not consider itself an immigration country. At the same time there was little political will to restrict the still-increasing influx of immigrants. Instead, remigration constituted an imported policy aim. In 1979, however, the Scientific Council for Governmental Policy published its "Ethnic Minorities" report, and the government finally acknowledged that remigration was a myth. It formulated the fundaments of a coherent policy in the 1983 minorities memorandum, characterized by two aims: a tolerant, multicultural society and social equality. The new minorities policy, as developed in the 1980s and 1990s, can be broken down into three categories: integration policy, policies with regard to legal position and discrimination, and cultural policy.

Integration policy concerns equality in the areas of employment, education, housing, and social security. The main problems have been with employment and education. In the 1980s the main goal was to establish equal starting positions through education. However, when unemployment among immigrants remained persistent, a political discussion arose about affirmative action. Though this idea met with resistance from employers, in 1993 a law to promote equal labor opportunities for immigrants was adopted. It sought to reduce unemployment by compelling employers to report on the ethnic composition of their staff.

The legal position of immigrants was regulated in the 1985 Citizenship Act. Immigrants were allowed to obtain a permanent residence permit after five years of legal residence; family members could do so after three years. Legal immigrants could acquire Dutch citizenship by choice or naturalization. The choice option was open to immigrants aged eighteen to twenty-five who had lived in the Netherlands all their lives. Naturalization was subject to fulfillment of a number of conditions and allowed for holding double nationality. Legal aliens received the right to vote in municipal elections after five years of residence.

Though the principle of nondiscrimination is laid down in the constitution and various civil and criminal laws, discrimination still exists. There are a few right-extremist political parties, which cannot be banned legally. The situation was less volatile than in neighboring Belgium and Germany. In the 1998 elections the parties of the far Right did not obtain a seat in parliament.

Cultural policy relates to culture, religion, and ethnic organizations. The overall goal has been a multicultural society. Ethnic minorities were given the right to organize and preserve their own culture, religion, and language. Government played a rather active role in this. But a problem concerns public opinion, which recently became more negative toward ethnic diversity. The goal of a multicultural society and the integration policies came under pressure. In 1994 acclimatization of immigrants to the Dutch culture (*inburgering*) became an important issue on the political agenda. In 1995 the government issued a notice on implementation of a program for acculturation (*inburgeringstraject*) for newcomers, consisting of an introduction to the Dutch society and Dutch language education. Municipalities were responsible for implementation of the policy, the frame of which was designed by the central government. The policy was formalized in the 1996 Acclimatization Act (*Inburgeringswet*), which involved an obligation for immigrants to take part in the *inburgeringstraject.*

Dutch policy on aliens (*Vreemdelingenbeleid*) was laid down in the New Dutch Aliens Act of 1994. In the same year, the secretary of justice issued the Aliens Circular 1994, which contained directives for policy implementation and has been updated yearly. Various other authorities have been involved in aliens policy. The Directorate of Aliens Policy develops policies for the Immigration and Naturalization Agency to carry out. The twenty-five Police Departments all have an Aliens Department.

Dutch law distinguishes among three main types of legal immigrants: migrant workers, family members of legal immigrants, and refugees/asylum seekers. Work permits are issued on the basis of the 1978 Aliens Employees Act, which sought to restrict admission of foreign workers. A work permit is only granted on the condition that a Dutch or European Union citizen cannot be found to fill the vacant position. The second type of immigration, family reunion/formation, has become an important ground for immigration. Dutch policy in this area is rather liberal, although attempts to restrict have been made. The third category of immigrants consists of invited refugees and individual refugees or asylum seekers, between whom Dutch policies distinguish. The former are recognized as such by the Dutch government and transferred to the Netherlands on its behalf; the latter are persons who seek asylum in the Netherlands. A last type of immigrant is illegal aliens. Their number in 1995 amounted to an estimated 50,000 to 100,000. In 1996, 51,000 aliens were expelled, one-third of whom were asylum seekers.

Until 1977, when a quota was established, admission of refugees was regulated ad hoc. In 1981 a centralized policy for invited refugees was introduced. However, there was no centralized admission policy for asylum seekers until 1987, when a new regulation on the Reception of Asylum Seekers (ROA) came into effect. It aimed at housing asylum seekers in municipal ROA houses and Centers for Asylum Seekers. The ROA can be characterized as austere but humane, designed to discourage asylum seekers from applying in the Netherlands. In 1992 a new, more restrictive asylum procedure was adopted, because of the ineffectiveness of the old procedure for the increasing number of applicants. Nonetheless, the amount of refugees and asylum seekers continued to increase. In the first half of the decade the influx skyrocketed, 1994 being a top year with 52,000 applicants. Since then, the number decreased again to around 20,000 a year. A new increase occurred in 1997, with 34,443 asylum seekers applying.

Invited refugees are received in the Central Refugee Center in Apeldoorn until they are allotted a house (formally within three months). Asylum seekers are first referred to a Reception and Investigation Center. The first decision on their application is taken within thirty days on the basis of an interview with an officer of the Department of Justice. Asylum seekers who will in all probability be admitted are housed in a regular Reception Center pending the conclusion of the procedure. All acknowledged refugees are granted a permanent residence permit.

BIBLIOGRAPHY

Gulbenkian, Paul, and Ted Badoux, eds. *Immigration Law and Practices in Europe.* London: Chancery Law Publishing, 1993.

Lucassen, Jan, and Rinus Penninx. *Nieuwkomers, Nakomelingen, Nederlanders: Immigranten in Nederland 1550–1993.* Amsterdam: Het Spinhuis, 1994.

Muus, Philip. "Shifting Borders: The Inclusion and Exclusion of Refugees and Asylum Seekers in the Netherlands," in Philip Muus, ed. *Exclusion and Inclusion of Refugees in Contemporary Europe.* Utrecht: European Research Centre on Migration and Ethnic Relations, 1997, 78–95.

Overdijk-Francis, J. E., G. M. Rutten, A. G. Smeets, C. A. Tazelaar, and J. A. C. Verheyden, eds. *Handboek Minderheden.* Lelystad, Netherlands: Koninklijke Vermande, 1993.

Ellen Mastenbroek

Catholicism

The Roman Catholic Church in the Netherlands was the basis for an intensely close-knit religious subculture until the early 1960s, yet it underwent a series of radical theological reforms in the 1960s and shortly thereafter witnessed a decline in membership and coherence unparalleled in Western Europe in its speed and scope.

In the early 1960s Catholics made up between 30 and 40 percent of the Dutch population. Of these approximately half lived in the overwhelmingly Catholic southern provinces of North Brabant and Limburg. The remainder was scattered throughout the small villages of the agrarian north and in the industrial cities of the west. Although Catholics in these regions lived side by side with their non-Catholic neighbors, they led lives detached from those of their neighbors and retained a remarkably coherent Catholic identity. In 1947 fewer than 7 percent of Dutch Catholics married non-Catholics. The figure for West German Catholics, by comparison, was 31 percent.

The Dutch use the term "pillarization" (*verzuiling*) to refer to the distinct subcultures that made up their society from the turn of the century onward. These "pillars" included Catholics, liberals, Social Democrats, and strict Calvinists, each led by a small elite and held together by a vast network of ancillary organizations that integrated daily life from the cradle to the grave. In the 1960s there were ten different Catholic youth organizations, forty-eight charity or charitable organizations, and thirty-two organizations representing almost every imaginable professional group: workers, shop owners, farmers, even Catholic goat breeders. The Catholic political party—Catholic People's Party (KVP)—likewise won the votes of over 80 percent of Catholics until the early 1960s, an astoundingly high figure without equal in Western Europe.

Yet by the late 1960s this picture of coherence and tradition was to change irrevocably. Already in the 1950s there were signs of waning interest among the young. The membership in Catholic youth organizations declined from nearly 885,000 in 1950 to 638,000 in 1963, while the number of new candidates for the priesthood also decreased. It was perhaps out of fear that Dutch Catholics were being left behind by changes in culture and society that the Dutch bishops introduced an ambitious, radical course of reform. They were strongly influenced by new ideas and theological ferment in the seminaries and universities. Instead of providing their flock with detailed guidelines on how to lead their daily lives, many clergy sought to open the church doors to outside influences, to legitimize critical debate within the church, and above all to instill new, more individualistic virtues of personal responsibility. These efforts to relax tight moralistic strictures on individual behavior were reinforced by the climate of ecumenism that arose during the Second Vatican Council (1962–65). And so in the mid-1960s, the Dutch bishops took a more open stance on issues such as birth control.

These new policies of tolerance, openness, and ecumenism in the Netherlands had enormous ramifications for Catholic institutions. The once vast network of Catholic ancillary organizations collapsed in a way that has often been referred to as "depillarization." By 1978 only seven of the ten youth organizations still existed; the national center for Catholic Youth Work dissolved itself in 1977. Of the 161 national Catholic organizations in 1960, little more than 60 remained in 1980. The percentage of Dutch Catholics voting for the Catholic People's Party accordingly dropped from nearly 84 percent in 1964 to less than 40 percent by 1974. By 1980 the KVP was forced to merge with two Protestant parties—the Anti-Revolutionary Party (ARP) and the Christian Historical Union (CHU). As attendance at Mass plummeted, some voters saw little point in voting for confessional parties; others, in light of the reforms of the 1960s, separated politics from religion.

The church in Rome responded dramatically to these changes. Against the wishes of the Dutch episcopate, two conservative bishops, Adrien Simonis and Jan Gijsen, were appointed to the diocese of Rotterdam and Roermond, respectively. Both were sympathetic to those who sought to uphold tradition and authority in the church. Gijsen's tenure in office proved so controversial (and evoked the ire of so many Dutch Catholics) that the Vatican was ultimately forced to transfer him in 1993 to Iceland, where he served as the Bishop for fewer than four thousand Catholics.

In the eyes of many contemporaries, Dutch Catholicism was transformed in under ten years from a subculture noted for being tradition-bound and narrow to one considered the most emancipated, progressive, and secular in Europe.

BIBLIOGRAPHY

Bakvis, Herman. *Catholic Power in the Netherlands.* Kingston, Canada: McGill-Queen's University Press, 1981.

Coleman, John A. *The Evolution of Dutch Catholicism, 1958–1974.* Berkeley: University of California Press, 1978.

Damberg, Wilhelm. *Abschied vom Milieu? Katholizismus im Bistum Münster und in den Niederlanden 1945–1980.* Paderborn, Germany: Schöningh, 1997.

Duffhues, Ton, and Joos Van Vugt. "Literatuur over 'Verzuilung en ontzuilung'," in *Jaarboek van het Katholiek Documentatie Centrum 1980* (1980) 160–70.

Mark Edward Ruff

Women's Movement

A traditional women's movement in the 1940s and 1950s, the Dutch women's movement was transformed into a feminist-inspired women's rights movement after 1967. Women in the Netherlands were traditionally assigned homemaking roles. In the 1930s this was stressed even by the enactment of laws restricting married women from working outside the home. But during the Second World War women came to assume other responsibilities. They took the jobs of men who were forced to work in Germany or became involved in the resistance movement. However, women in these years had a hard time finding enough food for their children and families.

After the war, most women gladly resumed their role as homemaker. The government even launched a political program to restore family life as the basis of Dutch society. The war was considered to have caused the moral decay of the family. In addition to being the object of a family politics, the family also became the basis of the government-initiated welfare-state programs. In 1960 the General Social Assistance Act was enacted; it based the level of social assistance on a family consisting of a man, a woman, and two children. If the male, the breadwinner, lost his job, the family would rely on social assistance. His wife was supposed to continue fulfilling her role inside the home. It is not surprising then, that the number of Dutch women working outside the home ranked among the lowest in the Western postwar world. Figures from 1947 show that no more than 10 percent of all married women in the Netherlands had a paying job. In the United States in 1947 the level was 35 percent. In 1960 the Dutch percentage was even lowered, to 7 percent. Although the figure has subsequently increased, in 1985 the percentage of women with paid jobs was still the lowest of any country in Europe.

The Dutch women's movement corresponded with the traditional family housewife pattern. The movement encompassed dozens of associations with different goals, varying from volunteer work or health care to children's issues. Political parties, churches, farmers, and workers' unions had their own women's organizations. All these groups were organized on the compartmentalized (pillarized) basis that characterized Dutch society as a whole since the early 1920s. Instead of being based on a class structure, the Netherlands until the 1970s was a segmented society consisting of at least four ideologically inspired segments (pillars), or social movements: Protestants, Catholics, Social Democrats, and Liberals. Thus, apart from Protestant and Catholic women's organizations, Socialist and Liberal counterparts existed. However, since the so-called second wave of emancipation overtook the Netherlands in the late 1960s, a women's rights movement developed. Women started asking for equal access to jobs, equal pay, equal educational opportunities, and equal chances in economic and social life. They also started to fight for a woman's right to choose abortion, as well as for social-service legislation that assigned benefits on an individual instead of a family basis. The first publicly visible form of the second-wave women's movement was the Mad Minnies (Dolle Mina), a group of militant feminists who provocatively found ways of demanding equal treatment of women. Man-Woman-Society (Man-Vrouw-Maatschappij) was an organization that tried to convince the Dutch establishment by argument and facts that women's rights had to be taken seriously. One consequence of these initiatives was that the government in the mid-1970s launched a women's emancipation policy. The Dutch women's movement developed contacts with the Dutch administration concerning emancipation, and many gains in equality were made. Women gained independent access to the labor market, and the prohibition of sexual discrimination was incorporated in the constitution.

In some areas, however, Dutch women have yet to catch up with women in other European countries. The Netherlands, as a member of the European Union (EU), is expected to follow European legislation. Since the late 1980s the EU has enacted five guidelines on equal treatment of men and women, and the Dutch government is obligated to implement these in national legislation. Nevertheless, it as been the slowest to date of all EU countries to comply.

BIBLIOGRAPHY

Bruijn, J. de, L. Derksen, and C. Hoeberichts. *The Women's Movement: History and Theory.* Avebury: Aldershot, 1993.

Gelb, J. *Feminism and Politics: A Comparative Perspective.* Berkeley: University of California Press, 1989.

Leijenaar, M. "Women in Public Administration in the Netherlands," in J. H. Bayes, ed. *Woman and Public Administration: International Perspectives.* New York: Harrington Park Press, 1991, 41–55.

Meehan, E., and S. L. Sevenhuijsen, eds. *Equality, Politics and Gender.* London: Sage, 1991.

Overzicht van de Archieven in het Internationaal Informatiecentrum en Archief voor de Vrouwenbeweging. Amsterdam: IIAV, 1991.

Hillie J. Van de Streek

Provos

One of the most creative and successful countercultural movements of the 1960s. Similar to the American Yippies in style, the Dutch Provos antedated them by several years and proved more effective in drawing widespread, and often sympathetic, public attention for their cultural and political aims.

Formed in May of 1965, the Provos were never an ideologically cohesive group. A few of them, like their leader Roel van Duyn, were theoretical anarchists; others were self-styled urban reformers. For example, the White Bicycle Plan, the most famous of the Provo "White Plans" (named after the Provos' favorite color), proposed prohibiting all cars from the center of Amsterdam, replacing them with thousands of free, public bicycles. Most of all, however, Provo was an impulsive movement that derived popularity from its playful opposition to authority. Provo "happenings" became the scene of a series of minor riots between police and public, and the Provos' hurling of smoke bombs during the 1966 wedding of Princess Beatrix and the German Claus von Amsberg proved the high point in their campaign to confound authority. Provo largely succeeded in making Dutch authorities seem both repressive and ridiculous.

Ultimately, however, Provo became the victim of its own success. Although none of their "White Plans" were directly implemented, sympathy among prominent citizens for the Provos' romantic, nonauthoritarian goals became so widespread that maintaining their oppositional stance became difficult. The police, too, developed more subtle tactics, avoiding open conflict. Partly for these reasons, Provo disbanded in May, 1967, although it retained a seat in the Amsterdam city council, and would inspire further countercultural activity, both at home and abroad.

BIBLIOGRAPHY

De Jong, Rudolf. "Provos and Kabouters," in David E. Apter and James Joll, *Anarchism Today.* Garden City: Doubleday, 1972.

Mamadouh, Virginie. *De stad in eigen hand. Provoís, kabouters en krakers als stedelijke sociale beweging.* Amsterdam: SUA, 1992.

Van Duyn, Roel. *Provo. De geschiedenis van de provotarische beweging.* Amsterdam: Meulenhoff, 1985.

James C. Kennedy

Euthanasia

Widely accepted medical practice with few effective legal restrictions. Although still technically illegal under the Dutch penal code, active euthanasia has been increasingly performed by the Dutch medical establishment since 1970, when the topic first became the subject of public debate.

In 1971 a Dutch doctor, G.E. Postma-Van Boven, administered a fatal dose of morphine to her mother, who, in chronic ill health, had expressed the wish to die. Found guilty of active euthanasia in 1973, the daughter was given a suspended sentence. Her case unleashed a movement, spearheaded by doctors, that sought the complete decriminalization of assisted suicide and active, voluntary euthanasia. This movement was supported mostly by socialists and liberals, and opposed by the Christian Democrats. Although the Dutch public has remained divided on the issue, the parameters of what might constitute morally acceptable euthanasia has generally widened since 1973, from use only on terminal patients, as argued by the Muntendam Commission of 1978, to those with a hopeless and painful prognosis, as argued by the State Commission report in 1985.

In the absence of any political consensus, Dutch doctors developed their own ad hoc procedures in which they often proved prepared to actively euthanize chronically ill patients who persistently asked to die. ("Passive euthanasia," not considered euthanasia in Holland, is widely practiced.) In 1981 a Rotterdam court established guidelines under which doctors could avoid being prosecuted under Article 293, such as consulting other doctors and seeking other options for the patient. But in reality doctors have executed euthanasia with little or no legal supervision. Most cases of active euthanasia have gone unreported, so that the number of related deaths is unknown. Both judges and politicians, unwilling to uphold a law for which public support has dwindled, have turned the matter over to the medical profession, which is highly esteemed in the Netherlands. They have counted on doctors themselves to "control" and "restrict" euthanasia. At the same time, politicians have resisted legalizing euthanasia for fear that it will increase the practice.

Dissatisfaction with this indeterminate situation, however, led to legislation in 1993 in which assisted suicide was conditionally legalized and in which euthanasia would not, under specific conditions, be prosecuted. In both cases, patient consent formed the basis of the conditions. The laws provided neither the full legal protection liberalizers desired nor the effective restrictions opponents demanded, and thus the euthanasia debate shows no sign of going away.

BIBLIOGRAPHY

Gomez, Carlos F. *Regulating Death: Euthanasia and the Case of the Netherlands.* New York: Free Press, 1991.

Hoogerkamp, Gijsbert. *Euthanasie op het Binnenhof: De euthanasiediscussie in politiek-historisch perspectief (1978–1992).* Utrecht: Utrechtse Historische Cahiers, 1992.

Keown, John. "The Law and Practice of Euthanasia in the Netherlands." *Law Quarterly Review* 108 (1992): 51–78.

Rapport van de Staatscommissie Euthanasie. The Hague: Staatsuitgeverij, 1985.

Van der Maas, P. J. *Euthanasia and Other Medical Decisions Concerning the End of Life.* Amsterdam: Elsevier, 1992.

James C. Kennedy

Nielsen, Holger K. (1950–)

Danish politician, chairman of the Socialist People's Party. Holger Nielsen, who was born in 1950, received a doctorate in social sciences from the University of Copenhagen in 1979. He was employed by the parliamentary group of Communists and related parties at the European Community (EC) Parliament from 1979 to 1981. He was a civil servant in the Ministry of Energy from 1981 to 1987.

Nielsen was chairman of the youth organization of the Socialist People's Party from 1974 to 1977. He was elected party chairman in 1991.

Nielsen represents the young generation of Danish socialists to the left of the Social Democratic Party who nevertheless do not espouse the Marxist-Leninist tradition and allegiance to the old Communist parties. He has written two books on the EC and a 1994 work, *Frihed i fællesskab* (*Freedom in Community*), in which he described his vision of the Socialist People's Party.

BIBLIOGRAPHY

Nielsen, Holger. *"Fornyelse i dansk politik": SF gennem 20 ar.* Copenhagen: SP Forlag, 1979.

Jørn Boye Nielsen

Noel-Baker, Philip (1889–1982)

British politician and disarmament advocate. Philip Noel-Baker was a Labour member of parliament (1929–31,

1936–70). He served as junior minister (1942–46), air minister (1946–47), Commonwealth relations minister (1947–50), minister of fuel and power (1950–51), and chairman of the Labour Party executive (1946–47). He became a life peer in 1977 as Lord Noel-Baker of Derby.

Noel-Baker, a Quaker, became interested in international disarmament while he was a League of Nations employee in the 1920s. He pursued this concern throughout his life. He was the author of numerous books, pamphlets, and articles on international law, disarmament, and the armaments trade, notably *The Private Manufacture of Armaments* (1936), and was well known for over fifty years as a lecturer on these subjects in many countries. Noel-Baker was awarded the Nobel Peace Prize in 1959.

As a Labour minister, Noel-Baker contributed to the organization of U.N. agencies, was a British delegate to U.N. bodies and international conferences, and had some input in British foreign and defense policy making. Despite acknowledged political skills, his uncompromising views on multilateral disarmament blocked his promotion, possibly to the Foreign Office in succession to Ernest Bevin.

Noel-Baker, a noted athlete in his youth, was active in the Olympic Games movement, often as a dissenting voice attacking commercial and political exploitation of sports.

BIBLIOGRAPHY

Gray, Tony. *Champions of Peace.* London: Paddington, 1976.

Whitaker, David J. *Fighter for Peace: Philip Noel-Baker, 1889–1982.* London: Sessions, 1989.

Don M. Cregier

Nomenklatura

The crucial mechanism of the Communist system of rule. "Nomenclatura" in Latin means a register or system of names. Although operation of the nomenklatura mechanism in Communist countries was highly institutionalized and even bureaucratized, it was never included in official proclamations on the system's working.

In practice "nomenklatura" had three interrelated meanings. First, it was a secret list of commanding positions in all spheres of social life that could not be filled without prior approval of a relevant committee of the Communist party. Party committees of various levels had assigned to them specific lists of positions that a unit of a given level was responsible for staffing. Beyond state administration positions, the list included numerous posts in the economy, media, cooperatives, labor unions, youth organizations, and voluntary associations. The list included positions that formally had electoral status (such as members of parliament) but could not be occupied without the approval of a proper party body. Second, it was a group of persons who held those positions in society, plus those perceived by the proper party bodies as suitable for taking such positions in case of vacancies, the so-called reserve cadre. When the Communist system matured, the nomenklatura in this sense became a separate rank of people granted certain rights and privileges. Those holding party posts that allowed them to make decisions about staffing the nomenklatura positions could be labeled members of the "inner party." There was an essential divide between those members of the apparatus (like secretaries of local, territorial units) who, once established in their positions, acted on a voluntary basis while retaining their earlier nonparty employment, e.g., school teachers, and those who became professional apparatchiks. The first group was excluded from circulation of some classified materials. Third, the nomenklatura was a system of societal control through the selection of cadres. Nomenklatura as a system of rule preferred ideological, organizational, and personal loyalty over competence. The system therefore promoted negative selection of cadres, since individuals were excluded for independence rather than incompetence. The mechanism secured the monolithic character of the Communist system. The policies of staffing the nomenklatura positions were regulated by secret directives issued by the political bureau of the central party committee. High political positions within the non-Communist, satellite parties also could be filled only through prior acceptance of a given Communist party committee. Occasionally directives from above encouraged lower-level party bodies to include ideologically "trustworthy" nonparty members in the nomenklatura to show the "democratic" nature of the party cadre policies. In the 1970s in Poland, an example of such top-down-directed personnel policies was the directive that the second secretary in regions (voivodships) should be a female.

Operation of the nomenklatura system was not legal even according to the Communists' own legal standards; there were, for example, no official legal provisions authorizing Communist party units to make direct decisions concerning the staffing of the managerial posts within state and cooperative enterprises. Only in the mid-1970s, after the principle of the ruling position of the Communist party in society was inserted into constitutions of the Soviet satellites, did some legal experts use this as a general justification for operation of the nomenklatura system. The nonconstitutional character of the nomenklatura system and the confidential nature of the cadre's recruitment procedures blurred the relationships between the state administration and the Communist party. It justified the use of the encompassing term "party-state."

BIBLIOGRAPHY

Ehrlich, Stanislaw. "Nomenklatura." *Panstwo i Prawo* 11–12 (1991).

Fleron, F. J. Jr. "Co-optation as a Mechanism of Adaption to Change: The Soviet Political Leadership System." *Polity* 3 (1969).

Garlicki, Andrzej, ed. "Nomenklatura." *Polityka* (September 8, 1990).

Harasimyw, B. 1969. "Nomenklatura: The Soviet Communist Party Leadership Recruitment System." *Canadian Journal of Political Science* 2, no. 3 (1969): 493–512.

Holmes, Leslie. *Politics in the Communist World.* Oxford: Clarendon Press, 1986.

Kaminski, Antoni Z. *An Institutional Theory of the Communist Regimes.* San Francisco: ICS Press, 1992.

Nove, Alec. "Is There a Ruling Class in the USSR?" *Soviet Studies* 34 (October 1975): 615–38.

Perzkowski, Stanislaw, ed. *Tajne dokumenty Biura Politycznego i Sekretariatu KC: Ostatni rok władzy 1988–1989* (*Secret Documents of the Politburo and the Secretariat of the Central Committee*). London: Aneks, 1994.

Podgórecki, Adam. "The Communist and Post-Communist Nomenklaturas." *Polish Sociological Review* 2 (1994).

Rigby, T. H. "Staffing USRR Incorporated: The Origins of the Nomenklatura System." *Soviet Studies* 40, no. 4 (1988): 523–37.

Andrzej Zybertowicz

Nordli, Odvar (1917–)

Prime minister of Norway (1976–81). Odvar Nordli was born November 3, 1917, in Stange. After studying business, worked briefly in the municipal auditor's office in Baerum before being appointed chief clerk in the Hedmark County auditor's office. He held that post from 1949 to 1957, when he became district auditor for the communes of Vang and Löten. Nordli was elected to the Stange Municipal Council in 1952. In 1960 he was elected chair of the municipal committee of the Hedmark Labor Party and was elected to parliament from the Labor Party in 1961. He was appointed a deputy member of the Labor Party's Central Committee in 1965 and chairman of the Hedmark Labor Party in 1968. Nordli served as minister of labor and municipal affairs in 1971–72. He was chosen to lead the Labor Party from 1973 to 1976. Nordli succeeded Trygve Bratteli, also from the Labor Party, as prime minister in 1976. Despite gains by Labor in the 1977 election, the party still depended on the vote of the Socialist Left Party to retain the government. After 1977 the party was increasingly weakened by foreign policy disputes and personal rivalries. Nordli rebuffed the left wing of the Labor Party when his government agreed to allow the United States to stockpile military equipment in Norway, and he resigned in February 1981. Gro Harlem Brundtland briefly replaced Nordli, but Labor was deeply divided and the Conservatives unanimously called for solidarity with NATO. In this climate the Conservatives won the 1981 parliamentary elections and formed a government under Kaare Willoch.

BIBLIOGRAPHY

Hvem er Hvem? 14th ed. Oslo: Kunnskapsforlaget, 1994.

Strute, Karl, and Theodor Doelken, eds. *Who's Who in Scandinavia.* Essen, Germany: Sutter Druckerei, 1981.

Bruce Olav Solheim
Bernard Cook

SEE ALSO Brundtland, Gro Harlem

North Atlantic Cooperation Council

After the fall of Communism in central and Eastern Europe in 1989, the North Atlantic Treaty Organization (NATO) took steps to establish relations with former member countries of the Warsaw Pact, the military alliance formed by the USSR with its satellites in 1955 and dissolved in 1991. As a culmination of these initiatives, the sixteen NATO members and nine countries from central and Eastern Europe with which NATO had established diplomatic liaison during 1990 and 1991 held the inaugural meeting of the North Atlantic Cooperation Council (NACC) on December 20, 1991. After the dissolution of the Soviet Union in December 1991 and the subsequent creation of the Commonwealth of Independent States (CIS), the weak association to promote economic and security cooperation among former republics of the Soviet Union, participation in the NACC was expanded to include all members of the CIS.

The NACC holds at least one regular meeting a year. It is aimed at promoting consultations among members on political and security-related issues, such as defense planning questions, principles and various aspects of strategy, military exercises, force and command structures, and civilian-military relations. The 1993 Work Plan included another range of topics and activities—nuclear disarmament, regional expert group meetings, crisis management, and peacekeeping. The range of activities was further expanded in the 1994 NACC Work Plan, with issues such as defense procurement as well as air defense and civil emergency planning.

The NACC in 1998 consisted of thirty-eight members. Activities of the permanent committees include political consultation, economic issues, informational matters, scientific and environmental issues, defense support issues, airspace coordination, civil emergency planning, and military cooperation. At the same time, efforts have been made to coordinate the activities of the NACC and the Partnership for Peace (PFP); a program set up in 1994 to establish cooperative links between NATO and former Warsaw Pact countries. At the same time, efforts have been made to coordinate the activities of the NACC and the Partnership for Peace (PFP), with a view to reinforcing security and stability in the Euro-Atlantic area.

BIBLIOGRAPHY

NATO Handbook. Brussels: NATO Office of Information and Press, 1995.

Tamás Magyarics

SEE ALSO North Atlantic Treaty Organization

North Atlantic Treaty Organization (NATO)

When the North Atlantic Treaty Organization (NATO) was established, in 1949, its fundamental tasks were to provide deterrence and defense against all forms of aggression directed toward the territory of any NATO member state, and to preserve a strategic balance within Europe. NATO was a product of the Cold War.

In the years immediately following World War II, most Western European governments drastically reduced their military forces. The Soviet Union, on the other hand, continued to maintain its military at near wartime strength. Between 1947 and 1949 a number of dramatic political events in Europe clearly showed that peaceful coexistence was not part of the Soviet agenda.

In March 1948 Belgium, France, Luxembourg, the Netherlands, and the United Kingdom signed the Brussels Treaty to develop a common defense system. The Brussels Treaty powers then opened talks with the United States and Canada for the creation of a single North Atlantic Alliance. Denmark, Iceland, Italy, Norway, and Portugal were also invited to participate in the negotiations, which culminated in the April 1949 Treaty of Washington and the creation of NATO. In 1952 Greece and strategically located Turkey joined the alliance. West Germany joined in 1955 and Spain in 1982, bringing NATO membership to sixteen.

NATO was created within the framework of Article 51 of the U.N. Charter, which affirms the rights of all states to engage in individual or collective self-defense. NATO is an intergovernmental organization in which each member retains full sovereignty and independence. NATO's basic underlying principle is that an attack against one of its members is an attack against all. Thus, the alliance is the linchpin of the transatlantic link, in which the security of North America is permanently tied to that of Europe. In practical Cold War terms, NATO brought Western Europe under the American "nuclear umbrella."

In March 1966 NATO faced one of its greatest crises when French President Charles de Gaulle announced that France would withdraw its military forces from NATO's integrated command structure. France continued, however, to remain part of NATO's political structure. As a result, all NATO military forces as well as NATO's various headquarters were asked to leave French territory. NATO's main headquarters relocated to Brussels, Belgium, in 1967.

The North Atlantic Council (NAC) is NATO's highest decision-making body. The NAC meets twice a year at the foreign minister level and periodically at the head of government level. In permanent session, the permanent representatives (ambassadors) to the NAC meet weekly. Each country's permanent representative is supported by a national delegation staff. Opening sessions of the NAC are presided over by the president, an honorary position that rotates annually among the foreign ministers.

The Defense Planning Committee (DPC) consists of representatives from those nations participating in NATO's integrated military command. (Currently France is the only NATO country that does not participate). The DPC also meets twice yearly at the defense minister level and in permanent session at the ambassadorial level. The Nuclear Planning Group is an organ of the DPC that consults on all matters relating to policy and force deployment of nuclear weapons.

NATO has a number of permanent organs and standing committees, supported by an international staff consisting of five divisions. The international staff is headed by the secretary-general, who is responsible for directing and coordinating consultation within the alliance. The secretary-general is also the chairman of the North Atlantic Council, the Defense Planning Committee, and the Nuclear Planning Group. In diplomatic protocol, he carries the rank of a prime minister.

The Military Committee (MC) is the highest military authority in NATO. It is composed of the chiefs of staff of all member nations participating in the integrated command structure. The chiefs of staff meet twice a year, and the MC functions in permanent session through permanent military representatives. The chiefs of staff elect a chairman of the MC from among the permanent military representatives. An international military staff serves as the Military Committee's executive agency, insuring that the policies and decisions of the committee are implemented as directed.

Under the Military Committee, the major NATO commands have the mission of carrying out actual military operations. For most of the history of the alliance there were three such integrated commands. Recently the major commands were realigned and one was eliminated. In addition to the major commands, the Canada-U.S. Regional Planning Group has responsibility for planning the defense of North America.

The Allied Command Europe (ACE) is responsible for the defense of Europe, from the northern tip of Norway to southern Europe, and from the Atlantic coast to the eastern border of Turkey. This includes all the Mediterranean. The headquarters of ACE is SHAPE (Supreme Headquarters, Allied Powers Europe), and the overall military commander is the Supreme Allied Commander, Europe (SACEUR). The largest portion of NATO's combat power comes under SHAPE.

The other Major NATO command is Allied Command Atlantic (ACLANT), headquartered in Norfolk, Virginia. Under the Supreme Allied Commander Atlantic (SACLANT), this command is responsible for the area from the North Pole to the Tropic of Cancer, and from the coastal waters of North America to the coasts of Europe and Africa, excluding the British Isles and the English Channel. ACLANT is primarily, but not exclusively, a naval command.

The third major command was Allied Command Channel (ACCHAN). Its area of responsibility was assumed by ACE in July 1994. During that reorganization of NATO, significant organizational changes also were made within ACE.

With the end of the Cold War and the demise of the overwhelming threat from the USSR, NATO went through a period of redefining itself and its mission. Out-of-area security and peacekeeping missions replaced the mass attack from the east scenario as the focus of military planning. Accordingly, NATO at the close of the twentieth century focused on four major security risks: ethnic unrest, especially in Eastern Europe; potential economic catastrophe in the former Communist countries, with the resulting westward migration of economic refugees; the resurgence of old forms of nationalist and religious extremism; proliferation of modern weapons, especially those of mass destruction, across unstable borders.

Many former East bloc countries expressed a desire to join NATO despite the significant difficulties involved. For one, almost none of the Eastern militaries had command and communications architectures compatible with NATO. Also, great care had to be taken to avoid making Russia feel that NATO, with expanded territory that might come right up to Russia's borders, was still an anti-Russian alliance.

On December 20, 1991, NATO inaugurated the North Atlantic Cooperation Council (NACC), composed of the NATO members, the three Baltic states, and six central and Eastern European countries. In March 1992, eleven states on the territory of the former Soviet Union joined the process, and by 1993 there were twenty-two NACC cooperation partners.

A key part of NATO's new look includes the Partnership for Peace (PFP) initiative, a program that is something of a halfway house for the former East bloc countries. The PFP includes the exchange of military contact teams, combined exercises on both Eastern and Western European territory, and limited support for modernizing and, most important, democratizing the old Warsaw Pact armies. The PFP does not, however, extend NATO security guarantees beyond actual member nations.

On July 8, 1997, NATO voted to accept Poland, Hungary, and the Czech Republic as candidates for membership. All three became full NATO members in March 1999. For information on NATO actions in Bosnia and Kosovo, see specific entries.

BIBLIOGRAPHY

Cook, Don. *Forging the Alliance: NATO 1945–1950.* New York: Arbor House/Morrow, 1989.

Davis, Brian L. *NATO Forces.* London: Blanford, 1988.

Dunn, Keith, and Stephen Flanagan. *NATO in the Fifth Decade.* Washington, D.C.: National Defense University Press, 1990.

Heller, Francis, and John R. Gillingham. NATO: *The Founding of the Atlantic Alliance and the Integration of Europe.* New York: St. Martin's Press, 1992.

NATO Handbook. Brussels: NATO Office of Information and Press, 1995.

David T. Zabecki

SEE ALSO Bosnia-Hercegovina, Bosnian War; Kosovo: Ethnic Cleansing and War; Supreme Headquarters Allied Powers in Europe

Norton, William (1900–1963)

Irish politician. Born in Kildare, William Norton was elected to the Irish parliament as Labour representative for County Dublin in 1926 but lost his seat in 1927. On his return to parliament for Kildare in 1932 he became leader of the Labour Party. This coincided with the election victory of the center-Right, anti-British, Fianna Fáil, led by Eamon de Valera. Labour supported the Fianna Fáil opposition to the Blueshirts, the pseudo-fascist paramilitary group founded by former Commissioner of Police Eoin O'Duffy, whom Norton denounced as Hitlerites.

The general election of 1943 was a critical test of Norton's leadership. He supported the return of James Larkin to the parliamentary party and was attacked by Larkin's old opponents in the Irish Transport and General Workers Union (ITGWU). Labour increased its representation from nine to seventeen seats. However, the ITGWU disaffiliated from the party and the union's members of the parliamentary party established a splinter party, National Labour. Following the general election of 1944, Norton led only eight deputies. Four years later the party secured fourteen seats and joined the first coalition government headed by John Costello of the Christian Democratically oriented Fine Goal party, in which Norton held the posts of vice premier and minister for social welfare. The breach between the Labour Party and National Labour was healed in 1950, a year before the end of the coalition government. Norton was again vice premier in the second coalition government in 1954 when Labour returned with nineteen seats. This time he held the ministry of industry and commerce. The party lost seven seats in the general election of 1957. Norton resigned the leadership three years later and was succeeded by Brendan Corish.

BIBLIOGRAPHY

Fanning, Ronan. *Independent Ireland.* Dublin: Helicon, 1983.

Farrell, Brian. *Chairman or Chief?* Dublin: Gill and Macmillan, 1971.

Keogh, Dermot. *Twentieth Century Ireland.* Dublin: Gill and Macmillan, 1994.

Lee, J. J. *Ireland, 1912–1985.* Cambridge: Cambridge University Press, 1989.

Michael J. Kennedy

SEE ALSO Costello, John

Norway

The history of Norway since 1945 has been one of remarkable growth and prosperity. Norwegians have successfully completed building a modern social welfare society amid the peril and difficulties of the Cold War.

At the end of World War II, King Haakon of Norway triumphantly returned to Oslo after five years of exile in Britain. With the Germans defeated and the country in disarray, the king asked Einar Gerhardsen, a Social Democrat who had been active in the resistance against the Nazis, to form a new government. As one of the first orders of business, more than ninety thousand Norwegians were investigated for their collaboration with the Germans during the war. Of those twenty-five, including the infamous Vidkun Quisling, were given the death penalty and over eighteen thousand were handed lesser sentences. Norwegians then settled in to rebuild their war-torn economy. The official foreign policy at the time was known as bridge building. Norway wanted to peacefully bridge the gap between the two superpowers: the United States and the USSR.

When the Storting (parliament) was reformed in 1945, 41 percent of the seats were taken by the Labor Party. The Conservatives held 17 percent of the seats, the Communist Party 12 percent, the Left Party 14 percent, the Center Party 8 percent, and the Christian People's Party 8 percent. The Labor Party was to dominate Norwegian politics throughout the rest of the twentieth century.

As the shadow of the world war lifted, new tensions emerged that took the form of the Cold War. Amid these tensions Norwegian statesman Trygve Lie settled into his post as the first secretary-general of the United Nations

Norway. *Illustration courtesy of Bernard Cook.*

in 1946. His high-profile position brought a great deal of attention to his small country. Lie faced the difficult task of guiding the new organization throughout the beginning of the Cold War.

In spite of such achievements as the establishment of the Scandinavian Airlines system (SAS) in 1946, the Norwegian economy needed a jump start in the first years after the war. In 1947 all Europe was in serious economic crisis. In a 1948 report the Norwegian Labor Party emphasized reconstruction as the country's paramount problem. Yet it was felt that reconstruction could not take place if the nation's security were threatened. Security and reconstruction were interrelated; foreign and economic policy concerns were inseparable. Government leaders realized that Norway had to be economically strong to maintain its freedom. The U.S.-sponsored Marshall Plan was one way of building up this strength. Norway's decision to participate in the plan indicated a clear choice of the West, a move away from bridge building, and had the effect of extending U.S. influence into Scandinavia.

In 1948, faced with the ominous implications of a Communist coup d'état in Czechoslovakia and with the Soviet-Finnish nonaggression pact, which led the Norwegians to fear that their Nordic neighbor would be the next country to fall prey to Soviet subversion, Norway decided that it could no longer remain on the fence of the East-West confrontation. Direct cooperation among the Nordic countries (Denmark, Iceland, Sweden) in 1948 in the form of the Scandinavian Defense Union (SDU) failed. Nevertheless, its security policies meshed with those of other Nordic countries. The Nordic region cooperated in the area of security, a concept known as the Nordic Balance. The Norwegians, however, believed that this was not by itself sufficient.

The German invasion of Norway on April 9, 1940, was still on many Norwegians' minds, and, with increasing Cold War tensions, they wanted security guarantees. Consequently, Norway opted for the North Atlantic Treaty Organization (NATO) in 1949. Both the United States and Norway were satisfied with the arrangement: the Americans liked it because Norway again chose the West, and the Norwegians liked it because it provided reassurance without the actual presence of U.S. troops on Norwegian soil. Membership in NATO became the dominant feature of Norwegian foreign policy during the Cold War.

Although Norway was definitely Western in orientation, its special adaptation to the Cold War environment—the dualist policy of allowing no foreign bases yet retaining NATO membership—was an effective tool in keeping both superpowers at a distance and ameliorating tensions in Norway and in northern Europe. Given that Norway shared a border with the Soviet Union, the no-bases policy was reassuring to the Soviets.

Norway's principal statesmen during the 1950s shaped policy in decisive ways. Oscar Torp of the Labor party was prime minister from 1951 to 1955, and Halvard M. Lange was foreign minister. After Torp resigned in 1955, Einar Gerhardsen returned to his prior position as prime minister. He was previously prime minister from 1945 to 1951, and served as the head of the Labor party until 1965. These tough-minded politicians personified the generation that had been hardened by World War II. They had resisted German domination and many had served terms in German concentration camps. The war had taught them the inadequacies of Norway's traditional neutrality policy and the importance of forming security bonds with likeminded allies.

In 1953, when NATO's strategy became more reliant on nuclear weapons, it was clear that the United States was to retain possession of these weapons. Norway was thereby placed beneath a nuclear umbrella since it did not allow such weapons on its soil. The Norwegian government was in favor of this strategy but also feared a public backlash if it were openly emphasized. By this time the nearby Kola peninsula buildup by the Soviets, with a nuclear submarine base and rocket-testing facilities, brought security in the northern flank to the forefront of U.S. and U.K. thinking. Norway was squeezed even harder between the two superpowers.

At the 1955 Labor Party Congress, many delegates felt that Norway's biggest concern was the need for effective international control of atomic weapons. In the eventuality of a major war in Europe, the NATO planners in April 1955 gave consideration to civil defense against nuclear attack. The Norwegian government followed up on these plans with the construction of shelters. In addition to civil defense, Norwegians had been monitoring radioactivity through their Defense Research Institute since the early 1950s. This involved a systematic measuring of radioactivity in collaboration with other Norwegian science institutes. In 1955 the alarm went off after Soviet testing in Novaya Zemlya and Semipalatinsk. Public pressure mounted as the results of this testing revealed fallout in Norway. But Norway's protests were of little immediate effect. Norway took the issue to the United Nations and NATO. In May 1957 Norway's full report of radioactivity measurements was disseminated throughout NATO. The Soviets stopped testing in 1958, partially because of Norway's international protests. Norwegian officials saw this as an example of how a small country could rely on international organizations to make its weight felt.

Because Norway was increasingly reliant on the international system, it became even more concerned with its image. It was especially aware of the need to overhaul the relationship between the First World and the Third. Because of what it considered the West's outdated relations with the Third World, and because the West's image was tarnished by its former colonialism, the Soviet system looked better to many in comparison. With Norway's increasing Western orientation came a desire to spread the nation's influence, especially to the Third World, to combat communism. On the domestic side, helping the Third World tended to take attention away from the rapid arms buildup with the NATO alliance.

While Norway was considering a U.S. Proposal to retain nuclear stockpiles and deploy IRBMs (intermediate-range ballistic missiles), Soviet Foreign Minister Nikolav Bulganin sent a threatening note to Prime Minister Gerhardsen. Bulganin pointed out that in case of hostilities, NATO bases in Norway and Denmark would be legitimate targets for Soviet hydrogen bombs. The Soviet view was that Norway's NATO membership, in spite of the country's no-base policy, meant it was a de facto base. Gerhardsen announced at the 1957 NATO meeting that Norway had no plans to let atomic stockpiles be established on Norwegian territory, or to construct launching sites for IRBMs.

U.S.-Norwegian relations were put to the test in the early 1960s. In May 1960 a pilot for the U.S. Central Intelligence Agency (CIA), Francis Gary Powers, was shot down in his U-2 spy plane over Sverdlovsk in the Soviet Union and was captured. Norway found itself in the middle of a potential superpower showdown. When it was discovered that the U-2 flight began in Pakistan and was to terminate at the Bodø Air Station in northern Norway, the Soviets threatened to destroy those bases that countries made available for aircraft that violated Soviet airspace. Norway responded with a diplomatic note that denied authorization of landing rights, and even requested that the United States not plan such flights again.

U-2 operations in Norway had gone on for some time before the incident in 1960. Only a few Norwegians were informed of these extremely sensitive operations at the Bodø airfield. The Norwegian government had consented to the U-2 operations only under the condition that they conduct no overflights of Soviet territory, a rather ill-conceived policy, since this aircraft was designed to conduct such missions. The Norwegian government did not really know what had happened until it heard Soviet Premier Nikita Khrushchev's accusations and U.S. President Dwight Eisenhower's explanation after Powers had been shot down.

Two months later the Soviets shot down another American plane, an RB-47 reconnaissance plane. This occurred off the Kola peninsula, territorial waters under the Soviet interpretation, and international waters according to the United States. The Soviets claimed that Norway had authorized landing rights for the flight. This the Norwegians denied. The Soviets concluded once again that, even if the Norwegian authorities had not authorized landing rights, the United States acted as if it did not need permission anyway. These two incidents brought Soviet-Norwegian relations nearly to the breaking point. Gerhardsen was also displeased with the United States over this incident, complaining that "they treat us like a vassal state." Although the Norwegian government was upset with the United States, defense collaboration continued. These incidents highlighted Norway's difficult position in the Cold War. Nevertheless, by the 1960s Communists had little influence in Norwegian politics. They held fewer than 3 percent of the seats in parliament and were not able to convince most Norwegians that a Western orientation was necessarily bad.

In discussions and planning for European economic integration in the 1950s, Norwegians' overwhelming concern was national security, not economic integration. Norwegians were generally skeptical of European integration strategies. Norwegians were inclined, however, to cooperate with other Nordic peoples because they felt strong kinship ties. Such Scandinavian integration was represented by the formation of the Nordic Council in 1953. The council handled domestic issues and was careful to avoid divisive foreign policy issues that would threaten the Nordic balance. Yet, the Nordic Council was a good example of functional integration.

Yet economic pressures and competition were mounting. Consequently Norway joined the European Free Trade Association (EFTA) in 1958 to seek economic protection from the developing European Economic Community. In 1972 Norwegians were asked to vote in a national referendum on whether or not to join the European Community (EC). Having traditionally feared continental European politics, Norwegians were concerned about a loss of sovereignty and the cultural impact that joining the EC might bring. In a referendum they turned down EC membership by 54 percent to 46 percent. EC membership was put to a vote again in Norway in November 1994. And again Norwegians turned down membership. The 1994 vote was narrower than the 1972 vote (52 percent against membership). Norway was the only Nordic country to reject EC membership. But Norwegians did not believe the argument that nonmembership would leave them outside the economic growth of Europe.

During the oil crises of the early 1970s Norwegians had already discovered and started development of their North Sea oil fields. It was estimated that Europe contained only 1 percent of all the world's oil, but 50 percent of that belonged to Norway. Norway formed a government oil company named Statoil in 1974. Oil revenues began to subsidize the increasing costs associated with the Norwegian social welfare system, which had been elaborated in the postwar period.

In the 1970s women dramatically increased their participation in Norwegian politics. Norway's remarkable achievement in promoting women in this area is partially due to the passing of its Equal Status Act in 1979, which prevented discrimination in job appointments and wages. An amendment to this act in 1988 required a minimum of 40 percent representation of both sexes on all public boards, councils, and committees. This 40 percent goal has since been incorporated into the organizational structure of political parties as well. Norway has a proportional representation electoral system that allows for more parties and, consequently, a greater number of women to participate and be elected. The result has been that in 1995 Norway had the highest percentage of women parliamentarians in the world, nearly 40 percent.

In February 1981, Gro Harlem Brundtland became prime minister of Norway and the leader of the Norwegian Labor Party. She was the first woman to hold the position of prime minister in Norway. In the 1980s, with so many women entering the labor market, greater emphasis was placed on childcare and parental leave policies. By the mid-1980s all major political parties shifted to a position supporting public funding for parental leave and state subsidies to promote childcare centers. Most political parties acknowledged that these new initiatives were a direct result of women's increased participation in politics.

Brundtland's second opportunity as prime minister came in May 1986. It was then that she formed what has been called the "women's government." Eight of the eighteen cabinet ministers were women. Brundtland's nineteen-member cabinet in 1990, her third term as prime minister, included nine women cabinet ministers. By 1991 the leaders of Norway's three major political parties were women—Prime Minister Brundtland of the Labor Party, Kaci Kullmann Five of the Conservative Party, and Anne Enger Lahnstein of the Agrarian Party.

Norway approached the twenty-first century with much promise and some mounting difficulties. Critics claim that Norway is riding high now on oil revenues that support its expensive welfare system, and that little is being done to maintain such a system when the oil runs out. Norway has also faced racial tensions as many guest workers and immigrants from Pakistan and other countries have arrived within the past twenty years and taken part in the social welfare system while forming ethnic enclaves within urban areas. Norway's homogeneous population is changing. Despite Prime Minister Brundtland's internationally renowned environmental leadership, Norway has faced severe criticism from environmental organizations over plans to resume whaling. The all-important fishing industry in Norway claims that fish harvests are diminishing owing to overpopulation of whales. Finally, Norway, in keeping with its being the home of the Nobel Institute, has maintained its central role as a supporter of U.N. peacekeeping missions and as a mediator in the Middle East peace process. The groundwork for the 1993 accord between Israel and the Palestine Liberation Front (PLO) was laid in Norway. The Norwegian government arranged secret talks in the country outside Oslo between representatives of the PLO and Israel, without the knowledge or participation of the United States or other states, and in those talks they worked out the accord that was formally ratified in Washington in August 1993 by the Israeli Foreign Minister Shimon Peres and the leader of the PLO Yasir Arafat.

BIBLIOGRAPHY

Bergh, Trond, and Helge Ø. Pharo, eds. *Vekst og Velstand: Nrosk Politisk Historie 1945–1965*. Oslo: Universitetsforlaget, 1989.

———. *Historiker og Veilder*. Oslo: Tiden Norsk Forlag, 1989.

Cole, Paul M., and Douglas M. Hart, eds. *Northern Europe: Security Issues for the 1990s*. Boulder, Colo.: Westview Press, 1986.

Cole, Wayne S. *Norway and the United States, 1905–1955: Two Democracies in Peace and War*. Ames: Iowa State University Press, 1989.

Derry, T. K. *History of Modern Norway*. London: Oxford University Press, 1973.

Holst, Johan J., ed. *Norwegian Foreign Policy in the 1980s*. Oslo: Universitetsforlaget, 1985.

Riste, Olav. *Isolasjonisme og Stormaktsgarantier: Norsk Tryggingspolitkk 1905–1990*, Vol. 3. Oslo: Institutt for Forsvarsstudier, 1991.

Skjeie, Hege. "The Uneven Advance of Norwegian Women." *New Left Review* 187 (May/June 1991): 79–102.

Solheim, Bruce O. *The Nordic Nexus: A Lesson in Peaceful Security*. Westport, Conn.: Praeger, 1994.

Tamnes, Rolf. *The United States and the Cold War in the High North*. Brookfield, Vt.: Dartmouth University Press, 1991.

Bruce Olav Solheim

European Community

Norwegians have traditionally avoided continental European politics. Consequently, in contemplating joining the European Community (EC), Norwegians were concerned about a loss of sovereignty and the cultural impact that EC membership would bring. In 1972 Norwegians, in a national referendum on whether to join the European Community (now the European Union, EU), voted no—54 to 46 percent. This popular rejection of the EC was accomplished even though a parliamentary majority favored membership. General divisions were clear. The south favored membership, while the north was largely against it. Urbanites favored it, rural inhabitants did not. The Labor Party government headed by Trygve Bratteli turned the referendum into a popular vote of confidence. The Left Party joined forces with the Agrarians and the Christian Party to oppose joining. When the majority of Norwegians voted no, the Labor government was forced to resign. But the issue would not go away.

EU membership was put to a vote again in November 1994. And again Norwegians turned down membership. The 1994 vote was narrower than the 1972 vote (52 percent against, 48 percent for). Norway was the only Nordic country, indeed the only European country besides Switzerland and Greenland, to reject EU membership. Opponents of EU membership had more time to campaign than supporters. EU supporters had only a few weeks between agreement on the proposal's details and the vote itself.

Many EU supporters worried about security in a Europe from which the United States was quickly disengaging. Most political and business leaders and nearly all national newspapers backed membership. The supporters' argument—that staying outside the EU would relegate Norway to the European periphery—was not convincing enough for the Norwegian people. Tariff barriers played little part in the debate because Norway already belonged to the European Economic Area (EEA), a Western European free-trade group, and was expected to continue to enjoy free trade with the EU. Opposition came mainly from farmers, other rural residents, and women.

Many Norwegians believed that joining the EU would mean giving up farm subsidies, which were the highest in Europe, opening the country to unrestricted EU immigration, and allowing foreign fishing trawlers in their waters. Norwegian rural life was largely sustained through huge government farm subsidies. But government officials said that if rural people moved en masse to the cities, the resulting pressure on social institutions, owing to increased social problems, would be more expensive than the farm subsidies.

One interesting difference between the 1994 debates and those in 1972 was that women, in large numbers, voted no in spite of Prime Minister Gro Harlem Brundtland's support for EU membership. Norwegian women, who enjoyed a great deal of equality, feared that closer ties to the continental Europeans, especially in a male-dominated institution like the EU in Brussels, could have had a negative impact on their rights and social guarantees.

Although the referendum vote was nonbinding, there was little chance that the Norwegian parliament would go ahead with membership in the face of rejection by a majority of voters, and Norway remains outside the EU.

BIBLIOGRAPHY

Allen, H. *Norway and Europe in the 1970s.* Oslo: Universitetsforlaget, 1979.

Archer, Clive. "Norway Says 'No'—Again." *World Today* 51 (February 1995): 23.

Einhorn, Eric S., and John Logue. *Modern Welfare States: Politics and Policies in Social Democratic Scandinavia.* Westport, Conn.: Praeger, 1989.

Miljan, Toivo. *The Reluctant Europeans: The Attitudes of the Nordic Countries Towards European Integration.* London: C. Hurst, 1977.

Orvik, Nils, ed. *Norway's No to Europe.* Pittsburgh: International Studies Association, 1975.

Bruce Olav Solheim

Political Parties

Modern political parties developed in Norway and the rest of Scandinavia during the latter part of the nineteenth century. The earliest parties, the Liberals and the Conservatives, developed along class lines. The Social Democratic Party emerged late in the nineteenth century representing the emerging industrial working class. It split from the Left Party after 1900. As in most other Scandinavian countries, Norway has had five basic types of political parties since World War I: conservative, agrarian, liberal, social democratic, and communist. Since 1980 nine parties have been active in Norway: Center Party (Senterpartiet), Christian People's Party (Kristelig Folkeparti), Communist Party (Norges Kommunistiske Partiet), Conservative Party (Høyre), Norwegian Labor Party (Norske Arbeiderpartiet), Liberal Party (Venstre), New People's Party (Nye/Leberale Folkepartiet), Progress Party (Fremskrittspartiet), and Socialist Left Party (Sosialistisk Venstreparti).

The Center Party (so named in 1959) was founded in 1920 as the Farmer's Party. Its traditional areas of strength have been the interior of east Norway and Trøndelag. Its philosophy has been generally conservative on economic, social, and religious issues, but it has favored state intervention in agriculture. The party was weakened in the 1970s when a rift developed over resurrecting a non-Socialist coalition. Voter support has declined considerably since the 1977 election.

The Christian People's Party, founded in 1933, did not gain national strength until after World War II. It has consistently received support from all regions of the country, but its real strength is in the west-southwest. The main objective of the party is to defend fundamentalist Christian values and beliefs. It takes strong stands on issues related to the sale of alcohol, religious instruction in schools, the family, and abortion. The party joined the non-Socialist coalition headed by the Center Party's Per Borten in 1965. The Borten government fell in March 1971 because of disagreements over membership in the European Community (EC), and the Christian People's Party turned to an anti-EC position. Its EC position, however, was not as divisive as in other parties, since the Christian People's Party did not consider it a central religious issue. The party has not gained considerably in strength since 1977 because of the deterioration of the center position in Norwegian politics. A hard line on abortion led to the exit of the Christian People's Party from the Conservative coalition in 1981.

The Conservative Party emerged in the 1880s, founded by higher-ranking civil servants and some business interests. Since that time it has become known more as a party of landowners and the middle class. Since 1940 the Conservative Party has accepted a concept of mixed economy where the state takes part in the regulation of industry and also provides and produces certain commodities. Conservatives accept the government's large role in the modern welfare state but have favored deregulation, tax cuts, and privatizing some functions now in government hands. The party has been a staunch supporter of NATO and favored EC membership. Party membership grew from 17.1 percent in 1973 to 30 percent in 1981. In 1981 the Conservatives formed a minority government.

The Norwegian Labor Party, the largest political party in Norway, was founded in 1887. After the advent of industrialization and suffrage reforms in the late 1890s, the party succeeded in electing representatives to the Storting (parliament). The Labor Party associated itself with the Soviet Union in 1919 when it joined the Communist International. Part of the membership broke away and formed the Social Democratic Party in 1920. The party's 1923 exit from the Comintern, or Communist International, established in Moscow in 1919 as a vehicle for Soviet domination of the international communist movement, caused another faction to leave, forming the Norwegian Communist Party. The Social Democrats and Labor reunited in 1927, becoming the single-largest party in Norway.

Norwegian politics in the twenty-year period after World War II was dominated by the Labor Party. Einar Gerhardsen, as prime minister, led Norway through some of the most difficult times during the Cold War. He established and completed formation of the modern welfare state in Norway. NATO issues, especially the "dual-track" question of membership in NATO while allowing no foreign bases on Norwegian soil, led to a split within the party in 1961. However, the Labor Party's biggest defeats were related to the EC referenda of 1972 and 1994. The ascendancy of Gro Harlem Brundtland propelled the Labor Party in the 1980s and 1990s. The party has moved toward the center in its efforts to maintain power, yet it has held firm on many social issues.

BIBLIOGRAPHY

Cole, Wayne S. *Norway and the United States, 1905–1955: Two Democracies in Peace and War.* Ames: Iowa State University Press, 1989.

Derry, T. K. *A History of Modern Norway, 1814–1972.* London: Oxford University Press, 1973.

Lundestad, Geir. *America, Scandinavia, and the Cold War, 1945–1949.* New York: Columbia University Press, 1980.

Bruce Olav Solheim

SEE ALSO Borten, Per; Brundtland, Gro Harlem; Gerhardsen, Einar

Economy

Since the end of World War II Norway has developed a version of what has become known as the Scandinavian social democratic economic model. As of 1945 a Labor government oversaw economic reconstruction and a substantial extension of state involvement in the economy. During the first phase of reconstruction (1945–47), Norway successfully neutralized the monetary overhang (a large surplus of circulating currency) inherited from the German occupation, and thus avoided hyperinflation. An Economic Coordination Council was established on May 4, 1945. It introduced indicative planning—the targeting of monetary policy, taxation, and state expenditures—to achieve full employment, income equalization, and economic growth. State ownership was extended through the expropriation of German investments in Norway, which resulted, for example, in majority state control of Norsk

Hydro, one of Norway's three energy companies and the country's largest manufacturer of chemicals. The government also founded two state-owned banks to reinforce its economic strategy.

The economic recovery of Norway led to a growing trade deficit, and foreign currency reserves reached a critically low level in 1947. During the second phase of reconstruction, however, 1947 to 1952, the American European Recovery Program (Marshall Plan) provided $400 million between 1948 and 1952. This helped relieve Norway of its external economic problem. As a result, substantial investment could be made in four key areas: rebuilding the merchant fleet, replacing the housing stock destroyed during the war, a substantial electrification program closely associated with an industrialization plan, and creation of large-scale industries in iron and steel and aluminum smelting.

The period 1950–70 was one of steady progress. Total output rose by an annual rate of 4.2 percent, unemployment averaged around 1 percent, and inflation rose by an annual rate of 4.3 percent. Total gross investment was above 30 percent of gross national product (GNP) during most of this time.

During the period Norway moved toward an open economy, which had been a condition for receiving Marshall Plan aid. In 1960 Norway became a founding member of the European Free Trade Association (EFTA). Seven years later, Norway applied to join the European Economic Community (EEC). After prolonged negotiations, a referendum was held in September 1972, in which Norwegians rejected membership in the EEC.

Norway's export-led economic growth strategy meant that its comparative advantage lay in exploiting its abundant natural resources (such as energy and forest products) or human capital. The development of cheap hydroelectricity was used to promote the growth of the aluminum smelting industry during the period from 1950 to 1970. Three traditional industries—forestry, shipping, and shipbuilding—also experienced strong growth. Manufactured goods increased as a percentage of merchandise exports, from 9.2 to 38 percent between 1949 and 1970. On the other hand, there was a significant increase in imports of goods in which Norway lacked comparative advantage, in particular mass-produced consumer items. The period also saw a relative decline in the contribution made by agriculture and fishing to the Norwegian economy, notwithstanding growing government subsidies in the case of the latter.

Since the early 1970s, the most important factor in the economic development of Norway has been oil and gas extraction. Drilling offshore in the North Sea began in 1966 after Norway established the required legal structure for the assignment of drilling rights and undertook the first round of leases to companies. From 1966 to 1971, international oil companies explored the southern parts of the Norwegian continental shelf, where Phillips Petroleum eventually discovered the giant Ekofisk field in December 1969. It proved that Norway had significant reserves of oil and gas. The government decided to take an active part in the development of oil and gas to ensure that as great a proportion of the benefits as possible went to all of Norway's people. For example, the Norwegian parliament created Statoil in 1972, a 100 percent–owned oil company, which has at least 50 percent ownership in new licenses. The 1970s saw huge investment in oil and gas, but the oil took some time to reach production. By the beginning of the 1980s, Norway was not yet an internationally significant producer but had developed an important domestic economic sector by overcoming major technological challenges to deep-water oil and gas extraction. During the 1980s oil production more than tripled. Norway became one of the world's largest oil producers and exporters. Gas production, on the other hand, remained at about the level reached in the early 1980s.

During the first half of the 1980s Norway experienced an oil bonanza as a result of the tripling of world oil prices in 1979–80 to over $40 a barrel. But when the international price of crude oil fell to eight American dollars a barrel in 1985–86, Norway experienced a severe shock that was exacerbated because the economy had already overheated. Norway was forced to devalue the krone by 12 percent to counteract a substantial loss of international competitiveness. Furthermore, a significant reduction in oil revenue cut Norway's real disposable income by 9 percent between 1985 and 1986.

The Norwegian government adopted a macroeconomic strategy to reduce the economy's dependence on oil revenue with a reduction in the growth of private and public consumption, while productivity was encouraged through supply-side reform. During 1989–90, a 6 percent increase in competitiveness was caused by a shakeout of labor in manufacturing. As a result Norway experienced a significant increase in unemployment. It doubled from 3.2 percent in 1988 to an average of 6 percent during the first half of the 1990s, the highest level since the 1930s.

During the late 1980s and early 1990s, a banking crisis resulted from the deregulation of Norway's financial institutions between 1984 and 1985. The government had to invest in the banking sector to prevent its collapse. Between 1988 and 1992 state ownership of the financial sector rose from the lowest level among the European members of the Organization of Economic Cooperation and Development (OECD) to one of the highest. However, as of 1993 the government gradually began to reprivatize the banks, after having reorganized them with only partial success.

The Norwegian economy began a strong recovery in 1991; from 1991 to 1995, average economic growth exceeded 3 percent per annum. However, once again, this growth was based largely on an oil bonanza. Manufacturing was now less than 15 percent of GDP and in relative decline. The Norwegian economy appeared to be in danger of overheating again as it did in the mid-1980s. Nonetheless, in 1993, with its per capita gross national product of $26,340, Norway was the fifth-richest country in the world.

On January 1, 1993, Norway became a member of the nineteen-nation free-trade zone, the European Economic Area. In the mid-1990s the question of the European Economic Community (now renamed European Union) arose again. Norway reapplied to join, but in a referendum of November 1994, Norwegians again declined to endorse membership. Between 1993 and 1997 Norway's level of unemployment was reduced to 3 percent, the lowest in Europe, and real wages grew by 6 percent.

BIBLIOGRAPHY

Hodne, Fritz. *The Norwegian Economy 1920–1980.* New York: St. Martin's Press, 1983.

Nelsen, Brent F., ed. *Norway and the European Community: The Political Economy of Integration.* Westport, Conn.: Praeger, 1993.

The OECD has published an annual survey of the Norwegian economy since 1960. The London *Financial Times* has also published a survey of Norway on an occasional basis since at least 1981.

Richard A. Hawkins

Labor Movement

As Norwegians increasingly fled rural poverty and migrated to cities seeking factory jobs, the first Norwegian labor unions were organized in the 1870s. By the end of the century, nationwide unions were organized. To coordinate these the Norwegian Confederation of Trade Unions (Landsorganisasjonen i Norge, LO) was founded on April 1, 1899. The LO became Norway's largest and most influential workers' organization. In 1998 more than eight hundred thousand workers belonged to the twenty-eight national unions affiliated with the LO, and there were approximately fifteen thousand local labor union branches. In 1900 employers responded to the formation of the LO by organizing what was later called the Confederation of Norwegian Business and Industry (Næringslivets Hovedorganisasjon, NHO).

The first nationwide labor dispute in Norway occurred in 1907, and it resulted in the first national wage agreement. The LO played a key role in agitating for the 1909 Sickness Benefit Act. The LO and the national unions are not affiliated with any party, but the LO has maintained a close relationship with the Norwegian Labor Party, which espouses many of the positions held by the LO. In 1916 the LO formed the first common program with the Labor Party, and in 1919 the Storting (parliament) approved an eight-hour working day and a weeklong paid vacation.

The Great Depression ushered in important changes for the labor movement in Norway. In 1932 the LO and the Labor Party issued a crisis program, demanding work for all. And in 1935 the first Basic Agreement between the LO and the employers' association was signed. The Basic Agreement has been called the Norwegian "Labor Charter." The agreements last for four years and define the rules that both labor and management must follow. The agreements have promoted industrial peace and good relations between labor and management. The Labor Party formed the first government with the participation of two LO members in the cabinet. This breakthrough was followed in 1936 by the Retirement Pension Act and in 1938 by the Unemployment Benefit and Worker Protection Act.

Following World War II, the Norwegian labor movement played a leading role in the construction of the social welfare state both through legislation and Basic Agreement negotiation. In 1947 paid vacation was increased to three weeks and in 1964 to four weeks. In 1956 a daily sickness benefit was established, and in 1961 another agreement established the principle of equal pay for women. This was followed by the 1978 Equal Status Act, giving the principle of equality in the workplace the sanction of law. In 1972 the LO gained the agreement of employers for worker representation on company safety and environment committees, and workers gained the right to choose representatives to sit on company boards and corporate assemblies. In 1973 the age of optional retirement was reduced to sixty-seven, and in 1976 workers over the age of sixty gained an additional week of paid vacation. The age of agreement-based pensions was reduced to sixty-five in 1989, to sixty-four in 1993, and to sixty-two in 1996. Parliament agreed in 1981 to the gradual introduction of a fifth week of paid vacation, but its implementation was made dependent on the performance of the economy. Only one day of the fifth week was subsequently implemented, in 1983. In 1986 the agitation of the LO for a 37.5-hour work week was answered by a lockout of 102,000 workers, but the LO prevailed.

In 1960 the LO developed in consultation with its members a Program of Action that is regularly updated. Its basic principles are work for all; equitable distribution of profits; good, safe conditions of work and pay; promotion of equal status, equal pay and equity; protection and development of the social (welfare) state; strengthening and further development of democracy, labor union rights, and codetermination in working life; national ownership of natural resources; maintenance and development of a strong, cost-conscious, service-minded public sector to counteract the privatization of public services; protection of national ownership in business and industry; continuance of residence and industry in the hinterland; an environmental policy that through international agreements contributes to a sustainable use of natural resources; international cooperation and solidarity; efforts for peace and disarmament; and counteraction of any form of racism.

A declaration of cooperation has been signed between the LO and the Confederation of Academic and Professional Unions in Norway (AF). The combined membership of the LO and the AF is about one million. Approximately 45 percent of the LO's members in 1998 were women. The LO also has cooperative agreements with the Norwegian Union of Teachers, the Norwegian Actors' Association, and the Norwegian Union for Dancers, Choreographers, and Dance Teachers.

BIBLIOGRAPHY

European Trade Union Institute. *The Trade Union Movement in Norway.* Brussels: European Trade Union Institute, 1987.

Galenson, Walter. *Labor in Norway.* New York, Russell & Russell, 1970.

Norwegian Joint Committee on International Social Policy (The Norwegian ILO Committee). *Labour Relations in Norway.* Oslo: Royal Ministry of Foreign Affairs, 1975.

Bernard Cook

Social Welfare

Norway has an extensive social welfare system. All residents of Norway are entitled to health, old age, and unemployment assistance. Norway commits approximately 37 percent of its budget to health and welfare.

The Norwegian welfare system is supported through a national insurance tax, paid by all wage earners and based on a fixed percentage of their wages. The self-employed pay a percentage of their income. Norwegians without income are nevertheless covered by the National Insurance Act and are entitled to full benefits. However, the amount of unemployment compensation, sick pay, and pensions depends on the individual's previous level of income and hence contribution.

The ill in Norway are all entitled to full, good quality medical care. Health care is based on need and no one pays more than 1,140 krone, or approximately $144, a year for health service. This amount is equivalent to only one-seventh of the average monthly wage of a factory worker. To ensure equal service throughout the country, the state carefully transfers funds to counties and municipalities to avoid differentials between richer and poorer areas. In addition to the general allocations, the health service devotes special contributions earmarked to address specific concerns such as telemedicine, suicide prevention, and rehabilitation.

General practitioners funded by the municipal health service provide preventive medicine and refer complicated problems to specialists. Counties operate hospitals, but the state health service has attempted to coordinate specialties to avoid redundancy. Five health regions have been assigned a coordinating role, and patients are allowed to choose between hospitals in their region. As to diseases for which Norwegian institutions lack expertise, the health program pays for treatment abroad. Apart from emergency cases Norwegians seeking treatment for non-life-threatening conditions enter a waiting list and are served in order. Priorities are set according to national guidelines, but anyone who is seriously ill is guaranteed treatment within six months.

All employed people are guaranteed sick pay, which begins with the first day of sickness-based absence. The employer pays for the first two weeks, then the cost passes to the national insurance. The pay for sickness is equal to the normal wage but there is an annual ceiling of approximately 39,230 krone ($4,974). At that point the state, municipalities, and employers step in and provide benefits equivalent to the person's previous salary. After a maximum of a year other national insurance schemes are activated. In the case of permanent disability, employers again step in, but many Norwegians carry supplemental private disability insurance. The state covers congenital disabilities or disabilities that develop at an early age. At retirement age old age pensions are activated. The social insurance scheme provides care at home and facilitating equipment, including specially equipped automobiles.

In the 1990s disability claims grew to 8 percent of work age Norwegians, a worrisome drain on resources. Of particular concern are the number of cases resulting from substance abuse.

The Social Care Act and its supervisory authority, the Ministry of Social Affairs, delineate the welfare rights of Norwegian residents. Assistance is provided to the young unable to gain employment, the unemployed who have exhausted their eighty weeks of unemployment benefits, and those who earn too little to subsist. During the 1990s a consensus developed for a reduction of assistance. The debate was concerned with the particulars—whether the able-bodied should be denied assistance and whether those who refuse work should be dropped from the rolls.

The municipal social services are required by the act to provide access to treatment for substance abusers. Abusers can be committed against their will for three months. Municipalities are also required to assist the mentally handicapped. Approximately 80 percent of persons with mental problems are dealt with outside of large institutional frameworks.

There is an ongoing effort to standardize care for the elderly. Twenty percent of Norwegians over age seventy require assistance at home, and 10 percent have to be institutionalized. With the elderly, as with the mentally disabled, home care is preferred. Day centers are provided and the elderly are given alarm equipment for the home to summon assistance in an emergency.

Norwegians may retire with benefits from the National Insurance Fund at sixty-seven. A minimum pension is guaranteed to all residents. Home workers, who care for children under seven, adults in need of care, and the mentally handicapped, receive credits toward a retirement pension even though they have received no salary. The minimum pension for a single person is 63,376 kroner, approximately one-third of an average factory worker's income, or about $8,022. But old age pensions depend on length of employment and level of income. Individual employers also often have private retirement plans.

The State Labor Office administers unemployment benefits for those who have been employed, but an increasing number of young Norwegians find entry into the job market difficult. The unemployed must register at a job center and take work if it becomes available. After the maximum eighty-week period, benefits are suspended for thirteen weeks before another eighty-week period commences. During the thirteen-week interlude the jobless can receive assistance from the municipalities' Social Care Act.

Women giving birth, if they have worked six of the previous ten months, are entitled to a maternity leave of forty-two weeks with full pay or fifty-two weeks with 80 percent of pay. Three weeks must be taken before the birth and four of the weeks must be taken by the father. Women who had not been employed receive a set payment equivalent to approximately $4,271. All children to the age of sixteen receive child benefits. Care is provided before and after school for children from ages six to ten. Norway has a special ministry for children's issues and a children's ombudsman. Municipal social welfare committees are required by the Child Welfare Act to supervise the living conditions of the young. In egregious cases, where assistance and advice is an insufficient remedy, children can be placed in foster care or in an institution.

BIBLIOGRAPHY

Ryen, Else. *Lov og lovmottaker: pragmatisk analyse av Lov om sosial omsorg.* Oslo: Universitetsforlaget, 1983.

Bernard Cook

Education

By the end of the nineteenth century, Norway had developed one of the most progressive education systems in the world, which reached large segments of the population. A comprehensive, unified school system has been an uncontroversial aim throughout the twentieth century. Ideals of equality and fellowship, self-realization, and free choice with respect to the path of education have been the dominant values of the postwar Norwegian school system. Since the 1980s, a stronger emphasis on efficiency and demands for increased individual efforts by pupils to some extent replaced this perspective of participation.

The number of young people applying to upper secondary education increased substantially after about 1950. From the late 1950s the number of students seeking higher education also increased drastically. To meet the challenges of this educational boom, a long reform period started in the mid-1950s. This period lasted until the mid-1970s. A nine-year compulsory basic school (for students from age seven to fifteen) was launched as an option in 1959, extending basic schooling by two years. In the same year, the division between urban and rural school systems was abolished. In 1969 nine years of education were made compulsory. A new curriculum was also implemented.

Another important part of the reforms was the integration of the various models for upper secondary education. The drive to coordinate the entire school system for the age group sixteen to nineteen ended with the upper secondary school law of 1974, which integrated general secondary schools and vocational schools. Further reforms took place throughout the education system in the 1990s. In 1997 the basic school was extended from nine to ten years, starting at age six. A new upper secondary school reform in 1994 sought increased integration between academic education and vocational training. Thirteen foundation courses were established, replacing the about one hundred previously available foundation courses. In the second and third years the number of courses available increased to ninety, then to approximately 250 occupationally related choices.

There has been a huge increase in the number of students in higher education since the 1960s. In the 1960s the number of students enrolled in universities tripled, from about ten thousand to thirty thousand. Since 1970 the number of university students has more than doubled. In 1995 40 percent of the students who completed upper secondary school enrolled in university-level education. The increase in the student body in the 1960s was countered by a decentralization of the university and college sector. New universities were founded in Trondheim and Tromsø. The development of regional colleges started in 1969. In 1994 a nationwide network was established to link the various institutions of higher education. To increase efficiency in the overall higher education system, specialization and division of educational tasks between the various universities and colleges was encouraged.

Higher education in Norway encompasses four universities, six specialized university colleges (architecture, agriculture, music, economics and business administration, veterinary medicine, and physical education and sport), and twenty-six regional colleges, offering medium- and short-term courses in fields such as technology, teaching, and health care.

An undergraduate university degree requires four years of study. A professional college education may be combined with additional courses from a college or university. At the graduate level, two years of advanced study leads to a master's degree. The master's degree includes exams and completion of a thesis.

BIBLIOGRAPHY

Bleiklie, Ivar. *Reform and Change in the Higher Education System.* Bergen: LOS-senteret, University of Bergen, 1996.

Dalin, Per. *Innovation in Education: Norway.* OECD/CERI publication of June 8, 1971.

Rust, Val D. *The Democratic Tradition and the Evolution of Schooling in Norway.* New York: Greenwood, 1989.

Solheim, R. G. *Reform 92, 94 and 97 in Norway.* Barcelona: Reforms of Education and Special Education, COST workshop, 1997.

Telhaug, Alfred Oftedal. *Norsk skoleutvikling etter 1945.* Oslo: Didakta, 1994.

Gisle Aschim

Language

Scandinavian languages are the northern branch of the Germanic language family. This northern group is further split into two geographical subgroups: East Scandinavian (Old Danish and Old Swedish) and West Scandinavian (Old Icelandic, Old Norwegian, and Old Faroese). Modern speakers of Norwegian, Swedish, and Danish can generally understand each other. Icelanders must use one of the mainland languages to be clearly understood by other Scandinavians.

Norway began to develop its own distinct language during the period from 900 to 1100. This was due to the arrival of Catholism and the Roman alphabet. The appearance of the Black Death in Norway in 1349 seriously interrupted the spread of written Norwegian and the development of a unified Norwegian language.

Norway was united with Denmark in the fourteenth century and the Danish language seriously influenced Norwegian. The upper classes spoke a Norwegian that took on Danish characteristics, while rural Norwegian dialects remained unchanged. After Norway split from Denmark following the Napoleonic Wars in 1814, there were two approaches to unifying the language. A moderate approach merged Norwegian into Danish. Called Riksmål, this was only a slight departure from Danish. Upper classes spoke this version. A more radical approach was to build a wholly Norwegian language based on rural dialects. This became known as Landsmål. Class divisions were exacerbated by the language differences. In 1885 parliament granted both dialects official status.

In the twentieth century, therefore, Norwegians have had two competing dialects—Landsmål and Riksmål—renamed in 1929 Nynorsk and Bokmål, respectively. The latter is the language of the cities and of the region surrounding Oslo. It is used in most newspapers and books, and is the language of the government and much business. Nynorsk is the language of the rural periphery. It has equal status in education and administration, however, and is used in some genres of literature.

BIBLIOGRAPHY

Haugen, Einar. *A Bibliography of Scandinavian Languages and Linguistics, 1900–1970.* Oslo: Universitetsforlaget, 1974.

———. *The Scandinavian Languages: An Introduction to Their History.* Cambridge, Mass.: Harvard University Press, 1976.

Bruce Olav Solheim

Press

The Norwegian press industry has lagged behind its neighbors, Sweden and Denmark. The first regularly published paper began in 1763. The first Norwegian daily paper, *Morgenbladet,* appeared in 1819. However, the break from Denmark in November 1814, when Norway became a constitutional monarchy, spurred the growth of many papers. Freedom of the press was granted also with the constitution of 1814. Circulations were small since most towns in Norway were small. As political arguments developed between Liberals and Conservatives, the press developed further. The first mass-produced newspaper, the *Aftenposten,* came out in 1860. Published in Oslo, it is conservative. The *Aftenposten* had the largest circulation in Norway until overtaken in 1981 by the Oslo *Verdens Gang,* which was founded in 1868. It is also conservative in its orientation. The Oslo *Dagbladet* and the *Bergens Tidende* are liberal.

Many newspapers ceased publication during the German occupation in World War II (1940–45). Papers flourished after the war, and there were eighty-one dailies by 1970. Norwegian papers are independent and no chains exist. This is due to geographic separation and circulations remain relatively small.

BIBLIOGRAPHY

Nordstrom, Byron J., ed. *Dictionary of Scandinavian History.* Westport, Conn.: Greenwood Press, 1986.

Bruce Olav Solheim

Refugees and Immigrants

Norway gives protection to refugees according to the principles of the U.N. Declaration on Human Rights, articles 13 and 14, and the U.N. Convention on Refugees of 1951. This means that Norway grants political asylum to persons who need protection because of individual prosecution due to race, religion, nationality, membership in a special social group, or political conviction as delineated in the 1948 U.N. Declaration on Human Rights.

According to the Norwegian immigration law, anyone who satisfies the U.N. criteria for refugee status has the right to asylum in Norway. The first organized group of refugees accepted by Norway consisted of 400 Jews who arrived in 1947. The next group, of 150 persons, arrived in 1948. These refugees all came from camps for displaced persons as a result of World War II. A Norwegian delegation went to the camps to select refugees who would be allowed to enter to Norway. In the 1950s three smaller groups of hard-core refugees from the camps, those with some kind of handicap or disease—arrived.

In 1948 a group of 175 Czechs arrived in Norway. The experience gained from the reception of the first refugees led Norwegian policymakers to emphasize refugees' ability to work. Now the needs of the labor market determined the selection of refugees, depending on their education and work experience.

Instead of being interned in special camps, smaller groups of refugees spent a short period in reception centers. The authorities believed that refugees would be forced to assimilate if they were required to take care of themselves.

In 1953 the Norwegian Refugee Council was established, and Norway again accepted hard-core refugees. The Norwegian Refugee Council collaborated with the State Institute of Rehabilitation. However, the Jewish Organization for Internees (JOINT), a Jewish charitable association, supported the refugees, economically and organizationally, even though refugee acceptance was formally organized by the Directory of Prisoners and Refugees under the Ministry of Social Affairs.

From 1953 to 1956, 236 refugees arrived in Norway. From 1947 to 1980, however, Norway received on average 300 refugees a year. The largest groups were Hungarians in 1956, Uganda Asians in 1972, and Vietnamese in 1979. In the 1980s approximately 1,000 asylum seekers arrived yearly, but in the "boom" year, 1987, 9,642 asylum seekers and refugees arrived.

Since the end of the 1970s, refugees and asylum seekers have gradually formed the larger part of immigration to Norway, owing to the prolonged end to normal immigration set in place in 1975. This regulation marked a new direction in Norwegian policy toward immigrants and refugees. Until 1975 immigration had followed the conjunctures of the labor market. After 1975, only those who qualified for political asylum or residence on humanitarian grounds have been permitted to stay.

The immigrant component of the Norwegian population has varied between 0.4 percent in 1950 and 5.5 percent in 1996. Compared with other European countries, the number of asylum seekers and refugees accepted by Norway is small. In 1995, while Sweden accepted 36,900 refugees and the Netherlands 30,800, Norway accepted only 1,460. Except for 1993 and the comparably large number of refugees who arrived that year, mainly from former Yugoslavia, the number of asylum seekers who have come to Norway has decreased during the 1990s. Norway had agreed to accept yearly one thousand refugees from United Nations High Commission for Refugees (UNHCR) refugee camps, but this limit was rarely reached. Norway was criticized in 1996 by the UNHCR for following a restricted interpretation of the U.N. refugee convention and the Declaration on Human Rights.

Because of the political situation in former Yugoslavia, which led to an increase in refugees who needed protection in Europe, Norway introduced a new approach in its refugee policy in 1994. Until that year, refugees had been granted permanent residence and were expected to remain in Norway. Bosnians, however, were given only temporary protection. This affected about twelve thousand who arrived in 1993. They could seek asylum on an individual basis only after four years of residence in Norway. Otherwise they were expected to repatriate to Bosnia when the Norwegian authorities considered it safe, but in November 1996, Minister of Justice Anne Holt gave assurances that no Bosnian refugees would be forced to repatriate.

Norway has sought to harmonize its refugee policy with the policy of EU member countries set down in the Dublin Convention and the Schengen agreement. Norway usually follows the example of Sweden. When Sweden introduced the obligation for Bosnian refugees to carry a visa, Norway initiated the same policy.

Although Norway's goal in the early 1950s was to assimilate refugees, the authorities now want them to integrate. Integration implies that the immigrants shall have the same possibilities, rights, and obligations as the Norwegian population, but can retain their own cultural identity. The board, consisting of humanitarian organizations that directed the refugee policy in the 1950s, emphasized that the time spent in the Norwegian reception centers should be short to prevent a camp mentality of alienation and hopelessness from setting in among refugees. All refugees who come to Norway however, are still automatically sent to refugee reception centers, where they spend up to two years while awaiting a decision on their asylum application. This has had a negative effect on the refugees' process of integration, because of the camp mentality syndrome.

Participation in the job market might be viewed as an indicator of integration. Unemployment rates are much higher for the immigrant population than for native Norwegians. While from February 1995 to February 1996 unemployment fell from 13.1 to 11.9 percent among immigrants, among the general population it decreased from 5.3 to 4.5 percent.

BIBLIOGRAPHY

Araldsen, Hege, Maria Gloria, and Ragnar Gloria. *Nfss: Det norske flyktningemottaket 1982–1988.* Oslo: Kommuneforlaget 1989.

Berg, Berit. *Bakerst i kxen. Om flyktningers deltakelse pe arbeidsmarkedet.* Trondheim: SINTEF-IFIM, 1992.

———. *Immigrants and the Norwegian Labour Market: A Meeting of Different Traditions and Concepts of Work. Institute of Social Research in Industry.* Trondheim: SINTEF-IFI, 1993.

Dolson, Stephen. *Don't listen to what they say, just see what they do: Refugee Policy in Norway.* Oslo: University of Oslo Press, 1990.

Hernes, Gudmund, and Knud Knudsen. "Norwegians' Attitudes toward New Immigrants." *Acta Sociologica* 35, no. 2 (1992): 123–39.

"Growth and Structure of Immigration Populations, Statistics Norway." *Arbeidsnotat,* no. 4. Lund: Tenth Scandinavian Demographic Symposium, 1992.

Ragnhild Sollund

Nouveaux Philosophes

Representatives of a minor French intellectual trend of the late 1970s. Epitomized by such thinkers as André Glucksmann (1937–), Jean-Paul Dollé (1939–), Jean-Marie Benoist (1942–), Guy Lardreau (1947–), Christian Jambert (1949–), and Bernard-Henri Lévy (1949–), "les nouveaux philosophes" (new philosophers, as journalists dubbed them) created a sensation in Paris through their much publicized critiques of Marxism, the Soviet Union, and the student-worker revolt of May 1968.

Whereas the Communist tendencies of the postwar French Left had already been denounced by a number of prominent intellectuals, notably by Raymond Aron, the new philosophers were viewed as unique insofar as their critique sprang from within the ranks of the Left itself. Indeed, while many had been students of Marxist philosopher Louis Althusser at the École Normale Supérieure and participated as Maoists in the events of 1968, all came to recant vigorously their earlier enthusiasm. Nevertheless, this disillusionment with Marxism did not lead to the wholesale acceptance of liberalism; most remained distrustful of modern states in general and continued to identify with the political Left.

Glucksmann is considered the most philosophically rigorous of the new philosophers. The son of refugees from Nazi Germany, Glucksmann was born in Boulogne in 1937 and graduated from the École Normale Supérieure de Saint Cloud with a degree in philosophy. In his work *The Cook and the Man-Eater* (1975), which was clearly inspired by Soviet novelist Aleksandr Solzhenitsyn's monumental study of the Gulag, Glucksmann surveys the history of the Soviet Union with special attention to the concentration camps. In his best-selling work *The Master Thinkers* (1977), Glucksmann shows how nineteenth-century philosophers like Fichte, Hegel, Marx, and Nietzsche contributed to the fascist ideology of the Nazi state.

Lévy emerged as the best known of the new philosophers. The son of a Jewish businessman, Lévy was born in Algeria and educated in Paris at the École Normale Supérieure. An editor at the Grasset publishing house, Lévy published *Barbarism with a Human Face* (1977), a book that became a best-seller in France and transformed the young philosopher into a media star. Despite the media attention devoted to them during the late 1970s, the new philosophers proved to be an ephemeral philosophical trend that failed to divert the dominant current of structuralism in French intellectual life.

BIBLIOGRAPHY

Glucksmann, André. *The Master Thinkers.* New York: Harper and Row, 1980.

Lévy, Bernard-Henri. *Barbarism with a Human Face.* New York: Harper and Row, 1979.

Christopher E. Forth

Novotný, Antonín (1904–75)

Czechoslovak Communist leader. Antonín Novotný, son of a bricklayer, was born in Letnany, near Prague, on December 10, 1904. Novotny's mother died when he was four. He was influenced politically by his father, an active social democrat and later a Communist Party functionary. A locksmith, Novotný belonged to the Social Democratic Party and joined the Czechoslovak Communist Party when it was formed in 1921. In 1928 he became leader of the Unified Proletarian Physical Culture Movement, a Communist sports organization. In 1929 he was appointed chairman of the Communist Party in the Karlin district. He worked in factories in the early 1930s, and in 1935 he was sent to Moscow as a delegate to the seventh congress of the Comintern, the Communist International established in 1919 to ensure Soviet control of international Communist parties. During the German occupation of Czechoslovakia in World War II, Novotný was leader of the Communist underground in Prague. He was captured by the Gestapo in September 1941 and imprisoned at the notorious Mauthausen concentration camp near Linz, Austria. After the war he was appointed regional secretary of the party in Prague. In 1946 he was brought into the Party's Central Committee. He played a leading role in the Communist coup of 1948, through which the Czechoslovak Communists gained complete control over the government, which previously had been a multiparty coalition. In 1951 he was promoted to the Central Committee and joined the party's politburo.

When Klement Gottwald died in 1953, Antonín Zápotocký became president. Zápotocký and the new prime minister, Viliám Siroky, desired a slight relaxation from the repressiveness of Gottwald's Stalinism. However, the riots precipitated in May 1953 by monetary reforms, which wiped out the savings of many farmers and workers, enabled Antonín Novotný to successfully oppose any liberalization. The Soviet leadership forced Zápotocký to accept collective leadership and in September 1953, Novotný became first secretary of the party. When Zápotocký died on November 13, 1957, Novotný became president. He retained leadership of the party, thus reuniting in his hands the control over party and state that Gottwald had possessed.

Novotný was a die-hard Stalinist, adamantly opposing liberalization and political innovation. By the early 1960s, Czechoslovakia's command economy had stagnated. Though in 1962 Novotný imprisoned minister of interior Rudolf Barak, a supporter of liberal reform, for fifteen years for embezzlement and "conspicuous consumption," the Central Committee the same year ordered an investigation of the Stalinist purges and the Stalinist purge and trial in 1952 of fourteen leading Czechoslovak Communists were ultimately denounced.

Novotný responded to growing criticism and pressure by dismissing supporters of his own policy of centralization who had roused the ire of Slovaks Karol Bacilek, first secretary of the Slovak Communist Party, and Viliám Siroky, Slovak premier. Alexander Dubček, a member of the Central Committees of the Slovak and Czechoslovak Communist Parties and a proponent of party and economic reform, succeeded Bacilek. Though Novotný was reelected president in 1964, Dubček denounced him at the end of 1967 for impeding economic reform and ignoring the desire of Slovaks for local autonomy. Novotný temporarily survived Dubček's denunciations and demonstrations in Prague by students and intellectuals because of support from Leonid Brezhnev, the General Secretary of the Communist Party of the USSR. But in early 1968 the Party's Central Committee separated the functions of first secretary and president. On January 5, 1968, Dubček assumed Novotný's post as first secretary of the party. In March Novotný resigned the presidency and was replaced by the national hero Ludvík Svoboda, who as a member of the Czechoslovak legion had fought against the Austro-Hungarians in World War I, and against the Germans as the head of the Czechoslovak army corps allied with the USSR. Novotný was subsequently stripped of his membership.

In May 1971, three years after the Soviet led Warsaw Pact invasion to suppress the Prague Spring, Novotný's party membership was restored but not his power. He died in Prague on January 28, 1975.

BIBLIOGRAPHY

Cerny, Rudolf. *Exprezident: vzpomínky Antonína Novotného.* Prague: Orego, 1998.

Renner, Hans. *A History of Czechoslovakia since 1945.* New York: Routledge, 1989.

Stone, Norman, and Eduard Stouhal, eds. *Czechoslovakia: Crossroads and Crises, 1918–88.* New York: St. Martin's Press, 1989.

Bernard Cook

SEE ALSO Dubček, Alexander; Slánský, Rudolf; Zápotocký, Antonín

Nuclear Non-Proliferation Treaty

Arms control agreement signed by over 160 nations. This treaty seeks to halt the spread of nuclear weapons to nations that do not possess them and thus limit the number of nuclear-armed states. It is formally titled the Treaty on the Non-Proliferation of Nuclear Weapons.

The treaty's major objective is to perpetuate the monopoly held by the five declared nuclear-armed states (United States, Russia, United Kingdom, France, China) and thus combat the "Nth nation" problem stemming from proliferation. The assumption is that each new nuclear state increases the likelihood of nuclear war. The treaty was signed by Great Britain, the Soviet Union, and the United States on July 1, 1968, and was initially ratified by forty nonnuclear states before it entered into force on March 5, 1970.

The core of the treaty concerns the transference of nuclear weaponry and technology. Nuclear-armed states and nonnuclear-armed states both have obligations to ensure that nuclear weapons do not proliferate, according to the treaty. The nuclear powers are obligated not to aid nonnuclear-armed states to acquire nuclear weaponry and to promote the peaceful uses of nuclear energy. Nonnuclear-armed states are to refrain from manufacturing or acquiring nuclear weapons and to accept the safeguards provided by the International Atomic Energy Agency regarding their peaceful nuclear pursuits.

The basing of nuclear weapons by a nuclear power on a nonnuclear state's territory is not affected by this treaty. The threat of "nuclear blackmail" for the nonnuclear states that sign the treaty is countered by the guarantee of assistance from the nuclear states if such a threat arises. Such assistance has not been specified, however. Any party may withdraw from the treaty by giving three months' notice.

China and France represented the two declared nuclear powers that for decades did not take part in this treaty. Not until March 9, and August 3, 1992 respectively, did China and France formally adhere to the treaty. On May 11, 1995, the NPT Extension Conference made this treaty permanent by acclamation. The conference also produced a commitment by the nuclear powers to a comprehensive test ban in 1996 and yearly compliance assessments beginning in 1997.

Criticism of the treaty has focused on its inherent inequality. The provisions are tougher on nonnuclear-weapons states than on the nuclear powers. This inherent inequality, it has been argued with limited success, is offset by the good-faith negotiations provision embodied in article 6, which ultimately seeks to establish a comprehensive test ban. Even harsher criticism, however, stems from Western arms control experts who view the treaty as irrelevant to arms control. States such as Liechtenstein and Haiti, which signed the treaty, had no chance of acquiring nuclear weapons anyway, and many nonsignatory states such as Pakistan, India, and Israel have recently acquired nuclear weapons.

BIBLIOGRAPHY

Epstein, William. "The Non-Proliferation Treaty and the Review Conferences," in Richard Dean Burns, *Encyclopedia of Arms Control and Disarmament,* Vol. 2. New York: Scribner, 1993.

Shaker, Mohamed I. *The Nuclear Non-Proliferation Treaty: Origin and Implementation 1959–1979,* 3 Vols. London: Oceana, 1980.

U.S. Arms Control and Disarmament Agency. *Arms Control and Disarmament Agreements: Texts and Histories of the Negotiations.* Washington, D.C.: Government Printing Office, 1990.

Robert J. Bunker

Nuclear Power

In a resolution adopted in 1975 focusing on energy and the environment, the Council of Europe stated that nuclear power was to become one of the principal sources of future energy supply. The council mandated the study of issues associated with the development of nuclear power, such as reactor safety, risks of radiation, release of heat, radioactive waste, and recycling of nuclear fuel. These issues began to be extensively researched starting in 1985 within the European Atomic Energy Commission (Euratom).

The prominent development of nuclear energy in Western Europe started in the early 1970s and intensified in 1973 following the Organization of Petroleum Exporting Countries' (OPEC) decision to place controls on the amount of oil produced in order to increase its price. This action led to a very steep rise in the price of oil, which, in turn, had an adverse impact on countries dependent on imported oil. As nuclear energy became a significant priority, it also produced a vocal protest movement. Nuclear power plants produce no carbon dioxide or other harmful airborne pollutants, and ordinary operation does not lead to harsh environmental effects, but low-level radiation is released during normal power plant operation, and there are routine environmental impacts of heated effluents. Nuclear power also introduces the dilemma of storage and disposal of radioactive waste, principally from spent fuel or waste processing, and the hazards of serious environmental effects from accidents such as at the Chernobyl nuclear reactor in the Ukraine in 1986.

Chernobyl was not a random disaster. Later investigations of Soviet reactors in Russia and Eastern Europe indicate that this catastrophe had a high probability of occurring, and that further incidents of this type are possible unless serious steps are taken to prevent them. There are potential hazards involved in the operation of a number of these reactors. Even if the current situation leaves the inhabitants of regions throughout Eastern Europe vulnerable, at the same time it facilitates significant openings for the nuclear energy enterprise in the West, offering compensation for flat domestic markets. The problem of nuclear safety generates a political struggle between supporters of procedures to guarantee that nuclear energy is produced safely in Eastern Europe or not used, and financial ventures wanting to profit through encouraging the development of nuclear energy in Russia and Eastern Europe.

The role of nuclear energy in fulfilling the need for electricity in Europe has increased expeditiously in recent years, though the rate of expansion is decreasing. Not every country has a nuclear energy program, and a number of countries have suspended plans for construction of new sites. The crucial element in deciding nuclear policy is the way in which the political system shapes the nuclear debate. In comparison with France, where the arrangement of political parties and the electoral system functioned to weaken the impact of groups opposed to nuclear reactors, in West Germany the parliamentary and electoral systems encouraged the effectiveness of the antinuclear Grünen, or Green Party. Disparate nuclear policies may be understood by focusing on the process of state policy making. The share of nuclear power in electricity generation varies a great deal among European Union (EU) members.

Usage of nuclear energy expanded in all countries during the 1970s and a good part of the 1980s, with major increases in the EU and the Soviet Union between 1980 and 1985. The EU has the maximal rate of development in electricity generation from nuclear energy. After 1985 the rate decreased in all countries, yet in the union utilization of nuclear energy for generation of electricity developed more rapidly than in central Europe, the European Free Trade Association (EFTA), or the USSR. The EU utilizes a higher proportion of nuclear energy—35 percent of its electrical production—than any other country group.

The nuclear accident at Chernobyl led to the most extensive release of radioactivity ever recorded in one technological calamity. After Chernobyl, public perception of nuclear energy would never be the same. Major reactor accidents such as this can have effects on a continental scale. The Chernobyl disaster produced the most widespread effect in Europe by increasing exposure to ionizing radiation, gamma rays. European states, especially in view of what they faced during Chernobyl as well as during subsequent Soviet mishaps, became anxious about radioactivity penetrating their borders through accident. This apprehension contributed to the need for areawide monitoring capacities.

Procedures for improving reactor safety are in place in a number of countries. Research and development are focused on advanced reactor design. Within the EU cooperation between the French firm Framatome and the German corporation Siemens on the European Pressurized Water Reactor is an instance of evolutionary design development. Yet while research proceeds into "inherently safe" nuclear reactors, the forecast for their utilization is unpredictable.

Long-term storage of radioactive waste is a principal cause of apprehension. The previous attention to the reprocessing of spent fuel has lessened in preference to research on secure procedures of long-term dry storage of spent fuel or waste. Anxiety also exists over the hazards of waste storage connected with the decommissioning of reactors at the completion of their lifetime.

Post-Communist Eastern Europe is confronted with a series of energy problems. The alternative of nuclear energy is compelling as the cleanest form of all and probably the least expensive for a country such as the Czech Republic, which possesses its own domestic uranium sources. Eastern Europe's comparatively meager endowment of primary fuels thus leads to a reliance on nuclear energy that appears environmentally dangerous after Chernobyl. The exigencies that mark Eastern Europe in terms of energy production are relative to the core issue of energy consumption. Coefficients of energy usage to national income are two or three times as high in Eastern Europe as in Western nations.

Yet even though nuclear energy is attractive, the first response to it after the fall of communism was negative. The reaction was influenced by Chernobyl and the sentiment that nuclear energy is a fundamental instance of regime unconcern for the environment and the security of its people. Environmental issues had catalyzed resistance to Communist governments throughout the Eastern bloc and were a serious policy consideration in post-Communist society. But the reality of energy dependence and the seeming lack of realistic alternatives appears to have altered public perceptions in preference for the nuclear option, an inclination apparent in the Baltic region as well as in Ukraine. Inspite of expanding awareness and citizen activism, the environmental crisis in the former Soviet bloc has not deminished since the collapse of communism. The proliferation of new states and the accumulation of economic dilemmas has complicated the attempt to find solutions.

For Western corporations, it is arduous to proceed with nuclear activity in Western countries because of public demands, and a number have contracted for increasing the security of nuclear plants in Eastern Europe or building new plants there. Because the funds for such large contracts are not obtainable from Eastern countries, the alternative for these corporations is to proceed with their enterprises in Eastern Europe supported by credits from Western organizations. In this situation, the function of the Nuclear Safety Fund, formed by the G-7 countries, is vital.

While safety is the alleged reason for acquiring funds from the government, more than twice as much money has been allotted for developing uncompleted nuclear power sites in central Eastern Europe than for upgrading the safety of existing ones. This financing frequently implies an increase in the generation of nuclear power, because Eastern Europe is induced to generate more electricity as a way of remuneration for the building of new sites. The attitude will receive the nuclear safety support the West offers through grants, but at the same time it encourages dependence on operative nuclear sites as the foundation of domestic energy policy.

The main point opposing the ongoing utilization of nuclear power is the large energy saving opportunity in central Eastern Europe. Modest amounts of money might eventuate in enormous savings in energy, in some areas as much as 40 percent. The inference is that even more of a cutback in energy consumption would make nuclear power outmoded.

Hungary, the Czech Republic, Slovakia, Russia, Ukraine, Lithuania, and Bulgaria are extremely reliant on nuclear energy. Nuclear sites in the region, though, have disparate features, in the context of criteria of construction, essential design, management, and operation. The outlook for shutting down the most dangerous central Eastern European reactors is a shifting one. Because of reliance on nuclear electricity, a number of countries are not able effortlessly to convert to alternative sources of fuel. The rapidity with which countries in central Eastern Europe are inclined to close plants is contingent on prospective need for electricity and on its cost. One of the reasons for the dependence of a number of countries on nuclear energy is that fossil fuels need to be purchased without resort to credit.

Another factor is that Western assistance programs seem to be keeping nuclear power plants in Eastern Europe in operation. Western donors execute temporary solutions, presumably to increase safety levels at hazardous sites until strategies can be developed to allow their definitive future shutdown without a concrete plan for closure. For this reason, these interim solutions are in danger of becoming permanent. It is critical for both central Eastern Europe and Western contributors to reform the management of nuclear plants, and to create low-cost investments that produce significant benefits in increased safety. Appropriate pricing for electricity is likewise crucial. Another dilemma is the safe disposal of nuclear wastes. Eventually, wastes will need to be stored and ultimately disposed of in their region of origin. Consequently, many states will need to build or enlarge waste storage and disposal plants.

In Russia, Chernobyl has resulted in reevaluation of the use of nuclear energy, with grassroots environmentalist demands opposing nuclear power sites emerging as a core element in the process of democratization. The energy plan for the future has been reworked to provide a decrease in the role of nuclear power, although nuclear power plants would nonetheless, according to projection, generate approximately 6.5 percent of Russia's energy by the year 2000.

Advocates of nuclear power predict that it will remain the main large-scale base-load energy source available to meet both increasing electricity demands and requirements to reduce or stabilize greenhouse emissions. Public sentiment in Europe is governed by the threat of serious accidents and the negative effects of routine emissions from nuclear power stations and waste facilities. No acceptable method exists for storing highly radioactive, high-level waste generated by nuclear reactors, some of which will remain radioactive for hundreds of thousands of years. Advocates of nuclear power are more hopeful about the ability to deal with these problems. It is probable that many nuclear power programs, the development of which has been halted since the late 1980s, will start up again. Global warming and other environmental modifications may lead governments to reevaluate nuclear energy.

Nuclear power represents the most significant dilemmas of advanced industrial society: the impact of technological change on traditional values, the industrialization of rural districts, and the centralization of decision making. In the conflict over nuclear energy, nuclear power is also a symbol for the debate about the ambiguities of a postindustrial future.

BIBLIOGRAPHY

DeBardeleben, Joan, and John Hannigan, eds. *Environmental Security and Quality after Communism: Eastern Europe and the Soviet Successor States.* Boulder, Colo. Westview Press, 1995.

European Parliament, Directorate General for Research, Energy and Research Series W4, EN-10-92. *Possibilities and Limitations of Alternative Energy Sources in the Context of EC Policy.* Luxembourg: 1992.

Friends of the Earth. *Russian Roulette: Nuclear Power Reactors in Eastern Europe and the Former Soviet Union,* 3d ed. Washington, D.C.: Friends of the Earth, 1993.

Nelkin, Dorothy, and Michael Pollak. *The Atom Besieged.* Cambridge, Mass.: MIT Press, 1981.

Pryde, Philip. *Environmental Resources and Constraints in the Former Soviet Republics.* Boulder, Colo.: Westview Press, 1995.

UNECE (199). *Annual Bulletin of General Energy Statistics for Europe 1997.* New York: United Nations, 1997.

U.S. Central Intelligence Agency. *Eastern Europe Electric Power Infrastructure.* Washington, D.C.: Central Intelligence Agency, 1991.

U.S. Congress Senate Committee on Energy and Natural Resources. *Nuclear Safety Assistance to Russia, Ukraine, and Eastern Europe.* Washington, D.C.: Government Printing Office, 1994.

Kenneth Keulman

Nuremberg Trials

The victorious Allied powers at the end of World War II established an International Military Tribunal to try German war criminals and document the horrors of their regime. The principal trial, of twenty-one defendants, lasted from November 1945 to October 1946 and resulted in eighteen convictions and three acquittals. Eleven defendants were sentenced to death and the remainder to prison terms.

Well before World War II ended, American, British, and Soviet leaders repeatedly promised postwar trials of "major war criminals," formalizing this commitment in the Moscow Declaration of November 11, 1943. With victory, hundreds of German political and military leaders were detained, and lists of potential defendants were discussed at the Potsdam Conference of July 1945. Those to be indicted included government leaders—Hermann Göring, Joachim von Ribbentrop, Martin Bormann, and Rudolf Hess—and secondary figures substituted for their recently deceased superiors—Ernst Kaltenbrunner for Heinrich Himmler and Hans Fritzsche for Joseph Goebbels, Himmler and Goebbels having committed suicide. Others had administered conquered territories (Hans Frank, Poland; Artur Seyss-Inquart, Netherlands; and Wilhelm Frick, Bolemia and Moravia;) exploited slave labor (Fritz Sauckel and Albert Speer), or commanded the German army (Wilhelm Keitel and Alfred Jodl) or the navy (Erich Raeder and Karl Dönitz). Robert Ley, head of the Nazi Labor Front, committed suicide before the trial began. Gustav Krupp, included to underline the collusion of German industry with Nazism, was found to be senile. Twenty-one defendants actually appeared in the courtroom.

While such a trial was unprecedented, the Allies in 1919 had debated trying the kaiser and other German leaders without reaching agreement. Individual soldiers had been tried for criminal acts in wartime, and a basis for judging the conduct of nations and leaders could be found in the medieval concept of "just war," the Hague and Geneva Conventions, the Kellogg-Briand Pact, and treaties defining neutrals' rights or banning particular weapons of war. No existing agreement criminalized aggression or war itself, or specified penalties, but the Allies, with the arguable exception of the USSR, hoped that trials would establish the responsibility of political and military leaders for similar conduct in the future.

The charges fell in three general categories: crimes against peace (planning and waging aggressive war), war crimes (murder and abuse of prisoners, wanton destruction, slave labor), crimes against humanity (religious and racial persecution, extermination of minorities), and conspiracy to commit these crimes. Defenses based on obedience to national laws or superiors were precluded in advance. The tribunal, with four judges—American, British, French, and Soviet—four alternates, and a British president, Justice Geoffrey Lawrence, permitted no challenges to its competence.

The trials were held in one of the few intact courthouses in Germany, the Palace of Justice in Nuremberg. The 25,000-word indictment and prosecution case were the work of more than 2,500 attorneys and staff who documented the charges with thousands of captured German documents, publications, films, and photographs. A total of 240 witnesses and 300 sworn statements would be heard, simultaneously translated into French, English, Russian, and German. The case included a lengthy review of the ideology of the Nazi Party and its rise to power, as well as the regime's wartime conduct and crimes.

The defendants' German attorneys labored under serious handicaps. Their access to the prosecution's evidence and their ability to travel were restricted, and they had only one month to enter pleas after the indictments were presented on October 18–19, 1945. The defense had little staff, the largely Anglo-American court procedures were unfamiliar, and many requested defense witnesses were not permitted to testify. Judges treated defense attorneys curtly, lectured them on procedural errors, and often badgered defense witnesses. Defense arguments based on the Versailles Treaty or the Nazi-Soviet Pact, treatment of German prisoners of war, Allied atrocities and bombing of civilian populations, or Allied deportation of German civilians was generally excluded, but some attorneys made effective points. Göring's counsel demonstrated that the Katyn Forest Massacre was a Soviet, not a German, atrocity, and Dönitz's attorneys proved that the "crime" of submarine sinkings without warning was common to all belligerents.

After a month of deliberation the tribunal announced its verdicts on September 30 and October 1, 1946. Three of the indicted organizations—SA, Reich cabinet, and High Command—were declared not to be criminal, and three of the defendants—Hans Fritzsche, Hjalmar Schacht, and Franz von Papen—were acquitted. Of the eighteen found guilty, eleven—Göring, Frank, Frick, Kaltenbrunner, Keitel, Jodl, Ribbentrop, Alfred Rosenberg, Fritz Sauckel, Seyss-Inquart, and Julius Streicher—were sentenced to death. Walter Funk, Rudolf Hess, and Raeder were sentenced to life imprisonment. Dönitz, Speer, Constantin von Neurath, and Baldur von Schirach were sentenced to ten to twenty years in prison. Though Göring succeeded in committing suicide, the other death sentences were carried out on October 16.

Although the trial of the Nazi leaders received the most publicity, thirteen subsequent war crimes trials were held in Nuremberg, though these were all conducted before American judges. In all, Allied courts in the western zones of occupation of Germany tried nearly 3,500 Germans for war crimes, and approximately 10,000 were brought before Soviet courts. After 1949 another 13,000 were tried in German courts.

The Nuremberg trials remain controversial. Critics have focused on the unavoidable bias of "victor's justice," the difficulty of disobedience in a totalitarian state, the incapacity of individuals to violate international law (which applies only to nations), the ex post facto character of the charges, and the evidence of comparable crimes by the prosecuting powers (particularly Stalin's USSR).

The educational value of the trials is undeniable, but it proved difficult to institutionalize the Nuremberg "precedents." The United Nations recognized seven principles derived from the trials in 1950, and the 1951 Genocide Convention and various international treaties have sought to prohibit war crimes and crimes against humanity. Enforcement mechanisms are lacking, and a generally accepted definition of "aggression" has yet to be formulated.

BIBLIOGRAPHY

Davidson, Eugene. *The Trial of the Germans.* New York: Macmillan, 1966.

Smith, Bradley. *Reaching Judgment at Nuremberg.* New York: Basic Books, 1977.

Taylor, Telford. *The Anatomy of the Nuremberg Trials.* New York: Little, Brown, 1992.

Trial of the Major War Criminals before the International Military Tribunal, 42 Vols. Buffalo, N.Y.: William S. Hein, 1995.

David Longfellow

SEE ALSO Wartime Conferences

O'Brien, Conor Cruise (1917–)

Irish commentator, journalist, politician, and diplomat. Few personalities have aroused such controversy in the debate about Irish nationality and the Irish question as Connor Cruise O'Brien. O'Brien joined the Department of Finance in 1942 and moved to External Affairs in 1944. In 1955 and 1956 he was the Irish ambassador to France. He was a member of the Irish delegation to the United Nations from 1956 to 1960. In 1960 O'Brien served as assistant secretary in the Irish Department of External Affairs. In 1961 he went to Katanga as the personal assistant of U.N. Secretary General Daq Hammarsbjold. Amidst the turmoil following Belgium's relinquishment of its Congo colony in 1960, Moise Tshombe, with the financial support of European mining interests, declared the mineral rich Katanga (Shaba) province independent from the new Congo state. O'Brien directed the United Nation's effort to oust European mercenaries in the service of Tshombe from Katanga and arrest Tshombe, and he and the organization came under criticism for taking sides in an internal political struggle. As a result of the controversy, O'Brien resigned from the United Nations and the Irish Foreign Service to write *To Katanga and Back,* an account of his role in the Congo crisis. From 1962 until 1965 he served as vice chancellor of the University of Ghana, and from 1965 until 1969 as professor of humanities at New York University.

O'Brien returned to Irish politics in 1969. He joined the Labour Party and served as Labour representative for Dublin North-East from 1969 to 1977. In the early 1970s he aroused controversy with his comments that Northern Ireland was a problem of Irish Republican Army (IRA) violence, that the two nationalities in Ireland should have the right to self-determination, and, therefore, that Northern Ireland had the right to remain apart.

O'Brien was minister for posts and telegraphs in the 1973–77 Fine Gael–Labour coalition government, with responsibility for radio and television. He reaffirmed and extended the ban against IRA and Sinn Fein, the political arm of the IRA, representatives appearing on Irish airwaves. The ban was lifted only in 1994. O'Brien lost his parliamentary seat in the 1977 election. Elected to the senate in 1977, he resigned in 1978 to devote his time to journalism and writing.

From 1978 to 1981 he was editor in chief of the *Observer* and a contributor to the *Times,* the *Irish Times,* and the *Irish Independent.* O'Brien asserted that the Irish middle classes were no longer interested in the republican ideal of a united Ireland. He also heightened awareness of the sectarianism of Irish society. O'Brien is an outspoken, courageous, and insightful commentator on Irish politics and current affairs.

BIBLIOGRAPHY

Jordan, Anthony J. *To Laugh or to Weep: A Biography of Conor Cruise O'Brien.* Dublin: Blackwater Press, 1994.

O'Brien, Connor Cruise. *Parnell and his Party.* Oxford: Clarendon, 1957.

———. *Conor Cruise O'Brien Introduces Ireland.* London: Deutsch, 1969.

———. *My Life and Themes.* New York: Cooper Square, 2000.

———. *States of Ireland.* London: Hutchinson, 1972.

———. *Reflections on Religion and Nationalism.* Cambridge, Mass.: Harvard University Press, 1988.

Young-Bruehel, Elisabeth. *Conor Cruise O'Brien: An Appraisal.* Newark: Proscenium Books, 1974.

Michael J. Kennedy

O'Brien, Edna (1932–)

Irish novelist. Edna O'Brien, born in County Clare, studied pharmacy in Dublin. She moved to London in 1958, where she still lives. Her first novel, *The Country Girls,* was banned in Ireland. It reflected the permissive society that was coming into Ireland in the early 1960s. Her next novel, *The Lonely Girl* (1962), was filmed as *The Girl with Green Eyes.* Along with *Girls in Their Married Bliss* (1964), these books form a trilogy on the maturation and disenchantment of an Irish country girl. Until 1982 O'Brien published a major work almost every two years, including, *August Is a Wicked Month* (1965), a collection of short stories, *The Love Object* (1968), *A Pagan Place* (1970), *Mother Ireland* (1976), and *Returning* (1982). Love is the dominant theme in these works. They are rich in the folklore of her native county Clare and Irish mythology. She has also written for cinema, *Zee & Co.* (1976), and theater, *The Gathering* (1974).

BIBLIOGRAPHY

Eckley, Grace. *Edna O'Brien.* Lewisburg, Pa.: Bucknell University Press, 1974.

Michael J. Kennedy

O'Brien, Flann (1911–66)

Irish journalist, writer, and Gaelic scholar. Flann O'Brien was the best known of many pseudonyms used by Brian O'Nolan. He was born in Strabane in Northern Ireland on October 5, 1911, and died in Dublin on April 1, 1966. After study at University College in Dublin, he worked as a civil servant while contributing the satirical column "Cruiskeen Lawn" to the *Irish Times* (1940–66) under the pen name Myles na Gopaleen.

His satire and social criticism ridiculed the provincialism and constrictions of modern Irish Catholic society, including the solemnities and sentimentality of the Gaelic revival. Focusing on local Irish peculiarities, O'Brien's humor and insight elevated the trivial to universal absurdity and transcended the Irish comic tradition with a trenchant wit compared to Jonathan Swift and Oliver St. John Gogarty.

Some of O'Brien's finest newspaper columns were collected in *The Best of Myles* (1968), and his growing popularity in Europe and the United States after his death led to a collection edited by Kevin O'Nolan in *The Hair of the Dogma: A Further Selection from "Cruiskeen Lawn"* (1977). Other selections from his columns for the *Nationalist* and the *Leinster Times,* written under the nom de plume George Knowall, were collected in *Myles Away from Dublin* (1985). However, Flann O'Brien's literary reputation rests on his novels, especially *At Swim-Two-Birds* (1939); *The Hard Life* (1961); *The Dalkey Archive* (1964); *The Third Policeman* (1966); and *The Poor Mouth* (1941 in Irish, English translation, 1973).

Critics agree his best book is *At Swim-Two-Birds,* which was well received in 1939 but vanished during the war, until reissued in 1960. This novel is widely regarded as a hilarious tour de force, a major work in twentieth-century fiction comparable to the work of James Joyce and Samuel Beckett.

BIBLIOGRAPHY

Clissmann, Anne. *Flann O'Brien: A Critical Introduction to His Writings.* New York: Barnes and Noble Books, 1975.

Cronin, Anthony. *No Laughing Matter: The Life and Times of Flann O'Brien.* London: Grafton, 1989.

Imhof, Rudiger, ed. *Alive Alive O!* Totowa, N.J.: Barnes and Noble Books, 1985.

O'Brien, Flann. *A Flann O'Brien Reader.* Ed. by Stephen Jones. New York: Viking, 1978.

———. *Stories and Plays.* London: Hart-Davis, MacGibbon, 1973.

Peter C. Holloran

O'Brien, Kate (1897–1974)

Irish novelist and biographer. Kate O'Brien was born in Limerick and educated at University College, Dublin. Initially she worked as a journalist in Britain for the *Guardian* and as a translator. Her first book, *Without My Cloak* (1931), won the Hawthornden prize and established her as a name in Irish fiction. It was followed by eight more novels. *That Lady* (1946) is her most popular book and was turned into a film of the same name in 1955 staring Olivia de Havilland. The 1950s saw the publication of *The Flower of May* (1953) and *As Music and Splendour* (1958). Two of her novels, *Mary Lavelle* (1936) and *The Land of Spices* (1941), were censored for alleged immorality by the Irish Censorship Board. Her travel books and biographies include *Farewell Spain* (1937), *English Diaries and Journals* (1943), a monograph, *Teresa of Avila* (1951), and *My Ireland* (1962). Her autobiography, *Presentation Parlour,* was published in 1962. The major characters in almost all of O'Brien's novels are women seeking to overcome the roles destined for them by society. In 1947 O'Brien was elected to the Irish Academy of Letters and as a Fellow of the Royal Society of Literature.

BIBLIOGRAPHY

Dalsimer, Adele M. *Kate O'Brien.* Boston: Twayne Publishers, 1990.

Reynolds, Lorna. *Kate O'Brien: A Literary Portrait.* Totowa, N.J.: Barnes & Noble, 1987.

Michael J. Kennedy

O'Casey, Sean (1880–1964)

Irish playwright and autobiographer, Sean O'Casey was born John Casey on March 30, 1880, in a lower-middle-class Protestant neighborhood in Dublin. He was the youngest child of Susan Archer and Michael Casey, and the third John, two other children of the same name having died, as had six other Casey infants. Life in the Casey household, while sometimes comfortable, was often turbulent and economically uncertain.

O'Casey's father died when he was only six years old, leaving the family financially dependent on the older Casey children. It was with his brother Isaac's help that O'Casey began to act, and in 1895, he was in a production of Dion Boucicault's *The Shaughraun,* a play that made a lasting impression on O'Casey because Boucicault was able to give the stock Irish character a roguish heroism.

Always a staunch Protestant, O'Casey argued for religious tolerance. In his own family, Isaac married a Catholic, changed his name to Joseph, and cut himself off from his Protestant family. The family tensions became for O'Casey political ones as Ireland became independent, and the Catholic clergy emerged as an oppressive force in Ireland. Like James Joyce, he began to feel that his country might never be free.

In his twenties O'Casey was politically active with the Gaelic League, learned Gaelic, and became involved with the Citizen's Army, a group formed to protect workers against police brutality during strikes and demonstrations. He worked closely with labor leader Jim Larkin, who was to remain a hero for the dramatist all his life. At that time, he changed his name from John Casey to Sean O'Cathassaigh, later changing it back to Sean O'Casey.

O'Casey's most famous trilogy of plays, produced at the Abbey Theatre in Dublin—*The Shadow of a Gunman* (1923), *Juno and the Paycock* (1924), and *The Plough and the Stars* (1926)—focuses on the tragic and troubled years of Ireland before independence. All three plays are set in Dublin tenements, and all three satirize romantic notions of Irish nationalism at the expense of the poor Irish worker. It is the women in the plays—Juno Boyle and Nora Clitheroe—who finally recognize that "The country is gone mad" (*Shadow of a Gunman*). Indeed, O'Casey's depiction of the Easter Rising in *The Plough and the Stars* led to riots because the Irish audience was not prepared for O'Casey's trenchant criticism of the newly emerging patriots. He managed to antagonize both the Catholics and the Nationalists with *The Plough and the Stars.*

O'Casey went to England in 1926, ostensibly to accept the Hawthornden Prize for *Juno and the Paycock.* His short trip turned into a lifetime exile when he met and married actress Eileen Carey Reynolds. When William Butler Yeats and the Abbey Theatre rejected his next play, *The Silver Tassie,* a caustic indictment of World War I, O'Casey severed his connections with Ireland.

Over the next thirty-seven years, O'Casey's political commitment to workers and his artistic commitment to the drama never flagged. He wrote and produced seventeen plays, among them the widely acclaimed dramas *Within the Gates, The Star Turns Red,* and *Red Roses for Me.* All have the signature O'Casey concern for the oppressed worker, and all signal O'Casey's enduring commitment to socialism as the answer to class and religious oppression. From 1939 to 1954 O'Casey also published a six-volume autobiography that merged imaginative sketches with his perceptive social criticism. *I Knock at the Door* (1939), *Pictures in the Hallway* (1942), *Drums under the Windows* (1945), *Inishfallen, Fare Thee Well* (1949), *Rose and Crown* (1952), and *Sunset and Evening Star* (1954) bring together imaginative prose of the highest order with a strong commitment to the language of social protest.

Always committed to the people of the tenements, O'Casey radically changed the course of modern drama because in art, as in politics, he trusted his own instincts and not the cant of critics and politicians.

BIBLIOGRAPHY

Ayling, Ronald. "Sean O'Casey." *Modern British Dramatists, 1900–1945, Dictionary of Literary Biography,* Vol. 10. Detroit: Gale Research Co., 1982, 71–90.

Krouse, David. *Sean O'Casey: The Man and His Work.* New York: Macmillan, 1975.

O'Connor, Garry. *Sean O'Casey: A Life.* New York: Atheneum, 1988.

O'Riordan, John. *A Guide to O'Casey's Plays.* New York: St. Martin's Press, 1984.

Mary A. McCay

Occhetto, Achille (1936–)

Leader of the Italian Communist Party (PCI). Achille Occhetto was born in Milan on March 3, 1936. He studied philosophy at the University of Milan but quickly turned his attention to the student movement, of which he was an officer until 1966. During that period he edited *Nuova Generazione* and *Città Futura.* During the Vietnam War he took part in an official PCI delegation lead by Giancarlo Pajetta that met labor leaders of Vietnam and the Communist leaders of China.

Occhetto, elected a member of the PCI's leadership in 1967, was positively influenced by the student movement of 1968. He decided that the struggle for a socialist transformation of society was not synonymous with labor union activity and that it did not have to conform to a predetermined model. He also realized that reform and socialism could be advanced outside the PCI.

From 1969 to 1977 he was secretary of the PCI's Sicilian Regional Committee in Palermo. He first entered parliament in 1976. With Gerardo Chiaromonte he wrote *Scuola e democrazia di massa* (Education and Mass Democracy, 1977), which linked educational change with social transformation. Occhetto became the PCI's assistant secretary in 1987 and general secretary in 1988 after Allessandro Natta's resignation. He attempted to introduce new perspectives and approaches into the party. He defined the PCI in terms of the European Left. In addition to meeting with Mikhail Gorbachev, the Soviet leader, he met with leaders of the Socialist International, the umbrella organization for socialist and social democratic parties, and the German Social Democratic Party. At the Eighteenth Congress of the PCI on March 18, 1989, he repudiated democratic centralism, the Leninist concept of a military-like discipline within the party and totalitarianism, or an all dominant one party state, and his position as general secretary was confirmed. In May he met with representatives of the U.S. Congress, and after the collapse of the Berlin Wall in November 1989 he initiated debate about the foundation of a new Italian party that would no longer be Communist. His political line, even though it met with dissent, was adopted at the Nineteenth Congress at Bologna in March 1990. Ochetto pushed for the party to be renamed the Democratic Party of the Left, but he was strongly opposed by the left wing of the PCI and many of its traditional supporters. The name was changed, but Ochetto was not re-elected as general secretary at the Twentieth Constituent Congress of the Democratic Party of the Left at Rimini on February 4, 1991, because of his opposition to the Gulf War of 1991. However, he was reelected at an extraordinary meeting convened in Rome on February 8, 1991. He subsequently resigned as general secretary in 1994 and was succeeded by Massimo D'Alema, but Ochetto continued to play a leading role in the Party of the Democratic Left as president of its foreign affairs committee.

BIBLIOGRAPHY

Ferrero, F. *Dal PCI al PDS: dalla questione sociale alla società civile.* Milan: F. Angeli, 1994.

Lorusso, M. Occhetto: *Il comunismo italiano da Togliatti al PDS.* Florence: Ponte alle Grazie, 1992.

Occhetto, Achille. *Silenzio, parla Achille: il meglio dell'Occhetto-pensiero.* Milan: Mondadori, 1994.

Occhetto a dieci anni dal'68. Rome: Editori Riuniti, 1978.

Adalgisa Efficace

SEE ALSO D'Alema, Massimo; Natta, Alessandro

O'Ceallaigh (O'Kelly), Sean T. (1883–1966)

Fianna Fáil politician, president of Eire (1945–49), and first president of the Irish Republic (1949–59). Sean T. O'Ceallaigh (O'Kelly), a founding member of Sinn Fein and the Irish Volunteers (an organization founded in 1913 to fight, if necessary, for a united Ireland against the Ulster Volunteers), fought in the 1916 uprising and was captured and imprisoned by the British. He was elected to the first parliament in 1918 and led an unsuccessful Irish delegation to the 1919 Paris Peace Conference. O'Ceallaigh opposed the 1921 treaty with Britain, which divided Ireland and set up the Irish Free State in the South. He was a founding member of Fianna Fáil, the party led by Eamon de Valera that called for severing all ties to Britain and the establishment of an Irish Republic, in 1926. When Fianna Fáil came to power in 1932, he served as vice president of the Executive Council. From 1932 to 1939, O'Ceallaigh was minister for local government and public health, and he instituted much-needed housing plans. From 1937 to 1945, he served as vice premier, and from 1939 to 1945, minister for finance.

O'Ceallaigh was a shrewd and independent politician, but he took the presidency in 1945 to allow Sean Lemass to become vice premier and eventual successor to Eamon de Valera. O'Ceallaigh was not prime minister material. There were other men better than he and he did not make a great mark despite his political ability. O'Ceallaigh was always on committees but never the dominant individual. He held his position because of being a founder of Fianna Fáil.

BIBLIOGRAPHY

Kee, Robert. *Ireland, a History.* Boston: Little, Brown, 1982.

Michael J. Kennedy

SEE ALSO de Valera, Eamon

Ochab, Edward (1906–89)

First secretary of the Central Committee of the Polish United Workers (Communist) Party (1956), one of the highest party functionaries (1944–68), an economist, and activist in the cooperative movement.

Before World War II, though a member of the Polish Communist Party, Edward Ochab was not a leading figure. His personality was shaped during his stay in the Soviet Union during the war. He co-organized the Union of Polish Patriots among Polish prisoners of war in the USSR, and Polish military units to fight on the side of the USSR against Germany. After his return to Poland in 1944, Ochab became a member of the Central Committee of the Communist Party, and in 1948, after the Socialists had been forced to merge with the Communists, of the Polish United Workers Party. Following the death of Bolesław Bierut, the party's first secretary, and with the support of Nikita Khrushchev, the general secretary of the Soviet Communist Party, Ochab became first secretary of the Polish United Worker's Party in March 1956. He held that position until October of that year. In addition to his party functions he also held various posts in the government: minister of public administration (1945), deputy minister of national defense (1949–50), minister of agriculture (1957–59), deputy prime minister (1961–64), and prime minister (1964–68).

Despite a rich political career Ochab remained an uninspiring leader, without authority in the party ranks or in society. Ochab suffered two major defeats. The first was his inability to face political renewal in 1956, when he was forced to hand over power to Władysław Gomułka. The second occurred in 1968 when Ochab, a Jew, was forced to withdraw from political life because of the anti-Semitic campaign initiated by Mieczysław Mozcar, the head of the security police, and Gomułka.

BIBLIOGRAPHY

Torańska, Teresa. *Oni.* London: Polonia Book Fund, 1985.

Ryszard Sudziński

SEE ALSO Bierut, Bolesław

O'Dalaigh, Cearbhall (1911–77)

President of Ireland from 1974 to 1976. Cearbhall O'Dalaigh was editor of the center-right Fianna Fáil Party–oriented *Irish Press* from 1931 to 1940. He served as attorney general from 1946 to 1948, and from 1951 to 1953. In 1953 he was appointed to the supreme court. From 1961 to 1973 he was chief justice and president of the supreme court. O'Dalaigh was a major legal reformer responsible for much of Ireland's law reform in the 1960s. When Ireland was admitted to the European Economic Community (EC) in 1973, O'Dalaigh became the Irish representative at the European Court of Justice. In 1974 he became Ireland's fifth president as an agreed candidate to succeed Erskine Childers. He resigned in November 1976 following criticism by Paddy Donegan, minister for defense of the 1973–77 coalition government, of his constitutional right to refer legislation to the supreme court. O'Dalaigh was succeeded by Patrick Hillery.

BIBLIOGRAPHY

Townshend, Charles. *Ireland: The Twentieth-century.* Oxford University Press, 1999.

Michael J. Kennedy

SEE ALSO Childers, Erskine; Hillery, Patrick

Oddsson, David (1948–)

Prime minister of Iceland and former mayor of the capital, Reykjavík. David Oddsson rose to prominence in Icelandic politics when he led the center-conservative Independence Party to a convincing victory in communal elections in Reykjavík in 1982. For the next decade he served as mayor of Reykjavík and ousted the vice chairman of the Independence Party in 1989. Two years later he was elected chairman of his party, leading it to victory in parliamentary elections in the spring of 1991. Oddsson then formed a coalition government with the Social Democratic Party, repeating a political pattern of the so-called reconstruction government of 1959–71. The government held its ground in the 1995 elections, but Oddsson decided to solidify his majority, electing to form a new government with the second-largest party in Iceland, the centrist Progressive Party, instead of the Social Democrats.

Oddsson earned respect in his party for his effective administration of Reykjavík, although his forceful political style aroused controversy, at least among his adversaries. As a politician on a national level, Oddsson united the Independence Party after a decade of internal disputes, and under his leadership the party seems to have solidified its position as the largest party in Iceland.

BIBLIOGRAPHY

Hjalmarsson, Jon R. *History of Iceland: From the Settlement to the Present Day.* Reykjavik: Iceland Review, 1993.

Gudmundur Halfdanarson

SEE ALSO Hermannsson, Steingrimur

O'Faolain, Sean (1900–1991)

Irish writer and journalist. Sean O'Faolain was born John Whelan in Cork, the son of a police constable. In 1918 he changed his name to the Gaelic form. His student days at University College, Cork, were interrupted by the Troubles (1919–23), the fight with the British for independence and then the civil war between supporters and opponents of the 1921 treaty that divided Ireland, during which he served as a courier and publicity officer for the Irish Republican Army. After he received an M.A. from Harvard University in 1926–29, he became well known for his short stories, especially his first collection, *Midsummer Night Madness* (1932). But these romantic, ironic tales of the Anglo-Irish War and the bitter civil war were banned in Ireland as obscene.

O'Faolain also wrote biographies of Eamon De Valera (1932), Constance Markievicz (1934), Daniel O'Connell (1938), Hugh O'Neill (1942), and John Henry Newman (1952). His first novel was *A Nest of Simple Folk* (1933); then *Bird Alone* (1936); *Come Back to Erin* (1940); and finally *And Again?* (1979). His autobiography, *Vive Moi,* appeared in 1964, followed by ten short collections, among the best of which were *The Heat of the Sun* (1966), *The Talking Trees* (1971), and *Foreign Affairs* (1976).

O'Faolain is acknowledged as Ireland's greatest contemporary storyteller writing in both Gaelic and English. His book *The Irish: A Character Study* (1947) was revised and published again in 1969. However, his short stories established his fame, especially when published in *The Collected Short Stories of Sean O'Faolain* (1983). O'Faolain's central concern was censorship and repression of the individual. As editor of *The Bell* (1940–46), a Dublin literary magazine, and as a short story writer, his acerbic observations targeted narrow-minded Irish society, self-consciously separated from European civilization.

BIBLIOGRAPHY

Bonaccorso, Richard. *Sean O'Faolain's Irish Vision.* Albany: SUNY, 1987.

Harmon, Maurice. *Sean O'Faolain: A Critical Introduction.* Notre Dame, Ind.: University of Notre Dame, 1966.

Rippier, Joseph S. *The Short Stories of Sean O'Faolain: A Study in Descriptive Techniques.* New York: Barnes and Noble, 1976.

Peter C. Holloran

Ohlin, Bertil (1899–1979)

Swedish economist and politician, winner in 1977 with English economist James E. Meade of the Nobel Prize in economics. Ohlin received the award fifty years after the publication of his *Interregional and International Trade,* which analyzed geographical patterns of commerce. Ohlin successfully challenged British economist John Maynard Keynes's belief that Germany would be unable to meet its post–World War I reparations payments. Assar Lindbeck of the Nobel selection committee called Ohlin the "originator of [the] modern theory of international trade." It was Meade who applied Ohlin's theories to questions of economic policy.

Ohlin was born into a large middle class family in a village in southern Sweden. He was educated at Lund University, the Stockholm Business School, the University of Stockholm, and Harvard University. An early article was rejected for publication by Keynes, who wrote that "this amounts to nothing." Ohlin was appointed to the University of Copenhagen in 1925. In 1931 he returned to Sweden with an appointment to the Stockholm School of Business, where he taught until 1965.

Ohlin was a member of the Swedish parliament from 1938 to 1970. He was minister of trade in 1944–1945. He became leader of the Liberal Party in 1944 and held that post until 1967. Under Ohlin's leadership the Liberal Party supported social reform but opposed nationalization and excessive state control of the economy. He died on August 3, 1979.

BIBLIOGRAPHY

Heckscher, Eli F., and Bertil Ohlin. *Heckscher-Ohlin Trade Theory.* Tr., ed., and introduced by Harry Flam and M. June Flanders. Cambridge, Mass.: MIT Press, 1991.

Ohlin, Bertil. *Interregional and International Trade.* Cambridge, Mass.: Harvard University Press, 1967.

———. *Some Insufficiencies in the Theories of International Economic Relations.* Princeton, N.J.: Princeton University, 1979.

Bernard Cook

Oi Music

Variant of punk rock, usually associated with the neo-Nazi skinhead movement in Europe, especially in Germany and the United Kingdom. The term "oi," a Cockney dialectal interjection (equivalent to "hey" in American English), was embraced by British youth in the late 1970s to designate their working-class youth movement, which, disheartened by depressed economic conditions, rejected the United Kingdom's social and political status quo. Loud, aggressive, and usually performed by players lacking technical proficiency, oi music has been aptly characterized by music critic Lester Bangs as "a version of 1977 punk stripped of its humor and vision." Although the term "oi" originally implied no specific political affiliation, it soon became primarily identified with right-radical skinheads and the British National Front. British oi bands such as the 4-Skins and Skrewdriver appeared on albums with titles such as "Strength Thru Oi," a play on Nazi Germany's "Strength through Joy" program. Oi music spread to Neo-Nazi circles in Germany and elsewhere in Europe, as well as in the United States. German skinheads developed their own oi bands, with names like Endstufe (Final Stage), Störkraft (Destructive Power), Radikahl (a pun on "radical" and "bald"), recording and performing songs with inflammatory titles such as "Swastika," "Saviors of Germany," and "Mercenary."

Performances by oi bands in the 1980s and 1990s were often associated with hooliganism and racial violence. In 1992 the German government banned the sale of many oi recordings to persons under eighteen, citing a connection between the music and outbreaks of violence against foreigners. In 1993 German authorities began seizing oi recordings from private homes as well as businesses, thereby ironically stimulating consumer interest in a marginal music form.

Mark P. Gingerich

SEE ALSO Neofascism in Western Europe

O'Kennedy, Michael (1936–)

Irish politician. Michael O'Kennedy served as a member of the Irish Seanad (senate), the upper house of the Irish parliament, from 1965 to 1969. From 1969 to 1979 he represented Tipperary North in the Dáil, the lower house of parliament. In 1972 and 1973 he was minister without portfolio. Between 1973 and 1977 he served as opposition front-bench spokesperson on foreign affairs, and from 1977 to 1979 was minister for foreign affairs. In 1979 and 1980 he was minister for finance and in 1981 and 1982 European Commissioner. O'Kennedy resigned as European Commissioner after reelection to the Dáil in 1982. From 1983 to 1987 he served as the center-Right Fianna Fáil party front-bench spokesperson on finance. From 1987 to 1991 he was minister for agriculture. In 1992 he again entered the senate.

BIBLIOGRAPHY

Townshend, Charles. *Ireland: The Twentieth-century.* Oxford University Press, 1999.

Michael J. Kennedy

Ollenhauer, Erich (1901–63)

Head of the Social Democratic Party (SPD) in the Federal Republic of Germany (1952–63). Born in Magdeburg on March 21, 1901, Erich Ollenhauer joined the socialist movement before the age of twenty. During the 1920s he served as secretary and chair of the socialist youth organization the Young Socialist Workers (Sozialistische Arbeiter–Jugend). Between 1933 and 1945 Ollenhauer joined the SPD Executive Committee in Exile first in Prague and later in London. Following the SPD's reestablishment in the British occupation zone of Germany in 1945, Ollenhauer was second only to Kurt Schumacher within the party. Confirmed as Schumacher's successor at the 1952 Dortmund SPD party convention, Ollenhauer pledged to continue traditional socialist goals. Throughout the 1950s, Ollenhauer opposed West German Chancellor Konrad Adendauer's policy of linking West Germany to the United States. He advocated nuclear disarmament and four-power negotiations as a more effective guarantee of peace and path toward German unity. Within the 1957 Ollenhauer Plan, Social Democratic notions of a system of collective security blended well with domestic security defined in terms of economic prosperity within a free market. As a candidate for chancellor, Ollenhauer led the SDP into the disastrous 1957 elections, in which the SDP won only 31 percent of the vote and the Christian Democrats won an outright majority for the first time. Following the elections Ollenhauer moved the party toward what became the Bad Godesberg reform program of 1959, which repudiated Marxism.

BIBLIOGRAPHY

Seebacher-Brandt, Brigitte. *Ollenhauer: Biedermann und Patriot.* Berlin: Sieder, 1984.

David A. Meier

SEE ALSO Brandt, Willy; Schumacher, Kurt

Olszewski, Jan (1930–)

Prime minister of Poland (December 1991–June 1992). Jan Olszewski received a law degree from the University of Warsaw in 1953. He worked in the Ministry of Justice in 1953–54. He then was a scholar at the Department of Law of the Polish Academy of Sciences and a member of the editorial staff of the journal *Po Prostu* (No Problem).

Olszewski gained popularity for his defense of Jacek Kuroń, Adam Michnik, Karol Modzelewski, and others accused of antistate activity, for their protests against policies of the Communist state. He also defended students arrested during the March demonstrations in 1968 and workers arrested for striking in Radom in 1978. In 1984 he was an auxiliary prosecutor in the assassination case of Jerzy Popieluszko, the pro-Solidarity priest murdered by members of the security police in October 1984.

Olszewski's early political career was connected with the Polish labor union Solidarność (Solidarity). As a member of the Committee for Defense of Workers (KSS) and adviser to Lech Wałęsa, the leader of the Solidarity movement, he participated in the Round Table with representatives of the government concerning the relegalization of Solidarity in February and April 1989. Later he was nominated as vice president of the Court of Justice and of the National Civil Committee.

With the collapse of Polish Communism in the Summer of 1989 he joined the Center Alliance, the rightist party formed to support Lech Wałesa's candidacy for president. The Central Alliance nominated him for prime minister. He formed a seven-party coalition in December 1991. Olszewski wanted to delay privatization and increase spending for social welfare. He also wanted to call informers of the former Ministry of Internal Affairs to account. Otherwise, he argued, they would threaten the structures of the state. However, both the parliamentary majority and Lech Wałesa, who had been elected president in December 1990, refused to support this. They argued that some records might have been faked, and the disclosure of the lists in question could demolish the present political system and bring about too dramatic a change in the top authorities. The only solution appeared to be Olszewski's dismissal, which occurred on June 5, 1992. After a split in the Central Agreement Party, Olszewski became a leader of a parliamentary club Movement for the Republic. Following a subsequent splintering of that organization, he formed his own faction, Jan Olszewski's Movement for the Republic. Parliament, according to him, was the most important governmental power in the state. He was an advocate of employee shareholding as the only form of privatization that would enable a wide range of social groups to benefit. In this Olszewski represented a social democratic point of view. He offered an alternative to the "Shock Therapy" or rapid privatization pursued by the Polish government in the early 1990s and which produced a large measure of social misery.

BIBLIOGRAPHY

Stachura, Peter D. *Poland in the Twentieth Century.* New York: St. Martin's Press, 1999.

Agnieszka Schramke

Olympic Politics

International politics have long intruded into the Olympic Games. The praiseworthy ideals of Baron Pierre de Coubertin, who established the modern Olympics in 1896, have been diluted. He sought to revive Greek humanitarian values through competitive international sport, but interfering international politics have created, in the words of George Orwell, an atmosphere of "mimic warfare."

The USSR quickly grasped the propaganda value of international sports. At the Helsinki Summer Games in 1952 the Soviets won seventy-one medals to seventy-six for the United States. They forged ahead at the 1956 Summer Games Melbourne, taking ninety-eight medals to the Americans' seventy-four. At these games the Hungarian water polo team defeated the Soviets in a brutal contest that left blood in the water, a presentiment of the Hungarian Revolution of later that year. The Rome Summer Games in 1960 marked the American nadir, when the U.S. track and field team fell far behind the Soviets. But Americans countered, accusing the USSR of "undisguised professionalism" in the form of salaries to the athletes, state-subsidized training schools, and drug enhancement. The 1964 Tokyo Games witnessed an American comeback, and at Lake Placid in 1980 the U.S. hockey team, composed of college students, defeated the Soviet professionals 4–3. The same year the United States and some sixty other nations boycotted the Moscow Games in protest against the Soviet invasion of Afghanistan in 1979. The Soviets in turn refused to participate in the Los Angeles Games of 1984. One final Cold War confrontation occurred at the Summer Games of 1988 in Seoul, South Korea. The spectacular TV coverage concealed the tense atmosphere caused by the military threat from North Korea. After communism's collapse in Europe, the Russian athletes at Barcelona in 1992 carried the Olympic flag, instead of the hammer and sickle, signaling the end of the Cold War.

Third World politics stirred at Rome in 1960 when black African athletes protested South Africa's all-white team as sanctioning that nation's apartheid policies. Then, four years later in Mexico City, protesting college students demonstrated against their poverty-stricken country's hosting of the 1964 games. Police suppression killed over two hundred. Two U.S. relay athletes gave the black power salute in support during the playing of the U.S. national anthem. Black African states again objected at the 1976 Montreal Games because New Zealand's rugby team toured expelled South Africa. At the same time, the People's Republic of China's complaints forced Taiwan's ouster.

International terrorism rammed its way into the Israeli wing of the Olympic Village at the Munich Games in 1972, when a Palestinian commando squad took nine athletes hostage. Police intervention at the airport left all the prisoners dead, killed by a terrorist's hand grenade. Lord Killanin, head of the International Olympic Committee after 1972, bemoaned: "alas, sport is intertwined with politics."

BIBLIOGRAPHY

Baker, William J., and John M. Carroll. "The Politics of the Olympics," in William J. Baker and John M. Carroll, eds. *Sports in Modern America.* St. Louis: River City, 1981.

Espy, Richard. *The Politics of the Olympic Games.* Berkeley: University of California Press, 1979.

William J. Miller

O'Malley, Desmond (1939–)

Irish politician. Desmond O'Malley, a solicitor, was elected to the Dáil (lower house of parliament) as a representative of the center-Right Fianna Fáil party for Limerick East in 1968. In 1969 and 1970 he served as parliamentary secretary to Prime Minister Jack Lynch, parliamentary secretary to the minister for defense, and government chief whip. As minister for justice (1970–73), O'Malley threatened to intern suspected terrorists in late 1970, and he introduced the Offences against the State Bill in December 1972, setting up the Special Criminal Court. From 1977 to 1980 he was minister for industry and commerce. O'Malley deferred to George Colley in the Fianna Fáil leadership struggle after Jack Lynch left office. Between the years 1981 to 1985, he was the leading challenger to Charles Haughey, who led Fianna Fáil from 1979 to 1992. In 1982 he served as minister for trade, commerce, and tourism. After his expulsion from Fianna Fáil in May 1985 because of his support for the Anglo-Irish agreement to confer and seek peace in Northern Ireland, O'Malley helped found the Progressive Democratic Party (PD), which advanced a more conciliatory approach to the Northern Ireland question. He led the Progressive Democrats from 1985–94. During the Coalition of Fianna Fáil and Progressive Democrats (FF-PD), O'Malley was minister for industry and commerce from 1989 to 1992. When Prime Minister Albert Reynolds accused O'Malley of giving deceptive information to an inquiry over alleged fraud in the beef export market, a resulting vote of no confidence in the government ended in the dissolution of the Dáil and the FF-PD coalition left office. O'Malley was defeated in the June 1994 election for the European Parliament by fellow PD Pat Cox in Munster.

BIBLIOGRAPHY

Smith, Raymond. *The Quest for Power.* Naas, Ireland: Aherlow, 1986.

Walshe, Dick. *Des O'Malley: A Political Profile.* Dingle, Ireland: Brandon, 1986.

Michael J. Kennedy

O'Malley, Donough (1921–68)

Irish politician. Donough O'Malley was born in Limerick, and was educated as an engineer. A member of the Dáil (lower house of parliament) for Limerick East from 1961 to 1968, O'Malley served as minister for health (1965–66); and minister for education (1966–68). One of Prime Minister Sean Lemass's new ministerial talents, O'Malley was an energetic minister who modernized the Irish educational system by establishing, with help from the international Organization for Economic Cooperation and Development (OECD), free primary and secondary education for all. He closed rural schools and bused pupils to larger schools. His proposed controversial merger between Trinity College, Dublin, and University College, Dublin, is still being debated. O'Malley was one of the forces of modernization, growth, and social change in Ireland of the 1960s. There was great public enthusiasm for his schemes and they took a decade to have complete effect. He realized that Irish economic development needed the development of human resources. He was the uncle of former Progressive Democrat leader Desmond O'Malley.

BIBLIOGRAPHY

Townshend, Charles. *Ireland: The Twentieth-century.* Oxford University Press, 1999.

Michael J. Kennedy

SEE ALSO Lemass, Sean

O'Neill, Terence (1914–)

Ulster Unionist politician and prime minister of Northern Ireland (1963–69). Terence O'Neill was born in London in 1914. A captain in the Irish Guards (1939–45), he was returned as MP for Bannside, County Antrim, in 1946. He was parliamentary secretary to the minister for health (1948–52), deputy speaker of the House (1953–56), and minister for home affairs (1956). As minister for finance (1956–63) his efforts to attract industries and foreign investment were quite successful. He succeeded Lord Brookeborough as leader of the Unionist Party and prime minister in 1963. Loyalists who did not want closer relations with the Irish Republic were opposed to his gesture of inviting Irish Republic Prime Minister Sean Lemass to take tea at Stormont, seat of the Northern Ireland government, on January 14, 1965. He returned the visit, to Dublin, later in the year. This policy of rapprochement was condemned by hard-liners, led by Ian Paisley, who were further alienated when the prime minister allowed peaceful commemorations of the fiftieth anniversary of the Easter Rising of 1916 during 1966. There was an increasing demand from the Catholic minority population for an end to the discrimination that characterized local government in Northern Ireland. O'Neill agreed to the abolition of the business vote but rejected other demands put forward by the Northern Ireland Labour Party and the Irish Congress of Trade Unions. Following demands by the Northern Ireland Civil Rights Association and the People's Democracy, he announced a five-point program of civil rights in November 1968. The division within the cabinet over his concessions became public when he dismissed Minister for Home Affairs William Craig in December. The disturbances that accompanied the socialist People's Democracy's march from Belfast to Derry in 1969 received widespread media coverage and led to harsh criticism of Paisleyites and the police. There was a public demand for an investigation of the attack at Burntollet on the marchers, and, under pressure from the British government, O'Neill announced the establishment of the Cameron Commission. This led to the resignation of Brian Faulkner, deputy leader of the Unionist Party and minister for commerce, on January 23, 1969. Challenged for leadership of the party and attempting to unify it, O'Neill called a general election for February 24. In his own constituency he was opposed by Paisley, who polled 6,331 votes to his 7,741. O'Neill secured twenty-three votes in the leadership contest, with Faulkner opposing him, Craig abstaining, and ten walking out. His position continued to be eroded, and when his cousin, Major James Chichester-Clark, minister for agriculture, resigned on April 23, O'Neill's moral authority within the party was shattered. He resigned on April 28. In the election for a new leader, when Chichester-Clark defeated Faulkner by one vote, the decisive vote was O'Neill's. He resigned from politics in January 1970 and his seat went to Paisley. Shortly afterward in January 1969, O'Neill was raised to the peerage as Lord O'Neill of the Maine.

BIBLIOGRAPHY

Arthur, Paul. *Northern Ireland since 1968,* 2d ed. Oxford: Blackwell Publishers, 1996.

Aughey, Arthur, and Duncan Morrow, eds. *Northern Ireland Politics.* London: Longman, 1996.

Bew, Paul. *Northern Ireland, 1921–1996: Political Forces and Social Classes.* London: Serif, 1996.

Gordon, David. *The O'Neill Years: Unionist Politics, 1963–1969.* Belfast: Athol Books, 1989.

Ricki Schoen

SEE ALSO Chichester-Clark, James; Faulkner, Arthur Brian Deane

Opus Dei

International Roman Catholic organization founded in Madrid in 1928 by Monsignor Josémaría Escrivá de Balaguer y Albas (1902–75). Opus Dei (OD), "Work of God" or, familiarly, "The Work," is composed of laity and priests. OD's purpose is to help lay people attain holiness in and through their everyday activities, especially through their professional work. OD underwent various stages of development before being designated the Catholic Church's first (and to date only) personal prelature, "Prelature of the Holy Cross and Opus Dei" (an autonomous group independent of regular diocesan church authority) by Pope John Paul II in 1982. In contrast to diocesan jurisdiction that extends over a circumscribed territory, the canonical status of personal prelature grants OD a certain measure of autonomy from ordinary ecclesiastical authority by placing its membership directly under the authority of the OD prelature in matters pertaining to spiritual and doctrinal formation and the apostolic activity freely undertaken through contractual bond with OD. OD develops its apostolates through a male division and a female division. The governing prelate is elected for life in a general congress summoned for that end and his election must be confirmed by the pope. The candidate has to be a priest with no fewer than five years of experience. The prelate resides in Rome and answers to the Sacred Congregation of Bishops. He governs OD with the assistance of two councils: the General Council helps in governing the male section; the female council is governed by the prelate with the general secretary vicar, who is the vicar of the women's section and the central office. All the directors serve terms of eight years. OD is divided into administrative units termed "regions." As a prelature, OD can train, ordain, and assign its own priests. These priests, about 2 percent of the total membership, exercise a special care for the spiritual, doctrinal, and apostolic formation of the lay membership.

The structure of OD indicates several different levels of commitment: (1) numeraries, who are celibate, live in the special centers and work full-time at the apostolate; separate male and female residential centers are maintained; female numeraries are often assigned to administrative and domestic tasks in the residences. (2) Oblates live a celibate life outside these centers. (3) Supernumeraries, who make up a majority of the membership, are married members who live independently and have professional careers. (4) Cooperators (who may be non-Catholic) support the work of OD in various ways. The priests under the jurisdiction of the prelature are responsible for the spiritual direction and sacramental life of the lay members. In addition, the Society of the Holy Cross is composed of diocesan priests who cultivate the spirituality of OD and support its programs, but they remain subject to their bishops. The overwhelming majority of OD members are married, live outwardly normal lives, and do not publicize their membership. Any lay Catholic over eighteen is eligible to join. By 1998, OD had spread to over ninety nations and numbered approximately 80,000 lay members, 1,649 priests, and 363 seminarians. Over half the membership is found in Europe, especially in Spain; another third are in the Americas; the rest are scattered throughout the world.

While refraining from corporate ownership, OD provides support and spiritual guidance for a number of public institutions. These include involvement in hundreds of universities and high schools and organs of the media. OD's notable apostolic works include the Catholic University of Navarre (founded in 1952), Pamplona, Spain; the Academic Center of the Holy Cross in Rome for advanced ecclesiastical studies by members and nonmembers (granted pontifical status in 1998); Strathmore College of Arts and Sciences, Nairobi, Kenya; Seido Language Institute, Osaka, Japan; universities in Mexico, Peru, and Colombia; various technical institutes and trade schools, and other institutions in the areas of health care and social welfare. OD operates student residences throughout the world, some of them international in character, and maintains conference centers. These residences and conference centers serve as hospitality sites for attracting, recruiting, and forming new members. The Work especially seeks to recruit intellectuals and the professorial class.

Escrivá stressed the universal call to holiness and ordinary work as a means of sanctification. To preserve the secular character of the organization, members do not incorporate themselves in OD by taking vows as traditional religious do in the Catholic Church, but they "contract" to commit themselves to the spiritual formation and the apostolic works sponsored by OD.

OD has been dogged by controversy. Its critics, some of whom are disaffected former members, accuse it of being overly secretive and manipulative. In 1981, Cardinal Basil Hume, archbishop of Westminster (London, England), felt compelled to issue guidelines to govern the activity of OD in his diocese. These include the requirement that families be notified, if at all possible, when one of their children desires to enter OD; that the liberty of individuals be respected, including the right to choose one's own spiritual director, even if the chosen director is not an OD member; and that the initiatives and activities of OD clearly indicate OD sponsorship. Critics have also charged that it is difficult to obtain the OD constitution (1982) and that even bishops in whose dioceses OD operates have not been able to peruse this document. In the realm of politics, critics have charged that OD members tend to favor authoritarian governments. In Spain, for example, OD members were well connected with the Franco regime. In Latin America, bishops associated with OD have a reputation for being inimical to the pastoral approaches associated with liberation theology. In response, OD states that its members are free to follow their own lights in the political realm. Other critics allege that OD sets its eye on the intellectual elite, the well-to-do, and the socially prominent. OD responds that people from all classes can be found within its membership. Finally, OD has been accused of establishing a "parallel church," thus undermining the unity of the local church. OD answers that its membership is faithful to the teaching authority of the church.

BIBLIOGRAPHY

Estruch, Joan. *Saints and Schemers: Opus Dei and its Paradoxes.* Tr. by Elizabeth Ladd Glick. New York: Oxford University Press, 1995.

Ghirlanda, G. "Natura della prelature personali e posizione dei laici." *Gregorianum* 69 (1988): 299–314.

Le Tourneau, D. "L'Opus Dei en prélature personnelle: dans le droit fil de Vatican II." *Revue de Sciences religieuses* 57 (1983): 295–309.

Messori, Vittorio. *Opus Dei: Leadership and Vision in Today's Catholic Church.* Tr. by Gerald Malsbary. Washington, D.C.: Regnery, 1997.

Rocca, Giancarlo. *L'Opus Dei: appunti e documenti per una storia.* Rome: Claretianum, 1985.

Walsh, Michael. *Opus Dei.* San Francisco: HarperSanFrancisco, 1992.

Peter J. Bernardi

Organization for European Economic Cooperation (OEEC)

Organization of European states set up to administer U.S. Marshall Plan aid for European reconstruction after

World War II. In response to U.S. Secretary of State George Marshall's June 5, 1947, Harvard University speech, in which he offered U.S. aid for the reconstruction of Europe provided that the countries of Europe join together and offer a coherent program for economic reconstruction, the United Kingdom and France jointly convened a conference for European Economic Cooperation at the French Foreign Ministry on July 11, 1947. This was the initial meeting of what would become the Council for European Economic Cooperation.

Georges Bidault, French foreign minister and Ernest Bevin, his British counterpart, had met with Vyacheslav Molotov, the Soviet foreign minister. When he left Paris on July 2, 1947, it was evident that the USSR would not participate in the Marshall Plan. The French and British, however, proceeded on their own on July 4 to invite twenty-two European countries (Albania, Austria, Belgium, Bulgaria, Czechoslovakia, Denmark, Finland, Greece, Hungary, Iceland, Ireland, Italy, Luxembourg, Netherlands, Norway, Poland, Portugal, Romania, Sweden, Switzerland, Turkey, and Yugoslavia) to attend the conference. The USSR was again invited to participate. Albania, Bulgaria, Finland, Hungary, Poland, and Romania refused the invitation. Czechoslovakia at first accepted but, owing to Soviet pressure, announced on July 10 that it would not participate. Subsequently Spain and Portugal were allowed to join.

The conference on July 12, 1947, established a working committee, chaired by Hervé Alphand, which drafted a plan for the new organization. The following day the plan was submitted to a conference consisting of the foreign ministers or ministers of trade from the individual states. The conference then established the Committee for European Economic Cooperation, which was to draw up a list of the resources and needs of the sixteen participating countries and of the western section of Germany. Claude Bouchinet-Serreules of France was appointed secretary-general.

Following the U.S. response to the report of this committee, the conference again met on March 15, 1948. A working party, chaired by Hervé Alphand, was instructed to draft a constitution for a permanent organization. On April 16 the Convention on European Economic Cooperation was signed and the Organization for European Economic Cooperation (OEEC) was constituted.

After the successful completion of the Marshall Plan, the members of the OEEC decided to continue their coordination and to extend the number of states involved. This decision produced the Organization for Economic Cooperation and Development (OECD) in 1961.

BIBLIOGRAPHY

The archives of the Organization for European Economic Cooperation are located in the Historical Archives of the European Communities at the European University Institute in Florence, Italy.

Ouin, Marc. *The OEEC and the Common Market; Why Europe Needs an Economic Union of Seventeen Countries.* Paris: Organization for European Economic Cooperation, 1958.

Bernard Cook

SEE ALSO Marshall Plan

Orkney Islands

Archipelago of more than seventy islands and rocky islets, with a total land mass of 377 square miles (974 sq km), fewer than twenty miles north of Scotland, from which they are separated by the Pentland Firth. The Orkney Islands, following the administrative reorganization of 1975, form one of the United Kingdom's three island regions; the other two are the Shetland Islands and the Outer Hebrides, or Western Isles. Kirkwall on Mainland (Pomona), the largest island in the group, is the seat of the area council. Twenty-five of the islands are inhabited and in 1991 their population was 19,450.

Settled by the Picts, the Orkneys were invaded by the Vikings in the eighth century. The Orkney Islands along with the Shetlands passed from Norse to Scottish rule in 1472. The Orkneys are a much more prosperous farming area than the Shetlands or the Hebrides. The holdings average thirty-five acres and are farmed by their owners, unlike the cofting (tenant farming) system predominant on the other two island groups. Beef and dairy cattle, pigs, chickens, and fodder are the chief agricultural concerns. Because of the good agricultural conditions, fishing is not as important as in the other two island areas. A major terminal for the Piper and Claymore North Sea oil fields has been constructed at Flotta in Scapa Flow, the enclosed anchorage south of Mainland, which was the base of Britain's Grand Fleet in World War I and became the graveyard of the German fleet scuttled there in 1918.

BIBLIOGRAPHY

Bailey, Patrick. *Orkney.* Devon: Pevensey Press, 1995.

Bernard Cook

SEE ALSO Hebrides; Shetland Islands

Orlando, Leoluca (1947–)

One of Italy's most important anti-Mafia politicians. Leoluca Orlando led anti-Mafia city administrations in Palermo from 1985 to 1990. Disappointed by the Christian Democratic Party's policy of weak opposition to the Mafia in southern Italy, Orlando left the party in 1990 and founded a new political movement, La Rete (The Network).

Orlando was born in 1947 in Palermo, Sicily, into a large, traditional Catholic family. He studied law at the University of Palermo and, briefly, international law at Heidelberg University in West Germany. Returning to Sicily, he became a professor of regional law at the University of Palermo.

Orlando entered politics as a Christian Democratic city councilor in Palermo in 1983. Two years later, promising to remove the Mafia from city business, he was elected mayor. Orlando reformed the process of awarding city contracts, removing an important source of income from the Mafia, and brought the city into an anti-Mafia trial as a damaged party in 1986. Orlando condemned the Italian Socialist Party in Palermo for accepting Mafia votes and hinted at high-level collaboration between politicians and organized crime.

Though Orlando received more votes than any other candidate in the May 1990 city council elections, he was not endorsed by his own party as mayor. Convinced that the Christian Democratic Party was no longer committed to defeating the Mafia, Orlando left the party at the end of the year. As leader of La Rete, Orlando was reelected mayor with 75 percent of the vote in November 1993.

BIBLIOGRAPHY

Haberman, Clyde. "The Ex-Mayor, the Mafia and Politics." *New York Times,* April 24, 1991, A7.

Montalbano, William. "Basta! The People of Sicily Say 'Enough' to the Cosa Nostra." *Los Angeles Times Magazine,* December 19, 1993, 36.

Suro, Robert. "The Men in Black Take on the Mafia." *New York Times,* November 27, 1987, A19.

David Travis

SEE ALSO Mafia

Osimo, Treaty of

Treaty of 1975 between Italy and Yugoslavia confirming the frontiers between the two countries. Following World War I a half million Slovenes were incorporated into Italy and there was tension between Italy and Yugoslavia over the city of Fiume until 1924 when Yugoslavia dropped its claim to the city. After the defeat of Yugoslavia by Germany in April 1941, Italy occupied Dalmatia and Bosnia. At the end of World War II Yugoslavia, attempting to take advantage of Italy's weakness, sought to push its frontier with Italy to the Isonzo River. In April 1945 Yugoslav forces occupied a large part of the province of Venezia Giulia but after six weeks were forced to withdraw by the Western powers. The Western powers were willing to concede much of the Istrian hinterland around the port of Trieste to Yugoslavia but not the city itself, the population of which was overwhelmingly Italian. The Big Four in July 1946 agreed to employ a "free territory" formula reminiscent of post–World War I Fiume or Danzig. This was acceptable to neither Yugoslavia nor Italy. Despite Yugoslav protests and obstruction on February 10, 1947, the Italian treaty, which included the Trieste compromise, was signed in Paris. In fact U.S. and British forces occupied and administered the city, which was promised on March 20, 1948, by Georges Bidault, the French foreign minister, speaking on behalf of the West, to Italy if the Communists were defeated in the upcoming Italian election.

After Yugoslavia lost the support of the Soviet Union (because of the 1948 rupture between the Yugoslav Communist leader Tito and Joseph Stalin), which had supported its claims, the West took matters into its own hands. In 1954 the Western powers unilaterally allowed Italy to annex Trieste and handed over the hinterland of the "free territory" to Yugoslavia. The arrangement was ratified in 1975.

In April 1994 Mirko Tremaglia, a deputy of the National Alliance, the successor of the neofascist Italian Social Movement, called for Italy to renounce the 1975 treaty. He said that since Yugoslavia no longer existed, the treaty should be regarded as a dead letter. He described Istria, the city of Rijeka (Fiume), and Dalmatia as "occupied territories" that were "historically Italian." He also stated that Italy should block the entry of the former Yugoslav republics Slovenia and Croatia into the European Union (EU). Although Tremaglia's position was widely denounced by Italian political figures, some agreed that Italy should block the entry of Slovenia and Croatia into the EU until a successful renegotiation of the Treaty of Osimo was completed. Slovenia and Croatia had agreed in 1993 to renegotiate, but Italian critics decried the lack of progress. Slovenia and Croatia should, they insisted, be required to compensate the approximately 150,000 Italians whose property was confiscated after World War II and to guarantee the rights of ethnic Italians.

BIBLIOGRAPHY

Wolf, Robert Lee. *The Balkans in Our Time,* rev. ed. New York: Norton, 1978.

Bernard Cook

Owen, David (1938–)

British physician, politician, and diplomat. A Cambridge University medical degree and posts at London hospitals prepared Owen for a career in psychiatry and neurology. His hospital work reinforced his concern for the plight of the poor, however, and in 1964 he was elected a Labour member of Parliament. Under the governments of Prime Minister Harold Wilson he held posts in the Ministries of Defense (1968–70) and Health (1974–76). An ardent supporter of British entry into the European Community (EC), Owen, with the prominent Labour MP and former cabinet member Roy Jenkins, defied Wilson's decision in 1972 to oppose British membership. In 1977, under James Callaghan, Owen became foreign secretary. After the defeat of the Labour Party in 1979, the rise of left-wing influence in favor of unilateral nuclear disarmament and the restructuring of the party to increase the labor unions' influence led him to join Jenkins, William Rodgers, and Shirley Williams to form the Social Democratic Party (SDP). The SDP's electoral successes were meager and its leadership fell into controversies over its principles and its relationship with the Liberal Party. Owen supported a British nuclear deterrent and a social democracy based on market economics and state-sponsored redistribution of wealth. He feared that alliance with the Liberal Party, a course favored by Jenkins, would compromise these principles and spoil the party's chances to elect a substantial number of its own candidates. Owen's energies and convictions carried him into political isolation. In 1987 he formed his own version of the SDP but it dissolved in 1990. In August, 1992 he became the European Community's chief mediator for the Bosnian crisis.

With Cyrus Vance, the former U.S. secretary of state, Owen proposed a peace plan in late 1992 that, while preserving a sovereign Bosnia, would have divided Bosnia between the Bosnian Serbs, on the one hand, and the Bosnian Muslims and Bosnian Croats, on the other. Owen was accused of rewarding ethnic cleansing because the Bosnian Serbs would have received approximately 70 percent of the territory. For his part, Owen blamed the United States for undermining the Vance-Owen Plan and condemning Bosnia to nearly three more years of war, and to an ultimate peace settlement, the November 1995 Dayton Accords, that, in effect, divided Bosnia.

BIBLIOGRAPHY

Jenkins, Peter. *Mrs. Thatcher's Revolution: The Ending of the Socialist Era.* New York: Random House, 1987.

Jenkins, Roy. *A Life at the Center: Memoirs of a Radical Reformer.* New York: Random House, 1991.

Owen, David. *Balkan Odessey.* New York: Harcourt Brace, 1995.

———. *Time to Declare.* London: Michael Joseph, 1991.

———. *David Owen, Personally Speaking to Kenneth Harris.* London: Weidenfeld and Nicholson, 1987.

Robert D. McJimsey

SEE ALSO Callaghan, James; Foot, Michael; Jenkins, Roy; Wilson, Harold

Paasikivi, Juho (1870–1956)

President of Finland (1946–56). Juho Kusti Paasikivi, born November 27, 1870, received a doctorate in law in 1901. He was a university teacher (1899–1903) but was appointed director of the State Financial Office (1903–14). From 1914 to 1934 he was a member of the board and managing director of the Kansallispankki, a leading business bank.

During his early political years Paasikivi was a member of the Eduskunta (parliament, 1907–9, 1910–13), a senator (1908–9), and deputy chairman of the Financial Committee of the Senate in 1918. Paasikivi wished to become Finland's first president, but finding little or no support, he preferred a monarchy. Consequently, he left the political stage but was chairman of the National Coalition Party in the 1930s.

Paasikivi's political comeback was related to his fellow Finns' increasing perceptions of the threat of war toward the end of the 1930s. He became Finnish ambassador to Sweden (1936–40) then to the USSR (1940–41). He was a member of the government during the Winter War (1939–1940). At the end of Finland's renewed war with the USSR (1941–44), the Continuation War, in 1944 Paasikivi became prime minister. Paasikivi and President Carl Mannerheim, in light with the military success of the Soviet Union were compelled to shift the nation from the war against the Soviet Union to war against its former ally, Germany. In 1946, according to Paasikivi's wish, Mannerheim resigned and the Eduskunta elected Paasikivi president.

In the 1950 presidential elections Paasikivi was expected to win without serious competition. This fact did not change when Urho Kekkonen, a close friend and partner, unexpectedly challenged him. Paasikivi was elected in the first round of balloting, and Kekkonen remained prime minister in most governments during Paasikivi's second term. Paasikivi did not wish to continue in office by 1956, at the age of eighty-five. However, some electors, mainly from the Conservative Party, persuaded Paasikivi to enter the second round in the Electoral College to prevent Kekkonen from becoming president. Paasikivi accepted the invitation because the delegation asking him promised a unanimous election. However, both big parties, the Agrarian Union and the Social Democrats, voted for their own candidates, Kekkonen and Fagerholm, respectively. Furthermore, the Communists divided their votes between Kekkonen and Fagerholm, who continued to the third round. Paasikivi, who was ultimately elected, died at the end of the same year.

Paasikivi, as chairman of the Finnish Peace Commission in 1940, prime minister, and president, concentrated on building working relations between Finland and the Soviet Union. He understood the Russian language and culture and had direct contacts with Soviet politicians during his years in Moscow. He adopted the conciliatory approach to Russian power politics of the Old Finns, who before independence in 1918 had been willing to comply with Russia interference in the internal affairs of the Grand Dutchy of Finland. As a result Paasikivi opened a new opportunity for Finnish foreign policy by maintaining that the Soviet Union had no inherent desire to occupy Finland or crush its Nordic political institutions, but only wished to guarantee Soviet security needs along its northwest border against aggressors, namely, Germany and its allies. Paasikivi's doctrine was important in establishing peaceful external relations for rebuilding the country after World War II and the depressed national identity. It also gave the Soviet Union a basis for accepting Finland's neutrality and democracy. The new foreign policy orientation soon acquired the name Paasikivi Line. During the 1956 presidential campaign Kekkonen's supporters coined the term Paasikivi-Kekkonen Line, implying that Kekkonen had formulated the line from the very beginning.

Paasikivi's domestic achievements were even greater. Both the Soviet Union and Finnish Communists wished him to become an interim leader in Finland's path toward a "people's democracy." Paasikivi did not share such aspirations. On the contrary, the postwar Finnish political atmosphere was colored by the power struggle between Paasikivi (supported by the nonsocialist parties and the SDP) and the Communists who had direct Soviet support. The last battle was fought in 1948. While Finland and the Soviet Union were negotiating the terms of a mutual assistance pact, Paasikivi refused to go to Moscow, fearing that he might be forced to sign an unacceptable treaty. Furthermore, he placed the police and army in the Helsinki area on alert to prevent a Communist coup. Paasikivi won the fight. The Soviet Union was persuaded to revise the text of the suggested treaty to make it acceptable to the Eduskunta, and the Communists lost the 1948 parliamentary elections.

A conservative politician and until the war a supporter of a German orientation in Finnish foreign policy, Paasikivi nonetheless convinced Soviet leader Joseph Stalin that he alone was able to redirect the Finns to establish working relations between Finland and the Soviet Union. Paasikivi saw Finland as belonging to the Western community, but his wish for neutrality was a way of keeping Finland's distance from the Soviet Union.

BIBLIOGRAPHY

Allison, Roy. *Finland's Relations with the Soviet Union 1944–1984.* Oxford: Macmillan, 1985.

Jakobson, Max. *Finnish Neutrality.* New York: Praeger, 1969.

Tuominen, Uuno, and Kari Uusitalo. *J.K. Paasikivi, A Pictorial Biography.* Helsinki: Otava, 1970.

Vilho Harle

SEE ALSO Kekkonen, Urho

Paisley, Ian (1926–)

Northern Irish Free Presbyterian clergyman and Democratic Unionist Party leader and MP for North Antrim (1970–); member of the European Parliament for Northern Ireland (1979–). Ian Richard Kyle Paisley was born in Armagh in 1926. He was awarded a diploma of the Theological Hall of the Reformed Presbyterian Church, Belfast, and, after a short seminar at the Barie School of Evangelism, South Wales, was ordained to the ministry by his father in 1946. He was a cofounder and moderator of the Free Presbyterian Church of Ulster (1951). During the 1950s Paisley became a noted opponent of Roman Catholicism and any form of liberalism in the Protestant churches. Paisley opposed ecumenism and, to this end, visited Rome to protest against the Second Vatican Council, (1962–65). On June 4, 1963, he held a mass meeting to protest the lowering of the flag on Belfast, City Hall as a mark of respect for the deceased Pope John XXIII.

The improvement in relations between Northern Ireland and the Republic of Ireland, due to meetings between Captain Terence O'Neill, the prime minister of Northern Ireland, and Sean Lemass, the prime minister of the Republic of Ireland, led to Paisley's to denounce O'Neill as a traitor. Paisley founded the Ulster Constitution Defence Committee and the Ulster Protestant Volunteers in April 1966 to oppose any commemorations in the North of the Easter Rising of 1916. His behavior was denounced by O'Neill on June 15, 1966, and Paisley was imprisoned from July 20 to October 19, 1966, for leading a banned march through a Catholic Section of Belfast. By now recognized as the champion of fundamental Protestantism, Paisley was awarded a doctorate of divinity by the Bob Jones University of Greenville, South Carolina.

Aided by Major Ronald Bunting, Paisley halted a civil rights march in Armagh on November 30, 1968. Militant Protestants, led by Bunting, also harassed the People's Democracy march that left Belfast on January 1, 1969, for Derry. On January 4, the loyalist faction made a concerted attack on the unarmed marchers at Burntollet Bridge. Later that month Paisley and Bunting were imprisoned for participating in an unlawful assembly. In the general election of February 24 Paisley, from prison, stood against O'Neill in the Bannside division, polling 6,331 votes to the prime minister's 7,745. In April O'Neill resigned and was succeeded on May 1 by Major James Chichester-Clark. Paisley strongly criticized Chichester-Clark's attempts to balance the Catholic demand for reforms of the police and the Unionist right-wing demand for maintenance of the Protestant-Unionist supremacy. He was released from prison under a general amnesty on May 6.

Paisley and his supporters were outraged by the disbandment of the Special Constabulary, an entirely Protestant supplementary police force, on April 1, 1970. He was returned to Stormont, the Northern Ireland parliament, for the Bannside division on April 16, 1970, as a Protestant Unionist and in June returned for the North Antrim seat. Chichester-Clark was replaced by Brian Faulkner as prime minister on March 1971. Six months later Paisley and Desmond Boal, a leading barrister and Ulster Unionist, founded the Democratic Unionist Party. Unionism continued to fragment as the pace of the war between the Irish Republican Army and the British army accelerated, and when Faulkner proved unable to restore peaceful government, the parliament of Northern Ireland was closed, and direct rule of Northern Ireland by the British government was introduced on March 30, 1972. Over the next few years, Paisley continued to demand the restoration of the Northern Ireland parliament and government but the British government was now committed to some sort of power sharing between the two communities in Northern Ireland. Paisley denounced this as antidemocratic. He was elected to the new Assembly of Northern Ireland where he was a member of the opposition to the power-sharing Executive that was to include representatives of the Catholic as well as Protestant community. He was a strong supporter of the strike by the Ulster Workers Council that brought about the collapse of the Executive in 1974.

As a member of the United Ulster Unionist Council, Paisely sat at the constitutional convention that succeeded the Assembly. He subscribed to the convention report, which effectively argued for the restoration of Stormont. The British government rejected these proposals and the convention was dissolved. In 1977, Paisley attempted to secure a change in British security policy on Northern Ireland by calling another general strike. The strike was a failure, however, as it did not involve the power-station workers, who led the ability if they struck to largely shut Northern Ireland down. He has consistently topped the polls in his Northern Ireland constituency in elections for the European Parliament of the European Community, later European Union. Paisley has controlled the *Protestant Telegraph* since its foundation in 1966. He bitterly opposed the 1998 Good Friday agreement, which paved the way for the formation of a government of Northern Ireland consisting of representatives of the major parties representing both the Protestant and Catholic Communities.

Paisley has been a negative force in Northern Irish politics. He has become synonomous with intollerant sectarianism.

BIBLIOGRAPHY

Arthur, Paul. *Northern Ireland since 1968,* 2d ed. Oxford: Blackwell Publishers, 1996.

Bruce, Steve. *God Save Ulster: The Religion and Politics of Paisleyism.* New York: Oxford University Press, 1986.

Cooke, Dennis. *Persecuting Zeal: A Portrait of Ian Paisley.* Dingle, Co. Kerry, Ireland: Brandon, 1996.

Marrinan, Patrick. *Paisley, Man of Wrath.* Tralee, Ireland: Anvil Books, 1973.

Paisley, Rhonda. *Ian Paisley, My Father.* Basingstoke, Hants, U.K.: Marshall Pickering, 1988.

Smyth, Clifford. *Ian Paisley: Voice of Protestant Ulster.* Edinburgh: Scottish Academic, 1987.

Ricki Schoen

Palme, Olof (1927–86)

Swedish prime minister (1969–76, 1982–86). Sven Olof Joachim Palme was born on January 30, 1927, in Stockholm. His wealthy family sent him to study in the United States, where he graduated from Kenyon College in 1948. He received a law degree from the University of Stockholm in 1951. He quickly made his mark in the Social Democratic Workers Party (SAP) and became Prime Minister Tage Erlander's private secretary in 1953. Palme was elected to parliament in 1958 and became a minister without portfolio in 1963. In 1965 he was appointed minister of communication and in 1967 minister of education and of ecclesiastical affairs.

When Erlander resigned his party and government posts in 1969, Palme succeeded his mentor as secretary of the SAP and prime minister. His attacks on the U.S. persecution of the war in Vietnam and his willingness to allow deserters from the U.S. military to seek haven in Sweden seriously dampened U.S.-Swedish relations. After the defeat of the SAP in the 1976 election, Palme continued to lead the party. He held a number of international posts during his party's interregnum. From 1979 to 1980 he was president of the Nordic Council. He chaired the Independent Commission on Disarmament and Security in Geneva, and he served as a special U.N. envoy in an effort to mediate the war between Iraq and Iran in the 1980s. After the victory of the SAP in the election of 1982, Palme again became prime minister. Succeeding a center-right government, Palme attempted to set the course once again toward his vision of a socialist Sweden.

Palme was shot to death on February 28, 1986, as he and his wife walked in downtown Stockholm after attending a film. Palme's death shocked Sweden not only because of his position but because of the criminal nature of the act. Controversy surrounded the investigation and the eventual arrest in December 1988 and prosecution in June and July 1989 of a man with a history of mental illness and violent criminal activity. The accused was convicted of the crime but subsequently acquitted because of insufficient evidence of guilt in October 1989. Conspiracy theories have abounded.

In 1996 Eugene De Kock, the leader of a South African "hit squad," claimed that a South African spy was involved in the assassination of Palme, an outspoken opponent of apartheid. Sweden was a main source of financial backing for the anti-apartheid African National Congress. However, the Swedish police at the end of the century had not solved the case.

Palme gained wide recognition, and, perhaps, notoriety in some U.S. circles, because of his impassioned opposition to war. He was deeply concerned about international development and remained committed to democratic Socialism.

BIBLIOGRAPHY

Antman, Peter. *Olof Palme, den granslose reformisten.* Stockholm: Tiden, 1996.

Haste, Hans. *Olof Palme.* Paris: Descartes, 1994.

Mosey, Chris. *Cruel Awakening: Sweden and the Killing of Olof Palme.* New York: St. Martin's Press, 1991.

Palme, Olof. *Socialism, Peace, and Solidarity: Selected Speeches of Olof Palme.* New York: Advent Books, 1990.

Bernard Cook

Palsson, Thorsteinn (1947–)

Minister of justice and fisheries and former prime minister (1987–88) of Iceland. Thorsteinn Palsson entered Icelandic national politics in 1981 when he was selected to the steering committee of the center-conservative Independence Party, becoming chairman of the party in 1983. The same year, Palsson was elected to parliament for the first time, and two years later he was appointed to his first ministerial post. From 1985 to 1987 he served as minister of finance, as prime minister from July 8, 1987 to September 28, 1988, and as minister of justice and fisheries in two cabinets since 1991.

Palsson rose quickly through the ranks of the Independence Party but proved unable to hold this largest political party in Iceland together in a difficult period. He was ousted from his post as chairman of the party in 1991 by David Oddsson. Palsson has retained a strong position in Icelandic politics, however, as he has held two of the most important ministries in Iceland in two successive cabinets.

Gudmundur Halfdanarson

SEE ALSO Oddsson, David

Pangalos, Theodoros G. (1938–)

Foreign minister of Greece (1996–). Theodoros G. Pangalos was born in Elefsis in August 1938. He graduated from the faculty of law and economics at the University of Athens in 1963. He was involved in left-wing student and youth organizations, and was a founder of the youth organization Grigoris Lambrakis. In 1964 he ran for parliament as a candidate of the United Democratic Left. Though he was not elected, he did receive a scholarship the same year from the French government. Eventually he received a master of science in politics and philosophy from the University of Paris.

He was in France at the time of the Greek military coup of 1967. He worked abroad during the seven-year dictatorship of the colonels to organize antiregime activity among Greek exiles, to assist exiled Greeks, and to rouse European public opinion against the colonels. Because of his activity and his antijunta articles, he was stripped of his Greek citizenship in 1968. From 1969 to 1978 he lectured on economic development at the Sorbonne. Since 1978 he has been active in the environmental movement.

In 1981 he was elected to the Greek parliament as a representative of the Panhellenic Socialist Movement (PASOK). He was reelected in 1989, 1990, 1993, and 1996. In July 1982 he was appointed under-secretary of commerce. In January 1984 he was made undersecretary of state for European Community affairs. In August 1985 he was appointed the alternate minister for foreign affairs and was appointed to that post again in October 1993. He was elected a member of PASOK's executive board in 1987. He represented the Greek parliament at the Council of Europe from 1989 to 1993. In July 1994 he became minister of transport and communication, and in January 1996, foreign minister.

Bernard Cook

Panić, Milan (1929–)

Prime minister of the truncated Yugoslav Federation, July to December 1992. Milan Panić was born in Belgrade on December 20, 1929. He was educated at the University of Belgrade, and became the champion cyclist of Yugoslavia. As a young man he emigrated to the United States, where he spent thirty years, becoming an industrialist in the pharmaceutical industry and a millionaire. He returned to Serbia and became prime minister of the Yugoslav Federation on July 2, 1992. He and Dobrica Cosić, the federal president, pursued a policy of conciliation. Panić proposed a dialogue with the different nationalities with a view to establishing a multinational and multiconfessional society. He also called for an end to the fighting that had erupted in the wake of the disintegration of Tito's Yugoslavia.

Panić challenged Slobodan Milošević in the Serbian presidential election of December 1992. Milošević, a former Communist, now became nationalistic and rallied the forces of ultra-Serbian nationalism and xenophobia. Panić was supported by Cosić but was defeated by Milošević, who promptly fired the prime minister. Panić then returned to the United States, where he chaired ICN Pharmaceuticals.

Catherine Lutard
(Tr. by B. Cook)

Pannella, Giacinto (1930–)

Italian lawyer and journalist, champion of civil rights. During his university studies Giacinto (Marco) Pannella became a student activist and a leader of student associations. He was one of the organizers of the Radical Party and is one of the founders of numerous leagues for the affirmation of civil rights. During the seventies he was engaged in the struggles for the right to divorce and abortion and for the right of conscientious objection to military service. At the end of the 1970s and during the 1980s he campaigned against preventive arrest and public financing of political parties. In the 1990s he encouraged initiatives for a change in the Italian political system from proportional representation to a majority system. He has been in the forefront of initiatives for the decriminalization of certain drugs and for the elimination of hunger. He has utilized nonviolent methods such as the hunger strike and actions of civil disobedience, and is a supporter of forms of direct democracy like the referendum.

Pannella has been elected numerous times as town and county counselor in Rome, Naples, Trieste, and to the Italian and European parliaments. During the 1994 elections Pannella promoted an alliance with the center-right party of Selvio Berlusceoni, Forza Italia. In the 1996 elections his party, Club Pannella-Riformatori, of which he was president, campaigned independently. Despite his party's small size, Pannella's political initiatives have gained considerable support and have been widely influential in Italian political life. He was elected to the E.U.'s European Parliament in 1999.

BIBLIOGRAPHY

Moncalvo, Gigi. *Pannella: il potere della parola.* Milan: Sperling and Kupfer, 1983.

Pannella, Marco. *Pannella su Marco Pannella.* Rome: Magma, 1977.

Suttora, Mauro. *Pannella: i segreti di un istrione.* Milan: Liber, 1993.

Daniele Petrosino

Papadimas, Lambros (1939–)

Lambros Papadimas was born in Lamia in central Greece on January 1, 1939. Following a family tradition he studied medicine at the University of Athens. From 1969 to 1972 Papadimas was director of clinical surgery at the General Regional Hospital of Yannitsa, and from 1972 to 1989 director of the General Regional Hospital of Lamia. From 1978 to 1982 he was president of the Panhellenic Association of Medical Specialists in the Provinces. He also served on a working group set up to revamp the Greek National Health Service.

In 1982 Papadimas was elected mayor of Lamia and was reelected in 1986 and 1990. From 1983 to 1990 he was president of the Local Union of Municipalities and Communities in the province of Fthiotida. From 1986 to 1990 he was a member of the executive committee of the Greek Central Union of Municipalities and Communities, and from 1990 to 1993 he served as president of the Association of Greek Municipalities. Papadimas was the first Greek local official to be elected vice president of the Council of Municipalities and Regions of Europe. He held that post from 1988 to 1990.

Papadimas, who served as a member and deputy secretary of the Panhellenic Socialist Movement's (PASOK) Local Government and Institutions Office, was elected to parliament in 1993 as a PASOK delegate for the Fthiotida district. He served in the Costas Simitis government in 1996 as undersecretary in the Ministry of the Interior, Public Administration, and Decentralization. In the 1996 election he was returned to parliament.

Bernard Cook

Papadopoulos, Georgios (1919–)

Military leader of the junta regime of the Greek colonels that ruled Greece between 1967 and 1974. Commissioned into the Greek army in 1940, Georgios Papadopoulos was promoted to the rank of colonel in 1960. An extreme right-winger and virulent anti-Communist, he served from 1959 to 1964 in the shadowy central Service of Information (KYP), a propaganda office in the Defense Ministry reportedly infiltrated completely by the U.S. Central Intelligence Agency (CIA) that had helped create it after the Greek civil war of 1946–49. A top military adviser in the office of Greek prime minister Georgios Papandreou, in 1967, Papadopoulos developed a loathing for his radical son, Andreas Papandreou, then a cabinet minister in his father's government, hostile to both King Constantine and the army. Later justified by an alleged need to stem the tide of communism in Greece, the military coup led by Papadopoulos in April 1967 was by far the most controversial and traumatic event in modern Greek politics since the civil war of the 1940s. Formally known as the Greek Revolutionary Junta, the colonels' regime was reportedly covertly co-organized and supported by the CIA, for whom Papadopoulos and his military coconspirators were agents of long standing.

Also aided in its power grab by King Constantine, who lost his throne because of it, the junta was an illegitimate body and a betrayal of Greek democracy. Dominated by Papadopoulos, who ran it as prime minister from 1967 to 1973, regent in 1972–73, and president of the republic in 1973–74, the junta was based on lawlessness and violent repression, including the mass arrest and torture of its opponents. Despite its illegal status, the junta enjoyed the de facto support of its main foreign sponsor, the United States. In 1974, after a disastrous attempt to annex Greek-controlled Cyprus, Papadopoulos and the junta fell from power after Turkey invaded and partitioned Cyprus de facto. Later tried and condemned to death for high treason in 1975, Papadoupoulos was subsequently given a commuted sentence of life imprisonment for his past crimes without hope of remission.

BIBLIOGRAPHY

Clogg, Richard, and George Yannopoulos. *Greece under Military Rule.* New York: Basic Books, 1972.

Veremis, Thanos. *The Military in Greek Politics: From Independence to Democracy.* Montréal: Black Rose, 1997.

Yannopoulos, George. *A Concise History of Greece.* Cambridge: Cambridge University Press, 1994.

Marko Milivojevic

SEE ALSO Constantine II; Cyprus; Karamanlis, Konstantinos

Papandreou, Andreas Georgios (1919–96)

Greek politician, prime minister of Greece (1981–89, 1993–96). Andreas Georgios Papandreou was born on the Greek island of Chios on February 5, 1919. His father was future prime minister Georgios Papandreou. The younger Papandreou studied law at the University of Athens. Before the Italian invasion of Greece in October 1940 during World War II, Papandreou went to the United States, where he earned a doctorate in economics in 1943. He then taught economics at Harvard University and became a naturalized U.S. citizen. After receiving a commission in the U.S. navy, Papandreou served as a naval officer for two years. During that time he was assigned as a technical adviser to the Greek delegation at the 1944 Bretton Woods Conference in New Hampshire concerning postwar international monetary and financial policies.

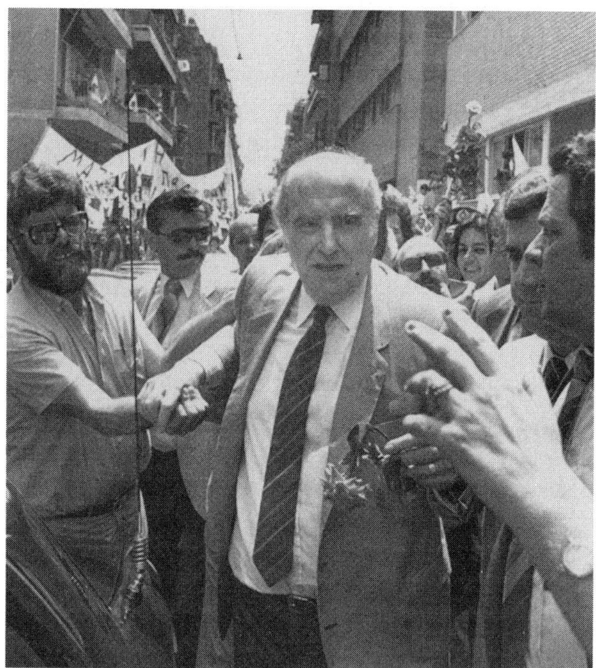

Prime Minister Andreas Papandreou of Greece, mobbed by his supporters ourtside the Electoral Center in Athens, June 2, 1985. *Illustration courtesy UPI/Bettmann Newsphotos.*

After his discharge from the navy, Papandreou again taught economics for a year at Harvard then at several other U.S. universities. In 1959 he returned to Greece and organized the Center for Economic Research in Athens. He became engrossed in Greek politics and resumed his Greek citizenship. He successfully ran for parliament in February 1964 on the ticket of his father's Center Union Party and became chief aide to his prime minister father. He was at first given the title minister to the premier, then deputy minister for economic coordination. In that post he directed Greece's economic policy.

His rapid rise, abetted by nepotism, roused the ire not only of his father's political enemies but also of some of his father's political allies within the Center Union. He was increasingly regarded by the United States as anti-American and anti-NATO. On November 15, 1965, he resigned because of allegations that he had granted a government contract to a friend without competitive bids. Nevertheless, within six months he reentered the government and resumed his old post.

On July 15, 1965, Premier Papandreou and his cabinet were ousted by King Constantine. The issue was control of the Ministry of Defense and the plan of the premier to purge rightists from the officer corps. Andreas Papandreou, at the center of this crisis, was accused of being in league with left-wing officers who had formed the anti-right-wing ASPIDA organization.

When Georgios Papandreou agreed to accept a caretaker government under Ioannis Paraskevopoulos until new elections scheduled for May 28, 1967, Andreas lambasted him for betrayal. In October 1966 the government issued a report accusing ASPIDA of plotting an antimonarchical coup, and twenty-eight officers were tried for treason. Andreas was mentioned in the indictment but was not brought to trial because of his parliamentary immunity, which the Union of the Center would not revoke.

When, despite the affair and the opposition of the monarchy and the military it appeared that the Center Union was headed toward a significant electoral victory, the military intervened with its coup of April 21, 1967. The Papandreous and six thousand others were jailed. Andreas was charged with high treason for his involvement with ASPIDA. He was released on December 24, 1967, however, in a Christmas amnesty. A month later Andreas left Greece and took a teaching post at the University of Stockholm then at York University in Toronto. But he never ceased to agitate against the military regime in Greece.

After the collapse of the junta in 1974, Andreas returned to Greece and organized the Panhellenic Socialist Movement (PASOK). The party won an overwhelming parliamentary victory in 1981. He campaigned against the continued presence of U.S. bases in Greece and agitated for Greece to leave NATO, but after the victory of his party he moderated both those positions. Papandreou's mixture of populism and strident anti-Americanism resonated well with the Greek electorate, and PASOK's vote increased in the 1985 election. But austerity measures dictated by economic exigencies and a financial scandal that led to the resignation of three cabinet ministers soured many voters. Papandreou's open relationship with Dimitra Liani, a young divorced Olympic Airline attendant, also offended some Greek voters. In the June 18, 1989, election PASOK lost its majority and Papandreou was forced to resign. He was charged with corruption in connection with Greek-American banker George Koskotas and brought to trial in 1991. In 1992, Papandreou was acquitted of four counts of bribery and breach of trust. PASOK then won a landslide in the parliamentary election of October 1993. Suffering from a serious heart condition, Papandreou was eventually able to work only a few hours a day. To the consternation of many, he appointed Dimitra, whom he had married in 1989 after divorcing his American second wife of thirty-eight years, his chief of staff in control of the prime minister's schedule and of access to him. His declining health forced him to retire in January 1996, and he died on June 23.

BIBLIOGRAPHY

Featherstone, Kevin, ed. *Political Change in Greece: Before and after the Colonels.* Kent, U.K.: Croom Helm, 1988.

Papandreou, Andreas. *Democracy and National Renascence.* Athens: Fexis, 1966.

———. *Democracy at Gunpoint: The Greek Front.* New York: Doubleday, 1970.

Papandreou, Margarita. *Nightmare in Athens.* Englewood Cliffs, N.J., Prentice-Hall, 1970.

Spourdalakis, Michalis. *The Rise of the Greek Socialist Party.* New York: Routledge, 1988.

Yannopoulos, George. *A Concise History of Greece.* Cambridge: Cambridge University Press, 1994.

Bernard Cook

SEE ALSO Papandreou, Georgios

Papandreou, Georgios (1888–1968)

Greek politician, three times premier of Greece. Georgios Andreas Papandreou was born in Patras on February 13, 1888. He received a doctorate in law from the University of Athens in 1911 and studied at the Universities of Berlin and Leipzig. In 1915 he was appointed prefect of Chios. In 1917 he joined Eleutherios Venizelos' government of national defense, which led Greece into World War I on the Allied side. From 1917 to 1920 he was governor of the Aegean Islands. In Colonel Nikolaos Plastiras brief government he was minister of the interior in 1923. From 1923 until 1936 he represented Lesbos in the Greek parliament, and from 1929 to 1933 he was minister of education under Venizelos. In 1933 Papandreou left the left wing of the Liberal Party for the Republican Socialist Party. During the dictatorship of Ioannis Metaxas from 1936 to 1940 Papandreou, because of his opposition to the military government, was sentenced to internal exile on the islands of Andros and Kythera. During World War II he was released from internal exile and helped organize the resistance under the Italian, German, and Bulgarian occupation and was arrested by the Germans. But he however, escaped and made his way to Cairo, where he joined the Greek government-in-exile.

He served as a minister in a number of governments between 1946 and 1952 but then entered the opposition. He led his Democratic Socialist Party, the postwar reincarnation of the Republican Socialist Party, into a union with the Liberal Party and in 1961 formed a center-left group, the Center Union. In 1964 the Center Union won a bare majority in parliament. Though Papandreou, as its leader, was appointed prime minister he promptly resigned to seek an increased majority. This he achieved in the 1964 election. He instituted a program of social reform and attempted to free Greece from what he regarded as subservience to the policy of the United States. In 1965 Papandreou was dismissed by King Constantine as result of the plan of his son Andreas, minister of defense, to dismiss rightists from the army. A period of instability followed. When it became apparent that Papandreou's party would win the ensuing election, the military staged a coup d'état on April 21, 1967. The military regime jailed Papandreou as the leader of the party that would have been victorious if an election had been permitted and his son. Papandreou was released because of his age and declining health in October but he died on November 1, 1968.

BIBLIOGRAPHY

Featherstone, Kevin, ed. *Political Change in Greece: Before and after the Colonels.* Kent, U.K.: Croom Helm, 1988.

Papandreou, Margarita. *Nightmare in Athens.* Englewood Cliffs, N.J., Prentice-Hall, 1970.

Yannopoulos, George. *A Concise History of Greece.* Cambridge: Cambridge University Press, 1994.

Bernard Cook

SEE ALSO Papandreou, Andreas

Parri, Ferruccio (1890–1981)

Italian political leader. He was born on January 19, 1890, in Pinerolo, Italy. After working as a secondary-school teacher and journalist, he fought in World War I and was decorated for valour. After the war, Parri directed the National Institute for Combatants and worked on the editorial staff of *Corriere della Sera.*

During the Fascist era of the 1920s and 1930s, he organized an underground movement and was arrested for the first time in 1927 and interned until 1930. From 1931 to 1933 he organized the group Giustizia e Libertà (Justice and Liberty) and the Action Party. After the collapse of Mussolini's regime in 1943 and the occupation of Italy by the German army, Parri, using the pseudonym of Maurizio, was one of the commanders of the resistance group Voluntary Corps for Liberation. Arrested by the Germans, Parri was released as part of an exchange of prisoners. In June 1945, after the end of World War II, Parri was elected premier of the coalition government of the Committee of National Liberation, but profound differences ended the unity achieved during the resistance. The efforts made by Parri's administration to overcome postwar problems were abruptly opposed by the Liberal Party, and his government fell in November 1945. The crisis within the Action Party led Parri together with Ugo La Malfa to found the Republican Democracy Party. After serving as a deputy of the Constituent Assembly, Parri joined the Italian Republican Party and was elected senator in 1948. Parri's reformist ideas led him to continue an ongoing critique of the more centrist Christian Democratic Party through his journalistic work. He died in Rome in 1981.

BIBLIOGRAPHY

Aniasi, Aldo. *Parri: L'avventura umana militare e politica di Maurizio. "I Padri della repubblica."* Rome: Nuova ERI, 1991.

Commemorazione del Senatore Ferruccio Parri. "Celebrazioni e commemorazioni." Rome: Tipografia del Senato, 1981.

La Navicella: I Deputati e i Senatori del 1 °Parlamento Repubblicano. Città di Castello: INI, 1948.

Fabio Marino

Partial Test Ban Treaty (1963)

Nuclear testing agreement, August 5, 1963, initially among Great Britain, the United States, and the Soviet Union. The official title of this agreement is the Treaty Banning Nuclear Weapon Tests in the Atmosphere, in Outer Space and Under Water.

The Test Ban Treaty was the first nuclear arms testing agreement reached during the Cold War, and took place in the aftermath of the Cuban Missile Crisis of 1962. For this reason the treaty was enthusiastically supported in the West as signifying a new era in East-West relations. In this agreement nuclear explosions for military or peaceful purposes are prohibited in the atmosphere, in outer space, and under water. Underground nuclear tests are allowed as long as radioactive debris does not leave the boundaries of the nation conducting the test. This treaty is of unlimited duration and has been extended to all the nations of the world. The majority of nations are participating; the openly proclaimed nuclear armed states of China and France were notable exceptions. States have the right to withdraw from this agreement, and voting mechanisms exist for its amendment.

Besides contributing to an East-West dialogue, the Test Ban Treaty significantly protected the global environment from ecologically devastating nuclear testing such as the type witnessed at the March 1954 Bikini atoll detonation, conducted by the United States. It was criticized, however, for undermining U.S. national security because it limited U.S. knowledge of Soviet nuclear development. It also limited the study of the effects of critical nuclear phenomena, such as electromagnetic pulse, which directly threatened the survivability of U.S. strategic force and command structures. The agreement is also known as the Limited Test Ban Treaty.

In September 1996, China and France joined Russia, the United States, and the United Kingdom in signing a comprehensive Nuclear Test Ban Treaty. India and Pakistan refused to sign. However, after both successfully tested nuclear weapons, they expressed their willingness to sign in 2000. In October 1999 the U.S. Senate refused to ratify the treaty, but President Bill Clinton did not believe that that rejection would be permanent.

BIBLIOGRAPHY

Seaborg, Glenn T. *Kennedy, Khrushchev, and the Test Ban.* Berkeley: University of California Press, 1981.

Terchek, Ronald J. *The Making of the Test Ban Treaty.* The Hague: M. Nijhoff, 1970.

Voss, Earl H. *Nuclear Ambush: The Test-Ban Trap.* Chicago: Henry Regnery, 1963.

Robert J. Bunker

Pasternak, Boris Leonidovich (1890–1960)

Russian poet and novelist, Nobel prize winner, and one of the greatest Russian poets of the twentieth century. Boris Pasternak was born in Moscow on February 10, 1890, the eldest of four siblings in a Jewish family. His father, Leonid Osipovich Pasternak, was a painter, and his mother, Rosalina Kaufman Pasternak, was a pianist. He married Yevgenia Vladimirovna Lurye Muratova in 1922, and divorced her in 1931. Three years later he married Zinaida Nikolaevna Neuhaus. He had three sons. Although at first considering music as a profession, he turned to poetry owing to a lack of musical talent and published his first collection in 1914. The usually cautious writer survived World War I and the Russian Revolution, and was able to publish his poems in the Soviet Union up to 1936, when he fell into disfavor. This led to government censorship of his work, and travel from his home in the writers' colony of Peredelkino, near Moscow was restricted. No one can fully explain why Pasternak was not exterminated like millions of others in Stalin's great purges of the 1930s, such as his famous contemporary Osip Mandelstam, but there are rumors that the Soviet dictator seemed to favor him. Pasternak was limited, however, to working on translations of noncontroversial literature. During World War II Pasternak contributed his literary skills to the national war effort. After Stalin's death in 1953, when Communist Party controls were relaxed somewhat, Pasternak's poems began to be published again. For several years Pasternak had been working on a novel, *Drozhivago,* that incorporated a romantic love story set against the historical backdrop of the chaos of World War I, the Russian Revolution, and the ensuing Civil War. The journal *Novy Mir* (*New World*) decided against publishing portions of the work when it was evaluated as indirectly challenging official views. The poet certainly knew that he was courting disaster by sending his work outside of the USSR to be published, but, like many other Soviet writers, he was not deterred, preferring to put his work above personal convenience and safety. He sent a copy of his manuscript to Italian Communist publisher Feltrinelli in Milan. Pasternak quickly became a pawn in a game between larger political forces, much like his hero Zhivago. The Kremlin tried to stop publication of the manuscript, but in an act of independence from a fellow Communist, the book was released to immediate success, and was quickly translated into several other languages. The publicity of the event was very galling for the Soviet government, and Pasternak was expelled from the Writer's Union and lost his title of Soviet Writer. When he was awarded the Nobel Prize in literature in 1958 for *Dr. Zhivago,* Pasternak was pressured by Soviet officials into refusing the award, which they saw as an attack by the West. However, the Swedes held the award on Pasternak's behalf. The movie version of the novel was released in 1965 to wide popular acclaim. Directed by filmmaker David Lean, the film started a new period of interest in Pasternak in the West. But the author never saw the visual embodiment of his work.

Pasternak died of cancer on May 30, 1960, at Peredelkino. Although the Communist authorities tried to keep his funeral a secret for fear of spontaneous demonstrations, some two thousand people showed up to honor the poet. The weakening of the Soviet empire in the late 1980s led to the publication of *Dr. Zhivago* in the USSR in 1987. Pasternak's home was turned into a museum, and on December 10, 1989, in Stockholm, his son Yevgeny accepted his father's 1958 Nobel prize.

BIBLIOGRAPHY

Conquest, Robert. *Courage of Genius: The Pasternak Affair: A Documentary Report on its Literary and Political Significance.* London: Collins and Harvill, 1961.

deMallac, Guy. *Boris Pasternak: His Life and Art.* Norman: University of Oklahoma Press, 1981.

Fleishman, Lazar. *Boris Pasternak: The Poet and His Politics.* Cambridge, Mass.: Harvard University Press, 1990.
Levi, Peter. *Boris Pasternak.* London: Hutchinson 1990.
Sendich, Munir. *Boris Pasternak: A Reference Guide.* New York: G.K. Hall, 1994.

Daniel K. Blewett

Patrascanu, Lucretiu (1900–1954)

Founding member of the Romanian Communist Party in 1921, its leading theorist, and a leader of the resistance during World War II who helped arrange the overthrow of the pro-Nazi Antonescu regime in August 1944. Born in Moldavia, son of respected satirist and professor D. D. Patrascanu, Lucretiu Patrascanu also became an intellectual. He studied in Paris, Leipzig, and Bucharest and held doctorates in economics and law. When not under arrest for his Communist activities in Romania, he frequently defended Communists. Additionally, he published several Marxist analyses of Romanian politics and economics. His election to the Romanian parliament in 1931 was invalidated by the Romanian government. In 1933 he was the Communist Party's delegate to the meeting of the Comintern in the USSR. Stalin's purges kept him there until 1935. The execution by the Soviet secret police of his Russian wife helps to explain his anti-Soviet attitude.

Since Patrascanu was a prominent Communist and from a respected family, King Michael and a few leading non-Communist politicians included him in their successful plot to overthrow Antonescu's regime on August 23, 1944, during World War II. Between 1944 and 1948, although the Communists refused him high party office, he held several government positions, including minister of justice, and in 1946 was a member of Romania's delegation that concluded peace with the Allies. During these early postwar years his popularity and tendency to place Romanian interests above those of the USSR cost his seat on the Politburo of the Romanian Communist Party and angered the Soviet dictator Stalin, who ordered his arrest in 1947. He and his wife were arrested on April 28, 1948, but he was not executed immediately because Ana Pauker protected him. Gheorghe Gheorghiu-Dej, fearing that the USSR's post-Stalinist leaders might promote him to high office, had Patrascanu executed on May 17, 1954, but spared his wife. In 1968, Nicolae Ceaușescu rehabilitated Patrascanu and recognized his contributions to Romanian communism.

BIBLIOGRAPHY

Deletant, Dennis. *Communist Terror in Romania: Gheorghiu-Dej and the Police State, 1948–1965.* New York: St. Martin's Press, 1999.
Georgescu, Vlad. *The Romanians; A History.* Columbus, Ohio: Ohio State University Press, 1991.
Ionescu, Ghita. *Communism in Rumania, 1944–1962.* Westport, Conn.: Greenwood Publishing, 1976.

Robert F. Forrest

SEE ALSO Pauker, Ana

Patsatsia, Otar (1929–)

Georgian politician and prime minister of Georgia (1993–95). Educated as an engineer at the University of Leningrad, Otar Patsatsia worked for over thirty years as a senior manager in a number of major Georgian enterprises in his native town, Zugdidi. Well known in the 1980s as a technocrat who got things done, he was then repeatedly praised by leaders of the Communist Party of Georgia for his management skills. Despite this, he was to clash with the local party after criticizing the endemic corruption in its ranks in Zugdidi. He was brought back into local government by the new Georgian president, Edvard Shevardnadze, in 1992, who then appointed him prime minister in September 1993. In October 1995, however, a new Georgian constitution abolished the office of premier, whereupon Patsatsia became a parliamentary deputy. During his term of office he was credited with laying the foundations of an economic revival and partial political stabilization.

BIBLIOGRAPHY

McGiffert Ekedahl, Carolyn, and Goodman, Melvin. *The Wars of Eduard Shevardnadze.* University Park, Penn.: Pennsylvania University Press, 1997.
Suny, Ronald. *The Making of the Georgian State.* Bloomington: Indiana University Press, 1994.

Marko Milivojevic

Pauker, Ana Rabinsohn (1893 [1894?]–1960)

Romanian foreign minister (1947–52) and vice premier (1949–52). The daughter of a Moldavian Jewish butcher, Ana Rabinsohn joined the socialist movement in 1915 before marrying Marcel Pauker. They joined the newly formed Romanian Communist Party in 1921; Pauker became a member of the Central Committee in 1922. Arrested in 1925, she escaped to the USSR and worked in the Comintern. She did not return to Romania until the early 1930s when she was arrested again in 1935 and sentenced to ten years in prison. In 1940 the Romanian government freed her as part of a prisoner exchange with the Soviets. She returned to Moscow and worked on the Executive Committee of the Comintern without her husband, whom Stalin had executed in 1937. Nevertheless, Stalin trusted her and let her organize the Tudor Vladimirescu division in 1943 from Romanian soldiers captured by the Soviets during World War II. At the time, Romania was allied with Nazi Germany. As a political commissar she accompanied the Red Army into Romania in 1944 along with other Romanian Communists termed "Moscow Stalinists" (they had passed the war in the Soviet Union), who competed for power with the group led by Gheorghe Gheorghiu-Dej led, who remained in Romania during the war. She had the support of Soviet Communists like Molotov, Beria, and Malenkov, while Stalin backed Gheorghiu-Dej. Placed on the Politburo in 1945, she was responsible for collectivization of agriculture and party organization, statutes, and recruitment of party members. In 1952 Gheorghiu-Dej, with Stalin's blessing, purged her as part of an anti-Semitic action aping Stalin's policies in the USSR. After having played a leading role in establishing Romania's postwar Communist regime, she lived in obscurity in Bucharest until cancer claimed her life in June 1960.

BIBLIOGRAPHY

Deletant, Dennis. *Communist Terror in Romania: Gheorghiu-Dej and the Police State, 1948–1965.* New York: St. Martin's Press, 1999.

King, Robert R. *History of the Romanian Communist Party.* Stanford, Cal.: Hoover Institution Press, 1980.

Robert F. Forrest

SEE ALSO Gheorghiu-Dej, Gheorghe

Paul VI (1897–1978)

Pope of the Roman Catholic Church from 1963 to 1978. Giovanni Battista Montini, who assumed the name Paul VI, was born in Concesio, a small village near Brescia, Italy, son of Giorgio Montini, an adviser to Pope Benedict XV (1914–22), member of the Chamber of Deputies from Don Luigi Sturzo's Popular Party, and editor of a Catholic daily, and of Giudetta Alghisi, who was also of an upper-middle class background. After studying at Milan and the Gregorian University in Rome, Montini was ordained a priest in May 1920 and proceeded directly to train for the church's diplomatic corps. His first assignment was in Poland in 1922, but because of poor health he returned to Rome and was assigned to the Vatican bureaucracy.

From 1923 to 1939 Montini served in the Papal Secretariat of State, where, after 1930, he worked closely with Eugenio Pacelli, the future Pius XII (1939–58), who was then Pius XI's (1922–39) secretary of state. At the same time, in his role as adviser to the University Federation of Catholic Action, Montini took a rather critical position regarding the fascist regime and befriended a number of antifascists including Alcide De Gasperi and Aldo Moro both of whom would be (future Christian Democratic prime ministers in postwar Italy). In 1937 Montini was appointed undersecretary of state and retained that position after Pius XII's election in 1939. During World War II Montini was charged with the care of Allied diplomats confined within the Vatican, and in that post he gained their respect and appreciation. He also played a significant role in the care of the many refugees who crowded into the confines of the Vatican and the papal residence of Castel Gandolfo, outside of Rome, during that period.

In 1953, when Pius created twenty-four new cardinals, it was announced that Montini, who apparently had fallen out with the pope, had declined that honor. In 1954 Montini left Rome to become archbishop of Milan. There he gained valuable pastoral experience that would be a factor in his later election to the Holy See. He took a particular interest in the industrial parishes, established a diocesan office for pastoral and social action, and gained a reputation as the "archbishop of the workers."

In 1958 Montini was at the top of the list of cardinals named by the new pontiff, John XXIII (1958–63). He welcomed the convening of the Second Vatican Council in 1962, and during the first sessions he lived at the Vatican, serving to some extent as a confidant and adviser to John XXIII.

Upon the death of John XXIII in June 1963, Montini, back in Milan, announced in a sermon that he believed the initiative taken by the deceased pontiff and, in particular, the council and its objectives must continue. The subsequent conclave in Rome elected Montini pope on June 21, 1963. He took the name Paul VI. A day after his coronation he announced that he would continue the work of John XXIII, especially in the areas of church reform and ecumenical interests.

On his 1964 pilgrimage to the Holy Land, Paul met with the Orthodox ecumenical patriarch of Constantinople, the first such meeting since 1439. In 1965 he brought the Second Vatican Council to a successful conclusion. He remained a staunch defender of the poor and Third World populations and issued the encyclical *Popolorum Progressio,* which called for the redistribution of the world's wealth. Despite the advice of a commission of experts that he had assembled, he issued his controversial encyclical, *Humanae Vitae,* condemning artificial birth control.

His significance lies in the implementation of the reforms of the Vatican Council, his advancement of ecumenism, and his concern for peace and justice. He died in 1978 and was succeeded by John Paul I.

BIBLIOGRAPHY

Guitten, Jean. *The Pope Speaks: Dialogues of Paul VI.* New York: Meridith Press, 1968.

Holmes, J. Derek. *The Papacy in the Modern World: 1914–1978.* New York: Crossroad, 1981.

William Roberts

Pavelić, Ante (1889–1959)

Fascist leader of wartime Croatia. Ante Pavelić was born on July 14, 1889, in Bradina, Bosnia. In 1920, as a member of the Croatian Party of Rights, he was elected to the Zagreb city council, Croatian nationalists objected to the centralized character of the newly created Kingdom of Serbs, Croats, and Slovenes (later, Yugoslavia). To the Croatian nationalists it was merely a cover for a greater Serbia. From 1927 to 1929 Pavelić was a representative in the parliament in Belgrade. When King Alexander assumed direct control of the country in 1929 following the assassination of Croatian nationalist Stepan Radić on the floor of parliament by a pro-Serb Montenegrin, Pavelić fled to Italy and established the radical nationalist Ustaša, the object of which was the destruction of the unitary Yugoslav state and the establishment of an independent Croatia.

Pavelić was able to assume power in Croatia with the support of the Germans after the German conquest of Yugoslavia in April 1941. Fascist Croatia included Herceg-Bosna, the predominantly Croat segment of Bosnia. Pavelić's extreme nationalists then conducted a campaign of terror against Serbs, Jews, and Gypsies. Their death camp at Jasenovac is infamous. With the expulsion of his German protectors, Pavelić fled to Italy and escaped to Argentina in 1948. He later sought refuge in Franco's Spain, where he died on December 28, 1959.

BIBLIOGRAPHY

Glenny, Misha. *The Fall of Yugoslavia: The Third Balkan War,* rev. ed. New York: Penguin, 1994.

Laurière, Hervé. *Assassins au nom de Dieu.* Paris: Éditions La Vigie, 1951.

Paris, Edmond. *Genocide in Satellite Croatia, 1941–1945: A Record of Racial and Religious Persecutions and Massacres.* Tr. by Lois Perkins. Chicago: American Institute for Balkan Affairs, 1961.

Pavelic, Ante. *Errori e orrori, comunismo e bolscevismo in Russia e nel mondo. Le teorie comuniste e la prassi bolscebica nella Russia sovietica e nella propaganda mondiale.* Varese: Istituto per gli studi di politica internazionale, 1941.

Bernard Cook

Pawlak, Waldemar (1959–)

Chairman of the Executive Committee of the Polish Peasants Party and prime minister of Poland (1993–95). Waldemar Pawlak was born on September 5, 1959, in Model. He graduated from Warsaw Polytechnic in the Department of Cars and Machines in 1983.

Elected to parliament in 1989, Pawlak was one of the youngest Peasants Party delegates. He served on the Committee for Local Government affairs and was chosen chairman of the party's Parliamentary Club, a position in which he served from November 1991 to May 1993. He resumed the party's chairmanship in September 1993.

A member of the United Peasants Party since 1985 and then the Polish Peasants Party since May 1990, Pawlak was elected chairman of the party at a special Congress in July 1991. He was reelected almost unanimously at the party's second congress in November 1992.

Designated prime minister by President Lech Wałęsa in July 1992, Pawlak was accepted by parliament but was unsuccessful in constructing a coalition government in July 1992. After parliamentary elections in September 1993, the victorious left-wing parties—Social Democrats and Polish Peasants Party—formed a governing coalition. Pawlak was nominated again, and on October 18, 1993, was sworn in as prime minister.

His government hoped, as Pawlak stated to parliament on November 8, 1993, to "create favorable conditions for the state administration and local governments to function properly." Within a year, however, reform stalled, the privatization program ground to a halt, and, though many personnel changes had taken place, the reconstruction of administrative districts was postponed. Local communities began to protest against the government's policy. Pawlak himself was highly inconsistent. He did not support his own officials and was hesitant and slow to make decisions. What was worse, according to his critics, in the midst of a critical economic situation he gave top priority to his own political party and his personal ambitions over the interests of the country. However, the last year of this government brought an increase in production and a slight improvement in the standard of living. Exports also rose and Poland's foreign debt was reduced.

In March 1995 parliament dismissed Pawlak, and Jozef Oleksy was charged with of forming a new government.

BIBLIOGRAPHY

Poznanski, Kazimierz. *Poland's Protracted Transition: Institutional Change and Economic Growth 1970–1994.* New York: Cambridge University Press, 1996.

Stachura, Peter D. *Poland in the Twentieth Century.* New York: St. Martin's Press, 1999.

Sławomir Przybułek

Peace and Liberty (Paix et Liberté)

Parallel government-sponsored anti-Communist "psychological warfare" agencies established in the late 1940s or early 1950s, first in France then in various other countries. Although their overt activities were devoted primarily to countering Soviet propaganda initiatives, several branches also carried out illicit covert "action" operations against domestic opponents.

In March 1949 the first branch was established in Paris as the Union Démocratique pour la Paix et la Liberté (Democratic Union for Peace and Liberty), apparently at the initiative of French Interior Minister Jules Moch. Jean-Paul David, a dynamic young leader of the minuscule Radical Socialist Party and high-ranking official in the umbrella Assembly of the Left Republicans, which brought together all the center-left "third force" parties opposed to both the Gaullists and the French Communist Party, was appointed to head the organization. With the help of a permanent staff of twelve, outside supporters recruited from the media and political class, and an unknown number of unofficial rank-and-file activists, David arranged for the production and display of numerous provocative leaflets and flyers designed to challenge Soviet-backed "peace" campaigns and depict French Communists, not without some justification, as an internal fifth column. Paix et Liberté also sponsored a weekly radio broadcast, made by David himself, and, less openly, several ephemeral publications warning of the dangers of Soviet expansionism. Perhaps more important, David headed an international committee that coordinated the activities of branches established in other countries, including Belgium, Britain, Greece, Italy, Netherlands, Norway, Turkey, Vietnam, and West Germany.

Along with the production and dissemination of aggressive, clever, and often effective propaganda against foreign and domestic Communists, all these Peace and Liberty agencies shared four primary characteristics. First, high-ranking government officials in various European countries facilitated their establishment and provided them with secret subsidies in conjunction with major industrial and financial companies such as Fiat in Italy and Brufina in Belgium. For example, in France the Council of Ministers, Interior Minister Moch, police chief Jean Dides, and elements of French intelligence were all actively involved in sponsoring or financing Paix et Liberté. The Italian Peace and Liberty, established in 1953, received similar support from Foreign Minister Carlos Sforza, Interior Minister Mario Scelba, General Giuseppe Pièche of the Carabinieri, the Italian militarized national police, and Colonel Renzo Rocca of Armed Forces Intelligence Service (SIFAR); the Belgian Paix et Liberté, established in 1951, received support from Interior Minister Albert De Vleeschawer and General Maurice Keyaerts of the army's General Intelligence Service; the West German Volksbund für Frieden und Freiheit (People's League for Peace and Freedom) established in 1950, received support from the Ministry for All-German Affairs, other departments of the German government, the Federal Intelligence Service, and perhaps the Military Protection Service.

Second, the leadership of the national branches was invariably entrusted to veteran anti-Communist activists who had adopted pro-Atlantic sentiments, sometimes opportunistically, in the postwar era. Many had formerly participated in non-Communist resistance movements that had worked closely with the Office of Strategic Services (OSS) and other Allied intelligence agencies during World War II, including David himself, Dides, future Italian NATO official and Peace and Liberty chief Edgardo Sogno, and André Moyen in Belgium. Others were instead recruited from among the ranks of former Axis collaborators or enemy officials, such as Dides's police colleague Charles Delarue, Belgian "black knight" Marcel De Roover, and Eberhard Taubert, an ex-Nazi court judge and key member of Josef Goebbels's Propaganda Ministry, who became head of the Volksbund. After the war all these figures maintained close relations with American intelligence officers, from whom they obtained aid, and actively recruited assorted right-wing extremists, including ex-Nazis and neo-Fascists, into their respective Peace and Liberty branches.

Third, these agencies were closely interlocked, often via overlapping personnel, with a host of other clandestine, covert anti-Communist organizations. Among others, these included the Gladio stay/behind networks set up under the aegis of NATO; the intelligence-linked, Taiwan-based World Anti-Communist League, an international umbrella organization encompassing both respectable conservatives and right-wing extremists; the secretive European "action" group Catena (Chain); the anti-Algerian counterterrorist group Main Rouge (Red Hand), a front created by the French Foreign Intelligence and Counterespionage Service; and certain U.S. Central Intelligence Agency (CIA)–funded non-Communist labor unions.

Fourth, several leading Peace and Liberty activists were directly implicated in anticonstitutional political activities, including serious acts of political violence and antigovernment coup plots. In Italy, for example, Sogno was among those involved in planning a 1974 coup whose aim was to install a Gaullist-style "presidentialist" regime; his erstwhile Peace and Liberty collaborator Luigi Cavallo carried out a number of provocations and violent actions against Communist union activists while in the employ of Fiat, and a self-described "anarchist" with links to SIFAR, neo-Fascist circles, and Peace and Freedom received a light sentence in prison after carrying out a grenade attack in front of Milan police headquarters in May 1973. In Belgium a member of Paix et Liberté confessed on his deathbed to the 1950 assassination of Julien Lahaut, head of the Communist Party of Belgium. For his part, in addition to authoring several anti-Communist and often blatantly anti-Semitic publications, Taubert later collaborated with the Central Intelligence Service of the Greek colonels' regime and reestablished contacts with his former Nazi Propaganda Ministry colleague, Gerhard Hartmut von Schubert, who had set up the mercenary Paladin Group in Spain. Finally, the French branch not only allegedly carried out violent union-busting activities but also played an important role in the Leakages scandal in 1954, whose aim was to discredit Interior Minister François Mitterrand and bring down the government of Pierre Mendés-France. As a result Paix et Liberté was formally disbanded, but the other national branches either continued to operate or mutated into new organizations with similar anti-Communist objectives, such as De Roover's International Committee for Information and Social Action in Belgium.

BIBLIOGRAPHY

Doorslaer, Rudi van, and Étienne Verhoeyen. *L'Assassinat de Julien Lahaut: Une histoire de l'anticommunisme en Belgique.* Antwerp: EPO, 1987.

Garibaldi, Luciano. *L'altro italiano, Edgardo Sogno: Sessant'anni di antifascismo e di anticomunismo.* Milan: Ares, 1992.

Gatti, Claudio. *Rimanga tra noi L'America: l'Italia, la "questione comunista": I segreti di 50 anni di storia.* Milan: Leonardo, 1991.

Hirsch, Kurt. *Rechts von der Union: Personen. Organisationen. Parteien seit 1945. Ein Lexikon.* Munich: Knesebeck & Schuler, 1989.

Sommer, René. " 'Paix et Liberté': La Quatrième République contre le PC[F]." *L'Histoire* 40 (December 1981): 26–35.

Wall, Irwin M. *The United States and the Making of Postwar France, 1945–1954.* Cambridge: Cambridge University Press, 1991.

Willems, Jan, ed. *Gladio.* Brussels: EPO/Reflex, 1991.

Jeffrey M. Bale

SEE ALSO Gladio

Peaceful Coexistence

Central tenet of Soviet foreign policy toward the West. Peaceful coexistence was a basic doctrine and policy that defined the relationship between the capitalist and socialist states. The evolution of the concept reflected developments in Soviet foreign policy from the Russian Revolution in 1917 to the demise of the USSR in 1991. A concept originally developed by Vladimir Lenin in the early years of the USSR, the doctrine of peaceful coexistence guided Soviet foreign policy. The interpretation of peaceful coexistence changed over time, but the basic concept remained. As developed by Lenin, "peaceful coexistence" posited that the class struggle between workers and capitalists, described by Karl Marx, had been transformed at the international level into a global struggle between socialism and capitalism, or two camps, with Soviet Russia (later the USSR) representing the socialist camp and the West representing the capitalist camp. These concepts were an outgrowth of Lenin's monograph *Imperialism: The Highest Stage of Capitalism,* written in 1916. After the Russian Revolution, when trying to reconcile the existence of a Soviet Union in a hostile world, Lenin argued that the USSR could cooperate with the West so long as it was understood that irreconcilable differences between the two systems underlay the relationship between the two camps. Lenin initially conceived of a breathing space for the USSR but later became convinced the "breathing space" could be a lengthy period. Lenin wanted trade with the West to ensure Soviet survival so he argued that the West and the USSR could cooperate, but eventually there would be a final showdown in which one or the other camp would prevail. Lenin introduced the formula "*Kto kogo?*" (Who will defeat whom?) to describe the process of the global struggle. Part of Lenin's theory of imperialism was the strategy of detaching colonial countries and less developed countries from the capitalist world, which he saw as a necessary step in the defeat of imperialism.

Lenin's conception of peaceful coexistence contained a fundamental challenge to the West but was coupled with the intention to cooperate. Joseph Stalin, Lenin's successor, reinterpreted the global struggle as one of permanent hostility toward the West although limited cooperation was possible. Except for World War II, the policy of peaceful coexistence that prevailed in the Stalin era (1924–53) proceeded from suspicion, hostility, and fear. Prior to World War II Stalin frequently warned that the capitalists were preparing to attack the Soviet Union. During World War II cooperation among the United States, Great Britain, and the USSR arose from their common struggle against Nazi Germany. After World War II the Cold War in Europe escalated tension between the USSR and the West.

After Stalin died in 1953, the USSR was a relatively isolated power. Stalin's policy of peaceful coexistence, although retaining a link to Lenin's formula for relations with the West, had emphasized the irreconcilable differences between the two systems. Stalin's successors changed Soviet policy toward the West and, therefore, the interpretation of peaceful coexistence. Nikita S. Khrushchev, first secretary of the Communist Party of the Soviet Union (CPSU, 1953–64), redefined "peaceful coexistence" at the Twentieth Party Congress in 1956. Khrushchev proposed a competitive approach to peaceful coexistence, maintaining that it was possible to cooperate with the Western powers without forgetting the fundamental class struggle between the two systems. Khrushchev predicted socialism would prove superior in peaceful competition between the two systems without a final military showdown.

The changes adopted during the Khrushchev era did not fundamentally change the doctrine of peaceful coexistence but altered the way the conflict between socialism and capitalism would be played out. The concepts of irreconcilable differences and class struggle between capitalism and socialism remained firmly in place. The idea that a military showdown could be averted was a reflection of the recognition that in the nuclear era war could mean the end of the world. Nonetheless, Khrushchev underscored the significance of vigilance and military preparedness in dealing with the West. Khrushchev's view of peaceful coexistence included competition for the loyalty of the newly independent former colonies as part of peaceful competition between the two systems. The idea of rivalry in the Third World originated in Lenin's ideas on imperialism, but the strength of the USSR in the 1950s made it possible.

The West never formally accepted Khrushchev's challenges but tacitly behaved over the next decades as if competition existed between the Soviet bloc and West. After the collapse of the Berlin Wall in 1989 and the breakup of the Soviet Union in 1991, some in the West discussed the defeat of Marxist socialism in Eastern Europe as proof of the superiority of capitalism and democracy.

Khrushchev's conception of coexistence was continued by his successors, Leonid Brezhnev and Aleksey Kosygin, although the post-Khrushchev leadership deemphasized the role of competition. The policy of détente, adopted during the Brezhnev years, was derived from peaceful coexistence. At times, the two terms appeared to be used interchangeably in Soviet statements. Détente was the hallmark of Brezhnev's policy toward the West. While the idea of direct economic competition with the West was dropped, the USSR continued to seek allies and client states in the Third World, thus continuing the idea originating with Lenin that a key to the defeat of global capitalism lay in diminishing its influence in the less developed states.

Détente marked a departure from Stalin's hostile peaceful coexistence and Khrushchev's confrontational, competitive peaceful coexistence. It was the most cordial form of coexistence since Lenin but still maintained a dyadic view of the world. Although the USSR extended its outreach during the Khrushchev and Brezhnev years, Soviet foreign policy retained the ideological context of peaceful coexistence. The world was divided into the capitalist and socialist systems while less developed countries were categorized by whether they were neutral, pro-Western, or pro-Soviet.

Only in the Gorbachev era (1985–91) was there a leap from the heritage of two camps and the dyadic Marxist-Leninist view into new thinking about the world. Détente in the 1970s may be viewed as a bridge between Khrushchev's competitive coexistence and Gorbachev's new thinking. Mikhail Gorbachev never officially dropped peaceful coexistence, but he reinterpreted and even transcended it. At the Twenty-seventh Party Congress in 1986 the idea of peaceful coexistence as a form of class struggle was dropped. Global interdependence was emphasized in an essentially humanistic approach to global problems. Gorbachev did not abandon the notion of competition between the two systems, although the USSR reduced support to its allies in the Third World, which had been part of global competition. In the Gorbachev era peaceful coexistence abandoned conflict but retained competition between the two systems. Gorbachev thus emphasized elements of Lenin and Khrushchev's approaches, while dropping vestiges of the Stalinist interpretation. Gorbachev to some degree dropped Lenin's concept of *Kto kogo?* although there remained an underlying belief that socialism would prove superior to capitalism in meeting human needs.

In the Gorbachev era, peaceful coexistence gradually withered away. The end of the Cold War seemed to make peaceful coexistence obsolete. After the collapse of the USSR, peaceful coexistence became a historical concept, no longer an active principle of foreign policy. Had the Soviet system survived, it is likely the concept of peaceful coexistence would have remained in some form. Gorbachev went much further than either Khrushchev or Brezhnev in abandoning the negative overtones of peaceful coexistence, but he retained the essential concept until the dissolution of the USSR.

BIBLIOGRAPHY

Brown, Archie. *The Gorbachev Factor.* Oxford: Oxford University Press, 1996.

Checkel, Jeffrey T. *Ideas and International Political Change: Soviet/Russian Behavior and the End of the Cold War.* New Haven, Conn.: Yale University Press, 1997.

George, Alexander, Philip J. Farley, and Alexander Dallin, eds. *U.S.-Soviet Security Cooperation: Achievements, Failures, Lessons.* New York: Oxford University Press, 1988.

Goldgeier, James M. *Leadership Style and Soviet Foreign Policy: Stalin, Khrushchev, Brezhnev, Gorbachev.* Baltimore: Johns Hopkins University Press, 1994.

Gorbachev, Mikhail. *Perestroika: New Thinking for Our Country and the World.* New York: Harper and Row, 1987.

Halliday, Fred. *From Kabul to Managua: Soviet-American Relations in the 1980s.* New York: Pantheon, 1989.

Kim, Young Hum, ed. *Patterns of Coexistence: USA vs. USSR.* New York: Capricorn, 1966.

Kull, Steven. *Burying Lenin: The Revolution in Soviet Ideology and Foreign Policy.* Boulder, Colo.: Westview Press, 1992.

Powaski, Ronald E. *The Cold War: The United States and the Soviet Union, 1917–1991.* New York: Oxford University Press, 1998.

Norma C. Noonan

SEE ALSO Détente

Pelikan, Jiří (1923–99)

Czechoslovak editor and publisher. He joined the Czechoslovak Communist Party in 1939 and during the German occupation of his country was jailed by the Gestapo for participating in the anti-Nazi resistance. As director of Czechoslovak Television in 1968, Jiří Pelikan played a key role in disseminating the messages and images of the Prague Spring, the brief period of reform spearheaded by the Communist Party. A Communist Party and student union functionary since 1948, Pelikan became well known in Slovakia as an editor and writer. He was appointed director of the state television services in 1963. A noted Communist reformer, Pelikan was elected to the party's Central Committee in 1968. He also served as chairman of the National Assembly's Foreign Committee that year. With his support and direction the Czechoslovak media broadcasted abroad images of the developments of the Prague Spring up to and throughout the invasion of the country by soviet-led Warsaw Pact forces in August 1968.

Pelikan emigrated from Czechoslovakia in 1969 and settled in Italy, where he gained prominence as a writer. He carried on the legacy of the Prague Spring by editing and publishing literary and scholarly works on the period. He died in Rome on June 26, 1999.

BIBLIOGRAPHY

Kusin, Vladimir V. *The Intellectual Origins of the Prague Spring. The Development of Reformist Ideas in Czechoslovakia, 1956–1967.* Cambridge: Cambridge University Press, 1971.

Pelikan, Jiří, ed. *Socialist Opposition in Eastern Europe: The Czechoslovak Example.* New York: St. Martin's Press, 1973.

Timothy C. Dowling

Penderecki, Krzysztóf (1933–)

Contemporary Polish composer. Krzysztóf Penderecki acted as rector of the Music Academy in Kraków from 1972 to 1987, and as art director of the Kraków Philharmonic Orchestra. In 1988 he became conductor of the Norddeutscher Rundfunk in Hamburg, Germany. He also taught in many foreign universities.

Penderecki graduated in 1958 with a degree in composition. He experimented in his early works with new ways of articulation in the group of string and drum instruments, he using among other things, whisper-sound techniques. In the 1960s, he turned to tradition, using old musical forms such as sonata, fugue, passacaglia, and to music of the second half of the nineteenth century, such as Wagner's first operas and his music theater. In the 1990s Penderecki began to experiment with pastiche and chamber music, writing religious music including oratorios and cantatas.

Penderecki rejected a vanguard approach to experimenting with sound and created a synthesis of achievements of twentieth century music. His more important works are *Ofiarom Hiroszimy—tren* (1960); *Anaklasis* (1960); *Sabat Mater* (1962); *Dies irae* (1967), an oratorio dedicated to the memory of Auschwitz victims; *Pasja wg. w. Łukasza* (*St. Luke's Passion,* 1965); *Diabły z Loudun* (*The Devils of Loudun,* 1969); *Kosmogonia* (1970); *Jutrznia* (1970–71); *Raj utracony* (*Paradise Lost,* 1978); *Te Deum* (1980), a composition dedicated to Pope John Paul II; *Polskie Requiem* (1980–84); *Czarna maska* (*The Black Mask,* 1984–86); *Veni Creator* (1987); *Ubu Król* (*King Ubu,* 1991); *V Symfonia* (*The Fifth Symphony,* 1992); *Kwartet* (1993); and *Il Koncert skrzypcowy* (Second Violin Concerto, 1994).

BIBLIOGRAPHY

Schwinger, Wolfram. *Krzysztof Penderecki: His Life and Work.* London: Schott, 1989.

Kinga Nemere-Czacowska

Pershing II Missile

U.S. army missile, the result of improvements in the Pershing Missile system first deployed in Europe by the United States in 1964.

The Pershing II (classified MGM-31A) was a land-based, highly mobile tactical missile system that provided NATO members with a reliable, all-weather deterrent to Warsaw Pact forces. The Pershing system was utilized by the U.S. army and the Federal Republic of Germany's air force. A total of 108 Pershing systems were active in Europe. Pershing missiles were on constant alert at fixed sites in Germany; their status was monitored by NATO headquarters and the national commands.

The NATO alliance and the USSR began talks in the late 1970s to reduce intermediate-range nuclear forces in Europe. By the end of the decade the talks had become stalemated. In 1979 the United States signed the Dual-Track Agreement with NATO, in which the United States committed itself to improve theater nuclear forces. This was in response to Soviet fielding of advanced missile and aircraft systems, specifically the Backfire bomber and SS-20 missiles. The protocol called for modernizing the Pershing system, and Pershing II was the direct result. The agreement also called for the United States to develop ground-launched cruise missiles (GLCM). As arms negotiations with the USSR continued, the systems were deployed to European bases.

Controversy erupted in Europe over the planned Pershing II missile deployment. Various activist groups in different countries protested the decision as an acceleration of the arms race. They argued that it would only bring more Soviet systems on line against Western Europe. U.S. missile sites in Germany were a scene of constant protests by antinuclear and peace groups. Meanwhile the United States and the USSR continued discussions concerning intermediate nuclear forces (INF) and moved closer to agreements in principle. The Soviets especially desired to have the Pershing II included in the INF agreement.

The Soviets were concerned over Pershing II's major technical improvements. The missile had a range of more than 1,000 miles and advanced, on-board targeting radar. That, coupled with its extended range, made precise strike options possible. The Circular Error Probable (CEP) was 120 feet as opposed to 1,200 feet for reentry vehicles on the Pershing 1A. This improvement permitted much less destructive warheads and reduced possible collateral damage associated with INF weapons systems. Improvements in missile ground support equipment made it the most advanced system of its type.

The Pershing II was assigned exclusively to the U.S. army. The 56th Field Artillery Brigade was the unit designated to operate the Pershing missiles; its headquarters were located at Schwabisch Gmünd, West Germany, with firing battalions at Schwabisch Gmünd, Neu Ulm, and Heilbronn. The Brigade comprised three artillery battalions (1-41 FA, 1-81 FA, and 3-84 FA) and one infantry battalion (2-4 IN). This unique, self-contained force was responsible for all U.S. Pershing operations.

The German air force's Pershing organizations were surface-to-surface missile wing (SSWW) 1 and 2. Supporting the wings were U.S. army artillery units (85th and 74th U.S. Army Field Artillery Detachments). NATO restriction precluded the German air force from receiving Pershing II, but it was scheduled to receive advanced missile ground support equipment. The German version was classified Pershing IB.

In late 1983 the first Pershing IIs were deployed to Europe and became operational in U.S. army units. Protests increased throughout Europe, but the deployment of Pershing II gave added impetus to Soviet-American negotiations concerning INF limits. The major stumbling block of these talks was U.S. insistence on on-site verification of withdrawal and destruction of missile systems. Deployment of missiles to Europe caused the Soviets to yield and agree on inspection protocols.

In 1987 both sides reached agreement, and on December 8, 1987, the Intermediate Nuclear Forces Treaty was signed in Washington, D.C. It provided for the withdrawal and destruction of all Pershing IIs and comparable

Soviet systems, and it provided for a thirteen-year program of on-site inspections at specified sites in Europe, the United States, and the USSR. In 1991 the last active Pershing II missile was destroyed and the five thousand U.S. troops who manned the missile units returned to the United States.

BIBLIOGRAPHY

Curtis, Myron F., Thomas M. Brown, and John C. Hogan. "Pershing—It Gave Peace a Chance." *Field Artillery Journal* (February 1991): 29–32.

Dastrup, Boyd. *King of Battle: A Branch History of the US Army's Field Artillery.* Ft. Monroe, Va.: U.S. Army, 1992.

Dorman, James, Jr. *The US War Machine.* New York: Crown, 1978.

Julius A. Menzoff

SEE ALSO Intermediate-Range Nuclear Forces Treaty

Pertini, Sandro (1896–1990)

Italian politician. Alessandro (Sandro) Pertini, a lawyer and journalist, took part in World War I, then devoted himself to politics, joining the Italian Socialist Party (PSI) and opposing fascism. Condemned to prison for his antifascist activity, Pertini escaped to France but returned to Italy in 1929, where he organized a Socialist Party underground. Arrested and condemned to eleven years' imprisonment, he also had the opportunity to become a close friend with other political prisoners, above all with Antonio Gramsci. Refusing to petition for a pardon from the Italian dictator Benito Mussolini, he was released only in 1943 after the fall of fascism. In September of the same year, fighting against the German occupation, he was arrested and sent to Regina Coeli prison in Rome, where he was condemned to death. Some months later he escaped together with Giuseppe Saragat and other patriots, reached Milan, where he became secretary of the PSI, and led the partisan war against the Germans.

After the war Pertini devoted himself to politics and journalism. He edited *Avanti!* in 1945–46 and from 1950 to 1952, and the *Lavoro* of Genoa in 1947. He was elected to the Constituent Assembly in 1946, and senator of the republic and president of the Socialist Parliamentary Group in 1948. After the election of 1953, Pertini entered the Chamber of Deputies and served as vice president of the Committee of the Interior and of the Committee of Constitutional Affairs.

In 1963 he was elected vice speaker of the chamber and in 1968 became speaker. After the failed effort to reunite the Italian Socialist Party and the Italian Social Democratic Party, he submitted his resignation, which was rejected by all factions within the party, and he was subsequently reconfirmed in office until 1976. Reelected to the Chamber of Deputies in 1976, Pertini, on July 8, 1978, was elected president of Italy. During his presidency he contributed to restoring public faith in government. In 1985, at the end of his term, he was elected senator for life.

BIBLIOGRAPHY

Ghirelli, A. *Caro Presidente.* Milan: Rizzoli, 1981.

Guidotti, M. *Sandro Pertini: Una vita per la libertà.* Rome: Editalia, 1988.

Jacobucci, M. *Pertini uomo di pace.* Milan: Rizzoli, 1985.

Milani, S. *Compagno Pertini.* Rome: Napoleone, 1978.

La Navicella: *I Deputati e i Senatori del 10° Parlamento Repubblicano.* Città di Castello: INI, 1988.

Fabio Marino

Peter (1923–70)

Last king of Yugoslavia. Peter (Petar) II, eldest son of Alexander I and Marie of Romania, was born in Belgrade on September 6, 1923. He succeeded his father on October 11, 1934, two days after the latter's assassination at Marseilles. Because Peter was a minor, a regency was established under his cousin, Prince Paul.

Paul was deposed by a coup led by General Dušan Simović on March 27, 1941. The coup, directed against the pro-Axis policy of the government, placed the young king in power for a few weeks until the Axis defeat of the Yugoslav army. The Yugoslav government capitulated on April 17, and Peter established a government-in-exile, first in Greece then in England. Events in his country developed without him. The Croats turned against the Serbs and were given independent status by Hitler. The underground resistance to the Germans acted independently of Peter.

Peter remained in England and studied international law at Cambridge University while the two groups of resistance fighters—the Chetniks under Draža Mihajlović and the Partisans under Josip Broz Tito—began to fight each other as well as the occupying Germans. Peter favored Mihajlović, whom the Allies suspected of collaborating with the enemy. Peter was strongly urged to abandon Mihajlović and to support Tito, whom the Allies increasingly supported, but he refused.

At the Tehran Conference the Allies officially recognized Tito and gave him their support. Tito assembled a national parliament, made up of members of his movement, and founded a temporary government. It deprived the Yugoslav government-in-exile of all power, and forbade Peter from returning to Yugoslavia. Following a single-party (uncontested) run by the Communist-dominated National Front election, the monarchy was abolished in November 1945, and Yugoslavia became a Communist republic.

After he was deposed Peter emigrated to the United States, where he worked in public relations in New York City and wrote his memoirs, *A King's Heritage.* He died in Los Angeles on November 3, 1970. His funeral was held at the monastery of the Serbian Church in Libertyville, Illinois. Peter married Princess Elizabeth of Greece, daughter of King Alexander of Greece on March 20, 1944, in the Yugoslav Embassy in London. They had one son, Alexander, the present claimant to the throne.

BIBLIOGRAPHY

Alexandra. *For Love of a King.* Garden City, N.Y., Doubleday, 1956.

Djilas, Milovan. *Wartime.* New York: Harcourt Brace Jovanovich, 1977.

Milazzo, Matteo J. *The Chetnik Movement and the Yugoslav Resistance.* Baltimore: Johns Hopkins, 1975.

Roberts, Walter R. *Tito, Mihailovic and the Allies, 1941–1945.* New Brunswick, N.J.: Rutgers University, 1973.

Martin J. Manning

SEE ALSO Mihajlović, Draža; Tito

Peterle, Lojzc (1948–)

Slovenian prime minister (1990–92). Lojzc Peterle was born in Cuznja Vas, Yugoslavia, on July 5, 1948. He graduated from the University of Ljubljana. He worked as a city planner and on projects in environmental protection and resource conservation. In 1989 he was a founder of the Slovenian Christian Democratic Party and has been the party leader since then. Peterle became prime minister after the April 1990 elections. His Christian Democrats were part of a six-party coalition—the Democratic United Opposition (Demos)—that won control of the Slovenian parliament. The Demos had campaigned calling for independence from the Yugoslav federation within a year. During Peterle's tenure as prime minister, Slovenia declared its sovereignty on July 2, 1990, and ultimately its independence on June 25, 1991. It fought a short war against the Serb-dominated Yugoslav army, temporarily suspended its declaration of independence, but reactivated it on October 7, 1991. Slovenia won recognition as an independent state from the European Union (EU) in January 1992. In April of that year, after the government of Peterle lost a parliamentary vote of confidence, Ivan Drnovsek, leader of the Liberal Democratic Party (LDP), became prime minister. Peterle served as foreign minister in 1993–94. He was elected vice president of the European Union of Christian Democrats in 1993.

BIBLIOGRAPHY

Gow, James, and Cathie Carmichael. *Slovenia and the Slovenes: A Small State and the Challenge of Internationalization in the New Europe.* Bloomington: Indiana University Press, 1999.

Bernard Cook

SEE ALSO Kucan, Milan

Pflimlin, Pierre (1907–)

French prime minister whose nomination signaled the end of the Fourth Republic. Born in Roubaix on February 5, 1907, Pierre Pflimlin studied law at Strasbourg University and the Catholic Institute of Paris. As a member of the Mouvement Républicain Populaire (Popular Republican Movement), he participated in the two post–World War II constituent assemblies and was elected a deputy to the French National Assembly (lower house of parliament) in 1946, 1951, and 1956. He also held several cabinet posts.

In the governmental crisis stemming from the war in Algeria, President René Coty in May 1958 asked Pflimlin to form a new government. French settlers and soldiers in Algiers, who feared that Pflimlin favored independence for Algeria, rioted in that city, set up a committee of public safety there, and seized control in Corsica.

The soldiers and settlers called for the return to power of General Charles de Gaulle. As fears increased of a paratroop attack on Paris, Pflimlin met with de Gaulle on May 26. De Gaulle's public announcement that negotiations had begun for a change in government infuriated Pflimlin. Fearful of civil war, however, Pflimlin resigned on the night of May 27.

Pflimlin was elected a deputy to the National Assembly in 1958 and 1962, and he served in governments of the Fifth Republic, which was established upon de Gaulle's return to power. He served in de Gaulle's government during 1958–59 and in the government of Georges Pompidou. He was also active in European politics, serving as vice president then, from 1984 to 1986, president of the European Parliament.

BIBLIOGRAPHY

Agulhon, Maurice. *The French Republic, 1879–1992.* Tr. by Antonia Nevill. Oxford: Blackwell, 1993.

Northcutt, Wayne, ed. *Historical Dictionary of the French Fourth and Fifth Republics, 1946–1991.* New York: Greenwood Press, 1992.

Michael R. Nichols

SEE ALSO Algerian War; Coty, René; De Gaulle, Charles

Philosophy, Post-1945 European

French Philosophy after 1945

The recent development of philosophy in France has traditionally been presented in terms of a passage leading from the generation after 1945, that of the "three H's" (Hegel, Husserl, Heidegger) to the post-1960s generation, that of the three "masters of suspicion" (Marx, Nietzsche, Freud).

Following Heidegger's attempt at a fundamental ontology (referring to the ontological-existential analysis preceding all other ontologies, or theories of reality), Jean-Paul Sartre and Maurice Merleau-Ponty reinterpreted Husserl's modification of the Hegelian account of phenomenology as the "science of the experience of consciousness." Their existentialization of Husserl's transcendental phenomenology (a phenomenology whose first principle is the transcendental ego), which was informed by the problematization of Cartesian dualism and some of its inherent oppositions (objective/subjective; empirical/transcendental; world/consciousness; self/other), opened up new possibilities for rewriting the experience of the self in terms of its being-in-the-world, its concrete relation with others, and its specific temporality.

While Sartre's conception of a phenomenological ontology, based on a critique of the transcendental ego, attempted to disclose intentional consciousness as an empty, differential field, as nothing or being-for-itself, thus stressing existence as free, projective, and temporal activity vis-à-vis a world of indifferent and inert objects, Merleau-Ponty, in his phenomenology of perception, emphasized the vitality of human experience and particularly our embodied existence as lived.

In contrast to Sartre's notion that we are condemned to freedom, Merleau-Ponty claimed that we are condemned to meaning. Understanding human experience, perception brings together our various senses as the body tends toward expression. Gesture, motility, and spatiality are all aspects of bodily expression—they constitute the phenomenal field in which the meanings of experience appear.

While the late 1940s and early 1950s were characterized by the dominance of existentially oriented philosophies—in addition to Sartre's philosophy of freedom and Merleau-Ponty's phenomenology of the body, one has to mention Albert Camus's philosophy of the absurd and Gabriel Marcel's dialogical philosophy. It was during that period that both Sartre and Merleau-Ponty gave new impetus and new directions to phenomenology as a philosophical enterprise. Merleau-Ponty's reorientation of phenomenology from a philosophy of the body to a metaphysics of visibility allowed him to reassess the dimension of meaning in the different fields of experience. Phenomenology, for Merleau-Ponty, came to be synonymous with the genesis and dialectics of expression as an originary experience of visibility. Merleau-Ponty understood this visibility that is situated somewhere between the visible and the invisible, the seeing and the seen, as a new dialectics and as an intertwining of appearance with what appears.

Like Merleau-Ponty, the Sartre of the late 1950s and 1960s concerned himself with the question of (individual) history and its relation to dialectics, but now in terms of the progressive-regressive method, which he offered as a way of reading historical figures such as the authors Genet and Flaubert, and contemporary thinkers such as Claude Lévi-Strauss and Jacques Lacan. This progressive-regressive method transformed his existential phenomenology into an existential Marxism that came to dominate his writings until his death in 1980.

While in the 1950s and early 1960s several French philosophers took phenomenological research into specific fields of philosophy (Mikel Dufrenne developed a phenomenology of aesthetic experience; and Emmanuel Levinas's "philosophy of the Other" remained singularly phenomenological in its concrete investigations and descriptions), it was Paul Ricoeur who supplemented French phenomenology with hermeneutic considerations (hermeneutics being the art of interpretation and understanding), thereby establishing himself as one of the foremost mediators among different philosophical traditions such as phenomenology, existential philosophy, analytic philosophy, psychoanalysis, and structuralism.

The generation active after 1960, however, taking its arguments from a rereading of Marx, Nietzsche, and Freud, came to see dialectical approaches toward history supported by a phenomenology of the subject, the body, and expression, as well as the different phenomenological conceptions of language, as mere illusion. The opposition between the prevailing postwar doctrine and what was soon to acquire for the public the name of structuralism (and poststructuralism) appeared to be total.

Deciphering dialectical conceptions of history and of consciousness in terms of a logic of identity that, by reclaiming the principle of the subject, could not fail to reduce otherness and difference to the same, the "*nouvelle vague*" in French philosophy attempted to accomplish a paradigm shift by appropriating and applying the semiological theory of Ferdinand de Saussure to different disciplines. And it was particularly language's differential meaning described in semiology that provided the backdrop for the emergence of the structuralisms of Lévi-Strauss in anthropology, Lacan in psychoanalysis, Roland Barthes in literary criticism, and Louis Althusser in political theory. Unlike (existential and hermeneutic) phenomenology, where its philosophy had crept into other fields, structuralism entered into philosophical research from related disciplines. Questions of methodology, the status (death?) of the subject or self, and the implications of a synchronic conception of history became important issues for structuralism.

The confluence of structuralism, phenomenology, Marxism, and psychoanalysis in post-1968 France led to philosophy's dispersal into a multiplicity of different philosophical styles and designations: Michel Foucault's archaeologies and genealogies; Gilles Deleuze's nomadologies; Jean-François Lyotard's libidinous economies; the deconstructions of Jacques Derrida, Philippe Lacoue-Labarthe, Jean-Luc Nancy, and Sarah Kofman; the feminist theories of Julia Kristeva, Hélène Cixous, and Luce Irigaray; and the postmodernism of Jean Baudrillard. All of them form a philosophical text that, by reading the gaps, margins, limitations, and frameworks of a problematized modernity and by articulating the differences in sexual, political, intellectual, and racist practices, marks the inscription of otherness and discontinuity in the traditional philosophical systems, thus driving and keeping alive the dynamics of contemporary French thought.

German Philosophy after 1945

The course of German philosophy after 1945 can be traced in terms of a temporal division into two main phases: the phase immediately after the Second World War until the mid-1950s marked by the elaboration and institutionalization of different versions of existential philosophy; and the phase from the end of the 1950s to the 1990s with its increasing pluralization of philosophical styles.

While it had been the existential philosophy of Martin Heidegger and Karl Jaspers, as well as its French versions personified by Jean-Paul Sartre and Albert Camus, that occupied the philosophical center stage left devastated by the war experience with topics such as existence, time, finitude, mortality, and freedom. The next ten years saw the gradual opening and internationalization of German philosophy accomplished by both a return of exiled logical empiricism and attempts at resuming certain philosophical traditions such as (neo-)Marxism and hermeneutics whose contours had already been sketched in the period preceding the war.

The 1960s were characterized by public debates among the three main philosophical theories, critical rationalism (Karl Popper), critical theory (Max Horkheimer, Theodor W. Adorno, Walter Benjamin, Herbert Marcuse), and hermeneutics (Hans-Georg Gadamer). Both the controversies concerning positivism and hermenutics/ideology critique were concerned with philosophy's self-understanding, its methods, and, in particular during the student movement of 1968–69, its political role in society. And it was this very "culture of discussion" of the late 1960s and early 1970s that, especially in the writings of Jürgen Habermas, Karl-Otto Apel, Albrecht Wellmer, Manfred Frank, Bernhard Waldenfels, and Odo Marquard, brought about a transformation of formerly exclusionary positions into a critical cooperation among those movements by means of detailed discussions and explorations of new philosophical possibilities in a climate of critical objectivity devoid of all effusive gestures.

This communicative discourse of a new philosophical generation emerging in the seventies and early eighties was characterized both by explicit references to the positions and thoughts of their predecessors and philosophical parents and the attempt at reestablishing contact with previously neglected or excluded philosophical conceptions. Here one has to mention the hermeneutic school of Gadamer, the neo-Hegelian school of Joachim Ritter, the constructivist school of Erlangen founded by Paul Lorenzer, the critical Frankfurt School, and the analytically oriented Munich school with Wolfgang Stegmüller as its most significant representative. In the 1970s and 1980s philosophy in Germany continued to open itself up toward styles of thought from abroad that had been cut off by the German tradition dominant during the Nazi era and the 1950s. Analytic philosophy with authors such as Wittgenstein, Gilbert Ryle, Willard Van Orman Quine, Nelson Goodman, John Austin, and John Searle, the discovery of American pragmatism, and neo-Marxist positions emerging in and after 1968, all found a philosophical home in Germany and served to bring an international face to the sometimes provincial bearing of German philosophy in the 1950s and early 1960s.

The reception of French philosophy in Germany was somewhat different. After Sartre's and Camus' respective philosophies had been in vogue in the 1950s, French structuralism of the 1960s was read only marginally; in the 1980s and early 1990s, however, French philosophy gained considerable significance under the influence of poststructuralism and postmodernism, an influence that, though sometimes fiercely combated, has acquired institutional form at some German universities.

As to the general development of German philosophy after 1945, one has to notice an increasing independence on the side of specific philosophical disciplines in relatively demarcated fields such as logic, the philosophy of science, epistemology, social philosophy, aesthetics, or ethics tending toward a dissociation from a unified philosophical meta-discourse. This has been accompanied by a new cautious, philological, and philosophical appropriation of "classic" philosophers both of antiquity and of modernity. In particular, German idealism has been reexamined in careful readings and interpretations for the validity of its arguments and insights as well as for the actuality of its questions and answers. This has also provided the context for large-scale editorial projects partly extending into the new millennium (for instance, historicocritical editions of Hegel and Schelling), as well as for elaborations of lexical and philosophico-historical foundations whose results have come to be appreciated as standard works.

Contemporary German philosophy has been informed by a willingness to transcend disciplinary borders and limits toward certain nonphilosophical subject areas. This applies, above all, to the philosophy of language, ethics, and aesthetics, but also to the ongoing debate over the political involvement of certain philosophers with National Socialism (Heidegger and others). In summary, the most recent philosophy in Germany has marked itself off from the philosophy prevailing in the two decades after the Second World War by its intensified internationalization, pluralization, and dispersion into partial disciplines and thematic orientations.

Italian Philosophy

While the first phase in the development of twentieth-century Italian philosophy had seen an indisputable prevalence of idealist philosophies, especially Giovanni Gentile's thought, the second phase was marked by a widespread violent reaction against idealist philosophy in general and "actual idealism" (Gentile's version of idealism) in particular, by setting against it not only the materialist, that is, Marxist conception of history, but also later tendencies of German thought such as Husserl's phenomenology and Heidegger's existential philosophy.

One can perhaps distinguish three main trends in Italian Marxism on the basis of their different relation to the idealist tradition. According to Antonio Gramsci, his conception of a philosophy of praxis is a reform and development of Hegelianism by historicizing the latter's speculative conception of the world. Opposed to this "subjective" conception of historical materialism elaborated by Gramsci was the interpretation of Marx's thought as a "logic of existence," or of "contingent reality," put forward by Galvano Della Volpe. The school of Della Volpe (Mario Rossi, Lucio Colletti) in opposition to any metaphysics or mysticism stressed the radical difference between thought and being and vindicated a "positive reality." On the other hand, the interpretation of Marxism articulated by the Milan phenomenological school founded by Antonio Banfi, whose most prominent exponent was Enzo Paci, shared with Gramsci the insistence on the "subjective," humanistic character of historical materialism, and supplemented the understanding of human subjectivity with the theoretical achievements of transcendental phenomenology.

Nicola Abbagnano's "positive existentialism" or "neo-illuminism" was based on an interpretation of Heidegger's existential ontology. Abbagnano emphatically denounced any possible return to metaphysics by grasping the method of existential analysis in terms of a mere empirical and contingent description of "limit-situations." Inaccessible to merely theoretical or rational approaches, the "irrational" nature of human existence must not be conceptualized in ontological categories expressing the essence of some pure rationality such as universality, necessity, or infinity, "progress," but rather in terms of "singular individuality" and its facticity, contingence, and finiteness.

While Enzo Paci's joining of the existentialist problematic to the phenomenology of the later Husserl and to some aspects of historical materialism moved within a markedly "atheistic" sphere of reflection, Luigi Payreson's version of Italian existentialism provided, with its central notion of "existential finitude," a possible answer to an ontological and religious question implying the possibility of a Christian existentialism, thereby reintroducing certain mystical elements found in Schelling, Kierkegaard, and Gabriel Marcel.

In the 1970s and 1980s a widespread "decline of ideology" took place that has to be understood as having begun largely before the "historical crisis" of Marxism, terminating in Italy with the internal division of the Left and the tragic experience of terrorism. Out of this very crisis, two conflictual positions have emerged. The first converges around the proposal of interpreting (late) Heideggerian thought by means of philosophical hermeneutics. This philosophical stance, sometimes described as "progressive desacralization," or "secularization" of metaphysics, includes thinkers like Gianni Vattimo who, well known for his "weak thought" meaning postfoundationalist modes of thinking, founded the important center for hermeneutic studies at the University of Torino; Mario Perniola; Pier Aldo Rovatti; Giorgio Agamben; Carlo Sini; and, as the representative of semiotics conceptualized not so much as critical theory, but rather as positive science, Umberto Eco (who founded the center for semiotics at the University of Bologna).

On the opposing side one finds the proposal to go beyond metaphysics. This position is willing to give up on the "radical" critique of the metaphysical tradition and attempts to confront the question of being in a more constructive sense. This second side of the recent Italian debate in philosophy, inaugurated by Emanuele Severino and continued by Massimo Cacciari, has taken up certain themes and modes of argumentation of medieval Scholasticism to revive certain central topics of Greek speculative thought.

Erik Vogt

SEE ALSO Adorno, Theodor; Althusser, Louis; Barthes, Roland; Baudrillard, Jean; Bloch, Ernst; Camus, Albert; Castoriadis, Cornelius; Derrida, Jacques; Eco, Umberto; Foucault, Michel; Frankfurt School; Gadamer, Hans-Georg; Guattari, Felix; Habermas, Jürgen; Heidegger, Martin; Horkheimer, Max; Kristeva, Julia; Lacan, Jacques; Levinas, Emmanuel; Lyotard, Jean; Marcel, Gabriel; Maritain, Jacques; Merleau-Ponty, Maurice; Nouveaux Philosophes; Pollock, Friedrich; Ricoeur, Paul; Sartre, Jean-Paul

Piasecki, Bolesław (1915–79)

Polish lawyer, politician, founder and leader of the movement of the "socially progressive" lay Catholics who declared themselves in favor of building socialism. They were gathered around the weekly *Dziś i Jutro* (Today and Tomorrow), founded in 1945, and the organization Pax (a Catholic movement set up to support the regime), founded in 1947.

Before World War II Bolesław Piasecki was active in the extreme rightist, profascist political organization Falanga. As of 1941 he was a commander of the underground right-wing Nation's Confederation, and he fought against Soviet-backed partisans during the war. In 1945, imprisoned by the Soviets, he gained the support of Władysław Gomułka, the Communist Party leader, and I. Sierov by offering to cooperate with the communist authorities. Piasecki, on the Communist payroll, carried out many tasks dealing with religious issues. His position was often contrary to the policy of the Catholic Episcopate. Sometimes, as in 1950, he acted as an intermediary in talks between the communist authorities and the Catholic Church. During the political crises of 1956 and 1968, Piasecki declared himself on the side of authoritarian rule and against the democratic opposition. He fully accepted political dependence on the USSR.

Despite Piasecki's efforts and his skillful political game, he never held government office, he was a member of parliament from 1965 to 1979 and a member of the National Council from 1971 to 1979.

BIBLIOGRAPHY

Bromke, Adam. *Poland's Politics: Idealism versus Realism.* Cambridge, Mass.: Harvard University Press, 1967.

Ryszard Sudziński

Pieck, Wilhelm (1876–1960)

First president of the German Democratic Republic (East Germany). A joiner by trade, Pieck was an active member of the pre-1914 Social Democratic Party (SPD) and trade union movement. Although he performed military service between 1915 and 1917, his left-wing political views led to several spells in prison. As World War I drew to its close he became associated with the Spartacists. During the Weimar Republic he was one of the central figures in German communism as a founding member of the German Communist Party (KPD), one of the party's Reichstag (lower house of parliament) deputies from 1929 to 1933, and a member of the Comintern Presidium as of 1931. During the fierce internal party disputes of the 1920s Pieck belonged to a circle of functionaries who sought to avoid committing themselves to a particular faction but eventually joined up with Ernst Thälmann's left wing, thereby bringing the KPD more under the influence of Soviet dictator Stalin at the end of the decade.

After Hitler came to power in Germany in 1933, Pieck took refuge in Paris and after January 1935 in Moscow. After Thälmann's imprisonment by the Nazis, Pieck was chosen in 1935 as caretaker leader of the KPD. Unflinchingly loyal to Stalin, he survived the purges between 1936 and 1938 and contributed to the development and implementation of the Soviet Union's plans for postwar Germany. On returning to a defeated Germany in July 1945 after World War II, Pieck was confirmed as KPD chairman and played a crucial role in the fusion of the KPD and the SPD into the Socialist Unity Party (SED). A more conciliatory figure than Communist Party leader Walter Ulbricht, Pieck was elected cochairman of the SED in 1946, and in October 1949 he became president of the German Democratic Republic. His political influence declined sharply after spring 1953 because of ill health.

BIBLIOGRAPHY

Voßke, Heinz, and Gerhard Nitzsche. *Wilhelm Pieck: Biographischer Abriß.* Frankfurt/Main: Verlag Marxistische Blätter, 1975.

Mike Dennis

SEE ALSO Ulbricht, Walter

Piñar López, Blas (1918–)

Spanish far-right political leader and parliamentarian. Blas Piñar has been an influential figure on the Francoist right throughout much of the postwar era, first as an official associated with the most "immovable" traditionalist wing of the Falange, then as the driving force behind an even more uncompromising party known as Fuerza Nueva (New Force, FN). He is also suspected of having secretly supported various acts of terrorism and military coup plots between the 1960s and the late 1980s.

Piñar was born in Toledo in 1918. His father was a career military officer who served in Morocco and later fought against republican forces during the Civil War, but Piñar himself spent most of the war hiding out in various foreign legations in Madrid. After Francisco Franco's Nationalist victory, he studied law at the University of Madrid and embarked a successful career as a lawyer and notary. In 1958, after gaining prominence as the national vice president for propaganda in the Catholic Action (*Acción Católica,* AC) organization, he was personally appointed by Franco to serve as a Falangist Party "national counselor" and deputy in the regime's rubber-stamp Cortes (parliament). He went on to occupy a succession of important posts in other government-affiliated and ultra-traditionalist organizations. Throughout the 1960s Piñar distinguished himself as an uncompromising opponent of every political development that seemed to threaten "pure" Francoism, including the liberalization measures promoted by the "technocratic" Opus Dei government ministers, the increasing activism of dissident left-leaning national syndicalists who accused "reactionary" Franco loyalists of having sold out the revolutionary potential of falangism, the outbreak of left-wing student protests and strikes, the resurgence of Basque separatism and terrorism, the abandonment of traditionalism by influential sections of the Catholic hierarchy in the wake of Vatican II, and the government's alleged subservience to British and American foreign policy initiatives. A persuasive orator, he regularly spoke out in the Cortes, against these trends in articles written for the rightist press, and in public speeches made at rallies organized by Francoist hard-liners. His bitter disillusionment about the ever-growing influence wielded by the regime's "traitorous" *aperturistas* (flexibles) prompted him to found a publishing company in 1966, a weekly magazine in 1967, a loose organizational network in 1968, a "political association" in 1969, and an official political party between 1974 and 1976, all of which were named Fuerza Nueva. In the process he began paying rhetorical homage to martyred Flangist leader José Antonio Primo de Rivera and established close links to violence-prone far-right groups such as Mariano Sánchez Covisa's Guerrilleros de Cristo Re (Guerrillas of Christ the King GCR).

During Spain's turbulent transition from Franco to a democratic system, Piñar and other civilian and military ultras, known collectively as "the Bunker," desperately sought to prop up the increasingly moribund Francoist regime and derail the democraticization process. Although he has always denied being involved in anticonstitutional violence, FN militants have repeatedly been arrested for carrying out acts of terrorism and accused of offering support to military personnel implicated in coup plots. Admiral Luis Carrero Blanco, Franco's designated successor and head of the Servicio Central de Documentación (Central Information Service, SECED), admired Piñar enough to recommend him as justice minister, and in 1970 he ordered his right-hand man, Colonel José Ignacio San Martín to recruit FN members into yet another action organization operating under the rubric of the Junta Coordinadora de Afirmación Nacional (National Affirmation Coordinating Committee JCAN), which was then involved in several demonstrations and violent confrontations with "subversives." After Basque terrorists assassinated Carrero Blanco in 1973, Piñar and his party actively collaborated with other far-right groups to impede the transition to democracy.

At the same time, Piñar and the FN pursued various legalist parliamentary strategies. These efforts to achieve "bourgeois" respectability and electoral success were viewed with disdain by the proponents of direct action within the party. On February 23, 1981, Guardia Civil officer Antonio Tejero Molina seized the parliament building, an action supported in Valladolid by Lieutenant Colonel Angel Campano López, an FN member. Only four months later in June ultras from FN allegedly planned to carry out "false flag" terrorist provocations to precipitate a new military coup organized by hard-line ex-Falangist labor minister and longtime Piñar associate José Antonio Girón, among others.

In 1983 Piñar formally dissolved his party and transformed it into a "study center" known as the Centro de Estudios Sociales, Políticos y Económicos (Center for Social, Political, and Economic Studies), but within three years he revived the party under a new name, the Frente Nacional (National Front), and shifted its emphasis from the nostalgic defense of Francoism to the promotion of traditional Catholic values. Since then he has unsuccessfully campaigned for election as a deputy in the European Parliament.

BIBLIOGRAPHY

Alvarez-Solis, Antonio. *Que es el búnker?* Barcelona: Gaya Ciencia, 1976.

Cadena, Ernesto (pseud. Ernesto Milá). *La ofensiva neofascista: Un informe sensacional.* Barcelona: Acervo, 1978.

Ellwood, Sheelagh. "The Extreme Right in Spain: A Dying Species?" In *The Far Right in Western and Eastern Europe.* Ed. by Luciano Cheles et al. London: Longman, 1995.

———. *Spanish Fascism in the Franco Era: Falange Espanola de las JONS, 1936–1976.* London: Macmillan, 1987.

Gilmour, John. "The Extreme Right in Spain: Blas Piñar and the Spirit of the Nationalist Rising," in *The Extreme Right in Europe and the USA.* Ed. by Paul Hainsworth. New York: St. Martin's Press, 1992.

La matanza de Atocha. Madrid: Akal, 1980.

Piñar, Blas. *Hacia un estado nacional?* Madrid: Fuerza Neuva, 1981.

———. *Combate por España.* Madrid: Fuerza Neuva, 1975.

Preston, Paul. *The Politics of Revenge: Fascism and the Military in Twentieth-Century Spain.* London: Unwin Hyman, 1990.

Rees, Philip. *Biographical Dictionary of the Extreme Right since 1890.* New York: Simon and Schuster, 1990.

Rodríguez Jiménez, José Luis. *Reaccionarios y golpistas: La extrema derecha en España dal tardofranquismo a la consolidación de la democracia, 1967–1982.* Madrid: Consejo Superior de Investigaciones Científicas, 1994.

Jeffrey M. Bale

SEE ALSO Terrorism, Right Wing

Pineau, Christian (1905–95)

French Socialist politician Christian Paul Francis Pineau was born in Chaumont-en-Bassigny. His father, a colonel, died when he was a child and his mother married playwright Jean Giraudoux. After receiving degrees in political science and law, Pineau worked in banking. During World War he was a Resistance leader and helped to found the Resistance paper, *Libération.* In 1943 he was arrested by the Germans and, before being sent to Buchenwald concentration camp in Germany, was tortured by the Gestapo (Secret police) in Lyon. Three weeks after his release from Buchenwald in 1945 he was appointed minister of food supply. In 1955 parliament gave its approval to Pineau to form a cabinet but his effort to negotiate a coalition failed. He was foreign minister from 1956 to 1958. He was instrumental in organizing the Anglo-French-Israeli coalition that precipitated the 1956 Suez crisis, and he signed the Treaty of Rome on March 25, 1957, initiating the European Economic Community.

After retiring from politics he wrote children's books as well as political memoirs. He died on April 5, 1995.

BIBLIOGRAPHY

"Lives of Note." *Evening Post* (Wellington, New Zealand:), April 20, 1995.

Pineau, Christian. *1956, Suez.* Paris: R. Laffont, 1976.

Saxon, Wolfgang. "Christian Pineau, French Hero and Foreign Minister, Dies at 90." *New York Times,* April 7, 1995.

Bernard Cook

SEE ALSO Suez Crisis

Pintasilgo, Maria (1930–)

Portuguese prime minister. Maria da Lourdes Pintasilgo was born in Abrantes on January 18, 1930. She studied at the Higher Technical Institute in Lisbon and worked as an industrial engineer. She founded the National Committee on the Status of Women in 1970 and chaired the group until 1974. In 1971–72 she was a member of the Portuguese delegation to the United Nations. Following the overthrow of the old regime in Lisbon in 1974, she became Portuguese minister of social affairs then in 1975 secretary of state for social security. She was appointed Portuguese ambassador to UNESCO and a member of UNESCO's executive board in 1976. On July 29, 1979, President Antonio Ramalho Eanes announced that he was appointing Pintasilgo to head an interim nonparty government of military officers and civilians. Pintasilgo's task was to guide the country to a parliamentary election, but she was responsible for a large number of important laws approved by presidential decree. Pintasilgo was the first female Portuguese prime minister and the second woman to hold such a post in Europe. Her prime ministership lasted from August 1, 1979, to January 1980. She ran in the presidential race in 1986 with the support of the Democratic Renewal Party, but she angered Eanes by taking this step without his approval. The party subsequently split and she ran as an independent, receiving only 7.6 percent of the vote.

In 1989 she became a member of the World Policy Institute and in 1990 chairman of the Helsinki World Institute for Developing Economies Research. From 1992 to 1996 she was president of the Independent Committee on Population and the Quality of Life. In 1993–94 she was the chair of the Council of Europe's working group on Equality and Democracy. In 1996 she chaired the intergovernmental committee on social and civic rights of the European Commission. A devout Catholic, she continues to be active in church organizations, particularly those dealing with women's issues.

BIBLIOGRAPHY

Bruneau, Thomas C. *Politics and Nationhood: Post Revolutionary Portugal.* New York: Praeger, 1984.

Bruneau, Thomas C. and Alex MacLeod. *Politics in Contemporary Portugal: Parties and the Consolidation of Democracy.* Boulder, Col.: Westview Press, 1986.

Mattoso, José, ed. *História de Portugal.* 8 vols. Lisbon: Editorial Estampa, 1993–1994.

Maxwell, Kenneth. *The Making of Portuguese Democracy.* Cambridge: Cambridge University Press, 1995.

Bernard Cook

Pipa, Arshi (1920–97)

Albanian intellectual. Arshi Pipa was born in Shkodër in 1920. He received a doctorate in philosophy from the University of Florence. When Italy invaded Albania in 1939, Pipa and his brother Myzafer returned to their occupied country, where Pipa taught in a secondary school. After the war he was a founder of the Albanian League of Writers. He and his brother, however, were branded reactionaries by the Albanian Communist Party. His brother was publicly executed and Pipa was sentenced to jail in 1946 for opposing Stalinist "socialist realism," He spent years in prisons and labor camps until his release in 1955. While in prison he watched as fellow prisoners Vincenz Prenushi, a poet and archbishop of Shkodër, and Ndoc Nikaj, a novelist arrested at the age of eighty-six for allegedly attempting to overthrow the Communist regime, die in their cells. After his release Pipa fled to Italy and the United States, where he taught at Georgetown, Berkeley, and the University of Minnesota. In 1990 he founded the review *Albanian Literature.* Pipa returned to Albania for a visit after the fall of communism and was honored by the new political authorities, but returned to the United States. He died in Washington, D.C. in August 1997.

BIBLIOGRAPHY

"Obituary of Arshi Pipa." *Daily Telegraph,* August 28, 1997.

Bernard Cook

Pire, Dominique (1910–69)

Belgian winner of the 1958 Nobel Peace Prize for his assistance to displaced persons in Europe after the Second World War. Dominique Georges Henri Pire was born on February 10, 1910, in Dinant. He entered the Dominican priory of La Sarte at Huy in 1928 and was ordained in 1934. He received a doctorate in theology from the Angelicum, the Dominican university, in Rome in 1936. He then spent a year studying social and political science at the University of Louvain (Leuven). He taught ethics and sociology at La Sarte from 1937 to 1947. Pire simultaneously served as pastor in a parish with many poor agricultural laborers. In 1938 he set up an organization to assist poor children throughout Belgium.

Pire was active in the resistance to the German occupation in the Second World War. He was part of a network that helped Allied airmen escape and provided intelligence to the Allies. For his service during the war he received the Belgian War Cross with palms, the Metal of Resistance, and the Medal of National Reconnaissance. After the war he set up camps for French and Belgian refugee children. In 1949 he founded Aide aux Personnes Déplacées (Aid to Displaced Persons) to provide assistance and support to displaced persons regardless of nationality or creed. His particular concern was hard-core refugees from Eastern Europe who could not find host countries because of age, illness, or disabilities. In the early 1950s Pire established four homes in Belgium for elderly refugees. He also inspired the construction of seven European Villages for refugees in Belgium, Germany, and Austria. His plan was not to establish refugee ghettos but real communities attached to cities.

After receiving the Nobel prize, Pire established the Mahatma Gandhi International Peace Center, or the University of Peace, at Huy as a peace education center for young people. He also established World Friendships to foster interracial understanding and World Sponsorships to assist African and Asian refugees. Pire died at Leuven on January 30, 1969.

BIBLIOGRAPHY
Schuffenecker, Gerard. *Une Révolution tranquille.* Huy: Fondation Dominique Pire, 1979.

Bernard Cook

Pithart, Petr (1941–)

Czech historian, legal scholar, and politician. Petr Pithart was born in Kladno on January 2, 1941. He received a law degree from Charles University in Prague and taught there from 1964 to 1970. In 1969 and 1970 he studied at Oxford University. However, in the aftermath of the repression by the Warsaw Pact forces of the Prague Spring reform movement in 1968, he lost his university position and was forced to work as a laborer for two years before being allowed to practice law. He was a signer of Charter 77 (a document protesting human rights abuses in Czechoslovakia), and as a result was forced to earn a living as a gardener. He worked as a warehouse clerk from 1979 to 1989. He was a close and trusted political adviser of playwright and future president Václav Havel during the Velvet Revolution, and served as the spokesman for the Civic Forum. From February 2, 1990, to July 2, 1992, he was a deputy to the Czech National Council and served as prime minister of the Czech Republic, at that time one of the constituent republics of Czechoslovakia. He replaced František Pitra, a member of the former Communist regime who resigned the previous week. Pithart became an advocate of liberal foreign investment in Czechoslovakia. He believed that the country lacked the domestic capital to finance the privatization process and to reconstruct its sluggish and outmoded economy. In November 1996 he was elected to the Czech Senate and became its chairman. He resumed teaching at Charles University in the faculty of law in 1994.

BIBLIOGRAPHY
"Former Dissident Appointed As Leader of Czech Republic." *New York Times,* February 7, 1990.
Kamm, Henry. "Premier of Czechs Seeks U.S. Capital." *New York Times,* July 19, 1990.

Bernard Cook

Pius XII (1876–1958)

Roman Catholic pope (1939–58). Eugenio Pacelli was born in Rome in 1876. After ordination to the priesthood in 1899 he served with the Vatican's secretariat of state. He also taught canon law at the Ateneo del Seminario Romano and the Accademia dei Nobili Ecclesiastici. At the same time he collaborated with Cardinal Gasparri, the papal secretary of state, in the preparation of a new code of cannon law. During World War I (1914–18) Pacelli was appointed apostolic nuncio to Bavaria. In 1920 he became nuncio to Germany. Pacelli negotiated individual concordats with Bavaria, Prussia, and Baden that formalized the church's relationships with these states. Pacelli was named a cardinal in 1929 by Pope Pius XI (1922–39) and soon succeeded Gasparri as secretary of state. One of his primary objectives was to defend the church against the Nazis, and as part of his diplomacy, he negotiated a concordat with the Hitler regime in 1933.

After the death of Pius XI, Pacelli was elected pope on March 2, 1939, the second day of the conclave. His first preoccupation as pope was to avert war. At the beginning of May he attempted to intervene with the heads of state of major European powers. After the August Non-Aggression Pact between the USSR and Germany, he made a last appeal to European governments. Once war began in September 1939, Pius XII sought to limit the extension of the conflict, to assist its victims, and to reach a just peace. In his first encyclical, *Summi Pontificatus* of October 20, 1939, his insistence that states abide by natural law was a pointed reference to the German-Soviet invasion of Poland. In May 1940 his public appeals for peace in the name of moral and legal principles caused a protest from Italian dictator Benito Mussolini, to which the pope answered that he feared no retaliation.

Pius, from the pages of *L'Osservatore Romano,* the official Vatican newspaper, expressed his solidarity with the Netherlands, Belgium, and Luxembourg at the moment (1940) of their invasion by Germany and openly denounced German aggression. For its part, the Nazi regime's attitude, notwithstanding the concordat of 1933, had always been hostile to the Vatican. During the war the church always protested against German treatment of ecclesiastical authorities and of people in the occupied countries. The Holy See openly took positions against Nazi ideology and against its policies of euthanasia of the mentally ill and against forced sterilization. The pontiff also tried to mitigate the consequences of the conflict on civilians and to gather news about people in German and Russian concentration camps.

Pius XII worked to save not only Rome but other major cities from destruction during World War II. At the end of the war he prompted the organization of an active aid system, the Papal Welfare Organization (PAO) to help ex-servicemen, repatriates, and refugees. But diplomatically his postwar concerns centered on the Soviet Union's imperialistic aims. In a radio message as early as 1942, the pope had condemned Communist ideology.

The encyclical *Orientales omnes* of December 23, 1945, denounced the destruction of churches in Ruthenia, which the USSR had incorporated from Czechoslovakia. In the fall of 1946 the trial and imprisonment of Bishop Stepinać in Zagreb, Yugoslavia, capped a series of killings and deportations that hit Yugoslav clerics. In 1948 persecution of the Hungarian church culminated in the trial against Cardinal József Mindszenty. A decree of the Holy Office of July 1949 reiterated the errors of Marxist ideology and elaborated the contents of Catholic social doctrine.

Pius XII made important contributions to dogmatic teaching. A series of his encyclicals gave defined various doctrinal questions. Pius also emphasized ethical and legal aspects concerning the family, whose protection the church considered paramount for a society based on Christian values. The pope believed that the state had the obligation to eradicate poverty from society and give people access to personal property and real estate. He defended private property as a milestone of a good social order while criticizing the mistakes of both communism and capitalism.

During his pontificate the church hierarchy was expanded with the establishment of many new archibishoperics or bishoperics, especially in non-European countries. Pius XII died in 1958 after a pontificate of more than nineteen years. He was succeeded by John XXIII.

Almost a half-century after his death, Pius's historical reputation remains clouded by the controversy surrounding his actions during the Nazi's Holocaust against the Jews of Europe during World War II. His detractors assert that Pius failed to use the power of the papacy to publicly denounce the extermination of the Jews. Instead, they claim, he remained silent in order to protect the interests of the Roman Catholic church from retaliation by the Nazis. Pius's defenders point out that the pope worked tirelessly through many different channels, and that it fact was responsible for sheltering and saving the lives untold numbers Jews.

The dispute over Pius XII and the Jews is one facet of a wider issue of the church's historic relationship with the Jews—a problematic and painful issue that has dogged Roman Catholicism into the twenty-first century.

BIBLIOGRAPHY

Angelozzi Gariboldi, Giorgio. *Pio XII, Hitler e Mussolini: il Vaticano fra le dittaure.* Milan: Mursia, 1988.

Giordani, Igino. *Pio XII, un grande papa:* Turin: S.E.I, 1961.

Konopatzki, I. L. *Eugenio Pacelli-Pius XII. Kindheit und Jugend in Dokumenten.* Salzburg: A. Pustet, 1974.

Lichten, Joseph L. *Pio XII e gli ebrei: un contributo per la storia.* Bologna: Edizioni Dehoniane, 1988.

Pacelli, Eugenio. *Discorsi e panegirici (1931–1938).* Milan: Vita e Pensiero, 1938.

Pius XII. *Discorsi (dal marzo 1939 al maggio 1940).* Modena: Immacolata concezione, 1940.

———. *Discorsi e radiomessaggi . . . ,* Vols. 1–13. Milan: Vita e Pensiero, 1941–1946; Vatican City: Tipografia Poliglotta Vaticana, 1947–51.

Bernard Cook

SEE ALSO John XXIII; Mindszenty, József; Stepinac, Alojzije

Pivetti, Irene (1963–)

Speaker of the Italian parliament (1994–96). Irene Pivetti was born in Milan in 1963. Her father was a theater director and her mother an actress. She was educated at the Catholic University of the Sacred Heart in Milan. While at the university Pavetti, an ardent Catholic, founded Dialogue and Renovation, a Catholic activist movement. After graduation in 1986 she remained active in the group while working at a publishing house and editing Catholic newspapers and journals. She married economist Paolo Taranta in 1988, but they separated in 1992, and she obtained an ecclesiastical annulment.

Following the victory in November 1990 of the Lega Nord (Northern League) a regionalist party that advocated autonomy for Northern Italy, in a by-election, Pivetti wrote an analysis of the campaign and mailed it to Umberto Bossi, head of the league. He was so impressed that he initiated political conversations that led to her entry into the league. Pavetti was elected to parliament in 1992 as a representative of the league. In April 1994 she was elected president of the Chamber of Deputies (lower house of parliament), and in that position she presided over the parliamentary proceedings that resulted in the fall of Silvio Berlusconi's government in 1995, when the Northern League pulled out of the governing coalition.

In parliament she became an admirer of President Oscar Luigi Scalfaro. Inspired by him, she wished to re-create a party based on Roman Catholic values. Though that project failed to materialize, Pivetti was ousted by the Northern League for her critical opposition to Bossi's proposal to declare the independence of "Padania" (Northern Italy) on September 15, 1996. She organized a new party, Italia Federale (Federal Italy), to promote a federal reorganization of Italy but not secession. In October 1997 Pivetti married Alberto Brambilla, a university student who worked for the Fondazione San Michele, the cultural center of her new party.

Pavetti, an admirer of the late Archbishop Lefebvre, the excommunicated French prelate who defied the reforms of the Second Vatican Council, continues to promote a conservative Catholic perspective.

Bernard Cook

Pleven, René (1901–93)

French premier and advocate of an integrated Western European army. René Pleven was born in Rennes on April 15, 1901. He received a doctorate in law from the University of Paris then became an industrial executive. He entered politics during World War II when he joined Charles de Gaulle's Free French government in exile, where he served successively as commissioner of finance, of colonies, and of foreign affairs. In 1944 he became colonial minister in the French provisional government.

After the war, as finance minister in de Gaulle's cabinet, he pursued liberal economic policies to encourage investment, industrial modernization, and increased productivity. Following formation of de Gaulle's Rassemblement du Peuple Français (Rally of the French People, RPF) in April 1947, Pleven urged a rapprochement between the Third Force parties of the center and the Gaullist RPF. However, the leaders of the Third Force parties, who feared de Gaulle's ambitions, were skeptical and unmoved.

From 1946 to 1953 Pleven was president of the newly created, left-centered Union Démocratique et Socialiste de la Résistance (Democratic and Socialist Union of the Resistance, UDSR). He was twice minister of defense (1949–50, 1952–54) and twice premier (July 1950–February 1951, August 1951–January 1952). As premier Pleven assembled a Paris conference in July 1950 to advance his proposal, the Pleven Plan, which called for the establishment of the European Defense Community (EDC) with an integrated European army to unify North Atlantic and Western European defense under a single command. However, the United States call for the rearmament of the Federal Republic of Germany frightened the French public. Pleven tried to reassure his countrymen by proposing on October 24, 1950, the formation of a European army under a European defense minister supervised by a European assembly. The German military would exist only as part of a larger European military structure. Proponents considered the EDC a companion to the Schuman Plan to integrate West Germany into a Western European community. After initial doubts, the Western allies signed the treaty in May 1952. It was ratified by the Benelux countries and by Germany, but it was rejected by the French National Assembly on August 30, 1954.

After his premiership, Pleven held ministerial posts in several governments during the remaining years of the Fourth Republic, including foreign affairs in the last government of May 1958. That same year Pleven and François Mitterand fought for leadership of the UDSR, a rivalry that reflected the confusion and political fragmentation at the end of the Fourth Republic. Pleven broke away from the UDSR to support de Gaulle's constitution, which established the Fifth Republic. He formed a new party, the Union pour une Démocratie Moderne (Union for a Modern Democracy) in 1959. This party usually supported the Gaullist government, but in 1966 Pleven criticized de Gaulle in the Chamber of Deputies for withdrawing France from NATO's military command structure.

Following de Gaulle's retirement in 1969, Pleven served as justice minister during the ministries of Jacques Chaban-Delmas and Pierre Messmer, but he lost his seat in the Chamber of Deputies to a Socialist candidate in the 1973 elections. Though this ended his national career, Pleven continued to participate in local politics in Brittany until 1976. He died on January 13, 1993.

BIBLIOGRAPHY

Bougeard, Christian. *René Pleven: un français libre en politique.* Rennes: Presses universitaires de Rennes, 1994.

Lambert, Bruce. "René Pleven." *New York Times,* January 20, 1993.

Papiers René Pleven: 560 AP: inventaire. Paris: Archives Nationales, 1995.

Pleven, René. *L'Union européenne.* Lausanne: Fondation Jean Monnet pour L'Europe, Centre de Recherches Européennes, 1984.

Rioux, Jean-Pierre. *The Fourth Republic, 1944–1958.* Cambridge: Cambridge University Press, 1987.

Martin J. Manning

SEE ALSO De Gaulle Charles; Monnet, Jean; Schuman, Robert

Podgorny, Nikolay Viktorovich (1903–83)

Chairman of the Presidium of the Supreme Soviet and president of the Soviet Union (1965–77). A political client of Soviet Premier Nikita Khrushchev, Nikolay Podgorny became, along with Aleksey Kosygin and Leonid Brezhnev, a member of the "troika" that exercised political leadership in the post-Khrushchev years, after 1964. His fall in 1977 marked the end of collective leadership in the USSR.

Podgorny's career was unremarkable until 1944, when he supervised the repatriation of Ukrainians from Poland as the Red Army drove the Germans back and portions of Poland were incorporated into the USSR. He rose rapidly thereafter, becoming by 1957 first secretary of the Ukrainian Soviet Socialist Republic. He was elected to the Soviet Communist Party's Central Committee in 1956, named a candidate member of the Presidium in 1958, and became a full member in 1960. Podgorny entered the Secretariat in 1963 and was regarded as a possible successor to Khrushchev. In 1965, however, he was "demoted" to chairman of the Presidium and, thereby, titular president of the USSR. Podgorny was removed from the Secretariat in 1966. Most of his official functions were assumed by Brezhnev in 1972, and he was removed from the presidential office in 1977. While many details remain unclear, Podgorny's career is representative of the second generation of Soviet "technocrat" politicians.

BIBLIOGRAPHY

Hadnett, Grey. "Nikolai Podgorny," in *Soviet Leaders.* Ed. by George Simmons. New York: Thomas Y. Cromwell, 1967.

Loewenhardt, John, James R. Ozinga, and Eric van Ree. *The Rise and Fall of the Soviet Politburo.* New York: St. Martin's Press, 1972.

Timothy C. Dowling

SEE ALSO Brezhnev, Leonid; Khrushchev, Nikita

Poher, Alain (1909–96)

French politician. Poher Alain-Émile-Louis-Marie, son of a railroad worker, was born in Ablon-sur-Seine, a village near Paris, on April 17, 1909. After studying engineering, he began work as a lower-level civil servant. During the Second World War he earned the War Cross and the Resistance medal. After the Liberation from German occupation, Poher was elected mayor of Ablon-sur-Seine, a post he held for twenty-three years. He entered national politics in 1946, serving as chief of staff to Premier Robert Schuman and winning a seat in the Senate (upper house of parliament). He quit the Senate in 1948 to assume the first of a number of cabinet posts, among which were minister of budget and secretary of state for finance. Poher was reelected to the Senate in 1952. There he was a consistent supporter of European integration.

While Poher was president of the Senate from 1968 to 1992, he was twice called on to serve briefly as president of the Fifth French Republic. When Charles de Gaulle resigned the presidency following the electoral defeat of April 27, 1969, referendum, in which he proposed a change in the composition of the Senate, a reduction of its power, and the granting of greater regional autonomy, Poher as head of the Senate stepped in for seven weeks until the election of Georges Pompidou in June. When Pompidou died in April 1974, Poher again assumed the presidency for seven weeks until the election of Valéry Giscard d'Estaing. Poher retired from the Senate in 1995, having served there as a representative of the center-right Centrist Union bloc for forty-nine years.

Poher was also president of the European Parliament from 1966 to 1969. He died on December 9, 1996.

BIBLIOGRAPHY

"Alain Poher." *The Herald* (Glasgow), December 12, 1996.

Simons, Marlise. "Alain Poher." *New York Times,* December 11, 1996.

Bernard Cook

Poland

Country of 120,727 square miles (312,683 sq km) and 38.4 million inhabitants, formerly the largest country of Eastern Europe, but now surpassed by Ukraine both in

Poland. *Illustration courtesy of Bernard Cook.*

size and population. Poland's history has been greatly affected by its position between Germany and the former Soviet Union. It regained its independence only because of the debility of those two states at the end of World War I. It was partitioned by Germany and the USSR following the Nazi-Soviet Pact of August 23, 1939. The country suffered greatly during the Second World War, when it was divided between Germany and the USSR and pillaged by the Germans.

The Red Army liberated German-occupied Poland between July 1944 and April 1945. Yet the "liberators" soon became the next occupying army. At the Yalta Conference of February 1945, Roosevelt, Churchill, and Stalin decided that the eastern Polish border would lie on the Bug River and that former German territory would become the new western boundary of Poland. As a result of this the territory of the country shifted westward, and Poland lost the cities of Vilnius and Lvov. It was also agreed that postwar Polish elections would be conducted without international supervision. The field would be limited to democratic and anti-Nazi parties, but exactly what this meant was not specified. This in effect put Poland under Soviet control.

The Polish underground state, whose 800,000-person Home Army was the largest in occupied Europe in 1944, was systematically destroyed by the new authorities. Brutal pacification of civilians, deportations of Home Army soldiers to the Soviet Union, and mass arrests were only the initial stages of Soviet Poles strategy aimed at intimidating the nation. By the end of 1945 about 80,000 remained underground. Liquidation of partisan units, court-sanctioned executions, assassinations, and intimidation led, by 1947, to the disappearance of the armed underground and the end of the civil war between remnants of the Home Army and the Communist Security forces.

The Potsdam Conference in July 1945 assigned to "Polish administration" former German territories east of the Oder and Neisse Rivers, together with Gdansk (German, Danzig) and the southern part of East Prussia. The northern part of East Prussia with the major city of Königsberg was given to the USSR. Two to four million Germans fled these territories as the Red Army advanced in 1944 and 1945. The victorious allies decided at Potsdam to expel all ethnic Germans from these territories. This resulted in the displacement of 2.5 million Germans between 1945 and 1947.

Between 1945 and 1947, 480,000 Ukrainians, and 56,000 Belarussians and Lithuanians were moved from Polish territory to the USSR. In February 1946 the population of the new Poland was 23.9 million, whereas it had been 35 million within the Polish frontiers of 1939. By 1947, 1.8 million Poles had moved to Poland from the USSR and by 1950, 800,000 had returned from the West. In 1950 1.6 million Poles still remained in the USSR and around 500,000 in the West. In all, between 1944 and 1955, 7 million people had to relocate. In Poland there remained only 200,000 Germans, 150,000 Ukrainians, 100,000 Belarussians, and 80,000 Jewish Holocaust survivors. As of 1996, though Poland's population had grown to 38.4 million, these proportions, with the exception of a dramatic decrease in the Jewish population, have remained constant.

The war caused many Poles to hate Germans, and some Poles were anti-Semitic as well. The stereotype of the Jewish Communist was widespread. That accounts for the success of the Internal Security Office provocation in Kielce. On July 4, 1946, the secret police staged a pogrom in which forty Jews were killed. Anti-Jewish propaganda was used by the government in March 1968 to create the impression that protesting students were not Polish and therefore should be expelled from the country. Despite all this, the Communists were never able to create strong anti-Jewish organizations. In the 1990s organizations with anti-Jewish programs were so marginal that they were not able to secure a single local election victory. With time, hatred toward Germans has subsided. In 1965 Polish bishops began the process of reconciliation by sending a letter to German bishops stating: "We forgive and ask for forgiveness." On December 7, 1970, West German Chancellor Willy Brandt and Polish Prime Minister Józef Cyrankiewicz signed a treaty normalizing relations between Poland and Germany. From that date onward the government's propaganda apparatus could no longer successfully exploit a German threat. In the 1990s a reunited Germany became Poland's most important trade and political partner.

The Communists' push to take power in Poland severely limited the number and activities of political parties. The ruling Polish Workers (Communist) Party (PPR) also directed other parties that adopted the names of traditional parties: Peasant Movement (SL), Democratic Movement (SD), and Polish Socialist Party (PPS). The Christian Democratic Work Movement was legalized only after it incorporated a group loyal to the Communists. The Polish Peasant Movement (PSL), created on August 22, 1945, and led by Wincenty Witos and Stanisław Mikołajczyk, in January 1946 had 540,000 members and thus became the largest political party in Poland. In spite of this fact it was allotted only 52 seats in the 456-seat Polish National Council. From the very beginning, the Communists censored publications of the PSL, and their activists were persecuted or even murdered (e.g., the PSL secretary Bolesław Óciborek was murdered in December 1945).

The PPR wanted to test the functioning of the state apparatus and propaganda and police machinery before the first parliamentary elections. To do that, the PPR organized a popular referendum on June 30, 1946. The questions concerned abolition of the Senate, rural reform, nationalization of industry, and Poland's western border. A "yes" vote would mean agreement with Communist rule. Mikołajczyk's call to vote no to the first question was answered by 80 percent of voters, but the authorities claimed their victory by falsifying the results. Before the elections the internal security officers murdered 118 PSL activists. On January 19, 1947, falsified results again gave the PSL 28 seats and the bloc parties (PPR, PPS, SD and SL) 394 mandates. In October 1947 Mikołajczyk secretly left Poland.

The new, pro-Communist authorities of the PSL in 1949 united with the SL creating the United Peasant Movement (ZSL). In December 1948 the PPR and the PPS united to create the Polish United Workers (Communist) Party (PZPR). In 1950 the Communists dissolved the Christian Democratic Work Movement. A system of one ruling party—the Communists—with two satellite parties (ZSL and SD) was created.

After liquidation of private land ownership (holdings over 50 to 100 hectares, depending on the part of the country) and nationalization of industry in 1947, all private trade was liquidated. In 1948 collectivization of farming began. On July 22, 1948, after staged national discussions, parliament approved a new constitution of the Polish People's Republic that had earlier been approved by Soviet dictator Joseph Stalin.

The thaw in the Soviet Union following Stalin's death in 1953 allowed by 1954 some criticism of the apparatus of repression in Poland. This was encouraged by radio Free Europe, financed by the United States. The Polish thaw was expressed by the publication of critical works such as Adam Ważyk's *Poemat dla Doroslych* (*Poem for Adults*) in August 1955. Political conflicts after the Twentieth Party Congress of the Communist Party of the Soviet Union in 1956 and growing discontent articulated by Polish Communist Party revisionists led to unrest in October 1956. Władysław Gomułka, released from prison in December 1954, took control of the party.

The suppression in October 1957 of the weekly *Po Prostu* meant the end of liberalization. Gomułka purged the Communist Party and organized a new secret political police. In 1959 he launched a new wave of industrialization. While in the early 1950s the government had concentrated on heavy industry, especially for the military, Gomułka concentrated on developing extractive industries, brown coal, copper, and sulfur mines. In the 1960s women were integrated into the workforce; the growth in GNP, however, was fueled by low wages. Gomułka's rule was a period of stabilization through fulfilling human needs on a minimal level with low-quality products. Small apartments with windowless kitchens became a symbol of those times.

The canceling of performances of Adam Mickiewicz's (1798–1855) nationalist drama, *Dziady* (*Forefather's Eve*) on January 30, 1968, evoked student demonstrations in Warsaw. The biggest one took place on March 8 at Warsaw University. The demonstration was stopped by so-called "worker activists" armed and directed by the Ministry of Internal Affairs. However, the demand to democratize the Communist system spread to all universities.

Despite criticism by the Catholic Church, the authorities imprisoned students, dissolved six faculties of Warsaw University, and fired some professors, among them the philosopher Leszek Kolakowski, and forced about 30,000 people of Jewish origin to immigrate. Gomułka stayed in power thanks to the backing of Edward Gierek, a leader of the economic administrators, adopting anti-Jewish slogans and retaining the support of the USSR.

Lack of popular support for Gomułka, the growth of the GNP through reinvestment of profits at the expense of consumption, with a concomitant increase of time spent in lines to buy essential items and a lowering of living standards, led to protests when food prices increases were announced on December 13, 1970. The next day demonstrators at the Lenin Shipyard in Gdansk were fired upon by the secret police, and in the afternoon the crowd attacked the party building in Gdansk.

By the second evening there were two competing centers of party power: Gomułka's collaborators and supporters of Mieczysław Moczar, minister of the interior and leader of the "partisan" coterie rooted in the tradition of the People's Army of World War II. On the morning of December 15 Gomułka decided to use force to crush the demonstrations. On the same day the crowd, after fights with the police, set fire to the party building. Other factories in Gdansk joined the strike. There were also demonstrations in the nearby port of Gdynia. On the evening of December 16 Gomułka's supporters directed workers to stay home while Stanisław Kociołek, a technocratic manager allied to Moczar, called on them via local television to return to work.

On December 17 at the Gdynia-Stocznia train station, the army killed several dozen people going to work. Fights broke out in Gdynia. On the same day the first secretary of the local party committee, despite Gomułka's order to defend the party building, followed Gierek's orders to leave it and hide in the military barracks. By December 18 the biggest factories of the Baltic region were on strike, and the strike committee took over the port of Szczecin. In the evening an agreement between Gierek and Moczar to replace Gomułka was worked out.

On December 20, during the Seventh Plenum of the Communist Party, Gomułka resigned. Gierek became first secretary and in June 1971 he eliminated Moczar from the party leadership. To limit the authority of local party functionaries, Gierek abolished the county (powiaty) administrative districts, and on June 1, 1974, he established forty-nine provinces to replace the previous seventeen.

On January 1971 Gierek averted a new strike wave in Szczecin by promising to engage in discussion with the workers. His slogan and implied promise was "Will you help—we will help." Four days after the beginning of strikes in Lodz on February 11, the decision to raise food prices was revoked. Gierek initiated a so-called "big leap" based on investments financed with Western credits. At the same time, the consumption level was kept relatively high. Salary increases led to increased demand for meat products. Discrimination against private farming, and an increase in feed imported for collective farms tremendously increased production costs. The cost increases combined with the system of state-regulated prices then led to meat shortages.

The threat of price increases led to many strikes, and in several cities to street demonstrations in June 1976. In the evening of June 25, Premier Piotr Jaroszewicz withdrew consideration of the projected price increases from the Sjemt (parliament). Protesters were threatened. The Communist Party organized rallies condemning the anti-price-rise demonstrations, and arrests, summary trails, and firings from work.

After the June events, dissenters decided to defend workers. On September 23, 1976, Jacek Kuron, a dissident leftist arrested in 1967 for advocating democratic socialism, together with twelve other people founded the Workers' Defense Committee (KOR). KOR activists believed in self-organization by the members of society. They supported publishing activities of independent publishers, the Society for Scholarly Courses founded in January 1978, the Independent Labor Unions founded in February 1978 in Katowice and in April 1978 in Gdansk, and the Students' Solidarity Committee founded on May 15, 1978, after a student Stanisław Pyjas, a KOR supported, was killed in Kraków, a murder many blamed on the secret police. On September 1, 1979, an illegal independent right-wing political party, the Confederation for Independent Poland (KPN), led by Leszek Moczulski was founded.

The pontificate of Karol Cardinal Wojtyla of Kraków, who became Pope John Paul II, the first Polish Pope on October 16, 1978, and his pilgrimage to his native Poland in June 1979 was a boost to the morale of Polish Catholics.

Growing internal fights resulting in Jaroszewicz's resignation from the premiership in February 1980 weakened Gierek's position. After the outbreak of two, he was removed as first secretary on September 6, 1980. Despite personnel changes and the pledge of the new secretary, Stanisław Kania, to carry out the agreements made with the strikers led by the electrician Lech Wałesa, the PZPR could not coexist with the independent Solidarity. Agreements signed between Solidarity and party cells in large factories and universities did not overcome the opposition of conservative party functionaries.

The culminating moment of social mobilization came in March 1981, when, after 200 police stormed the prefecture at Bydgoszcz and clubbed workers, over 80 percent of the nation's workforce were ready to participate in a general strike. Among the party elite there was a clash between two factions: the pragmatic so-called liberal one centering around Kania and the army led by General Wojciech Jaruzelski, the minister of defense, and the hardliners directed by Stefan Olszowski. The latter pushed for Soviet intervention, while the former wanted to defeat the growing opposition by introducing martial law. On December 13, 1981, Jaruzelski who became premier on February 11, 1981, and first secretary of the Communist Party on December 15, imposed martial law.

This decision and its consequences, including the shooting of workers at the Wijek coal mine who were striking in protest against the Suppression & Solidarity and a number of Solidarity activists, divided Poland into a small minority supporting the Communist Party leadership and the so-called underground society convinced of the necessity for changes. After 1982 social protests diminished but the degree of alienation from the political system remained unchanged. The murder of Father Jerzy Popieluszko by secret police officers on October 19, 1984, resulted in support for the underground organizations by the Catholic Church. Discovering the murderers and their conviction in 1985 allowed Jaruzelski to remove leaders of the faction opposed to him without arousing the ire of the Soviet Union.

Between 1982 and 1987 the GNP, according to official statistics, went up by 15 percent but was still lower than in 1978. There were no new credits available, ecological devastation of the country increased, the rural population was becoming smaller and older, and the number of people awaiting a new apartment increased by an additional 500,000. About 250,000 Poles emigrated during this period. Basic goods were rationed and others were not available at all.

The carefully prepared Round Table talks between representatives of the Communist government and of the outlawed union, Solidarity, resulted in the signing of an agreement on April 5, 1989, legalizing Solidarity. Parliamentary elections held on June 4, 1989 brought victory to Solidarity electoral committees, winning all of the 161 seats they were allowed to contest in the lower house, the Sejm (65 percent were reserved for the Communist Party), and all but 1 of the 100 seats in the new upper house, the Senate. The PZPR was not able to form a government. In the beginning of July 1989 the historian, journalist, and former dissident, Adam Michnik, published an article, "Your President our Premier," in the first Polish independent daily *Gazeta Wyborcza,* which he edited. A compromise led to the installing of Jaruzelski as president and Tadeusz Mazowiecki a Catholic intellectual and advisor of Solidarity as premier on August 24, 1989.

The Deputy Premier and Finance Minister Leszek Balcerowicz took steps to slow down hyperinflation, created monthly state budgets, and prepared economic reforms. Besides allowing individual citizens to establish enterprises, he introduced interest on credit above the expected inflation rate, tied the value of the Polish zloty to the U.S. dollar, limited subsidies for coal and gasoline, and initiated the privatization of state-owned enterprises. Factories began to base their production and employment on market demand. Unemployment became common (three million workers at its peak in 1994), disparity of income grew, but inflation fell from 76 percent in January 1990 to 6 percent in March.

On December 29, 1989, parliament changed the name of the country from People's Republic of Poland to Polish Republic and described it in the constitution as a democracy in which supreme power belonged to the nation, not as in the Communist constitution to to the working masses. The article on the leading role of the Communist Party and Poland's alliance with the USSR was removed. These constitutional changes became a symbolic expression of Poland's struggle for complete independence and the desire to create a democratic political system.

The fall of communism in Europe brought improved possibilities to Polish foreign policy. A treaty between Poland and a reunified Germany was signed on November 14, 1990; it finally confirmed Poland's western borders on the Oder and Neisse (Polish, Nysa) Rivers. In April 1990 the Soviet government finally admitted that the Katyn Forest massacre of World War II was perpetrated by the NKVD (secret police). On September 17, 1993, the last Russian troops withdrew from Poland. In May 1991 President Lech Wałesa asked in the Israeli parliament, the Kneset, for forgiveness for each act of violence against Jews committed by Poles. Since 1994, Poland has signed friendship and co-operation agreements with its seven neighbors. Poland became a member of NATO on March 12, 1999 and wants to join the European Union (EU), of which it became a candidate member in 1999. At the same time Poland has co-authored regional agreements with the Czech Republic, Hungary, and Slovakia and supports free trade in central Europe.

A multiparty system is slowly emerging. Elections held on May 27, 1990, established elected local governments on the county level. On December 9, 1990, Lech Wałesa was elected in the second round of presidential elections. Tadeusz Mazowiecki, who had opposed Wałesa's candidacy, and desired a more gradual process of privatization, resigned as premier in January 1991 and was succeeded by a free-market liberal, Jan Krzysztof Bielecki. On October 27, 1991, the first truly free parliamentary elections took place. Twenty-nine political parties and factions were represented in the new parliament. After two month of negotiations, a coalition government was formed with Jan Olszewski, a lawyer who had defended dissidents under the Communist regime, as premier. On June 4, 1992, after Olszewski's conflict with Wałesa over the control over the army, the process of decommunization, and the initiation of legal proceedings against members of the former Communist leadership, his government fell, repudiated by the Sejm.

On July 10, 1992, parliament asked Hanna Suchocka from the Democratic Union to form a new government. On October 17, 1992, a temporary constitution was voted into existence. It defined the authority of the president, comparable to the French model, the Council of Ministers, the National Assembly, and local governments. Work on a new constitution began in 1994 and it went into effect in October 1997.

BIBLIOGRAPHY

Davies, Norman. *God's Playground: A History of Poland,* Vol. 2, *1795 to the Present.* Oxford: Oxford University Press, 1981.

Kaminski, Bartlomiej. *The Collapse of State Socialism: The Case of Poland.* Princeton, N.J.: Princeton University Press, 1991.

Ost, David. *Solidarity and the Politics of Anti-Politics: Opposition and Reform in Poland Since 1968.* Philadelphia: Temple University Press, 1990.

Raina, Peter K. *Political Opposition in Poland 1955–1977.* London: Poets' and Painters' Press, 1978.

Roman Bäcker

Polish Question

At the major conferences of the Big Three (Great Britain United States, USSR) that led the coalition against Nazi Germany during World War II, the boundaries of Poland and its place in Europe, and consequently the postwar political system of the country, were decided. Soviet territorial and ethnic aspirations did not arouse much resistance from the Allies, nor did the eastern border of Poland desired by Stalin.

The fate of Poland was determined at the Teheran Conference of November 28–December 1, 1943. By agreeing to a second front in Western Europe, the Allies assured that Poland and other countries of central and Eastern Europe would come under the domination of the Soviet Union. Premier Stalin, Prime Minister Churchill, and President Roosevelt assumed that conditions of the postwar peace treaty would be defined by the Big Three alone. In a top secret resolution they agreed that the postwar territory of Poland would stretch from the so-called Curzon line in the east to the Oder (Polish, Odra) River in the west. To compensate Poland for its lost territory, it was to be given Opole Silesia and Eastern Prussia, which were part of Hitler's Reich.

Soon afterward Stalin revised the Curzon line to Poland's advantage the cities of Białystok, Łomża, and Przemyśl were to be left within Poland, but Vilnius and Lvov (Polish, Lwów) were to be incorporated into the Soviet state. In accord with the secret amendment imposed on the Polish Committee for the National Liberation on July 26, 1944, the general resolution of Teheran for the western border was specified to be the Oder and Neisse (Polish, Nysa Łużycka Rivers). The former German cities of Stettin (Szczecin), Swinemünde (Świnoujście), and Breslau (Wrocław) were to be on the Polish side.

At the Yalta Conference (February 4–11, 1945), Roosevelt and Churchill agreed to the demands of Stalin. The eastern border of Poland followed the Curzon line with a slight deviation to Poland's advantage. The western border was to be decided definitively only at the peace conference. Adjustments were made so that the new Polish Provisional Government of National Unity could be approved by the three powers. Stalin and his foreign minister, Vyacheslav Molotov, suggested that the provisional government, which had operated in Poland since 1944, would be "democratically organized with the contribution of all democratic leaders in the country and abroad." The government was obliged to "carry out, as soon as possible, free general elections based on a general ballot." All democratic and anti-Nazi parties were to be allowed to field candidates.

At the Potsdam Conference (July 17–August 2, 1945), Stalin, President Harry Truman, and Prime Minister Clement Attlee recognized the Provisional Government of National Unity formed in Moscow on June 21, 1945. The Curzon line had been accepted but the definitive determination of the western border was again postponed until the peace treaty. For the time being German territories east of the Oder and Neisse Rivers were to be "the protectorate of the Polish state." The former free city of Gdansk (German, Danzig) and part of German East Prussia were incorporated into Poland. Despite the temporary protectorate status, the German population was expelled by the Red Army from East Prussia and by the Poles from the western border transferred to Poland and German property was claimed as reparations by both the Soviets in the northern section of East Prussia and by the Poles elsewhere.

BIBLIOGRAPHY

Churchill, Winston. *The Second World War,* Vol. 5, *Closing the Ring* (1951); Vol. 6, *Triumph and Tragedy.* Cambridge, Mass.: Houghton Mifflin, 1953.

Feis Herbert. *Between War and Peace: The Potsdam Conference.* Princeton N.J.: Princeton University Press, 1960.

Kersten, Krystyna. *Jalta w polskiej perspektywie.* London: Ameks, 1989.

Rozek, Edward. *Allied Wartime Diplomacy: A Pattern in Poland.* Boulder, Col.: Westview Press, 1989.

Woodward, Lewellyn. *British Foreign Policy in the Second World War,* Vols. 1–5. London: H.M. Stationery Office. 1970.

Ryszard Sudziński

Censorship

In Poland and other Eastern European countries after World War II, institutionalized control of expression was introduced as they fell under Soviet influence. In Poland the first Department of Censorship was organized by the pro-Soviet Polish Committee of National Liberation in August 1944, then transformed into the Main Office for the Control of Press, Publications, and Public Performances in July 1945. The socialist state, controlled by the Communist Party, used censorship systematically to combat political opponents, support ideological objectives, and manipulate society. Censorship in Poland had a mostly preventive character, operated beyond societal control, and involved almost everything: printed matter, television, radio, all kinds of performances, exhibitions, motion pictures; even mimic performances, personal cards, match boxes, obituaries, and comics were strictly controlled. Censorship was facilitated by nationalization of television, radio, printing offices, paper factories, publishing houses, and networks of distribution. Ubiquitous state censorship generated an interesting phenomenon, self-censorship. Many authors, to avoid the repression of censorship, tried to anticipate its interventions and censored their own works themselves. Other authors strove to "cheat" the system by using subtle hints and metaphors instead of explicit statements. Censorship led to independent underground publishing, the so-called second circulation, particularly popular and strong after 1976, when the Workers Defense Committee (KOR) was established. After the first half-free election in 1989, which brought the defeat of the Communist Party, censorship became weak and powerless and was definitively eliminated in April 1990.

BIBLIOGRAPHY

Bagilski, Kazimierz. *Cenzura w Polsce.* Warsaw: Nowa, 1981.

Curry, Jane. *The Black Book of Polish Censorship.* New York: Random House, 1984.

Drygalski, Jerzy, and Jacek Kwalniewski. *(Nie)realny socjalizm.* Warsaw: PIECHUR, 1988.

Kostecki, Janusz, and Alina Brodzka, eds. *Pilmiennictwo—systemy kontroli—obiegi alternatywne.* Warsaw: Biblioteka Narodowa, 1992.

Peleg, Ilan. *Patterns of Censorship around the World.* Boulder, CO: Westview Press, 1993.

Schopflin, George. *Censorship and Political Communication in Eastern Europe:* A Collection of Documents. London: Pinter, 1983.

Krzysztof Olechnicki

October 1956

Period of mass social protest in Poland tied to changes in the policy of the United Polish Workers (Communist) Party, as well as radical changes in its ranks. The main actors of the October events were two factions in the leadership of the party: the neo-Stalinist "Natolinians" (named after chateau, Natolin, where they met) and the more flexible and responsive "Puławians" (named after the Puław district), or revisionists or proponents of a democratic form of socialism, drawn from young party activists from the universities, big factories, and theoretical journals, especially *Po Prostu.*

On June 28, 1956, a strike began in Poznan. Its slogan was "bread and freedom," and it soon produced street demonstrations that were bloodily suppressed by the militia and the army. This led to a radicalization of the young revisionists. They began to establish workers' councils that were taking over power in factories. The first one was at the auto factory at Żerań outside Warsaw. In the tension created by the threat of Soviet intervention and the threat of a coup d'état by the "Natolinians," the Eighth Plenum of the party's Central Committee on October 19 elected Władisław Gomułka as candidate for first secretary.

Nikita Krushchev, the Soviet first secretary and much of the Soviet leadership flew to Warsaw on October 19 to try to bring the Poles in line. Krushchev withdrew Soviet troops concentrated around Warsaw. On the next day Edward Ochab resigned as first secretary and head of state and Gomułka, thanks to the "Puławians" support, was elected his successor as first secretary, the post in which power resided. In his inaugural address Gomułka criticized the lack of economic reality of Poland's six year plan, reliance on outdated technology, and the decline of productivity to pre-1918 levels. According to him the Poznan events were not an act of sabotage but legitimate workers' protests against distortions of socialism. He denounced the cult of personality and promised to separate the administration of the state from the direct control of the party to base Polish-Soviet relations on the principle of sovereignty, and to introduce workers' co-management of factories and the freedom to farm privately for individual farmers. The last promise was an attempt to sanction the process of dissolving previously forced food production cooperatives. Out of 10,510 cooperatives registered on September 30, 1956, there were only 1,534 by December 31. At the same time peasants failed to deliver 40 percent of their compulsory quota and 20 percent of their taxes.

Unrest continued in cities and towns across the land. Demonstrators showed support for the new party leadership and elected new local authorities while demanding democratization of the political system. On October 24, during a rally of about four-hundred thousand in Warsaw, Gomułka called for return to work. Gomułka restored the freedom of the Catholic Church to appoint bishops and gave the church the right to provide religious instruction in state schools. He also allowed limited representation for Catholics in the Sejm (parliament). In elections of January 1957, it was still possible to present personal views, but it was becoming apparent that the degree of freedom achieved in October 1956 was being limited. The closing of *Po Prostu* by the authorities on October 2, 1957, symbolized the end of the October reforms.

BIBLIOGRAPHY

Hiscocks, Richard. *Poland: Bridge for the Abyss?* London: Oxford University Press, 1963.

Syrop, Konrad. *Spring in October: The Polish Revolution of 1956.* London: Weidenfield and Nicholson, 1957.

Zinner, Paul E. *National Communism and Popular Revolt in Eastern Europe: A Selection of Documents on Events in Poland and Hungary February-November 1956.* New York: Columbia University Press, 1956.

Roman Bäcker

SEE ALSO Gomułka, Władisław; Ochab, Edward

March 1968

Political crisis from fall 1967 until spring 1968, that involved a conflict between the Communist Party and elements of society opposing its rule, with an attempted coup d'état by forces opposed to the rule of Władysław Gomułka, the first secretary of the United Polish Workers Party (Communist Party).

The events were triggered by popular dissatisfaction with unfulfilled promises and hopes in the wake of the political crisis of 1956. This dissatisfaction was spurred by the subsequent limitation of concessions that had been wrested from the government in 1956 (workers' councils, freedom of speech, lessening of censorship) and the return to authoritarian methods of governing as well as government action against pro-reform intellectual elites who were accused by the party of revisionism.

Using Polish-Soviet relations as a pretext to attack the intelligentsia, party leaders associated with Gomułka suppressed a performance of Adam Mickiewicz's *Dziady* (*Forefathers*) that, they claimed, was "anti-Russian and full of religion." This provoked student demonstrations and protests by literary circles. The high point of the protest took place in March 1968 at Warsaw University. Demonstrators were eventually arrested, expelled from the university, and tried for political offenses.

During a March 28 protest at the university, a "Declaration of the Students' Movement" was disseminated and approved by a student assembly. The declaration asserted the right to organize; demanded the end to preemptive censorship; and called for openness in economic life, democratic control over the authorities, extending the authority of parliament, constitutional guarantees of the basic rights of citizen, creation of a constitutional tribunal, and independence of the courts. These were the most radical political demands formulated during Communist rule in Poland. Yet they were of importance to student and intellectual circles only. For workers the basic issue was improvement of living conditions.

In addition to this discontent there was also a struggle within the government elite, between Gomułka and his people and the party group of the so-called "partisans" gathered around security police general Mieczysław Moczar. Moczar combined patriotic phraseology with an anti-Jewish campaign, skillfully egging on the students who were to be used as a force to overthrow Gomułka. The anti-Semitic campaign resulted in the expulsion from Poland of about two hundred thousand individuals of Jewish descent, especially political activists and intellectuals. It was implied by the "partisans" that Jews were responsible for the repression of the Stalinists era. Polish society, however, remained indifferent to the inner-party conflicts, not understanding the ramifications of the conflicts that were taking place.

Gomułka, although married to a Jew, went along with the anti-Semitic campaign and received renewed Soviet moral support for his assistance in their campaign against the process of liberalization in Czechoslovakia against Alexander Dubček's "Prague Spring." Despite the opposition of Moczar, Edward Gierek, and their backers, he was subsequently reelected leader of the party. Yet, he was a spent force whose ouster was delayed only to December 1970.

The events of 1968 were a decisive turning point for the Polish intelligentsia. After 1968 they no longer believed that the Communist system could be democratized and transformed. The hopes of reform rooted in the concessions of Gomułka in 1956 were destroyed.

BIBLIOGRAPHY

Checinski, Michael. *Poland, Communism, Nationalism, Anti-Semitism.* New York: Karz-Cohl, 1982.

Lendvai, Paul. *Anti-Semitism Without Jews: Communist Eastern Europe.* Garden City, New York: Doubleday 1971.

Raina, Peter. *Political Opposition in Poland 1954–1977.* London: Poets and Painters Press, 1978.

Stokes, Gale. *The Walls Came Tumbling Down: The Collapse of Communism in Eastern Europe.* New York: Oxford University Press, 1993.

Ryszard Sudziński

SEE ALSO Gomułka, Władysław

December 1970

Political crisis that took place on December 14–20, 1970. It began with a protest by workers against sharp food price increases, but it was used as a pretext by a group of leading Communists headed by Mieczysław Moczar, head of the security police, and Edward Gierek, the party secretary in the industrial region of Upper Silesia to remove Władysław Gomułka and his supporters from power within the Communist Party.

The authorities used the favorable occasion of the signing of a treaty with West Germany recognizing the western boundaries of Poland established at Potsdam to introduce food price hikes. These increases caused strikes and demonstrations. Escalation of the unrest, including the burning of the Communist Party headquarters in Gdansk and the looting of shops, was fueled by the elements in the police and party that hoped to bring about the removal of Gomułka. On December 15, police opened fire on workers in Gdansk, and the next day Gomułka ordered the use of fire arms against workers who had "betrayed People's Poland." To obscure the real cause of the events and to cloud responsibility for the repression, independently operating command centers were set up in the areas of unrest. The dispersal of authority led, among other things, to a massacre on December 17 of shipyard workers in Gdynia who were on their way to work. Besides in Gdansk and Gdynia, riots took place in Szczecin, Słupsk, and Elbląg. Some 27,000 soldiers, 550 tanks, 750 armed personnel carriers, 2,100 trucks, 108 planes and helicopters, and 40 ships were used to restore "law and order" in the Baltic region. According to official statistics, 45 people were killed and 1,165 wounded.

After intense intrigue within the party and after the support of the Kremlin was withdrawn in a December 18 letter, Gomułka resigned as first secretary on December 20 and Gierek took his place.

BIBLIOGRAPHY

Cescherson, Neal. *The Polish August.* New York: Penguin, 1982.

Domanski, Pawel, ed. *Tajne dokumenty Biura Politycznego: Grudzień 1970.* London: Aneks, 1991.

Ryszard Sudziński

SEE ALSO Gierek, Edward; Gomułka, Władysław

Workers Defense Committee (KOR)

Opposition organization founded in 1976 in Poland. The direct impulse for its foundation was government repression of workers who participated in protests over the increase in food prices in Radom and Ursus. KOR was founded on July 17, 1976, the day when trials of those arrested for strikes in the Ursus factory began. On September 23 the founders sent an open letter to the Polish parliament informing its members that the committee had been founded.

The committee sought to organize collective assistance for repressed workers, to criticize and discredit the party-government authorities through petitions and protest letters, and to collect and disseminate uncensored information. There were also attempts to create independent organizations among the workers, the peasants, and the intelligentsia.

On July 19, 1977, owing to increasing protests organized by KOR, an amnesty for all convicted in the Radom and Ursus trials was announced. Even though it seemed that the main aim of the organization had been achieved, its members decided to widen KOR's program and transform it into an institution to defend human and citizen rights. It also changed its name to the Committee for the Self-Defense of the Workers (KSS KOR). The new organization focused on fighting against political repression and working for a reform of the system so that citizens' rights and freedoms would be guaranteed institutionally.

KOR established its own publishing house, NOWA. By publishing papers, pamphlets, and books, KOR tried to overcome the state monopoly on information. The intervention office of KSS KOR played the important role of verifying and documenting cases of people who were in conflict with the authorities and intervening on their behalf, mainly through legal and financial aid.

On January 22, 1978, inspired by KSS KOR, the Society for Scholarly Courses was founded. Its members were prominent representatives of the world of culture and science who sought the end of censorship. In the beginning of 1978, KSS KOR activists established free labor unions. In August 1979 the KSS KOR magazine, *Robotnik* (*Worker*), published a Charter of Workers' Rights. The program included workers' demands and identified possible forms of protest. KSS KOR was also involved in creating independent farmers' unions.

KSS KOR's activities increased during the wave of strikes in August 1980, precipitated by a conjuncture of an increase in the price of meat and the firing by the Lenin Shipyard in Gdansk of a popular activist, when it added demands for political reforms to workers' economic demands. After the agreements between the Communist state authorities and the Interfactory Strike Committee (MKS) set up by Lech Wałęsa and the other leaders of the August strikes, were signed, KSS KOR activists, who had held advisory functions and had organized publishing and financial help, began to organize branches of the independent labor union that was formed by the MKS during the August strikes. On September 28, 1981, during the first Solidarity congress in Gdansk, the oldest

KOR member, Edward Lipinski, recalled the history of the organization and announced its self-dissolution. Most KOR members then joined Solidarity.

The total number of KOR members was thirty-eight. The founders and main activists included Jerzy Andrzejewski, Stanisław Baranczak, Ludwik Cohn, Leszek Kolakowski, Jacek Kuroń, Edward Lipinski, Jan Józef Lipski, Jan Litynski, Antoni Maciarewicz, Adam Michnik, Piotr Naimski, and Henryk Wujec.

BIBLIOGRAPHY

Lipski, Jan Józef. *KOR: A History of the Workers' Defense Committee in Poland, 1976–1981.* Tr. by Olga Amsterdamska and Gene M. Moore. Berkeley: University of California Press, 1985.

Stokes, Gale. *The Walls Came Tumbling Down: The Collapse of Communism in Eastern Europe.* New York: Oxford University Press, 1993.

Zuzowski, Robert. *Political Dissent and Opposition in Poland: The Workers' Defense Committee "KOR."* Westport, Conn.: Praeger, 1992.

Adam Zdunek

August 1980

Period of social protest that led to the creation of the Solidarity labor union and ultimately to the collapse of communism in Poland. The developments of August 1980 were caused by an economic crisis, the widespread hope for a better life evoked by John Paul II's first pilgrimage to Poland in 1979, internal fights within the Communist Party, and the existence of organized opposition to the party.

The first wave of protests began on July 1, 1980, and continued until August 15. Workers' demands were mainly centered on welfare issues. The strikes began because of a price increase for meat at the Warsaw Ursus Tractor Factory canteen. Strikes in Świdnik soon spread to Lublin, where railroad employees joined in. By the end of July work stoppages took place in Wrocław, Świdnica, Stalowa Wola, Poznań and many other cities. According to official statistics, 82,000 people in 177 factories were on strike in July alone. In the beginning of August strikes spread to Lodz; on August 14 the sit-down strike at the Gdansk shipyard began. Sympathy or solidarity strikes of public transport workers began in Gdansk on August 16. These initiated the second stage of the August protests—the formation by workers of a number of centers of coordinated activity. This phase continued until September 3. As the strikes progressed centers for solidarity and coordination were created. These provided organizational and symbolic unity and pushed for the formulation of common political demands. A central role was played by worker crews dominated by young, educated workers, many of whom were radical in their outlook and inspired by democratic values.

On August 16 the Interfactory Strike Committee (ISC) led by Lech Wałęsa was created. On the same day it formulated twenty-one demands, the most important of which called for labor unions independent of party and state. There were also demands for the right to strike, freedom of speech and press, release of political prisoners and reinstatement of those fired after the strikes. The economic demands included free Saturdays, pay increases, and automatic cost-of-living adjustments. On August 18 similar demands were issued by the strike committee in Szczecin.

Edward Gierek, first secretary of the party, in a TV speech rejected the workers' political demands. At the same time he sent Deputy Premier Tadeusz Pyka to Gdansk to mediate the ending of strikes in return for economic concessions. In Gdansk the ISC, however, broke off the talks after some opposition leaders were arrested. On August 21 a new government commission was sent to the tricity region of Gdansk, Gdynia, and Sepet. On August 24 Catholic activists led by Tadeusz Mazowiecki and lectures of the so-called "flying university" led by Bronisław Geremek joined striking workers in Gdansk. They established a commission of experts to assist the ISC. On the same day, the Fourth Party Plenum removed many of Gierek's supporters from power, accepted talks with striking workers, but established a military headquarters to prepare for the suppression of the strikes.

After August 20 solidarity strikes intensified through the country. Strike centers in Elbląg and Wrocław issued their own demands and continued to strike in support of Gdansk demands. An ISC founded in Jastrzębie on August 29 added to the Gdansk demands specific issues associated with the situation in the mining industry. According to official statistics, 700,000 people participated in strikes in 750 factories located in all 49 Polish provinces. The Baltic region, Upper Silesia, Wrocław, Kraków, Warsaw, and Toruń experienced the most intensive strikes.

On August 30 Barcikowski's commission signed an agreement with the Szczecin ISC, and on the next day a similar agreement was signed in Gdansk. In return for confirmation of "the Party's leading role," the ISCs became founding committees of new "independent and self-governing labor unions." Agreements with the ISC in Jastrzębie were signed on September 3. The signing of August-September agreements launched a new phase in the history of communism. For the first time, ruling

Communist parties admitted that the claim of official, party-sponsored unions to represent the workers was hollow. That brought in question the whole ideological basis of the system. However, the party leadership was forced to choose between bloody intervention by Soviet-led Warsaw Pact troops or agree to worker demands with stipulations that buttressed the party's role. To limit the importance of the systemic concessions, the party tried to personalize the accusations contained in the demands of striking workers. On September 6 the party removed Gierek and many of his supporters from their posts. But this did not quell the disturbances.

From the very signing of the agreements, the third phase of the strike process began and was completed at the beginning of October. During this period strikes began to break out in medium-sized and small factories in provinces that had only small concentrations of heavy industry. These areas were characterized by a strong and autonomous party-state apparatus. Strikes usually broke out there because local authorities did not respect the August-September agreements. In September about one million workers in eight hundred factories were on strike.

August 1980 became a symbolic month in the Polish tradition of protest against Communist rule. It initiated the process of questioning the bases of Polish society, and created a new political situation involving conflict between the party and Solidarity.

BIBLIOGRAPHY

de Weyenthal, Jan B., et. al. *August 1980: the Strikes in Poland.* Munich: Radio Free Europe Research, 1980.

de Weyenthal, Jan B. "Workers and Party in Poland." *Problems of Communism.* (November–December 1980): 1–22.

Sabbat, Anna, and Roman Stefanowski. "Poland: A Chronology of Events, July-November 1980." RAD Background Report 91 (Poland), *Radio Free Europa Research,* March 31, 1981.

Roman Bäcker

SEE ALSO Geremek, Bronislaw; Gierek, Edward; Mazowiecki, Tadeusz; Wałęsa, Lech

Solidarity

Independent Polish labor union, established in 1980. This independent, mass, antitotalitarian social movement was outlawed on December 13, 1981, but re-legalized in April 1989. It spearheaded the transformation of Poland to a non-Communist society.

Solidarity was able to develop as a result of an agreement signed with the Polish government after strikes in August–September 1980 along the Baltic coast and in Upper Silesia. In September 1980 representatives of spontaneously formed interfactory committees and interenterprise workers' councils followed the advice of lawyer Jan Olszewski to register all these committees as a single labor union. The name was suggested by "solidarność" Wrocław historian and former political prisoner Karol Modzelewski. The union was organized into a federal system based on regions. Lech Wałęsa, an electrician, supported by a group of advisers from the Catholic intelligentsia and the lay left—the Workers Defense Committee (KOR)—became head of the National Coordination Board. Until the end of 1980 organizations were set up in factories and nearly all other institutions except the Citizens' Militia and army.

Supporters of presidential candidate Lech Wałęsa wave a Solidarity banner outside his campaign headquarters on the eve of his election as president of Poland (December 1990). *Illustration courtesy Reuters/Mascierzynski/ Archive Photos.*

Nearly ten million wage earners, about 80 percent of the employed population, joined Solidarity. At this time the Polish people enjoyed freedom of thought and discussion stimulated by a spontaneously emerging independent press. Their main instrument of pressure was the strike. Human dignity, democratic self-government, and revival of national traditions were the basic goals of this movement. Such a vast independent social movement threatened the existence of the state-party machinery. That is why it had to be destroyed or at least split and incapacitated. The means to achieve this were constantly provoked clashes to show the fruitlessness of sit-in strikes and other disturbances. The result was a general mood of fatigue, apathy, and helplessness.

On October 24, 1980, the Warsaw District Court registered the Solidarity union but inserted a paragraph asserting the party's leading role and revoked the right to strike. The negotiations that followed this assertion resulted in a compromise. On November 10 the Supreme Court removed the offensive amendments that the District Court had inserted. However, part of the Gdansk Agreement, negotiated by representatives of the Interfactory Strike Committee and the government on August 31, 1980 in Gdansk, which stated that the new union would recognize the leading role of the Communist Party, was included in the form of an appendix. After the statutes had been registered, the regions canceled a planned "step-by-step" general strike.

On December 10 the National Coordinating Committee of Solidarity set up the Committee for the Defense of those Imprisoned for their Beliefs. Aleksander Hall, a former leader of a national-Christian opposition movement Mloda Polska (Young Poland), served as its president. The committee sought to assist imprisoned activists of the Confederation of Independent Poland, led by Lech Moczulski.

On December 16–18 to honor the tenth anniversary of the brutal suppression of the Baltic workers' protest in Gdansk, Szczecin, Gdynia, and Elbląg, representatives of Solidarity, the government, and the church unveiled a monument in front of the Gdansk shipyard for the December victims. However, despite the fact that Leonid Brezhnev canceled plans for military intervention in Poland by Warsaw Pact troops, the party did not take advantage of this admittedly risky opportunity to build consensus with the now structurally developed organization.

The Jastrzębie agreement in Silesia guaranteed Saturdays without work, but the government limited this privilege to miners only. In protest, on Saturday, January 10, 1981, many Polish employees did not go to work. After the preceding Saturday protest both the government and Solidarity accepted a forty-two-hour work week with one Saturday of eight-hour work a month.

On March 19 Solidarity members were refused the right to speak at the Provincial National Council meeting in Bydgoszcz. Those who protested were removed from the meeting hall. Three of them, including the president of the Regional Inter-factory Founding Committee, were beaten. This Bydgoszcz provocation led to popular indignation, and three provinces went on a two-hour strike the following day, while a four-hour warning strike throughout the country was supported by many local Communist party organizations and Communist labor unions. The labor union began preparations for an unlimited general strike scheduled for March 31. However, on March 30 the Warsaw Agreement was signed and the government announced that the authorities responsible for the violence at Bydgoszez would be punished. The agreement permitted Solidarity's access to the mass media, with permission to begin publishing a national weekly on April 3. In addition, the Farmers' Union was registered in May, but the Bydgoszcz offending—functionaries from the Security Service—remained "unknown." The Bydgoszcz conflict was the climax of popular involvement and support for Solidarity. Subsequently distrust toward the union's leaders began to grow.

When on July 23 meat rations decreased, women in the clothing factories of Lodz organized "starvation marches" to protest against food shortages. The Solidarity demonstration on August 3–5 in Warsaw, which was refused permission to pass near Communist Party headquarters, blocked the city's main streets and brought about an immense traffic jam in the center of town.

The first National Congress of Solidarity, which met from September 5 to October 7, accepted a proposal for a "Self-managed Republic" and called for a referendum on self-management. It also called for democratic elections of local governments. The congress addressed a "Letter to the Working People of Eastern Europe" supporting them in their efforts to set up independent labor unions. Lech Wałęsa was again elected chairman of the National Coordinating Committee.

From October 21 to November 4 workers in Zyrardow went on strike to protest shortages of food. Both their protest and the strike in Zielona Gora were intentionally prolonged by the authorities. The Security Service provoked sit-in strikes at the Engineering College in Radom on October 26, which spread to all universities and academic institutions and lasted until December 10.

In response to the rumors that parliament was going to agree to emergency measures against Solidarity, the National Coordination Committee followed the lead of its presidium in Radom and on December 3 announced a twenty-four-hour protest strike to be followed by a general strike on December 11–12 if these special powers were put into effect.

Thanks to its censorship-free bulletins, the freedom of speech at rallies, and its democratic procedures at meetings, Solidarity created civil consciousness in society. The initial slogan—"Socialism, yes, distortions, no," which was understood as control over the authorities through social agreements—was abandoned after the Bydgoszcz provocation, and socialism itself, in spite of attempts to reform it into a system of democratic and autonomous self-governments, was rejected.

On the night of December 12–13, before martial law was declared at 6:00 A.M. on December 13, the Citizens' Militia and Security Service detained and interned most of the National Committees' members. Altogether 10,131 labor union activists were interned and kept in forty-four internment camps and prisons until the end of 1982.

From the summer 1981, as a result of the growing "demobilization" of its members, Solidarity was able to organize strikes only in big factories: the Lenin Shipyard at Gdansk, the Katowice Steelworks, factories at Swidnik and Wrocław, and a few coal mines. On December 16 nine miners were shot by a special unit of the Citizens' Militia in the Wujek coal mine. The last strike ended on December 28 in the Piast coal mine.

On December 17 the first issue of an underground newsletter, "Wiadomości", (News) in Warsaw launched an illegal publication. From December 13, 1981, to 1988, thousands of illegal papers and books were published. No fewer than 1,907 underground titles appeared in the field of fiction and literary review alone. The goal of each underground Solidarity group was to publish its own paper. The most popular magazine was the *Mazowsze* weekly. The Wrocław weekly *Z Dnia Na Dzie (From Day to Day)* had the highest circulation. Also Solidarity Radio broadcast its programs at irregular intervals.

On January 13, 1982, two members of the National Coordination Committee, Eugeniusz Szumiejko and Andrzej Konarski, founded the National Committee of Resistance, but it was not supported by the underground. The factory, regional, and ideological underground groups were subordinated to the Provisional Coordination Committee, which was set up on April 22, 1982, by the chairmen of the Mazowsze region—Zbigniew Bujak, chairman of Silesia; Władysław Frasyniuk, chairman of Gdansk; Bogdan Lis; and the chairman of Malopolska, Władysław Hardek.

In February Jacek Kuroń, still interned, wrote an article advocating a well-organized resistance movement, disciplined, and ready for a concerted effort to remove the centers of authority from power. Following the example of the August strikes, advisers of the union, the Catholic primate of Poland, Cardinal Glemp, intellectuals, and Solidarity activists, mainly Wałęsa and later Kuroń, advocated a compromise with the authorities and social agreement achieved through peaceful pressure.

Independent demonstrations were organized every year, but the number of demonstrators continually declined. Neither the anniversary demonstrations to celebrate the Jewish uprising of 1943 in the Warsaw ghetto, the August uprising of 1944 in Warsaw, the June events of 1956 in Poznan, December 1970 in the Baltic region, or Liberation Day on November 11 gained much support.

Following the assassination of the priest Jerzy Popiełuszko by Security Service officers in October 1984, over five hundred priests started giving homilies that severely criticized the government. But attempts to legalize human rights associations in several cities were unsuccessful. The response to Solidarity's demand to boycott parliamentary elections of October 18, 1985, was also lukewarm.

On his third pilgrimage to Poland, June 8–14, 1987, Pope John Paul II gave a homily in Gdansk that emphasized the importance of both Solidarity and the Gdansk Agreement for the history of Poland and for the growth of social consciousness, and expressed hope that these social expectations would soon come true.

The strike at the Lenin Steelworks in Kraków in April 1988 was the first in a series of spring demonstrations to defend sacked Solidarity activists. The strike at the Gdansk Shipyard on May 2 gave birth to another slogan, "No freedom without Solidarity," which meant that if Solidarity was not legalized the government could expect strikes. The response of the authorities was quick. Troops suppressed the strikes in the Lenin Steelworks on May 5, and the Lenin Shipyard in Gdansk was simply closed. Only following the strikes in Szczecin in June and Stalowa Wola in July were workers allowed to return to work. Strikes in the coal mines on August 15 did not lead to other factory strikes.

The Communist Party's Central Committee on January 18, 1989, agreed again to legalize independent labor unions, enabling the round table discussions to commence. The moment the round table talks started, Solidarity organizations emerged from underground and began to open their offices. Thus this process of legalization took several years. The victory of the Civil Solidarity Committees in the parliamentary elections of June 4, 1989, and the formation of the first non-Communist government under Tadeusz Mazowiecki proved again the power of the factory and regional structures of Solidarity, which initially was able to insist on economic guarantees to serve as a "protective umbrella" to soften the market reform of Leszek Balcerowicz, who served as ministers of finance from 1989 to 1991 and launched a rapid transition to a market economy, known as "shock therapy." On the other hand, new political parties and the opportunity to make a career in the state and the newly created local administrations attracted former underground Solidarity activists. Barely two million members joined the union after its legalization. Thus, Solidarity became merely the second-biggest labor union, behind the post-Communist National Alliance of Trade Unions.

The Second Solidarity Congress in April, 1990 elected Wałesa chairman of the union again. Half a year later, after bitter competition, Wałesa won the first presidential election on December 22, 1990, and was sworn in as president of Poland. Marian Krzaklewski, an activist from Silesia, was chosen the new leader of Solidarity.

In the September 19, 1993, vote Solidarity did not win the necessary 5 percent to gain representation in parliament. The new government was formed by post-Communist parties, and Solidarity was pushed to the periphery of political life. However, the victorious strikes organized by Solidarity in the electrical industry in spring 1994 and its draft proposal for a new constitution signed by a million people returned the union to the political scene.

The early Solidarity (August 1980 to December 13, 1981) was a broad national movement of people fighting for their dignity within the framework of group and national solidarity. From December 13, 1981, until the establishment of the round table in early 1989, Solidarity was an underground organization. It was then transformed into a movement seeking peaceful and democratic but radical change to supplant totalitarianism in Poland. After 1989 Solidarity was transformed from a dual reform/labor movement into a traditional labor party.

BIBLIOGRAPHY

Ash Garton, Timothy. *The Polish Revolution: Solidarity 1980–1982.* London: Jonathan Cape, 1983.

Goodwyn, Lawrence. *Breaking the Barrier: The Rise of Solidarity in Poland.* New York: Oxford University Press, 1991.

Kaufman, Michael T. *Mad Dreams, Saving Graces: Poland, A Nation in Conspiracy.* New York: Random House, 1989.

Lopinski, Maciej, Marcin Moskit, and Mariusz Wilk. *Konspira: Solidarity Underground.* Tr. by Jane Cave. Berkeley: University of California Press, 1990.

Ost, David. *Solidarity and the Politics of Anti-politics.* Philadelphia: Temple University Press, 1990.

Staniszkis, Jadwiga. *Poland's Self-limiting Revolution.* Princeton, N.J.: Princeton University Press, 1984.

Touraine, Alain. *Solidarity: The Analysis of a Social Movement: Poland, 1980–1981.* In collaboration with Grazyna Gesicka. Tr. by David Denby. New York: Cambridge University Press, 1983.

Walesa, Lech. *The Struggle and the Triumph: An Autobiography.* New York: Arcade Publishing, 1992.

Roman Bäcker

SEE ALSO Jaruzelski, Wojciech: Popiełuszko, Jerzy Aleksander; Wałęsa, Lech

Round Table

Series of talks between Lech Wałęsa, his proxies, and the Polish United Workers Party (Communist) on the legal status of the Solidarity labor union and its place in a new political system. "Round table" was later applied to describe other negotiations between dissenters and the Communist parties in Hungary, East Germany, and Bulgaria during the so-called people's fall of 1989.

The idea of the round table was first proposed by Wałęsa's adviser Bronisław Geremek in 1987, but he used the terminology "anticrisis pact." In August 1988, when workers on strike demanded that Solidarity be legalized, one of the secretaries of the Communist Party's Central Committee, Józef Czyrek, and the chairman of the Warsaw Club of Catholic Intelligentsia held secret talks to discuss the meeting of a "round table." On August 31, Wałęsa and General Czesław Kiszczak, minister of internal affairs, agreed to talks that would cover political and social problems as well as economic reforms.

Although the first meeting was scheduled for mid-October, it had to be postponed because of the hesitation of Mieczysław Rakowski, who had just taken over as prime minister on September 27. The first indication that the prime minister had acceded was the contact established by Alfred Miodowicz, leader of the official Communist trade unions who had opposed the idea, with Wałęsa.

Negotiations were possible only after a plenary meeting of the party's Central Committee on January 18, 1989, agreed to accept a "constructive opposition" in the political system and to lift restrictions against the formation of new labor unions. The round table talks presided over by Kiszczak and Wałęsa were divided into three teams dealing with economic and social policy, labor union pluralism, and political reform. The most sensitive matters were discussed at confidential meetings in Magdalenka. General Wojciech Jaruzelski, first secretary of the Central Committee, played a decisive role in the talks. He set targets on the government's side, accepted the results of the talks, and sought the consent of the Kremlin.

It was agreed that Solidarity, Rural Solidarity (the union of private farmers), and the independent students' union would be legalized and incorporated into a redefined political system. Executive power would still be in the hands of the Communist Party, which with its allies would retain 65 percent of the seats in the Sejm (lower chamber of parliament). These seats would give the Communists 53 percent of the votes in the National Assembly, consisting of the Sejm and the Senate, which was to elect a new president with slightly less power than the French president. The opposition was allowed to contest 35 percent of seats in the Sejm and all hundred seats in the newly created Senate, which would enable them to balance the power of the executive and to play a significant role in the legislative process. The Senate had the right of veto, which, in turn, could be rejected by a two-thirds majority in the Sejm. This was calculated to force the two sides to seek compromise.

The round table agreement was approved by the Communist Party of the Soviet Union, which expected Solidarity to become an ordinary labor union and the status and prestige of the Communist Party to increase. The agreements resulted in the parliamentary election of June 4, 1989, however, which was won by the Civil Committees of Solidarity. Solidarity, in addition to fielding candidates who swept the 35 percent that they were allowed to contest, backed individual members of the Communist Party for seats allotted to the Communists and their allies. Therefore the bloc in power was not able to form a government and the resolutions of the round table lost their validity. On August 24 the Catholic intellectual and supporter of Solidarity, Tadeusz Mazowiecki, formed a coalition of Solidarity, Peasants Party, and Democratic Party.

The Communist Party lost its power, and state authority was now taken over by parliament and a government dependent on it. The round table talks thus led to a peaceful, evolutionary assumption of power by a previously illegal opposition.

BIBLIOGRAPHY

Stachura, Peter D. *Poland in the Twentieth Century.* New York: St. Martin's Press, 1999.

Stokes, Gale. *The Walls Came Tumbling Down: The Collapse of Communism in Eastern Europe.* New York: Oxford University Press, 1993.

Roman Bäcker

Martial Law

Marital law was imposed by Wojciech Jaruzelski the first secretary of the Polish Communist Party (Polish United Workers Party), minister of defense, and prime minister, on the night of December 13, 1981, as a result of constant disagreements between the Solidarity labor union and the Communist Party, as well as a consequence of the growing threat since autumn 1980 from Communist Party and

Street demonstration in Poland around the time martial law was declared in 1981. *Illustration courtesy of Polish Embassy, Washington, D.C.*

military authorities in the Soviet Union of military interference, euphemized as "allied help," by armies of the Warsaw Pact, of which Poland was a member.

Under the leadership of General Wojciech Jaruzelski, who was first secretary of the party's Central Committee, prime minister, and minister of national defense, a Military Council of National Salvation was set up. It consisted of fifteen generals in addition to Jaruzelski, five colonels, and the minister of internal affairs, Czestaw Kiszczak. The council also had department, provincial, urban, and communal delegates who were commissioned as military commissars. The Proclamation of the State of War, the Polish version of martial law, called on the public to keep the peace and abide by the decree of martial law decreed by the Council of State on December 12, 1981. Thus all social gatherings, marches, and demonstrations were banned. All forms of public entertainment, sporting events, or publishing activities required permission of the local administrative authority. Also tourism and sailing or rowing at sea were considerably restricted. All associations, trade and student unions, and social organizations, except churches and religious institutions, were suspended. On September 8, 1982, Solidarity was formally banned. Young men of military age could be recruited without advance notice. Administrative and economic institutions, particularly those important for the defense and security of the state, were subject to orders of a military commissar. All mail and telephone calls were censored, and communications equipment and shotguns had to be surrendered to the authorities. No military or police, their equipment, or key components of the infrastructure could be photographed or filmed. In addition, traveling and transport were curtailed, inhabitants of some provinces were forbidden to leave their place of residence, and other areas could not be visited. To prevent people from staying out late, a night-time curfew was imposed. After a while, however, these rigors were commuted.

During the period of martial law, people who violated these regulations, restrictions, or obligations were subject to on-the-spot fines or instant arrest. Civil and courts-martial, as well as other local administrative bodies, applied summary convictions. Summary convictions included temporary detention, and the courts were empowered to levy sentences of three, fifteen, or twenty-five years or even capital punishment. Verdicts of summary courts could not be appealed. Courts-martial replaced civil courts in many political, economic, and state security and order cases. Under the martial law decree all Polish citizens over seventeen suspected of "violating or threatening the security or defense of the state" could be isolated in special internment centers that could accommodate as many as 5,200 people at a time. A total of 10,554 were interned. In the case of "direct threat to the life, health or freedom of citizens or social property, administrative buildings, headquarters of political organizations, industrial or military and defense centers," not only the police but also military troops were empowered to "bring direct pressure on violators." Pacification efforts resulted in several deaths and hundreds of casualties.

On December 31, 1982, martial law in Poland was suspended and the restrictions were eased by the decree of December 1982. On July 22, 1983, martial law was abolished and martial law legislation was replaced by the Act of July 21, 1983, which provided "special legislative regulations for the period necessary to overcome the socio-economic crisis," to prevent strikes and maintain labor discipline.

BIBLIOGRAPHY

Garton Ash, Timothy. *The Polish Revolution: Solidarity 1980–1982.* London: Granta, 1991.

Haig, Alexander. *Caveat: Realism, Reagan and Foreign Policy.* New York: Macmillan, 1984.

Jaruzelski, Wojciech. *Stan wojenny: Dlaczego?* Warsaw: BGW, 1992.

Labedz Leopold, ed. *Poland under Jaruzelski.* New York: Scribner, 1984.

Meretik, Gabriel. *La Nuit du Général: enquête sur le coup d'État du 13 décembre 1981.* Paris: P. Belfond, 1989.

Ryszard Sudziński

SEE ALSO Jaruzelski, Wojciech

Citizens' Committees

Citizens' Committees were founded by the Executive Committee of the Solidarity labor union to carry out organizational tasks for the elections of June 4, 1989, which had been approved in the Round Table between representatives of the Polish Communist government and Solidarity, the independent labor union outlawed since the imposition of martial law in December 1981. The agreement re-legalized Solidarity and set free elections for June. Regional branches of Solidarity founded regional Citizens' Committees in cities, towns, and villages where rural or worker adherents of Solidarity were active.

On June 17, 1989, after the elections, the Executive Committee ordered the regional committees dissolved. This decision was not carried out and was eventually revoked. The committees were transformed from campaign organizations into stable territorial structures that prepared for local elections. But their work in communities went beyond electioneering. They performed multiple self-help actions including organizing financial help for the needy. They promoted economic activity through creation of enterprises and local banks and cooperation with foreign partners. They also monitored the government in the areas of privatization and fraud. In carrying out these undertakings, the committees acted as coordinators, supporters, or organizers.

The Citizens' Committees' importance was confirmed in elections to local governments on May 27, 1990, in which they received about 40 percent of the vote. Paradoxically, victory in elections led to the demise of the committees because the newly elected local councils sought to solve problems without seeking support from the committees. The committees also faced contention over the splits in the Solidarity camp over the presidential election when some of the Solidarity camp refused to support the founder of the movement, Lech Wałesa, for president and soon ceased to function. Their collapse was demonstrated in the parliamentary elections of October 27, 1991.

BIBLIOGRAPHY

Stachura, Peter D. *Poland in the Twentieth Century.* New York: St. Martin's Press, 1999.

Stokes, Gale. *The Walls Came Tumbling Down: The Collapse of Communism in Eastern Europe.* New York: Oxford University Press, 1993.

Marek Jeziński

Economy

The socialist system was implemented in Poland after World War II. The socialist economy was based on three principles: nationalized ownership of the means of production, a centralized directive system of planning and management, and political control over the economy.

In 1946 nationalization of industry and agrarian reform was pushed through. Over one million family farms were established. Their average size was 17.28 acres (7 hectares). Until 1949 a small private sector in industry, services, and trade was allowed to operate in firms having up to fifty employees.

One of the tools used by the Communist Party to exercise political power over the economy was the system of economic planning. Only the first three-year plan, of 1947–49, was fully realized. The next six-year plan of 1950–55 and the following five-year plans were changed many times during their course and were always only partly successful.

The six-year plan was implemented during the period of Stalinization. The Communist Party attempted to conform the Polish economic system to the Soviet model. They proclaimed a "battle of trade" that resulted in the liquidation of the private sector in commerce. During the same time a program of collectivization of agriculture was attempted but unsuccessfully implemented. In 1954 only 9 percent of Polish cultivated land belonged to state-owned farms. Poland remained the only European socialist country with a private sector in agriculture. In the first half of the 1950s restrictions were placed on private craftsmen's workshops. Many of them were closed but later reopened. In 1985 there were around three hundred thousand of them, and in the next four years their number doubled.

At the beginning of the 1950s enforced industrialization was launched. Its main characteristics included the primacy of the production of producer goods, reduction of consumption, central planning along with the domination of administrative commands over the economy strong involvement of the Communist Party apparatus in all aspects of the economy, multiplication of the forms of institutional control over production, and limitation of popular input by of workers and consumers.

Bottlenecks rapidly emerged throughout the economy. There were a number of causes: the rapid acceleration of industrialization, mostly because of the necessity of investment in military industry during the Korean War (1950–53); its one-sidedness, along with the lack of balance between mandated quotas and possibilities of fulfilling them; the failure to correlate effectively investments with the production capabilities of the existing enterprises; imbalances between agriculture and industry; and lack of coordination between the demand for raw materials and energy, on the one hand, and their production and importation, on the other. The domination of producer goods was determined ideologically in line with the Soviet model of development. The services and housing sectors were particularly underdeveloped. This situation led to control of the distribution of consumer goods in various forms—from the allocation of apartments and coupons for cars, through coupons for TV sets, refrigerators, and washing machines (in the 1950s and 1960s), to coupons for sugar, butter, meat, soap, shoes, and other basic consumer goods in the 1980s. As a consequence a black market appeared in the 1980s.

Increasing market imbalances and the necessity to maintain a high level of investments at the expense of the standard of living led to a high level of inflation and to social unrest. The socialist economy continually generated crises, the most severe of which occurred in 1956, 1970, and 1980.

The economic crises may be represented by the following four-phase model. The first phase was a period of rapid and intensive industrialization with investment mostly in the producer good sector. Transition from the first to the second phase coincided with emerging barriers to economic growth and an emerging limit of popular endurance. The main characteristic of the second phase was the declaration of a new, pro-consumption policy. It was to be implemented by the freezing of investments and changes in the assortment of produced goods. The authorities declared their intention to pay much more attention to agriculture and to craftsmanship. These so-called economic maneuvers were never successful. The first reason was the inertia difficulty of establishing new priorities for the economy. Moreover, strong interest groups emerged, connected with various branches of heavy industry and with the highest levels of management. All of them profited from the existing state of affairs. Internal contradictions within the power elite in the broadest sense be also negatively impacted the attainment of economic goals. The competing groups within the Communist Party intending to take over political power attempted to weaken the ruling group that made it more difficult to carry out the "shift of economic focus." The third phase of the cycle was the overt social conflict resulting from the failures of this economic policy. The fourth phase was actually another pro-consumption stage. It lasted until the new power elite made sure that it was really in charge. Then, the new cycle was ready to begin.

The cyclic model shows that crises were built into the system. The working of the economy seems to have been secondary to politics and ideology. Signs of the economic crisis constantly surfaced: the permanent budget deficit, market imbalance, decreased industrial production (e.g., in 1982 GNP decreased by 15 percent in comparison with 1980), foreign trade, deficit inflation, and inefficiency of management.

During the period from 1945 to 1989, enforced industrialization transformed the economy in the sense of increasing the number of existing enterprises and the volume of production, but it did not lead to the essential modernization of the economy. It was inefficient and energy-consuming, for example, in the 1980s, to realize one dollar of GNP in Poland, three times more energy was used than in West Germany. Natural resources were exploited extensively. The concentration of enterprises impacted the environment and the surrounding inhabitants negatively.

In the entire post–World War II period there were almost no universally accepted and functioning rules and norms regulating economic. It is difficult to estimate the damage to the work ethic done by the socialist economic system. Nevertheless, the standard of living, especially for peasants and factory workers, became much higher than in the prewar period. Yet the standard of living of the intelligentsia decreased. This caused vast numbers of well-educated Poles to emigrate.

The final outcome of this process was the complete collapse of the socialist economy and its inability to support the socialist political system.

Maria Nawojczyk

Economic Transformation in the 1990s

At the beginning of the year 2000, the economy of Poland appeared in substantially better shape than before the collapse of Communism in the late 1980s. Goods and services that previously were in short supply were now easily available, if one had the money. New markets were developed. No longer was there the heavy trade dependence on the Soviet Union or its successor states. Symbolic of the changes was Poland's admission to NATO in 1999. The Poland of Wojciech Jaruzelski, Edward Gierek, and Wladysław Gomułka no longer existed, and in its place there was a Western-oriented, capitalistic republic. The last decade of the twentieth century saw a noticeable improvement in the standard of living, and economic growth even reached seven percent per annum.

In order to understand the dramatic changes in Poland, one should briefly look at the Communist dimension in the People's Republic before the Revolution of 1989 when no one could have predicted the present prosperity. Each successive regime since World War II wrestled with the problem of economic reform, but always within the limited confines of Communism. Although the population did not suffer overtly from malnutrition after the close of the Stalinist era in the mid-1950s and the basic reconstruction of Poland from the devastation of the Second World War, the people faced shortages of important foods and household necessities like meat and even toilet tissue, which resulted in regular rationing of foodstuffs throughout the 1980s. Only those who had access to Western currencies like dollars and marks were able to supplement their larders with items obtained from special "hard currency" stores called Pewex.

Despite more than four decades of Communist control, Poland was never molded completely in the Marxist model. Some limited versions of capitalism flourished, whether with government approbation or not. For example, many small shops, which provided everything from cut flowers (a necessity in Polish society!) to fresh produce and clothing, operated under licenses from the government. Many Poles preferred to shop at these establishments rather than at those owned and controlled directly by the authorities. This was especially prevalent in the larger cities like Kraków and Warsaw. A nonregulated, obviously illegal market, which provided everything from gasoline to meat and currency exchange also flourished. In addition, it must be pointed out that not all of the agricultural lands of Poland had been confiscated by the government. Communes similar to those in the Soviet Union were common in the lands annexed to the country after World War II, i.e. those east of the new western border with Germany. Private farms remained the norm in central and southern Poland. These remnants of capitalism provided some of the seeds of the Polish miracle of the 1990s.

The spirit behind the reforms was the Finance Minister Leszek Balcerowicz who combined formidable managerial skills with economic leadership by spearheading a drive to reform investment laws and regulations that simplified and encouraged foreign investment in Poland. A cursory examination of the Polish Embassy's web-page in the United States will demonstrate that point. And his work was continued by his successors. Unlike other former Communist regimes in eastern Europe where ex-communists reversed some of the efforts towards privatization, Poland maintained the basics of the Balcerowicz program throughout the 1990s. Other reasons for Polish economic success included the overwhelming popular support of the Solidarity movement and a willingness by many of its members to dismantle Communism and institute reforms, even difficult ones like wage controls (early in the 1990s, inflation soared beyond 800 percent!). Poles were also disenchanted with socialism as they experienced it, because of shortages and its concomitant rationing, and they desired to create what many of them experienced in their trips to the West or heard about from friends or perhaps even saw on television (the ubiquitous satellite dishes on apartment balconies might have played a role!). Very quickly after the collapse of General Jaruzelski's government in 1989, numerous Poles took advantage of their new found freedom to form their own small businesses, thereby adding substantially to the private sector economy and giving it additional strength during the difficult transition. Significant in this process was the creation of the Polish American Enterprise Fund that was organized to make small loans (with a limit of $20,000) enabling many to start small, but promising businesses. Until the banks were reorganized, they did not ordinarily make this type of loan. It was indeed fortunate for the new government as it instituted difficult reforms that the Soviet markets collapsed. The severe economic problems that Poles at first experienced caused them to blame these export losses rather than the reforms.

Some of the main characteristics of the Balcerowicz program included floating the złoty, the Polish currency. This action in turn eliminated the black market in currency exchange that permeated the country. It was also an effort to rejuvenate the zloty that had been weak or non-convertable since World War II. Other features of the reforms were the end of government restrictions on private business as well as on imports. Food subsidies were abandoned and almost immediately more products in large quantities were available throughout Poland. This new competition forced the state-owned enterprises to adopt Western-style merchandising techniques or face bankruptcy. Most important was debt-restructuring with foreign countries and private banks who agreed to forgive almost one-half of the debt. The result was a dramatic improvement in Poland's credit rating. Finally, these reform-minded governments of the 1990s reorganized the banks, worked successfully to correct many past mistakes, and instituted modern banking regulations. Rather than attempting to create a stock market and other financial institutions from scratch, Poles decided to borrow extensively from the West where these institutions prospered or at least faithfully fulfilled their charges. For example, its Security and Exchange Commission, closely mirrors its counterpart in the United States. The Warsaw Stock Exchange, established in 1991 now list over 250 companies, with more than a majority of the investors from Poland itself, a situation that buttresses the stability of the new economy. Also, reform of business regulations enabled large scale foreign investment without the interminable red tape so common in other eastern European countries. However, in this area, it must be noted that because government employees are paid substantially less that those holding similar positions in the private sector, noticeable corruption still exists. But at least, Poland has been able to avoid the mafia-style "protection" practices that exists in other former Communist countries.

In the early days of "shock therapy," the Solidarity government did not attempt to reform several important sectors of the economy: iron and steel, mining, and power. These were considered not just difficult to re-organize, but also dangerous to the stability of the government. Workers in these industries have been highly politicized and have been willing to demonstrate their ire openly, even in the streets. Not until 1998 did the government pass a mining reform bill that was designed to make that industry profitable in five years. The work force was bloated and the working conditions execrable. Thanks to a one-billion dollar loan from the World Bank, the government was also able to offer miners the equivalent of three years wages as a buy-out program. Within a year more than 20,000 miners accepted these conditions, many of whom entered re-training programs or sought employment in the new industries like General Motors. This was especially the case in Silesia, Poland's most important coal center. Such actions have been necessary and remain crucial if Poland's economy is to be privatized and subsidies to various industries terminated.

In a little more than a decade, Poland has taken on a Western image, although the reforms are less than complete. Wages, production, and efficiency continue to improve. Significant reforms have made Poland the focus of much international investment. The illegal markets of Communist days helped to train many in free market techniques, thereby providing one more basis for a vibrant economy of the year 2000. Nonetheless, not all industries have been privatized. Even the financial problems on the international scene, especially in eastern Asia and Brazil, did not undermine the new Polish economy. They merely slowed its growth down from more than 7 percent to about 3 percent per annum.

The health system remains under government auspices with all health care-givers, including physicians and nurses, on its payroll. Poor salaries severely affects negatively this aspect of Polish social programs. Also, economic reforms threaten the stability of the government because no party is able to maintain a majority in the Sejm (Parliament). Coalitions are obviously the norm, often with the inclusion of ex-communists. Nonetheless. Poland entered the year 2000 with confidence because of the revolutionary changes it has directed: a modern, western-style economy has been taking shape.

BIBLIOGRAPHY

Simpson, Peggy, "Why Poland Is Making It," *Foreign Service Journal,* (June 1999): 20–29.

Thomas C. Sosnowski

Worker Self-Management

Employee self-management, as an idea and to some extent as a social practice, was a unique, Polish phenomenon of the immediate post–World War II period.

Employee self-management in Poland and its institutional forms developed in three main cycles. The first cycle began in 1944 and ended in 1950. The second began with the process of de-Stalinization in 1956. This cycle formally ended in June 1980. The third cycle began in 1980 with the emergence of the independent and self-governing labor union solidarność (Solidarity). This cycle ended in January 1990, with the beginning of the transition from the centralized and socialist economy to the free-market and capitalist economy. Therefore, the important thresholds are the years 1944, 1956, 1980, and 1990.

The immediate postwar years, lasting until 1948, were a period of dramatic socialist reforms. During these years management was nearly totally exerted by employees themselves, mostly factory workers. The situation became legally recognized by the decree of February 6, 1945, "on the institutionalization of the plant councils." According to this law, plant councils were granted authority to control and supervise all activities of the enterprises.

However, the Stalinist centralized, directive system of planning and management of the economy opposed the idea of employee self-management. The centralizing trend was eventually reflected in a new decree "on plant councils," issued on January 16, 1947. Despite this, between 1946 and 1948, employee self-management councils, even if their role was weakened, still participated in the decision-making process. Only during the next period, the so-called Six Year Plan (1949–54), did the directive system of management became absolutely dominant.

In 1956 the first overt conflict between the working class and the Communist authorities occurred. A new political elite, still representing the Communist Party, took over. Workers' councils began to emerge spontaneously, and various plans for employee self-management were discussed. According to estimates, between April and December of 1956, about three thousand workers' councils emerged in about seven thousand state-owned enterprises.

The law on workers' councils was passed on November 19, 1956. But in 1958 the situation began to change again, and once more employee self-management was eliminated. In 1958 parliament passed a new law on workers' self-management. Many articles of this law made possible the actual liquidation of the self-management movement. The number of elected and operating workers' councils continuously decreased. At the beginning of the 1970s, there were about six thousand workers' councils, and in the second half of the 1970s only six hundred. In January 1980 there were only six workers' councils, and in June 1980 the last of them were dissolved.

The next overt conflict between the central Communist authorities and civil society took place in 1980. The independent and self-governing labor union Solidarity emerged. The idea of a "self-management reform," with particular stress on the financial and organizational independence of state-owned enterprises, was the foundation of the proposal of economic reform put forward by Solidarity.

The "August Agreements" signed in 1980 changed workers' attitude to participation in management from negative or, at least indifferent, to positive. By October 1980 the first employee self-management councils emerged. The "battle for self-management" became the power struggle between the state authorities and Solidarity.

On September 25, 1981, parliament passed two laws: "On State-owned Enterprises" and "On Employee Self-management in State-owned Enterprises." The law on self-management stated that "employee self-management of a state-owned enterprise [the employees' council] makes decisions concerning crucial problems of the enterprise, presents its opinions, takes initiative and presents motions as well as controls the activities of the enterprise."

The decree on martial law of December 13, 1981, stated that any activities of the organs of employee self-management in state-owned enterprises and in other institutions would be suspended. At the end of the martial law period, on December 31, 1982, however, employee self-management councils were partially reconstructed. Their potential activities, however, were to be extremely limited because they were regulated by the law "on special legislation during the period of overcoming the socio-economic crisis."

This form of "employee self-managing," with different details from plant to plant, existed until the transformation period that started in the economy at the beginning of 1990. Many economists believed that the self-managing system was a good solution to various problems of a centrally planned economy. In a market economy, however, it had to be dispensed with because it was incompatible with the new economic system. The process of privatization and commercialization thus eliminated a phenomenon that for at least thirty-five years, to a greater or lesser degree, was an important facet of the Polish public arena.

BIBLIOGRAPHY

Gąclarz, Barbara. "Employee Self-Management in the 1980's," in Jerzy Hausner and Tadeusz Klementewicz, eds. *The Protracted Death Agony of Real Socialism.* Warsaw: ISP PAN, 1992.

Morawski, Witold. "Self-Management and Economic Reform," in Jadwiga Koralewicz, Ireneusz Białecki, and Margaret Watson, eds. *Crisis and Transition: Polish Society in the 1980's.* New York: St. Martin's Press, 1987.

Nawojczyk, Maria. "The Rise and Fall of the Self-Management Movement in Poland." *Polish Sociological Review* 4 (1993): 343–54.

Maria Nawojczyk

Privatization

Movement in Poland away from the state-controlled economy of the Communist period. The issue of privatization was advanced in 1989 in the program of the first non-Communist cabinet. As of the beginning of 1990 the Sejm (parliament) passed several laws changing the way the economy operated. The issue of privatization was dealt with by two laws passed on July 13, 1990.

The law on privatization of state-owned enterprises defined two main paths toward privatization. The first was "capital privatization," based on the classic privatization techniques in market economies. This procedure was used in the case of large state-owned companies. The first step was so-called commercialization, meaning the transformation of a state-owned enterprise into a commercial company owned by the state. The commercialized enterprises were to be administered by the Ministry of Property Transformations, which represented the state as the owner. According to the same law the ministry had the right to sell shares of the company to third persons. By 1997, 183 state-owned enterprises had been privatized in this way, including 29 sold directly via the stock exchange market. An additional 550 companies had already been commercialized and prepared for sale.

The second way of privatizing state-owned enterprises was the privatization that followed the liquidation of the firm in question. This procedure was used in the case of small and medium-sized companies. It gave the firm's employees a chance to buy a part or even the whole company that was being liquidated. This kind of privatization led to employee ownership. By 1997, 2,700 state-owned enterprises had been liquidated in this way, and 1,040 employee-owned companies were established in their place. This turned out to be the most efficient form of privatization.

With the process of privatization the problem of distribution of property rights emerged. Several programs of "universal privatization" mostly done by a free distribution of coupons (vouchers) among citizens were advanced. Finally in 1993, the Sejm accepted the program authored by Janusz Lewandowski, minister of property transformations in the cabinets of Jan Krzysztof Bielecki and Hanna Suchocka, establishing the National Investment Funds. The government selected 512 state-owned enterprises for this program. They were commercialized and their shares were distributed among fifteen funds.

Since 1997 the shares of the funds have been quoted on the Warsaw stock exchange. During 1996 every citizen over eighteen years old had the right to buy one government bond that he or she could sell on the market or exchange for shares of the funds.

In 1997 around three thousand enterprises were still state-owned, including the 240 largest companies, which have a monopolistic position in their markets. During the left-wing rule of 1995–97 through coalitions of Social Democracy of the Republic of Poland (the former Communists) and the Democratic Left Alliance, privatization was slower than in previous times of much more liberally oriented post-Solidarity cabinets. Privatization still remains a contentious political issue, however, despite the liquidation of the Ministry of Property Transformations during the reform of the state bureaucracy that started in 1997.

The process of Property transformations in Poland consist not only of the privatization of already existing state-owned enterprises but also of establishing new private companies. By 1997 over two million private firms, mostly small and medium-sized, had been established.

BIBLIOGRAPHY

Poznanski, Kazimierz. *Poland's Protracted Transition: Institutional Change and Economic Growth, 1970–1994.* New York: Cambridge University Press, 1996.

Stachura, Peter D. *Poland in the Twentieth Century.* New York: St. Martin's Press, 1999.

Maria Nawojczyk

Polish United Workers' Party

Marxist-Leninist party that ruled in Poland from the end of World War II until the fall of communism. Founded on December 15, 1948, by the merger ordered by Soviet dictator Joseph Stalin of the Polish Workers' Party and the Polish Socialist Party, which had been completely dependent on the Communists. Also called the Communist

Party, it was dissolved on January 28, 1991, during its Eleventh Congress; the delegates then founded the Social Democracy of Poland. Only a small group led by Tadeusz Fiszbach founded the marginal and short-lived Polish Social Democratic Union.

From 1948 until his death on March 12, 1956, Bolesław Bierut led the Communist Party. He was succeeded by Edward Ochab, who was in power only until October 21, 1956. Władysław Gomułka was party leader until December 20, 1970, and was succeeded by Edward Gierek. On September 6, 1980, Gierek was replaced by Stanisław Kania. Kania was succeeded by Wojciech Jaruzelski on October 18, 1981. Jaruzelski resigned from his post on July 29, 1989, after he was elected president of Poland. Until the party was dissolved it was led by Mieczysław Rakowski.

Until the twentieth Congress of the Communist Party of the Soviet Union (CPSU), the Polish party was ruled by a group supported by the secret police and fully subordinated to the CPSU. In 1956 the "Puławians"—activists, named after the Puław district of Poland, who tried to adjust propaganda and programs to meet popular social demands—were opposed by the "Natolinians," named after the palace of Natolin where they met, who used anti-Semitic slogans against them. Gomułka's faction within the party gradually eliminated the Puławians, and the remnants of the Natolinians joined the ranks of the head of the security police Mieczysław Moczar's followers, who were called "partisans" because of his role as a partisan leader in German occupied Poland. Provoking students' unrest in March 1968 and fueling demonstrations in December 1970, Gomułka lost his fight for power with the "technocrats" led by Edward Gierek.

In spite of Gierek's creation of a balance of influence within the party and trimming of the sails of the security police headed by the Minister of the Interior Franciszek Szlachcic, worker unrest of August 1980 led to his fall. He had to give in to Kania and Jaruzelski, who controlled the army.

At the moment of its founding the Communist Party had 1,367,000 members. Despite a stiff admission policy, it developed into a mass organization. In 1980 there were 3,092,000 members. However, that year 800,000 members, mostly workers and intelligentsia, all supporters of the Solidarity earlier union, left the party. During 1989 a mass exodus from the party took place. Only about 60,000 people joined the ranks of its successor the Social Democracy of Poland (SdRP).

The Communist Party had the right to appoint all management personnel in the state and society and to control and to change all administrative decisions. It thus ruled over the state and many aspects of social life. Its full-time workers were the core of a centralized party-state apparatus. In times of crises, however, it ceased to be a typical apparatus (Marxist-Leninist) party since there were, at those times, always members who opposed the party's position. In 1956 the "revisionists" sought democratization of the system. In 1980 and 1981 proponents of "horizontal structures" forced democratic elections and demanded talks with Solidarity. The so-called Movement of July 8, institutionalized in mid-1989, led to the transformation of the Polish United Workers Party into the Social Democracy of Poland.

BIBLIOGRAPHY

Dziewanowski, M. K. *The Communist Party in Poland: An Outline of History.* Cambridge, Mass.: Harvard University Press, 1959.

Roman Bäcker

SEE ALSO Bierut, Bolesław; Gierek, Edward; Gomułka, Władysław; Jaruzelski, Wojciech

Political Parties Since 1989

Before 1989 Poland was dominated by a hegemonic party, the Polish United (Communist) Workers' Party. It tolerated satellite parties, such as the Peasant Movement and the Democratic Movement. But after 1980 the clandestine Solidarity labor union movement and a variety of groups loosely associated with it challenged the party's claim to represent the Polish people. Associated with Solidarity were the pacifist movement Freedom and Peace founded in April 1985; Jan Józef Lipski's Polish Socialist Party, founded in November 1987 the Polish Peasant Movement, continuing traditions of Mikołajczyk's Polish Peasant Movement, founded in June 1988; and the Confederation of Independent Poland (KPN), led by the right-wing nationalist Leszek Moczulski, founded in September 1979.

This dual political system collapsed in 1990. On November 26, 1989, the Peasant Movement was transformed into the Polish Peasant Movement "Odrodzenie" (Revival) (PSL). It took over the property, press, and four hundred thousand members of the old party and thus became the Polish political party with the largest number of members. After unification with one of the small post-Solidarity peasant parties, the modifier "Odrodzenie" (Revival) was dropped. Roman Bartoszcze, a leader of one of the smaller parties, became its chair. His attempt to supplant the leaders of the former Peasant Movement led in 1991 to a conflict with Roman Jagieliński, chairman of the party's Supreme Council. Bartoszcze was replaced as PSL chair by Waldemar Pawlak; Józef Zych became chairman of the Supreme Council. Bartoszcze founded the Polish Peasant–Christian Forum, Rola, in July 1991, but it did not play an important role.

As a result of the demise of the Communist Party in January 1990, the Social Democracy of Poland (SdRP) was created, led by Aleksander Kwaśniewski and Leszek Miller. In February 1990 it was transformed into the Alliance of the Democratic Left (SLD), which united it with the labor unions and social movements with roots in the old Communist Party.

The Citizens' Committee, founded by Lech Wałęsa, the leader of Solidarity in December 1988, which initially functioned as an advisory body to Wałęsa and from April 1989 as the Solidarity Citizen Committee, overseeing the election campaign of Solidarity candidates in elections of June 4, 1989, became the political arm of Solidarity. In February 1991 it attempted to resume operation under its old name but soon afterward ceased to exist. This was the result of the fight initiated in June 1990 when Wałęsa declared a "war at the top" between himself and Premier Tadeusz Mazowiecki.

At the same time parties defined by specific programmatic and personal preferences were being founded. In May 1990 a coalition, Liberal-Democratic Congress (KDL), was founded. The Center Alliance (PC), an alliance of various peasant, Catholic, and Solidarity activists led by Jaroslaw Kaczyński, soon followed. The Alliance supported Wałęsa's candidacy for presidency. The creation of the Citizen Movement–Democratic Action was a response to the Alliance. At the beginning of October 1990 activists of the Movement together with liberal conservatives led by Aleksander Hall and a group associated with *Tygodnik Powszechny the Catholic newspaper* (Universal Weekly) founded an election committee for Tadeusz Mazowiecki. After his failure in the presidential election on December 2, 1990, they founded the Democratic Union (UD), led by Mazowiecki. The PC had support among workers and residents of small towns while Mazowiecki and the UD were supported by white-collar workers, intelligentsia, and residents of big cities.

Wałęsa's candidacy was also supported by the Christian National Union (ZChN), founded on September 15, 1989, and led until 1994 by Wiesław Chrzanowski, and then by Ryszard Czarnecki and Marian Piłka. The Social Democratic Alliance was also pro-Wałęsa. It was headed by Ryszard Bugaj and Karol Modzelewski. In August 1993 it changed its name to the Work Union (UP).

Wałęsa's opponent in the second round of presidential elections on December 9, 1990, was former emigrant Stanisław Tymiński, an entrepreneur from Canada and Peru with unclear sources of campaign financing. In March 1991 he registered his election committees as the populist "X" Party.

Although there were 160 registered political parties in the elections of October 27, 1991, only 65 parties participated and only 30 election committees secured places in the Sejm (parliament). The splitting of parties and the moving of representatives from one parliamentary club to another was slowed down by the introduction in 1993 of a 5 percent election threshold. On April 23, 1994, the UD united with the KLD creating the Freedom Union (UW). Led by Mazowiecki and later Leszek Balcerowicz, it slowly adjusted to the role of an opposition party.

Rightist organizations, although together receiving 30 percent of the vote, did not manage to get into parliament. They founded three political alliances. Ultra liberal supporters of Janusz Korwin-Mikke together with conservative-Christian democrats founded the Alliance of November 11. The Center Alliance, the Christian National Union, and several lesser parties created the Alliance for Poland. Much less important were the so-called patriotic and independence parties gathered around the Secretariat of Center-Right Groups.

The presidential elections of fall 1995, in which there were seventeen registered candidates, increased the fracturing of the party scene. Strength was shown by the post-Communist SLD, the social democratic UP, the liberal democratic UW, the peasant PSL, and the rather populist but nevertheless pro-market reform Wałęsa camp.

BIBLIOGRAPHY

Pridham, Geoffrey, and Tatu Vanhanen, ed. *Democratisation in Eastern Europe: Domestic and International Perspectives.* London: Routledge, 1994.

Roman Bäcker

Ethnic Groups

Ethnic and national minorities in Poland, which between the world wars constituted such a significant presence and were regarded to be a threat to the integrity of the Polish state, after World War II constituted only about 3 to 4 percent of the population. They live mainly near the eastern and southern borders of the country. The principal minorities have their own political representatives, but these are of marginal importance.

There are between 450,000 and 600,000 Belorussians, who live mainly in "Western Belorussia," which is a part of the Białystok region and also in the Suwalki and Biala Podlaska regions. This minority is usually associated with underdevelopment and poor rural areas. With government support, Białystok Public Television broadcasts programs in Belorussian, and local folk and cultural festivals are organized to maintain the minority's traditions.

The Belorussian minority is closely connected with the Orthodox Church. There are occasional conflicts with the Catholic majority, such as the controversy over the ownership of Suprasl, a rebuilt monastery. Nevertheless, relations between the Orthodox Church and the state appear to be generally good and improving.

There are approximately 300,000 Ukrainians. Other than the Germans, they are the most active minority from the point of view social, political, and cultural activities. A number of local conflicts have arisen from this. The memories of war are still alive and they influence the relations between Poles and Polish Ukranians. In 1947 there were massive compulsory relocations of Ukrainians from the Bieszczady Mountains and eastern boundary regions to the western lands gained as a result of the Yalta Conference of February 1945. This forced removal, called the "Vistula" action, still evokes bitter feelings among the Ukrainians of Poland, Between relocated Ukrainians lie the Lemkos, some of whom consider themselves a separate nation.

The state has not solved all the problems raised by the representatives of the Ukrainian minority. Impassioned political conflicts have arisen such as the problem of ownership of forests formerly belonging to Ukrainian highlanders or the demand for a resolution condemning the Vistula action. Only in 1996 was a separate Greek Catholic diocese approved by the authorities of the Roman Catholic Church in Poland.

There remain approximately 600,000 Germans in Poland. The existence of this minority after the war is an interesting phenomenon. After many but not all Germans left postwar Polish territory, Polish authorities long refused to admit that such a minority still existed in Poland. Later, after parliament passed the post-1989 act on associations, German efforts to register their associations were resisted by local authorities. Since 1990 the Polish Germans are represented by the Union of German Social and Cultural Associations.

Most of the Germans live in the Regions of Opole, Katowice, Częstochowa and Wałbrzych. In Mazury (northeast Poland) about 50,000 mainly elderly Germans reside. A large number of Germans, in many cases after administrative pressures, left the former German territory of East Prussia in the 1950s and again in the 1980s. The higher standard of living in Germany attracted many. The Polish Germans are mostly Roman Catholic, though, some in the southeast are Lutherans.

There are between 3,000 and 7,000 Polish Jews, and they constitute an influential group mainly in the common consciousness. Traditionally Jews inhabited Galicia, a region in southeast Poland, where in some towns they constituted as much as 80 percent of the population. The only remains of that community today after the decimation of the German occupation are synagogues, now frequently converted cultural centers and libraries, and old cemeteries.

In 1946 in Kielce there was a pogrom. That event has still not been explained, and some people regard it as a provocation by the secret police. Nevertheless, it is frequently cited as an example of Polish anti-Semitism. An additional instance are the events of 1968, which caused many Jews to emigrate to Israel. Lack of reaction of the authorities to outbursts of anti-Semitic graffiti is sometimes interpreted as a sign of the Polish national attitude toward Jews. Anti-Semitic attitudes are still fostered by rightist extremist from such parties as Wspolnota Narodowa (National Community).

The breakthrough in Polish-Jewish relations was the reestablishment of diplomatic relations with Israel in 1990 and the establishment of the post of main rabbi of Poland, held by Menachem Joskowicz. There are three functioning synagogues: one in Warsaw and two in Kraków.

Gypsies living in Poland come from four tribes: Lowari, Polska Roma, Bergitka Roma (mostly from the Carpathian Mountains), and Keldareshies. In the 1960s they were forbidden to camp and were forced to settle down permanently. Their different style of living has been a constant cause of conflict with other Poles. In the 1980s and 1990s there were a number of cases of anti-Gypsy arson in Poznan and Mława. The lack of Gypsy schools has been attributed to absence of coordination and differences in dialects among the various Gypsy groups. Certain steps have been undertaken by the Roman Catholic Church to remedy the situation. The church conducts an organized Ministry for Gypsies.

A Lithuanian minority of about 30,000 lives in the north of the Suwałki Region in the north eastern corner of Poland around Sejny and Punsk. Polish Lithuanians have their own schools and maintain close contacts with neighboring Lithuania.

There are about 7,000 Polish Armenians, descendants of the Armenians who came to Ukraine in the Middle Ages. They are now mostly a Polish-speaking minority, and all that differentiates them from other Poles is their historic memory and the services in the Catholic Church held in their ritual. Similarly, the Tartars are a small group of about 6,000 who live mainly in the east of the Białystok region close to the Belorussian border. After World War II they spread over the whole country. Relatively numerous communities grew up in Gdansk and Gorzów Wielkopolski. Polish Tartars are mainly Muslims. In 2000 there were six mosques; two eighteenth century mosques in the villages of Bohoniki and Kruszyniany in the Podlasie region of eastern Poland and newly constructed ones in Gdansk. Rzeszów Warsaw in Białystok. The new mosques were built with financial support from Arab countries.

An even smaller group differentiated only by religion is the Karaims. Their religion is a mixture of Christianity and Judaism. They are descendants of the members of this unique religious group who settled in Lithuania in the Middle Ages. At the moment the group consists of about two hundred people living in big cities. They maintain a small cemetery in Warsaw. Their main house of worship is in Wrocław.

Kashubians are a group differentiated by language (an old Polish dialect) and culture, although they consider themselves Poles. They live in the regions of Gdansk, Słupsk, and north of Bydgoszcz. In 1994 they founded their own high school. A problem was the choice of a single local dialect as the official language. Kashubians are basically Roman Catholics. They have a quite extensive literature.

Descendants of Czech weavers live in Zelów, near Piotrków Trybunalski. There are also small groups around Cieszyn and Kłodzko. Slovaks live in the Orava and Spish regions, near Nowy Sącz. Some intellectual representatives of that minority live in Kraków, Katowice, and Warsaw. Their common organization is the Socio-Cultural Association of Czech and Slovaks.

BIBLIOGRAPHY

Ficowski, Jerzy. *The Gypsies in Poland: History and Customs.* Warsaw: Interpress Publishers, 1989.

Paluch, Andrzej K., ed. *The Jews in Poland.* Cracow: Jagiellonian University, 1992.

Szczepanski. Marek S., ed. *Ethnic Minorities and Ethnic Majority: Sociological Studies of Ethnic Relations in Poland.* Katowice, Poland: Wydawnictwo Uniwersytetu Slaskiego, 1997.

Tomasz Marciniak

The Abortion Issue

Controversy that deeply divided Polish society after the fall of communism in 1989. In the People's Republic of Poland abortion was legalized by a law of April 27, 1956. Abortion was permitted in the case of rape or incest and for medical or economic/personal reasons. Abortions could be performed both in state-owned hospitals and in private clinics. The issue of abortion was not widely or publicly discussed during the Communist period. In 1989, after partially free national elections, members of the upper house of parliament began an effort to ban abortion. This ignited one of the longest and most hard-fought legislative battles in post–World War II Poland. During the long media campaign, nearly all significant actors in Polish society presented their views.

Public opinion polls indicated that a substantial majority of the public opposed the proposed restrictive measures, and there was strong pressure for a public referendum on the issue. President Lech Wałesa stated that he was against a referendum and that he would not sign any law legalizing abortion. The Roman Catholic bishops published a letter declaring that a referendum should not be a source of law in Poland. They declared their support for members of parliament who were faithful to "Christian values."

Following considerable debate and parliamentary negotiation, restrictive abortion legislation was passed in January 1993. It permitted abortion only if the woman's life or health was in danger, if the fetus was irreparably damaged, or if pregnancy had resulted from rape or incest.

Owing to strong public support for liberalization of the abortion law, this issue remained politically volatile. Elections in September 1993 ushered in a more left-oriented parliament, and the Parliamentary Caucus of Women presented an amendment to the abortion law to legalize abortion for economic or personal reasons. President Wałęsa, however, vetoed liberalizing amendments to the 1993 law passed by parliament in 1995. After Aleksander Kwaśniewski was elected president in 1995, both chambers of parliament passed a liberalizing amendment again and the president signed the measure into law.

In August 1996, the lower house, following the lead of the former Communists, Social Democracy of the Republic of Poland, voted to permit pregnancies before the twelfth week to be terminated because of economic hardship or personal problems. But the amendment, required counseling and a three-day waiting period. Severe penalties were also imposed on anyone performing an abortion on a viable fetus. Although the upper house of the Polish parliament voted against the legislation, the lower house on October 24, overturned the Senate veto. President Kwaśniewski then signed the law.

BIBLIOGRAPHY

Fuszara, Malgorzata. "Legal Regulation of Abortion in Poland." *Journal of Women in Culture and Society* 17 (1991): 117–28.

McCutcheon, Allan L., and Maria Nawojczyk. "Making the Break: Popular Sentiment toward Legalized Abortion among American and Polish Catholic Laities." *International Journal of Public Opinion Research* 3 (1995): 232–52.

Maria Nawojczyk

Roman Catholic Church

Largest religious body in Poland. Poland was Christianized in 966. The Roman Catholic Church has been closely connected with both the statehood and the culture of Poland for over one thousand years. Some 93 to 94 percent of Poles declare their affiliation to the Catholic Church.

During the Second World War Poland lost one-fifth of its population. Compared to other social groups the clergy were, after the Jews, the second-most affected community, with 1,932 priests, 6 bishops, 850 monks, and 289 nuns killed. These figures do not cover those persecuted and those who survived the German death camps but died after the war.

In September 1939—after the German invasion—under the agreement between the Polish government and the papal nuncio, Primate of Poland August Hlond left the country and the church worked on with overall authority. In spite of the new social and political system established in postwar Poland and the policy of the Communist authorities that aimed at the creation of an atheistic society, the church began to reconstruct religious life and church administration. The episcopate of Poland consisted of twenty bishops, compared with one hundred of 1990, after the fall of the communist regime.

At the beginning of the establishment of the Communist regime the state authorities showed remarkable restraint in its attitude toward the church. Both the Polish Committee for National Liberation on July 22, 1944, and the Sejm (parliament) on February 22, 1944, recognized freedom of religious beliefs. Part of the church's property was legally recognized and the first university in the Polish People's Republic, the Catholic University of Lublin, was established.

On July 20, 1944, Primate Hlond returned to Poland, empowered to reorganize the church system in the country. After taking over the church jurisdiction from the German church in the territories annexed from Germany in the west and north east, he set up a Polish church administration there. On September 12, 1944, the concordat between Poland and the Vatican was invalidated because of the Vatican's war policy under which some jurisdictions of the Polish church were handed over to the administration of the Roman Catholic Church in Germany. The Polish government found this decision to be a formal breech of the concordat.

On November 12, 1948, after the death of Hlond, Pope Pius XII named bishop Stefan Wyszyński primate of Poland. The new primate inherited all special powers from his predecessor. Showing conciliatory gestures toward the Communist authorities, he was unyielding as far as theological priorities were concerned. Under his administration the church founded numerous institutions, theological seminaries, church courts, bishop's curias, charities, religious buildings, and convents that provided both theological and educational or medical and charity services. Catholic activists presented their opinions and attitudes in diocesan press and other Catholic periodicals—*Znak* (*Sign*), *Tygodnik Powszechny* (*Universal Weekly*), and *Tygodnik Warszawski* (*Warsaw Weekly*).

With no major obstacles, the church carried out its religious works. There was relative freedom of worship, and catechism lessons were taught at state schools. The state provided some financial support to reconstruct churches destroyed in the war. The Catholic press was published and representatives of the hierarchy participated in public life while politicians took part in some religious services. The church itself functioned as a relatively independent social institution not affected by the political system. The Roman Catholic Church enjoyed the status of primus inter pares (first among equals) among other religions. Its broad autonomy allowed a strong influence on social life. Until 1948 relations between church and state were relatively smooth.

However, the fall of Wladysław Gomułka, the first secretary of the Polish Workers Party (Communist Party) and a National Communist, the new leadership of the Polish Workers' Party, and, after December 1949 when the Socialists were forced to merge with the Communists, subservient to Moscow the Polish United Workers' Party as it was called, launched a severe Stalinization process in many fields of social life and declared an open war against the church and religion itself. The hierarchy was accused of a hostile policy toward the state stimulated by the Vatican and Western political centers.

On March 1, 1949, Pope Pius XII sent a letter to the German Episcopate announcing that the transfer of German territory in the East to Poland was still an open issue. This again worsened the relations between state and church. The decree of the Holy Office of July 13, 1949, that anathematized Roman Catholics who collaborated with the Communist authorities did not help the situation. The state authorities began to slander the clergy and expelled some bishops from their dioceses. The work of church schools and associations was restricted, and the

Catholic press and publications were censored. *Tygodnik Warszawski* and *Znak* were closed, and *Tygodnik Powszechny* put under strict control. Monastic hospitals were nationalized, pro-church political groups were dissolved, and the church's ability to administer its institutions was impaired.

At the end of 1949 the Communist government brought into being the Committee of Priests, which organized so-called priests-patriots. The movement, supported by a regime-sponsored lay association called PAX, enrolled about two thousand clergymen.

At the same time opposition to the dictatorship of the party grew. Avoiding open, antisocialist declarations and promoting political neutrality, the church turned into an important, well-organized oppositional center. To settle the conflict, Wyszyński initiated the meeting of the so-called Combined Committee representing both the church and the regime. The government was represented by Franciszek Mazur, a member of the Communist Party's Political Bureau responsible for church affairs; the church's spokesman was Bishop Zygmunt Choromański, a secretary of the episcopate. Although the negotiations were not very successful, on April 14, 1950, a limited agreement was signed, the signatories of which were the members of the Combined Committee: Bishops Choromański, Michal Klepacz, and Zakrzewski, and, apart from Minister Wolski, Edward Ochab and Mazur on the government's side. The Polish government promised to respect freedom of religious beliefs and the episcopate promised its consideration for so-called Polish state interests. In spite of these declarations, catechism lessons were often suspended, the work of Catholic associations was restricted, and priests were often forbidden to say mass in prisons, hospitals, and other venues.

In January 1951 the apostolic administrators in the Regained Territories were replaced by chapter curates. To avoid a direct conflict and schism, Wyszyński empowered them with necessary church jurisdiction and appointed them his personal curates. The state authorities dismissed some bishops, and many officials of the church were arrested.

On July 16 some minor theological seminaries and monastic novitiates were closed. Wyszyński took precautions to prevent other persecutions. Not only did he take part in the parliamentary elections of October 1952, but he allowed the ringing of church bells on the day of Soviet dictator Stalin's funeral as well.

On February 9, 1953, the authorities issued a decree taking over crucial church posts, including that of bishops. The decree was often in conflict with the church administration's regulations. In September 1953 Primate Wyszyński was detained and interned. His successor for the time was Bishop Michal Klepacz, who remained chairman of the episcopate until October 28, 1956, when Wyszyński was released.

October 1956 witnessed a return of Gomułka, who again became first secretary of the party, and the process of liberalization in political life. Wyszyński regained his post and the Combined Committee was replaced by the Common Committee of Government and Episcopate. In December 1956 a State-Church Agreement was signed that considerably improved relations. The decree on church posts was changed, and religious instruction was reintroduced in the schools. The church regained some works of art, Catholic journals could be published again, and licences to build religious buildings were issued. In January 1957 Prime Minister Józef Cyrankiewicz, who wished for a large turn-out to indicate Polish acceptance of the regime, sought Wyszyński's support in parliamentary elections and received it. Wyszyński went to vote and even changed the Sunday mass schedule to allow Catholics to vote to conform to the situation.

On July 15, 1961, a new educational law came into force according to which state education was to have an exclusively lay character. Thus religion lessons were again taught outside of school in parishes where about twenty thousand special centers were opened.

From 1962 to 1965 the Second Vatican Council met. The Polish church before this council was sometimes regarded by proponents of reform in the Catholic Church as a "folk church" because of its traditionalism and authoritarianism, which resulted in unquestioning obedience of parishioners and uniformity of behavior and attitudes. Polish Catholicism was dominated by folk forms of worship. The Vatican Council was followed by essential changes in the Polish Catholic Church. The laity grew in importance. The liturgy was reformed, and Latin was replaced by the Polish language. Services became a dialogue between priest and parishioner. Folk religious practices began to diminish. This religious revival produced new religious movements and associations. One of them was the Light-Life Movement, which developed fully in the 1980s.

November 18, 1965, brought another turn in church-state relations. When an effort to hold talks between Polish and German bishops did not materialize, Polish bishops sent a letter to their German colleagues in which they "forgave and sought forgiveness." Forty-two German bishops answered the letter, but Poland's Communist government found it to be an interference in political affairs and refused permission for Pope Paul VI to visit Poland.

From 1945 to 1970 over one thousand two hundred churches were built or reconstructed and the number of priests grew by some 60 percent. The 1970s and the 1980s brought many newly conceived projects and investments in theological education, as well as some important changes in church-state relations. When the government ruthlessly suppressed workers' protests, Wyszyński called for bloodshed to be prevented, and the church assumed the role of mediator in the December 1970 conflicts. That certainly helped to preserve social stability. In return for this several buildings in the territories gained from Germany at the end of World War II were transferred by the government to the church and meetings of a "working group" from Poland and the Vatican began.

Cardinal Wyszyński at age seventy-five wanted, in accordance with canon law, to retire. The government asked the Vatican to delay his resignation. In the mid-1970s the economic situation in the country considerably worsened. In July and August 1980 workers went on strike and Wyszyński mediated again. The new leaders of the Communist Party sought an agreement with the church and gave up ideological confrontation.

Wyszyński died on May 28, 1981. On July 9 bishop Józef Glemp was elected primate of Poland. When several months later the regime, in an effort to crush Solidarity, imposed martial law, the anti-Communist labor union, Solidarity, found strong support from the church and the cardinal himself. The episcopate of Poland, a main political mediator, was soon to take the side of Solidarity in the contest between the union and the regime. The assassination of the priest Jerzy Popiełuszko was followed by a break between the church and the government. The church became a center of independent criticism and at the same time because of its status and backing a deterrent against the use of arbitrary force by the regime. The church won social support and strengthened its educational function.

A new wave of strikes in April 1988 resulted in the so-called Round Table talks in February and April 1989 in which the church was represented by Bronisław Dembowski and Alojzy Orszulik. The parliamentary elections of June 4 brought an overwhelming victory to Solidarity.

In the new post-Communist state the church enjoyed the privileged status of a stimulator of social change. Initially its sociopolitical involvement was fully approved by society. However, some of its political initiatives were far from accepted. In September 1990 the Common Government-Episcopate Committee agreed to reintroduce religious instruction in the schools. The minister of education decreed this in April 1992. The decree, however, was taken to the Court of the Constitution by the state civil rights ombudsman Tadeusz Zielmski. In answer to this some members of the hierarchy demanded the spokesman's dismissal.

Then in parliamentary elections of 1991 the church declared its neutrality but soon started its own moral and political campaign in which the issue of abortion became the defining litmus test for church support or opposition as far as candidates were concerned. The Catholic Electoral Action and some electoral committees could rely on priests for advice and support. Moreover, the hierarchy pressured the government to promulgate regulations that compelled Christian values to be "respected" in mass-media, and, taking advantage of the amendment to the State-Church Agreement of May 1989, it regained most of its former property.

The Catholic Church, in both its declarations and its actions, began a campaign of political and social pressures and demands that resulted in a remarkable change in social attitudes toward this once highly respected institution. Poles in general, and part of the church hierarchy as well, have not accepted church interference in purely political affairs.

In the early 1990s the church in Poland had not yet defined its place in the new society.

BIBLIOGRAPHY

Stachura, Peter D. *Poland in the Twentieth Century.* New York: St. Martin's Press, 1999.

Stehle, Hansjakob. *Eastern Politics of the Vatican 1917–1979.* Tr. by Sandra Smith. Athens: Ohio University Press, 1981.

Stokes, Gale. *The Walls Came Tumbling Down: The Collapse of Communism in Eastern Europe.* New York: Oxford University Press, 1993.

Paweł Załęcki

SEE ALSO Glemp, Józef; Popiełuszko, Jerzy; Wyszyński, Stefan

Press

The Polish press after 1947 was totally controlled by the Communist Party. Preemptive censorship and the party's direct influence on printed material did not allow a free portrayal of the information in the legal press.

Together with the strengthening of the party's hegemony after 1945, attempts to limit the development of the press were undertaken. The liquidation of the relatively independent local press began in 1947. To control the mass media, the party limited the number of publications associated with its political opponents. On April

25, 1947, the party created the Workers' Publishing Cooperative (RSW), or Prasa, which was to carry out the party's informational policy. The aim of this decision was to concentrate all party publications and writers in one organization. The rest of the press, however, had to be associated with the RSW as well.

In 1951 the RSW absorbed the press division of the Czytelnik publishing house. (Czytelnik had been set up in 1944 to attract and neutralize untrustworthy groups of intelligentsia and journalists.) With elimination of the opposition, Czytelnik was no longer needed. Its absorption increased the Communists' share of the press from 53 to 80 percent. This completed their monopolization of the press.

In 1973 the RSW absorbed Ruch, which controlled press distribution, and the publishing house Książka i Wiedza. The conglomerate RSW "Prasa-Książka-Ruch," owned by the Communist Party, was created and soon controlled 85 percent of total press production in Poland.

The RSW allowed the Communists to control almost the entire press of the country. The party could also select journalists on political grounds and control distribution and promotion of the press. The syndicate was especially convenient to the party's needs. It ended all financial independence of publishers, subjected the local press to central and local party authorities, and limited the number of titles and increased their circulation, which led to the standardization of the content of the press.

Yet it was difficult for the party to monopolize the press in Poland because of readers' opposition. To achieve this goal, the party introduced forced subscriptions.

By 1952 each province had a local paper that was the party's organ. The party assumed that its effectiveness in manipulating the press would increase with the decreased opposition among journalists. The party, therefore, began to control personnel policy by controlling promotions and benefits, recruitment, salary administration, and professional training.

Beside the RSW, which the party owned, the only other publications allowed were those of the Catholic Church, movements allied with the party, the military, and a few specialized interest areas. There was also the illegal press associated with the opposition. It had limited distribution, and the authorities combated it with police and administrative methods. Among the legal Catholic newspapers but independent from the special role assigned to that sector by the Communists was *Tygodnik Powszechny.* It was founded in March 1945 and closed by the Communists in 1953 when it refused to publish a eulogy upon the death of Soviet leader Stalin. It was reopened in 1956 during temporary liberalization of press control. This short thaw ended in October 1957 with the suppression of *Po Prostu,* the magazine associated with the Marxist revisionists, who called for greater democratization and liberalization of the regime.

The founding of Solidarity caused another liberalization of the press control. That period, however, ended with martial law in December 1981, which brought about the suppression of many publications. At the same time the party purged journalists. Another period of liberalization began in the mid-1980s. Democratic changes initiated by the Round Table agreements produced by negotiations between representatives of the regime and Solidarity in early 1989 required changes in the functioning of the press. The collapse of the Communist Party in 1990 led to the liquidation of the RSW. Some of its magazines and newspapers were taken over by cooperatives founded by former RSW employees or by various political parties. The rest fell into the hands of foreign or Polish businesses.

Piotr Skuz

Independent or Underground Publications

Materials usually dealing with sociopolitical, historical, and literary issues were published by independent organizations, publishing houses, and various social groups (students, trade unions) in Poland between 1976 and 1990 and circulated outside approved channels to circumvent state censorship.

Until the mid-1970s the Communist government had controlled all mass media, education, and culture; all performance halls, cinemas, theaters, printing machines, and radio and television broadcasts; and the production and distribution of paper. The emergence of underground publications was prompted by the events of 1976 when price increases led to strikes and clashes with the police and the arrest of workers and the founding of such dissident organizations as the Workers Defense Committee (KOR), the Movement for the Defense of Human and Civil Rights, and the Confederation for an Independent Poland. Democratic opposition organizations and movements began to publish and circulate censor-free journals and books. Soon movements independent of the Communist Party were set up by students, the Student Solidarity Committee including an underground university, the Young Poland Movement, and Free Trade Unions. Independent publishing houses, such as Niezależna Oficyna Wydawnicza (Independent Publishing House, NOWA), Krag, KOS, and CDN, were also set up. Regular bulletins, "Biuletyn Informacyjny" and "Robotnik," and large literary and political magazines—*Zapis, Krytyka, Opinia, Puls, Głos, Spotkania*—were published. Books and journals were printed on rather primitive presses brought illegally to Poland from the West. Runs of independent publications from 1976 to 1980 never exceeded one thousand copies.

Famous Polish writers, poets, scholars, and journalists whose works were stopped by censorship published underground, using either pseudonyms or their real names. Many reprints of books published abroad and banned by Polish censorship were also available from underground publishers. Translations of works by Western and Eastern European writers were also published underground. The subject matter of underground-published books ranged from literature to political science, sociology, history, philosophy, education, handbooks, children's stories, and cartoons. Audio and video cassettes were also published. The principal consumers of independent publications were the intelligentsia, students, organized workers, and independent libraries. Funds for these projects came principally from Polish émigrés through the Instytut Literacki in Paris, the Polish American Congress, and the Polish Canadian Congress. After the founding of the Solidarity labor union in 1980, and especially during the period of martial law (1981–83), circulation of independent publications grew. Book editions ran to 5,000 copies and journals up to 30,000. The biggest circulation was that of *Tygodnik mazowsze,* with 60,000 copies. It is calculated that from 1976 to 1990, with a special concentration in 1981–85, about 6,000 different books and 4,000 journals and bulletins were published. The underground publishing movement owned secret printing shops, developed distribution channels, established libraries, and even produced printing machines.

It is estimated that about 250,000 Poles read independent publications. In 1990 the Main Office of Control of Press, Publications and Performances in Warsaw was closed, and independent publishers were legalized.

BIBLIOGRAPHY

Blumsztajn, Seweryn. *Une Pologne hors censure.* Paris: Association Solidarité France-Pologne, 1988.

Mastny, Vojtech, ed. *Soviet/East European Survey, 1983–84.* Durham, N.C.: Duke University Press, 1985.

Papierowa rewolucja: *Underground publishing in communist Poland.* Fribourg, Switzerland: Bibliotheque Cantonale et Universitaire, 1992.

Preibisz, Joanna M. *Polish Dissident Publications.* New York: Praeger, 1982.

Mirosław Supruniuk

Art

Polish art after World War II was closely connected with political life. Right after the war artists attempted to continue the prewar tradition. But shortly afterward, art fell under strong Soviet influence. The era of socialist realism was officially proclaimed and, by definition, that kind of art was intended to serve Communist ideology. Conceptual art was heavily criticized and artists were meant to fulfill the directives of the Communist Party. Literature was similarly affected.

Architecture of that period was characterized by monumental buildings resembling those built in the Soviet Union. An example is the Joseph Stalin Palace of Culture and Science, which dominates the landscape of Warsaw. Officially the palace was a "gift" of the Soviet Union to Poland. However, all the materials came from destroyed palaces in the north and west of Poland, lands transferred by Germany to Poland after World War II. A number of high-rise residential quarters and towns such as Nowa Huta, near Kraków, were intended to be a working-class counterweight to conservative and Catholic Kraków.

Some artists voluntarily joined the Communist Party to build a new system or further careers. Among these were sculptor Alfons Karny, who created monuments of anonymous welders and miners, and Stefan Zechowski, known for paintings that created scandal before the war. Painters began to paint portraits of Stalin and leaders of other Communist countries as well as pictures of workers and farmers at everyday work. Today this embarrassing period is documented in the in Kozłówka museum near Lublin.

Despite the severely limited flow of information from Western countries the period witnessed the beginning of the Polish style of posters. The most outstanding representatives were Waldemar Swieży, Franciszek Starowieyski, and Andrzej Pągowski, who would later become art manager of the Polish edition of *Playboy.* This utilitarian art was the only group achievement of postwar art in Poland.

The works of Polish illustrators are well known. These include Daniel Mroz and Jan Marcin Szancer, the representatives of the older generation; and Janusz Stanny, Janusz Grabiński, Bohdan Butenko, and Sławomir Jezierski of the younger generation.

The political change of 1956 opened Poland to the influence of Western art. That influence was reflected almost immediately in literature, film, and plays.

After Edward Gierek came to power (1970) relations between church and state improved. A number of modern churches were built, and in Hajnówka the first postwar Orthodox church in Eastern Europe was constructed.

Comics, a combination of fine art and literature, are the only element of Western culture not developed extensively in Poland. In the 1950s comics were decried along with jazz as counter revolutionary. Later, however, they were used as an element of official propaganda, dealing with matters such as World War II, criminal stories, and science fiction. Since 1991 national conventions of comics authors has been held in Lodz. The most important authors are Henryk Jerzy Chmielewski (*Tytus, romek i A'Tomek*), Janusz Christa (*Kajko i Kokosz*), and Boguslaw Polch. Grzegorz Rosiński (*Thorgal*) lives in Switzerland.

The best-known contemporary Polish painters are Jerzy Duda-Gracz, Stanisław Get-Stankiewicz, and Zdzisław Beksiński. The sculptures of Magdalena Abakanowicz are well known. Władysław Hasior is a controversial precursor of avant-garde pop art.

Political changes at the end of the 1980s that created a private market economy also produced a private market for art. A high number of privately owned art galleries and foundations have been established. The film and theatrical director Andrzej Wajda, for example, created an outstanding Center for Japanese Culture in Kraków.

There are state as well as privately owned institutes of higher education offering studies in a variety of art disciplines. A number of periodicals are also devoted exclusively to art, such as the bilingual *Art and Business, Architektura,* and *Sztuka i wychowanie.*

BIBLIOGRAPHY

Olszewski, Andrzej K. *Dzieje sztuki polskiej 1890–1980.* Warsaw: Interpress, 1988.

Thomas Marciniak

Cinema

On November 13, 1945, the Communist government decreed the establishment of a state-owned company Film Polski (Polish Cinema). Film Polski was awarded a monopoly for all motion picture activities including production, distribution, and exhibition. Nationalization of the film industry served mostly the party's ideological control. State and Communist Party officials exerted considerable influence over the subjects treated by films and even over the composition of film crews. This control was especially strong during the late 1940s and early 1950s. In 1949 the Higher School of Film at Lodz was established. Eventually, its graduates exercised profound influence on the shape and future of the industry.

The first films of the 1940s were wartime memories: Leonard Buczkowski's *Zakazane piosenki* (*Forbidden Songs,* 1947), Wanda Jakubowska's *Ostatni etap,* (*The Last Stage,* 1948), Aleksander Ford's *Ulica graniczna,* (*Border Street,* 1949).

Also in 1949 the congress of filmmakers at Wisla proclaimed the principles of socialist realism. It required the arts to contribute strongly to the socialist reeducation of society. In the first half of the 1950s few films were produced. Most were schematic and full of ideology. However, a new direction was launched in 1954 with Ford's *Piątka z ulicy Barskiej* (*Five Bays with Barska Street,* 1954). In 1955 the period of de-Stalinization began in politics as well as in the fine arts. On May 1, 1955, the Creative Film Unit came into being. Under this system, which was to survive various political vicissitudes, directors, scriptwriters, cameramen, production managers, and assistants came together in separate companies. Each unit made up something like a cooperative that attempted to realize the projects of its members. Finance, distribution, and promotion were in the hands of the state. Also by 1955, noted filmmakers Andrzej Wajda, Andrzej Munk, Kazimierz Kutz, and Janusz Morgenstern had all graduated from the Lodz Film School. All those factors created conditions of intellectual ferment, artistic adventure, and critical approach. The first results of all this atmosphere were films and directors that were later called the Polish School. As an artistic phenomenon the Polish School ended in the mid-1960s. The best films of this school include Wajda's *Kanał* (*Canal,* 1957), *Popiół i diament* (*Ashes and Diamonds,* 1958), and *Lotna* (1959); Munk's *Eroica* (1958) and *Zezowate szczęście* (*Bad Luck,* 1960); Jerzy Kawalerowicz's *Pociąg* (*Night Train,* 1959), and *Matka Joanna od Aniołów* (*Mother Joan of the Angels,* 1961); Wojciech Has's *Pętla* (*The Noose, 1958*); Kutz's *Krzyż walecznych* (*Cross of Valor,* 1959); Stanisław Różewicz's *Wolne miasto* (*Free City,* 1958); and Czesław and Ewa Petelskis' *Kamienne niebo* (*A Sky of Stone,* 1959), and *Ogniomistrz Kaleń* (*Sergeant-Major Kalen,* 1961). The success of the Polish School was also due to cameramen such as Jerzy Wójcik and Jerzy Lipman; scriptwriters such as Jerzy Stefan Stawiński, Tadeusz Konwicki, Andrzej Ścibor-Rylski, and Józef Hen; and actors such as Zbigniew Cybulski, Edward Dziewoński, Gustaw Holoubek, Bogumił Kobiela, Tadeusz Janczar, and Ewa Krzyżewska.

The 1960s were called in Poland "a small stabilization" period. The films of that era did not deal with large social events; instead they became rather simple stories about various issues. There were still remnants of the Polish School: Munk's *Pasażerka* (*The Passenger,* 1963), Has's *Jak byc kochana* (*How to Be Loved,* 1963), Rozewicz's *Swiadectwo urodzenia* (*The Birth Certificate,* 1961) and *Westerplatte* (1967), and Konwicki's *Salto* (1965). Historical spectacles based on classic national literature were produced: Kawalerowicz's *Faraon* (*The Pharaoh,* 1965), Wajda's *Popioły* (*Ashes,* 1965); and Has's *Rękopis znaleziony w Saragossie* (*The Saragossa Manuscript,* 1966) and *Lalka* (*The Doll,* 1968). A new generation of directors also appeared: Roman Polański with his *Nóż w wodzie* (*Knife in the Water,* 1961); Jerzy Skolimowski with his *Rysopis* (*Identification Marks, None,* 1964), *Bariera* (*The Barrier,* 1966), and *Ręce do góry* (*Hands Up!,* 1968 but censored and released for showing only in 1985); Krzysztof Zanussi with his *Struktura kryształu* (*Structure of Crystal,* 1969).

As of the early 1960s documentaries developed into a strong branch of the Polish film industry. In Kraków the Festival of Short Films was established, and in the 1980s this became international. During the 1960s the best documentaries were made by Jerzy Bossak, Kazimierz Karabasz, and Roman Wionezek. In the late 1960s and the first half of 1970s interesting documentaries were produced by Marek Piwowski, Grzegorz Królikiewicz, Krzysztof Kieślowski, and Tomasz Zygadło. When they later started to make full-length features, they brought to them a new perspective. At this time the "old masters" made more universal films: Wajda's *Wszystko na sprzedaz* (*Everything for Sale,* 1969), *Brzezina* (*Birchwood,* 1970), and *Ziemia Obiecana* (*Land of Promise,* 1975); Has's *Sanatorium pod klepsydrą* (*Hospital under the Hourglass,* 1974); and Zanussi's *Życie rodzinne* (*Family Life,* 1971), and *Illuminacja* (*Illumination,* 1973).

With Wajda's *Człowiek z marmuru* (*Man of Marble*) and Zanussi's *Barwy ochronne* (*Camouflage*), 1976 saw the beginning of the second important period of Polish film — the Cinema of Moral Concern. The style of the films of this movement was derived from documentary tradition. The content showed a concern for moral issues related to political and social problems. From them, it appears that moral consciousness had but one safety valve, the cinema, and the films offered the viewer a system of positive values. The most representative films of this movement are Wajda's *Bez znieczulenia* (*Rough Treatment,* 1978) and *Człowiek z żelaza* (*Man of Iron,* 1981); Zanussi's *Spirala* (*Spiral,* 1978), *Konstans* (*The Constant Factor,* 1980), and *Kontrakt* (*Contract,* 1980); Piwowski's *Przepraszam, czy tu biją?* (*Foul Play,* 1976); Zygadło's *Rebus* (1977), *Ćma* (*The Moth,* 1980); Feliks Falk's *Wodzirej* (*Top Dog,* 1977); Kieślowski's *Amator* (*Film Buff,* 1979); Agnieszka Holland's *Aktorzy prowincjonalni* (*Provincial Actors,* 1979); and Wojciech Marczewski's *Dreszcze* (*Shivers,* 1981). These films featured a new generation of actors: Krystyna Janda, Jerzy Stuhr, Jerzy Radziwilowicz, and Marek Kondrat.

After the 1981 declaration of martial law, censorship prevented the distribution of some films: Kieślowski's *Przypadek* (*Coincidence,* 1981, not released until 1987); Jerzy Domaradzki's *Wielki bieg* (*The Big Race,* 1981, not released until 1987); Ryszard Bugajski's *Przesłuchanie* (*Interrogation,* 1981, not released until 1989); and Janusz Zaorki's *Matka Króláw* (*Mother of Kings,* 1982, not released until 1987). Some directors turned again to literature-based stories: Wajda's *Danton* (1983) and Kawalerowicz's *Austeria* (1983). Relatively popular were comedies made by Juliusz Machulski, Sylwester Chęciński, and Janusz Majewski. Kieslowski turned back from the political and social issues toward more universal problems to produce *Dekalog* (*Decalogue,* 1987) and consequently in the 1990s *Podwójne życie Weroniki* (*The Double Life of Veronika,* 1991) and *Trzy kolory—Niebieski, Bialy, Czerwony* (*Three Colours: Blue, White, Red,* 1992–93).

In the late 1980s decentralization of distribution started and the repertory of Polish movie theaters became dominated by foreign, mostly American, films. This process was accelerated in the 1990s because of privatization of distribution.

The political transformation that has taken place in Poland since the beginning of the 1990s has not found its reflection in films. The new films made by the younger generation are very much like American action films. However, new talented directors such as Jan Jakub Kolski, Filip Zylber, and Dorota Kędzierzawska show promise.

BIBLIOGRAPHY

David, Paul, ed. *Politics, Art and Commitment.* London: Macmillan, 1983.

Fuksiewicz, Jacek. *Polish Cinema.* Warsaw: Interpress, 1973.

Historia filmu polskiego (*History of Polish Film*). 6 Vols.: Vols. 1–4 ed. by Jerzy Tooplitz; Vols. 5–6 ed. by Rafał Marszałek. Warsaw: Wydawnictwo Artystyczne i Filmowe, 1966–94.

Michałek, Bolesław, and Frank Turaj. *The Modern Cinema of Poland.* Bloomington: Indiana University Press, 1988.

Maria Nawojczyk

Theater

Polish theater mirrored and at times affected the political and cultural currents of Poland after World War II.

Between 1944 and 1948 there was a reconstruction of Polish theater life according to the projects devised by the Theater Council, which functioned underground during the war, but this was limited in scope because of the new political reality as the Communists consolidated their monopoly of power. It focused on the rebuilding of old theaters and the creation of new ones, especially in the western provinces of the country that were taken from Germany at the end of World War II and the organization of drama schools. That time was also characterized by the nationalization of theaters by the Communist regime.

During this period the major theaters were in Lodz, the Theater of the Polish Army and the Kameralny Theater; Kraków, Juliusz Słowacki's Theater, the Old Theater, and the Rhapsodic Theater; Toruń, Wilam Horzyca; and Gdansk, Iwo Gall. The repertoire consisted of Polish and foreign classical works, especially comedy, contemporary world drama, especially the famous premiere of Jean Giraudoux's *Electra,* and contemporary Polish plays dealing with issues of war, history, and politics. A great debate centered around Jerzy Szaniawski's *Dwa teatry* (*Two Theaters*).

Artists of the older generation, fully formed before World War II, played an important role in the early postwar theater. Among the directors were Wilam Horzyca; Leon Schiller, founder of Polish fundamental theater; Edmund Wiercinski and Iwo Gall, both associated with Juliusz Osterwa's *Reduta;* and Bohdan Korzeniowski. Among art directors were Karol Frycz, A. Pronaszko, and Władysław Daszewski. The major actors were Ludwik Solski, Karol Adwentowicz, and Aleksandr Zelwerowicz. Mieczysław Kotlarczyk's original Rhapsodic Theater functioned until 1967; Karol Wojtyła, later Pope John Paul II, was associated with it. Erwin Axer's "literary" theater also began at that time; it was based on contemporary Western and Polish repertoire and "hidden" directorship. Great performances by Stefania Perzanowska, I. Eichlerówna, Jacek Woszczerowicz, Tadeusz Fijewski, Zofia Mrozowska, A. Śląska, Adam Łapicki, Tadeusz Łomnicki, Zbigniew Zapasiewicz, M. Komorowska, and Julius Englert took place there. Axer continued his "theater for the intelligentsia" until 1981.

The period from 1949 to 1956 was characterized by the Communist Party's proclamation of the doctrine of socialist realism and the centralization of cultural policy, which forced ideological and stylistic unity on theaters and all the arts. The Festival of Russian and Soviet Art, begun in 1949, and the Festival of Polish Contemporary Drama, launched in 1951, were used to stage standard-setting productions. The repertoire consisted of classical productions, limited by the criterion of class struggle and a primitive rationalism, contemporary pieces dominated by social drama, creating the model for a new positive protagonist—the so-called industrial intelligentsia. Leon Kruczkowski became the most famous Polish playwright during this period, and Warsaw became the main center for Polish theater.

Young actors under the direction of Kazimierz Dejmek signaled the first symptoms of the ideological-aesthetic changes of October 1956. The turning point was preceded by the visit of Bertold Brecht's Company from Berlin in 1952, participation of Polish theaters in the Paris Festival of the Nations in 1954, and the appearance of a new political theater critical toward reality exemplified by J. Lutkowski's *Ostry Dyżur,* directed by Axer; Władimir Władimirawlicz Majakowski's *Laznia;* and Jerzy Andrzejewski and Jerzy Zagórski's *Święto Winkelrida,* directed by Dejmek. Dejmek also prepared Stanisław Wyspiański's *Noc listopadowa* in 1956), the second production of a Polish classical work after the Polish Theater's *Dziady* in 1956.

The period 1956–68 witnessed the new cultural policy of thaw. Besides criticism of Stalinism, the introduction of new topics such as Polish military participation in the West during the war and the activities of the wartime Home Army, as well as various creative initiatives, helped to reinvigorate the Polish theater. There was also decentralization of theater life. The placing of theaters under local administration promoted development of theaters throughout the country. There were soon sixty active theaters. Provincial theaters, to promote their achievements, organized the Festival of Theaters of Northern Poland in Toruń in 1959 and the Kalisz Theater Meetings in 1961. The former initiative continued for over thirty years; the latter is still functioning. New, more widely organized festivals also began to emerge: the Festival of Polish Modern Art at Wrocław and the Festival of Russian and Soviet Art at Katowice. The former still continues, along with the associated Polish Theater Confrontations–Polish Classical Works in Opole. The repertoire during this period became more diverse. It consisted of foreign classical works, from antiquity to the first part of the twentieth century, with special emphasis on Shakespeare and Polish classics, from early Polish plays to Stanisław Ignacy Witkiewicz and Witold Gombrowicz, with special emphasis on the romantics—Adam Mickiewicz, Juliuz Słowacki, Zygmunt Krassiński, Cyprian Norwid, and the neoromantic Stanisław Wyspiański. A broad spectrum of new plays was also introduced: Bertolt Brecht, Jean Paul Sartre, Samuel Beckett, Eugene Ionesco, Max Frisch, Friedrich Dürrenmat, Jean Genet, as well as Polish authors Sławomir Mrożek, Tadeusz Różewicz, Jerzy Broszkiewicz, Roman Brandstaetter, and Stanisław Grochowiak.

Two important theaters of that time were the People's Theater in Nowa Huta under directors Krystyna Skuszanka and Jerzy Krasowski, and the Dramatic Theater of Warsaw under directors L. Ren, L. Zmkow, and Konrad Swinarski and with actors Ida Kaminska, Halina Mikołajska, Ryszarda Hanin, Barbara Krafftówna, Jan Świderski, and E. Czyżewska. At the end of this period the National Theater began to play a special role. Its director, Dejmek, and art director Andrzej Stopka attempted to develop a Polish theatrical style. This consisted of a synthesis of the old Polish theater with peasant culture. Their attempts resulted in the staging of *Dziady (Forefathers' Eve)* in 1967. The ban of this production was a direct cause of the March events of 1968.

In the area of classical repertoire there was a transition from great actor creations and pure theater effects toward a contemporary, usually political, interpretation of plays. Producers begin to use aesthetic expressions of the grotesque, traditionally associated only with a contemporary repertoire. They were supported by the achievements of art directors who broke with the service function of theater scene design and became sources of the most revolutionary changes in the theater. The two competing scene design schools were the Warsaw school with Jan Kosiński, A. Sadowski, Zofia Wierchowicz, Ewa Starowieyska, and Jerzy A. Krassowski; and the Kraków school with Tadeusz Kantor, Józef Szajna, Wojciech Krakowski, Andrzej Majewski, Krystyna Zachwatowicz, Krzysztof Pankiewicz, and Kazimierz Wiśniak.

The "hegemony of fine arts in the theater" was manifested by the phenomenon of "staging of fine arts" represented by Józef Szajna's kinetic set design and Kantor in the Cricot-2 Theater. In the Kraków puppet theater "Grotesque," Zofia and Władysław Jarema together with art directors Lidia and Jerzy Skarżyński and surreal painter K. Mikulski created a mask theater. For adult audiences they presented Sławomir Mrożek, A. Jarr (Alfred Jarry?), and Michel de Ghelderod. The Pantomime Theater of Henryk Tomaszewski was established in 1958. In 1959 Jerzy Grotowski created his "poor theater," based on the relation of an actor with the audience.

Between 1968 and 1981 the theater, like the rest of Polish culture, was placed under intensified censorship and functioned in an atmosphere of recurring political unrest. At that time Polish theater went through its "golden period" of development. From 1968 to 1978, Wrocław was host to the International Festival of Student Theater Festivals and became one of the most important European forums for representing "open," alternative theater. In 1975 the Season of Nations' Theaters was organized in Warsaw. In the repertoire of this period Polish and foreign classical works dominated, and there was growing interest in Gombrowicz. In the contemporary repertoire, the so-called neoproductions written by both Soviet and Polish authors become popular. Also historical drama, in which reconstruction of facts from the past was less important than contemporary political allusions, developed under Jerzy Zurek, Tomasz Lubienski, Jerzy Mikke, and Jerzy S. Sito. In 1980 the works of émigré Polish authors Czesław Miłosz, Marek Hłasko, Tadeusz Konwicki, Stanislaw Barańczak, and Zbigniew Herbert returned in the form of adaptations. Also dramatic works of the future pope, Karol Wojtyła, reemerged.

At the beginning of that period a generation of "young and talented directors" appeared who followed the current of reinterpretation of classical repertoire, but, rather than updating its contents, searched for new aesthetic approaches. M. Prus, Helmut Kajzar, Jerzy Grzegorzewski and Izabella Cywińska belong to this group. Grzegorzewski founded his "visionary" theater, which continues on the stage of the Old Theater and the Studio Theater. At the National Theater Adam Hanuszkiewicz presented classical repertoire in the style of the "young and talented." In staging solutions he directly referred to the audience whose artistic sensitivity was shaped by mass media. But the Old Theater in Kraków, thanks to three directors—Arthur Swinarski, Andrjez Wajda, and Jerzy Jarocki—stood out. This theater became the premier stage in Poland. Jarocki distinguished himself as a producer of contemporary repertoire—Stanisław Ignacy Witkacy, Witold Gombrowicz, and Tadeusz Różewicz—while Swinarski and Wajda specialized in Polish romantic and neoromantic plays. The former directed Shakespeare and the latter adaptations of Dostoyevski.

Throughout the 1970s an alternative theater movement developed. It was inspired by Western experience of counterculture theater, and grew as a protest against the theater-institution and the social-political "unreality" of that period. The most renowned companies were associated with student communities—the Calambur Theater from Wrocław, the Theater of 100 and the Pleonazmus from Kraków, the Theater of the Eight Days from Poznan, and the Academy of Movement from Warsaw. From the experiences of Grotowski the Theatrical Association Gardzienica also emerged in 1977. Its founder, Wlodzimierz Staniewski, sought the new environment for theater in the sphere of traditional culture.

The period 1981–89 was marked by a repressive cultural policy and growing opposition. During martial law all theaters were closed, their management subjected political scrutiny, many productions were banned, and actors boycotted TV and radio. The theater escaped toward a repertoire for children and light entertainment. The plays of B. Schffer became popular. At the beginning of that period a new generation of directors—Krystian Lupa, R. Major, K. Zaleski, Krzysztof Babicki, M. Grabowski, Janusz Wiśniewski, and Tadeusz Bradecki—joined the ranks of the young and talented. Despite many aesthetic differences, they were similar in that they did not negate theater tradition and wanted the theater to become a place for searching for the truth about reality; they preferred ethics over aesthetics. The (alias of Witkacy) Stanisław Ignacy Witkiewicz Theater in Zakopane under the direction of Andrzej Dziuk, which attempted to marry the aesthetic ideal of alternative theater with the pragmatism of the institutional theater, became popular.

The year 1989 ushered in a transformation of Polish theater on both the aesthetic and the organizational planes. Theaters remained state owned, but, to a large extent, were funded by local authorities. The theater became increasingly commercial, and theaters in smaller towns closed. Liberated from political and national pressures, the theater sought a place in the new Polish society.

Janusz Skuczynski

Music

The socialist political system allowed only for state patronage of culture, including music. The state supported musical institutions and awarded scholarships. After World War II there were nine opera theaters in Poland, nine operetta and music theaters, twenty philharmonic orchestras, and three radio orchestras, the Symphonic Orchestra of the Polish Radio and TV in Katowice, and ensembles in Kraków and Warsaw. Music education was conducted by eight music academies and a network of primary and secondary music schools. Musicology also flourished. Polish music publishers played an important role in the development of music in postwar Poland. Among many music festivals and competitions worth mentioning are the International Frederick Chopin Piano Competition, reactivated in 1949 and after 1955 organized every five years; the International Henryk Wieniawski Violin Competition, reactivated in 1952 and held every five years; the International Modern Music Festival Warszawska Jesien, founded in 1956; and the oratory-cantata festival Vratislavia Cantans.

Postwar musical life in Poland can be divided into four periods. The first reconstruction (1945–48). The second is real socialism (1948–56), during which music served the ruling ideology. Music inspired by local folklore was preferred. Access to Western musical culture was strictly limited. Foreign avant-garde music and the search for new means of expression by Poles were severely criticized. The third period came with the political thaw of 1956 (1956–89) and allowed the development of musical techniques and concepts. Creative freedom allowed Polish musicians to join the European vanguard. The fourth period begins as of 1989. With the fall of communism state patronage over culture decreased, placing many cultural institutions in serious financial difficulties. As one effect the tempo of musical life in Poland slowed.

After World War II many Polish composers produced music influenced by national traditions; they used Polish dance rhythm and folk tunes as themes for their symphonies, suites, and concertos. Polyphonic music was important. The dodecaphonic (twelve-tone) technique was also used. Aleatory concepts were also influential. The founding of the Center of Experimental Music in the Polish Radio was a direct result of interest in electronic music. Since the 1980s religious elements have entered Polish music. A recent addition to world-class chamber music ensembles is the Silesian Quartet.

After 1945 a group of composers continued their prewar activities, including Grazyna Bacewicz, Witold Lutosławski, Artur Malawski, Jan Maklakiewicz, Zygmunt Mycielski, Kazimierz Sikorski, and Tadeusz Szeligowski. After the war, new composers on the scene were Tadeusz Baird, Henryk Mikolaj Górecki, Wojciech Kilar, Włodzimierz Kotoński, Andrzej Panufnik, Krzysztof Penderecki, Kazimierz Serocki, and Bogusław Schaeffer. Górecki, whose *Third Symphony of Sorrowful Songs* (1977) became one of Poland's most popular classical music pieces, acquired international fame. Lutosławski, Penderecki, Roman Maciejewski, Roman Palester, and Panufnik, whose *Katyn Epitaph* (1967) was banned in Poland, also enjoy international recognition.

Conductors Jerzy Maksymiuk and Agnieszka Duczmal; singers Teresa Żylis-Gara, Stefania Woytowicz, and Wiesław Ochman; and performers Kristian Zimerman, Henrk Szeryng, Konstanty Andrzej Kulka, and Wanda Wiłkomirska gained world recognition.

As of the 1960s popular music became increasingly important, but, only Polish jazz made an impact in the international arena. Initially, the Communist authorities considered jazz to be synonymous with "reactionary American culture." Krzysztof Komeda, the best Polish jazz player, made his first steps, with the Melomani, a jazz group founded after the war. After 1956 jazz ceased to be regarded as politically unacceptable and this enabled it to develop. In 1956 the *Astigmatic* was recorded (Krzysztof Komeda, Tomasz Stańko, Zbigniew Namysłowski). Even today it is considered the best Polish jazz album. In the 1960s Tomasz Stańko's Quintet was established, specializing in jazz improvization. In the 1970s there were interesting attempts to connect Polish folk music with jazz (Zbigniew Namyslowski). At that time such artists as Urszula Dudziak, Adam Makowicz, and Michał Urbaniak began their careers, subsequently continuing them in the United States. In the 1980s the most famous Polish jazz band was Krzesimir Dębski's String Connection. Until 1989 the Jazz Jamboree held annually in Warsaw was the only important jazz festival in central and Eastern Europe.

Other important figures of Polish jazz include Czesław Bartkowski, Wojciech Karolak, Mieczysław Kosz, Sławomir Kulpowicz, Janusz Muniak, Zbigniew Seifert, Tomasz Szukalski, Jaroslaw Śmietana, and Jan Ptaszyn Wróblewski.

Other genres of Polish music did not excite wider interest even though Ewa Demarczyk (art song) and Czesław Niemen (rock) received positive reviews. Recently, Zbigniew Preisner's film music, especially for Krzysztof Kieślowski's films, has acquired international critical acclaim.

BIBLIOGRAPHY

Bacuiewski, Krzysztof. *Polska twórczość kompozytorska 1945–1984.* Kraków: PWM, 1987.

Dziebowska, Elzbieta, ed. *Polska współczesna kultura muzyczna.* Kraków: PWM, 1968.

Kowal, Roman. *Polski jazz,* Vol. 1. Kraków: AM, 1996.

Olechno-Huszcza, Gillian. *Polish Music Literature, 1915–1990.* Los Angeles: University of Southern California Press, 1991.

Kinga Nemere-Czachowska

Poles in Exile, 1939–90

Polish refugees after the German and Soviet invasions of 1939 created a sort of Poland in exile in which, especially in Great Britain, almost all the institutions of public, political, and cultural life necessary for the existence of a normal state functioned. The president of the Polish Republic was the leader of the government-in-exile. From September 1939 to April 1940, the presidency was located in France; in April it moved to Great Britain. The first President was Władysław Raczkiewicz and the last was Ryszard Kaczorowski. A government was elected, and its first premier was General Władysław Sikorski. The National Council played the role of a parliament. Various political parties were founded and dissolved, constituting coalition governments or remaining in opposition.

The Polish army continued to fight against the Axis. In 1945 there were 200,000 Polish soldiers in the Polish armed forces, among whom were members of the Polish air force, which had participated in the Battle of Britain (1940). After the war Polish soldiers were stationed in Great Britain and the American occupation zone of Germany.

Polish emigrants have had their own schools extending to higher education, with institutions such as the Polish School of Medicine at the University of Edinburgh (Scotland), the Polish School of Law at Oxford (England), the Polish University College, and the Polish University Abroad. There were Polish theaters, museums, orchestras, galleries, libraries, publishing houses, as well as a daily and a literary press, including Mieczysław Grydzewski's *Wiadomości,* published from 1940 to 1981, and *Kultura,* still edited and published by Jerzy Giedroyc and Zofia Hertz in France. Many of the best Polish writers have lived and produced in exile, among them Czesław Miłosz, Nobel Prize in literature recipient in 1980; Witold Gombrowicz, Gustaw Herling-Grudziński; and Marek Hłasko. Programs of the Polish sections of Radio Free Europe, BBC, Voice of America, Radio France International, or Radio Madrid were discussed in Polish coffeehouses and clubs in London and Chicago. In many European capitals and in the United States there are Polish churches and Polish cemeteries.

Polish emigrants created their own foundations; labor unions; professional associations of writers, artists, doctors, architects, veterans organizations; institutes; and learned societies, such as the Polish Learned Society in London, the Polish Institute of Arts and Science of America in New York City, and the Institut Littéraire in Paris.

Since 1945 more Poles lived abroad than the entire populations of many European countries. The size and destination of Polish emigration were decided during World War II. War migrations were initiated by soldiers, officers, and civilians, mainly to Romania, Hungary, Lithuania, and Latvia. About 150,000 Poles fled. Half of them joined the Polish army in France (and after the defeat of France in April 1940, in Great Britain) and in the Middle East. Over 40,000 of the Polish soldiers interned in Romania went to German POW and forced labor camps. About 1.2 to 2 million people were transported to Soviet labor camps. Only 115,000 from that group left the Soviet Union in 1942, along with the evacuation of the Anders army created from freed Polish prisoners of war in the USSR, after the outbreak of the Soviet-German war in June 1941. Over three million Poles were ultimately taken to forced labor and concentration camps in Germany and Austria. Over 200,000 Poles were inducted into the German army; many of them deserted and joined the Polish armed forces in the West. Altogether during World War II about five million people emigrated from Poland, and only two million returned after the war. Between 1945 and 1947 over one million Poles left Europe, emigrating to 113 different countries, mostly the United States (110,000), Australia and New Zealand (60,000), Israel (55,000), Canada (47,000), South and East Africa (25,000), Brazil (7,000), and Argentina (5,000). Only about 170,000 Poles remained in the United Kingdom, and 30,000 settled in France.

In Great Britain, and partly in the United States, the Polish government-in-exile continued its activities. After 1945 it was not recognized by most countries, but Spain, Cuba, the Vatican, and a few others continued to recognize it. Between 1946 and 1948 10,000 Jews who survived the Holocaust left Poland at their own request. Then in the late 1960s several thousand people of Jewish origin were forced to leave Poland due to an anti-Sematic campaign launched by a section of the party leadership. Between 1981 and 1983 about 50,000 Poles left the country, after the Polish government imposed martial law in December 1981 and outlawed the independent trade union, Solidarity.

Polish political activists in exile cooperated with representatives of other emigration groups from Eastern Europe, mainly within the framework of the Free Europe Committee and the Congress for Cultural Freedom. Polish writers were active in the PEN–Club in Exile. Emigrants several times organized political campaigns to direct the attention of international opinion to the Polish cause, for example, the huge demonstration in the center of London in May 1956 during Soviet Premier Nikita Krushchev's visit in the United Kingdom. Emigrants supported activities of the underground liberation movement in Poland between 1944 and 1953 and the political opposition, especially the Solidarity labor union, between 1956 and 1990. As a result of free elections in June 1989 and the establishment of a non-Communist government in August political changes in Poland in 1989, political organs of the Polish state in exile gradually ceased operation. In 1990 President Lech Wałęsa received in London the insignia of the presidency in exile.

The biggest and best archives dealing with the history of Polish emigration are in the possession of the Polish Institute and Sikorski Museum in London, the Polish Libraries in London and Paris, as well as the Polish Institute of Art and Science of America in New York City. In addition rich collections are held at the libraries and archives: of Yale, Harvard, Stanford and the University of California at Berkeley. In Poland the richest collection can be found at Nicolas Copernicus University in Toruń.

BIBLIOGRAPHY

Habielski, Rafal. *Emigracja.* Warsaw: Wydawnicturo Szkolne i Pedagogiczne, 1995.

Zybrzycki, Jerzy. *Polish immigrants in Britain.* The Hague: M. Nijhoff, 1956.

Miroslaw Supruniuk

SEE ALSO Sikorski, Władysław

Pollock, Friedrich (1894–1970)

German economist and a founding member of the Institut für Sozialforschung (Institute for Social Research). The son of assimilated Jewish parents, Friedrich Pollock was born in Freiburg in 1894, and received a doctorate in economics at the University of Frankfurt in 1923. The same year he founded the institute with Leo Lowenthal, Walter Benjamin, Theodor Adorno, and lifelong friend Max Horkheimer, and served as its administrative director and financial officer during the 1930s. Forced into exile with his colleagues to New York in 1934 by the rise of Nazism, Pollock returned to Frankfurt after the war with Horkheimer and Adorno to rebuild the institute.

Pollock broke with classical Marxian economics by arguing that the collapse of the world economy in 1929 signaled not an automatic transition to socialism but the rise of capitalist planned economies. This "state capitalism," he argued, provided for the temporary stabilization of its own internal crises at the expense of a liberal free market. Pollock's analyses were crucial for the development of the critical theory of Horkheimer, Adorno, and Herbert Marcuse, who agreed that classical Marxism could not fully account for developments in modern capitalist societies.

BIBLIOGRAPHY

Jay, Martin. *The Dialectical Imagination: A History of the Frankfurt School and the Institute of Social Research, 1923–1950.* Boston: Little, Brown, 1973.

Kellner, Douglas. *Critical Theory, Marxism, and Modernity.* Baltimore: Johns Hopkins University Press, 1989.

Wiggershaus, Rolf. *The Frankfurt School: Its History, Theories, Political Significance.* Cambridge, Mass.: MIT Press, 1994.

Christopher E. Forth

Pompidou, Georges (1911–74)

French politician and president (1969–74). Born in Montiboudif in south-central France on July 1, 1911, Georges Pompidou, the child of schoolteachers, excelled as a student. He graduated first in his class at the École Normale Supérieure in Paris. Pompidou pursued advanced studies at the École des Sciences Politiques. After performing his required military service, he taught first in Marseilles then at the exclusive Lycée Henri IV in Paris.

With the Second World War Pompidou was called into the army as an infantry lieutenant. After the armistice with Germany in June 1940, he returned to teach at the lycée in Paris. He was the exception among future Gaullist leaders in that he never joined the wartime Resistance. As he put it later, "My resistance was exclusively verbal."

In August 1944 General Charles de Gaulle who had led the Free French abroad, returned from Algeria to Paris and set up a provisional government. With the assistance of a friend, Pompidou secured a modest post on de Gaulle's staff and from that time his destiny was linked with that of the general. When, in January 1946, de Gaulle abruptly resigned as provisional president, Pompidou continued in his service. He arranged for publication of the general's wartime memoirs and headed a charity set up by the de Gaulles for the mentally retarded.

In 1954 Pompidou moved to the Rothschild Bank, becoming a general director two years later. However, he continued to make himself indispensable to de Gaulle; when the general returned to power in 1958, Pompidou became his chief of cabinet. After helping with the transition to the newly created Fifth Republic he returned to the Rothschild bank. In 1961 de Gaulle gave Pompidou the task of establishing ties with representatives of the Algerian National Liberation Front (FLN) in Switzerland. Secret talks there eventually led to settlement of the Algerian War in 1962 and Algeria's independence from France.

In April 1962 de Gaulle named Pompidou premier with jurisdiction over domestic affairs. There was criticism at the time that Pompidou had never held elective office and was a mere technician. However, he developed into an effective administrator and speaker. The student unrest of May 1968, followed by widespread worker strikes across France, gave Pompidou the chance to prove himself. He was responsible for the plan of a wage increase for workers, and, after dissuading de Gaulle from a referendum, he managed the new election campaign that led to a Gaullist triumph.

Pompidou had performed so well at a time when de Gaulle displayed some indecisiveness that a few days later de Gaulle rewarded him by asking him to resign. When he left office in July 1968, Pompidou had been premier (1962–68) longer than any other Frenchman since François Guizot in the mid–nineteenth century. He remained a deputy in the National Assembly but was denied leadership in the Union of Democrats for the Fifth Republic (UDR). In January 1969 Pompidou announced that he would be a candidate in the next presidential election. De Gaulle responded that he intended to stay in office until the end of his term in 1972.

At the beginning of 1969 de Gaulle announced a national referendum on a proposal to reorganize France on a regional basis. A number of vested interests already opposed the plan when de Gaulle said that he would regard the referendum as a personal vote of confidence. In April French voters defeated the proposal by a narrow margin and de Gaulle resigned. Pompidou ran for the presidency in a special June elections, and strong Gaullist backing led to his election.

President Pompidou's leadership style was much different from that of his illustrious predecessor; he proceeded cautiously and calmly. Within the government there was much more freedom of discussion and, unlike de Gaulle, Pompidou did not lecture his ministers.

Although he had a solid majority in the National Assembly (lower house of parliament), Pompidou broadened the government by bringing in non-Gaullists and surrounding himself by competent technocrats. He was much interested in achieving economic growth. His government devalued the franc and began a program of austerity. It also pushed ahead with university reform. The economy did well until the energy crisis brought on by the Arab oil embargo at the time of the 1971 Yom Kippur War between Egypt and Israel. This led to high inflation, and Pompidou was forced to float the franc.

International affairs also reflected Pompidou's low-key, pragmatic style. He continued de Gaulle's efforts to build relations with China and the USSR, and he pushed France's influence in the Middle East. Perhaps under Pompidou French policy more accurately reflected actual French power than de Gaulle's vaunted ambitions, and he demonstrated a willingness to compromise. In several areas he reversed the policies of his predecessor. He allowed Britain to enter the European Community (EC) and he worked to restore good relations with the United States, which had frayed considerably under de Gaulle.

Pompidou also helped transform Paris. This included an underground shopping center at the western suburb of La Défense, and the Pompidou Center, the French National Art and Cultural Center, with industrial looking exterior on the rue Beaubourg. More controversial was the development of the 56-story Montparnasse Tower, which purists argued defiled the skyline of Paris.

Pompidou's last year and a half was marked by economic problems and his illness. He died of cancer on April 2, 1974, and was followed in office by his minister of finance, Valéry Giscard d'Estaing. Pompidou had shown that Gaullism and the Fifth Republic could continue without the general.

BIBLIOGRAPHY

Alexandre, Philippe. *The Duel: De Gaulle and Pompidou.* Tr. by Elaine P. Halperin. Boston: Houghton Mifflin, 1972.

Bromberger, Merry. *Le Destin secret de Georges Pompidou.* Paris: Fayard, 1965.

Roussel, Eric. *Georges Pompidou.* Paris: Lattès, 1984.

Spencer C. Tucker

SEE ALSO De Gaulle, Charles

Poos, Jacques F. (1935–)

Foreign minister of Luxembourg (1994–). Jacques Poos was born in Luxembourg City on June 3, 1935. He received a licentiate in economic and commercial studies from the University of Lausanne, Switzerland, in 1958, a superior diploma in comparative economics from the International University of Luxembourg in 1960, and a doctorate in economics and commercial sciences from the University of Lausanne in 1961.

Poos served as an attaché at the Economics Ministry of Luxembourg from 1959 to 1962. He was director of research at the Center for Research and Economic Statistics (STATEC) from 1962 to 1964. From 1964 to 1976 he was director of the Coopérative printing house and editor of the newspaper *Tageblatt.* He was president of the Luxembourg Society of Editors from 1964 to 1976.

In 1969 Poos entered politics, serving as a municipal councillor for Esch/Alzette, a post he held until 1976. He was elected to parliament in 1970, served as president of the parliamentary socialist caucus in 1975–76, and was president of the Finance and Budget Commission during that same period. In 1976 he was elected to the executive committee of the Socialist Workers Party (POSL) and became the party's vice president in 1982, a post he held until 1975. He headed the POSL electoral list in 1984 and 1989.

Poos was minister of finance and governor of the World Bank from 1976 to 1979. From 1980 until 1982 he was director of the Banque Continentale du Luxembourg, and from 1982 until 1984 director of the Banque PARIBAS (Luxembourg). In 1984 he returned to the government, where he was appointed vice president and held multiple ministerial responsibilities as minister for foreign affairs, trade and cooperation, economy, middle-class, and finance. From 1989 to 1994 he served as assistant prime minister and minister of foreign affairs, trade and cooperation, and interior. He held these posts through successive governments, until he was succeeded in 1999 by Lydie Polfer, the chair of the Democratic Party.

BIBLIOGRAPHY

Poos, Jacques F. *Crise économique et petites nations : le modèle luxembourgeois.* Lausanne: Centre de recherches européennes, 1977.

———. *Le Luxembourg dans le marché commun.* Lausanne: Centre de recherches européennes, 1961.

Bernard Cook

Popiełuszko, Jerzy Aleksander (1947–84)

Priest supporter of the Solidarity labor union, murdered by Polish security officers. Jerzy Popiełuszko was pastor of St. Stanisław Kostka parish in Warsaw. In August 1980 he became a spiritual leader to Warsaw steelworkers involved in the Solidarity movement. After the imposition of martial law in December 1981, he organized aid for families of jailed Solidarity activists. In June 1984 he was accused of abusing religious freedom by giving pro-Solidarity sermons and possessing a gun and illegal Solidarity literature. Although he claimed that these items had been planted by the police, he was jailed. Released in the general amnesty given to jailed Solidarity members in mid-1984, Popiełuszko continued his support of Solidarity, and his parish served as a rallying point for pro-Solidarity opposition to the regime. Jerzy Urban, a spokesman for the Communist Party, continually denounced the priest and his activities. On October 19, 1984, as Popiełuszko was returning to Warsaw after giving a sermon at Bydgoszcz, he and his driver were stopped at Przysiek, near Toruń. Though the driver escaped, the priest was beaten, bound, weighted, and thrown into the Vistula River near Włocławek. After his body was found eleven days later, nearly a million people attended his funeral. General Wojciech Jaruzelski publicly disassociated himself and his regime from the killing. He ordered the four implicated—three officers of the security police and their superior, a colonel—tried in televised proceedings. This was the first prosecution of political police in a Communist country. During the trial the defendants referred to repeated pressure to "silence Popiełuszko." Sentenced from eleven to twenty-five years, all were amnestied early but the reputed ring-leader, Capt. Grzegorz Piotrowski. The martyred Popiełuszko served in death, probably more than he had in life, as an indictment and challenge to the regime.

BIBLIOGRAPHY

Daszkiewicz, Krystyna. *Uprowadzenie i morderstwo ks. Jerzego Popiełuszki.* Poznan: SAWW, 1990.

Moody, John. *The Priest Who Had to Die.* London: Victor Gollanz, 1986.

Nitecki, Piotr. *Znak zwyciestwa: ksiadz Jerzy Popiełuszko, 1947–1984.* Wrocław: Wydawn. Wrocławskiej Ksieg. Archidiecezjalnej, 1991.

Popieluszko, Jerzy. *Kazania patriotyczne.* Paris: Libella, 1984.

———. *The Way of My Cross: Masses at Warsaw.* Chicago: Regnery, 1986.

Proces o uprowadzenie i zabojstwo ksiedza Jerzego Popiełuszki. Warsaw: Niezalezna Oficyna Wydawnicza Nowa, 1992.

Tomasz Stapf

Popov, Dimitar (1937–)

Bulgarian prime minister without party affiliation, approved overwhelmingly by the Grand National Assembly (parliament) as premier of a coalition government from December 20, 1990, to November 8, 1991. An expert in criminal and transport law, Dimitar Popov became chairman of the Sofia Municipal Court in March 1990. He gained prominence and respect for his efficient and evenhanded performance as a secretary of the Central Electoral Commission during the June 1990 general elections. Zhelev appointed Popov premier. The government he headed included members of the former ruling Bulgarian Socialist Party (political heir of the Bulgarian Communist Party), Union of Democratic Forces (UDF), and Bulgarian Agrarian People's Union, the traditional coalition partner of the Bulgarian Communist Party since the advent of the Communist regime in Bulgaria. Popov's government had to offer a program for the survival of the nation at a moment of deep economic crisis, intensified by insufficient monetary reserves and the rupture of Bulgaria's international economic links, which had predominantly been with the USSR and Eastern Europe. Bulgaria was now required to pay Russia hard cash for the natural gas and oil that it received from that country and its old markets in Eastern Europe dried up. His government attempted to start economic reform while safeguarding the interests of the most vulnerable members of society and preserving an active partnership with the labor unions. He will be remembered by the majority of Bulgarians for his appeal, "For God's sake, sisters and brothers, don't buy!" when he tried to make consumers understand that the first serious jump of prices could be controlled if they stopped shopping for a couple of days.

BIBLIOGRAPHY

Crampton, R. J. *A Short History of Modern Bulgaria.* Cambridge: Cambridge University Press–Open Society Foundation in Bulgaria, 1994.

Lyudmila Iordanova Dicheva

Popov, Gavril Kharitonovich (1936–)

Mayor of Moscow, economist, and advocate of market economic reform. Gavril Popov was born in Moscow on October 13, 1936. He received a doctorate in economics from Moscow State University, where he taught from 1960 to 1989, and was dean of the economics faculty from 1977 to 1980. He became a member of the Congress of People's Deputies of the USSR, a new 2,250-member representative body elected in March 1989 on the basis of a competitive ballot, and the city council of Moscow in 1989. He chaired the city council in 1990–91 and was popularly elected mayor of Moscow in 1991. He was an early ally and adviser of future President Boris Yeltsin. In 1990 Popov resigned his membership in the party, which he had held since 1959. In 1992 he stepped down as mayor of Moscow in order to devote his efforts to national politics. He became chair of the Russian Democratic Reform Movement and leader of the Social Democratic bloc in 1995.

BIBLIOGRAPHY

"Popov, Gavril." *Russia and the Commonwealth A to Z.* Ed. by Andrew Wilson and Nina Bachkatov. New York: HarperPerennial, 1992.

Bernard Cook

SEE ALSO Luzhkov, Yuri

Porkkala

Naval base fewer than fifteen miles west of Helsinki. In the Interim Peace Treaty (1944) through which Finland ended its Continuation War (1941–44) with the Soviet Union, launched in conjunction with Germany's invasion of the USSR, had to lease the Porkkala Peninsula to the Soviet Union for a period of fifty years. The military value to the Soviets was small, but the presence of Soviet forces in Porkkala guaranteed that Finnish decision makers paid attention to Soviet interests.

The death of Soviet leader Joseph Stalin in 1953 led to a gradual decrease in international tension, culminating finally in the 1954–55 "Spirit of Geneva," or the new approach of peaceful coexistence advancedly First Secretary Nikita Krushchev. Through an international agreement Austria became a neutral country, and Soviet forces were withdrawn. This left Porkkala as the sole point outside the East bloc where Soviet forces remained after World War II. In addition to an improved international atmosphere, changes in Soviet foreign policy toward Finland had been emerging since the failure of the attempted Communist coup in 1948 and the loss of influence domestically by Finnish Communists. The Soviet leadership realized that Finland would not become a "people's democracy" and member of the Soviet bloc. Therefore, they decided to maintain friendly relations with the most influential political forces in that country, President Juho Paasikivi and the Agrarian Union, especially its leading figure, Urho Kekkonen. A Soviet proposal was published in 1955 responding favorably to the Finnish policy of friendship toward the USSR. The proposal suggested the return of Porkkala to Finland on the condition that the mutual assistance treaty of 1948 be extended for twenty more years.

The agreement was concluded during a visit of President Paasikivi to Moscow in September 1955. The Soviets wished to demonstrate their appreciation for the Finnish president. Their timing was also intended to boost the political fortunes of Prime Minister Kekkonen, who was responsible for the negotiations and was a candidate in the 1956 presidential elections. The special relationship between Finland and the Soviet Union was therefore frequently referred to in Finland as the "Paasikivi-Kekkonen line."

In accord with the preamble of the mutual assistance treaty, Finland had declared itself neutral to give the West the impression that it was not a Soviet satellite. Yet, in the strictest sense, as long as the Soviets had a base at Porkkala, Finland could not be considered neutral. The return of Porkkala made a policy of neutrality possible. In fact, the withdrawal of Soviet troops from Finland made Finland a fully sovereign country. As a result Finland became more active in international affairs, especially by joining the United Nations and the Nordic Council in 1955.

BIBLIOGRAPHY

Allison, Roy. *Finland's Relations with the Soviet Union 1944–1984.* Oxford: Macmillan, 1985.

Jakobson, Max. *Finnish Neutrality.* New York: Praeger, 1969.

Väyrynen, Raimo. *Conflicts in Finnish and Soviet Relations.* Tampere, Finland: University of Tampere, 1972.

Vilho Harle

SEE ALSO Finland; Kekkonen, Uhro; Paasikivi, Juho; Karelia

Portugal

Republic in southwestern Europe sharing the Iberian Peninsula with Spain. Portugal is bordered on the north and east by Spain and on the south and west by the Atlantic

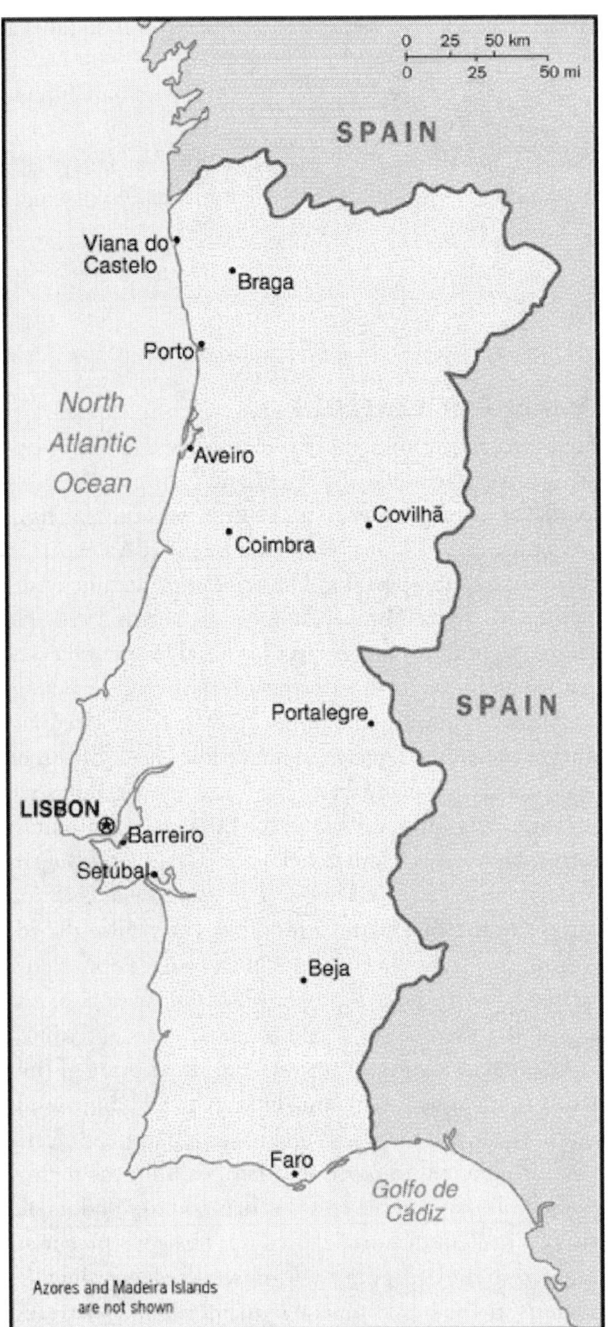

Portugal. *Illustration courtesy of Bernard Cook.*

Ocean. In 1945 Portugal was ruled by António de Oliveira Salazar, who had exercised a dictatorship over Portuguese politics since 1928. The son of lower-middle-class parents from central Portugal, Salazar was a pious Catholic and a lifelong bachelor who led an austere personal life. He participated in various conservative intellectual groups under the Republic (1910–26) and, after a conservative military regime came to power through a coup in 1926, he was appointed minister of finance and was given a veto over the expenditures of other ministries. In

1932, he was not a fascist but rather an authoritarian conservative. His policies emphasized depoliticization of body politic, a stratified hierarchical society, thrift and a suspicion of modernity. He believed that bourgeois democracy as practiced in Western Europe was equivalent to mob rule. Only one party, Salazar's National Union, was permitted.

Portugal entered the postwar world with the hope that the triumph of the Western democracies over fascism would result in major changes within its so-called New State and possibly the restoration of democracy to the nation. Even Salazar began to talk of Portugal as an "organic democracy." In 1945 Salazar dissolved the parliament and called for elections in November in which the opposition would be allowed to participate. After almost twenty years of dictatorship and censorship, Salazar came to believe his own propaganda that the regime was fully supported by the nation. With the slight opening in the system allowed during the month of October preceding the elections, a torrent of opposition emerged; but when the government refused to guarantee fair elections, the opposition refused to participate. During the years of Salazar's rule (1933–68), Portugal held more elections than any other country in Europe. This frequent use of the polls served the dual propose of legitimizing the regime to foreign opinion and discovering who the regime's opponent were. After any election, those who had emerged as part of the opposition were prosecuted and marginalized.

In the late 1940s Salazar was forced to deal with internal dissension from some of the regime's supporters. Marcelo Caetano, the leading theorist of the regime, became a critic of Salazar. In 1947 President António Óscar de Fraqoso Carmona and members of the army were involved in a plot to overthrow Salazar. This attempt was discovered by the secret police and the conspirators were retired from the armed forces or moved to distant parts of the empire. Salazar, realizing that Caetano was a critic who should be integrated more closely into the regime's political structure in order to co-opt or control him, gave him major nonpolicy-making posts in the União Nacional Party, while the elderly president was allowed to continue in office.

In the 1949 presidential election Carmona again ran as the regime's candidate, and General Norton de Matos, a leading figure of the republican period (1910–1926) was the opposition candidate. Matos conducted a vigorous campaign and used the preelection period to effectively challenge Salazar, attacking the regime's repression and censorship and declaring that he favored Salazar's dismissal. Matos withdrew before the election because since the regime would give no guarantee of honest elections, he was unwilling to give the appearance of legitimacy to a fraud. Carmona was easily reelected. Carmona died in 1951 and the election that followed was of little consequence. The new president, General Craveiro Lopes, proved to be less amenable to Salazar, and he was not allowed to run again in 1958. In 1958 the regime nominated, Admiral Americo Tomás, and the opposition ran the charismatic General Humberto Delgado. Delgado's popularity was so great that Salazar prepared military action in case Delgado's supporter would refuse to accept a negative tally by the government. When the results were in, Tomás was declared president, but many Portuguese believed that Delgado had really won. Shortly afterward Delgado was forced to go into exile. He continued to protest against the regime from Brazil and was assassinated by the secret police in 1963 near the Portuguese-Spanish border following a meeting with fellow oppositionists. Salazar immediately changed the constitution. Hereafter, the president would be chosen by an electoral college. In the aftermath of the election many people were forced to reside under police supervision in remote parts of the country or expelled from Portugal altogether, including Bishop António Ferreira Gomes of Porto, who had openly criticized Salazar's policies.

In the 1950s Salazar strengthened the instruments of repression. In the 1930s the purpose of the secret police was to uncover plots, put down coup attempts, and break strikes. Originally, the government dealt with rebels by deporting them to other parts of the empire, and, after 1936, to the Tarafal concentration camp in the Cape Verde Islands, which Portugal owned. The most repressive legislation of the New State came only after 1945, when fascist control of Europe had ended and the regime launched a repressive campaign against Communists. In 1945 the secret police (PIDE) was given power to arrest and jail without trial for up to ninety days "anyone suspected of political activities." In addition, the police were given discretionary powers over the release or prosecution of such people. In 1956 the secret police was granted the power to use "preventive measures against criminality" against "vagrants and other persistent delinquents." These "security measures" of six months to three years of detention were renewable if the criminal continued to appear dangerous. This meant that after completing a sentence, a person might still remain in prison for many years.

The Portuguese economy, already improving in the 1930s, greatly benefited from World War II. Salazar maintained a policy of "belligerent neutrality," selling wolfram used for hardening steel, and maintaining open trade relations with both sides. By 1945 Portugal had the second-strongest currency in Europe, a stable political system, cheap labor, and an infrastructure that should have allowed rapid economic development. However, Salazar's fear of modernization and vehement opposition to borrowing the capital that Portugal needed for industrial investment squandered the opportunity for economic development. As the years passed, Portuguese state became increasingly dependent on colonial resources and markets rather than developing into a modern industrial economy. Only in the 1960s, faced with its colonial wars in Angola, Mozambique and Guinea-Bissau, did Salazar permit foreign investment in Portugal.

The last decade of Salazar's life saw an increase in opposition activity, beginning with the highjacking of the cruiseship *Santa Maria* in 1961 by Captain Henrique Galvão and the April Conspiracy (*Abrilhada*), which involved the ministers of defense and of the army, former president Lopes, and other high-ranking officers. They hijacked the ship to bring world attention to bear on the Portuguese dictatorship. They hoped to reach Angola and begin a revolution against Salazar. The ship was blocked by U.S. warships and the plot failed. The conspirators were dispersed to distant outposts of the empire, but in subsequent years there were periodic coup attempts and minor revolts. However, the major crisis was the colonial rebellions. In December 1961 India invaded and annexed the Portuguese territories of Goa, Damão, and Diu, on the west coast of India and anticolonial revolts started in Angola (1961), Guinea-Bissau (1963), and Mozambique (1964) in Africa. Because of its economic dependence on the colonies, Portugal dared not give them up. The colonial wars soon began to take an increasingly larger share of the budget and became a heavy burden for the nation both financially and in human casualties.

Salazar's political career came to an end in September 1968 when, at age seventy-nine, he fell from a chair and suffered a stroke from which he did not recover. President Tomás appointed Marcelo Caetano as prime minister. Salazar retained the title of president of the Council of Ministers and in fact was never told he had been replaced.

Caetano entered the political scene as a right-wing activist in the 1920s. He had been responsible for some of the major legal reforms of the 1930s but after 1945 became an in-house critic of the regime. Caetano had served as minister of the colonies (1944–49) and deputy prime minister (1955–59). In 1961–62 he was rector of the University of Lisbon but resigned in protest against Salazar's ordering the police to enter the university to crush demonstrations in 1962 in violation of the corporate autonomy of the university. Once appointed prime minister he began a series of reforms to bring more openness to the system. He permitted hundreds of exiles to return, curbed the powers of the secret police, permitted greater freedom of the press and the arts, and, for the first time, permitted the opposition freer participation in elections. Although the opposition did not win any seats in the 1969 election, the liberal wing of the regime had some victories. However, having no one on the left on which to rely, Caetano had to be careful of the extreme right, which, under the leadership of President Tomás, was exerting pressure on policy decisions. Since 1959 the Portuguese economy had expanded considerably because of foreign investment. By 1974, however, it still remained inefficient. Agriculture used one-third of the labor force but produced less than 20 percent of GNP. Portugal's major exports remained cork, canned fish, and wine while it imported machinery and foodstuffs. Portugal had the lowest per capita income of Western Europe and a poor health and educational system. The middle class, which under Caetano began to aspire to some luxuries, was hard hit by the economic recession caused by the OPEC oil crisis of 1973. It was also alienated by the draft for the colonial wars, which after a decade continued to intensify. By 1973, having failed to solve the colonial question, Caetano's reforms where thwarted by the conservatives and the system of repression intensified.

In 1973 some members of the military began to express the desire for a nonmilitary solution to the colonial question. In February 1974 General António de Spínola published his book *Portugal and the Future,* which called for a federalist solution in the colonies and, between the lines, advocated a coup against the Caetano regime. Because of pressure from the right, Spínola and the army chief of staff, General Francisco da Costa Gomes, were dismissed on March 14. On March 16 a military revolt was quickly suppressed, but on April 25, 1974, a military movement of middle-level officers brought down the government in a revolution called the Carnation Revolution because it occurred just as florist shops in Lisbon were offering red carnations for sale, and Caetano and Tomás exiled to Brazil.

The middle-level officers of the Armed Forces Movement (MFA) who brought down the regime had no coherent program for government. Rather, in the aftermath of the coup a series of items pulled together from various platforms (Communist, Socialist, as well as liberal groups) were used to organize a plan for governing the new democracy. This program was designed to distance the movement from the Salazar/Caetano regime by emphasizing decolonization, democratization, and economic development. General Spínola was the only officer with enough prestige to take over the movement and was appointed interim president in May 1974 by the MFA. But he was too conservative to disassociate himself completely from the former regime. Spínola favored gradual change from within and opposed complete decolonization. This immediately led to conflict between the MFA and Spínola. Spínola's conservative ideas alienated the MFA, which originally had not been leftist, and now was pushed to the left. The new Prime Minister Adelinoda Palma Carlos, was forced to resign in July, and Spínola appointed Col. Vasco Gonsalves of the MFA as premier. As the summer wore on Gonsalves and the MFA moved further left. Spínola resigned in September and was replaced by General Costa Gomes. On March 11, 1975, Spínola and the right attempted a coup. Though the effort failed, it further radicalized the MFA, which by now, with the help of the Communist Party, was attempting to institutionalize itself with a preponderant stake in the political future of Portugal. During the summer of 1975 the situation became increasingly complicated as the MFA moved further and the army began to disintegrate into factions. Portugal was on the brink of civil war.

In September 1975 Vasco Gonsalves resigned as premier and was replaced by admiral Pinheiro de Azevedo. During autumn 1975 the situation turned more chaotic, until on November 12–14 protesting workers held the government and the Constitutional Assembly prisoners at parliament's São Bento palace. From November 14 to 18 the government went on strike, demanding full support from the MFA. In early November a group of moderates in the military began organizing to countermand any action by the left. On November 25 leftist units initiated a move to take over the centers of military power. The moderates under Lieutenant Colonel António Ramalho Eanes outmaneuvered and defeated them. Eanes was made army chief of staff and proceeded to reorganize the MFA and the military in such a way that neither would be able to return to the political arena.

In April 1976 the assembly that had been elected following the revolution to draw up a new constitution, completed its works and the new constitution became law and the Socialist Party received 40 percent of the vote in parliamentary elections of April 25. On June 27 Eanes was elected president by popular vote and took office in July. He received the support of the three non-Communist parties and was elected president with 61.54 percent of the vote. After taking office on July 14, he appointed Socialist Party leader Mário Soares as prime minister.

During the two-term presidency of Ramalho Eanes (1976–86), the Portuguese government was dominated by minority or coalition governments, either the Socialists in coalition with the right, or a coalition of the right (Aliança Democratica). With the Communist Party firmly out of power since November 1974, the other parties led the country along a moderate path revising some of the radical legislation of 1974–75 while protecting the advantages gained from the social legislation of the revolution. During his tenure President Eanes was instrumental in providing stability and in consolidating democratic institutions. After the April 25, 1976, election parliament was divided among four major parties, with the Socialist Party holding only 107 of the 260 seats. President Eanes and a series of prime ministers were faced with political instability resulting from two years of revolutionary excesses, a stagnant economy, and high trade deficits. The inability of Soares's minority government to deal with these problems led to its collapse in December 1977. Eanes encouraged Soares to form a coalition with the Center Democratic Party, but it, too, fell apart in July 1978. Faced with the inability of any party to form a government, Eanes named a nonpartisan technocrat, Alfredo Jorge Nobre da Costa, as premier. When Nobre da Costa failed to receive parliamentary approval, Eanes again took the initiative by naming Carlos Alberto da Mota Pinto, a law constitutional expert, and political independent as prime minister. The new government won approval, but as the political infighting worsened, it resigned in June 1979. Eanes next appointed Maria de Lurdes Pintasilgo as premier, dissolved parliament, and called for new elections. In the elections that followed, the conservative Aliança Democratica won a bare majority and Eanes appointed its leader, Francisco de Sá Carneiro, premier. In December 1980 Sá Carneiro died in a plane crash and Eanes appointed the new head of the coalition, Francisco Pinto Balsemão, as premier. Also in December 1980 Eanes won election to a second term as a nonparty candidate, although with the informal support of the Socialists and Communists, despite the bitter opposition of the Aliança Democratica.

During his second term as president, Eanes saw his powers curtailed by the constitutional revision of 1982, especially with reference to his ability to appoint prime ministers by presidential initiative. This revision concluded the transition to democratic institutions indicated by the Revolution of April 1974, when it abolished the Council of the Revolution and substituted in its place the Council of State, thus ending the role of the military in politics. This was made possible by Eanes's efforts in reforming and depoliticizing the military during the period 1976–79, in which he was both president and chief of the general staff. In the winter of 1983 the Balsemão coalition fell apart and Eanes was forced to call early elections. The Socialists received only a plurality of seats but remained in office until June 27, 1985, through an informal coalition with the Social Democrats. On June 12, 1985, Portugal signed the treaty of admission to the European Community. When in 1985 it became clear that within the context of the existing assembly it was impossible to form a government, Eanes again called elections. Unlike previous elections, in addition to the four established political parties, a new party, the Democratic Renewal Party, created with the support of President Eanes, participated in the elections. Despite this, the Social Democrats won a plurality and formed a government.

In early 1986 Eanes's second term ended, and on March 9, 1986, former prime minister and secretary-general of the Socialist Party Mário Soares was elected president. He was reelected in 1991. He became the first civilian president since Bernardino Machado was deposed in 1926. He was succeeded by Jorge Sampaio, former mayor of Lisbon, in 1995. The minority government of Anibal Cavaco Silva collapsed in 1987. In parliamentary elections of July 1987 his PSD party received an absolute majority and formed the first majority government of the Second Republic. The PSD retained its majority in the 1991 parliamentary elections but lost it to the Socialists in 1995.

After 1986 the governments of Anibal Cavaco Silva and António Guterres initiated policies to develop the Portuguese economy and bring it into compliance with European Community (EC) standards. In 1985 Portugal was admitted to the EC (later, European Union) and with other Western European nations is a full participant in the economic and political union formed in 1992. In 1998 Portugal hosted the World Exposition —Expo 98. By the mid-1990s democratic institutions had stabilized, with center parties alternating in power.

BIBLIOGRAPHY

Bretell, Caroline B. *Men Who Migrate, Women Who Wait: Population and History in a Portuguese Parish.* Princeton, N.J.: Princeton University Press, 1986.

Bruneau, Thomas C. *Politics and Nationhood: Post Revolutionary Portugal.* New York: Praeger, 1984.

Bruneau, Thomas C., and Alex MacLeod. *Politics in Contemporary Portugal: Parties and the Consolidation of Democracy.* Boulder, Colo.: Westview Press, 1986.

Dicionário Ilustrado da Historia de Portugal, 2 Vols. Lisbon: Publicações Alfa, 1985.

Figueiredo, Antonio. *Portugal: Fifty Years of Dictatorship.* New York: Homes and Meier, 1975.

Gallagher, Tom. *Portugal: A Twentieth-Century Interpretation.* Manchester, England: University of Manchester Press, 1983.

Graham, Lawrence S., and Harry M. Makler, ed. *Contemporary Portugal: The Revolution and Its Antecedents.* Austin: University of Texas Press, 1979.

Graham, Lawrence S., and Douglas L. Wheeler, eds. *In Search of Modern Portugal: The Revolution and Its Consequences.* Madison: University of Wisconsin Press, 1983.

Herr, Richard, ed. *Portugal: Democracy and Europe.* Berkeley: International and Area Studies and the University of California at Berkeley, 1992.

Marques, Antonio H. de Oliveira. *History of Portugal,* 2d ed., 2 Vols. New York: Columbia University Press, 1976.

Mattoso, José, ed. *História de Portugal,* 8 Vols. Lisbon: Editorial Estampa, 1993–94.

Maxwell, Kenneth. *The Making of Portuguese Democracy.* Cambridge: Cambridge University Press, 1995.

Medina, João, ed. *História Contemporanea de Portugal,* 7 Vols. Camarate, Portugal: Mutilar, 1990.

Robinson, Richard A. H. *Contemporary Portugal: A History.* London: George Allen and Unwin, 1979.

Rosas, Fernando, and J. M. Brandão de Brito, eds. *Dicionário de Historia do Estado Novo,* 2 Vols. Lisbon: Circulo de Leitores, 1996.

Serrão, Joel, ed. *Dicionário da Historia de Portugal,* 6 Vols. Porto: Livraria Figueirinhas, n.d.

Paul Brasil

Armed Forces Movement

The Armed Forces Movement (Movementos das Forcas Armadas, MFA) was a principal military and political player in Portugal from 1973 to 1982. Formed at first to protest the regime's handling of internal military matters, it eventually became a left-wing revolutionary body interested in fundamental transformations of Portuguese society.

The Portuguese right-wing dictatorship known as the Estado Novo (New State) was led by António de Salazar from 1933 to 1968, then by Marcello Caetano from 1968 to 1974. When the colonial war broke out in Angola in 1961, Salazar, then Caetano, insisted on a military victory at any cost. Other colonial wars also raged, notably, in Mozambique and Guinea-Bissau. The burden of the colonial wars fell on junior-ranking officers, many of whom were stationed in one of Portugal's African colonies for long periods of time. These officers yearned for a negotiated settlement to the conflict. By the early 1970s many of them had been forced to spend ten or more years in Africa.

The trigger that led to the formation of the MFA was the Decree Law 373-73 announced on September 9,

1973. That decree permitted conscripted officers special privileges, including moving quickly up the slow-moving seniority line. Facing manpower shortages, the regime calculated that this could attract more officers to fight. The junior officers already fighting wars in Africa resented this special treatment, especially the idea that newcomers could be promoted ahead of them. They started organizing to petition the regime to protect their rights.

The first meeting of what would become known as the Armed Forces Movement was secret. It took place on September 9, 1973, in Evora, Portugal. Some 136 officers requested the regime to repeal the law. They met for a second time on October 6, 1973, in Lisbon, and voted to ask the regime to pursue a political settlement to the colonial wars, and improve their pay. At their third meeting, on December 1, 1973, in Obidos, Portugal, they considered a petition to organize a coup d'état against the regime. They opted to continue negotiating, but also asked Colonel Otelo Saraiva de Carvallo, a founding members of the Armed Forces Movement to plan a coup, in case they could not come to an agreement with the regime.

The regime finally repealed the offending law in December 1973, but the Armed Forces Movement had decided to demand that the regime reach a political settlement with the rebels. The MFA soon discovered they had an unexpected ally with the February 1974 publication of a book entitled *Portugal and the Future,* by General António de Spínola. Known for his conservative politics, Spínola surprised most observers with his call for a negotiated end to the colonial wars. He was concerned about the erosion of military hierarchy caused by unending war and felt that military victory was unlikely. The prime minister, Marcello Caetano was outraged by the book, dismissed Spínola, and insisted on military victory.

On hearing that Spínola had been dismissed, a group of MFA officers in Caldas da Rainha, led by Colonel Vasco Lourenço, marched on Lisbon. This first effort to overthrow the regime failed on March 16, 1974, when loyal forces blocked an MFA march on Lisbon. Five weeks later the MFA tried again. On April 25, 1974, the MFA, with Otelo commanding, successfully overthrew the Caetano regime. Once in power, the MFA exhibited ideological divisions, with four main factions. The Reformers supported conservative Spínola, who was not in the MFA, and sought gradual change. *Portugal and the Future* had criticized the regime's colonial policy and sketched a moderate path for the country. The other MFA groups felt that Spínola's ideas did not go far enough. The Radicals, led by the ranking MFA officer General Vasco Gonçalves, favored the implementation of an Eastern European Communist political and economic model for Portugal. The Populists, led by Major Otelo de Saraiva Carvalho, favored a revolutionary model along the lines of Fidel Castro's Cuba or Gama Abdel Nasser's Egypt. The MFA-Moderates, led by Melo de Antunes, preferred a German or Swedish socialist and democratic model. These factions fought over the next two years, and the Moderates ultimately won out.

The MFA-Moderates delegated their power to the Council of the Revolution (CR), and included a provision in the 1976 constitution assigning the CR the right to veto any legislation passed by the National Assembly (parliament) that it deemed contrary to the objectives of the April 25, 1974, revolution. This oversight role was ended with the 1982 amendment of the constitution, which eliminated the CR. The remaining officers formed the Association of 25 April, which has acted as a retired officers' club. The MFA played a vital and historical role in the transition to democracy in Portugal.

BIBLIOGRAPHY

Graham, Lawrence S., and Douglas L. Wheeler, eds. *In Search of Modern Portugal: The Revolution and Its Consequences.* Madison: University of Wisconsin Press, 1983.

Mattoso, José, ed. *História de Portugal.* 8 vols. Lisbon: Editorial Estampa, 1993–1994.

Maxwell, Kenneth. *The Making of Portuguese Democracy.* Cambridge: Cambridge University Press, 1995.

Medina, João, ed. *História Contemporanea de Portugal.* 7 vols. Camarate: Mutilar, 1990.

Robinson, Richard A. H. *Contemporary Portugal: A History.* London: George Allen and Unwin, 1979.

Paul Christopher Manuel

SEE ALSO Spínola, António de

Junta of National Salvation

The Junta of National Salvation (JSN) was formed as an interim governing body following the April 25, 1974, coup d'état in Portugal. It was appointed by the Coordinating Committee of the Movement of Armed Forces (MFA), the organization of junior officers who engineered the coup against Portuguese dictator Marcelo Caetano. The JSN was composed of seven officers: General António de Spínola, General Francisco da Costa Gomes, and Brigadier Jaime Silveiro Marques from the army; Admiral António Rosa Coutinho and Admiral Jose Baptista Pinheiro de Azevedo from the navy; and Brigadier Manoel Diogo Neto and Colonel Carlos Galvao de Melo from the air force.

The JSN chose Spínola to be the interim president of Portugal and promised to implement "the three d's" political program of the MFA, which called for democracy, development, and decolonization. Specifically, among other measures, this political program called for elections for a constituent assembly to be held within one year of the April 25, 1974, coup; the end of censorship; the abolition of the regime's secret police, the Directorate of General Security (DGS); amnesty for political prisoners; and the right to form political parties and other associations.

Soon, ideological differences appeared between the relatively moderate Junta for National Salvation and the MFA Coordinating Committee. The Spínola-led JSN sought slow change as opposed to demands from the MFA that their political program be implemented immediately. At first Spínola successfully appointed conservative professor of law from the University of Lisbon, Adelino da Palma Carlos, to be the country's prime minister. By May 1974, however, the leftist MFA Coordinating Committee had gained the upper hand, replacing Palma Carlos with the communist-leaning General Vasco Gonçalves. As prime minister Gonçalves outmaneuvered António de Spínola, who resigned on September 29, 1974. Gonçalves took this opportunity to appoint a new JSN, which reflected his leftist views. By the beginning of 1975 the JSN ceased to be an important political body as power shifted to the MFA Coordinating Committee.

BIBLIOGRAPHY

Graham, Lawrence S., and Douglas L. Wheeler, eds. *In Search of Modern Portugal: The Revolution and Its Consequences.* Madison: University of Wisconsin Press, 1983.

Mattoso, José, ed. *História de Portugal.* 8 vols. Lisbon: Editorial Estampa, 1993–1994.

Maxwell, Kenneth. *The Making of Portuguese Democracy.* Cambridge: Cambridge University Press, 1995.

Medina, João, ed. *História Contemporanea de Portugal.* 7 vols. Camarate: Mutilar, 1990.

Robinson, Richard A. H. *Contemporary Portugal: A History.* London: George Allen and Unwin, 1979.

Paul Christopher Manuel

SEE ALSO Gonçalves, Vasco

Decolonization

Portugal, the first European country to acquire a modern colonial empire that extended beyond the Mediterranean region, was also the last to decolonize, stubbornly resisting the independence movements of the mid–twentieth century until the bitter end. Beginning with the capture of Ceuta on the North African coast in 1415, the Portuguese Empire was built over five hundred years, but after Goa was lost to India in 1961, it took fewer than fifteen years to unravel.

The empire was acquired during three periods of exploration and diplomatic activity: an early exploratory phase involving the acquisition of small island and coastal possessions in Africa and along the sea route to Asia, and Brazil in South America; a middle phase of territorial gains and losses from the sixteenth to the early nineteenth century, culminating in Brazilian independence in 1822; and a final phase resulting from the carving up of Africa by the European powers in the late nineteenth century. It was not until after 1890, in response to a British ultimatum setting conditions of ownership, that Portugal began to consolidate its control through the pacification, settlement, and economic development of the interior regions of the huge African territories of Angola and Mozambique (14 and 8.5 times, respectively, the size of Portugal), as well as the smaller Guinea—the gems of its twentieth-century empire and also the main theaters of its colonial wars.

In 1945, as World War II ended, Portuguese overseas possessions consisted of East Timor, Macao, and Goa, Diu, and Damão in Asia; and Portuguese Guinea (Guinea-Bissau), Angola, Mozambique, Cape Verde Islands, São Tomé and Príncipe, and São João de Ajudá (a few-acre estate in Dahomey) in Africa.

This far-flung empire was never administered uniformly, but a common underlying philosophy always characterized Portuguese colonialism as it passed through various legal changes over time. Viewed as a "civilizing mission," begun by Prince Henry the Navigator and the fifteenth-century explorers, Portuguese rule intended to elevate less-developed peoples via their adoption of Portuguese culture. As such, it was assimilationist in nature and favored economic integration.

The distinct legal character of the modern empire was first set by the Colonial Act of 1930 and the statutes of António de Oliveira Salazar's Novo Estado (New State), which began in 1933. The Novo Estado distinguished among Portuguese territorial entities, designating all but the metropolis, the Azores, and the Madeiras as "colonies" instead of the previous "provinces." It also reversed a decentralizing trend, concentrating administrative control in the Colonial Ministry in Lisbon. Through the Estatuto do Indígenato (Native Statute), standards were set for natives to become *assimilados,* or Portuguese citizens with full rights. Native education was entrusted to the Catholic Church, essentially re-Catholicizing imperial policy. Subsidized by the government, the church was no longer a mere "civilizer," but an agent of the Portuguese political presence, specifically encharged with instilling good work habits for colonial enterprises. And, finally, the Novo Estado organized the colonial economies as suppliers of raw materials and cheap labor and, ultimately, markets for Portuguese products, all for the benefit of the metropolis. Colonial budgets were balanced and approved in Lisbon. The inferior legal status of non-*assimilados,* or *indígenas,* fit well into this economic construct, since the *Indígenato,* as the system came to be known, called them to obligatory labor for public purposes.

By 1950 all colonialisms, but particularly the Portuguese system, faced rising international criticism. In Portuguese Africa little progress had been made toward the lofty ideal of a race-neutral Lusophile nation. In that year only .75 percent had qualified for *assimilado* status in Angola, and .076 percent in Mozambique. Assimilation was a complicated bureaucratic procedure, and many who could have had the status did not choose it to avoid becoming Portuguese taxpayers. Scant value was placed on the franchise in a dictatorial regime. Moreover, the system of compulsory labor was dubbed a form of modern slavery by Lisbon's critics, who were not only foreigners but Portuguese liberals and clerics in Africa.

The response of the government was to try to blunt criticism and to preserve the empire through minimalist legal changes. In 1951 the Colonial Ministry was renamed the Overseas Ministry, and the colonies became "overseas provinces" with representation in the national legislative bodies back in Lisbon. The former "colonies" were now said to be integral parts of Portugal, no longer subject to decolonization. New provincial administrative structures accorded greater status to *assimilados* and tribal chiefs, and some of the harsher aspects of "forced labor" were eliminated. However, none of these changes could still international disapproval, which grew only louder as Portugal assumed its seat in the United Nations in 1955. In 1960 the new Third World and Eastern bloc majority declared the Portuguese "provinces" "non-self-governing territories" and demanded their independence. Again on the defensive, Portugal initiated significant reforms this time, ending forced labor in 1960, abolishing the *Indígenato* in 1961, and protecting native farmlands from seizure in 1961. By this point, nevertheless, the winds of change proved irreversible.

Despite the focus on Africa, Portuguese decolonization began, somewhat ironically, with Goa and the other small Indian territories, Damão and Diu. Although of little economic or strategic importance to the metropolis, Goa was of great sentimental value since it dated to 1510 and was the city where the early Jesuit, St. Francis Xavier began his missionary work in Asia in 1542, and where he was buried. Claimed by newly independent India since 1950, Prime Minister Jawaharlal Nehru's government did not act until December 1961, after repeated attempts to negotiate with Salazar had failed. Massively outnumbered and with no allies or reinforcements, General Manuel António Vassalo e Silva gave up the struggle in two days on December 19, 1961. India officially annexed the three former Portuguese territories in March 1962. The loss of Goa was a tremendous psychological blow, ranking with that of Brazil earlier, for a large percentage of Goans, although not subject to the *Indígenato,* had adopted Portuguese culture and many had attained prominence in Lisbon. In fact, Salazar never accepted the loss while he was still living, in Portuguese literature and textbooks Goa remained Portuguese and "temporarily" occupied, and Goan representatives sat in the National Assembly until the dictatorship fell on April 25, 1974. A lasting consequence was the dismissal of Vassalo and his fellow officers, producing a resentment in the military that would carry over to the African wars. Two other Portuguese areas would be easily taken over by their newly independent neighbors: São João de Ajudá in 1961 and East Timor in 1975. Macao reverted to China by treaty in 1999.

The fighting in Africa began in Angola in 1961, in Guinea in 1963, and in Mozambique in 1964. The Novo Estado, under Salazar until 1968 and under Marcelo Caetano until 1974, would be embroiled in Africa until the regime's end. In Angola three rival groups conducted the independence effort: the Angolan Popular Liberation Movement (MPLA) led by Agostinho Neto, the Union of Populations of Angola (UPA) of Holden Roberto, and Jonas Savimbi's National Union for the Total Independence of Angola (UNITA). Although they did not cooperate, their guerrilla tactics, bases outside Angola, and assistance from the East bloc allowed initial successes that forced Portugal to pour sixty thousand troops into the field. The Portuguese were able to stabilize the situation and turned to a campaign, which would be repeated in Mozambique and Guinea, to win the hearts and minds of the natives through development projects that improved infrastructure, education, and medical care. Nonetheless, it was impossible to control so vast a land, and by the 1970s the war in Angola was a standoff. In Mozambique, by contrast, one coalition, the Mozambique Liberation Front (FRELIMO) of Eduardo Mondlane, dominated and came to control large areas in the north. But with the war going well in Angola, the Portuguese army could raise troop levels in Mozambique, where it contained the guerrillas by 1970, reducing FRELIMO activity to ambushes and sabotage. Actually it was in Guinea that the war proved the most intractable. There the Guinea and Cape Verde Independence Party (PAIGC) had in Amílcar Cabral probably the most talented of the African independence leaders. By 1968 PAIGC controlled 70 percent of the territory and 50 percent of the population. The Portuguese army was engaged on three fronts, with indefensible borders, against a popular leader with broad-based international support. General António de Spínola was named commanding officer and governor that year, and began to warn the Lisbon government that the wars in Africa could not be won militarily. Yet the regime would not abandon Guinea to concentrate elsewhere because of an ideology, expressed by President Américo Thomaz in 1968, that attached as much importance to Guinea as to any "other sacred portions of national territory." PAIGC championed the cause of Cape Verdean independence and Kwame Nkrumah of Ghana that of São Tomé and Príncipe, but Portuguese rule was never militarily threatened on these tiny islands, where guerrilla warfare was impossible.

It took the end of the Portuguese dictatorship and the democratization of Portugal itself to end the colonial system. Although they had no clear political program, the junior officers who made the Carnation Revolution, the revolution that overthrew the conservative-authoritarian state in April 1974 (so called because it occurred as red carnations were available in florist shops), favored a democratic political system, decolonization, and the breakup of the old economic monopolies. The African experience contributed greatly to the demise of the regime as war-wearied soldiers and economically burdened civilians were no longer willing to support the fight. Some observers, Spínola among them, argued that Caetano, who had favored a federative state, sold out his ideas to conservative political forces when taking over for Salazar, wasting a critical opportunity to create some sort of commonwealth and save the empire. Most observers dissent, however, believing that by that time all Africa was destined to become independent. Caetano, furthermore, embraced the traditionalist integrist ideology that precluded total independence and, like Salazar, believed that the survival of the regime depended on retaining the colonies and their economic benefits, regardless of the costs of war. With the revolution of 1974 the African empire was liquidated in fewer than two years, via painful negotiations, during which time thousands of European settlers, the *retornados,* returned to Portugal as refugees from violence.

BIBLIOGRAPHY

Bruce, Neil. *Portugal: The Last Empire.* New York: Wiley, 1975.

Costa Pinto, António, ed. *Modern Portugal.* Palo Alto, Calif.: Society for the Promotion of Science and Scholarship, 1998.

Ferreira, Hugo Gil, and Michael W. Marshall. *Portugal's Revolution: Ten Years On.* Cambridge: Cambridge University Press, 1986.

Guerra, João Paulo. *Descolonizcão portuguesa: o regreso das caravelas.* Lisbon: Publicaçoes Dom Quixote, 1996.

Robinson, R. A. H. *Contemporary Portugal: A History.* London: George Allen and Unwin, 1979.

Salazar, António de Oliveira. *The Road to the Future.* Lisbon: NSI, 1963.

Regina A. Mezei

SEE ALSO Spínola, António de

Political Parties

During the Salazar/Caetano regime, Portugal had no political parties. Oliveira Salazar, who had risen to dominance within the military lacked government in 1928 and had been appointed premier by the military on July 5, 1932, was a traditionalist who believed that political mobilization would undermine institutions and social structures. In a speech in November 1932, Salazar, who was in effect a dictator, informed the country that the military, which had seized power in 1926 and imposed a dictatorship, had dissolved all political parties. However, the constitution of 1933 did not prohibit political parties, nor did any laws. Rather, the government prevented their existence by regulating the right to association. In 1930 the government established the União Nacional (National Unity) as a government nonparty or civic association to garner public support for the regime. During the period 1930–45, when political parties of mass mobilization were a feature of the European political scene, the União Nacional had no political importance. It was reactivated as a political movement after the rebirth of opposition in the aftermath of World War II. In the late 1940s and early 1950s, it served as a forum for internal debates among the leadership over the question of restoring the monarchy, which Marcelo Caetano was instrumental in defeating. Until its end in 1974, the União Nacional organized the regime's candidates in the periodic elections that were held. By the 1960s it was unable to attract younger members and had lost the ability to rejuvenate itself. In 1969 Caetano renamed it Acção Nacional Popular (National Popular Action, ANP) and attempted give it a more active character. But with the retrenchment of political forces and the consequent failure to replace Americo Tomás as president in 1972, the ANP rapidly lost its energy. It was abolished on April 25, 1974, when the Armed Forces Movement staged a successful coup.

During the same period there were several opposition entities. In the 1930s to the right of the regime was the National Syndicalists, or Blueshirts (Fascist), and on the left the Portuguese Communist Party and several republican groups. Salazar crushed the Syndicalists and incorporated their remnants into the União Nacional in 1934. After 1945 the organized opposition on the left was made up of the Portuguese Communist Party (PCP) and various small moderate opposition umbrella groups. The United Democratic Movement (MUD) formed in 1945 was an attempt to coordinate the efforts of various opposition groups, including the moderate opposition, former supporters of the regime, and the PCP. It challenged the regime in the 1945 parliamentary elections. It was declared illegal in 1948, and its remnants joined the presidential campaign of Norton de Matos in 1949. During the 1950s and 1960s various opposition groups emerged, but ideological and personal disagreements prevented the appearance of a united opposition. The efforts of opposition candidates in the 1969 elections were coordinated by several umbrella organizations, including the CDE (Communists), CEUD (Socialists and Social Democrats), and CEM (monarchists).

The Portuguese Communist Party was founded in 1921 and is the longest-existing political party in Portugal. It was reorganized in 1940–41 along Stalinist lines and has retained that orthodox ideology despite the collapse of the Soviet Union. During the Salazar/Caetano regime it operated clandestinely among labor organizations. In 1949 it joined with the moderate opposition in supporting Norton de Matos as its presidential candidate. In 1951 it presented its own presidential candidate, Ruy Luis Gomes, but was refused recognition by the regime. In the 1958 elections it supported the artist and opposition politician Arlindo Vicente (1906–1977). It also joined other opposition groups in supporting candidates in parliamentary elections between 1945 and 1973. In the 1960s several groups that rejected the PCP's Stalinist orthodoxy broke away to form their own parties. Those with Maoist tendencies formed the MRPP Marxist Revolutionary Peoples Party in 1969 and PCP-LM Leninist Marxis in 1970. The Trotskyites formed the LCI International Communist League in 1973. Other small splinter parties were organized after the 1974 coup, including another three Maoist parties and another Trotskyite party.

Although the Communist Party did not participate in the coup of April 25, 1974, it had the prestige of half a century of fighting the dictatorship and good grassroots organization. After an initial cautious phase during the presidency of António de Spínola, the PCP followed a revolutionary strategy that brought Portugal to near civil war. As members of the interim government and leading supporters of the Armed Forces Movement (MFA), they attempted to implement socialism in Portugal through nationalization of industry, land reform, and consolidation of labor unions into a PCP-dominated union (the General Confederation of Portuguese Worker, CGTP). With the failure of the radical-left coup attempt in November 1975, the PCP lost its hold on power. In the aftermath, the PCP focused on consolidating the gains achieved by the revolution rather than pushing for extending it. Since 1975 the PCP parliamentary policy has been to attack the various governments' capitalist policies as anti–working class. The PCP achieved its greatest share of the vote in 1983 (18 percent) and declined since to 8.6 percent in 1995.

The Socialist Party (PS) was organized at a conference in Bad Münstereifel, Germany, in 1973 by Mário Soares, who subsequently served as prime minister, 1976–78 and 1983–85, and president, 1986–96. Although its origins can be seen in the Socialist Party of the monarchy, which was overthrown in 1910, and the First Republic (1910–1925), it had its roots in the Portuguese Socialist Action Group (ASP) founded in 1946 by Francisco Ramos Costa and Manuel Tito Morais. Before 1974 it had established cells among Portuguese exiles abroad and among dissenters from the PCP in Portugal. In April 1974 the PS existed mostly on paper, but it had strong connections with the Socialist parties of other European countries, which helped it financially during its early existence. Its leader, Soares, joined the first three provisional governments as foreign minister and was instrumental in implementing decolonization. It broke with the PCP over the issue of a single labor union and left the government in July 1975. The PS won the largest block of votes in the Constitutional Assembly of 1975, and the constitution it helped frame incorporated provisions that ensured a transition to socialism.

In the parliamentary elections of 1976, the PS won a plurality of votes and Soares was appointed prime minister. The PS held power from 1976 to 1978, from 1983 to 1985, and again in 1996. Each time it held power, the PS followed policies supporting democratization, modernization, and economic growth, including a harsh austerity package demanded by the International Monetary Fund (IMF) in 1978. The IMF extends credit to countries facing financial difficulties but demands that corrective measures be implemented, such as the curtailment of government subsidies and excessive spending so that inflation can be controlled. Since 1976 the PS share of the vote has fluctuated considerably. However, its presidential candidates, Mário Soares, won election in 1986 and 1991, and Jorge Sampiao in 1996.

After forty-eight years of right-wing government the return to democracy led the right-wing to obfuscate their political character by using left-sounding labels. The first major right-of-center party to form in May 1974 was the Popular Democratic Party (PPD), later renamed the Social Democratic Party (PSD). The PSD drew support from moderate opposition groups and liberals. It also benefited because there were no other democratic conservative parties in summer 1974 that could be viewed as an alternative to the PCP and the PS. Among its founders were several members of the liberal wing of the 1969 Caetano legislature, such as Francisco de Sá Carneiro and Francisco Pinto Balsemão, each of whom served as prime minister. Sá Carneiro in 1980, and Pinto Balsemão from 1981 to 1983. It looked for support from non-Marxist leftists alienated by the Marxism of the PCP and the PS. A second party, the Social Democratic Center (CDS), renamed the Popular Party (PP) in 1992, was formed in July 1974 by conservatives from the former regime and people who disliked Sá Carneiro or the PSD leftist rhetoric. Both parties built their organization among the traditional *caciques* (political bosses) of the north and center. Neither party was effective in building a strong network in the industrial and latifundist regions of the country.

The CDS participated in the second PS government in 1977–78 and in the coalition governments (Aliança Democratica, AD) of Sá Carneiro and Pinto Balsemão. In parliamentary elections its share of the vote has declined progressively. It received 9 percent in the October 1999 parliamentary elections.

The PSD gained 26 percent of the vote in the elections of 1975 and 24 percent in 1976. In coalition with the CDS and Monarchists (Aliança Democratica), it received 42 percent in 1979 and 44 percent in 1980. The PSD running alone received 27 percent of the vote in 1982 and 29 percent in 1985. In 1987 and 1991 it received 50 percent of the vote, declining to 35 percent in 1995. Its presidential candidates lost the elections in 1980, 1986, and 1995. In 1975 it supported General António dos Santos Ramalho Eanes and in 1990 Socialist Soares. The PSD held power under the AD coalition in 1979–83 and by itself from 1985 to 1996. Since 1976 the PSD had held its place as the right-of-center alternative to the PS, and when in power it has followed conservative policies promoting economic growth and modernization.

Several other lesser parties have held seats in parliament since 1974. The most significant alternative party was the National Renewal Party (PRN), which formed around President Eanes in 1985. It was supported by those disaffected by the policies of the PS and the PSD, receiving a dramatic 18 percent of the vote in 1985, mostly at the expense of the PS, but it declined to 4.5 percent in 1987 and subsequently faded from the scene. The Communist-controlled MDP/CDE, an umbrella organization established in 1973 that combined the remnants of various 1969 opposition organizations, became a political party in 1974 and received five seats in the Constitutional Assembly election, but subsequently has held seats only in coalition with the Communist Party. Among other minor parties is the União Democratica Popular (Popular Democratic Union, UDP), a Maoist party that won a seat in parliament in 1976, 1979, and 1980, thus making it the only minor party able to win seats in parliament on its own. The Monarchist Party has held seats (five in 1979, six in 1980) in parliament as part of a coalition ticket of the Aliança Democratica in 1979–83 but its share of the popular vote has remained consistently at 0.5 percent. The MRPP and the Greens have also held seats in parliament in coalition tickets with the PCP. There are about a dozen other minor parties including on the extreme left Maoists, Trotskyists, several Communist and Socialist splinter parties, and also several groups on the extreme right. None of these small parties have won seats on their own. Since 1987 the Portuguese political system has stabilized, with the PS and the PSD alternating in power.

BIBLIOGRAPHY

Bruneau, Thomas C., ed. *Political Parties and Democracy in Portugal: Organizations, Elections, and Public Opinion.* Boulder, Colo.: Westview Press, 1997.

Bruneau, Thomas C., and Alex MacLeod. *Politics in Contemporary Portugal: Parties and the Consolidation of Democracy.* Boulder, Colo.: Westview Press, 1986.

Gaspar, Carlos. "Portuguese Communism Since 1976: Limited Decline." *Problems of Communism* (January–February 1990): 45–63.

Mattoso, José, ed. *História de Portugal,* Vols. 7–8. Lisbon: Editorial Estampa, 1993–94.

———. *História de Portugal dos Tempos Pré-Históricos aos Nossos Dias,* Vol. 15. Alfragide, Portugal: Ediclube, 1994.

Opello, Walter C., Jr. *Portugal's Political Development: A Comparative Approach.* Boulder, Colo.: Westview Press, 1985.

Rosas, Fernando, and J. M. Brandão de Brito, eds. *Dicionário de Historia do Estado Novo,* 2 Vols. Lisbon: Circulo de Leitores, 1996.

Paul Brasil

Portuguese Social Democratic Party. The Portuguese Social Democratic Party (PSD), first christened the Popular Democratic party (PPD), was organized as a political party in early May 1974. Informed by the country's political, social, and economic realities, PSD leaders formulated a sufficiently vague and moderate (non-Marxist) program that provided practical, not ideological, ways to bring democracy and modernization to Portugal. Under the charismatic leadership of Francisco Sá Carneiro, the PSD developed into a populist, national mass-based political party. The PSD drew support from a diverse range of moderate opposition forces formerly associated with the former authoritarian regime: liberals, university student movements, Masons, Catholic associations, cooperatives, and other semilegal opposition groups.

Within a populist, "very Portuguese" party such as the PSD, charismatic leaders were not only important but vitally necessary. Leaders served as a common reference point, given the party's diverse membership and electorate, ill-defined, nonideological program, and flexible political strategies. This personalization of politics, however, also became a source of party vulnerability. Competition among elites for power has been an underlying factor of internal conflicts throughout the party's history. The PSD's participatory organic structures created the conditions for the formation of tendencies led by powerful barons. But the PSD developed into more than a party of "barons," as it gradually achieved a nationwide structure linking party militants to the leadership. This ensured that the bases remained intact even when disgruntled local barons opted to abandon the PSD for personal, ideological, or opportunistic reasons. The party's leadership has ideologically been located in between its bases (more to its left) and its electorate (more to its right). In the initial stages of the party's evolution, Sá Carneiro's strong leadership and charismatic personality helped unite this eclectic party organization.

The PSD pursued different, often contradictory policies and strategies during the transition period in order to win political power. Party choices were logically defined more by survival and power considerations than by ideological or programmatic rigidity. In the first constituent elections of April 1975, the PSD garnered 26.7 percent of the vote, second to the Socialist Party led by Mário Soares.

The predominance of leftist political forces and the nature of the electoral system limited the PSD's political fortunes at the national level until the party decided to run in a conservative coalition, the Aliança Democratica (Democratic Alliance, AD), with the Social Democratic Center Party (CDS) and the small Popular Monarchy Party (PPM). That the minority Socialist government from 1976 to 1979 became identified with the severe austerity measures, aimed at reducing governmental expenditures in order to control inflation, imposed on Portugal by the International Monetary Fund (IMF), which were prerequisites to additional IMF credits and were accepted by the Socialist government, helped to advance the political successes of the center-right in Portugal. After the demise of Soares's governments and several failed attempts at presidentially supported governments, the AD won the early elections of December 1979 with 44.9 percent of the vote. For the first time the democratic right had won power in postauthoritarian Portugal.

The AD parties set out to legitimize the ideology and politics of the right in their own liberal agenda; they supported private initiative, criticized state socialism, and wanted to limit presidential intervention in the legislative arena. The AD enjoyed continued electoral successes at the local level and won even more seats in the regularly scheduled October 1980 election, with 47.5 percent of the vote. The AD governing coalition faced many internal challenges after the untimely death of AD founders Sá Carneiro and Amaro da Costa, in a possibly sabatoged plane accident on December 4, 1980. PSD leader Francisco Pinto Balsemão took over the reins of power but lacked the necessary charisma and strength to keep the coalition and his own party united.

Once the conservative alliance broke up in December 1982, the PSD remained in government by allying with the Socialists in the Central Bloc lasting from 1983 to 1985. As a governing party, the PSD would continue to enjoy the fruits of power and oversee negotiations with the European Community (EC) on Portugal's terms of accession on January 1, 1986. Neither the PS nor the PSD was willing to jeopardize nearly ten years of arduous dealings with the EC (European Union as of 1993, EU). As soon as the treaty was signed in June 1985, however, the new PSD leadership under the charismatic Aníbal Cavaco Silva broke with the PS, and the coalition government came to an end.

In the early elections of October 1985 the PSD won the most votes and opted to form a minority government. Prime Minister Cavaco Silva demonstrated his strong leadership qualities and efficiency in developing policies to improve the domestic economic situation. A successful motion of censure in 1987 brought the minority PSD government to an end, and the next elections gave Cavaco Silva the governing majority he had demanded.

The PSD's performance in the 1987 election presented the center-right with an unprecedented landslide victory, with 50.2 percent of the vote. During its first full governing mandate, the PSD worked to revise the country's constitution, specifically the socialist economic features. The 1989 constitution embodied a neoliberal economic orientation for the quickly modernizing country. As one of the poorer members of the EU, Portugal was beginning to catch up with its European neighbors in terms of economic development.

Even more significant was the PSD's increase in its base of support in the 1991 elections to 50.4 percent. The PSD received these majorities because it attracted votes from all the other parties to its left and right. By reducing the role of the state in society, the PSD hoped to modernize Portugal's economy and strengthen its democratic institutions.

The October 1995 legislative election results marked the end of the PSD's hegemonic position. The final years of Cavaco's government were marked by a worsening domestic economic situation, increasing charges of corruption, and complications in the relations between the prime minister and President Soares. And as if these conditions were not enough, the PSD contested the elections with a new leader, Fernando Nogueira, who lacked the charisma and authority of his predecessor.

The PSD lost its broad electoral appeal as disgruntled voters in the center opted for the Socialists and those more to the right gave their support to the rejuvenated CDS, now called the Popular Party (PP). When compared with the PSD's level of electoral support before the "Cavaco phenomenon," the 1995 results were not all that catastrophic. The PSD enjoyed a solid electoral base of 35 percent. The average PSD voter is female; is a practicing Catholic; lives in a town with fewer than two thousand inhabitants; is older than forty-five; and resides in the northern and central littoral. The electoral map today reflects how the left still dominates south of the Mondego River, in the littoral and in the large cities; the right continues to prevail in the north, the interior, and the countryside.

The PSD as a party in opposition already has survived its first internal crisis. Nogueira, linked to the party's social democratic wing, resigned as party leader when the PSD's former leader and presidential candidate, Cavaco Silva, lost his bid to become president to Socialist Jorge Sampaio in January 1996. The party's March congress elected Marcelo Rebelo de Sousa, associated with the PSD's liberal wing, to lead the party in opposition and, most important, to prepare to win back power. The PSD remains a divided party ideologically among social democrats, liberals, and conservatives, but its real weakness lies in its many competing personalities.

BIBLIOGRAPHY

Bruneau, Thomas, ed. *Political Parties and Democracy in Portugal: Organizations, Elections and Public Opinion.* Boulder, Colo.: Westview Press, 1997.

Frain, Maritheresa. *O PPD/PPD e a Consolidacao do Regime Democratico.* Lisbon: Diario de Noticias Editorial, 1998.

Opello, Walter C., Jr. *Portugal's Political Development: A Comparative Approach.* Boulder, Colo.: Westview Press, 1985.

Maritheresa Frain

Constitution

Following the April 25, 1974 coup d'état by the Armed Forces Movement (MFA) against the dictatorship of Prime Minister Marcelo Caetano, a key aim of political life was to implement a new constitution. A constituent assembly was elected on April 25, 1975, and dedicated itself to the preparation of the constitution. The results of their work was the constitution of 1976, passed by the Constituent Assembly on April 2, 1976. Of note, this constitution did not have to be ratified by the citizenry. Rather, once the Constituent Assembly voted in the affirmative, President Francisco da Costa Gomes simply signed it into existence.

Unlike the American constitution, which seeks to limit governmental power, this constitution envisioned a positive role for the state to achieve various rights for its citizens. Among other rights, the constitution guaranteed citizens rights to a job, housing, and health care.

The first ten articles proclaim Portugal to be a free and democratic country, and protect the basic freedoms of speech, association, and religion. They also acknowledge the pivotal role of the MFA and carve out a space for the Council of the Revolution (CR) to monitor the activities of the democratically elected National Assembly and of the president. It grants the unelected CR the right to veto any legislation it deems contrary to the goals of the April 25, 1974, revolution. Article 9 commits the country to the eventual adoption of a socialist economic structure: the nationalization of the means of production.

The constitution was designed with three key objectives in mind. First, it was framed to provide for a democratic regime that was neither excessively unstable nor fraught with party divisions. Second, it grant political parties a central role in the new regime. Third, it feature a dual-executive arrangement, with both a president and a prime minister. The president is elected by universal suffrage for a five-year term, and presidents are prohibited from serving more than two consecutive terms. The president is also authorized to monitor the activities of the government and to veto legislation. The prime minister and the National Assembly are given the responsibility to write, debate, and vote on legislative bills.

The Constitution provides for the election of 250 deputies, using the d'Hondt system of proportional representation, which has a tendency to give more seats to large parties and reduce the chance for small parties to gain representation. It also specifies that only officially recognized political parties can present candidates for the National Assembly. Amendments to the constitution require a two-thirds' majority.

There have been two significant amendments to this constitution. In 1982 the National Assembly amended it to remove the last vestiges of the MFA from political life—the Council of the Revolution (CR). The original constitution had granted the CR veto power over any legislation it deemed contrary to the goals of the April 25, 1974 revolution. By 1982 the political parties in the National Assembly decided that a true democracy should not function under such a supreme unelected military body. So with the support of all political parties except the Communists, the CR was eliminated in 1982. This constitutional amendment of 1982 also reduced presidential powers regarding the dismissal of the prime minister, and placed more powers with the prime minister and the National Assembly. A second amendment passed in 1989 removed all the constitutional provisions adopted in 1976 that had required the government to adopt measures leading to socialism.

Portugal currently functions under a democratic constitution, which has successfully and peacefully framed political life since 1976.

BIBLIOGRAPHY

Graham, Lawrence S., and Douglas L. Wheeler, eds. *In Search of Modern Portugal: The Revolution and Its Consequences.* Madison: University of Wisconsin Press, 1983.

Mattoso, José, ed. *História de Portugal.* 8 vols. Lisbon: Editorial Estampa, 1993–1994.

Maxwell, Kenneth. *The Making of Portuguese Democracy.* Cambridge: Cambridge University Press, 1995.

Medina, João, ed. *História Contemporanea de Portugal.* 7 vols. Camarate: Mutilar, 1990.

Robinson, Richard A. H. *Contemporary Portugal: A History.* London: George Allen and Unwin, 1979.

Paul Christopher Manuel

Labor Union Confederations

The two main labor union confederations in Portugal are the General Confederation of Portuguese Workers—Intersindical (CGTP-IN) and the General Workers Union (UGT). As in other southern European political systems, each of the union confederations tends to be aligned with, if not penetrated by, a major political party. The CGTP-IN is closest to the Portuguese Communist Party (PCP), while the UGT is allied with the more reformist Socialist Party (PS) and the center-right Social Democratic Party (PSD). There is also a much smaller group of independent unions not affiliated with either the CGTP or the UGT. Although exact numbers are difficult to ascertain, clearly union density has generally declined in Portugal in recent years, as elsewhere in Europe. Overall unionization rose from 52.4 percent in the period 1974–78 to 58.8 percent in 1979–84. Since then, however, substantial declines have occurred. A most recent estimate points to an average of 36 percent in the 1991–95 period, but much lower density rates have also been suggested. In any case, it seems clear that unionization rates dropped by at least 50 percent in the 1980s, and the power of organized labor has declined accordingly.

Before Portugal's transition to democracy, which began on April 25, 1974, the formation of autonomous labor organizations was severely constrained by a network of authoritarian corporatist policies. These policies and the institutions they created effectively co-opted potentially significant political groups in both urban and rural areas, and channeled social and economic concerns into a limited number of district interest groups that were compulsory, monopolistic, hierarchically ordered and functionally differentiated. By the early 1970s the corporatist system was losing its legitimizing functions, and during a brief period of liberalization workers' organizations were allowed a small amount of greater autonomy. Intersindical was created in October 1970 and, despite persistent regime repression, managed to survive as a semiclandestine resistance movement to the dictatorship.

Following the 1974 military coup that toppled the Salazar/Caetano dictatorship, the unions emerged as critical actors in the revolutionary transition to democracy. The PCP, which was the only political party with any presence in Portuguese society at the time of the revolution, was already well represented within Intersindical. But there were other currents both to the left and to the right of the Communists within the union movement; these included syndicalist or far Left elements seeking a more decentralized popular democracy, as well as more reform-minded elements who sought to capture the non-Communist opposition and move away from what was seen as excessive radicalism. Following the defeat of the far Left at the national level after 1975, the labor movement was increasingly split between the pro-Communist and pro-PS wings. Eventually, by January 1979, the split was made official with the recognition of the confederation of the UGT.

Despite the problems of inflated membership statistics, the CGTP clearly took the lead as Portugal's most important union federation, with 149 of the country's 293 affiliated unions as of 1983. In 1989 the CGTP's membership was reported to be 500,000, while the UGT's was 350,000. The leading sectors represented by the CGTP were public employees and metalworkers, while in the UFT they were bank workers.

Given the differences in their membership structures and party affiliations, it is not surprising that there are strong differences in the behavior and tactics of each of the main federations. Although the CGTP claims to be completely autonomous from the PCP, its policies, analyses, and actions tend to parallel closely those of the PCP. Likewise, while the UGT has attempted to remain autonomous from direct party control, it has inevitably reflected rivalries within and between the two main governing parties. Given its more reformist stance, the UGT has also been more likely to sign social accords with recent governments than the CGTP. However, these divergences within the labor movement have not necessarily prohibited collective action. General strikes to protest the government's economic liberalization plans were called by both confederations throughout the 1980s, with the last general occurring in 1989.

Union membership continued to decline in the late 1980s and the 1990s. One study suggested a union membership rate of only 29 percent in 1989 and in a national poll conducted in 1993 only 11 percent of the total population reported being members of a union.

BIBLIOGRAPHY

Bacalhau, Mário. *Atitudes, Opiniões e comportamentos políticos dos Portugueses: 1973–1993.* Lisbon: FLAD, 1994.

Bruneau, Thomas C., and Alex Macleod. *Politics and Contemporary Portugal: Parties and the Consolidation of Democracy.* Boulder, Colo.: Lynne Rienner, 1986.

Cerdeira, Manuela C. "A Sindicalização Portuguesa de 1974 a 1995." *Sociedade e Trabalho,* no. 1 (October 1997).

Nataf, Daniel. *Democratization and Social Settlements: The Politics of Change in Contemporary Portugal.* Albany: SUNY, 1995.

Schmitter, Phillipe. "Organized Interests and Democratic Consolidation in Southern Europe," in *The Politics of Democratic Consolidation: Southern Europe in Comparative Perspective.* Ed. by Richard Gunther, P. Nikoforos Diamandouros, and Hans-Jürgen Puhle. Baltimore: Johns Hopkins University Press, 1995.

Stoleroff, Alan D. "Between Corporatism and Class Struggle: The Portuguese Labour Movement and the Cavaco Silva Government." *West European Politics* 15 (1992): 118–50.

Michael A. Baum

Retornados

Term meaning "returned ones" applied to European settlers who returned to Portugal in 1974–76 as refugees from the African wars of independence. From the 1920s on, Portuguese citizens were encouraged to migrate to Africa, especially to Angola and Mozambique; however, the Salazar dictatorship made the population of the colonies a constitutional goal in 1933 and developed schemes to carry it out. One such project was the settlement of poor white farmers in the Angolan central highlands beginning in the 1940s. Many of them failed, however, ending up in the capital, Luanda, engaged in menial occupations alongside indigenous peoples. In fact, most Portuguese migrants of all economic levels would live in the largest cities of Angola, Guinea, and Mozambique. The incidence of miscegenation has been romantically exaggerated. Racial mixing was not extensive, occurred mostly out of wedlock, and tapered off as the white population grew in the 1950s and 1960s. Whites, furthermore, always enjoyed a superior legal status as Portuguese citizens, and also benefited from informal discrimination in jobs and other business matters.

Amid the mélange of demographic statistics available, those of R.A.H. Robinson appear the most credible. He put the European population of Angola at 300,000 in 1970 and that of Mozambique at 250,000 in 1973. By 1974 these numbers were surely higher, so that these two areas, along with Guinea and the offshore Portuguese islands, the Cape Verde Islands and São Tomé and Principe, produced 650,000 *retornados* by May 1976, with more to come before the reverse migration was finally over.

By the time the Salazar-Caetano dictatorship fell on April 25, 1974, and the Armed Forces Movement (MFA) announced its commitment to decolonization, some Portuguese settlers had already experienced thirteen years of guerrilla wars of liberation. Racial confrontation had become commonplace, in a conundrum of revenge and counterrevenge, and the violence only intensified until November 1975, when Angola became the last colony to achieve independence. The flow of *retornados* to the mother country began from Mozambique in May 1974 and continued from all the Portuguese territories until the end of 1976. Some of the former settlers made dangerous escapes by sea; almost all arrived destitute, having left everything they owned behind.

The plight of the *retornados* attracted international attention and contributions; the United States, for instance, provided funds and airlift help. The unstable provisional governments in Lisbon, following the revolution of 1974, which overthrew the authoritarian regime but produced no immediate consensus of the type of government that should replace it, did create several commissions (the first on January 21, 1975) to resettle the refugees. Most *retornados* were assisted by their own relatives rather than the government, however, and were bitterly resentful toward the leftist-leaning regime that had abandoned them. The reintegration of the *retornados* was further complicated by the recession produced by the international oil crisis of 1973–74, as Portuguese migrants returning from northern Europe and soldiers returning from Africa competed with the *retornados* for jobs in a struggling economy.

What is remarkable is the relatively small impact of the *retornados* on the developing Portuguese political system. Anti-Communist and anti-center by philosophy, they became politically active in the north. In 1975 they participated in the rightist Democratic Liberation Movement of Portugal, led by ex-President António de Spínola from exile, and the Portuguese Liberation Army, which operated in Africa. Both conspired, unsuccessfully, against the MFA. In the first elections under the new constitution of April 1976, the *retornados* supported the Party of the Social Democratic Center, which came in third. They remained active in separatist protests until about 1980. By 1984 most *retornados* had been absorbed into Portuguese society, becoming influential in the small-business sector.

BIBLIOGRAPHY

Ferreira, Hugo Gil, and Michael W. Marshall. *Portugal's Revolution: Ten Years On.* Cambridge: Cambridge University Press, 1986.

Guerra, João Paulo. *Descolonizcao portuguesa: o regreso das caravelas.* Lisbon: Publicacoes Dom Quixote, 1996.

Robinson, R. A. H. *Contemporary Portugal: A History.* London: George Allen and Unwin, 1979.

Regina A. Mezei

Education

The educational system in Portugal has undergone dramatic change since the end of the Second World War, and the changes continue through to the present. Under the dictatorial regime of Antonio de Oliveira and later Marcello Caetano, frequent attempts to revive a moribund educational system were made with little result. However, as Portugal moved away from its past as an expansionary colonial power through a stage as a repressive dictatorship to its present democratic status as a member of the European Union, its educational system was adjusted in an effort to meet the country's demands.

During the first five hundred years of Portugal's history as an independent state, formal education was conducted first in cathedral schools, and later in monastic schools. In 1555 the monarchy granted the Society of Jesus (the Jesuits) a monopoly in Portuguese education that continued until the expulsion of the society from Portugal in 1759. The next one hundred and thirty years were a period of experimentation and attempts at reform of a system unsure of its purpose or direction, a period that ended with the Jaime Moinz Reform of 1895. This system was explicitly modeled on the contemporary German educational structure, and continued with modification until the Republic was proclaimed in 1910.

Popular clamor about the new government's failed educational policies led to the passage of the Reform of 1936, intended to modernize the educational system to meet the needs of the industrial age. This was the last major, overarching reform of the system until the revolution of 1974, and by all accounts it was considered another in a nearly unbroken two hundred year series of failed initiatives intended to bring Portugal's educational system in line with its European counterparts.

After the revolution of 1974, reform of the educational system was deemed a top priority. The new republic's constitution of 1976 declared the right of all Portuguese to equal opportunity for access to and success in education, although implementation of this proviso has been markedly uneven. The General Law on Education, the basic document governing education policy in Portugal, was not implemented until 1986.

Portugal's educational system has been faced with the daunting task of coping with rapid globalization with a paucity of resources. It has attempted to address these issues in a number of ways, including: a new emphasis on foreign language instruction, beginning at the primary school level; providing internet access to primary schools, enabling linkage to world-wide information repositories; and official encouragement of both students and educators to participate in international exchanges.

Today, compulsory education in Portugal is conducted from the ages of 6 to 15, while secondary education is voluntary. Approximately 1.2 million pupils attended nearly 13,000 primary schools in the late 1980's, instructed by more than 75,000 teachers. Secondary schools accounted for another 650,000 students in 1500 schools staffed by approximately 54,000 teachers.

Higher education has a long history in Portugal, with two of Europe's oldest universities, the University of Coimbra in Coimbra, and the University of Lisbon, both dating to the late thirteenth century. Post-secondary educational enrollment totaled nearly 110,000 students in the late 1980's and continues to expand due to increasing numbers of students completing secondary school and a heightened consciousness of the value of a university degree.

Student unrest has recently grown to levels not seen since the period of Portugal's decolonization, although the targets of the protests have shifted from international politics to issues closer to home, such as higher education costs and university entrance exams. With cries of "No more fees!," university students took to the streets in the early 1990s. Protesting increasing costs and difficult entrance examinations, mass student demonstrations led to the resignation of the minister of education, in large part due to his inability to address student concerns and quell the disturbances.

The educational system of Portugal faces a number of daunting challenges if it is to meet the demands for competitiveness in an integrated Europe. While literacy and secondary school graduation rates continue to increase on an annual basis, the increased student populations at all levels and improving vocational programs require large investments in capital and staffing.

BIBLIOGRAPHY

Commission of the European Communities, Directorate General for Employment, Social Affairs and Education. *Social Europe: Information Technology and Social Change in Spain and Portugal.* Luxembourg: Office for Official Publications of the European Communities, 1987.

Grilo, E. Marcal. *Vocational Education and Training in Portugal.* Luxembourg: Office for Official Publications of the European Communities, 1996.

Melo, Alberto and Ana Benavente. *Experiments in Popular Education in Portugal 1974–1976.* Paris: United Nations Educational, Scientific and Cultural Organization, 1978.

Organization for Economic Co-operation and Development. *Reviews of National Policies for Education:* Portugal. Paris: OECD, 1984.

Patrocinio, J. Tomas, and Luis Valadares Tavares. *New Information Technology in Education in Portugal.* Luxembourg: Office for Official Publications of the European Communities, 1993.

Michael A. Ross

Pozsgay, Imre (1933–)

Hungarian politician. Imre Pozsgay held various senior positions in the Hungarian Socialist Workers (Communist) Party and the government in the 1970s and 1980s. He headed the ministry of culture from 1976 to 1980 and of education from 1980 to 1982.

Pozsgay graduated from the Lenin Institute in Moscow and worked in the Communist Party in various junior positions in the late 1950s and in the 1960s; he was editor in chief of a sociological journal in the early 1970s. He was promoted to deputy minister of cultural affairs in 1975 and became minister of culture in 1976, a post he held until 1982. That year he was demoted to secretary-general of the Popular Front, a group of nominally independent organizations and parties operating with the sanction of and in cooperation with the Communist Party. He served as a minister without portfolio between 1988 and 1990. He was the Party's presidential candidate in 1989, but his candidacy was thwarted by the emerging opposition parties, as Hungary was shaken by the general collapse of Communism in Eastern Europe in 1989. The anti-Communist Árpád Göncz of the Free Democrats Alliance was elected. He was one of the founders, and later president, of the Movement for a Democratic Hungary a populist movement advocating cooperation with the Communists. However, resigned from the Communist Party in October 1990 and the next year helped found the National Democratic Alliance, which slipped into insignificance and ceased to exist in 1996. In 1997, Pozsgay became an adviser to the Hungarian Democratic Forum a centrist party.

Pozsgay was the leading member of the so-called reform Communists in the late 1980s and after the breakup of the party he joined a succession of center or right-of-center movements and parties. He was also active in the academic world as a professor of political science at Kossuth Lajos University at Debrecen and rector of the Saint Ladislaus Academy.

Tamás Magyarics

SEE ALSO Antall, József; Nemeth, Miklós

Primakov, Yevgeny M. (1930–)

Russian foreign minister. Yevgeny Primakov was born in Kiev in Soviet Ukraine but spent his youth in Tbilisi, capital of Soviet Georgia. He trained as an Arabist at the Institute of Oriental Studies in Moscow. Primakov was a reporter for the Communist Party's newspaper *Pravda* in Cairo in the 1960s and, reputedly, a KGB (secret police) agent. He became a foreign policy adviser to General Secretary Leonid Brezhnev, and served on the Central Committee of the Communist Party and the Politburo. He subsequently helped General Secretary Mikhail Gorbachev implement his policy of perestroika (restructuring). In an attempt to assert the power and influence of the USSR, he tried to use his influence with Iraqi leader Sadam Hussein to prevent the Gulf War by encouraging voluntary Iraqi evacuation of Kuwait. Primakov stood by Gorbachev during the attempted coup by hard-liners attempting to prevent the loss of power by the Communist Party and the break-up of the Soviet Union in August 1991, but in its aftermath he shifted loyalties to President Boris Yeltsin, under whom he directed Russia's foreign intelligence service. Primakov has been described as a loyal pragmatist rather than an ideologue.

Yeltsin appointed Primakov foreign minister in January 1996 in the aftermath of the victory of the Communists and nationalists in the December 1995 parliamentary elections. Primakov's predecessor, Andrey Kozyrev, had been excoriated by nationalists for being too accommodating to the West. Kozyrev was forced to resign on January 5, 1996. Primakov, who was appointed on January 9, quickly expressed his opposition to the expansion of NATO into Eastern Europe. He was expected to project Russia's image abroad and to concentrate on building stronger relations with the former republics of the USSR.

On August 23, 1998, a week after Sergey Kiriyenko's government devalued the ruble in an effort to avert financial collapse, President Yeltsin dismissed him and announced that he was reappointing Viktor Chernomyrdin as prime minister. However, Yeltsin's attempt to replace Kiriyenko with Chernomyrdin was rejected by the Duma (Parliament). Rather than push the nomination for the third vote, which if rejected again would have plunged the country into a political campaign in the midst of an economic and social crisis and perhaps might have led to civil conflict, Yeltsin retreated. On September 10, following negotiations with the Communist leadership, Yeltsin withdrew Chernomyrdin's nomination and nominated Primakov instead, who was acceptable to the Communists. In the first months of his government, composed of a mixture of centrists, reformers, and Communists, no coherent policy emerged to deal with the crisis of Russia. Money was printed to keep the government and the economy operating and to begin payment of workers' wages that had been in arrears. To warnings of inflationary pressures, the government responded that it was controlling the amount of money placed in circulation. Nevertheless, IMF loans, which were necessary to continue servicing Russia's international debt, were temporarily suspended because of Russia's violation of IMF monetary conditions.

On May 12, 1999, Yeltsin, whose own popularity had shrunk drastically, fired Primakov, who at the time was ranked the most popular politician in Russia. Yeltsin replaced Primakov with Sergey Stepashin, a Yeltsin loyalist, who also controlled the Russian police and security forces.

BIBLIOGRAPHY

Stanley, Alessandra. "Russia Spy Chief to Join Cabinet." *New York Times,* January 10, 1996.

———. "Russia's New Foreign Minister Sets a More Assertive Tone." *New York Times,* January 13, 1996.

Bernard Cook

SEE ALSO Kiriyenko, Sergey; Kozyrev, Audrey; Yeltsin, Boris

Prodi, Romano (1939–)

Founder of the Olive Tree coalition, Italian prime minister from April 1996 to October 1998, and president of the European Commission. Romano Prodi was born in Scandiano, Italy, in 1939. He studied economics at the University of Bologna under Beniamino Andreatta, an influential Catholic intellectual and member of the left of the Christian Democratic Party (DC), who would later become defense minister in his former pupil's government. Prodi pursued postgraduate studies at the London School of Economics and in the United States at Harvard University.

He returned to Italy to teach at the University of Bologna and in the mid-1970s became director of the famous Center for Industrial Economics or Nomisma at Bologna. In 1978 Prodi briefly served as minister of industry under Prime Minister Giulio Andreotti. He went on to become president of the Institute for Industrial Reconstruction (IRI), the state holding company. Although he would later describe this as his "personal Vietnam," Prodi managed to turn IRI around, leaving it in 1989 with a profit of over a trillion lira or approximately $772,000. He briefly returned to that post in 1993, following the removal of IRI chairman Franco Nobili in the wake of *Tangentopoli,* the so-called Clean Hands scandal.

Asked by his former mentor Andreatta to serve as leader of the Partito Popolare (Popular Party, PPI), the inheritor of the left of the Christian Democrats, Prodi finally agreed to enter politics only when, in January 1995, Rocco Buttiglione, leader of the PPI, declared that his party would join the former fascist party, Alleanza Nazionale, in a right-wing coalition. While Buttiglione left the PPI, bringing only a small faction with him to form the United Christian Democrats (CDU), committees for "the Italy we want" were spontaneously formed all over the country. An electoral program of the new center-left coalition, named the Olive Tree, was also elaborated by these committees, while Prodi visited Italy on a one hundred-day coach tour.

Following the legislative elections of April 1996, Prodi's Olive Tree coalition was supported in parliament by the Rifondazione Communista (Communist Refoundation Party), formed by members of the old Communist Party, who disagreed with the formation of the Democratic Party of the Left and he became prime minister. He remained in power until October 1998, when he lost a vote of confidence that he had called to pass the annual budget. Replaced by the leader of the major party of the Olive Tree coalition, Massimo D'Alema of Democrats of the Left, Prodi was then successfully nominated by the D'Alema government to become president of the European Commission, a position he is expected to hold until 2005.

Federiga Bindi

Proletarian Internationalism

Socialism is the wave of the future—thus ran the Communist slogan proclaimed throughout the "socialist third" of the world, and widely outside. This form of socialism entailed, in Soviet parlance, the dictatorship by a Communist nomenklatura. Doctrinal differences regarding socialism, thus understood, differed, of course, widely. Soviets, Chinese, Vietnamese, North Koreans, Cubans all vied with one another in asserting the special validity of their own brand. But at least there was general agreement that socialism was immensely superior to capitalism economically, morally, politically, even aesthetically. Marx and Lenin were universally honored as the Founding Fathers of an all-conquering ideology that ultimately would create a new society, a new world, and a "new man." The battle would be won under the command of a self-appointed vanguard that would lead the backward masses to eventual triumph. The end of history would be a new Messianic age within a classless society. A sign outside of Moscow once proclaimed, "We are living in an age in which all roads lead to Communism."

But "peaceful coexistence" applied only to the foreign relations between sovereign states. There could be no "peaceful coexistence" between competing social systems, between socialism and capitalism. On the contrary, "peaceful coexistence" implied the intensification of the international class struggle by all means—economic, propagandistic, cultural, diplomatic, even military. Military intervention in Third World states was justified, therefore, by a new doctrine of "proletarian internationalism" according to which the embattled working class of one country might be rightfully supported by armed force and the liberation struggle in another. The Soviet Union continued to consider itself as the center of a great revolutionary movement, with an intricate, far-flung network of intelligence and propaganda organizations in the West. More important, the Soviet Union continued to expand its military and long-range missile forces.

Determined not to suffer another diplomatic defeat such as it sustained over Cuba in 1962, the USSR, during the later 1960s and 1970s, built a powerful navy. In addition Moscow, under the guise of proletarian internationalism, supported so-called liberation wars in various parts of the world, in Africa particularly by Cuban proxy forces and by East German specialists in military matters and police procedures.

Marxist-Leninists made major political gains under proletarian internationalism. The peace treaty negotiated for the purpose of ending the Vietnam War soon foundered, and in 1975 South Vietnam fell to the Communists; Cambodia and Laos soon followed. The breakdown of the Portuguese Empire (1974) led to the creation of two self-proclaimed Marxist-Leninist republics, Angola and Mozambique, both led by "vanguard parties" in close touch with the Communist Party of the Soviet Union (CPSU). Cuban soldiers were deployed in Angola and also in Ethiopia, where the monarchy had fallen in 1973, to be replaced later by another Marxist-Leninist dictatorship. Marxist-Leninist revolutionaries also seemed to make good progress in the New World. Aided by Cuba and the Soviet Union, the Sandinistas seized power in Nicaragua in 1979. They were committed to the international class struggle, and dedicated to helping other revolutionaries in Central America. Above all, Soviet forces in 1979 invaded neighboring Afghanistan. For the first time since World War II the Soviet Union intervened directly with its own military forces in a foreign country, without even bothering to use proxies—whether soldiers from Cuba or police and security experts from East Germany.

Nevertheless, the tide was turning against proletarian internationalism. The new Marxist-Leninist states all ran into desperate economic difficulties. Angolan forces and their Cuban allies failed to subdue the armed opposition organized by the National Union for the Total Independence of Angola (UNITA) rebels, who were in turn supported by South Africa. In Mozambique the government could not control widespread revolts nominally coordinated by the National Resistance of Mozambique (RENAMO), again sustained with South African help. The Sandinista experiment in Nicaragua depressed the economy and could not defeat its opposition. Marxism-Leninism likewise ran aground in Ethiopia. Above all, the Soviet empire—as the British Indian empire before—proved unable to subdue the mountaineers of Afghanistan, a defeat fraught with much graver consequences for the Soviets in the twentieth century than it had been for the British in the nineteenth.

The Soviet Union could not quiet discontent at home by victories abroad. The empire in Eastern Europe proved costly to sustain, as did "fraternal" help to Cuba and other pro-Soviet states. At long last the ice broke. The first major crack may have opened when Konstantin Chernenko took power as Communist Party General Secretary in 1984. Chernenko tried to improve relations with the United States. In 1987, almost unnoticed by the world at large, Mozambique, a Soviet ally in the Third World, concluded at Nkomati an accord with South Africa whereby the two signatories agreed not to foment subversion beyond their respective borders. Even a few years earlier such an arrangement would have seemed inconceivable, given the Marxist-Leninist assumption that South Africa was a Western financial colony, run by a reactionary, racist clique doomed to speedy extinction. In 1985 Chernenko died, to be replaced by Mikhail Gorbachev, and relations with the West thereafter underwent a fundamental change.

Gorbachev's reputation has declined. Critics within and without the Soviet Union stress his vacillations, his inability or unwillingness to take his initial reforms to their predestined conclusion. These objections are well taken. Yet, when all is said and done, it was under Gorbachev that Soviet citizens secured for themselves what they had ardently desired—freedom of speech, assembly, religion.

The strategy of direct intervention carried out under the banner of "proletarian internationalism," had far-reaching consequences. The Soviet Union and its allies worked out a military division of labor in which the USSR provided the higher strategic direction, logistic support, and arms; East Germany supplied experts, technicians, and instructors (especially those to train intelligence agents and secret police officers); and Cuba became responsible for the bulk of the combat forces. This formula had been applied with much success to Ethiopia, where the Soviet Union and Cuba airlifted large numbers of troops and heavy supplies over great distances in an impressive display of military strength, enabling the Ethiopians to defeat a Somali invasion in 1977–78 and largely suppress a widespread rebellion in Eritrea. Ethiopia became to them a testing ground for the ability of a Marxist-Leninist revolution to survive in a hostile world; a touchstone for the efficacy of proletarian internationalism as a revolutionary instrument in a backward society; a strategic bastion in the Horn of Africa; and a potential labor power reservoir for military operations in other parts of Africa, the Persian Gulf, and Saudi Arabia.

However, having waged a long, bloody, unpopular, and inconclusive counterinsurgency war, the Soviet armed forces withdrew from Afghanistan in 1988. In the same year the Soviet Union, South Africa, and Cuba negotiated a treaty providing for the Cuban army's withdrawal from Angola. Class struggle and proletarian internationalism were virtually repudiated as the basis of Soviet foreign policy. Addressing the Council of Europe at Strasbourg in July 1989, Gorbachev announced that the Red Army would no longer intervene in domestic disorders in the "socialist" of central and Eastern Europe. Henceforth "real existing socialism" and proletarian internationalism were doomed, for the various Quisling regimes could no longer rely on their own armies.

BIBLIOGRAPHY

Duignan, Peter, and L. H. Gann. *The Rebirth of the West: The Americanization of the Democratic World, 1945–1958.* Oxford: Basil Blackwell, 1992.

Gann, L. H., and Peter Duignan. *Hope for South Africa?* Stanford, Calif.: Stanford University, Hoover Institution Press, 1991.

Peter Duignan

Provos

One of the most creative and successful countercultural movements of the 1960s. Similar to the American Yippies in style, the Dutch Provos antedated them by several years and proved more effective in drawing widespread, and often sympathetic, public attention for their cultural and political aims.

Formed in May 1965, the Provos were never an ideologically cohesive group. A few of them, like their leader Roel van Duyn, were theoretical anarchists; others were self-styled urban reformers. For example, the White Bicycle Plan, the most famous of the Provo "White Plans" (named after the Provos' favorite color), proposed prohibiting all cars from the center of Amsterdam, replacing them with thousands of free, public bicycles. Most of all, however, Provo was an impulsive movement that derived popularity from its playful opposition to authority. Provo "happenings" became the scene of a series of minor riots between police and public, and the Provos' hurling of smoke bombs during the 1966 wedding of Princess Beatrix and the German Claus von Amsberg proved the high point in their campaign to confound authority. The Provos largely succeeded in making Dutch authorities seem both repressive and ridiculous.

Ultimately, however, the Provos became the victim of their own success. Although none of their White Plans were directly implemented, sympathy among prominent citizens for the Provos' romantic, nonauthoritarian goals became so widespread that maintaining their oppositional stance became difficult. The police, too, developed more subtle tactics, avoiding open conflict. Partly for these reasons, Provo disbanded in May, 1967, although it retained a seat in the Amsterdam city council and would inspire further countercultural activity, both at home and abroad.

BIBLIOGRAPHY

De Jong, Rudolf. "Provos and Kabouters," in David E. Apter and James Joll. *Anarchism Today.* Garden City, N.Y.: Doubleday, 1972.

Mamadouh, Virginie. *De stad in eigen hand: Provos, kabouters en krakers als stedelijke sociale beweging.* Amsterdam: SUA, 1992.

Van Duyn, Roel. *Provo: De geschiedenis van de provotarische beweging.* Amsterdam: Meulenhoff, 1985.

J. C. Kennedy

Pugo, Boris Karlovich (1937–91)

Soviet interior minister (1990–91). After having served as head of the KGB (Secret police) in Soviet Latvia and head of the Control Committee of the Communist Party of the USSR, Boris Pugo was appointed interior minister of the Soviet Union in December 1990 by President Mikhail Gorbachev. His appointment was part of the conservative shift of which Eduard Shevardnadze warned when he resigned as foreign minister in December 1990. Pugo played a leading role in ordering the attacks by Soviet Interior Ministry Troops on separatists in Latvia and Lithuania in early 1991 in a futile effort to intimidate the supporters of independence for those Soviet Republics. He was one of the central conspirators in the unsuccessful coup launched on August 19, 1991, against Gorbachev. With the failure of the coup, he shot his wife and committed suicide.

BIBLIOGRAPHY

"Pugo, Aleksander Sergeyevich," in Andrew Wilson and Nina Bachkatov. *Russia and the Commonwealth A to Z.* New York: Harper Perennial, 1992.

Bernard Cook

Pujol i Soley, Jordi (1930–)

Leader of the moderate nationalist coalition, Convergencia i Unió (Convergence and Union), who became president of the Catalan Autonomous Government in 1980. Jordi Pujol i Soley was born in Barcelona in 1930. Originally a businessman and founder of Banca Catalana in 1959, he was an active member of the nationalist Catholic opposition under Francisco Franco. He was sentenced to a seven year prison-term in 1960 but was freed on bail in 1963. His main activity then became promotion of Catalan cultural enterprises. Founder of Convergencia i Unió in 1974, he abandoned all entrepreneurial activities to dedicate himself to politics. He has written extensively on Catalan national identity and on the need to integrate immigrants into Catalan society. His political leadership has been characterized by stability and a great ability to negotiate concessions from Madrid for Catalan autonomy.

BIBLIOGRAPHY

Conversi, Daniele. *The Basques, the Catalans and Spain: Alternative Routes to Nationalist Mobilization.* London: C. Hurst, 1996.

Daniele Conversi

Putin, Vladimir V. (1952–)

President of Russia. On August 10, 1999, Prime Minister Sergey V. Stepashin was fired by President Boris Yeltsin after less than three months in office and replaced by Vladimir V. Putin, the head of Russia's domestic security. Putin was born on October 7, 1952, in Leningrad. He graduated in law from Leningrad State University. He then worked in the foreign intelligence service of the KGB (the secret police and intelligence service) principally in Germany and rose to the rank of lieutenant colonel. He returned to Leningrad and taught in the international affairs department of the Leningrad State University. In 1990, Putin resigned from the KGB to join the team of his former law professor, Anatoly Sobchak, who had become mayor of Leningrad. Putin headed the city's external relations committee and in March 1994 became the deputy mayor. In September 1996, after Sobchak's electoral defeat, Putin, who had headed the St. Petersburg branch of the pro-Yeltsin "Our Home is Russia Party," moved to Moscow and became the deputy head of management in President Yeltsin's administration. In 1998, Putin was appointed deputy head of presidential administration and the head of the federal security service, the domestic division of the former KGB. He retained the latter position when he was simultaneously appointed secretary of the presidential security council. Gennadi Zyuganov, the Communist leader, criticized Putin as a carbon copy of Stepashin. Some commentators, however, surmised that Yeltsin replaced Stepashin because the latter seemed to have developed little potential as a presidential candidate for the 2000 election. Yeltsin, they believe, was desperate to have one of "his" men succeed him in order to offer presidential protection for Yeltsin and his entourage. Yeltsin apparently found both requisites in Putin.

Putin launched a military campaign against breakaway Chechnya at the end of September. The Russian invasion was in response to Chechen attacks in Dagestan and the bombing of three apartment buildings in Russia, attributed by the Russian government to the Chechens. Though the Russian campaign did not proceed as swiftly as predicted by the government and the army, the decisive action directed by Putin won him wide popularity. On December 31, 1999, Yeltsin unexpectedly announced that he was stepping down and handing the presidency over to Putin on January 1, 2000. Putin had made a number of concessions to Yeltsin. Yeltsin was promised immunity from prosecution, a generous retirement allowance, and a number of perquisites. A presidential election was held March 2000, and Putin was elected president in his own right.

BIBLIOGRAPHY

Bohlen, Celestine, "Gray Eminence Compels Respect and Even Fear," *New York Times,* August 10, 1999.

Bernard Cook

SEE ALSO Yeltsin, Boris

Quasimodo, Salvatore (1901–68)

Italian poet, translator, and critic; winner of the 1959 Nobel Prize in literature. Born in Modica, Sicily, Quasimodo entered engineering school but for lack of funds worked as a technical designer, store clerk, then civil engineer in the army. In 1930 he published three poems in the journal *Solaria,* through the aid of his brother-in-law, and published his first collection, *Acque e terre* (*Waters and Lands*). These simple, subtle fragments showed the symbolist influence of Giuseppe Ungaretti and the hermetic poets. Quasimodo published subjective, pessimistic poetry in *Oboe sommerso* (*Submersed Oboe,* 1932), *Odore di eucalyptus, ed altri versi* (*Scent of eucalyptus, and other verses,* 1933), *Erato e Apollion* (1935), *Poesie* (1938), and *Ed è subito sera* (*And Suddenly It Is Evening,* 1942). In 1939 he left engineering to become a drama critic; in 1941 he became a literature professor in Milan.

After the end of World II War and the fascist regime in Italy, Quasimodo adopted a more accessible, less personal voice in his collections *Con il piede straniero sopra il cuore* (*With the Foreign Foot on the Heart,* 1946), republished as *Giorno dopo giorno* (*Day after Day,* 1947); *La vita non è sogno* (*Life Is Not a Dream,* 1949); *Il falso e vero verde* (*True and false green,* 1954, 1956); *La terra impareggiabile* (*The Incomparable Earth,* 1958, 1962); and *Dare e avere* (*To Give and to Have,* 1966).

The Nobel Committee cited Quasimodo's social voice in awarding him the 1959 literature prize. With guilt and censure he confronted death under fascist rule, in battle, in extermination camps, and in nuclear war. Other lyrics pined with nostalgia for an ideal, lost land: his native Sicily with its Greek heritage. He saw Greek poetry as the keystone of Mediterranean culture; his *Lirici greci* (1940) updated Sappho and Alcaeus with a modern treatment. He later translated Homer, Virgil, Ovid, Catullus, Sophocles, Aeschylus, Euripides, Shakespeare, Molière, Ruskin, E. E. Cummings, Pablo Neruda, and the Gospel of John. Despite his leftist criticism of hermeticism as anachronistic for the new postwar age, he returned to neohermeticism with his later poems of love and personal tragedy.

BIBLIOGRAPHY

Quasimodo, Salvatore. *Complete Poems.* Introduced and tr. by Jack Bevan. New York: Schocken Books, 1984.

Salibra, Elena. *Salvatore Quasimodo.* Rome: Edizioni dell'Ateneo, 1985.

Salina Borello, Rosalma. *Salvatore Quasimodo: Biografia per immagini.* Cavallermaggiore, Italy: Gribaudo, 1995.

Mark Choate

Raab, Julius (1891–1964)

Austrian chancellor. During his entire political career the conservative and pious Catholic Raab acted as the champion of business, particularly craftsmen and small businessmen. His political persona paralleled that of the transformation of the First (1918–33/38) and Second Austrian Republics (1945–). Deeply immersed in the political antagonisms between the main political camps until the *Anschluss* (1938), when Nazi Germany absorbed Austria, he emerged as a great pragmatist and consensus builder in the postwar coalition governments between the formerly hostile camps. As the chancellor who regained full Austrian sovereignty after World War II, he entered the history books as the "State Treaty Chancellor."

Raab was born into a bourgeois family on November 29, 1891, in St. Pölten in Lower Austria. He matured in the waning years of the Habsburg monarchy. Military service during World War I interrupted his studies in civil engineering at the Technical University in Vienna. As a young, highly decorated lieutenant, Raab distinguished himself throughout the war on the Russian and Italian fronts in a sapper regiment, which by the end he commanded. At war's end he finished his studies and joined his father's construction company.

After working his way up in the Christian Social Party in Lower Austrian local politics, he was elected to parliament in 1927 as its youngest member. Chancellor Ignaz Seipel asked him to act as a moderating force in the radicalized Lower Austrian home defense formations (Heimwehr). As Heimwehr leader, Raab engaged in the politics of anti-Communism and anti-Semitism. He once attacked the Socialist leader, Otto Bauer, on the floor of parliament as an "insolent Jewish pig." Raab supported the authoritarian Dollfuss/Schuschnigg corporate state (1934–38) and acted as minister of trade in the final weeks before Germany's annexation of Austria on March 12, 1938. Raab kept a low profile during World War II and made it through the war unharmed in the construction business.

In April 1945 Raab quickly reemerged as a founding father of the Second Republic. He was present at the formation of the new conservative People's Party (ÖVP). Chancellor Karl Renner appointed him minister of reconstruction in his provisional government (April–November 1945). Raab played a crucial role in cleaning away the rubble and starting to rebuild war-torn Vienna. The Soviets, who occupied a zone of "liberated" Austria along with the American, British, and French zones after the war (1945–55), perhaps bearing his independence and opposition to Soviet economic demands, vetoed Raab's appointment as minister of trade in the newly elected national unity government led by his old party friend Leopold Figl.

Raab emerged as the éminence grise among conservatives, pulling the strings of domestic politics behind the scenes. He acted as Figl's floor leader in parliament, chaired the People's Party from 1952–60, and acted as president of the Chamber of Business and conciliator among the various ÖVP interest groups. In 1952 Raab instigated a tighter currency and economic policy and precipitated both a budget crisis and a new election from which he emerged as the new chancellor in spring 1953.

After Soviet leader Joseph Stalin's death in March 1953, Raab became a champion of easing tensions with the new leadership in the USSR. Against the advice of the new Eisenhower administration in the United States, he initiated behind-the-scenes bilateral diplomatic contacts with the Soviets and tested the feasibility of Austrian neutrality. The Western powers watched with trepidation as Raab's bold policy departure brought Austria its State Treaty in spring 1955, which ended the postwar occupation. Soviet concessions leading to the "Austrian solution" of neutrality also helped ease East-West tensions during the Cold War and led to the Geneva Summit of July 1955.

During his final six years as chancellor, Raab was a solid manager of the grand coalition government and a consensus builder with the Socialists. In foreign policy he carefully shepherded Austrian neutrality through Cold War crises in Hungary (1956) and Lebanon (1958). Domestically he acted as one of the principal architects of the Sozialpartnerschaft, the widely admired postwar Austrian model of preserving the social peace among the principal interest groups. A set of interlocking institutions was designed to control wages and prices and to manage the Austrian economy with its huge public-sector industries.

After recovering from a stroke Raab resigned in 1961. He was not successful in his campaign for the Austrian presidency in 1963. He died on January 8, 1964.

Like Eisenhower, Raab was highly popular in the 1950s, presiding over an age of growing expectations and widening middle-class prosperity. In the corridors of power he was an authoritative figure who practiced a military style of decision making, frequently going against majority opinion. His idea of statesmanship was not to do what the people wanted but to induce the people to do what he felt was good for them.

BIBLIOGRAPHY

Bischof, Günter. "The Making of the Austrian Treaty and the Road to Geneva," in Günter Bischof and Saki Dockrill, eds. *Cold War Respite: The Geneva Summit, July 1955.* Baton Rouge: Louisiana State University Press, 1998.

Bischof, Günter, and Anton Pelinka, eds. *Austro-Corporatism: Past-Present-Future.* New Brunswick, N.J.: Transaction, 1996.

Brusatti, Alois, and Gottfried Heindl, eds., *Julius Raab: Eine Biographie in Einzeldarstellungen.* Linz: R. Trauner, 1986.

Gerlich, Peter. "Julius Raab," in Herbert Dachs et al., eds. *Die Politiker: Karrieren und Wirken bedeutender Repräsentanten der Zweiten Republik.* Vienna: Manz, 1995.

Rauchensteiner, Manfried. *Die Zwei: Die Groze Koalition in Österreich 1945–1966.* Vienna: Österreichischer Bundesverlag, 1987.

Günter Bischof

Rajk, László (1909–49)

Hungarian Communist politician and interior minister (1946–49). László Rajk taught at the University of Budapest until he was expelled for his Communist activities. As a member of the Federation of Building Workers, he was involved in organizing nationwide strikes in Hungary in 1935. During the Spanish Civil War (1936–39) Rajk was party secretary in the Hungarian Battalion of the International Brigade. With the victory of the Nationalist forces, he sought refuge by crossing the Pyreness, and was interned in France but fled to Hungary, where as secretary of the illegal Hungarian Communist Party, he was interned again. When the Germans took control of Hungary in late 1944 he was deported to Germany but survived to return to Hungary as the secretary of the Budapest section of the Hungarian Communist Party (1945–46) and then vice general secretary of the national party from 1946 to 1949.

Rajk replaced Imre Nagy in the postwar Hungarian coalition government as minister of the interior in February 1946. In 1949, he became minister of foreign affairs and general secretary of the newly organized Hungarian Independence Front. In May 1949, however, Rajk was arrested by the Communist secret police. In a show trial he confessed to national deviation, that is, pursuing a path in opposition to the Soviet Union and its leader Joseph Stalin, and to having been a traitor in Spain. He was sentenced to death. Rajk was posthumously rehabilitated in 1955. The trial of Rajk was part of the power struggles and political purges of the late 1940s through which Mátyás Rákosi, the general secretary of the Hungarian Workers Party (Communist Party), and his allies and followers consolidated power. Altogether twenty Hungarian Party Communist leaders were arrested at the beginning of July 1949 and later sentenced to death or prison.

BIBLIOGRAPHY

Molnár, Miklós. *A Short History of the Hungarian Communist Party.* Boulder Colo.: Westview Press, 1978.

Soltész, István. *Rajk-dosszié.* Budapest: Láng Kiadó, 1989.

Heino Nyyssönen

SEE ALSO Rákosi, Mátyás

Rákosi, Mátyás (Róth, Mátyás) (1892–1971)

Hungarian Communist leader. Mátyás Rákoski was born Mátyás Róth on March 14, 1892 in Ada, Serbia. He served in the Austro-Hungarian army in World War I and became a Communist while a prisoner of war in Russia. During the Hungarian Soviet Republic of 1919, Mátyás Rákosi was the people's commissar of commercial affairs, one of the commissars of social production, and commander of the Red Guard, the army of the short lived

Hungarian Soviet. After the collapse of the Hungarian Soviet, Rákosi fled to Moscow and became a secretary in the Comintern, the international Communist organization set up in 1919 to assure Soviet dominance of the world Communist movements, from 1921 to 1924. In 1925 he was arrested after returning to Hungary and was sentenced to nine and a half years in prison. At the end of his term Rákosi was rearrested and sentenced to life imprisonment for his activity as a people's commissar during the Hungarian Soviet.

Through diplomatic arrangements Rákosi was expatriated to the Soviet Union in 1940, where he became leader of the Communist emigrants, the Muscovites. After returning to Hungary in 1945, following the Soviet occupation of the country, Rákosi became minister of state and vice prime minister (1945–49) in the coalition government that the non-Communist Smallholders had promised the Soviets they would establish after free elections were held in 1945. From 1952 to 1953 he was premier.

Rákosi was secretary-general of the Hungarian Communist Party from 1945 to 1948. After the fusion of the Communists and the Social Democrats, he was general secretary of the new Hungarian Workers Party until 1953, and from 1953 to 1956 first secretary, when the title was changed.

Between the world wars Rákosi was a well-known figure in the world Communist movement. Later he was described as the most faithful student of Stalin, and he subsequently followed a Stalinist policy in Hungary. He is noted for his "salami tactics," through which he eliminated his enemies slice by slice. He carried out a policy of purge and terror. Almost half of all party officials were removed in late 1951, and more than 350,000 party members had lost their membership by August 1954. Rákosi, wishing Hungary to become a "land of iron and steel," also brutally attempted to force industrialization on Hungarian society in only a few years.

After the death of Stalin in 1953, Rákosi was among the Communist leaders of the Soviet satellite states summoned to Moscow by the new Soviet leadership in June 1953. Rákosi was forced to relinquish the premiership to Imre Nagy by Georgy Malenkov, the new Soviet party premier, but was allowed to remain first secretary. The following two years witnessed a struggle between the reformers clustered around Nagy and the followers of Rákosi. When Malenkov lost his contest with Nikita Khrushchev, the first secretary of the Communist Party of the USSR, Nagy was ousted from his position by the Rákosists.

Rákosi had consolidated his power by attacking his rivals within the party as Titoists. Under Khrushchev however, the Soviet relationship with Tito, who had severed Yugoslavia's ties to Joseph Stalin's USSR in 1948, improved. After the June 1956 riots in Poland, Anastas Mikoyan, an influential Soviet presidium member and supporter of Khrushchev, went to Hungary to urge the ouster of the hard-line Rákosi in order to facilitate reforms in Hungary and forestall the kind of popular unrest that had prompted Soviet concessions in Poland. Rákosi was forced to resign and was summoned to the Soviet Union. In 1962, during the era of János Kádár he was expelled from the Hungarian Socialist Worker's Party. Rákosi managed a paper factory in Soviet Kazakhstan for a while and died in the Soviet Union in 1971.

BIBLIOGRAPHY

Fejtö, François. *A History of the People's Democracies.* New York: Praeger, 1971.

Molnár, Miklós. "The Communist Party of Hungary," in *The Communist Parties of Eastern Europe.* Ed. by Stephen Fischer-Galati. New York: Columbia University Press 1979.

Pünkösti, Ărpád. *Rákosi a hatalomért 1945–1948.* Budapest: Európa, 1992.

Nemes, János. *Rákosi Mátyás születésnapja.* Budapest: Láng Kiadó, 1988.

Rákosi, Mátyás. *Der Weg Unserer Volksdemokratie: Vortrag auf der Parteihochschule der Partei der Ungarischen Werktätigen am 29. Februar 1952.* Berlin: Dietz Verlag, 1952.

Heino Nyyssönen

SEE ALSO Gerö, Ernö; Kádár, János; Nagy, Imre; Rajk, László

Ramadier, Paul (1888–1961)

Moderate French Socialist and, the first prime minister of the Fourth Republic (January–November 1947). Paul Ramadier's unstable left-of-center coalition faced a succession of crises: food shortages, fighting in France's colony of Indochina, budget deficits, inflation, labor unrest, and the beginning of the Cold War. In May Ramadier expelled the Communists from his cabinet after they refused to endorse his economic policies, an event that marked a decisive rupture between French Communists and other parties of the Left.

Beginning his career as a lawyer for consumer and marketing cooperatives, Ramadier was elected mayor of Decazeville in 1919. A right-wing Socialist in parliament from 1928 to 1940, he served in Léon Blum's first cabinet. An opponent of Marshal Philippe Pétain's Vichy regime during World War II, he actively worked for the Resistance. After resigning as premier, Ramadier served as Henri Queuille's defense minister from 1948 to 1949, and as Guy Mollet's finance minister from 1956 to 1957. He opposed General Charles de Gaulle's return to power in 1958, and retired from politics after losing his seat in the 1958 parliamentary election. Ramadier was recognized as a competent man of determination and integrity, but not as an outstanding leader.

BIBLIOGRAPHY

Auriol, Vincent. *Mon Septennat, 1947–1954.* Ed. by P. Nora and J. Ozous. Paris: Gallimard, 1970.

Ouilliot, Roper. *La S.F.I.O. et l'exercice du pouvoir, 1944–1958.* Paris: Fayard, 1972.

Rioux, Jean-Pierre. *La France de la Quatrième République,* 2 Vols. Paris: Le Seuil, 1980–83.

Thomas T. Lewis

Rapacki Plan

Polish disarmament project stimulated by the idea of disengagement that sought to limit military forces in a Europe divided at the time into unfriendly military blocs.

On October 2, 1957, at the twelfth General Assembly of the United Nations, Adam Rapacki, Polish minister of foreign affairs, proposed the creation of a nuclear-free zone in central Europe. The zone, controlled by the Soviet-led Warsaw Pact and NATO, would include Poland, Czechoslovakia, and both German states. In the zone the production, transportation, storing, and deployment of nuclear weapons was to be forbidden. Rapacki's plan, elaborated in a February 14, 1958, memorandum of the Polish government, was presented to the respective states. Although the socialist countries approved the project, the Federal Republic of Germany followed by other Western states rejected it. According to them, nuclear disarmament in central Europe without reduction in conventional weapons would give military superiority to the USSR and its allies.

Having taken into account the reservations of the Western countries, Rapacki prepared a revised version of the plan. On November 4, 1958, he suggested two stages for the process of disengagement. Nuclear weapons were to be deactivated, then removed, and conventional armies subsequently reduced considerably. The plan was much discussed at the Geneva Disarmament Conference, which met intermittently from 1958, and gained considerable support from the Scandinavian countries, Finland in particular. The NATO states, however, were still opposed, fearing that the plan would confirm the division of Europe into two blocs. The subsequent suggestion of Polish Communist Party First Secretary Władysław Gomułka in 1963 that nuclear and thermonuclear armaments should be banned in central Europe found much praise.

BIBLIOGRAPHY

Graebner, N. A. *The Cold War: Ideological Conflict or Power Struggle.* Boston: Heath, 1963.

Ryszard Sudzinski

Rasmussen, Poul Nyrup (1943–)

Danish Social Democratic politician who became prime minister in 1993. Poul Nyrup Rasmussen was born into a working-class family in Esbjerg, a port town in the west of Denmark. Early in life he was politically active in the local youth section of the Social Democratic Party. He received a doctorate in economics from Copenhagen University in 1971. After graduation he was employed as an economic adviser to the National Trade Union Congress (LO). From 1980 to 1986 he served as chief economist in the LO. This important job brought him into contact with the leading Social Democratic ministers and politicians. From 1986 to 1988 he was director for a private pension fund, LD Pension. He was elected to the Folketing (parliament) in 1988, served as vice chairman of the Social Democratic Party from 1987 to 1992, and became party chairman in 1992.

Rasmussen became prime minister in 1993 in a four-party coalition government. After the general election of September 1994, he was leader of a three-party coalition minority government. Since 1971 minority governments—a government without a majority in parliament but without a majority against it—have been characteristic of the Danish parliamentary system. Of the twelve governments between 1971 and 1996, eleven have been minority governments. The only exception was Rasmussen's government in 1993–94.

Jørn Boye Nielsen

Rau, Johannes (1931–)

Minister president of the West German Land (state) of North Rhine-Westphalia (1978–), Rau unsuccessfully sought, as the Social Democratic candidate, the offices of federal chancellor against Helmut Kohl in 1987 and president against Roman Herzog in 1994. Rau served as president of the Bundesrat (upper house of parliament) in 1982–83 and 1994–95. A leading figure in the Social

Democratic Party (SPD), Rau became a member of its national executive committee in 1968. He has also held a seat on the party's Presidium since 1978. He chaired the national party briefly in 1993. Within North Rhine-Westphalia Rau's policies combined a pro-labor social welfare foundation with contemporary demands for ecologically sound economic growth. Under his leadership the SPD maintained an absolute majority in the state parliament from 1980 to 1995. After 1995 Rau worked to preserve a difficult coalition with the Bündnis 90/Die Grünen (Alliance 90/Green Party).

Born January 16, 1931, in Wuppertal-Barmen, Johannes Rau developed a career in business management and by 1954 ran a publishing company. Rau also worked as a free-lance journalist for the *Westdeutsche Rundschau* and other daily papers. Co-editor of the journal, *Politische Verantwortung—Evangelische Stimmen* (*Political Responsibility—Evangelical Voices*) since 1957, Rau has maintained close links with the Evangelical Church throughout his career.

Rau's political life in North Rhine-Westphalia began with the Gesamtdeutsche Volkspartei (All German People's Party, GVP) in 1952. Joining the SPD in 1957, Rau entered North Rhine-Westphalia's state parliament in July 1958. He headed Wuppertal's SPD (1959–68), was elected a member of Wuppertal's City Council (1964–78), and later mayor (1969–70). On the state level Rau chaired the SPD's parliamentary faction (1967–70), served as minister for science and research (1970–78), and beginning in 1977 chaired the state party. In 1990 Rau became North Rhine-Westphalia's minister for federal affairs.

On May 23, 1999, with the expiration of the term of Roman Herzog, Rau was elected president of the Federal Republic. His competitors were Dagmar Schipanski, of the Christian Democratic Union, and Uta Ranke-Heinemann, of the Party of Democratic Socialism. Some German newspapers expressed the hope that Rau, who is fond of the saying "versöhnen statt spalten" (reconcile rather than divide), would be able to narrow the divide between east and west Germans.

BIBLIOGRAPHY

Für eine Kultur der Gerechtigkeit: Positionen des christlich-sozialistischen Dialogs: Johannes Rau zum 60. Wuppertal: Hammer, 1991.

Rau, Johannes. *Lebensbilder.* Gutersloh: Gutesloh Verlagshaus Mohn, 1992.

———. "Nährboden für rechtsautoritäre Kräfte: Die Grünen aus der Sichte der SPD," in Jörg R. Mettke, ed. *Die Grünen.* Reinbek bei Hamburg: Spiegel-Verlag, 1982.

David A. Meier

Rauti, Giuseppe (1926–)

Italian neofascist leader, journalist, and parliamentarian. Giuseppe ("Pino") Rauti has long been an important figure in both extraparliamentary radical right circles and the hard-line Evolan faction within the neofascist electoral party, the Movimento Sociale Italiano (Italian Social Movement, MSI). He has also been implicated in various acts of anticonstitutional subversion and terrorism.

Rauti was born in Cardinale in the province of Cosenza in southern Italy in 1926. In 1943 he enlisted in Guardia Nazionale Repubblicana, (Republican National Guard, GNR). Rauti attained the rank of second lieutenant before being captured by the British on the Po River front in 1944. After escaping to Spanish Morocco he was recaptured and imprisoned at Taranto for several months before being amnestied in 1946. In 1948 he joined the newly founded MSI, was appointed a provincial youth leader, and became a key figure in the radical-right current inspired by philosopher Giulio Cesare ("Julius") Evola's uncompromising so-called "conservative revolutionary" doctrines. In 1954 he founded the Centro Studi Ordine Nuovo (New Order Studies Center) as a discussion group for militants from the MSI's youth organizations, but after the 1956 internal seizure of power by the MSI's moderate faction, he broke with the party along with the bulk of his activist-oriented followers. The newly autonomous Ordine Nuovo (New Order, ON) group thence served as a useful cover for an antidemocratic activism until fall 1969, when increasing legal problems caused Rauti to rejoin the MSI. This precipitated a schism within the ON between Rauti's supporters and the more radical, violence-prone elements led by Clemente Graziani, whose renamed Movimento Politico Ordine Nuovo (New Order Political Movement, MPON) faction increasingly resorted to clandestineness and terrorist violence.

Meanwhile, Rauti exploited the shelter provided by the MSI and the parliamentary immunity he obtained after his 1972 election to the Chamber of Deputies (lower house of parliament) to help intransigent party chairman Giorgio Almirante carry out a two-track strategy. On the one hand, this involved an attempt to attract centrist votes by portraying the party as the last bastion of law and order in the face of social chaos and Communist subversion, and on the other, to seize control of the streets by provoking disorders and violently confronting the extraparliamentary Left. This dual strategy eventually backfired, and after the government belatedly cracked down on the most notorious neofascist paramilitary groups (including the ON) in 1974, Rauti began to promote a subtler, less violent strategy designed to wrest cultural and intellectual "hegemony" from the far left. He supported the formation of an iconoclastic youth counterculture whose aim was to escape from the fascist ideological ghetto by adapting novel concepts from across the entire political spectrum, including the New Left. In the process he helped preside over the mid-1970s creation of a new Italian Right that both paralleled and borrowed elements from the French *nouvelle droite* (New Right). At the same time, he sought to achieve a dominant position within the MSI to shift the party away from its conservative, "bourgeois," pro-Atlantic orientation toward a more radical "third force" position. After his patron Almirante's death, Rauti struggled with Giorgio Fini for leadership of the party but was defeated by his moderate rival in the early 1990s. During the past decade Rauti gradually outgrew his extremist image by holding a succession of bureaucratic positions in the MSI, including deputy secretary, the Council of Europe, the European Parliament, and the recently established Alleanza Nazionale (National Alliance) bloc.

In 1951 he was arrested and tried, along with Evola and other key militants, for his involvement in a series of terrorist actions carried out by the Fasci d'Azione Rivoluzionaria (Revolutionary Action Groups, FAR). After his release from prison, he established close links to an international neo-Nazi network headed by Gaston-Armand Amaudruz, the editor since 1946 of the racist and revisionist periodical *Le Courier du continent,* in Switzerland, the Nouvelle Ordre Européenne (New European Order, NOE). Following the creation in 1961 of the terrorist Organisation de l'Armée Secrète (Secret Army Organization, OAS) in French Algeria, Rauti and his group secretly provided OAS members with logistical support in Italy, in exchange for which ON personnel received paramilitary training from seditious French military experts. As a result of this collaborative arrangement, Rauti also established connections with other right-wing action groups like Jeune Europe (Young Europe, JE) in Belgium, Aginter Presse in Lisbon, and the Kinema tes 4 Augoustou (Fourth of August Movement, K4A) in Greece.

These connections with right-wing militants abroad also led to direct or indirect collusion between Rauti and secret service personnel from Italy, Portugal, Spain, and the colonels' regime in Greece. In the mid-1960s he, along with his neofascist comrade and fellow journalist Guido Giannettini, was enlisted by the Servizio Information Forze Armate (Armed Forces Intelligence Service, SIFAR) to direct the Agenzia A press agency. In that capacity he gave a presentation at a Rome conference on French-inspired counterrevolutionary warfare doctrine (*guerre révolutionnaire*), sent seditious leaflets to selected military officers, and wrote a polemical booklet, "Le mani rosse Sulle Forze armate" (Red Hands on the Armed Forces) supporting hard-line general Giuseppe Aloja against his bitter rival, General Giovanni De Lorenzo, who was himself later investigated for allegedly planning a coup in 1964. Following the 1967 military coup in Greece, Rauti became a key intermediary between Italian neofascist circles and officials in the new junta. Several years later, an insider testified that Rauti personally met with members of the Italian neo-fascist Franco (Giorgio) Freda's terrorist cell in Padua to plan the neofascist bombing campaign that culminated in the December 1969 Piazza Fontana massacre in Milan. This accusation prompted investigating magistrates to formally charge the ON leader with participating in a subversive plot against the state. Although these charges were later dropped owing to a lack of substantive evidence, suspicion remained that Rauti was involved behind the scenes in various phases of the terrorist "strategy of tension" carried out by neofascist ultras in Italy between 1968 and 1974.

BIBLIOGRAPHY

Bale, Jeffrey M. "The 'Black' Terrorist International: Neo-Fascist Paramilitary Networks and the 'Strategy of Tension' in Italy, 1968–1974. (Ph.D. diss., University of California at Berkeley, 1994.

Beltrametti, Eggardo, ed. *La guerra rivoluzionaria: Il terzo guerra mondiale e gia comciato.* Rome: Volpe, 1965.

Ferraresi, Franco, ed. *La destra radicale.* Milan: Feltrinelli, 1984.

Flamini, Gianni. *Il partito del golpe: Le strategie della tensione e del terrore dal primo centrosinistro organico al sequestro Moro,* 4 Vols. in 6 parts. Ferrara: Bovolenta, 1981–85.

Messala, Flavio (pseudonym for Pino Rauti), and Guido Giannettini. *Le mani rosse sulle Forze armate.* Rome: Savelli, 1975.

Raisi, Enzo. *Storia ed idee della Nuova destra italiana.* Rome: Settimo Segillo, 1990.

Rauti, Pino. *Le idee che mossero il mondo.* Rome: Europa, 1976.

Jeffrey M. Bale

SEE ALSO Terrorism, Right Wing

Raznatović, Zeljko (1952–2000)

Commander of Serbian volunteers in Bosnia who has been accused of atrocities connected with ethnic cleansing. Zeljko (Arkan) Raznatović was born in Slovenia in 1952. He commanded the Serbian Volunteer Guards (SDG), the "Tigers," who were particularly noted for murderous activities during the fighting in Croatia and Bosnia-

Herzegovina, and the Serbian campaign of ethnic cleansing in Kosovo in 1999.

By 1975 Raznatović had gained a reputation as one of the most dangerous criminals in Europe. He was wanted in six counties for bank robberies and other crimes. He shot his way to freedom from a courtroom in Sweden, was re-arrested in the Netherlands, and then escaped from jail and made his way back to Yugoslavia. Before the Bosnian war he was a major figure in the Serbian underworld and is alleged to have carried out assassinations abroad for the Yugoslav government in the 1980s.

Raznatović and his paramilitary "Tigers" have been accused of carrying out a campaign of torture, rape, and murder, during the wars in Croatia and Bosnia after the breakup of the Yugoslavian Federation. After the Bosnian war he became rich through the protection racket and violating the economic sanctions against Yugoslavia.

Raznatović was named a suspected war criminal by the US State Department. After the beginning of NATO operations against Yugoslavia in March 1999 the War Crimes Tribunal at the Hague announced that Raznatović had been secretly indicted by Tribunal in 1995. NATO sources claimed that he was in Kosovo giving orders in two towns where Albanians were being rounded up and their property looted and destroyed. Raznatović denied this.

On January 15, 2000, Raznatović, along with a friend and a policeman, was shot and killed in the lobby of Belgrade's Intercontinental Hotel. Speculation about the motive of the killing ran the gamut from political intrigue to the criminal underworld of Belgrade.

BIBLIOGRAPHY

"Butcher of Bosnia is back in the business of ethnic cleansing." *Australian,* March 30, 1999, 13.

Catherine Lutard
Bernard Cook

SEE ALSO Ethnic Cleansing in Croatia and Bosnia

Reitz, Edgar (1932–)

German film director and writer, best known for the sixteen-hour "cinematic event" *Heimat* (Homeland, 1984), which chronicled the daily life of a family in the fictional Rhineland town of Schabbach from 1919 through the early 1980s.

Edgar Reitz was born in Morbach in the Rhineland and grew up during the Third Reich. He was young enough to escape military duty in World War II and came of age during the West German economic miracle of the 1950s. In the 1960s, he became a doyen of the New German Cinema. He signed the 1962 Oberhausen Manifesto with twenty-five other young filmmakers who "vowed to create the new German feature film"; he co-founded, along with Alexander Kluge, the Institute for Film Formation in Ulm (Germany's only film school prior to the establishment of institutions in Munich and Berlin); and he contributing a segment to the momentous film anthology *Deutschland in Herbst* (Germany in the Fall, 1978), a highly critical view of the West German political establishment. He and other proponents of the New German Cinema wanted their works "to bear the unmistakable signature of an 'author' " as they "rejected the ideological and commercial exploitation of the film medium."

Reitz's masterpiece, *Heimat,* engages the history of the twentieth century by focusing on the daily lives of three generations of the Simon family. The outside world—including war, financial fluctuations, and technological developments—gradually impinges on the village. Other narrative developments, such as automobile accidents and illicit births, are the stuff of dramas (or soap operas) and stand apart from the broader historic contours. The vivid film, which contains memorable performances by both professional and nonprofessional actors, in the words of one critic, "is not only the fulfillment of all the hopes of the New German Cinema over the past few decades, but should also go down as a milestone in contemporary film history." Others have stressed its importance as a critique of the popular *Heimatfilm* genre that flourished from the 1930s through the 1950s. His subsequent twenty-six-hour television series from 1992, *Die Zweite Heimat* (The Second Homeland), concentrated more on the existential tribulations of the autobiographical artist hero; it was seen as TV entertainment by many critics.

Reitz's other film credits include *Mahlzeiten* (Meals, 1966), *Die Reise nach Wien* (The Trip to Vienna, 1973), *Stunde Null* (How Zero, 1976), and *Der Schneider von Ulm* (The Taylor from Ulm, 1978).

BIBLIOGRAPHY

Birgel, Franz. "You Can Go Home Again: An Interview with Edgar Reitz." *Film Quarterly* 39, no. 4 (Summer 1986): 210.

Elsaesser, Thomas. *New German Cinema: a History.* New Brunswick, N.J.: Rutgers University Press, 1989.

Kaes, Anton. *From Hitler to Heimat: The Return of History as Film.* Cambridge, Mass.: Harvard University Press, 1989.

Reitz, Edgar, and Peter Steinbach. *Heimat: eine Deutsche Chronik.* Nordlingen: Greno, 1985.

Reitz, Edgar. *Die Zweite Heimat: Chronik einer Jugend in 13 Büchern.* Munich: Goldmann, 1993.

Scheib-Rothbart, Ingrid, and Richard McCormick. "Edgar Reitz: Liberating Humanity and Film," in Klaus Phillips, ed. *New German Filmmakers.* New York: Ungar, 1984.

Jonathan Petropoulos

Religion

In most of continental Europe at the end of the Second World War, organized Judaism had ceased to exist. Physical damage to Christian churches was widespread, and the leadership of the various denominations had lost its moral voice because of the collaborationist, or at best the silent, stand that it had taken during the Nazi era. Nevertheless, during the first twelve years of the postwar period, Western European religious denominations were optimistic, looking to recapture their leading roles in society, discerning a religious revival, and even hoping for increased church attendance. Sociological studies and public opinion polls indicated that the overwhelming majority of the population claimed church membership.

This period was a golden age for the Christian Democratic and other religious parties in Italy, France, West Germany, Belgium, and the Netherlands. Reacting to the Cold War and the challenge from the mass-based French and Italian Communist parties, the churches for the most part supported center-right parties (save in Spain and Portugal, where the Roman Catholic Church endorsed Francisco Franco's and António Salazar's traditionalist dictatorships). In Britain, the coronation of Elizabeth II in June 1953 epitomized the sense of restoration. Church, monarchy, and nation came together in what also was the first experience of television for many in Britain itself and in the English-speaking world. There, church leaders supported the moderate leadership of the Labour and Conservative Parties.

In doctrinal terms, the churches were animated by orthodoxy. Within Roman Catholicism, Pope Pius XII, pope from 1939 to 1958, maintained the doctrinal orthodoxies of his namesakes Pius IX, X, and XI. In 1950, he made official the doctrine of the Assumption (the belief that Mary, Jesus' mother, had bodily ascended into heaven immediately after her death). Church authorities encouraged the laity to participate in the traditional faith activity of making pilgrimages to sites where Mary was thought to have appeared, such as the shrines at Lourdes and La Salette in France, Fatima in Portugal, and Knock in Ireland. The high point of postwar pilgrimage culture was reached in 1958, when the centenary of the Lourdes apparition drew six million visitors. Within the Protestant churches, neoorthodoxy, which rejected nineteenth-century liberal theology in favor of an altogether transcendent God, was ascendant under the influence of theologians Karl Barth (1886–1968), Reinhold Niebuhr (1892–1971), and Paul Tillich (1886–1965). American evangelist Billy Graham's "crusade" in London in 1954 was the first of several efforts at mass evangelization that later included the Continent. Graham preached a traditional theology of personal conversion and individualistic, internal religion. The popularity of his preaching also reflected the growing cultural influence of the United States.

Europe's Jewish communities saw the most radical change during this period. The Holocaust had destroyed the centers of Continental Judaism in central and Eastern Europe. The intellectual centers of Jewish life now were to be found in the English-speaking world, in the United States above all. The Holocaust also combined with the emergence of Israel and the Cold War to limit Jewish political and social options; assimilationism was discredited and socialism was problematical, leaving Zionism the most respectable of the Jewish ideologies.

If the religious face of Western Europe appeared to have been restored, that of Eastern Europe appeared to have changed out of all recognition. The Slavic world without exception was ruled by atheistic governments that viewed the churches as tools of the prewar regimes. Most Communist governments were content to marginalize the churches by restricting religious education, monitoring the activities of clergy, and limiting denominational autonomy. The power of the Polish Roman Catholic Church was such that the government had to come to an accommodation with it. By contrast, the Hungarian government arrested the Roman Catholic cardinal, József Mindszenty (1892–1975), whose imprisonment and later self-immurement in the U.S. Embassy in Budapest turned him into a Cold War icon. Antireligious policies were the most successful in the Czech lands of Czechoslovakia with their strong tradition of free thought and association of Roman Catholicism with Habsburg rule, and in East Germany, where a third of the population declared itself to have no religion.

Church attendance began to decline in Western Europe after the war, and especially after the mid-1950s, when most economies had recovered from postwar austerity. This decline was part of the larger change in religious habits that characterized the industrial era, but it also owed much to postwar intellectual developments. The certitudes of traditional religion offered less workable answers to the human predicament than did the philosophy of existentialism. The latter view, by calling for people to construct their own authenticity, seemed better to fit the mood of postwar reconstruction and the reality of improving economic conditions.

The score of years after the death of Pope Pius XII (1958) saw the dramatic transformation of European religious behavior. This transformation occurred against the backgrounds of the decolonization movements of the 1950s and 1960s that eliminated formal empires in Africa and Asia, and the height of the Cold War during the Cuban Missile Crisis (1962) and the Vietnam War. The decline of Western prosperity owing to energy crises and stagflation in the 1970s brought this period to a close.

Elected to be a caretaker, Pope John XXIII, pope from 1958 to 1963, surprised both the Roman Catholic Church and the world by calling the Second Vatican Council (1962–65); his successor, Paul VI, pope from 1963 to 1978, implemented the council's reforms. Vernacular liturgies replaced the Latin Mass, conferences of bishops gained more authority, and the role of the laity was enhanced.

Protestantism and Roman Catholicism drew together in two ways. First, the ecumenical movement made its mark. The immediate postwar period saw the creation of the Church of South India in 1947 and the foundation of the World Council of Churches in 1948. After John XXIII became pope, the Roman Catholic Church slowly reduced its isolation from other Christians. John signaled the change by referring to Protestants in 1958 as "separated brethren," by creating the Secretariat for Unity in 1960, by meeting the Anglican archbishop of Canterbury, Geoffrey Fisher, also in 1960, and by sending observers to the World Council of Churches in 1961, the same year that Eastern Orthodox churches joined the organization. Protestant churches responded to these openings by moderating their traditional anti-Catholicism.

The second point of convergence was the rise of liberation theology. Originating among Roman Catholic thinkers in Latin America, this movement rejected the Christian Democrats' gradual reformism within the capitalist context and constructed a theology of Christianized Marxism, dependency analysis, and idealization of the poor. Liberation theology grew influential in the established Protestant churches of Europe and served to draw Protestantism and Roman Catholicism together. Although not endorsing liberation theology, Pope John XXIII captured the spirit of the age with his encyclical letters *Mater et Magistra* (1961) and *Pacem in Terris* (1963), which called for social justice and world peace.

The liturgical and theological ferment of the period failed to stem the continuing decline in church attendance among Christians; European Jewish communities continued to dwindle because of continuing assimilation. The youth culture of the 1960s and 1970s eroded religious orthodoxy by challenging traditional moral teachings and by promoting the mainstream popularity of Eastern mysticism. Mass popular culture offered an alternative value system to that of traditional Christianity. The erosion of traditional Christian restraints on behavior is exemplified by the liberalization, during the 1960s, of attitudes and laws relating to artificial methods of birth control, abortion, divorce, and consensual sexual activity between adults. Mores also changed with respect to gender roles. The popularization of feminism during the period challenged the notions that the husband was the head of a proper Christian family and that women should be excluded from priestly roles in the churches.

The European churches were faced with increasingly severe pastoral problems related to these changing social mores. Although Pope Paul VI continued to support the ecclesiastical reforms within Roman Catholicism, he spoke against the personal liberation of the age in his encyclical *Humanae Vitae* (1968), which condemned the use of artificial contraception as sinful and maintained the church's bans on abortion and divorce. The Protestant and Anglican churches were somewhat more liberal on these matters, coming to tolerate under certain circumstances artificial contraception and divorce, and even coming to consider the possibility of abortion and remarriage after divorce. During the 1960s, the number of men entering the priesthood dropped, especially in Roman Catholicism. As women began to feel a calling to the Christian priesthood, the Protestant churches and some branches of Anglicanism began admitting them, but not Roman Catholicism.

The same period saw several contrary developments that later were to become important. In reaction against the liberating religious and social views of the day, small movements sprang up within Roman Catholicism, Protestantism, and Judaism that emphasized emotionalism, biblical literalism, rejection of contemporary society, and often extremely conservative politics. Some of these movements (Jewish Hasidism, Protestant Fundamentalism) had roots in earlier centuries, while others (the Roman Catholic Opus Dei movement and the Society of St. Pius X) were twentieth-century creations. Simultaneously there was the quiet growth of non-Western immigrants (Algerians to France, Turks to Germany, Indians and Pakistanis to Great Britain) who brought their religions with them, especially Islam, Hinduism, and Sikhism.

The election of Pope John Paul II (1978–) marked the closing of one era and the opening of another in the history of European religion. The 1980s in the Western world saw a decisive turn against the political, economic, and social spirit of the postwar world. In politics, both socialist and Christian Democratic ideologies were rejected in favor of neoconservatism. In economics, Keynsian demand-side economics gave way to Chicago school supply-side monetarism. In social policy, the commitment to the welfare state began to weaken. Moreover, postwar economic and political certainties dissolved with the rise to industrial power of Japan, Taiwan, and other Asian states in the 1980s and with the collapse of communism between 1988 and 1991.

The new pope at first appeared to continue the spirit of his immediate predecessors. He praised the social goals of liberation theology, traveled more widely than any pope before him, and professed his commitment to ecumenism by worshipping with the archbishop of Canterbury in 1982. He proved to be a doctrinal traditionalist, rejecting married clergy and women priests; narrowing the limits of allowable theological speculation; denouncing abortion, artificial contraception, and homosexual love; and promoting devotion to Mary. He declared himself on the side of the poor and castigated the West for its alleged materialism; but in 1986 he declared it "criminal" for Christians to use popular piety to promote "a purely earthly plan of liberation." His traditionalism erected major barriers against deeper ecumenical relations and alienated liberal Catholics, but satisfied the desires of many for certitude and security in an era of rapid change (desires also satisfied by the reported sightings of the Virgin Mary at Medugorje in Bosnia that began in 1981). A similar conservative reaction in Protestantism took the forms of biblical literalism, Evangelicalism, revivalism, and the charismatic movement. Yet at the same time, many practicing Roman Catholics ignored papal teachings on proper sex, women increasingly occupied leadership roles in the churches, and Protestantism in practice if not in theory abandoned its opposition to divorce.

In Eastern Europe, organized Christianity played an important role in the fall of communism. Polish Roman Catholicism had continued its historical function as definer and protector of the national identity. Roman Catholicism in Hungary, Czechoslovakia, and East Germany, and Protestantism in East Germany and Romania, provided environments from which to resist oppressive governments. Roman Catholic devotion played a major role in the Polish Solidarity labor movement; the especially vigorous repression of Roman Catholicism in Czechoslovakia fostered the development of underground lay leadership and the ordination of married men. As economic conditions worsened in the 1980s, religious-based resistance became sharper.

By the mid-1990s, however, the situation began to return to older patterns. In Poland, with communism overthrown, the Roman Catholic Church assumed the role of a state church by persuading the government to impose mandatory sectarian religious training in the schools. In the Czech Republic, married priests were summarily laicized and newly appointed bishops hastened to reassert hierarchical authority. In Slovakia, nationalists exhumed as a hero the priest Josef Tiso, who had headed a pro-Nazi puppet state during the Second World War. A similar development occurred in Hungary, where the corpse of prewar dictator Miklós Horthy was given a state funeral, and where politicians found that attacks against "cosmopolitanism" (i.e., Jewishness) appealed to the public. Attendance at religious services declined during the 1990s, suggesting that religion had been a means to the end of attaining the Western good life, rather than an end in itself.

The most profound shift in European religion was the growth of non-Western religions, and especially their emergence into the public consciousness. By the 1980s, immigrant communities had become prosperous and confident enough to build their own houses of worship. In some places, contributions from the Middle East aided the construction of mosques. The children of postwar immigrants began to become visible in the professions. This development was most marked in Great Britain, which was well on the way to becoming a multiracial, multicultural society, having in 1985 twice as many Muslims as Methodists. The host societies made some accommodation to these communities; in Britain, for instance, Sikh police and soldiers were permitted to wear turbans in place of helmets. In France, on the other hand, the state's insistence on banning religious symbols from the schools led to conflict with fundamentalist Muslim parents' insistence that their daughters wear veils. Throughout Europe religious and cultural minorities became targets for skinheads and others cast adrift by the massive changes of the 1980s.

As Europe approached the end of the twentieth century and the second Christian millennium, the religious landscape had changed. Governments paid lip service to the importance of traditional churches and hierarchies, and even maintained religious establishments in some countries. The number of regular Sunday worshippers, however, was in decline, and many of the regular attenders picked and chose for themselves which beliefs to accept and which to ignore. The non-Western religions, especially Islam, grew, but the growth was due primarily to the growth of immigrant communities rather than to conversions.

BIBLIOGRAPHY

Chadwick, Owen. "Great Britain and Europe," in *The Oxford Illustrated History of Christianity.* Ed. by John McManners. Oxford: Oxford University Press, 1990.

Davie, Grace. *Religion in Britain Since 1945: Believing Without Belonging.* Oxford: Blackwell, 1994.

Edwards, David L. *Religion and Change.* London: Hodder and Stoughton, 1969.

Lannon, Frances. *Privilege, Persecution, and Prophecy: The Catholic Church in Spain, 1875–1975.* Oxford: Oxford University Press, 1987.

Monticone, Ronald C. *The Catholic Church in Communist Poland, 1945–1985: Forty Years of Church-State Relations.* Boulder, Colo.: East European Monographs, 1986.

Vidler, Alec R. *The Church in an Age of Revolution: 1789 to the Present Day,* Vol. 5 of *The Pelican History of the Church,* 3d ed. Ed. by Owen Chadwick. New York: Penguin, 1974.

Wedel, Janine, ed. *The Unplanned Society: Poland During and After Communism.* New York: Columbia University Press, 1992.

Denis G. Paz

Renner, Karl (1870–1950)

Austrian chancellor and federal president, leader of the Social Democratic Party. Born in 1870 in Southern Moravia (today part of the Czech Republic), Karl Renner died shortly after his eightieth birthday during the last hours of 1950 in Vienna.

Renner played an important, even decisive role during different periods of Austrian history. As a member of the lower house of Reichsrat (parliament) between 1907 and 1918, Renner represented the more pragmatic wing of the Social Democratic Workers Party. In 1918 he became chancellor of the provisional government established on November 12, 1918 after the defeat of the Austro-Hungarian Empire in the First World War, and he led the Austrian delegation to the Peace Conference of St. Germain in 1919. Between 1920 and 1933 Renner was one of the prominent figures of the Social Democratic Party in opposition. When the Nationalrat (parliament) was dissolved on March 4, 1933, by the authoritarian conservative government of Engelbert Dollfuss, Renner was president (speaker) of the house but could not prevent the authoritarian takeover.

Karl Renner, president of Austria. *Illustration courtesy of the Austrian Press and Information Service.*

During the years of the authoritarian regime (1934–38) Renner joined neither the socialist underground nor the exiled, nor did he do anything to legitimate the dictatorship imposed by Dollfuss and, after his assassination on June 25, 1934, continued by Kurt von Schuschnigg. In 1938 Renner was briefly utilized by Nazi propaganda to give Germany's occupation of Austria (*Anschluss*) a pseudodemocratic pretext. His support for the Anschluss reflected Renner's pan-German feelings, which were typical of the Austrian Social Democrats of his time. During World War II Renner lived as a pensioner, again avoiding any involvement in the resistance.

Immediately after the liberation of Austria in 1945, Renner became active again. He formed a coalition cabinet of a Provisional Government and was chancellor once more. In December 1945 the newly elected Nationalrat unanimously chose Renner to be federal president.

The son of poor farmers, Renner joined the labor movement and graduated from the law school of Vienna University. He published extensively during all periods of his life: Academic studies of the Habsburg monarchy's ethnic conflicts and of the social meaning of property laws, analyses of the Marxist theory of state and government, and sociological reflections on human development. These underline Renner's great abilities to combine the role of scholar with that of politician.

Throughout his intellectual life, Renner was considered the most important figure of his party's right wing. However, even the right wing of the Austrian Social Democrats framed its positions within the context of Marxism. In that respect, Renner, together with Otto Bauer and Max Adler, represented the theoretical school of "Austromarxism." Renner wanted to enrich Marxism with modern sociology. He was the Austrian equivalent of the German proponent of an evolutionary, reformist Socialism, Eduard Bernstein, but disguised as a Marxist. Renner was the most important representative of "revisionism, the transformation of Marxism from a revolutionary ideology to a reformist political movement," in Austria while claiming not to be a "revisionist" at all.

He represented especially the moderate Left's dominant interest in governing. When the Austrian imperial government at the end of World War I wanted to save the empire by broadening its basis, Renner was the first candidate to be discussed as a possible Socialist minister in the emperor's cabinet. This speculation did not materialize because the Social Democratic Workers Party strongly opposed such a coalition. But one year later, when the empire collapsed and the German-speaking remnant became a republic, Renner was the man of the hour.

This interest in governing was the motor behind his ideological flexibility. Renner was pan-German when this perspective seemed to carry the day: in 1918, when the newly constituted republic declared itself part of the German Republic; and in 1938, when he declared his support of the already dictated *Anschluss,* although this was not his concept of a democratic integration of Austria into a democratic Germany. But when pan-German attitudes were outdated, Renner was the first to change. Renner with the backing of the Soviet occupation forces became chancellor of a provisional government set up on April 25, 1945. In 1945 he declared Austria's independence from Germany and developed a theory of an Austrian national identity separated from Germany. He was also one of the first Austrians to picture his country after 1945 as a second Switzerland, a small, neutral democracy among the powers.

His pragmatism made him the whipping boy of communists. Lenin and Stalin used him as an example of the "opportunistic" attitude of the social democrats. Renner figured prominently among the "traitors" the Leninists wanted to expose. However, it is one of the jokes of history that Josef Stalin decided to put his weight behind a Renner-led government in Austria immediately after liberation. The usual explanation for this peculiarity is that Renner wrote an extremely flattering letter to Stalin in April 1945 and Stalin thought Renner to be already senile. But once more Renner's influence was important in the strategic decision of Austrian Social Democracy to prefer the coalition with the conservative People's Party to a possible alliance with the Communists. Austria's Western orientation after the war was not the least of Renner's accomplishments.

BIBLIOGRAPHY

Hannak, Jacques. *Karl Renner und seine Zeit: Versuch einer Biographie.* Vienna: Europa, 1965.

Pelinka, Anton. *Karl Renner zur Einfüehrung.* Hamburg: Junius, 1989.

Rauscher, Walter. *Karl Renner: Ein Österreichischer Mythos.* Vienna: Überreuther, 1995.

Anton Pelinka

Reuter, Ernst (1889–1953)

Social Democratic mayor of West Berlin from 1948 until his death in 1953. Through his determined leadership Ernst Reuter symbolized West Berlin's resistance to Soviet and East German efforts to curtail the city's autonomy.

Reuter was born in Apenrade, Schleswig-Holstein, on July 29, 1889. After his university studies he entered politics by becoming an instructor in the adult education program of the Social Democratic Party (SPD). Reuter's Weimar-era activity (1919–1933) included a term as Reichstag (lower house of parliament) deputy. Arrested by the Nazis, he owed his release from a concentration camp to the intervention of British Quakers. He lived in Turkey from 1935 to 1946, teaching at Ankara University and serving as an adviser to the Ministry of Economics.

Reuter moved to Berlin early in 1947 and soon emerged as an outspoken anti-Communist and leader of the city's SPD. Overwhelmingly elected mayor in December 1948, Reuter was the most visible symbol of West Berlin's struggle for survival. During the Berlin Blockade (1948–49), wearing his trademark beret, he frequently rallied hundreds of thousands of Berliners. Reuter supported the creation of the Federal Republic of Germany and its economic and military integration into Western Europe. His views on these issues coincided closely with those of West Germany's first chancellor, Konrad Adenauer, but differed from those of Kurt Schumacher, leader of the SPD. A strong pro-Western stance, Schumacher feared, could hinder the chances of German reunification.

To remove doubt about the future status of West Berlin, Reuter insisted on its full incorporation into the Federal Republic. Adenauer found this objective politically unacceptable since it would further emphasize the division of Germany; moreover, it could possibly undermine the Four-Power agreements supporting the Western presence in the city after the war. A compromise solution defined West Berlin as a Land (state) of the Federal Republic "in principle," though legally it remained occupied territory.

Reuter's administration had to deal with a difficult economic situation. Employment rose significantly after 1949 because of the stimulus of U.S.-sponsored Marshall Plan aid and matching West German funds. However, the influx of East German refugees, both before and after the abortive anti-Communist East Berlin uprising of June 1953, proved a continuing burden on the city's resources. Reuter's hope that Stalin's death in March 1953 would make the Soviet Union more accommodating with regard to German reunification proved unfounded. Nor did Reuter achieve his ambition to become foreign minister in a coalition government in Bonn. Reuter died suddenly of a heart attack on September 29, 1953, at the age of sixty-four.

BIBLIOGRAPHY

Brandt, Willy, and Richard Lowenthal. *Ernst Reuter: ein Leben für die Freiheit. Eine politische Biographie.* Munich: Kindler Verlag, 1957.

Schwenger, Hannes. *Ernst Reuter: ein Zivilist im Kalten Krieg.* Munich: Piper, 1987.

Sheldon Spear

SEE ALSO Berlin; Brandt, Willy; Schumacher, Kurt

Reynolds, Albert (1932–)

Irish prime minister and leader of Fianna Fáil (1992–94). Before embarking on a political career Albert Reynolds was a dance hall owner in the west of Ireland and a successful businessman in the pet foods industry. He was first elected to parliament in 1977 for Longford-Westmeath. He held the posts of minister for posts and telegraphs and minister for transport from 1979 to 1981, minister for industry and commerce in 1982, minister for industry and commerce from 1987 to 1988, and minister for finance from 1988 to 1991. During his term at finance he maintained the pattern of improving economic conditions established under his predecessor, Ray McSharry. The country continued to break out of a low-growth cycle and borrowing by the government declined. Reynolds took over from Charles Haughey as prime minister and leader of Fianna Fáil in 1992 after a period of prolonged political, financial, and economic scandals in which Haughey was implicated. In 1993 tensions with his coalition partners, the Progressive Democrats, over an investigation into corruption in the Irish beef industry led to the collapse of his first coalition government. After the ensuing general election Reynolds remained prime minister in a Fianna Fáil–Labour coalition. Reynolds short-lived (1993–94) government will be remembered for its contribution to the peace process in Northern Ireland with the December 1993 Downing St. Declaration and the 1994 declaration of a ceasefire by the Irish Republican Army, which had been waging a campaign of terror against the British. Scandals over the appointment of the attorney general and malpractice in the Department of Justice led to the fall of his second coalition in December 1994. He resigned to be replaced by John Bruton, who led a Fine Gael/Democratic Left/Labour coalition. Reynolds was replaced as leader of Fianna Fáil by Bertie Ahern.

BIBLIOGRAPHY

Ryan, Tim. *Albert Reynolds: The Longford Leader.* Dublin: Blackwater Press, 1994.

Michael J. Kennedy

SEE ALSO Bruton, John; Haughey, Charles

Ricoeur, Paul (1913–)

French philosopher. Born in the southern French town of Valence in 1913, Paul Ricoeur studied theology under Gabriel Marcel in Paris, and joined the Esprit group around Catholic thinker Emmanuel Mounier in 1932. After studying at the universities of Rennes and Paris, Ricoeur received an *agrégation de philosophie* in 1935. His interest in philosophy increased after discovering Edmund Husserl's phenomenology as a prisoner in Germany during World War II, and he received a doctorate in 1950. A professor at the University of Strasbourg until 1956 and at the Sorbonne in Paris until 1966, he elected to teach at the newly formed University of Paris X (Nanterre). Ricoeur was forced to resign from that post in 1970 for taking strong public political positions against both conservatives and revolutionaries whose differences had led to the student demonstrations and violence in May 1968. In recent years he has divided his time between the University of Paris and the Divinity School of the University of Chicago.

Typically at odds with the main currents of French intellectual life, Ricoeur has striven to integrate modern rationality and hermeneutics with Christian morality and the belief in a higher spiritual order. Despite his growing interest in linguistics since the 1960s, Ricoeur remains deeply committed to Husserlian phenomenology, and has adhered to this philosophical method despite its eclipse by the ascendant structuralism of the 1960s and 1970s. He is widely regarded as the world's foremost living phenomenologist.

BIBLIOGRAPHY

Kurzweil, Edith. *The Age of Structuralism.* New York: Columbia University Press, 1980.

Ricoeur, Paul. *Freud and Philosophy.* New Haven, Conn.: Yale University Press, 1978.

———. *Time and Narrative,* Vol. 1. Chicago: University of Chicago Press, 1984.

———. *Fallible Man.* Chicago: Regnery, 1965.

Wood, David, ed. *On Paul Ricoeur: Narrative and Interpretation.* London: Routledge, 1991.

Christopher E. Forth

Rizhkov, Nikolay Ivanovich (1929–)

Chairman of the Council of Ministers (Prime Minister) of the Soviet Union (1985–1991). Nikolay Rizhkov was born in 1929 in the Urals. He started working in 1950 at the Ural Heavy Machine Producing Plant (Ordzhonikidze Uralmash) and joined the Communist Party in 1956. He graduated from the S.M. Kirov Urals Politechnical Institute in 1959 and became the chief engineer of Ordzhonikidze Uralmash in 1965. In 1970, Rizhkov became director of the plant and later advanced to the position of general director of the Uralmash Enterprise.

In 1975 he was appointed first deputy minister in the Heavy and Transport Machine Building Ministry, and in 1979 became the first deputy of the State Planning Body (Gosplan) of the USSR. Because of his success in the economic sector and his well-liked personality, he was elected a member of the Central Committee of the Communist Party in 1981. In the November 1982 plenary session of the Central Committee of the Communist Party, he was elected a Secretary of the Central Committee and at the same time was nominated the head of the Economic Department of the Central Committee, a post he held until 1985.

In April 1985 at the plenary session of the Central Committee following General Secretary Konstantin Chernenko's death, the Gorbachev era started and Rizhkov was elected as a member of Politiburo. From September 1985 till November 1991 Rizhkov was the chairman of the Council of Ministers of the USSR and was included to the Presidential Council.

When he was dismissed by Gorbachev as chairman of the Council of Ministers on January 14, 1991, and replaced by Valentin Pavlov, Rizhkov made a speech at the session of the Supreme Soviet of the USSR saying that the government led by him had managed to do the best it could and would be remembered as one of the best in Soviet history. After the speech he was nicknamed "a crying bolshevik."

Rizhkov ran for president of the Russian Soviet Socialist Republic in the summer of 1991 but was not elected. In 1993 he was elected a deputy of the State Duma that was set up by a special decree of President Boris Yeltsin as the legislative body and the Lower Chamber of the Federal Assembly of Russian Federation (Parliament).

BIBLIOGRAPHY

Ryzhkov, Nikolai Ivanovich. *IA iz partii po imeni "Rossiia."* Moscow: Informatsionno-analiticheskoe agentstvo "Obozrevatel," 1995.

———. *Perestroika: istoriia predatel'stv.* Moscow: Novosti, 1992.

Suny, Ronald Grigor. *The Soviet Experiment: Russia, the USSR, and the Successor States.* New York: Oxford University Press, 1998.

Oleg N. Kozhin

Robertson, George (1946–)

British minister of defense in the cabinet of Labour prime minister Tony Blair, and later secretary general of the North Atlantic Treaty Organization (NATO). George Robertson, the son of a policeman, was born on April 12, 1946, in the house-police station in Port Ellenon on the island of Islay, Scotland. He was educated at Dunoon grammar school, which counts a number of political figures among its alumni, including John Smith, former leader of the Labour Party, and the former Tory Lord Chancellor, Lord Mackay. At the age of fifteen Robertson briefly joined the Scottish National Party. Ironically, Robertson's entry into political activity was spurred by his opposition to the stationing of U.S. nuclear submarines at Holy Loch. He studied at Dundee University, where he contributed a political column for the student newspaper. After graduating in economics he became a trade union organizer for a distillery workers' union.

He was elected to parliament from the Labour Party in 1978. Robertson became shadow Scottish Secretary in

1993 and led the Labour campaign for devolution. With Labour's victory in 1997, however, the post of Scottish Secretary went to Donald Dewar, and Robertson was appointed defense secretary. Robertson gained recognition during the Kosovo conflict (1999) as one of the most forceful supporters of the NATO campaign against Serbia.

On August 4, 1999, Robertson was selected by the NATO allies to succeed Javier Solana, as secretary-general of the alliance. After his appointment, Robertson, who, despite his support for the transatlantic link, is committed to an active European defense, said that "one of the clear lessons of the Kosovo conflict is the need for Europe to enhance its military capabilities." He decried the fact that despite a military spending level equivalent to 66 percent of the United States, the military capabilities of the European allies were only 20 percent those of the United States. In his mind it was a question of how the European defense budgets were spent. He contends that European forces must be modernized so that they can meet "the threats of tomorrow rather than the enemies of the past."

BIBLIOGRAPHY

Bruce, Ian, "New NATO chief must persuade governments to commit themselves in shaping a resourceful alliance," *The Herald* (Glasgow), August 5, 1999.

Dahlburg, John-Thor, and Marjorie Miller, "NATO Selects No-Nonsense Leader," *Los Angeles Times,* August 5, 1999.

Nicoll, Alexander. "Robertson appointed head of NATO," *The Financial Times* (London), August 5, 1999.

Whitney, Craig. "NATO appoints British Defense Chief to its top civilian post," *New York Times,* August 5, 1999.

Bernard Cook

Robinson, Mary (1944–)

Elected president of Ireland in 1990. Mary Robinson was born in Ballina, County Mayo. She was educated at Trinity College, Dublin, and at Harvard University. She is a barrister, and was professor of constitutional and criminal law and of European Community law at Trinity College. She has published in many legal journals on family and constitutional legal issues. An outspoken defender of human rights and civil liberties, Robinson came to prominence in the 1970s when seeking the liberalization of Irish contraception laws. She has since continued to be associated with liberal causes. She served on many international and national legal and advisory committees, such as the Irish Parliamentary Joint Committee on Marital Breakdown (1983–85), the New Ireland Forum (1983–84), the Irish Committee for European Law (1988), and the International Committee of Jurists (1987–90).

Robinson was the youngest person ever to sit in the Irish Senate, where she served from 1969 to 1985. She was a Labour Party member in the 1970s and stood twice, unsuccessfully, as a Labour general election candidate. She left Labour in 1985 after disagreeing with the party's support of that years' Anglo-Irish Agreement, feeling that it did not take into account the sensitivities of the Northern Irish Unionists, who wished to preserve the tie between the province and the U.K. and distrusted any involvement of the Republic of Ireland in the affairs of Northern Ireland.

As a surprise Labour-backed candidate, Robinson defeated Brian Lenihan of Fianna Fáil and Austin Curry of Fine Gael to win the 1990 presidential election. This heralded the existence of a large liberal constituency after the conservative constitutional referenda of the 1980s. Her election also broke the mold of a Fianna Fáil–dominated presidency. She entered office wishing to use its ceremonial nature to the benefit of the public. Robinson also used her constitutional powers forcefully. Her presidency provided a sharp contrast to that of Patrick Hillery, president from 1976 to 1990, who preferred to stay in the background. Robinson had wide nonpolitical popular support. As Ireland's first woman president, and with a background outside the two civil war–based political parties, she has been viewed as representing the new modern Ireland of the late twentieth century.

BIBLIOGRAPHY

O'Sullivan, Michael. *Mary Robinson: Portrait of an Irish liberal.* Dublin: Blackwater Press, 1993.

Michael J. Kennedy

Rocard, Michel (1930–)

French prime minister (1988–91). Michel Rocard led the French Socialist movement to reformulate its ideas around themes of *autogestion* (self-empowerment) and decentralization. Both notions differed sharply with the statist approach to socialism that dominated traditional French socialist ideology during most of the twentieth century.

In 1930 Rocard was born into a middle-class Parisian family to a Protestant mother and a lapsed Catholic father. During World War II Rocard's father joined the non-Communist Resistance movement and later participated in the physics research team that developed the

French atomic bomb. From his formative years Rocard drew important lessons on the value of pluralism and a wariness about simplistic assumptions about the nature of technology and economic progress. Distrustful of the Stalinist French Communist Party, Rocard as a student joined the Socialist Party (officially the French Section of the Workers' International, SFIO) youth movement. By 1950 he became its national secretary. In 1955 Rocard entered the prestigious École Nationale d'Administration in Paris to prepare for a career in the civil service. The Algerian War was to prove a great watershed for Rocard, forcing him to interrupt his studies for military service. He subsequently joined the antiwar movement and began a thoughtful reexamination of Socialist Party doctrines. By 1959 his break with the socialism of Guy Mollet, secretary general of the SFIO from 1946 to 1969, was complete. Rocard helped organize the Parti Socialist Unifié (United Socialist Party, PSU) that sought to redefine the essence of French socialism in antistatist terms.

As an inspector of finance in the Finance Ministry, Rocard promoted decentralization and a greater degrees of autonomy in official decision making. The great upheaval of May 1968 thrust Rocard and the PSU into the center of the political crisis that seemed to repudiate long-standing statist approaches to governance common to both right-wing and left-wing traditional political movements in France. Rocard stood as the PSU candidate for president in 1969 following the surprise resignation of General Charles de Gaulle. Rocard garnered less than 4 percent of the national vote, he won a seat in the National Assembly (lower house of parliament) during the following year by ousting longtime Gaullist loyalist Maurice Couve de Murville from his district in the Yvelines, a Paris suburb. The PSU proved to be too weak a vehicle to support Rocard, however, and in 1973 he lost his reelection bid. A year later he threw his lot with François Mitterrand, the first secretary of the PS from 1971 to 1981, when he became president of France, in hopes of reforming the Socialist Party.

While less than half of the PSU followed Rocard into the Socialist Party (PS), as the reformed SFIO was renamed in 1969, Rocard and the new recruits played a pivotal role in securing the presidential nomination for Mitterrand in the 1981 election. Despite his reliance on Rocard's considerable influence within the Socialist Party, Mitterrand became wary of Rocard's own political ambitions. Thus during Mitterrand's first term Rocard received only the minor Ministry of Planning. Compounding the slight, the early Mitterrand policies were cut full measure from the old statist formulas of traditional socialism. However, as the French economic crisis deepened, Mitterrand finally abandoned his initial policies and in 1983 adopted a program closer to Rocard's liberalizing strategy.

In 1988 Rocard reaped the rewards of a career built on debunking traditional Socialist ideas. His rising popularity finally compelled Mitterrand to appoint him prime minister. Despite frequent clashes with Mitterrand, Rocard served as prime minister for three years. Mitterrand took advantage of his own popularity at the end of the Gulf War (1990–91) to replace Rocard with Édith Cresson. Freed of the responsibilities of government, Rocard threw himself into party politics and quickly worked to establish himself as the dominant contender for the Socialist presidential nomination in 1994. However, following the parliamentary electoral debacle of the PS in 1993, Rocard decided not to challenge the apparently invincible Jacques Chirac, the Gaullist mayor of Paris. The Socialist Lionel Jospin was left to challenge Chirac. Though Jospin lost the presidential vote, his effort enabled him to lead the PS in the 1997 parliamentary election, which enabled him to become premier. Rocard was elected to the EU's European Parliament in 1994.

BIBLIOGRAPHY

Andreani, Jean-Louis. *Le Mystère Rocard.* Paris: Laffont, 1993.

Rocard, Michel. *Le Coeur à l'ouvrage.* Paris: Odile-Jacob, 1987.

Peggy Anne Phillips

SEE ALSO Cresson, Édith; Mitterrand, François

Rohwedder, Detlev Carsten (1932–91)

President of the Treuhand, the German privatization agency. Detlev Carsten Rohwedder was born on October 16, 1932, in Gottia, Germany. Together with his wife, Hergard, who later became a judge, he studied law in Hamburg and Mainz. In 1959 he went to the University of California at Berkeley as a Fulbright and Ford Foundation scholar. Shortly after Rohwedder returned to Germany he joined a health resort firm and became a partner. In 1970 he went to Bonn and worked as one of the youngest undersecretaries for the minister of trade and commerce, Karl Schiller. Over the years Rohwedder advised Helmut Schmidt, the Social Democratic chancellor from 1974 to 1982, Hans Friedrichs, and Graf Lambsdorff, minister of economics and head of the Free Democratic Party. After ten years in Bonn Rohwedder joined the private sector again and, as head of the Duisburger steel company Hoesch, became immersed in a major industrial conflict. Thanks to Rohwedder's successful crisis management, the Duisburg Consensus between the unions and the employer enabled Hoesch to survive this critical period. Rohwedder stayed with the company for the next twelve years, becoming one of Germany's most successful managers. In 1990 Rohwedder, despite being a member of the Social Democratic Party, was asked by Christian Democratic Chancellor Helmut Kohl to head the board of directors of the newly created German privatization agency, the Treuhand. The Treuhand was founded in April 1990, shortly before German reunification. By the time Rohwedder took over in August 1990, it was structured like a private joint stock company with the aim of selling East Germany's state-owned companies to the private sector.

The idealistic Rohwedder and his 3,800 mostly East German subordinates faced immense problems. The privatization of an entire economy was without precedent. Some 95 percent of East German property had to be sold, many lawsuits by former owners were still pending, and Rohwedder had to combat cases of fraud committed against the Treuhand by organizations controlled by former Communists (soon labeled *Seilschaften,* or Roped parties). By 1992 the cases of fraud amounted to two billion German marks. The main problem was that many East German factories were run down and their products were unable to compete on the international market. Rohwedder reacted with closures that produced a sharp rise in unemployment. As a consequence he faced growing criticism for his emphasis on speeding up privatization without taking into account the resulting social problems. It was this criticism of the Treuhand and its head that the left-wing terrorist group Rote Armee Fraktion (Red Army Faction, RAF) wanted to use for its own ends. Shortly before midnight on April 1, 1991, while working at his home in Düsseldorf, Rohwedder was shot by members of the RAF. The murderers were never caught. After a state funeral attended by President Richard von Weizsäcker and Chancellor Kohl, Rohwedder's deputy, Birgit Breuel, successfully took over the management of the Treuhand on April 15, 1991.

BIBLIOGRAPHY

Schipke, Alfred, and Alan M. Taylor, eds. *The Economics of Transformation: Theory and Practice in the New Market Economics.* Berlin: Springer-Verlag, 1994.

Karina Urbach

Roma

The people, who in addition to the Jews, represent Europe's largest traditional nonterritorial minority. Known by a variety of names (Gypsies, Gitanes, Zigeuner, Gitanos, Manouches, Sinti, etc.) in the different countries of Europe, the identity of the Rom, whether romanticized or more frequently excoriated, has challenged Europeans for at least five hundred years.

Though present historically in nearly every European country, and forming a near majority in some regions, the Rom have never had a firm politico-territorial identity. Though this can be attributed in some measure to the migratory lifestyle practiced by some groups of Rom, by far the major factor has been the unwillingness of others to accept the Rom as a real "people" and the harshness, persecution, and even enslavement that has characterized the relationship between the Rom and other European peoples. Since their arrival in Europe the Rom have been treated with nearly unrelenting hostility and suspicion, often culminating in violent attacks upon them. Though reaching its most recent climax in Nazi Germany's attempt to exterminate them during the Second World War (the Holocaust, or Porajmos), violence against the Rom continues in Europe and has recently increased again. The history of the Rom in post-1945 Europe is then a continuation of much that went before. The history of the Rom is important in itself, but it is also important for what it tells us about the history of Europe as a whole. Though often associated with "darkness," the history of the Rom in fact illuminates much of the darker side of past and contemporary Europe.

While known collectively as Rom, the Rom people are composed of several distinct groups divided on the basis of their national "origins" and other criteria of traditional occupation or "clan" relationships. Even though these distinctions are extremely important to the Rom as well as to outsiders, the Rom share a commonality of origin and of early history that provide aspects of unity despite their very evident contemporary divisions. Shared origins and shared persecution provide the essential links in the unity of the Rom. Though still the subject of some academic debate, the origins and early history of the Rom have now been largely accepted. Originating in the Punjab of northwest India, the Rom left India in groups about the eleventh century A.D., speaking their own language of Romani, which is related to Hindi, and migrated westward through Persia and Armenia into the Byzantine Empire. The reasons for their migration are not clear, though the wars in the Punjab at that time were probably the precipitating factor. Likewise their social "caste" (whether warriors, craftsmen, entertainers, or some composite of the three) is still unclear. Their arrival in Europe coincided with the invasions of the Seljuk and then Ottoman Turks, so that they were greeted with suspicion by some as infidels or spies and with grudging acceptance by others for the additional labor power and skills they brought. This pattern was to continue as some groups of Rom moved into central and western Europe.

Small groups of Rom scattered around Europe in the fourteenth century establishing the bases for the "national" Rom populations of northern Europe in Britain, Scandinavia, and the Baltic. Other groups established themselves in France and Italy. A further substantial group of Rom settled in Spain. Greater concentrations could be found in central and eastern Europe in Germany, Poland, and Russia, with the greatest numbers being found in or on the borders of the Ottoman Empire, especially in Hungary, Slovakia, and the Balkans. An especially large concentration of Rom was located in Moldavia and Wallachia (in present-day Romania), where they were enslaved from the fifteenth century until the middle of the nineteenth century.

Though some contact was maintained between "national" groups, they largely developed separately. Their individual histories form the basis for the existence of the different groups to the present day. Each group intermarried to varying degrees with other peoples, and each group developed national dialects of Romani and "Para-Romani" (i.e., a mixture of Romani and another language in which many elements of Romani have been displaced), which are frequently mutually unintelligible. Some groups lost Romani altogether and, as a preliterate people, there was no means of retaining much of their initial unity as a people. That unity was provided in large measure by their common place in the social hierarchy of whichever country they were in and by the hostility directed against them.

The advent of the industrial revolution and the rapid political changes of the nineteenth century effected the Rom dramatically in every country in which they lived, though the nature and extent of these effects varied from place to place. One common factor was the pressure felt by the Rom as the nomadic or seminomadic lifestyles of some groups of Rom became increasingly at odds with the social organization of European countries. In addition, the largely rural world in which the "traditional" skills of many Rom had been practiced (horse trading, tinsmithing, copper work, etc.) was giving way to a more urbanized environment with large-scale production answering to many economic needs. Finally, the political ideologies of nationalism had little place for the Rom as an "alien" people. Though the Rom of southern and western Europe were not immune from hostile political nationalism, the pressures were greatest in central and eastern Europe, where an often aggressively *völkisch* nationalism coincided with political insecurity and large populations of Rom. This mixture was to prove literally fatal for many Rom.

The post–World War One "settlement" of Europe set the seal on these developments and created a variety of difficult environments for the Rom. In western Europe the economic insecurity and political uncertainty led to much official and unofficial harassment of Rom in countries such as Great Britain and France alongside the progressive dislocation of their way of life and economic base. The Russian Revolution (1917) officially created some space for the Rom of Soviet Russia and the Ukraine, but this was always tenuous and, owing to the changing economy and continuing popular hostility, inherently unstable. The Soviet thrust to collectivize the land and to make the Rom into peasants and workers was highly disruptive to the Rom; on the other hand, the Soviets stimulated a renaissance in Rom culture with the creation of a modest literature in Romani and various state-funded institutions to foster Rom music and theater. In western Europe, likewise, the conduct of much of the public and of government officials was in a small measure counterbalanced by the rise of scholarly interest in the Rom, a romantic affection for "traditional" facets of Rom life (the famous painted caravans, etc.), and the acceptance of the importance of individual Rom, especially musicians such as Django Reinhardt.

In central and eastern Europe, though here too Rom music, especially in Hungary, was seen as part of the national heritage, the situation was far worse. In addition to the substantial "national" populations of Rom, the freeing of the Rom of Romania from slavery in the mid–nineteenth century led to an outmigration of Rom, the Vlach Rom, to many neighboring countries and eventually around the world. These new populations of Rom were no better adapted to the changed economic and political environment of the time than were the "national" groups and further exacerbated the perception of there being a "Gypsy problem." The worsening economic situations of these countries and their political instability led to the rise of right-wing movements that often had an explicitly racial element to their ideologies. In Germany, Hungary, Romania, and other countries of central and eastern Europe the Rom were subject not only to explicit attempts to eradicate their culture, urbanize their lives, and "proletarianize" their work but also to an array of measures aimed at either "integrating" them or expelling them. The common element was that Rom had to disappear as a distinct people either through assimilation, should that be possible, or expulsion. The "right approach" was discussed in political and governmental circles though no firm conclusions were reached. Life for the Rom was always lived in uncertainty.

Beginning in the 1930s that uncertainty gave way to a far worse form of certainty. Led by the Nazi regime in Germany, the Rom were subject to ever harsher measures culminating in a determined effort to eradicate them as a people. The Nazi racial laws were enforced with great rigor against the Rom. These measures progressed rapidly from efforts to register all Rom and those with even remote Rom ancestry to shipping them out to concentration and extermination camps. Everywhere in German-dominated Europe the Rom were harried and killed; even in western Europe officials in countries such as Belgium and France collaborated in the German efforts. In central and eastern Europe indigenous fascist movements participated alongside the Germans in their efforts to finally solve the Gypsy problem. After 1941 the Rom of the occupied USSR, including the Ukraine and the Baltic states, were accorded similar treatment. In some areas, though often treated harshly, Rom fared somewhat better at least until the Germans actually arrived. In Bulgaria, thanks to Boris III, in Slovakia, thanks to Father Tiso, the premier, and in parts of former Yugoslavia, especially Macedonia, which was annexed by Bulgaria, significant numbers of Rom survived. In Hungary, Rom were persecuted by the indigenous fascist Arrow Cross, but many of the worst acts of violence happened after the German occupation, which, fortunately for the Rom, was mercifully short. In Romania the Iron Guard fascist group spearheaded attacks on Rom and many were deported or killed. However, Romania's shifting political alliances enabled many Rom to survive.

The Rom communities of Europe were devastated by the Holocaust. The Germans assisted by their local collaborators both killed at random and systematically exterminated whole groups of Rom. Local pogroms were the backdrop to the mechanical violence of Auschwitz and Ravensbruck. While figures must remain inexact, more than a million Rom died in this period, representing significantly more than half the Rom population. Though the clear basis for this violence lay in racism, the Rom of much of Europe, and especially of Germany, were also persecuted as "asocials." Because of this designation the Rom have been consistently denied their status as victims of the Nazi German racial laws and thus of financial and social compensation. The Rom world that emerged from the rubble of the Second World War was, like the rest of Europe, divided into two main zones: the Communist-dominated bloc and the West. In addition, owing to the significant Rom population of Yugoslavia, that country represented a "third way" for the remaining Rom.

In western Europe only the Rom communities of the British Isles and Iberia escaped the violence of the Germans. In Britain the Rom remain a small minority of around eighty thousand who, with significant exceptions, have largely accommodated themselves to contemporary life. Though "traditional" Rom life is viewed with some "folkloric" affection and scholarly activity is high, the actual life of Rom is often harsh and squalid, and the efforts of the authorities to get Rom to "move on" contrasts with various assimilationist efforts. The Rom, though still distrustful of outsiders (*gadzje*), have intermarried with other people from Britain, both sedentary and indigenous seminomadic groups such as the Tinkers. They have continued to maintain a tenuous existence, albeit with an attenuated culture and the loss of much of the Romani language. The Rom, however, do have recognized status as an ethnic minority within the legal system. In Iberia, most noticeably in southern Spain though Rom can be found throughout the peninsula, a related though different pattern emerges. Most of the Rom of Spain (the Calé) are not nomadic, and in fact their most famous communities, such as Guadix, demonstrate many centuries of the nonnomadic life. The slower pace of industrialization in Spain isolated these communities from much of the dislocation experienced in other parts of Europe. Likewise the Francoist regime, though far from being truly benign, was not wedded to racist ideas, as were the other fascist regimes. The association of the Calé with music and entertainment, most notably Flamenco and *cante jondo*, further insulated them. Despite the latter, the life of the average Calé has remained one of unremitting struggle, poverty, and illiteracy. The increasing prosperity of Spain has left the approximately 750,000 Calé largely behind. The formation of cultural and social organizations whose objects are political and practical rather than folkloric indicates the possibility of a better future for the Calé.

For most of the rest of western Europe, including the very small Rom populations of Scandinavia, the position is much like that of Britain, though again with significant local variations. For the approximately three hundred thousand Roma of France and Italy (largely Rom, Sinti, and Manouche, though reinforced by Vlach and other Rom from eastern Europe and the Balkans), life since the Second World War has oscillated between official neglect and interventionism, along with continuing pressure to assimilate. There has not been any substantial effort, however, on the part of the authorities to fully address the needs of the Rom or even begin to attempt to fund them. Though the two countries differ as to the zeal with which the bureaucracy implements its policies, the tendency has been the same. The recent influx of Rom from eastern

Europe (especially Macedonia) has exacerbated the problems of "indigenous" Rom and has also fed into the increase in right-wing racism and attacks on foreigners. The undoubted poverty and marginality of these immigrants has provided the "evidence" that was needed for contentions about the criminality of the Rom and their threat to society. The weakness of civil society, especially in Italy, and the economic and political climate of uncertainty have worsened the situation.

Germany, especially following reunification, lies at the crossroads of western and central Europe and is subject to both unique pressure and unique scrutiny. More than 80 percent of German Rom (Rom and Sinti) were killed during the Second World War. The shattered remnants of these communities have struggled with the twin legacies of continued discrimination and continued denial of the fact of racial persecution, rather than persecution based on collective "asocial" characteristics. With the German "economic miracle" increasing numbers of foreign workers (*Gästarbeiter*) were required to supplement the existing German workforce, and many of these, whether categorized as Turkish or Yugoslav, were Rom. Their treatment was often less than positive, but still Rom believed that they were better off declaring themselves as Yugoslav rather than Rom, since the Rom were still not welcome. With the collapse of communism, large numbers of refugees have entered Germany, and many of these from Romania and Yugoslavia are Rom. They have been subjected to the same hostility and occasional violent attacks as have other refugees in Germany. The rise of the new aggressive Right, whether of the respectable or less respectable type, has been marked by violent attacks on Rom in Germany and in Austria, where a pipe bomb killed several Rom in the Bürgenland in 1995. In most German-speaking areas attacks on Rom have become a part of a more general xenophobia.

Yugoslavia represented a different environment for the Rom. Nearly a million Rom live in the former Yugoslavia, with particularly large groups in Serbia and Macedonia. Though considerable pressures were brought to bear in favor of assimilation, the Rom of Yugoslavia benefited from widespread recognition of their identity as a people and from the effort to create a Yugoslav nationality in which they too could be members. The poverty of many areas of Yugoslavia, especially those in which the Rom live, such as Kosovo and Macedonia, undermined these efforts and still left the Rom at the bottom of the employment and social structures. Individual events, such as the Skopje earthquake of 1963, made these limitations clear and prompted new outmigration of Rom to other countries, especially West Germany. There they were accepted not as Rom but as Yugoslavs. The death of Tito (1980) and the consequent implosion of Yugoslavia made matters far worse as the rise of ethnic nationalism in Serbia and Kosovo and the weakened situation of Macedonia once more left the Rom outside the political calculus. The future remains very uncertain for the Rom of former Yugoslavia, and the high hopes expressed by Rom intellectuals and politicians in the 1970s now seem very likely to be frustrated.

Within the Soviet bloc, the pressure to assimilate has been relentless, albeit with occasional efforts, most noticeably in Hungary and the former Czechoslovakia, to encourage literacy in Romani as a way to achieve this assimilation. Central planning meant the attempt to move large numbers of Rom from the countryside into urban areas to work in industrial production. The inability of many Rom to adjust to this process (work habits, apartment living, etc.) often served only to exacerbate tensions between Rom and the other populations of the cities. An additional complication in the case of Czechoslovakia was that much of the Rom population was born in Slovakia. With the separation of Slovakia from the Czech Republic, on January 1, 1993 their lives were doubly complicated. Throughout the Soviet bloc assimilation led to widespread abandonment of the use of Romani (it is estimated that some 65 percent of Hungarian Rom do not know the language) without any comparable rise in economic and social status or acceptability. Even in the former Soviet Union itself, though 70 percent of the Rom used Romani as their native language and the growth of a Rom intelligentsia, though attenuated, was significant, the Rom were still a largely embattled minority with little respect or security. In Romania the nearly one million Rom throughout the 1970s officially did "not exist," and their problems were only grudgingly addressed in the 1980s. Urbanization and assimilation were the goals of the Ceauşescu regime, and, as in other areas, this not only failed to address the real concerns of Rom but further exacerbated tensions with other Romanians.

With the collapse of the USSR and Yugoslavia, the fate of the Rom took another turn for the worse. Collapsing economies left the Rom particularly vulnerable, nationalism left them not only excluded but subject to xenophobic attacks, and attempts at emigration to western Europe exposed them to further such attacks, most noticeably in Austria and Germany. The resulting dislocation of Rom communities has weakened them at their base without giving them a more positive image in their new host countries. Romanian and other eastern European Rom have been violently attacked in refugee hostels, while the criminal activities of Yugoslav Rom in Italy and elsewhere have heightened public hostility and aroused many traditional concerns and fears. The attempts of the Czech authorities to label most of the Rom as "Slovaks" and then deport them to their "home" has far worsened the situation of Rom in those two countries. The reports of Human Rights Watch on the Rom of Bulgaria and Romania indicate how quickly conditions have deteriorated in those two countries. The civil wars in the former Yugoslavia and the continuing tensions and poverty of Kosovo and Macedonia have rendered the life of the Rom communities in these two areas completely unstable.

It would not be right to conclude solely by indicating the problems that the Rom of Europe now face, however serious they may be. The Rom have made very real gains in the twentieth century, and especially in more recent years, in terms of establishing a solid basis for contemporary Rom culture and a respect for it among others. Though substantial disagreements remain, a solid basis for a standardized written Romani that could unite all Rom has been laid. A not insubstantial literature in Romani has been produced, and Romani culture, especially in music, is given at least some of the impartial recognition that it deserves. Rom political activism, though varying from one country to another, has been substantial, and the work of the World Romani Congress has helped to form a consciousness of the unity of the Rom people that has been long suppressed. Religion remains a strong force among Rom and, whether expressed in "traditional" forms or as part of the Evangelical Revival in France or the English-speaking world, augments and protects Rom identity. Though the immediate future for the Rom of Europe is uncertain, they have experienced many worse times. Their resilience and the respect that this must engender have carried them through much poverty and oppression. Perhaps the future Europe will give them at least some measure of the respect they deserve and recognize the important contribution that they have made to Europe in the last five hundred years.

BIBLIOGRAPHY

Crowe, David. *A History of the Gypsies of Eastern Europe and Russia.* New York: St. Martin's Press, 1994.

Crowe, David, and John Kolsti, eds. *The Gypsies of Eastern Europe.* Armonk, N.Y.: M.E. Sharpe, 1991.

De Gila-Kochanowski, Vania. *Parlons Tsigane.* Paris: Éditions l'Harmattan, 1994.

Djuric, Rajko, et al. *Ohne Heim, ohne Grab.* Berlin: Aufbau Verlag, 1996.

Fraser, Angus. *The Gypsies.* Oxford: Blackwell Publishers, 1993.

Hancock, Ian. *The Pariah Syndrome.* Ann Arbor, Mich.: Karoma Press, 1989.

Reemtsma, Katrin. *Sinti und Roma.* Munich: Verlag Beck, 1996.

Míchál Thompson

Roman, Petre (1946–)

Romanian political leader and prime minister (December 1989–September 1991). Petre Roman was born in Bucharest on July 22, 1946. His father, Valter Roman (Ernest Neulander), was Jewish and his mother, whom Valter had met as a member of the International Brigades organized by Comintern, the Soviet dominated Communist organization, fighting in the Spanish Civil War during the 1930s, was Spanish. Later Valter Roman rose to membership in the Romanian Communist Party's (RCP) Central Committee and directed the party publishing house at the time of his death in 1983. Valter's status in the RCP meant that his son received privileges, such as permission to study abroad. After graduating from the University of Bucharest in 1968 with a degree in engineering, Roman obtained a doctorate from the University of Toulouse, where he studied from 1971 to 1974. He then became a professor of hydraulic mechanics at the Bucharest Polytechnical Institute, a post that he has retained. Although Roman joined the RCP, he never held any party positions, displayed no political ambitions, and never joined any groups conspiring against dictator Nicolae Ceaușescu. His acquaintance with Ion Iliescu, the president of Romania from December 26, 1989 to November 29, 1996, who also studied hydraulics, dates back to the early 1980s when they belonged to an informal group that Roman's father had organized to investigate planning, management, and scientific problems. Since Iliescu directed the press that published some of Roman's books, they met occasionally after 1983.

Roman entered politics on December 22 as one of the crowd that surged into the Central Committee building in Bucharest while Ceaușescu and his wife, Elena, fled from the roof in a helicopter. He and a few others hastily drafted a declaration on behalf of an ad hoc anti-Ceaușescu group, the People's Unity Front, which he read to the masses gathered outside from the building's second-floor balcony. This act established him as revolutionary leader. That and the support of dissident Communist Silviu Brucan, a close friend of the Roman family, persuaded Iliescu to make Roman prime minister in the National Salvation Front (NSF), formed by former Communists to replace the government of Ceaușescu, which had the backing of the military's leaders and some sections of the Securitate (secret police).

January 1990 found Romanians desperately needing a stable government and economic reform, but the NSF's supporters, which now included Communist bureaucrats whom Iliescu needed to govern, had no interest in reform. The NSF cautiously refrained from removing any but the highest Communist officials and preferred to implement democracy and a market economy gradually, ostensibly to lessen any hardships they might have caused Romanians. The NSF created the impression of rapid economic improvement during the first half of 1990 by spending the foreign hard currency Ceauşescu had amassed on exports during the 1980s, while strictly limiting foreign investment.

Initially Roman accepted these policies and remained Romania's prime minister following the NSF's controversial victory in the May 1990 general elections. He also acquiesced in the NSF's violent repression of its opponents in Bucharest during June 14–16, 1990, and its tolerance of the authoritarian ultranationalist groups that emerged during 1990. In fact, Roman publicly referred to members of the ultra-nationalist political organization, Vatra Românească, as "harmless patriots." During the summer and fall of 1990 Roman began to diverge from the former Communists surrounding Iliescu. In the company of several politically uncompromised technocrats, he assumed control of the reform process when the false prosperity ended. His group wanted to move rapidly toward a market economy as Poland and Hungary had done in the belief that Romania's overvalued currency, the leu, and numerous inefficient and unprofitable state-owned industrial plants made inflation and unemployment unavoidable. The way to lessen this was to hasten Romanian integration into the world economy through "shock therapy" rather than to postpone it with gradualism. Furthermore, Romania could ease the economic consequences of reform by encouraging foreign investment and loans from international financial institutions. However, foreign assistance depended on the regime's accepting political pluralism and ending its connections with xenophobic ultranationals, which Iliescu could not do without threatening his power base. Displaying a faith in social engineering left over from the Communist era, Roman urged extensive price deregulation and privatization but did not call for cuts in spending on social welfare programs despite the regime's budget deficit.

Iliescu accepted Roman's "shock therapy" because he knew that reform could no longer be postponed. Roman neither explained his policies well to the public nor heeded his critics, who found them chaotic, improvised, and uncoordinated. Roman managed to remove most price controls and subsidies by April 1991, which caused inflation to increase sharply. Privatization proceeded more slowly, although the February 1991 Land Law did result in about 80 percent of Romania's farmland reverting to private hands by late 1991. Public opinion polls taken during the first half of 1991 revealed that Roman was more popular than Iliescu. The same polls also showed that the majority of Romanians feared Roman's shock therapy and desired more moderate change.

The bureaucracy resisted the reforms and the labor unions engaged in numerous, usually successful, strikes for higher wages. At the end of March 1991 Roman was elected president of the NSF at its convention despite evidence that his reforms had divided the party and created a personal rivalry between himself and Iliescu. At the end of September 1991 miners from the Jiu Valley traveled to Bucharest and rioted for higher wages. They demanded the resignation of Roman and Iliescu, and at the urging of Virgil Magureanu, head of Romania's new secret police, Iliescu dismissed Roman, although only parliament could legally remove a prime minister.

In the following months the two men feuded bitterly in the media, which climaxed at the NSF's March 1992 convention when Roman blocked Iliescu's nomination as the NSF's presidential candidate for the fall elections. The party then split. Those supporting Iliescu and his gradualism formed the Democratic National Salvation Front, which triumphed in the fall elections. Roman's proreform NSF, tainted by the economic hardship it was thought to have caused, finished third. Roman, who was elected to the Senate, the upper house of the parliament, successfully defended himself against charges of corruption while in office, and endured anti-Semitic slurs. In May 1993, hoping to distance himself further from Iliescu, Roman merged the NSF with the Democratic Party, creating the Democratic Party–National Salvation Front, which claimed to stand for a confusing mixture of social democracy and liberalism in an effort to attract members. In 1994 the party became simply the Democratic Party and Roman ran against Iliescu for president in the October 1996 elections. He finished third with 20.5 percent of the vote, but he was reelected to the Senate and was expected to remain a force in Romanian politics in the years ahead.

Robert Forrest

SEE ALSO Brucan, Silviu; Iliescu, Ion

Romania

Romania is a republic located in the eastern part of the Balkan Peninsula. It consists of 91,699 square miles

Romania. *Illustration courtesy of Bernard Cook.*

(237,500 sq km) and is bordered by the Black Sea, Ukraine, Moldava, the Slovak Republic, Hungary, Serbia of the Yugoslav Federation, and Bulgaria. Much of Romania is dominated by the Carpathian Mountains that separate Moldavia in the east and Wallachia in the south from Transylvania in the center and north-west of the country. The Danube River forms the frontier between Romania and Serbia, and part of Romania's frontier with Bulgaria. Before the Danube reaches the Black Sea, it flows north through Romania past the city of Galati to the frontier with Moldava and Ukraine. There it turns abruptly to the east creating the frontier between Romania and Ukraine, eventually forming a delta before entering the sea. The population of Romania in 1998 was 22,491,000. Ethnic minorities constitute 9.3 percent of the population, of these the Hungarians, principally in Transylvania are the most numerous. They constitute 7.2 percent of Romania's population or approximately 1.7 million people. Until 1989 there was a sizable German ethnic community, numbering between 300,000 and 400,000. Most Romanians are Romanian Orthodox Christians, but 5.1 percent, principally Hungarians, are Roman Catholic. There are also Calvinists and Unitarians among the Hungarians of Romania. But since the collapse of Communism there has been a large migration of these people to Germany. In 1998, Bucharest, the capital city, had a population of 2,080,363. Constanta on the Black Sea is the second largest city with 348,575 inhabitants. The next three cities in size are Lasi with 339,889; Timisoara with 327,830; and Galati with 326,728. In 1919–20 Romanian nationalists realized their dream of a Greater Romania. The victorious Allies awarded to the Old Kingdom (consisting of Moldavia and Wallachia) territories from Russia (Bessarabia), Bulgaria (southern Dobruja), and Austria-Hungary (Transylvania and Bukovina). Greater Romania contained a diverse population consisting of about 72 percent Romanians, 8 percent Hungarians, 5 percent Roma, 4 percent Germans and Jews, 3 percent Ukrainians, and 2 percent Russians and Bulgarians. Preserving Greater Romania took precedence over all other problems facing Romania in the interwar period. Accordingly, Romanian leaders largely ignored such domestic issues as land reform for peasants, social equality, and corruption.

Except for Transylvania's leaders, political power during the interwar period remained concentrated in the hands of the monarchy and a few Old Kingdom nobles who kept the government centralized at the capital, Bucharest. Their attempt to unify Greater Romania with Romanian nationalism failed because it alienated non-Romanians and nourished a populism that preached anti-intellectualism and rural mistrust of urban Romania. Furthermore, since Romanian nationalists were frequently xenophobes, they restricted foreign investment needed for Romania's industrialization.

During the tumultuous 1930s Romanian nationalism and populism amalgamated into a powerful fascist movement, the Iron Guard, dedicated to defending Orthodoxy and Greater Romania. Faced with such opposition Carol II established a royal dictatorship designed to defend both the monarchy and Romania from their enemies, but in 1940 he abdicated in favor of his son, Michael, after Hitler and Mussolini had forced him to return northern Transylvania to Hungary and Soviet dictator Joseph Stalin had grabbed Bessarabia and northern Bukovina. Marshal Ion Antonescu, who had been fired as minister of defense by King Carol in 1938 but was appointed prime minister on September 4, 1940 by the King two days before his abdication, ignoring young King Michael, established a semifascist dictatorship and committed Romanian troops to Germany's war against the USSR in return for regaining Bessarabia and northern Bukovina. With German defeat certain in 1944, King Michael enlisted the help of a few Communist and non-Communist political leaders to depose Antonescu on August 23, before the Red Army invaded Romania. Having "liberated" themselves from fascism, Romania's leaders sought the Allies' favor by establishing a democratic coalition government and helping the Soviets drive the Germans from Romania and Hungary.

The Allies still considered Romania a defeated enemy and largely left the peace terms to Stalin. The Soviets exacted heavy reparations from the Romanians and exploited them with joint Soviet-Romanian ventures called Sovroms until shortly after Stalin died in 1953. They also stationed Soviet troops in Romania until 1958. Stalin repartitioned Greater Romania by returning northern Transylvania to Romania, reclaiming Bessarabia and northern Bukovina for the USSR, and restoring southern Dobruja to Bulgaria.

Stalin imposed communism on Romania slowly because forcing the small, unpopular, and internally divided Romanian Communist Party (RCP) on Romanians in 1944 could have precipitated a civil war. Step by step the Soviets pressured Romania's coalition government to grant the RCP control of its key ministries. Meanwhile the RCP increased its popularity by advocating social and economic reforms desired by many Romanians since defeat had rendered the concept of Greater Romania obsolete. The converted, along with opportunists, rushed to join the party, swelling its ranks from one thousand in 1944 to several hundred thousand by 1947. On December 30, 1947, the now dominant Communists forced King Michael to abdicate and declared Romania a "people's republic." These actions completed Romania's isolation from the non-Communist world.

That the Western Allies only protested Stalin's actions in Romania has produced a myth that U.S. President Franklin Roosevelt gave Stalin Eastern Europe in February 1945 at the Yalta Conference. This interpretation ignores the fact that the West still needed Stalin's help to win the war against Japan, and that Roosevelt hoped for his cooperation in the postwar world. Furthermore, Romania's geographic location prevented either Britain or the United States from occupying it before the Red Army arrived in August 1944.

Between 1947 and 1952 the RCP (renamed Romanian Workers Party from 1948 until 1965), now the sole Romanian political party, revolutionized Romania and sought to impose the strictest Stalinism on it. The RWP substituted class struggle for nationalism, which terminated public discrimination against Romania's minorities and xenophobia, although the party's ideological condemnation of the West preserved the concept in a different context. Romania's small, wealthy, and powerful elite perished under social leveling designed to make Romania egalitarian. Socialism, including a comprehensive social security program copied from the USSR, replaced private enterprise. Romania's new Stalinist economy emphasized heavy industrialization, energy production, and collectivized agriculture rather than consumer goods. Economic growth would come through centralized planning in the form of goals set by five-year plans, the first of which began in 1950. This approach to industrialization preserved Bucharest's predominance in Romanian affairs. The RWP controlled its opposition, real and potential, by suppressing freedom of expression, limiting the practice of religion, controlling education, and using terror. In the last case, before 1953 its security force, the Securitate, arrested at least three hundred thousand peasants who resisted collectivization.

In 1952 Gheorghe Gheorghiu-Dej acquired total control of the RWP and the Romanian government. He tried to preserve his power by maintaining the party's incoherence and its patron-client nature that made personal relationships more important for advancement than competence. In fact, the weak economy threatened his power more than the party. Peasant resistance to collectivization became so severe that he temporarily suspended it. The economic situation also intensified his fear that intellectuals and technocrats, however necessary to industrialization, had little faith in communism; thus he refused to relax restrictions on freedom of expression. In 1955 the economy entered a period of strong growth that lasted until 1980. Prosperity enhanced the party's popularity and created confidence in the soundness of its methods. Consequently, Gheorghiu-Dej resumed collectivizing agriculture, completing it in 1962.

Soviet Premier Nikita Khrushchev's de-Stalinization campaign in 1956 and insistence on a socialist division of labor within the Soviet-controlled Comecon, the Council for Mutual Economic Assistance, set up in 1949 to coordinate the economic activities of the Eastern Bloc countries, to avoid costly industrial duplication posed serious problems for Gheorghiu-Dej's Stalinist dictatorship. The latter policy would have required Romania to curtail its industrialization and concentrate on producing raw materials and food. In defense of himself and his regime, Gheorghiu-Dej veered Romania toward the course it had followed prior to 1944 by reviving nationalism. A sharp debate has occurred over whether Gheorghiu-Dej introduced nationalism in 1962, when he officially announced it, or earlier. The historian Stephen Fischer-Galati maintains that Gheorghiu-Dej actually formulated the policy in 1945 but began cautiously pursuing it only around 1955. On the other hand, the historian Kenneth Jowitt concludes that prior to 1962 the regime merely obeyed Khrushchev's desire that each socialist country follow its own path to socialism. Romania's independent stance, in Jowitt's, view did not emerge until after the party had finished collectivizing agriculture in 1962, a prerequisite for seeking industrial autarky. The evidence supports

Fischer-Galati, although many historians would prefer 1957–58 to Fischer-Galati's 1955.

A strong sense of nationalism was latent in many Romanians, even RWP members, until Khrushchev's policies reactivated it. The Soviet invasion of Hungary in 1956 convinced Gheorghiu-Dej that Khrushchev represented a real threat to himself and to Romanian Stalinism. Consequently, to fashion and protect an independent, prosperous, and egalitarian Romania achieved through Stalinism, he decided in 1957 to act independently of Moscow in foreign affairs and in 1958 to become as economically self-sufficient as possible. The latter decision led to the public break with Comecon in 1962 that amounted to freeing Romania from its status as a Soviet satellite without de-Stalinization.

Gheorghiu-Dej based his new foreign policy on peaceful coexistence and the unity of the socialist camp, in which every member was equally independent and free to pursue its own course to socialism without interference from any other state. In practice this meant that Romania recommenced trade and limited cultural exchanges with the West and remained neutral in the ideological conflict between Mao Tse-Tung's China and the USSR, mainly to gain leverage against the Soviets. These positions caused the world to recognize Romania as a "third force" in the socialist camp. Since socialist states surrounded Romania and the RWP had no intention of abandoning communism, the Soviets tolerated Romania's independence.

The party also successfully used independence to increase its popularity with Romanians by appealing to their anti-Soviet feelings and linking itself to the historical goal of national unification. The RWP also revived Greater Romania in the guise of questioning the USSR's right to Bessarabia. By 1964 nationalism had also produced limited freedom of expression and the rehabilitation of earlier authors, as well as renewed discrimination against Romania's minorities, partly because the Soviets had used them to control the RWP.

Gheorghiu-Dej died in 1965, and a collective leadership, headed by Nicolae Ceauşescu, succeeded him. It continued his policies without question except for the lessening of oppression. The debate over continuing or halting liberalization ended in the negative when Ceauşescu became Romania's dictator after 1968. Following the death of Gheorghiu-Dej, he had been the most prominent member of a genuine collective leadership. In 1967 he became president of the State Council, head of the government, and titular head of the party. He used those positions to gain control of the Securitate, the secret police, and expel his enemies from the party, enabling him to establish himself as dictator. Ceauşescu was an unimaginative man who rose to power through his skill as a tough negotiator and by ruthlessly outmaneuvering his rivals in the RWP. During his time in power he carried Gheorghiu-Dej's policies to and beyond their logical limits by seeking to transform Romania into a "multilaterally developed socialist state"—a slogan meaning the simultaneous creation of a new person as well as economic abundance. After 1971 Ceauşescu began using an increasingly perverse cult of personality to style his rule as the "golden age" of Romanian history, and himself as the only person wise enough to achieve Romania's Communist and national goals. In this era the party, the government, and Gheorghiu-Dej's legacy disappeared from view as he took personal credit for communism's successes and blamed its failures on the Romanian people. For example, while Ceauşescu skillfully continued his predecessor's foreign policy objectives, he personalized them by substituting "Ceauşescu the maverick Communist" for Romania the "third force" in the socialist camp.

Under Ceauşescu heavy industrialization remained the key to prosperity and independence, and he expanded it through diversification and ever larger enterprises designed more for their demonstration effect than their productivity. Capitalizing on his reputation as a maverick, he borrowed money and purchased technology from the West to realize these projects. By 1980 a combination of poor investments and higher energy costs had halted Romanian economic growth. In 1982, faced with a stagnant economy and a $10 billion dollar debt, Ceauşescu, who never lost faith in Stalinist economics, raised production quotas rather than reform the economy and slashed imports while exporting whatever the West would buy, mostly food, to repay the loans. Nevertheless, the economy worsened throughout the 1980s, and Romanians had to endure numerous hardships such as shortages of food, heat, and light (energy went to the factories), and poor health care owing to restrictions on imports of medical supplies. An unfortunate consequence of these deprivations was to revive the corruption checked by the Communists since they had seized power.

Ceauşescu used social engineering to complete the party's goal of social leveling. Rows of concrete apartment blocs in which the size of a family's apartment depended on the number of members in the family came to symbolize most prominently this social engineering. At the end of the 1980s Ceauşescu also announced a plan, called systematization, to demolish over half of Romania's villages and replace them with agro-alimentary centers consisting of apartment complexes like those in the cities. The plan aimed to erase urban-rural differences and make agriculture more productive, but little was done to implement this before the dictator's fall in 1989.

The weak opposition to Ceauşescu's dictatorship has sparked ongoing controversy. Some claim that Romanians never resist authority or that they accepted his regime out of opportunism. These oversimplifications omit several crucial factors. Between 1955 and 1981 economic growth made socialism acceptable to most Romanians. The utilization of nationalism had increased that popularity, especially with the military, because Romanian independence enhanced the military's importance. Ceauşescu controlled the party by improving on Gheorghiu-Dej's methods. He made the party's institutions unwieldy by enlarging their memberships and rotated the nomenklatura to different positions in different locations to prevent any organized opposition from developing.

The worsening economy in the 1980s, and Ceauşescu's increasingly draconian responses to the crisis, magnified his fear of opposition. To justify his methods and turn the West and Romania's minorities into scapegoats, he revived the xenophobia and populism with its anti-intellectualism that characterized pre-1944 Romanian nationalism. At the same time, he intensified Securitate intimidation and infiltration of dissident groups. The anti-Soviet element in Romanian nationalism caused many Romanians to hope that Ceauşescu would eventually abandon the Soviet paradigm, making opposition unnecessary. The West's praise for Ceauşescu's independent stance until around 1985 caused most dissatisfied Romanians to conclude that the West would not support them; thus they preferred to emigrate rather than to resist the dictator. Finally, Ceauşescu controlled the party and government through more rapid rotation of cadres and by appointing as many members of his large family as possible to important positions. In the process, he isolated himself from Romanians and Romania from the world.

The Romanian people, mostly youths and workers, seeking personal freedom and prosperity, which they equated with democracy and capitalism, finally revolted against Ceauşescu in December 1989. A group of Communists seized control of the spontaneous uprising and, calling themselves the National Salvation Front, selected Ion Iliescu, a reform Communist who had fallen out of favor with Ceauşescu in 1984, as their president. He headed Romania's government until November 1996. Romanians obtained their freedom immediately, and, after a shaky start, democracy, but prosperity has eluded all but a small minority. Partly to delay the inflation and unemployment made unavoidable by the Communists' practice of basing economic policy on nationalism and partly to prolong the careers of former Communist bureaucrats, the government privatized Romania's economy very slowly. This continued politicization of economic decisions has contributed greatly to the further deterioration of Romanians' standard of living. It has also perpetuated corruption, forcing most people to use bribery or influence to found new businesses or to obtain profitable state properties. These successful individuals, frequently former Communist officials, by becoming extremely wealthy while the bulk of Romanians suffer from poverty, are restratifying Romanian society along pre-Communist lines. Extremists, also mostly former Communists, have played on Romanian's fears with the worst aspects of Romanian nationalism, populism, and xenophobia, which has prolonged ethnic strife and dissuaded former investors from helping Romania end its economic crisis. The hope of annexing Bessarabia, now the independent country of Moldova, has existed in Romanian nationalist aspirations to recover at least part of Greater Romania, but Moldovans have rejected the idea. Last of all, the world's condemnation of Romania's ethnic violence coupled with the West's unwillingness to accept the vast number of Romanians wanting to emigrate has delayed Romania's reintegration into mainstream European culture. In 1996 Romanians rejected extremism when they elected Emil Constantinescu, the rector of the University of Bucharest, as their president, with a mandate to halt Romania's slide into its past that threatened to destroy totally the more egalitarian society that the Communist Party had tried to introduce. Constantinescu started to achieve this difficult task by attacking corruption and closing unprofitable factories.

BIBLIOGRAPHY

Deletant, Denis. *Ceausescu and the Securitate: Coercion and Dissent in Romania, 1965–1989.* Armonk, N.Y.: M. E. Sharpe, 1995.

Fischer-Galati, Stephen. *Twentieth Century Rumania,* 2d ed. New York: Columbia University Press, 1991.

Gilberg, Trond. *Nationalism and Communism in Romania: The Rise and Fall of Ceausescu's Personal Dictatorship.* Boulder, Colo.: Westview Press, 1992.

Jowitt, Kenneth. *Revolutionary Breakthroughs and National Development: The Case of Romania, 1944–1965.* Berkeley: University of California Press, 1971.

Rady, Martyn. *Romania in Turmoil: A Contemporary History.* London: IB Tauris, 1992.

Robert Forrest

Securitate

Secret Police, which used terror, intimidation, and propaganda against Romanians to help the Communist regime achieve its objectives.

In the fall of 1944 during World War II, the Red Army occupied Romania, and by 1945 the Soviets controlled both of Romania's secret services—the military's Special Information Service (SSI) and the Ministry of the Interior's Directorate of Security Police (Siguranta). In August 1948 Romania's Communist regime replaced the Siguranta with the General Directory of People's Security (Securitate) and assigned the SSI to the Ministry of the Interior. The Securitate was ordered "to defend the democratic conquests and to ensure the security of the Romanian People's Republic against the plotting of internal and external enemies." The Ministry of the Interior also received authorization from the regime with Soviet blessing to absorb the police, who were renamed the militia, and raise security troops to maintain order and quash anti-Communist resistance. Finally, the regime forced the courts to sustain the Ministry of the Interior's activities.

Most of Interior's initial key personnel were Soviet citizens; some even assumed Romanian names to conceal their origins. These Soviet agents recruited, trained, and monitored the activities of Romania's security specialists. Not until 1952 did the Soviets allow a Romanian, Alexander Draghici, to head the Ministry of the Interior. In December 1964, two years after Romania declared its autonomy within the socialist camp, the Soviets reluctantly withdrew their last "advisers" from Romania's Ministry of the Interior, making Romania the first Warsaw Pact country to emancipate its security forces from the Soviet KGB (secret police). Nevertheless, the Securitate continued to collaborate with the Soviets on security and intelligence matters.

The Soviets selected brutal leaders for Romania's security forces. The Securitate, militia, and security troops, assisted by thousands of informants, used terror to turn Romania into a police state. Freedom of expression, religion, and movement, except for reasons of work or health, ended. Romanians could no longer choose their own jobs or places of domicile. All who resisted the regime, such as the thousands of peasants who demonstrated against the collectivization of agriculture or whom the Securitate suspected of opposing communism, were susceptible to relocation or arrest and arbitrary imprisonment, where they might be tortured and brainwashed. Beginning in 1950 the Securitate also resorted to forced labor, making the Ministry of the Interior one of Romania's largest "employers." For example, the infamous Danube–Black Sea Canal project used around 40,000 such prisoners in the early 1950s. Scholars estimate that, all told, the Communist regime arrested 282,000 people, of whom 190,000 died in confinement.

The Soviet Union withdrew its occupation troops from Romania in 1958, and Gheorghe Gheorghiu-Dej, Romania's Communist first Secretary and from 1961 to 1965, head of state, intensified the terror, fearing that their absence might encourage open rebellion. The Securitate's random enforcement of the new, little publicized draconian procedures frightened Romanians intensely. However, arrests declined probably because Gheorghiu-Dej's difficulties with Moscow, which had adopted an anti-Stalinist line, prompted him to rely more on Romanian nationalism and less on communism to legitimize his rule. Having sought popularity through nationalism, the Communists could not maintain that approval and continue to arrest Romanians indiscriminately for ideological reasons. Consequently, the Securitate curtailed its terrorism and released 12,750 political prisoners between 1962 and 1964.

Nicolae Ceauşescu succeeded Gheorghiu-Dej in 1965. He also emphasized Romanian nationalism; therefore the Securitate continued to rely on fear more than terror. Until Ceauşescu gained firm control of the Communist Party (RCP) and the government by 1971, party leaders also restrained the Securitate with judicial supervision ("socialist justice"). Fear meant subjecting dissidents, Baptists, and Romania's ethnic minorities to surveillance, harassment, loss of employment, intimidation, relocation, and occasionally arrest. Although mass arrests ceased, terror did not disappear and even reemerged in 1965, when the Securitate started to place the party's most troublesome opponents in psychiatric hospitals, where it drugged and tortured them.

Ceauşescu relied on the Securitate to uphold his despotism in more ways than Gheorghiu-Dej had done, especially after 1971. Besides employing fear, he enlarged the Securitate's military arm and increasingly used these elite troops to keep order. To the Securitate's censorship duties Ceauşescu added the task of propagating his cult of personality, especially abroad. Furthermore, he placed the Securitate in control of foreign trade. In return for their loyalty, Ceauşescu favored Securitate agents with access to foreign products denied ordinary Romanians, better food and housing, and special vacations. These privileges, plus the fact that many of these agents had neither talent nor education, won the dictator their allegiance. An unknown number of Securitate troops and agents unsuccessfully defended Ceauşescu during the 1989 revolution, which toppled the leader, the Securitate, and communism.

In the aftermath of the revolution the Securitate was dissolved but many of its officers were, because of their connections, able to manage quite successfully during the transition.

BIBLIOGRAPHY

Constante, Lena. *The Silent Escape: Three Thousand Days in Romanian Prisons.* Tr. by Franklin Philip. Berkeley: University of California Press, 1995.

Deletant, Denis. *Ceausescu and the Securitate: Coercion and Dissent in Romania, 1965–1989.* Armonk, N.Y.: M.E. Sharpe, 1995.

Robert Forrest

Revolution of 1989

Rising of December 15 to 25, 1989, in which Romanians overthrew the tyranny of their Communist ruler, President Nicolae Ceauşescu.

By 1989 widespread discontent over a declining standard of living and fear of Ceauşescu's police apparatus gripped Romanians and insulated Ceauşescu from the people. Thus, with communism in Eastern Europe collapsing all around him, Ceauşescu announced his intention not to introduce any reforms in October 1989 at the Fourteenth Congress of the Romanian Communist Party. Furthermore, Ceauşescu, convinced of numerous foreign plots against him, had deliberately isolated Romania internationally, hoping in part to revive his regime's flagging legitimacy by buttressing Communist ideology with nationalism. In fact, Ceauşescu had proved that a government could survive for years with little or no legitimacy. The reasons were the unpredictable ways Ceauşescu used power and, paradoxically, economic failure. Unpredictability meant that no one could feel secure in a job and free from arrest or harassment. With the unpalatable choice between the apparently impossible revolutionary course of opposing the nature of Ceauşescu's rule rather than the easier path of attacking his policies, most did nothing. Ceauşescu also proved that a sufficiently depressed economy can enhance political power because people become so involved with physical survival that they cannot form an opposition. Last, Ceauşescu was careful to keep the forces of coercion loyal through high salaries, generous perquisites, and the selection of mediocre individuals who could never merit such rewards on their own. The result was an unyielding Ceauşescu and a fragmented population incapable of threatening his regime because neither the few workers who struck nor the few intellectuals who plotted and protested had a following or any support among Ceauşescu's coercive forces.

It seems very unlikely that a plot of any type—foreign, domestic, or combination thereof—overthrew the dictator in December 1989, despite claims to the contrary, most notably by Michael Castex, a French journalist, and Anneli Ute Gabanyi, a German analyst of Romanian origin. The revolt arose spontaneously from a people who had collectively reached the limit of their profound ability to endure hardship. For the first time since 1940 they also had the opportunity to seize control of their destiny without fear of outside interference from a great European power and its allies in southeastern Europe. Secret groups of conspirators existed, such as the one including Ion Iliescu, that had explored means to seize control of the state should the opportunity arise, but they all lacked the power to create that opportunity.

A routine police attempt to discipline László Tökes, a Hungarian Reformed Church assistant pastor in the western Romanian city of Timisoara, precipitated the revolution. For objecting to state interference in his ministry and criticizing Ceauşescu's systematization policy for agriculture, the police in May 1989 had ordered Tökes transferred to Mineu, a small Transylvanian town where he could not become a focal point for opposition to the regime. Tökes refused to leave, and on October 14 the police set December 15 as the date for his eviction. On December 10 Tökes informed his congregation of the imminent deadline, and on the appointed day a mostly Hungarian group of them prevented the Securitate (secret police) from evicting Tökes by forming a human chain around his home.

The next day the Securitate summoned the mayor of Timisoara, but neither he nor Tökes could disperse the crowd, which swelled during the afternoon with the addition of many Romanians, most of them high school and university students. After nightfall much of the crowd drifted away from Tökes's home and turned an act of religiously inspired civil disobedience into political rebellion. Crying "down with Ceauşescu," the demonstrators virtually seized control of the city from the police, who could not receive permission from the minister of interior and the minister of defense to fire on the demonstrators. The failure of these ministers to authorize police action has elicited contradictory speculation. Instead the ministers called in Securitate and army troops, who restored order by the morning of December 17. The Securitate grabbed Tökes during the night and transported him and his family to Mineu, ending the pastor's role in the revolution.

While Securitate and army units held Timisoara, a furious Ceauşescu met in Bucharest with the party's Politburo and ordered it to crush the riot immediately by slaughtering the demonstrators if necessary. Throughout the day protesters clashed with the troops occupying Timisoara. Sporadic shots were fired until around 5 P.M., when the army and Securitate troops began shooting at the demonstrators in earnest. They killed between 70 and 90, wounding a further 210. A satisfied Ceauşescu placed his wife, Elena, in charge and flew to Iran partly to prove that such incidents could not force him to change his schedule and partly because of his ignorance of his countrymen's mood.

Ceauşescu's tyranny depended on a fear derived from secrecy that intensified people's insecurity through false rumors often spread by the Securitate. In this case the secret was between the government and the population of Timisoara; however, unlike past incidents the foreign press publicized this one. Hungarian and Yugoslav journalists witnessed the events in Timisoara and sent reports home that Romanian troops had killed thousands. Immediately, their stories attracted international attention, and many Romanians living in the western part of the country viewed reports broadcast on Yugoslav and Hungarian television. They learned that although Timisoara's young demonstrators had lost the fight for the city center, the struggle continued in the suburbs, where workers had started strikes that would develop into a general strike on December 20. Riots also erupted in the Transylvanian cities of Arad, Cluj, Sibiu, Brasov, and Tirgu Mures. Elena Ceauşescu hoped to conceal the violence by bringing the dead to Bucharest for cremation and to contain the disturbances by closing Romania's boarders, which only lent credence to the rumors of massacres entering Romania by television and foreign shortwave radio broadcasts.

The spreading violence prompted Ceauşescu to shorten his state visit to Iran and return to Bucharest on the afternoon of December 20. While he denounced the demonstrators on Romanian television that evening as hooligans and fascists incited by a Hungarian plot to partition Romania, a crowd of about one hundred thousand gathered in the center of Timisoara, but the troops, having lost their desire to shoot their fellow citizens, either did nothing or joined the crowd. That night army commanders withdrew their contingents from the city. In his television speech Ceauşescu made the mistake of publicly admitting and taking responsibility for the deaths of Romanians by thanking the army and Securitate for their restraint before having taken such action. He also threatened to use more force against future rioters, and, to prove the supposed popularity of his stand, called for a mass rally the next morning at the Communist Party's Central Committee building in the center of Bucharest.

Ceauşescu's speech made further confrontation unavoidable. He offered Romanians nothing but foreign threats and fear as reasons to support him, but his countrymen wanted an end to fear and economic hardship. The crowd at the ill-advised rally on December 21 did not cheer him as in the past but jeered. Shocked, he withdrew from the balcony only to return shortly with a promise of wage increases, which failed to satisfy a crowd that, sensing his weakness, would settle only for an end to his regime. Ceauşescu again retreated inside the Central Committee building and instructed the military and Securitate to use force to restore order. In so doing he condemned his country to a brief but bitter civil war.

Following the rally's collapse, thousands of young people poured into the center of Bucharest, and during the night of December 21–22 they fought with Securitate and army troops who regained control of Bucharest's center. Defense Minister Vasile Milea mitigated the fighting's intensity by again refusing to give the army explicit orders to shoot the demonstrators, which sowed confusion throughout the army. The next morning workers by the thousands poured from their homes and moved toward the center of Bucharest to join the fray. The army did little to stop them, and in some cases army and Securitate troops joined their ranks, so that by 9 A.M. the center of Bucharest began to fill with protesters again. When Ceauşescu learned of Milea's insubordination, he had him executed around 9:30 A.M. The announcement of Milea's death, called a suicide, cost Ceauşescu his remaining support in the army, leaving the dictator with only the Securitate's military units to protect him. While they were less numerous, they were better trained and equipped than those in the regular army.

With his defenses evaporating and the crowd beginning to storm the Central Committee building, Ceauşescu activated a long-standing plan to evacuate the government from Romania in the event of foreign invasion. At about noon, he, Elena, and two of their closest supporters fled in a helicopter that picked them up from the Central Committee building's roof. The military refused to play its part in the plan, and the escape turned into a farce that ended with the Ceauşescus' confinement at an army post near Tirgoviste. During the next hour the police joined the revolt and the crowd occupied the Central Committee building. Demonstrators, acting jointly with the army for the first time, seized the state television station in Bucharest, while others rushed to fill the power vacuum that Ceauşescu's departure had created.

Television, which had played a key role in publicizing the events in Timisoara and welding individual discontent into a spontaneous general uprising, now became central to establishing a new order in Romania. Renamed Romanian Free Television, it became the primary means by which the new leaders introduced themselves and their goals to the country and the rest of the world. Furthermore, although its nonstop coverage was selective, it also allowed everyone to watch the remainder of the revolution.

Of the various groups seeking power, the one led by Iliescu seized the opportunity to proclaim itself on television the National Salvation Front. Iliescu sought popular support by including a cross section of Romanian society in the Front, but his real legitimacy came from the support of military leaders, who held the balance of power. Iliescu had proven qualities of leadership and a reputation as a moderate reformer that appealed to the military and the nomenklatura, who wanted changes that would not disturb their careers and perquisites too much. Thus, Iliescu compromised the revolutionaries' desire to move toward a free market economy to insure the revolution's success and to become its leader.

That night, fighting resumed suddenly, mainly in Bucharest and Sibiu, initiating the most controversial stage of the revolution. A few Securitate units associated so closely with Ceauşescu that they had little future in the new Romania choose to resist. Television announcers dubbed them "terrorists" and revived Ceauşescu's foreign invasion myth by incorrectly claiming that many were foreigners. Securitate troops concentrated in the center of Bucharest, at its airport, and at the television station, but for still unexplained reasons they did not attack the Central Committee building where the Front was meeting and did not try to destroy the television station, which they may have wanted for their own use. The fighting raged throughout December 23 and 24, with sixty thousand deaths reported on television. During the night of December 24 the Front decided to convene a military tribunal on the morning of December 25 to try and execute Nicolae and Elena Ceauşescu, hoping that their deaths would end the violence and prevent the couple from causing any further problems. Although sporadic shooting lasted until December 29, the execution of the leader and his wife ended the fighting, which took 1,033 lives, 889 of them after Ceauşescu had tried to flee.

BIBLIOGRAPHY

Deletant, Dennis. *Ceausescu and the Securitate: Coercion and Dissent in Romania, 1965–1989.* Armonk, N.Y.: M.E. Sharpe, 1995.

Ratesh, Nestor. *Romania: The Entangled Revolution.* Westport, Conn.: Praeger, 1991.

Robert Forrest

SEE ALSO Ceauşescu, Nicolae; Iliescu, Ion

Political Parties (1945–50)

Between 1945 and 1947, the Romanian Communist Party (RCP) was transformed from a minor party in Romanian politics to the controlling party of the country. During the early interwar period (1918–1939), the two major political parties had been the Liberal Party (LP) and the National Peasant Party (NPP). The RCP is reported to have had one thousand members during this period. The small RCP was pursued in the 1930s and the early 1940s, first by Carol II, then by the fascists under Marshal Ion Antonescu.

Following the August 23, 1944 coup against the Antonescu government ordered by King Michael as the Soviet army approached Bucharest and the subsequent Soviet occupation of Romania in August 1944, one of the first tasks of the RCP was to create a broader base of support. Gheorghe Gheorghiu-Dej, leader of the RCP, used the coup to legitimize his power within the party and to marginalize RCP members who had spent the interwar period in Moscow, namely, Ana Pauker and Vasile Luca. During that period the Soviet Union allowed King Michael to form several coalition governments that included members of the LP, NPP, and RCP. However, no genuine coalitions were formed. During the first three postwar Romanian governments, most of the important ministerial positions were usually given to RCP members.

In October 1944 the National Democratic Front (NDF) government was formed; it included members from the RCP, the Social Democratic Party, the Union of Patriots, and the Plowman's Front. The Union of Patriots was an amalgamation of intellectuals, professionals, and other groups that had never had significant political influence. The Plowman's Front had been particularly popular in Transylvania during the 1930s, and its leader, Petru Groza, had participated in the governments of the 1920s. In March 1945 the NDF government under Groza was installed. By this time the Plowman's Front had become an extension of the RCP, which was heavily recruiting members. By March 1945 RCP membership had increased to well over thirty-five thousand.

In November 1946 national elections were marked by fraud and manipulation of the press. Not surprisingly, the RCP enjoyed a huge electoral victory, and the Groza government continued in power. By 1947 it had abolished the LP and the NPP. On December 31, 1947, it forced King Michael to abdicate and proclaimed the creation of the Romanian Peoples' Republic. Following this proclamation the NDF was renamed Popular Democratic Front. The Social Democratic Party was absorbed by the RCP, and by 1948 these two parties had merged to form the Romanian Workers Party (RWP). This merger increased the membership of the RWP by more than 250,000.

The Communist leadership was engaged in two campaigns to eliminate political opposition. The first campaign, which lasted from March 1945 until December 1947, focused on the destruction of traditional political forces. The second campaign was waged within the RWP itself. A so-called "verification campaign" was launched in 1948 to eliminate "opportunist elements," people who had joined the party for the social and economic advantage connected with membership rather than ideological commitment, within the RWP. However the purge allowed the removal of members, regarded as undesirable for any number of reasons from personal to political. By the end of the verification campaign, in May 1950, almost 350,000 individuals had been purged from the party.

BIBLIOGRAPHY

Fischer-Galati, Stephen. *Twentieth Century Rumania.* 2nd ed. New York: Columbia University Press, 1991.

Gilberg, Trond. *Nationalism and Communism in Romania: The Rise and Fall of Ceausescu's Personal Dictatorship.* Boulder, Colo.: Westview Press, 1992.

Rady, Martyn. *Romania in Turmoil: A Contemporary History.* London: IB Tauris & Co. Ltd., 1992.

Scott Burris

SEE ALSO Gheorghiu-Dej, Gheorghe; Groza, Petru; Pauker, Ana

Political Parties (1989–97)

Following the events of December 22, 1989, when a spontaneous uprising erupted against Nicolae Ceausescu, the Communist Dictator of Romania, a group of Communists formed the National Salvation Front and took control of the situation. Within days non-Communists were added to the FSN and it scheduled multi-party elections to be held in May. The FSN proclaimed a provisional government with Ion Iliescu, a reform Communist who had fallen out of favor with Ceausescu in 1984, as president of the FSN Council and interim president of the country, and Petre Roman was named interim prime minister. Some of the first parties to officially register after December 1989 included interwar parties such as the National Peasants Party–Christian Democratic (PNT–CD), National Liberal Party (PNL), and Social Democratic Party of Romania (PSDR).

Following the FSN's decision to form a party along Social Democratic lines and nominate candidates for the upcoming national elections, leaders of the PNT–CD, PNL, and PSDR protested. The FSN and members of other parties agreed to form a Provisional Council of National Unity, which became the de facto parliamentary body until the elections in May 1990, when FSN candidates won over 66 percent of the parliamentary seats, and Iliescu won over 85 percent of the presidential vote. The Hungarian Democratic Union of Romania and the PNL each won over 7 percent of the parliamentary seats. A total of eighteen parties won seats to parliament, and nine minority parties were given seats in the lower house, the Chamber of Deputies.

Following the overwhelming victory of the FSN, Romanian opposition parties formed an alliance for the March 1992 local elections. Several opposition parties including the PNT–CD, PNL, UDMR, PSDR, Civic Alliance Party (PAC), Liberal Party 1993 (PL93), the Romanian Ecological Party, and the National Liberal Party–Democratic Convention formed the Democratic Convention, later renamed Democratic Convention of Romania (CDR) in November 1991. The CDR did extremely well in the March elections, winning mayoral elections in Bucharest as well as Constantsa, Brasov, and Timisoara. Also in March, a split in the FSN caused members loyal to President Iliescu to leave the party to form the Democratic National Salvation Front (FDSN). The FSN members loyal to former Prime Minister Roman, who was replaced by Theodore Stolojan in September 1991, later renamed the FSN Democratic Party-FSN.

The CDR continued as the main opposition to the FDSN into the September 1992 national elections. While the FDSN did not enjoy an absolute parliamentary majority following these elections, it formed a coalition government with the assistance of several right-wing parties, including the Greater Romania Party, Socialist Party of Work, and Party of Romanian National Unity. Presidential candidate Iliescu did not receive an absolute majority in the first round of voting, so a second round was held, in which he defeated CDR presidential candidate Emil Constantinescu. President Iliescu nominated Nicolae Vacariou as prime minister.

In July 1993 the FDSN renamed itself Party of Social Democracy of Romania (PDSR). In May 1994 several parties left the CDR, including the PAC, PSDR, and PL93. Despite these defections the CDR reorganized and did extremely well in 1996 local elections, winning once again the mayoral elections in Bucharest, Brasov, and Timisoara, as well as many city and county council seats. Besides the CDR a new opposition coalition called the Social Democratic Union (USD) contested the local elections. The coalition of the Democratic Party–FSN and the PSDR received approximately 11 percent of the city and county council seats. The success of the CDR continued through the November 1996 national elections. The CDR received approximately 30 percent of the parliamentary vote and formed a coalition government with the USD. The CDR presidential candidate was once again Constantinescu, and in the 1996 presidential elections he defeated Iliescu in the second round. Constantinescu received approximately 53 percent of the vote.

BIBLIOGRAPHY

Rady, Martyn. *Romania in Turmoil: A Contemporary History.* London: IB Tauris & Co. Ltd., 1992.

Scott Burris

Democratic National Salvation Front Political party of Romanian President Ion Iliescu, which controlled parliament between October 1992 and November 1996.

The Democratic National Salvation Front (DNSF) split off from the National Salvation Front (FSN), which had been formed in December 1989, following that party's third national convention held from March 27 to 29, 1992. At that convention Petre Roman, president of the NSF, prevented President Ion Iliescu from running for a second term as the FSN nominee. Iliescu did not head his own party because Romanian law prohibited a political leader from being president of both Romania and a political party. Consequently, Roman, who was lliescu's prime minister until lliescu dismissed him in September 1991, headed the FSN. The two had become personal rivals for control of the party, and they disagreed over how to reform Romania's economy and politics.

Iliescu and his DNSF supporters maintained that Roman's policies for rapid transition to a market economy and democracy placed unnecessary burdens on the population. They preferred moderately paced economic reforms and increases in social security spending to dampen the impact of inflation and unemployment. The DNSF also wanted to minimize foreign investment to protect Romania's sovereignty. Politically the party vaguely depicted itself as centrist-left, committed to social democratic principles similar to those of Western European social democratic parties. Lastly, the party refused to attack former Communists or openly discuss Romania's Communist past because so many of its members were exnomenklatura.

Playing on Romanians' fears of the intentions of the Hungarian minorities and the future, Iliescu was reelected president and the DNSF won the largest proportion of seats in parliament, but, being short of a majority, the party had to form a coalition to govern. On July 10, 1993, the DNSF changed its name to Party of Social Democracy in Romania to emphasize its commitment to a form of social democracy, though the party failed to spell out exactly what it meant by "Social Democracy". After four years of economic stagnation and inflation, the PSDR lost control of parliament in the fall 1996 elections and Iliescu failed to win a third term as president.

BIBLIOGRAPHY

Rady, Martyn. *Romania in Turmoil: A Contemporary History.* London: IB Tauris & Co. Ltd., 1992.

Robert Forrest

SEE ALSO Iliescu, Ion; Roman, Petre

National Salvation Front Political group that replaced Romania's Communist regime in 1989. The National Salvation Front (FSN) was formed in the wake of the December 22, 1989, popular rising against Nicolae Ceauşescu, the Romanian dictator. It emerged from the need to unite the youth and intellectuals who had toppled Ceauşescu and to provide them with enough military power to prevent his return. The army's price for joining the revolution that ousted Ceausescu was that serious politicians, not artists or intellectuals, head the new government. Ion Iliescu, a moderate reformer whom Ceauşescu had demoted, became the Front's leader because both the generals and the revolutionaries trusted him. He chose Petre Roman, an engineering professor, as his assistant. The Front included generals, bureaucrats, intellectuals, and artists to obtain a consensus capable of restoring order.

It was a fragile consensus. The concerns of the generals and bureaucrats for their careers conflicted with the desires of the technocrats and the young intellectuals to purge more than just the top Communist leaders to bring democracy, freedom, and capitalism to Romania. When the Front decided to perpetuate itself by becoming a political party in January 1990, the intellectuals left it. Since they were the least-organized part of the consensus, their loss did not destroy the Front.

Because of the Front's victory in the May 1990 elections, Roman became prime minister and Iliescu president. While Iliescu's policy of gradual reform did not threaten former Communist officials, he still faced the aspirations of Roman and the technocrats for rapid, sweeping reform. Iliescu's policy prevailed when he dismissed Roman in September 1991, but Roman split the NSF in March 1992. Most of its members created a rival Democratic National Salvation Front, and Roman's FSN finished third in the fall 1992 general elections. Roman merged it with the small Democratic Party in May 1993 to distance himself from Iliescu and gradualism. By 1996 the Democratic Party-FSN DP-FSN had shortened itself to the Democratic Party.

BIBLIOGRAPHY

Rady, Martyn. *Romania in Turmoil: A Contemporary History.* London: IB Tauris & Co. Ltd., 1992.

Robert Forrest

SEE ALSO Iliescu, Ion; Roman, Petre

Economy

Romania is one of the poorer countries of eastern Europe. It entered the transitional period from communism with a distorted economy and an obsolete industrial infrastructure.

At the end of World War II, Romania was an overwhelmingly agricultural country. What industry existed, other than oil, was centered principally around the capital, Bucharest. Collectivization of agriculture was completed by 1962, but there was a further organizational arrangement of multivillage agri-complexes. Some private retail marketing was permitted in town markets run by the state, and agricultural produce increased markedly between 1970 and 1977. Approximately one-third of Romania's agricultural production came from the 9.4 percent of Romanian farmland held by private farmers and the plots allotted to members of collectives. After 1979, however, shortages developed as President Nicolae Ceauşescu sought hard currency to pay back the loans taken out to finance additional industrial expansion in the early 1970s by increased exports of food, especially meat, from the collectives.

With the consolidation of agriculture into collectives, many rural workers were rendered redundant. They provided a surplus labor force for the rapid state-sponsored industrialization championed by the Stalinist model adopted by Romanian Communists. As much as 35 percent of GDP was reinvested in industrial expansion. The obverse of this was the low level of consumption, but the goal of Romanian communism was heavy industry rather than production of consumer goods. In the 1980s massive hydroelectric projects were constructed. A nuclear power plant was constructed and the expansion of giant steel complexes were also undertaken.

Toward the end of his regime, despite evident problems, including the shortage of raw materials, Ceauşescu stubbornly persisted with his centralized, heavy-industrial model. Romania's external debt was eliminated, with a concomitant increase in popular misery. During Ceauşescu's last years food was rationed and cities regularly went without electricity and gas.

After paying off the country's external debt in April 1989, Ceauşescu, instead of easing up on the people, whose dire plight led workers in Brasov to riot in November 1987, continued his scheme of razing villages and constructing agro-industrial centers. He also demolished a historic section of Bucharest to construct a grossly monumental presidential palace in a country overwhelmed by misery.

After the overthrow of Ceauşescu, there was no effort to restructure the economy for some time. Ceauşescu's budgetary surplus amassed in the last year of his reign was depleted within two years when the new government used it to finance food imports. Finally, in 1996, a government was elected committed to economic restructuring. The government introduced emergency measures to promote social and political stability but ultimately placed its hope in privatization, fiscal and monetary reform, and the attraction of foreign investment.

Romania's per capita GDP in 1996 was estimated to be $5,200. As much as 36.4 percent of its labor force was still employed in agriculture. Its inflation rate ran at an annual 56.9 percent.

Romania at the end of the 1990s was continuing its difficult transition to a market economy. Its GDP contracted by approximately 6.6 percent in 1997 and by 7.3 percent in 1998. As a result of a tight monetary policy, inflation in 1998 declined to 41 percent from its level of 152 percent in 1997. A large current account deficit, however, persisted as did high payments on external debt.

BIBLIOGRAPHY

Shoemaker, M. Wesley. *Russia, Eurasian States, and Eastern Europe 1994.* Harpers Ferry, W.V.: Stryker-Post, 1994.

Bernard Cook

România mâre (Greater Romania)

Influential extremist weekly newspaper launched in June 1990 by Eugen Barbu and Corneliu Vadim Tudor, who had been hagiographers of the Ceauşescu dictatorship. It articulated the fears and uncertainties of a range of social groups discomfited by rapid political change. From the outset it made an impact by its capacity to shock as well as to amuse and titillate. The formula for the paper was devised by trained propagandists who had gained experience in spreading sublimated nationalist images among a desensitized population.

România mâre not only alleged numerous foreign conspiracies against the country, but claimed that it had been under continuous siege from enemies like Hungary as well as "internal occult forces" in the pay of the Vatican or unnamed Western interests. The paper attacked those who advocated a democracy based on civic values and promoted instead an ethnically based state. It lauded national institutions such as the military and the Orthodox Church as embodiments of the national will. It defined liberty only in terms of freedom from foreign rule, and sought to exploit disillusionment with the new freedoms acquired after 1989 in the midst of collapsing living standards.

BIBLIOGRAPHY

Gallagher, Tom. *Romania after Ceausescu: The Politics of Intolerance.* Edinburgh, Scotland: Edinburgh University Press, 1995.

Tom Gallagher

SEE ALSO Barbu, Eugen; Tudor, Corneliu Vadim

Rommel, Manfred (1928–)

Christian Democratic mayor of Stuttgart, Germany. The only son of Lucie Maria Mollin and Field Marshal Erwin Rommel, Manfred Rommel was elected mayor of Stuttgart in 1974. From the liberal wing of the Christian Democratic Party, Rommel governed in a cordial coalition with the Social Democrats. Through a pragmatic mixture of liberalism and conservatism, he helped to transform the city into a dynamic economic and social center of the Federal Republic of Germany. The voters of Stuttgart showed their overwhelming approval of his policies by electing him to a second term in 1982 with 69.8 percent of the vote.

James L. Newsom

Ronchi, Edo (1950–)

Italian Green politician. Edo Ronchi was born in Treviglio on May 31, 1950. He studied electrical engineering at the Politecnico di Milano. He joined the Lega per l'Ambiente (League for the Environment) in 1983 and became a member of its national steering committee in 1989. He was elected to the Chamber of Deputies (lower house of parliament) in 1983 and became a member of the Commission on the Environment and Public Works. In parliament he led battles against unauthorized construction and pollution. In 1987 he became a member of Democracza Proletaria (Proletarian Democracy).

In 1989 Ronchi, with Francesco Rutelli, at that time a member of parliament for the Radical Party and subsequently mayor of Rome, founded the environmentalist Verdi Arcobaleno (Green Rainbow), and he was its national spokesman until its fusion with the Green List and development of a national federation in 1991. To pursue this project in 1989, he resigned his seat on the European Parliament after only one month. After the 1992 election he was the leader of the Greens in the Italian Senate. Following the 1996 election Ronchi, who drafted the environmental position of the Olive Tree alliance, a center-left electoral coalition victorious in the 1996 parliamentary election became part of the government of Romano Prodi as minister of the environment.

BIBLIOGRAPHY

"Intervista con il ministro dell'ambiente. Edo Ronchi, Gli incentivi 'verdi.'" *La Lettera d'Automobile,* September 1997.

Bernard Cook

SEE ALSO Rutelli, Francesco

Rugova, Ibrahim (1944–)

Leader of the Kosovar Albanians of Kosovo. Ibrahim Rugova was born in 1944 in the village of Cerce, in the Ostog district of Kosovo. When he was an infant his father and grandfather were shot by Communist Yugoslav Partisans as they re-established Yugoslav control over Kosovo after the Germans and Italians, who had occupied Kosovo during World War II, were driven out. He studied literature in Pristina and won a scholarship to the University of Paris, Sorbonne, in 1975. After receiving a Ph.D. in literary studies in Paris he taught and wrote in Kosovo. He is a specialist in literary history and wrote a study of the writings of a seventeenth century Albanian archbishop, Pjetër Bogbani.

After the stripping of autonomy from Kosovo by the Serbian nationalist Slobodan Milošević in 1990, Rugova became president of the Democratic League of Kosovo (DSK) and in 1992 was elected president of the "Republic of Kosovo." Rugova was at the same time the coordinator of an organization based in Pristina that represented all of the Albanian parties of Kosovo, Montenegro, and Macedonia.

The Republic of Kosovo did not receive recognition from the international community, but that did not prevent Rugova from declaring that, if the Serbs in Bosnia confederate with Serbia, Kosovo will confederate with Albania. He recommended an international protectorate as a transitional solution. For Rugova, the Albanians are Illyrians, an ancient Indo-European people, who have been in place for two millennia and are the true indigenous people of the region. He counted on the bad international image of the Serbians to bring about the recognition of his party.

Rugova and the Albanian Democratic League of Kosovo (LDK) urged the Albanians of Kosovo to limit themselves to peaceful protests. However, Kosovo and the plight of its majority was ignored in the Dayton-Paris Peace Accords. 1996 and 1997 witnessed the growth of a Kosovo Liberation Army (KLA, UCK in Albanian), which staged numerous armed attacks on Serbian police and civilians and on Albanians accused of collaborating with the Serbs. The activity of KLA, supported by a growing number of LDK leaders, was countered by a policy of repression by the Serbians. After prolonged and fruitless negotiations with the US special envoy Richard C. Holbrooke, Milošević was finally swayed by a credible threat of NATO bombing. On October 13 he agreed to withdraw his forces, to allow NATO verification of this, to permit 2,000 unarmed civilian monitors into Kosovo, and to grant partial autonomy to the province. This, however, proved to be merely a tactical retreat. His forces launched a new effort in January 1999 against the KLA and the Albanian peasant communities. The atrocities committed by the Serbs were aimed at driving the Albanian population from the province. After futile negotiations in France, NATO, which had once again thought that the threat of bombing would be enough to prevent Milosevic from destablizing the area and, perhaps, provoking a wider war, was forced, for the sake of its credibility to act. During the war Rugova's credibility with the KLA was undermined as he appeared on Serbian television with Miloševič and made conciliatory statements. After the war, Rugova, who is still regarded as president by the LDK, returned to Kosovo and attempted to regain his leadership role, and though supported by many moderate Kosovar Albanians, was marginalized by the KLA and its leader, Hashim Thaci.

BIBLIOGRAPHY

Carlen, Jean Yves, Stève Duchêne, and Joël Ehrhart. *Ibrahim Rugova: le frêle colosse du Kosovo.* Paris: Desclée de Brouwer, 1999.

Glenny, Misha. "Bosnia II," *New York Times*, December 9, 1997, A21.

———. *The Fall of Yugoslavia: The Third Balkan War.* New York: Penguin, 1993.

Hall, Brian. *The Impossible Country: A Journey through the Last Days of Yugoslavia.* New York: Penguin, 1994.

Hedges, Chris, "In New Balkan Tinderbox, Ethnic Albanians Rebel against Serbs," *New York Times*, March 2, 1998.

Malcom, Noel. *Kosovo: A Short History.* New York: New York University Press, 1998.

Catherine Lutard
Bernard Cook

SEE ALSO Kosovo: Ethnic Cleansing and War; Vllasi, Azem

Rumor, Mariano (1915–90)

Several times prime minister in the center-left governments of Italy from 1968 to 1974. Mariano Rumor played outstanding roles as minister of agriculture, and of home and foreign affairs. From 1964 to 1968 he was also secretary of the Christian Democratic Party. In 1979 he was appointed senator and was elected to the European Parliament.

Rumor's cultural and political background was rooted in the social Roman Catholic movement. An activist in Catholic associations, he joined the resistance against the Germans during World War II and was a member of the National Liberation Committee. A member of the Constituent Assembly and elected to the first parliament in 1946, Rumor was one of the Christian Democratic Party's "second generation" and implemented a new political trend by mediating between those who had not participated in the old Popular Party and the policy of Alcide De Gasperi, the founder and leader of the post-war Christian Democratic Party.

As a statesman he demonstrated remarkable qualities, characterized by balance and resoluteness, in a historical period tormented by the Hot Autumn, a wave of Strikes in 1969, the 1968 student movement, the 1969 Piazza Fontana outrage, a terrorist attack in Milan, and various forms of terrorism.

BIBLIOGRAPHY

Ghirotti, Gigi. *Rumor.* Milan: Longanesi, 1970.

Graziani, Pier Antonio. "Mariano Rumor," in *Il Parlamento Italiano 1861–1988,* Vol. 20. Milan: Nuova CEI, 1992, 297–314.

Malgeri, Francesco, ed. *Stòria della Democrazia Christiana,* 5 Vols. Rome: Cinque Lune, 1987–89.

Rumor, Mariano. *Memorie 1943–1970.* Ed. by Ermenegildo Reato and Francesco Malgeri. Vicenza: Neri Pozza, 1991.

Sbalchiero, Pino, ed. *Grazie Mariano Rumor.* Quaderni de "Il momento vicentino", no. 1, Vicenza: Il momento vicentino, 1990.

Rumor's Archives are kept by his family and are being catalogued in Vicenza.

Walter E. Crivellin

SEE ALSO Fanfani, Amintore; Movo, Aldo

Russell, Bertrand (1872–1970)

English philosopher and writer who used logical analysis to define his views on metaphysics and ethics and attempted to use logic as a moral persuader. One of the twentieth century's most vocal champions of freedom and liberty, Bertrand Russell won the Nobel Prize in literature in 1950.

Orphaned at three, Russell was raised by his grandmother in Richmond Park, where he was privately tutored. He went on to Trinity College, Cambridge, where he so distinguished himself that, after a short stay in Paris as a diplomat at the British Embassy, he was made a fellow of his college in 1895. He was invited to join the Royal Society in 1908, and in 1910 he became a fellow at Trinity College.

Russell's thought and writing was influenced by the liberalism of John Stuart Mill and his friendship with Alfred North Whitehead, with whom he produced Principia Mathematica, in which they attempted to demonstrate that mathematics can be deduced from a small number of logical principles. During World War I he lost his lectureship at Trinity College because of his pacifist views. He was offered a post at Harvard University but was refused a visa. Pacifist ideals would continue to mark his later life and politics. Russell published his wartime thoughts as *Political Ideals* and served a six-month prison term for a pacifist article that appeared in the *Tribunal* during World War I.

On his release from prison Russell earned his living by lecturing and writing. When his brother died in 1931, Russell became the third earl of Kingston. He returned to Britain in 1944 after a prolonged stay in the United States and gave a series of radio lectures on philosophy. He continued these in the after World War II period as he sounded the alarm against nuclear war, calling it "man's peril." In 1945 he produced *A History of Western Philosophy,* followed by *Human Knowledge, Scope and Limits* (1948) and *Unpopular Essays* (1950). His utopian instincts were expressed in *New Hopes for a Changing World* (1951) and *Human Society in Ethics and Politics* (1954).

With the explosion of the hydrogen bomb by the United States in 1952, Russell increasingly became an antinuclear activist. He organized the Pugwash conferences in Nova Scotia, which brought together scientists from the West and East to discuss the nuclear threat and world security, and in 1958 the Campaign for Nuclear Disarmament. He was arrested in England in 1961 during an antinuclear war demonstration but later played a less directly confrontational role by organizing the antinuclear Bertrand Russell Peace Foundation. In his later years he lived in North Wales and wrote his *Autobiography* (1967).

BIBLIOGRAPHY

Blackwell, Kenneth. *A Bibliography of Bertrand Russell.* London: Rutledge, 1994.

Kuntz, Paul Grimley. *Bertrand Russell.* Boston: Twayne, 1986.

Moorehead, Caroline. *Bertrand Russell: A Life.* New York: Viking, 1992.

Russell, Bertrand. *My Philosophical Development.* New York: Simon and Schuster, 1959.

Barbara Bennett Peterson

Russia

Successor state to the Russian Soviet Federated Socialist Republic. Russia (Russian Federation) became an independent political entity as a result of the collapse of the Soviet Union, sealed by the December 8, 1991, Minsk Agreement among Boris Yeltsin, president of the Russian Federation; Leonid Kravchuk, president of Ukraine; and Stanislav Shushkevic, president of Belarus, which established the Commonwealth of Independent States (CIS).

Russia is the largest country in the world. Its 6,592,800 square miles (17,075,400 sq km) make it almost two times the size of either the United States or China. With 147 million inhabitants, in 1998 it is the sixth most populous country in the world. It is bordered on the north by the Arctic Ocean; on the east by the

Russia. *Illustration courtesy of Bernard Cook.*

The autonomous regions of Russia. *Illustration courtesy of Bernard Cook.*

Bering Sea, the Pacific Ocean, the Sea of Okhotsk, and the Sea of Japan; on the south by North Korea, China, Mongolia, Kazakhstan, the Caspian Sea, Azerbaijan, Georgia, the Black Sea, and Ukraine; and on the west by Belarus, Latvia, Estonia, the Gulf of Finland, Finland, and Norway. Its discontinuous appendage, the Kaliningrad Oblast, is bordered by the Baltic Sea, Poland, and Lithuania.

On December 25, 1991, President Mikhail Gorbachev, the last leader of the USSR, resigned, turning over control of the former USSR's nuclear arsenal to President Boris Yeltsin, and Russia stepped into the former USSR's seat in the U.N. General Assembly and its seat on the Security Council. The CIS had agreed to keep conventional forces as well as nuclear forces under a single command, but as the former Soviet republics of Ukraine, Moldova, and Azerbaijan organized their own national armies, the unified command idea fell by the way. The CIS agreement also envisioned the members forming an economic unit, but this plan faltered as well. When a severe imbalance of trade developed in Russia's favor with the other members of the CIS, Russia, concerned with their excessive spending, abandoned its support for a single ruble zone in mid-1992. In Russia Yeltsin freed prices in accord with the free-market policy being preached by the shock therapists. The subsequent rapid increase in prices hurt many and led to opposition in the Supreme Soviet (Parliament), which had granted Yeltsin the power in December 1991 to rule by decree for a year. Its speaker, Ruslan Khasbulatov, became the leader of the anti–shock therapy majority. With opponents of Yeltsin's policy in charge of the State Bank, a flood of currency was issued to permit inefficient state enterprises to operate and pay their workers. Led by Khasbulatov, the Congress of People's Deputies, the lower house of parliament established by the Soviet Constitution of 1988, denied Yeltsin an extension of his power to rule by decree and failed by only a few votes to transform him into a figurehead. It repudiated the reform program of acting Prime Minister Yegor Gaidar and refused to endorse him as prime minister. When Yeltsin threatened to organize a referendum on his reform policy, the Congress backtracked. With Valery Zorkin, chairman of Russia's Constitutional Court, acting as mediator, a compromise was reached. Yeltsin was allowed to retain his emergency powers for four more months and a referendum on a new constitution would be held in April 1993. Yeltsin also agreed to appoint a prime minister acceptable to the Congress majority. His choice, Viktor Chernomyrdin, who had served on the staff of the Central Committee of the Communist Party of the USSR, however, continued the economic policy of his predecessor. When members of the Supreme Soviet, the upper house of the parliament, developed misgivings about a referendum that might put an end to their jobs, and Yeltsin was warned by the heads of the regional governments, the governors and presidents of the 21 republics, 49 regions, six territories, and ten autonomous areas, which constituted the Russian Federation of Federal Republic, that the referendum might ignite a popular explosion, Khasbulatov and Yeltsin agreed to delay the referendum and work together. The full Congress, which reconvened on March 10, was less malleable. It voted to rescind Yeltsin's right to vote by decree. Yeltsin responded by announcing a referendum that would serve as a vote of confidence for his presidency. It would be held on April 25 and in the meantime Yeltsin affirmed that he would ignore the Congress and the Supreme Soviet. Vice President Aleksandr Rutskoi and Justice Zorkin denounced Yeltsin's action as unconstitutional, a judgment confirmed by the full Constitutional Court. A vote for impeachment in the Congress gained a majority but fell short of the necessary 66 percent. The referendum went forward, with added questions relating to elections for the president and a new parliament. Yeltsin won the support he was seeking. He then attempted to take advantage of his victory at the polls to circumvent the Congress. He called representatives from the regional governments to Moscow on April 29 and presented them with a draft constitution. He asked for their comments and for the appointment of two delegates from each republic and region to meet at the end of May to modify and ratify the draft. After a month of deliberation, more than two-thirds of the members of the constituent assembly approved a modified draft, which was submitted to the republics and regions of the Russian Federation for ratification.

The Supreme Soviet moved to preempt the president by vastly increasing the level of state spending in the government's proposed budget, which they labeled "antisocial." The president was powerless against this threat to destroy his reform through hyperinflation. He vetoed the budget twice, but the Supreme Soviet was prepared to override his veto by passing it for a third time on September 22. On September 21 Yeltsin announced that parliament had been disbanded and that a new parliament would be elected on December 11 and 12. The Supreme Soviet, led by Khasbulatov, voted almost immediately to remove Yeltsin and replace him with Rutskoi. Yeltsin was supported by Chernomyrdin and his cabinet, the police, and the army. After a two-week standoff, when the parliamentarians collected arms and barricaded themselves in the parliament building, Yeltsin ordered the police to surround the building and ordered the heat, water, and electricity cut off.

On October 3 a crowd of parliamentary supporters broke through the police lines. Urged on by Rutskoi, they attempted to seize the main television broadcast center. Yeltsin then ordered the army to attack the parliament with troops and tanks. Rutskoi and Khasbulatov were taken prisoner. Yeltsin then proceeded with the December election and broadened it into a referendum on the new constitution. The results were a repudiation of Yeltsin. Of the 450 seats in the lower house of the new parliament, the State Duma, half were to be filled by proportional representation. Radical nationalist Vladimir Zhirinovsky's misnamed party, Liberal Democratic Party (LDPR), won the largest number of proportional votes, 22.8 percent. Russia's Choice, the party of market reformer Yegor Gaidar, won 15.4 percent of the proportional votes, but because of its individual representative vote and the subsequent adherence of individuals elected as independents, it emerged with the largest contingent, 76 seats. The New Regional Policy, comprised of 65 centrist independents, formed the second-largest electoral group. Zhirinovsky's party was third with 64. But the Communists (CPRF) won 48 seats, and its allies the Agrarian Party and Women of Russia, 33 and 23, respectively. The only other firm supporter of Yeltsin's reforms besides Russia's Choice was the economist and proponent of economic reform Gregory Yavlinsky's Yabloko, an electoral group that promoted free reform and the rooting out of corruption, with 25 seats. The other parties all opposed shock therapy or even liberal market reform. The tenor of the parliament can be measured by the fact that a Communist, Ivan Rybkin, was elected speaker. The upper house, the Federation Council, was more supportive of Yeltsin, but after the election all the economic reformers left the government. Chernomyrdin, nevertheless, proceeded with a program that gained the support of the International Monetary Fund (IMF).

In January 1994 Yeltsin gradually formed a new government, with Chernomyrdin remaining as prime minister. But reformers Boris Federov and Gaidar were forced out. The Duma granted amnesties to Rutskoi, Khasbulatov, and other leaders of the parliamentary rebellion but also for the leaders of the attempted hard-line coup of August 19, 1991, against Gorbachev.

Despite the promotion of the reform-minded champion of privatization Anatoly Chubais to first deputy chairman of the government in November, the government moved away from further economic reform and sought to distract the public from dramatic inflation and counter its opponents in the Duma by a military victory. In December 1994, after the humiliating failure the previous month of an attempt to oust the breakaway regime of Dzhokhar Dudayev in the rebellious Russian province Chechnya, utilizing some dissident Chechens aided by Russia armor, Yeltsin's advisers decided to stage a major campaign that they thought would easily overwhelm the Chechens and give the Yeltsin administration a needed boost with the Russian public. Their faulty evaluation of the task before them and the inadequacy of their preparations brought disaster. Instead of bolstering the Yeltsin government, the Chechen war proved to be a humiliating defeat that cast its shadow over the Yeltsin government.

The results of the December 17, 1995, elections for the State Duma reflected the disenchantment of the Russian electorate with Yeltsin. The Communist Party emerged first of the forty-three contending parties and electoral blocs, while Zhirinovsky's Liberal Democrats were second. Chernomyrdin's Our Home is Russia and Yabloko also made a respectable showing. None of the other parties reached the 5 percent necessary to gain proportional seats. The Communists also won the largest number of single-seat constituencies and were therefore the largest party by far, with 157 delegates. A Communist, Gennady Seleznev, was elected chairman of the Duma, but the Communists did not have enough votes to pass legislation without the backing of the Agrarians and independents.

Nevertheless, in response to the success of the CPRF and the LDPR, Yeltsin restructured his government. Andrey Kozyrev, who had been criticized by the opposition for being too accommodating to the West, was replaced as foreign minister by Yevgeny Primakov, who was perceived as being more inclined to defend Russia's interest against the West. Chubais was replaced as first deputy chairman by Vladimir Kanannikov, a critic of the latter's privatization program, and Yegorov replace the liberal Sergey Filatov as head of the Presidential Administration. However, Aleksandr Kazakov, who supported reform, was appointed in place of Sergey Belyayev as chairman of the State Committee for State Property Management.

As the conflict in Chechnya dragged on, the incompetence and brutality of the Russian forces became glaringly evident. Following the successful forays of Chechen fighters led by the field commander Shamil Basayev at Budyonnovsk in Southern Russia in June 1995 and by Salman Raduyev, a Chechen rebel leader, at Kizlyar-Pervomayskoye in Dagestan, next to Chechnya, in January 1996, Yeltsin's embarrassment was total. Despite the killing of Dudayev in April 1996, the war dragged on and cast its shadow over the impending presidential election. In mid-February, despite serious questions about his health, Yeltsin formally announced his intention to seek a second term as president. His principal rivals were Communist Zyuganov and Aleksandr Lebed, former commander of the Fourteenth Russian Army in a Section of Moldava east of the Dnester River. In the June 16 primary Yeltsin received 35.8 percent of the vote, but close behind was Zyuganov with 32.5 percent. Lebed received 14.7, trailed by Yavlinsk and Zhirinovsky. To secure the support of Lebed, Yelstin appointed him secretary of the Security Council of the Russian Federation and national security adviser, empowered to solve the war in Chechnya. Defense Minister Pavel Grachev, who had been a proponent of the attack on Chechnya and an advocate of a military solution, was dismissed, as were several other members of the government and seven generals. Despite attempts by military leaders and civilian politicians to sabotage his effort, Lebed negotiated a cease-fire with the new Chechen leadership in August 1996.

In the second round of the presidential vote on July 3, 1996, Yeltsin with the support of Lebed and Yavlinsky, won 54 percent of the vote to Zyuganov's 40 percent. Despite, or perhaps because of, Lebed's success he came under attack. Yeltsin, in consummate ingratitude, publicly took Lebed to task for not settling the crisis more quickly and openly expressed his support for Anatoly Kulikov. Kulikov, who had commanded Russian forces in Chechnya, had been appointed minister of internal affairs in July 1995 after the humiliating display of Russian weakness and ineptitude at Budyonnovsk. Lebed had demanded his replacement and Kulikov, for his part, had stridently denounced the settlement negotiated by Lebed. The publicly acknowledged recurrence of Yeltsin's heart problems and the announcement that he would undergo surgery opened the possibility of a factional struggle between the supporters of Chernomyrdin and Lebed within the government. Unrest and strikes over unpaid wages and food and power shortages were accompanied by warnings from Lebed of the danger of an upheaval in the military. In the middle of October 1996 Lebed was suddenly dismissed by Yeltsin following the claim by Kulikov that Lebed was plotting a coup. If Yeltsin had hoped to consign Lebed to political oblivion the move miscarried. In May 1998 Lebed successfully challenged Valery Zubov, the incumbent governor of Krasnoyarsk, a politically and economically important region in Siberia. Despite support for Zubov from Yeltsin and the CPRF, Lebed, who had explicitly stated that he intended to use the post as a launching pad for the 2000 presidential campaign, won 57 percent of the vote.

When Yeltsin underwent heart surgery in early November, he transferred presidential powers to Chernomyrdin. Yeltsin reassumed presidential duties late in December, but was hospitalized shortly afterward for pneumonia. There were growing demands for his resignation or impeachment. Yeltsin's physical incapacity was all the more troublesome because of continuing economic problems and the unrest generated by them. In March 1997 Yeltsin blamed Chernomyrdin for failing to prevent a worsening of the conditions of most Russians and for failing to stem widespread corruption. Nevertheless, unwilling to face a confirmation vote in the Duma for a new prime minister, Yeltsin retained Chernomyrdin but reshuffled the cabinet to emphasize reform. Chubais became first deputy chairman and minister of finance, and Boris Nemtsov, the successful governor of Russian region (oblest) of Nizhnii Novgorod, entered the government as first deputy chairman with responsibility for privatizing state monopolies. After two million demonstrators took to the streets toward the end of March to protest unpaid wages, Yeltsin spoke out against corruption in the government and the government-controlled sector of the economy.

On March 23, 1998, Yeltsin dismissed his entire government, including Chernomyrdin, to establish a government that would respond better with "energy and efficiency to economic reforms." Observers, however, suggested that the move had been in response to pressure from powerful business interests, which objected to the policies of Chernomyrdin and Chubais. Chubais, in particular, had sought to limit the influence exerted by business on the government. Politically well-connected industrialist Boris Berezovsky was at odds both with Chubais and Chernomyrdin, who had recently approved the sale of the state-owned petroleum concern, Rosneft, to business rivals. Perhaps the move was also motivated by Yeltsin's pique at the idea that he had been rendered irrelevant because of his illnesses. Yeltsin appointed Sergey Kiriyenko, who had been earlier dismissed from his post as minister of energy, to succeed Chernomyrdin. The day after the ouster of the government, Yeltsin backtracked and it was announced that Yevgeny Primakov would retain the foreign ministry and that Igor Sergeyev would retain the ministry of defense. When some in the Duma balked at Kiriyenko's youth (thirty-five) and his inexperience, Yeltsin threatened to dissolve the Duma. Though the Duma twice voted against Kiriyenko, it retreated on the third vote rather than face dissolution and a new election.

On August 23, a week after Kiriyenko's government devalued the ruble in an effort to avert financial collapse, Yeltsin dismissed him and announced that he was reappointing Chernomyrdin as prime minister. Nevertheless, the crisis deepened. The ruble dropped rapidly; foreign investors pulled funds from the country; and Russian banks faced currency shortages. The government moved to restructure state bonds and as a result cost foreign investors and Russian banks billions of dollars. After a futile effort to support the ruble, which cost the central bank additional billions of dollars, the effort was halted. On August 27 the central bank suspended trading in the ruble to prevent its collapse. Reformer Nemtsov, who had been Kiriyenko's political mentor, blamed Kiriyenko's exit on an oligarchy of bankers and oil company executives who feared reforms by the prime minister.

Yeltsin's attempt to replace Kiriyenko with Chernomyrdin was rejected by the Duma. Rather than push the nomination for the third vote, which if rejected again would have plunged the country into a political campaign in the midst of an economic and social crisis and perhaps might have led to civil conflict, Yeltsin retreated. On September 10, following negotiations with the Communist leadership, Yeltsin withdrew Chernomyrdin's nomination and nominated Primakov, who was acceptable to both the Communists and Yeltsin. In the first months of his government, composed of a mixture of centrists, reformers, and Communists, no coherent policy to deal with the country's many crises emerged. Money was printed to keep the government running and to begin the payment of wage arrears. To warnings of inflationary pressures, the government responded that it was controlling the amount of money placed in circulation. Nevertheless, IMF loans were temporarily suspended.

On May 12, 1999, Yeltsin, whose own popularity had shrunk to the low single digits, fired Primikov, who at the time was ranked the most popular politician in Russia. Primakov's popularity and independence contributed to his ouster. Wishing to maintain power Yeltsin replaced Primakov with Sergei Stepashin, a thorough Yeltsin loyalist. On August 10, 1999, Stepashin was fired by Yeltsin, after less than three months in office, and replaced by Vladimir V. Putin, the head of Russia's domestic intelligence service. Stepashin's ouster can be attributed to his failure to become a credible presidential candidate capable of winning the up coming 2000 presidential election and protecting Yeltsin and his associates from prosecution for corruption. Yeltsin apparently found both requisites in Putin. Putin launched a military campaign against breakaway Chechnya at the end of September. The Russian invasion was in response to Chechen attacks in Dagestan and the bombing of three apartment buildings in Russia, attributed by the Russian government to the Chechens. Though the Russian campaign did not proceed as swiftly as predicted by the government and the army, the decisive action directed by Putin won him wide popularity. On December 31, Yeltsin unexpectedly announced that he was stepping down and handing the presidency over to Putin on January 1, 2000. Putin had made a number of concessions to Yeltsin. Yeltsin was promised immunity from prosecution, a generous retirement allowance, and a number of perquisites. A presidential election was held March 2000 and Putin was elected to a full term of office.

Yeltsin was the dominant figure in Russia from 1991 to 2000. His best hour was his defiance of the attempted hard-line coup on August 19, 1991. He will be remembered as the destroyer of the Soviet Union and the creator of the Russian Republic. Though Yeltsin retired from the presidency with Russia's new formal democracy intact, he did not direct Russia's transion to a market economy well or consistently, and he did not effectively deal with the problems of crime and corruption.

BIBLIOGRAPHY

Shoemaker, M. Wesley. *Russia, Eurasian States, and Eastern Europe, 1995.* Washington, D.C.: Stryker-Post, 1995.

Suny, Ronald Grigor. *The Soviet Experiment: Russia, the USSR, and the Successor States.* New York: Oxford University Press, 1998.

Wegs, J. Robert, and Robert Ladrech. *Europe since 1945: A Concise History,* 4th ed. New York: St. Martin's Press, 1996.

Bernard Cook

SEE ALSO Chechnya

Political Parties

Democracy based on participatory political parties as understood in the United States and Western Europe has not been comprehensible to most Russians. Democratic political values, attitudes, and beliefs as well as the skills necessary to implement them have only begun to take root since 1989. In Russia to date there are no historical or behavioral inclinations toward the creation of a full-fledged competitive political party system. The historical gulf that separated the governed from the governors—whether czars, Politburo members, or current governors—has not been bridged. The largest number of Russians have no obvious sense of political efficacy. Even late-twentieth-century rulers seem more concerned with maintaining their power than providing for Russians' general welfare. The government is faced with the daunting dual challenge of creating a unique democratic state at the same time as it needs to produce policies that will satisfy Russians' fundamental need for security at the international level and the desire for domestic well-being. Most successful democracies have decades to deal with the challenge of developing a participatory political system and establishing a legitimate means for insuring national security and their citizens' ability to share in the economic benefits of nationhood. Russia has had no such leeway. On the contrary, the task of Russia's leaders has become all the more difficult because of the expectations associated with its former superpower-nuclear status. Russian leaders are trapped by the rhetorical expectations of their immediate, ideologically dominated past, and the yet-to-be fulfilled hopes of the new Russia. In the tumultuous transition from the USSR to the successor states, there have been civil wars, insurrections, and an attempted coup. It is no wonder that the Russian political party system is as unique as Russia's political social history.

There is no majority political party in Russia, nor is there one type of political party that can be readily compared with dominant types of political parties found in the United States and Western Europe. Instead, there are groups of political sentiments that are apparent precursors to aggregative political parties. Among the traditional Marxist-Leninist parties is the successor to the Communist Party of the Soviet Union (CPSU), the Communist Party of the Russian Federation (CPRF); a number of smaller Communist-oriented parties centering on Communist leaders; and a rural reflection, the Agrarian Party, which articulates nostalgic sentiments for collective agriculture. The roots of these parties are singular and they are heirs to the conspiratorial party model created by V. I. Lenin as an engine to drive the Russian Revolution of 1917. Under the Soviet regimes the CPSU was a relatively small party, carefully recruiting and currying members, often more times for loyalty to Marxist-Leninist ideology than for competence. Because it was the only party permitted by law, it could and did penetrate every aspect of Soviet society. According to the last Soviet constitution, the Soviet state was still the handmaiden of the party. Given this historically preeminent status, high level of discipline, and tight organization, Communists endured a government-inspired backlash to their long, desultory rule. They managed to survive the chaotic transition to the current regime as the largest although not majority party in the Russian Duma, the lower house of the bicameral legislature, with 157 seats out of 450. In the 1996 presidential elections, their candidate and the CPRF party head, Gennady Zyuganov, came in second behind Boris Yeltsin, who is not a formal member of any political party. Ideologically, the platforms of the various Communist successor parties represent reformed communism, at times verging on the position of the more left-wing socialist parties of Western Europe. The policy positions of the CPFR tend toward slowing down the "shock therapy" reforms generated by reform-minded government leaders and their legislative allies.

The other various, incipient political parties that competed for Duma seats, by and large, reflect the personalization of current Russian politics, and are characterized by a lack of organizational depth. This collection of quasi parties clustered around "notables" inhabit the right traditionalist/nationalist, center-right, reform, and center-left of the Russian political spectrum, along with whimsical groups such as the Beer Lovers' Party, which attracted 400,000 votes but won no seats in the legislature, given minimum vote numbers for representation there. In the 1996 Duma election the option "Against all Parties" received 2.75 percent of the total vote, suggesting political anomie and citizen alienation from the whole process.

Each of the groupings in the 1996 Duma election had front-runners. Among the former CPSU remnants, the CPRF received the largest number of votes and largest number of Duma seats, 157. In the right-traditionalist/nationalist group, the Liberal Democrats led by Vladimir Zhirnovsky received 51 seats. Zhirnovsky and his cohorts generally represented a romantic fixation with the czarist empire and restoring Russia to its "rightful" place in the international arena. Included in their free-form positions was regaining Alaska from the United States and reincorporating Ukraine and Belarus into Russia. The center-right was dominated by Our Home Is Russia, represented by 55 seats. This party supported President Boris Yeltsin and has worked closely with the government of Prime Minister Viktor Chernomyrdin supporting moderate reforms. Reformists splintered among ten groups, the largest of which was Yabloko, receiving 45 seats. Led by Grigory Yavlinsky, Yabloko offered a platform that focused on democratic principles and market-driven economics. This group, indicative of the personalistic nature of current Russian parties, derived its name from its founders' names, rather than any ideological vector. The center-left portion of the political spectrum was shared by eight groups, the largest of which was Women of Russia, represented with three seats. In addition to the obvious feminist orientation, the group's platform included commitments to "equal rights, equalization of opportunity, and partnership."

The number of parties represented in the Duma declined from the 1993 election to the 1996 elections, while the number of seats held by successful parties increased. Forty-three organizations applied to the election commission to run in the 1996 election. Some were hardly electoral organizations, with names such as Generation of the Frontier, Stable Russia, and For the Motherland. Others, in addition to those already mentioned, represent the beginnings of a multiparty system, pretending stability. These included Democratic Choice and the Congress of Russian Communities, now headed by former general, presidential candidate, and Yeltsin national security adviser, Aleksandr Lebed.

BIBLIOGRAPHY

Suny, Ronald Grigor. *The Soviet Experiment: Russia, the USSR, and the Successor States.* New York: Oxford University Press, 1998.

Conrad Raabe

Economy

Russia continues to experience severe difficulties associated with its attempt to shift from a centrally directed economy to a market economy. While 75 percent of Russia's industry has been privatized, agriculture has yet to be affected to any great degree by reform. The process of privatization has often been effected in a manner that witnessed the transfer of state assets to private holders with little social recompense. The rights of stockholders remain tenuous and corruption and criminality are widespread. Many enterprises operate in a legal and financial never-never land. Barter, increasing debts, and unpaid workers are widespread. According to state statistics, in 1996 the Russian economy declined for the fifth straight year. Gross domestic product (GDP) fell that year by 6 percent and industrial output by 5 percent. The anti-inflationary effort, however, had some success. Inflation fell from 131 percent in 1995 to a more manageable but still significant 22 percent in 1996. However, the level of unreported economic activity, estimated to run between 20 and 50 percent of Russia's GDP, probably means that the situation is not as dire as official statistics indicate. Real average incomes, inflated by the obscene profits of some "New Russians," (those who profited from the economic changes, sometimes by legally questionable means) grew by 8 percent from the beginning of 1993 to the end of 1996. The number of Russians living below the official poverty level was reported to have dropped from 33 percent to 28.6 percent by the end of 1998. Few Russians, according to the government, lacked basic necessities. The accumulation of consumer goods appeared to be growing significantly.

The government has been plagued by low tax collections, and government expenditures continue to be excessive in light of revenue. The outflow of capital is a serious problem. In fact, capital flight in the mid-1990s exceeded the inflow of foreign capital.

In 1998, suffering from the ramifications of the Asian economic crisis, the government let the ruble fall dramatically. In January 1997 a U.S. dollar could purchase 5,785 rubles. In January 1998 it required 9,7051 rubles to purchase a dollar, and by January 1999 the figure was 22,2876. The decline in oil prices hurt Russia's trade balance, tax delinquency continued to be a major problem, and the GDP contracted by a further 5 percent in 1998.

Bernard Cook

Cinema

Russian cinema was Soviet cinema, a state-controlled and Communist Party–monitored industry until the end of the Soviet Union in 1991. If we include the post-Communist present, we should thus speak of Russian cinema as having experienced five quite distinct periods since 1945. Cinema received a strong vote of confidence from the beginning from Vladimir Lenin the founder of the USSR who felt it was "the most important art" for its power to reach a basically illiterate public everywhere. Sergei Eisenstein, Vertov, and Pudovkin were just a few of the many filmmakers who brought silent Soviet cinema international praise.

World War II brought much Soviet filmmaking to a halt, while that which survived focused on producing patriotic, anti-German works to help the war effort. But a more profound change was that Moscow-based filmmakers, Russians for the most part, moved to the various Soviet republics and helped insure that almost invisible film industries in places such as Uzbekistan and Kazakhstan suddenly became creative and highly professional—an influence that helped these "non-Russian" cinemas long after the war.

The postwar period was still influenced by the doctrine of socialist realism developed in the 1930s for all Soviet art. These generally simplistic, often anticapitalist films were the standard fare until Stalin's death in 1953.

With Premier Nikita Khrushchev's denunciation of Stalin in 1956, a true thaw began that lasted until Leonid Brezhnev came to power in 1964. During this period the Soviet Union's most noted filmmaker of the past thirty years came of age. Andrey Tarkovsky was immediately seen as an important artist in 1962 when his *Ivan's Childhood* appeared. This highly personal, poetic look at World War II seen through the eyes of a young boy mixes memory, dreams, and reality in startling and haunting black-and-white photography. Clearly Tarkovsky's film suggested what could never have been implied before Stalin's death: it includes much spiritual and religious imagery and works overall as an antiwar film rather than as a traditional anti-German propaganda vehicle.

Despite difficulties with officials and frequent censorship of various forms, Tarkovsky became the undisputed film artist of his generation in a remarkable series of films that won much international attention and praise, including *Andrei Roublev* (1966), a long-banned portrait of one of Russia's greatest icon painters; *Solaris* (1972), *Mirror* (1975), *Stalker* (1979), *Nostalghia* (1983), and *The Sacrifice* (1986). Tarkovsky became a symbol of what a filmmaker could accomplish within and in spite of the Communist system to keep his own integrity and express a personal vision.

The "thaw" seen from today's perspective is all the more impressive for the variety of fine and often daring films made. Mikhail Kalatozov's *The Cranes Are Flying* (1957) was a sensitive portrayal of the hardships of the war seen from a woman's point of view; this "revisionist war" genre also included the much admired *Ballad of a Soldier* (1958, Grigory Chukhria), which tells a simple tale powerfully and with great humanity of a young soldier's journey home from the front to visit his mother during which he falls in love and meets a wide cross section of people.

The late 1950s and 1960s were a period for creating filmed classics and adaptations done with taste, talent, and depth. Grigory Kozintsev's *Hamlet* (1964) and Sergey Bondarchuk's eight-hour version of Tolstoy's masterpiece, *War and Peace* (1964), were part of this movement.

But the 1960s also saw the development of a truly popular comic and satirical tradition quite different from the rigid pro-regime films during the Stalinist period. The most loved of all Russian comic directors has been Eldar Riazanov, who, since *Carnival Night* (1957), has found a large audience for films that have made Soviet citizens laugh about the absurdities of everyday life.

Outside Moscow, where the most important studio, Mosfilm, was located and where most important filmmakers worked, a name that, along with Tarkovsky, became recognized as representing original and controversial work was that of Armenian director Sergo Paradzhanov. Unlike Tarkovsky, he was frequently imprisoned for his films and behavior. *Shadows of Forgotten Ancestors* (1964), shot in the Ukraine, concerns the life of the Huzul people of that area in the 1800s. Paradzhanov's film and subsequent works as well, including *The Color of the Pomegranate* (1969), are like tapestries or folk legends come to life. Lyrical, painterly, and full of rituals, passions, and yet highly stylized renderings, Paradzhanov's cinema owes much more to folk culture than to the influence of American, European, or even Russian cinemas.

The 1970s under Brezhnev came to be known as a third era after 1945, the period of *Zastoi* (stagnation), and yet a number of talented directors were working including Nikita Mikhalkov (*An Unfinished Piece for a Player Piano,* 1977), his talented brother Andrey Mikhalknov-Konchalovskii (*Siberiada,* 1978), Elem Klimov (*Agony,* 1975), and Otar Loseliani (*The Summer in the Country,* 1976). Georgian comedy proved a bright spot also during the 1970s as Leonid Gaidai directed the ever popular *The Twelve Chairs* (1971), and Georgy Danelia filmed *Don't Grieve* (1970) and the touching satire *Autumn Marathon* (1979), about the midlife crisis of a Leningrad intellectual writer who is having an affair and satisfying no one, least of all himself.

Soviet leader Mikhail Gorbachev announced the policy of glasnost (openness) in 1985, and by 1986 the Soviet film industry throughout the various republics began to take up the challenge and produce a remarkable series of documentaries and feature films that dared for the first time since the Russian Revolution of 1917 to tell the truth on subjects that had been covered up or prohibited. Initially the documentary filmmakers rushed in to take advantage of the new freedom of information and expression to make films about Stalin's gulags (*Solovki Regime,* 1988, Marina Goldovskaya), disillusioned youth on drugs and fed up with the whole system (*Is It Easy to Be Young?* 1987, Juris Podnieks), the effects of the Afghanistan war (1979–1989) for families and loved ones (*Pain,* 1988, Sergey Lukyanchikov), and the Chernobyl nuclear disaster (*Chernobyl: Chronicle of Difficult Weeks,* 1986, Valadimir Shevchenko), among countless other topics.

In terms of feature fiction films, fresh young voices began to be heard and seen as the monolithic Soviet film industry crumbled and the Filmmakers' Union took power into its own hands. Vasily Pichul shocked millions with the first portrayal of sex on the Soviet screen in the neorealist *Little Vera* (1988), while Rachid Nougmanov from Kazakhstan spearheaded a "Kazakh New Wave" of young directors with his influential *The Needle* (1988), starring pop rock star Victor Tsoi, in a drug narrative. Some directors started to work on films coproduced with foreign money, including Pavel Loungin, whose *Taxi Blues* (1980) was a hard-nosed look at the ugly side of Russian nationalism and anti-Semitism, while Alexander Proshkin put American Western formulas to original use in depicting the immediate lawlessness after Stalin's death in the powerful *The Cold Summer of '53* (1987). In Leningrad (St. Petersburg) Yuri Manin shot finely tuned satirical barbs at the crumbling Soviet empire in *The Fountain* (1988).

The brief bright moment of importance for these filmmakers was swiftly clouded, however, by a number of factors including the flood of cheap films and black market videos from the West, the closing of many cinemas, the breakdown of the distribution system, and the collapse of government subsidies for filmmaking. The pressure to become "commercial" meant that many filmmakers tried to make American or Hong Kong–styled sex-and-violence films, for the most part with little luck. Others tried to combine art and commerce as Western filmmakers have long been forced to do. *Intergirl* (1989) was veteran director Pyotr Todorovsky's effort to make a "significant" film about the new prostitution, while Yuri Kara's *The King of Crime* (1988) paved the way for Russian mafia gangster films that have followed in ever increasing numbers.

The overall picture of Russian cinema in the fifth and current post-Soviet post-Communist stage is not encouraging. The breakdown of all areas of society including filmmaking have meant that while Russia and the Soviet Union used to make and distribute about 150 feature films a year, fewer than 50 were made in 1994, and only a handful of those ever made it to the screen in Russian cinemas. In 1993 Russian films captured only 14 percent of the home box office.

And yet talented filmmakers such as Kira Muratova, Vladimir Khotinenko, Eldar Ryazanov, Sergey Bodrov, Aleksandr Sokurov, Sergey Solovyev, Evgeny Tsymbal, and Nikolay Dostal somehow have found a way to keep making films. That, of course, is the hope for the future.

BIBLIOGRAPHY

Horton, Andrew, ed. *Inside Soviet Film Satire: Laughter with a Lash.* New York: Cambridge University Press, 1993.

———. *The Zero Hour: Glasnost and Soviet Cinema in Transition.* Princeton: Princeton University Press, 1992.

Horton, Andrew, and Michael Brashinsky, eds. *Russian Critics on the Cinema of Glasnost.* New York: Cambridge University Press, 1994.

Lawton, Anna. *Kinoglasnost: Soviet Cinema in Our Time.* New York: Cambridge University Press, 1992.

Leyda, Jay. *Kino: A History of the Russian and Soviet Film.* Princeton, N.J.: Princeton University Press, 1960, reprint 1983.

Zorkaya, Neya. *The Illustrated History of Soviet Cinema.* New York: Hippocrene Books, 1989.

Andrew Horton

Russia at the End of the Twentieth Century

On December 31, 1999, Russian president Boris Yeltsin, unexpectedly announced his immediate resignation and the appointment of his newly chosen prime minister, Vladimir Putin, as interim president. Observers were surprised not so much by the resignation as by its timing. Yeltsin, in poor health for most of his time in office, had declared that he would not seek reelection in upcoming elections, but few expected such an early departure from a politician who had clung to power so tenaciously. Yeltsin's sudden resignation prompted speculation about Russia's future. The departing president left Russia with markets failing and war raging in Chechnya. In his resignation speech, Yeltsin stressed that the country needed a new leadership for the new millennium, but his resignation was clearly the last act of an ailing, weary president who sought to guarantee an orderly succession. Recent events, including Yeltsin's resignation, Putin's rise, and the Second Chechnyan War illuminate the web of economic woes, political crises, internal struggles, and geopolitical challenges in which Russia was caught. Since 1991, Russia had struggled to create new political and economic systems, while facing worsening problems. Conflict was inherent in independent Russia, which inherited unresolved political disputes from the late Soviet era. Power struggles tested the strength of political reforms in 1993, 1996, and again in 1999. In 1993, Yeltsin became involved in a standoff with Soviet-era legislators and responded by ordering the shelling of the parliament building, in which his armed opponents were challenging his power. The assault on the parliament building caused many Russians to lose their confidence in Yeltsin as a guarantor of freedom and stability, and in December 1993, voters expressed their disillusionment with reforms by giving Vladimir Zhirinovsky's extremist Liberal Democratic Party the largest number of seats in the State Duma, the lower house of the legislature. By the middle of 1995, soaring prices and unemployment had also made the reestablished Communist Party a force to be reckoned with. The party fared well in elections to the State Duma, and in 1996, Communist Party candidate, Gennady Zyuganov, challenged Yeltsin for the presidency, only to be defeated in a run-off election. In 1993 and 1996, Yeltsin overcame challenges to his leadership and programs but not without paying a heavy price.

Events in 1999 also raised questions about the future of reform. Given Yeltsin's history of abrupt promotions and demotions, Putin's appointment as prime minister was interpreted by many as a sign of instability and a turn away from reform. Nevertheless, despite initial questions about motivations, the appointment helped perpetuate the Yeltsin political legacy. In the State Duma elections of December 1999, the Putin-Yeltsin Unity Party received the largest number of seats, while the All Fatherland Party, formed by Moscow mayor Yuri Luzhkov and former prime minister Evgeny Primakov, failed at the polls. Within weeks of his appointment, Putin announced that his Unity Party would form a coalition with the Communists in the State Duma, and shortly thereafter, Primakov announced that he would not run for the presidency.

By early 2000, with their opponents fading, Yeltsin and Putin appear to have been quite successful in arranging a succession. The "brown-red" alliance that many feared has not come to pass, insofar as Communists and extreme nationalists are as divided and fragmented as Russia's reformers. Perhaps the most important achievement of the last decade is that Russians have become accustomed to contested elections and peaceful political transitions. Beneath Russia's placid political waters, a turbulent economy and a tumultuous society churn. Despite the optimism in the early 1990s, the collapse of the Soviet Union has reduced many to poverty, and other facts such as falling life expectancy and natural population decline point to deeply entrenched social problems. Conditions have worsened over the past decade. Citing rates of inflation and economic decline that were decreasing in 1995, many both inside and outside Russia declared that the country had turned the corner, only to retract their optimistic predictions when in 1998 fall-out from the Asian economic crisis and long-standing internal weaknesses brought about another currency collapse.

Russia has suffered the effects of failed and misguided policies. Already in 1993, many Russians insisted that "shock therapy" reforms were "all shock and no therapy." Some argued that Russian politicians and foreign market-reform advisors had made a fundamental mistake: they had confused processes (liberalization and privatization) with desired outcomes (democracy and free markets). Stressing that liberalization and privatization did not create the markets and democracies of the West, these critics faulted advisors and reformers for following programs with no historical basis. Reforms, according to some, did irreversible damage to the cause of reform. Privatization wound up concentrating the country's wealth in the hands of a few, and many of those most favorable to Westernization, including Russians in the educational and cultural sectors, took the brunt of reforms, going unpaid for months or losing their jobs. By the mid-1990s, many Russians who were once enthusiastic about Western ideas denounced the West and blamed its influence for everything from the soaring prices of bread to the proliferation of pornography.

For many, Russia appeared as it had in earlier eras. As in late Czarist history, the governing power (*vlast*) in the 1990s was increasingly distant from society (*obshchestvo*), and the gulf between those above (*verkhi*) and those below (*nizy*) was widening. The second-place finishes of the Communist Party and its candidates in 1996 and 1999 pointed toward an increasingly polarized country. For some, Yeltsin's flurry of promotions, demotions, and firings from 1996 to 1999 hearkened back to Czar Nicholas II's pattern of "ministerial leap frog" during World War I and signaled the government's imminent collapse. The abrupt staffing changes were widely regarded as a series of haphazard moves to deflect blame for Russia's troubles and appease interest groups. Less than a decade after the collapse of the Soviet Union, polarization and cleavages split the new Russia, and worsening economic and social crises undermined continuity in government and policy.

Throughout the 1990s, corruption, in all of its definitions and ambiguity, played an important role in the politics and economy of Russia. The notorious corruption of the mature Soviet Union, usually summed up by anecdotes about favoritism and bribery, was joined by new forms of corruption closely tied to the breakdown of government and law enforcement in Russia. Market reforms, particularly privatization, served as a catalyst in the processes of corruption and collapse. By the mid-1990s, many former apparatchiks had figured out how to get their hands on state property and sell it abroad, making the word "privatization" synonymous with theft. Organized crime quickly penetrated the highest echelons of government, blurring the lines between street and incumbent crime. In the late 1990s, economists assessing Russian economic performance made large allowances for "black" or "gray" commerce, and conservative estimates placed the value of state property stolen or misappropriated in the billions of dollars. Recent revelations, such as the 1999 uncovering of a money-laundering scheme involving a US bank, only hint at the extent of the problem of corruption and capital flight in Russia. The set of phenomena lumped together and loosely defined as corruption has taken a heavy toll on Russia.

The convergence of politics, money, organized crime, and a collapsing state have prompted some to use the terms "kleptocracy" and "mafiacracy" to describe Russia's system of government. Crime, corruption, and skimmed funds have created a class of millionaires who wield tremendous power, and according to some, these "kleptocrats" were behind the murders of Vladislav Listev, an investigative journalist, and Galina Starovoitova, a St. Petersburg parliament member who was leading an investigation of political corruption and organized crime. Persistent rumors circulate about the Swiss and offshore bank accounts of political figures. Public perceptions of corruption in government were furthered by Putin's declaration of a pardon for Yeltsin for any wrongs committed while in office. Corruption has not only siphoned off capital necessary for a successful transition, but it undermined public confidence in the political system. The devolution of power has led to the rise of regionalism in Russia. Even overwhelmingly Russian regions of the country have asserted their autonomy vis-à-vis Moscow, and a once highly centralized state has been replaced by strong regional administrations. Regional administrators have withheld taxes and ignored federal decrees. Impressed by the power of centrifugal forces in the new Russia, many predicted that the collapse of the Soviet Union would be followed by the collapse of the Russian Federation. Although predictions of warlords splintering the federation into fiefdoms have not come to pass, regional bosses are frequently more influential and wealthier than their federal counterparts.

Russia's economic and social problems have been complicated by internal and external challenges, best exemplified by the two Chechnyan Wars. In 1991, the small Chechno-Ingush Republic declared its independence from the Soviet Union, and in 1992, Russia responded to the breakaway effort by dividing the Caucasian republic into a Chechen republic and an Ingush republic. The newly created Chechen republic became a haven for bandits and hijackers, and fighting in and around the republic escalated. In the fall of 1994, the Russian military began to aid opponents of the Chechen government, and in the December of 1994, Russian military leaders convinced Yeltsin to support a full-scale assault on the republic. Russian forces captured the Chechen capital Grozny in January 1995, but not without taking heavy casualties and inflicting heavy civilian casualties. The following year, Chechen guerrillas retook the capital, and the Russian military was forced to negotiate a withdrawal. The clear loser in the war was the Russian government, which lost Chechnya and deeply disturbed Western leaders, whose sensibilities included human rights. Compounding the Russian government's popularity problems, many Russians joined foreign leaders in condemning the Russian military's disregard for human life.

In the First Chechnyan War, Moscow failed to bring Chechnya under its control, and by 1997, members of a militant Islamic movement had taken power in the republic. In the fall of 1999, the Russian leadership took military action in response to the attack of Chechen Islamic militants on villages in neighboring Dagestan. In marked contrasted to the first military action in Chechnya, the government's military response to the new situation in the Caucasus enjoyed widespread public support. Russians, who blamed Chechen immigrants for a crime wave and a mysterious series of bombings in Russian cities, cheered the invasion. In early February 2000, Russian forces took Grozny and routed their opponents. As in the first war, the military's treatment of the civilian population quickly came under attack in the West, and Russian forces took heavy casualties when they engaged their opponents. Unresolved as of February 2000, the Second Chechnyan War shows that Russia is far from stability and even further from the world of Western sensibilities. Recent elections and military victories have guaranteed Russia short-term stability and a temporary reprieve, but widening gaps within Russia and between Russia and the West make long-term prospects unsure. Decreasing military and economic might have made it difficult for Russia to maintain a credible presence on the world stage, and internal controversies over empire and nation coupled with the absence of a compelling ideology have only further confused Russia's policy toward Russian territories, the "Near Abroad" neighbors, and its "Far-Abroad."

In early 2000, Russia seems much further away from its goal of becoming of a "normal, civilized country" than it was in 1991, and observers who spoke about a transition period of five years now speak of a transition period of five decades. Prosperity, civil society, and rule of law have eluded Russia.

Anthony Amato

Rutelli, Francesco (1954–)

Italian Green politician and mayor of Rome, (1993–). Francesco Rutelli was elected to parliament in 1983 as a member of Marco Pannella's Radical Party. Rutelli joined the Italian Federation of Greens in 1989. He served as speaker of the movement until March 1992, when he was succeeded by Carlo Ripa, a former commissioner of the environment for the European Union. Rutelli was named Italian minister of the environment on April 28, 1993, but he resigned after a few hours to protest the refusal of the government to revoke the parliamentary immunity of Bettino Craxi, the former Socialist prime minister accused of accepting illegal contributions to his party. On December 5, 1993, Rutelli was elected mayor of Rome in a runoff election in which he defeated Gianfranco Fini, the leader of the right wing National Alliance party.

Bernard Cook

SEE ALSO Craxi, Bettino; Pannella, Giacinto (Marco)

Rutskoi, Aleksandr (1947–)

Russian vice president (1991–93). Aleksandr Rutskoi, an air force colonel, hero of the war in Afghanistan, and a prominent figure in Russian nationalist circles, was chosen as a running mate by Boris Yeltsin in 1991 to mollify conservatives troubled by Yeltsin's cortege of pro-Western market reformers. Rutskoi aided Yeltsin in countering his Communist and right-wing opponents. After the June election, however, serious differences arose between Yeltsin and his vice president over questions of foreign and economic policy. Rutskoi quickly sided with Yeltsin's opponents in the Supreme Soviet (parliament). When Yeltsin attempted unconstitutionally to dissolve parliament in September 1993, its chairman, Ruslan Khasbulatov, refused to comply. Parliament, led by Khasbulatov, proclaimed Rutskoi president. The anti-Yeltsin majority, consisting of Communists, nationalists, and conservatives led by Rutskoi and Khasbulatov, resisted. Yeltsin regarded their effort as an attempted coup d'état. They depicted themselves, however, as defenders of the constitution against presidential effrontery. The anti-Yeltsin parliamentarians took control of the parliament building, from which Yeltsin had led resistance to the August 19, 1991, attempted coup against President Mikhail Gorbachev, before the breakup of the USSR. The parliamentary forces attempted to seize communication centers, but Yeltsin called out tanks and ordered the parliament building shelled. The fighting, which began on October 3, lasted for two days, and approximately 150 were killed. The resisters were ultimately forced to submit and were jailed.

Following the victory of the nationalists and Communists in the December 1993 parliamentary election, Rutskoi was pardoned. On October 21, 1996, he was elected governor of the Kursk region by an overwhelming majority. As governor he entered the Federation Council (upper house of parliament) and gained an additional podium from which to challenge Yeltsin.

BIBLIOGRAPHY

Rutskoi, Aleksandr. *Afganistan . . . Kreml . . . Lefortovo..?: epizody politicheskoi biographii Aleksandra Rutskogo* (Afganistan . . . Kremlin . . . Lefortovo..?: Episodes in the Political Biography of Aleksandr Rutskoi). Moscow: Lada-M, 1994.

Bernard Cook

Rüutel, Arnold (1928–)

Chair (president) of the Supreme Council of Estonia (1983–92). Arnold Rüutel was the only leading member of the Communist establishment to retain his position during and after Estonia's transition to independence from the Soviet Union. However, in the first two presidential elections after independence (1992 and 1996), Rüutel was defeated by Lennart Meri, the first president of Estonia after it regained its independence. Though leader of the Rural People's Party, which, with the Party of Consolidation, formed the victorious electoral coalition in the 1995 parliamentary election, he failed to gain a ministerial portfolio, becoming instead a deputy speaker of parliament.

An agronomist and one-time rector of the Estonian Agricultural Academy, Rüutel became deputy prime minister of Estonia from 1979 to 1983 and was elected chair of the Supreme Council (the legislative body in the Estonia Soviet Socialist Republic) (president) in 1983. In 1990 he was reelected following the victory of the Popular Front, a political organization formed in April 1988 to work for the independence of Estonia, in the elections to the Supreme Council.

His abilities as a media performer, his capacity to distance himself from the economic problems associated with transition to a market economy, and his willingness to offer public support for greater autonomy for Estonia in 1987–88 when most of the Communist hierarchy opposed it, helped him to remain president during the transition to independence. He strengthened his position with ethnic Estonians by becoming more hard-line on the question of citizenship, to impose language requirements to make it difficult for ethnic Russians and other Slavs who had settled in Estonia during the Soviet era to become citizens, and by supporting the Supreme Council's declaration that Estonia was an occupied country in transition to independence.

Rüutel gave the impression of being above politics by leaving the Estonian Communist Party and concealing his affiliation with the Free Estonia group of former Communists. In March 1991 he was the most popular politician in Estonia among ethnic and nonethnic Estonians alike. Against the majority view, he supported a presidential rather than a parliamentary form of government in the debates on the constitution.

In 1992 in the first direct election for the presidency after independence, Rüutel ran against Meri, Rein Taagepera a professor of Baltic Studies at the University of California-Irvine, and Lagle Parek. Although he obtained the highest number of votes, his failure to secure a majority threw the election into the predominantly right-wing parliament, which voted against Rüutel as a former Communist.

Rüutel used his time in opposition (1992–95) to form the Estonian Rural Union, a political party reflecting his long-standing interest in the agricultural sector. He supported the restoration of private farming as a means of reviving traditional Estonian values, and advocated a policy of agricultural protection in the form of tariffs, cheap loans, and tax relief for private farmers.

In the 1995 parliamentary election the Rural Union entered into a coalition agreement with the Party of Consolidation, led by Tiit Vahi, and the Association of Pensioners and Families. Composing the largest single grouping in parliament, the coalition formed the government, first in alliance with the Center Party, then with the Reform Party. Failing to obtain the agricultural portfolio, Rüutel was elected deputy speaker of parliament and played a major role in the presidium of the Baltic Assembly, uniting MPs from all three Baltic states (Estonia, Latvia, Lithuania) to discuss issues of common concern. He ran for president in 1996 and was again defeated at the second stage by Meri. In March 1997 Rüutel withdrew his candidacy for deputy speaker but continued to serve as his party's chair.

BIBLIOGRAPHY

Hiden, John, and Patrick Salmon. *The Baltic Nations and Europe: Estonia, Latvia, and Lithuania in the Twentieth Century.* Harlow, England: Longman, 1991.

Lieven, Anatol. *The Baltic Revolution: Estonia, Latvia, Lithuania and the Path to Independence.* New Haven, Conn.: Yale University Press, 1993.

Norgaard, Ole, et al. *The Baltic States after Independence.* Cheltenham, England: Edward Elgar, 1996

Smith, Graham, ed. *The Baltic States: the National Self-Determination of Estonia, Latvia and Lithuania.* Basingstoke, England: Macmillan, 1994.

Taa'gepera, Rein. *Estonia: Return to Independence.* Boulder, Colo.: Westview Press, 1993.

Thomas Lane

SEE ALSO Meri, Lennart

Rybakov, Anatoly N. (1911–98)

Soviet novelist, a consistent romantic revolutionary who portrayed the Great Terror as a Stalinist perversion of the Russian Revolution. Anatoly Rybakov, who was born in Chernigov, Ukraine, in 1911, moved to Moscow with his assimilated Jewish family when he was eight. In 1933, when he was an engineering student at the Institute of Transport, Rybakov was arrested for "counterrevolutionary propaganda." He had written a lampoon of the party line in a school newspaper, for which he was exiled for three years to Mozgova, a remote Siberian village on the Angara River. At the end of the three-year period he was forbidden permission to live in any large city. He kept a low profile, working as a truck driver, longshoreman, and dancing instructor. His rehabilitation came with World War II. After four years of combat that took him to Berlin, he returned to his old Moscow district, the Arbat. Most of his friends had perished in Stalin's purges and the war. To preserve their memory, he decided to devote himself to his love of writing. Rybakov published his first book in 1948. *The Knife* recounts the lives of children in the 1920s after the Russian Revolution. It was subsequently published in forty languages. In 1951 Rybakov won the Stalin Prize for his novel *Drivers.* However, Rybakov's most important work, *Children of the Arbat,* could not be published until Mikhail Gorbachev became Communist Party leader in 1985 and launched his policy of glasnost (openness). The book, which became a 2.4 million copy rage in the Soviet Union, traces the lives of a dozen families whose stories illustrate the fate of millions of Soviet citizens enveloped in the web of Stalin's terror. Its publication was an important indication of Gorbachev's intent to reform the Soviet Union. Rybakov's *Dust and Ashes* is a sequel to *Children of the Arbat.* Especially notable among his ten books is *Heavy Sand,* a novel about small-town life in the Soviet Union and the fate of the country's Jewish population.

In 1989 Rybakov was elected head of the Soviet branch of the international writers' organization PEN. Rybakov, who had a home in New York as well as Moscow, died in New York City on December 23, 1998.

BIBLIOGRAPHY

Cushman, John H. Jr., and Richard Hallgran. "Washington Talk: Briefing; Mr. Rybakov Regrets." *New York Times,* May 31, 1988.

Folkart, Burt A. "Anatoly Rybakov, 87; Russian Novelist." *Los Angeles Times,* December 25, 1998.

Mitgang, Herbert. "Popular Soviet Author visits U.S. with Wife." *New York Times,* April 26, 1986.

Bernard Cook

Rybkin, Ivan Petrovich (1946–)

Russian politician. Ivan Rybkin was born in Semigorovka in the Voronezh region of the USSR on October 26, 1946. He studied at the Volgograd Institute of Agriculture and received a doctorate from the Academy of Social Sciences of the Central Committee of the Communist Party in Moscow. After working briefly as an agricultural engineer, he was appointed lecturer at the Volgograd Institute of Agriculture, where by 1987 he had become professor, chair, then dean.

In 1983 he became secretary of the Volgograd Communist Party committee. From 1987 to 1991 he was first secretary of the party's district committee in Volgograd and second secretary of the Volgograd regional committee. He became head of the divisional Central Committee of the Communist Party of the Russian Soviet Federated Socialist Republic in 1991.

Rybkin served as a deputy in the Russian Congress of People's Deputies, the Soviet era Russian parliament, from 1990 until the congress was suppressed by Boris Yeltsin in 1993 at the culmination of his power struggle with its leadership who opposed the president and his desire to exercise executive power. In 1991 he was a founder and co-chair of Communists of Russia, the reorganized Communist Party. He then joined the Agrarian Party and simultaneously helped found the Socialist Party of Workers (SPW). Rybkin subsequently transformed a segment of the SPW into the Socialist Party of Russia. He was elected to the State Duma, the lower house of the parliament, established by the 1993 Constitution, in December 1993 as a representative of the Agrarian Party, and with the support of the Communist Party and the nationalists was elected speaker. Rybkin soon broke with the Agrarian Party, however, and allied himself and the Socialist Party with Yeltsin. As speaker in 1994–95 Rybkin steered the Duma away from confrontation with the president. As a result Yeltsin appointed him to the Russian Security Council, a presidential commission to advise the president and assist him in the management of internal and external security issues, in 1994. With the dismissal of Aleksandr Lebed as National Security Adviser and head of the Security Council on October 17, 1996, Rybkin was appointed secretary, a post he held until 1998, and placed in charge of Russia's negotiations with the leaders of the breakaway region of Chechnya. Lebed contemptuously asserted that the new security chief would serve Yeltsin's purpose of transforming the Security Council into a weak bureaucratic office. Nevertheless, on assuming the task Rybkin asserted his determination not to let the peace brokered by Lebed collapse.

In March 1998 Yeltsin appointed Rybkin a deputy prime minister in the government of Sergey Kiriyenko. Rybkin was assigned to oversee Russia's relations with the republics of the former USSR. The cabinet shift was regarded by some as an indication of the power and influence of financier Boris Berezovsky, who was Rybkin's deputy on the Security Council and who remained closely linked to Rybkin.

BIBLIOGRAPHY

Bennet, Vanora. "Yeltsin Appoints a Moderate." *Los Angeles Times,* October 20, 1996.

Erlanger, Steven. "Russia's New Parliament Chooses Ally." *New York Times,* January 15, 1994.

Stanley, Alessandra. "Yeltsin Picks an Unassuming, Loyal Legislator." *New York Times,* October 20, 1996.

"Yeltsin Continues Ministerial Musical Chairs." *Financial Times* (London), March 3, 1998.

Bernard Cook

SEE ALSO Lebed, Aleksandr

Saami

The Saami (formerly called Lapps, or Laplanders) are the indigenous people living for several thousand years in the northernmost part of what today is Norway, Sweden, Finland, and western Russia. The earliest Saami presence in Arctic Europe, as nomadic hunters, predates that of Scandinavians, Finns, and Russians. During the past four centuries, Saami have ceased their dependence on hunting, becoming nomadic reindeer herders, settled farmers, and ocean fishers. More recently, since World War II, Saami have entered every other occupation and the mainstreams of their national societies as well, and are represented in education, business, tourism, and government.

Altogether, the Saami people number perhaps 80,000, with about half speaking the Saami language, a Uralic-Altoic language, in addition to their dominant national languages. At the present time about 7,000 Saami practice reindeer management, herding 450,000 head of livestock that graze for the most part on public lands.

While it may be unwise to generalize about the Saami condition throughout all four countries, there are overwhelming common features, both intrinsic and extrinsic. Until 1945 most Saami subsisted on traditional livelihoods and lived in nomadic bands or mono-ethnic settlements. They experienced World War II, while theoretically remote, in distinct contexts (Sweden being neutral, Finland being at war at different times with both the USSR and Germany, and Norway being German-occupied even in the Arctic). In each case the infrastructure left by the war changed Saami society as much as did various technological developments and political agendas following the war, including boundary adjustments between Finland and the USSR. Hence, 1945 is a cusp separating an era of autonomous primary subsistence, each community distanced from each other and from state control, and the contrastive contemporary situation of sedentary mixed communities, with fixed dwellings and transportation systems.

Traditionally shamanism was the sole religion, while today these shamanistic practices are overshadowed by Saami participation in their national Lutheran-related churches. Public schooling follows state curricula, but instruction may be in the native language. Publications and media abound in the Saami language. In all countries but Russia, Saami have established parliaments to advise their governments about cultural, economic, and ecological issues. One current crisis concerns the consequences of the 1986 Chernobyl nuclear accident in Soviet Ukraine, but the patchiness of the fallout has led to local strategies complementing those at national and international levels.

Saami have also cooperated with each other across their national boundaries, and with other indigenous "Fourth World" peoples around the world. The Fourth World movement may be the most significant extranational political development, but the emergence of grassroots political agendas coupled with media linkages affect more persons on a daily basis.

BIBLIOGRAPHY

Anderson, Myrdene. *Saami Ethnoecology: Resource Management in Norwegian Lapland.* Ann Arbor, Michigan: University Microfilms, 1978.

Beach, Hugh. *Case of Tuorpon Saameby in Northern Sweden.* Uppsala Studies in Cultural Anthropology, 3. Uppsala: Almqvist and Wiksell, 1981.

Ingold, Tim. *Skolt Lapps Today.* Cambridge: Cambridge University Press, 1976.

Paine, Robert. *Coast Lapp Society,* Vol. 2, *Study of Economic Development and Social Values.* Oslo: Universitetsforlaget, 1965.

Pelto, Pertti J. *Individualism in Skolt Lapp Society.* Kansatieteellinen Arkisto, 16. Helsinki: Suomen Muinaismuistoyhdistys, 1962.

Vorren, Ørnulv, and Ernest Manker. *Lapp Life and Customs.* Oxford: Oxford University Press, 1962.

Myrdene Anderson

Sačirbey, Mohamed (1956–)

Bosnian ambassador to the United Nations from 1992 to 1995 and then foreign minister. Mohammed Sačirbey is from a prominent Sarajevo Muslim family who left Communist Yugoslavia during his early childhood. After 1967 he grew up in Ohio and became a U.S. citizen in 1973. He earned a law degree and had a meteoric career as a corporate lawyer on Wall Street, serving as a senior vice president of the merchant bank Security Pacific.

In May 1992, Sačirbey became Bosnia's first ambassador to the United Nations. In television studios across the world he proved a formidable advocate of what, at many points, seemed the lost Bosnian cause. His familiarity with American life enabled him to champion the Bosnian cause before the U.S. Congress, while his religious orientation enabled him along with Prime Minister Haris Silajdžić to mobilize the Islamic world. His mastery of the media and his clean-cut, moderate image that was the antithesis of the customary political Islamic image were vital in what became a media as well as a territorial war. In June 1995 he became foreign minister after his predecessor, Irfan Ljubijanivic, was shot down by Bosnian Serbs while riding in a helicopter.

Sačirbey had close ties to President Alija Izetbegović and was supported by confessional Muslims engaged in a power struggle with secularists inside the ruling Democratic Action Party.

Tom Gallagher

Sakharov, Andrey (1921–89)

Soviet physicist and human rights activist. After key contributions to the first Soviet hydrogen bomb, Andrey Sakharov challenged official policies, speaking out for human rights and disarmament. He won the Nobel Peace Prize but also incurred the disfavor of the authorities and was sent into internal exile. Released from this exile at Gorby by Mikhail Gorbachev, Sakharov continued to promote democratic reform in the USSR.

Born May 21, 1921, in Moscow, Sakharov was an outstanding physics student at Moscow State University from 1938 to 1941 and after evacuation due to the German invasion of the USSR in June 1941 to Ashkhabad, in Soviet Turkmenistan. He performed laboratory work instead of military service during the war. His marriage in 1943 to Klavdya Vikhireva produced three children; she died of cancer in 1969.

In 1945 Sakharov enrolled at the Physical Institute of the Academy of Sciences in Moscow under Igor Tamm, earning a candidate (Ph.D.) degree in 1947. In 1948 he joined a special group under Tamm working on thermonuclear fission and fusion, moving to the top-secret Soviet atomic facility, Arzamas-16, in 1950. Sakharov created a key design for the successful Soviet hydrogen bomb test in August 1953 and the TOKAMAK concept for controlled thermonuclear fusion.

For that accomplishment he won the first of three Hero of Socialist Labor awards, the Stalin Prize, a country house, and in 1953 was the youngest member ever elected to the Academy of Sciences. In Moscow after 1953, Sakharov continued work on nuclear weapons, also studying elementary particles, astrophysics, and cosmology. Although he earlier believed that Soviet nuclear parity with the United States would help ensure world peace, by 1957 he cited the dangers of fallout from Soviet as well as American nuclear tests.

On July 22, 1968, Sakharov's "Reflections on Progress, Peaceful Coexistence and Intellectual Freedom," proclaiming the necessity of "freedom of thought," appeared in the New York Times. He was banned from defense work but kept his academician's privileges. Sakharov continued his physics research while speaking out forcefully on behalf of writers, national minorities, Jews, and religious believers subjected to harassment by Soviet authorities. In 1970 he helped found the Moscow Committee of Human Rights and called for gradual democratization to remedy the Soviet Union's "economic breakdown and stagnation." Earlier he had hoped for a convergence of capitalism and socialism, but *My Country and the World* (1975) published in English by Alfred A. Knopf labeled Soviet totalitarianism the primary obstacle to nuclear disarmament. In 1972 he married Yelena Bonner, a physician whom he met at a dissident rally.

When Sakharov was awarded the Nobel Peace Prize in 1975, he was called a "Judas" and a "laboratory rat of the West." But he only intensified his advocacy of human rights and criticism of the regime, terming it in 1977 a "centralized and essentially militaristic structure of control." After attacking the 1979 Soviet invasion of Afghanistan and urging a boycott of the 1980 Moscow Olympics, Sakharov was arrested on January 22, 1980, accused of divulging state secrets and slandering the Soviet Union, stripped of his decorations, and banished to Gorky (Nizhni Novgorod).

Never formally charged with a crime, Sakharov remained under close surveillance, his apartment raided and papers and books seized, and was forbidden all contact with foreigners. Nevertheless, with the support of Yelena Bonner, he continued protesting, including three hunger strikes, and sending out appeals, in 1981 against the "false and dangerous messianism of the USSR" and in 1983 stressing "the interrelatedness of international security and defense of human rights."

On December 16, 1986, Gorbachev told Sakharov to "go back to your patriotic work," to which he now devoted his failing energies wholeheartedly as the most prominent Russian human-rights activist. He became chairman of Memorial, a group commemorating Stalin's victims, and in 1989, as a member of the new Congress of Peoples' Deputies, with 2,500 elected members established by Gorbachev, reached millions at home and abroad through television, charging that Gorbachev was enacting "democratic reforms through undemocratic means." Although opposed by conservatives in the Congress and once abruptly cut off by Gorbachev, Sakharov worked unremittingly for genuine democracy as a leader of the reform Inter-Regional group of deputies until his death on December 14, 1989.

Official obituaries were only grudgingly favorable, but there was widespread dismay that the Soviet Union's "moral compass" was gone; one hundred thousand people paid their respects at his bier at the Academy of Sciences. Sakharov enjoys universal admiration for his humanistic vision, moral witness, and belief that science has an ethical imperative "to make good the demands of reason and create a life worthy of ourselves." Sakharov commissions in Moscow and at Brandeis University preserve his papers and continue his work.

BIBLIOGRAPHY

Academy of Sciences of the USSR. *Andrei Sakharov: Facets of a Life.* Gif-sur-Yvette, France: Éditions Frontières, 1991.

Babyonyshev, Alexander, ed. *On Sakharov.* New York: Knopf, 1982.

Bailey, George. *Galileo's Children: Science, Sakharov and the Power of the State.* New York: Arcade, 1990.

Bonner, Elena. *Alone Together.* Tr. by Alexander Cook. New York: Knopf, 1986.

Sakharov, Andrei. *Memoirs.* Tr. by Richard Lourie. New York: Knopf, 1990.

———. *Moscow and Beyond, 1986 to 1989.* Tr. by Antonina Bouis. New York: Knopf, 1991.

Daniel L. Schlafly Jr.

Salan, Raoul (1899–1984)

Highly decorated French officer who fought in both world wars and numerous campaigns in the French Empire. After service in Indochina, he was posted to Algeria. General Raoul Salan became a focal point for French Algerian resistance to Arab nationalism and President Charles de Gaulle's policy of an Algerian Algeria.

Salan was France's most highly decorated soldier this century, but he had the personal misfortune to be closely involved in France's military withdrawal from its empire. He was commander of French forces in Indochina from 1952 to 1954, and presided over the end of the French presence in the region. That failure convinced Salan, along with many in the French army, that there should be no more defeats for the French Empire.

Salan was posted as Commander of the French forces in Algeria in 1956, where the army was fighting a brutal war against Arab nationalists. Initially seen by die-hard French Algerians as a threat to the idea of *Algérie française* (French Algeria), Salan narrowly escaped an assassination attempt. However, he became the hero of the *pieds noirs* (French Algerians) when he agreed to lead an insurrection in May 1958.

The Algerian problem threatened to bring civil war to metropolitan France until General de Gaulle came out of retirement to found France's Fifth Republic. As Salan hoped, de Gaulle appeared to support the idea of *Algérie française.* However, when it became apparent that de Gaulle's policy was for an Algerian Algeria, the *pieds noirs* and elements of the army turned against him. Salan retired from the army in 1960 and became even more closely identified with the cause of *Algérie française.* In April 1961 he was involved, along with Generals Maurice Challe, Jouhaud, and Zeller in a coup attempt in Algeria, the "General's Putsch." The aim was to overthrow de Gaulle and reaffirm the French presence in Algeria. The putsch collapsed in three days, and Salan went into hiding, becoming the head of the recently created terrorist organization, the Secret Army Organization (OAS).

Salan did not, in fact, have much control over the day-to-day activities of the OAS, which were in the hands of Jean-Jacques Susini, its director, but Salan took responsibility for their actions. The OAS mounted a vicious terror campaign, killing 2,360 people and wounding 5,418 in less than a year in Algeria. They also took their campaign to metropolitan France, mounting a number of assassination attempts against de Gaulle. But the killings were to no avail, and an Algerian Algeria came into being in 1962 when France granted independence to its North African appendage.

Salan was captured in April 1962 and put on trial for his life. Defended by extreme-right-wing lawyer Jean-Louis Tixier-Vignancour, Salan was sentenced to life imprisonment. He was granted amnesty at the time of the May crisis in 1968.

BIBLIOGRAPHY

Henissart, Paul. *Wolves in the City: The Death of French Algeria.* New York: Simon and Schuster, 1970.

Horne, Alistair. *A Savage War of Peace: Algeria 1954–1962.* London: Macmillan, 1977.

Stephen M. Cullen

SEE ALSO Algerian War; Terrorism, Right Wing

Salazar, António de Oliveira (1889–1970)

Portuguese prime minister and dictator for thirty-six years. Critics have often judged António de Oliveira Salazar without regard to the problems that existed under Portugal's First Republic (1910–26), but perhaps the cost in freedom that Portuguese citizens were forced to pay during the dictatorship was too high. He created the corporatist, or corporativist, "New State," which continued under his successor, Marcelo Caetano, until the Portuguese revolution of 1974 restored democracy.

António Salazar was born on April 28, 1889, in the village of Vimieiro, near the small town of Santa Comba Dão. His political views were most influenced by St. Thomas Aquinas, Pope Leo XIII, Charles Maurras's *Action française,* Pope Pius XI, and António Sardinhas's integralism, a conservative Roman Catholic perspective favoring monarchy. After the 1926 military coup ended the First Republic, Salazar played an increasingly important role in government. By 1932 the military regime had transferred power to a civilian government with Salazar as prime minister. He set about framing the constitution for the New State, ratified in a 1933 referendum, which declared Portugal to be a corporatist and unitary, rather than pluralist, republic.

Salazar offered a new system based on strong authoritarianism that would maintain order rather than allowing a reversion to the instability of the republican period. He felt that Portuguese political culture required a "national revolution" creating a more ordered political system dominated by corporatist ideology. In the New State political parties and trade unions were abolished, censorship was applied, political power was centered on the executive branch, and the values of God, country, and family were inculcated. While Salazar theoretically espoused corporatism, in reality he preferred to maximize his personal power rather than mediate. He also sided with business over workers' interests.

Many have labeled Salazar a fascist, but the label did not accurately fit him. He did not, for example, create a government party. He also did not believe in mass mobilization. Although a secret police existed, it was relatively small. His views were more traditional and restrained than those of fascists such as Mussolini and Hitler.

Salazar believed that Portugal had to steer a middle course between looking to the past and focusing on the future. He attacked what he saw as the endemic Iberian trait of pursuing elaborate, expensive development schemes before attending to the nation's essential needs—infrastructure, development.

During the Spanish Civil War (1936–39) Salazar supported General Francisco Franco and the Nationalists for geostrategic reasons and because of his staunch anti-Communism. The war led Portugal further toward authoritarianism with intensified secret police activity, censorship, and repression of the left, especially the Communist Party. As a result, resistance increased throughout the decade in reaction to Salazar's human rights and economic policies.

Salazar maintained Portuguese neutrality, and was influential in maintaining Spanish neutrality, throughout World War II. He did not like the German Nazis but appreciated their defense against Communist insurgency. For six years Salazar walked a tightrope between neutrality and alliance, managing to maintain the former. His policies were neither pro-Axis nor pro-Allies but pro-Portuguese. One of his major concerns was with German desire for territory in Africa and the fear that the United Kingdom would negotiate away Portuguese colonies in exchange for peace in Europe. While maintaining its neutrality, Portugal profited handsomely by selling goods, especially the strategic mineral wolfram, to both sides.

By the 1950s Portugal was ready for economic takeoff because of infrastructure developments and substantial foreign currency reserves, but Salazar refused to allow economic expansion. He feared that modernization, which would accompany development, would imperil his attempt to preserve Portugal's traditional values. Economic stagnation led to waves of foreign emigration. In the end, Salazar sacrificed growth and welfare for stability. By 1965 he felt compelled to move in a different direction as he began allowing foreign investment.

After World War II the major foreign policy issues that concerned Salazar dealt with were primarily related to the Portugal's overseas colonies. Portugal's colonial policy blocked its effort to gain membership in the United Nations until 1956. Salazar's policies made industrial and economic development in the African colonies peripheral to the needs of the mother country. By the 1960s wars of national liberation had begun throughout its African colonies, and Portugal also lost its Indian colonies.

On June 9, 1968, Salazar fell off of a deck chair while at his seaside residence near Estoril and developed a blood clot in the brain, which eventually led to an incapacitating stroke. He died two years later in Lisbon on July 27, 1970. Despite his low visibility, Salazar left his mark internationally as a result of his policies during World War II and because of his response to other foreign events. Opinions still vary on whether Salazar was a good or bad leader.

BIBLIOGRAPHY

Derrick, Michael. *The Portugal of Salazar.* Freeport, N.Y.: Books for Libraries Press, 1939.

Ferro, António. *Salazar: Portugal and Her Leader.* Tr. by H. de Barros Gomes and John Gibbons. London: Faber and Faber, 1939.

Figueiredo, Antonio de. *Portugal: Fifty Years of Dictatorship.* New York: Homes & and Meier, 1976.

Fryer, Peter, and Pinheiro, Patricia McGowan. *Oldest Ally: Portrait of Salazar's Portugal.* London: D. Dobson, 1961.

Gallagher, Tom. *Portugal: A Twentieth Century Interpretation.* Manchester: Manchester University Press, 1983.

Garnier, Christine. *Salazar: An Intimate Portrait.* New York: Farrar, Strauss and Young, 1954.

Kay, Hugh. *Salazar and Modern Portugal.* New York: Hawthorn Books, 1970.

Rosas, Fernando. "Salazar, António de Oliveira," in Fernando Rosas and J. M. Brandão de Brito, eds. *Dicionário de História do Estado Novo,* Vol. 1. Venda Nova, Portugal: Bertrand Editora, 1996.

Carlos A. Cunha

Salvadori, Bruno (1942–80)

Valle d'Aostan regionalist and theorist of regionalism, Bruno Salvadori, though he died when he was only thirty-nine years old, was a decisive influence not only on politics in the Valle d'Aosta in north eastern Italy but also on other European ethnic-nationalist movements and on the rise of the so-called new regionalism in Italy. Born in 1942 in Aosta, Italy, Salvadori was active from an early age in Aostan journalism and the politics of the region. In 1965 he helped reestablish the *jeunesse valdôtaine,* the "Valle d'Aostan Youth," a pro-autonomy regionalist organization, which had provided much of the initial impetus for the formation of the Union Valdôtaine, a Valle d'Aostan regionalist political party, and became the editor of their journal, *Le Drapeau rouge et noir.*

Though an activist and a journalist, Salvadori was primarily concerned with creating a consistent ideology for the Union Valdôtaine that would enable it to build on its history and on existing "regionalist" sentiment, but also to incorporate ideas of ethnonationalism and federalism in a less parochial context. His major statement of these ideas was published in 1967 as *Pourquoi être autonomiste.* This short work provided an overview of the history of the Valle d'Aosta and its politics, but also firmly placed these not just in the context of the Italian nation-state but in that of Europe as a whole. The Union Valdôtaine was not a strictly local movement for him but represented part of the wider phenomenon of the regionalism throughout Europe. The guiding principles rested on respect for the individual, the natural community, and a European federalism based not on the nation-state but on a thoroughgoing practice of local control. His breadth of vision united the original ideas of the founder of the Union Valdôtaine, Émile Chanoux, with the broader spectrum of federalist and Catholic social thought. Though warmly welcomed by many in his party, their very breadth contrasted sharply with the current practice of the party as it became bogged down in local, internecine infighting under the increasingly autocratic leadership of Séverin Caveri. The tension between ideology and practice eventually proved too strong and Salvadori was instrumental in creating the Union Valdôtaine Progressiste, which broke away from the original party. Salvadori never intended to divide the movement and worked for the next few years to reunite it, but with the idea of *fédéralisme intégral* as its center. In 1976 he succeeded and the movement was reunited. Salvadori took a central role in the new party, and in 1977 he became the first editor of the party journal, *Le Peuple valdôtain,* which he edited until his death in a motor accident in 1980.

His ideas put him into contact with similar movements. In 1979 he fought the first election to the European Parliament not only for the Union Valdôtaine but as the candidate of a whole slate of regionalist and ethnonationalist movements from all over Italy. One of his campaign staff was the young Umberto Bossi, who later went on to found the Northern League. Salvadori was thus instrumental not only in recreating the Union Valdôtaine and reinforcing similar movements in other parts of Europe but also contributed significantly to the ongoing debate about the future shape of Italy and Europe.

BIBLIOGRAPHY

Salvadori, Bruno. *Pourquoi être autonomiste.* Aosta: Duc, 1967.

Míchál Thompson

SEE ALSO Bossi, Umberto; Nationalism and Regionalism

Sampaio, Jorge (1938–)

Portuguese opposition activist in the latter years of the Salazar/Caetano regime. After the restoration of democracy in 1974, Jorge Sampaio served as a member of the National Assembly, Socialist Party parliamentary leader, and mayor of Lisbon. He became president of Portugal in March 1996.

Sampaio was born in Lisbon on September 18, 1939. He studied law at the Faculty of Law of the University of Lisbon. Stimulated by the presidential campaign of Humberto Delgado in 1958, he became a political activist. As president of the Faculty of Law Academic Association in 1960–61, and as secretary-general of the Conference of Academic Associations in 1961–62, he played a key role in the academic crisis of 1961–62, when Salazar ordered the police to enter the University of Lisbon to crash protests. During the 1960s he served as defense attorney of several political prisoners.

During the Caetano liberalization in 1969, Sampaio was a candidate of the Democratic Electoral Commission to the National Assembly. But like other opponents of the regime, he refused to participate in the 1973 elections because of the lack of guarantees of a genuinely free election. In the aftermath of the April 1974 revolution, he participated in the organization of the Movimento da Esquerda Socialista (the Movement of the Socialist Left) but left it when it adopted a Marxist ideology and became a political party. In March 1975 he joined the fourth provisional government as secretary of state for external cooperation. In July he resigned along with the ministers of the Socialist, Social Democratic, and Center Democratic Parties to protest the radicalization of the government by the Armed Forces Movement, the military organization that had engineered the revolution, had moved further to the left, and now, with the support of the Communist Party, was attempting to institutionalize itself as the government of Portugal. He formally joined the Socialist Party in 1978 and was elected deputy in 1980, 1985, 1987, and 1991. In 1987 he was elected head of the parliamentary delegation and two years later he was elected secretary-general of the party. In 1989 he was elected mayor of Lisbon and was reelected in 1993. He resigned as mayor in 1995 to run for the presidency. Elected president in 1996, he succeeded Mario Soares and became the second civilian president since 1926.

BIBLIOGRAPHY

Bruneau, Thomas C. *Politics and Nationhood: Post Revolutionary Portugal.* New York: Praeger, 1984.

Bruneau, Thomas C., and Alex MacLeod. *Politics in Contemporary Portugal: Parties and the Consolidation of Democracy.* Boulder, Col.: Westview Press, 1986.

Maxwell, Kenneth. *The Making of Portuguese Democracy.* Cambridge: Cambridge University Press, 1995.

Paul Brasil

SEE ALSO Soares, Mario

Sands, Bobby (1954–81)

Irish political activist, prisoner, and prison protest leader; Northern Irish MP for Fermanagh–South Tyrone, April–May 1981. Bobby Sands was born in Belfast in 1954. In 1973 he was arrested and imprisoned on a weapons charge as an Irish Republican Army (IRA) terrorist struggling to end the union of Ulster with Great Britain and to unite it to the Republic of Ireland. He served three years of his five-year sentence and during this time had special-category (political prisoner) status while he was in the Belfast Maze Prison. In 1977 he was back in police custody as an I.R.A. suspect and was eventually sentenced to fourteen years' imprisonment. As soon as he was in the Maze, he joined the republican (IRA) prisoners who were campaigning for the restoration of special category status. During the hunger strike in 1980 he became the leader of the republican prisoners in the Maze. The following year he began his fatal hunger strike in support of the demand for political-prisoner status. His cause was gaining support which was illustrated by the fact that he was elected MP while in prison in the 1981 by-election for the Fermanagh–South Tyrone seat. This election victory translated into more widespread support for the republican movement. Although there was much pressure on Sands to abandon his hunger strike from both politicians and churchmen, he remained on it for sixty-six days. On his sixty-sixth day of fasting, Sands became the first of ten republican prisoners to die during this protest.

BIBLIOGRAPHY

Sands, Bobby. *Bobby Sands, Irish Rebel: A Self-Portrait in Poetry and Polemics, Issued on the 10th Anniversary of His Death.* Ed. with a preface by Robert West. Lewiston, N.Y.: E. Mellen Press, 1991.

———. *One Day in My Life.* Intro. by Sean MacBride. Chicago: Banner Press, 1985.

———. *Skylark Sing Your Lonely Song: An Anthology of the Writings of Bobby Sands.* Introduction by Ulick O'Connor. Dublin: Mercier Press, 1982.

Ricki Schoen

SEE ALSO Ireland, Northern: Political Parties: Irish Republican Army

San Marino

Independent state completely surrounded by Italian territory. San Marino with its 23.5 square miles (62 sq km) and 23,400 inhabitants is a city-state that survived the process of Italian unification. It was reputedly allowed to continue its separate existence because of the refuge it provided to nineteenth-century Italian revolutionaries, including Giuseppe Garibaldi. Its constitution dates from 1600, with revisions in 1929 and 1939. The sixty members of the Great and General Council (parliament) are elected every five years by a suffrage that, since 1960, has been universal. In 1945, the Sanmarinese elected a Communist government. In 1957, for a period of two months, two rival bodies—one Communist, the other anti-Communist—claimed to be the legitimate government. In 1988, the Communist Party and the Christian Democrats running on a combined ticket won the parliamentary election. The General Council elects two captains regent who serve as head of state for a six-month term.

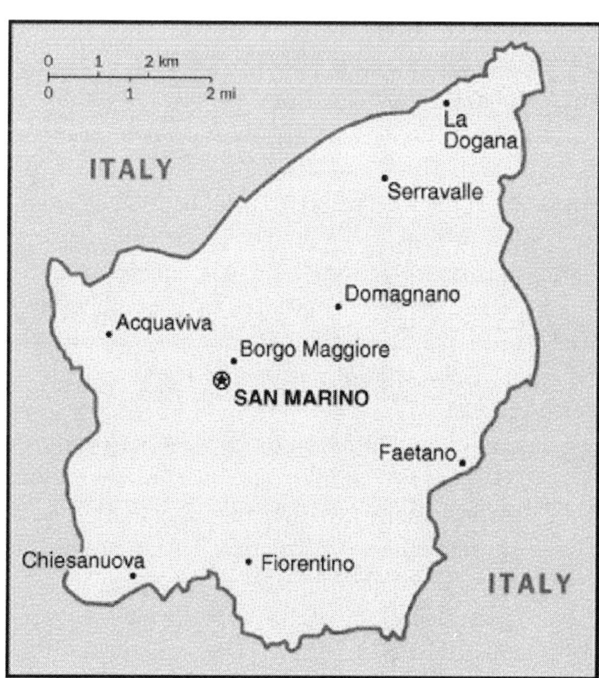

San Marino. *Illustration courtesy of Bernard Cook.*

Women were allowed to run for public office as of 1973. In 1981, Maria Lea Pedini Angelini became the first female elected to the Captains Regency. The General Council also elects from its ranks ten secretaries of state, who exercise executive power in an executive council, the Council of State. The secretary of state for foreign affairs and the secretary of state for internal affairs are the leaders of the government. In 1989, Gabrielle Gatti was elected secretary of state for internal affairs. Finally, the General Council also elects the Council of Twelve, in effect a Supreme Court, which hears judicial appeals.

San Marino, whose economy is fueled by tourism, provides a generous social welfare system. The Sanmarinese receive free health care and free education through the university level. San Marino guarantees all its citizens work or compensation amounting to 60 percent of an individual's usual salary. It also pays up to 75 percent of the cost for citizens residing abroad to return to vote in general elections.

San Marino, which has no standing army, is tied to Italy by a customs union and a treaty of friendship dating from March 22, 1862. In 1992 it joined the United Nations and, although not a member, it has been granted free trade with the European Union.

BIBLIOGRAPHY

Bent, James T. *A Freak of Freedom or the Republic of San Marino.* Port Washington, N.Y.: Kennikat, 1970.

Rossi, Giuseppe. *A Short History of the Republic of San Marino.* San Marino: Artioli-Modena, 1954.

Bernard Cook

Sant, Alfred (1948–)

Prime minister of Malta. Alfred Sant was born on February 28, 1948. After receiving a masters degree in physics at the University of Malta, he earned a diploma from the Institute International d'Administration Publique in Paris, an M.B.A. from the University of Boston, and, finally, a doctor of business administration from Harvard University in 1979. In the early 1970s he had been the second, then the first secretary at the Maltese mission to the European Community, but he resigned from Malta's foreign service in 1975 to undertake studies in the United States.

In 1977–78 Sant was a financial adviser at the ministry of parastatal and people's industries, and in 1979–80 he was managing director of Medina Consulting Group, which advised businesses. Between 1980 and 1982 he was executive deputy chairman of the Malta Development Corporation, set up by the Maltese parliament in 1967 to promote industry and attract foreign investment to Malta.

In 1982 Sant was appointed chairman of the information department of the Malta Labour Party (MLP). He was elected party president in 1984 and held that post until 1988. From 1984 to 1988 Sant was chairman of an educational foundation supported by the MLP and the General Workers Union, the largest general union in Malta, the Guze' Ellul Mercer Foundation. He was elected to parliament in 1987. In 1992 he was elected leader of the MLP. With the victory of the MLP in the 1996 election, Sant became prime minister.

Under the leadership of Sant the MLP shifted away from its previous socialist and sometimes violently confrontationalist stance toward a more liberal economic position and has severed its formal ties with the General Workers Union.

Following disagreements within his party Sant was forced to call an early election, which he lost, in September 1998; but he was reconfirmed as party leader and consequently as leader of the opposition.

A playwright and man of letters, Sant is one of the few Maltese intellectuals to become a prominent politician and arguably the only one to become premier. Although Dominic Mintoff, Sant's maverick, militant predecessor, largely caused Sant to call and to lose such an early election, the election also marked Mintoff's own disappearance from the political scene after half a century. Sant was reconfirmed as Labour leader after the electoral defeat and has since led the opposition.

BIBLIOGRAPHY

Dobie, E. *Malta's Road to Independence.* Norman, Okal.: University of Oklahoma Press, 1967.

Bernard Cook
Henry Frendo

Santer, Jacques (1937–)

Prime minister of Luxembourg from 1984 to 1994, and president of the European Commission, the administrative council of the European Union. Jacques Santer was born in Wasserbillig, Luxembourg, on May 18, 1937. He received a doctor of law degree from the University of Strasbourg and a certificate from the Institut d'Études Politiques in Paris. He then served as a barrister of the Court of Appeal in Luxembourg from 1961 to 1965. He was elected to parliament and served as parliamentary secretary of the Christian Social Party from 1966 to 1972. From 1972 to 1974 he was secretary-general of the Christian Social Party, and from 1974 to 1982 party chairman. In 1972 he entered the government as secretary of state for cultural and social affairs. From 1979 to 1984 he was minister of finance, labor, and social security. From 1984 to 1989 he was prime minister and minister of state for finance. During this period he was responsible for the post and telecommunications, the country's national computer center, the mass media, religious affairs, and regional planning. He simultaneously (1984–9) served as governor of the World Bank. From 1989 to 1994 he was prime minister, minister of state for finance, and minister for cultural affairs. He was simultaneously governor of the International Monetary Fund from 1989 to 1994, and from 1991 to 1994 governor of the European Bank for Reconstruction and Development.

Santer was elected to the European Parliament in 1975 and from 1975 until 1977 served as its vice president. He was chair of the center-right political group in the European parliament, the European People's Party, from 1987 to 1990. On July 15, 1994, Santer was unanimously nominated by the leaders of the European Union (EU) to succeed Jacques Delors as president of the European Commission. The EU leaders had met in June at Corfu and deadlocked over a choice. Santer's election had been contested in the European Parliament, and he had also been opposed by the Greens, who complained that the Council's desire to appoint a colorless president was part of its plan to increase the Commission's power. Nevertheless, he was endorsed on July 21, 1994.

Bernard Cook

Saragat, Giuseppe (1898–1988)

Italian politician, president from 1964 to 1971. Born in Turin in 1898, Giuseppe Saragat was a volunteer in the Italian army during World War I. After the war he studied economics at the University of Turin. In 1922 he joined the Unitary Socialist Party and became one of its leaders. During the fascist period (1926–43) he was exiled to France, where he joined other Italian political refugees like Pietro Nenni. Saragat, together with Nenni, directed the paper *Nuovo Avanti!* and favored rejoining the two socialist parties.

Soon after Italy's surrender to the Allies in September of 1943, he returned to Italy. However he was arrested and placed in custody by the Germans, who now occupied the northern two-thirds of Italy, but he escaped. In 1944 he was an executive member of the Italian Socialist Party of Proletarian Unity (PSIUP) and a minister without portfolio during the time of Ivanoe Bonomi's nonparty government from June 1944 to June 1945, which reunited all antifascist forces. After the war Saragat returned to France for one year as the Italian ambassador. In 1946 he was elected to the Constituent Assembly and became its president. In January 1947 he resigned from this office to lead a faction that withdrew from the PSIUP because of opposition to the idea of a coalition with the Communist Party. Saragat founded the Italian Socialist Party of Italian Workers (later, Italian Social Democratic Party, PSDI), of which he was undisputed leader.

Saragat favored the entry of Italy into NATO and advocated European integration. Thanks to his sharp differentiation from the Nenni-led Italian Socialist Party, he could collaborate with the Christian Democratic Party (DC). From 1947 to 1949 he was minister in the government of Alcide De Gasperi, and from 1954 to 1957 he was vice president in governments presided over by Christian Democrats Mario Scelba and Antonio Segni. The latter government failed because of Saragat's distrust; at that time he tried to disengage himself from the DC to establish better contacts with the Italian Socialist Party (PSI), led by Nenni.

The Hungarian Revolution of 1956 put an end to the PSI's sympathies with the Soviet bloc and with the Italian Communist Party. That change created the conditions for a center-left government with the participation of the PSI. This took place in 1963, was presided over by Aldo Moro. Saragat was elected to the presidency in 1964. He achieved this office thanks to Communist support, according to a coalition that Saragat himself had favored in the name of "antifascist values." When Saragat's term of office expired he returned to parliament as a life member of the Senate (upper house). He died in Rome on June 10, 1988.

BIBLIOGRAPHY

Casanova, Antonio. *Saragat.* Turin: ERI, 1991.

Delzell, Charles F. *Italy in the Twentieth Century.* Washington, D.C.: American Historical Association, 1980.

Indrio, Ugo. *Saragat e il socialismo italiano dal 1922 al 1946.* Venice: Marsilio, 1984.

Dario Caroniti

Sarajevo

Capital of Bosnia-Hercegovina, this city of 450,000 endured the longest siege in modern times following the outbreak of war in Bosnia on April 6, 1992. By 1994 over ten thousand of its residents had been killed and at least sixty thousand wounded by shells and sniper fire from rebels loyal to the Serbian Republic of Bosnia who had encircled the city.

Bombing resulting in the "water queue" massacre of May 27, 1992; the market massacre of February 4, 1994, which killed sixty-nine people; and the deaths of thirty-four others on August 28, 1995 drew the United Nations and, finally NATO, deeper into the conflict. NATO launched a two week bombing campaign that together with a Bosnian and Croat offensive broke the ability and will of the Bosnian Serbs to continue fighting. The duration of the siege—from April 6, 1992 until November 1995—and the suffering endured by a city whose reputation for multiethnic tolerance was part of its distinctiveness, was widely felt to have undone much of the progress that had resulted in Europe from the ending of the Cold War.

The Dayton Peace Accords of November 1995 assigned control over Sarajevo and its suburbs to the Bosnian government. Before the Serb suburbs were handed over, most of their inhabitants, encouraged by the Bosnian Serb leaders, fled to areas assigned to the Serbs. They took what they could and some set fire to their homes before leaving.

BIBLIOGRAPHY

Filipovic, Zlata. *Zlata's Diary: A Child's Life in Sarajevo.* Intro. by Janine Di Giovanni, tr. by Christina Pribichevich-Zoric. New York: Viking, 1994.

Karahasan, Dzevad. *Sarajevo, Exodus of a City.* Tr. by Slobodan Drakulic, afterword by Slavenka Drakulic. New York: Kodansha International, 1994.

Tom Gallagher

Sardinian Autonomism

Sardinian autonomism has its roots in the nineteenth century and found its full political expression in the Partito Sardo D'Azione (Sardinian Party of Action), the PSDA in 1921. The PSDA attracted people who fought during the First World War, among them Emilio Lussu and a substantial part of the Sardinian intelligentsia. The victory of the fascist regime in Italy increased divisions in the party between those who thought it possible to obtain a large degree of autonomy for Sardinia from the fascists and those who decidedly rejected fascism. Other political groups also held autonomist ideas. Of distinctive importance was the formation of an autonomist current in the Sardinian Communist Party and in the Catholic movement. At the end of the Second World War almost all Sardinian political forces had adopted an autonomist position, but their internal divisions prevented Sardinia from obtaining true autonomous status from Italy. Sardinia was recognized as a region with autonomous status by the

Italian constitution, but this nominal autonomy was far from what the autonomists had done. In the 1950s and 1960s Sardinian autonomism was identified chiefly with Christian Democracy. A plan of Sardinian economic development, which required financial interventions from the Italian government, was charted.

In the 1970s there was resentment among many Sardinians at the low level of development, and autonomism became an issue for the forces of the left. The PSDA again accentuated the call for independence. In the meantime a movement for the defense of the Sardinian language and culture developed, advocating recognition of a Sardinian national identity. The PSDA in the 1980s obtained important electoral support but was not able to maintain it. The autonomist demand became the patrimony of all Sardinian political forces. So far none has succeeded in advancing a successful proposal in the debate on the federal reform of the Italian state that animates the political discussion in the 1990s.

BIBLIOGRAPHY

Brigaglia, Manlio, ed. *Enciclopedia della Sardegna.* Cagliari: Edizioni della Torre, 1982.

Cubeddu Salvatore, Sardisti. *Viaggio nel Partito Sardo d'Azione tra cronaca e storia.* Vols. 1–3. Sassari: Edes, 1993–95.

Del Piano, Lorenzo, ed. *Antologia storica della questione sarda.* Padua: CEDAM, 1962.

Murru Corriga, Giannetta, ed. *Etnia Lingua Cultura: Un dibattito aperto in Sardegna.* Cagliari: Edes, 1977.

Sechi, Salvator. *Il movimento autonomistico in Sardegna (1918–1925).* Cagliari: Fossataro, 1975.

Daniele Petrosino

Sartre, Jean-Paul (1905–1980)

French philosopher, playwright, and novelist, the predominant voice of French existentialism, and epitome of the engaged intellectual. Jean-Paul Sartre articulated his philosophy of existentialism in an early novel, *Nausea* (1938), and the demanding essay, *Being and Nothingness: An Essay on Phenomenological Ontology* (1943). These two works established individual freedom and responsibility as the primary themes of his intellectual journey, in which he embraced Marxism and, in the *Critique of Dialectical Reason* (1960), sought to synthesize it with existentialism. His writings embody many of the major themes of Western thought since the Enlightenment: secularization, consciousness, historicism, materialism, and concern with the ethical.

Sartre was born into a bourgeois family and educated in La Rochelle and Paris. His education culminated at the École Normale Supérieure in Paris, where he studied philosophy and met his lifelong companion, Simone de Beauvoir. After completing his military service, he taught philosophy at lycées in Le Havre and Paris, interrupting his career with a year in Germany (1933–34) to read the phenomenology of Edmund Husserl and Martin Heidegger. In 1939 he was drafted and fought the invading Germans in May, 1940. Made a prisoner of war in 1940 by the victorious Germans, he was released in 1941. He spent most of World War II in Paris, writing, contributing to Resistance newspapers, and becoming the center of the intellectual world of Left Bank Paris.

After the Liberation he helped launch and edit the journal, *Les Temps Modernes* (1945) and published perhaps his most widely read essay, Existentialism and Humanism (1946). This was also his most significant literary period. A volume of short stories entitled *The Wall* (1939) had appeared after *Nausea* and was followed by his three-volume novel, *The Roads to Freedom* (1945–49). And he produced his major theatrical works at this time: *The Flies* (1943), *No Exit* (1945), *Dirty Hands* (1948), and *The Devil and the Good Lord* (1951). Fiction and drama, in depicting characters facing ethical choices in concrete situations, brought his philosophy to life. Though he continued to write plays, the most important of which is *The Condemned of Altona* (1960), he increasingly turned from literature to the political.

During the 1950s Sartre moved toward a commitment to communism, causing a break with his friend Albert Camus. Sartre was jolted by the Soviet invasion of Hungary in 1956, and his intellectual evolution toward an existential Marxism continued. As he examined the relation of the individual to history and developed an existential, anti-Freudian psychoanalysis, he wrote biographies—*Baudelaire* (1946), *Saint Genet: Actor and Martyr* (1952), and *The Family Idiot: Gustave Flaubert* (1971–72)—and his autobiography, *The Words* (1964). Ten volumes of his critical and political essays have also appeared under the title *Situations* (1947–76). Sartre was awarded the Nobel Prize in literature in 1964 but refused it, citing the need to retain an uncompromised political independence. He was, indeed, constantly engaged in radical political activity, condemning American conduct in Vietnam, supporting anticolonial struggles, participating in the French uprising of 1968 (Events of May), and flirting with Maoism.

Sartre's existentialism insisted that existence precedes essence; that is, humans are born into a world of contingency, without intrinsic meaning or necessity, and are thus "condemned to be free." Humans create themselves. For Sartre, one is what one does—one is the sum of one's actions. Responsibility and anxiety accompany freedom, for humans are alone, without God or a priori certainties to guide them. There is no freedom not to choose, and one chooses oneself again and again through one's actions. Standards of choice are not grounded or objective but are themselves a matter of choice. Only retrospectively, through reflection on the "look" of others and what Sartre called "the lived," is one able to discern a meaning in one's choices. Though humans desire necessity or "being," Sartre rejected such objectification, as well as the reification of ethical categories, as "bad faith."

As Sartre increasingly considered the relation of individual freedom to social and historical context, he called the writer to be engaged in the world and write for the present. The critical task of the intellectual, and of literature, was to subject society and its bad faith to a penetrating look, and to affect change. His biographies reveal a central tension in his thought as they point both to his search for examples of individuals appropriating the circumstances in which they live and altering them in an exercise of their freedom, and to his growing preoccupation with the unrelenting historical conditioning that limits those individuals. By the time of the *Critique* his focus was no longer on the individual but on the group-in-fusion. Isolated individuals could be transformed by theory, that is, by the imagination that projects a future derived from examining the concrete present and creates a possible unity for life and experience, into a group, with the agency previously given to the individual, and a common, historically progressive project. For Sartre the model of such a group was the Marxist revolutionary proletariat struggling to transform its historical situation.

Throughout his intellectual evolution Sartre's thought remained intensely ethical and consistently committed to the centrality of freedom and of the imaginary. The philosopher of unabated human responsibility, Sartre remains today one of the most widely read and cited writers of the twentieth century.

BIBLIOGRAPHY

Cohen-Solal, Annie. *Sarte: A Life.* Tr. by Anna Cancogni. New York: Pantheon, 1987.

Flynn, Thomas R. *Sartre and Marxist Existentialism: The Test Case of Collective Responsibility.* Chicago: University of Chicago Press, 1984.

Howells, Christina, ed. *The Cambridge Companion to Sartre.* Cambridge: Cambridge University Press, 1992.

William E. Duvall

Sartzetakis, Christos (1929–)

Greek lawyer and president. Christos Sartzetakis is known for his principled interpretation of the law. The highlight of his career was to serve as premier of Greece from 1985 to 1989 during the rule of the Panhellenic Socialist Party (PASOK) government.

Sartzetakis was born in Thessaloníki in 1929. He studied law at the University of Thessaloníki and practiced law for one year before becoming a judge. In the judiciary he distinguished himself through his skill in combining legal expertise with ethical values. He rose quickly through the judicial ranks.

He received nationwide publicity in May 1963 when, as chief justice of Thessaloníki, he was assigned as examining judge in the Lambrakis murder case. Gregoris Lambrakis, a member of parliament for the Greek Democratic Left party (EDA), had been attacked and killed by ultra-right-wingers at a peace rally in Thessaloníki. Sartzetakis was pressured to keep a low profile in the proceedings, but succeeded in maintaining a high legal and judicial standard throughout the case, despite the public attention. His investigation showed links between the assassins and highly placed state officials. This affair served as the basis for Vasiles Vasilikos's novel *Z* and the film *Z,* directed by Costa-Gravas.

In 1965 Sarzetakis received a government scholarship to pursue studies in the field of international and comparative law. His studies were cut short, however, when following the successful military coup d'état in Athens he was asked to return to Greece by the authorities. Sarzetakis refused to comply with the guidelines that the military government imposed on the judicial branch and the practice of law. This resulted in his dismissal on May 29, 1968, from the judicial body and marked the beginning of a period of persecution and imprisonment by the junta. The authorities released him in November 1971 following the protests of the international community, especially the French government. When democracy was reinstated in Greece in 1974, Sarzetakis returned to the legal profession as a judge in the Court of Appeals of Athens. In 1981 he became president of the syndicate of judges of the Court of Appeals of Nafplion, and shortly thereafter was promoted to the highest legal honor as a Supreme Court judge. Having reached the pinnacle of his legal career, he was recommended by the Panhellenic Socialist Party (PASOK) for the position of president of Greece. He held the highest post in government following a vote in parliament on March 29, 1985. He held that position until May 4, 1990.

BIBLIOGRAPHY

Vasilikos, Vasiles. *Z.* New York: Four Walls Eight Windows, 1991.

Stelios Zachariou

Savisaar, Edgar (1950–)

Founding member of the Popular Front, an organization founded on April 13, 1988 to work for the restoration of Estonian independence, and prime minister of Estonia (1990–92). Edgar Savisaar was a critically important figure during the Estonian independence period, but he was increasingly isolated by the growing nationalist movement among ethnic Estonians, who distrusted his attempts at conciliation with Moscow and the ethnic Russians living in Estonia. He played a key role in the transition from communism to liberal democracy as Estonia achieved its independence from the USSR. After his resignation as prime minister, he formed the Center Party out of the rump of the Popular Front. He entered a coalition government led by Tiit Vahi after the 1995 elections until he was forced to resign his office because of a scandal.

After receiving a Ph.D. in social philosophy, Savisaar worked part-time at the Estonian Academy of Sciences and as a planner in the capital, Tallinn. He became a department head in the State Planning Committee in 1985 and its chair in 1989. A leading figure of the reformist wing of the Estonian Communist Party, he was one of the four authors of an economic plan that sought to achieve economic autonomy of Estonia (*Ise-Majandav Eesti,* Self-Managing Estonia, IME) in 1987.

Taking a position between the radicals who sought to abolish the Soviet regime and the Communists, Savisaar pursued his reform agenda within the established Soviet framework. In 1988 he took the initiative in the formation of the Popular Front for the Support of Perestroika (its original name) and became one of the five members of its executive committee. When the Soviets agreed in principle to Estonian economic autonomy in July 1989, Savisaar became deputy prime minister in charge of economic reform, preparing the country for economic self-government and a market economy.

In the elections to the Estonian Supreme Soviet, the Communist era "representative" body in 1990, the Popular Front, with help from pro-independence ethnic Russian voters, achieved a two-thirds' majority, enabling the Supreme Soviet to enact constitutional changes, declare that Estonia was moving to full independence, and elect Savisaar prime minister with a cabinet composed largely of former Communists like him.

Savisaar faced acute problems associated with economic transition, including fuel and food shortages, high inflation, and growing unemployment. He tried to steer a course between the aggressive Soviet tactics and the increasingly radical policies of Estonian nationalists. He sought compromise with ethnic Estonian Russians, particularly over citizenship and language policies, and lost support from the radicals as a result. He maintained good links with Soviet military commanders, averting the kind of attacks by Soviet forces that took place in Latvia and Lithuania. He was in office when independence was achieved as a result of the failed Moscow coup attempted in August 1991 against President Mikhail Gorbachev. However, his government fatally lost support among ethnic Estonians over his willingness to compromise with the Russians over the states of the Russian majority in the city of Narva, and over his demand for emergency powers to tackle the fuel crisis in 1992. The outrage that greeted the realization that his small majority in the Supreme Council, as the legislative was now called, depended on ethnic Russian votes led to his defeat in parliament and his resignation as prime minister.

Once out of office, he turned what was left of the Popular Front into a center-left party that, though reformist, attempted to protect ordinary people from the worst effects of adapting to the free market. In the 1995 parliamentary election this Center Party polled strongly, drawing on the support of the urban working class, and became part of the government coalition with the Consolidation Party of Vahi and the Rural Union of Arnold Rüutel. The coalition collapsed when Savisaar had to resign over a taping scandal. After the local elections of 1996, he became chair of the Tallinn City Council, and remains an MP. He and his party should continue to play a significant part in Estonian politics.

BIBLIOGRAPHY

Hiden, John, and Patrick Salmon. *The Baltic Nations and Europe: Estonia, Latvia and Lithuania in the Twentieth Century.* Harlow, England: Longman, 1991.

Lieven, Anatol. *The Baltic Revolution: Estonian, Latvia, Lithuania and the Path to Independence.* New Haven, Conn.: Yale University Press, 1983.

Norgaard, Ole, et al. *The Baltic States after Independence.* Cheltenham, England: Edward Elgar, 1996.

Smith, Graham, ed. *The Baltic States: The National Self-Determination of Estonia, Latvia, and Lithuania.* Basingstoke, England: Macmillan, 1994.

Taagepera, Rein. *Estonia: Return to Independence.* Boulder, Colo.: Westview Press, 1993.

Thomas Lane

Scalfaro, Oscar Luigi (1918–)

Italian president (1992–99). Oscar Luigi Scalfaro was born in Novara on September 9, 1918. He obtained a law degree at the Università Cattolica Sacro Cuore in Milan. During the Second World War he sided with the antifascists and was highly active in diocesan organizations and in the lay Catholic Action organization, which, for a time, he directed. In 1945 he became public prosecutor in the Special Courts of Assizes of Novara and Alessandria. He was elected as a Christian Democrat to the Constituent Assembly in 1946. He was elected to the Chamber of Deputies (lower house of parliament) in the 1948 elections and held his seat until he assumed the presidency.

Scalfaro belonged to the moderate faction of the Christian Democrats (DC) and distinguished himself in several campaigns for raising of moral standards in politics. He obtained his first government appointment during the Mario Scelba cabinet (1954–55) when he was deputy to the prime minister and deputy minister at the Ministry of Labor and Social Security. From 1955 to 1958 he served as deputy minister at the Ministry of Justice, and as deputy minister at the Ministry of the Interior from 1959 to 1962. He was vice secretary for the DC from 1964 to 1966.

Scalfaro was minister of transportation during the third government headed by Aldo Moro (1966–68). He held the same position during the second government of Giovanni Leone (1968) and in the first government of Giulio Andreotti (February 1972). He was organizing secretary for the DC from 1970 to 1972, served as minister of education during the second government of Giulio Andreotti (1972–73), and vice deputy speaker of the Chamber of Deputies from October 1975 to July 1983. He returned to the government during the two cabinets headed by Bettino Craxi (1983–87) with the prestigious post of minister of the interior. In July 1984 Scalfaro suspended two officials from the department of police suspected of abuse of office during the interrogation of several mafia suspects following the murder of commissioner Guiseppe Montana. A heated controversy that followed led Scalfaro's resignation, which was, however, rejected by the government. As minister of interior Scalfaro in 1986 defended the legitimacy of the religious organization Opus Dei, which had been challenged as a secret society, and which would have made it illegal.

In spring 1987, President Francesco Cossiga asked him to form a new government, describing Scalfaro as the right man in the right place as he was an ex-member of the Constituent Assembly, deputy speaker of the Chamber, and "a person not part of any faction inside his own party." But Scalfaro refused the appointment.

As a member of parliament Scalfaro presided over the commission of inquiry on measures taken for reconstruction of the territories in Basilicata and Campania destroyed by earthquakes in 1980–81. In this role he roused the ire many DC leaders, who were accused by the commission of having misappropriated for their own use the financial aid given to the earthquake victims.

Between 1991 and 1992 his defense of the constitution and of the prerogatives of parliament against President Cossiga, who in his defense of the paramilitary organization, Gladio, had roused intense parliamentary opposition, and as a consequence sought to increase the power of the presidency at the expense of parliament, brought him into open disagreement with Cossiga. On April 24, 1992, Scalfaro was elected president of the Chamber of Deputies by a narrow majority. On May 24, 1992, the Mafia assassinated Judge Giovanni Falcone, an incident that shook public opinion. Parliament, which had been sitting for several weeks to elect a new president, responded by agreeing on Scalfaro, who was elected president on May 25, 1992.

In March 1993, he refused to countersign a law that tried to save political leaders involved in the *Tangentopoli* (bribe city) scandal by depenalizing the crime of illicit party financing. In October the public prosecutor of Rome ordered the arrest of some officers and executives of the Italian secret service, accused of having illegally managed slush funds. The following November a defendant implicated all ministers of the interior from 1982 to 1992, with the exception of Amintore Fanfani. Scalfaro vigorously rejected the accusation by means of a live televised personal message to the nation. He refused to be tried and spoke of a plot against the institutions of the state, he implying that there was a plot to avoid an early election, allowing in this way numerous members of parliament implicated in the bribes scandal, and who at that time were covered by parliamentary immunity, to avoid prison. The polemic against the head of state did not subside, so Scalfaro dissolved parliament and called new elections.

In May 1994, he asked Silvio Berlusconi, leader of the center-right formation that won the parliamentary elections, to form a new government. Scalfaro's relationship with this new government, however, soon deteriorated. In December 1994, a minister openly accused him of conspiring against the government, and at the same time rekindled the polemics on his involvement in the secret service scandal. Scalfaro survived the attack serving out the rest of his term to May 15, 1999. The Berlusconi government, however, faired less well. It fell on January 17, 1995.

BIBLIOGRAPHY

Buonadonna, Sergio, and Roberto Ginex. *Guida alla seconda Repubblica.* Palermo: Arbor, 1994.

Montanelli-Cervi, Indro. *L'Italia degli anni di fango.* Milan: Rizzoli, 1994.

Vespa, Bruno. *Il cambio: Uomini e retroscena della nuova Repubblica.* Milan: Mondadori, 1994.

Dario Caroniti

SEE ALSO Berlusconi, Silvio

Scargill, Arthur (1938–)

British coal miner and labor union leader. Arthur Scargill was active in the National Union of Mineworkers (NUM), serving as the president of the Yorkshire area from 1973 to 1982, when he became national president. He led a yearlong strike over pit closures in 1984–85 and mounted vigorous campaigns for the preservation of the coal industry in the early 1990s.

Scargill gained national attention as leader of the 1984–85 coal miners' strike. This protest against the National Coal Board's decision to close several pits proved unsuccessful. The growing reliance on other forms of fuel and the stockpiling of coal at power stations meant that such a strike no longer had the same potential to destabilize the government as it had in the 1970s. The strike was also hampered by internal divisions that resulted in the formation of the Union of Democratic Mineworkers, a moderate group dissatisfied with Scargill's leadership.

In 1988 Scargill was elected to another five-year term as president of the NUM by a very narrow margin. However, he soon became embroiled in scandal involving funds that had been donated to the NUM by Soviet miners during the strike and did not make their way into NUM coffers. He managed to hold on to his post after arranging for the transfer of funds. In 1992 an announcement was made by the National Coal Board to scale back coal production by 60 percent and close thirty-one of fifty pits. Scargill mounted a renewed campaign to preserve the coal industry. He resisted his own inclination to call a strike and instead mobilized a cross section of middle England to protest the policy. This effort led to the Secretary of State for Industry and the President of the Board of Trade Michael Heseltine's announcement that the closure program would be reviewed and a Department of Trade Industry investigation would explore new markets for coal. In the wake of this policy change, Scargill gained a new international reputation and became active in European meetings on the management of energy resources. The reprieve for the pits proved short-lived as British Coal, the former nationalized British coal company, which was privatized under Major, announced more closures in spring 1993. Scargill ordered two one-day strikes that proved unsuccessful and, in May, the high court paved the way for the closures to be carried out.

BIBLIOGRAPHY

Routledge, Paul. *Scargill: The Unauthorized Biography.* London: Harper Collins, 1993.

Samuel, Raphael, et al., eds. *The Enemy Within: Villages and the Miners' Strike of 1984–85.* London: Routledge and Kegan Paul, 1986.

Eileen Groth Lyon

Schärf, Adolf (1890–1965)

Austrian vice chancellor (1945–57) and president (1957–65). Adolf Schärf was born into a working-class family in Nikolsburg, Moravia (in the present-day Czech Republic), on April 20, 1890. His family moved to Vienna, where he joined a socialist youth organization while in secondary school. He earned a doctorate in law at the University of Vienna. After completing his studies he fought as an officer in World War I. In 1918 he became secretary to the Social Democratic parliamentary leaders, among whom was Karl Renner. In July 1933 Schärf was elected to the upper house of parliament, but when Engelbert Dollfuss, the chancellor of Austria from 1932 to 1934 suppressed the Social Democratic Party, he was arrested and sent to the Wöllersdorf concentration camp for nine months. After his release he worked as a lawyer but was secretly the leader of an underground revolutionary branch of the socialist movement. Following the *Anschluss* (union with Nazi Germany), Schärf was twice imprisoned by the Nazis. After Germany's defeat in 1945, Schärf helped found the Austrian Socialist Party (SPÖ). He became its provisional chairman in April 1945 and its actual chair in December.

Renner appointed Schärf State Secretaries (minister) in the provisional government of Austria on April 27, 1945. Schärf was elected to the upper house and became vice chancellor on December 20, 1945, in the coalition government of the People's Party and the SPÖ, headed by Leopold Figl. When Julius Raab became chancellor in 1953, Schärf continued as vice chancellor until his election on May 5, 1957 as president, a largely ceremonial post, the most important political function of which is to commission the leader of one of the parliamentary parties to form a government. As vice chancellor Schärf played an important role in the negotiation of the 1955 Austrian State Treaty, which restored the sovereignty of Austria and ended the four power occupation dating from the end of World War II. When President Theodor Körner died in January 1957, Schärf defeated the candidate of the People's Party, Wolfgang Denk. He was elected to a second term on April 28, 1963, but died on February 28, 1965.

BIBLIOGRAPHY
Bischof, Günter. *Austria in the Nineteen Fifties.* New Brunswick, N.J.: Transaction Publishers, 1995.
Sully, Melanie A. *A Contemporary History of Austria.* New York: Routledge, 1990.

Bernard Cook

SEE ALSO Figl, Leopold; Raab, Julius; Renner, Karl

Scharping, Rudolf (1947–)

Minister-president of the German Land (state) of Rhineland-Pfalz (1991–94) and successor to Björn Engholm as Social Democratic Party (SPD) chair in 1993. Born on December 2, 1947, in Niederelbert, Rudolf Scharping studied political science, law, and sociology at the University of Bonn. Joining the SPD in 1966, he directed the SPD's youth organization (Jungsozialisten) in Rhineland-Pfalz from 1969 to 1974 before moving to its national committee (1974–76).

A member of the state legislature in Rhineland-Pfalz (1975–94), Scharping served as the secretary the SPD's parliamentary membership (1979–85) and, subsequently, chaired the party's parliamentary group (1985–91). During Scharping's chairmanship (1985–93) state elections in 1987 gave the SPD 44.8 percent of the vote and ended forty-four years of Christian Democratic rule in Rhineland-Pfalz, the home state of then Chancellor Helmut Kohl.

Scharping's regional successes propelled him onto the national scene in 1988 and landed him a seat on the SPD's executive committee. A Bundestag (lower house of parliament) representative since 1994, Scharping became a key leader of the SPD parliamentary delegation and rose to the highest party position, chairman. In the general elections of 1994, Scharping led the SPD in a surprisingly successful campaign, moving the party within a few percentage points of ending Chancellor Kohl's center-right coalition. Electoral failure split party loyalties among Gerhard Schröder, Oskar Lafontaine, and Scharping. In 1995 Oskar Lafontaine replaced Scharping as party chair and as the SPD's next candidate for chancellor.

BIBLIOGRAPHY
Leonhard-Schmid, Elke. *Aus der Opposition an der Macht: wie Rudolf Scharping Kanzler werden will.* Cologne: Bund-Verlag, 1995.
Lief, Thomas. *Rudolf Scharping, die SPD und die Macht eine Partei wird besichtigt.* Reinbek bei Hamburg: Rowohlt, 1994.
———. *Rudolf Scharping: der Profil.* Düsseldorf: ECON, 1994.

David A. Meier

Scheel, Walter (1919–)

Foreign minister of the Federal Republic of Germany (1969–74) and president (1974–79). Walter Scheel became leader of the Free Democratic Party (FDP) in 1967. He brought flexibility to his party's traditional agenda of strong laissez-faire capitalism and limiting the growth of the welfare state. As co-architect of the social-liberal coalition in 1969 and as Chancellor Willy Brandt's foreign minister, Scheel helped prepare and implement Brandt's policy of *Ostpolitik,* his eastern policy of building relations with the Communist states of Eastern Europe in order to put pressure on the East German Communist regime. Scheel played a prominent role in relaxing relations with the Soviet Union and with the German Democratic Republic (East Germany). As party leader he also helped prevent the FDP's right wing from undermining his coalition arrangements with the Social Democrats, even at the price of several party members defecting to the Christian Democrats. Scheel's reward came in 1972 when the FDP almost quadrupled its seats in the Bundestag (lower house of parliament) in the November elections.

After Brandt's resignation over a spy scandal within his staff in 1974 and the succession of Helmut Schmidt to the chancellorship, Scheel was elected president, replacing Gustav Heinemann in that highly visible, albeit largely ceremonial, office. He pursued an activist yet statesmanlike presidency and restored much of the dignity the office had lost in the 1960s under Heinrich Lübke, when evidence surfaced that raised doubts about his personal and political integrity under the Nazis. In openly attacking political radicalism and embracing a broad historical perspective, Scheel set the tone and example for his widely esteemed successors, Karl Carstens and Richard von Weizsäcker.

BIBLIOGRAPHY
Baring, Arnulf. *Machtwechsel: Die Ära Brandt-Scheel.* Stuttgart: DVA, 1982.

Schneider, Hans R. *Walter Scheel.* Stuttgart: Bonn Aktuell, 1974.

Eric C. Rust

Schiller, Karl (1911–94)

West German Social Democratic politician. A professor of economics at the University of Hamburg since 1947, Karl Schiller, who joined the Social Democratic Party (SPD) in 1946, was senator (minister) of economics and traffic in Hamburg (1948–53), a member of the Hamburg Bürgerschaft (parliament, 1949–57), and senator of economics in West Berlin (1961–65). In 1965 Schiller became a Berlin delegate in the German Bundestag (lower house of parliament) and deputy chair of the SPD parliamentary caucus. He was minister of economics, first in the grand coalition with the Christian Democrats (1966–69), then in the coalition with the Free Democrats (1969–72). During 1971–72 he was also minister of finance.

Schiller is best known for his close cooperation during 1966–69 with Franz Josef Strauss, the Christian Social minister of finance. Schiller initiated major innovations in economic policy, including *Globalsteuerung,* a model for state intervention at the macroeconomic level to influence the economic cycle; *Mittelfristige Finanzplanung,* or medium-term financial and budgetary planning; *Konzertierte Aktion,* a policy to encourage close cooperation among government, labor unions, and employers; and, finally, the 1967 *Stabilitäts-und Wachstumsgesetz,* a Keynesian-inspired law for an anticyclical government spending policy.

After 1969 Schiller quickly became disillusioned with his party's public spending policies. He resigned in 1972 over his suggested public spending cuts. Schiller left the SPD and, together with Ludwig Erhard, his Christian Democratic predecessor as minister of economics and former chancellor, campaigned for the Christian Democrats in the 1972 general election, only to rejoin the SPD in 1980. Schiller remained active as an international economic adviser and was the SPD's liberal economic conscience. He was highly critical of the economic management of German reunification in 1990 and also of European monetary union, which went into effect on January 1, 1999, summarizing his views in the book *Der schwierige Weg* (*The Difficult Path*).

BIBLIOGRAPHY

Schiller, Karl. *Der Ökonom und die Gesellschaft: Das freiheitliche und das soziale Element in der modernen Wirtschaftspolitik. Vorträge und Aufsätze.* Stuttgart: Gustav Fischer Verlag, 1964.

———. *Der schwierige Weg in die offene Gesellschaft: Kritische Anmerkungen zur deutschen Vereinigung.* Berlin: Siedler, 1994.

Scholz, Robert. "Karl Schiller und die West-Berliner Wirtschaftspolitik 1961–1965," in Otto Busch, ed. *Beiträge zur Geschichte der Berliner Demokratie 1919–1933/1945–1985.* Berlin: Colloqium Verlag, 1988, 231–72.

Schiller's personal papers are located in the Bundesarchiv (Federal Archives) in Koblenz, Germany, N 1229.

Wolfram Kaiser

Schlöndorff, Volker (1939–)

German filmmaker. Volker Schlöndorff learned his filmmaking in France, where he studied and assisted some of the most prominent directors of French New Wave, Louis Malle, Alain Resnais, and Jean-Pierre Melville. Schlöndorff's work reflects the formal influence of this school of realist filmmaking.

When he returned to Germany after his apprenticeship, Schlöndorff directly addressed some troubling issues, particularly Germany's recent fascist past and the causes and consequences of National Socialism. To answer these questions, Schlöndorff, at least initially, turned to German twentieth-century literature. To be sure, Schlöndorff's interest in the literary had a practical side to it: Germany's film subsidy board looked favorably on literary adaptations thus assuring funding for his filmmaking. His first film, an adaptation of Robert Musil's classic novella from 1906, *Young Törless,* marked a new juncture in German film history: the rise of New German Cinema.

Internationally praised but notorious in Germany, the film presents a complex dialectic of victim and perpetrator that takes place in a young boy's military preparatory school. In many ways, this film can be read as a critical "prequel" to the Third Reich. In this institution, which is responsible for educating and socializing the leaders, officers, and state officials of tomorrow, the protagonist is fascinated and repulsed, and ultimately does nothing, as two of his cohorts mercilessly taunt and torment a Jewish classmate. The movie ends with the Jewish boy's suicide. Despite the horror of these events, the film's social and political critique is aimed at the educational institution that remained unchanged even after this acknowledged brutality and tragedy. *Young Törless* exposes the brutality, oppression, and tacit complicity that remained at work in

Germany during the Third Reich and even into the post-war era.

The Sudden Wealth of the Poor People of Kombach (1971), co-directed with his then wife and acclaimed film-maker, Margarete von Trotta, presents a critical spin on the genre of *Heimatfilme,* an indigenous genre of democratizing Germany that casts Germany as a lost, bucolic, provincial paradise. This savage mockery of an extremely popular genre of early postwar German film served as the swan call for the genre as it faded away into a distant landscape of kitsch.

Schlöndorff made many psychological dramas and other film adaptations of twentieth century German classics: Heinrich Böll's *The Lost Honor of Katharina Blum* (1975), and Günther Grass's *The Tin Drum* (1979), which won gold prize at Cannes and then an academy award in 1980. His more recent work, *Voyager* (1990), which stars Sam Shepard, is based on *Homo Faber,* the novella of Swiss writer, Max Frisch. Schlöndorff also filmed a version of Michel Tournier's allegory of fascism, *The Ogre.*

His films raise politically progressive issues and present them through an aesthetically conventional mode of realism. His topics are social, political, and historically pertinent issues. His contribution to the politically invested collaborative film, *Germany in Autumn,* provided an ironic commentary on the state of German current events. Schlöndorff's joint collaboration with Heinrich Böll was a staged debate about the circumstances that had supposedly prevented the broadcasting of *Antigone* on television. The television executives decide that the political and moral questions raised by this classic would be too inflammatory for contemporary Germany, because of the controversy surrounding Gudrun Ensslin's sister, whose ceaseless efforts to rally public awareness of the circumstances of the death of her sister, the jailed Red Army Faction terrorist, rendered a play about age-old themes of conflict between family and state loyalty too hot to touch.

Schlöndorff's films describe social reality as a historical dialectic. Despite the social commitment and historical mindedness of his films, they have enjoyed continued mass reception and Hollywood recognition. Schlöndorff seems to have achieved the balance of critical vision and popular appeal. What his representational techniques lack in formal daring, they make up in accessibility. Schlöndorff, who ascribes to Bela Belaz's description of the art of film as making "everything look what it is," uses film to promote a political realism. Being firmly within a realist tradition makes his films accessible. Schlöndorff, unlike his uncompromising counterparts Rainer Werner Fassbinder, Alexander Kluge, and Jean-Marie Straub, remains a critical and yet popular filmmaker of the New German Cinema.

BIBLIOGRAPHY

Cook, David A. *A History of Narrative Film.* New York: W. W. Norton, 1981.

Corrigan, Timothy. *New German Cinema: The Displaced Image,* rev. ed. Bloomington: Indiana University Press 1994.

Elsaesser, Thomas. *New German Cinema: A History.* New Brunswick: Rutgers University Press, 1989.

Rentschler, Eric, ed. *German Literature on Film: Adaptations and Transformations.* New York: Methuen, 1986.

Jill Gillespie

SEE ALSO Fassbinder, Rainer Werner

Schlüter, Poul (1929–)

Danish Conservative politician, prime minister from 1982 to 1993. Poul Schlüter, a lawyer, was chairman of the Conservative Youth from 1952 to 1955. He served as a member of the Folketinget (parliament) from 1964 to 1994 for the Konservative Folkeparti (Conservative People's Party). He was chairman of the party's parliamentary group from 1974 to 1982 and political spokesman for his party from 1971 to 1981. He served as national president of the party from 1974 to 1977 and again from 1981 to 1993. He was prime minister and leader of several non-Socialist minority governments from 1982 and 1993, the longest tenure of any prime minister after World War II. Schlüter was, during this whole period, dependent on the support of other parties in parliament. This situation resulted in frequent general elections, in 1984, 1987, 1988, and 1990. In the area of economic policy he broke the long Social Democratic tradition of expanding the welfare state, often financed with foreign loans. Schlüter's governments pursued an anti-inflationary economic policy, reducing both public and private consumption. The competitiveness of Danish business was improved, and 200,000 new jobs were created. However, the level of unemployment continued to increase as well as Denmark's foreign debt during the 1980s. At the end of the 1980s international economic conditions and Denmark's trade balance improved. The foreign debt also started to decrease at the beginning of the 1990s as a consequence of Denmark's near self-sufficiency in oil and natural gas from the North Sea.

Schlüter's career as prime minister came to an end in January 1993. A report by a group of Supreme Court judges came to the conclusion that his former minister of justice, Erik Ninn-Hansen, had violated the immigration act by personally preventing family reunifications of Tamil refugees, a right they had according to the law. Schlüter resigned, hoping that a successor from his own party could replace him. But one of the parties in his coalition decided to leave and aligned itself with the Social Democratic Party. This paved the way for a new center-left government under Poul Nyrup Rasmussen.

In 1994 Schlüter was elected from the Conservative People's Party list to the European Parliament, the parliament of the EU, parliament and was subsequently elected vice-president of the European Parliament.

BIBLIOGRAPHY

Boelsgaard, Kurt. *Poul Schlüter, politikeren der samlede det borgerlige Danmark.* Copenhagen: Schultz, 1984.

Fonsmark, Henning B. *Schlüters Danmark.* Copenhagen: Borsen Boger, 1992.

Kristiansen, Michael. *Poul Schlüter.* Copenhagen: Spektrum, 1992.

Schlüter, Poul. *Den lange vej—fra nederlag til fremgang.* Copenhagen: Peter la Cour, 1980.

Jørn Boye Nielsen

Schmid, Carlo (1896–1979)

West German Social Democratic politician and Bundestag member (1949–72). A former professor of international law and political science, Carlo Schmid was one of the intellectual leaders of the postwar Social Democratic Party (SPD). As a member of the party's national committee (1949–72) and one of its most prominent speakers on foreign affairs, Schmid was a key figure in the SPD's modernization and eventual emergence as a governing party in the Federal Republic of Germany (West Germany).

Born in southwest Germany, son of a German father and a French mother, Schmid began his career as a political outsider, representing a new breed of cosmopolitan Social Democratic politician. He was known for his intelligence and his joie de vivre, which earned him the nickname "Monte Carlo." His intellectual reputation and personality distinguished him from the often lackluster SPD leadership. His appeal to voters beyond traditional SPD worker strongholds signaled a change in German social democracy toward more tolerant left-liberal policies, which he then helped codify at the SPD's watershed party conference in Bad Godesberg in 1959.

Schmid was intimately involved in the reconstruction of West German democracy after 1945. After serving as justice minister of the new state of Württemberg-Hohenzollern, Schmid went on to serve as a member of the Parliamentary Council, which drafted the West German Basic Law. As the leading SPD representative on the Council, Schmid chaired the executive committee that worked out the main legal details of the new state structures. After his election to the first Bundestag (lower house of parliament) in 1949, Schmid rose to national prominence as an advocate of bipartisan cooperation, especially on foreign policy. He accompanied Chancellor Konrad Adenauer on his historic trip to Moscow in 1955. In 1959 he unsuccessfully ran as the SPD candidate for the federal presidency. His efforts to move the SPD into governmental responsibility were rewarded with the creation of the grand coalition cabinet of Social and Christian Democrats in which he served (1966–69). Beginning as an outsider, Schmid retired from the Bundestag in 1972 as one of the grand old men of the SPD.

BIBLIOGRAPHY

Carlo Schmid's personal Papers are in the Archiv der Sozialen Demokratie of the Friedrich-Ebert-Stiftung, Bonn, Germany.

Hirscher, Gerhard. *Carlo Schmid und die Grundung der Bundesrepublik: eine politische Biographie.* Bochum: Studienverlag N. Brockmeyer, 1986.

Schmid, Carlo. *Erinnerungen.* Bern: Scherz Verlag, 1979.

Ronald J. Granieri

Schmidt, Helmut (1918–)

Social Democratic (SPD) chancellor of the Federal Republic of Germany (1974–82). Helmut Schmidt continued the reforms of his predecessor, Willy Brandt, in a moderate fashion. As an economic expert above all, he achieved success in monetary policy. He also dedicated himself to a continued easing of international tensions and was concerned over the price to Germany of additional armaments. If he was referred to as the "Iron Chancellor," this was based on the adverse circumstances he confronted in the areas of international politics and the economy. His particular character traits, including self-assured determination, and inclination to describe himself as a "doer," who got things done, were also factors.

Schmidt's formation in his home city, Hamburg, and his experiences as a front-line soldier during World War II deeply influenced his professional development. The son of a teacher, he grew up in Barmbek, a traditional working-class district of Hamburg, which was reduced to soot and ash during the war. Born in 1918, Schmidt was destined for years of combat in Hitler's armies. Promoted

Helmut Schmidt, chancellor of the Federal Republic of Germany from 1974 to 1982. *Illustration courtesy of the German Information Service.*

to the rank of lieutenant, Schmidt ended the war as a prisoner of the British. After his release he returned to Hamburg and studied economics at the University of Hamburg. After receiving a doctorate in 1949, a professor arranged for him to enter the Hamburg city administration. He worked in the office of business and traffic until his election to the Bundestag (lower house of parliament) in 1953.

In 1961 he returned from Bonn to Hamburg. As a municipal senator he earned a national reputation the following year. During the catastrophic Hamburg flood of 1962 he demonstrated his remarkable talent for organization. Into the 1970s with the help of his ubiquitous Hamburg peaked Seaman's cap Schmidt cultivated the picture of the intrepid helmsman in the storm. He went again to Bonn in 1965 and assumed the top position in the SPD parliamentary caucus before becoming its chair in 1967. In 1969 he became defense secretary in the first Brandt cabinet and was already the uncontested crown prince.

Although the same age, the two Social Democrats personified two completely opposed political types. In the five years before 1974 they nevertheless worked together smoothly. Schmidt lacked Brandt's vision, which led West Germany to the new orientation of *Ostpolitik;* Brandt, on the other hand, was less comfortable than Schmidt in dealing with economic issues. When Schmidt became chancellor in 1974, the halcyon years of the social-liberal coalition had already passed. Under Brandt, large-scale social-political reforms had been launched that brought important advances in social and educational policies as well as in legislation on behalf of workers and wage policies. For a large portion of the working class the standard of living advanced rapidly. However, the recession of 1974 brought seemingly uncontrollable economic problems for the first time since the 1950s. The number of unemployed soared from three hundred thousand to over a million in 1975. Under these conditions coordination of expenditures and social welfare policies was the necessity of the hour and no longer a matter of political debate.

Schmidt as finance minister since 1972 initiated a successful stability program in 1973 that limited the German inflation rate to the lowest level of any western industrialized state. Together with his French counter-part and friend, President Valéry Giscard d'Estaing, he initiated the European currency system in 1979. It helped establish confidence in currency stability in the European Community because it replaced a system troubled by prolonged dollar weakness with a system of solid exchange rates. The harmonious finance policies established by France and Germany fell apart in 1981 as Giscard's successor, François Mitterrand, destroyed the French stabilization policy through excessive expenditures.

Schmidt was forced to endure the greatest test of his endurance in 1977. Terrorists kidnapped Hans-Martin Schleyer, the president of the German employers' association, and in the process killed his escort. They then demanded the release of imprisoned comrades. In the course of the negotiations Arab terrorists hijacked a Lufthansa plane with German tourists, flew it to Zomalia, murdered the pilots, and threatened to blow up the plane if their demands were not met. Schmidt finally ordered the storming of the plane by an elite German anti-terrorist squad, the GSG 9, and as a consequence, the terrorists already in detention in Germany began to kill themselves, and the kidnappers killed Schleyer. This antiterror strategy culminating in the incidents of 1977 brought Schmidt to the verge of resignation.

Relaxation of Cold War tensions ended in the mid-1970s, and a new phase of the Cold War emerged with an increasing arms buildup. The Soviet Union had supplemented its military superiority in conventional arms with SS-20 medium-range missiles, which threatened to further undercut the balance of deterrence in central Europe. Because the American security policy for Europe had been based solely on protection through intercontinental rockets, a threatening gap developed in deterrence. Could West Germany still assume that the United States would use its atomic weapons against the Soviet Union if the USSR used "only" conventional troops and medium-range rockets against the federal republic? Schmidt answered this question with a clear no.

Therefore, he pushed the leading Western power to modernize its medium-range weapons in West Germany and elsewhere in Western Europe. In 1979 NATO came to a similar decision, calling for an arms buildup if the United States and the USSR could not come to an agreement on a cutback of their medium-range missiles. However, neither Soviet leader Leonid Brezhnev nor U.S. Presidents Carter or Reagan were interested in responding to the pressure initiated by Schmidt for negotiations. In 1981, however, there were U.S.-Soviet negotiations that, after a successful beginning, came to nothing. Simultaneously, the West German policy of détente collapsed under the renewed flare-up of East-West confrontation following the Soviet invasion of Afghanistan in 1979 and the imposition of martial law in Poland in 1981.

As disagreements on economic-political questions increased, Schmidt's coalition partner, the Free Democratic Party (FDP), under the leadership of Foreign Minister Hans-Dietrich Genscher, sought a coalition change in favor of the Christian Democratic Union/Christian Social Union. Internal political tensions reached their high point with a massive demonstration of 300,000 to 500,000 protesters in Bonn on June 10, 1982, organized by the German peace movement against U.S. deployment of new medium-range missiles. Also the left wing of the SPD further distanced itself from the deployment agreement and in its opposition was supported by Brandt, the party's general-secretary.

Schmidt was ousted through a vote of no confidence in the Bundestag. He remained a member of parliament until 1987. Earlier, in 1983, became a coeditor of the most important German weekly, *Der Zeit.* He has also written several books on foreign policy issues.

His popularity with the German people, rooted in his role as a crisis manager and a leader of European integration, remained steady after 1977.

BIBLIOGRAPHY

Carr, Jonathan. *Helmut Schmidt: Helmsman of Germany.* London: Weidenfeld and Nicolson, 1985.

Lahnstein, Manfred, ed. *Leidenschaft zur praktischen Vernunft: Helmut Schmidt zum Siebzigsten.* Berlin: Siedler, 1989.

Schmidt, Helmut. *Eine Strategie für den Western.* Berlin: Siedler, 1986.

———. *Menschen und Machte.* Berlin: Siedler 1987.

———. *Die Deutschen und ihre Nachbarn.* Berlin: Siedler 1990.

Steffahn, Harald. *Helmut Schmidt.* Hamburg: Rowohit, 1990.

Georg Wagner
(Tr. by B. Cook)

SEE ALSO Brandt, Willy

Schnur, Wolfgang (1944–)

Lawyer and politician in the German Democratic Republic (GDR, East Germany). Wolfgang Schnur was born on June 8, 1944, in Stettin (now in Poland). He grew up an orphan. He studied law and became lawyer in Binz and later in Rostock. Schnur pleaded the cases of dissidents, conscientious objectors, and church members accused by the Communist East German State of various offenses against the regime. He was also a member of the Synod of the Federation of the Protestant Churches of the GDR. From the early 1970s he kept contact with the Ministerium für Staatssicherheit (Ministry for State Security, MfS; also known as the Stasi). Under the cover name "Torsten" he reported on his clients.

In October 1989 Schnur became cofounder and chairman of the opposition group Demokratischer Aufbruch (Democratic Start), a relatively conservative organization. In the GDR parliamentary election of March 18, 1990, Schnur's Christian Democratic Party and the German Social Union formed the conservative Allianz für Deutschland (Alliance for Germany). Schnur was the leading candidate of this alliance. But some days before the election his MfS membership became known and he resigned. Later he left the party, but in 1993 his license was revoked as a result of a new law on legal credentials. This decision was confirmed by the Bundesgerichtshof (Federal Court of Justice) in 1994. In 1996, Schnur was sentenced to a year's probation as a result of denunciations by former clients.

Jürgen Streller

Schröder, Gerhard (1910–89)

West German minister of the interior (1953–61), foreign affairs (1961–66), and defense (1966–69). A lawyer by training, Gerhard Schröder emerged in the 1950s as a skillful and popular Christian Democrat (CDU) politician and administrator who helped shape postwar German history, especially as foreign minister in the 1960s. After serving in two cabinets under Chancellor Konrad Adenauer, whose fourth and last term he opposed, Schröder stayed on as Chancellor Ludwig Erhard's foreign minister. In this capacity he helped move West Germany from its francophile position in the 1950s toward increased independence and flexibility in international relations. While favoring close affinity to the United States in such matters as the Cuban Missile Crisis (1962) and the developing war in Vietnam, he managed to maintain cordial relations with France without selling out West Germany's foreign policy to French President Charles de Gaulle. Notably he was an early proponent of British membership in the European Economic Community. Schröder also undercut the rigid Hallstein Doctrine that required the severing of West German diplomatic relations with any state other than the USSR that maintained diplomatic relations with East Germany with his own "policy of movement" by arranging trade agreements between West Germany and a number of Eastern European countries in the early 1960s.

Schröder later became defense minister in Kurt Georg Kiesinger's grand coalition government (1966–69). Subsequently, he ran in 1969 without success as the CDU's candidate for the office of president, losing to Social Democrat Gustav Heinemann. After almost two decades in prominent cabinet posts and with many accomplishments to his credit, Schröder retired in 1969 upon the formation of Willy Brandt's center-left coalition.

BIBLIOGRAPHY

Hanrieder, Wolfram F. *Germany, America, Europe: Forty Years of German Foreign Policy.* New Haven, Conn.: Yale University Press, 1989.

Kuper, Ernst. *Frieden durch Konfrontation und Kooperation.* Stuttgart: Fischer, 1974.

Schröder, Gerhard. *Decision for Europe.* London: Thames and Hudson, 1964.

Eric C. Rust

Schröder, Gerhard Fritz Kurt (1944–)

Social Democratic chancellor of Germany (1998–). Gerhard Schröder was born on April 7, 1944, in Mossenburg, Lower Saxony. His father died in World War II and his mother supported Schröder and his four siblings by working as a cleaning woman. Schröder became an apprentice salesperson at fourteen. He returned to school, however,

Gerhard Schröder, chancellor of the Federal Republic of Germany since 1998. A Social Democrat, he succeeded Helmut Kohl, a Christian Democrat who had been in office since 1982. *Illustration courtesy AFP/Corbis.*

and earned a law degree in 1976 from the University of Göttingen.

While working as a lawyer he became active in the Social Democratic Party (SPD), and in 1978 he became leader of the SPD youth group, the Young Socialists. He was elected to the Bundestag (lower house of parliament) in 1980. In 1986 he was appointed to the national executive board of the SPD. Schröder, who at first was associated with the left wing of the party, moved to a more centrist position. In the 1990s he was regarded sufficiently sympathetic to business to be selected a member of the board of Volkswagen.

In 1990, following the success of his SPD slate in the state elections, he became the minister president of Lower Saxony after forming a coalition between his SPD and the Green Party. In April 1998 he became SPD candidate for chancellor. In the September 27, 1998, election, Schröder and the SPD defeated Helmut Kohl and his Christian Democrats. The SPD victory can be attributed to a numbers of factors. Schröder projected an image of youthful vigor in contrast to Kohl. Some voters had tired of Kohl's leadership. Others were disaffected by continuing high levels of unemployment, especially in the East. Others reacted against the long and costly process of integrating the East into the federal Republic. The Christian Democrats won 28.4 percent of the vote and their Christian Social Union allies garnered 6.7 percent. The Social Democrats won 40.9 percent and Schröder formed a coalition with the Greens who won 6.7 percent of the vote.

Oskar Lafontaine, the chairman of the SPD, who played a central role in orchestrating the SPD's electoral victory was appointed minister of finance. Under increasing criticism for attempting to interfere with the Eurobank's fiscal policy and after fierce attacks from the British yellow press in particular, his tenure came to an abrupt end on March 11, 1999, when he resigned his ministerial post and simultaneously resigned as chairman of the SPD. Lafontaine's left-oriented economic policy, including the advocacy of higher taxes and wage increases calculated to stimulate demand, had upset financial and industrial interests in Germany and had been at odds with Schröder's economic pragmatism. Schröder also resented Lafontaine's independence, which was rooted in his position as chairman of the party.

Schröder, despite the resentment of the party's left wing, was able to win the support of a majority to succeed Lafontaine as party chairman. His national popularity dipped in 1999. He had campaigned promising to remove regulations from business in order to encourage job creation. In practice, however, Schröder vacillated between cuts to the social welfare budget and concessions to SPD's labor constituency. Nevertheless, by the end of the year Schröder profited from the scandal concerning unreported campaign contributions that tarnished the reputation of former chancellor Helmut Kohl and left the Christian Democratic Party in disarray.

BIBLIOGRAPHY

Schröder, Gerhard. *Und weil wir unser Land verbessern—:26 Briefe für ein modernes Deutschland.* Gerhard Schröder with Reinhard Hesse. Hamburg: Hoffmann und Campe, 1998.

———. *Reifeprüfung: Reformpolitik am Ende des Jahrhunderts.* Gerhard Schröder with Reinhard Hesse. Cologne: Kiepenheuer & Witsch, 1993.

Schröder, Gerhard, and Oskar Lafontaine. *Innovationen für Deutschland.* Göttingen: Steidl, 1998.

Bernard Cook

SEE ALSO Lafontaine, Oskar

Schumacher, Kurt (1895–1952)

West German Social Democratic leader. Kurt Schumacher, son of a merchant, was born in Kulm (later in Poland) on October 13, 1895. He studied at the Universities of Halle, Leipzig, Berlin, and Münster. While studying law and economics at the outbreak of World War I, he was commissioned as a subaltern and lost his right arm fighting against the Russians near Lodz in December 1914. After his recovery he returned to his studies and received a doctorate from the University of Münster in 1920.

In 1920 Schumacher became political editor of the Stuttgart Social Democratic newspaper *Schwäbische Tagwacht.* He was elected to the Württemberg state legislature in 1924 and to the Weimar Republic's parliament in 1930. He was unrestrained in his attacks on the Nazis and the Communists. When the Nazis came to power in 1933, he went into hiding but was soon arrested. He spent ten years in concentration camps. He was confined in an underground cell in Kuhberg for seventeen months, refusing an offer of release if he would convert to Nazism. He was released in 1943 but forbidden to return to Stuttgart. He was temporarily rearrested after the July 20, 1944, plot to kill Hitler but then again released.

After World War II, in October 1945, he convened a Social Democratic Party congress in Hanover. Delegates from the three western zones of occupied Germany attended and elected Schumacher party chairman. His position as chairman of the Sozialdemokratische Partei Deutschlands (Social Democratic Party, SPD) for all Germany was confirmed in May 1946, following the forced merger of the Social Democrats in the Soviet occupation zone with the Communists to form the Socialist Unity Party (Sozialistische Einhertsparter Deutschland SED). In March 1946 Schumacher was appointed to the Zonal Advisory Council by the British Military government to provide responsible German input concerning the British administration of its zone of occupation in Germany.

Schumacher attempted to broaden the support of the SPD by courting the middle class and people of religious conviction, but his adherence to a policy of socialization and his opposition to the West limited the party's appeal. Nevertheless, despite the efforts of the SED, the SPD won more votes in the 1947 Berlin elections than it had ever won before. Following the amputation of his left leg in 1948, Schumacher's tenuous health rapidly declined. He was embittered by the success of his Christian Democratic opponents, whom he felt had usurped the role that should rightly have been that of the SPD because of its opposition to Hitler. With the formation in 1949 of the Federal Republic of Germany (West Germany), led by Chancellor Konrad Adenauer and the Christian Democrats, Schumacher headed the Social Democratic opposition in the Bundestag (lower house of parliament). He rejected Adenauer's choice of an alliance with the West. To Schumacher this would have prevented any hope of German reunification, which was for him a paramount concern. He was opposed to the Schuman Plan, to NATO, and to German rearmament, seeing German nonalignment as the path to reunification. His promotion of neutrality, adherence to socialization, and general negativism cast a shadow over the party even after his death on August 20, 1952.

BIBLIOGRAPHY

Albrecht, Willy. *Kurt Schumacher: ein Leben für den demokratischen Sozialismus.* Bonn: Verlag Neue Gesellschaft, 1985.

Edinger, Lewis Joachim. *Kurt Schumacher: A Study in Personality and Political Behavior.* Stanford, Calif.: Stanford University Press, 1965.

Merseburger, Peter. *Der schwierige Deutsche, Kurt Schumacher: eine Biographie.* Stuttgart: Deutsche Verlags-Anstalt, 1995.

Schulz, Klaus-Peter. *Adenauers Gegenspieler: Begegnungen mit Kurt Schumacher und Sozialdemokraten der ersten Stunde.* Freiburg im Breisgau: Herder, 1989.

Zitelmann, Rainer. *Adenauers Gegner: Streiter für die Einheit.* Erlangen: D. Straube, 1991.

Bernard Cook

SEE ALSO Brandt, Willy

Schuman, Robert (1886–1963)

Premier (1947–48) and foreign minister (1948–53) of the Fourth French Republic. A prominent statesman during the early postwar years, Robert Schuman emphasized the importance of Franco-German rapprochement, and this goal was the basis for the so-called Schuman Plan, his proposal that became the European Coal and Steel Community. From the beginning of the Cold War he vigorously supported the American policy of containment of the USSR, and he played a significant role in the formation of the North Atlantic Treaty Organization (NATO).

Robert Schuman, the foreign minister of France, signs the treaty creating the North Atlantic Treaty Organization (NATO), Washington, April 4, 1949. *Illustration courtesy the Bettmann Archive.*

Born in Luxembourg to prosperous parents from Lorraine, Schuman grew up in Metz when it was under German rule, and he studied law at Bonn, Munich, and Berlin. He entered politics after Lorraine was returned to France and was elected deputy to the National Assembly (power house of parliament) from Metz in 1919. A devout Catholic, he aligned himself with the Christian Democrats, and in parliament he gained a reputation as an expert in public finances. After the beginning of World War II, in 1940, Premier Paul Reynauld appointed him minister for refugees and displaced persons. On June 27, 1940, although voting to confer full powers on Marshal Pétain, Schuman soon resigned from the Vichy government and worked for a short time with the Resistance.

Following the Liberation from the Germans in 1944, Schuman joined the Mouvement Républicain Populaire (Popular Republican Movement, MRP), a centrist Christian Democratic party. In 1945 he was reelected deputy of the Moselle, and he quickly rose to prominence because of the key role of the MRP in the volatile coalitions of the period. He was appointed finance minister by Premier Georges Bidault in 1946 and by Paul Ramadier in 1947. Committed to balanced budgets, Schuman attempted to promote fiscal restraint to limit inflation and to defend the franc.

From November 24, 1947, to July 19, 1948, he served as premier over a "third force" coalition that excluded Communists on the left and Gaullists on the right. When he faced a difficult financial crisis and industrial unrest, his government's margin for maneuver was severely constrained by the necessity to compromise with coalition partners. Schuman took a hard line against Communist-led strikes, and he worked for a close relationship with the United States as the Cold War developed. During his term the U.S. Congress voted for "stopgap aid" until the U.S.-sponsored Marshall Plan was finally approved. Economic hardship and anxiety about the resurgence of German power as the Western Allies prepared to re-establish a German government were the two major causes for the fall of his government.

From July 1948 to January 1953, Schuman headed the Ministry of Foreign Affairs in ten successive governments, providing continuity within an unstable political climate. As foreign minister, he strongly defended the European Recovery Program as well as French participation in the Atlantic Alliance and NATO. Recognizing that the

French were unable to prevent the United States and Great Britain from promoting the economic and military development of West Germany, Schuman decided that the best way to preserve peace in Europe was to integrate the German economy into a larger multinational system. On May 9, 1950, he proposed the Schuman Plan (actually drafted by Jean Monnet), which offered to merge the coal and steel industries of France and Germany under a common authority. The resulting Treaty of Paris, signed in 1951, established the European Coal and Steel Community, which later evolved into the European Economic Community (1957) and eventually the European Union (EU, 1993). On colonial issues Schuman supported more flexible arrangements that eventually resulted in the independence of the French North African colonies of Morocco and Tunisia. He was also one of the principal spokesmen for the unsuccessful Pleven Plan, which would have included German regiments within a European Defense Community (EDC). The bitter debates over the negotiations and ratification of the EDC treaty led to his resignation as foreign minister in 1953.

In 1955 Schuman was appointed minister of justice by Premier Edgar Faure. Although fading from the political spotlight after Charles de Gaulle's return to power and the founding of the Fifth French Republic in 1958, he served as first president of the European Parliamentary Assembly from March 1958 to March 1960, and continued as honorary president until February 1963. He died on September 4, 1963.

BIBLIOGRAPHY

Hitchcock, William. "France, the Western Alliance, and the Origins of the Schuman Plan, 1948–1950." *Diplomatic History* 21 (1997):603–30.

Hostiou, Réne. *Robert Schuman et l'Europe.* Paris: CUJAS, 1969.

Poidevin, Raymond. *Robert Schuman: Un homme d'état, 1886–1963.* Paris: Imprimerie Nationale, 1986.

Schuman, Robert. *Pour l'Europe,* 2d ed. Paris: Nagel, 1960.

Thomas T. Lewis

SEE ALSO European Defense Community; European Union; Marshall Plan; Monnet, Jean; North Atlantic Treaty Organization; Schuman Plan

Schuman Plan

Established a free-trade area for coal and steel among six European states. The European Coal and Steel Community (ECSC) formally came into being on July 25, 1952, and operated until July 1, 1967, when its functions were subsumed by the European Economic Community (EEC). The aim of the ECSC was to abolish all customs barriers against the trade of coal and steel among Belgium, France, West Germany, Italy, Luxembourg, and the Netherlands, and to promote greater average productivity and efficiency in the coal and steel industries through regional specialization. The ECSC was the model for later projects toward European integration such as the European Defense Community (EDC), the European Atomic Energy Community (Euratom), and the EEC itself.

The significance of the ECSC lay less in its economic objectives—previous attempts had been made in the 1920s to conjoin Franco-German coal and steel production—than in its novel political framework. The ECSC, designed by Jean Monnet, the French economic expert who devised the Monnet Plan for French economic recovery of the World War II, and formally proposed by French Foreign Minister Robert Schuman on May 9, 1950, comprised a supranational High Authority that worked in conjunction with national representatives in a Council of Ministers. A Court of Justice, whose decisions were binding, governed the procedures of the ECSC. Thus, the ECSC did not simply express the will of its member states. Instead, each state agreed to give a considerable degree of its decision-making powers to the ECSC, which in turn made final decisions about policies concerning the production and trade of coal and steel.

The innovative structure of the ECSC reflected the political objectives behind the founders of the treaty. Since the end of World War II, French leaders hoped to place lasting constraints on German economic and political power in Europe. This had led France to champion both coercive policies under the Allied occupation of Germany and constructive efforts visible in the establishment of the Organization of European Economic Cooperation and the Council of Europe. However, as West Germany became ever more important to the Western alliance in the early years of the Cold War, the United States and the United Kingdom grew less sympathetic to French calls for policies that would inhibit German economic recovery. Indeed, the United States and the United Kingdom by 1950 had begun to consider a policy of rearming West Germany to integrate it into the Western defense system. The French feared that a rearmed and economically powerful Germany might emerge as the leader of the new Europe and diminish French influence. One of the principal goals of the Schuman Plan was to create a long-term balance of economic power between France and Germany to inhibit German domination of the European economy.

Yet there were other motives behind the Schuman Plan. Jean Monnet, its chief architect, believed the modernization of the French coal and steel industries to be vital to the future health of the nation. This modernization could not proceed behind the traditionally high protectionist walls that France had erected in the interwar years. Monnet argued that a larger market for coal and steel would boost production, raise living standards for labor, eliminate inefficiency, and allow further investment in new manufacturing capacity. Furthermore, a sector-specific agreement such as the ECSC could provide a model for future integrative experiments and promote the ideal that Monnet espoused: an integrated European community.

German Chancellor Konrad Adenauer accepted the plan chiefly because it offered a means to end the unpopular Allied controls over West German industry, and because within the ECSC West Germany would be treated as an equal in a genuinely European enterprise. Through the ECSC West Germany could begin to demonstrate its willingness to act as a "good citizen" of Western Europe. Italy, not a major producer of coal or steel, sought inclusion in the Community to ensure equal political footing with France and Germany in the new Europe. The Benelux countries, which had already committed themselves to a three-way customs union in 1948, supported the scheme, though they feared Franco-German domination of the Community and so urged the establishment of the Council of Ministers to check the power of the High Authority. Of Western Europe's major producers, only the United Kingdom refused to join the scheme, unwilling to subject its very large coal and steel industries to the control of a supranational authority based on the continent.

The signature of the ECSC treaty on April 18, 1951, was not universally applauded in the signatory nations, and during the ratification debates industrial and political interests raised concerns. The Belgian coal industry and French steel manufacturers, for example, complained that the High Authority would have too much power and that open markets would bring unwelcome and damaging competition for their products. They worried especially about the long-term prospect that Germany would come to dominate the industry in Europe and swamp smaller producers. German industrialists meanwhile feared that the ECSC would perpetuate the unpopular decartelization policies of the occupation, which they saw as discriminatory. Conversely, left-wing opinion in Europe criticized the plan chiefly for consolidating the division of Europe into hostile blocs. These criticisms did not derail ratification but demonstrated significant opposition in various quarters.

The years 1952 to 1959 constituted something of a golden age for the ECSC. Under the presidencies of Jean Monnet (1952–55), René Mayer (1955–57), and Paul Finet (1958–59), the ECSC began significant work in removing trade barriers, harmonizing transportation costs, reducing unfair state subsidies, controlling pricing practices, coordinating national investment policies, and restricting the formation of cartels and concentrations. For all that, the quantitative impact of the ECSC in these years remains difficult to measure. While production of steel in Europe doubled in the 1950s, the direct responsibility of the Community for this development has not been proved. Trade in coal and steel among the member states rose significantly in these years, with trade in steel nearly tripling. But again, overall trade among ECSC members in nontreaty products doubled in this period, demonstrating a general expansion of trade in the region.

The ECSC revealed its weaknesses during the early 1960s. A serious coal crisis caused by overproduction and by increased competition from oil and gas led to a collapse of prices in 1959. Nations tried to protect their industries and their market shares by pursuing policies that conflicted with the efforts of the High Authority to seek a sharing of the burden among all member states. Further, the very purpose of the ECSC was placed in doubt by the establishment of the EEC in 1958, with its broad mandate to harmonize overall European economic policies. Under the presidencies of Piero Malvestiti (1959–63) and Rinaldo Del Bo (1963–67), the ECSC never recovered the influence it had in the mid-1950s.

While the economic impact of the Community is difficult to demonstrate, the political contribution looms much larger. In 1950 Franco-German relations had hit a postwar low, owing to wrangling about the Saar, disagreements about a range of occupation policies, and conflict over West Germany's future role in the security of Western Europe. The Schuman Plan of 1950 broke the deadlock by creating a mutually acceptable balance of economic and political power between the two former enemies and thus lay the foundation for further experiments in economic integration in postwar Western Europe.

BIBLIOGRAPHY

Diebold, William. *The Schuman Plan: A Study in Economic Cooperation 1950–1959.* New York: Council on Foreign Relations, 1959.

Gillingham, John. *Coal, Steel and the Rebirth of Europe, 1945–1955: The Germans and French from Ruhr Con-*

flict to Economic Community. New York: Cambridge University Press, 1991.

Poidevin, Raymond, and Dirk Spierenburg. *The History of the High Authority of the European Coal and Steel Community.* London: Weidenfeld and Nicolson, 1994.

Schwabe, Klaus, ed. *Die Anfange des Schuman Plans, 1950–1951.* Baden-Baden: Nomos, 1988.

William I. Hitchcock

SEE ALSO European Union; Monnet, Jean; Schuman, Robert

Scotland: Devolution

On May 6, 1999 residents of Scotland turned out to vote in the first elections for a Scottish parliament in almost three hundred years. The parliament was created following a referendum win in September 1997 in which Scots voted first, for a parliament, and second, to give it tax-assessing powers. The referendum victory in the devolution campaign had been the effort of Labour, Liberal Democrat and Scottish National Party (SNP) supporters, but it was also the result of years of campaigning by organizations such as the Scottish Constitutional Convention and the Campaign for a Scottish Assembly.

Following the referendum, Labour established a consultative steering group to provide structural guidelines for the parliament. Many of the recommendations followed from the Scottish Constitutional Convention report "Scotland's Parliament, Scotland's Right," produced in 1995. Among the most significant changes, was a system of proportional representation that combined single-member constituencies and a number of regional seats to provide a degree of proportionality. This "Additional Member System" (AMS) would provide the parliament with a 129-member chamber. The 72 existing constituencies representing Scots in the British parliament would be the basis for the constituency element. An additional constituency was added with the division of the Orkneys and the Shetlands into two seats. The remaining 56 seats were divided among the eight European regional constituencies, to provide the proportional element. Under the AMS electoral system, it would have been difficult for any one party to gain an overall majority of seats. As a result, the Liberal Democrats were virtually assured a position in a coalition government, whether with Labour of the pro-independence SNP. Additional changes included a horseshoe shaped chamber to facilitate debate, family-friendly nine-to-five working hours, school holidays for the parliament, and a strengthened committee system that combined standing and select committee functions.

The May 1999 parliamentary campaign was fought by four main parties: Labour, the Liberal Democrats, the Conservatives, and the SNP. Left without any British parliamentary representation in the 1997 general election, the Conservative Party was left battling a combination of difficulties, not least of which were the legacy of former prime minister Margaret Thatcher, the perception of a weakened party, and a recent history of opposing devolution. In response to such challenges, the party convened a "listening exercise" in which the party members traveled around Scotland to better understand the interests of voters. The resulting party manifesto began with a recognition that the party had "got it wrong." In the face of such a turnaround, the Scottish media were quick to label the Conservative manifesto the longest apology in history. For Labour, the task of campaigning for parliamentary elections that it had supported consistently since the 1970s was a comparatively easier task. That said, the party faced strong criticism of the policies of its British counterpart. Its decision to implement tuition fees for postsecondary education and its support of the private-finance initiative, a private-public partnership in which private companies would help fund public projects such as schools and hospitals, drew heavy criticism from political opponents. For the Liberal Democrats, the task was to emphasize distinct policies without angering either of its potential coalition partners, Labour, or the SNP amidst charges from the Conservative Party that its policies would be ignored when coalition talks necessitated compromise. In certain respects, the SNP was in the easiest position, campaigning for a parliament that it supported as a step toward independence. If the parliament worked, the SNP could argue that independence was now justifiable. If it did not, the party could blame the lack of sufficient autonomy. In May, Labour failed to elect an outright majority of MSPs (Member of the Scottish Parliament) and quickly entered coalition talks with the Liberal Democrats. The Conservative Party, despite its opposition to proportional representation, and to the parliament, benefited from the AMS electoral system since, as in 1997, the party failed to elect a single representative in a constituency seat.

Labour won 53 constituency seats and three AMS seats; the SNP seven and 28; the Conservatives 18 AMS seats; the Liberal Democrats 12 and five; the Green Party one AMS seat; the Scottish Socialist Party one AMS seat; and one Independent constituency seat. The first group of members of the Scottish Parliament is not different from its United Kingdom or Westminster counterparts by most measures. In part this was due to the presence of a number of present and former politicians. The parliament contained sixteen dual mandate politicians who are sitting in Westminster and in Holyrood, the seat of the Scottish Parliament. Intended to provide experience in the first term of the parliament these politicians, including First Minister Donald Dewar (Labour), Deputy First Minister Jim Wallace (Liberal Democrats) and SNP leader Alex Salmond, were not expected to campaign in the next Westminster elections. The chamber also contains a number of local councilors and two former Members of the European Parliament. One distinguishing characteristic is the presence of three representatives from smaller parties. Dennis Canavan, a Labour MP in Westminster, was not selected to stand for the party. Canavan ran as an Independent candidate in his Westminster constituency, beating the candidate approved by the Labour Party. Robin Harper, leader of the Green Party was elected from the Lothians electoral list around Edinburgh, and Tommy Sheridan, of the Scottish Socialist Party, was elected off the Glasgow regional list.

The election campaign also marked the beginning of what was to have been the start of "new politics" in Scotland. In the creation of a new Scottish Parliament campaigners hoped to eradicate the worst excesses of the Westminster system. Perceiving the British Parliament as a centralized, aggressive, and male-dominated institution caught in outmoded customs and traditions, organizations such as the Scottish Constitutional Convention and the Consultative Steering Group called for a more open style of politics. The four principles of the Consultative Steering Group were accountability, accessibility, equal opportunities, and power-sharing. It was hoped that political parties, the media, and the parliament itself would embrace these principles in an effort to create a new type of politics in Scotland. Perhaps the most striking example of such principles in practice is in the area of gender representation. Labour was alone in employing an overt mechanism to ensure the representation of female candidates in the election. The party relied on a twinning mechanism in which male and female candidates were paired in similar and equally winnable constituencies. For the SNP and the Liberal Democrats, a combination of training workshops and informal mechanisms increased the number of female candidates. The Conservative Party stressed that the merit principle dictated the selection of its candidates. Following the election, Labour was left was represented by 28 female Members of the Scottish Parliament, exactly 50 percent of its total number of seats. The SNP was represented by 28 women, or 40 percent of their seats. The Liberal Democrats and Conservative Party were represented by two and three percent women respectively.

Ailsa Henderson

Scottish Nationalism and the Scottish National Party

Scottish nationalism has taken different forms since 1945, and the Scottish National Party (SNP) represents just one aspect of Scottish national sentiment. Following the Act of Union in 1707 Scotland lost its independent parliament and was governed through the British parliament at Westminster but retained many aspects of its national identity. Since 1945, however, Scottish national sentiment has become more pronounced. Changing economic conditions for both Britain and Scotland brought increasing strains to the union. This has been reflected in the growth of support for constitutional change, along with the collapse of the Scottish Conservative Party, which is the political expression of unadulterated unionism. With the overwhelming victory of the Labour Party in Scotland and Britain in the 1997 general election, it became clear that Scotland would once again see a Scottish Parliament in Edinburgh.

In the mid-1940s Scottish nationalists created a broad-based movement, the Scottish Convention, that they hoped would succeed where the tiny SNP had failed. In 1949 the Scottish Convention organized a surprisingly successful petition, the Scottish Covenant, that gathered over two million signatures calling for a Scottish home rule parliament. But the Labour and Conservative Parties ignored this call, while the Liberal Party, which had long favored constitutional change, had no parliamentary representation in Scotland.

Other manifestations of Scottish national sentiment centered on the cultural and sporting life of the country. Rivalry between Scotland and England in soccer and rugby helped maintain a sense of Scottish national identity, although it brought bitter accusations from SNP activists that their fellow countrymen and -women were no more than "90 minute patriots." In literature Scotland developed a self-consciously Scottish literary canon. Much of this was the result of the leadership of individual writers, such as Hugh MacDiarmid, Neil Gunn, Hamish Henderson, and Compton Mackenzie. On a broader front, Scotland has maintained its separate legal, educational, and ecclesiastical institutions, which underpin its people's strong national feeling. Finally, individual Scottish nationalists have staged symbolic acts to keep alive the political cause of nationalism. Most famous of these was the removal of the Stone of Destiny, the Stone of Scone, the symbol of Scottish authority, from Westminster Abbey in 1950, and its return to Scotland.

Although the SNP was founded in 1933 and won its first parliamentary seat in a by-election in 1945, it did not come to widespread notice until it won the Hamilton by-election in November 1967. It followed this success by notable advances in local government elections in Scotland. This 1960s groundswell of support for the SNP developed into a major advance for the nationalists during the 1970s, peaking in the October 1974 general election, when the SNP won eleven parliamentary seats. The strength of nationalism, and the parliamentary weakness of the Labour government, led to proposals for a devolved Scottish assembly, preceded by a referendum in Scotland. But the referendum went against devolution, and the SNP slumped at the 1979 election, winning only two parliamentary seats. Following its 1979 defeat, the SNP was beset by internal feuding, and it was not until the late 1980s and the early 1990s that it reestablished its position on the Scottish political scene.

Led by Alex Salmond, the SNP entered the 1992 election calling for independence in Europe under the slogan "Free in '93," but it was not to be, and the SNP performed poorly. Frustration at the victory of the Conservatives in 1992 led to the formation of several popular movements aimed at agitating for constitutional change, but these groups faded after a few years. The SNP once again promised full independence for Scotland at the 1997 general election, but could do no more than take six seats in Scotland, compared with the victorious Labour Party's fifty-five, out of the total of seventy-two Scottish seats at Westminster. The results of the election indicated that although the Scottish people had once again rejected the option of independence for Scotland, they were keen to see some form of devolved government. The Labour Party has promised to deliver this option, on the basis of the work of the Scottish Constitutional Convention, a cross-party body that had been preparing for constitutional reform since 1989.

On September 11, 1997, a vote was held on devolution for Scotland in which 74.3 percent of those who went to the polls voted to establish a 129-member Scottish parliament. Scottish voters also voted 63.5 percent in favor of giving the new Scottish parliament taxing powers. Prime Minister Tony Blair, whose Labour government had supported the measure, touted the victory as an indication of the end of big centralized government. Under the new arrangement the British parliament in London would retain control over international questions but the Scottish parliament in Edinburgh would control Scotland's annual budget, and its competence would extend to legal, social, and criminal matters. It would have control over health, education, and employment.

BIBLIOGRAPHY

Finlay, Richard. *Independent and Free: Scottish Politics and the Origins of the Scottish National Party, 1918–1945.* Edinburgh: John Donald, 1994.

Harvie, Christopher. *No Gods and Precious Few Heroes: Scotland since 1914.* Edinburgh: Edinburgh University Press, 1993.

———. *Scotland and Nationalism: Scottish Society and Politics, 1707–1994,* 2d ed. London: Allen & Unwin 1994.

MacKenzie, Gordon. "Jubilant Scots Dance in Streets." *Toronto Star,* September 13, 1997.

Marr, Andrew. *The Battle for Scotland.* Harmondsworth: Penguin, 1992.

Stephen H. Cullen

Sedivy, Jaroslav (1929–)

Czech foreign minister. Jaroslav Sedivy was born on November 12, 1929, in Prague. He graduated from the philosophy faculty of Charles University in Prague in 1952. He began working at the Slavonic Languages Institute of the Czechoslovak Academy of Science in 1954. He worked at the archives of the Institute for International Politics and Economics from 1957 until he was dismissed in February 1970 in the purges that followed the suppression of the Prague Spring as of 1968. In 1971 Sedivy was imprisoned and sentenced to eighteen months for subversion. After his release, unable to continue his work as an intellectual, Sedivy worked as a logger, truck driver, and window cleaner.

Sedivy was one of the signers of the dissident indictment of the regime, Charter 77, and he wrote two histories that were published in Czechoslovakia under a friend's name. Finally, he was employed in 1989 as an economic analysts at the Institute of Economic Forecasting in Prague. Later that year in the midst of the Velvet Revolution, which saw the fall of communism, Sedivy was assigned the task on November 17, 1989, of assembling a group of foreign affairs experts for the Civic Forum (CV), the political association of anti-Communist human rights organization that overturned the Czechoslovak Communist regime in December 1989. In December, as the CV sought a foreign minister from its ranks, the choice was between Sedivy, Jiří Hajek, and Jiří Dienstbier. When the choice fell upon Dienstbier, he chose Sedivy as his adviser. Sedivy's first priority was the removal of Soviet troops from Czechoslovak soil. In 1990 Sedivy was appointed ambassador to France. He intended to leave the foreign service in 1994 but was persuaded to go to Brussels as ambassador to Belgium. He also was the chief Czech representative to NATO during the negotiations for the inclusion of the Czech Republic in an expanded NATO. On October 23, 1997, Sedivy succeeded Josef Zieleniec as Czech foreign minister.

BIBLIOGRAPHY

RJC. "Profile of Jaroslav Sedivy, New Czech Foreign Minister." Czech News Agency (CTK) National News Wire, October 23, 1997.

Bernard Cook

Segni, Antonio (1891–1972)

President of Italy (1962–64). Antonio Segni was born into a deeply Catholic rural middle-class family in Sassari, Italy, in 1891. He received a law degree in 1913 and started in the profession with support from the diocese of Sassari, where the church encouraged groups of young people inspired by the political and social ideas of the church. In World War I he became an artillery officer. He joined the Italian Popular Party (PPI), founded by Luigi Sturzo, at its inception in 1920, and was a delegate to its national congress in Naples. That same year he began teaching law at the University of Perugia, where he remained until 1925. At the elections of 1922, when the PPI split over participating in the Fascist leader Benito Mussolini's coalition cabinet or opposing it, Segni assumed the intransigent line of the Sardinian Catholics, who followed the political program of the weekly magazine *Libertà*.

At the regional congress of 1923, Segni and other young Catholics upheld the defense of Christian moral values in the struggle with extreme ideologies. His firm opposition both to fascism and socialism was expressed clearly in the elections of 1924. The same year, after the murder of the Socialist parliamentary leader Giacomo Matteotti, Segni organized the opposition committee now supported not only by Catholics but even by some of the Socialists. As Mussolini's fascist dictatorship consolidated itself, Segni had to retire from active political life. He continued his academic carrier, but for political reasons he was not approved in 1932 to teach civil legal procedure at the University of Naples.

In 1942–43, during World War II and the final period of the fascist regime, Segni resumed political activities with other Sardinian Catholics. At a national meeting in Naples in 1944 Segni became a member of the national council of the new Catholic party, Christian Democracy (DC). Shortly afterward he took part in the Socialist Ivanoe Bonomi's government (June 1944–June 1945) as undersecretary in the Agriculture Department. He retained that post in Ferruccio Parri's government (June 1945–December 1945) and in the first ministry of De Gasperi. In 1946 Segni was elected to the first Italian republican parliament, and served again as agriculture minister in the De Gasperi governments until 1951.

During that period Segni developed a project for agrarian reform. His aim was to keep farmers from being manipulated by the left-wing parties and involved in social struggles with revolutionary consequences. He promoted the expropriation of uncultivated areas belonging to large land owners in order to create small land owners and to make the country productive. This will to reform met with obstacles, not only from right-wing political groups who rejected the concept of a limitation of property rights, but also from the left who viewed it as a move to undermine their effort to gain support from the country people. The projected law was rejected. Only with De Gasperi's support and that of the left-wing of the DC was the law partially approved in October 1950. Some 121,000 families with a total of 300,000 workers were able to take possession of expropriated lands. Nevertheless, the hopes of developing agricultural activity through a redistribution of the properties were frustrated by the gradual abandonment of the lands in the 1950s and 1960s by the same farmers, attracted by jobs in the industry in the northern part of Italy. Between July 1951 and January 1954 (except in the government formed only by the DC from July 16 to August 17, 1953), Segni served as minister of public education. He dedicated most of his energies to the struggle against illiteracy.

Segni led his first government, formed by the DC, Social Democrats (PSDI), and Liberals (PLI), from July 6, 1955, until May 19, 1957, with Aldo Moro at the Department of Justice. In these two years Italy was admitted to the United Nations and joined the European Economic Community (EEC, later EC). This government fell because of the EEC agrarian pacts supported by Segni. He rejoined Prime Minister Amintore Fanfani's DC-PSDI government from July 1, 1958, to February 15, 1959, as assistant prime minister and defense minister.

After the fall of Fanfani's government a single-party DC government led by Segni, who also held the office of internal affairs, lasted from February 15, 1959, until March 25, 1960. After the fall of this second Segni government at the initiative of the PLI, the issue of working with the Socialists arose again. Segni retained the foreign ministry in the third and fourth Fanfani ministries, between July 1960 and June 21, 1963.

Segni, though distinguishing between the incompatibility of Catholicism and Marxism and the compatibility of Catholicism with a nonauthoritarian socialism, became leader of the opposition to any opening to a center-left policy. But Aldo Moro pushed the DC in the other direction. Segni stressed that Italy should remain faithful to NATO and to the integration of Europe. On this platform Segni, thanks to the DC and to the right-wing parties, was elected as third president of the republic in May 1962.

Segni resigned from the presidency in December 1964 in the wake of the DiLorenzo coup. But Aldo Moro, a fellow Christian Democrat and the leader of the first Italian center-left government, subsequently stated that Segni had not behaved in an unconstitutional fashion.

Segni's political orientation can be characterized as very centrist. He was a traditionalist rather than a conservative, both anti-Communist and antifascist and willing to promote agrarian reform.

BIBLIOGRAPHY

Di Salvo, Settimio. *L'azione meridionalistica dei cattolici democratici e A.S. Conferenza tenuta nella sede del Centro studi "Nuovo Mezzogiorno" di Pomigliano il 31 marzo 1973.* Naples: Edizioni Nuovo Mezzogiorno, 1973.

Giovagnoli, Agostino. "1964–1968: Il Centro-Sinistra. La 'stagione' di Moro e Fanfani," in *Il Parlamento italiano: 1861–1988,* Vol. 20. Milan: Nuova CEI, 1992, 245–65

Malgeri, Francesco. "Alcide De Gasperi," in *Il Parlamento italiano,* Vol. 15. Milan: Nuova CEI, 1992.

Segni, Antonio. *Scritti giuridici [1915–1961],* Vols. 1–2. Turin: Utet, 1965.

———. *Comunità europea e problemi del Mezzogiorno: Conferenza tenuta al Palazzo di Città di Catania il 17 settembre 1960.* Catania: Centro Studi per i Problemi dell'Unità Europea, 1960.

———. *Europa, oggi e domani: Celebrazione del quinto anniversario della firma dei trattati della CEE e della CEEA.* Rome: Giovane Europa, 1962.

Valentino, Nino, *L'elezione di Segni.* Milan: Edizioni di Comunità, 1963.

Paolo Pastori

SEE ALSO Fanfani, Amintore; Italy; Moro, Aldo; Tambroni, Fernando

Seifert, Jaroslav (1901–86)

Czech poet, writer, and translator; winner of the Nobel Prize in literature (1984). Jaroslav Seifert, born on September 23, 1901, grew up poor in Zizkov, a working-class district of Prague. That is the explanation for his career and his profile, which were different from his colleagues and contemporaries, such as Vitezslav Nezval and Karel Teige, of the surrealist group Devetsil. Seifert's leftist orientation was not the result of a generational conflict affecting children from bourgeois families. His father was a blue-collar worker, and this environment had a decisive impact on Seifert. He attended the Zizkov high school, not the famous high school in Kremencova Street. Before graduating he left school and started to work for the Communist daily *Rude Pravo* (*The Red Law*) and the Brno *Revnost* (*Equality*), first as an apprentice then as a journalist for cultural affairs.

His first published poetry, *Mesto v slzach* (*The Weeping City,* 1921), is an example of his youthful proletarian orientation. In 1920 Seifert founded in cooperation with Jaroslav Havlicek, Adolf Hoffmeister, K. Teige, and Vladislav Vancura the leftist association for artists, Devetsil. At the beginning Devetsil represented proletarian art and magic realism. Later the group became the voice of constructivism and poetism and established a new feeling for life and creativity in all variations of art. Between 1923 and 1925 Seifert traveled as a cultural delegate to France, Switzerland, Italy, and the USSR.

Seifert was excluded from the Communist Party and from Devetsil in 1929, after he and six other artists protested against the new leadership of the party under Klement Gottwald. During the Nazi occupation (1939–45) and also the first years of Communist dictatorship Seifert wrote philosophically reflexive poetry. His orientation did not fit into the concept of socialist realism, and he was forbidden to publish in 1950. After Soviet dictator Joseph Stalin's death in 1953, he was allowed to publish again and for his lyrical publication *Maninka* (*The Mother*) he received the State prize in 1955. In 1956, at the second Czechoslovak Congress of writers, he asserted that most of the writers had not fulfilled their function as the consciousness of the nation. He asked for the rehabilitation of writers who were still imprisoned or not allowed to publish. At this time his health deteriorated and the first signs of paralysis were seen.

During the Prague Spring, 1968, Seifert chaired the rehabilitation commission of the Writers' Association. After the invasion he refused to welcome the occupation. As a result, from 1970 to 1979 he was again forbidden to publish. His poems were distributed secretly and his older works censored.

After 1981 some of his newer poetry was published, but only with some changes by censors. His memoir, *Vsecky krasy sveta* (*All the Beauties of the World*) was published in Toronto in 1981, but in Prague in 1982, only after being censored. On the occasion of Seifert's eightieth birthday, the regime put out an omnibus volume, *Ruce Venusiny* (*Hands of Venus*), with transcripts of his poems. A couple of them were new but not until 1984 could a new book —*Nejkrasnejsi byva silena* (*The Most Beautiful Is Usually Crazy*), with new poems, his love poems — be published openly in Czechoslovakia. When the Nobel Prize Committee decided to award him with the prize for literature in 1984, his daughter Jane went to Stockholm to receive the honor. By the time he died on January 10, 1986, Seifert and his poetry were considered part of the Czech identity. Today a street in Prague-Zizkov is named for him.

BIBLIOGRAPHY

Seifert, Jaroslav. *The Casting of Bells.* Iowa City: The Spirit That Moves Us Press, 1983.

———. *Mozart in Prague.* Iowa City: The Spirit That Moves Us Press, 1985.

———. *The Plague Column.* London: Terra Nova Editions, 1979.

———. *The Selected Poetry of Jaroslav Seifert.* New York: Macmillan 1986.

Marta Marková

Serbia

One of the six republics of the former Yugoslavia. With Montenegro it forms the Federal Republic of Yugoslavia. The capital of the federation is Belgrade, which is also the capital of Serbia. The national language is Serbo-Croatian. Serbia combined with Kosovo and Vojvodina, two provinces of Serbia stripped of their autonomy in 1989, joined with the former Yugoslav republic of Montenegro on April 27, 1992, to form the Federal Republic of Yugoslavia. Serbia opens in the north onto the great Danubian plain and constitutes the heart of the Balkan Peninsula. Serbia has an area of 21,609 square miles (88,361 sq km). It is bordered on the north by Hungary, on the east by Romania and Bulgaria, on the south by Macedonia and Albania, and on the west by Montenegro, Bosnia-Hercegovina, and Croatia. It has no direct access to the sea. The Danube, however, provides a main avenue of commerce. Serbia has a heterogeneous ethnic population and is multiconfessional (Orthodox, Muslim, and Roman Catholic). According to the census of 1991, its 9,791,475 inhabitants are 65.8 percent Serb, 17.2 percent Albanian, 3.5 percent Hungarian, 3.2 percent who identified themselves as Yugoslavs, 2.4 percent who identified themselves as Muslim, 1.4 percent Montenegrins, 1.1 percent Croats, and 1.4 percent Rom. According to the same census, 24.6 percent of Serbs lived outside Serbia. Serbia played a preponderant role in the wars that erupted in the breakup of the former Yugoslavia in 1991 and 1992. Because of its role, it was subjected to stringent international economic sanctions by many western nations. Its politics have been characterized by a centralist nationalist and authoritarian regime led by Slobodan Milošević, the president of Serbia from 1989 to 1997 and from 1997 the federal president.

Serbia. *Illustration courtesy of Bernard Cook.*

BIBLIOGRAPHY

Judah, Tim. *The Serbs: History, Myth and the Destruction of Yugoslavia.* New Haven, Conn.: Yale University Press, 1999.

Catherine Lutard
(Tr. by B. Cook)

SEE ALSO Croatia; Milošević, Slobodan; Montenegro

Economy

A UN economic embargo was imposed on the Republic of Yugoslavia from May 1993 until November 1995. Contrary to its objectives, though it resulted in the pauperization of the people, it only reinforced the authoritarian system of Milošević. However the economic situation in Serbia had profoundly deteriorated even before the UN resolution. The causes were many but they were above all political: the incapacity of authorities to carry out effective reforms; the carving up of Titoist Yugoslavia; the heavy spending on war; and the development of a parallel economy controlled by a mafia that shared its spoils with the leaders. The gross domestic product had begun to fall in 1989. At that time Yugoslavia belonged to the bottom ranks of the semi-industrialized countries. Its per capita national product amounted to about

$2,100. Three years later this figure had fallen to $900, a decline of 60 percent.

Hyperinflation struck the middle class very hard, increasing the gulf that separated the majority of the poor or those people of modest means from the class of leaders and the mafia who knew how to profit from the "benefit" of war, the embargo, and from the commerce tied to the parallel economy. Mismanagement of the economy was exacerbated by the UN embargo because of Serbia's involvement in the war in Bosnia. Although the embargo was lifted partially after the Dayton Peace Accords (1995), further chaos resulted from NATO air attacks on Yugoslavia in 1999 because of its ethnic cleansing of Albanians in Kosovo. With much of its infrastructure damaged, Serbia faced economic disaster.

Catherine Lutard
(Tr. by B. Cook)

Nationalism

Serbian nationalism played a leading role in the breakup of Yugoslavia and the subsequent wars in Croatia and Bosnia-Herzegovina. After the nationalist excesses of World War II, Yugoslavia's ruling Communist Party, under Marshal Tito, attempted to suppress Serbian and Croatian nationalism. However, Tito's death in 1980 hastened a resurgence of Serbian nationalism, a movement that would prove useful for Slobodan Milošević's waning Communist Party. Serbian nationalism helped trigger the secessionist movements in Slovenia and Croatia that eventually led to war in Yugoslavia in 1991. Extreme Serbian nationalism has aimed at joining all Serb-held areas to a "greater Serbia."

Serbian nationalism was one of the first nationalist movements to emerge in southeastern Europe in the late eighteenth and early nineteenth centuries. After the establishment of a small, autonomous Serbia in 1815, its leaders focused on expansion. The prime target was the declining Ottoman Empire, of which Serbia had once been a part. By the eve of World War I the Serbian population in the ever-weakening Ottoman Empire came under Serbian control. Serbia then shifted its aim toward the Habsburg Empire to add Bosnia-Herzegovina and other areas to the Serbian state. A Serbian nationalist assassinated Archduke Franz Ferdinand, heir to the Austro-Hungarian throne, in Sarajevo in 1914, setting of the Great War. The creation of Yugoslavia after World War I included, for the first time in modern history, all the Serbs in one state.

The Serbs' suppression of other nationalities included in the new Yugoslav state prevented the creation of a stable country. With World War II's German-Italian occupation of Yugoslavia in 1941, instability deteriorated into a bloody civil war among Croatian Fascists (Ustaša), Communist Partisans led by Tito, and Serbian nationalist Chetniks.

The Partisans, won the civil war largely because of their appeal across national lines. After their victory in 1945, the Communists persecuted the Chetniks and executed their leader, Draža Mihajlovic. Despite the Partisans' antinationalist stance, Serbian nationalism persisted in Communist Yugoslavia. Aleksandar Ranković, minister of the interior and head of the secret service, was notorious for persecuting non-Serbs and demanding a high degree of centralization. After his demise in 1966 and the federalization of Yugoslavia in the 1970s, Serbs felt increasingly disadvantaged in the state. The high degree of autonomy granted to two provinces of Serbia—Vojvodina, an area populated by a wide range of minorities, especially Hungarians, and the mostly Albanian Kosovo—considered the cradle of the Serbian nation, caused widespread dissatisfaction among Serbs.

Serbian nationalism reentered the political arena with clashes between Albanians and Serbs in Kosovo over the status of the province in the early 1980s. Leading Serbian intellectuals wrote a memorandum in 1986 calling for protection against what they called a genocide of Serbs in Kosovo. In this volatile atmosphere Slobodan Milošević, head of the Serbian League of Communists (Communist Party), utilized Serbian nationalism to diffuse its potential threat to Communist Party authority.

Milošević and leading Serbian nationalists called for a centralization of Yugoslavia and blocked any political and economic liberalization already underway in the republics of Slovenia and Croatia. Through mass rallies of nationalist supporters, Milošević installed political leaders in Montenegro, Vojvodina, and Kosovo who shared his views. The reaction against the rise of Serbian nationalism brought secessionist and nationalist parties to power in Slovenia and Croatia during the first free elections there in 1990. Serbian nationalists grew more insistent over the establishment of a greater Serbia, to consist of large parts of Croatia, Bosnia-Herzegovina, Montenegro, and parts of Macedonia.

In the years leading up to the outbreak of war, Serbian and Croatian nationalism mutually reinforced each other, increasing the perception of threat from the other. Between 1990 and 1991 Serbs in Croatia and Bosnia were armed by the Yugoslav army. As Croatia and later Bosnia prepared to secede from an increasingly Serb-dominated Yugoslavia, many Croatian and Bosnian Serbs, especially those living in rural areas, created autonomous enclaves. The Serbian Democratic Party, led by Jovan Rasković in

Croatia and Radovan Karadžić in Bosnia, carried out this organization, setting the foundation for the Serbian breakaway republics.

With the outbreak of war in June 1991, the Serb-held areas withdrew from the control of the Croatian and later the Bosnian government. Serbian paramilitaries joined the Yugoslav army in their offensive against Croatia. These irregular contacts were forged by influential politicians in Serbia, such as Vojislav Šešelj, head of the fascist Serbian Radical Party.

Although Serbian nationalists failed to secure the entire territory, they managed to conquer a third of Croatia and 70 percent of Bosnia after the March 1992 outbreak of war there. Despite the military successes that created Greater Serbia, Milošević turned against Serbian nationalists in 1995 to secure his position against the rising popularity of Karadžić. Consequently, most Serb-held lands in Croatia fell between May and August 1995, and the Dayton peace accords bringing peace to Bosnia were signed in December 1995.

While Serbian nationalism reemerged in confrontation with ethnic Albanians in Kosovo, its main target was Croats and Muslims. Serbian nationalist perception depicted Croats as genocidal descendants of the World War II Ustaša, and thus justified the conquest of Serb-populated lands in Croatia. Bosnian Muslims were equated with Turks, and their Islamic religion was ostracized as alien to the region.

Even before the outbreak of war in the former Yugoslavia, Serbian nationalism was expansionist and hostile to its neighbors. The defeat however, of the Serbs in Croatia and Bosnia and internal divisions over Serb-nationalist aims, however, led to a more self-centered nationalism in the late 1990s. The war marked an end to centuries of Serbian settlement in Croatia. Thus, Serbian nationalism continued to redefine itself. The large number of Serb refugees from Croatia and Bosnia in Serbia formed a potential source for extreme Serbian nationalism in the future.

BIBLIOGRAPHY

Djilas, Aleksa. "A Profile of Slobodan Milosevic." *Foreign Affairs* 72, no. 3 (Summer 1993): 81–96.

Judah, Jim. *The Serbs: History, Myth and the Destruction of Yugoslavia.* New Haven Conn.: Yale University Press, 1997.

Lederer, Ivo J. "Nationalism and the Yugoslavs," in *Nationalism in Eastern Europe.* Ed. by Peter F. Sugar and Ivo J. Lederer. Seattle: University of Washington Press, 1969.

Ramet, Sabrina P. *Nationalism and Federalism in Yugoslavia, 1962–1991.* Boulder, Colo.: Westview Press, 1992.

Sardamov, Ivelin. "Mandate of History: Serbian National Identity and Ethnic Conflict in the Former Yugoslavia," in *State and Nation Building in East Central Europe: Contemporary Perspectives.* Ed. by John S. Michiel. New York: Institute on East Central Europe, Columbia University, 1996, 17–37.

Silver, Laura, and Allan Little. *The Death of Yugoslavia.* London: BBC Books & Penguin Books, 1995.

Florian Bieber

SEE ALSO Karadžić, Radovan; Kosovo; Milošević, Slobodan; Šešelj, Vojislav; Vojvodina

Political Parties

Serbian political parties other than the Communist Party emerged only in 1990, but they remained sidelined by the dominant Socialist Party—the renamed Serbian Communist Party. Communist Yugoslavia hosted one party, the League of Communists. With the first multiparty elections in 1990, other parties emerged, all small, weak, and mostly nationalist. Their programs and alliances changed frequently and most of their appeal depended on their leaders. In the subsequent years the Communist Party, renamed Socialist Party, has continued to control the political sphere of Serbia as the Socialist Federative Republic of Yugoslavia disintegrated in 1991–92 and was succeeded by the Serbian dominated Federal Republic of Yugoslavia.

Until 1990 the Serbian branch of the Yugoslav League of Communists dominated the Serbian political scene. Revolutions in Eastern Europe in 1989, political liberalization in the other Yugoslav republics, as well as internal pressures in the region forced the party, under the leadership of Slobodan Milošević, to hold free elections and to allow the establishment of other political parties.

In July 1990 the Communist Party merged with its front organization, the Socialist Alliance of the Working People of Serbia, to form the Socialist Party of Serbia (SPS). Although it attracted former dissidents, including leading dissident Mihajlo Marković, it underwent little change and remained under the firm leadership of Milošević. With 46 percent of the vote, it was well ahead of all other parties and continued to dominate the country's political life.

The main opposition party was the Serbian Renewal Movement (SPO), led by nationalist writer Vuk Drašković. Drašković originally favored the breakup of Yugoslavia to establish a greater Serbia that would incorporate parts of the neighboring republics. The SPO also took a strict anti-Communist line, at least until the beginning of the war in 1991. Then it abandoned its nationalist stance for a moderate program, seeking a settlement with the other republics. It captured 15 percent of the vote in 1990, making it the second-largest party in the Serbian parliament.

The second early opposition party was the Democratic Party (DS). Originally lead by Dragoljub Micunović, it comprised the liberal part of the political spectrum and appealed to a constituency of intellectuals and the minuscule middle class. The DS received only 7.5 percent of the vote in the first election.

Other groups also organized for the first election. The last prime minister of the former Yugoslavia, Ante Marković, sought to rally support for a nonnationalist platform in his Alliance of Reform Forces of Yugoslavia but failed to gather more than 1.5 percent of the vote. While the political parties of the Muslim minority Party of Democratic Action (SDA) and the Hungarian minority in the Vojvodina, the Democratic Community of Vojvodinan Hungarians (DCHV), participated in the first and subsequent elections, Albanian parties from Kosovo boycotted all elections in Serbia, holding independent elections instead.

Large opposition protests, led by the SPO in March 1991 protesting irregularities in the election and the authoritarian tactics of Milošević, were put down with the help of the army. The next large-scale demonstrations of opposition parties took place in November 1996, after the end of the wars in Croatia and Bosnia protesting, the expulsion of Serbs from the Krajina of Croatia in August 1995 and the Dayton Peace Accords of November 1995.

With the beginning of the war in Croatia in July 1991, the Serbian Radical Party (SRS), under the leadership of Vojislav Šešelj, emerged as a strong political force on the ultraright extreme of the political spectrum. In the 1992 elections smaller opposition parties joined the SPO to form the Democratic Movement for Serbia (DEPOS) coalition, but it came in only third behind the Socialist and Radical Parties. As the Socialists lost their absolute majority in parliament, they entered a coalition with the Radical Party.

The Socialist Party abandoned its nationalist course in 1993, seeking to portray itself as a peacemaker. Consequently, its coalition with the Radical Party broke apart, and new elections reestablished the SPS's absolute majority. This prompted the SPO and the DS, under the new leadership of Zoran Djindjić, to revert to a more nationalist program and ultimately to cooperate with Radovan Karadžić, leader of the Serbian Democratic Party in Bosnia, subsequently indicted for war crimes by the International Criminal Tribunal for the Former Yugoslavia.

By war's end, with over two hundred thousand Serbian refugees in Serbia proper and a devastated economy, the dominance of the Socialist Party was threatened for the first time. Zajedno (Together), a new coalition of the SPO, DS, and smaller opposition parties, captured many cities and towns in local elections in November 1996. Milošević's ruling Socialist Party falsified the election results, stirring an unprecedented series of protests that brought the government to the verge of collapse. After Milošević conceded the fraud in early 1997, the coalition fell apart. Though Drašković participated in the subsequent presidential elections, the other opposition parties boycotted them.

The Socialist Party's firm grip on the police force and media has prevented the development of a democratic political system in Serbia. Furthermore, Serbian nationalism and war inhibited the emergence of an effective opposition. Parties are largely vehicles for political leaders such as Šešelj, Drašković, and Djindjić. With their agendas characterized by opportunism instead of integrity, the political landscape remains in flux. Parties that adopt a clearly antinationalist platform, such as the Civic Alliance of Vesna Pesić, remained sidelined and risked being branded as traitors.

BIBLIOGRAPHY

Brankovic, Srbobran. *Serbia at War with Itself: Political Choice in Serbia.* Belgrade: Sociological Society of Serbia, 1995.

Judah, Jim. *The Serbs: History, Myth and the Destruction of Yugoslavia.* New Haven, Conn.: Yale University Press, 1997.

Miller, Nicholas J. "A failed Transition: The Case of Serbia," in *Politics, Power, and the Struggle for Democracy in South East Europe.* Ed. by Karen Dawisha and Bruce Parrott. Cambridge: Cambridge University Press, 1997, 146–88.

———. "Searching for a Serbian Havel." *Problems of Post-Communism* 44, no. 4 (July/August 1997): 3–11.

Silver, Laura, and Allan Little. *The Death of Yugoslavia.* London: BBC Books & Penguin Books, 1995.

Torov, Ivan. "The Resistance in Serbia," in *Burn This House: The Making and Unmaking of Yugoslavia.* Ed. by Jasminka Udovicki and James Ridgeway. Durham, N.C.: Duke University Press, 1997, 245–64.

Florian Bieber

SEE ALSO Drašković, Vuk; Milošević, Slobodan; Šešelj, Vojislav

Šešelj, Vojislav (1954–)

Radical Serbian nationalist political figure and paramilitary leader. Vojislav Šešelj was born in 1954 in Sarajevo, at that time the capital of the Bosnian Republic of the Socialist Federated Republic of Yugoslavia. At the age of 25, after writing a dissertation on the Marxist theory of military defense, he became the youngest Ph.D. in the history of Communist Yugoslavia. In 1984 he was convicted of propagating nationalism and sentenced to eight years in prison. He was released from prison after twenty one months of reputedly brutal treatment with his nationalism intact and deepened.

As the Socialist Federated Republic of Yugoslavia began to fall apart in 1991, Šešelj, then a lawyer, organized a private militia, first called the Chetniks in honor of the Serbian royalist guerrillas who fought the Germans and Tito's Communist partisans during World War II. His force fought the Croatians and sought to separate Serb-inhabited territory from Croatia and add it to a Greater Serbian state. His Chetniks have been accused of killing non-Serbs or expelling them from territory desired by the Serbs. During the war launched by Bosnian Serbs following the Bosnian proclamation of independence in April 1991, Šešelj commanded a paramilitary force called the White Eagles. The White Eagles, who were armed by Serbian Ministry of Internal Affairs, were reputedly involved in ethnic cleansing, torture, and mass killings in Bosnia. These paramilitaries are also accused of bringing loot taken from their victims back to Serbia.

In Serbia, Šešelj founded the Serbian Radical Party in 1990 and became its president. He, at first, supported the nationalist policies of Serbian President Slobodan Milošević, but later accused him of not adequately supporting the Serbs of Croatia and Bosnia. In 1998, Šešelj's Radical Party, with 82 seats in the 250-seat Serbian parliament was second in strength only to Milošević's Serbian Socialist Party (the renamed Communist Party) with 110 seats. In the 1997 Serbian presidential election, Seselj ran against Milošević's designated successor for that post, Milan Milutinović, and won 39 percent of the vote. Though he had opposed Miloševićand his Serbian Socialist Party in that election, he was, at the direction of Milošević, appointed deputy prime minister of Serbia. Milošević, who was elected president of Yugoslavia in 1997 at times found Šešelj's rabid nationalist invective useful. He could point to Šešelj to demonstrate his own relative moderation to the West. Šešelj was a strong proponent of Serbian repression of the ethnic Albanians in Kosovo. He resigned as deputy prime minister in opposition to Milošević's submission to NATO and its demands with regard to that province during the 1999 war, but later agreed to stay on. He is regarded as a potential challenger and successor to Milošević.

BIBLIOGRAPHY

Glenny, Misha. *The Fall of Yugoslavia: The Third Balkan War.* New York: Penguin, 1994.

Silber, Laura, "Serbia's Ultranationalist Leader Emerges as Formidable Political Force," *Los Angeles Times,* August 3, 1993.

Bernard Cook

Shehu, Mehmet (1913–81)

Albanian military leader and premier. Born into the family of a Tosk Muslim priest in southern Albania, Mehmet Shehu was enrolled in the Tirana Albanian Vocational School funded by the American Red Cross. He graduated in 1932 with a diploma in agriculture. Shehu was unsuccessful in finding employment within the Albanian Ministry of Agriculture, but an Albanian government scholarship did permit him to attend the Naples Military Academy. But he was expelled for pro-Communist sympathies after only a few months. In 1936 he gained entry to the Tirana Officers School but left in the following year after volunteering to fight for the republican side in the Spanish Civil War. He joined the Spanish Communist Party and rose to command the Fourth Battalion of the Garibaldi (Twelfth) International Brigade fighting against General Francisco Franco's forces. The crushing defeat of the republican cause forced Shehu and his men to retreat across the border into France in early 1939, where he was interned. He was later transferred to an Italian internment camp, where he joined the Italian Communist Party. Shehu returned to Albania in 1942, now occupied by Italian forces, where he immediately joined the fledgling Communist Partisan movement. He rose swiftly to command the First Brigade, created in August 1943. During the Nineteenth day Battle of Tirana in October and November 1944, Shehu directed the fighting in and around the city as commander of the First Storm Division.

An acknowledged military tactician, without whose leadership the Communist Partisans may well have failed in their battle to win Albania for the Marxist cause, Shehus was ruthless and exhibited an Albanian ideological zeal that singled him out for rapid promotion in the postwar "people's republic." In 1945 he married his wartime vice commissar, Fiqret Sanxhaktari, and later the same year attended the Voroshilov Military Academy in Moscow, returning home in the summer of 1946 as chief of staff of the Albanian army. Shehu supported Enver Hoxha against Koci Xoxe in the power struggle that took place in the country in 1947 and 1948. Following the Tito Stalin split in October 1948, Shehu replaced Xoxe as interior minister. In the same year he was elected to the Politburo of the Albanian Workers (Communist) Party, thus enjoying high office in both party and state.

In 1954 Hoxha relinquished the premiership to Shehu and for the next twenty-seven years the two men jointly controlled the destiny of the Albanian state and in the process created the most rigidly centralized authoritarian system of government in Eastern Europe. A regular succession of purges of party and government personnel through the years maintained the Hoxha-Shehu duumvirate in supreme power. It is generally assumed that Shehu, whose power base was the Interior Ministry and the much feared Sigurimi (secret police), headed by members of the Shehu clan since 1954, arranged the "practicalities" of such purges, while Hoxha, as party leader, provided the ideological justifications in each case.

During their joint rule of more than a quarter century, all agriculture was collectivized, all commerce and industry nationalized, all artistic life molded by ideology, religion "abolished," and all dissent—real and imagined—mercilessly crushed. On the credit side, a system of universal education and health care was created, but the price exacted in human suffering for the creation and maintenance of the regime was colossal.

On the night of December 17–18, 1981, Shehu died. According to official account, the premier committed suicide, but it is generally assumed that Hoxha personally ordered the murder of his long-standing second in command to smooth the path for his anointed successor as party leader, Ramiz Alia. The entire Shehu family was eventually physically eliminated or incarcerated in the notorious Burrel prison camp. Hoxha accused his former right-hand man of being a multiple agent of foreign powers, both West and East, and Shehu's name was excised from the 1982 edition of the party history.

BIBLIOGRAPHY

Costa, Nicolas J. *Albania: A European Enigma.* Boulder, Col.: East European Monographs, 1995.

O'Donnell, James S. *A Coming of Age: Albania under Enver Hoxha.* Boulder, Col.: East European Monographs, 1999.

Philip E. Wynn

SEE ALSO Hoxha, Enver; Alia, Ramiz

Shelest, Petro (1909–96)

Head of the Soviet Ukrainian Communist Party (1963–72). Petro Shelest was a doctrinaire hard-liner, but he encouraged a flowering of Ukrainian culture. Shelest has been credited with laying the cornerstone for Ukrainian statehood. The brief Ukrainian cultural renaissance, which his promotion of the use of the Ukrainian language and his defense of Ukrainian culture encouraged, won him disfavor within the Politburo in Moscow. In 1972 he was accused by the Soviet leadership of encouraging Ukrainian nationalism and removed as Ukrainian party leader. His successor, Volodymyr V. Shcherbitsky, a bitter rival and a protégé of General Secretary Leonid Brezhnev, demanded that Russian be used in education and in public. Repression of Ukrainian cultural expression followed.

After his dismissal, Shelest was appointed a deputy prime minister of the USSR, but owing to Brezhnev's animosity was removed from that post after one year. He then became director of a military enterprise near Moscow until his retirement. He died in Moscow in January 1996. Petro Tolochko, vice president of the Ukrainian Academy of Sciences, credited Shelest with being "one of the first in the Soviet era to lay the cornerstone for Ukrainian statehood."

Bernard Cook

SEE ALSO Podgorny, Nikolay

Shetland Islands

Group of 100 islands, 20 of which are inhabited, 130 miles north of Scotland. The total land mass of the Shetland Islands, a constituent part of the United Kingdom, is 552 square miles (1,430 sq km). The administrative center is Lerwick, the most northerly town of the United Kingdom. This town of almost 8,000 is located on the largest island, Mainland. It is the seat of the Shetland Islands Area Council, which exercises greater authority than comparable bodies on the mainland. Picts settled on the islands around 200 B.C. The islands, invaded and settled by the Norse in the eighth and ninth centuries, were annexed to the Scottish Kingdom in 1472. They have continued until today, however, to have a largely local existence. In 1989 there were 22,170 inhabitants. A combination of tenant farming (crofting), sheep raising, and fishing have traditionally sustained the islanders. The principal fishing port is Scalloway, located on Mainland. The discovery and development of the Brent and Ninian North Sea oil fields to the northeast slowed the persistent problem of depopulation. An oil depot connected to the fields by a pipeline was constructed at Sullom Voe on the north coast of Mainland in the 1970s.

The Area Council has gained control of oil development in the area of the islands themselves, and there has been a growing demand for completely autonomous local administration.

BIBLIOGRAPHY

Scott Moncrieff, George. *The Scottish Islands,* 2nd ed. Edinburgh: Oliver and Boyd, 1963.

Venables, Ursula. *Life in Shetland, A World Apart.* Edinburgh: Oliver and Boyd, 1956.

Bernard Cook

SEE ALSO Hebrides; Orkney Islands

Shevardnadze, Eduard (1928–)

Foreign minister of the Soviet Union (1985–90, and 1991) and head of Georgia first as chairman of the council of state and then as president (1992–). Eduard Shevardnadze, a native Georgian, was chosen by Mikhail Gorbachev, the General Secretary of the Communist Party of the Soviet Union, in 1985 to serve as Soviet foreign minister. Shevardnadze played a central role in implementing Gorbachev's new political thinking abroad. Before returning to Georgian politics in 1992, following the disintegration of the USSR in December 1991, he facilitated both the liberation of Eastern Europe from Soviet control and the ending of the Cold War.

Shevardnadze was born on January 25, 1928, in Mamati, a village in the Georgian Soviet Socialist Republic. His father, a schoolteacher, encouraged Shevardnadze to become a physician, and he entered Tbilisi Medical College in 1946. That same year he joined the Communist Party of Georgia (CPG), serving as secretary of the college chapter of the Komsomol (Communist Youth). By 1948 he had abandoned medicine in favor of politics. In 1951 he graduated from the party school in Tbilisi, and in 1960 took a degree in history from Kutaisi Pedagogical Institute. In the following decade he rose rapidly through the party hierarchy, serving as Pervomaisky regional secretary (1961–64), deputy minister of Georgian internal affairs (1964–65), then minister (1965–72) and, finally, first secretary of the Central Committee of the CPG (1972–85).

Eduard Shevardnadze (right), president of Georgia and former foreign minister of the USSR, shaking hands with Russia's foreign minister, Andrei Kozirev, in Tibilisi, April 1992. *Illustration courtesy of Reuters/Bettmann.*

Shevardnadze's ascent to the top CPG post owed much to his campaign against corruption in Georgian politics and his growing reputation as an innovative reformer. As minister of internal affairs, he exposed several of the most corrupt and powerful figures in Georgia. As first secretary he initiated campaigns against black marketeering and bribery. Shevardnadze's success in reducing corruption was accompanied by economic reform. Under his guidance, both industrial and agricultural output rose considerably. While most Soviet republics saw food queues growing longer, Georgia's disappeared. Shevardnadze's innovations extended to a balanced approach to the question of Georgian nationalism. He embraced a Georgian cultural renaissance while protecting the republic's ethnic minorities. As critics have often pointed out, Shevardnadze's reforms were accompanied by widespread repression. Under his anticorruption campaigns, thousands of Georgians were arrested, tortured, and executed.

With his dual persona of reformer and hard-liner, Shevardnadze had by the early 1970s attracted the attention of the Soviet ruling elite. General Secretary Leonid Brezhnev cited Shevardnadze's policies of rooting out graft as exemplary, while General Secretary Yuri Andropov's anticorruption campaign, cut short by his death, was largely modeled on the Georgian blueprint. Mikhail Gorbachev, in one of his first acts as general secretary of the Communist Party of the Soviet Union, brought Shevardnadze to Moscow in July 1985, making him Soviet foreign minister and a full member of the party's Politburo.

The appointment of Shevardnadze to replace the seasoned Andrey Gromyko sent shockwaves through diplomatic circles at home and abroad. Shevardnadze had no experience in world diplomacy. He knew no foreign languages, spoke Russian with a heavy Georgian accent, and had rarely traveled. His only qualifications were a longstanding friendship with Gorbachev and a common vision of reform. Many initially believed that the Georgian would merely become the general secretary's mouthpiece. Shevardnadze soon belied such assumptions, revealing himself to be a welcome change from his grim and confrontational predecessor. He possessed an unmistakable flair for diplomacy, lighting the world stage with charm, ironic humor, and a dynamism rarely associated with a Soviet envoy.

As foreign minister, Shevardnadze became one of the most effective proponents of Gorbachev's reform policies of glasnost (openness) and perestroika (restructuring). His key foreign policy achievements included overseeing the withdrawal of Soviet troops from Afghanistan in 1988, negotiating historic arms control agreements with the United States, and, most spectacularly, the repudiation of the Brezhnev Doctrine, the USSR's self-proclaimed right to intervene militarily in the affairs of its allies. Thus Shevardnadze presided over the fall of Communist regimes across eastern Europe during 1989–90. Removing any doubts that the Cold War had indeed ended, during the 1990–91 Persian Gulf War, Shevardnadze facilitated cooperation between the Soviet Union and the U.S.-led coalition forces against the Iraqi regime of Saddam Hussein.

Despite his successes in foreign affairs, Shevardnadze encountered continuous resistance at home from Russian nationalists and unreconstructed Communists. His critics blamed him for surrendering the fruits of Soviet victory in World War II. In the wake of mounting criticism from hardliners within the party leadership, Shevardnadze resigned in December 1990, warning that the right was in ascendancy and dictatorship was imminent. After the 1991 failed coup attempt by hard-liners who were trying to preserve the Soviet Union and the dominance of the Communist Party, he returned briefly to the foreign ministry, only to be rendered obsolete by the dissolution of the Soviet Union in December 1991.

In March 1992, Shevardnadze returned to Georgia, now an independent state but leaderless and racked by civil war. For many Georgians Shevardnadze represented the best hope for political stability. In October 1992 he was elected chairman of parliament, a position equivalent to president. As head of state Shevardnadze sought to find solutions to separatist violence in the Georgian provinces of South Ossetia and Abkhazia. While these endeavors met with only limited success, his international stature won Georgia considerable foreign aid and investment.

Shevardnadze, who after Soviet dictator Joseph Stalin is only the second native Georgian to achieve international fame, leaves a legacy that is difficult to exaggerate. A politician of consummate skill, he bided his time as a regional party bureaucrat, rising through the ranks and awaiting an opportunity (to leave a lasting mark). As the last foreign minister of the Soviet Union, Shevardnadze played a key role in the most tumultuous political upheaval of postwar Europe.

BIBLIOGRAPHY

McGiffert Ekedahl, Carolyn, and Melvin Goodman. *The Wars of Eduard Shevardnadze.* University Park: Pennsylvania University Press, 1997.

Shevardnadze, Eduard. *The Future Belongs to Freedom.* New York: Free Press, 1991.

———. *My Choice: In Defense of Democracy and Freedom.* Moscow: Novosti, 1991.

Suny, Ronald. *The Making of the Georgian State.* Bloomington: Indiana University Press, 1994.

Daniel Kowalsky

SEE ALSO Abkhazia; Brezhnev Doctrine; Georgia

Shushkevich, Stanislau (1934–)

Chairman of the Supreme Soviet (parliament) of Belarus (1991–94). In this capacity Stanislau Shushkevich was acting head of state, however, with little real power. He was born in Minsk on December 15, 1934. His father was a Belarusan poet who spent the years 1937–54 in labor camps, a victim of Stalin's repression. Shushkevich graduated from the Belarusan State University in 1956, earned a doctoral degree in technical sciences in 1970, and became a respected physicist at the university. He authored several monographs and more than 150 articles on radio electronics and computer science. He joined the Communist Party (CPB) in 1968 but entered politics only after the Chernobyl nuclear disaster in neighboring Soviet Ukraine. The Belarusan Popular Front, a broad political movement agitating for independence and change in Belarus supported him, although he was still a member of the CPB until 1991. This helped him to be elected in 1989 to the Congress of People's Deputies of the USSR, the new Soviet parliament established by President Mikhail Gorbachev, and in March 1990 also to the Supreme Soviet of the Belarusan Soviet Socialist Republic, of which he became the first deputy chairman. In September 1990 the centrist Shushkevich was elected first chairman of the Belarusan Supreme Soviet, replacing Mikalai Dzemyantsei. Shushkevich was one of the few prominent politicians who spoke Belarusan instead of Russian. On December 7, 1991, he joined Boris Yeltsin and Leonid Kravchuk of Ukraine in the formation of the Commonwealth of Independent States (CIS) and was instrumental in the decision to locate its main offices in

Minsk, the Belarusan capital. He was voted out of office in January 1994. The reason for the negative vote in the Belarus Supreme Soviet was an alleged failure to combat corruption, but the real issue was that most deputies found him not conservative enough. By this time, the chairmanship of the Supreme Soviet was little more than a figurehead position, overshadowed by the premiership held by Vyachaslau Kebich.

BIBLIOGRAPHY

Urban, Michael, and Jan Zaprudnik. "Belarus: A Long Road to Nationhood," in Ian Bremmer and Ray Taras, eds., *Nation and Politics in the Soviet Successor States.* Cambridge: Cambridge University Press, 1993, pp. 99–120.

Zaprudnik, Jan. *Belarus: At a Crossroads in History.* Boulder, Col.: Westview Press, 1993.

Karel C. Berkhoff

SEE ALSO Dzemyantsei, Mikalai; Kebich, Vyachaslau

Sicilian Autonomy

Regional autonomy was conferred on the island of Sicily in May 1946 through the approval of the Sicilian Special Statute of the constitution of the Republic of Italy (1946). The first regional elections took place in April 1947, a year before the first free Italian parliamentary elections after the demise of the fascist regime. The Special Statute for Sicily was ratified when Italy approved a Sicilian constitution in 1948, granting the island legislative power on a wide range of matters such as control of police forces, local administration, and taxation. Thanks to its special autonomy, Sicily enjoys the status of an autonomous political entity. Provided that Sicilian autonomy does not infringe on the superior jurisdiction of the national state, it exists as an autonomous entity inside the Italian state and not as an independent sovereign entity federated to the Italian Republic. Yet Sicily's political autonomy is considerable compared with other forms of local autonomy in Italy and elsewhere in Europe.

The motivations for such particular treatment can be found in the history of Sicilian parliamentary institutions. The first Sicilian parliament was founded by the Normans around 1130. In modern times the parliament in Palermo twice exercised legislative and constitutional initiative. The first time was in 1812, when it approved a constitution inspired by the English example, and again in 1848 during the liberal rising against the Bourbon monarchy.

After unification with Italy in 1860, integration within the new Italian nation was not as easy as expected. Large groups of the Sicilian population regarded the new state as another foreign domination, not unlike the many that had already occurred in the history of the island. Peasant revolts followed at regular intervals until the end of the nineteenth century, often bloodily repressed. The fear of a separatist movement in Sicily until the end of World War II was the main reason that Italy awarded the island such a wide measure of self-government.

BIBLIOGRAPHY

Atti della Consulta siciliana. Palermo: Regione Siciliana 1946.

Bobbio, N. *Introduzione alla costituzione.* Bari, 1951.

Dolci, D. *The Man Who Plays Alone.* New York: Pantheon, 1969.

Gangi, M. *Il 1948 e la costituzione siciliana del 12 gennalo.* Palermo: Regione, Siciliana, 1972.

Guccione, E. *Dal federalismo mancato al regionalismo tradito.* Turin: G. Giappichelli, 1998.

Stefania Mazzone

Sigua, Tengiz (1934–)

Nationalist Georgian politician and twice prime minister (1990–91 and 1992–93) of the Georgia before his political demise in 1995. Educated as an engineer at the Metallurgy Institute of the Georgian Academy of Sciences, Tengiz Ippolitovich Sigua was a leading member of the Round Table–Free Georgia Alliance, which won the first multiparty elections to the Georgian Supreme Soviet (Parliament) in 1990. His anti-Russian nationalist sympathies were then attested to by his chairmanship of the All-Georgia Rusteveli Society, a group set up by the Communist Party in Georgia to promote the Georgia language and culture. Appointed premier by independent Georgia's first leader, Zviad Gamsakhurdia (chairman of the State Council) in 1990, he resigned in 1991 because of his opposition to Gamsabhurdia's growing authoritarianism. A key participant in the armed rebellion that deposed Gamsakhurdia in January 1992, Sigua was then appointed premier by a new Military Council dominated by the Georgian National Guard and the Mkhedrioni (Horsemen) militia. He continued as premier under President Edvard Shevardnadze, but he and his miltia leader allies fell out with the leader they had put in power in 1993. In 1994 he and Tengiz Kitovani, a militia leader who had also fallen out with Shevardnadze in 1993, formed an opposition National Liberation Front (NLF) that then mounted an unsuccessful attack against the rebel Georgian province of Abkhazia in 1995. Also implicitly aimed at toppling Shevardnadze, the NLF was later banned by the Georgia government and its leaders charged with inciting civil war, a development that finished Sigua's political career in Georgia.

Marko Milivojevic

SEE ALSO Gamsakhurdia, Zviad

Sik, Ota (1919–)

Deputy prime minister of Czechoslovakia (1968). A professor of economics, Ota Sik was the leading architect of economic policy during the Prague Spring, the period of liberalization under First Secretary Alexander Dubček that was crushed in 1968 by the soviet-led Warsaw Pact invasion. Appointed to head a government commission for economic reform in 1961, Sik advocated use of market factors and a shift in emphasis toward consumer goods. He was elected a member of the Central Committee of the Communist Party in 1962, and appointed director of the Economic Institute of the Czechoslovakia Academy in 1963. He became deputy prime minister in April 1968 under Dubček. Forced to resign in the aftermath of the Warsaw Pact's invasion of Czechoslovakia in August 1968, Sik was expelled from the Communist Party dominated by the new conservative first secretary Gustáv Husák in 1969. He was allowed to emigrate to Switzerland and was appointed professor of comparative economic systems at the University of St. Gallen. Sik's theories on economic reform in a socialist system were a catalyst for the Prague Spring and a major part of the Action Program prepared by Dubček's government.

BIBLIOGRAPHY

Sik, Ota. *For a Humane Economic Democracy.* New York: Praeger, 1985.

Svitak, Ivan. *The Czechoslovak Experiment, 1968–69.* New York: Columbia University Press, 1971.

Timothy C. Dowling

SEE ALSO Dubček, Alexander

Sikorski, Władysław E. (1881–1943)

Polish general, prime minister, and commander in chief of the World War II Polish government-in-exile. Although Władysław Sikorski perished in 1943, his initiatives as wartime prime minister had a profound impact on postwar Poland. Sikorski was born east of Kraków, in what was then Austrian territory. During World War I he served in the Austrian army, commanding Polish units. With the post–World War I rebirth of Poland, Sikorski played a prominent role in the 1919–21 Polish-Soviet War. He later became chief of the General Staff, and in 1922 he was appointed prime minister by President Joseph Piłsudski and held the post until replaced in 1923.

Sikorski's career went into eclipse after Józef Piłsudski seized power in 1926. During his years as a leading opponent of the Piłsudski regime, Sikorski played little direct role in Polish affairs. In 1934 he published *The Future War,* a brilliant book that predicted the coming roles of armored vehicles and air power. The book was ignored in Poland but studied closely by other armies, especially the Soviet.

Sikorski did not participate in the campaign of September 1939 when Poland was faced by an overwhelming invasion by Nazi Germany. When the Polish government fled the Germans and was interned in Romania, he established a Polish government-in-exile in Paris on September 30, 1939—with himself as both prime minister and commander in chief of the armed forces. After France fell in June 1940, Sikorski's government moved to London.

When the Germans invaded the Soviet Union in June 1941, Sikorski reestablished relations with the Soviets who had also invaded Poland in September 1939 and seized the eastern third of the country. The resulting controversial Sikorski-Maisky Agreement provided for the formation of a Polish army in the Soviet Union composed of Polish POWs captured by the Soviets in September 1939.

One of the enduring myths of World War II is that the establishment of the Oder-Neisse Line as postwar Poland's western boundary was purely a Communist contrivance, designed to penalize Germany and to compensate Poland partially for large tracts of territory "returned" to the Soviets in the east. Sikorski, was in fact, the first Polish statesman to propose such a boundary in a December 4, 1942, memorandum to U.S. President Franklin Roosevelt. Sikorski anticipate that postwar Poland would loose the eastern areas to the Soviets. But his justification for the western border was based more on Poland's strategic needs and historical claims to Silesia, which came under German control only when Frederick the Great seized it in the 1740s.

Sikorski also advocated a postwar Polish-Czechoslovak confederation, in which the small states of central Europe would play a balance-of-power role between East and West. Sikorski's diplomatic initiatives began to fall apart with the April 1943 discovery of the mass graves of Polish officers in the Katyn Forest in the western USSR. From that point on, relations with the Soviets were on a crisis footing, eventually resulting in the establishment of a rival

Polish government-in-exile in Moscow. The conflict with the Soviets also weakened the position of Sikorski's government with Great Britain and the United States both of whom went to great lengths to maintain smooth relations with their Soviet allies during the war. In the middle of the crisis, Sikorski and his closest aides were killed on July 4, 1943, in an airplane crash off Gibraltar. The apparent accident occurred under somewhat mysterious circumstances, resulting in considerable speculation ever since.

After Sikorski's death, the London Polish government without his leadership went into a decline from which it never recovered. The West eventually yielded to Stalin's demands for most of prewar eastern Poland, and the Soviets and the Moscow Poles took up the call for the Oder-Neisse Line to become Poland's western boundary. As a result, Poland remained tightly bound into the Soviet orbit throughout the Cold War.

BIBLIOGRAPHY

Garlinski, Jozef. *Poland in the Second World War.* Houndmills, U.K.: Macmillan, 1985.

Sword, Keith, ed. *Sikorski: Soldier and Statesman.* London: Orbis, 1990.

Terry, Sarah Meiklejohn. *Poland's Place in Europe: General Sikorski and the Origins of the Oder-Neisse Line, 1939–1943.* Princeton, N.J.: Princeton University Press, 1983.

David T. Zabecki

SEE ALSO Katyn Forest Massacre; Wartime Conferences

Silone, Ignazio (1900–1978)

Italian writer who made a pilgrimage from Catholicism through communism, which eventually left him a Christian without a church and a socialist without a party. Ignazio Silone, baptized Secondo Tranquili, was born into a smallholding peasant family at Pescina in the Abruzzi on May 1, 1900. He was educated in the local Catholic seminary. His socialism was an outgrowth of his Catholic social values. He became secretary for a local organization of agricultural workers and in 1917 joined the Socialist Youth League.

He enthusiastically embraced the radicalism of the Italian Communist Party (PCI) when it was organized in 1921. He was first sent to Trieste to write for a Communist newspaper, then to Spain, where he changed his name to Ignazio Silone and was twice arrested for political activity. In 1927 he and Palmiro Togliatti, the general secretary of the PCI from 1927 to 1964, represented the PCI at a meeting of the Communist International (Comintern) in Moscow. Josef Stalin wanted the backing of Comintern in his campaign to isolate his political enemy, Leon Trotsby. When told to sign a denunciation of Trotsky, which he had not read, Silone, despite verbal abuse, refused. His refusal to ignore the abuse of power and the betrayal of ideals by his own PCI and the Soviet Communist Party, and his denunciations of those faults led to his expulsion from the PCI in 1931.

During the 1930s, suffering from poor health and isolation, he spent his exile in Switzerland writing. In 1941, Silone was appointed to the executive committee of the Italian Socialist Party (PSI) and headed its headquarters in exile. He returned to Rome in late 1944 as editor of the PSI newspaper *Avanti!* and in 1946 was elected to parliament from his district in the Abruzzi.

Silone's democratic socialist aspirations for Italy and Europe were confounded. He was deeply disappointed by the territorial and ideological barriers of the Cold War. When the 1947 Rome Congress of the PSI chose to cooperate with the PCI, Silone emerged again without a party. He was associated with the pro-American Congress for Cultural Freedom but never lost faith in socialism. Until his death in Geneva on August 22, 1978, he continued to stress the themes of justice and freedom in his writings.

BIBLIOGRAPHY

Crossman, Richard, ed. *The God That Failed.* New York: Bantam, 1965.

Guerriero, Elio. *L'inquietudine e l'utopia: Il racconto umano e cristiano di Ignazio Silone.* Milan: Jaca, 1979.

Marelli, Sante. *Silone: intellectuale della libertà.* Rimini: Panozzo, 1989.

Silone, Ignazio. *Fontamara.* [1993]. New York: Signet, 1981.

———. *Bread and Wine.* (*Pane e Vino,* 1936). New York: New American Library, 1963.

———. *Handful of Blackberries* (*Una Manciata di More,* 1952). New York: Harper and Row, 1953.

———. *Emergency Exit.* (*Uscita di Sicurezza,* 1965). New York: Harper and Row, 1968.

Bernard Cook

Simenon, Georges (1903–89)

Belgian francophone author. Georges Simenon, creator of the legendary Commissaire (Inspector) Maigret, was one of the most productive and popular novelists of the twentieth century. Many of his novels have been adapted for cinema or television.

Simenon spent his youth in Liège before settling in Paris. At the end of World War II he moved to the United States. Returning to Europe in 1955, he lived in Lausanne, Switzerland, until his death in 1989.

The main features of Simenon's world are its special atmosphere, the oddness of the characters, and a determination on the part of the author not to judge them—features that reappear in the diversity of places, human types, and situations evoked in hundreds of novels. Simenon has been compared to Balzac. His themes have been described as the typical concerns of a petite bourgeoisie whose strengths and weaknesses provide the authenticity and set the limitations to a work that, through its size and international success, is unique in modern literature.

The last phase of Simenon's work, written after his decision to give up the novel, remains almost unknown. The *Dictées* (1975) are intimate monologues in which the man reveals his inner life; the *Mémoires intimes* (1981), the huge book derived from the terrible crisis caused by his daughter Mary-Jo's suicide, conflate an apparently sincere confession with an attempt at self-justification. Critical opinion is divided over these works. But whether masterpieces or mere gossip, they have been more or less neglected by the admirers of his other works.

BIBLIOGRAPHY

Assouline, Pierre. *Simenon—Biographie.* Paris: Julliard, 1992.

Eskin, Stanley G. *Simenon: A Critical Biography.* Jefferson, N.C.: McFarlan, 1987.

Fabre, Jean. *Enquête sur un enquêteur, Maigret: Un essai de sociocritique.* Montpellier: Études sociocritiques, 1981.

Lemoine, Michel. *L'autre Univers de Simenon.* Liège: C.L.P.C.F., 1991.

Piron, Maurice, and Michel Lemoine. *L'Univers de Simenon.* Paris: Presses de la Cité, 1983.

Paul Delbouille

Simon, Claude (1913–)

French writer of the *nouveau roman* group and recipient of the Nobel Prize in literature. Born in Antananarivo, Madagascar, the year Marcel Proust published *Du Côté de chez Swann,* Claude Eugène Henri Simon was educated in French secondary schools in Perpignan and at the Collège Stanislas, a private school situated in the Montparnasse neighborhood of Paris. In England he studied briefly at Cambridge and Oxford Universities but received no formal university degree. Mobilized in the Second World War, he was taken prisoner by the Germans. After he revealed his supposed tribal origins to the Germans, they sent him to a POW camp in France. In 1940 he escaped and joined the French Resistance in Perpignan. During the early 1960s Simon was politically involved in protesting France's presence in Algeria. Though participating in the literary life of France with its many conferences, he continued a life of solitude on his wine-producing estate.

His novels, considered difficult for many readers, have been translated into numerous languages. First distinguished by French literary prizes, Simon won the Nobel Prize in literature in 1985. Categorized as a member of the *nouveau roman* (new novel) group of writers, which includes among others Michel Butor, Alain Robbe-Grillet, and Nathalie Sarraute, who are often studied as writers in search of a subject or novel, Simon himself seems to be more faithful to the traditional representation of reality. In many ways the heir of Gustave Flaubert, whose definition of style was that of vision, Simon has pushed the play of the visible in its myriad forms into an intellectual construct. His novels have developed away from the more traditional French psychological text, with its call for concise and orderly expression, and indeed away from a Cartesian tradition that would posit meaning in a thinking subject, into a play of words whereby the reader becomes an important decipherer and cooperative producer of the text.

Simon's novels have become the resource for literary theoreticians of the new novel as well as for those concerned with formalism and Derridian deconstruction. Simon's own style developed with the appearance of *The Wind* (1957) and became more recondite with novels such as *Triptyque* (1973). In his later work readers and critics perceived a return to earlier themes. Given the stylistic adventure that writing was for him and for his reader, Simon will continue to belong to that tradition of novelists, such as Proust and Flaubert, known for their emphasis on the task of writing for oneself.

BIBLIOGRAPHY

Britton, Celia. *Claude Simon: Writing the Visible.* Cambridge: Cambridge University Press, 1987.

Fletcher, John. *Claude Simon and Fiction Now.* London: Calder and Boyars, 1975.

Sarkonak, Ralph. *Understanding Claude Simon.* Columbia: University of South Carolina Press, 1990.

Peter S. Rogers

Sindona, Michele (1920–86)

Sicilian-born financier who climbed to the top of the Italian banking world during the 1960s, accumulating a fortune of more than $450 million in banks and real estate.

Michele Sindona came from a poor family in Patti, Sicily. A good student with an aptitude for mathematics and business, Sindona received a scholarship and earned a degree in tax law from the University of Messina in 1942. He rose quickly to the top of the legal and financial community in Sicily and moved to Milan to pursue new opportunities. As a Sicilian, Sindona was often the victim of discrimination as he struggled to acquire wealth and respect in an attempt to be accepted by the Italian and American banking communities. Sindona's financial genius was heralded by the international banking community when he opened banks such as his Banca Privata Italiana and purchased corporations such as Libby and McNeil & Libby. Sindona believed strongly in the American free-market system, often speaking out against the tendency toward nationalization promoted by influential Italian business leaders such as Enrico Cuccia. Sindona enjoyed a fruitful partnership with the Vatican when Pope Paul VI made him the main financial adviser for the Vatican. As a member of the highly secretive Masonic group Propaganda Due (P-2), Sindona received support and protection. He was also connected to the Sicilian Mafia, which eventually turned on him, wounding and kidnapping him in 1979.

In 1974 the New York–based Franklin National Bank, in which Sindona had purchased a controlling interest in 1972, collapsed. Authorities charged him with causing the bank's failure—the largest to date in American history—and sentenced him in 1980 to twenty-five years. In 1984 Sindona was extradited to Italy, where he was convicted on fraud charges and received a fifteen-year sentence. This was followed by a conviction and life sentence in 1986 for ordering the murder by Mafia assassins in 1979 of Giorgio Ambrosoli, a bank liquidator who was investigating Sindona. Sindona attempted suicide numerous times as his legal difficulties increased and finally succeeded in March 1986, when he ingested a fatal dose of potassium cyanide.

BIBLIOGRAPHY

Di Fonzo, Luigi. *St. Peter's Banker.* New York: Franklin Watts, 1983.

Spero, Joan Edelman. *Failure of the Franklin National Bank: Challenge to the International Banking System.* Washington, D.C.: Beard Books, 1999.

Tosches, Nick. *Power on Earth.* New York: Arbor House, 1986.

Wendy A. Pojmann

SEE ALSO Gelli, Licio; John Paul

Sinowatz, Fred (1929–)

Austrian chancellor, chairman of the Social Democratic Party. Fred Sinowatz was born in 1929 into a rural working-class family in Burgenland, Austria's easternmost province. He studied history, graduated from the University of Vienna, and began his political career as the secretary to the SPÖ's provincial party leader for the Burgenland. After some years as the state minister for culture in Burgenland, he was appointed federal minister for education in 1971 and kept this position until 1983 during all the remaining years of the Chancellor Bruno Kreisky's tenure. Between 1981 and 1983 he was Kreisky's deputy as vice-chancellor and in that capacity his heir apparent. When the SPÖ lost its overall majority in 1983 and Kreisky resigned, Sinowatz became chancellor of the coalition cabinet with the Freedom Party (FPÖ) and party chairman.

As successor to such a dominant figure, Sinowatz tried to free himself from Kreisky's shadow. When the SPÖ-FPÖ coalition became increasingly less popular, Sinowatz prepared for his own exit. Against Kreisky's wish he appoints Franz Vranitzky minister of finance and, after the SPÖ's defeat in the presidential elections in 1986, he resigned and threw his support to Vranitzky, who became chancellor with the backing of the SPÖ. Sinowatz was well aware that Vranitzky did not want keep the alliance with the FPÖ, an alliance that Kreisky considered his own strategic recipe. Sinowatz stayed for two more years as party chairman before Vranitzky succeeded also to this position.

Sinowatz is the link between two periods, the Kreisky era, characterized by social democratic domination, and the Vranitzky era, the revival of the coalition between the SPÖ and the ÖVP.

BIBLIOGRAPHY

Cap, Josef. *Sozialdemokratie im Wandel.* Vienna: Jugend und Volk, 1989.

Pelinka, Anton. *Die Kleine Koalition: SPÖ-FPÖ 1983–1986.* Vienna: Boehlau, 1993.

Anton Pelinka

Sinyavsky, Andrey Donatovich (1925–97)

Soviet writer condemned for alleged subversion. Andrey Sinyavsky, who wrote under the pseudonym Abram Tertz, was born in Moscow on October 8, 1925. He studied literature at the University of Moscow and taught at the Gorky Institute of World Literature in Moscow. He wrote for *Novy Mir,* a literary journal. His novels, none of which appeared in the Soviet Union, were published in the West. *Sud idyot,* (*The Trial Begins*), which dealt with the trumped up 1953 Doctors' Plot, was published in London in 1960. A collection of short stories, *Fantastic Stories,* was published in English in 1963. It broached such taboos as tyranny and the emptiness of the experience of the Soviet man.

The Brezhnev era (1964–82) brought renewed repression of Soviet artists and intellectuals. On September 13, 1965, Sinyavsky and the dissident author Yuli Daniel were arrested and subsequently convicted of anti-Soviet propaganda. Sinyavsky was released from prison in 1971. Two years later he received permission to emigrate to France with his wife and son, and taught at the Sorbonne. He died on February 25, 1997, at his home in Fontenay-aux-Roses outside Paris.

BIBLIOGRAPHY

Dalton, Margaret. *Andrei Siniavskii and Julii Daniel: Two Soviet Heretical Writers.* Würzburg, Germany: Jal-Verlag, 1973.

Lourie, Richard. *Letters to the Future: An Approach to Sinyavsky–Tertz.* Ithaca, N.Y.: Cornell University Press, 1975.

Sinavsky, Andrei. *Strolls with Pushkin.* Tr. by Catharine Theimer. New Haven, Conn.: Yale University Press, c1993.

———. *Unguarded Thoughts. Mysli vrasplokh.* Tr. by Manya Harari. London: Collins, Harvill Press, 1972.

Bernard Cook

Siroky, Viliám (1902–71)

Premier of Czechoslovakia from 1953 to 1963. Viliám Siroky was born in Bratislava on May 31, 1902. He was a founding member of the Czechoslovak Communist Party in 1921. When the Czechoslovak President Klement Gottwald died in 1953, Antonín Zápotocký, who had been premier, became president, the principal political post in the country. Siroky then became premier. When Zápotocký died in 1957 he was succeeded as president by Antonín Novotný, who like his predecessor was an unreformed Stalinist. As pressure mounted in Czechoslovakia after 1960 for liberalization on charges of corruption and economic decentralization, Novotný was able to engineer the conviction of one of his most vociferous critics and advocate of liberal reform, the minister of interior Rudolf Barak, in 1962. When this did not silence opposition, Novotný in 1963 sacrificed Karol Bacilek, leader of the Slovak branch of the Communist Party, and Siroky, both of whom had roused the ire of the Slovaks by supporting the centralization espoused by Zápotocký and then by Novotný. Siroky was replaced by Josef Lenart, an apparently more acceptable Slovak, and Bacilek was replaced by Alexander Dubček. These appointments temporarily calmed the situation, and Novotný was elected president again in 1964. Siroky died in Prague on October 6, 1971.

BIBLIOGRAPHY

Shoemaker, M. Wesley. *Russia, Eurasian States, and Eastern Europe 1994.* Harpers Ferry, W.V.: Stryker-Post, 1995.

Bernard Cook

Skvorecky, Josef (1924–)

Editor, writer, author of film scripts, translator, literary critic, and professor of literature at the University of Toronto. Josef Skvorecky, born in Nachod, Czechoslovakia, on September 27, 1924, graduated from high school in Nachod in 1943. During the German occupation of World War II, he worked as an unskilled worker. Between 1945 and 1949 he studied at Charles University in Prague. He began medical studies but shifted to English and philosophy. He taught high school while completing his Ph.D. thesis on Thomas Paine (1737–1809), the English-American radical writer. His military service from 1951 to 1953 was the background of his book *Tankovy prapor* (*The Republic of Whores*), his best-known novel. In its style this book is a neo-Schweikian story, a confrontation full of absurdities. Similar to the Czech writer Jaroslau Hašek's *The Good Soldier Schweik* that mocked unreasonable authority and dehumanized bureaucracy. Today it is considered a classic interpretation of the 1950s in Czechoslovakia.

The *Republic of Whores* is the story of politically unreliable young men with bourgeois backgrounds, with relatives in the Western emigration, some of them active in Allied armies during World War II, some religious. They are "punished" by being forced into a special tank battalion to face particularly dangerous tasks during their military service. The book was printed but not distributed because of the Soviet occupation in 1968. It was published in 1971 in Toronto, and in 1989 the story became a script for a movie.

From 1953 to 1955 and again from 1959 to 1963 Skvorecky was editor at the state-owned publisher Odeon. Between 1956 and 1958 he was editor for the bimonthly magazine *Svetova literature* (*World Literature*). In 1961

Communist President Antonín Novotný prohibited the shooting of Skvorecky and Miloŝ Forman's film script, *A Little Jazz Music*. After 1963 Skvorecky was self-employed.

Skvorecky's literary work is the expression of a generation who spent their youth under a totalitarian regime. During this time his stories were a kind of bible for his contemporaries, especially for those who were opposed to Communism. Skvorecky's experience with life in a small town during World War II, his beloved but forbidden jazz music, the Nazi occupation, and the political and social turmoil following the war and the impact of all these things on ordinary Czechs are the topics of his work.

In 1949 he wrote his autobiographical novel, *Zbabelci* (*The Cowards*), about the last days of World War II in his hometown. This book was not published until 1958 but even then was immediately prohibited and confiscated. Unofficial copies became best-sellers on the black market. In its revised edition this book was officially published again in 1964. Skvorecky is also known for his novels with Jewish topics, like *Legende Emoke* (1963) and *Sedmiramenny svicen* (1964) that deals sensitively with the memories and views of survivors and fellow travelers. During this period Skvorecky was considered the best translator of Anglo-American literature in his Country. He was also one of the leading Czech experts on jazz. In cooperation with Lubomír Doruzka a Czech musicologist, he published studies on jazz. In his 1986 book on the Bohemian composer Antonín Dvořák (1841–1904), *Scherzo capriccioso—Dvořak in Love,* he describes the influence of American music on Dvořák's music, but also the impact of Dvořák on jazz.

His personal activity on behalf of *Svetova literatura* was enormous. This journal had a small circulation and the demand for it was never satisfied. It was during a time when traveling abroad was practically impossible for the average Czechoslovak and when censorship was active. Even at the beginning of the 1960s readers had to wait for the death of a subscriber to get a subscription.

Skvorecky and his wife, Zdena Salivarova, emigrated to escape this repression. They lived for a brief period in 1968 in the United States. After 1969 they lived in exile in Toronto. In 1969 Skvorecky and his wife—a dancer, singer, actor, writer, script writer and author—founded the publishing house Sixty-Eight. Its main purpose was the publication of literature forbidden under the regime of first secretary of the Communist Party and then president, Gustáv Husák (1969–1989) in Czechoslovakia. Skvorecky also began teaching at Toronto University in 1968. In 1973 he started broadcasting regularly for the Voice of America. In 1978 his Czechoslovak citizenship was revoked for political reasons but after the Velvet Revolution of 1989, President Václav Havel decorated Skvorecky and Zdena Skvorecky-Salivarova with the highest Czechoslovak decoration, the Cross of the White Lion.

BIBLIOGRAPHY

Skvorecky, Josef. *Headed for the Blues.* Hopewell, N.J.: Ecco Press, 1996.

———. *Jeri Menzel and the History of the Closely Watched Train.* Boulder, Colo.: East European Monographs, 1982.

———. *The Republic of Whores.* London: Faber and Faber, 1994.

———. *The Return of Lieutenant Boruvka.* New York: Norton, 1991.

———. *Talkin's Moscow Blues.* New York: Ecco Press 1990.

———. *The Tenor Saxofonist Story.* Hopewell, N.J.: Ecco Press, 1996.

———. *Vsichni ti bystri mladi muzi.* (*An Essay about Czechoslovak Cinema*). Prague: Horizont, 1991.

Skvorecky, Josef, Papers 1949–94. Hoover Institutions Archives. Stanford University, Palo Alto, Calif.

Marta Marková

Slánský, Rudolf Salzmann (1901–52)

Secretary-general of the Czechoslovak Communist Party (1946–51). Rudolf Slánský was the second-most powerful member of the Communist Party of Czechoslovakia at the time of his arrest in 1951. A founding member of the party, Slansky was elected to the National Assembly (parliament) in 1935. He fled to the USSR in 1938 and remained until 1944, returning to Czechoslovakia as a partisan in the final stages of the Second World War. He reentered parliament in 1945 as a representative of the Communist Party and played a key role in the Communist takeover of the government in 1948. In November 1951, however, Slánský was accused by the party of leading a Titoist-Zionist plot to assassinate Klement Gottwald, the Czechoslovak premier and Slánský's rival for power. Slánský was tried publicly as part of the purges ordered by Soviet leader Josef Stalin. Found guilty, he was hanged December 2, 1952. He was rehabilitated legally in 1963 and fully exonerated in 1968. Slánský's name, however, remains synonymous with the show trials of the Stalinist era in Eastern Europe.

BIBLIOGRAPHY

Pelikán, Jirí, ed. *The Czechoslovak Political Trials, 1950–1954: The Suppressed Report of the Dubcek Govern-*

ment's Commission of Inquiry, 1968. Stanford: Stanford University Press, 1971

Slánská, Josefa. *Report on My Husband.* New York: Atheneum, 1969.

Timothy C. Dowling

SEE ALSO Gottwald, Klement; Slánský Trial

Slánský Trial

Largest Stalinist purge trial of post–World War II Europe. In the trial held in Czechoslovakia in 1952, Rudolf Slánský, general secretary of the Czechoslovak Communist Party, and thirteen other defendants were branded as bourgeois nationalists, Titoists, Zionists, or Western imperialist agents. Although there is little doubt that Slánský was a loyal Stalinist, all were found guilty of treason and other high crimes against the state. Eleven, including Slánský, were executed. The remaining three received life imprisonment.

From 1949 to 1954 Stalinist terror in the form of purge arrests and trials reached its height in Czechoslovakia. It is estimated that tens of thousands were arrested, and well over a hundred thousand lost jobs or government and party positions. Among the targeted "bourgeois nationalists" were Roman and Greek Catholic religious leaders, lawyers, doctors, small shopkeepers, merchants, and the leadership of the wartime Slovak Communist Party. Most accused "Titoists" were persons having extensive international contacts: Spanish Civil War veterans or foreign trade and foreign policy specialists assigned to the West during the 1930s and World War II. Jews who were seen as antistate "Zionists" were then labeled, through Zionism, as agents of American foreign policy. Of the fourteen persons charged in the Slánský trial, twelve were Jews. The state of Israel's alignment with the United States, along with Stalin's personal anti-Semitism, opened to suspicion all Czechoslovaks of Jewish ancestry.

Although purges often followed from power struggles within the Eastern European Communist parties, the Slánský trial, like the majority of that era's purges and other show trials, resulted more broadly from Cold War pressures. The growing U.S. presence in Western Europe, seen in the Truman Doctrine, Marshall Plan, and NATO, led Stalin to create the Cominform, designed to unify the international Communist movement and subordinate it to Soviet needs. Czechoslovakia's flirtation with the Marshall Plan, along with the failure evident in the late 1940s of its five-year plan, in conjunction with Tito-led Yugoslavia's breakaway from the Cominform, provoked in the Soviet leadership a fear of all national independence movements. Zhdanovism—the Soviet Union's version of McCarthyism—generated a need for internal enemies in order to bolster strict obedience within the bloc. The 1949 purge trial of László Rajk in Hungary had already set the tone for the Slánský trial.

The fourteen Slánský defendants were arrested in 1950–51. From the time of their arrest until their trial in late 1952, they were physically and psychologically tortured. They were forced to confess and to memorize statements of guilt. The trial was conducted as a piece of theater, with scriptwriters, actors, and directors. Czechoslovak President Klement Gottwald was informed that the trial would begin at 9:00 A.M. on November 20, with sentencing to be handed down on the eighth day between 9:00 and 11:00 A.M. The state prosecutor charged the following with sabotage, espionage, and high treason: Vladimír Clementis (1902–52), Otto Fischl (1902–52), Josef Frank (1909–52), Ludvík Frejka (1904–52), Bedrich Germinder (1901–52), Vavro Hajdů (1913–), Evžen Löbl (1907–), Artur London (1915–), Rudolf Margolius (1913–52), Bedřich Reicin (1911–52), André Simone (1895–1952), Rudolf Slánský (1901–52), Otto Šling (1912–52), and Karel Šváb (1904–52). Slánský and ten others were hanged on December 30, 1952. Hajdů, Löbl, and London were given life sentences. All were legally exonerated in 1963. The Slánský trial epitomized the brutality and inhumanity of Stalinism in Eastern Europe and sowed the seeds there of rebellion against communism in the 1980s and 1990s.

BIBLIOGRAPHY

Kaplan, Karel. *Report on the Murder of the General Secretary.* Columbus: Ohio State University Press, 1990.

Loebl, Eugene. *Sentenced and Tried: The Stalinist Purges in Czechoslovakia.* London: Elek Books, 1969.

London, Artur. *On Trial.* New York: Morrow, 1970.

Zilliacus, Konni. *A New Birth of Freedom?: World Communism Since Stalin.* London: Secker & Warburg, 1957.

Ken Millen-Penn

SEE ALSO Clementis, Vladimír; Cominform; Rajk, László; Zilliacus, Konni

Slovakia

On January 1, 1993, Czechoslovakia split into the Czech Republic and Slovakia. Slovakia, with its capital at Bratislava, has five million inhabitants, half the population of the Czech Republic. Generally speaking the Slovaks took their Catholic religion more seriously, were more

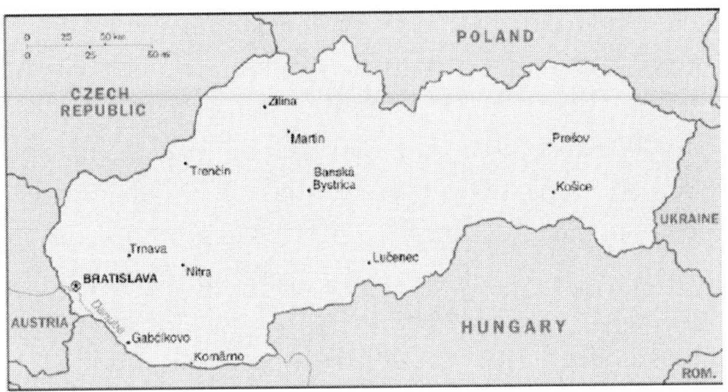

Slovakia. *Illustration courtesy of Bernard Cook.*

conservative, and were not as well educated as their western neighbors.

The dominant figure in the breakup of Czechoslovakia was Vladimír Mečiar, a former Communist and leader of the party named the Movement for a Democratic Slovakia, made up largely of former Communists. Mečiar was viewed by many as antidemocratic, despite his party's name. He and his supporters pushed through the breakup of the country despite public opinion polls that showed a majority of Slovaks wanted to remain in a federation with the Czechs. Mečiar became Slovakia's first prime minister and held power, after October 1993, in coalition with the Slovak National Party.

Trends in Slovakia have been in marked contrast to those in the Czech Republic. Slovakia has had higher unemployment and inflation, and poorer economic growth than the Czech Republic. Part of this was the loss of traditional markets resulting from the collapse of the Soviet Union, but it was also because of poor management by the Mečiar government. Slovakia was the site of many large industries, which produced military equipment or were inefficient by Western standards. Mečiar played on the fear of many that privatization would result in massive unemployment.

Slovakia increasingly moved toward one-man, one-party rule. Mečiar was seen as an erratic leader and was criticized by intellectuals as well as other political parties, and even by Slovak President Michal Kováč, who repeatedly called on Mečiar to bring more parties into his two-party coalition government. Through early 1994 Mečiar held all the main economic posts, including minister of privatization, made vacant when Lubomír Dolgos quit because Mečiar balked at privatization. The issue of privatization united opposition parties against Mečiar.

This was critical because Mečiar refused to relinquish ownership of the largest state-owned companies, and the economy was based on heavy industry, still owned by the state. By February 1994 only about 5 percent ($4.7 billion) of its state-owned enterprises had been privatized, and many of these were sold at bargain rates to Slovak officials and allies of Mečiar from the old Communist Party. In early 1994 virtually the entire economy remained in state hands. Many Western firms interested in investing in Slovak factories, especially heavy engineering, were turned away. Meanwhile, foreign investment in the Czech Republic totaled more than $2 billion, and 40 percent of state enterprises had been privatized. In early 1994 unemployment in Slovakia was 15.1 percent, compared with only 3.5 percent for the Czech Republic. Inflation was also ahead of that in the Czech Republic, 22 to 18 percent.

In addition to dominating the economy, Mečiar controlled Slovak foreign policy as well. This was marked by strident nationalism and deteriorating relations with neighboring Hungary. Some six hundred thousand Hungarians lived in southern Slovakia and their status was the subject of strident and contradictory statements from both Bratislava and Budapest. There was also controversy over a large Slovak hydroelectric project involving the flow of water, and hence navigation, on the Danube River. Mečiar did not hesitate to invent a military threat from Hungary to unite public opinion behind him as a strong leader capable of defending Slovak interests against a more powerful neighboring state.

In March 1994 Mečiar and his cabinet were nevertheless ousted in a parliamentary vote of no confidence. Slovakia faced a transition government headed by Jozef Moravčik, former foreign minister and leader of the Christian Democratic Party on the political right, who had led the revolt against Mečiar. Moravčik pledged nonconfrontation and policies more likely to allow Slovakia "to join European political and economic structures." However, in October 1994 in the first Slovak national election since independence, Mečiar and his Movement for a Democratic Slovakia won 35 percent of the vote and far outstripped all other parties. During the campaign Mečiar, who called himself "father of the nation," made anti-Hungarian comments and promised to cut taxes by 25 percent, limit foreign investment, and end privatization.

The civil service and the government-run media were purged of people accused of insufficient loyalty. The withholding of state funding was used against recalcitrant communities. In November 1995 parliament passed a law requiring that the Slovak language rather than Hungarian be used in many circumstances even in predominantly Magyar towns. Proposals were introduced in parliament to give Mečiar, the prime minister, increased power. These developments led Western governments to complain that Slovakia was falling short of democratic standards. František Sebej, leader of a small opposition party and the former chairman of the foreign relations committee of the parliament of united Czechoslovakia, expressed the concern that Slovakia, though led by individuals without a specific ideology, was becoming increasingly authoritarian because of the insatiable desire of some of its leaders for power.

BIBLIOGRAPHY

Kinzer, Stephen. "West Says Slovakia Falls Short of Democracy." *New York Times,* December 26, 1995, A3.

Kirschbaum, Stanislav J. *A History of Slovakia: The Struggle for Survival.* New York: St. Martin's Press, 1996.

Leff, Carol Skalnik. *National Conflict in Czechoslovakia: The Making and Remaking of a State, 1918–1987.* Princeton, N.J.: Princeton University Press, 1988.

Spencer C. Tucker

SEE ALSO Czechoslovakia; Czech Republic; Durzinda, Mikulas; Mečiar, Vladimír; Moravick, Josef

Hungarian Minority

Slovakia's largest ethnic minority and, after the Hungarian community in Romania, the largest group of Hungarians living outside Hungary. Ethnic Hungarians have lived in Slovakia since they arrived in central Europe in the ninth century. When Slovakia was part of the Kingdom of Hungary, its Hungarians belonged to the dominant ethnic group of the state. After the Treaty of Trianon in 1920 separated Slovakia from Hungary, Hungarians became a threatened and often persecuted minority there. Since Slovakia's independence in 1992, the treatment of its Hungarians has been a major human rights concern for the new country. Hungarians live mostly on the southern border of Slovakia, and are overrepresented in urban areas.

Slovakia has always been ethnically mixed, both because people of many different ethnicites lived in a given region or town and because many individuals possessed multiple allegiances. In 1920 a census taker in Slovakia reported a peasant who called himself a "Hungarian Slovak," and who then elaborated this answer with the explanation "I speak Hungarian, and also Slovak." The fact that Jews and Rom in Slovakia sometimes identify themselves as Hungarians further complicates the statistics. For these reasons, census figures on nationality must be examined with skepticism.

The census figures themselves depict many changes in nationality. In 1880 there were some 540,000 Hungarians in Slovakia, 22 percent of the population. In 1910, owing either to Magyarization or irregularities in the 1910 census, the number of ethnic Hungarians had increased to 900,000, or 30 percent of the population. Some of these "new Magyars" reverted to Slovak identities under Czechoslovak rule: the Czechoslovak authorities counted 640,000 Hungarians in Slovakia in 1921, and only 600,000 Hungarians in 1930, about 18 percent of Slovakia's population. In addition 370,368 Hungarians were counted in Ruthenia (Subcarpathian Ruthenias), a region that was part of Hungary before World War I, autonomous under Czechoslovak rule between the world wars, and annexed by Soviet Ukraine in 1945.

After Trianon Hungarians assimilated to Slovak identity for the same reasons that Slovaks had assimilated to Hungarian identity before it: membership in the dominant nationality was economically advantageous, and because of nationalist educational policies. The dominant nationality, whether Hungarian or Slovak, conducted official business in its own language and hindered education in other languages. While Czechoslovakia's treatment of the Hungarians under its jurisdiction was noticeably better than Hungary's treatment of the Slovaks before World War I, there were several infringements of basic civic rights. The Czechoslovak administration withheld pensions and citizenship papers from Hungarians and printed street signs and official notices only in Slovak, even in predominantly Hungarian districts.

The Hungarian community, previously the dominant group in Slovakia, suffered a large drop in status and influence when the Czechoslovak era began. Hungarians under Slovak rule remained more loyal to their town or region than to an abstract idea of Hungary, and few Hungarians moved to live under a Hungarian government. Yet in 1935, 73 percent of Hungarians living in Slovakia voted for separatist parties, the highest percentage of any of Czechoslovakia's minorities. (German separatist parties won 68 percent of the German vote.) Unsurprisingly, when the Czechoslovak state collapsed in 1938, when the Germans occupied the Czech region, the Hungarians occupied part of Slovakia, and the remainder of Slovakia became a German protectorate. Hungarians in Slovakia preferred Hungarian rule to continued minority status in an independent Slovakia. The Hungarian army occupied the southern fringe of Slovakia during World War II, including the second-largest town, Kosice.

At the end of World War II the Hungarians of Slovakia were deprived of their rights as citizens. Czechoslovakia in the immediate postwar years expelled some 160,000 Hungarians, along with the better-known expulsion of some 3,000,000 Sudeten Germans, and would have expelled more had not the great powers, particularly the United States, expressed disapproval.

The situation of the Hungarian community in Slovakia improved after the Communist coup d'état in 1948. Decree 33, which prohibited Hungarian language schools in Slovakia, was rescinded, and schools that offered instruction in Hungarian were reopened in 1950. By this time, only 350,000 people in Slovakia declared themselves ethnic Hungarians—only 10 percent of Slovakia's population. This figure increased as the memory of persecution abated: the 1961 and 1970 censuses counted 520,000 and 550,000 Hungarians, respectively—both around 12 percent of the population. While the Hungarian community produced its dissidents, most prominently Mikloš Duray, a geologist imprisoned for signing Charter 77, the document in which Czechoslovak dissidents protested the human rights record of the Czechoslovak Communist regime, and for criticizing Czechoslovakia's treatment of Hungarian minority, these infringements of civil liberties occurred in the context of general despotism and injustice under Czechoslovakia's Communist government.

After the collapse of communism in 1989 and Slovakia's independence in 1993, new tensions arose over Slovakia's Hungarian minority. Prime Minister Vladimír Mečiar suggested a population exchange with Hungary, and also a law that would compel all Hungarian women to add the suffix "ova" to their names, in the Slovak style. Neither proposal was implemented, but Hungarians and human rights monitors found them worrying. Duray organized a political party, Egyutteles (Coexistence), which allied with the Hungarian Christian Democratic Movement, a Catholic party, and the Hungarian Civic Party to form the Hungarian Coalition. The Hungarian Coalition won 10 percent of the vote in the 1994 elections and has played an important role in Slovak politics.

The European Union has often criticized Slovakia's human rights record, and has devoted much attention to the grievances of the Hungarian minority. Most of Slovakia's Hungarians speak Slovak as well as Hungarian, and intermarriage is common. The Hungarians are not a clear majority in the districts they inhabit, which is the main reason why no international support exists for a 1994 proposal to establish a Hungarian autonomous zone in southern Slovakia. Recently human rights observers have devoted more attention to Slovakia's Rom population. Despite many troubling incidents, particularly the harassment of Hungarian journalists, the fact that of the 570,000 Hungarians counted in the 1991 census, fully 150,000 are thought to be Rom declaring themselves Hungarians to avoid discrimination illustrates the relatively secure place Hungarians occupy in post-Communist Slovakia.

BIBLIOGRAPHY

Hacszar, Edward, ed. *Hungarians in Czechoslovakia: Yesterday and Today.* Astor, Fla.: Danubian Press, 1988.

Janics, Kalman. *Czechoslovak Policy and the Hungarian Minority, 1945–1948.* New York: Social Science Monographs, 1982.

Krejci, Jaroslav, and Pavel Machonin. *Czechoslovakia, 1918–92, a Laboratory for Social Change.* New York: St. Martin's Press, 1996.

R. W. Seton-Watson and his Relations with the Czechs and Slovaks, Documents 1906–1951, Vol. 1. Ed. by John Rychlik. Ustav: T.G. Masaryka, 1995.

Stevcek, Pavol, ed. *Slovaks and Magyars: Slovak-Magyar Relations in Central Europe.* Bratislava: Ministerstvo kultury Sloveskej republiky, 1995.

Alexander Maxwell

Political Parties

Although the only genuine parliamentary democracy in East-central Europe during the interwar period, which ended with its annexation by Germany in 1939, the first Czechoslovakia nevertheless was dominated more by Czech than Slovak interests. This neglect of Slovakia was to result in a radical approach by the Slovaks on this key issue even before the end of the first Czechoslovakia at the hands of Nazi Germany in 1939. The main prewar Slovak party, the Hlinka Slovak National People's Party, was thus a clericofascist grouping that used the demise of Czechoslovakia to strike a deal with Hitler to create a puppet Slovak state under the leadership of a Catholic priest, Josef Tiso, from 1939 to 1945. An extremely controversial period of modern Slovak history at a time when the Czech lands were under direct German occupation, Slovakia's wartime "autonomy" was to cast a long shadow over its postwar politics. Immediately after the war, however, some powers were devolved to a new Slovak National Council (SNC), but even this small degree of federalization was revoked when the Communist Party of Czechoslovakia seized power in an unconstitutional and Soviet-backed coup in 1948. That move was then justified by the Communists on the pretext of preventing the alleged reemergence of the fascist supporters of the former Tiso regime in Slovakia.

Far less popular in Slovakia than in the Czech lands, where it gained 30 percent and 38 percent of the popular vote, respectively, in the first postwar democratic elections in 1946, the Communist Party of Czechoslovakia (CPC) adopted an extremely hard-line policy toward any manifestation of Slovak nationhood after 1948. Not until the 1968 Prague Spring, led by reformist First Secretary of the Czechoslovak CPC Communist Party Slovak Alexander Dubček, did the issue of Slovak autonomy reemerge in public debate in Czechoslovakia. In that year the CPC approved a federal system of two equal republics for the government of the country. Despite the subsequent Soviet-led Warsaw Pact invasion of Czechoslovakia and the purging of the CPC, this system was formally introduced in 1969. It was to remain an empty shell in practice, however, for the next twenty years. Compared with the Czech Republic, where an influential Charter 77 grouping of human and civic rights activists emerged in Prague during the mid-1970s, Slovakia was relatively quiet politically during the two decades of so-called normalization by the CPC in Czechoslovakia. Yet at a deeper level, the still unresolved political and economic disparities between the Czech and Slovak Republics meant that Slovak national grievances continued to fester during the 1970s and 1980s. Once the power monopoly of the CPC collapsed during the Velvet Revolution of November 1989, the Slovak national question reemerged to dominate Slovak politics throughout the 1990s.

Formed in opposition to the Communist regime at the same time as Civic Forum in the Czech Republic, Public Against Violence (PAV) quickly became the dominant political force in Slovakia after the events of 1989. Closely allied to Civic Forum at the federal level of government, PAV also became the single-largest party in the SNC after Slovakia's first post-Communist multiparty parliamentary elections in June 1990. Its leader, Vladimír Mečiar, a former boxer who had been ousted from his position in the Communist youth movement and expelled from CPC for supposedly supporting the reforms of Dubček, was thus then elected prime minister of the Slovak Republic. Like Civic Forum in the Czech Republic, PAV was more a broad-based movement bound together by little more than anti-Communist sentiment than a political party ready for government. In 1991 PAV split into a number of new political parties, mainly because of lack of agreement over the central issue of the sort of relations that should exist between the Slovak and Czech Republics. Forced to resign from the premiership over this central issue in 1991, Mečiar strongly supported an independent Slovakia from the very beginning. In 1991 he founded his own party, the Movement for a Democratic Slovakia (MDS). Concomitantly, a new Christian Democratic Movement (CDM) founded in 1990 and the second-largest party in the SNC formed a new government in 1991. An explicitly nationalist party opposed to the free-market economics then being introduced by Czech leaders like Václav Klaus, Mečiar's MDS established itself as the dominant political force in Slovakia at the time of the parliamentary elections of June 1992. Once reinstated as premier, Mečiar quickly moved Slovakia toward full independence and hence the formal dissolution of Czechoslovakia on January 1, 1993. This was an arguably hasty rush to an unnecessary divorce that was also then supported by Mečiar's counterpart in the Czech Republic, Klaus.

Post-1989 party politics in independent Slovakia were far more controversial than in the Czech Republic. Partly the result of the dominant position of the MDS in the SNC, where it held half the seats after 1992, these political problems were also exacerbated by the party's extremist policies and Mečiar's highly abrasive and thuggish performance. Unlike the situation in the Czech Republic, where former Communist and left-wing parties were influential in opposition, the successor to the former Communist Party of Slovakia, the Party of the Democratic Left (PDL), was in the political wilderness during the early years of post-Communist Slovakia. Therefore, there was little real opposition to the triumphalism of Mečiar's MDS. The Slovak leader's only real opponent was President Michal Kováč, a former colleague of Mečiar's in both the MDS and PAV before it. Elected president of the newly independent Slovak Republic in February 1993, Kováč was henceforth to block Mečiar's MDS government at every turn, a policy of obstruction that was to be fully reciprocated by the premier. Mečiar's poor management of his own party resulted in the rise of rival factions that could not be counted on to vote with the government in parliament, thereby forcing the Slovak premier to enter into pacts with politically disreputable groupings like the fascist Slovak National Party (SNP) in 1993. Despite such moves, Mečiar's government lost a working majority in the SNC in early 1994.

Supported by the CDM, PDL, and rebel MDS deputies, a successful no-confidence motion in the SNC in March 1994 resulted in Mečiar's resignation as premier and the fall of his government, a development openly approved of by Kováč. Following new parliamentary elections later the same year, however, Mečiar became premier for a third time, at the head of a new MDS-led coalition that also included the SNP and the equally politically suspect Association of Workers of Slovakia (AWS), a far-left grouping that openly called for a Communist restoration. On the Slovak national question, Mečiar's willingness to ally his party with avowed fascists created even more controversy, thereby further worsening relations with Slovakia's large ethnic Hungarian minority represented in the SNC by the Hungarian Christian Democratic Movement (HCDM) and the Hungarian People's Party (HPP). Externally, Mečiar's authoritarian populism and rabid nationalism severely damaged Slovakia's international standing in relation to both the European Union (EU) it aspired to join and the United States. By the mid-1990s it became clear that Slovakia, unlike the Czech Republic, was not to be considered for membership in Europe's premier grouping by 2000.

Domestically, Mečiar's undignified feud with Kováč finally ended when his rival's five-year term as president expired in March 1998, and this key office was controversially left vacant by the Slovak premier. Such a development strongly suggested that Mečiar aimed to stay in power indefinitely, regardless of future election results. If such a scenario unfolds, Slovakia's multiparty democracy will turn out to be a sham with no deep roots in the country's authoritarian political culture. This very real possibility now sharply separates Slovakia from the Czech Republic, where a genuine multiparty parliamentary democracy has emerged since 1989.

BIBLIOGRAPHY

Shepherd, Robin H. E. *Czechoslovakia: The Velvet Revolution and Beyond.* New York: St. Martin's Press, 2000.

Szomolányi, Sona, and John A. Gould, eds. *Slovakia, Problems of Democratic Consolidation and the Struggle for the Rules of the Game.* Bratislava: Slovak Political Science Association and Friedrich Ebert Foundation, 1997.

United States Congress. *Commission on Security and Co-operation in Europe. Human Rights and Democratization in Slovakia.* Washington, D.C.: CSCE, 1997.

Marko Milivojevic

SEE ALSO Mečiar, Vladimír; Kováč, Michal

Slovenia

Independent republic formed from the Socialist Republic of Slovenia of the former Yugoslavia. Slovenia consists of 7,819 square miles (20,296 sq km). It is bordered on the west by Italy, on the north by Austria, on the northeast by Hungary, and on the south by Croatia. Most of its border with Italy runs through the Julian Alps, but Slovenia also includes the northeastern part of the Istrian Peninsula as a thirty-two-km section of Adriatic Sea coast. The border with Austria lies in the Karavanke Mountains. The Kamnik Mountains lie to the south of the Austrian frontier. The country is crossed by the Sava and the Drava Rivers. Most of Slovenia apart from the mountains consists of forested hilly terrain. Ten percent of the country's area is arable; 2 percent is devoted to orchards; meadows and pastures constitute 20 percent; and 45 percent is forest. Slovenia possesses reserves of lignite, lead, zinc, mercury, uranium, and silver. The Sava is polluted by industrial and human waste, while heavy metals and toxic chemicals pollute coastal waters. Forests near the coastal city of Koper have been damaged by pollution from metallurgical and chemical factories. The capital, Ljubljana, is home to 323,291 of Slovenia's 1,972,227 inhabitants (1994), 91 percent of whom are Slovene, 3 percent Croat, 2 percent Serb, 1 percent Muslim, and 3 percent other. Some Italians live in the west. The growth rate of the population in 1994 was 0.23 percent. The archbishop of Ljubljana set up the first government-licensed Slovenian grammar school in 1905.

Slovenia. *Illustration courtesy of Bernard Cook.*

After the collapse of Austria-Hungary in World War I, Slovenian leaders supported Slovenia's inclusion in the new Kingdom of Serbs, Croats, and Slovenes. Slovene General Rudolf Maister seized the town of Maribor from the Austrians for Slovenia on November 1, 1918, but when the Italians occupied Primorska, 300,000 additional Slovenes were included in Italy. Following the German conquest of Yugoslavia in April 1941, Slovenia was divided among Germany, Italy, and Hungary. A Slovene Liberation Front was formed and fought as an ally of Tito's Yugoslav Partisan army, but some Slovenes—the clerical anti-communist homeguard, the *domobranci*—fought on the side of the Germans against the Communists. Many *domobranci* and their families fled with the retreating Germans to Austria. Approximately ten thousand were turned over to the Partisans by the Allies after the war and executed.

During the era of Tito's Yugoslavia (1945–91) Slovenia was the most prosperous and developed of the Yugoslav republics. Nevertheless, there was unrest even during the Tito era. In January 1958 miners in Trbovlje and Zagorje waged the first strikes in Communist Yugoslavia. In June 1968 students at the University of Ljubljana gave voice to the student discontent that so marked Europe that year. Ljubljana students demanded that Communist doctrine be taken seriously and a truly egalitarian society be established. Student idealism cooled, however, when the government increased student stipends. In December 1968, at the Seventh Congress of the League of Slovenian Communists (Communist Party), Slovenian Prime Minister Stane Kavšić advocated development of small- and medium-scale industry and the service sector in preference to heavy industry; he also proposed the introduction of limited private ownership. But the Slovenian administration in 1972 agreed to accept the national economic policy that favored heavy industry with minor provisions for small independent businesses. During this period the national policy promoted the immigration of workers from other Yugoslav republics into Slovenia to provide workers for the growing industry and to mix the population and dilute to overwhelming Slovenian majority.

In November 1972 conservatives in the Slovenian Communist Party led by Eduard Kardelj, Mitja Ribišić, Andrej Marinć, and Stane Dolanć, as part of an all-Yugoslav campaign against reformism and "nationalism" within the republics of Yugoslavia leaders, forced the ouster of Kavšić. The 1974 Yugoslav constitution appeared to give the individual republics more local control but at the same time provided for party control of all political bodies. A new Yugoslav constitution in 1976 stressed economic self-management but still maintained the primacy of politics in practice. In 1978 Slovenian banks were merged into Ljubljanska Banka (the Bank of Ljubljana) that was required to provide loans at low interest rates for politically determined investments. Before Tito's death in 1980, there was growing resentment in Slovenia that it was being forced to pay excessive contributions to the underdeveloped republics and of Yugoslavia that much of the contribution was wasted on political display in Serbia rather than true development. After Tito's death Slovenes were inspired by the growing decrepitude of the Communist system to press for multiparty elections. At the same time they were disturbed by the growing nationalist pretensions of Slobodan Milošević in Serbia.

The growth of Slovenian self-assertion can be traced through a number of developments. In February 1987 intellectuals associated with the journal *Nova Revija* issued a call in the journal for democracy and respect for human rights, which they labeled the new "Slovenian National Program." In February 1988 the weekly *Mladina* of the Socialist Youth Association, in the first public criticism of the Yugoslav People's Army (YPA), denounced Yugoslav Defense Minister Branko Mamula for traveling to Ethiopia to broker an arms deal. *Mladina* followed up with increasing criticism of federal authorities and denunciations of corruption within the Slovenian Communist bureaucracy. In May 1988 *Mladina* published the minutes of a secret session of the Slovenian Communist Party's Central Committee during which plans were disclosed for the YPA to use force against the growing opposition in Slovenia. Janez Jansa, a *Mladina* journalist, was arrested by the Slovenian Intelligence Service. Jansa and three others were charged by the military court in Ljubljana with possessing a classified military document. The trial before a military court was closed to the public. While the Slovene Communist Party remained silent, Igor Bavsar, an official of the Socialist Alliance, which had previously served as a Communist front organization, an organization permitted as useful by the Communist regime, organized the Committee for the Defense of Human Rights to protest the trial. The organization of this committee, though its scope was limited to the issue of human rights rather than a transformation of the system, is regarded by many as the beginning of the Slovenian Spring, a counterpart to the reformist Czechoslovak Prague Spring. In February 1989 Serbia's repression of its Kosovo region's autonomy and the imposition of martial law there led to protests in Ljubljana. In May a large public protest in Ljubljana produced the May Declaration, which called for an independent and democratic Slovenia with respect for human rights and political pluralism. The protest itself was organized by the Slovenian Writers' Association, the Slovenian Democratic Union, the Slovenian Farmers' Union (which would become the People's Party), the Slovenian Christian Social Movement (which would become the Christian Democrats), and the Social Democrats. The May Declaration can be regarded as the foundational document for the Democratic Opposition of Slovenia (DEMOS), which was formally organized on November 27. On September 27, 1989, the one-party Slovene Assembly asserted Slovene sovereignty and the right of Slovenia to secede from Yugoslavia and authorized opposition parties.

In January 1990 the Slovenian delegates to the Fourteenth Congress of the League of Communists of Yugoslavia (LCY) withdrew when the congress refused to approve of multiparty elections and greater autonomy for the constituent parties and republics of the Yugoslav state. Serbia instituted a boycott of Slovenian products and Slovenia retaliated by imposing sanctions against Serbia. The League of Communists of Slovenia broke with the LCY and became the Party of Democratic Reform (PDR).

The first multiparty election in post-Tito Slovenia was held in April 1990. The DEMOS won a slight majority in two out of three chambers. On May 15 they formed a government with Christian Democrat (SDC) Lojze Peterle as prime minister. However, Milan Kukan, the former president of the Central Committee of the Slovenian

Communist Party and now the leader of the PDR, was elected president, and the PDR was the single-largest party in the legislature. Peterle's government, nevertheless, laid the groundwork for independence. Further declarations of sovereignty by the legislature in July 1990 and an amendment to this effect and the assumption of republic control over the territorial defense force still did not persuade the Serbs to consent to reform the federation. As a consequence 89 percent of voters in a December 23, 1990, referendum, gave their assent to Slovenian independence.

Slovenia signed a mutual assistance agreement with the Yugoslav republic of Croatia in January 1991 and began secretly to form a Slovenian army. When Serbia remained adamantly opposed to the establishment of a new federation of sovereign states and in May 1991 blocked the scheduled rotation of the Yugoslav federal presidency to Croatian Stipe Mesić, the Slovene legislature asserted its determination to secede from Yugoslavia. Despite diplomatic pressure from the United States against secession and its apparent sanction of action by the Yugoslav People's Army (YPA) to maintain Yugoslav territorial integrity, Slovenia and Croatia declared their independence on June 25, 1991.

By June 27 the troops of the YPA were on the move. A column of Yugoslav tanks headed toward Slovenia from Karlovac, Croatia, and shots were fired in a war that lasted ten days. Sporadic fighting ensued despite efforts by the European Community (later, European Union, EU) to negotiate a cease-fire. After several days of fighting in which the Slovenes surprised the YPA by their determination and ability to fight, Slovenia unilaterally declared a cease-fire on July 2. Negotiations sponsored by the EU produced the Brioni Declaration on July 7 between Slovenia and Yugoslavia. Slovenia agreed to suspend its act of secession for three months and YPA forces were to withdraw to their barracks. There was a cease-fire and two weeks later the YPA, which Slobodan Milešović, the president of Serbia, wished to concentrate against Croatia, began to withdraw. When the suspension expired on October 8 with no indication of any change of heart on the part of the Serbs, Slovenia renewed its secession, and a new constitution that delineated the functions of the newly independent state went into effect on December 23.

The Vatican recognized Slovenian and Croatian independence on January 13, 1992. Recognition from the EU came on January 15. The subsequent history of Slovenia was much less traumatic than that of any of its former fellow Yugoslav republics that seceded from Yugoslavia. The last federal military forces had withdrawn from Slovenian territory on October 26, 1991. The new country contained no significant minorities and no further trouble with Serbia. The United States recognized Slovenia in April, and the new country was admitted to the United Nations in May.

When it became evident that Slovenia would not have to fight a prolonged battle for independence, internal political divisions surfaced. The Slovenian Democratic Union, one of the principal components of DEMOS, split into two factions in October: the Democratic Party and, on the right, the National Democratic Party. Undermined by factional strife, DEMOS collapsed in December and Peterle suffered a vote of no-confidence in April 1992 and resigned. The new prime minister was Janez Drnovsek of the Liberal Democratic Party (LDP).

In the December 1992 elections the LDP emerged as the largest party, but it lacked a majority. In January Drnovsek formed a coalition composed of the LDP, SCD, United List, Greens of Slovenia, and Social Democratic Party of Slovenia. Peterle became minister of foreign affairs. Drnovsek formed a new government in 1994. His LDP, which had merged with Greens and Democrats to form the Liberal Democracy of Slovenia (LDS), joined with the SCD and the United List of Social Democrats to form the governing coalition. In September 1994 Peterle resigned, accusing LDS of attempting to concentrate too much power in its hands.

In the November 1996 election the LDS claimed 45 of the 90 delegates through the support of the ULSD, the Democratic Party of Pensioners of Slovenia (DESUS), the SNP, and representatives of the Italian and Hungarian minorities. However, a newly formed electoral alliance, Slovenian Spring, composed of the Slovenian People's Party, the SCD, and the SDPS, controlled the other 45 seats. Kucan nominated Drnovsek to form a government, but in the standoff he was unable to gain a majority. The formation of a coalition, however, proved equally difficult. In late February a coalition consisting of the LDS, SPP, and DESUS was confirmed.

Following the collapse of Yugoslavia and Slovenia's independence, the new country had to establish new relations with its neighbors and develop new economic ties. In May 1992 it signed an agreement of cooperation with the European Free Trade Association and in April 1993 it entered into a trade and economic cooperation agreement with the EU. In May 1993 it became a member of the Council of Europe and in December was granted observer status by the Western European Union. In 1994 it joined NATO's Partnership for Peace program. In June 1995 it became an associate member of the EU. In January 1996 Slovenia was admitted by Poland, Hungary, the Czech Republic, and Slovakia into the Central European Free Trade Association.

Following the November 1995 Dayton Peace Accords, which ended the war in Bosnia and laid the foundation for the normalization of Croatian and Serbian relations, Slovenia recognized the Federal Republic of Yugoslavia (Serbia and Montenegro, FRY) and began efforts to establish formal diplomatic relations between itself and that successor state to the SFRY.

Relations with Slovenia's neighbor Croatia were clouded by several issues, including border disputes concerning the waters of the Bay of Piran and coastal territory in Istria. In June 1995 the two countries settled the issue with regard to 98 percent of the disputed land and sea frontier.

Strained relations with Italy temporarily impeded Slovenia's effort to develop closer ties with the EU. Both Croatia and Slovenia opposed Italy's efforts to revise the 1975 Treaty of Osimo, which defined the Italian-Yugoslav frontier and provided compensation to Italians who had lost property in the transfer of territory to Yugoslavia in 1947. Italy delayed consideration of EU associate member status for Slovenia but in March 1995 lifted its objection. In June 1996 Slovenia, with Italian support, became an associate member of the EU and immediately applied to become a full member.

Slovenia has the highest standard of living among the states of the former Yugoslavia. It will have less difficulty than the other successor states of Yugoslavia in making a successful transition to a market economy. Even during the difficult transition period, the state has been able to provide pension and welfare payments and fund education. Education from preschool through the age of fifteen is free and compulsory. In ethnically mixed areas students are given a choice of bilingual education or education in the minority language. There are two universities—Ljubljana, with 30,529 students in 1994; and Maribor, with 13,064. There are also thirty-four other institutions of higher education.

BIBLIOGRAPHY

Fink-Hafner, Danica, and John R. Robbins, eds. *Making a New Nation: The Formation of Slovenia.* Brookfield, Vt.: Dartmouth, 1997.

Hocevar, Toussaint. *Slovenia's Role in the Yugoslav Economy.* Columbus, Oh.: Slovenian Research Center, 1964.

Maganja, Nadja. *Trieste 1945–1949: Nascita del movimento politico autonomo sloveno.* Trieste, Italy: Krozek za druzbena vprasanja Virgil Scek, 1994.

Svetlik, Ivan, ed. *Social Policy in Slovenia: Between Tradition and Innovation.* Aldershot, England: Avebury, 1992.

Znidarsic, Joco. *The Battle for Slovenia.* Tr. by Dejan Susnik and Mark Valentine. Ljubljana, Slovenia: Cankarjeva Zalozba, 1991.

Bernard Cook

Economy

Slovenia was by far the most prosperous of the republics of the former Yugoslavia, and its economic prospects after independence were positive.

After a period of economic instability following World War II, Slovenia experienced rapid economic growth. Development of new state-controlled heavy industry and energy production spurred a 7.7 percent growth in employment between 1946 and 1953, and by 1953 Slovenia's rate of economic growth was 15 percent. The development of excess hydroelectricity and nuclear power capacity and infrastructure are the positive legacies of the socialist period. Excessive concentration on heavy industry and pollution are negative ones. In 1995 Slovenia agreed to share equally with Croatia the electricity produced by its single preindependence era nuclear power plant.

Slovenia's per capita income more than doubled the Yugoslav average and was not far behind that of Slovenia's neighbors Italy and Austria. Slovenia suffered short-term dislocations as a result of its conflict with the Serbian republic and the dissolution of the former Yugoslavia, with patterns of trade and sources of raw materials disrupted. As a result industrial production declined by approximately 26 percent between 1990 and 1994. The iron and steel, machine-building, chemical, and textile industries were especially hard hit. Exacerbating the country's economic situation was the influx of refugees from the wars in Croatia and Bosnia. On the positive side, there was little material damage during Slovenia's short war for independence. At that time, Slovenia already had, strong ties with Western and central European countries. It also possessed a well-educated skilled workforce, a developed infrastructure, and many citizens with a Western-style economic outlook, and it produced far more electricity than it used. In 1992 its principal trading partners were Germany, Croatia, Italy, and France. Slovenia's principal products were ferrous metallurgy and rolling mill products, aluminum reduction and rolled products, lead and zinc smelting, electronic equipment, trucks, electric power equipment, wood products, textiles, chemicals, and machine tools. In 1993 its gross domestic product was $15 billion, or $7,600 per capita. By 1995 the GDP had grown to $16.3 billion.

In 1995 agriculture constituted only 5 percent of gross domestic product but employed 10.4 percent of the country's workers. Stock breeding and dairy farming were predominant. The main crops included cereals, potatoes, sugar beets, grapes, hops, hemp, and flax. Still, Slovenia has had to import much of its food.

In 1995 Slovenia had a visible trade deficit of $953.5 million but a surplus of $36.5 million in its balance of payments. In 1996 the country had an overall budget surplus, but its external public debt amounted to $3.5 billion. Inflation, which had averaged 21.2 percent between 1992 and 1995, was brought down to 9.7 percent in 1996. On September 1, 1995, the tolar—the Slovenian currency—became completely convertible.

A program for the privatization of industrial firms was set in place in 1992 but implementation was slow. The problems associated with the formation of a new government after the elections of 1996 delayed necessary legislation, including a new law concerning the ownership of property.

Slovenia is a member of the World Bank and the International Monetary Fund (IMF). In 1995 Slovenia signed a free-trade agreement with the European Free Trade Association and joined the World Trade Association. In June 1996 it became an associate member of the European Union (EU) and applied for full membership.

BIBLIOGRAPHY

Ferfila, Bogomil, and Paul Phillips. *Slovenia: On the Edge of the European Union.* Lanham, Md.: University Press of America, 2000.

Gow, James, and Cathie Carmichael. *Slovenia and the Slovenes: A Small State and the Challenge of Internationalization in the New Europe.* Bloomington: Indiana University Press, 1999.

Heffner, Krystian, and Vladimir Klemencic. *Small Regions in United Europe: Macroregional and Social Policy.* Opole, Poland: Governmental Research Institute, Silesian Institute in Opole, 1995.

Mrak, Mojmir, Janez Potocnik, and Matija Rojec. *Strategy of the Republic of Slovenia for Accession to the European Union: Economic and Social Part.* Ljubljana, Slovenia: Institute of Macroeconomic Analysis and Development, 1998.

Phillips, Paul Arthur, and Bogomil Ferfila. *The Canadian and Slovene Economies: Systems Theory and Political Economy Approaches.* Halifax, N.S.: Fernwood, 1994.

Svetlik, Ivan, ed. *Social Policy in Slovenia: Between Tradition and Innovation.* Aldershot, England: Avebury, 1992.

World Bank. *Slovenia: Economic Transformation and EU Accession.* Washington, D.C.:World Bank, 1999.

Bernard Cook

Slyunkou, Mikalai (1929–)

First secretary of the Communist Party of Belarus (CPB) from 1983 to 1987, and a full member of the Politburo of the Central Committee of the Communist Party of the Soviet Union (CPSU) from 1987 to 1990. Mikalai Slyunkou was in charge of Soviet leader Mikhail Gorbachev's program of economic reform.

Born on April 26, 1929, to Belarusan peasants in Haradzets, Slyunkou graduated from the Belarusan Institute of Mechanization of Agriculture in 1962, and started a career as plant director in Minsk. A member of the CPB since 1954, he was a full member of its Central Committee from 1966 to 1976. From 1972 to 1974, he was also first secretary of the Minsk city party committee.

From 1974 to 1983 Slyunkou was in Moscow as a deputy chairman of the State Planning Commission (Gosplan), responsible for machine building. In the mid-1980s he was back in Belarus leading the CPB, while also sitting on the presidiums of the Supreme Soviets (parliaments) of the Belarusan Soviet Socialist Republic and the USSR. In 1986 he became a candidate member and in 1987 a full member of the Politburo. In 1987 and 1988 Slyunkou headed the CPSU Central Committee's Economic Department, and as of September 1988 its new Commission on Questions of Social and Economic Policy. Like Gorbachev, he was unable to formulate a clear program of economic reform. Probably because of ill health, he resigned from politics in July 1990.

Karel C. Berkhoff

Smirnov, Igor Nikolaevich (1941–)

President of the unrecognized Transnistrian Moldovan Republic declared on September 2, 1990, in the eastern part of the Republic of Moldova. Igor Smirnov was born in 1941 to an ethnic Russian family in Petropavlovsk, in the Russian republic of the USSR. After graduating from a machine-building institute in Zaporozhe, Smirnov joined the Elektromash machine-building works in Zaporozhe in 1959 as an electrical worker. He joined the Communist Party of the Soviet Union (CPSU) in 1963. Smirnov remained at Elektromash until 1987, rising to the position of factory director. In 1987 he moved to Tiraspol, in the Transnistria region of the Moldovan Soviet Socialist Republic (MSSR), to manage the Elektromash factory there.

As a prominent figure in Moldovan industry, Smirnov was elected in August 1989 to chair the United Council of Work Collectives (OSTK) in Tiraspol, a group formed to protest the pro-Romanian cultural reforms launched by the Moldovan government. As head of OSTK Smirnov organized a number of protests against the central Moldovan government, including strikes and the blockage of railroads from Transnistria to the rest of Moldova. Denounced by the Communist Party as a separatist, he was expelled from the party in April 1990. By this time, however, Smirnov and the Transnistrians had begun to form their own quasi-state structures based on existing institutions of local government.

Smirnov was elected chair of the Tirsapol city executive committee in May 1990, and in November 1990 became chairman of the newly created Supreme Soviet of the Transnistrian Moldovan Soviet Socialist Republic, which had been declared on September 2, 1990. Smirnov and his associates were strong supporters of the coup in August 1991 by hardliners trying to busy Gorbachev and opposed the breakup of the Soviet Union. For supporting the coup, Smirnov was arrested by the Moldovan police in August 1991 but quickly released. On December 1, 1991, with 65 percent of the vote he was elected president of the Transnistrian Moldovan Republic, which had declared independence from Moldova when Moldova declared independence from the Soviet Union on August 27, 1991. Smirnov was reelected to that position in December 1996.

Under Smirnov's leadership the Transnistrians continued to develop separate state structures, including a well-equipped army. A brief civil war was fought between Moldovan and Transnistrian forces in 1992, with Smirnov having taken the position of Transnistrian commander in chief in January 1992. Smirnov was the main spokesperson for the Transnistrian side in negotiations on the future status of Transnistria. He represented the most radical of Transnistrian separatists, intent on creating an independent Transnistrian state rather than settling for autonomy within a united Moldova. In 2000, Transnistria, though unrecognized by any country, was still asserting its independence and refusing to submit to Moldovan.

Charles King

SEE ALSO Transnistrian Moldovan Republic

Smith, John (1938–94)

British politician. John Smith assumed leadership of the Labour Party from Neil Kinnock after the party's loss to the Conservatives led by John Major in the April 1992 election. He presided over a resurgence in popularity of the Labour Party until his death on May 12, 1994.

Smith was born on September 13, 1938, in Ardrishaig, Scotland. His father, a headmaster, was a committed socialist, and Smith joined the Labour Party when he was sixteen. Smith ran unsuccessfully for parliament twice while he was a student at the University of Glasgow. He received a law degree in 1967, and in 1970 won the parliamentary race in Lanarkshire North. Smith was a Labour member of parliament for that Scottish constituency from 1970 to 1983, and for Monklands East from 1983 to 1994.

After the completion of his legal training and a brief period in practice, Smith entered parliament in 1970. He was one of the Labour MPs who defied a three-line whip (strongest order to follow the party's line) and voted in favor of Britain's application to join the European Community in 1971. Despite his participation in this revolt against the party hierarchy, he was offered various junior positions in government when Harold Wilson returned to office as prime minister in 1974. His first cabinet post came in 1978 when Prime Minister James Callaghan appointed him secretary of state for trade.

The defeat of Labour in the general election of 1979 initiated a long period in opposition. Smith held various posts in the shadow cabinet: spokesman on trade (1979–82), energy (1982–83), employment (1983–84), trade and industry (1984–87), treasury and economic affairs (1987–92), and leader of the opposition (1992–94).

As leader of the Labour Party, Smith moved cautiously in seeking to reform the role of the labor unions within the party structure. He was successful in introducing a "one member one vote" policy in the party elections of 1993. This began the process of modernization that was to be accelerated under the leadership of Prime Minister Tony Blair.

Eileen Groth Lyon

Smyth, Martin (1931–)

Ulster Unionist MP for Belfast South (1982–); grand master of the Grand Orange Lodge of Ireland (1972–). Martin Smyth was born in Belfast in 1931. He was ordained as a Presbyterian minister in 1957 but resigned his church ministry when he was elected MP in 1982. His party, the Ulster Unionist Party (UUP), received a much needed boost with his by-election victory in 1982 because the UUP had been losing ground to the Democratic Ulster Party. He opposed the Anglo-Irish Agreement in 1985 through which the British and Irish governments agreed to work together concerning Northern

Ireland. Two years later he advocated a new federal structure that would have involved all parts of the British Isles, even the Republic of Ireland. As part of this arrangement, he argued for a more integrated place for Northern Ireland within the United Kingdom. He was spokesman for health and family policy within the UUP and chief party whip.

BIBLIOGRAPHY

Arthur, Paul. *Northern Ireland since 1968,* 2d ed. Oxford: Blackwell Publishers, 1996.

Aughey, Arthur, and Duncan Morrow, eds. *Northern Ireland Politics.* London: Longman, 1996.

Bew, Paul. *Northern Ireland, 1921–1996: Political Forces and Social Classes.* London: Serif, 1996.

Ricki Schoen

Snegur, Mircea (1940–)

First popularly elected president of the independent Republic of Moldova (1991–96). Born in 1940 to an ethnic Moldovan/Romanian family in Trifanesti village, in the formerly Romanian region of Bessarabia, Mircea Snegur graduated from the Frunze Agricultural Institute in Kishinev (Romanian, Chisinau) in the Moldovan Soviet Socialist Republic (MSSR). He made much of his early career in the republic's large agricultural sector. From 1961 to 1968 he worked as chief agronomist and chairman of the Path Toward Communism collective farm in Floresti, MSSR. He later completed a doctorate in agronomy at the Frunze Agricultural Institute and, from 1973 to 1981, served in various posts within the MSSR Ministry of Agriculture and the Institute for Agricultural Research.

Snegur began work within the Communist Party of Moldova (CPM) in 1981, initially as first secretary of the Edinet raion party committee and, as of 1985, as a secretary on the Central Committee of the CPM. In 1989 he was elected chairman of the Supreme Soviet (parliament) of the MSSR, and in 1990 became the first president of the MSSR—a post newly created by the Supreme Soviet. Both as chairman of the Supreme Soviet and as MSSR president, Snegur was an important figure in the reform movement in the late 1980s and early 1990s. Under his leadership the Supreme Soviet adopted laws making Moldovan/Romanian the state language of the MSSR instead of Russian and mandating its transition to the Latin from the Cyrillic alphabet. After Moldova's secession from the Soviet Union in August 1991, Snegur also became the first popularly elected president of the independent state, receiving 98 percent of the vote in the December 1991 elections in which he was, however, the only candidate.

During Snegur's tenure as president, tensions increased between the central Moldovan government and separatist forces in the Transnistrian Moldovan Republic, an unrecognized breakaway republic in the eastern part of Moldova with a majority of Ukrainians and Russians. As president, Snegur was also responsible for the violence that erupted in eastern Moldova in 1992—a brief civil war between Moldovans and Transnistrians that was quelched by Russian troops. Snegur was instrumental in the transition from centralized economic planning and the development of an independent foreign and security policy for Moldova; while the republic joined the Commonwealth of Independent States (CIS), Snegur insisted that Moldova not participate in many of the CIS's main economic and military conventions.

In the presidential elections in 1996 Snegur received 39 percent of the vote in the first round, but was defeated by Petru Lucinschi, speaker of the Moldovan parliament, in the second round. After his defeat Snegur remained active in Moldovan party politics and emerged as an important figure in the center-right Party of Reconciliation and Concord.

BIBLIOGRAPHY

Helsinki Watch. *Human Rights in Moldova: The Turbulent Dniester.* New York: Human Rights Watch, 1993.

King, Charles. *Post-Soviet Moldova: A Borderland in Transition.* London: Royal Institute of International Affairs, 1995.

Kolsto, Pal, and Andrei Edemsky with Natalya Kalashnikova. "The Dniester Conflict: Between Irredentism and Separatism." *Europe-Asia Studies* 45:6 (1993), 973–1000.

Charles King

Soares, Mario (1924–)

Lawyer, prime minister, and president of Portugal, and a founding member of the Portuguese Socialist Party. Mario Alberto Nobre Lopes Soares played a critical role during Portugal's democratic transition. A leading opposition figure to the Salazar/Caetano regime in the 1960s and 1970s, he was imprisoned and exiled. While in exile, he formed the Portuguese Socialist Party in Bonn, West Germany, in 1973. At that time he pledged that one day the Portuguese Socialist Party would lead the way to a equitable and democratic Portugal. Although his words were warmly greeted, few actually believed that he would be so successful.

On returning to Portugal after the April 25, 1974, coup, which brought down the conservative regime of Prime Minister Marcelo Caetano, Soares participated in the May Day celebrations with the head of the Communist Party, Alvaro Cunhal, and other notable political figures, in front of thousands of supporters. He was appointed minister of foreign affairs in the provisional government, and played an important role in negotiating the independence of the Portuguese colonies in Africa.

By the end of 1974 Soares became concerned that the Communist Party had gained undue influence with the Armed Forces Movement (MFA), the organization of radical middle-level officers who had spearheaded the coup and were attempting to institutionalize itself as the government of Portugal. He insisted that the MFA hold elections for the Constituent Assembly. Over the objections of Cunhal, the MFA agreed to hold elections. On April 25, 1975, the Soares-led Socialist Party gained a plurality, with 37.87 percent of the vote.

After these elections Soares used his political success to contest decisions by the Communist-leaning MFA prime minister of the provisional governments, Vasco Gonçalves. In particular, during the "hot summer" of 1975, when the MFA forced the resignation of Prime Minister Adelino da Palma Carlos, and the new premier Col. Vasco Gonsalves and the MFA moved to the left, Soares appeared at pro-democratic political rallies and warned of the dangers of Soviet-style communism. By the end of 1975 Soares and the moderates in the MFA had defeated the Communists and other leftist forces, and constructed a new democratic regime. In the elections for the first constitutional assembly on April 25, 1976, the Soares-led Socialist Party once again gained a plurality. In July 1976, Soares was sworn in as the first prime minister under the 1976 constitution by the newly elected president, Ramalho Eanes.

Soares served as prime minister for three governments between 1976 and 1985. Of note, he applied for Portugal's membership in the European Economic Community in 1977. Later, Soares was elected the country's first civilian president in sixty years in 1986, and was reelected in 1991. As president, he played a key role consolidating the new democracy, especially after the 1987 and 1991 victory of the rightist Social Democratic Party (PSD), which was led by Prime Minister Anibal Cavaco Silva. Soares retired from political life in 1996.

Soares was a critical figure in the transition and consolidation of Portuguese democracy. He also played a key role in the country's economic transition from reliance on the colonies to membership in the European Economic Community (now the European Union).

BIBLIOGRAPHY

Janitschek, Hans. *Mário Soares: Portrait of a Hero.* New York: St. Martin's Press, 1986.

Maxwell, Kenneth. *The Making of Portuguese Democracy.* Cambridge: Cambridge University Press, 1995.

Paul Christopher Manuel

SEE ALSO Cavaco Silva, Anibal

Sobchak, Anatoly A. (1937–2000)

Russian political figure, mayor of St. Petersburg (1990–96). Anatoly Sobchak, son of a railroad engineer, was born in Leningrad (present-day St. Petersburg) on August 10, 1937. He grew up in Chita, Siberia, close to the Chinese frontier. He studied law at the University of Leningrad and worked as a lawyer in Stavropol. He returned to Leningrad and taught law at the Institute of Technology while completing a doctorate. His doctorate was delayed for eight years until 1981 because of the controversial nature of his thesis—on the advantages of a free-market economy. In 1983 he was appointed professor of economic law at Leningrad State University, where he eventually became dean of the law faculty. Despite his contempt for the Communist system, Sobchak joined the Communist Party in 1988. He believed at the time that there was no possibility for change except within the framework of the party system. This was at a time when Soviet leader Mikhail Gorbachev had launched his program of reform.

Sobchak was elected to the Congress of People's Deputies in April 1989. In June he was elected to sit in the Supreme Soviet. In the Supreme Soviet he led a refusal to rubber-stamp the nomination of party bureaucrats to high posts, joining Boris Yeltsin, and others to form a nascent opposition to the Communist Party. Sobchak headed the committee that held Yegor Ligachev, a member of the Politburo, and other party leaders responsible for deadly violence against demonstrators in Tbilisi, Soviet Georgia, in April 1991. He also attacked Prime Minister Nikolay I. Ryzhkov for corruption on national television. In 1989, to the dismay of Gorbachev, Sobchak came within two votes of engineering a repeal of article 6 of the Soviet constitution, which assigned to the Communist Party the leading role in Soviet society. In March 1990, however, Sobchak's motion succeeded in the Congress of People's Deputies.

Sobchak at first rejected an appeal to run for the city council of Leningrad in the city's first free municipal election, but in May 1989 ran for an open seat and won. He was then elected mayor, a choice ratified by 66 percent of the city's voters on June 13, 1990. He attempted to address the city's growing economic problems by transforming it into a free economic zone. On July 13, 1990, he followed the lead of Yeltsin and, with Gavril Popov, mayor of Moscow, resigned from the Communist Party.

On January 20, 1991, he was a leader of a march in Moscow protesting the Soviet crackdown on separatists in the Soviet Baltic States of Latvia and Lithuania. On July 1 he joined with Eduard Shevardnadze, who had resigned as Soviet foreign minister at the end of 1990, and others to launch a formal democratic opposition, the Movement for Democratic Reform. At the time of the hardliners' coup against Gorbachev on August 19, 1991, with an armed guard, Sobchak barged into a meeting of the KGB, police, and military leaders in Leningrad to threaten them if they cooperated with the coup. He then went on television and called hundreds of thousands of people into the streets. The military district commander of the Leningrad region, Viktor Samsonov, backed down and did not occupy the city.

In the aftermath of the coup, Sobchak following the approval of the city's voters in a referendum rechristened the former Russian capital St. Petersburg in November. However, he opposed the breakup of the old Soviet Union. He also opposed the rapid lifting of price controls and economic shock therapy. Some accused him of being too autocratic. Sobchak was narrowly defeated in the mayoral contest on June 2, 1996, by his former deputy, Vladimir Yakoviev. Yakoviev, who made overtures to the Communists, capitalized on popular discontent with shrinking services, unemployment, and a collapsing infrastructure. Sobchak, who was under investigation for corruption, left Russia in 1997 and sought medical care in Paris. When the case was dropped in 1999 he returned to St. Petersburg.

Sobchak moved to Kaliningrad, the discontiguous Russian enclave on the Baltic, following the resignation of Russian President Boris Yeltsin on December 31, 1999, where he hoped to direct the presidential campaign there of Vladimir Putin, the acting president. When Sobchak had been mayor, Putin was his deputy and close adviser. Sobchak, who had suffered from a deteriorating heart condition, suffered a fatal heart attack on February 20, 2000.

BIBLIOGRAPHY

Bennett, Vanora. "Tale of Fallen Mayor Evokes Russian Classics." *Los Angeles Times,* November 2, 1997.

"Obituary of Anatoly Sobchak," *The Daily Telegraph* (London), February 22, 2000.

"Sobchak, Anatoly A.," in Andrew Wilson and Nina Bachkatov, eds., *Russia and the Commonwealth A to Z.* New York: Harper Perennial, 1992.

Bernard Cook

Soccer Hooliganism

Disruptions at soccer matches have greatly concerned authorities as they increased markedly in intensity and destruction since the conclusion of World War II. Often stimulated by drugs and alcohol, hooligans frequently attended just to cause trouble. Many appear to protest what they regard as their inferior social status, using the games to vent their resentment. The question of order at the great soccer matches, therefore, has grown to be more and more of a problem.

A decisive opportunity for hooligans lies in the popularity of soccer, the world's leading sport. There are probably 120 million players in 190 countries. When the World Cup was shown on television in 1990, it set a record of 1.06 billion viewers.

At international soccer matches fans sit in their own sections by nation, whirl flags and scarves, show off their grease paint and tattoos, and make plenty of noise in a deluge of excitement, offering hooligans their chance for disruption. Much of this surfaced in the first postwar World Cup final at Maracana Stadium in Rio de Janiero before 200,000 in 1950. Brazil was so heavily favored over Uruguay that Brazilian fans were already preparing for their victory march. However, Uruguay won two to one, and in Rio's new stadium. False rumors quickly circulated that some Brazilian players had taken their own lives. Riots shattered the city. Brazil's coach, rightly fearful for his life, went into hiding.

In 1982 at a game in Moscow a rioting crowd caused the collapse of the stands, killing some 340. Ten years later in Bastia, Corsica, the wooden stadium gave way, killing 52 and injuring 200. But the attack of hooligans on rivals at Heysel Stadium in Brussels on May 29, 1985, stands out. There, just before the final game for the European Cup, which pitted Liverpool against Juventus of Turin, a large crowd of drunken Britishers attacked Italian fans. Under the weight of the overloaded stands, a retaining wall collapsed, crushing 39 to death, while injuring 200. TV showed the bedlam to a horrified audience. Team captains appealed to the crowd over loudspeakers. Amazingly, the game went on after eighty-five minutes' delay. But the European Football Association suspended the British team for three years.

Another horrendous episode occurred at the British Football Association Cup semifinal on April 15, 1989, which brought Liverpool against Nottingham Forest. Although the nearest grandstand was already full, the police opened a gate where a surly mob of fans had gathered, unable to buy tickets. Chaos followed, killing about 95 and injuring 180. Many children were crushed against the railings. Somehow play started but stopped after six minutes. Bill Shankley, former manager of the Liverpool Football Club, offered this explanation: "The way some people talk about Soccer, you'd think the result of one game was a matter of life and death. They don't understand: it [life] is much more than that." To many unprivileged hooligans, however, their hooliganism is a justified protest through which they flaunt themselves and challenge society.

BIBLIOGRAPHY

Baker, William J. *Sports in the Western World.* Urbana: University of Illinois Press, 1988.

Trifari, Elio, and Charles Miers. *Soccer! The Game and the World Cup.* New York: Rizzoli International, 1994.

William J. Miller

Socialist International

International organization of socialist and social democratic parties established in 1951 to exchange information and promote cooperation among its members.

The Socialist International has had a number of precursors: the First International (International Working Men's Association), 1864–76; the Second International, 1889–1914; and the Third International (the Communist International, or Comintern), 1919–43. A Fourth International, founded in 1938 by Leon Trotsky, one of the principal leaders of the 1917 Bolshevik Revolution in Russia, expelled from the Communist Party and the USSR by Joseph Stalin, Lenin's successor as head of the Party, has remained small and separate from the Socialist International.

The current International was originally organized in Frankfurt, West Germany, and has tended to represent social democratic parties of Western Europe, Asia, the Americas, and Africa. It was not allied with the former Soviet Union. Indeed, its founding declaration emphasized pluralism within socialist views and rejected Soviet communism as the only true form of Marxism. With the demise of the Communist governments of the former Soviet bloc, socialist parties from Eastern Europe, which had previously been parties in exile, have joined the International as official representatives of those states.

Since the 1970s the International has become even more pro-West in its orientation, and many of the European socialist parties have accepted fundamental tenets of capitalist economic theory and practice. For instance, the governing French and Spanish socialist parties in the 1980s pursued liberal market and budget policies, and the British Labour Party has in recent years moderated its reformism. Socialist leaders such as Helmut Schmidt, François Mitterrand, Felipe Gonzáles, and Bettino Craxi have also brought the foreign policies of their parties closer to those of NATO and the United States. At the same time, socialist leaders have also been among the most outspoken against U.S. intervention in Latin America.

The International is governed by a council, elected by a congress that meets every three years. The council appoints a bureau and a secretariat, based in London. The organization also has affiliated with labor union and women's councils.

While much of the contemporary business of the International concerns issues outside Europe, many of its European parties have used its structures to build the solidarity they deem necessary to face the challenges and opportunities of European integration. The members of the International are also concerned with retaining electoral support, given the growing prosperity and broadening of the middle class in European society. Consequently, these parties have attempted to broaden their appeal to the middle and professional classes, and have attempted to accommodate social movements such as feminism and environmentalism.

BIBLIOGRAPHY

Boggs, Carl. *The Socialist Tradition from Crisis to Decline.* New York: Routledge, 1995.

Kitschelt, Herbert. *The Transformation of European Social Democracy.* Cambridge: Cambridge University Press, 1994.

Pelinka, Anton. *Social Democratic Parties in Europe.* New York: Praeger, 1983.

Przeworski, Adam, and John Sprague. *Paper Stones: A History of Electoral Socialism.* Chicago: University of Chicago Press, 1986.

Sturmthal, Adolf. *Left of Center: European Labor since World War II.* Urbana: University of Illinois Press, 1983.

Wilde, Lawrence. *Modern European Socialism.* Aldershot, U.K.: Dartmouth, 1994.

Eric Gorham

Solana, Javier (1942–)

Spanish foreign minister and secretary-general of NATO. Javier Solana was born in Madrid on July 14, 1942. Solana earned a doctorate in physics and was a professor at the Complutense University in Madrid. He was also a Fulbright scholar at several U.S. universities. He joined the Spanish Socialist Party in 1965 and was elected to parliament in 1977. He served as a government minister as of 1982 until assuming the NATO post in December 1995. He was minister for culture from December 1982 until July 1988, and from 1985 to 1988 he was also spokesman for the government. He served as minister for education from 1988 until July 1992, when he became minister of foreign affairs.

After the resignation of Willy Claes as NATO's secretary-general in 1995 because of a political scandal, there was bickering among the members, especially the United States and France, over his successor. The United States vetoed the choice of France and Britain—former Dutch prime minister Ruud Lubbers. The United States opposed Lubbers, even though as prime minister he had taken the politically unpopular step of backing the U.S. plan to deploy Pershing missiles in the Netherlands. U.S. opposition stemmed from the feeling that France and other countries had not taken the United States into their counsel. France, for its part, blocked the U.S. candidate, former Danish Foreign Minister Uffe Ellemann-Jensen, declaring that his knowledge of French was insufficient, but he had also openly criticized French nuclear tests in the Pacific. Solana was a compromise candidate for the post, which traditionally is held by a European while an American holds the top military post.

BIBLIOGRAPHY

Simons, Marlise. "NATO Picks Spanish Foreign Minister for Secretary General." *New York Times,* December 2, 1995.

Bernard Cook

SEE ALSO Claes, Willy; North Atlantic Treaty Organization

Solzhenitsyn, Aleksandr (1918–)

Soviet writer and dissident. Aleksandr Solzhenitsyn used his years of prison and exile to create a devastating indictment of Marxism-Leninism and the Soviet regime. He earned domestic and international acclaim, but also official wrath. Deported in 1974, he returned to Russia in 1994, but his uncompromising call for spiritual regeneration met with less support in the post-Communist era.

Born in Kislovodsk in 1918, Solzhenitsyn married Natalya Reshetovskaya in 1940. After completing university studies in mathematics and physics, he enlisted in July 1941, the month following Nazi Germany's invasion of the USSR. A decorated artillery officer, he was arrested in February 1945 for criticizing Stalin in a personal letter. Solzhenitsyn spent eight years in labor camps, including two prison research institutes later described in *The First Circle* (1968), and a special camp in Kazakhstan, the setting for *One Day in the Life of Ivan Denisovich* (1962). He was freed in 1956 after three more years of exile in Kazakhstan, almost dying of stomach cancer, as portrayed in *The Cancer Ward* (1968). After his release Solzhenitsyn taught secondary-school mathematics at Ryazan, but writing remained his passion. Besides the above works, he wrote *The Gulag Archipelago* (1973–75), a massive chronicle based on hundreds of personal stories of the Soviet slave labor system, and *Laroue rouge* (*The Red Wheel*) (1983–98), a multivolume exploration of Russia's path to the October Revolution (1917). In 1957 Solzhenitsyn remarried Reshetovskaya, whom he had divorced in 1952.

Solzhenitsyn's combat service during World War II, and especially his experience of prison and exile, turned him against not just the Stalinist terror but also the revolutionary ideology in general of Lenin and Marx. Like Dostoevsky, who also underwent a prison conversion, Solzhenitsyn defended personal freedom, championed Russia's cultural and religious heritage, and saw himself as a moral and historical prophet.

Premier Nikita Khrushchev's de-Stalinization campaign allowed *One Day in the Life of Ivan Denisovich* to appear in the liberal literary journal *Noviy Mir* in 1962. This firsthand account of Stalin's slave labor camps made the provincial schoolteacher an instant celebrity but also a target for Communist Party hard-liners and the KGB (secret police). Solzhenitsyn chronicled his subsequent harassment by security organs in this period in *The Oak and the Calf* (1975). Until 1988 only occasional short pieces of his were published in the Soviet Union.

Solzhenitsyn's determined public protests and the publication abroad of *The Cancer Ward* and *The First Circle,* both banned at home, won him growing international acclaim, culminating in the Nobel Prize in literature in 1970. When the first volume of *The Gulag Archipelago* appeared abroad in 1973, Soviet hostility to Solzhenitsyn, already expelled from the Writers' Union in 1969, intensified. In February 1974, Solzhenitsyn was charged with treason, stripped of his citizenship, and forcibly exiled. A month later he was joined by his sons and his wife, Natalya Svetlova, whom he married in 1973 after divorcing Reshetovskaya in 1972.

After a brief stay in Switzerland, Solzhenitsyn settled in Cavendish, Vermont, in 1976 where, except for rare excursions, he worked with considerable passion and self-discipline. His ambitious goal has been the recovery and reinterpretation of the authentic history and soul of the Russia he believed was distorted and crippled by seventy-five years of Marxism-Leninism and later threatened by what he called "Western-Pagan" forces. Particularly after his harsh criticism of Western materialism and individualism in a 1978 Harvard University speech, "A World Split Apart," Western opinion of Solzhenitsyn became less favorable.

Solzhenitsyn's major effort in exile was the continuation of *The Red Wheel,* focusing on key turning points, which he called "knots." The first, *August 1914,* was published in Paris in the Russian language in 1971, with an enlarged version appearing in 1981. Since then, *October 1916* (1982), *March 1917* (1986–88), *April 1917* (1991), and *November 1916* (1998) have appeared, but he has abandoned plans to carry the story to 1922, as well as epilogues going to 1945. In the eleven published volumes, Solzhenitsyn interweaves historical events and figures with the fates of ordinary people in a brilliant attempt to recreate a world torn by cataclysmic change.

Although Solzhenitsyn always believed he would return to Russia, this seemed unlikely until the era of Mikhail Gorbachev; as late as 1988, his works were banned in the Soviet Union. But in 1989 the first short piece was published and he was readmitted to the Writers' Union. In 1990 his citizenship was restored, and the reason charges were dropped in 1991. Solzhenitsyn then turned to contemporary issues; *Rebuilding Russia* (1990) argued for the spiritual regeneration of the Slavic and Orthodox core, allowing the other areas to leave the union. He scorned Gorbachev for temporizing and clinging to discredited Marxist concepts. He also criticized the crony capitalism and indifference to social needs of the Yeltsin era.

In May 1994 Solzhenitsyn finally returned to Russia, taking up residence in Moscow after an eight-week train trip across the country from the Pacific, meeting with numerous groups to buttress his analysis of Russia's "spiritual crisis." Rejecting a direct political role, Solzhenitsyn continued to attack Marxism-Leninism, false Western values, and Russia's post-Communist authorities in *The Russian Question at the End of the Twentieth Century* (1994), *Russia in Collapse* (1998), addresses, and a short-lived television show.

Solzhenitsyn continues to urge spiritual renewal and the gradual development of local democratic institutions, based on authentic Russian traditions. This message now finds less resonance among nationalists, who once saw him as a potential political leader or an increasingly cynical general public preoccupied with day-to-day economic survival. But Solzhenitsyn's stature as a moral and prophetic writer whose literary talent and personal courage did more than anything else to expose the true nature of the Soviet system remains unchallenged.

BIBLIOGRAPHY

Dunlop, John B., Richard Haugh, and Alexis Klimoff, eds. *Aleksandr Solzhenitsyn: Critical Essays and Documentary Materials.* New York: Macmillan, 1975.

Dunlop, John, and Richard Haugh, eds. *Solzhenitsyn in Exile: Critical Essays and Documentary Material.* Stanford, Calif.: Hoover Institution, 1985.

Ericson, Edward E. *Solzhenitsyn and the Modern World.* Washington, D.C.: Regnery Gateway, 1993.

Pontuso, James F. *Solzhenitsyn's Political Thought.* Charlottesville: University Press of Virginia, 1990.

Scammell, Michael. *Solzhenitsyn: A Biography.* New York: Norton, 1984.

———, ed. *The Solzhenitsyn File.* Chicago: University of Chicago Press, 1995.

Daniel L. Schlafly Jr.

Soustelle, Jacques (1912–90)

French politician and anthropologist, most noted for his opposition to Algerian independence. Jacques-Émile Soustelle, son of a railroad worker, was born in Montpellier on February 3, 1912. He studied at the École Normale Supérieure in Paris and in 1937 earned a doctorate at the Sorbonne. He became a professor of anthropology at the Collège de France in 1938 and was active in left-wing political activity, becoming secretary-general of the Vigilance Committee of Antifascist Intellectuals.

On June 18, 1940, Soustelle responded to General Charles de Gaulle's appeal from London to continue resistance to the German invaders. He went to London and served as an envoy of the Free French to Latin America. In 1943 he became head of the Free French secret service. With the liberation of France in 1945, Soustelle was appointed by de Gaulle minister of information then minister of colonies. In 1947 he became secretary-general of de Gaulle's Rally of the French People. After his election to the National Assembly (lower house of parliament), Soustelle served as the Rally's parliamentary leader (1951–52). In 1955 Prime Minister Pierre Mendès-France appointed Soustelle governor–general of Algeria. There he became a strong supporter of Algeria remaining a constituent part of France. In February 1956 Premier Guy Mollet recalled Soustelle to France, but as leader of the pro-de Gaulle element in the assembly from 1956 to 1958, Soustelle made Algeria the litmus test for its support of governing coalitions and won the appellation "destroyer of ministries." In May 1958 he went to Algeria and became a leader of the rebellious French who supported the Committee of Public Safety, formed by rebels in the military to prevent France from abandoning Algeria. Soustelle played a role in forcing Pierre Pflimlin to resign as premier and bringing de Gaulle to power. De Gaulle appointed him minister of information on July 7, 1958, and in January 1959 minister for Sahara and atomic affairs. He broke with de Gaulle and left the government in February 1960 over what he perceived as de Gaulle's betrayal of the cause of French Algeria.

Soustelle with Georges Bidault and General Raoul Salan formed the Secret Army Organization (OAS) to fight what it regarded as the betrayal of French interests in Algeria. When he was charged in 1962 with "attempts against the state," Soustelle went into exile. He did not return to France until 1968, when following an agreement between de Gaulle and General Jacques Massu during the student and worker protests in May that threatened to topple de Gaulle's government, an amnesty was declared for the OAS participants. Soustelle became director of the École Pratique des Hautes Études. In 1973 he was elected to the National Assembly, serving there until 1978. In 1973 he was France's representative to the Council of Europe.

Soustelle, an expert on the pre-Colombian civilization in Mexico, was elected to the Académie Française in 1983. He died on August 7, 1990.

BIBLIOGRAPHY

Cook, Joan. "Jacques Soustelle, Leader in Fight for a French Algeria." *New York Times,* August 9, 1990.

Ullmann, Bernard. *Jacques Soustelle: le mal aimé.* Paris: Plon, 1995.

Bernard Cook

SEE ALSO Algerian War; De Gaulle, Charles; Massu, Jacques; Salan, Raoul

South Ossetia

Autonomous region of the former Georgian Soviet Socialist Republic of the USSR, located in north central Georgia along the Caucasian border with Russia's republic of Alania (North Ossetia). During the period of Georgian independence (1918–21), the Ossetians sided with the Russians, and several Ossetian risings were crushed by the Georgian social democratic government. After the victory of the Soviets in Transcaucasia, Joseph Stalin, as Soviet commissar of nationalities, divided the Ossetians between the Soviet Socialist Republics of Russia and the Georgia. On April 20, 1922, South Ossetia became an autonomous region of the Georgian Soviet Socialist Republic. In 1979 ethnic Ossetians constituted 66 percent of the region's population. According to the 1989 census, 175,000 Ossetians lived in Georgia, but some resided outside the autonomous region in other parts of Georgia, particularly in the eastern portion of the province of Kakheti.

The Orthodox Christian Ossetians are an Indo-European people related to the Iranians. The Ossetians had settled in the north Caucasus, in the area of what is today North Ossetia, by the sixth century. Between the twelfth and eighteenth centuries, groups of Ossetians emigrated across the Caucasus Mountains into the area now known as South Ossetia. Georgian nationalists assert that North Ossetia (now called the Republic of Alania) is the true home of all Ossetians and that they have no "national" rights to traditional Georgian territory.

The animosity of the Georgians for the Ossetians is rooted in both language and the pro-Russian sentiments of the Ossetians. In 1989, fearful of being separated from the Ossetians to the north in Russia and of being submerged in an ethnocentric nationalist Georgia in which their non-Georgian-speaking youth would have limited prospects, the Ossetians of South Ossetia demanded Autonomous republic status within the USSR as a prelude to unification with North Ossetia and hence inclusion in the Russian Federated Soviet Socialist Republic.

In 1989 violent clashes erupted in South Ossetia between local Georgians and Ossetians. Thousands of young Georgians mobilized by the Georgian President Zviad Gamsakhurdia converged on Tskhinvali, capital of South Ossetia, and committed atrocities against Ossetians. Order was restored by forces of the Soviet Ministry of Internal Affairs. However, in August 1990 the Georgian Supreme Soviet (parliament) attempted to outlaw the South Ossetian Popular Front and other separatist political organizations by passing an electoral law banning parties whose activities were limited to one region. In September the South Ossetian Autonomous Region Soviet responded by declaring the region the South Ossetian Democratic Republic and appealed to Moscow to recognize it as an independent component of the Soviet Union. The Georgian Supreme Soviet responded by declaring the proclamation null and abolishing the region's autonomous status.

In early January 1991 the Georgian parliament voted to refuse to comply with Soviet President Mikhail Gorbachev's presidential decree that, while annulling the South Ossetian declaration of independence, denounced the Georgian abolition of South Ossetia's autonomous status as unconstitutional. It also ignored his demand that Georgia remove its troops from the area. Violence continued. In March Georgian authorities boycotted the all-union referendum on the future of the USSR, but against the instructions of the Georgian government polling stations were opened in South Ossetia and Abkhazia, an autonomous region in north western Georgia. In South Ossetia, voters overwhelmingly approved the preservation of the USSR.

In December 1991, when the Georgian government sent additional troops to the region, the Ossetian Supreme Soviet responded by renewing its declaration of independence and its demand for inclusion in the Russian Federation. An Ossetian referendum in January 1992 overwhelmingly supported these measures. Despite Georgian overtures after the ouster of Gamsakhurdia, on January 6, 1992, because of his authoritarian proclivities fighting continued. Georgian forces shelled Tskhinvali, and North Ossetian volunteers poured in to assist their southern conationals. The fighting took 400 Georgian and 1,000 Ossetian lives and forced thousands of Ossetians to flee to the north. Some estimate that as many as 120,000 Ossetians from Georgia sought refuge in North Ossetia. In late 1992 a more permanent cease-fire was negotiated by the new Georgian leader, Eduard Shevardnadze and Russian President Boris Yeltsin. In July monitors from Russia, Georgia, and South Ossetia were installed and armed forces were withdrawn or demobilized. In November 1992 the South Ossetian legislature affirmed its secession from Georgia, a position again endorsed by popular referendum, and in December 1993 a new constitution was adopted in South Ossetia that declared the region's sovereignty. In July 1995, however, under the supervision of the Organization for Security and Cooperation in Europe (OSCE), the security and human rights monitoring organization of European State, the U.S., and Canada, a quadripartite control commission consisting of representatives from Russia, Georgia, North Ossetia, and South Ossetia launched discussions in search of a political settlement.

In May 1996 Shevardnadze and Lyudvig Chibirov, chairman of South Ossetia's parliament, signed an agreement to resolve the status of South Ossetia peacefully. In November 1996 Chibirov was elected president of South Ossetia but neither Georgia nor the international community recognized the validity of the election.

BIBLIOGRAPHY

Goldenberg, Suzanne. *Pride of Small Nations: The Caucasus and Post-Soviet Disorder.* London: Zed Books, 1994.

Bernard Cook

South Tyrol

Border region of Italy and Austria. The Brenner Pass, which connects the two neighbors, is the major point of access between central and southern Europe and is the principal reason for the contested history of the South Tyrol (German, Tirol). The unification of Italy in 1870 was posited on two principles: bringing together all "Italians" and achieving the "natural" geographical boundaries of the state. The South Tyrol, which was inhabited by German speakers, did not fit the first criterion. As the South Tyrol and the Italian-speaking province of Trento to the south were part of the Hapsburg Empire, they, like Friulia-Venezia Giulia, today an Italian region bordering the Austria province of Kärntan (Corinthia) and Slovenia, were regarded by Italian nationalists as "unredeemed" territories. The continued reluctance of Austria to cede the South Tyrol to Italy was instrumental in Italy's entering the First World War on the side of the Entente, which promised the South Tyrol to Italy as part of the London Treaty of 1915.

Despite the wishes of the population, the South Tyrol was given to Italy at the Paris Peace Conference of 1919. With the rise to power of Italian fascism, the South Tyrol was subjected to intense Italianization campaigns. The German language was banned in all areas of public life, and German surnames were even Italianized. In addition, Italians were encouraged to migrate to the area. In spite of Hitler's avowed ambitions to unite all Germans into the Third Reich, he reached an agreement with Italian leader Benito Mussolini that allowed the Italianization of the region to continue. German speakers were subsequently allowed the "option" of moving to the Reich, and some seventy-five thousand chose to do so. After Mussolini was reduced to a German puppet in the northern Italian Social Republic (1943–45), Germany annexed the South Tyrol in late 1943. But this acquisition was short-lived—the region was returned to Italy after the Second World War. The South Tyrol—the Italian Province of Bolzano—became part of the "special region" of Trentino-Alto Adige in 1948. However, since Trentino formed part of the region, the "special region" was two-thirds Italian-speaking.

The desire of German speakers to be separate or united to Austria led to much agitation, culminating in outbursts of armed terrorism in the 1960s. In 1969 an agreement was reached between Austria and Italy whereby considerable administrative and legislative autonomy was granted to the South Tyrol. Inhabitants were given the right to appeal against Italian administrative decisions and laws to the International Court of Justice, and Austria agreed to a policy of nonintervention. The Südtiroler

Volkspartei, founded in 1945 to act as the political voice of German speakers in Trentino-Alto Adige, has long dominated the political life of Bolzano at the national and regional electoral levels. Though it cooperated with the Italian Christian Democratic Party from the 1960s to 1980s, it did so always to gain concessions for the German speakers of the province. With the advent of the European Union, in which both Austria and Italy are now members, the struggle for a return to Austria has become largely irrelevant. Likewise, the rise of regionalism has encouraged more concessions. In 1992 further legislation guaranteed additional educational rights and civil service representation to German speakers. Though grievances remain, the South Tyrol has moved toward de facto autonomy.

BIBLIOGRAPHY

Alcock, Antony Evelyn. *The History of the South Tyrol Question.* London: Michael Joseph, 1970.

Míchál Thompson

Spaak, Paul-Henri, and Western European Unity

Paul-Henri Spaak was Belgium's greatest statesman after World War II. He helped draft the U.N. charter in 1945 and served as president of the U.N. General Assembly in 1946, foreign minister of Belgium in 1947, and prime minister from 1947 to 1951. He was a leader of various movements toward European cooperation and integration: the formation of Benelux, the customs union of Belgium, France, Britain, the Netherlands, and Luxembourg, then, in 1949, by adding the United States to the group, the formation of the North Atlantic Treaty Organization (NATO)—the transatlantic military alliance—and in 1957, the European Economic Community (EEC, later, European Union, EU), an economic customs union.

Many Americans would have been content to give no more than general support to the Brussels Treaty signed on March 17, 1947, by Britain, France, and the Benelux countries. But on their own, the forces of the resultant Western Union alliance would clearly have been inadequate. The Western European Union moreover placed a disproportionately heavy burden of defense on an ailing Great Britain. British Foreign Minister Ernest Bevin, as a consequence, saw the Brussels Treaty and Western Union as a device to lure the Americans into giving Western Europe full military backing in much the same way as the joint Western European response to the Marshall Plan had procured U.S. economic aid. According to Spaak, Belgian foreign minister at the time and another of NATO's architects, the new April 1949 Washington treaty, which created NATO, would become on the Atlantic scale what the Brussels Treaty, that is, Western European Union, was on the European scale. Skillful British, Canadian, and Benelux diplomacy thus played a major part in getting the United States to commit itself to an Atlantic alliance. Once President Harry Truman was reelected in 1948, hesitation within the U.S. administration ended. A number of additional hurdles were overcome. For instance, Norway rejected a Swedish offer to join a neutral Scandinavian bloc. The Soviets gave additional impetus by their blockade of Berlin (1948–49) and by crude attempts to intimidate Norway. NATO formally came into being on April 4, 1949. NATO formed, and continued to form thereafter, one of the most successful alliances in history, and Spaak played a major role in its formation before becoming NATO's secretary-general (1957–61).

From 1948 to 1952 Spaak led several other organizations for European political and economic cooperation, such as the European Coal and Steel community (ECSC), the European Atomic Energy Community (Euratom), in 1957, and the European Economic Community (EEC), which created the Common Market. The resultant treaties were signed by the six in March 1957 and came into force on January 1, 1958. The agreements represented the political compromise between advocates, especially West German, of an unfettered market economy and spokesmen for a market economy modified by national planning and government intervention. The treaties likewise constituted an accommodation between those who favored integration on intergovernmental lines and those who pleaded for supranational unification. Frenchmen Robert Schuman and Jean Monnet and Spaak laid the foundation for a United States of Europe in the ECSC, Euratom, and the EEC, integrating friends and foes of World War II into a cooperative free-trading system and common market that integrated a rehabilitated Germany into associations of peaceful cooperation with the countries of Western Europe. NATO had created a supranational organization to allow military equipment, trucks, pipelines, and communications systems to cross national borders and to organize a supranational defensive force to keep the Soviets out, the Germans cooperative, and the United States involved in Europe.

A leftist socialist, Spaak retired from the Socialist Party in 1966 to pursue business interests. He died in 1972 after a distinguished career in Belgian and European politics dedicated to cooperation and integration of the nations of Western Europe.

BIBLIOGRAPHY

Duignan, Peter, and L. H. Gann. *The Rebirth of the West: The Americanization of the Democratic World, 1945–1958.* Oxford: Basil Blackwell, 1992.

Peter Duignan

Spadolini, Giovanni (1925–94)

Italian journalist, historian, and statesman. He was the first non-Christian Democratic prime minister of Italy.

Giovanni Spadolini was born in Florence on June 21, 1925. Spadolini was a contributor to numerous dailies, including *Il Messaggero* and *La Stampa,* as well as weeklies *Il Mondo* and *Epoca.* At the age of thirty he became director of the *Il Resto del Carlino* (1955–68) and then of *Il Corriere della Sera* (1968–72). In 1961 he was appointed professor of contemporary history at the University of Florence. He subsequently served as president of Bocconi University of Milan and the Italian Institute of Historical Studies of Naples. In 1980 he transformed the historical journal Nuova *Antologia,* founded in 1821, to maintain its continuation and independence. In 1992 he was granted membership in the Accademia Nazionale dei Lincei (the National Academy of Lincei).

In 1972 Ugo la Malfa, leader of Italian Republican Party, nominated Spadolini as a candidate for the Senate (upper house of parliament). Because of his success, la Malfa nominated him as minister in the new Ministry of Culture and Environment. Spadolini's second experience as a minister was in August 1979 as head of Education in Giulio Andreotti's cabinet. After la Malfa's death in 1979, Spadolini became his natural heir, and therefore secretary of the Republican Party from September 1979 until July 1987. His political orientation placed him in the political spectrum somewhere between the Socialist Party and the Christian Democratic Party. From June 1981 to November 1982 he was twice prime minister. His two governments consisted of an alliance of the Socialist, Republican, Social Democratic, and Liberal Parties with the Christian Democratic Party. These political alliances obtained an anti-inflation agreement and helped reduce the foreign trade deficit. The two Spadolini cabinets have been credited with the defeat the right and left-wing terrorism that plagued Italy in the 1970s. They supported the Atlantic alliance (NATO) and promoted European integration. Spadolini emphasized the cultural, historical, and political common interests between Europe and the United States. His cabinet decided to begin installation of NATO "euromissiles" on Italian territory to balance forces against Soviet SS-20 missiles.

In summer 1981 during his first cabinet, Spadolini was confronted with the crisis caused by the P-2 Masonic Lodge scandal. In response he purged the heads of the military and the secret and intelligence services. From August 1983 to April 1987 Spadolini was secretary of defense during Bettino Craxi's cabinet. Spadolini established the fundamental principles for the modernization of the Italian army and resolved the crisis when the cruise ship *Achille Lauro* was detained by Palestinian terrorists and one of its American passengers was murdered.

In 1987 Spadolini was elected president of the Senate and was reelected in 1992. In 1991 he was appointed senator for life.

Among Spadolini's numerous historical and political writings are *Lotto sociale in Italia* (1948); *L'opposizione cattolica* (1955); *I repubblicani dopo l'Unità* (1960); *Le due Rome. Chiesa e Stato fra '800 e '900* (1978); *Il mio debito con Gobetti: 1948–1981* (1981); *Tradizione garibaldina e storia d'Italia* (1982); *Bloc-notes 1988–1990* (1990); *Il debito con Croce* (1990); and *Il disordine mondiale. Bloc-notes 1992–1994* (1994).

Spadolini died in Rome on August 4, 1994.

BIBLIOGRAPHY

Sabelli Fioretti, C. *Spadolini: Il potere della volontà.* Milan: Sperling and Kupfer, 1983.

Valiani, L. *Spadolini e la storia dell'Italia contemporanea.* Florence: Le Monnier, 1991.

Claudia Giurintano

Spain

Spain is a constitutional monarchy located on the Iberian Peninsula in Western Europe. It is bordered by Gibraltar, the Atlantic Ocean, Portugal, the Bay of Biscay, France, Andorra, and the Mediterranean Sea. It consists of 194,898 square miles (504,784 sq km) and has a population of approximately 39 million. Its capital, Madrid, has over four million inhabitants. In addition to the Castilian dialect of Spanish there are the regional languages of Catalan, Basque, Galician, and Valencian.

The history of Spain in the postwar period is that of the aftermath of the Civil War (1936–1939), which ended the democratic Second Spanish Republic (1931–36). Often thought of as the opening act of World War II in Europe, the Spanish Civil War began on July 18, 1936, with an organized uprising by a segment of the military backed by a nationalist coalition of monarchists, conservative Catholics, and fascists (represented in the Spanish Fascist party, the Falange). The war quickly became a staging ground for the looming confrontation in

Europe. Germany and Italy intervened militarily in support of the nationalist insurgents, but the republican government failed to attain similar support from France and Britain. The inaction of the French and British governments stacked the odds against the republic and gave an increasingly important role to the Soviet Union, which became the republican government's major external supplier. It also increased the influence of the Spanish Communist Party (PCE) on the republican side, polarizing the conflict and contributing to its intensity. The war ended in April 1939 with the fall of Madrid and led to the establishment of a conservative dictatorship under the leader of the nationalist side, General Franciso Franco (1892–75), that was to last almost four decades.

Franco opted for neutrality when Britain and France declared war on Germany in 1939 and kept Spain out of the war for its duration. His close association with the Axis powers that had supported him in the civil war, his equivocal stance after 1940 when he changed Spain's position from neutrality to nonbelligerence on Mussolini's advice, and his espousal of the fascist discourse of his Falangist supporters at home, however, all spelled a period of intense isolation for Spain at the end of World War II. In 1946 the United Nations passed a resolution recommending a diplomatic boycott of Spain, and most member countries withdrew their ambassadors from Madrid. Spain was also excluded from NATO and the Council of Europe, as well as from U.S. Marshall Plan funding. The regime's ostracism was mitigated, however, by the onset of the Cold War, which led the United States to orchestrate an end to the U.N. boycott and to send an ambassador to Madrid in 1950. Three years later the Eisenhower administration signed a defense pact with Spain whereby the United States was granted use of three land bases and one naval base on Spanish territory in return for a package of military and economic aid amounting to over $1 billion from 1963 to 1973.

In the domestic political sphere Franco used the exceptional circumstances that World War II created for Spain to cement his control over the disparate political factions, or "families," that had supported his victory in the Civil War. This objective involved two principal tasks: neutralizing through skillful use of cabinet appointments possible challenges to his personal rule from conservative generals, some of whom sought a restoration of the monarchy, and domesticating the national syndicalist wing of the Falange, which ascribed to a program of radical economic reforms set out by the party's charismatic founder, Jose Antonio Primo de Rivera, who was captured and executed by the republican side in 1936. Franco partially achieved the latter objective during the civil war. In 1937 he imposed a decree of unification on the Falange in which the party was forced to merge with Carlist (conservative monarchist) organizations that ascribed to a far more conservative vision of Spain than the national syndicalist welfare state advanced by Primo de Rivera. Shortly thereafter, he sentenced to death Primo's successor as party leader, Manuel Hedilla. After the war, the now renamed Falange Española Tradicionalista was turned into an instrument of the state directly responsible to Franco. It provided the regime with an ideological identity but no longer served as the base for the advancement of radical policy alternatives.

In the economic sphere, the Franco regime pursued an inward-looking strategy of economic nationalism during its first two decades. This strategy, known as the *autarquia,* allowed for the significant acceleration of industrialization. But it also proved unsustainable. In 1956 the Falangist minister of labor, José Giron, instituted a large wage increase in response to worker unrest in the industrial north. The result was an inflationary surge that set off a balance-of-payments crisis. Franco responded by appointing a cabinet that gave control over economic policy to a group of neoliberal technocrats. Two years later the regime agreed to a stabilization plan sponsored by the International Monetary Fund (IMF) to solve its persisting balance-of-payments crisis. At the same time, it initiated a new, outwardly oriented policy course (*nueva ordenacia*) by liberalizing prices, external trade, and inward capital flows, and by adopting a French-styled framework of indicative planning, that is targeting specific sectors of the economy for investment and development. These changes allowed Spain to become a member of the Organization for European Economic Cooperation (OEEC, later OECD), the IMF, and the World Bank.

The 1959 policy turn made possible Spain's economic miracle of the 1960s. A massive tourism boom, inward capital flows, and cheap credit policies served to finance the second stage of industrialization, allowing Spain to become the tenth-largest industrialized economy in the early 1970s. This success in the economic sphere was accompanied by an easing of political repression and some measure of political liberalization. Strike activity by workers was depenalized and collective bargaining between employers and the official trade union, which was overseen by the *Movimiento,* or Falange, was legalized. In 1966, the government passed a new press law that significantly reduced the level of censorship. Reformist ministers also began to put forth calls for an opening of the political system (*apertura*) that would allow for some form of competing political organization to the *Movimiento* and for a legislature elected by universal suffrage. Finally, in 1969,

Franco nominated Prince Juan Carlos of Bourbon, grandson of Spain's last monarch, Alfonso XIII, to be his successor. The move was backed by reformers within his regime and tacitly condoned by the United States, the Vatican, and democratic governments in Europe. It was opposed by Falangists; supporters of the Prince's father, Don Juan, who favored a monarchy based on the traditional line of succession; and much of the democratic opposition in exile. The political moderation that the Franco regime underwent during the 1960s was intended to facilitate the government's application for association with the European Community (EC) in 1962. However, in contrast to the United States, which supported Spain's integration into a variety of international bodies and often acted as an ally, European governments insisted that participation in the EC would require an end to autocratic rule. Although the regime eventually negotiated a preferential trade agreement with the EC in 1970, European governments continued to condemn openly the regime's authoritarianism.

In the early 1970s external and internal opposition to the regime intensified just as Spain was hit by economic crisis. The oil shock of 1973 coincided with the assassination of Franco's right-hand man, Admiral Luis Carrero Blanco, the prime minister. The assassination was carried out by members of the radical Basque separatist organization, Euskadi Ta Askatasuna (ETA), which during the regime's last years initiated what was to become a long-lasting campaign of terrorist acts. The following year opposition forces of vastly different ideological strains began to come together to demand a democratic break with the past, and strike activity by workers rose dramatically. The regime was also confronted with an unprecedented wave of international condemnation, including that of the Vatican, once an important supporter, when Franco decided in September 1975 to carry out the death sentences of five ETA militants and of another leftist terrorist organization, the Frente Revolucionario Antifascista Patriatico (FRAP). The executions led fifteen European governments to recall their ambassadors from Madrid. They also ended any hope that Franco might step aside to allow his successor to initiate a transition to democracy: a solution advanced now more urgently by the United States and by reformers within the regime, who feared that the regime might otherwise become the victim of the kind of revolutionary end that befell the long-standing authoritarian dictatorship in neighboring Portugal in 1974. However, Franco's death in November 1975 finally made such a transition possible.

The two most often noted features of the transition to democracy that followed Franco's death are its negotiated character and its implementation within the existing legal framework of the authoritarian regime. In accordance with Franco's political will, Juan Carlos de Bourbon ascended to the throne and became the head of state two days after the dictator's death. The new king first reappointed Franco's last prime minister, Carlos Arias Navarro, but soon replaced him when it became clear that Arias was failing to carry out serious political reforms. Arias's successor, Adolfo Suárez, submitted a proposal for free elections based on universal suffrage to the Cortes (parliament), which had rubber-stamped the government's decisions in the past. The proposal was accepted by the regime's representatives, who thus in effect voted themselves out of existence, and was approved in a referendum in December 1976. Suárez then set out to negotiate a framework for free elections with the main opposition parties, including the Spanish Socialist Workers Party (PSOE) and the Spanish Communist Party (PCE), which had formed a common platform in early 1976. A critical test was overcome with the legalization of the PCE in April 1977, a move that many feared might set off a reaction by the military, and free elections to a constituent assembly were held in July.

The winner of the 1977 elections was the Union de Centro Democratico (Union of the Democratic Center, UCD), a centrist party formed by Adolfo Suárez that brought together a wide spectrum of reformers from within and outside the regime. Renominated prime minister, Suárez now set out to negotiate a constitution with opposition party leaders, including Catalan and Basque nationalist leaders who sought to reestablish the kind of regional autonomy that Catalonia had enjoyed under the republic. In October 1978 the Cortes approved a constitution that allowed for the creation of autonomous communities—regional governments based on independent assemblies with powers over a wide range of policy areas.

The constitution was approved by an overwhelming majority in December. The "historical communities"—Catalonia, the Basque Country (now called Euskadi), and Galicia, along with Andalucia—were allowed to attain their statutes of autonomy in a short time by holding local referenda. Their regional governments were also granted the right to dissolve their assemblies and call new regional elections at their own discretion. The remaining thirteen communities attained their statutes by way of a slower constitutional route in the following years and received a somewhat more limited set of powers. In 1978 the Suárez government also reached an incomes policy agreement with the main opposition parties—the Moncloa Pact—that assured wage restraint by the unions. This allowed the government to break the inflationary surge that had taken place in the 1975–77 period. The pact and the agreement on regional devolution enshrined in the constitution are commonly regarded as the cornerstones of the consensus politics that underpinned the Spanish regime transition.

The UCD won a second term in parliamentary elections of 1979. Intense infighting among the party's differing factions and a rapidly worsening economic crisis, however, led to Suárez's resignation as prime minister in 1981. The following year Spain experienced its first democratic alternation in power when the PSOE swept to power in a new round of parliamentary elections. Under the premiership of its charismatic young leader, Felipe González, the PSOE would go on to win absolute majorities of parliamentary seats in two further elections in 1986 and 1989, and held on to power in one additional election in 1993 by forming a minority government with the support of the two principal regionalist parties: the Convergencia i Uniõ, (Catalan Convergence and Union, CiU) and the Basque Nationalist Party (PNV). The party finally lost to the main conservative opposition, the Partido Popular (Popular Party, PP), in 1996.

The PSOE's first action in power was a devaluation of the peseta coupled with the imposition of a severe austerity program. At the same time, the new government moved to resolve a mounting crisis in the banking sector, which had enjoyed a high degree of protection under the Franco regime. The party had abandoned its adherence to Marxism at a special party congress in 1979. It now set out to prepare the Spanish economy for membership in the European Community (EC) by cutting inflation and the public deficit and by restructuring ailing public industrial firms. These actions would raise the level of unemployment in Spain above 20 percent in 1985 and eventually brought the government into open confrontation with the main Socialist labor union, the Union General de Trabajadores, (General Union of Workers, UGT). Having lent its support to González's economic program during his first term in office only to see a sharp rise in the level of unemployment, in 1988 the UGT joined the rival Communist labor confederation, the Comisiones Obreras (Workers' Commissions, CC.OO), in calling a general strike and in the 1989 elections refused to campaign in favor of the PSOE. In 1986 González overcame a crucial hurdle when Spaniards voted in a referendum not to leave NATO, which Spain had joined under the UCD government in 1982. The PSOE had campaigned in 1982 on the promise of putting the issue to referendum, given the strong anti-American sentiment among a large segment of the population with left-wing sentiments. Now González found himself in the awkward position of campaigning in favor of continued membership. On the other hand, the government used the unresolved question of NATO membership as a way to speed negotiations with other European governments over Spain's entry into the EC. These negotiations had been initiated by the UCD government but had been stalled by British concerns about the implications of Spanish membership for the status of Gibraltar (owned by Britain, claimed by Spain) and the French government's concern about the impact on French agriculture. With the threat that Spanish citizens might reject NATO membership looming in the background, EC governments agreed to a treaty of accession for Spain in June 1985, and Spain officially joined the EC six months later. Nonetheless, the Spanish government had to accept a number of unfavorable provisions as part of the treaty, including a seven-year transition before Spanish fruits and vegetables could freely be sold in the community, and strict limits on the number of Spanish fishing boats that could have access to EC waters. Spain joined the Exchange Rate Mechanism (ERM) of the European Monetary System (EMS) in 1989.

The PSOE's last two terms in office were marked by growing disenchantment over the results of the government's economic policies, which included a record unemployment rate of 24 percent in 1994, as well as by a series of major political scandals. The most important scandal involved allegations that the government had financed a clandestine counterterrorist organization, the GAL, that had carried out assassinations of suspected ETA members in the 1980s. The scandal played an important role in the PSOE's loss of a parliamentary majority in the 1993 elections and its eventual defeat by the PP in 1996.

Yet the PP victory fell short of a parliamentary majority. The new conservative government, under the leadership of prime minister José María Aznar, was therefore forced, as the PSOE had been during its last term, to reach a parliamentary alliance with the two main regionalist parties, the Catalan CiU and the Basque PNV. This placed the central government in the position of having to renegotiate the distribution of powers and resources to regional governments. The conservative government was also struck by an intense campaign of assassinations of regional and municipal PP representatives by ETA. This wave of assassinations heightened tension between the government and the PNV over the question of negotiations with Herri Batasuna (HB), a political party ascribing to a radical separatist agenda and generally considered to represent ETA's political wing. In the late 1990s Spain thus saw the reemergence of many of the regional issues that the 1978 constitution had sought to put to rest.

BIBLIOGRAPHY

Carr, Raymond, and Juan Pablo Fusi. *Spain, Dictatorship to Democracy.* London: Allen and Unwin, 1981.

Gillespie, Richard, Fernando Rodrigo, and Jonathan Story, eds. *Democratic Spain: Reshaping External Relations in a Changing World.* New York: Routledge, 1995.

Jackson, Gabriel. *The Spanish Republic and the Civil War, 1931–39.* Princeton, N.J.: Princeton University Press, 1965.

Maravall, José María. *Dictatorship and Political Dissent: Students and Workers in Franco's Spain.* London: Tavistock, 1978.

Payne, Stanley G. *The Franco Regime: 1936–75.* Madison: University of Wisconsin Press, 1987.

———. *Spain's First Democracy: The Second Republic, 1931–1936.* Madison: University of Wisconsin Press, 1993.

Preston, Paul. *Franco: A Biography.* New York: Harper Collins, 1993.

———. *The Triumph of Democracy in Spain.* New York: Methuen, 1986.

Thomas, Hugh. *The Spanish Civil War.* New York: Hamish Hamilton, 1986.

Tortella Casares, Gabriel. *Desarollo de la España contepor-anea: historia econimica del siglo 19 y 20.* Madrid: Alianza Editorial, 1995.

Sofia A. Perez

Political Parties

Spain's present-day political parties are the outcome of the democratic transition of 1976–78, which ended almost four decades of authoritarian dictatorship. The party system includes a number of national-level parties alongside parties that represent regionalist or separatist agendas and whose support is based in one of the autonomous communities created by the constitution of 1978.

In the decade (1975–85) following the transition from Francoism, the party system remained in flux largely because right-wing political groups, burdened by their association with the authoritarian Franco dictatorship, were unable to organize a credible electoral alternative to the Left. The party that won the first two parliamentary elections in 1977 and 1979, the Union of the Democratic Center (UCD), was a loose coalition of centrist forces, including social democrats, liberals, and Christian democrats, that was brought under the leadership of prime minister Adolfo Suárez in early 1977. From its inception the UCD was marred by internecine conflict among its ideologically disparate factions. Following the defeat of the UCD by the Spanish Socialist Workers Party (PSOE) in 1982, the UCD fell apart, leaving a major political vacuum on the right of the political spectrum. This allowed the PSOE to win parliamentary majorities in two subsequent elections, in 1986 and 1989. After winning an additional election in 1993 but loosing its parliamentary majority, the PSOE remained in power for one additional term by forming a minority government with the support of the two principal regionalist parties in the lower house of the national legislature (Cortes): the Basque Nationalist Party (PNV) and the Catalan Convergence and Union (CiU). In 1996 the PSOE's dominance over Spanish politics came to an end when the conservative Popular Party (PP) staged its first national electoral victory. The PP, nonetheless, also failed to win an absolute majority of seats in the lower house and was forced into a similar parliamentary alliance with the PNV, CiU, and a smaller regional party, the Canary Islands Coalition.

Along with Spain's history of regional nationalisms, the other major influence on the party system has been the electoral system introduced during the transition of regimes. The system is based on the principle of proportional representation with closed and blocked party lists, but it also imposes a number of correctives to this principle, including a minimum number of seats per district irrespective of population, the d'Hondt system for counting votes, and a 3 percent threshold in large districts. These features favor rural electoral districts over urban districts and generally produce a strong overrepresentation of the two parties that receive the largest number of votes within any given electoral district. The system was intended to protect conservative constituencies represented in the UCD and to favor the emergence of a national two-party system that would produce parliamentary majorities. However, with the absence of a viable conservative opposition during the 1980s, the system favored the PSOE in much of Spain while leading to the emergence of distinct local party systems in Catalonia and the Basque country (Euskadi). The upshot in the 1990s was a regionally fragmented "few" party system that made it difficult for any of the national-level parties to form a government without the support of the regionalist parties.

The major players in this "few" party system are the PSOE, PP, PNV, CiU, and United Left (IU). The latter is an alliance of leftist parties organized in the 1980s under the leadership of the Spanish Communist Party (PCE). Two general ideological tendencies can be observed within the party system: the competition to capture the political center between the two main national-level parties—PSOE and PP— and the entrenchment of the regionalist cleavage in national elections.

The centrist tendency can clearly be observed in the evolution of the national-level parties since the political transition of regimes. The PSOE, founded in 1879 as a socialist party and the principal party of the Left during the Second Republic, declared itself a Marxist party at its 1976 congress. After its second electoral defeat in 1979, the party's leader, Felipe González, forced the party to abandon its Marxist label, and in its 1982 electoral program the party also dropped a promise of nationalizations in favor of a more moderate program of economic reforms. Once in power, González appointed a neoliberally minded economic team that imposed a strict austerity program and geared economic policy toward the goal of membership in the European Community. These policies brought the party into direct conflict with the socialist trade union, the UGT. Yet, the party's shift to the center was popular with large segments of the electorate that sought a moderate leftist political alternative.

The success of the PSOE's centrist electoral strategy was also reflected in the fate of its main rival to the left, the Spanish Communist Party (PCE). Still under the leadership of historical figures such as Santiago Carillo and Dolores Ibárruri (la Pasionaria), the PCE received around 10 percent of the vote in the 1977 and 1979 elections. Sectarian conflict within the party and voter defections to the PSOE, however, led to a decline in the PCE's share of votes to 4 percent in 1982. In 1986 the party formed an alliance with a number of small leftist groups, including pacifists who opposed Spanish membership in NATO, and began to run under the label of the United Left (IU). In the following elections in 1989, 1993, and 1996, the IU drew a considerable share of votes away from the PSOE. But the representational bias against smaller national parties imposed by Spanish electoral rules, which limited the IU's number of seats in the Chambers of Deputies, and the radical posture maintained by the party's leadership, kept the party from becoming a viable coalition partner for the PSOE in 1993 and 1996.

The centrist trend in the Spanish political system is also reflected in the evolution of the PP. Originally called the Popular Alliance (AP), the party was founded in 1976 by reformist members of the Franco regime under the leadership of Manuel Fraga Iribarne. Because of these origins, the AP was seen by much of the electorate as a party of the far right, and in the first two parliamentary elections it received a meager 8 and 6 percent of the vote, respectively. In 1982, with the dramatic decline of the UCD, the AP's share of the vote rose to 26 percent, and it became the main opposition party. Thereafter, however, the party's vote stagnated. In 1988 Fraga changed the party's name to Popular Party, and soon thereafter he named a young politician without a past in the Franco regime, José María Aznar, as the party's candidate for prime minister. These changes were reflected in a sharp rise in the party's vote in 1993. When it came to power in 1996 with Aznar as prime minister, the party shifted further away from its conservative origins by agreeing to devolve more powers and resources to the regions as part of its alliance with the PNV and CiU, and by seeking agreement with the labor unions to support its economic program.

While the Spanish electoral system encourages centripetal electoral competition among the national parties, it has also supported the position of the major regionalist parties in national parliamentary elections. In Catalonia, the nationalist center-right coalition, CiU, became the party that receives the second-largest share of votes in national parliamentary elections early during the transition. This allowed its leader, Jordi Pujol, to become the principal power broker in national politics once the PSOE lost its absolute majority in 1993. In the Basque country, the center-right PNV has played a similar role in national elections. However, the nationalist vote in Euskadi has been more fragmented than in Catalonia, with a larger share going to the leftist nationalist party Euskadiko Ezkerra (Basque Left) and the radical separatist party Herri Batasuna (Popular Unity).

BIBLIOGRAPHY

Colomer, Josep M., ed. *Political Institutions in Europe.* New York: Routledge, 1996.

Gunther, Richard, Giacomo Sani, and Goldie Shabad. *Spain after Franco: The Making of a Competitive Party System.* Los Angeles: University of California Press, 1986.

Morlino, Leonardo. *Democracy between Consolidation and Crisis: Parties, Groups, and Citizens in Southern Europe.* New York: Oxford University Press, 1998.

Sofía A. Pérez

SEE ALSO González, Felipe; Pujol, Jordi

Regionalism

In 1978 the Spanish constitution established the Estado de Autonomías (State of the Autonomies), officially recognizing the regionalist tradition of the nation. Today, seventeen autonomous communities (and two small enclaves in North Africa) constitute the political system.

Many of the current regions existed as political entities long before the formation of modern Spain in 1479; it was during the common effort of the Reconquest that they pledged their loyalty to the crown of Castile in exchange for a royal oath to their local constitutions, or *fueros*. As the Spanish government became more centralized over time, especially after the Bourbons took over in 1700, *fueros* were reduced or eliminated, creating tensions between Madrid and the historic regions. During the politically turbulent nineteenth century much of the violence, whether by Basque Carlists or the urban proletariat of Catalonia, had to do with center-periphery conflicts over home rule. Even the alignments during the Spanish Civil War were skewed by autonomist desires, as Basque Catholics sided with the anticlerical Second Republic that had granted them an autonomy statute on October 13, 1936.

Under the Franco dictatorship (1939–75), regional protests developed into a major source of opposition to the regime. The intensity of Basque-Navarrese, Catalan, and Galician regionalism is explained by three factors: the peripheral isolation of these areas nurtured regional languages and distinct cultures; their relative wealth (or poverty in the case of Galicia) increased the desire to control their own financial affairs; and their *foral* regimes (those with special privileges) had been either the most enduring or the most cherished. Obsessed that Spain would fall apart, Franco severely repressed the regionalists. He prohibited public use of their languages and "occupied" their lands with national forces of public order, so that the regionalists turned to violence. The most dangerous regionalist group by far was the Basque ETA (Basque Country and Freedom). In the 1960s and 1970s ETA violence was considerable, accompanied by spectacular public trials of its members accused of killings. In 1973, ETA assassinated Prime Minister Luis Carrero Blanco, and in 1975 a new set of antiterrorist laws covered all sorts of complicity as martial law was imposed on the Basque country.

After Franco's death on November 20, 1975, the transition became twofold: from dictatorship to parliamentary democracy and from the unitary state to one of autonomous communities, each with its own regional parliament. While this extra layer of government was costly, it also proved popular, for all fifty provinces had voluntarily joined in the formation of seventeen autonomous communities by 1983, following procedures outlined in the constitution of December 29, 1978. The autonomous communities range in size from Andalusia, which covers a large portion of southern Spain, to one-province autonomous communities such as Cantabria.

The devolution of powers from the center to the autonomous communities was at first negotiated individually, but now by law self-governing rights granted must be uniform in all the communities. Catalonia has been the forerunner of late in gaining local control for all the regions over health, education, prisons, ports, roads, police systems, and a larger portion of income tax revenues because its president, Jordi Pujol, has become a deciding factor in national politics. In 1996 sixteen Catalan votes in the Cortes, along with five from Basque nationalists, allowed José María Aznar to become prime minister.

Any assessment of the Estado de Autonomías has to be positive. ETA has been discredited and violence is rare, separatism is implausible, and the overwhelming majority of Spaniards are satisfied with the current political system. Three Spanish sociologists conducted a study in 1990 to measure regional versus national loyalties. They found that while regional attachments have strengthened since 1978 in both the historic and nonhistoric regions, the parallel phenomenon of dual identity, as a Spaniard and as an autonomous community citizen, has emerged to become the dominant sentiment in Spain. Furthermore, only in Basque-Navarra and Catalonia did as many as 20 percent consider that autonomy included the right to choose independence (which is illegal). When asked directly about progress in the devolution of powers to the regional governments, the majority were satisfied with the present level of rights. This information bodes well for the stability of the Spanish state, proving perhaps that the resolution of the regionalist problem was crucial in the transition to democracy.

BIBLIOGRAPHY

Arango, E. Ramón. *Spain: Democracy Regained,* 2d ed. Boulder, Col.: Westview Press, 1995.

Clark, Robert P. "The Basques, Madrid and Regional Autonomy: Conflicting Perspectives between Center and Periphery in Spain," in William D. Phillips Jr. and Carla Rahn Phillips, eds. *Marginated Groups in Spanish and Portuguese History.* Minneapolis: Society for Spanish and Portuguese Historical Studies, 1989.

Conversi, Daniele. *The Basques, the Catalans and Spain.* Reno: University of Nevada Press, 1997.

Ferrando, Manuel García, et al. *La conciencia nacional y regional en la España de las autonomías.* Madrid: Centro de Investigaciones Sociológicas, 1994.

Regina A. Mezei

SEE ALSO Basque Country; Catalonia; Galicia; Pujol, Jordi

Economy

Despite occasional setbacks, the period since 1945 was for Spain one of economic expansion and modernization. The development of the Spanish economy can be divided into four distinct periods: 1939–59, marked the arduous process of rebuilding following the civil war and characterized by strong autarkic policies; 1959–70, a period of rapid growth sometimes referred to as the Spanish miracle; 1970–85, a slowdown of growth and the onset of recession in part due to international factors; 1985–97, a return to equilibrium and increasing prosperity.

The destructive effects of the Spanish Civil War (1936–39) left the economy in ruins. Industrial installations and infrastructure were destroyed or heavily damaged, agricultural production was stagnant, and the flood of refugees and exiles drained the country of both human and economic capital. In addition, international antipathy toward the dictatorship of Francisco Franco led to an economic embargo sanctioned by the United Nations; Spain was also denied access to U.S.-sponsored Marshall Plan aid. Economic isolation combined with nationalist rhetoric committed the Franco regime to pursue autarkic policies.

Shortages of foodstuffs, energy, and capital equipment were commonplace during this period. Serious price inflation resulted from increased public spending, static agricultural production, and inordinately high wages. Elevated production costs and a gradually worsening trade deficit prevented modernization. Finally, a highly centralized and inefficient administration hampered economic development.

By the late 1950s the failure of autarkic planning seemed clear and the regime began to modify economic policy. The National Stabilization Plan of 1959 marked the end of autarky and the beginning of a period of rapid expansion up to 1970. The plan aimed to encourage internal growth and reestablish external balance. The elimination of public subsidies combined with strict limits on credit and government spending helped curb inflation. The plan increased external trade by fixing currency exchange and lowering restrictions on foreign investment. Franco's decision to abandon protectionism in favor of a more open economy also coincided with a general period of growth in the Western economies.

The plan began to pay dividends as rapid economic growth developed by 1961. The liberalization of import restrictions brought a much needed influx of capital and modern equipment. This led to increased industrial production and efficiency as Spanish firms rapidly modernized. Investment rose owing to elevated levels of foreign capital and the remittances of Spanish workers abroad. The balance of trade improved further during the 1960s as tourism became the country's most valuable source of foreign currency. Economic growth provided jobs for many, particularly female workers, who had remained unemployed or underemployed since the Civil War. The number of women employed outside the home grew by almost one million between 1960 and 1970. These new workers became a key factor in the sustained economic expansion of the 1960s.

The period was not a complete success, however, and its limitations combined with a deteriorating international situation, plunged Spain into crisis from 1970 to 1985. Terms of trade, although improved during the 1960s, remained unfavorable. They continued to decline as prices of raw materials and energy products rose precipitously in the 1970s. In particular Spain's dependency on oil imports triggered a rise in consumer prices. Government policy also contributed to the rapid growth of inflation. The practice of linking salary increases to the rate of inflation resulted in enormously high production costs. Furthermore, an inequitable and inefficient taxation system led to rampant evasion and the growth of a large-scale underground economy. In addition, the ineffectiveness of continual government intervention in the economy further exacerbated the crisis.

Political uncertainty limited government reaction to the growing recession. The assassination of Admiral Luis Carrero Blanco, the expected candidate to succeed as leader, and the death of Franco himself in November 1975, paralyzed nearly all government activity. The new head of government, King Juan Carlos I, was committed to economic and political reform. But owing to the difficult and uncertain transitional period, little was done to alleviate economic difficulties.

The first serious attempt to deal with the crisis occurred following the national elections of 1977. The 1977 Moncloa Pact was an all-party agreement designed to introduce reform and stimulate growth. A key component was to remove government intervention and move toward an open-market economy similar to those of other Western European nations. The agreement also revised the old tax code, reduced the growth of wages, and limited public spending. Adjustment and change continued following the election of Felipe González as prime minister in 1982. Economic liberalization continued as Spain completely abandoned the protectionism that had characterized the economy since 1939. González also pushed for stronger integration in the European Community (EC).

Anticipation of Spain's full partnership in the EC in 1986 ushered in a new period of growth in economy from 1985 to 1997. This period was characterized by reduced inflation, structural and technical modernization of industry, and improved financial markets.

Sustained growth continued into the late 1980s but not without problems. High production costs encouraged growing inflation, and the unemployment rate skyrocketed. By 1990 the percentage of unemployed was almost twice the average rate of EC nations. These factors weakened the international competitiveness of Spanish firms and resulted in diminishing investment and expanding public debt. Following larger international trends, the Spanish economy slipped into a brief period of recession during 1992–93.

However, by 1995 key economic indicators signaled improvement. Continued growth was due in part to a change in political leadership and the resulting drive to achieve integration into the European Economic and Monetary Union. In 1996 a conservative government led by José María Aznar entered office. It embarked on a program to reduce public spending, increase productivity, and lower domestic prices. Largely successful, these policies cut inflation and the public deficit by half in fewer than two years. These levels positioned Spain to enter into the first phase of monetary union that began on January 1, 1999.

The current economic position of Spain is not completely positive. Rigid employment regulation has kept the official unemployment rate at three times the European average. In addition, wage growth continues to influence negatively the cost of production and domestic prices. Potentially more problematic is rapid deindustrialization brought on by low investment, high production costs, and decreasing competitiveness.

The development on the Spanish economy since 1945 has largely been one of growth and modernization despite occasional periods of crisis brought on by internal mismanagement and external pressures. The transformation from an isolated, protectionist economy to a true free-market system took almost forty years. Real gains were achieved to raise Spain from one of the most economically backward Western European nations to one of the richest. Nevertheless, key problems and challenges must be overcome if Spain is to continue to be economically healthy in the next century.

BIBLIOGRAPHY

Alonso Zaldivar, Carlos. *Spain beyond Myths.* Madrid: Alianza Editorial, 1992.

Carreras, Albert, Jordi Nadal, and Carles Sudrià, eds. *La economía española en el siglo XX: Una Perspectiva histórica.* Barcelona: Ariel, 1987.

Garcia Delgado, J. L., ed. *La economiá española de la transición y la democracia.* Madrid: CIS, 1990.

Harrison, Joseph. *The Spanish Economy in the Twentieth Century.* London: Croom Helm, 1985.

Lieberman, Sima. *Growth and Crisis in the Spanish Economy 1940–1993.* London: Routledge, 1995.

Brian D. Bunk

Labor Movements

The history of Spanish labor movements since 1945 must be viewed in two distinct periods: that under the dictatorship of Francisco Franco (1939–75) and the other within the democratic system that evolved following his death.

Franco designated control of the labor movement to the Fascist Party, the Falange, and therefore created a single union firmly under the control of the state. Representation was highest within industry, while agricultural sectors were less organized. The labor movement followed principles of Catholic state corporatism, attempting to eliminate class conflict while promoting Catholic social principles. Despite being under governmental control, the syndicates held some authority over certain aspects of economic production, and a system of factory councils of elected workers provided limited representation.

This system of labor organization controlled the workers but failed to generate true loyalty. The movement was weak in areas of the country such as Catalonia and Asturias where worker organization had been the strongest before the civil war. In many of these areas outlawed pre–civil war organizations continued to operate clandestinely.

In the 1960s a series of measures began reorganizing the official movement. The Organic Law of 1966 removed elements of fascist doctrine but did not significantly alter the function or structure of the organization. Two separate Syndicate Laws in 1969 and 1971 improved the system of worker representation, broadened social assistance, and granted other economic concessions. These changes were partly a reaction to growing labor unrest and the rise of a powerful new union called the Workers Commissions.

The Workers Commissions were a clandestine organization founded during the 1950s by Marcelino Camacho in the northern province of Asturias. They were politically independent but did have close ties to the Communist Party. The commissions were instrumental in directing numerous strikes in the 1960s and 1970s. Although strikes remained technically illegal during this period, the amount of time lost because of work stoppages increased tenfold between 1966 and 1975. The activities of the commissions contributed to the breakdown of the

Franco regime in its final years, and the organization was considered by security officials to be the single greatest threat to the stability of the government.

The second stage of labor organization began following the death of Franco. Several newly legalized labor unions helped negotiate the Moncloa Pact of 1977, an attempt to improve labor relations and stimulate economic growth. Owing to its prominent role in the disturbances of the Franco era, the Workers Commissions became the largest labor organization in Spain. However, during the 1980s, the pre–civil war General Union of Workers began to reassert itself and eventually superseded its rival by 1982.

A series of agreements between 1980 and 1986 stabilized labor relations. But the system broke down by the late 1980s as the government promoted economic policies favorable to employers. For the first time the Workers Commissions and the General Union of Workers began cooperating and staged a series of joint actions including a successful one-day general strike in 1988. Although lesser general strikes were called in 1992 and 1994, the power of the unions was already on the decline. Economic liberalization reduced the role of government in labor negotiations and introduced greater flexibility in employment practices. This, combined with government programs aimed at reducing unemployment by creating temporary or low-paying employment, limited the effectiveness of the organizations. By 1994 the groups officially represented only 10 percent of workers, and their real influence was limited to industrial wage bargaining.

Throughout much of the period after 1945, Spanish labor movements were fully subjugated and controlled by the state. However, the rise of the Workers Commissions in the 1960s led to serious mobilization and demonstrations by workers. These disturbances and strikes represented a real threat to the Franco dictatorship and helped prevent any chance of a continuation of the regime following the dictator's death. The labor organizations enjoyed a brief renaissance in membership and power during the late 1970s and early 1980s, culminating in the general strike of 1988. However, structural changes in the economy and declining membership have weakened both the strength and the influence of the unions.

BIBLIOGRAPHY

Aparicio, Miguel. *El sindicalismo vertical y la formación del estado franquista.* Barcelona: Eunibar, 1980.

Fishman, Robert M. *Working Class Organization and the Return to Democracy in Spain.* Ithaca, N.Y.: Cornell University Press, 1990.

Payne, Stanley G. *The Franco Regime, 1936–1975.* Madison: University of Wisconsin Press, 1987.

Pérez Díaz, Victor. *The Return of Civil Society: The Emergence of Democratic Spain.* Cambridge, Mass.: Harvard University Press, 1993.

Wozniak, Lynne. *Industrial Modernization and Working-class Protest in Socialist Spain.* South Bend, Ind.: University of Notre Dame, 1991.

Brian D. Bunk

Education

Spain's educational system remained virtually unchanged from the mid-nineteenth century until 1970. In the 1980s and 1990s, a series of reforms were introduced to decentralize and democratize education and to adapt it to the needs of the European postindustrial economy. The Education Act of 1857, or Moyano Law, introduced a centralized system, that left education in the hands of the private sector (mainly Catholic institutions). The state played a subsidiary role, providing schooling only where the private sector did not. Education, in part due to the lack of public resources, became a privilege of the economic elite.

The attempts by the authorities of the Spanish Second Republic (1931–39) to promote the construction of public schools, equality, secularism, and coeducation were overturned in 1939, with defeat of the Republic by the Nationalists in the Spanish Civil War. The dictatorial regime of Francisco Franco centralized education even more, using it for the ideological indoctrination of pupils. Education was to serve as the basis for the building of a new social and political order, inspired by Catholic principles. Between the 1940s and the 1960s, private schools flourished.

The process of economic industrialization promoted by Franco's technocratic regime set in motion forces that worked against its educational model. As modernization ensued, the number of Spaniards joining religious orders declined, decimating the staffs of the private schools, and forcing the schools to hire growing numbers of non-religious teachers. Since religious schools did not pay salaries to religious teachers, the secular teachers became an economic burden. Moreover, industrialization required the education of laboring people (especially for technical positions) to serve the needs of the market, but the system provided deficient technical education.

The government responded with the approval of Ley General de Educación (General Law of Education) in 1970, which introduced a unitary, free system of Educación General Básica (General Basic Education). The reorientation of the state's role in education caused a significant increase in teachers' wages, which had been historically neglected, and, as a result, also pushed up the salaries of teachers in private schools, thus adding to the financial difficulties of the private schools. As a means of compensation, the private sector lobbied to obtain a system of grants from the state to subsidize private education.

The government established a generous program of subsidies in the 1970s, thanks to which 96 percent of the students in the ages of compulsory education (six to sixteen), either in public schools or in subsidized private schools, received free education. The grants provided a system of sticks and carrots that the government could manipulate to bring about reforms in the grant-aided schools: democracy in management through participation of teachers, parents and students on governing bodies, adherence to state-defined norms, and freedom of conscience for both teachers and students. With the collapse of Francoism with the death of Franco in 1975, religion was removed from the curriculum as a compulsory subject in the 1980s.

With these reforms, the technocratic administration expected to meet the needs of new industrial employers and to facilitate the incorporation of migrants who had settled in the industrial fringes in the cities. Between 1939 and 1964, the number of children receiving pre-school education and compulsory basic education in state schools remained constant at 2.5 million. In the late 1970s, it surpassed four million. At the Bachillerato (high school) level, children in state schools grew from 82,000 in the 1960–61 academic year, to 700,000 in 1980–81. Attendance at private schools remained stable.

The priority in the early 1980s was decentralization, to increase the scope for communities, provinces, and individual schools and teachers to modify the curriculum in light of local or individual needs, and to teach in a community language other than Spanish. At school level, governing bodies comprised roughly equal numbers of teachers, on the one hand, and parents and pupils on the other, all of them elected from their constituencies. However, these governing bodies normally focused on management issues, leaving curriculum development to the teachers' councils. The reform of the curriculum emphasized consultation, research and development, as opposed to educational theory, and rests on constructivist notions of learning and skill-related processes rather than the transmission of important knowledge. Educational ideology no longer gave weight to Catholic nationalist doctrine, as in the Franco period. Instead, it focused on a set of values that emphasized democracy, Europeanization, modernization, prosperity, equality of opportunity, and individual development.

The Spanish school system consists of several levels: preschool, elementary school (ages 6 to 13), secondary school (ages 14 to 16), technical and vocational, preuniversity or bachillerato (16 to 18), and university. Education is compulsory until the age of sixteen. The main curriculum areas of primary education are language (Spanish and/or the community language, e.g. Basque) and literature, mathematics, natural and social environment, arts (including music), physical education, religion (voluntary), and, after the age of eight, a foreign language. In secondary education, the main areas are natural sciences, physical education, art, geography, history and social sciences, foreign languages, language (Spanish and/or the community language) and literature, mathematics, music, religion (voluntary), and technology.

The bachillerato has a common core comprised of language and literature (Spanish and the community language, where appropriate), a foreign language, mathematics, history, geography, natural sciences, philosophy, and physical education. Students must also choose one of four modules: arts, natural and health sciences, humanities and social sciences, or technology. The bachillerato in human and social sciences, for instance, includes options in Latin, Greek, epistemology, economics and sociology, history and geography, and history of art. After completion of the bachillerato, students must take a university entrance test that evaluates their academic maturity, as well as their skills and knowledge in each major subject area. The grades attained are averaged with those of the bachillerato, and submitted to the universities the student wishes to attend.

The curriculum of the vocational schools, called educación técnico profesional, is designed jointly by the educators and the business sector. Starting at the first phase of compulsory secondary education, it emphasizes technology as a foundation subject, as well as professionally related activities, and combines these courses with some others from the bachillerato. Thus, the vocational schools prepare students either for university and/or professional modules of the highest grade. The second module of formación profesional específica, is made up of professional modules related to specific professions.

The Spanish university system was one of the most centralized of Europe until the first important reform of 1970. University education was a state monopoly, it functioned mainly to channel the children of the elite into the professions, and its curricula was mandated by the Ministry of Education, neglecting research. Franco purged university ranks of those who were not sympathetic to the new regime. Teachers had to be members of the national Falangist movement, and to possess certificates of loyalty to the regime. The Church had a strong influence. Students were obliged to belong to the approved student union and to study religious, political, and physical education.

University syllabi had to be approved by the Ministry of Education, following consultations with an advisory committee made up by the presidents of the universities (rectores), and the oldest professors (catedráticos) had a lot of power in their departments. The classrooms were overcrowded and there was little interaction between teachers and students. The Law of University Reform (Ley de Reforma Universitaria) of 1983 tried to make the university system more democratic, by addressing the issue of the balance of power between the State, the autonomous communities, community interests, and the university (through the Consejos Sociales and the Consejo de Universidades, or Social Councils and Council of Universities), as well as the balance of power within the university. Autonomous communities (regions) were given authority to approve the creation of new universities, within certain guidelines established by the central government. In the early 1980s, sixty percent of the teachers were non-tenured. In 1988 many tenure track positions were opened, but ninety percent of them were filled internally, some times at the expense of recognized professors. Between 1983 and 1993, over 500 curriculum plans were standardized.

A report by the Organization for Economic Co-Operation and Development, commissioned by the Ministry of Education in 1987 to explore Spain's need to increase its competitiveness in the European market, concluded that the Spanish system had to add a strong international dimension to its curricula, to adapt them more effectively to professional demands, to reinforce scientific and technical research, eliminate the overcrowding of some campuses, and attract more students away from the humanities and social sciences to basic sciences and technology. However, the growth of the university system has been dramatic. In 1960, there were twelve universities, all of them public. In the year 2000, there were 69, sixteen of them private. Access to the universities has also risen. In the 1980s, almost half of Spain's university students had parents who had not received more than elementary school education. In 1991, twenty percent of the Spanish population held a Bachelor's degree (the second highest percentage in Europe).

In the 1999–2000 academic year there were 8,555,321 students in Spain. Of those, 1,119,740 were in pre-school education, 2,519,041 in primary education, and 2,035,002 in compulsory secondary education. Sixty percent of them attended public schools. 1,278,781 studied non-compulsory secondary education (75 percent of them in public schools). 27,757 received special education (50 percent in public schools). And 1,575,000 attended universities (93 percent to public institutions).

BIBLIOGRAPHY

Boyd-Barrett, Oliver, and Pamela O'Malley, eds. *Education Reform in Democratic Spain.* London: Routledge, 1995.

Council of Europe. *Secondary Education in Spain.* Strasbourg, France: Council of Europe, 1996.

Lawlor, Teresa, Mike Rigby, and Manuel Per Yruela, eds. *Contemporary Spain: Essays and Texts on Politics, Economics, Education and Employment, and Society.* Massachusetts: Addison-Wesley Pub., Co., 1998.

Organization for Economic Co-Operation and Development. *Reviews of National Policies for Education: Spain.* Washington, D.C., OECD, 1987.

Pablo Toral

Press

For much of the period after 1945, the liberty of Spanish journalists was sharply limited by government regulation; complete freedom of the press was established only in 1977.

In 1938 Francisco Franco enacted a law giving control of the press to the Fascist Party, the Falange. This decree called for heavy censorship and government appointment of editors and senior staff. With only minor changes this system remained in effect until 1966. Following even tighter controls during World War II, some restrictions were lifted in 1945. Although it still called for prior censorship, the modified code allowed for the expression of ideas as long as they did not attack the fundamental tenets of the state. Throughout the period of Franco's rule the press served as a means of promoting and legitimizing the dictatorship while espousing an ideology of unity, security, and opportunity.

While the limitations on the press remained virtually unchanged for the next two decades, the official tone shifted during the 1950s as the regime sought to distance itself from fascism. In the early 1950s a movement led in part by the Catholic Church attempted to modify restrictions and eliminate prior censorship. This effort proved ineffectual at ending controls, and it was only with the Press Law of 1966 that things began to change decisively.

In large part the work of Minister of Information and Tourism Manuel Fraga Iribarne, the law ended the system of censorship that had existed since 1938. While still banning attacks on the regime and other particular subjects, the measure did give editorial control over to journalists. Furthermore, publishing companies were given the freedom to appoint editors and staff without government approval.

The new freedoms led to an increase in the number of periodicals and their readership. Within a few years 129 new publications appeared in Madrid alone, with 8 of them being dailies. Total newspaper circulation in the entire country grew from 500,000 in 1945 to 2,500,000 by 1967. The new publications and increased readership played a key role before and during the transition from dictatorship to democracy. For the first time journalists could report freely on political and social questions without prior government censorship.

The Press Law of 1966 was viewed by conservative elements of the regime as a disaster. As political and social disturbances grew in the late 1960s and early 1970s, many hard-liners blamed the Press Law for producing or exacerbating them. By 1968 some limitations of the law were implemented but without fundamentally altering its basic structure or reimposing prior censorship. The government reserved the right of inspection and retained control over foreign news. Those who violated the law faced suspension of publication as well as heavy fines. The leading proponent of the measure, Manuel Fraga, was dismissed from his cabinet position.

Following the death of Franco in 1975 regulation of the press changed dramatically. Just six months later, in May 1976, *El Pais* became the first new independent newspaper to be established since the 1930s. The final legal restrictions on publication were eliminated in 1977, allowing for complete and unfettered coverage of the first free democratic elections since 1936. Finally, the constitution of 1978 included an article guaranteeing freedom of the press.

Because Spain was ruled by a dictator for much of the period following 1945, freedom of the press was severely limited. Only the Press Law of 1966 created a more open and independent press. The effects of the Press Law are difficult to underestimate. The limited, but real, freedoms that the measure provided enabled the Spanish press to play a key role in promoting democratic principles and norms. The role of the press helped insure that the transition to democracy was peaceful.

BIBLIOGRAPHY

Barrera, Carlos. *Periodismo y franquismo: de la censura a la apertura.* Barcelona: Ediciones Internacionales Universitarias, 1995.

Haywood, Paul. *The Government and Politics of Spain.* New York: St. Martin's Press, 1995.

Maxwell, Kenneth. ed. *The Press and the Rebirth of Iberian Democracy.* Westport, Conn.: Greenwood Press, 1983.

Payne, Stanley G. *The Franco regime, 1936–1975.* Madison: University of Wisconsin Press, 1987.

Sinova, Justino. *La censura de prensa durante el franquismo, 1936–1951.* Madrid: Espasa Calpe, 1989.

Terrón Montero, Javier. *La prensa en España durante el régimen de Franco.* Madrid: CIS, 1981.

Brian D. Bunk

Water Law

Irrigation has always played an important role in the agriculture of Spain, a semiarid country with a dry, Mediterranean climate. Spanish irrigation systems have an extraordinary history, dating in many instances to the Roman and Islamic presence. Since the late nineteenth century the Spanish state has intervened vigorously in water policy, beginning with a comprehensive water law in 1879, and followed by the creation of watershed management authorities in 1926. In 1985 a new water law was implemented to correct deficiencies of the earlier law and to adjust water policy to the creation of regional autonomous communities established in the 1978 constitution.

The 1985 water law distinguished water renewed through the hydrological cycle and subject to state ownership from nonrenewable water capable of being privatized. The use of ground water, relatively unfettered under the 1879 water law, became highly circumscribed by the state. Watershed management authorities were given key powers under the law. Their control over watersheds exceeds the territorial boundaries of the autonomous communities created in the 1978 constitution. Regional watershed authorities are authorized to elaborate, modify, and revise watershed management plans; administer and control public hydraulic property; plan, construct, and manage water works funded through their own funds and through state funds; and contract public works with other public and private organisms.

Another distinction of the 1985 water law is its emphasis on water-use planning. Population growth, changes in lifestyle, urbanization, industrialization, and a series of serious droughts dramatically increased water demand since the 1960s. To meet the challenge, the 1985 water law charged a newly created National Water Council with overseeing the drafting of a National Water Plan and balancing the interests of regional autonomous communities and the central government. When a draft plan was released in 1993, it triggered a national debate over whether to pursue a traditional course of increasing water supply by constructing dams and transferring water from water-surplus basins to water-deficit basins, or a new one of instituting measures to manage demand and save water.

Autonomous communities have tended to lay claim to water that originates within their boundaries and to object to the central government's specifying where such water should flow. Family farmers found an effective voice in the National Federation of Irrigation Communities for their resistance to demand management. An incipient environmental movement gained strength during the 1990s and constituted an important force in its own right. Environmental concerns parallel European Union (EU) pressures to establish water quality standards and minimum levels for rivers to maintain biotic diversity. The environmental components of the water law synthesized five EU directives that link surface and underground water together as part of the public domain. Environmentalists criticized the high economic and environmental costs of dam construction, and parliament questioned the wisdom of expanding irrigated land in an era when the EU and the General Agreement on Tariffs and Trade were (GATT) pressuring countries to reduce cultivated land. Interbasin water transfers, while logical economically, caused immense political and administrative problems. Both surface and groundwater cross municipal, *comarcal* (district), provincial, and autonomous community boundaries. These political units exert conflicting claims over water, making it difficult to equalize distribution in the case of surface water and quell the overuse of acquifers and contamination of groundwater reserves.

The 1985 water law has opened a new era of water policy reflecting global trends toward demand management and away from supply augmentation. It marks the end of Franco-era policies of large-scale dam construction, a laissez-faire approach toward ground water, and top-down, nonparticipatory, policy making.

BIBLIOGRAPHY

Embid Irujo, Antonio, et al. *El plan hidroloaico nacional.* Madrid: Editorial Civitas S.A., 1993.

Martin-Retortillo, Sebastian. "Competencias constitucionales y autonomicas en materia de aguas." *Revista de Administracion Publica* 128 (1992): 23–83.

Naylon, J. "An Appraisal of Spanish Irrigation and Land-settlement Policy since 1939." *Iberian Studies* 2 (1973): 12–19.

Silvers, George Matthew. "The Natural Environment in Spain: A Study of Environmental History, Legislation, and Attitudes." *Tulane Environmental Law Journal* 5 (1991): 285–316.

Tens, Ortiz de, and Maria del Carmen. *Planificacion hidroloaica.* Madrid: Marcial Pons, 1994.

David Guillet

Späte, Margarete (1958–)

German politician. Margarete Späte was born in Leipzig, East Germany, on February 26, 1958. She grew up in Kayna, and completed her *Abitur* in 1976. She trained as a stone mason and restorer and then studied sculpture at the Superior School for Art and Design in (Hochschule Burg Gielschenstein) Halle. In 1980 she took over her father's stone mason and sculpture workshop in Kayna and was placed in charge of the reconstruction project for the local church.

In 1990, the year of the demise of the German Democratic Republic and the reunification of Germany, she entered politics as a municipal official in Kayna, and in 1994 she became mayor. She joined the Christian Democratic Union in 1991. In 1992 she became a member of the party's district council, vice president of the league of cities and communities in the eastern German state of Saxony-Anhalt, and a member of the managing committee of the League of Municipal Officials of Saxony-Anhalt. She was elected to the Bundestag (lower house of parliament) in 1994, where she served on the committee for construction and urban development.

Bernard Cook

Späth, Lothar (1937–)

German Christian Democratic politician, prime minister of the Land (state) Baden-Württemberg (1978–91). Lothar Späth, son of a stockroom administrator with a liberal as well as Protestant background, was born on November 16, 1937, in Sigmaringen. After completing high school in Heilbronn without passing the final examinations, he spent his apprenticeship in the administration of Baden-Württemberg. He began his professional career in 1960 in the field of financial administration. In 1967 he joined the Christian Democratic Union (CDU) and gained immediate popularity with the constituents in Ludwigsburg II during the 1968 elections for the state parliament. He was elected mayor of Bietigheim in 1967 and was appointed chairman of the state caucus of the CDU in May 1972. Späth, an ambitious politician, henceforth played an important role in several organizations, such as the building society, Neue Heimat, (new Homeland) of Baden-Württemberg, as well as in political life. As a result of public opinion pressure following a series of suicides by terrorists, primarily members of the

Rote Armee Fraktion (Red Army Faction) in the prison of Stammheim in 1978, the state government of Baden-Württemberg was forced to restructure the cabinet. Späth was appointed minister of the interior. In that same year, Späth became deputy to Hans Filbinger, chairman of the South-Western German CDU.

The next step on Späth's career path was the position of prime minister of Baden-Württemberg. Filbinger had to resign on August 7, 1978, because of decisions he had made as a judge toward the end of the Third Reich. Späth was nominated as a candidate to succeed Filbinger, as was the mayor of Stuttgart, Manfred Rommel, son of World War II hero General Erwin Rommel. Späth won to become the youngest prime minister of any state of the Federal Republic of Germany (West Germany).

At the beginning of his term Späth continued to support the ideas of less state control and less bureaucracy. In 1979, Späth defeated Filbinger and became state chairman.

Increasingly, Späth became a rival of Chancellor Helmut Kohl by advocating the changing federal policies, such as a revision of the right of political asylum and forcing young people reluctant to work to do so. Späth became a stand-by chancellor (*Reservekanzler*) for the CDU, trying in vain to bring down Kohl. Späth's previously dominant position, however, was delivered a setback at the federal party conference of the CDU in Bremen in September 1989. There he reverted to a state-centered policy. In the second half of the 1980s the South-Western German CDU lost votes. Consequently, Späth tried to rally new support for the CDU. He set up a Ministry of Environment, but he was thwarted in his plan to create a new tax to support a cleaner environment.

May 1990 marked the political demise of Späth. He had to appear as a witness in a trial in the Stuttgart district court concerning party contributions. At the beginning of 1991 he again had to appear in court at the trial of the former head of the SEL, one of Germany's biggest telecommunications manufacturers. It was disclosed that companies had paid for trips made by Späth and his family. The prosecuting attorney made inquiries and the state parliament appointed a parliamentary investigative committee. In spite of that, Späth was acquitted of any charges of wrongdoing, and, the final outcome of the investigation proved that he was not guilty. Yet, people were still under the impression that he had benefited from some economic advantage and he was forced to resign as prime minister on January 13, 1991. After his political demise, Späth became an adviser to the state government of Thüringen, became chairman of the Jenaoptik Ltd., a manufacturers of high quality cameras, and eventually worked as an economic manager on the board of several firms.

BIBLIOGRAPHY

Filmer, Werner. *Lothar Späth.* Düsseldorf: ECON, 1987.

Graw, Ansgar. *Lothar Späth: Politik, Wirtschaft und die Rolle der Medien.* Zurich: Orell Fussli, 1991.

Späth, Lothar. *Die Chancen der Vielfalt: Föderalismus als Moderne Staatsform.* Stuttgart: Verlag Bonn aktuell, 1979.

———. *Facing the Future: Germany Breaking New Ground.* Berlin: Springer-Verlag, 1986.

———. *Politische Mobilmachung: Partnershaft statt Klassenkampf.* Stuttgart: Seewald, 1976.

Annette Biener

Spiegel Affair

Political crisis in West Germany resulting from a charge of treason against the German news weekly *Der Spiegel* in October 1962. The case was widely seen as a test of the viability of the West German parliamentary system and its commitment to civil liberties and freedom of the press. Irregularities in the arrest and investigation of publisher Rudolf Augstein and leading *Spiegel* journalists drew widespread public criticism and threatened to break up Chancellor Konrad Adenauer's Christian Democratic Union–Free Democratic Party (FDP) governing coalition. The outcome of the affair, however, showed that West German institutions functioned effectively in the defense of civil liberties.

The immediate cause of the action against *Der Spiegel* was an October 10, 1962, cover story on the recently completed NATO military exercise "Fallex 62," based in part on a classified Defense Ministry study. The article revealed that the Bundeswehr (West German army) had been placed in the lowest category of readiness by NATO inspectors. The article was also highly critical of Defense Minister Franz Josef Strauss, who favored a nuclear response to any Soviet attack and increased reliance on tactical nuclear weapons rather than conventional forces. A day after the appearance of the article, federal attorneys and police began a criminal investigation based on a Defense Ministry affidavit. Minister of Justice Wolfgang Stammberger, a member of the FDP, was not informed of the impending operation until October 24. On October 26 federal police launched the operation with nighttime raids on *Der Spiegel* offices in Hamburg and Bonn in search of classified materials. Copies of a forthcoming issue were confiscated. Eleven persons were eventually arrested, including Augstein; Conrad Ahlers, *Der Spiegel* military affairs correspondent; and Colonel Alfred Martin, a member of the Defense Ministry, accused of leaking documents. Ahlers was arrested while on vacation in Spain with the help of the Spanish police.

Public protests erupted against an operation that reminded many government critics of Nazi methods used to suppress freedom of the press. The case was uncomfortably reminiscent of the conviction of journalist Carl von Ossietzky for betraying military secrets in the last years (1927–31) of the Weimar Republic. Suspicion arose that the case was a politically motivated act of retaliation for *Der Spiegel*'s repeated criticisms of Strauss. Under heavy questioning in the Bundestag on November 9, Strauss admitted that he had personally called the military attaché in the German Embassy in Madrid to initiate Ahlers's arrest. It was later revealed that he did so on his own initiative after finding out that the Federal Criminal Office could not execute the arrest warrant because the charge against Ahlers was a political crime. The defense minister was also implicated in the decision to withhold information on the case from Stammberger. On November 30 Strauss announced his resignation as minister of defense, and the government crisis was resolved in December when Adenauer agreed to retire by October 1963.

The *Spiegel* affair demonstrated the strength of public concern about freedom of expression and inquiry. Most of the West German press rallied to the defense of *Der Spiegel*. No convictions resulted from the case. Augstein was released on February 7 after a confinement of 103 days. All charges against Augstein and Ahlers were dismissed by the Federal High Court in 1965. The court, however, upheld the constitutionality of the government's action against *Der Spiegel* on a tie vote of four to four in 1966.

BIBLIOGRAPHY

Bunn, Ronald F. *German Politics and the Spiegel Affair: A Case Study of the Bonn System.* Baton Rouge: Louisiana State University Press, 1968.

Schoenbaum, David. *The Spiegel Affair.* Garden City, N.Y.: Doubleday, 1968.

Seifert, Jürgen, ed. *Die Spiegel-Affäre,* 3 Vols. Olten, Germany: Walter-Verlag, 1966.

Rod Stackelberg

SEE ALSO Adenauer, Konrad; Augstein, Rudolf; Strauss, Franz Josef

Spínola, António de (1910–96)

Leading Portuguese general in the African colonial wars and first president of democratic Portugal following the 1974 coup. António de Spínola was born in Estremoz on April 11, 1910. His father served as inspector general of finance in the government of Antonio De Oliveira Salazar the dictator of Portugal, and it was the dictator who encouraged the young Spínola's army career. Spínola rose quickly in the ranks, fighting in the Spanish Civil War as part of Portugal's aid to Franco's nationalists, acting as a military observer with German forces in World War II on the Russian front, and attaining a high post in Portugal's Republican National Guard. He first gained national attention fighting against the Angolan rebels (1961–64) as a lieutenant colonel and battalion commander. Spínola later stated that it was in Angola that he began to believe that Portugal's African colonies could not be held by military means.

In 1968 Spínola, then a general, was named commanding officer and governor in the west African colony of Guinea-Bissau, where Portuguese forces had lost control. There he would have great influence over a corps of young officers whom he appointed to help him study the situation and try to win over the local population. When he requested permission to negotiate a settlement with the liberation movement, PAIGC, however, he was refused by Prime Minister Marcelo Caetano, Salazar's successor. Infuriated, Spínola saw the military relegated to a no-win scenario as it had been in the Portuguese Indian colony of Goa in 1961.

Despite strained relations with the regime, Spínola returned to Lisbon in 1973 as a patriotic hero, and in January 1974 he was named deputy chief of staff of the armed forces. But within two months on March 14, 1974, he was dismissed for failing to give full support to the Caetano government.

Spínola had already tested the limits of the regime's censors by securing the publication of his book *Portugal e o futuro* on February 22, 1974. The book was a popular sensation and provided ideological content for the Carnation Revolution (so called because it occurred at the time that red carnations were available) made by junior officers left disenchanted by the African experience. In his book Spínola called for a federation of African states with Portugal democratically formed and organized. He believed the African territories would choose to remain in such a Lusitanian (Portuguese) community, and the fruitless guerrilla wars could finally be ended. Implied in his writing was the need for the democratization of Portugal itself and economic liberalization.

Spínola's military rank was too high for him to be an overt conspirator, but he was willing to lend his prestige to the Armed Forces Movement (MFA), which unseated the dictatorship on April 25, 1974. The Junta of National

Salvation elected him president, and he was inaugurated on May 15, 1974.

But Spínola's position was shaky from the start for legal and ideological reasons. Since he had obtained his office from a revolutionary junta, he lacked a democratic base and could not act independently. The Council of Ministers was a conglomeration of people of competing ideologies, and the MFA refused to disband and reintegrate itself into the regular military structure. Instead it forged links with left-wing parties and was able to control political developments. Spínola was a political moderate who did not favor total independence for the African colonies, nationalization of banks, promotion of organized labor, and other MFA positions. He could not tolerate the waves of strikes and worker unrest that disrupted the nation. He survived one confrontation with the MFA in mid-June 1974, but when he tried to take his case to the people through a "silent majority" demonstration in late September, leftist roadblocks forced him to cancel it. He resigned on September 29, 1974. After a failed countercoup attempt in March 1975, he went into exile.

The Spínola presidency represented a critical stage in the transition to modern Portugal. During his brief term Spínola ushered in democratic reforms, released political prisoners, allowed exiles to return, dismantled the political police, and ended press censorship. He presided over the independence of one African colony, appropriately Guinea-Bissau, and welcomed it into the community of free nations on September 11, 1974. Once the Portuguese revolution stabilized into a more moderate mode, Spínola's role as a bridge to democracy was better appreciated. In late 1976, he retired from political life, participating only in celebrations of the revolution.

BIBLIOGRAPHY

Guerra, João Paulo. *Descolonizcao portuguesa: O regreso das caravelas.* Lisbon: Publicacoes Dom Quixote, 1996.

Insight Team of the London Sunday Times. *Insight on Portugal, the Year of the Captains.* London: André-Deutsch, 1975.

Spínola, António de. *Ao servico de Portugal.* Lisbon: Atica/Livraria Bertrand, 1976.

Wheeler, Douglas L. *Historical Dictionary of Portugal.* Metuchen, N.J.: Scarecrow Press, 1993, 169–70.

Regina A. Mezei

SEE ALSO Caetano, Marcelo; Gonçalves, Vasco; Salazar, António

Sports (Professional)

Sports undoubtedly played a part in the rehabilitation of the European spirit after World War II. Europeans cheered their teams and fellow nationals as they pursued traditional sports in increasingly popular competitions—the World Cup in soccer, the Olympic Games, auto and bike races, and international matches in tennis and golf. Soccer is undoubtedly the world's most popular sport, but nowhere is it more enthusiastically followed than in Europe. There its greatest events are the World Cup, held every four years; the European Cup, scheduled annually; and the Football Association Finals, contested every year in Britain's Wembley Stadium, in a suburb of London. Although soccer originated in England, where the Football Association (hence the sport's name) set the first rules in 1863, that country did not participate in the World Cup before World War II because of policy differences with Europe's Fédération Internationale des Football Associations (FIFA). Finally, joining in 1950, Britain did poorly at first in its very own game, but when Sir Alf Ramsey became coach of the British team, he promised: "We shall win the World Cup." Thus, Ramsey set his team's objective. The day came in 1966 when the British team, starring Bobby and Jackie Charlton, Captain Bobby Moore, and their incomparable goalie, Gordon Banks, scored a thrilling triumph in the first World Cup ever held in Britain. The Germans countered with their great leader "Kaiser" Franz Beckenbauer and the iron determination of Helmut Haller. Goeff Hurst, however, scored three goals for the British in an amazing 4-2 victory. Queen Elizabeth II presented the trophy to the team before a gallery of one hundred thousand super enthusiasts. Although the West Germans reversed that decision by winning in 1974, the World Cup's future seemed at times to belong to Third World countries. The great Eusébio from Mozambique, who scored nine goals in the 1966 games, starred for the Portuguese team. Another figure was Argentina's Diego Maradona. But it was the magnificent Pelé, playing for Brazil, who amazed everyone. His career spanned the years 1956–77, over which he scored a record 1,284 goals in 1,363 games. The media labeled him the "Black Pearl" and "O'Rey." During the Pelé epoch the Brazilian team won three World Cup titles, in 1958, 1962, and 1970. Italy, led by its great Paolo Rossi, won notably in 1982. By 1994 West Germany and Italy had three titles as European leaders. But in 1994 Brazil beat Italy in the first World Cup played in the United States. A tragic episode erupted from that competition, however; Andrés Escobar of the Colombia team accidentally kicked a goal into his own net, which resulted in a Colombian defeat. Back home, near Medellín, he was murdered by angry fans.

Baron Pierre de Coubertin, the French nobleman who founded the modern Olympic Games in Athens in 1896, sought to bring the classic Greek humanitarian ideals to a pre–World War I Europe torn by social Darwinism, ravenous imperialism, contentious alliance systems, and a perilous arms race. His heart today is buried on the field of Olympia, in Greece, where the games began in 776 B.C. After World War II the games resumed at London in 1948, where Emil Zatopek, the Czech track and field athlete, was the outstanding European participant. At the Melbourne games in 1956, the Soviet Vladimir Kuts set the 10,000-meter record in track and field. At Rome, in 1960, a bit of irony occurred in that competition when the Ethiopian Abebe Bikila won the Marathon running barefoot! Interestingly, Bikila's father had fought in the Ethiopian army that unsuccessfully resisted Mussolini's invasion of his country in 1935–36.

The Munich Summer Games in 1972 featured outstanding American swimmer Mark Spitz. He won a record seven gold medals, but his achievements were overshadowed by terrorist attacks on the Olympic Village. The winter games in 1984 at Sarajevo, Yugoslavia, saw skilled Finnish skier Maria Liisa Hämälainen win three gold medals and one bronze, the best for her country in half a century. Then there were the Winter Games at Calgary in Canada in 1988, where Katarina Witt of East Germany repeated her 1984 Olympic gold medal performance in figure skating, the first athlete for two generations to accomplish consecutive golds in figure skating. In the Winter Games of 1994 at Lillehammer, Norway, that country's crack speed skater, Johann Olav Koss, achieved the unbelievable—three golds in new world record times—after having already set a mark at the 1992 Winter Games at Albertville, France. After the competitions Koss made a $30,000 contribution from his victory bonuses to the Olympic Fund with the understanding that a substantial portion of it go to relieve the suffering of war-ravaged Sarajevo, site of the Winter Games in 1984. Finally, there was Russian cross-country skier Yegorova Lyubova, who in the 1992 and 1994 Winter Games won a total of six gold medals and three silvers.

Tennis had European origins, its name derived from the French word *tenez* (hold, take heed). The British contributed also when Major Walter J. Wingfield set the first rules and established the oldest competition at Wimbledon in 1877. The French established their competition in 1891, then the Australians in 1905, while the United States set up the Forest Hills competition in 1914 in Queens, New York. The International Lawn Tennis Association (ILTA) had already been organized in 1912. The European and American competitions together became known as the Grand Slam, the ultimate achievement of great tennis stars. Because of World War II, European players for some time failed to make a world impact, although Frenchman Yvon Petra won his nation's tourney in 1946. The immediate postwar era was dominated mostly by Americans, notably by Jack Kramer and then "Pancho" Gonzalez. Then, after 1950, the Australians surged: Frank Sedgman, Ken McGregor, and later Ken Rosewall and left-handed star Rod Laver. The Australians were students of masterful coach Harry Hopman. Among the women, the American Maureen Connolly won the Grand Slam in 1953; later it was American Billie Jean King. Virginia Wade proved the most capable of the British women when she took the Wimbledon crown in 1977.

Tennis shed its country club image in 1968, when the ILTA permitted amateurs and professionals to compete together, thus shattering the legalistic "amateurism" ideal, which long burdened the Olympics. By that time European tennis players were hitting their stride, especially when Manuel Santana became the first Spaniard to capture Wimbledon in 1966 before adding the Italian title in 1972. But the European climax arrived in the person of a young Swedish prodigy with an uncanny consistency to his game, Björn Borg.

After winning both the Italian and French titles in 1974 at barely eighteen years of age, Borg tore his way between 1976 and 1980 to virtually every tennis title, while earning at least $2 million a year in endorsements. Following Borg came Czech star Ivan Lendl, and the Swede Mats Wilander, who at seventeen was the youngest to take the French title. West German Boris Becker also won at Wimbledon at seventeen, and he would repeat at Wimbledon twice more in 1986 and 1989.

Martina Navratilova was the truly dominant figure in the post–World War II tennis era. She won some 158 tournaments, a record for both men and women. Born in Prague, Czechoslovakia, in 1956, she won her first of nine Wimbledon titles in 1978. Because she had departed her country and assumed U.S. citizenship in 1975 to enhance her playing opportunities, the Czech government forbade her return, nor would it permit her family to leave their country. Navratilova won the Grand Slam in 1983 and 1984, and won six successive Wimbledon tourneys. She retired after losing in the finals there in 1994 at age thirty-seven.

Navratilova's successor was West German Steffi Graf, who defeated her in the Wimbledon finals in 1988, the year that Graf won the Grand Slam at just nineteen years. She shared the first-place tennis ranking with Ivan Lendl for 1990. Soon both met challengers in Monica Seles, the "ferocious young Yugoslav," and Greek-American Pete Sampras. Seles was attacked in 1993 by a knife-wielding spectator during a Hamburg tournament. Her resultant back injury retired her temporarily. Sampras won at Wimbledon in 1993 and 1994, the U.S. Open in 1993, and the Australian Open in 1994. Spain's Conchita Martinez took the Wimbledon women's title from Navratilova in 1994 in Seles's absence.

Golf has both Dutch (*kolf,* or club) and Scottish origins. James I, the first Stuart King of England, brought the game from Scotland. The Royal and Ancient Golf Club was established in 1754 at St. Andrews, Scotland, near Edinburgh and the first British Open took place at Prestwick Course in England in 1860. Following World War II American golfers prevailed, especially Arnold Palmer and Jack Nicklaus. The former was designated "athlete of the decade" in the 1960s by the Associated Press, while Nicklaus won each of the four great competitions: the British Open, U.S. Open, Masters, and PGA—Golf's "Grand Slam"—no fewer than three times each between 1962 and 1978. Mildred "Babe" Didrikson, another American, won 33 tourneys out of 88 in women's competition, but European players soon challenged the American dominance in golf.

One of the most successful, Tony Jacklin of England, won the British Open in 1969, the first from that country to capture his own national tourney in almost two decades. Then Jacklin took the U.S. Open in 1970, the first Briton ever to take that title, adding the Canadian Cup in 1972. Some years later Jacklin captained the British team. Under his instruction the improvement continued. Nick Faldo proved one of Britain's great achievers when he took the French Open and five lesser tournaments in 1983. He captured the British Open in 1987, then the Masters and three European championships in 1989. Faldo took the British Open and the Masters again in 1990, and finally the British Open once more in 1992, gaining top European ranking. Eminence in the game they had helped develop historically had returned to the British.

A capable West German, Bernhard Langer, took the Masters in 1985 and again in 1993. The European golfer whom the largest galleries followed along the course, however, was the Spaniard Severiano Ballesteros, who had turned pro at just seventeen. At nineteen he tied Jack Nicklaus for second place in the 1976 British Open. For 1977–78 he was the leading European money winner, and he won the British Open in 1979, 1984, and 1988. He won six tournaments in 1987 alone, and he was number one in the Volvo Order of Merit in 1991. As a sequel, his fellow countryman José María Olazabel won the Masters in 1994.

Notice should be taken of three players from the former British Commonwealth—Gary Player of South Africa, who won three British titles by 1974, and Greg Norman from Australia, who took that same British Open in 1986 at Ayrshire, Scotland, and again in 1993. Norman scored a 267 in that tournament, including a 64 for his last round, both records for the British Open. Finally, there was Nick Price from Zimbabwe, who won the British Open and the Masters to earn the distinction of best golfer for 1994. Prominent also was Penny Grice Whittaker of the United Kingdom, who won the British Women's Open Championship in 1991, and Helen Alfredsson of Sweden, who took the same title the previous year.

Racing has many followers in Europe. When Édouard Michelin invented detachable tires and inner tubes, the bicycle was born to sports competition. The Tour de France started in 1904, and its races over the Alps and Pyrenees cover all of 2,500 miles. The Tour of Italy commenced in 1909. Also, there was the Tour of Spain. After World War II, however, the Tour de France was still supreme. Jacques Anquetil, the dashing young Frenchman, won consecutive races from 1961 to 1964. His first Tour covered over 2,730 miles and lasted twenty-two days.

The presiding executive body, the Union Cyclistes Internationale (UCI), was concerned about drugs after World War II. Tests took place despite bitter complaints from cyclists. When Tom Simpson of England, who had won the Tour of Spain in 1965, the first Briton to do so, collapsed and died during the French races, drugs were blamed. Some participants, however, found them attractive because their stimulation overcame fatigue and depression, while firing determination to win. Drugs remained a serious problem for competitive cycling.

Cycling was also part of the Olympics. At Barcelona in 1992 Britisher Christopher Boardman won the Gold Medal, and the next year he set a new speed record of 52.270 kmph. in a Bordeaux race. In the meantime, Belgian Eddie Marckx had won the Tour de France for all four years from 1969 to 1972. Then it was the turn of Spain's Miguel Indurain, who duplicated that accomplishment from 1991 to 1994. The 1992 competition was expanded to cover six countries as Europe opened more frontiers. Indurain added the Tour of Italy title that year as well.

Auto racing paralleled cycling in development. The Grand Prix was first run in France in 1905. The Monte Carlo Rally was begun in 1911. Finally, Le Mans was set up in 1923 for two driver cars. The Fédération Internationale de l'Automobile presided. Some very outstanding drivers in the post–World War II era included American

Phil Hill, who won the Italian Grand Prix at Monza in 1960; then he teamed with Olivier Gendebien, driving a Ferrari, to take the 24-hour race at Le Mans in 1961 and again in 1962, averaging a speed of 115.90 mph. Jim Clark of Scotland won the honors for 1963 by winning seven races, ranging from France and Belgium to South Africa and Mexico. Much later the Grand Prix became completely international, growing to sixteen races, when British driver Nigel Mansell won the designation "World Champion" for 1992. A crash in 1977 had broken his neck, and his doctors told him to forget about racing. But he left the hospital on his own to crown his ambitions fifteen years later. Yet Mansell did not repeat, for Frenchman Alain Frost won in 1993 with Brazilian Ayrton Senna a close second. Tragically, the next year in the San Marino Grand Prix, Senna's car crashed into a wall at 186 mph, and he was killed instantly, at just thirty-four years of age. Senna's disaster proved the hazards of auto racing for drivers and spectators alike.

Horse racing as we know it today originated in Britain, where it was literally "the sport of kings." Restored Stuart monarch Charles II established the turf at Newmarket, a center for racing and breeding. Soon after, Queen Anne founded the Royal Ascot. The Jockey Club, established about 1750, administered by aristocratic owners, set the rules. Racing was strictly for the privileged. Races founded at St. Leger in 1776 and the Derby in 1780 are still held today. The sport emigrated to the British Empire, especially Australia and New Zealand, to the United States, where Churchill Downs was opened in 1875, and to the European continent. At present Queen Elizabeth II keeps her own stable. In 1954, she knighted the jockey Gordon Richards, the first to be so honored, who on his retirement had ridden 4,870 winners. On the continent France today enjoys racing at the Grand Prix de Paris at Longchamps and the Prix d'Arc de Triomphe, climaxing with the Grand Criterium in October.

BIBLIOGRAPHY

Baker, William J. *Sports in the Western World.* Chicago: University of Chicago Press, 1988.

Killanin, Lord, and John Rodda, eds. *The Olympic Games: Eighty Years of People, Events and Records.* New York: Macmillan, 1976.

Thraves, Andrew, ed. *The History of the Wembley FA Cup Final.* London: Weidenfeld and Nicolson, 1994.

Trifari, Elio, and Charles Miers. *Soccer! The Game and the World Cup.* New York: Rizzoli International, 1994.

William J. Miller

SEE ALSO Olympic Politics; Soccer Hooliganism

Spring, Dick (1950–)

Irish politician. After briefly practicing law, Dick Spring was elected in 1981 to the Dáil (parliament) as a Labour representative for Kerry North. In 1981 and 1982 he served as minister of state for justice. In 1982 he replaced Michael O'Leary as leader of the Labour Party. He was vice-prime minister from 1982 to 1987 in the Fine Gael–Labour coalition. He was minister for the environment (1982–83) and minister for energy (1982–87). He served as leader of the Labour delegation to the New Ireland Forum, a year-long series of meetings of the parties of the Irish Republic to try to work out a proposal on Northern Ireland that would be acceptable to the vice-prime minister, the Protestants, and Catholics of the North. Spring nominated Mary Robinson for president in 1990. He served as minister for foreign affairs and vice-prime minister from 1992 to 1994 in the Fianna Fáil-Labour Coalition Government and minister for foreign affairs and Tanaiste in the 1994 Fine Gael–Labour-Democratic left coalition. Following the Downing St. Declaration of 1993, Spring played a major role in the peace process in Northern Ireland.

Despite an uncertain beginning, the Labour Party grew in support and parliamentary strength under Spring's leadership. The election of Mary Robinson to the presidency in 1990 and Labour's 33 seats of the 166 seats, an increase of 17 seats in the November 1992 election over the 1989 election demonstrated the party's increased profile in Irish political life. The high-profile foreign affairs portfolio and the peace process in Northern Ireland greatly added to Spring's personal standing.

BIBLIOGRAPHY

Ryan, Tim. *Dick Spring: a Safe Pair of Hands.* Tallaght, Ireland: Blackwater Press, 1993.

Michael J. Kennedy

Springer, Axel (1912–85)

West Germany's most powerful conservative publicist from the 1960s through the 1980s. Springer published the largest German daily paper, the *Bild-Zeitung,* a scandal sheet with yellow press leanings, but at the same time with important political influence. Springer also published many other papers and popular magazines, including the conservative *Die Welt* and *Die Welt am Sonntag,* popular magazines such as *Twen, Kicker, Bravo, Eltern,* and two major Berlin dailies, the *Berliner Zeitung* and the *Berliner Morgenpost;* in addition, Springer controlled other publishing houses, including Ullstein and Propyläen. In the 1960s Springer became a symbol of conservative Germany and was the target of much criticism from the Left, even after his death in 1985. The Springer empire, now much smaller, continues his political legacy, though certainly less stridently than under his leadership.

He worked diligently and successfully for good relations with Israel and for positive relations between Germans and Jews; at the same time he was an aggressive opponent of the division of Germany and of the East German regime (German Democratic Republic, DDR), to which his newspapers always referred in quotation marks ("DDR") as a way of demonstrating his view of its tentative and illegitimate character. He symbolically moved his main offices from Hamburg to Berlin in 1967 and built a modern glass skyscraper directly next to the Wall in the center of West Berlin. The *Bild-Zeitung*'s ever more aggressive attitudes toward the GDR, politically active leftist students, and Chancellor Willy Brandt's *Ostpolitik,* or attempt to establish relations with the Communist countries of Eastern Europe, made Springer's Berlin headquarters the target of student attacks in 1967 and of riots following the shooting of the radical student leader Rudi Dutschke in 1968. In 1972 West German terrorists bombed the publisher's Hamburg offices, injuring seventeen. In 1974, Heinrich Böll, the Nobel Prize—winning German novelist, skewered Springer's tactics and the *Bild-Zeitung* in his novel *Die verlorene Ehre der Katharina Blum* (*The Lost Honor of Katharina Blum*). The East German propaganda machine devoted much energy to a slanderous television series about Springer. Even a decade later, in 1980, several hundred prominent German writers, led by novelist Günter Grass, began an organized action against Springer publications, refusing to write for them on the grounds that they were antidemocratic and monopolistic, and restricted free speech. At about the same time, however, Springer received the Adenauer Peace Prize from the West German government for his work toward German-Israeli relations, his dedication to the city of Berlin, and his philanthropy in the arts. Springer received numerous honors and awards in Germany and abroad, with those from Israeli universities being perhaps the most significant for this powerful person who was one of the most influential and controversial figures in postwar German society.

BIBLIOGRAPHY

Lohmeyer, Henno. *Springer: Ein deutsches Imperium.* Berlin: Edition Q, 1992.

Müller, Hans Dieter. *Der Springer-Konzern: Eine kritische Studie.* Munich: Piper, 1968.

Naeher, Gerhard. *Axel Springer: Mensch, Macht, Mythos.* Erlangen: Straube, 1991.

Springer, Axel. *Reden wider den Zeitgeist.* Berlin: Ullstein, 1993.

Scott Denham

SEE ALSO Dutschke, Rudi; Springer Publishing House

Springer Publishing House

Largest German publishing house. Founded in 1946, the Axel Springer Publishing House is renowned for its innovative journalism as well as for its size and its clear political orientation.

With the help of British and German authorities after World War II, Axel Springer founded several newspapers modeled after British examples. He launched the monthly and later weekly *Hör zu!* in 1946, followed by the daily *Hamburger Abendblatt* in 1948. In 1952 the *Bild-Zeitung* was established. This tabloid with its yellow journalism became the biggest success of the publishing house. One year later the British authorities sold Springer their zonal newspaper, *Die Welt.* All these papers still belong to the publishing house. Moreover, Springer founded and bought several others. He also introduced the Anglo-Saxon form of Sunday papers to Germany.

In general, Springer's papers copied the style of British and American journalism. They were more sensational and less theoretical than other German newspapers. Articles were written to connect political events with the experiences of the readers. The papers were mainly designed for women and the working class.

On the whole, the publishing house's papers spread the same message. The most important thing is to be friendly toward one another. But the papers cautioned that, though everybody is basically good-hearted, people are easily misled. This message fit perfectly into the 1950s, when most Germans wanted harmony and to stay out of politics. It was supplemented by a rigid rejection of communism. All the papers demanded early reunification of Germany, but negotiations with leaders of Soviet-bloc countries were rejected. Ideas, persons, and politics within West Germany that did not fit into the ideology of the publishing house were usually condemned as having a Communist background or as being supportive of the Communists. The United States was depicted as a helpful friend who defended West Germany against the danger of communism.

Because of the hierarchical organization of the company, all its newspapers represented an identical ideology. Springer, together with the chief editors, outlined the general course all papers had to follow. In 1963 the essentials of this course were support for Germany's reunification;

reconciliation between Germans and Jews and the support of Israel as a sovereign state; rejection of political extremism; and support for the social market economy. These essentials still apply. The first, however, was changed to "struggle to strengthen German unity" after the reunification of the country.

During the 1960s the message of the publishing house increasingly met with disapproval. While the papers stressed the things worth maintaining, German youth preferred change. At this time the company published around 40 percent of the country's dailies and reached an even higher percentage in the press's publishing centers—Hamburg and Berlin. Because of its size and its uniform message, the publishing house was reproached for manipulating its readers. Allegedly, its journalism prevented people from thinking independently. The freedom of the German press was supposed to be endangered. At Easter 1968 the reproach turned aggressive. Demonstrators prevented the delivery of the newspapers from Berlin and burned down parts of the publishing house in Berlin. Four years later two bombs exploded at the company's Hamburg branch, injuring seventeen employees.

Despite allegations that the papers of the publishing house, which spread the same basic message, manipulated their readers, their success was based on their ability to adopt opinions already predominant within the German public as well as on their innovative journalistic style.

BIBLIOGRAPHY

Jürgs, Michael. *Der Fall Axel Springer: Eine deutsche Biographie.* Munich: List Verlag, 1995.

Lohmeyer, Henno. *Springer: Ein deutsches Imperium.* Berlin: Edition Q, 1992.

Müller, Hans Dieter. *Der Springer-Konzern: Eine kritische Studie.* Munich: Piper, 1968.

Naeher, Gerhard. *Axel Springer: Mensch, Macht, Mythos.* Erlangen: Straube, Verlag, 1991.

Main archival site: Historische Verlagsdokumentation des Axel Springer Verlages, Hamburg.

Gudrun Kruip

SEE ALSO Springer, Axel; Zehrer, Hans

Stalin, Joseph (1879–1953)

Dictator of the Soviet Union, 1929–53. Joseph Stalin, born Iosif Vissarionovich Djugashvili, won supreme power in the USSR through a bitter political struggle after the death of Vladimir Lenin. He transformed the Soviet Union into an industrial power, defeated Nazi Germany in alliance with the major Western powers, and subjugated Eastern Europe at a cost of tens of millions of lives.

Stalin was born a shoemaker's son in Georgia. Educated to be an Orthodox priest, he left the seminary in 1899 to become a professional revolutionary. His revolutionary activities as a party organizer led to his arrest and exile in 1902, the first of many brushes with tsarist Russia's police.

Stalin associated himself with Lenin's Social Democratic Labor Party, (Bolshevik) party, attracted by Lenin's authoritarian and uncompromising approach to Marxism. Lenin established his Bolshevik faction in 1903 in opposition to the Menshevik faction of the Russina Social Democratic Labor Party. Lenin's faction, which he labeled Bolshevik, or majority, at first did not actually represent the majority of Russian Marxists. However, under Lenin's leadership, the faction that became a party by mid-1917 was actually larger than the Mensheviks. It differed from the Mensheviks in its conception of the party as a disciplined group of full-time professional revolutionaries. By 1912 Stalin had become a member of the party's Central Committee. He had ironically carved a niche for himself as the party expert on nationality and ethnicity. Georgian by birth, Stalin identified himself with the Russian people, though he would always speak Russian with an accent. He gave up his Georgian surname, Djugashvili, in favor of the nom de guerre Stalin—man of steel.

As World War I broke out, Stalin was in Siberian exile. When Tsar Nicholas II's regime collapsed under the pressures of war and revolution in 1917, Stalin raced back to Petrograd (St. Petersburg) to rejoin party life. A ramshackle provisional government, splitting power with a network of soviets (workers' councils), had taken over after the fall of the tsar. Stalin, like most members of the Bolshevik Party, was reluctant to push for an immediate seizure of power. Lenin, however, returned from Swiss exile and cajoled the party into moving as quickly as possible to bring down Russia's provisional government. Lenin proved correct: the Bolsheviks overthrew the provisional government with surprising ease in November 1917.

Seizing power was simple; keeping it was not. The Bolsheviks fought and won a bitter, bloody civil war against other socialists, peasants, and supporters of the old regime. Throughout the civil war (1918–20) Stalin was a troubleshooter, turning from crisis to crisis at Lenin's behest. During this period Stalin forged many of the personal connections that would serve him well in his climb to power after the war ended in 1920.

Lenin suffered the first of a series of debilitating strokes soon after the Bolshevik victory. Stalin and the rest of the party leadership then jockeyed for the right to inherit Lenin's mantle well before he finally died in 1924. By taking over personnel assignments and the party bureaucracy, Stalin built a network of clients and grateful supporters. Masterfully making and breaking alliances, Stalin defeated his rivals until, by 1929, his grip on political power was absolute. He then began the total transformation of Soviet society. Ordinary peasants were forced into collective farms while more prosperous peasants, the kulaks, were stripped of their property and sent into internal exile. The resulting disruption of agriculture produced a famine in 1933 that took the lives of six to seven million in the Ukraine, the north Caucasus, the lower Volga, and Kazakhstan.

April 1929 marked the official beginning of the First Five-Year Plan, a massive program of investment in heavy industry intended to make the Soviet Union an economic and military power virtually overnight. In a frenzy of ever-higher production targets, millions of citizens worked on new construction projects in hopes of building socialism while suffering abysmal living standards.

Stalin's revolution also radically changed Soviet culture and society. The rapid expansion of industry and the state bureaucracy required a flood of new managers and administrators. Peasants, workers, and army veterans poured into cities and universities to occupy the new positions created by Stalin's policies. The social advancement this offered created an important constituency who saw Stalinism as their route to a bright future. To ensure loyalty Stalin created a cult of personality that portrayed him as the infallible, all-powerful leader of the Soviet people. The relative cultural pluralism that had survived in the Soviet Union through the 1920s came to a rapid end.

The strains of Stalin's revolution caused growing opposition within the party. At the 1934 Seventeenth Party Congress, more than one hundred of the delegates voted in a secret ballot against Stalin's membership in the Central Committee. That same year, Leningrad party boss Sergey Kirov was assassinated. Some evidence suggests that Stalin arranged the killing to remove a possible rival, but he used Kirov's murder as a pretext to unleash state terror, allowing summary executions for those accused of treasonous conspiracy against the party. Stalin quickly linked Kirov's assassin to old-time party leaders who had opposed his struggle for power. In August 1936 Grigory Zinoviev and Lev Kamenev were put on trial on trumped-up charges and shot.

This was only the first step in a massive terror campaign. A second trial in January 1937 condemned former Trotskyites Iuri Piatakov and Karl Radek, and in June some of the Red Army's most talented officers were tried and shot for treason. The final great show trial in March 1938 settled accounts with Nikolay Bukharin, executed for plotting with the Germans to overthrow the Soviet regime. With no evidence to support these outlandish charges, the defendants were made to confess through torture and threats to their families.

Besides the show trials, Stalin personally approved death sentences for hundreds of people at a time. At the local level, party and secret police functionaries followed the example set at the center and began their own witch hunts for supposed traitors and saboteurs. Though estimates vary widely, at least seven hundred thousand lost their lives in the great purges, including some of the Communist Party's leading figures, the flower of the Soviet military's high command, and the USSR's most talented artists and scientists. Millions more went to the regime's vast network of slave labor camps.

While Stalin waged war against his own society, European war was approaching. Through most of the 1930s Soviet Foreign Minister Maksim Litvinov advocated collective security through the League of Nations to contain Adolph Hitler's Nazi Germany. But Stalin kept his options open by maintaining back-channel contacts with Germany. The Czech crisis of 1938 seems to have convinced Stalin that Britain and France could not be relied on, and he explored an alliance with Hitler. Historians dispute when precisely Stalin decided to cast his lot with Hitler, but it seems he toyed with both Germany and the Allies as long as possible to make the best deal he could, carrying on simultaneous negotiations with both as the European crisis deepened in 1939.

The Molotov-Ribbentrop Pact, signed in Moscow in the early morning of August 24, 1939, between the Soviet Union and Nazi Germany, gave Hitler the free hand he needed to attack Poland on September 1. Secret clauses in the pact partitioned Poland and the Baltic states between Germany and the Soviet Union, and Soviet troops accordingly moved into eastern Poland on September 17. Over the next two years the USSR would supply Germany with raw materials needed for its war machine. After overrunning Western Europe in the spring of 1940, however, Hitler decided to turn east against his soviet ally. By 1940 he called off plans to invade Britain and began planning an attack on the Soviet Union.

On June 22, 1941, the German army launched Operation Barbarossa to crush the Soviets in a short campaign. Stalin's purges of the Soviet officer corps left the Red Army ill-prepared for the German onslaught, and Hitler's betrayal caught Stalin by surprise. The Soviet Army suffered staggering losses, and German troops quickly cut off Leningrad, took Kiev, and reached the outskirts of Moscow. The Russian winter, dogged resistance by the Soviet people, and the timely transfer of Siberian reserves saved Moscow in the winter of 1941–42. This bought time for the Soviet Union's immense human and material resources to rebuild a military machine that would eventually crush the Germans.

Victory in war required Stalin to compromise with Soviet society. The military regained some of its independence and prestige, and Stalin became with time and experience a more effective commander in chief. He also eased restrictions on religion and Russian nationalism to bolster resistance to the Germans.

The need to maintain solidarity against Germany kept the wartime coalition of the Soviet Union, United States, and United Kingdom intact despite strains over burden sharing, postwar spheres of influence, and the fate of Germany. With the defeat of the Third Reich in sight, however, suppressed tensions resurfaced. To make matters worse, Harry Truman, who became U.S. president after Roosevelt died in office in April 1945, was far less willing to compromise with Stalin than his predecessor.

After the war Stalin would settle for nothing less than docile, pro-Soviet governments in Eastern Europe. As became increasingly apparent, however, Eastern European states could be either free or pro-Soviet, but not both. The problem was worst in Poland, for the Soviets had executed tens of thousands of Polish officers and social elites in 1940. Even Yugoslavia's Josip Broz (Tito), who had seized power without Soviet help, found that being communist was not enough. Too independent for Stalin, Tito broke from the Soviet camp in 1948. One by one, Stalin imposed Communist rule on the countries of Eastern Europe, irrevocably damaging relations with the West.

Stalin refused to permit the Eastern European satellites to participate in the U.S.-sponsored Marshall Plan for European postwar economic recovery. In summer 1948 Soviet occupation forces cut off land communications to West Berlin, an island of American, British, and French control completely surrounded by Soviet-run East German territory. By so alarming the West, Stalin's heavy-handed tactics led to the creation of the North Atlantic Treaty Organization (NATO) for defense against Soviet encroachment and the creation of a West German state out of the American, British, and French occupation zones.

The Cold War became a military conflict in the summer of 1950, when North Korea invaded South Korea. As recently available documents make clear, Stalin personally gave Kim Il-sung, dictator of North Korea, the go-ahead to invade the South. The United States immediately committed troops under U.N. auspices and began an immense military buildup to repel the North Korean invaders.

Despite the opening of Soviet archives, Stalin's last years remain shrouded in mystery. His isolation and paranoia worsened as he aged. Having eliminated any followers who could threaten him, he left an inner circle of sycophants constantly plotting against one another over the succession.

For the Soviet people, expecting some reduction in their cruel burdens after their Herculean sacrifices to defeat Nazi Germany, the postwar years brought only intensified repression. Leningrad party boss Andrey Zhdanov led a ruthless campaign against any deviations from orthodoxy in literature and culture. Prominent Soviet Jews became the targets of increased persecution, including arrests and executions. Stalin seems to have been preparing a last purge and pogrom that was cut short only by his death.

Details of Stalin's final days remain unclear. When he suffered a stroke, his bodyguards and inner circle are reported to have been too terrified to call for immediate medical assistance. He died on March 5, 1953.

Stalin's eventual successor as Soviet premier, Nikita Khrushchev, in a 1956 secret speech to the Twentieth Party Congress, denounced Stalin's crimes in detail as part of a process of de-Stalinization. Stalin's embalmed body was removed from Lenin's tomb for reburial, and as the contents of the secret speech became common knowledge throughout the Soviet bloc, statues to Stalin disappeared. Memories of his terror and the graves of his victims could not be erased as easily.

BIBLIOGRAPHY

Bullock, Alan. *Hitler and Stalin: Parallel Lives.* New York: Knopf, 1992.

Conquest, Robert. *Stalin: Breaker of Nations.* New York: Viking, 1991.

Deutscher, Isaac. *Stalin: A Political Biography.* New York: Oxford University Press, 1949.

Khrushchev, Nikita. *Khrushchev Remembers.* New York: Little, Brown, 1970.

Medvedev, Roy. *Let History Judge: The Origins and Consequences of Stalinism.* New York: Knopf, 1971.

Tucker, Robert. *Stalin as Revolutionary: A Study in History and Personality, 1879–1929.* New York: Norton, 1973.

———. *Stalin in Power: The Revolution from Above, 1928–1941.* New York: Norton, 1990.

Volkogonov, Dmitri. *Stalin: Triumph and Tragedy.* New York: Grove Weidenfeld, 1991.

David Stone

SEE ALSO Beria, Lavrenty; Khrushchev, Nikita; Malenkov, Georgy; Marshall Plan

Staller, Ilona (1952–)

Hungarian-born porn star elected to the Italian Chamber of Deputies (lower house of parliament) in June 1987. Ilona Staller, better known as Cicciolina, gained notoriety during her campaign on behalf of the small, left-wing Radical Party. Staller's public appearances, in which she often disrobed, generated a media blitz and provoked both excitement and controversy.

Staller's father was a minor bureaucrat and her mother a gynecologist. After completing high school in Budapest, Staller married an Italian man in order to emigrate to the West. She divorced him shortly after moving to Italy and began an acting and modeling career. A young photographer, Riccardo Schicchi, became Staller's manager and encouraged her to pursue a career in the adult entertainment industry. Her explicit films, photos, and public exhibitions in the 1980s made Cicciolina famous throughout Italy.

When a coalition of the Socialist and Christian Democratic Parties collapsed in 1987, requiring new elections, the Radical Party asked Staller to run for parliament as a representative of Pomezia, an industrial town near Rome. The party's leaders hoped Staller would attract voters. They also believed that running a porn star run for office would exemplify the absurdity of existing political practices. No one, however, expected her to win. Staller, who had developed a platform of issues ranging from abolishment of the modesty act to animal rights, secured enough votes to gain a seat in parliament. Staller left politics in 1992. She married then divorced an American sculptor with whom she had a son. Though no longer a member of parliament, Staller set an unusual precedent in Italian politics. An assortment of other celebrities and porn stars have run for office in Italy since Staller. In 1994 the Italian government changed the electoral laws to make it more difficult for those who are not serious politicians to enter the legislature.

BIBLIOGRAPHY

Baldwin, Alan. "Italian Elections Low on Celebrities and Color." *Reuters,* April 17, 1996.

Lee, Andrea. "Letter from Rome." *New Yorker* 63 (1987): 133–36.

Lilla, Mark. "The Body Politic." *New Republic* 197 (1987): 14–16.

Wendy A. Pojmann

Starodubtsen, Vasiliy Aleksandrovich (1931–)

Soviet and Russian political figure, member of the State Committee for the State of Emergency (GKChP), which launched the August 1991 coup against President Mikhail Gorbachev, and later a member of the state duma of the Russian Federation.

Vasiliy A. Starodubtsen was born to a peasant family on December 25, 1931, in a small village of Volovchik in Volovsk region. He started working in 1942 on a collective farm during World War II and soon became a brigade leader of a collective farm in the Lipetsk Oblast. Following the war he moved to the small town of Zhukovskiy in Moscow Oblast and became a miner at the Stalinogorskugol mine, where he worked till 1964. Starodubtsen then became the chairman of the V. Lenin Collective Farm in Tula Oblast. In 1987 he was elected as the chairman of an agro-industrial enterprise, Novomoskovskoye, in Tula Oblast.

In August 1991 Starodubtsen became a member of GKChP during the coup, but with its failure he was arrested. When he was released in June 1992 he returned to his position as the chairman of Novomoskovskoye and as chairman of the V. Lenin Collective Farm.

He was a deputy of the Supreme Soviet of the USSR (1989–1992), and in 1997 was elected as the governor of Tula Oblast and became a member of the Federal Council of Russian Federation.

Oleg N. Kozhin

Stefanopoulos, Costis (1926–)

President of Greece (1995–). Costis Stephanopoulos was elected president by the Greek parliament and assumed office on March 9, 1995. He was born in Patras in 1926 and received a law degree from the University of Athens. Stefanopoulos was elected to parliament in 1964 as a representative of the National Radical Union. With the reestablishment of democratic government in Greece in 1974 Stefanopoulos entered parliament as a member of the conservative New Democracy political party founded by Constantinos Karamanlis and joined the government as undersecretary of commerce. He joined the New Democracy Party and was continuously elected to parliament as one of its representatives until 1985. He was minister of internal affairs, minister of social services, and minister of the presidency in various Karamanlis governments.

He unsuccessfully sought to become leader of New Democracy in 1981 and 1984. After the resounding electoral defeat of New Democracy in 1985, the opposition of Stefanopoulos to the leadership of Constantinos Mitsotakis led him to leave the party. He set up a new party with fifteen other New Democracy MPs, Democratic Renewal. As the leader of Democratic Renewal Stefanopoulos was again elected to parliament in June 1989. The party faltered in the 1990 elections, however. Stefanopoulos lost his seat and withdrew temporarily from politics. In 1995, the Pan Hellenic Socialist Movement (PASOK) proposed him as its presidential candidate and he was elected on the third ballot.

BIBLIOGRAPHY

Allison, Graham T., and Kalypso Nicolaïdis. *The Greek Paradox: Promise vs. Performance.* Cambridge, Mass.: MIT Press, 1997.

Clogg, Richard. *Parties and Elections in Greece: The Search for Legitimacy.* Durham, N.C.: Duke University Press, 1987.

Clogg, Richard, ed. *Greece, 1981–89: The Populist Decade.* New York: St. Martin's Press, 1993.

Featherstone, Kevin, and Dimitrios K. Katsoudas. *Political Change in Greece: Before and After the Colonels.* New York: St. Martin's Press, 1987.

Pappas, Takis Spyros. *Making Party Democracy in Greece.* New York: St. Martin's Press, 1999.

Bernard Cook

Stepan, Miroslav

Head of the Communist Party organization in Prague at the time of the Velvet Revolution of 1989. Miroslav Stepan was considered a possible successor to Miloš Jakeš, the general secretary of the Czechoslovak Communist Party until the Velvet Revolution, the peaceful protest that shoved the Communist regime aside in November and December 1989. After he ordered police action against student demonstrators on November 17, 1989, in which 167 were injured, he became a liability to the Communist Party. On November 25 Stepan resigned as leading secretary of the Prague city committee of the Communist Party. On November 27 he, along with Miroslav Zavadil, head of social policy for the party's Politburo, and Jozef Lenart, chief of foreign policy, was ousted from the Politburo.

On July 9, 1990, Stepan was convicted of abuse of power for ordering the police to forcibly disperse demonstrators in October 1988. He was charged with ordering them to use dogs, water cannon, and tear gas to disperse several thousand demonstrators commemorating the seventieth anniversary of the founding of Czechoslovakia and of ordering the police to seize approximately two hundred dissidents, among them the dissident playwright and future president of Czechoslovakia Václav Havel, in January 1989, when they attempted to mark the twentieth anniversary of the self-immolation of the student Jan Palach who set himself on fire to protest the Warsaw Pact suppression of the liberal reforms of Alexander Dubček, the first secretary of the Communist Party. He appealed the conviction and went on to found the Party of Czech Communists.

Bernard Cook

Stepinac, Alojzije (1898–1960)

Roman Catholic prelate, archbishop of Zagreb, Croatia. Alojzije Stepinac, was born into a peasant family near Krasic, Austria-Hungary, on May 8, 1898. Despite his belated denunciation in March 1943 of the persecution of the Serbs, Jews, and Gypsies by the Croatian fascist Ustaša regime of Ante Pavelić, he was prosecuted by the new Communist regime in October 1946. However, during the trial Stepinac was not condemned for his collaboration with the extreme right-wing regime, but, because he represented the very symbol of the anti-Communist struggle, he constituted a threat to the new regime of Tito, the founder and leader of the Communist Yugoslav state. Stepinac was sentenced to sixteen years in prison. This was commuted to house arrest in 1951 and was forbidden by the government to resume his apostolic functions. He was made a cardinal by Pope Pius XII in 1953. Stepinac has recently been rehabilitated by the Croatian parliament and a canonization process has begun in Rome.

BIBLIOGRAPHY

Bulajic, Milan. *The Role of the Vatican in the Break-up of the Yugoslav State: The Mission of the Vatican in the Independent State of Croatia: Ustashi Crimes of Genocide.* Belgrade: Ministry of Information of the Republic of Serbia, 1993.

Cavalli, Fiorello. *Il processo dell'arcivescovo di Zagabria.* Rome: La Civilta cattolica, 1947.

Landercy, M. *Le cardinal Stepinac: martyr des droits de l'homme.* Paris: Apostolat des Éditions, 1981.

Prcela, John. *Archbishop Stepinac in His Country's Church-State Relations.* Scottsdale, Ariz.: Published for the Croatian Holocaust Information Center by Associated Book Publishers, 1990.

Stepinac, Alojzije. *Stepinac govori; zivot i rad te zbirka govora, propovijedi, pisama i okruznica velikog hrvatskog rodoljuba i mucenika dra Alojzija Stepinca. Napisao i tekstove priredio: Eugen Beluhan Kostelic.* Valencia, Spain: 1967.

Catherine Lutard
(Tr. by B. Cook)

Stikker, Dirk (1897–1979)

Secretary-general of NATO (1961–64). Dirk Uipko Stikker was born in Winschoten, Netherlands on January 5, 1897. He received a doctorate in law from the University of Groningen in 1922. Stikker achieved prominence in banking and business. During the German occupation of World War II, he promoted cooperation between the organizations of employers and workers. His efforts after the war helped create the Foundation of Labor, which he chaired. In 1946 he spearheaded the formation of the Freedom Party, which he led for two years and represented in the parliament. In 1948 he was a founder of the People's Party for Freedom and Democracy, formed by an amalgamation of the Freedom Party and elements of the Labor Party, led by P. J. Oud, mayor of Rotterdam. Stikker was elected president of the new party and Oud served as vice president.

From August 7, 1948, to September 1952, Stikker was foreign minister in the coalition government of Willem Drees. In that post, he supported the formation in January 1949 of the Council of Europe, a step toward European integration, and the 1952 European Coal and Steel Community. He furthered the Benelux agreement and participated in the formation of a single North Atlantic Alliance, the Atlantic Pact established with the NATO treaty signed on April 4, 1949. In September he participated in the first meeting of the North Atlantic Council. In 1948–49 he also represented the Netherlands in negotiations that resulted in the Dutch acceptance of Indonesian independence on December 27, 1949. In February, 1950 he was elected political mediator of the Organization for European Economic Cooperation (OEEC), set up in 1948 to coordinate U.S.-sponsored Marshall Plan aid. From late 1950 to 1952 Strikker served as chairman of the Council of the OEEC.

Following a reorganization of the Dutch cabinet, Strikker was appointed ambassador to Great Britain from 1952 to 1956, and ambassador to Iceland from 1956 to 1958. In 1958 he was appointed permanent Dutch ambassador to NATO and the OEEC, and to the latter's 1961 successor, the Organization for Economic Cooperation and Development (OECD). On April 21, 1961, he succeeded Paul-Henri Spaak as secretary-general of NATO and chairman of the North Atlantic Council. He presided over a NATO buildup during the Berlin Crisis in 1948 and 1949. He resigned his NATO post in 1964 and died in 1979.

Stikker played an important role in the effort to establish a cooperation relationship between the countries of Western Europe after World War II.

BIBLIOGRAPHY

Stikker, Dirk U. *Men of Responsibility: A Memoir.* New York: Harper & Row, 1966.

Westers, Marnix F. *Mr. D.U. Stikker en de na-oorlogse reconstructie van het liberalisme in Nederland: een zakenman in de politieke arena.* Amsterdam: Bataafsche Leeuw, 1988.

Bernard Cook

Stolojan, Theodor (1944–)

Romanian prime minister (October 1991–October 1992). Theodor Stolojan, an economist, served in President Nicolae Ceauşescu's regime as a director in the Hard-Currency Department of the Finance Ministry from 1982 to 1987. He was also a deputy secretary of the Finance Ministry's Romanian Communist Party branch. Following the fall of communism in Romania in December 1989, Stolojan resigned from the Communist Party and refrained from joining any of the numerous political parties that sprang up in post-Communist Romania. Nevertheless, because of his economic expertise and his personal contacts, he was appointed the Minister of Finance in Romania's first post-Communist government and held the post until April 1991, when he was appointed head of the National Privatization Agency, which was charged with breaking up some of the huge Communist-created industrial enterprises. By September 1991 Stolojan had become a widely respected financial expert. He was also considered a more ardent adherent of radical economic reforms than Prime Minister Petre Roman. In March 1991 Stolojan resigned from Roman's cabinet because he considered its price deregulations insufficient. While committed to replacing communism with free enterprise, he wanted social protection for Romanians whom privatization would affect adversely.

For three days in September 1991 Bucharest endured its third invasion of militant miners from the Jiu Valley since February 1990. This time a number of local residents joined their rampage, which culminated in an unsuccessful storming of President Ion Iliescu's residence. The most prominent victim of this crisis was Prime Minister Roman, whom Iliescu forced to resign. On October 1 Iliescu announced that he had selected Stolojan to head a caretaker government until national elections could be held in 1992. Stolojan's credentials as a reformer appealed to Iliescu, who, in order to gain economic assistance and credit, needed to reassure the West that Romania's reform program would continue; he also wished to improve Romania's violence-tarnished international image. Stolojan's administration sought economic stability and more market reform during his year in office, but with mixed results. In May 1992 he removed 25 percent of state subsidies on a number of consumer products, including food staples, and on essential services, such as electricity. Gasoline prices were raised in October 1992. These measures contributed to the inflation rate of 8 to 12 percent per month that Romanians suffered during Stolojan's administration. To keep inflation under control, Stolojan accepted higher rates of unemployment, which rose from 2.7 percent in October 1991 to 8.6 percent in October 1992. During this same time Romanian industrial production fell 23.5 percent despite an increase in exports. Foreign investments, plus credits and loans from the World Bank, the International Monetary Fund, and the United States Export-Import Bank, prevented the economy from deteriorating further, but an estimated 50 percent of Romanians were living in poverty by October 1992. Privatization proceeded slowly, although the government distributed vouchers to eligible citizens for their individual share of state property and gave preferences to small investors and employees of firms being privatized.

Stolojan's other main goal was to oversee genuine democratic elections in 1992, which he achieved despite some charges of fraud. Since the elections, Stolojan has worked as a top official of the World Bank in Washington, D.C.

BIBLIOGRAPHY

Jackson, Marvin R. *The Romanian Economy and Political Economy after Ceausescu.* Cologne: Bundesinstitut für Ostwissenschaftliche und Internationale Studien, 1990.

Organisation for Economic Co-operation and Development. *Romania: An Economic Assessment.* Paris: Organisation for Economic Cooperation and Development, 1993.

Ovidiu, Cernei Florin. *The Transition to Market Oriented Economy: Case of Romania, the Present Facts and Situations.* Tokyo, Japan: Dept. of Research Cooperation, Economic Research Institute, Economic Planning Agency, 1995.

Stan, Lavinia. *Romania in Transition.* Brookfield, Vt.: Dartmouth, 1997.

Robert Forrest

SEE ALSO Iliescu, Ion; Roman, Petre

Stolpe, Manfred (1936–)

Minister-President of the Land (State) Brandenburg, Germany. Manfred Stolpe was born on May 16, 1936, in Stettin. After obtaining his *Abitur* at the secondary school in Greifswald in the German Democratic Republic (East Germany), Stolpe studied law at Jena and Berlin. In 1959 he began working with the Evangelical Church (EKD) in Berlin-Brandenburg and from 1962 to 1969 held the post of chief legal council for the EKD. In 1962 Stolpe secretly entered the ranks of the East German secret police (Stasi). Resisting state pressure to subordinate the church to socialism, Stolpe in 1969 cofounded the Bund Evangelischer Kirche (United Evangelical Church of Germany, BEK) and subsequently directed its secretariat. In 1982, Stolpe became the BEK's vice chair as well as president of the Consistory of the Berlin-Brandenburg Church. During these years Stolpe resolved many disputes among state authorities, the church, and East German youth. In recognition of his actions in the former East Germany, Stolpe was asked to give the keynote address to the joint Bundestag-Volkskammer meeting of the West and East German parliaments in anticipation of the forthcoming reunification of Germany (October 3, 1990), on June 17, 1990. Joining the Social Democratic Party (SPD) in June 1990, Stolpe became Brandenburg's minister-president on November 22, 1990. Plagued by revelations of his ties with the secret police, Stolpe acknowledged his Stasi past in December 1990 but denied that the Stasi had influenced his actions. Nevertheless, his center-left coalition fell apart in March 1994 when the Alliance group of Greens and civil rights activists left, accusing Stolpe of lying about his links with the Stasi. Stolpe governed thereafter through a minority SPD-Free Democrat government.

BIBLIOGRAPHY

Stolpe, Manfred. *Schwieriger Aufbruch.* Berlin: Siedler, 1992.

David A. Meier

Stoltenberg, Thorvald (1931–)

Norwegian politician and diplomat. Thorvald Stoltenberg was born in Oslo on July 8, 1931. He joined the Norwegian Foreign Service in 1959 and served at a number of foreign posts. In 1970–71 he was the international secretary for the Norwegian Federation of Trade Unions. Stoltenberg was undersecretary of state in the Foreign Ministry (1971–72, 1976–79), and in the ministry of commerce (1974–76). He also served as minister of defense (1979–81) and minister of foreign affairs (1987–89, 1990–93). In 1989–90 he was Norwegian ambassador to the United Nations. Stoltenberg served as U.N. high commissioner for refugees in 1989–90. He became the U.N.'s chief negotiator in the former Yugoslavia, serving first as the special representative of the U.N. secretary-general in the former Yugoslavia in 1993–94, then replacing Cyrus Vance as cochair, with Lord David Owen, of the International Conference on the Former Yugoslavia from 1994 to 1996. In 1996 he became Norwegian ambassador to Denmark.

BIBLIOGRAPHY

Hvem er Hvem?, 14th ed. Oslo: Kunnskapsforlaget, 1994.

Bruce Olav Solheim
Bernard Cook

Stoph, Willi (1914–)

Chairman of the Council of Ministers of the German Democratic Republic (GDR, East Germany). Willi Stoph, a bricklayer and the son of a blue-collar worker, joined the German Communist Party in 1931. Although involved in antifascist activities after Hitler came to power in 1933, he served in the armed forces during World War II until wounded. After the war, as a department head in the German Central Administration for Industry, Stoph was instrumental in the development of the administrative-command system in the Soviet zone of Germany, the precursor to the GDR. The austere Berliner was a member of the Socialist Unity (Communist) Party (SED) Politburo from 1953 to 1989, and the holder of key economic and security posts such as minister of the interior (1952–55), minister of national defense (1956–60), and chairman of the Council of Ministers (1964–73, 1976–89).

At one time in line to succeed Walter Ulbricht as SED general secretary Stoph took a backseat when Erich Honecker became general secretary in 1971, and he was demoted in 1973 to chairman of the Council of State. Returning three years later to the Council of Ministers, Stoph continued to operate as the arch bureaucrat. Although in general agreement with Honecker over the basic principles of state socialism in the GDR, he was concerned about the perilous state of the country's finances and its debt during the 1980s and played a crucial role in Honecker's overthrow. As chairman of the Council of Ministers he introduced a surprise item into the agenda of the October 17, 1989, meeting of the SED Politburo calling for the removal of Honecker as general secretary and his replacement by Egon Krenz. After German reunification in 1990, he was imprisoned temporarily on a charge of misuse of office and corruption. An attempt to charge him with complicity in the shootings of East Germans attempting to cross West Germany had to be abandoned.

BIBLIOGRAPHY

Stoph, Willi. *DDR—Staat des Sozialismus und des Friedens: Ausgewählte Reden und Aufsätze.* Berlin: Dietz, 1984.

Mike Dennis

SEE ALSO Honecker, Erich; Ulbricht, Walter

Stoyanov, Petar (1952–)

President of Bulgaria. Petar Stephanov Stoyanov was born on May 25, 1952, in Plovdiv. He received a degree in law from Sofia University. Until 1992 he was a lawyer, specializing in divorce processes, in Plovdiv. In 1989 Stoyanov was involved in the Club for "Glasnost and Perestroika." He was a member of the Union for Democratic Forces, the strongest component of the anti-Communist opposition in Bulgaria. He was elected to the National Assembly in 1990, and during the elections to the National Assembly in 1991 Stoyanov was a member of the Coordination Committee for the campaign of the anti-Communist opposition in the city of Plovdiv. He was appointed deputy minister of justice in Philip Dimitrov's government, the first government of the Union of Democratic Forces a coalition of thirteen political parties that had been organized in opposition to the former communists in 1992–93. In 1993, Stoyanov became vice president of the National Club for Democracy and in 1995 vice president of the Union of Democratic Forces. In the 1996 National Assembly election, Stoyanov was elected from the town of Montana. He was then chosen to be vice president of the parliamentary group of the Union of Democratic Forces. At the Union's March 1996 national conference, Stoyanov was named the party's candidate in the forthcoming presidential election, and on November 3, 1996, he was elected president of Bulgaria.

Dimiter Minchev

Strásky, Jan (1940–)

Jan Strásky was born in Plzeň on December 24, 1940. He received a Ph.D. in economics from Charles University in Prague in 1970. He worked at the State Bank in Prague from 1968 to 1989. In 1990–91 he was director of the Commerce Bank. From 1991 to 1992 Strásky, a member of Václav Klaus's center-right Civic Democratic Party (ODS), served as the deputy prime minister of the Czech government. In 1992 when he served as prime minister from July 20 to December 31, Strásky simultaneously became the last prime minister of the Czech and Slovak Federated Republic. Following the division of the country on January 1, 1993, Klaus became prime minister of the Czech Republic. From 1993 to 1995 Strásky was minister of transportation. In 1995 he became minister of health. In February 1997, in an effort to stave off the bankruptcy of two prime teaching medical facilities, Strásky introduced controversial cost-cutting and consolidating measures.

Bernard Cook

Strategic Arms Limitation Talks I

The Strategic Arms Limitation Talks (SALT I) resulted in a treaty limiting antiballistic missile (ABM) systems and an agreement limiting strategic offensive arms. These accords were signed on May 26, 1972, after two and a half years of negotiation between the United States and the USSR. A number of "agreed statements" that clarified specific provisions or parts of the negotiating history were attached.

The ABM Treaty sought to preclude the development of national missile defense systems. This treaty is of unlimited duration but allows either party the right to withdraw on six-months notice if it believes its national interests are jeopardized.

Two ABM deployment areas were allowed for each nation and were so restrictive that a nationwide ballistic missile defense system could not be developed. Each side was allowed a system to defend its capital and another to protect an intercontinental ballistic missile (ICBM) launch site. These systems must be at least 1,300 kilometers away from each other, and each could have one hundred interceptor missiles and one hundred launchers. New generations of early-warning radars may be deployed, but they must be sited along the periphery of each country and directed outward so as not to facilitate an ABM defense. As agreed, the ABM Treaty is reviewed every five years.

A protocol to this treaty was signed on July 3, 1974, reducing the number of ABM deployment areas to one for each nation. The ABM Treaty was criticized by conservatives in the United States for terminating the Safeguard ABM system, which was to be deployed in twelve locations throughout the United States to protect ICBM sites, and for erasing the U.S. lead in ABM research and development. It was further criticized for encouraging the Soviet Union to create a counterforce capability that threatened U.S. land-based deterrent forces.

The agreement was to remain in force for five years, and was a stopgap measure to limit the offensive strategic arms race while further negotiations would be carried out under SALT II. Under this agreement, strategic land-based ballistic missile launchers, including those under construction, were frozen at current levels. Further, submarine-launched ballistic missiles (SLBMs) could be increased to greater levels only if accompanied by the destruction of an equal number of older ICBM or SLBM launchers. Soviet strategic force ceiling levels were set at 1,618 ICBMs and 950 SLBMs (740 then existed). U.S. strategic force ceiling levels were set at 1,054 ICBMs and 710 SLBMs (656 then existed).

Although mobile ICBMs, multiple-independently-targetable-reentry-vehicle (MIRV) ballistic missiles, and strategic bombers, of which the United States enjoyed an advantage, were not covered in the Interim Agreement, it was criticized for conceding to the USSR an advantage in strategic ballistic missile launchers in return for the continuance of East-West arms control negotiations.

BIBLIOGRAPHY

Labrie, Roger P., ed. *SALT Handbook: Key Documents and Issues 1972–1979.* Washington, D.C.: American Enterprise Institute for Public Policy Research, 1979.

Smith, Gerard C. "The Treaty's Basic Provisions: View of the U.S. Negotiator," in Walter Stützle, Bhupendra Jasani, and Regina Cowen. *The ABM Treaty: To Defend or Not to Defend?* Oxford: Oxford University Press, 1987.

U.S. Arms Control and Disarmament Agency. *Arms Control and Disarmament Agreements: Texts and Histories of the Negotiations.* Washington, D.C.: Government Printing Office, 1990.

Robert J. Bunker

SEE ALSO Strategic Arms Limitation Talks II

Strategic Arms Limitation Talks II

Second stage of strategic arms limitation talks (SALT II) between the USSR and the United States. The primary focus of these talks was the replacement of the SALT I Interim Agreement of May 26, 1972, with a more complete and balanced treaty.

These talks resulted in the signing on June 18, 1979, of a Treaty, Protocol, and Joint Statement of Principles that were never ratified by the U.S. Senate. Following the Soviet invasion of Afghanistan that year, President Jimmy Carter withdrew the treaty from Senate consideration, where it had come under considerable opposition. The Reagan administration, in turn, never resubmitted the treaty because of Soviet violations, such as the Krasnoyarsk radar site and the development of the SS-25 ICBM, and growing tensions as the Cold War heightened.

The treaty would have provided for an initial overall limit of 2,400 strategic nuclear delivery vehicles for each nation and a limit of 1,300 multiple-independently-targetable-reentry vehicles (MIRV) carrying ballistic missiles. The protocol would have banned the deployment of air-to-surface ballistic missiles (ASBMs) and ground- and sea-launched cruise missiles (GLCMs and SLCMs) with ranges in excess of 600 kilometers, while the Joint Statement of Principles would have provided for subsequent SALT III negotiations.

Still, the SALT II accords were observed by both the USSR and the United States on a voluntary basis until May 1986, when President Ronald Reagan announced that the United States would no longer be bound by its ceilings. In the meantime, a new round of arms control negotiations had already been initiated by the Reagan administration in July 1982 under the Strategic Arms Reduction Talks (START I).

BIBLIOGRAPHY

Labrie, Roger P., ed. *SALT Handbook: Key Documents and Issues 1972–1979.* Washington, D.C.: American Enterprise Institute for Public Policy Research, 1979.

U.S. Arms Control and Disarmament Agency. *Arms Control and Disarmament Agreements: Texts and Histories of the Negotiations.* Washington, D.C.: Government Printing Office, 1990.

U.S. Congress, Committee on Foreign Relations. *The SALT II Treaty.* Report and Hearings. 96th Congress, 1st Session. Washington, D.C.: Government Printing Office, 1979.

Robert J. Bunker

SEE ALSO Strategic Arms Limitation Talks I; Strategic Arms Reduction Treaty

Strategic Arms Reduction Treaty

Arms control talks (START I) between the USSR and the United States that replaced the Strategic Arms Limitation Talks (SALT). These talks were carried out from June 1982 until July 1991, resulting in the Treaty Between the United States and the USSR on the Reduction and Limitation of Strategic Offensive Arms.

These talks were initially conducted by the United States with the goal of reducing large numbers of Soviet multiple-independently-targetable-reentry-vehicled (MIRVed) intercontinental ballistic missiles (ICBMs), while at the same time keeping intact U.S. submarine-launched ballistic missiles (SLBM) and air-launched-cruise-missiles-(ALCM)-based strategic forces. Soviet delegates countered these proposals with their own demands, which included a total ban on all long-range cruise missiles. These talks were broken off by the USSR in November 1983. They resumed only in March 1985, under the bilateral Nuclear and Space Talks forum, after an easing of tensions over U.S. basing of ground-launched cruise missiles (GLCMs) and Pershing IIs in Western Europe. The START I Treaty was finally reached on July 31, 1991. The Russian Federation, Republic of Belarus, Ukraine, and Kazakhstan—four successor states of the former Soviet Union—became parties to this treaty with the signing of the Lisbon Protocol in May 1992.

In this treaty an agreed limit of 1,600 "deployed" strategic nuclear delivery vehicles (SNDVs) and 6,000 "accountable" warheads (that is, warheads on the SNDVs) was set. For these warheads, limits were set at 4,900 for deployed ICBMs/SLBMs, 1,100 for deployed mobile ICBMs, and 1,540 for deployed heavy ICBMs. Reductions to the agreed upon limits were to take place in three phases over the course of seven years. The treaty itself would be in force for fifteen years, at the end of which an option for extension exists.

The first phase of reductions took place no later than thirty-six months after treaty entry into force and witnessed a lowering of SNDVs to 2,100 and warheads to 9,150 (of which only 8,050 could be deployed on ICBMs/SLBMs). The second phase of reductions was slated to take effect no later than sixty months after the treaty's entry into force and would achieve a lowering of SNDVs to 1,900 and warheads to 7,950 (of which only 6,750 could be deployed on ICBMs/SLBMs). The third phase of reductions would take place no later than eighty-four months after the treaty's entry into force and represents the target numbers agreed upon in this accord. Separate agreements to this treaty limited SLCMs with ranges above 600 kilometers at 800 for each nation and limited Soviet Backfire bombers to 500.

Three major criticisms of the START I Treaty exist. First, it fails to take into account immense Soviet ICBM/SLBM reload capabilities (i.e., strategic SNDV reserves). Second, the lack of parity between Soviet and U.S. SNDVs was not given consideration. The Soviet ICBM force was far more lethal than its U.S. counterpart, yet both sides' ICBMs were counted equally. Last, the concept of "accountable" warheads deployed on SNDVs is flawed. Photoreconnaissance suggests that the Soviet SS-18 force, which represented most of the Soviet's ICBM throw weight, was capable of being outfitted with additional warheads per missile in violation of treaty terms.

Because of these criticisms, it has been argued that the START I Treaty allowed the Soviets to use the rubric of arms reductions to achieve strategic offensive force modernization while at the same time denying such an option to the United States. With the demise of the USSR and the signing in January 1993 of the START II agreement as yet unratified, many of these criticisms may be alleviated. The START II treaty eliminates all MIRV-equipped ICBMs and limits the overall number of warheads to 3,500 or fewer.

BIBLIOGRAPHY

Clark, Mark T. "START and the Bush Initiative." *Global Affairs* (Winter 1992): 132–49.

Kartchner, Kerry M. *Negotiating START: Strategic Arms Reduction Talks and the Quest for Strategic Stability.* New Brunswick, N.J.: Transaction Publishers, 1992.

U.S. Arms Control and Disarmament Agency. *START: Treaty Between the United States of America and the Union of Soviet Socialist Republics on the Reduction and Limitation of Strategic Offensive Arms.* Washington, D.C.: Government Printing Office, 1991.

Robert J. Bunker

Strategic Defense Initiative

The Strategic Defense Initiative (SDI) was a research and technology development program established by the United States in January 1984. The Strategic Defense Initiative Organization (SDIO) was created in April 1984 to explore five research concepts relating to a defense against ballistic missiles. Two of these concepts were based primarily on forms of advanced nonnuclear weaponry, directed-energy weapons (DEW): lasers and particle beams, and kinetic energy weapons (KEW): electromagnetic and rail guns. The three other research concepts were surveillance, acquisition, tracking and kill assessment (SATKA), systems analysis and battle management (SA/BM), and survivability, lethality, and key technologies (SLKT).

The Reagan administration's primary rationale behind SDI was originally to protect the population of the United States and that of its allies by a "missile shield"; however, the emphasis shifted to one of deterrence and thereafter to lower Soviet capacity for preemptive strike capability against U.S. retaliatory forces.

The USSR did not respond to the SDI. Rather, the SDI was a response by the United States to the strategic missile defense program of the USSR. For years prior to the SDI, the Soviets had been actively creating and deploying strategic missile defenses, at times in violation of the 1972 Anti-Ballistic Missile (ABM) Treaty. Defenses for the Soviet capital, Moscow, represented the only fully operational ABM system deployed in the world.

Soviet doctrine and strategy emphasized strategic defense as a complement to the use of overwhelming offensive forces. The SDI directly challenged Moscow's preemptive strike capability and, as a result, placed its entire military strategy in jeopardy. Further, the SDI threatened to take the Cold War to a new threshold and place the USSR in a no-win situation. A ballistic missile defense race would place such an immense strain on the Soviet economic and political system that it would be unable to compete effectively against a technologically advanced West unless it adopted a market economy. The adoption of this type of economic system would discredit and ultimately undermine the ideology of the Soviet Communist regime.

In response, an intensive propaganda and disinformation campaign was directed against the SDI by the USSR. This well-coordinated campaign was conducted on a number of levels, including overt government arms control efforts, propaganda, and KGB-promoted active measures that focused on the SDI.

The SDI program was reoriented in 1991 under the Bush administration to defend against limited ballistic missile threats and became known as global protection against limited strikes (GPALS). This program in turn was reorganized under the Ballistic Missile Defense Organization (BMDO) by the Clinton administration. The BMDO focused on theater missile defense (TMD) and contained very modest strategic ballistic missile defense research.

The SDI was also known derogatorily as "star wars" because of the science fiction-like weaponry it would require. This type of weaponry, of which lasers are one example, is currently beginning to be deployed by U.S. ground forces.

BIBLIOGRAPHY

Clark, Mark T. "The Soviet Political Campaign Against the U.S. Strategic Defense Initiative." (Ph.d diss, University of Southern California, 1989.

Mikheev, Dmitrii. *The Soviet Perspective on the Strategic Defense Initiative.* Washington, D.C.: Pergamon-Brassey's International Defense Publishers, 1987.

Yost, David S. *Soviet Ballistic Missile Defense and the Western Alliance.* Cambridge, Mass.: Harvard University Press, 1988.

Robert J. Bunker

SEE ALSO Arms Control Treaties and Agreements

Strauss, Franz Josef (1915–88)

Conservative West German political leader from 1946 to 1988. Franz Josef Strauss exercised great political influence as head of the Christian Social Union (CSU), the Bavarian State counterpart of the Christian Democratic Union (CDU), from 1961 to his death in 1988. A member of the Bundestag (lower house of parliament) for almost thirty years, he held important ministerial posts in several national governments from 1953 to 1969, became the CDU/CSU candidate for chancellor in the Bundestag election of 1980, and served as minister-president (governor) of the Land (state) of Bavaria from 1978 until his death. His outspoken anticommunism and advocacy of military and nuclear power endeared him to the right, while his authoritarian, impulsive, bellicose style dismayed, angered, and frightened liberals and the Left.

A former member of the National Socialist Student Association though not the Nazi Party, Strauss completed his training as a high school teacher before serving in World War II as a soldier at the front and as an officer responsible for strengthening military morale. He became a founding member of the CSU in 1945 and served as the chairman of the regional party organization before becoming chief administrator of his home district of Schöngau in Bavaria and senior civil servant in the Bavarian Ministry of Culture in 1946. In 1948 Strauss was promoted to director of the youth bureau in the Bavarian government, and was one of the officials selected to represent Bavaria in the Economic Council of the newly amalgamated Western zones of occupation in Frankfurt. Named secretary-general of the CSU in December 1948, Strauss was elected to the first Bundestag of the newly founded Federal Republic of Germany (FRG) in August 1949. Impressed by his talent for politics, Chancellor Konrad Adenauer called him into the cabinet as minister for special tasks in 1953. In 1955, the year that the FRG regained full internal sovereignty, Strauss was appointed by Adenauer to head the newly created Ministry for Atomic Affairs, a position he used to attack the policies of his colleague Theodor Blank, whose post as minister of defense he coveted. After some vacillation Adenauer supported Strauss's demands that Germany's newly created army, the Bundeswehr, be equipped with nuclear weapons as part of a European nuclear force. As Adenauer's minister of defense from 1956 to 1962, Strauss presided over the stationing of tactical nuclear weapons under American control in West Germany in 1960, but failed in his clandestine efforts to reverse the government's 1955 renunciation of nuclear arms for the Bundeswehr. Strauss's (nuclear obsession) provoked a public protest authored in 1957 by physicist Friedrich von Weizsäcker and signed by seventeen colleagues, including Nobel prize winners Otto Hahn, Max von Laue, Werner Heisenberg, and Max Born. Strauss's nuclear ambitions and Cold War militancy were also severely criticized in *Der Spiegel,* Germany's leading news magazine, edited by Rudolf Augstein. A highly critical article in October 1962 on Strauss's nuclear policy and the Bundeswehr's alleged lack of preparedness for conventional war led to the arrest of Augstein and several journalists on the charge of revealing military secrets. Strauss's personal role in *Der Spiegel* affair, which was widely perceived as a heavy-handed attempt to suppress the critical voice of the press, forced his resignation from the Adenauer government in November 1962.

After firming up his political base in Bavaria as the newly elected head of the CSU, Strauss returned to the government from 1966 to 1969 as minister of finance in Kurt-Georg Kiesinger's grand coalition with the Social Democrats (SPD). These were administratively among the most successful years of his career. Together with Economics Minister Karl Schiller (SPD), Strauss introduced reforms that led to renewed economic growth, but he opposed the revaluation of the undervalued deutsche mark, which occurred over Strauss's opposition in 1969. Strauss also made no secret of his opposition to German participation in the Nuclear Non-Proliferation Treaty (to which west Germany did not adhere until 1974). His advocacy of repressive measures against the student movement and his support for the Vietnam War may have cost the CDU/CSU the necessary votes to prevent Willy Brandt's coalition from coming to power in 1969. Nor could Strauss's fierce criticism of *Ostpolitik,* Brandt's policy to establish relations with the Communist countries of Eastern Europe, prevent Brandt's triumphant reelection in 1972.

In Bavaria, Strauss's support continued to grow as the CSU won a record-breaking 62 percent of the vote in state elections in 1974. But his hard-line, right-wing positions, which included opposition to the 1975 Helsinki Accords, made him unacceptable to moderates in the CDU, who united behind Helmut Kohl as the CDU/CSU chancellor candidate in the 1976 national election. After Kohl's defeat by the SPD's Helmut Schmidt, Strauss used the threat of launching the CSU as a national party to the right of the CDU and thus breaking up the twenty nine-year old CDU/CSU alliance to put himself at the head of the CDU/CSU ticket for the 1980 election. Strauss's efforts to convey a more moderate image in the election campaign failed to convince the German public, however, and Strauss's defeat once again strengthened

Kohl, who became chancellor after the breakup of the Social-Liberal coalition in 1982.

Disappointed in his quest for national power and unable to secure the desired post of foreign minister in Kohl's government because of the coalition partner FDP's claim to that office, Strauss used his position as minister-president of Bavaria to launch several personal diplomatic initiatives, the most startling of which was the negotiation of a billion-mark West German bank loan to East Germany in 1983. His efforts to steer the CDU/CSU policies to the right in the 1987 election did not meet with success, however, and precluded his return to national office. Strauss died in 1988 at the age of seventy-three.

BIBLIOGRAPHY

Bickerich, Wolfram. *Franz Josef Strauss: Die Biographie.* Düsseldorf: Econ Verlag, 1996.

Krieger, Wolfgang. *Franz Josef Strauss: Der barocke Demokrat aus Bayern.* Goettingen: Muster-Schmidt Verlag, 1995.

Schöll, Walter, and Wilfried Scharnagl, eds. *Franz Josef Strauss: Der Mensch und der Staatsmann. Ein Porträt.* Percha: Verlag R.S. Schulz, 1984.

Strauss, Franz Josef. *Die Erinnerungen.* Berlin: Siedler Verlag, 1989.

Rod Stackelberg

SEE ALSO *Spiegel* Affair

Strougal, Lubomír (1924–)

Czechoslovak premier (1970–88). Lubomír Strougal was born in Veseli nad Luznici on October 19, 1924. He became a member of the Communist Party of Czechoslovakia in 1945, the year he began the study of law at Charles University in Prague. He received a doctorate in law in 1949. He was admitted to the party's Central Committee in June 1958. He was a member of the Party Secretariat from June 1958 until June 1961, when he became interior minister.

Strougal supported the reforms of the Prague Spring and was appointed deputy prime minister on April 8, 1968. At the time of the Soviet-led Warsaw Pact invasion of Czechoslovakia on August 20, 1968, he signed a formal protest denouncing it and demanding a withdrawal of the troops. He soon adopted a cooperative attitude, however.

Strougal was appointed prime minister in 1970 by Gustav Husák, at the time first secretary of the Communist Party and who was presiding over the elimination of the liberalization that had occurred during the Prague Spring. By 1988 Strougal had become the leading party advocate for the sort of changes being promoted by Soviet leader Mikhail Gorbachev in the USSR. In early 1988 Strougal said that the party leadership was divided into those who opposed change, those who wanted slow change, and those who desired prompt reform. While Strougal advocated rapid reform, Miloš Jakeš, who had become the general secretary of the Communist Party in December 1987, desired a slow approach to prevent the process from escaping the control of the party. Besides his criticism of the economy, Strougal had opposed the decision of party leaders in June of that year to break up a Prague human rights conference and to use police against demonstrators.

On October 10, 1988, Strougal relinquished his eighteen-year hold on the prime ministership and resigned from the party Presidium. His departure resulted from his differences with Jakeš. He was succeeded by Ladislav Adamec. Strougal has been credited by some with being a proponent of change who was forced to temper his views after the Warsaw Pact invasion. In the opinion of others he was an opportunist.

BIBLIOGRAPHY

Tagliabue, John. "Czech Premier Quits Over Policy Rift." *New York Times,* October 11, 1988.

———. "Prague Journal: The Czechs' Fate." *New York Times,* July 8, 1988.

Bernard Cook

SEE ALSO Husák, Gustav; Jakeš, Miloš

Stuart, Francis (1902–)

Irish novelist, journalist, and poet. Francis Stuart is the author of more than twenty mainly autobiographical, novels, the most famous remains *Black List section H* (1971). He was born in Australia in 1902, but his family returned to Ireland. He spent his childhood in Derry and Meath, but was educated in England, finally at Rugby, which he left without graduating. His early marriage to Iseult Gonne was unhappy. He fought on the republican side during the Irish Civil War (1922–23) and was imprisoned in 1923.

Stuart was a convert to Catholicism and was influenced by mysticism. He had mixed literary and poetic success during the 1920s and 1930s. Following a lecturing contract, Stuart spent the years of World War II at Berlin University and as a broadcaster for German radio, believing that his status as the citizen of a neutral state allowed him to do this. In 1945 he was arrested and imprisoned without charge by the French. After his release he lived in Germany until 1958 when he returned to Ireland. His novels *The Pillar of Cloud* (1948) and *Redemption* (1949) marked the rebirth of his career, which saw six more novels including *The Flowering Cross* (1950) and *Victors and Vanquished* (1958). He reached his peak popularity in recent years and has attained something of a cult status among Irish intellectuals.

Michael J. Kennedy

Sturzo, Luigi (1871–1959)

Italian priest, political figure, and political theorist. Luigi Sturzo was born in Caltagirone, Sicily, on November 26, 1871. He was a sociologist and one of the most original political thinkers produced by Catholic culture in the nineteenth and twentieth centuries. He was a critic of his time. He clearly understood the dysfunctions of Western democracy and the bankruptcy of communism, both as a doctrine and as a system of government, while it appeared to be endowed with political and military power. Some of his essays published during his exile by American newspapers then collected in the volume *La mia battaglia da New York (1943–1946)* looked to the future, predicting, amid general skepticism, the collapse of the Soviet Union and the advent of a new era with the federation of all the states of Europe from the Atlantic to the Urals.

Sturzo's father was Felice Sturzo, baron of Aldobrando, a member of the landed aristocracy. The family had produced a number of distinguished political figures, magistrates, and administrators. After his ordination as a priest, Sturzo received degrees in philosophy and theology from the Gregorian University in Rome. There he became acquainted with Giuseppe Toniolo a proponent of Christian Syndicalism (unions) and the corporate state, a state organized according to economic functions to blunt this dursiveness of class struggle, and Romolo Murri, a priest proponent of church involvement in social issues. With those two, he became a proponent of the new ecclesiastical direction launched by Pope Leo XIII, and immersed himself in local political activity. Sturzo founded and directed *La Croce di Constantino,* a social Christian weekly. Inspired by *Rerum Novarum* the 1891 social encyclical issued by Pope Leo XIII he organized the first Catholic cooperatives of tenant farmers and workers. In 1904 he was named the prefectural commissioner of Caltagirone, and in 1905 he obtained a pontifical dispensation, successfully forming an electoral list for the communal council. For the next fifteen years he simultaneously held the offices of mayor and provincial counselor. From 1912 to 1924 he was vice president of the Association of Italian Towns. In addition, from 1915 to 1917 he was secretary-general of the Catholic Action movement.

Following the First World War, when Italy though victorious was in the grip of economic and political crisis, Sturzo founded the Italian Popular Party, the first Catholic political party, on January 18, 1919. As its secretary until 1923 he defined it as nonconfessional, centrist, and interclass in character. He rejected every effort to compromise with dictator Benito Mussolini and tried in vain to resist the influence of the fascist apparatus. He was forced by the church hierarchy to resign as director of the party, however, and to go into exile in 1924, first to Paris, then London, and finally Jacksonville, Florida, and New York City. He returned to Italy on September 5, 1946, after twenty two years of forced absence.

To his prolific writing in exile, he added in his final period in Rome parliamentary discourses on the "compelling necessity" for institutional reform and a lively journalistic campaign against the dangerous growth of communism, which he regarded as immoral. He envisioned his effort as a battle for liberty when the young Italian democracy was in danger of degenerating into demagoguery or a tyranny of the majority.

Among his numerous philosophical, political, and sociological works are *Italy and Fascism* (1926), *La comunità intentazionale e il diritto di guerra* (1928), *La Società: sua natura e leggi* (1935), *Politica e morale* (1936), *Church and State* (1939), *La vera vita, Sociologia del soprannaturale* (1943), *L'Italia e il nuovo ordine internazionale* (1944), *Problemi spirituali del nostro tempo* (1945), and *Nazionalismo e intemazionalismo* (1946).

In accord with Christian principles, Sturzo did not respond critically to the proponents of Christian Democracy who regarded themselves as the heirs of the Popular Party. He would have preferred that they be more faithful to their professed ideals, less compromising, and without a sense of inferiority with regard to their adversaries. Many points, nevertheless, divided him from the new Christian Democratic Party. He was, for example, still convinced of the need for a nonconfessional lay party. As an advocate of a clear distinction between religion and politics, he always opposed calling a party of Christian inspiration Christian Democracy. And eighteen days before his death, writing in *Il Giornale d'Italia,* Sturzo condemned statism, which he regarded as the most lethal viruses of democracy.

Sturzo was named senator for life in 1953 by President Luigi Einaudi. In the Senate Sturzo always sought to promote his idea of the common good rather than the interests of any political party. In 1954 he was named vice president of the Istituto dell'Enciclopedia Italiana di

Scienze, Lettere ed Arti, which was founded in 1925 by industrialist and publisher Giovanni Treccani degli Alfieri and was directed by philosopher Giovanni Gentile. He died in Rome on November 26, 1959. In 1962 his remains were transported back to his native Caltagirone. His political thought, rooted in the principle of solidarity and strongly critical of totalitarianism, has served as the inspiration for post-Communist parties of Christian inspiration.

BIBLIOGRAPHY

Campanini, Giorgio, and Nicola Antonetti. *Luigi Sturzo, il pensiero politico.* Roma, Città Nuova, 1979.

De Rosa, Gabriele. *Luigi Sturzo.* Turin: Utet, 1977.

Di Giovanni, Alberto. *Attualità di Luigi Sturzo.* Milan: Massimo, 1987.

Di Lascia, Alfred. *Filosofia e storia in Luigi Sturzo.* Rome: Cinque Lune, 1981.

Guccione, Eugenio. *Municipalismo e federalismo in Luigi Sturzo.* Turin: Società Editrice Internazionale, 1994.

Morra, Gianfranco. *Luigi Sturzo, il pensiero sociologico.* Rome: Città Nuova, 1979.

———. *Sturzo profeta della seconda Repubblica.* Bologna: Monduzzi Editore, 1995.

Piva, Francesco, and Francesco Malgeri. *Vita di Luigi Sturzo.* Rome: Cinque Lune, 1972.

Eugenio Guccione

Suárez González, Adolfo (1932–)

Spanish premier (1976–81). Adolfo Suárez was born on September 1932 in Avila. He studied law at the University of Madrid, where he eventually received a doctorate. Almost immediately after his studies he began a career in government service that would last most of his life. During the 1960s he held a series of positions in the bureaucracy of the regime of Francisco Franco, including procurator of the Cortes (parliament), vice secretary-general of the *Movimiento,* and director general of radio and television. In this last post, which he held for two tenures between 1965 and 1973, he was noted for improving the quality and relaxing the censorship of the state-sponsored media. Perhaps more important, it brought him into close contact with Franco's designated heir and Spain's future king, Juan Carlos.

Suárez, along with many other highly placed government officials, recognized the need for reform as Franco's regime waned with the leader's health. In 1975 Suárez was appointed secretary-general of the *Movimiento,* a Francoist umbrella for a plethora of political, social, and religious movements, and used his position to ease restrictions on the formation of political associations. Following Franco's death that year, the government of Carlos Arias Navarro failed to satisfy the growing demands for reform, the king's among them. Juan Carlos asked Arias Navarro to step down and in July 1996 named Suárez premier. Initial reaction to the king's appointment was cool. Suárez was not as well known as other potential candidates, and those who did know of him generally expected him to be too gradualist in his approach to reform. Spain's most prominent daily, *El Pais,* branded Suárez and his cabinet too young and too Francoist. Juan Carlos knew, however, that Suárez's pedigree would placate conservatives but that he shared the king's own vision of the post-Franco transition. In fact, the king had carefully orchestrated the nomination of Suárez by the Council of the Realm, a small body intended by Franco to ensure that the government that followed him would remain true to Francoism, through the former royal mentor, Torcuato Fernández Miranda.

After his selection, Suárez promised sweeping democratic reforms but proposed to enact them within the context of the Fundamental Laws, Spain's piecemeal Francoist constitution. In other words, Suárez, with the encouragement of Juan Carlos, set out to undo Francoism by using the mechanisms set forth in Franco's own laws. In a referendum held in 1976, his proposals for universal suffrage, a redesigned Cortes, and legalization of political parties were overwhelmingly approved. He formed the Democratic Center Union party (UCD), which won a sweeping victory in the 1977 elections, the first free elections in Spain since 1936, and was again named premier. He presided over the Cortes as it devised the constitution of 1978, which also won a landslide referendum victory.

Suárez and the UCD were again victorious in the elections of 1979 as Spain continued its successful transition to democracy. Government became increasingly difficult for him, though, as the economy slowed and regionalist violence threatened Spain's stability. In addition the coalition he built in the UCD began to fracture as party conservatives demanded more concessions. Finally, in 1981, he resigned. In the wake of his resignation an abortive right-wing coup attempted to seize power but was thwarted by the determination of Juan Carlos. While the UCD remained in power, Suárez sought several times to return to office but failed. Eventually he left the UCD to form his own party, the Social and Democratic Center (CDS). Both the UCD and the CDS were relegated to opposition roles after the victory of Felipe González and the Spanish Socialist Workers Party (PSOE) in 1982. González ruled for thirteen years, though the CDS enjoyed electoral success in 1986 and 1989, winning the third-highest number of seats in the Cortes each time. However, Suárez and the center-right parties steadily lost ground thereafter to the resurgent Popular Party (PP), the conservative party that eventually subsumed most of Spain's right and center-right political movements and came to power in 1996. Suárez retired from active political life in 1991, though he continued to speak and write about Spanish politics. In 1996 he published his memoir of and reflections on Spain's transition to democracy, *Fue Posible la Concordia.*

Steven P. James

Šubašić, Ivan (1892–1955)

Croatian politician. Following the formation of the Kingdom of the Serbs, Croats, and Slovenes in 1919, Ivan Šubašić was a member of the Croatian Peasant Party (HSS). An ally of Vladimir Maćek, the leader of the Croatian Peasant Party, Šubašić was elected to the Yugoslav parliament in 1938. He was *ban* (governor) of the Croat district (*banovina*) after the Serb-Croatian Cvetkovic-Macek Accord (1939) that reorganized Yugoslavia as a federal state. Hostile to the fascism of wartime Croatian leader, Ante Pavelić, Šubašić followed the royal government into exile to London, where he became its president. He concluded an accord with Tito, the Communist leader of the wartime Partisans in Yugoslavia in June 1944 in which he agreed that the government in-exile would cooperate with Tito. When Tito's Partisans in conjunction with the advancing Soviet army liberated Yugoslavia, it was theoretically still a monarchy, but actual power rested in the hands of Tito and the Communists. Šubašic became the foreign minister of the Yugoslav Popular Front a coalition government, dominated by the Communists, in 1945, but he resigned the same year in protest against the total seizure of power by the Communist Party.

Catherine Lutard
(Tr. by B. Cook)

Suchocka, Hanna (1945–)

Prime minister of Poland (July 1992–October 1993).

Hanna Suchocka received a Ph.D. in law from Adam Mickiewicz University in Poznan in 1975. From 1980 to 1985 she was an MP from the Democratic Party and belonged to the small opposition fraction in the Sejm (parliament). In the parliament's Committee for Legislative Agenda she voted against martial law in, and at one of a plenary session in 1982 she protested against the outlawing of Solidarity, against a repressive penalty law, and against forced labor. Suchocka's protest over Solidarity resulted in the suspension of her membership in the Democratic Party. She left the organization in 1984.

Since 1980 Suchocka has been a member of Solidarity, for which she served as a legal expert. In the parliamentary elections of 1989, as a representative of Lech Wałesa's team, she won the support of 72 percent of the voters in her constituency. In parliament she was elected to head the Civic Parliamentary Club a democratic caucus and elected vice-chairman of the Legislative Committee. With the support of the Democratic Union, founded by Tadeusz Mazowiecki, the first non-Communist prime minister, who had broken with Wałesa and became an opponent of his, Suchocka was elected to parliament for a second term. She was also elected head of the Polish delegation for the Parliamentary Assembly at the European Council and then became president of the council itself.

The post of prime minister was awarded to her at the instigation of Solidarity, which played the role of mediator among the seven coalition parties. Under her government Poland carried on political and economic reforms. The recession was overcome and Polish economic growth rose from 1.5 percent in 1992 to over 4 percent in 1993. Social peace was maintained; the law regulating the three branches of government was passed; employment in the private sector increased by 60 percent in 1992; demand for goods and services stabilized and exports increased. On the other hand, Suchocka's government failed to reform health care and the social insurance system. Many saw their standard of living decline, and more felt insecure. A crisis within the government coalition brought about the replacement of its prime minister. On May 28, 1993, the Sejm passed by one vote a vote of no confidence put forward by Solidarity.

Arkadiusz Kubalewski

Suez Crisis

In response to the nationalization by Egypt of the Suez Canal in July 1956, Great Britain, France, and Israel invaded Egypt in November in an operation halted by financial and diplomatic pressure from the United States. The Suez crisis contributed to the fall of the British government led by Anthony Eden, resulted in a temporary breach in the Anglo-American alliance, and both illustrated and reinforced trends in British and French foreign and imperial policies that had been evident since the end of World War II.

The roots of the crisis lay in Britain's long-standing interest in the Middle East. The Suez Canal, which links the Mediterranean with the Red Sea, was completed in 1869 by the French Suez Canal Company. The canal soon became a vital commercial and strategic link between Britain and its Indian and Asian territories. In 1875 the British government purchased a substantial interest in the company; in 1881 Britain intervened in Egypt, and in 1914 Egypt became a formal British protectorate. The 1936 Anglo-Egyptian Treaty terminated the British occupation while granting Britain control of the Suez Canal base.

World War II confirmed the British in their belief that, to remain a world power, they needed to control the Middle East, its oil, and the canal. After the war the British government was confronted by a dilemma: it realized that, without American assistance, it did not have the financial resources to support the commitments of a world power, yet it was determined to remain one, and to consolidate its position in the Middle East even as it slowly decolonized. Given American antipathy to policies redolent of overt British colonialism, and the rise of nationalism in Britain's formal and informal empire, the internal contradictions of these aims were not likely to remain untested for long.

In July 1952 a military junta took power in Egypt. In March 1954 Colonel Gamal Abdel Nasser became president of Egypt and, in October, a new Anglo-Egyptian Treaty was signed, under the terms of which British troops were to leave the Suez base by June 1956. Throughout 1955 relations among Egypt, Britain, and the United States deteriorated; the Western powers feared the Soviet Union was seeking to destabilize the Middle East by using Nasser as a pawn, or that Nasser himself was seeking to unite the Arab world against the West.

In December 1955 Britain and the United States agreed to fund the construction of the Egyptian High Aswan Dam. They hoped to use financial aid to pressure Nasser into aligning Egypt with the West. But by April 1956 this strategy was believed to have failed and was abandoned. When the United States failed to provide weapons for the Egyptian army, Nasser turned to the Communist bloc. In its place, the Western powers adopted a policy of seeking to isolate Nasser. On July 19, 1956, U.S. Secretary of State John Foster Dulles withdrew the offer of aid. In response, on July 26 Nasser announced the nationalization of the Suez Canal Company, which held the concession to operate the canal.

British Prime Minister Anthony Eden, together with the rest of the cabinet, believed that Nasser posed a serious threat to the British Empire, Britain's world role, and the fragile status quo with the Soviet Union. The cabinet, as well as the opposition Labour Party, was also strongly influenced by the analogy of appeasement. Eden, who as foreign secretary had resigned from the government in 1938 over British policy toward Italy, argued that Nasser was another Mussolini: a potentially dangerous dictator who, if the Western democracies acted in time, could be stopped with relative ease. This combination of Cold War fears and dubious lessons from history proved potent in both Britain and France. On August 10, 1956, Britain approved Operation Musketeer, an Anglo-French military plan to remove Nasser from power.

For the next three months the British insisted in public that they wanted only to internationalize the canal; in private, they continued to plot Nasser's downfall. The nationalization of the canal was not illegal, and France and Britain therefore needed a pretext to intervene against Egypt. This need was all the more urgent because, although Labour accepted the appeasement analogy, it wanted Britain to refer the crisis to the United Nations, not take unilateral action. Even more important, U.S. President Dwight Eisenhower made it clear to Eden that he would not support the use of force by Britain, which, he feared, would turn the nonaligned world against the West.

The United States sought to defuse the crisis. On September 10 the British government accepted an American proposal to form a Suez Canal Users Association. It regarded the association not as an attempt to seek a diplomatic solution to the crisis, however, but as a ploy that would fail and thus allow the Americans to support the use of force by Britain and France. When Eden and Foreign Secretary Selwyn Lloyd visited French Prime Minister Guy Mollet and Foreign Secretary Christian Pineau on September 26–27, all agreed that Nasser had to be removed.

Yet American diplomatic efforts to resolve the dispute continued. On October 12 the U.N. Security Council adopted "Six Principles" to govern the operation of the canal; on October 14 Eden proposed further negotiations with Egypt in Geneva. The Six Principles satisfied the British government's publicly professed aims, and formed the basis for the final disposition of the Canal in 1957, but did not meet its private desire to remove Nasser. Tthe, hours after proposing the Geneva negotiations, Eden met French envoys and agreed to plan an Anglo-French-Israeli operation against Egypt.

The scheme was worked out at talks among officials from the three conspiring nations on October 22 and 24: Israel was to invade Egypt, and Britain and France, posing as peacemakers but in reality intent on overthrowing Nasser, would seize the canal to "protect" it from the combatants. On October 29 Israel invaded, and on October 30 Britain and France issued an "ultimatum" to Egypt and Israel. The next day the European powers began bombing Egypt. On November 5 and 6 an Anglo-French force landed in the Canal Zone.

World opinion reacted strongly against Britain and France. Soviet Prime Minister Nikolay Bulganin condemned the Western powers and threatened rocket attacks on Britain; in view of the simultaneous Soviet invasion of Hungary, this was rank hypocrisy. Labour opposed the government in the House of Commons; Eden chose to lie to the House by denying that Britain had colluded with Israel. Most important of all was the reaction of the United States. Harold Macmillan, chancellor of the exchequer, had known since August that the pound sterling would come under extreme pressure and would not receive American aid if Britain resorted to force. Yet for reasons that remain unclear, he supported military action and did not fully inform the cabinet of the economic situation until November 6, when financial and diplomatic pressures orchestrated by the United States forced Britain to agree to stop military operations at midnight. On December 3 the cabinet, desperate for U.S. economic assistance, announced the complete withdrawal of British forces from Suez.

The immediate consequences of the crisis were surprisingly limited. On January 9, 1957, Eden resigned; he was ill and had lost the support of his senior cabinet colleagues. He was replaced by Macmillan, who had remarkably emerged from the crisis with the reputation as a man who could take tough decisions. In the long run, the crisis confirmed existing trends in British and French policies. Both before and after Suez, Britain needed the support of the United States and could not afford the world status it desired. It continued to try to bring its commitments in line with its resources by decolonizing. France also decolonized and sought to identify itself with other continental nations in the European Economic Community to retain a world role, a policy Britain adopted in the early 1960s. Yet the Suez crisis also demonstrated that Britain and France were reluctant to accept these trends, and that both nations did not adjust immediately to the changed circumstances of the postwar world.

BIBLIOGRAPHY

Carlton, David. *Britain and the Suez Crisis.* Oxford: Blackwell, 1988.

Epstein, Leon. *British Politics and the Suez Crisis.* Urbana: University of Illinois Press, 1964.

Gorst, Anthony, and Lewis Johnman. *The Suez Crisis.* London: Routledge, 1997.

Hahn, Peter. *The United States, Great Britain, and Egypt, 1945–1956: Strategy and Diplomacy in the Early Cold War.* Chapel Hill: University of North Carolina Press, 1991.

Kunz, Diane. *The Economic Diplomacy of the Suez Crisis.* Chapel Hill: University of North Carolina Press, 1991.

Kyle, Keith. *Suez.* New York: St. Martin's Press, 1991.

Louis, William Roger, and Roger Owen, eds. *Suez 1956: The Crisis and Its Consequences.* Oxford: Clarendon Press, 1989.

Lucas, W. Scott. *Divided We Stand: Britain, the United States and the Suez Crisis.* London: Sceptre, rev. ed., 1996.

Nutting, Anthony. *No End of a Lesson: The Story of Suez.* London: Constable, 1967.

Ted R. Bromund

SEE ALSO Eden, Anthony

Supreme Allied Commander Europe (SACEUR)

Military head of Allied Command Europe (ACE), one of the two NATO major military commands. The other major command is Allied Command Atlantic (ACLANT), commanded by the Supreme Allied Commander Atlantic (SACLANT). The operational headquarters of ACE is Supreme Headquarters Allied Powers in Europe (SHAPE), located at Casteau, Belgium.

Under the overall authority of NATO's North Atlantic Council and Defense Planning Committee, the Supreme Allied Commander Europe (SACEUR) is responsible for identifying and requesting the forces required to promote stability in Western Europe, to contribute to crisis management, and to provide effective defense. In the event of aggression directed against Western Europe, the SACEUR is responsible for executing all necessary military measures to preserve or restore Allied territorial integrity. Like the SACLANT, the SACEUR has direct access to the chiefs of staff, defense ministers, and heads of government of the NATO member states.

The first SACEUR was General Dwight D. Eisenhower. The first Deputy SACEUR was Field Marshal Viscount Montgomery. By common consent the SACEUR is always an American general. Since August 1952, the Commander in Chief, U.S. European Command (USCINCEUR) has also served as the SACEUR. In military organizational terms, the SACEUR and the USCINCEUR are "double hatted." With the exception of U.S. Air Force General Lauris Norstad, the SACEUR/USCINCEUR has always been a U.S. army general.

Since the end of the Cold War, NATO has made major changes in its military command structure, and its strategic focus has shifted from east-west to north-south. In July 1994, the Allied Command Channel (ACCHAN) was disbanded, and its operational responsibility was assumed by ACE. By mid-1999, ACE had undergone a complete internal reorganization and was redesignated Strategic Command Europe. The SACEUR's operational headquarters was, and will remain, Supreme Headquarters Allied Powers in Europe (SHAPE), located at Casteau.

Supreme Allied Commanders Europe

General Dwight D. Eisenhower	Dec. 1950–May 1952
General Mathew B. Ridgeway	May 1952–July 1953
General Alfred M. Gruenther	July 1953–Nov. 1956
General Lauris Norstad	Nov. 1956–Jan. 1963
General Lyman L. Lemnitzer	Jan. 1963–July 1969
General Andrew J. Goodpaster	July 1969–June 1974
General Alexander M. Haig	June 1974–June 1979
General Bernard W. Rogers	June 1979–June 1987
General John R. Galvin	June 1987–June 1992
General John M. Shalikashvili	June 1992–Aug. 1993
General George A. Joulwan	Aug. 1993–Jul 1997
General Wesley Clark	July 1997–April 2000
General Joseph Ralston	April 2000–

BIBLIOGRAPHY

Davis, Brian L. *NATO Forces.* London: Blandford, 1988.

Dunn, Keith, and Stephen Flanagan. *NATO in the Fifth Decade.* Washington, D.C.: National Defense University, 1990.

Heller, Francis, and John R. Gillingham. *NATO: The Founding of the Atlantic Alliance and the Integration of Europe.* New York: St. Martin's Press, 1992.

NATO Office of Information and Press. *NATO Handbook.* Brussels: NATO Information Service, 1995.

SHAPE. *SHAPE and Allied Command Europe: In the Service of Peace and Security.* Fleurus, Belgium: Bietlot, 1973.

David T. Zabecki

SEE ALSO Supreme Headquarters, Allied Powers in Europe

Supreme Headquarters, Allied Powers in Europe (SHAPE)

Headquarters of the Allied Command Europe (ACE), one of the two major military commands of NATO. Both ACE and Supreme Headquarters, Allied Powers in Europe (SHAPE) were established on December 18, 1950. Presently located in Casteau, Belgium, SHAPE is responsible for coordinating and controlling the defense of Europe, from the northern tip of Norway to southern Europe, and from the Atlantic coast to the eastern border of Turkey, including all the Mediterranean.

Until July 1994 SHAPE consisted of four major subordinate commands: Allied Forces Northern Europe (AFNORTH); Allied Forces Central Europe (AFCENT); Allied Forces Southern Europe (AFSOUTH); and the United Kingdom Air Forces (UKAIR). Under the Cold War scenario of a massive armored attack by the Warsaw Pact, the main defensive burden would have been born by AFCENT. The two main ground combat forces available to the AFCENT commander, usually a German general, were the Northern Army Group (NORTHAG) and the Central Army Group (CENTAG). NORTHAG usually was commanded by a British general, and CENTAG was commanded by the Commander in Chief, U.S. Army Europe (CINCUSAREUR).

In 1989 AFNORTH had a deployable strength of five divisions, 115 tanks, and 520 artillery pieces. AFCENT was capable of fielding 37 divisions, 9,900 tanks, and 5,900 artillery pieces. In the northern and central regions combined, SHAPE had 2,035 tactical aircraft. In addition, France could field 15 divisions, 1,340 tanks, 1,430 artillery pieces, and 435 tactical aircraft. In the southern region (Italy, Greece, and Turkey), AFSOUTH could field 25 divisions, 6,470 tanks, 6,450 artillery pieces, and 1,065 tactical aircraft.

With the 1994 reorganization of NATO, ACE also assumed the responsibility for the territory previously defended by Allied Command Channel, which was disbanded. ACE was realigned internally, with three major subordinate commands. UKAIR was disbanded. The new Allied Forces North West Europe (AFNORTHWEST), which is always commanded by a British general, is responsible for Norway and the United Kingdom. AFCENT, commanded by a German general, continued to remain responsible for central Europe but acquired responsibility for the Baltic approaches as well. AFSOUTH, commanded by an American admiral, remains responsible for Greece, Turkey, Italy, and the entire Mediterranean. NATO operations in Bosnia came under the command of AFSOUTH.

BIBLIOGRAPHY

Davis, Brian L. *NATO Forces.* London: Blandford, 1988.

Dunn, Keith, and Stephen Flanagan. *NATO in the Fifth Decade.* Washington, D.C.: National Defense University, 1990.

Heller, Francis, and John R. Gillingham. *NATO: The Founding of the Atlantic Alliance and the Integration of Europe.* New York: St. Martin's Press, 1992.

NATO Office of Information and Press. *NATO Handbook.* Brussels: NATO Information Service, 1995.

SHAPE. *SHAPE and Allied Command Europe: In the Service of Peace and Security.* Fleurus, Belgium: Bietlot, 1973.

David T. Zabecki

SEE ALSO North Atlantic Treaty Organization; Supreme Allied Commander Europe; Warsaw Pact

Süssmuth, Rita (1937–)

Christian Democratic speaker of the German Bundestag (lower house of parliament). She has been called the voice of conscience within the Christian Democratic Party (CDU). Rita Süssmuth was born at Wupperthal on February 17, 1937. She was educated at the universities of Münster, Tübingen, and Paris. She taught at the universities of Stuttgart and Osnabrück and the Pedagogical High School of the Ruhr before becoming a professor at the Ruhr University at Bochum, the Pedagogical High School, and finally the University of Dortmund. She was director of the research Institute on Women and Society in Hanover. From 1971 to 1985 Süssmuth was a member of the committee on family affairs sponsored by the Ministry for Youth, Family Affairs, and Health. She successfully ran for the Bundestag in 1983. She served as minister for youth, family, and health from 1985 to 1988. From 1986 to 1988 she also held the portfolio for women's affairs. In 1988 she was elected president of the Bundestag. Süssmuth often found herself at odds with Chancellor Helmut Kohl. Repudiating the nationalism of the extreme right, she frequently reiterated the need for German reconciliation with Jews and Poles because of Germany's behavior toward them in World War II. She unstintingly supported women's issues and expressed concern for pressures exerted on the families of Germany's unemployed. She also called for a more liberal drug policy and for measures to deal with the problems associated with the spread of AIDS.

BIBLIOGRAPHY

Diekmann, Kai, Ulrich Reitz, and Wolfgang Stock, eds. *Rita Süssmuth im Gespräch.* Bergisch Gladbach, Germany: Bastei Lübbe, 1994.

Glotz, Peter, Rita Süssmuth, and Konrad Seitz. *Die planlosen Eliten: Versäumen wir Deutschen die Zukunft?* Munich: Edition Ferenczy bei Bruckmann, 1992.

Süssmuth, Rita. *Kämpfen und Bewegen: Frauenreden.* Freiburg, Germany: Herder, 1989.

———. *Wenn die Zeit den Rhythmus ändert: persönliche und politische Erfahrungen im Amt der Bundestagspräsidentin.* Munich: Vertrieb, Moderne Verlagsgesellschaft, 1991.

Süssmuth, Rita, and Helga Schubert. *Gehen die Frauen in die Knie?: über Rollen und Rollenerwartungen im vereinigten Deutschland.* Zurich: Pendo-Verlag, 1990.

Süssmuth, Rita, and Konrad Weiss. *Neuland: Dialog in Deutschland.* Cologne: Kiepenheuer & Witsch, 1991.

Bernard Cook

SEE ALSO Kohl, Helmut

Sutherland, Peter (1946–)

Director general of the General Agreement on Tariffs and Trade (GATT), European Commissioner, and Irish attorney general. Peter Sutherland, a lawyer, served as the policy strategist and election policy director of Fine Gael, the Irish moderate political party, in late 1970s. He was attorney general in 1981, 1982, and again in 1982 to 1984. From 1985 until 1988 he was European commissioner with responsibility for competition and for relations with the European Parliament. From 1989 to 1993 he was chairman of Allied Irish Banks Group. As director general of GATT (1993–), he was crucial to the success of the Uruguay Round.

Michael J. Kennedy

Svalbard

Norwegian archipelago in the Arctic Ocean. It is 24,209 square miles (62,924 sq km) in size and consists of nine principal islands, the largest of which, Spitsbergen (formerly Vestspitsbergen), 15,075 square mile is (39,044 sq km). In 1992, there were 3,116 inhabitants, of whom 1,958 were Russian and 1,148 Norwegian.

On February 9, 1920, an international accord signed by forty-one states recognized Norwegian sovereignty but provided for international access to the archipelago's mineral resources. Svalbard was incorporated into the Kingdom of Norway in 1925 and is administered by a governor who resides at Longyearbyen on Spitsbergen. A mining code set up by Norway in 1925 for the islands and their waters to a distance miles of (7.4 km) is administered by a commissioner of mines.

Due to the German threat in World War II, the population was evacuated by the British in 1941. In 1944 the Soviet Union's request for a condominium over the archipelago was rejected by Norway. Today Russia has two coal mines, a helicopter base, and a radar station on Spits-

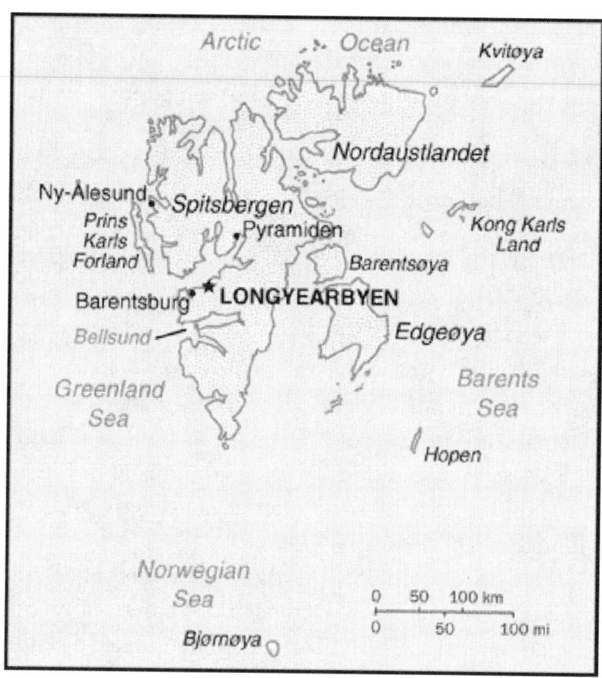

Svalbard. *Illustration courtesy of Bernard Cook.*

bergen. Norway also operates two mines, which, despite their unprofitability, are maintained to affirm Norway's rights in the archipelago. Expectations of oil deposits have led to a dispute between Norway and Russia concerning the maritime boundaries in the area. Russia has refused to recognize the 230-mile (370-km.) protected fishing zone declared by Norway in 1977.

BIBLIOGRAPHY

Greve, Tim. *Svalbard: Norway in the Arctic Ocean.* Oslo: Grondahl, 1975.

Norderhaug, Magnar. *Svalbard.* Oslo: Universitetsforlaget, 1984.

Risanger, Otto. *Russerne pa Svalbard: hvem er de?: hva gjor de?* Longyearbyen: Sampress, 1978.

Bernard Cook

Svoboda, Ludvík (1895–1979)

Czechoslovak president (1968–75). Ludvík Svoboda was born in Hroznatín, Moravia, on November 25, 1895. He deserted the Austro-Hungarian army in World War I and joined the Czechoslovak Legion fighting on the side of Russia against Austria-Hungary. After the war he pursued a career in the Czechoslovak military. After Nazi Germany seized the remainder of Czechoslovakia on March 15, 1939, he went to Poland and organized Czechoslovak units there. Following the fall of Poland he went to the USSR, where he eventually headed a Czechoslovak corps to fight the Germans. Following the liberation of Czechoslovakia in 1945, he was appointed minister of defense by President Edvard Beneš.

Svoboda was well disposed to communism and joined the Czechoslovak Communist Party in 1948. But he fell victim to the Stalinist antinational communist purges. Svoboda was expelled from the army in 1950 and imprisoned in 1951. Rehabilitated under pressure from Soviet First Secretary Nikita Khrushchev, Svoboda was appointed head of the Klement Gottwald military academy. When Svoboda retired in 1959, he was proclaimed a hero of the USSR and of the Czechoslovak Socialist Republic. Svoboda was chosen president of Czechoslovakia on March 30, 1968, during the Prague Spring, the short-lived attempt to liberalize the Communist system in Czechoslovakia. At the time of the Soviet-led Warsaw Pact invasion in August aimed at suppressing the reforms, his refusal to accept a new Soviet sponsored conservative leadership, headed by Alois Indra, or even to negotiate until he had seen Czech leader Alexander Dubček is credited by some with saving the life of Dubček, Prime Minister Oldrich Cernik, and others. Svoboda was flown to Moscow and Dubček survived but not the Prague Spring because Dubček's program of liberalization was ended and the changes implemented under him reversed. Svoboda retired from the presidency in 1975, and he died on September 20, 1979. In the words of Alexander Dubček, his final years were "increasingly passive, subdued, and even detached." He had no further impact except to provide legitimization of the repressive measures of the new head of the Communist Party, Gustav Husák, who had formally replaced Dubček as party leader in 1969.

BIBLIOGRAPHY

Dubček, Alexander. *Hope Dies Last: The Autobiography of the Leader of the Prague Spring.* New York: Kondasha International, 1993.

Bernard Cook

Sweden

Country dominating two-thirds of the Scandinavian Peninsula in northwestern Europe. The Kingdom of Sweden is bordered by Norway on the west and north, Finland on the northeast, the Gulf of Bothnia and the Baltic Sea on the east, the Sound, the Skagerrak, and the Kattegat on the southwest. Denmark, especially at Helsingør, is only a short distance across the Sound. A 10 mile (16 km) bridge across the Öresund strait at the bottom of the Sound is scheduled to be completed in 2000 and thus to link Malmö, Sweden, with Copenhagen, Denmark. Swe-

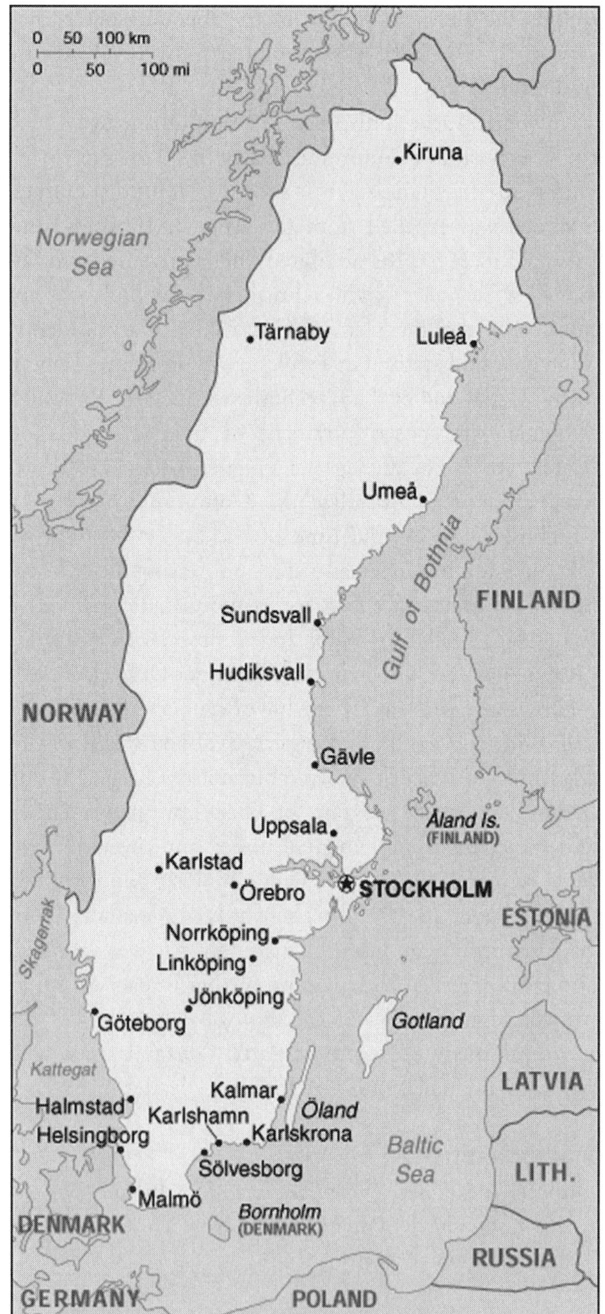

Sweden. *Illustration courtesy of Bernard Cook.*

den, with an area of 173,654 square miles (449,793 sq km), is approximately 1,000 miles (1,600 km) from north to south and approximately 300 miles (500 km) wide at its widest part. Fifteen percent of Sweden is above the Arctic Circle. However, more than 90 percent of the population lives in the southern half of the country and over half in the bottom third. Sweden has a population of approximately 8.8 million. Swedish is the official language but there are small Finnish and Lapp (Saami) minorities. Toward the end of the nineteenth century, only 10 percent of Swedes lived in towns. At the end of the twentieth century, approximately 83 percent live in towns and cities. Approximately a third of the population lives in the capital, Stockholm (1.4 million), Göteborg (700,000), and Malmö (450,000). The Evangelical Lutheran Church of Sweden counts 86.5 percent of the population as at least nominal members.

Sweden evolved into a constitutional monarchy in the nineteenth century. Full parliamentary government, however, was not achieved until 1917. Universal suffrage was established in 1921. Since the Napoleonic Wars Sweden has not fought nor has it belonged to any military alliance. It obtained Norway from Denmark in the 1814 Treaty of Kiel, as compensation for its loss of Finland to Russia. But Norway was allowed internal autonomy and was granted independence in 1905.

From 1932 until 1976, with the exception of a short time in 1936, the Social Democratic Workers Party (Socialdemokratiska Arbetareparti, SAP) dominated Swedish politics. Its base of support lay in its links with and support from the Swedish Confederation of Trade Unions (Landsorganisationen i Sverige, LO), whose twenty-five unions represent approximately 90 percent of Swedish workers. The SAP governed alone apart from 1936–45 and 1951–57, when it headed coalition governments in alliance with the Farmers Party, which changed its name to Center Party in 1957. During the long period of SAP dominance, only three individuals served as prime minister—Per Albin Hansson (1932–36, 1936–46), Tage Erlander (1946–69), and Olof Palme (1969–76). These Social Democratic administrations advanced the "Swedish Model" of administered capitalism through consensus among government, employers, and labor unions. The guiding principles were full employment and improvement of the economic and social conditions of the majority of the people.

Palme, who became leader of the SAP and prime minister after the resignation of Erlander, formed a minority government after the election of September 1970. He presided over a constitutional reform that went into effect in January 1971, transforming the old bicameral Riksdag (parliament) into a single-chamber assembly. In January 1975 a revised constitution completed the transformation of the Swedish monarchy into a figurehead. Carl XVI Gustaf (1946–), who became king at the death of his grandfather Gustav VI Adolf (1882–1973), saw his power to name the prime minister pass to the speaker of the Riksdag.

In the September 1976 election the SAP maintained its plurality, but the opposition together won enough seats to form a government. Sweden has one of the highest per capita levels of energy consumption in the world.

Hydroelectric plants produce 15 percent of the country's energy needs, and domestically produce wood, coal, coke, and waste generated another 14 percent. The remainder is supplied by imported oil. In the wake of the oil crisis after 1973, the SAP had planned to build twenty-four nuclear power plants. This became a key issue, strenuously opposed by the Center Party, and cost the SAP votes. Other voters were disenchanted by the high level of taxation necessary to fund the elaborate Swedish welfare state. The nuclear issue, however, which had provided the opposition with its victory, proved to be its downfall.

Thorbjörn Fälldin, leader of the Center Party, formed a center-right coalition in October 1976. As prime minister, Fälldin refused to approve the fueling and start-up of the country's seventh and eighth nuclear power plants. This led to serious differences with the Center's coalition partners—the Liberals, or People's, Party (Folkspartiet, FP) and the Moderate Unity Party (Moderata Samlingspartiet, MS), which until 1969 was called the Conservative Party. The FP and the MS endorsed a recommendation by an independent commission to continue to use nuclear power and rejected Fälldin's proposal to submit the issue to a referendum. Fälldin's government resigned in October 1978 and Ola Ullsten (1931–), leader of the FP, formed a minority government. After the September 1979 election Fälldin returned as head of a government consisting of the Center, the MS, and the FP. But their majority, consisted of one seat. In a referendum on nuclear power held in March 1980, 58 percent of voters approved the completion of twelve reactors at four plants, but all reactors would be shut down at least by 2010. In 1995 a parliamentary commission recommended that the 2010 deadline be dropped because of the cost of alternative energy, but it also recommended that one reactor be decommissioned before 1998.

During the 1980s the political debate centered around economic issues. Sweden was challenged not only by the price of energy and the cost of its welfare programs but by changes in the international economy. Textiles, steel, and shipbuilding were all hard pressed by foreign competition, and the low wages of the newly industrializing countries. Sweden experienced troubling inflation and unemployment. Unemployment, intensified by the economic slump of 1980–83, was a central issue in the 1982 election. Also at the forefront was a proposal by the SAP in conjunction with the LO to establish a "workers' fund." Swedish industry was dominated by fifteen to twenty corporations, many family-owned. While 89 percent of Swedish households owned no stock, 1 percent of households owned 75 percent of the country's stock, and 0.3 percent of families owned 50 percent of the stock. Labor's proposal was that each year a portion of a firm's profits and wages be transferred to five boards nominated by the government but controlled in fact by the unions. The boards could purchase up to 80 percent of a firm's stock, thus eventually passing control of Sweden's production to labor unions.

The SAP won 45.6 percent of the vote and 166 of the Riksdag's 349 seats, a three-seat majority over the three nonsocialist parties. The election witnessed an increasing polarization of the electorate. The Conservatives increased their representation while the Liberals lost half their seats. Palme formed a new minority government after the Left Communist Party (Vänsterpartiet-Kommunisterna, VpK) announced its support. In office Palme moved to address the problems of the economy. To stimulate exports and hinder imports the krona was devalued by 16 percent and employers were pressed not to accede to demands for higher wages.

In the midst of an economic recovery the September 1985 election was held. Palme strengthened the position of his government. The SAP and the VpK together won 50 percent of the vote and 178 seats. The three nonsocialist parties won 48 percent and 171 seats. The Liberals, now led by Bengt Westerberg, stressing their simultaneous support for a market economy and a socially responsible welfare program, increased their seats from 21 to 51. The Christian Democrats (Kristdemokratiska Samhällsparteit, KdS), in alliance with the Center, won a seat for the first time.

On February 28, 1986, Palme was assassinated on a Stockholm street by an unknown gunman. Controversy surrounds the investigation and the eventual prosecution of a man with a history of mental illness, who was convicted of the crime but subsequently acquitted. Deputy Prime Minister Ingvar Carlsson (1934–) became prime minister and assumed acting leadership of the SAP. He announced that he would continue Palme's effort to fight inflation and economic recession while maintaining social benefits.

In the September 1988 election the Green Party (Miljöpartiet de Gröna, MpG) made its entry into the Riksdag with 5.5 percent of the vote, surpassing the required 4 percent barrier, and a respectable 20 seats. The success of the environmental party was preceded by two ecological disasters caused by pollutants. An algae bloom along the west coast devastated aquatic life there, and an epidemic virus destroyed approximately 66 percent of the North Sea and Baltic seals. The SAP lost three seats but was supported by the VpK, which with 21 seats had gained 2. The MS won 66 seats and was still the second-largest party. In February 1990 the VpK, now transformed into the Left Party (Vänsterpartiet, VP), and the MpG announced that they would not support Carlsson's anti-inflationary austerity measures. Carlsson was forced to resign but reconstituted his minority government by moderating his proposed austerity measures.

Compelled by a new recession in 1990, however, the government resorted to new austerity measures and retreated from the SAP's traditional and central commitment to full employment and preservation of the full-blown welfare system. In 1991 income taxes were reduced, and the value-added tax on goods and services was increased. The government also moved to deregulate financial institutions.

In the September 1991 election the SAP lost 18 seats. It remained the largest party with 138 seats, but it did not have sufficient strength to form a government. The MS led by Carl Bildt (1949–), won 22.1 percent of the vote and 80 seats. The KdS won 26, and a new right-wing party, New Democracy (Ny Demokrati, ND), won 25. Though the Center party and the FP lost votes to the upstarts, they were represented as well. The Greens failed to break the 4 percent threshold and were denied representation. With the assistance of the VP the SAP could muster only 154 seats to the 170 seats of the combined nonsocialist parties. Therefore Carlsson resigned. Bildt, as leader of the largest nonsocialist party, formed a coalition composed of his Moderates, the Center, the FP, and the KdS. Pooling all their seats, these parties still did not possess a majority; therefore Bildt was compelled to rely on the ND to enact legislation. Bildt had promised to transform Sweden's economy from a socialistic to a free-market system. He quickly moved to further deregulate the economy. He also introduced proposals to cut taxes and government spending, to privatize thirty-five state-owned companies, and to allow foreign ownership of Swedish companies.

The years from 1992 to 1994 were not good for Bildt's government or for Sweden. In 1992 the continuing recession caused increased budgetary deficits. International money market speculation damaged the krona, and there was an outflow of capital. The government responded by letting the krona float, in effect devaluing it by 10 percent. As of March 1993 the Bildt government was plagued by the ND, which created continuous problems by refusing to support government measures.

In the September 1994 election the SAP, assisted by a negative reaction against the cutting of welfare benefits by Bildt's government, won 45.6 percent of the vote and 161 seats. The other left-wing parties fared well also. The VP increased its seats from 16 to 22, and the MpG reentered the Riksdag with 18 seats. The MS held its position with voters but its coalition partners did not maintain theirs. Bildt resigned and Carlsson formed a minority SAP government. In spite of opposition within the SAP to joining the European Union (EU), a key project of Bildt, Carlsson stated his government's intention of securing membership. The Riksdag in December 1990 had approved a decision by Carlsson's government to apply for EU membership, and Carlsson's government formally applied for membership in July 1991. Back in power, he now followed through with his earlier intention. A national referendum was held on November 13, 1994. The EU had granted concessions allowing the continuation of Sweden's stricter environmental standards and the subsidies that it provided to agriculture in the remote sections of the country. Despite the bitter opposition of many, 52.2 percent of those voting expressed their support for joining. The Riksdag ratified Sweden's acceptance in December, and on January 1, 1995, Sweden became a member of the EU. But the country reasserted its intention not to join NATO. Sweden had announced in 1992, nevertheless, that in response to instability in the former Soviet Union, it was increasing its military expenditures for a five-year period. It also expressed its desire to cooperate with Finland, Denmark, Norway, and the new Baltic states on security issues.

Strong steps were taken late in 1994 to stabilize the budget deficit while at the same time reducing unemployment and maintaining the welfare system. In August 1995 Carlsson announced that as of March 1996 he would retire from politics, stepping down from the office of prime minister and his post as leader of the SAP. Mona Sahlin, the deputy prime minister, was regarded as heir apparent, but she was forced to resign from the government in November 1995 due to allegations that she had improperly used her government issued credit card. Góran Persson (1949–), the minister of finance, subsequently moved into the government and party posts vacated by Carlsson in March 1996.

Following an inconclusive election in 1998, Persson's minority Social Democratic government was returned to power. Business and labor interests were at odds. Employers complained of extremely high rates of personal taxation and restrictive labor market rules. Labor for its part called for measures to cut unemployment rather than cutting taxation or public spending. Nevertheless, Sweden's situation at the end of the century was in many ways very positive. Inflation was low, and the economy was growing at a rate of between 2.2 and 2.6 percent annually.

BIBLIOGRAPHY

Childs, Marquis William. *Sweden, the Middle Way on Trial.* New Haven, Conn.: Yale University Press, 1980.

Elstob, Eric. *Sweden, a Political and Cultural History.* Totowa, N.J.: Rowman and Littlefield, 1979.

Miles, Lee. *Sweden and European Integration.* Brookfield, Vt.: Ashgate, 1997.

Scott, Franklin Daniel. *Sweden, the Nation's History.* Carbondale: Southern Illinois University Press, 1988.

Thompson, Wayne C. *Western Europe 1996.* Harpers Ferry, W.V.: Stryker-Post, 1996.

Viklund, Daniel. *Sweden and the European Community: Trade, Cooperation, and Policy Issues.* Uppsala: Swedish Institute, 1989.

Bernard Cook

Political Parties

The Social Democratic Workers Party (Socialdemokratiska Arbetareparti, SAP) is the largest Swedish political party. After a six-year hiatus the SAP returned to government under Palme from 1982 until his assassination in 1986, and under Ingvar Carlsson from 1986 to 1991. After another period of nonsocialist government, Carlsson returned from 1994 to 1996, then stepped aside and transferred the government to Göran Persson of the SAP in 1996.

The other parties of the Left are the Left Party and the Green Party. They have both at times provided support to SAP minority governments. The Party of the Left originated in 1917 as the breakaway Swedish Social Democratic Left Party. This party then split in 1921. The larger of the two splinters was the Swedish Communist Party. To stress its Eurocommunist stance, the party changed its name in 1967 to Left Communist Party (Vänsterpartiet-Kommunisterna, VpK). With the collapse of communism across Eastern Europe, it underwent another name change, becoming the Left Party (Vänsterpartiet, VP). Its party leader is Gudrund Schyman.

The Green Party (Miljöpartiet de Gröna, MpG) has its roots in the environmental, antinuclear, women's rights, and peace movements. A party was formed in 1981 and the name Green Party was adopted in 1985. In 1991 the MpG failed to break the 4 percent threshold and was denied representation. In the September 1994 election the MpG reentered the Riksdag with 5.2 percent of the vote.

The Center Party was, at that moment, the largest of the nonsocialist parties, with roots in the 1913 Farmers Union. It gained its first seats in parliament in 1918 as the Farmers Party. It changed its name in 1958. It is supported by the Farmer's Organization, with which it shares an overlapping leadership. Seventy percent of Sweden's farmers vote for the Center Party, and the party's members, leadership, and members of parliament are predominantly farmers. But numerically more workers than farmers vote for the Center. The Center, which espouses a guided market economy, sympathizes in many regards with the notions of the SAP. The Center Party in 1976, however, profited from its strenuous opposition to the SAP plan to extend Sweden's production of nuclear power. Other voters were disenchanted by the high level of taxation necessary to fund the elaborate Swedish welfare state. The nuclear issue that had provided the opposition with its victory proved to be its downfall.

The Liberals, or People's Party (Folkspartiet, FP) was founded in 1934 but has its roots in a liberal party led by Karl Staaff early in the twentieth century. Its supporters are a heterogeneous group centered in the large cities, especially Stockholm and Göteborg. Although it does receive some assistance from the Confederation of Employers (SAF), it is not the official party of any large organization. The FP was the only nonsocialist party to participate in all the nonsocialist governments after 1976. Although nonsocialist, the FP has always been at odds with the conservatism of the MS. It cooperated with the SAP from 1973 to 1976. Its sympathy for the SAP cost it conservative voters, but it was unable to improve its position with the electorate when it shifted to the right in 1982. Another shift was made under the leadership of Bengt Westerberg, under whom it stressed both dedication to the free market and social responsibility. In 1985 it drew voters from all other principal parties. In the 1994 election, however, it again sagged, dropping to 7.19 percent.

The Moderate Unity Party (Moderata Samlingspartiet, MS) has its roots in the conservative groups that coalesced in the Swedish parliament at the end of the nineteenth century. The General Coalition of Voters (Allmänna Valmansförbundet) was formed during the debate on universal suffrage in 1904. It formed its first government in 1906 with Arvid Lindman serving as prime minister. In 1938 it adopted the name Conservative Party and in 1969 changed its name to Moderate Unity Party. The MS draws its support from large and small businesses, large farmers, the higher ranks of the civil service, and increasingly from young voters. It is assisted financially by the Confederation of Employers. Its leader, Carl Bildt was prime minister from 1991 to 1994. The MS themes stressed by Bildt were the end of collectivism, centralized decision making, and high taxes, and in their place greater individual freedom. In 1994 it received 22.37 percent of the vote, making it second only to the SAP.

The other nonsocialist parties are the Christian Democratic Party (Kristdemokratiska Samhällsparteit, KdS) and the right-wing New Democracy Party (Ny Demokrati, ND). KdS was founded in 1964. ND's leader is Count Iam Wachmeister, an ardent advocate of individual freedom and opponent of state controls. In 1985 KdS formed an electoral alliance with the Center and won a seat for the first time. In September 1991 the KdS won 26 seats and the new right-wing party, New Democracy, won 25. Bildt had to bring the KdS into his government and was compelled to rely on the ND for support to enact legislation. In 1994 the KdS won 15 seats but the ND received only 1.2 percent of the vote and received no seats.

BIBLIOGRAPHY

Aylott, Nicholas. *Swedish Social Democracy and European Integration: The People's Home on the Market.* Brookfield, Vt.: Ashgate, 1999.

Esaiasson, Peter, and Sören Holmberg. *Representation from Above: Members of Parliament and Representative Democracy in Sweden.* Tr. by Janet Westerlund. Brookfield, Vt.: Dartmouth, 1996.

Meyerson, Per-Martin. *The Welfare State in Crisis, the Case of Sweden: A Critical Examination of Some Central Problems in the Swedish Economy and Political System.* Stockholm: Federation of Swedish Industries, 1982.

Milner, Henry. *Sweden: Social Democracy in Practice.* New York: Oxford University Press, 1989.

Persson, Inga, ed. *Generating Equality in the Welfare State: the Swedish Experience.* New York: Norwegian University Press, 1990.

Petersson, Olof. *Swedish Government and Politics.* Tr. by Frank Gabriel Perry. Stockholm: Fritzes, 1994.

Bernard Cook

Economy

Sweden's export-oriented economy has an integrated system of labor relations and state intervention that has started to fragment.

Sweden, a relatively small industrialized country, is dependent on international trade to maintain its high living standard. In 1996 exports amounted to 40 percent of gross domestic product (GDP). Exploitation of extensive forests, rich iron ore deposits, and abundant waterpower resources as well as a relatively skilled labor force enabled a fast transition from a poor agrarian country to a modern industrial society.

A shift has taken place from manufacturing based on domestic raw materials to the production of various goods requiring a highly skilled labor force. Forest production is still an important industrial sector, but sectors such as iron mining, steel production, textiles, and shipyards have declined. Investments in raw material–based industries created demand for engineering products and provided an impetus for new engineering companies. In the late 1990s industrial products accounted for more than 80 percent of total exports. Large multinational companies such as Ericsson, ABB, Electrolux, Volvo, and Saab accounted for nearly 60 percent of employment in manufacturing and more than 80 percent of manufactured products. Engineering has expanded sharply and accounted for about half of manufacturing exports. Other important exports were pulp, paper, paper products, wood products, and chemical products including pharmaceuticals. The most important export markets are countries within the European Union. Exports from the raw material industries are primarily sold to markets in Europe, but engineering products are exported to markets outside the continent.

A distinctive feature of the Swedish economy is its dependence on a limited number of very large multinational companies that are especially dominant in manufacturing. Around 8 percent of the multinational corporations in the world are headquartered in Sweden. Around 90 percent of the sales of these multinational corporations are in foreign markets, and more than 60 percent of their staff is employed outside Sweden. Swedish multinationals are among the highest spenders on research and development, and most of that work has taken place in Sweden. Despite this fact, knowledge-based industries have grown slowly. Until the 1990s Swedish investments abroad greatly exceeded foreign investment in Sweden. The situation changed during the 1990s as foreign investment started to show a sharp increase. This is perhaps related to the fact that Sweden decided to join the European Union in the early 1990s and became a member in January 1995.

In the early 1950s a comprehensive system of labor regulations and state intervention was developed that is often termed the "Swedish model." The underlying principles of the model were developed by Gösta Rehn and Rudolf Meidner, two economists associated with the Swedish Trade Union Confederation (Landsorganisationen i Svergie, LO). The model was based on a restrictive monetary-fiscal policy to avoid excess demand pressures; an active labor market policy to ensure full employment; wage policy to achieve pay equality; and welfare capitalism to pursue equality beyond the market. Swedish welfare capitalism involved a growing provision of services accompanied by progressive taxation and egalitarian wage policy. However, production was to remain in the hands of private, capitalist enterprises as individual firms were considered to be efficient producers of products and profit, even though the market system was regarded as an inefficient mechanism for the establishment of priorities and the distribution of returns. Finally, economic growth at the national level and paid work at the individual level were considered the primary paths to gender equality. Various policy reforms were undertaken during the 1980s and early 1990s aimed at improving the function of the Swedish economy and reducing large budget deficits. These reforms involved fundamental changes in the Swedish model. The deregulation of the centralized bargaining system (1983–) and a less progressive tax system (1991) led to an increase in inequality. The commitment to full employment has also been weakened by large cuts in public employment during the 1990s.

Until the mid-1970s Sweden experienced a high economic growth rate compared with other members of the Organization for European Cooperation and Development (OECD). Industries and infrastructures were largely undamaged by World War II, and the economy could take full advantage of the upswing in world trade during the postwar period. After the mid-1970s economic growth slowed and lagged behind the OECD average. The economic slowdown was primarily due to a loss by Sweden of 25 percent of its world market share for manufacturing exports. During the 1980s and 1990s the deindustrialization of the Swedish economy was regarded as a natural step toward a more service-based economy. Yet the economy continued to be dependent on manufacturing exports. Hence, by the late 1980s and early 1990s the government implemented various measures intended to strengthen the competitiveness of the economy, especially the manufacturing sector. These measures included deregulation of the capital market to stimulate private investment and savings, tax reforms, and a reduction in employers' payroll fees. Swedish manufacturing output continued to fall until 1992 but rose sharply thereafter. Due to the stimulative measures in 1996 industrial output was 17 percent higher than in 1990.

The public sector since the 1960s has been the main source of employment growth. The lack of employment growth in the private sector may be attributed to the solidaristic wage policy aimed at "pricing-out" low-productivity firms and the progressive taxation of small firms that hindered the entrance of new family firms. The centralized bargaining system was used to achieve a relatively compressed wage structure. The government encouraged the growth of large firms through a discriminatory tax policy and the legalization of cartels. Until the late 1980s, small firms were taxed proportionally more heavily than large firms. Until the early 1990s it was legal to make cartel agreements concerning prices and market divisions.

Private ownership of the business sector is more than 85 percent. During the 1980s the private service sector started to grow in importance, but it was hard hit by the recession of the early 1990s. Major employment reduction occurred when the postal services, telecommunications, and civil aviation were privatized. Since 1993 the private service sector has had a strong production growth but the employment level is still at the pre-recession level. Growth in service-oriented business is partly due to contracting out of tasks previously performed by the public sector. The expansion of the public sector during the 1960s and 1970s opened up new job opportunities for women, which in turn put pressure on the state to provide services previously performed at home. In 1996, 50 percent of all employed women worked in the public sector while the share of men was only 15 percent. The largest percentage of women worked for local governments in the care service sector. Although extensive tax reform has taken place, the public sector is still large and Sweden's tax revenues amount to more than half of its GDP, which is higher than that of most other OECD countries.

Economic growth during the postwar period was translated into greater employment growth in Sweden than in the other Western European countries. In 1996 around half the population was in the labor force. This high participation rate was due to the fact that 75 percent of women aged sixteen to sixty-four were gainfully employed but their working hours were shorter than those of men. The increase in women's real pay, paid parental leave (1974), subsidized public child care, and individualization of taxation (1971), along with very progressive taxation, facilitated women's labor force participation. Temporary immigration of foreign labor has not been encouraged, but a common Nordic labor market has been in existence since 1954, and around half the foreign nationals are from other Nordic countries. During the postwar period unemployment was low by international standards because of the expansion of the industrial sector, growth of the public sector, and Sweden's active labor market policy. The economic recession of the early 1990s brought about a tremendous increase in the level of unemployment. Registered unemployment climbed from 1.6 percent to 8.2 percent in 1993, when it peaked. Those hardest hit were young people, immigrants, and other groups with weak labor market positions. Women have been less susceptible than men to unemployment. Sweden is now investing large sums in education and training, both in the formal school system and in employment training. In 1996 unemployment was 8.1 percent but 12.6 percent if those enrolled in labor market programs are included. The responsibility for administration of the various programs for the unemployed lies with the National Labor Market Board (Arbetsmarknadsstyrelsen, AMS), county labor boards, and local employment service offices. The labor market policies stress active measures rather than cash benefits for the unemployed. The aim of the active measures is to generate employment, enhance the employability of the unemployed, and improve the matching of workers and jobs. The measures include subsidized in-house training, wage subsidies, creation of temporary jobs, mobility grants, vocational training, and an extensive job placement service.

The Swedish currency, the krona, was pegged at a more or less fixed rate during the postwar period. As a result of severe structural problems in the manufacturing sector, the government was forced to devalue the krona several times in the late 1970s and early 1980s. That resulted in an effective depreciation of more than one-third the value of the krona. Deregulation of the capital market was undertaken during the late 1980s; this stimulated foreign investment in real estate and insurance companies. In the autumn of 1992 the Swedish central bank was forced to abandon fixed rates and to allow the krona to float. The change to a floating rate resulted in an immediate devaluation of around 20 percent. Sweden decided not to join the EU's Economic and Monetary Union (EMU), although it has managed to fulfill the convergence criteria for membership in the EMU.

BIBLIOGRAPHY

Bosworth, Barry P., and Alice M. Rivlin. *The Swedish Economy.* Washington, D.C.: Brookings Institution, 1987.

Mahon, Rianne. "From Solidaristic Wages to Solidaristic Work: A Post-Fordist Historic Compromise for Sweden?" *Economic and Industrial Democracy* 12 (1991): 295–325.

Persson, Inga, ed. *Generating Equality in the Welfare State: The Swedish Experience.* Oslo: Norwegian University Press, 1990.

Statistical Yearbook of Sweden. Stockholm: Statistics Sweden, 1998.

Lilja Mósesdóttir
Gudny Björk Eydal

Labor Movement

Sweden is the most unionized of OECD members, but industrial disputes are infrequent by international standards. Unionization went from 80 to 90 percent during the recession of the early 1990s. The centralized bargaining system was a central feature of the Swedish labor market during the postwar period until 1983, when it was gradually replaced by agreements at the sectoral level. The Swedish Confederation of Trade Unions (Landsorganisationen i Svergie, LO) has held a central position among the national trade unions because of its close ties to the Social Democratic Party, which has been in power during most of the postwar period. A large number of laws regulate the labor market that cover employment security, the status of shop stewards, work environment, and employee participation in decision making.

At the organizational level there is a division between manual, or blue-collar, workers in the Swedish Trade Union Confederation LO on the one hand and white-collar workers in the Confederation of Professional Employees (Tjänstemännens Centralorganisation, TCO) and the Swedish Confederation of Professional Association (Sveriges Akademikers Centralorganisation, SACO), on the other. The LO was established in 1898 by a number of unions. In 1902 employers formed the Swedish Employers Confederation (Svenska arbetsgivareföreningen, SAF), which cooperated closely with the LO from 1938 onward after a period of much industrial unrest. In the famous 1938 agreement between the LO and the SAF at Saltsjöbaden, both parties agreed to conduct centralized, collective negotiations without direct government intervention and the LO would recognize the management right to manage. In 1944 two white-collar confederations representing private-sector employees, founded in 1931, and other civil servants, founded in 1941, merged into the Confederation of Professional Employees (TCO). In 1947 university graduates established the Swedish Confederation of Professional Association (SACO), which later opened its membership to related groups.

The LO has about 2.2 million members, organized in twenty-one nationwide labor unions with 928 branches and about 11,000 local sections. The largest unions are the Swedish Municipal Workers Union (Svenska Kommunalarbetareförbundet), Metal Workers Union (Svenska Metallindustriarbetareförbundet), State Employees Union (Statsanställdas förbund), Commercial Employees Union (Handelsanställdas förbund), and the Building Workers Union (Svenska Byggnadsarbetareförbundet). The TCO covers about 70 percent of all white-collar or clerical employees, and the membership is about 1.3 million. The largest of the twenty national union affiliations are the Swedish Union of Clerical and Technical Employees in Industry (Svenska Industritjänstemannaförbundet), Teachers Union (Lärarförbundet), and Union of Municipal Employees (Kommunalanställdas förbund). The third union confederation is SACO, with 385,000 members; most of these are employed in the public sector. The largest national unions within SACO are the Association of Graduate Engineers (Civilingeniörsförbundet) and the National Union of Teachers (Lärarnas riksförbund). The LO and to some extent the TCO are organized on the industrial principle that employees belong to national unions determined by the economic sector where they work, rather than by their profession. Although women constitute 45 to 60 percent of the members in the three confederations, they still hold only a small proportion of member-elected posts within all unions, especially at the higher positions.

Centralized bargaining did not become a regular practice until the mid-1950s. The bargaining system involved negotiation between representatives of large labor union confederations, e.g., the LO, and representatives from different employer associations, e.g., SAF, on how much all workers in a particular confederation of unions should receive. The sectoral organizations then signed collective agreements on wages and general conditions of employment based on the framework laid down by the LO and the SAF. The role of the labor unions was to set a wage level sufficiently high to provide wage increases and equality but not so high as to endanger full employment. Wage rates were not set according to the ability of the industry to pay but according to what was regarded as a "just wage." Wage solidarity was transformed into a broader idea of economic equality during the 1960s, and the gender wage gap narrowed considerably until the mid-1980s. However, wage drift was allowed in the private sector, where it experienced difficulties in recruiting and retaining workers.

To make wage restraint more acceptable to workers in high-profit firms, in 1976 the LO Congress adopted the economist Rudolf Meidner's proposal for wage-earner funds to be financed by the extra profits that arose when employees refrained from claiming higher wages than agreed on in centralized bargaining. By establishing wage-earner funds, capital was expected to remain within the firms, but the ownership should be successively transferred to employees as a collective. Not until 1984 did the Act on Employment Investment Fund come into existence, owing to the resistance of employers and the nonsocialist government of 1976–82. The 1984 legislation was a watered-down comprise as only five regional wage-earner funds of very limited size were introduced, and contributions came from only around 10 percent of all companies in Sweden and from a payroll tax of 0.2 percent of the total wage bill.

In 1983 employer representatives in the engineering industry managed to divide LO unity when they got the powerful Metal Workers Union to agree to bargain separately in order to achieve higher-than-average wage increases in profitable industries. The union accepted separate negotiations against the wishes of the LO because it wanted to get concessions on various grievances that had accumulated through the years of central negotiations. The SAF, on the other hand, had hoped to achieve a more differentiated wage policy by bargaining separately with the metalworkers. The LO gradually accepted this development and proposed a modified wage solidarity policy of "different pay for different work." In 1990 the SAF abandoned the centralized level of bargaining and resorted to negotiations at the sectoral or industry level.

BIBLIOGRAPHY

Ryner, Magnus. "Assessing SAP's Economic Policy in the 1980s: The 'Third Way,' the Swedish Model and the Transition from Fordism to Post-Fordism." *Economic and Industrial Democracy* 15 (1994): 385–428.

Standing, Guy. *Unemployment and Labor Market Flexibility: Sweden.* Geneva: International Labor Office, 1988.

Lilja Mósesdóttir
Gudny Björk Eydal

Swedish Confederation of Trade Unions

Principal federative organization of Swedish labor unions. The Swedish Confederation of Trade Unions (Landorganisationen i Sverige, LO) was established in 1898. It was organized to coordinate the efforts of the various unions to protect the interests and improve the conditions of Swedish workers. The LO, though it has affirmed its independence, has maintained a close relationship with the Swedish Social Democratic Workers Party (SAP). It supports the SAP by providing financial aid, campaign workers, and backing in the labor press, and the chairman of the LO is a member of the executive board of the SAP. Many member unions of the LO require their members to be members of the SAP, and most Swedish workers willingly vote for the SAP. The LO has grown from a membership of forty-three thousand in 1900 to approximately two million members at the end of the century. In the early 1960s its affiliate unions numbered forty-four, but owing to consolidation through the formation of single unions to represent all the workers in a particular industry, there were only twenty-five affiliated unions in 1976. These unions, however, represent approximately 80 percent of Swedish workers. That means that 40 percent of the Swedish population belong to unions.

Approximately 4.3 million Swedes, half the population, are in the labor force. That figure is so large because 75 percent of all women between the ages of sixteen and sixty-four work for wages. However, around a quarter of the labor force, principally women, work part-time.

In addition to the LO, white-collar workers are organized in the Confederation of Salaried Employees (TCO), and professional white-collar workers are organized in the Confederation of Professional Associations (SACO).

The LO has been one of the most important groups affecting economic, political, and social life in Sweden. Since an agreement at Saltsjöbaden in 1938 between the LO and the Confederation of Employers (SAF), relations between the two organizations and their members have, in general, been cooperative rather than confrontational. Representatives of the LO and the SAF between 1939 and 1984 met every year or two to agree on wage guidelines, which were generally accepted by their respective members. However, the LO concept of "solidarity wages"—the same pay for the same type of work regardless of the condition of the specific employer—suffered a challenge in 1984 when centralized wage bargaining was abandoned. In 1991 the conservative government proposed completely abolishing the practice. Pay negotiations, however, are still conducted by the SAF with the LO, the TCO, and the SACO. In addition, employment security, the status of shop stewards, worker participation in decision making, and the working environment are all guaranteed by law.

BIBLIOGRAPHY

Carlson, Bo. *Trade Unions in Sweden.* Stockholm: Tidens, 1969.

Johnston, T. L. *Collective Bargaining in Sweden.* Cambridge, Mass.: Harvard University Press, 1962.

Nordstrom, Byron J. "Swedish Confederation of Trade Unions," in *Dictionary of Scandinavian History.* Westport, Conn.: Greenwood Press, 1986, 603–4.

Thompson, Wayne C. *Western Europe 1996.* Harpers Ferry, W.V.: Stryker-Post, 1996.

Bernard Cook

Taxation

During the postwar period the Swedish tax system was used to achieve greater income equality and to facilitate industrialization. Taxes on individuals and small enterprises were highly progressive, while large firms were taxed proportionally. From 1985 to 1991 fundamental changes were made to the tax system. These changes involved less progressive taxation and a broader tax base on, the one hand, and a more uniform taxation of large and small enterprises, on the other. After the tax reforms, working hours increased slightly.

The Swedish tax system includes various direct and indirect taxes and charges. The most important direct levies are the national and local income taxes and the national tax on capital. Inheritance taxes and the gift tax are also direct. In addition, there is an extensive system of employer contributions (social security charges) that covers pensions, health benefits, and other social insurance. Indirect taxes are the value-added tax and excises on selected commodities, which go almost exclusively to the state. The value-added tax on most goods and services is between 6 and 25 percent.

For individuals, the national income tax in 1996–98 was 25 percent on all income earned each year above a certain level. In 1997 this dividing line was 209,100 kronor and the national income tax on income below that point was only 100 kronor. The threshold amount has been fixed as a multiple of the base amount defined in the Social Security Act. The base amount is increased for inflation (60 percent of inflation increases) and is used for calculation of various social benefits. The local income tax is proportional. Local governments decide each year what fixed percentage of taxable income is payable. The average local tax rate is about 31 percent of taxable income. Individuals are allowed to make certain deductions from their total taxable income. The basic deduction or personal exemption is at least 24 percent of the base amount. In 1997 this deduction was around 8,700 as the base amount stood at 36,300. The basic deduction is higher on annual taxable incomes between around 67,900 and 202,900. There is also a special basic deduction for retired people, the total of which is at least 1.5 the base amount in the case of single persons and 1.325 the base amount in the case of married persons. The special basic deduction is not to exceed the national basic pension plus pension supplements that retired persons receive but these are tax free.

Income from capital is taxed at a flat national rate of 30 percent. Capital income includes interest, dividends, capital gains and losses, and income from certain real estate and other similar income. The basic deduction is not allowed against capital income. A deficit in the capital income category results in a tax reduction of 30 percent on the deficit up to 100,000.

Corporations and economic associations constitute independent subjects for taxation. On the other hand the owners of sole proprietorships and partnerships are taxed directly for income from these sources, together with earned income from any other sources.

All income of corporations and economic associations is taxed in a single income category. The corporate tax rate is a flat 25 percent. Corporate profits are subject to double taxation, i.e., first the corporation pays tax on them, then the shareholders pay tax on dividends. Enterprises may allocate tax free a maximum of 25 percent of their annual profits to a tax-equalization reserve. The reserve must be returned to taxable status no later than the fifth year of allocation. If an owner of a sole proprietorship participates actively in the enterprise, the resulting income is classified as active income and the owner pays social insurance charges. In 1997 these social insurance charges totaled 31.35 percent of the income. Losses from the sole proprietorship may generally not be offset against income from employment but may be offset against future business income without any limits. As other enterprises, a sole proprietorship has the right to allocate 25 percent of its profit to a tax equalization. For both private business owners and companies, depreciation is allowed for the declining value of machinery and other equipment intended for continuous use. The deductions amount to 30 percent of the book value of the equipment per year.

Swedish employers are obliged to pay social welfare contributions to the public sector. In 1996 these contributions were 40 percent of blue-collar workers' annual wages and 42 percent of the salaries of clerical employees. These contributions go to finance the national supplementary pension system, the health insurance system, and the basic pension.

BIBLIOGRAPHY

McLure, Charles E., and Erik Norrman. "Svensk skattepolitik", in Richhard B. Freeman, Birgitta Swedenborg, and Robert Topel. *Välfärdsstat i omvandling. Amerikanskt perspektiv på den Svenska modellen.* Stockholm: SNS Förlag, 1995.

Lilja Mósesdóttir
Gudny Björk Eydal

Press

Swedes, who enjoy a literacy rate of 99 percent, purchase more newspapers per capita than any other Europeans except Icelanders. Though the number of newspapers is declining, Sweden, with a population of 8.8 million, still has nearly 100 daily and around 80 weekly newspapers. (Switzerland, which has approximately seven million inhabitants, has 231 newspapers, the largest number per capita of any European country.) Most Swedish newspapers are identified with a specific political party or ideology. Nearly 75 percent of them support the centrist and conservative parties, and around 20 percent support the Social Democratic Party (SAP). Except for the more successful commercial newspapers, Swedish newspapers receive direct subsidies and tax breaks from the government. The top Swedish newspapers in circulation are *Aftonbladet* (daily circulation in 1997, 408,300), *Dagens Nyheter* (347,900), and *Expressen* (339,000), all of Stockholm; the *Göteborgs-Posten* (261,600) of Göteborg; and the Stockholm *Svenska Dagbladet* (194,500), the Malmö *Sydsvenska Dagbladet* (122,800) and the Stockholm Dagens *Industri* (102,000). After these dominant newspapers, daily circulation drops significantly. The daily circulation of the next three largest Swedish newspapers—*Nerikes Allehanda, Östgöta Correspondenten,* and *GT*—is fewer than 70,000 each.

BIBLIOGRAPHY

Thompson, Wayne C. *Western Europe 1995.* Harpers Ferry, W.V.: Stryker-Post, 1995.

Bernard Cook

Welfare System

The Swedish welfare state includes an extensive system of social security schemes and service provisions.

The goals of the Swedish health-care system according to the Health and Medical Service Act of 1982 is to provide medical and health service of good quality to all Swedish citizens on equal terms. All citizens have a right to free or subsidized care. The system is run and financed by the public sector but administered by the landsting (county councils).

There are twenty-three county councils in Sweden, each of which is responsible for ensuring that all the county's residents have access to good health care. The county councils own and operate health-care centers and hospitals and employ most health-care and medical staff. Most doctors with independent practices are remunerated by the county councils. The county councils are also responsible for providing dental services, which are free of charge for children nineteen years and younger and heavily subsidized for persons twenty years and older. If hospital care is required, medical services are provided at both county and regional level in eighty hospitals.

Health-care centers provide extensive primary health-care services. Beside doctors, professionals such as nurses, auxiliary nurses, midwives, and physical therapists are employed at the health centers. Primary care is also provided by private doctors and at clinics for children and for maternity health care. At children's clinics, services are provided free of charge to all children under school age. Expectant mothers are also served free of charge at maternity clinics. In addition, primary care is provided free of charge at schools.

Apart from free services for children and expecting mothers, patients usually do have to pay users fees for primary care as well as for hospital care. Patients also pay for medicines but they are subsidized by the state. There is a cost ceiling on health-care costs to limit expenses incurred by patients. A patient or a family whose payments have reached the threshold amount is entitled to free health service for the rest of the twelve-month period counting from the day the first user fee payment was paid. The same system applies for the cost of medicine.

The social security system expanded during the postwar period, but its main features had developed earlier. Social expenditure as a percent of GNP rose from 16 percent in 1962 to 39 percent in 1992. The social insurance system has undergone two major changes. The first change involved the implementation of earnings-related benefits in addition to the universal flat-rate benefits. This development contributed to the dual character of the Swedish social insurance system, which includes both flat-rate and earnings-related payments. The second change involved the position of women, who gradually gained the same status as men. The last sign of formal differentiation between men and women disappeared in 1990, when the pension system for widows was abolished and a system of survivors benefits was implemented.

The social insurance benefits (except unemployment benefits) are administered by local social insurance offices that in turn are supervised by the National Social Insurance Board. The social insurance offices have no funds of their own as the system is financed through taxation.

The pension system covers elderly, disabled, and survivors. Pension payments are twofold, including, on the one hand, a universal flat-rate payment and, on the other hand, supplementary pension payment. The universal basic pension system was originally intended to guarantee basic security for everyone in old age. The compulsory supplementary pension system (ATP), which was introduced in 1960, is based on compensation according to the loss-of-income principle. Over the years the ATP has become the more important of the two pension systems.

All insured persons who become sick or have to stay at home to care for sick children are entitled to sickness benefits. The benefit is a taxable daily allowance that amounts to 75 to 85 percent of lost income. The national occupational injury insurance system pays all health-care costs for work-related accidents. Workers are covered by unemployment insurance through their membership in labor unions. Unemployment benefits amount to 80 percent of previous earnings. Unemployed people without such coverage are entitled to a lower benefit paid by the state. Extensive employment measures such as job training are utilized to enhance the employability of the unemployed.

Parents are entitled to a total of 360 days of paid leave from work. The parents can decide if and how to share the parental leave. However, at least one month is reserved for each parent. The leave can be taken at any time until the child is eight years old. Since 1994 each parent is entitled to 30 days with benefit equaling 85 percent of regular earnings. For the following 210 days, the benefit rate is 75 percent of regular earnings, and for the remaining 90 days, the rate is 60 kronor a day. When taking care of a sick child, parents are entitled to 120 days annually at 75 percent of previous income. Child allowances are also paid to parents until the child is sixteen years old; children who then continue their education are entitled to study allowances.

The roots of the system of social assistance can be traced back to the old system of poor relief. All persons are entitled to assistance from the social services committee if their needs cannot be satisfied in any other way. Social assistance is regarded to be the ultimate safety net in the welfare system. The system of social assistance differs in fundamental ways from the social insurance schemes. First, the system of social assistance has always been financed and administered at the local instead of the state level. Second, social assistance is means-tested and the family is the benefit unit. The social insurance system, on the other hand, is based on individual rights and benefits, which are either flat rate and/or income-related. Third, social assistance is not taxable as is the case with most other benefits.

Major parts of the Swedish welfare system are the various schemes of social services. The main character of the social services is that they are universally provided to all citizens in need. The services are either free of charge or user fees are charged. The history of social services can be traced back to the so-called poor houses, were persons unable to provide for themselves where institutionalized. During the twentieth century social services expanded rapidly and the major areas include childcare services, services for the elderly, and services for the disabled.

Day care services have been provided primarily by the public sector. Not until 1944 did the state grant regular state subsidizes to private childcare organizations. During the 1960s the demand for childcare expanded as women's labor force participation increased. In 1973 laws were passed encouraging municipalities to create a large number of day-care facilities. Since the 1960s their number has expanded almost fiftyfold. Beside the pedagogical aims of public day care, it has also been an important part of family, equality, and labor market policies. In 1995 municipalities were obliged by law to provide daycare for children from one to six years of age and school care children from the age of six to twelve if the parents were working or studying. As the provision of day care is the responsibility of each municipality, the organization of day care, the number of children enrolled, and the fees paid by parents vary considerably. Private day care is subsidized by municipalities. Parental cooperatives and family day care are the most common forms of private day care. Children from the ages of seven to nine can attend special leisure centers during after-school hours.

Services for the disabled have changed dramatically during the postwar period. In the 1960s there was a shift away from institutionalization toward integration and active participation of the disabled in society. Various services for the disabled have been organized to ensure their integration into society. In 1994 new laws on Support and Service for Persons with Certain Functional Impairments (LSS) came into force. These laws have been described as a human rights statute. One of the most important implications of the laws is that the disabled are now entitled to publicly paid personal assistance in accordance with need. In addition, it is no longer permissible to admit people with intellectual impairments to mental institutions.

BIBLIOGRAPHY

Björnberg, Ulla, and Gudny Björk Eydal. "Family Obligations in Sweden," in Jane Millar and Andrea Warman, eds. *Defining Family Obligations in Europe.* Social Policy Papers No. 23, Bath, England: University of Bath, 1995.

Spilä, Jorma, ed. *Social Care Services—The Key to the Scandinavian Model.* Aldershot, England: Avebury, 1996.

Lilja Mósesdóttir
Gudny Björk Eydal

Swinarski, Konrad (1929–75)

Theatrical director, apart from Leon Schiller the most important artist in the Polish theater of the last fifty years. Having completed his arts and staging studies in Sopot and Warsaw, Swinarski made his stage director's debut in 1955. This was followed by special training in the Berliner Ensemble from 1955 to 1957. Swinarski directed in many Polish theaters focusing on modern drama, primarily Brecht, Dürrenmatt, and Weiss. His production of *Marat/Sade* in the West Berlin Schiller Theater was voted the most distinguished production in Germany. Swinarski's best Polish productions were staged in the Old Theater in Kraków. Notable were the romantic *Nie-Boska komedia* (*Non-divine Comedy*) by Zygmunt Krasiński in 1965, and *Dziady* (*Halloween*) by Adam Mickiewicz in 1973; and the neoromantic *Wyzwolenie* (*Liberation*) by Stanislaw Wyspiański in 1974. Swinarski created his own theatrical style, called "barocco" or polyphonic, which meant rich, multiple theatrical staging. He sought to reveal versatility and discrepancies in presenting phenomena using irony and contrast techniques. Swinarski paid much attention to his work with actors, from whom he evoked great creativity. His productions dealt with basic issues of human existence confronting historical and natural forces, and made audiences ask themselves questions concerning fundamental values.

BIBLIOGRAPHY

Walaszek, J. *Konrad Swinarski i jego krakówskie inscenizacje.* Warsaw: PIW, 1991.

Maria Kalinowska

Swiss Banks and Jewish Funds

In 1995, the question of what became of Swiss bank accounts belonging to Jewish victims of the Holocaust surfaced in the world media. The controversy took three years to resolve, and it led to many more questions, including those of Swiss purchases of Nazi gold, unclaimed insurance policies for victims of Nazism, and looted art. It also caused a reexamination of concepts of political neutrality and how these were sacrificed on the altar of economic collaboration in Switzerland as well as other neutral nations.

Faced with increasing anti-Semitic measures in Germany after Adolf Hitler came to power in 1933, Jews of all social ranks started considering options for safeguarding their savings. Nazi economic policy followed a peculiar model of autarky and consequently restricted any export of capital on the part of all Germans. In so doing, Hitler's government relied on a 1931 law that the Weimar Republic had instituted to stop German capital from being sent abroad. The law imposed a heavy fine on anyone who exported currency without authorization. Thus, to place savings in a secure area, Germans in general and Jews in particular faced considerable challenges. In Switzerland, a 1934 law guaranteed bank secrecy. As a result, the country attracted many banking customers from all over Europe. Jews took great risks to get their money out of Germany, using false names and other business subterfuges, such as having money from foreign sales sent directly to bank accounts in Switzerland (an illegal procedure in Germany at the time).

Nazi customs agents, assisted by the Gestapo (the German secret police) and German diplomats, sought to check such exports by either obtaining the account number and forging signatures of the owners, or by dealing directly with Swiss bankers. Once such "illegal" accounts (under German law) were located, the Jewish account owner's bank generally agreed to transfer funds into an account controlled by the German government. Very few Swiss banks ever opposed such practices, despite warnings up to 1939 from the Swiss National Bank, which feared an overflow of foreign currency and gold on the Swiss market would hurt the Swiss economy and lead to inflation. As of 1939 all such warnings stopped as Switzerland, facing a potential blockade situation, became overly accommodating to German interests and ignored many illegal activities on the part of private Swiss banks, which had benefited from German and Jewish accounts. Thus, between 1933 and 1945, several banking institutions in Switzerland either cooperated knowingly with Nazi investigators. Nonetheless, German authorities failed to locate and expropriate thousands of accounts.

After 1945, surviving victims began to appear in Switzerland in search of accounts opened either by themselves or by family members who had perished in the Holocaust. In some cases, they were informed that such accounts had been closed as a result of the owner's signature (forged), or by a decision of the bank's board. In other cases, the inability to provide highly detailed information concerning an account led banks to reject a claim. Several cases were brought before the courts, but the great majority of claimants eventually gave up.

In March 1946, a Swiss delegation composed of banking and diplomatic representatives arrived in Washington to negotiate an agreement concerning funds Switzerland had accepted from the Nazi government. Accused of harboring gold stolen from countries under Nazi control, Switzerland found itself facing Allied demands for reparations reaching billions of dollars. The head of the Swiss delegation, Walter Stucki, negotiated an agreement whereby Switzerland would pay 250 million Swiss francs as compensation for the Nazi gold it had stored. The Washington accords of May 1946 also contained a note whereby Switzerland agreed to consider "with sympathy" the question of unclaimed bank accounts of Jewish victims of the Holocaust. Yet, the issue did not resurface for fifty years.

The Swiss government, eager to remain on good terms with the Allies early in the Cold War, sought to establish legislation that would require banks to deal with the problem of dormant accounts. Individuals in the government and in the Swiss National Bank sought time and again to have legislation passed in 1953, 1954, and 1957, but their resolve quickly evaporated when facing strong opposition led by the Swiss Banking Association (SBA). By then, a few hundred thousand Swiss francs worth of dormant accounts had been located, and in some instances liquidated under unilateral bank rules specifying that "inactive" accounts could be closed.

In December 1962, however, a federal Swiss mandate to deal with "the property in Switzerland of foreigners or stateless persons persecuted on religious, racial or political grounds" went into effect, requiring Swiss banks to locate dormant accounts and match these to owners. Some 9.5 million francs suddenly appeared, 75 percent of which were designated as belonging to specific individuals. However, of the 7,000 estimated names on lists, only 1,000 people showed up to claim funds. While the 1962 law constituted an attempt to deal with a thorny problem, it fell far short of expectations. Surviving victims or their descendants had until 1974 (when the mandate expired) to make a claim, but many living in Communist Eastern Europe were unable to do so. In the case of Hungary, for example, a lump sum payment of 325,000 Swiss francs was made to the Hungarian government, but the latter then paid 500,000 to Switzerland for confiscation of Swiss property by the Communist regime in Hungary. No individuals were compensated. In the 1970s and 1980s, at the height of the Cold War, nobody had any interest in questioning Switzerland's World War II behavior: although neutral, Switzerland was clearly a friend of the West. Following the end of the Cold War in the early 1990s, however, Switzerland underwent a crisis of identity.

Things came to a head in early 1995, when, on the heels of the celebrations of the fiftieth anniversary of the end of World War II and the liberation of the Nazi death camps, several Israeli newspapers covering the commemoration demanded in their editorials that funds of deceased victims be either given to their inheritors, the state of Israel, or to Jewish organizations. Swiss banks were heavily criticized for their past behavior. The SBA at first reacted with indecision and denied that "billions" might still be stored in Switzerland. However, under pressure of the World Jewish Congress, and with involvement from the American Senator Al D'Amato of New York, the first of several commissions to deal with the banking scandal was formed.

A Memorandum of Understanding of May 2, 1996, between the SBA, the World Jewish Restitution Organization, and the World Jewish Congress (representing the Jewish Agency and Allied organizations) established the Independent Committee of Eminent Persons (ICEP) consisting of six members and four alternates, half appointed by the Swiss Bankers Association and half appointed by Jewish Organizations. Paul A. Volcker, former

Chairman of the Board of Governors of the U.S. Federal Reserve System, served as the committee's chairperson.

Such measures were insufficient, however, as new evidence came to light regarding Swiss economic cooperation with Nazi Germany. In the United States, Senator D'Amato demanded a reexamination the Washington agreement (a request later rejected by U.S. State Department), while the media began questioning Swiss behavior in World War II. Consequently, a psychology of encirclement gripped the Swiss political and banking communities, leading to defensive and inflammatory comments by several Swiss officials. In January 1997, for example, the Swiss ambassador to United States, Carlo Jagmetti, was forced to resign following his complaints about a "war with organized Jewry" that appeared in a leaked confidential report. Similarly inflammatory comments by Swiss Federal Councilor and former President Jean-Pascal Delamuraz led to public apologies for his behavior.

By spring 1997, however, the three main Swiss banks (UBS, SBS, and Crédit Suisse) proceeded to set aside 100 million Swiss francs to start paying damages to Holocaust victims. They were soon joined by several Swiss corporations. Meanwhile, the Federal Council decided on the creation of a Swiss Solidarity Fund with a funding of seven billion francs to help alleviate human misery around the world. The money came from the sale of gold from the Swiss National Bank. At the same time, a specially appointed international group of experts, the Bergier Commission, first met in March 1997 to investigate Switzerland's economic dealings with Nazi Germany.

Several scandals continued to shake the reputation of Swiss banks, such as when Zürich bank guard Christoph Meili discovered that UBS was destroying archival material pertaining to World War II. Acrimonious accusations on all sides slowed further negotiations. In Switzerland, it also led to generational conflicts, which were characterized on the part of the defenders of Switzerland's past behavior by a mixture of anti-Semitism, anti-Americanism, and the rise of nationalistic isolationism among several political parties.

In July 1997, the first list of dormant accounts was published but was quickly revised because of multiple inaccuracies. Concurrently, negotiations concerning the amount of damages to be paid out to victims continued. Due to resistance on the part of the SBA and growing impatience on the part of several Jewish organizations, there were public calls for a boycott of Swiss banks in New York and California.

In October 1997, Rolf Bloch, head of the Swiss Federation of Jewish communities and director of the Swiss Fund for Victims of the Holocaust, handed out the first check, to Riva Schefer, a 75-year-old survivor from Latvia. By then, banks had located 80 million Swiss francs worth of funds.

By early 1998, multiple lawsuits had been filed against Swiss banks and the Swiss government. In March, however, collective law suits were dropped when Swiss banks reached an agreement with plaintiffs' lawyers on damages. Nevertheless, individual lawsuits continued. Eventually, steps taken by the World Jewish Congress, the U.S. government, and the SBA resulted in an agreement signed on August 13, 1998, whereby banks would pay out between 1.2 and 1.9 billion dollars beginning in the summer of 2000. The special fund of 273 million francs set up in 1997 was depleted within two years after having served to pay some 110,000 Holocaust victims.

The ICEP held its seventeenth and last meeting in Zürich on February 23, 2000. In its final report, it mentioned that the total number of identified pre-1945 dormant accounts would likely be reduced from 53,000 to 45,000 due to duplication during the investigative process. The ICEP also called for the establishment of a centralized archive for the documentation of the investigation, and the publication of the accounts that can be linked to victims of Nazism, roughly 26,000 in all, so that the Swiss Claims Resolution Tribunal can adjudicate the ownership of claims of these victims or their heirs.

While the crisis of the Swiss banks and Jewish dormant accounts has now subsided, it also opened the door to questioning neutral countries' behavior in World War II. Insurance companies are now being investigated, and the historical analysis of this aspect of Swiss history remains a point of argument among historians.

BIBLIOGRAPHY

Bower, Tom. *Nazi Gold.* New York: HarperCollins, 1998.

Independent Committee of Eminent Persons. *Report on Dormant Accounts of Victims of Nazi Persecution in Swiss Banks.* Berne: Staempfli Publishers, 1999.

Rickman, Gregg J. *Swiss Banks and Jewish Souls.* New Brunswick, N.J.: Transaction, 1999.

Vincent, Isabel. *Hitler's Silent Partners: Swiss Banks, Nazi Gold, and the Pursuit of Justice.* Toronto: Vintage Canada, 1998.

Guillaume de Syon

Switzerland

Country in the center of Europe with an area of 15,943 square miles (41,292 sq km) and a population of 6.91 million Switzerland is bordered on the west by France, on the north by Germany, on the east by Austria and Liech-

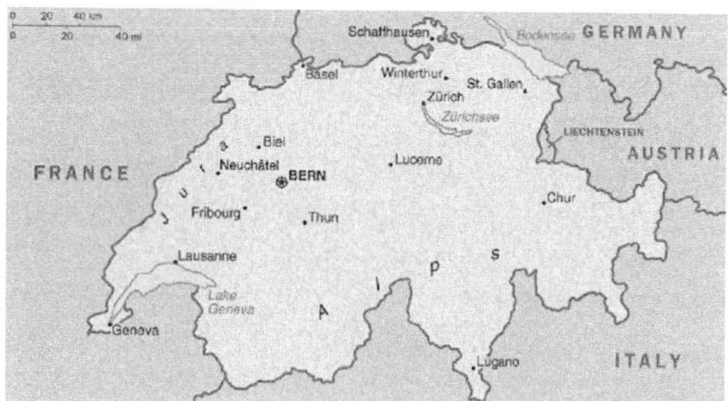

Switzerland. *Illustration courtesy of Bernard Cook.*

tenstein, and on the south by Italy. Its citizens are roughly 74 percent German-speaking, 20 percent French-speaking, 4 percent Italian-speaking, and 1 percent Romansch-speaking. Seventeen percent of the population consists of resident foreigners. The largest number is from Italy, but there are also large numbers of Germans, Spaniards, and Turks. Swiss nationals are 55 percent Protestant and 43 percent Roman Catholic; if resident foreigners are included, the total population is 49.4 percent Catholic and 47.8 percent Protestant.

Switzerland is a decentralized plebiscitary democracy. To understand Swiss political policy, one must take into account its predominant feature: direct democracy. Among Western democracies in the postwar period, Switzerland is the only state in the world to apply direct democracy to every sphere of government activity. From 1848 to 1990 Swiss citizens have been called to polls on 1,837 issues (148 obligatory referenda; 183 popular initiatives; and 1,506 optional referenda). Swiss voters are called on to decide between seven and fourteen national questions yearly, which are typically spread over three or four separate ballots. In addition, they are asked to vote in numerous cantonal and communal referenda. When elections of national, cantonal, and communal representatives are added to these, an average Swiss citizen is called to the polls more times in a single year than any other European citizen in a lifetime. Only in Australia, California, and a few other western U.S. states do referenda play such an important role in daily political life.

The explanation for Swiss attachment to direct democracy is its long-standing experience of direct vote, documented as existing in the canton of Schwyz since 1294. Popular Landsgemeinden (legislative assemblies) were used in several mountain cantons from the thirteenth century onward. But population growth in the nineteenth and twentieth centuries rendered the Landsgemeinden impractical in most cantons. Referenda and initiatives on key issues covering external and domestic policy came into common usage as a way of preserving the tradition of direct legislation. Major changes that have marked the postwar evolution of Swiss society are, without doubt, linked to this constraining element of power sharing, which is quite different from the Anglo-Saxon winner-take-all pattern.

In 1947 the introduction of an important federal social welfare bill, the AVS/AHV, an old age insurance scheme, which was an old Social Democratic demand, figured as the key issue to be solved so that the trend toward widening participation in the Federal Council could be negotiated. This participation was temporarily interrupted when the Social Democrats (SPS) withdrew from government between 1953 and 1958. A solution was found in 1959 when a majority of the Swiss political parties approved of the "Magic Formula." The governmental Magic Formula set up a new Federal Council made up of two Radicals, traditionally the Protestant anti-clerical party (FDP); two Social Democrats, a reformist party rooted in a socialist tradition (SPS); two Christian Democrats, traditionally Catholic (CVP); and one member of the Agrarian Bourgeois, which, in 1971, became the Swiss People's Party (SVP). The model has survived, up to now, irrespective of election results, although the latter have been remarkably stable over the past years. This, together with labor peace introduced in 1937, are often described as being the main steps in Switzerland toward creating a collaborative democracy (Konkordaz) in which all major political tendencies are represented, and collaborate.

A further step was taken when the right of women to vote after a first failure in 1959, was finally changed through an all-male referendum in 1971. Women obtained the right to vote at the federal level. However, it was only in 1981 that a constitutional amendment introduced legal, social, and economic equality for women. If the representation of women in the cantonal parliaments and the federal chambers is slowly progressing, women in Switzerland are still concentrated in lower-level jobs and sometimes do not obtain equal pay for equal work.

On the political agenda of the last fifty years there have been a number of distinctive Swiss issues. One is the constitutional revision, in particular the nature of the balance between federal and cantonal power (Switzerland has twenty-two cantons, and federal power is weak); another is the role of the Swiss army, the extent to which it should be supported financially, and whether civilian service alternatives should be provided for conscientious objectors. On November 26, 1989, more than a million voters, 35.6 percent of those going to the polls, supported an initiative to abolish the Swiss military, exceeding even the expectations of the antiarmy militants. Even though the proposal was defeated, it nevertheless compelled government reforms. Since 1995 citizens obliged to serve have seen their military service diminish from 360 days, divided between a four-month boot camp and a series of three- or two-week courses up to the age of forty-five, to 300 days of service. In addition to cuts in the size of the Swiss army, there were widespread demands for a civilian service option for men unwilling to enter the military. In 1990 the government passed a law decriminalizing conscientious objection to military service. It was approved at the polls in June 1991 and a constitutional amendment was ratified in May 1992.

Environmental protection is probably the most intensely debated political issue of all, especially in the aftermath of Chernobyl and the Rhine chemical disaster at Schweizerhalle in 1986. In the 1970s the antinuclear movement successfully stopped the construction of a power plant after several months of occupation of the site. When Ecologist Party and the Social Democrats (SPS) opposed the construction of new nuclear power plants, the issue was divisive. A popular initiative against the construction of new power plants failed in 1979, but the margin was razor thin. And protagonists of nuclear power were unable to win enough support for the continuation of the program. When in 1985 the federal chambers authorized the resumption of the construction of a nuclear power plant in Kaiseraugst, it encountered unanimous protest throughout Switzerland. The work was not resumed, and in 1989 the federal parliament dropped the project, paying over sfr 350 million Swiss francs in indemnities. In 1990 a compromise was finally found: the cantons and the people accepted a popular initiative for a ten-year moratorium on the authorization and construction of new plants.

The Swiss referenda that have attracted the most interest around the world have dealt with either foreign policy or the implementation of restrictive measures on foreigners working in Switzerland. Switzerland suffered no major visible damages during the Second World War. Nevertheless, the old "hedgehog mentality" of isolation, neutrality, and nonparticipation in international or multinational organizations, endured, and it was some time before the country started to open up under the slogan "Neutrality and Solidarity." Switzerland provided minor aid for "destroyed European countries," before collaborating within the Organization for European Economic Cooperation (OEEC) and the European Economic Community in the 1950s, and finally joining the European Free Trade Association (EFTA) in 1960. In June 1945 Switzerland was initially disposed to join the United Nations, provided that Swiss neutrality would be formally guaranteed by the organization. After U.N. Secretary-General Trygve Lie declared "that international organization and neutrality were on two separate planes which could not meet," Switzerland decided against membership. On March 16, 1986, the Swiss overwhelmingly rejected U.N. membership again. On May 17, 1992, Swiss voters with 55.8 percent of the vote agreed to become a member of the International Monetary Fund and Switzerland was given a seat on the executive board of the World Bank. Finally, on December 6, 1992, 50.3 percent of Swiss voters rejected joining the European Economic Area (EEA), after, as a member of the European Free Trade Association (EFTA), having participated in the negotiations for an enlarged single market with the European Community (EC, now European Union).

The other much published referendum issue was how the numbers of foreigners in Switzerland could be stabilized or reduced, and the extent of their rights. Foreigners number more than one million, 17 percent of the total population, and most of them work in jobs that the Swiss avoid if they can. An anti-alien movement developed, in the 1970s demanding a severe reduction in the number of foreigners allowed to work in the country. This movement launched unsuccessful several constitutional initiatives, which if they had been accepted, would have forced hundreds of thousands of foreigners to leave the country. Each one of these initiatives compelled the Federal executive to introduce stricter measures tightening up immigration.

In addition to tension between the Swiss and foreign workers, there has been some tension between Switzerland's indigenous peoples. The creation of the canton of Jura represents an exception to Swiss integration of cultural minorities. Historical factors and language, religious, cultural, and socioeconomic differences led to its separation from the canton of Bern. The Jura region, which is mainly Catholic and French-speaking, was incorporated into Protestant, German-speaking Bern in 1815. As a minority located at the northern periphery of the canton, the people of Jura felt they were being discriminated against both politically and economically. An escalation of political clashes after the Second World War gave rise to a separatist movement that triumphed in 1978, when the new Jura Canton was created. The conflict was complicated by the fact that the population of the Jura was itself divided: three southern districts had been Protestant since the sixteenth century, were economically better off, and had traditionally better relations with the old canton. Thus the deepening conflict was not only between Jura and Bern, but also between "separatists" and Bernese "loyalists" within the population of Jura.

The 1990s have brought forward a new series of much debated questions dealing with parochial cultures. German cantons have experienced a renaissance of dialects that are barely understood by Swiss French or Italian speakers. Doubts have also arisen about the fiscal competence and general effectiveness of the federal government. Among the debated issues are the state of the social security system and the need for economic revitalization and new measures to combat unemployment. The growing problems of drug use and AIDS have also drawn much public attention. Nevertheless, the Swiss are discovering, as is the rest of the world, that they cannot escape the tendencies of market liberalization and globalization, and that domestic policy and foreign affairs are more and more interdependent.

BIBLIOGRAPHY

Kobach, Kris W. *The Referendum: Direct Democracy in Switzerland.* Brookfield, Vt.: Dartmouth, 1993.

Linder, Wolf. *Swiss Democracy: Possible Solutions to Conflict in Multicultural Societies.* London: St. Martin's Press, 1994.

New, Mita, ed. *Switzerland Unwrapped: Exposing the Myths.* London: I.B. Tauris, 1997.

Steiner, Jörg. *European Democracies,* 3d ed. New York: Longman, 1995.

Julian Thomas Hottinger

European Community

In July 1947 Switzerland accepted the invitation extended by France and Great Britain to participate in the Paris Conference on the reconstruction of Europe. This reflected its standpoint that an interest in strengthening the economic unity of Europe was compatible with Switzerland's neutral status. On the eve of the conference, to anticipate any misunderstandings, the Swiss government addressed a note to the French and British legations stating that it would enter into no commitment that could affect its traditional neutrality. Moreover, any decisions taken at the conference concerning the Swiss economy would be binding only after these decisions had received official approval. Finally, Switzerland claimed its rights to continue or negotiate trade agreements with third countries at its own discretion. These three conditions, established in the immediate postwar period, have come to be a national and economic creed to which Switzerland still adheres in its approach to international agreements and organizations.

They were expressly repeated in negotiations or statements of position, for example, when the Organization for European Economic Cooperation (OEEC) was reorganized as the Organization for European Cooperation and Development (OECD) in 1960; when Switzerland refrained from joining the European Economic Community (EEC) in the 1950s; when it signed the General Agreement on Tariffs and Trade (GATT) in 1966; when it concluded the free-trade agreement with the EEC and the European Coal and Steel Community (ECSC) in 1972; and in the Federal Council's report in 1988 on the Swiss economy.

An analysis of the reservations made by the Swiss government during the various integration phases shows that there has been a shift of emphasis over the years. In the 1950s the overall aims of the EEC were judged incompatible with the principles laid down in Switzerland's constitution and thus formed an insuperable obstacle to Swiss membership. The 1988 integration report of the Swiss government is less absolute in its wording and admits that it would be "legitimate and credible" today to pay the political price for the political objective of helping to shape Europe, provided that there were signs among the population of "a credible basic desire for accession." This new approach is apparent not only in political matters but also in economic policy. If in the 1950s the main focus was on the disadvantages of joining the EEC, such as the high EEC customs tariffs, which would make Switzerland less competitive, contrariwise the most recent integration report suggests that possible risks for the Swiss economy lie not in joining the European Union (EU), but much more in remaining outside it. The completion of the EU internal market would lead to fiercer competition both within the single market and in non-EU markets.

Since the narrowly rejected referendum on the European Economic Area (EEA) membership in December 1992, the Federal Council has struggled to find a new relationship with the EU, through new bilateral agreements, while being very cautious as the European question is one of the most divisive issues in Swiss politics.

BIBLIOGRAPHY

Church, Clive. "The Paradoxical Europeanisation of Switzerland." *European Business Journal* 2 (1996): 9–17.

Saint-Ouen, François. "Facing European Integration: The Case of Switzerland." *Journal of Common Market Studies* 3 (1988): 273–85.

Julian Thomas Hottinger

Political Parties

Swiss political parties are highly distinctive, characterized both by intense localism and diversity of political forms and structures. While major cantonal parties are represented at the national level, they remain a cantonal structure. Quite often these parties are denominated the same way, but their representatives tend to defend cantonal interests at a federal level in detriment to classical cleavages. Concerned with local electoral considerations and patronage, a national focus is obscured, as congress members go to Bern, the federal capital, "to defend their canton's interests." This adds up to enhanced polarization inside the system, complicated by having twenty-six cantonal party systems represented in parliament, then the diversity of Swiss political parties is accentuated by a number of linguistic and religious splits.

The linguistic cleavages are probably the least important in explaining the current structure of political parties, although some of the smaller parties are based in one linguistic area or the other. Nevertheless, the four biggest parties—the Radical Party (FDP), Social Democratic Party (SPS), Christian Democratic Party (CVP), and Swiss People's Party (SVP)—are represented in French, German, Italian, or Romansch Switzerland. Any differences among the linguistic zones are due mostly to a cultural nature. Direct democratic forms are more characteristic of the German-speaking cantons, and sometimes there is differential voting among linguistic communities. For example, the European Economic Area Referendum received strong support in French Switzerland but much less in German and Italian Switzerland, while opposition to nuclear energy is stronger in German and Romansch cantons. The surprisingly resistant cleavage among parties remains that of religion.

Unlike its German counterpart, the CVP has remained overwhelmingly Catholic. On the other hand, parties such as the Evangelicals (EVP) or the Liberals (LPS) are overwhelmingly Protestant in membership. The Protestant Party (EDU) is the counterpart of the Christian Democrats, but without its large electoral support. The Radicals (FDP) have a Protestant tradition but also represent the formerly anticlerical forces in Catholic cantons such as Ticino or Solothurn. In a canton such as Luzern the old clerical/anticlerical division still exists to a considerable degree, and political differences are largely due to the persisting "pillarisation" (compartmentalization) of society.

Class differences, on the other hand, have been of less significance. There is little heavy industry in Switzerland, and the parties of the Left—the SPS or the Communists (PdA)—have always had to look outside the few industrial areas such as Basel or Zurich to get an adequate level of support. The SPS enjoys close relations with labor unions. Urban/rural differences have been more significant, and the small farmers' SVP party has remained influential, especially in the Protestant mountain cantons and in Bern, where the CVP is marginal. If Switzerland is the only Western European country outside Scandinavia where peasants' parties have developed and survived, a unique urban opposition to ecologists (GPS) has flourished these last few years with the "Motorists' Party," now known as the Swiss Freedom Party (FPS).

But the main complexity of the Swiss political party system is to be found elsewhere. Localized differences are still pertinent. Over thirty-seven of the parties running in the 1995 federal elections were restricted to one canton, as is the case for the Lega dei Ticinesi (LdT). Each canton and many communes have their own specific tradition and personalities, with an extensive use of direct democratic forms, such as the meeting of citizens in the annual Landsgemeinden, which still exists in certain cantons, and the widespread use of referenda and initiatives, at both the cantonal and the federal levels, often challenging laws and constitutional amendments or proposing new ones. This has had several effects on Swiss political parties. First, it has weakened the political parties (whose membership tends to represent 20 percent of voters) and strengthened instead sectoral associations and interest groups. Second, it has enabled parties such as the Social Democrats (SPS) to be both governing and opposition parties at the same time, participating in government decisions, while challenging them through referenda and initiatives. A third effect is that the direct popular control and the part-time and localized nature of much of Swiss politics have not contributed to the emergence of many dominant political figures.

Switzerland is unique in Western Europe in having a collegiate leadership of seven members who emanate since 1959 from the four main political parties—FDP, CVP, SPS, and SVP. There still is no prime minister, and the honorary president who changes every year is chosen from among the seven federal ministers.

BIBLIOGRAPHY

Jacob, Francis. *Western European Political Parties: A Comprehensive Guide.* New York, Longman, 1989.

Kerr, Henry. "The Swiss Party System: Steadfast and Changing," in Hans Daalder, ed. *Party Systems in Denmark, Austria, Switzerland, the Netherlands and Belgium.* London: Frances Printer, 1987.

Julian Thomas Hottinger

Economy

The Swiss economy, since the end of the Second World War, has been a success story. In terms of prosperity and macroeconomic indicators, its performance has been very positive.

During the nineteenth century, despite its scarce resources and because of its heavy dependence on international markets, Switzerland developed a variety of export-oriented industrial sectors such as textiles, watchmaking, and, later, chemicals and engineering; these sectors remained very competitive during the twentieth century. During the same period, the status of neutrality, the political stability of the country, combined with its noninvolvement in the two world wars and the discretion of banking regulations all favored the development of the financial sector throughout the century.

In addition to these general factors, the success of the Swiss economy is also based on economic policies followed by the authorities. Economic growth after the Second World War made it possible to complete the public infrastructure and to develop a welfare state that nevertheless, remained one of the smallest in comparison with other OECD countries. During the period of economic instability in the 1970s and 1980s, the economy maintained excellent performance in comparison with other OECD countries: low unemployment, low inflation and a positive balance of payments, and, to a lesser degree, the persistence of economic growth after the hard recession of the mid-1970s.

Two factors that contributed to economic development after the Second World War are particularly noteworthy. Because of an extremely tight labor market, Swiss employers hired many foreign workers to satisfy the constant economic growth. The total number of foreign workers (seasonal, annual, and transborder commuters) accounted for almost 20 percent of the whole working population, despite restrictive measures taken since 1964. During the recession of the mid-1970s, which hit the Swiss economy very hard, employment dropped by 11 percent. But three-fourths of this reduction was absorbed by foreign workers with temporary work permits. This partly explains the extremely low unemployment rate in Switzerland until the 1990s.

Another basic characteristic of the Swiss economy is the peaceful, stable cooperation between employers and labor unions that takes its origin in the "Labor peace" signed between employers and labor unions of the main industrial sectors (engineering and watchmaking) in 1937. These collective agreements were extended to many other sectors after the Second World War. Swiss labor relations are characterized by decentralization, the flexibility of wage formation, and the quasi absence of industrial conflicts. At the political level also, the Left was integrated into the government in 1959. During the 1970s and 1980s, despite the rising tension between employers and labor unions, the "labor peace" was maintained without difficulties.

Since the beginning of the 1990s, characterized by the rise of unemployment, European integration, and the Uruguay round of the GATT, many aspects of the Swiss economy, such as agricultural subsidies, aloofness from the European Union, and a disposable and rotating force of guest workers, were questioned. The old recipes are no longer suited to the new economic context, with its growing competition in a global economy.

The domestic sectors of the economy (agriculture, small businesses often cartelized) that benefited from hidden protectionism have been under severe pressure and have become progressively liberalized. In addition, it has become impossible to send home the foreign workers who, since the mid-1970s, have increasingly benefited from permanent residence permits. With the recession at the beginning of the 1990s, this factor explained the dramatic rise of unemployment in Switzerland. Closer ties with the European Union, liberalization of the sheltered sectors, and the rise of unemployment seem to constitute a turning point for the Swiss economy.

BIBLIOGRAPHY

Bairoch, Paul, and Martin Körner, eds. *La Suisse dans l'économie mondiale.* Geneva: Droz, 1990.

Bergier, Jean-François. *Histoire économique de la Suisse.* Lausanne: Payot, 1983.

Danthine, Jean-Pierre, and Jean-Christian Lambelet. "The Swiss Recipe: Conservative Policies Ain't Enough." *Economic Policy* 2 (1987): 147–79.

Katzenstein, Peter. *Corporatism and Change: Austria, Switzerland and the Politics of Change,* Ithaca, N.Y.: Cornell University Press, 1984.

Linder, Wolf. "Entwicklungen, Strukturen und Funktionen des Wirtschafts- und Sozialstaates in der Schweiz," in Alois Riklin, ed. *Handbuch Politisches System der Schweiz,* Vol. 1. Berne: Haupt, 1983.

André Mach

Female Suffrage

Although the Swiss constitution of 1848 granted universal suffrage to men, suffrage for women evolved slowly in Switzerland. After the founding in 1909 of a Swiss Association for Women's Right to Vote, several attempts were made to include women in the franchise. Petitions for such an amendment failed in 1920 and in 1929, as did other efforts in the 1930s and 1940s. In an unsuccessful 1957 referendum that proposed drafting women for civil defense training, Swiss females voted in the towns of Unterback, Lugano, Sierre, and Martiny-Bourg for the first time. In 1959, however, a national referendum of male voters rejected a law that would have given Swiss women the right to vote and hold office. Roman Catholic German-speaking cantons generally rejected the measure. Protestant French-speaking cantons were more supportive; in Vaud a local amendment granted Swiss women voting and office-holding rights on the cantonal level for the first time.

A 1971 constitutional amendment granting females the right to vote in federal elections and the right to hold public office found broad support; it reversed the 1959 referendum by a similar margin of votes. But the federal government did not guarantee local voting rights until 1990. In ten of the nation's twenty-five cantons and half-cantons, including all the French and Italian ones, women already possessed local voting privileges in 1971. Residents of the central and eastern cantons who voted against the measure spoke German. It had been supported by the nation's major political parties, both houses of the legislature, and numerous social organizations, newspapers, businesses, and churches. An estimated 1.5 million women qualified to vote in federal elections, while only 1.2 million men were currently eligible.

The 1981 equal rights amendment confirmed a growing acceptance of women's rights. The measure granted Swiss women far more privileges than women enjoyed in many countries with long-established female suffrage. It gave men and women equality in training and education as well as in hiring and work. Additionally, it granted equal pay for equal or equivalent work, causing some business interests to claim that the provision would bankrupt many companies. Major political parties, unions, and religious organizations, however, supported the measure. They believed that the new amendment might facilitate local female suffrage in the three cantons still withholding it.

Studies have suggested that Switzerland's consociational form of democracy, which emphasizes unity within a plural society, influenced the national government's reluctance to override the federal rights of individual cantons. The principles of federalism, however, conflicted with fairness to minorities.

Women finally achieved local suffrage in the holdout half-cantons of Outer Appenzell and Inner Appenzell in 1989 and 1990, respectively. On April 29 the men of Inner Appenzell, as they had done twice before since 1971, registered their clear majority against women's votes by raised hands at the traditional annual open-air meeting of the Landsgemeinde (assembly). As expected, in November 1990 the Federal Tribunal ruled that women could raise their hands at the next Landsgemeinde. Whether women would act on this right in the conservative canton was questionable. In December 1990, responding to the petition of two Appenzell women, the Federal Tribunal confirmed that the 1981 equal rights amendment superseded cantonal legislation. The court guaranteed the right of all Swiss women to vote in local elections.

Several factors were involved in Appenzell's delay in granting full female suffrage, a situation that appeared inconsistent with the participation of women in other local leadership roles and with Switzerland's democratic traditions. Displacing the issue of women's rights was concern with rural to urban demographic changes in Appenzell that threatened its traditional male-dominated Landsgemeinde. An additional factor was the success achieved by conservative women's groups, who prevailed over feminist groups in the canton.

BIBLIOGRAPHY

Bendix, John. "Women's Suffrage and Political Culture: A Modern Swiss Case." *Women and Politics* 12, no. 3 (1992): 27–56.

Camille Dean

Military

Switzerland has one of the oldest and strongest military traditions in Europe. Ever since their defeat in 1515 by the French at Maringano, the Swiss have pursued a policy of armed neutrality. Although the French revolutionary armies occupied Switzerland in 1798, Swiss neutrality was ratified at the Congress of Vienna in 1815. The Swiss army was mobilized in 1847 for a minor civil war, the Sonderbund war; in 1856 and again in 1870 in the face of threats from Prussia relating to the status of the canton of Neufchâtel; and during World Wars I and II to prevent violations of Swiss neutrality by both sides.

Swiss defense policy is based on deterrence through demonstrated readiness to fight and to destroy anything that might be of value to an invader. The Swiss military has no contingency plans for operating outside the country. Its doctrine of aggressive defense is based on launching powerful counterattacks against the flanks of any invader, combined with air interdiction against the lines of communication. Some six thousand industrial and communications sites in the country are prepared for demolition, if necessary. The alpine heartland contains a national redoubt, consisting of a series of fortresses manned by specialized mountain divisions.

The total active armed forces number only about 6,000, but the entire military of over 600,000 can be mobilized in forty-eight hours. This force is backed up by a paramilitary civil defense force of 480,000, with an extensive shelter program that can provide cover for up to 5.5 million people. (Of Switzerland's 6.91 million inhabitants, 5.9 million are citizens.)

All adult male citizens are subject to compulsory and virtually lifetime military service. Resident aliens are required to pay a hefty tax in lieu of military service. There is no provision for conscientious objection. As precisely defined in the federal constitution of 1874, Swiss nationhood is military even before it is cultural or political.

The military is organized into three classes. The Aufzug consists of men between the ages of 20 and 32. The Aufzug is considered the elite of the military, and it supplies the bulk of the units for the Field Army. The Landwehr consists of men from 33 to 42, and provides the units for the border, fortress, and national redoubt brigades. The Landstrum consists of men up to age 50; it provides supply and transportation units for the territorial brigades.

At the age of 19 all Swiss males are evaluated for military service. Those qualifying (about 80 percent) are selected for the various branches of the service and sent through a 118-day training cycle. The first 70 days consist of an initial recruit school, followed by three weeks of training in the field at the platoon and company level, and another three weeks of collective training at the battalion level. The final week of training is spent on demobilization.

Once released from initial training, Swiss soldiers keep their uniforms, equipment, and weapons at home. While members of the Aufzug, they undergo three weeks of annual training with their units. Members of the Landwehr perform annual training tours every two years, the Landstrum every four years. Soldiers who volunteer and are selected for officer or noncommissioned officers training attend those schools in addition to their unit training obligations. In the strictest sense, Swiss soldiers are never discharged; rather, they are sent home "on leave." Thus they technically are always members of the Swiss army, rather than part of its reserves. The practical effect of the three military classes, however, is the formation of a reserve system.

During the late 1980s and the 1990s, radical groups within Switzerland actively campaigned for the abolition of the Swiss army. Among the reasons they cited was the lack of any real external threat with the ending of the Cold War. More significantly, they objected to the army's all-pervasive influence on Swiss society, where selection as an officer can often be the path to future success in business. In November 1989 these groups placed the issue on the ballot of a national referendum and received one-third of the vote. The shock wave this sent through the country resulted in many long-overdue military reforms.

The Swiss maintain a small, highly selective cadre of full-time soldiers. Regular officers are trained at the Military Academy in Zurich, and return throughout their careers for higher-level training. The Swiss military has no supreme commander or commander in chief, except in time of full mobilization. Routine administration of the armed forces is a joint federal and cantonal responsibility, under the overall supervision of the federal minister of defense. In a time of crisis, both houses of the Federal Assembly would elect a commander in chief, who then would become Switzerland's only full general. Only four have been appointed since 1846.

The Field Army consists of three army corps of one mechanized and two infantry divisions each, and one mountain corps of three mountain divisions. Total mobilization strength (Aufzug and Landwehr) is 650,000, with an additional 400,000 in the Landstrum. Under the new Army Plan 95 the mobilization strength of the Field Army will be reduced to 450,000. The Field Army is well equipped with Leopard II tanks, M-113 armored personnel carriers, and 155 mm M-109 self-propelled howitzers.

The Swiss air force, which operates as an integral part of the army, has a full-time strength of 3,700 and a mobilized strength of 45,000. Its four interceptor squadrons are manned by full-time airmen, and equipped with top-of-the-line French Mirage IIIS and US F/A-18C/D fighters. The remaining fifteen squadrons of reconnaissance, transport, and ground-attack aircraft are manned by a combination of full-time and part-time airmen.

Despite the peaceful image of modern Switzerland and its long tradition of neutrality, the Swiss military would present a significant obstacle to any would-be invader.

BIBLIOGRAPHY

Keegan, John. *World Armies,* 2d ed. Detroit: Gale Research, 1983.

Switzerland, Department of Defense Information Service. *The Army of a Small, Neutral Nation: Switzerland.* Bern: Department of Defense, 1993.

David T. Zabecki

Social Services

The development of the Swiss social system is not comparable to that of other European countries. Switzerland cannot be classed as a welfare state. Its hybrid system, however, is by no means the result of haphazard planning; it hovers between the universalistic concept (the Beveridge model) and that of assurance (the Bismarck model).

Three main factors account for the syncretism of the Swiss system of social services. First, strong resistance, particularly from the cantons, to the centralization of power and the rights entailed in direct democracy, which is the corollary of the cantonal system, for over a hundred years hindered the implementation of compulsory health insurance. Second, there has been a tendency to reject the principle of obligatory insurance, thus preventing a universal system and directing social responses to immediate needs. Third, the influence and pressure exerted by professional corporations on political activities tend to favor vested economic interests at the expense of others.

Switzerland played a pioneering social role in several respects in the nineteenth century. It was the first state to pass a law on factory work, and in 1877 it legislated the length of the working day. With the progressive weakening of the reformist Radical Party, however, the social dimension of the state remained embryonic until World War II. Even then the generalization of the welfare state in Western Europe exerted only an indirect influence on Switzerland. Today, compared with the rest of Europe, Switzerland dedicates less than 23 percent of its gross national product to social protection. This is one of the lowest budgetary expenditures in Europe.

The Swiss social landscape presents a multifaceted medley of which certain elements are clearly defined, such as the protection of the aged and the unemployed, whereas there is no clear social policy for issues such as family policy and salary loss during maternity leave. The old-age pension scheme, one of the strong points of the system, has existed since 1947. It is obligatory and is deducted from all salaries. The retirement age for women is sixty-two or sixty-four and for men, sixty-five. However, the objective of guaranteeing a pensioner revenue to cover the basic necessities has never been attained. The state old-age pension was thus supplemented in 1985 by the introduction of a salary-related pension scheme based on a capitalization principle to which all employees must pay one part and the employer must contribute the other part; a minimum annual salary is a condition of participation. Finally, compulsory saving, within clearly defined limits, is encouraged by linked tax relief. This combined protection for the old is called the "three pillar" system. Since 1956 the disabled have been protected from a loss of effective earnings, and medical expenses incurred by their condition are paid for by the state. The system, however, is noted for its cumbersome bureaucratic procedures. Protection against unemployment was not generalized in Switzerland until 1982, by absence of necessity, as the country had been largely spared this social ill until 1990. The emergence of unemployment in the 4 to 5 percent range led to an effort to make the existing system more efficient by focusing on reinsertion, while at the same time limiting the overall costs. All salary earners must make a set contribution of 1.5 percent of their salary. The replacement rate ranges between 70 to 80 percent of the previous salary. The payments are for a limited period of time and vary according to age.

These insurance schemes fall within the competency of the federal government and their administration is centralized. However, the application depends on the individual cantons as relay points. This can result in significant discrepancies in actual benefits paid. The cantons exercise their competencies in two reserved areas: health and education. This is largely due to cultural factors. On the level of education, owing to the plurilinguistic nature of Switzerland, the main prerogatives have remained on the cantonal level. But agreements between different regions exist in an endeavor to harmonize both curricula and standards.

Health insurance, which is still evolving, has been compulsory for most of the country only since 1996. Every inhabitant is registered with a mutual health insurance company; the latter are in turn subsidized by the federal government. Contributions are calculated on a per capita basis and independent of the salary or the social situation of the insured. While the membership costs of all insured persons within one company are identical, they vary among companies themselves and among the cantons. This can lead to considerable disparities among cantons in cost, up to double for what are in theory the same benefits. Because of soaring health costs, individual state aid cannot be claimed by persons whose earnings fall below a certain level. Property dedicated to the collective good, such as hospital infrastructures, is financed by tax revenue. Parallel to the public sphere is a private sector reserved for holders of private insurance policies. Doctors of private patients charge fees on a different scale and, under the auspices of powerful professional medical organizations, they zealously guard their professional independence. The overall quality of medical services provided in Switzerland is highly regarded, although the public health system costs about 8 percent of the gross national product.

Social welfare is administered by the communes with financial help from the cantons. They are backed up in this task by private voluntary organizations and are encouraged and supported by public institutions, which strive to integrate them into the general concept of the distribution of social responsibility.

Building up a system of social protection has turned out to be a highly complex task. The intricacies of the bureaucracy and the law make it difficult for insured persons to take full advantage of the benefits to which they are entitled.

The fiscal system is equally complex. Taxation rates vary from canton to canton so much so that taxpayers in certain cantons pay up to twice as much as their counterparts in the more prosperous ones. Cantonal resources stem mainly from direct taxes. The federal revenue offices draw on indirect taxes (a value-added tax was introduced in 1995). The bulk of it is redistributed to the cantons, either as subsidies or as a means of realignment.

BIBLIOGRAPHY

Gilliand, Pierre. "Politique sociale" in Schmid Gerhard, *Manuel Système politique de las Suisse.* Bern: Haupt, 1993.

René Knüsel

Symons, Elizabeth Conway (1951–)

British undersecretary of state for foreign and commonwealth affairs (1997–). Elizabeth Conway Symons was born in April 1951. Following her studies at Cambridge University, she was employed in the Department of the Environment from 1974 to 1977. She became a leading figure in the labor union movement. In 1989 she was elected general secretary of the Association of the First Division of Civil Servants. In 1996 she was made a life peer, the Baroness of Vernham Dean. With the victory of Labour in 1997, she entered the cabinet.

Rosemary Cook

Szczypiorski, Andrzej (1924–)

Polish author and political activist. Andrzej Szczypiorski was born in Warsaw. He was incarcerated in Sachsenhausen concentration camp in Germany for his participation in the Warsaw Uprising of 1944 against the German occupiers during World War II. In his novels *Czas przeszly* (*Past Time,* 1961), *Godzina zero* (*The Zero Hour,* 1961), *Ucieczka Abla* (*Abel's Flight,* 1962), and *Za murami Sodomy* (*Behind the Walls of Sodom,* 1963) he introduced the issue of the Germans' responsibility for fascism. The ideological dilemmas of the young generation living under the postwar Stalinist regime in Poland are shown in the novel *Podroz do kranca doliny* (*Journey to the Edge of the Valley,* 1966). In the novel *I omineli Emaus* (*And they passed Emaus,* 1974), he analyzed contemporary dramatic existential situations. In a famous novel *Msza za miasto Arras* (*A Mass for Arras,* 1971), based on the events of mid–fifteenth century, Szczypiorski showed in symbolic parable-like pictures a history of the plague that resulted in mass madness: lack of tolerance, abuse of power, and laxity of morals. Besides references to totalitarian systems (fascism and communism), there are also indirect references to the official anti-Semitic campaign in Poland in 1968. In the novel *Zlowic cien* (*To Catch a Shadow,* 1976), through the prism of memory he described the spiritual education of a boy growing up in the period proceeding World War II. His best novel, *Poczatek* (*The Beautiful Mrs. Seideman,* 1986), is an unconventional picture of the German occupation of Poland and a departure from stereotypical approaches to persecution of Jews. As a moralist writer, Szczypiorski uses Catholicism as the basis of his ethical values.

Literary success and opposition political activity helped him to earn a seat in the Senate, the new upper house of the Polish parliament, in 1989. For many years he has been an advocate of Polish-German dialog and cooperation.

BIBLIOGRAPHY

Bugajski, Leszek. *Szczypiorski.* Warsaw: Authors Agency, 1991.

Matuszewski, Ryszard. *Literatura polska 1939–1991.* Warsaw: WSiP, 1992.

Szczypiorski, Andrzej. *The Polish Ordeal.* London: Croom Helm, 1982.

Jerzy Z. Maciejewski

Tabone, Vincent (Censu) (1913–)

Maltese politician. Vincent (Censu) Tabone was born at Victoria on Gozo on March 30, 1913. He studied at the University of Malta and at Oxford. After serving in the Royal Malta Artillery during World War II, he held the senior ophthalmic post at several Malta hospitals. Dr. Tabone did several consultancies for the World Health Organization, especially in southeast Asia and Taiwan, and was instrumental in the antitrachoma campaign against the viral eye disease, rampant in parts of the developing world, which often leads to blindness. In 1961 he became a member of the executive committee of the Nationalist Party. He served as its secretary general (1962–72), its first deputy leader (1972–77), and its president (1978–85). He was elected to parliament in 1966 and became minister of labour, employment and welfare in Dr. Borg Olivier's administration. In the 1987 election, the Nationalists won 50.9 percent of the vote and were able to form a government. From 1987 to 1989, Censu Tabone served as foreign minister and, in contrast to the policy of the previous Labor government, pursued a pro-EC policy. In 1989, Tabone was chosen the president of Malta. In April 1994 he was succeeded by another Nationalist, Ugo Mifsud Bonnici.

Bernard Cook

Tajikistan, Republic of

Independent successor state to the Tajik (Tadzhik) Soviet Socialist Republic of the former USSR. The Republic of Tajikistan, the smallest of the Central Asian states, consists of 57,250 sqare miles (143,100 sq km). It is surrounded by China, Pakistan, Afghanistan, Uzbekistan, and Kyrgyzstan. A long projection along its northern frontier extends into Uzbekistan and part of the agriculturally productive Fergana valley through which the Syr Darya river flows. Ninety percent of Tajikistan is mountainous. It contained the highest point in what was the former Soviet Union, the 24,585-ft Communism Peak.

Only 6 percent of Tajikistan's area is cultivated, and only 23 percent is pasture. Much of its arable land is devoted to the monoculture of water-intensive cotton, which makes large-scale irrigation a requisite. In the 1980s, Tajikistan was, despite its small size and limited arable land, the third largest producer of cotton in the USSR.

Excessive irrigation has led to the salinization of the soil and the depletion of water in the Amu Darya and Syr Darya rivers, which are also used for irrigation by other Central Asian states and that ultimately serve as the sources for the Aral Sea. To control mountain runoff, a large number of dams have been constructed. The quality of some is uncertain, and others are threatened by the proximity of fault lines. In March 1987 a dam in the Kulab region collapsed. The resulting wall of water killed thirty-six and left 500 people homeless. The largest dam in Central Asia is located just east of Dushanbe, the capital.

The population of Tajikistan is approximately 5.7 million, of whom 62 percent are Tajik, 23 percent Uzbek, and 7 percent Russian. The Uzbeks live predominantly in the northwestern part of the country. Another 8 percent consists of Ukrainians, Tartars, Germans, Kyrgyz, and Jews, all of whom reside primarily in the cities. The capital, Dushanbe, has 602,000 inhabitants. A total of 900,000 Tajiks live in Uzbekistan, and three million in Afghanistan.

Because of the mountainous terrain, more than half of the country is higher than 10,000 feet above sea level and divided into isolated valleys.

The Tajiks are divided into rival tribes with disparate dialects. The two most important subdialects are Yaghnabi and Pamir Tajik, which includes Bartang, the language in the Gorno-Badakhshan autonomous region. The Cyrillic alphabet has been used in written Tajik since 1940, but the teaching of the prior Arabic script was begun again in 1989. Most Tajiks and Uzbeks are Sunni Muslims, but the Pamiris of Gorno-Badakhshan in the eastern part of the country adhere to the Ism'ili sect.

The sedentary nature of the Tajiks and their language set them apart from their nomadic Turkic neighbors. Their semi-independent territories were absorbed by an expanding Russia and by the emirate of Bukhara in the nineteenth century. The northern section came under the control of the Bolsheviks in 1918, and was initially made part of the Turkistan Autonomous Soviet Socialist Republic. The Bolsheviks did not subdue the Bukharan section until 1921. Resistance by the *Basmachi* guerrilla forces endured until 1925 in the southeast. The Tajik Autonomous Soviet Socialist Republic was set up in October 1924 as part of the Uzbek Soviet Socialist Republic. In January 1925 the southeastern part of Tajikistan became a special Pamir region, later designated the Gorno-Badakhshan autonomous region, within the Tajik ASSR. On October 5, 1929, the Tajik ASSR, augmented by the addition of the Kokand region of the Uzbek SSR, became a full-fledged Union Republic of the USSR, the Tajik Soviet Socialist Republic (TSSR). However, some Tajik areas along the border with Uzbekistan and the old Tajik centers of Bubhara, Samasgand, and Tashbent remained in Uzbekistan.

There were some economic and social advances during the Soviet era, but Soviet investment in Tajikistan was the lowest per capita among the republics of the USSR. Hence, the TSSR remained a very poor area. In 1994, Tajikistan's per capita gross national product was $350, the lowest of all the former Soviet republics. Collectivization disrupted the uplands, where society was built around cattle husbandry. Disagreement with the way in which collectivization was being carried out arose within the Communist Party. Nasratullah Maksum and Abdurakhim, two ethnic Tajik local Communist leaders, were purged because of their opposition to collectivization. A series of purges rose to a crescendo in 1934 when as many as ten thousand Tajiks were killed, and resulted in the removal of almost all Tajiks from the administration of the TSSR. In 1937, Dimitrii Protopopov, a Russian, was appointed first secretary, and many Russians were brought into the republic to staff party posts. In 1990, Tajiks were still a minority in the Tajik Communist Party (CPT). In 1945, however, Protopopov was succeeded by Bobojan Gafurov, a Tajik Stalinist, who lasted until 1956. Gafurov, who touted the Russian conquest of Central Asia as a progressive development, hoped to transcend ethnic rivalries by advocating the use of the Russian language by all Tajiks. In 1961, Tursunbai Uljabaev, another Tajik, was removed for corruption. His successors, Jabar Rasulov and Rakhmon Nabiyev, were also Tajiks and were little interested in reform. During the 1970s an Islamic reaction grew, and there was violence against non-Tajiks. In 1978 there was a large anti-Russian riot, and after the 1979 invasion of Afghanistan, anti-Russian activists were arrested.

After the accession of Mikhail Gorbachev in 1985, his campaign against corruption resulted in the removal of Rakhmon Nabiyev (1930–1993) who had headed the CPT since 1982. His successor, Kakhar Makhkamov, complained about the republic's levels of unemployment and poverty. The relaxing of censorship unleashed expressions of grievance, including the charge of discrimination against Tajiks in Uzbekistan. In 1988, Loiq Sherali, the secretary of the Tajik Writers' Union, attacked Uzbek intellectual imperialism. He accused the Uzbeks of attempting to abrogate the work of Tajik or Farsi philosophers and poets. Though perhaps esoteric, the complaint publicly aired ethnic hostilities. Authorities were concerned. In January 1988 the editor of the Tajik party newspaper, *Komsomoli Tochikiston,* was dismissed for allowing ethnically divisive articles to appear in the paper. During debates over the issue of Nagorno-Karabakh, Gorbachev explicitly tied the Azeri-Armenian dispute to his concern that Tajiks might be encouraged by Armenian success in Nagorno-Karabakh to press claims against Uzbekistan. As Gorbachev feared, violence erupted in 1989 among villagers along the borders with Kyrgyzstan, and there were calls in the press for the rectification of the frontier with Uzbekistan. However, a parallel problem existed, raising the possibility of counterterritorial claims: a million Uzbeks reside in Tajikistan.

In February 1990, following rumors that Armenian refugees were to be resettled in Dushanbe, aggravation over unemployment and the shortage of housing led to an explosion of frustrated desire for political and economic reform. Besides being the poorest state in Central Asia, Tajikistan had the highest birthrate. Since 1959 its population had grown by over 3 percent a year, and between 1959 and 1979 the population doubled. The Soviet response was an antinatal campaign, which the Tajiks perceived as anti-Tajik. Housing, jobs, and infrastructure became desperate issues, which fueled ethnic animosities. In 1989, a total of 66 percent of the inhabitants of the TSSR lived in small and impoverished rural villages. Many of those lured to the cities in the 1980s by a campaign to augment urban labor resources found that they had not improved their conditions but had merely changed the locus of their poverty. When three thousand Tajik demonstrators fought with police in Dushanbe in February 1990, Makhkamov declared a state of emergency and requested reinforcements from the USSR's ministry of internal affairs. Five thousand interior ministry troops and militia units restored order, killing twenty-two people and injuring 565 in the process. This event played a crucial role in mobilizing political opposition. When two developing opposition parties, the popular movement Rastokhez (Renewal), which had played a role in the demonstrations, and the Democratic Party of Tajikistan (DPT) sought official registration, they were refused. The Islamic Revival Party (IRP), falsely depicted by Makhkamov as a radical fundamentalist group, was denied permission to hold a congress. Despite growing support for these organizations, opposition politicians were not allowed to stand in the March election for the Tajik Supreme Soviet (TSS).

On August 24, 1990, the TSS, responding to growing politicization and growing Tajik assertiveness, passed a declaration of sovereignty, and in November it elected Makhkamov executive president of the republic. The sovereignty declaration stressed the equality of all residents, but the upsurge of Islamic sentiment and interest in the Tajiks' Iranian heritage prompted a growing emigration, not only of non-Tajiks, but of educated Tajiks as well.

Concerned about the potential of being surrounded by nationalistic Turkic states, the Tajiks supported the new Union Treaty. A total of 90.2 percent of the electorate voted its support for the preservation of the USSR in the March 1991 referendum. The August coup, however, intervened. Makhkamov supported the coup, and his resignation on August 31 was forced by massive demonstrations organized by the DPT, the IRP, and Rastokhez. On September 9 the TSS voted a declaration of Tajikstan's independence as a democratic state based upon the rule of law, the Republic of Tajikistan. Continuing demonstrations, however, demanded the abolition of the CPT and the holding of new multiparty elections. The chairman of the TSS, Kadriddin Aslonov, as acting president, outlawed the CPT and ordered its assets seized. However, the CPT, which had just changed its name to the Socialist Party, survived and even reverted to the CPT label in January 1992. The CPT/Socialist Party majority in the TSS canceled Aslonov's decrees and demanded his resignation. He stepped down, and Rakham Nabiyev became acting president. But due to continued public pressure, the TSS, at the beginning of October, was again forced to ban the CPT. The IRP, which had been outlawed as a religious party, was legalized.

Seven candidates, including Nabiyev, who had given up his office to campaign, competed in the direct presidential election on November 24, 1991. With heavy backing from the countryside, Nabiyev won 58 percent of the vote. Daviat Khudonazarov, the head of the Soviet Cinematographers' Union and the joint candidate of the DPT and IRP, won only slightly more than 25 percent. Despite charges of electoral corruption, Nabiyev assumed the presidency in December. He promptly signed the accord establishing the CIS, and in January appointed Akbar Mirzoyev prime minister.

In March 1992 antigovernment demonstrations erupted in Dushanbe when Nabiyev fired Mamadayez Navzhuvanov, the minister of internal affairs. Navzhuvanov was a Badakhshani (Pamiri), and the dismissal was protested by the Pamiri organization, Lale Badakhshon, which agitated for greater autonomy for the Pamiri of the Gorno-Badakhshan autonomous region. Following the April arrest of Maksud Ikramov, the mayor of Dushanbe, who was sympathetic to the opposition, Rastokhez, the IRP, and the DPT threw their support to the demonstrations and demanded the ouster of Nabiyev. Anti-Nabiyev protesters camped in the center of Dushanbe for about two months. Nabiyev brought in counterdemonstrators from traditional CPT centers, Kulyab and Leninabad, and there were clashes. Nabiyev's National Guard eventually fired on his opponents and killed eight. The National Security Committee (the renamed KGB) reputedly distributed guns to the communists, and civil war erupted.

Fighting in the capital ended after Nabiyev agreed to a truce with the opposition and established a "Government of National Reconciliation," with Mirzoyev serving as prime minister and with members of opposition parties appointed to eight of the twenty-four ministries. Violence, however, spread in the southern section of the Kulyab region where pro-communists, who opposed the compromise, clashed with members of Islamic and democratic groups.

While the communists were centered in Kulyab in the south and Leninabad in the north, the Islamic and democratic opposition centered in the Kurgan-Tyube region in the south and the Garm valley east of Dushanbe. In the latter part of May, Sangak Safarov, a character with a long criminal record, invaded the Kurgan-Tyube region with a force from Kulyab, the Tajik People's Front (TPF). He claimed that the Islamic group was receiving support from Islamic fundamentalists in Afghanistan. The alliance of democratic and Islamic groups asserted that the TPF was receiving assistance from the Russian garrisons that had remained in Tajikistan after the collapse of the USSR.

At the end of August, antigovernment elements seized the presidential palace. Although Nabiyev escaped, he was captured at the airport on September 7 and forced to resign. Akbarsho Iskandarov, chairman of the TSS, became temporary head of state, and Abdumalik Abdullojonov (1949–), a communist from Leninabad, became acting prime minister.

Iskandarov was supported by the principal democratic and Islamic groups, but his authority was largely limited to the capital. Most of the south was under the control of the TPF, and leaders from Leninabad, which has a large Uzbek population, threatened to secede if an Islamic state were established. In late October, the city of Dushanbe was threatened by a pro-Nabiyev force led by Safarali Kenjayev, a former chairman of the TSS. Though driven back, he surrounded and blockaded the city for two months.

Unable to end the civil war, Iskandarov and the government resigned on November 10, 1992. The TSS met in Khokand, the capital of Leninabad, to try to form a new government and end the civil war. It abolished the presidency and chose Imamali Rakhmonov, the director of a Kulyab collective farm, to head the state as chairman of the TSS. A new government was formed under Abdullojonov, but all of the opposition ministers were replaced by supporters of Nabiyev from Kulyab.

In December 1992 units supporting this new government overran the Islamic-Democratic coalition military, the Popular Democratic Army, and complemented their control of Dushanbe with atrocities. Elements of the opposition withdrew to the mountains to the east of the city. They attempted to declare an Islamic republic there, but by March the government, openly assisted by Russian and Uzbek forces, had gained control of most of Tajikistan. The Uzbek government was deeply concerned over the possible ascendancy of an Islamic fundamentalist movement in its neighbor. As a result, it provided Rakhmonov military and political support. In January 1993, Russia, Uzbekistan, Kazakhstan, and Kyrgyzstan agreed to defend Tajikistan's border with Afghanistan. Thus they all openly sided with the Tajik government, and the Russians defended the frontier. In August, Russia, Uzbekistan, Kazakhstan, and Kyrgyzstan signed an agreement with Tajikistan to provide a CIS "peacekeeping" force to police the Tajik-Afghan frontier. By December, twenty-five thousand CIS troops, principally Russian, had been deployed.

According to the government, approximately 20,000 people were killed during the civil war, and another 600,000 were displaced. Independent estimates place the number at 70,000. In the month following the capture of the capital, 80,000 Tajiks, including Akbar Turajonzoda, a leading member of the IRP and the country's leading Moslem cleric, sought refuge in Afghanistan. Though government forces were able to pacify the interior, cross-border raids from Afghanistan and an active insurgency in Gornyo-Badakhshan continued.

Freedom of the press and broadcast media were suspended, and the Supreme Court officially banned the IRP, Lale Badakhshon, Rastokhez, and the DPT. Until individuals associated with the government later in the year spawned new parties—the Party of Economic Freedom, the People's Democratic Party, and the People's Party of Tajikistan (PPT)—the CPT was the sole legal political party.

At this point a split emerged between the leaders from Leninabad and the ascendant Kulyab fighters. In December 1993, Abdullojonov stepped down, but was replaced as prime minister by another political figure from Leninabad, Abdujalil Ahadovich Samadov. In March 1994, Rakhmonov, who had assumed personal control of the ministries of defense and interior and of the NSC, indicated his willingness to initiate discussions with the Islamic-Democratic opposition. Two weeks of talks in Moscow sponsored by the UN produced a joint commission on refugees and an agreement on additional talks.

Despite additional negotiations in Teheran, border clashes intensified. An important impulse for this fighting was to control drug-smuggling routes from Pakistan and Afghanistan to Russia and Western Europe. Individuals and groups had profited from the Tajik turmoil by making Tajikistan a major link in a new opium pipeline.

Apparently pressed by the Russians, the presidential election scheduled for September was delayed by the Tajik government to allow for opposition participation. However, when the election was held on November 6, only Rakhmonov and Abdullojonov ran. Rakhmonov won 58 percent of the votes of the 85 percent of the electorate who participated. A new constitution was also ratified by 90 percent of those voting. Abdullojonov, who dominated the voting in Leninabad and Gornyo-Badakhshan, protested rampant fraud and intimidation. Though his accusations were seconded by international observers, they were denied by Rakhmonov and his government. Rakhmonov assumed his new term and appointed Jamshed Karimov (1940–) prime minister.

The IRP and the DDT refused to participate in the February 26 parliamentary election. When Abdullojonov was not allowed to run, his Popular Party of Unity and Accord (PPUA) also withdrew. The OSCE, declaring the election fatally compromised, refused to send observers. Though there was but a single candidate in 40 percent of the districts, 84 percent of the voters participated in the election. The CPT took 60 of the 181 seats and the PPT, 5.

In September two government units, in what amounted to a turf war, engaged each other in serious fighting in Kurgan-Tyube. There was also major fighting in early 1996 following the murder of the mufti Fatkhullo Sharifzoda, who had replaced Turajonzoda after his flight into exile. Not only did the opposition launch a major attack, but two government commanders, both ethnic Uzbeks, rebelled, citing government corruption and incompetence. One, Makhmoud Khudoberiyev, the commander of the first brigade of the Tajik army, seized control in Kurgan-Tyube. Rakhmonov acquiesced and dismissed the prime minister and other officials. Yakhyo Azimov (1947–), a plant director in Leninabad, became the new prime minister. However, the government's effective control was limited to Dushanbe and the north.

In 1994 and 1995 the Russians became increasingly impatient over the failure of the Rakhmonov regime to arrive at a political settlement with its opponents. In 1995 and 1996, Kazakhstan and Kyrgyzstan cut back their participation in the CIS border force, and Kazakhstan said that it would completely exit the conflict unless there were meaningful talks. President Karimov of Uzbekistan also complained of the unwillingness of the Tajik government to compromise and of the treatment of Tajikistan's Uzbek minority.

Negotiations and violated cease-fires continued until June 1997. Rahmonov's government then signed a peace agreement with the main opposition groups. Included in the terms of the peace agreement were an amnesty, the legalization of the opposition parties, the exchange of prisoners of war, and the repatriation of the refugees who had fled to Afghanistan. A National Reconciliation Commission, to which each side would name thirteen members, would oversee the eventual formation of a new government. The commission had the power to appoint opposition leaders to positions in the central government and regional administrations. It was also to propose amendments to the constitution. The opposition fighters would turn in their arms and be integrated into the Tajikistan military. It was also agreed that Rakhmonov would continue to serve as president until the end of his term in 1999. When elections were held in November 1999, Rakhonov claimed an overwhelming victory with 96 percent of the vote. Despite accusations of fraud by his main opponent, Daval Usmon of the Islamic Resistance party, Rakmonov retained the presidency.

Although the larger rebel groups agreed to end the civil war, some smaller rebel factions refused to accept the accord. Intermittent clashes followed. The peace agreement called for the inclusion of representatives from all regions in the new government, but the old government in Dushanbe was determined to exclude the Leninabad faction led by Abdullojonov. He and his followers remained an uncertain part of the equation. This was also true of Colonel Khudoberiyev, the Uzbek commander of the first brigade. His forces launched an unsuccessful attack on Dushanbe in August 1997. On October 16, another group estimated to have numbered more than seventy attacked the headquarters of the presidential guard in Dushanbe and killed fourteen guards. Daviat Usmon, a leader of the opposition, said that the attack was the work of renegade rebel groups that did not accept the authority of the government.

The poorest republic of the USSR Tajikistan was negatively affected by the collapse of the USSR. The civil war exacerbated the country's economic difficulties. Tajikistan's gross national product declined between 1985 and 1994 at an annual rate of 11.7 percent. In 1995 it decreased by 12.4 percent. Apart from mineral extraction and the production of energy and aluminum, there is little heavy industry. Though hydroelectrical production accounted for 75 percent of the country's electricity needs prior to the civil war, the country's dependence on imported petroleum and natural gas led to energy shortages. Agriculture and forestry employed 51.2 percent of the population in 1993. Due to the disruption of agriculture by the civil war, food shortages occurred in the cities. Inflation averaged 1,157 percent annually in 1992, and 2,195 percent in 1993, but only 240 percent in 1994. At the end of 1994, a total of 31,800 people were officially unemployed, but this figure gives no real indication of the level of unemployment or underemployment and economic misery in Tajikistan.

BIBLIOGRAPHY

Atkin, Muriel. "Tajikistan's Civil War." *Current History* 96, October 1997 (612): 336–340.

Batalden, Stephen K., and Sandra L. Batalden. *The Newly Independent States of Eurasia: Handbook of Former Soviet Republics.* Phoenix, AZ: Oryx, 1997.

Shoemaker, M. Wesley. *Russia, Eurasian States, and Eastern Europe 1995.* Harpers Ferry, WV: Stryker-Post, 1995.

"Tajikistan." *The Europa World Year Book 1996.* London: Europa, 1996. II: 3071–76.

Bernard Cook

Tambroni, Fernando (1901–63)

Italian Christian Democrat leader and prime minister. Fernando Tambroni Armaroli was born in Ascoli Piceno on November 25, 1901. He studied law in Rome. He joined the Italian Catholic University Federation (FUCI), and was elected its vice-secretary in 1921. During the elections of 1919, he supported the Catholic Partito Popolare. With the arrival of fascism, he abandoned politics and concentrated on a career in forensic science. Following the ouster of Benito Mussolini on July 25, 1943, he reentered politics and was one of those who promoted the foundation of Christian Democracy (DC). He became provincial and regional secretary for the DC and was elected to the National Council of the DC in 1946. He was elected to the Constituent Assembly the same year. In 1950 he became undersecretary at the ministry of the navy. In 1953 he was undersecretary at the Justice Department and then minister of the navy until 1955. From 1955 to 1959 he was secretary of state for home affairs. As such he was responsible for laws relating to electoral campaigns, public safety, and the reorganization of the fire service. After the Hungarian uprising, he quelled the violent demonstrations against the Italian Communist Party. In 1959 he became head of the Treasury Department. He opposed nationalization and was responsible for the National Loan System and for the introduction of a sliding scale of salaries tied to inflation.

Tambroni belonged to the left wing of the DC led since 1945 by Giovanni Gronchi. In 1960 the political direction of the DC became an issue again, with the choice between the center-left and the center-right. With the fall of Antonio Segni's government on February 21, 1960, Tambroni was entrusted with forming a new government. His cabinet was "technical"—that is, it had objectives that were purely administrative and it was supported by the Italian Social Movement (MSI). Even though Tambroni emphasized that these votes did not influence his policy, a crisis resulted. He obtained the support of Gronchi and the National Council of his party, but unrest followed. He was accused of being a putschist due to the support of the MSI and his authoritarian bearing. Everything came to a head at the end of June during the national congress of the MSI in Genoa, a left-wing city with strong resistance traditions. The Italian Communist Party organized riots against the conference, which resulted in death and injury throughout Italy. The National Council of the DC asked Tambroni to resign. His resignation was accepted by Gronchi, and the third Amintore Fanfani government followed. Tambroni left politics and died of a heart attack in 1963 at the age of sixty-two.

BIBLIOGRAPHY

Baget-Bozzo, G. *Il partitio cristiano e l'apertura a sinistra: la DC di Fanfani e di Moro, 1954–1962.* Florence: Vallecchi, 1977.

Mammarella, G. *L'Italia dopo il fascismo.* Bologna: Il Mulino, 1974.

———. *L'Italia dalla caduta del fascismo ad oggi.* Bologna: Il Mulino, 1978.

Radi, Luciano. *Tambroni trent'anni dopo: il luglio 1960 e la nascita del centrosinistra.* Bologna: Il Mulino, 1990.

Tambroni, F. *Il senso dello Stato.* Ed. by Cesare D'Angelantonio. Milan: Bompiani, 1960.

Tamburrano, G. *PCI e PSI nel sistema democristiano.* Bari: Laterza, 1978.

Gabriella Portalone

SEE ALSO Gronchi, Giovanni; Italy

Teitgen, Pierre-Henri (1908–97)

French politician. Pierre-Henri Teitgen, the son of Henri Teitgen, a vice president of the National Assembly, was born in Rennes on May 29, 1908. After graduating with a law degree from the University of Nancy, Teitgen joined its law faculty and edited the journal *Droit Social.* Captured by the Germans while serving on the Maginot line, Teitgen escaped to Vichy France, where he became a professor of law at the University of Montpellier. Under the code name Tristan, he established the Resistance organization Combat with the Christian Socialist François de Menthon. In 1943, Teitgen was appointed provisional minister of information by Charles de Gaulle. Teitgen was captured by the gestapo on June 8, 1944, but he escaped and joined de Gaulle in Paris. De Gaulle appointed him minister of information in September. In this post, Teitgen was faced with the challenge of renovating the French press, besmirched by collaboration. He is credited with the establishment of *Le Monde* and the appointment of Hubert Beuve-Mery as its first editor.

In November 1944, Teitgen was a founder of the Popular Republican Movement (*Mouvement Républicain Populaire,* MRP). This Catholic party's social program was influenced by the progressive Resistance Charter, and it provided a political home for many of de Gaulle's prominent supporters, among whom were Georges Bidault, Robert Schuman, and Michel Debré. In the October 1945 election for the constituent assembly, in which Teitgen was elected to represent Rennes, the MRP, with 141 seats, emerged with the Communists and Socialists as one of the three dominant political parties. Teitgen became minister of justice, and as such, he insisted on the execution of Pierre Laval, who had been convicted of treason. Teitgen disagreed with de Gaulle's stubborn resistance to the constitution being formulated by the assembly, and after the resignation of de Gaulle, he became the vice-premier in the government formed by Paul Ramadier in January 1947. When Ramadier ousted the Communists from his cabinet in May 1947, Teitgen told Maurice Thorez and his three colleagues, "We will miss you!" Thorez took the remark as an ironic insult. Teitgen was a moderate socialist in his socioeconomic outlook and a strong proponent of European integration. In the French parlance of the time, he was labeled a member of the "extreme center."

During the tumultuous political period of 1947 and 1948, Teitgen was minister of the armed forces. He then served as vice-premier in the 1948 government of André Marie (1897–1974), minister of information in the 1949–1950 government of Georges Bidault, and vice-premier in the 1953–1954 government of Joseph Laniel (1889–1975). Teitgen was then elected head of the MRP, but the party had entered a fatal decline. The war in Algeria was a factor. As Teitgen's power base evaporated, his last ministerial post was as minister for overseas territories from 1955 to 1956 in Edgar Faure's government. It was a thankless political task.

Teitgen remained true to the "extreme center," even when his principles eventually relegated him to a rather lonely isolation. Teitgen's adherence to his political principles and to his vision of justice earned him the appellation "Robespierre" from his detractors. True to form, after de Gaulle returned to power in June 1958, Teitgen did not hesitate to take issue publicly with what he regarded as the general's absolutist proclivities. In 1965, Teitgen gave his support to Gaston Defferre, who attempted to unite the Socialists and Christian Democrats to challenge de Gaulle in the presidential election.

In 1976, Teitgen was elected to the European Court of Human Rights. He died in 1997.

BIBLIOGRAPHY

"Obituary of Pierre-Henri Teitgen French Vice-Premier nicknamed Robespierre for his implacable pursuit of justice." *Daily Telegraph,* April 10, 1997.

Bernard Cook

Ter-Petrossian, Levon (1945–)

President of Armenia, 1991–98. Levon Ter-Petrossian was born in 1945 in Syria. His father, Hakop Ter-Petrossian, was a leftist political activist. His family had been part of the Armenian community around Mount Mousa Ler, who successfully resisted the Turkish onslaught in 1915 and were transported by a French ship to Syria. In 1946, Ter-Petrossian's family was one of the many who accepted Stalin's offer of repatriation to Armenia. The returning Armenians were regarded with suspicion by many of the indigenous Armenians, and in 1949 many were targeted by Joseph Stalin's agents as nationalist and independent socialist enemies of his regime. After the death of Stalin, however, the new Armenians successfully merged into the general population.

Ter-Petrossian studied history at Yerevan State University, writing his thesis on the early relations between the Armenians and the Nestorians of Syria. In 1965 on the fiftieth anniversary of the Armenian holocaust, Ter-Petrossian participated in the student demonstrations in which the call for the reunification of Western Armenia with the Armenian Republic was voiced. After completing his studies at Yerevan in 1968, Ter-Petrossian attended the Institute of Oriental Studies in Leningrad. There he received an M.A. in 1972 and, after completing his dissertation, a Ph.D. in 1987. He returned to Armenia to work at the Manouk Abeghyan Literature Institute of the Armenian Academy of Sciences. In 1978 he was appointed the senior researcher at the Matenadaran Depository and the Institute for the Preservation, Study and Publishing of Ancient Manuscripts. He remained there until the Azeri assault in February 1988 on the Armenian community in Sumgait in the Nagorno-Karabakh, following the call by the enclave's Armenians for secession and union with Armenia.

Ter-Petrossian played a leading role in the formation of the Karabakh Committee and became one of the most prominent and eloquent proponents of national awakening in Armenia. The committee organized a republic-wide strike and a massive demonstration in Yerevan attended by a million Armenians. The committee assumed a leading role in the rescue effort following the massive earthquake of December 7, 1988, which devastated the Shirak and Lori districts. Soviet authorities then acted in an attempt to stem the development of the committee into a vanguard for an independent Armenia. The eleven leaders of the Karabakh Committee—among them Ter-Petrossian, Hambartsoum Galstyan, Raphael Ghazaryan, Vazgen Manoukyan, Ashot Manoucharyan, and Khachik Stamboultsyan—and more than two hundred followers were arrested and transported to Russia. The move completely backfired, and the eleven became national heroes.

Despite the imposition of martial law in Yerevan, the Armenian Pan-National Movement (ANM) was launched in April 1989, and nationalist demonstrations were organized both in Armenia and in Nagorno-Karabakh. The imprisoned members of the Karabakh Committee were released on May 31, 1989, and received a hero's welcome in Yerevan. On June 16, 1989, a total of 310 delegates from various groups met at Yerevan State University and formalized the ANM, which was recognized by the Armenian Supreme Soviet on June 28. At the party's first congress on November 4–5, Ter-Petrossian and the ten other leaders of the Karabakh Committee were elected to the thirty-six-member executive board of the ANM. The aims of the party were national self-determination, the joining of the Karabakh with Armenia, and a mixed economy. Ter-Petrossian was elected in a special election to the Armenian Supreme Soviet (ASS) in August. He and three other ANM members won four of the five contested seats. Ter-Petrossian was elected chairman of the presidium of the supreme council of the ASS and in that position guided the movement for independence. The ANM appeal for autonomy was echoed by the ASS on August 24, 1990, and affirmed in an independence referendum on September 21, 1991. In October 1991, Ter-Petrossian was elected the first president of the independent Republic of Armenia. His tenure witnessed the consolidation of Armenian independence and the gaining of de facto independence by Nagorno-Karabakh. However, his administration was accompanied by internal political turmoil and accusations of authoritarianism. On February 3, 1998, Ter-Petrossian was forced from office due to a number of factors: the economy, his increasingly authoritarian style, and his willingness to compromise with the Azerbaijanis on the issue of Nagorno-Karabakh.

Bernard Cook

SEE ALSO Armenia

Terrorism, Right-Wing

Organized political violence carried out for psychological effect by right-wing radicals. Although media attention has generally been focused on left-wing terrorism, transnational terrorism sponsored by various Middle Eastern networks, or separatist terrorism as in Northern Ireland and Spain, the terrorist actions carried out in postwar Europe by lesser-known right-wing extremists had both historical and political significance.

The importance of organized right-wing terrorism in postwar Europe derives from three main factors. First, it has frequently been carried out by international paramilitary networks operating beyond the confines of any one national or continental border. Second, its perpetrators have often been covertly protected, logistically supported, and used instrumentally by "hawkish" factions within various Western intelligence and security agencies, as well as by the dictatorial regimes that held power in Spain (until 1975), Portugal (until 1974), Greece (1967–74), and various Latin American countries (most notably, postcoup Chile and Argentina). Third, the neofascist ultras who carried out the most significant acts of terrorism had almost all been directly or indirectly exposed to sophisticated French unconventional warfare doctrines and techniques (*guerre révolutionnaire*). Therefore, since 1945, right-wing terrorism has consisted of a complex combination of genuine oppositional terrorism and covert state-sponsored or state-manipulated terrorism.

Since neofascist extremists have frequently been provided with institutional support by the most secretive apparatuses within various national governments, it has understandably proven difficult to extract reliable information about their violent and subversive operations. Furthermore, an essential feature of modern unconventional warfare is the systematic use of covert "false flag" operations, which are specifically designed to conceal the identity of the real perpetrators and sponsors and thereby ensure "plausible deniability." This is accomplished most often by implicating opposing political groups in serious crimes and other unsavory activities. Indeed, the most serious campaigns of right-wing terrorism in postwar Europe have fallen into this manipulative category, because the aim was to stir up public hostility against elements of the radical left that could legitimately be suspected of having committed such atrocities. By contrast, left-wing and separatist terrorists have more frequently, though by no means always, claimed responsibility for their acts of political violence.

If one excludes the state-sponsored paramilitary formations created during the Greek civil war, such as George Grivas's Organization X, and a number of shadowy anticommunist "action" groups established in the 1950s by the United States, NATO, or various European regimes, including the "Gladio" stay/behind paramilitary networks, organized right-wing terrorism of a truly dangerous sort did not emerge in Europe until the establishment of the Secret Army Organization (Organisation de l'Armée Secrète, OAS). The OAS was formed by disaffected French military officers and their rightist civilian supporters in Algeria and metropolitan France. The OAS conducted its brutal campaigns of terrorism aimed at maintaining French control over Algeria and, ultimately, at bringing down the Fifth Republic. The diaspora of fugitive OAS personnel laid the groundwork for the training of subsequent generations of neofascist extremists in the arcane arts of French counterinsurgency doctrine.

The most important result of this process was the creation of the so-called black International during the mid-1960s. From 1966 to 1974, the linchpin of this loosely organized transnational network was a press agency headquartered in Lisbon, Aginter Presse. The press was created by French army "dirty tricks" specialist and OAS veteran Yves Guérin-Sérac; "covered" and financed by the Portuguese secret police (the International Police for the Defense of the State, Policía Internacional e de Defesa do Estado, PIDE); and used as a convenient front for a center of international right-wing subversion and terrorism. The most important operations carried out by parallel networks of this sort can be broadly divided into three categories: (1) playing a key preparatory role and otherwise participating in outright military coups; (2) carrying out antidemocratic acts of violence and repression at the behest of state security forces or right-wing dictatorships in southern Europe and the Third World; and (3) systematically conditioning the political environment of various European democracies by conducting a wide variety of clandestine influence and terrorist operations.

The first of these types of operations is perhaps best exemplified in Greece (1967) and Turkey (1971, 1980). In both countries, right-wing paramilitary groups—in particular, Kostas Plevris's neofascist Fourth of August Movement (Kinema tes 4 Augoustou, K4A) in Greece and Alparslan Türkes's neofascist Nationalist Action Party (Milliyetcilik Hareket Partisi, MHP) in Turkey—helped precipitate and provide a pretext for military coups by initiating campaigns of terrorism and by making it appear as though the extra parliamentary left was primarily responsible. They were covertly aided and abetted in these particular instances by anticonstitutional factions within the armed forces and the intelligence services, which were then able to pose as "national saviors" who had rescued their respective nations from political violence and chaos. Similar operations were carried out by extremist paramilitary groups in Italy. In these cases the projected coups were either aborted or sabotaged before being brought to fruition. So it was with the December 1970 coup launched by Junio Valerio Borghese's National Front (Fronte Nazionale) and with the rash of coup plots fostered in 1973 and 1974 by groups such as Edgardo Sogno's Democratic Resistance Committee (Comitato di Resistenza Democratica, CRD), Carlo Fumagalli's Movement for Revolutionary Action (Movimento d' Azione Rizoluzionaria, MAR), and the Rosa dei Venti (Compass Rose) network; factions of the armed forces and secret services were implicated in all of these. Finally, neofascist ultras from several European countries participated directly in the Portuguese Liberation Army (Exercito de Liberataçao Português, ELP) efforts to overthrow the leftist government in Portugal after 1974, as well as in the July 1980 "cocaine coup" in Bolivia.

The second type of operation was even more widespread. To provide only a few examples, Aginter Presse participated in counterguerrilla campaigns in Portuguese Africa and infiltrated the Portuguese opposition in Europe; it also provided unconventional warfare training to right-wing militants and organized various other acts of terrorism and provocation. In Greece, Turkey, and Bolivia, the neofascists served in parallel intelligence and security organizations in the wake of the coups they helped provoke. Moreover, fugitive members of various paramilitary organizations—including the two principal Italian neofascist groups, Pino Rauti's New Order (Ordine Nuovo, ON) and Stefano Delle Chiaie's National Vanguard (Avanguardia Nazionale, AN); the OAS; José López Rega's Argentine Anti-Communist Alliance (Alianza Anticomunista Argentina, AAA) death squad; and anti-Castro Cuban groups—collaborated with their Spanish comrades from Mariano Sánchez-Covisa's Guerrillas of Christ the King (Guerrilleros de Cristo Rey, GCR). They joined in several antileftist and anti-Basque Fatherland and Freedom (Euzkadi ta Askatasuna, ETA) actions organized by the Spanish police and security services, under the cover of rubrics such as the Spanish Basque Battalion (Battallón Vasco Español, BVE) and the Anti-Terrorist Liberation Groups (Grupos Antiterroristas de Liberación, GAL). Delle Chiaie and other European extremists carried out propaganda and terrorist operations on behalf of General Augusto Pinochet's Chilean secret police and the Argentine military intelligence service.

The most clear-cut example of the role played by neofascist terrorists in covertly conditioning a democratic political environment occurred in Italy, which was subjected to the most sustained campaign of right-wing terrorism and subversion in the history of postwar Europe. This campaign, which has been dubbed the "strategy of tension," was designed to precipitate an authoritarian transformation of the Italian political system and in the process prevent the Italian Communist Party (Partito Comunista Italiano, PCI) from joining the ruling governmental coalition. It was characterized by a combination of public bombings, assassinations, coup initiatives, infiltrations of left-wing groups, provocations, and psychological warfare operations. These were exploited by rival sub rosa political factions: those seeking to precipitate an outright military coup; those seeking to modify the Italian constitution and political system by increasing the power of the chief executive at the expense of a divided, intensely partisan parliament (the so-called presidentialists); and those seeking to make instrumental use of the subversive and terrorist actions sponsored by the other two groups in order to maintain and strengthen their own privileged positions within the existing system. The seriousness of the situation was reflected in Italian police records, which attributed 83 percent of the 4,384 officially registered acts of political violence from 1969 to 1975 to the extreme right.

Prior to the end of the Cold War the importance of right-wing terrorism can be attributed primarily to the de facto operational alliance, in the name of anticommunism, between more or less independent neofascist bands and hard-line factions within the security forces of various democratic and authoritarian states. Yet even though neofascist terrorists were not entirely autonomous, much less marginal, political actors, it would be wrong to depict them as the simple agents or instruments of far more powerful conservative forces operating behind the scenes. They are best characterized as misguided revolutionaries who were regularly manipulated and duped by ostensibly sympathetic elements of the state into working against their own proclaimed interests and goals. These goals were the destruction of "bourgeois" democratic society and the creation of a powerful, united Europe as a "third force" able to regain its independence and influence in a postwar international order dominated by the hated capitalist and communist superpowers. In the end, the tactics of violent destabilization, which they habitually employed, almost invariably ended up stabilizing the established power structure, much to the chagrin of the real radicals. Even when their actions did help to provoke an actual military coup, the ultras involved were typically marginalized or suppressed as soon as they displayed any resistance to the new government's policies. Thus this complex, Janus-faced phenomenon not only sheds light on the complexity of the neofascist milieu, but also on the little-known covert networks that played an important role in surreptitiously waging the Cold War.

BIBLIOGRAPHY

Archival material can be found at the Istituto Cattaneo, Bologna; the Biblioteca della Camera dei Deputati, Rome; the Institut für Zeitgeschichte, Munich; and the Hoover Institution at Stanford University.

Bale, Jeffrey M. The "Black" Terrorist International: Neo-Fascist Paramilitary Networks and the "Strategy of Tension" in Italy, 1968–1974. Unpublished Ph.D. thesis: University of California at Berkeley/Department of History, 1994.

Bjorgo, Tore, ed. *Terror from the Extreme Right.* London: Frank Cass, 1995.

Chairoff, Patrice [Ivan-Dominique Calzi]. *Dossier néonazisme.* Paris: Ramsay, 1977.

Flamini, Gianni. *Il partito del golpe: Le strategie della tensione e del terrore dal primo centrosinistro organico al sequestro Moro, 1964–1978.* 4 vols. in 6 pts. Ferrara: Bovolenta, 1981–1985.

Harris, Geoffrey. *The Dark Side of Europe: The Extreme Right Today.* Edinburgh: Edinburgh University, 1994.

Laurent, Frédéric. *L'orchestre noir.* Paris: Stock, 1978.

Linklater, Magnus, et al. *The Fourth Reich: Klaus Barbie and the Neo-Fascist Connection.* London: Coronet, 1985.

Miralles, Melchor, and Ricardo Arques. *Amedo: El estado contra ETA.* Barcelona: Plaza & Janes/Cambio 16, 1989.

Willan, Philip. *Puppetmasters: The Political Uses of Terrorism in Italy.* London: Constable, 1991.

Jeffrey M. Bale

SEE ALSO Borghese Coup; Neofacism in Western Europe; Rauti, Giuseppe

Thatcher, Margaret (1925–)

Conservative prime minister of the United Kingdom from 1979 to 1990. Margaret Thatcher was Britain's longest serving prime minister in the twentieth century. Breaking with the post–World War II consensus in British politics, she advocated a new economic and political direction, hailed as Thatcherism by her followers. The Iron Lady of the Cold War, she developed a warm personal relationship with U.S. president Ronald Reagan and earned the respect of Soviet president Mikhail Gorbachev, thus putting herself in a position to conduct diplomacy with the superpowers during a historical epoch. As Third World and ex-Communist states began to rethink the statist policies of the past, Thatcherism presented an alternative.

Thatcher was born Margaret Roberts on October 13, 1925, in Grantham, Lincolnshire. Her father, Alfred Roberts, was a shopkeeper and a Grantham alderman. Margaret Thatcher always proudly acknowledged his influence, while neglecting to mention her housewife mother, Beatrice. For father and daughter alike, hard work and political involvement were values that not only supplied the formula for decency but for improving one's circumstances in Britain's rigid, class-based society. Thatcher had her father to thank for never having learned her place in society as a woman or as a member of a specific class. Later, her husband Denis, whom she married in 1951, provided the same strong backing for her ambitions. A graduate of Somerville College, Oxford, in chemistry in 1947, Thatcher first worked as a scientist before becoming a barrister with a specialization in tax law. From the constituency of Finchley, she went to Parliament in 1959. She established herself in a legal career and in politics while mothering twins, Mark and Carol, born in 1953.

Thatcher rose to ministerial prominence as the parliamentary secretary at the Ministry of Pensions and National Insurance from 1961 to 1964, and as the secretary of state for education and science from 1970 to 1974. Once she became party leader in 1975, she won three general elections in 1979, 1983, and 1987. In 1992 her successor, John Major, prepared the way for her political retirement in the House of Lords, awarding her a life peerage. The title she assumed was Baroness of Kesteven, the name of her grammar school, and thus she became Lady Thatcher.

Epitomizing the self-made woman, Thatcher became convinced that people must accept responsibility for shaping their lives for better or for worse and that government should not interfere in the conscious choices of its citizens. Individualism formed the platform for her vehement antisocialism. She rejected the indiscriminate lumping together of people into something called "society" to justify social engineering and, consequently, to deny their ability to help themselves. Although she denied the existence of "society" to oppose the political purposes of the Left, she remained deferential to Britain's social hierarchy, leaving it unchallenged, but redefining access to the upper ranks in terms of personal success and service. In her view, the celebration of individual achievement deserved the highest distinction. Thus, she surprisingly broke with the practice established in 1964 by former prime minister harold Wilson, who refused to appoint hereditary peers to the House of Lords. While Thatcher appointed hereditary peers, John Major, her successor, announced in 1993 his intention to appoint only life peers, refusing to join Thatcher in turning back the clock on this issue. Traditional in her outlook on the monarchy (and perfecting her own monarchical style), Thatcher was anything but reverent to haughty Conservatives. Indeed, the ascendancy of the Thatcherites dethroned the nobles in the leadership of the Conservative Party.

Thatcher was perhaps motivated more by the social constraints she overcame than by the gender constraints she faced, although both undoubtedly influenced her drive and determination. That she, herself, might have been class-bound led her to promote enterprising people. In her version of Britain, the economically successful deserved to keep their newly acquired wealth (from the state) as much as old-monied Britons had previously deserved to inherit wealth. A woman championing, initially, a marginal viewpoint was an oddity in Britain's political establishment. Her determination, therefore, would accept nothing less than fundamental change. Through personnel changes, she aimed to create a mainstream for her new ideology and to insure its dominance. Therefore, her ambition was not only to defeat socialism in elections but to eliminate it totally from the world's political landscape. In the beginning of her premiership, she had to live with the so-called wets in her own party, believers in the country's post–World War II compromise between Left and Right. Resigned to political realities, she carefully designed an inclusive first cabinet but made sure her followers were in the economic positions. As soon as she consolidated power, she purged her cabinet of wets and brought in people with whom she more closely identified. Toward the end of her tenure she surrounded herself predominantly with like-minded people. Her relations were also rocky with the "establishment" civil service, one of the targets of budget-cutting and held closely in check by a prime minister who would not tolerate resistance to her reforms by the bureaucracy.

At the outset, Thatcher's was a domestic political agenda, with a failing economy the subject of intense focus. She had a clear economic strategy to put in place—"monetarism"—which purported to control the economy through the money supply. Anti-Keynesian, the strategy was not concerned with the employment situation except as it stood to benefit eventually from an improved economy, only after "correct" policies were enacted and a steady reform course maintained. As monetarists believed they knew the kinds of policies required, a clear and definite course of action was possible (i.e., setting monetary targets), which must have appealed to Thatcher's scientific instincts and preference for tidiness. As the Thatcher government implemented the program, it included reductions in deficit spending by financing spending through taxation. This ended up shifting the burden from income taxes to indirect taxes (whereas the tax cuts during the administration of Ronald Reagan in the United States were done more experimentally and not, as in Britain, out of regard for the size of the deficit). In addition, the government administered the harsh medicine of serious reductions in government spending. In short, the adjustment was full of pain. Detractors of monetarism were not so convinced that it was foolproof, and they rejected its dogmatic aspects, especially the way it privileged certain economic priorities (and groups) over others in the name of economic necessity. With the same resoluteness, Thatcher pursued additional economic goals. She became known for extensive privatizations coupled with actions favorable to the private sector, especially market-freeing measures. Finally, she broke the power of the unions, culminating in the miners' strike from March 1984 to March 1985, which she successfully defeated.

As economic indicators were initially slow to legitimatize monetarism, it took a foreign-policy crisis to firmly establish Thatcher's leadership. Her electability soared as a result of the success on June 14, 1982, of the British military effort to rescue the Falkland Islands from an attempted Argentine takeover. Subsequently, foreign policy was very much tied to her political fortunes and misfortunes. Thatcher most significantly imprinted two foreign-policy arenas, that of East-West relations and that of the European Community (EC), now the European Union. In the former arena she established a secure place in history by being among the first leaders to recognize the inevitability of change and the necessity for the West to support change in the former Soviet Union. This change of heart in an avowed anticommunist who prided herself on being a "conviction politician" convinced even the U.S. president, Ronald Reagan. Thatcher delivered the capitalist's seal of approval on Soviet president Mikheil Gorbachev, identifying him as a man with whom she could do business. The important unilateral role the United Kingdom played in East-West relations during her premiership owed more to the personal inroads she made than to the world position of the United Kingdom. Thatcher clearly relished superpower politics.

European politics had the opposite effect, providing a source of continuous frustration. In the EC, Thatcher initially concerned herself unsuccessfully with wresting influence away from France and Germany, whose leaders saw themselves as the joint architects of the EC. She labored for nearly half a decade to correct the serious imbalance between Britain's contributions to and receipts from the EC budget. Ultimately, she scored a victory in the British budget dispute of 1980 to 1984, only to see the other EC heads of government steel their determination to stand up to her the next time. The ability to wield in European affairs the strong leadership she exercised at home eluded her. In the EC her country was no more than one of the big five, with an economy smaller than that of France, Germany, and Italy and challenged by an up-and-coming Spain. Instinctively, Thatcher resisted the EC process as overly bureaucratic and not sufficiently democratic; as consensus-governed and bound to produce mediocre, weak, and unprincipled decisions; and as damaging to Britain's vital sovereignty. Ideologically, the EC offended Thatcher as a vehicle for creeping socialism, all the more insidious to her because the organization insulated itself from national parliaments and their electorates. Reacting to the potential sovereignty infringements from a European central bank and single currency, Thatcher responded "not in my lifetime" to plans for the European Monetary Union (EMU). Undeterred, EC Commission President Jacques Delors continued to push for new EC policy competencies. On the subject of giving the EC a social dimension, the two personalities clashed. Thatcher felt personally betrayed by Delors's address to the British Trade Union Congress (TUC) in September 1988, in which he advocated the development of EC social policy. The Labour Party was able to use the TUC's receptiveness to Delors to announce its new course as the party of Europe. Not only did Thatcher react against Delors' interference in British politics, she also disagreed with the Commission trying to extend its own powers and social engineering at any level. Thatcher became more determined than ever to challenge Delors's vision with one of her own. The debate exploded into public with Thatcher's 1988 Bruges speech, in which she opposed a centralizing, superstate Europe. The collapse of the Soviet Union and the East bloc reinforced Thatcher's objections to the EC and provided her with powerful references and imagery to counter the integrationists. "If there was ever an idea whose time had come and gone it was surely that of the artificial megastate," she would write in her memoirs, *The Downing Street Years.*

Her combative style not only wore on relations with EC officials and politicians but affected relations with members of her own party, especially as policy disagreements became more serious. The generalists in the Foreign Office never inspired in her, the scientist, the respect they thought they deserved. The conflict came to a head over EC policy, and the obstructions she posed to EMU caused further harm to an already personally strained relationship between herself and the foreign secretary, Sir Geoffrey Howe. Along with Howe, the chancellor of the exchequer, Sir Nigel Lawson, favored Britain's closer integration with Europe. The policy Lawson followed, keeping the British pound stable in relation to the deutsche mark, caused friction with the prime minister. Lawson saw himself preparing sterling for entry into the Exchange Rate Mechanism (ERM) of the European Monetary System on which EMU intended to build. That Britain had not joined the ERM had been a sore point in European relations since Thatcher became prime minister in 1979. The consensus-based arrangements for currency stability in the ERM were hard enough for Thatcher to accept, much less the more ambitious plans EMU represented for giving important economic decision making to a European central bank. At the meeting of EC heads of government in Madrid in June 1989, Britain agreed to eventually join the ERM under carefully prescribed conditions, and it appeared that Howe and Lawson had won the day. However, Thatcher was only playing for time and remained as skeptical as ever of the economic logic that underpinned EMU and continued unwilling to cede Britain's sovereignty. It did not take long for Thatcher to respond to the pressure tactics of her ministers. In July 1989, Thatcher and Howe unsmoothly negotiated his move to the position of leader of the House, and finally Howe resigned from the cabinet altogether in November 1990.

Against the background of a disunified government, the economy had begun to perform badly in 1988. As long as Lawson insisted on linking sterling's value to that of European currencies, exchange-rate policy could not be used to relieve the economic recession Britain experienced. Amidst so many pressures, Thatcher decided to recall her trusted economic adviser, Sir Alan Walters, who was widely known to share her skepticism about the ERM. Lawson decided his authority was under assault and gave Walters's return as his reason for resigning in October 1989.

Increasing worry about Thatcher's European policy manifested itself among party elites and foreign office officials, many of whom had dedicated themselves to EC membership since Edward Heath's proud entry into the Community, and in the more cosmopolitan elements of the British public. City bankers predicted that Frankfurt would take over London's lead in financial services if Britain stayed out of EMU. However, the European issue did not cause the public discontent that arose as the result of the community charge, or poll tax.

Thatcher fell victim to the strong ideological and perfectionistic sides of her personality in insisting on the hugely unpopular poll tax, the damaging label her critics gave the community charge. In order to provide part of the financing for local councils, the prime minister was determined that a shift be made from the previous system, which taxed property owners, to one in which every voter paid a flat rate. The government believed that the poll tax would make local government more accountable, because every voter should feel the pinch if councils spent too much. Partly because of her influence, the voters had already begun to rein in the socialist-controlled, high-spending councils that were the targets of Thatcher's action. In 1985 her government, unflinching in face of the House of Lords' opposition, had already succeeded with legislation abolishing outright the Greater London Council. Why Thatcher returned again to this issue can also be explained in terms of her not being comfortable with a job unfinished. The "good housekeeping" mentality the continentals tended to deride continued to inspire her. In her last term, she was as preoccupied as ever with putting the national household in shipshape condition. Certainly it was important that she had promised to do away with property rates as early as 1974; it was also important to her that the chore still remained to be done. As the public, in general, found means of financing local government hard to relate to, it could not relate to this issue as a routinely necessary task. However, the public understood well the ideological battle the poll tax represented. They refused to go so far in rejecting socialism that they accepted equal taxation, regardless of wealth. The tradition of progressive taxation was too ingrained. Besides, it was clear this would not be the last battle. The public could less well tolerate the pain caused by reforms taken during an economic downturn and compounded by the cumulative pain of over a decade of reforms.

When it seemed Thatcher could no longer lead the party to victory in a general election, party elites had the most legitimate reason possible in the British system to remove the leader. It was a reason for which many had been waiting. Thatcher's leadership style had grown too prime ministerial, some would say presidential, for British tastes. Coupled with Lawson's resignation, Howe made a damning speech in Parliament on November 13, 1990, perfectly timed to influence the party's annual leadership contest on November 20. Howe exposed his differences with Thatcher concerning Europe and his objections to her governing style. There was no longer any doubt that she would have to face her rivals in the internal party election, which eventually forced her resignation on November 28. Failing on the first ballot to win against Michael Heseltine, who had been waiting for revenge since he left her cabinet in 1986 due to his disagreement with her reserve toward strengthening the European Community and over the way that she dominated the cabinet, she refused to go on to the second ballot. Therefore, the way opened for others to join the contest and for the candidate she handpicked, John Major, to become the next prime minister.

In an age of technical decision making, Thatcher had a grasp of details and was well known for mastering her briefs. Thatcher tended to take personal responsibility for issues that other heads of government delegated to their officials. Her hands-on governing style, the opposite of Ronald Reagan's detachment, required wide knowledge and enormous energy, which few heads of government are able to muster. If the strain showed on Thatcher toward the end, her initial burst of energy created an enduring image of a political leader hard at work. Owing to Thatcher's self-sufficiency, she could economize, as she was so fond of doing, in not needing a host of officials to accompany her on her foreign visits. One did not have to worry that "technocrats," not politicians, made policy under her leadership. In addition, she knew how to translate complex issues into common language. Thus, in educating Britons about the job she was doing, she was highly skilled. However, what was for her "plain speaking," sometimes came across as infuriating and undiplomatic, especially among both foreign and national elites. Besides being in daily control, Thatcher was a competent crisis manager. She knew how to inspire confidence by breathing new life into traditional symbols and was unafraid of making decisions under pressure.

While her loyalty, directness, and steadfastness were perhaps comforting, she could be as threatening as well. Hers was predominantly an assertive leadership style. Flattered by comparisons to Charles de Gaulle, enjoying the company of Henry Kissinger, and associating her own achievements with those of Winston Churchill, she saw herself belonging to the tradition of strong leaders. Thatcher's modus vivendi with nuclear weapons—her scientific grasp of the technology and her secure judgment that the policy of nuclear deterrence was stabilizing—was undiluted political realism. This point of view served her well most of the time, grounding her foreign policies, but she lost her bearings when the world did not correspond to her understanding of it. Just as the EC had been difficult for her as an issue that could not be processed in the regular way, so was German unification. Her response was to immediately look for a "balancer" where there was none, with France unavailable because of its close ties to Germany, the Soviet Union in a state of collapse, and the United States shifting its attention from Europe.

She was as fascinated by the "high stakes" world of business as she was by "high politics." Thatcher always promoted British commercial interests in her travels. When European subsidiaries of U.S. companies stood to lose contracts because the Reagan administration forbid them to supply technology to the natural gas pipeline proposed to link West Germany and the Soviet Union, Thatcher came to their defense. Cold War considerations notwithstanding, the U.S. action was a case of "extraterritoriality" and against international law, she informed Reagan.

It was the assertive side that enabled her to rise to the top of the British political establishment, and this was the side that eventually erred. Crisis management was appropriate in certain situations: for example, the Argentine invasion of the Falklands, the distress of the British economy at the start of her premiership, and the miners' strike. The style, however, exacted a price from the nation and the prime minister and, thus, was not successful over the long haul. Similarly, Thatcher's complete disdain for consensus might have served her well in key decisions, but eventually it cost her the support of the elites in her party who rediscovered their belief in cabinet government. In addition, certain forums required a minimum of consensus, if decisions were to be made at all. So it was with the EC and, increasingly, in international negotiations in the absence of dominant powers, or of powers who chose to exercise their dominance.

As prime minister, Thatcher presided over the renewal of the special relationship with the United States, the successful waging of a war, the 1980s recovery of the British economy, the fulfillment of her predictions about communism, and the adoption of Thatcherite economic principles by much of the world. It looked as if events had combined to give her a superhuman dimension. Upon closer examination, however, not all of these events were of her own making, and few of them were permanent trends and or had uncomplicated results. Whereas the "special relationship" with the United States revealed itself to be strictly a Thatcher-Reagan creation, it also revealed itself to be short-lived, with the William J. (Bill) Clinton presidency (1993–1997) favoring the relationship of the United States with a unified Germany. Certainly Thatcher turned back the clock on the issue of nationalizations, with the Labour Party's leadership anxiously awaiting the consent of activists to purge government ownership from its own party program. Indeed, as a result of her crusade, governments everywhere were more concerned with economic efficiency and accountability for public spending. However, the economic orthodoxy of unfettered markets and private initiative was advanced as much by the International Monetary Fund (IMF) as it was by Thatcher. Indeed, in relation to Russia's democratic striving, as a former prime minister, Thatcher expressed her concerns about the stringency of IMF measures there and the need to be mindful of the goal of political stability. After Thatcher's premiership, Western Europe entered a recession as decision makers considered the grim prospect that the economic problems they experienced were no longer cyclical but structural—in other words, unresponsive to the old policy manipulations. Under John Major, Britain continued to cut military spending, while the horrors of the former Yugoslavia, combined with the refusal of the United States to take a leadership role in Europe, belied the mighty Britain of the Thatcher era. The Balkan crisis also underlined the utility of regional solutions, especially in an age of declining resources and ineffective unilateral pressure. Last, communist regimes were not so easily converted into democracies or even good citizens of the European system. Internally, the large-scale corruption that capitalism afforded, among other evils, demoralized reformers and made some nostalgic for the petty corruption of party apparatchiks.

Thatcher's legacy will continue to be debated. Polls consistently showed that she did not have majority support for many of her policies, and in none of the three general elections did she win a majority of the British vote, although the electoral system awarded her party solid majorities in Parliament. According to this evidence, Thatcher's preeminence was a fluke. Evidence pointing strongly in a different direction is that the British electorate knew very well how to deprive the governing party of its majority in Parliament. Moreover, Parliament could vote no confidence (though it rarely does), and party elites could withdraw their support, as they eventually did. It is beyond dispute that Thatcher provided executive stability, which other British governments in the 1970s failed to provide.

In conclusion, it is likely that Britons were skeptical of a woman leader spouting monetarism, lecturing on age-old values, and carrying a big stick. For a time, her leadership convinced them otherwise. It is a rare brand of leadership that overcomes institutional resistance, moves the public, and restores confidence in the ability of government to bring about change, and in the end, gives the leader historical prominence. All this occurred in a democratic context to which Thatcher was genuinely, if sentimentally, committed.

BIBLIOGRAPHY

Cloke, Paul, ed. *Policy and Change in Thatcher's Britain.* Oxford: Pergamon, 1992.

King, Anthony, ed. *The British Prime Minister.* Durham, N.C.: Duke University Press, 1985.

Lewis, Russell. *Margaret Thatcher: A Personal and Political Biography.* London: Routledge & Kegan Paul, 1983.

Ogden, Chris. *Maggie: An Intimate Portrait of a Woman in Power.* New York: Simon and Schuster, 1990.

Smith, Geoffrey. *Reagan and Thatcher.* London: Bodley Head, 1990.

Thatcher, Margaret. *The Downing Street Years.* New York: HarperCollins, 1993.

———. *In Defense of Freedom: Speeches on Britain's Relations with the World, 1976–1986.* Buffalo, NY: Prometheus, 1987.

Young, Hugo. *The Iron Lady: A Biography of Margaret Thatcher.* New York: Noonday, 1990.

Mary Troy Johnston

SEE ALSO Falklands War; Major, John

Theater

European theater since 1945 can be labeled postmodern simply because the modern age from Henrik Ibsen through Bertolt Brecht looms undeniably as one of the great ages of world drama. Everything after Ibsen, John August Strindberg, Anton Chekhov, Luigi Pirandello, Federico García Lorca, Oscar Wilde, George Bernard Shaw, John Millington Synge, Sean O'Casey, Eugene O'Neill, and Brecht seems "post," an afterthought, by comparison.

Two of the most experimental moderns exercise the greatest and the most evident sway on post-1945 European theater: Pirandello and Brecht. Pirandello did not invent the-world-is-a-stage metaphor, but he brought it to a pitch of intensity in a series of plays that totally break down the conventional boundaries between stage and audience, sanity and madness, reality and illusion. Brecht put his "epic drama" at the service of a social vision, but his "alienation effect," whereby the audience is not allowed to dwell too easily on dramatic illusion because that illusion is continually broken and defied, has proved compelling to innumerable theatrical writers who were not consciously in service of a definable cause. A case in point, where both the Pirandellian and Brechtian influences are at play, would be Peter Weiss's (1916–) *The Persecution and Assassination of Marat as Performed by the Inmates of the Asylum of Charenton under the Direction of the Marquis de Sade* (1964), a work based on French history by a German émigré living in Sweden that received its most triumphant production in English translation in London and New York by the Royal Shakespeare Company under Peter Brook. In the-world-turned-upside-down tradition of absurdist drama, the entire action of *Marat/Sade* occurs in a madhouse that represents the world. Drama is employed as therapy, but the well-meant experiment gets out of hand when the inmate actors under de Sade's direction (the play is based on an actual historical event) truly inhabit their roles as Jean-Paul Marat, Charlotte Corday, and the Paris mob, and go on to foment a revolution in the asylum.

If this pattern of late-twentieth-century drama deriving from, and building on, the great exemplars of the modern era holds any truth, the twenty-year dramatic oeuvre of Samuel Beckett (1906–89) fractured the pattern. Beckett is sui generis. His roots are Modernist. Following James Joyce from Ireland to exile to Paris, and reversing the journeys of Joseph Conrad and Vladimir Nabokov from the margins to the center, he wrote dramas in an assumed language, French, but then did his own translations into English and collaborated in the early productions of his plays, which moved from Paris to London to New York. His career of minimalist theater bears out the key modernist precept: less is more. Beckett's oeuvre displays a steady pattern of diminution, as the number of characters is reduced, their mobility is limited, and stage running time is curtailed. *Waiting for Godot* (1953) has five characters in two acts; *End Game* (1957) has four characters; *Act without Words* (Part I, 1957, Part II, 1960) is done entirely in mime; *Krapp's Last Tape* (1958) has one character communing with his tape recorder; in *Happy Days* (1962) the character Winnie is at first buried up to her waist in a mound, which reaches to her neck in Act II; in *Play* (1964) three characters immobilized in urns speak only when a light shines on them; *Breath* (1970) consists of one minute of disembodied cries and breaths; and *Not I* (1972) shows only the mouth of a woman speaking. Beckett starts with very little and moves to test the boundaries of our imagination by annihilating all that is conventionally theatrical. Instead of Job in dialogue with his inscrutable God (who by the twentieth century has become *deus absconditus*), in *Waiting for Godot* Beckett shows us two Irish tramps with vaguely Russian-sounding names, Estragon and Vladimir (made clownish by being diminutized into Gogo and Didi), who do vaudeville turns as they await—or endure—the millennium. Instead of King Lear regressing from power in a palace to penury on a blasted heath, Beckett's characters start and end there, or in a bunker at the end of the world, as in *End Game.* In the tableau ending that play, which is like a movie freeze frame, the audience cannot know whether Clov will leave, and if he does, if there is anywhere to go. In these circumstances, is anyone his brother's keeper? In the drama of Beckett, "Everyman" becomes the Last Man in No Man's Land.

A further qualification of the generalization that recent drama is derivative of modernist innovations would take note of the absurdist eruption, primarily of the 1950s and 1960s. Martin Esslin's study, *The Theatre of the Absurd* (1961), heralded the movement. According to Esslin, the absurdists' acute sense of the malignancy, meaninglessness, or sterility of existence led them to reject previously accepted realistic conventions such as psychologically motivated characters and plots, logically consistent dialogue, and familiar Western styles of presentation. The Romanian/Parisian playwright, Eugène Ionesco's (1912–94) *The Bald Soprano* (1950) took off from his experience of language-learners' phrase books, whose out-of-date colloquialism and indeed outright errors led him to recognize the arbitrariness of language. In *The Lesson* (1951) a young female student's one-hour tutoring session with a respectable, aged professor, meant to prepare her for the Total Doctorate exam, degenerates into verbal bullying eventuating in her rape and murder. Ionesco could decline into parable, as in his *Rhinoceros* (1960), in which the Everyman-protagonist, Béranger, manfully resists all other people's metamorphoses into the brutal pachyderms. At his best he brought to wide audiences the psychological and metaphysical insights of the Surrealists (for example, Guillaume Appolinaire's *The Breasts of Tiresias,* 1917) and Dadaists (for example, Alfred Jarry's manic schoolboy parodies in the *Ubu* trilogy, 1896–1901). In a series of plays featuring perverts (a valorized term in his lexicon), prostitutes, and pimps, the lifetime French criminal Jean Genet (1910–86) brought to the stage a vision from society's underside (*The Maids,* 1947; *Deathwatch,* 1949; *The Balcony,* 1956; *The Blacks,* 1957; and *The Screens,* 1961) suggesting that any true social revolution must include revolutions in race and gender relations. The Englishman Harold Pinter (1930–) has sometimes been considered an heir of Beckett. In his "theater of menace," violence or at least the strong implication of violence is always present, although usually suggested rather than manifest. His career has stretched from his first full-length work for the stage, *The Birthday Party* (1957), to the present, when he is generally accorded to be the most skillful adapter of literary classics for the screen. In the opinion of many his best full-length stage work is *The Homecoming* of 1965. The viewer or reader of this play would be hard put to determine in terms of conventional motivation why Ruth, the wife of the émigré philosophy professor, Teddy, agrees to act as the live-in prostitute to three other male members of his family. Pinter is the master of the not-said, the innuendo, and the silence. Heir to the metaphysical side of Beckett would be the Czech-born British playwright Tom Stoppard (1937–). Like so many dramatists he tends to be defined by his first popular success, *Rozencrantz and Guildenstern Are Dead* (1967), not so much a play-within-a-play as a play-beside-a-play, in which two very minor characters in *Hamlet* view Shakespeare's tragedy from below stairs, with the concomitant dramatic ironies of being ignorantly involved in a plot whose outcome the audience knows.

Despite the foregoing litany of elements of recent theater in which a skeptical observer could cast recent playwrights not as innovators but as epigones of their great modern forebears, mining rich but depleting veins of theatrical experiment, it is possible to identify a handful of respects in which the period 1945 to 2000 is not 1880 to 1945. Although film was a lively art in the 1920s, '30s, and '40s, the era from 1945 to 2000 has seen alternative media for the projection of drama—film, radio, television, and the Internet—challenge but also stimulate the legitimate theater. Literary history has long accorded women fiction writers an important place in the rise of the novel to the prevalent literary form, from the eighteenth through the early twentieth centuries. But Shakespeare truly did not have the sister Virginia Woolf lamentingly imagined for him, and it was not until recently that a significant number of female playwrights began writing about and for women. The theater has always been open to cross-cultural influences, but it became apparent after World War II that the Theater of Dionysus in Athens was not the font and origin of all subsequent dramatic practice and that the great traditions of, for instance, Japan, China, and India were a major available source of various dramatic practice. The great national capitals have long been magnets for their countries' talent and money, but it was not until the post–World War II period that the cultural capitals (New York in particular), with their star system and fixation on hits, threatened to totally commercialize the theater and choke off development.

The great challenge of the radio, film, and television media is that they can reach audiences of millions, and thus, although the production costs of the latter two in particular are staggering, the rewards of success can be more than commensurate, while the costs to consumers range from modest to apparently nil. The threat of electronic media is that they will totally displace stage performance, debasing popular taste and thoroughly marginalizing all other tastes. Yet radio, film, and television also stimulate stage drama, not just to incorporate mixed media in stage productions, but to adapt film technique to stage uses—flash back and forward, montage, and an expectation of flexibility and alacrity in thought on the part of audiences educated by decades of movie-going. Adaptation into film can give extremely wide distribution to stage classics, as the Englishman Laurence Olivier (1907–89) and most recently the Irish-born Kenneth Branagh (1960–) have proved with Shakespeare. The new media have an unending appetite for dramatic material; a significant portion of the output of Pinter and Stoppard is radio and TV scripts—the pot boilers of their careers. The mass media open up alternative careers for stage actors, allowing them, in a sense, to bankroll their own forays into less lucrative stage ventures. Very significant crossover careers are possible for directors as well as writers: Ingmar Bergman (1918–) is as important as a stage director in Sweden as he was as a film director for the rest of the world, and his decades-long career enabled him to develop a magnificent repertory company for stage and screen—in summer he made films and in winter directed plays, and his film scripts are read as people read drama.

A crude distinction could be drawn concerning plays created by women in the past half century. Plays consciously advancing a women's social and political agenda and directly and critically exposing male hegemony could be called "feminist theater," whereas plays written and at least partly produced, directed, and acted by women, which see women and men as co-partners in the human condition who share mutual problems, prominent among which are their relations with one another, could be called "women's theater." But the distinction is difficult to maintain, for the most successful plays do both. France's María Irene Fornés' (1930–) *Fefu and Her Friends* (1977) has a definite feminist theme; although there are male characters in the play, none ever appears on stage; certainly many of the men alluded to are monstrous oppressors, but others are fellow-sufferers (Fefu's husband Philip is as tormented by their twisted relationship as she is); and the eight women in the play control their own fate. When Britain's Caryl Churchill's (1938–) *Top Girls* was first produced in 1982 it was an aggressively up-to-date attack on British Prime Minister Margaret Thatcher's political and social policies; the chief antagonists are two sisters who have made startlingly different accommodations to life in Thatcher's Britain; the play opens with a fantasy scene, and it violates chronological sequence in ways that would do Stoppard or Pinter proud; there is doubling of rolls; there are no male characters on stage, but some of the women are working quite effectively at making themselves into men. British playwright Timberlake Wertenbaker's (1946–) *Our Country's Good* (1988) is a play whose historical setting is just-settled Australia, with a strong social message about British class relationships and penal practices; there is cross-gender doubling of roles; but the play is most notable for an instance of self-referentiality and the world-stage metaphor worthy of Pirandello: the plot turns upon whether the convicts will be able to stage a production of George Farquhar's Restoration comedy *The Recruiting Officer*. The five "women's" plays discussed above form something of a continuum, from most to least evidently feminist. These female dramatists were certainly well aware of their foremothers, but their greatest influences as dramatic practitioners came from their own contemporaries and the great moderns and they represent an important new direction in the theater.

It may be true that non-Western theater has had a greater influence on production, staging, and scene design in European and American theaters than on dramatic writing per se. Earlier in the century dramatists set their fantasies—Puccini's *Turandot*—and their parables—Brecht's *Good Woman of Setzuan*—in the exotic East. Latterly, playwrights have been fascinated with the histrionic possibilities they saw in masks, stylized acting, the use of puppets of different scales, and the integrating of music and dance, in Oriental theatrical traditions.

The commercialization of the theater is no new concern. Since the near-mythical time when it was a communal religious celebration, theater has involved the exchange of money. But concentration in national cultural capitals such as New York has encouraged an emphasis on name-recognition stars playing in prohibitively expensive vehicles that are either overpowering hits or relative flops. The result is an intense focus on popularity that tends to squeeze out whatever is unusual, challenging, experimental, or dangerous. (The movie industry suffers the same syndrome, also complicated by American cultural domination of the world's screens.) The problem is particularly exacerbated with the musical theater, which is inherently costly because of the large forces required—musicians, dancers, etc.—and elaborate production values. Every financial backer wants, expects, and requires another *Cats, Phantom of the Opera,* or *Les Misérables.* One positive result of the hit syndrome has been the efflorescence of alternative venues, such as Off Broadway, The Fringe at the Edinburgh Festival, and equally importantly the renaissance of regional theater, even more in Britain than the United States. The Continental antidote has been state support for the arts, the U.S. version perhaps being theater supported by a widespread higher education infrastructure.

From the perspective of the century's end, then, apparently in the past fifty-five years there has been no revolution, no denial of the advances of the Modernist movement, but instead a consolidation, a degree of dependency on the practices of the giants of the first half of the century, and in particular a capitalization on their precedent. Samuel Beckett stands as the greatest innovator and the one whose example and influence are most profound and yet perhaps also least superficially evident.

BIBLIOGRAPHY

Artaud, Antonin. *The Theater and Its Double.* Tr. by Mary Caroline Richards. New York: Grove Press, 1958.

Bentley, Eric. *The Playwright as Thinker: A Study of the Modern Theatre—Shaw, Ibsen, Strindberg, Pirandello, Brecht, Sartre.* Rev. ed. Cleveland: World Publishing Company, 1955.

Brecht, Bertolt. *Brecht on Theatre: The Development of an Aesthetic.* Tr. by John Willett. New York: Hill and Wang, 1964.

Clurman, Harold. *Seven Plays of the Modern Theater.* New York: Grove Press, 1962.

Esslin, Martin. *The Theatre of the Absurd: Beckett, Ionesco, Adamov, Genet, Albee, Arrabal, Grass, Pinter, Simpson.* New York: Doubleday, 1961.

Gilbert, Miriam, Carl H. Klaus, and Bradford S. Field, Jr., eds. *Modern and Contemporary Drama.* New York: St. Martin's Press, 1994.

Ted Cotton

SEE ALSO Beckett, Samuel Barclay; Bergman, Ernst Ingmar; Brecht, Bertolt

Theodorakis, Mikis (1925–)

Greek composer and political figure, who gained broad recognition for his score of the film *Zorba the Greek* (1964). Michalis (Mikis) Theodorakis was born on the island of Chios on July 29, 1925. He was early drawn to the music of the Greek church and served as a cantor. While studying violin at the Paris Conservatory of Music, he began composing songs for his own band.

His political interests developed simultaneously with his musical ability. At fourteen he joined the paramilitary National Youth Organization of General John Metaxas. When he was refused entry into the Athens State Conservatory, he turned single-mindedly to politics. On March 25, 1942, he was arrested at a Resistance Day rally and tortured by Italian soldiers before his release. As he began preparing for law school in Athens, he succeeded in winning a scholarship to the Athens Conservatory. At the conservatory, Theodorakis joined the Pan-Hellenic Youth Organization (EPON) of the communist National Liberation Front. While directing the EPON cultural center in Athens, he wrote the oratorio *Third of December* to commemorate the twenty-eight partisans killed by the British on "Bloody Sunday" in 1944. During the Greek civil war, Theodorakis was arrested in July and imprisoned on the island of Ikaria. He was released temporarily but then returned to Ikaria and subsequently to the concentration camp Makronisos, where he was beaten and tortured. Released in August 1949 with severe tuberculosis, he later attempted suicide when it appeared that he would be returned to the camp.

His developing musical ability gained him a three-year scholarship to the Paris Conservatory from the French government. From 1954 to 1960 he composed twenty-one works while in Paris. His score for *Antigone* convinced him to return to his Greek musical roots. Greek folk music became his guiding inspiration. His song-cycle *Epitaphios* established his popularity. While he composed scores for films and theater music, he became leader of the United Democratic Left in 1963. Following the assassination of his best friend, the leftist legislator Grigoris Lambrakis, in Thessaloníki in May 1963, Theodorakis formed the Lambrakis Youth. The group became a powerful political force. Theodorakis, its president, was elected to Lambrakis's former seat in Parliament. He composed the score to Costa-Gravas's movie *Z*, which was based upon the assassination of Lambrakis. This was followed by his score to Costa-Gravas's *State of Siege* (1973). In January 1966, Constantine II banned Theodorakis's music on the state-owned radio, and the military junta imposed a complete ban on his music in June 1967. When the colonels seized power on April 21, 1967, Theodorakis went underground but was arrested on August 21. The regime responded to international pressure and released him in January 1968, but then rearrested him in August. With his family he was subjected to house arrest in the mountain village of Zatouna. In October 1969 he was sent to Oropos, a maximum-security prison. On April 13, 1970, due to international pressure, Theodorakis was released and sent to Paris for medical treatment. After his release from hospital, he continued his agitation against the junta.

After the collapse of the military dictatorship and the establishment of democracy, Theodorakis was elected to Parliament several times, and from 1990 to 1992 he served in the government of Konstantin Mitsotakis. He then returned as music director of the Symphony Orchestra and Chorus of Hellenic Radio and Television.

BIBLIOGRAPHY

Holst-Warhaft, Gail. *Theodorakis: Myth & Politics in Modern Greek Music.* Amsterdam: Hakkert, 1980.

"Theodorakis, Mikis," *Current Biography 1973,* 409–412.

Bernard Cook

Thorez, Maurice (1900–1964)

Leader of the French Communist Party. Maurice Thorez was born into a coal-mining family in 1900 in the impoverished department of the Nord. He died an unrepentant Stalinist in 1964. Over the course of his long career in the French Communist Party (Parti Communiste Français, PCF), Thorez rose through the ranks from a founding member of the PCF at the Congress of Tours in 1920 to general secretary in 1932. His rise within the party was captured in his mostly ghostwritten 1936 autobiography, *Fils du peuple.* It became required reading for all French Communists as Thorez' cult of personality took off during the heyday of Stalinism.

Thorez maintained an iron grip on the leadership of the PCF throughout his career, shaping PCF dictates in concert with the Stalinists in the Communist Party of the Soviet Union. Thorez firmly believed that the USSR represented the most advanced form of government in the world and that it was the moral duty of every communist to preserve the Soviet Union at all costs, including the defeat of one's own nation. When the Nazi-Soviet Pact was announced in 1939, Thorez deserted the French army and spent the war years in exile in Moscow. He was granted amnesty and returned to France in 1944. Thorez resumed leadership of the PCF and participated in the tripartite governments of the early Fourth Republic as the minister for labor. After the massive strike wave of May 1947, Thorez was dismissed from the government, and the PCF became a major force in the opposition. In Moscow the newly formed Cominform condemned Thorez for right-wing deviations and for his foray into parliamentarism, and he submitted to Moscow party discipline.

After a stroke in 1950, Thorez convalesced in Moscow, where he remained a virtual prisoner until Stalin's death in 1953. He returned to a France that was plunging deeper and deeper into the abyss of the Algerian War. He refused to support the independence movement of the National Liberation Front (Front de Libération nationale, FLN) on the grounds that they exercised extreme cruelty in their terror campaign against the French colonists. This position put him at odds with the Moscow party under Nikita Khrushchev.

Despite his rough treatment in the early 1950s, Thorez remained a loyal Stalinist. Upon his return to France, he used every opportunity to thwart Khrushchev's efforts to reform communism. In 1961, Thorez succeed in purging the anti-Stalinist faction of Marcel Servin and Laurent Casanova from the PCF. By casting the PCF firmly in the Stalinist traditions of his youth, Thorez created an enormous gulf between the PCF and the emerging New Left of the 1960s. His tenacious grip on the party and his uncanny ability to hold it fast to the Stalinist line made the PCF what it is today, a small, feeble anachronism.

Symbolically enough, Thorez died in 1964 while on vacation at a party dacha on the Black Sea.

BIBLIOGRAPHY

Thorez, Maurice. *Les grands combats de notre époque: paix-democratie, independance nationale, socialisme: résolution du Comité-central, I Ivry 15 decembre 1960.* Paris: Parti communiste francais, Comité central, 1960.

———. *Pour changer de politique, Unité d'action de la classe ouvriere: base du rassemblement des forces populaires: discours de Maurice Thorez et rapport de Jacques Duclos au Comité Central des 16 et 17 juin 1953 à Issy-les-Moulineaux.* Paris: S.E.D.I.C., 1953.

———. *Pour un parti communiste toujours plus fort au service du peuple: discours à la Journée d'étude des militants communistes des departements de l'Est, Moyeuvre-*

Grande, 23 juin 1963. Paris: Parti communiste français, 1963.

Mer, Jacqueline. *Le parti de Maurice Thorez: ou, Le bonheur communiste français: étude anthropologique.* Paris: Payot, 1977.

Robrieux, Philippe. *Maurice Thorez: vie secrete et vie publique.* Paris: Fayard, 1975.

Sedykh, Voleslav Nikolaevich. *Trois vies: Marcel Cachin, Maurice Thorez, Jacques Duclos.* Moscow: Editions du Progres, 1981.

Peggy Philips

Thoroddsen, Gunnar (1910–83)

Icelandic politician and diplomat. Gunnar Thoroddsen's political career was both long and complex. He entered politics in 1934, when elected to parliament at the age of twenty-four. There he represented the center-conservative Independence Party (IP) for all but three years from 1934 to 1965, when he retired from politics to become Iceland's ambassador to Denmark. Until then, he had been a prominent leader of the IP, serving as mayor of Reykjavik from 1947 to 1959 and minister of finance from 1959 to 1965. After suffering a crushing defeat in the 1968 presidential elections, Thoroddsen reentered public life in Iceland. He was appointed justice of the Supreme Court of Iceland in 1970, but resumed his political career when elected to parliament in the following year. He quickly regained his former status in the IP; he was elected vice-chairman of the IP in 1974, and was appointed minister of industry and social affairs in the same year. In 1980, Thoroddsen broke the party ranks, however, leading a small splinter group of IP representatives to form a coalition government with the parties to the left of the IP. Thoroddsen served as prime minister in this government until just before his death in 1983.

Gudmundur Halfdanarson

Threshold Test Ban Treaty (TTBT)

An arms-testing agreement, also known as the Treaty between the United States of America and the Union of Soviet Socialist Republics on the Limitation of Underground Nuclear Weapon Tests. This treaty, signed on July 3, 1974, was the second arms-testing accord between the superpowers. It directly built upon the agreements reached in the Partial Test Ban Treaty (PTBT), which was signed in August 1963.

The Threshold Test Ban Treaty (TTBT) established a nuclear "threshold" of 150 kilotons (150,000 tons of TNT) for underground weapons tests. This was militarily significant because it limited the testing of preexisting and new nuclear weaponry beyond the fractional-megaton range. It was intended to preclude the USSR or the United States from developing the warheads necessary for a first strike. The treaty also included a protocol concerning the exchange of technical data and the designation of specified testing sites for verification purposes. To regulate all underground nuclear explosions, the PNE Treaty, which addressed peaceful underground nuclear explosions, was negotiated in April 1976 as a complement to the TTBT.

Criticisms of the TTBT centered on numerous Soviet violations, the need for more effective verification procedures, and the 150-kiloton testing threshold, which, it was argued, was too high and would only result in a delay of a comprehensive test ban. After new verification protocols were signed in June 1990, the treaty was ratified by the U.S. Congress in December 1990, along with the PNE Treaty.

BIBLIOGRAPHY

U.S. Arms Control and Disarmament Agency. *Arms Control and Disarmament Agreements: Texts and Histories of the Negotiations.* Washington, D.C.: Government Printing Office, 1990.

U.S. Congress, Committee on Foreign Relations. *Threshold Test Ban and Peaceful Nuclear Explosions Treaty.* Report and Hearings. 100th Cong., 1st sess. Washington, D.C.: Government Printing Office, 1987.

U.S. Congress, Committee on Foreign Relations. *Threshold Test Ban and Peaceful Nuclear Explosion Treaties with the U.S.S.R.* Report and Hearings. 101st Cong., 2d sess. Washington, D.C.: Government Printing Office, 1990.

Robert J. Bunker

SEE ALSO Partial Test Ban Treaty

Tildy, Zoltán (1889–1961)

President of the Hungarian Republic, 1946–1948. Zoltán Tildy, a minister of the Reformed Church, was one of the founders of the Smallholder's Party in 1930 and served as its vice president until 1941. From 1945 to 1948 he was its chairman.

During World War II, Tildy planned for the Smallholders and the Social Democrats to cooperate after the war. His plans, however, were confounded by the Red Army. In 1945, Tildy supported cooperation and compromise with the Left. After the elections in November, he became prime minister of the coalition government, and in 1946, he was elected president of the new republic.

In 1948, Tildy's son-in-law was accused of spying and was executed. As a consequence, at the beginning of August, Tildy, under attack by the Communists, had to resign. Until May 1956, he was subjected to house arrest in Budapest.

During the uprising of 1956, Tildy became the minister of state in the government of Imre Nagy. For this, Tildy was subsequently sentenced to six years in prison, but he was released for health reasons in 1959. Tildy was posthumously rehabilitated in 1989.

BIBLIOGRAPHY

Céry, Dezsö. *Tildy Zoltán.* Budapest: Griff, 1946.

Nagy, Ferenc. *The Struggle behind the Iron Curtain.* Tr. by Stephen K. Swift. New York: Macmillan, 1948.

Vigh, Károly. *Tildy Zoltán életútja.* Békéscsaba: Tevan, 1991.

Heino Nyyssönen

Timisoara

The ethnically mixed city in western Romania where a revolt was begun against the dictator Nicolae Ceauşescu, which led to his overthrow on December 22, 1989. A local democracy movement with a significant following subsequently defied efforts by the ruling National Salvation Front, composed mainly of former communists, to claim for itself the mantle of the anti-Ceauşescu revolution. In March 1990 a Timisoara Proclamation was issued by the democracy movement. It called for decentralization, condemned chauvinism, and demanded that power holders from the pre–1989 era be barred from politics. It was a rallying cry for anticommunist forces nationwide during the politically disturbed period that lasted until the summer of 1990. In all of the elections since 1989, the reformist opposition has done far better in Timisoara than anywhere else in Romania. The government has sought to penalize the city for its nonconformism and radicalism, but despite lying only a few miles from the Serbian frontier, it remains a stronghold of interethnic coexistence and civic values.

Tom Gallagher

Tindemans, Leo (1922–)

One of the leading Belgian politicians in the 1970s and 1980s, and prime minister of Belgium from 1974 to 1979. Leo Tindemans was born on April 16, 1922, in Zwijndrecht. He studied at the University of Ghent and the Catholic University of Louvain, where he received a doctorate in economics and later became a professor of social sciences.

Tindemans joined the Belgian People's Christian Party (CVP) and served as its president from 1979 to 1981. He was elected to the chamber of deputies in 1961 and held his seat until 1989. He also served as mayor of Edegem (1975–76). Tindemans was minister of community affairs (1968–71), minister of agriculture (1972–73), and deputy prime minister and minister for the budget and institutional reform (1973–74). As minister of institutional reform he had to deal with the issue of national devolution in Belgium, or the division of Belgium into the French and Dutch linguistic communities with separate administration areas. Tindemans became prime minister in 1974 and served until October 10, 1979. His coalition collapsed over the issue of restructuring Belgium into a federal state, organized according to language communities. Tindemans, however, continued to play a dominant role in Belgian politics. He served as foreign minister (1981–89) and as minister of state (1992).

Tindemans was president of the European People's Party from 1976 to 1985. In January 1992 he was chosen to be president of the delegation of the European People's Party to the European Parliament. He held that post until July 1994.

Bernard Cook

Tischner, Jozef Stanislaw (1931–)

Polish Catholic priest, philosopher, and theologian. Jozef Tischner began teaching philosophy at the Department of Papal Theology at Theological Academy in Kraców in 1968. He began teaching at the Jagiellonian University in Kraków in 1979. In 1981 he became the president of the Institut für die Wissenschaften von Menschen. He also served as an adviser to Pope John Paul II. A disciple of the phenomenologist Roman Ingarden, Tischner has been mainly interested in the axiological foundations of Christianity.

He was a preacher and spiritual leader of the Polish underground movement, Solidarity. He created the so-called ethics of Solidarity as a kind of philosophical commentary on the formation of Solidarity, the independent Polish labor union in August 1980. He took the words of St. Paul as a motto: "Take the burden of your brothers on your shoulders and you shall fulfill the word of God." In his essays Tischner's philosophy centers on the themes of hope, work, and dialogue.

His main works include *The World of Human Hope* (1975), *Ethics of Solidarity* (1981), *The Polish Shape of*

Dialogue (1981), *Thinking in Agreement with Values* (1982), *Philosophy of Work* (1985), *The Polish Mill* (1991), *The Divine Mill* (1992), *The Confession of a Revolutionary* (1993), and *A Wretched Gift of Freedom* (1993).

Agnieszka Leńska

Tito (Broz, Josip) (1892–1980)

President of socialist Yugoslavia from its inception in 1945. Tito was without doubt the decisive personality in its authoritarian system, and simultaneously the promoter and the grave digger of the idea of Yugoslavia. Facets of his life are still obscure. Born at Kumrovac to the northeast of Zagreb in the Austro-Hungarian Empire to a Croatian father and a Slovene mother, he was a citizen of that state from his birth until the death of the empire in 1918. He volunteered for the Austro-Hungarian army during the First World War.

As a prisoner of war in Russia, he was swayed by the Bolsheviks. Upon returning to the new state of Yugoslavia, he rose rapidly in the ranks of the Yugoslav Communist Party (KPJ). He replaced Josip Cizinski (Milan Gorkic) in August 1937 as the secretary of the KPJ. His role in the execution of Gorkic during Stalin's purge remains a delicate point, but is illustrative of the ambitious character of Tito, who did not wish to share power.

Tito, postwar ruler of Yugoslavia until his death in 1980. His country survived him by a mere ten years. *Illustration courtesy of Archive Photos.*

During the Second World War Tito was leader of the partisans, the Communist resistance movement. He was declared marshal and chief of state by the Constitution of 1946. By virtue of "the historic role of Tito in the war of popular liberation and the Yugoslav revolution" (article 333 of the Constitution of 1974), Tito was elected president for life. He was incapable of imagining an eventual sharing of power. He felt this way his whole reign, skillfully using his charisma and eliminating, when it was necessary, associates who became too critical. Faithful to Stalinism, he nevertheless split with Joseph Stalin in 1948. Distancing himself from Moscow, Tito was then obliged to develop an alternate path to socialism to justify his break with Stalin and the USSR. The centerpiece of Tito's model was "self-management," the participation of the people in the organization of their communities and workplaces. Pragmatic and wise enough to surround himself with competent advisers, he took pains to construct an important international role for Yugoslavia, gaining in turn favors from the West and the Soviets. He was, along with Jawaharlal Nehru and Gamal Abdel Nasser, one of the architects of the nonaligned movement. Fostering the development of the cult of his personality, he scheduled Youth Day to coincide with his birthday, May 25. In the realm of internal policy, the absence of a satisfactory national policy compounded by an authoritarian regime contributed to the progressive but irreversible dismantling of Yugoslavia, and put into doubt the veracity of the Yugoslav slogan, "After Tito—Tito."

When he died in May 1980, this charismatic individual of eighty-eight had no successor. Most of his prewar colleagues, including Evard Kardelj and Vladimir Bakarić, were dead or like Milovan Djilas and Aleksandar Ranković, had fallen into disgrace. The collective presidency, which Tito had crafted, functioned for a while, but his Socialist Federal Republic of Yugoslav did not long survive his death.

BIBLIOGRAPHY

Lindsay, Franklin, and John Kenneth Galbraith. *Beacons in the Night: With the OSS and Tito's Partisans in Wartime Yugoslavia.* Stanford, Calif.: Stanford University Press, 1993.

Pavlowitch, Stevan K. *Tito, Yugoslavia's Great Dictator: A Reassessment.* Columbus: Ohio State University Press, 1992.

Catherine Lutard
(Tr. by B. Cook)

SEE ALSO Yugoslavia

Todorov, Stanko (1920–96)

Bulgarian prime minister, 1971–1981. Stanko Todorov was born in the Bulgarian village of Klenovik (Kolosh) in the district of Pernik on December 10, 1920. In 1936 he became a member of the Union of the Revolutionary Youth (URY), and in 1943 he joined the Bulgarian Communist Party. While a soldier in the Bulgarian army he participated in the organization of illegal URY groups. In 1943, Todorov deserted the army and worked with the Sofia District Committee of the URY to organize combat groups. In February 1944, during a skirmish with the police, he was wounded, arrested, and imprisoned, but he succeeded in escaping. Todorov participated in the preparation for and the execution of a coup d'état against the new neutralist government of Kosta Muraview of the Agrarian Union Party, on September 9, 1944. From the end of 1944 until 1947 he worked in the Sofia District Committee of URY and in its Central Committee (CC). From 1947 until 1950 he was secretary of the CC of the Union of the People's Youth (UPY). From February to October 1950 he was secretary of the Sofia District Committee of the BCP, and then first secretary of the Bourgas District Committee of the BCP; from January to August 1952, he was chief of the Agricultural Department of the CC of the BCP, and he served as minister of agriculture (1952–57). At the Sixth Congress of the BCP in 1954, Todorov became a member of the CC; in 1957 secretary of the CC; and in 1959 a member-candidate of the Politburo of the CC of the BCP and vice-chairman of the Council of Ministers of the People's Republic of Bulgaria. From 1959 to 1962, he was chairman of the Commission for State Planning. At the November 1961 Plenum of the CC, Todorov was elected a member of the Politburo of the CC of BCP. From the beginning of 1960 until 1966, he was the permanent representative of Bulgaria in the Council for Mutual Economic Support. In 1966 he became secretary of the CC of the BCP. In 1971, when Todor Zhivkov became president of the State Council, Todorov became chairman of the Council of Ministers. On June 16, 1981, he was replaced by Grisha Filipov, who was prime minister until 1986 when he was replaced by Georgi Atanasov. As pressure for change grew, Todorov was among the proponents of reform on the Politburo who toppled Zhivkov in November 1989. Todorov served as acting president of Bulgaria from July 6 until July 17, 1990. He died on December 17, 1996.

BIBLIOGRAPHY

Crampton, R. J. A. *A Concise History of Bulgaria.* Cambridge, U.K.: Cambridge University Press, 1997.

Dimiter Minchev

Togliatti, Palmiro (1893–1964)

Leader of the Italian Communist Party (PCI). Palmiro Togliatti was born in Genoa, Italy, on March 26, 1893. Togliatti graduated with a degree in law from the University of Turin in 1915. He met Antonio Gramsci while studying in Turin and joined the Italian Socialist Party. Togliatti was influenced in turn by idealism, economic liberalism, Marxism, Leninism, and the *meridionalismo* ("Southernism" or the unique impact of an undeveloped peasant Southern Italy) of Gaetano Salvemini. He was a founder of *Ordine Nuovo* (New Order) in 1919 and of the PCI in 1921. He served on its central committee from 1922, and successfully opposed the maximalism of Antonio Bordiga in 1924. Togliatti escaped fascist repression by emigrating to the USSR. He was an active member of the Comintern and supported its shift to the left in 1929. During the Spanish Civil War (1937–39), he worked in support of the Spanish Republic in Algiers and Paris, where he was imprisoned for six months in 1939.

Togliatti returned to Italy in 1944. By expressing support for the monarchy, he facilitated the formation of the Pietro Badoglio government, in which he was minister without portfolio (April–June 1944), and of the Ivonoe Bonomi government, in which he was again minister without portfolio (June–December 1944). Togliatti began to edit *Rinascita* in June 1944. He was deputy prime minister in the second Bonomi government (December 1944–June 1945), and minister of justice in the Ferruccio Parri government (December 1945–July 1946).

His strategy, which he spelled out for the PCI at that time, contradicted three fundamental principles of Leninism. Togliatti's idea of progressive democracy, or post-parliamentary democracy, precluded any proximate move to socialism; his advocacy of a "new party" was designed to reinforce an alliance with the middle classes of Italy; and he finally rejected the establishment of a revolutionary state based on the dictatorship of a single class.

Togliatti was a deputy in the Constituent Assembly (1946) and was elected to the Chamber of Deputies (1948), where he continued to serve until his death in 1964. After the Twentieth Party Congress of the Communist Party of the Soviet Union, Togliatti argued against the inevitability of war; he criticized the Soviet Union; and he declared the integral commitment of the PCI to the Italian constitution (VIII Congress of PCI, December 1956). He affirmed PCI's opposition to the center-left coalition following the Christian Democrats' "Opening to the Left", when the Christian Democrats and the Socialist Party joined in a common program (1958) and eventually a coalition government (1963), and he called for a dialogue with the Chinese Communists in 1962. His essays include *Politica comunista* (Communist Politics) (1945); *A. Gramsci* (1955); *Discorsi alla Costituente* (Speechs in the Constituent Assembly) (1958); *Il Partito comunista italiano* (The Italian Communist Party) (1958); *Momenti della storia d'Italia* (Moments in the History of Italy) (1963); *La via italiana al socialismo* (The Italian Road to Socialism) (1964); and the posthumous *Sul movimento operaio internazionale* (On the International Workers' Movement) (1965) and *Comunisti e cattolici* (Communists and Catholics) (1965).

BIBLIOGRAPHY

Agosti, Aldo. *Palmiro Togliatti.* Turin: UTET, 1996.

Togliatti, Palmiro. *Opere Scelte* (Selected Works). Rome: Editori Riuniti, 1974.

Vacca, Giuseppe. *Togliatti sconosciuto* (The Unknown Togliatti). Rome: Editori Riuniti, 1994.

Adalgisa Efficace

Tomášek, František (1899–1992)

Archbishop of Prague, 1977–1991. Frantisek Tomášek was born into a peasant family in Studénka, Moravia, near the Polish frontier, on June 30, 1899. He was ordained a Catholic priest in 1922. He received two doctorates from the Theological Faculty of Saints Cyril and Methodius in Olomouc. He taught there before its suppression by the Nazis in 1940 and again before it was closed by the Communists in 1948. He was consecrated bishop of Olomouc in 1949, but shortly afterward was condemned to a labor camp. After his release from imprisonment in 1954, Tomášek served as a parish priest.

Tomášek was the only Czechoslovak bishop allowed to attend the Vatican Council. Josef Cardinal Beran, the archbishop of Prague, who had been confined in monasteries by the Communists since 1949, was exiled to Rome in 1965. When Beran was forbidden to return to Prague by the Communist authorities, Tomášek was appointed by the Vatican to administer the diocese. Tomášek supported the attempt to liberalize Communism, the Prague Spring of Alexander Dubček in 1968, and appealed for religious liberty for Czechoslovakia. After the suppression of the reforms in August 1968, Tomášek continued to seek concessions from the Czechoslovak government, but he avoided clashes with it. His criticism of Catholic participation in the Charter 77 human rights campaign, which took the Czechoslovak government to task for its failure to adhere to the human rights provisions of the 1975 Helsinki Accord, dismayed dissident Catholic intellectuals and members of the clandestine church formed by priests forbidden by the regime to publicly exercise their ministry.

Tomášek was secretly made a cardinal in 1976, and his role as archbishop was publicly announced in 1977. Encouraged by the election of a fellow Slav, the Polish cardinal Karol Wojtyla, to the papacy in 1978, Tomášek condemned the government-sponsored and -controlled group of priests, *Pacem in Terris.* In 1988, Tomášek gave his support to a petition demanding religious freedom, which ultimately gained the signatures of 300,000 Czechoslovaks. His support of this successful protest is credited with contributing to the Velvet Revolution, the peaceful overthrow of Czechoslovakian Communism in December 1989. In December 1988 he announced his support for the "justified yearning of citizens to live in a free environment." On November 21, 1989, in a statement read to 150,000 demonstrators in Prague, Tomášek declared, "We are with you." On November 25, in the first mass televised in Czechoslovakia, Tomášek said, "In this historic moment in the fight for truth and justice, I and the Catholic Church are on the side of the people."

Tomášek retired on March 27, 1991, and died on August 4, 1992.

BIBLIOGRAPHY

Steinfels, Peter. "Cardinal Tomášek Is Dead." *New York Times,* August 5, 1992.

Bernard Cook

Tomaszewski, Henryk (1924–)

Polish actor, dancer, choreographer, and director. Henryk Tomaszewski, born on November 20, 1924, graduated from the Drama Studio of I. Gall and the Ballet Studio of F. Parnell. From 1949 to 1954 he worked as a dancer in the Wroclaw Opera Ballet. He then formed his own Pantomime Studio in the Polish Theater in Wrocław. In 1958 this became the Wrocław Pantomime Theater, and Tomaszewski was its managing director. The company gave performances in Europe, America, and Africa. For Tomaszewski the years 1956–65 were a period of experimenting with form and movement as a means of expression and search for inspiration in literature. Tomaszewski prepared *The Bell-ringer of Notre Dame,* based on Victor Hugo's *The Hunchback of Notre Dame; The Exchanged Heads,* based on Thomas Mann's *Transposed Head's: A Legend of India;* and *Woyzeck* based on Georg Büchner's drama. His later productions, such as *Marathon* and *The Post Office,* were no longer dominated by plot, but were characterized by "pure movement."

In 1965 the Pantomime Theater became a fully independent institution of visual art. Dramaturgy of movement became the basic raw material of the shows, which expressed through symbol the conflict between individual and society. The starting point was always movement of a group of mimes, stimulated and inspired by literature interpreted freely and according to the whims of imagination. The performances presented various pantomime styles, for which scene, music, and light were of equal importance.

Janusz Skuczyński

Toome, Indrek (1943–)

Prime minister of Estonia (1988–90). Indrek Toome was an important political figure in Estonia's transition to independence in the late 1980s, but he was replaced by more radical leaders, and he dropped out of politics in the early 1990s to enter private business.

Toome had an orthodox career as a Communist official, joining the Communist Party (CP) in 1973 and holding senior party and government positions in Soviet Estonia, among them first secretary of the Estonian Komsomol (Communist Youth Organization), deputy prime minister (1984–87), and ideology secretary (1988). In June 1988 he played a part in the Kremlin's dismissal of the reactionary Estonian CP First Secretary, Karl Vaino, and in November he became prime minister upon the resignation of Bruno Saul.

Toome was one of the few Communist leaders to attend reform meetings in 1988. He established his reform and nationalist credentials by supporting the endorsement by the supreme council in November of the plan, initially supported by Mikhail Gorbachev, for Estonian economic sovereignty (Ise-Majandav Eesti, IME, Self-Managing Estonia), which Toome believed would pave the way for Estonian economic independence. He also backed the laws to make Estonian the official language of the country and to restrict the voting rights of recent immigrants, who were mainly Russians.

However, the increasingly nationalist and pro-independence mood in Estonia led to Popular Front victories in elections to the USSR Congress of People's Deputies in 1989 and to the new Estonian Supreme Council in 1990, which replaced Toome with Edgar Savisaar as prime minister. When the Estonian CP split in 1989, many reform communists joined the Popular Front, but a number of senior party figures formed the Free Estonia group, which was chaired by Toome. This organization of former communists fought the 1992 parliamentary election as the Secure Home Party (Kindel Kodu) and obtained the second highest number of seats. By this time Toome had retired from politics for a business career. Unlike his colleague Arnold Rüutel, he seemed unwilling or unable to adjust to the politics of an independent Estonia. In 1994 he was arrested for allegedly bribing a security policeman to recover the confiscated passports of business associates.

BIBLIOGRAPHY

Lieven, Anatol. *The Baltic Revolution: Estonian, Latvia, Lithuania and the Path to Independence.* New Haven: Yale University Press, 1983.

Norgaard, Ole, et al. *The Baltic States after Independence.* Cheltenham: Edward Elgar, 1996.

Smith, Graham, ed. *The Baltic States: The National Self-Determination of Estonia, Latvia and Lithuania.* Basingstoke: Macmillan, 1994.

Taagepera, Rein. *Estonia: Return to Independence.* Boulder: Westview, 1993.

Thomas Lane

SEE ALSO Estonia; Rüutel, Arnold

Tourism

During the 1920s, an average of a quarter of a million American tourists, businessmen, and expatriates flocked to Europe each year. Many of them were attracted more by the strength of the American dollar in Europe than by the artifacts of Old World culture. American tourism to Europe resumed after the end of World War II; more and more Americans swarmed into Europe as countries that suffered heavy destruction in the war began to rebuild their cities and restore their monuments. For most American travelers, it was a chance to rediscover Europe. Tourism, in turn, had a positive impact upon the economies of the countries being visited. The negative side that developed among Europeans was an anti-Americanism that was heightened by U.S. tourists who were perceived as unappreciative and ignorant of other cultures. The "American tourist," with his or her various quirks and personalities as well as enthusiasm became a stereotypical character.

When World II ended, some well-known Americans went to Europe as temporary (or sometimes permanent) residents: American writers in postwar Europe included Gore Vidal, Tennessee Williams, Truman Capote, Ralph Ellison, and Mary McCarthy. Paris was Richard Wright's permanent home as well as an intermittent refuge for James Baldwin. From 1948 to 1950, Saul Bellow resided in Paris on a Guggenheim fellowship.

Americans in temporary residence in Europe reproduced the kinds of institutions that they knew from home, such as American-run churches, schools, hospitals and medical clinics, newspapers, university alumni associations, and sporting events. However, Europeans sometimes reacted with hostility, accusing American tourists of being loud, arrogant, materialistic, and provincial. The combined effect of American exports, investments, and tourism led many Europeans to define the meaning of Americanism and Americanization in negative terms. According to Richard Pells's *Not Like Us,* Rome in the 1950s developed what was, in effect, an American ghetto, with American newspapers, magazines, and posters that advertised American movies along with expensive, American-style hotels, American cocktail bars, gasoline stations, fast-food restaurants and, at its center, the American Embassy, an "American Rome." The negative aspect of this situation was the resentment of Americans by Europeans and the inability of Americans to appreciate foreign cultures.

However, the U.S. government made serious attempts to use this Americanization to boost its own tourist industry. In 1974, the United States Information Agency (USIA) implemented a tourist promotion program for its overseas posts to encourage trade and tourism in the United States to help improve the U.S. balance of payments. The next year, in an attempt to promote tourism in the United States by foreign citizens, USIA produced 60-second spots for foreign television that targeted gateway cities, such as Miami and New Orleans, which were considered prime cities for prospective tourists.

Because of the growth of tourism, American lawyers compiled a code of ethics for the tourism industry while other countries, such as Australia, New Zealand, and the members of the European Community, worked to develop their own tourism codes, possibly based on an American model. In an attempt to establish guidelines and regulations, the World Tourism Organization (WTO) was established. It started in 1925 as the International Union of Official Tourist Publicity Organization, set up in The Hague, Netherlands. It was renamed International Union for Official Tourism Organizations (IUOTO) after World War II and moved to Geneva, Switzerland. In 1970, IUOTO became the World Tourism Organization (WTO), headquartered in Madrid. IUOTO, an inter-governmental body of the United Nations, is the leading international organization in the field of travel and tourism; it serves as a global forum for tourism policy issues and a practical source of tourism expertise. Its membership includes 138 countries and territories along with 350 affiliate members representing local government, tourism associations, and private sector companies, including airlines, hotel groups, and tour operators.

In 1983, the United States took the lead in establishing an "open borders" travel and tourism policy among all nations. The policy was promoted by the United States Tour Operators Association, which recognized that the outbound and overseas travel operations of U.S. firms as well as inbound and domestic travel services are essential for maintaining American competitiveness in a globalized economy.

BIBLIOGRAPHY

Ashworth, G. J., and P. J. Larkham, eds. *Building a New Heritage: Tourism, Culture, and Identity in the New Europe.* London: Routledge, 1994.

Boissevain, Jeremy, ed. *Coping With Tourists: European Reactions to Mass Tourism.* Providence, R.I.: Berghahn, 1996.

Montanari, Armando, and Allan M. Williams, eds. *European Tourism: Regions, Spaces, and Restructuring.* New York: Wiley, 1995.

Pells, Richard. *Not Like Us: How Europeans Have Loved, Hated, and Transformed American Culture Since World War II.* New York: BasicBooks, 1997.

Richards, Greg, ed. *Cultural Tourism in Europe.* Wallingford, U.K.: CAB International, 1996.

Martin J. Manning

Trade Fair

Temporary market or commercial enterprise, organized to promote trade, where buyers and sellers gather to transact business, that assumed an increasingly important role in international trade during the twentieth century. Trade fairs are organized at regular intervals, generally at the same location and time of year, and usually last for several weeks. In Europe and Asia, they are very popular; nearly every country on these continents holds at least one major annual international exposition for one industry or branch of industrial production or for general exhibits of goods and merchandise.

More than seven hundred trade fairs are held each year, especially in Europe, and they provide access for American corporations to a market of over $3 trillion, which buys over $80 billion in U.S. goods and services annually. Among the most familiar are the Paris Air Show, which displays the latest in aviation technology; the Hannover Fair, perhaps the world's largest industrial show; and the International Spring Gift Fair at Birmingham, England, that country's largest consumer-products trade show. Other well-known commercial fairs are the Leipzig Fair, the Swiss Industries Fair, the International Trade Fair of Thessaloníki, the Zagreb International Trade Fair, and the Paris International Fair. Some popular specialized fairs include the International Textile and Clothing Industry Exhibition in Ghent, Belgium, and the International Furniture Fair in Cologne, as well as the Frankfurt Book Fair, the Nuremberg Toy Fair, and the Berlin Tourism and Travel Fair.

Most of the first-class international trade fairs are held in Germany, whose economy is dependent on them; they grew out of the medieval fairs, and actual business transactions are the central component.

BIBLIOGRAPHY

Auger, Hugh A. *Trade Fairs and Exhibitions.* London: Business Publications, 1967.

Cartwright, Gillian. *Making the Most of Trade Exhibitions.* Oxford and Boston: Butterworth Heinemann, 1995.

Martin J. Manning

Transcarpathia

An oblast, or province, located in far western Ukraine along its borders with Slovakia, Hungary, and Romania. The province has been known by several names in the past, including Carpatho-Russia, Carpatho-Ruthenia, Carpatho-Ukraine, and Subcarpathian Rus'. It covers 12,800 sq km, and according to the 1989 census had a population of 1,246,000. The population is ethnically diverse, including Ukrainians, also known as Ruthenians/Rusyns (78.4 percent), Hungarians (12.5 percent), Russians (4 percent), and Romanians (2.4 percent). Nearly 60 percent of the population lives in rural areas, usually small villages whose inhabitants are engaged in small-scale farming, sheepherding, and forestry. Industrial enterprises were for the most part established after 1945 and include machine-building, lumbering and forest products, building materials, and food processing.

The vast majority of the population is comprised of East Slavs, whether they be indigenous inhabitants (Rusyns or Ruthenians) or newcomers from other parts of Ukraine and Russia who settled there after 1945. The Hungarian and Romanian populations in the southern part of Transcarpathia are minorities who are culturally and linguistically related to the state nationalities in neighboring Hungary and Romania. In the past there was also a sizable Hasidic Jewish minority living in the region's cities and towns as well as in rural villages, but this community was almost entirely destroyed during World War II. The most important religions are Greek (Uniate) Catholicism and Orthodoxy, although there is also a Roman Catholic and Reformed Calvinist presence (among the Hungarians) and a Baptist and other evangelical minority (among the Russians and the indigenous Rusyns).

Transcarpathia has never had political independence, although it has enjoyed at various times autonomous status, in particular in the twentieth century. For most of its existence, from the eleventh century to 1918, Transcarpathia was an integral part of the kingdom of Hungary, which in turn had by the early eighteenth century become part of the Habsburg Austrian, later Austro-Hungarian, Empire.

Following the fall of Austria-Hungary in October 1918, Transcarpathia was incorporated into the new state of Czechoslovakia. Known at the time as Subcarpathian Rus', it was guaranteed autonomy by two of the treaties concluded at the Paris Peace Conference (Saint-Germain in 1919 and Trianon in 1920). In practice, the Czechoslovak government granted it only limited self-rule until the fall of 1938, when, following the Munich Pact, Subcarpathia Rus' (soon to be renamed Carpatho-Ukraine) formed its own government and elected a parliament. Full Subcarpathian autonomy was short-lived, however. As part of Adolf Hitler's dismantling of Czechoslovakia, Germany's ally Hungary was permitted to invade and annex Subcarpathian Rus' in March 1939. Renewed Hungarian rule lasted until the arrival of the Soviet Red Army in September 1944.

Initially, the Soviet Union and other allied powers agreed to restore Subcarpathian Rus' as part of Czechoslovakia. However, the Soviet authorities, backed by the Red Army, organized a campaign whereby in November 1944 the local population "voluntarily" declared its desire to "reunite" with "mother Ukraine." The province's name was changed to Transcarpathia, and on June 29, 1945, Czechoslovakia formally ceded the region to the Soviet Union. In January 1946 it became the Transcarpathian oblast of the Ukrainian Socialist Soviet Republic.

The Soviets brought to Transcarpathia centralized rule dictated by a centrally directed, state-controlled, command economy. This included the abolition of all political organizations except the Communist Party; the nationalization of land, industry, and private property; and the undermining of traditional cultural values, including the forcible dissolution of the Greek Catholic Church. The Soviets also tried to resolve the nationality question.

Ever since the national revival during the second half of the nineteenth century, local leaders had remained divided over whether the East Slavic majority of the population should be considered Russian, Ukrainian, or a distinct Rusyn nationality. After 1945, the Soviets banned any idea of a Rusyn nationality and administratively classified all the indigenous East Slavs as Ukrainians. However, when Soviet rule began to weaken after 1989 and eventually ended two years later, Transcarpathia witnessed calls for the legalization of a Rusyn nationality and for the reinstitution of autonomy. As part of the referendum on Ukrainian independence held on December 1, 1991, over 78 percent of the province's inhabitants voted for autonomy (self-rule) within an independent Ukraine. To date, the government of Ukraine has neither granted autonomy nor recognized a Rusyn nationality. The autonomy and nationality questions, together with the general economic crisis that plagues all former Soviet lands, are the main problems that continue to dominate life in Transcarpathia.

BIBLIOGRAPHY

Hranchak, Ivan, ed. *Narysy istorii Zakarpattia, Vol. I: z naidavnishykh chasiv do 1918 roku.* Uzhhorod: Uzhhorods'kyi derzhavnyi universystet/Instytut karpatoznavstva, 1993.

Istoriia mist i sil Ukrains' koi RSR; Zakarpats'ka oblast'. Kiev: Ukraïns'ka radians'ka entsyklopediia AN URSR, 1969.

Magocsi, Paul Robert. *Carpatho-Rusyn Studies: An Annotated Bibliography,* Vol. I: 1975–1984. New York: Garland, 1988.

———. *The Shaping of a National Identity: Subcarpathian Rus', 1848–1948.* Cambridge: Harvard University Press, 1978.

Pekar, Athanasius B. *The History of the Church in Carpathian Rus'.* New York: Columbia University Press/East European Quarterly, 1992.

Paul Robert Magocsi

Transnistrian Moldovan Republic

Unrecognized republic established in the eastern portion of the Republic of Moldova on September 2, 1990. The Transnistrian Moldovan Republic (PMR) (Russian: Pridnestrovskaia Moldavskaia Respublika, PMR; Romanian: Republica Moldoveneasca Nistreana) (Also known in English as the Dniester Republic or Transdniester) consists of six counties (raions) of the former Moldovan Soviet Socialist Republic (MSSR), plus the city of Tiraspol, located east of the Dniester River. These counties have a total area of 4,118 sq km and a population of 546,000 (12 percent of Moldova's total land area, and 13 percent of its total population). According to the 1989 Soviet census, the major ethnic groups included Moldovans/Romanians (40 percent), Ukrainians (28 percent), and Russians (25 percent). The PMR leadership, centered in Tiraspol, also claims some territory to the west of the Dniester, including the city of Bender with 138,000 inhabitants, of whom 42 percent are Russian, 30 percent Moldovan/Romanian, and 18 percent Ukrainian.

After 1990 the PMR established an array of local institutions, including a presidency, legislative assembly (Supreme Soviet), and army (Dniester Guards) separate from those of the central Moldovan government. In 1995 the PMR introduced its own currency, the PMR ruble, known colloquially as the suvorov, after the picture of the Russian military leader whose image appears on the bills. Rampant inflation in the PMR made it virtually worthless. Whereas in the rest of Moldova, democratization and economic reform took root after the breakup of the Soviet Union, local authorities in the PMR continued to call for a return of the Soviet state or, failing that, integration of the region into the Russian Federation. Despite the active involvement of the Organization for Security and Cooperation in Europe (OSCE) as a mediator in the dispute, Moldova remained a divided state.

BIBLIOGRAPHY

Helsinki Watch. *Human Rights in Moldova: The Turbulent Dniester.* New York: Human Rights Watch, 1993.

King, Charles. *Post-Soviet Moldova: A Borderland in Transition.* London: Royal Institute of International Affairs, 1995.

Kolsto, Pal, and Andrei Edemsky with Natalya Kalashnikova. "The Dniester Conflict: Between Irredentism and Separatism." *Europe-Asia Studies* 45, no. 6 (1993), 973–1000.

Charles King

SEE ALSO Bessarabia; Lebed, Aleksandr Ivanovich; Moldova; Smirnov, Igor Nikolaevich

Transylvania

Region bounded by the Carpathian Mountains to the north and east, the Transylvanian Alps to the south, and the Apuseni Mountains to the west, and located within present-day Romania. The neighboring Romanian areas of Maramures, Crisana, and Banat are sometimes also considered part of Transylvania. It is an area of some 21,000 square miles. Major rivers include the Mures, Somes, and the Olt, which flow either west toward the Tisza or south toward the Danube. Major cities include Cluj-Napoca (Kolozsvár, pop. 330,000), Sibiu (Hermannstadt, 188,000), Brasov (Kronstadt, 364,000), and Tirgu-Mures (Marosvásárhely, 172,000).

The region's name, (Romanian: *Transilvania* or *Ardeal:* Hungarian: *Erdély;* German: *Siebenbergen*)—literally, the land beyond the forest (Latin, *Transsilvania*)—first appeared in written documents in the twelfth century. It formed the center of the ancient kingdom of the Getae (Dacii) from roughly the first century B.C. to the first century A.D. From the Roman conquest (A.D. 106) to the withdrawal of the Roman legions (A.D. 270), it formed part of the Roman province of Dacia. After the removal of Roman troops, the indigenous population either retreated into the mountains or migrated southward beyond the Danube. Hungarian and Romanian historians differ over the fate of the Latinized communities left behind after the retreat of the Roman legions. Magyars (Hungarians) moved into the region over the next six hundred years.

In 1003, Stephen I of Hungary established control over the region and introduced Székely (Szeklers, a group related to the Magyars) and German Saxons into the region to encourage local development and to serve as border guards. Transylvania developed its own autonomous status within the Hungarian kingdom, and after the defeat of the Hungarians by the Turks at the Battle of Mohács in 1526, Transylvania became a fully autonomous entity subject to Turkish suzerainty. In the seventeenth century, under the powerful Báthory dynasty, the Transylvanians managed to retain their autonomous status situated between Hungary and the Ottoman Empire. But with the defeat of the Turks during their second siege of Vienna in 1683, Transylvania came under the sway of the Habsburgs. Under the Treaty of Carlowitz in 1699, the Turks recognized Habsburg control over Transylvania, and by 1711 the region had become a part of the Hungarian portion of the Habsburg empire.

A strong movement for magyarization developed throughout the eighteenth and early nineteenth centuries, and many of the traditional social structures that had developed during the period of autonomy, such as the power of the Szekler and Saxon nobles, began to disappear. The local Romanian population also began to agitate for full political and cultural rights, since the Magyars, Szeklers, and Saxons were the only communities recognized as "privileged nations." The Hungarian Revolution of 1848 further divided communities in Transylvania, with the Magyars supporting the revolutionaries and the local Romanians taking the side of the Habsburgs. After the revolution, Transylvania was removed from Hungarian control and became a separate Habsburg crown land and, later, an autonomous province, with the local Romanians arguing for full political rights as the "fourth nation" of Transylvania. But after the Ausgleich (Compromise) of 1867, Transylvania once again came under the direct control of Budapest, and a policy of full-scale magyarization was launched.

With the demise of Austria-Hungary after the First World War, local Romanians proclaimed the region's unification with Romania at Alba Iulia on December 1, 1918. Despite Hungarian protests, the region was recognized as part of Romania under the Treaty of Trianon in 1920. Portions of northern Transylvania once again came under Hungarian control as a result of the Vienna Diktat of 1940, but were returned to Romania as part of the postwar peace settlement in 1947. Tensions over Transylvania existed between Hungary and Romania throughout the communist period. A small Hungarian Autonomous Region was created in central Transylvania in 1952, but its powers were strictly limited, and it was eventually eliminated in 1968. The Romanian government encouraged the settlement of ethnic Romanians in Transylvania, diluting the region's Hungarian component.

In the 1980s, Hungary launched numerous protests against the treatment of local ethnic Hungarian communities by the regime of Nicolae Ceausescu. The anticommunist revolution of December 1989 began with protests in the city of Timisoara in support of an outspoken ethnic Hungarian minister, Lászlo Tökés, and his efforts to resist dismissal from his post by the Romanian authorities. The protests were met with violence by Romanian security forces, and news of the atrocities in Timisoara galvanized support for anti-Ceausescu demonstrations in Bucharest.

Relations between Romanians and Hungarians in Transylvania remained the subject of serious concern even after the demise of communism. Hungarians accounted for 7.9 percent of the total Romanian population in the 1977 census, and 7.1 percent in 1992, totaling some 1.6 million in the latter year. Most Hungarians were concentrated in Transylvania, in the counties of Harghita, Covasna, Mures, Satu-Mare, and Bihor. In Transylvania as a whole, Hungarians formed approximately a quarter of the population, although Hungarian leaders contended that these figures were too low. Communal violence in Tirgu-Mures in March 1990 and the refusal of local officials in Cluj-Napoca and other cities to allow multilingual street signs created an atmosphere of confrontation between local Romanians and Hungarians throughout the 1990s. On the international level, however, relations between Hungary and Romania improved considerably, with the two countries signing a bilateral treaty in 1996 that renounced any mutual territorial claims and committed both sides to respecting the rights of ethnic minorities. Moreover, the appointment of two ministers from the main Hungarian political organization, the Democratic Union of Hungarians in Romania, after the November 1996 parliamentary elections represented an improvement in intercommunal relations in the country.

BIBLIOGRAPHY

Gallagher, Tom. *Romania after Ceausescu.* Edinburgh: Edinburgh University Press, 1995.

Hitchins, Keith. *Orthodoxy and Nationality: Andrei Saguna and the Rumanians of Transylvania, 1846–1873.* Cambridge: Harvard University Press, 1977.

———. *The Rumanian National Movement in Transylvania.* Cambridge: Harvard University Press, 1969.

Kligman, Gail. *The Wedding of the Dead: Ritual, Poetics and Popular Culture in Transylvania.* Berkeley: University of California Press, 1988.

Macartney, C. A. *A History of Hungary, 1929–1945.* New York: Praeger, 1956.

———. *Hungary and Her Successors: The Treaty of Trianon and Its Consequences, 1919–1937.* New York: Oxford University Press, 1937.

———. *The Habsburg Empire, 1790–1918.* New York: Macmillan, 1969.

Verdery, Katherine. *Transylvanian Villagers: Three Centuries of Political, Economic, and Ethnic Change.* Berkeley: University of California Press, 1983.

Charles King

SEE ALSO Hungary; Romania; Timosoara

Travkin, Nikolai Ilyich (1946–)

Russian politician. Nikolai Ilyich Travkin, born on March 19, 1946, trained as a builder. He completed a correspondence course from the Kolomenskiy State Pedagogical Institute in physics and mathematics. In 1970 he joined the Communist Party of the Soviet Union (CPSU). In 1988–89 he attended the Advanced Party School in Moscow. He was elected to the Supreme Soviet of the Soviet Union in 1989 as a representative of Shchelkovskiy in the Moscow oblast. In 1990 he was elected to the Supreme Soviet of the Russian Soviet Federated Socialist Republic. There he joined the Reform Coalition bloc and became a member of the Democratic Platform of the CPSU. In March 1990, however, he withdrew from the CPSU and joined the CPSU Democratic Party. In May the party dropped all pretexts of continuity with the Communist Party and was formally established as the Democratic Party of Russia, with Travkin as its chairman. The party combined nationalism and populism, complaining about the impact upon Russian consumers of the decontrol of prices. The following April, the party splintered as members protested that Travkin's rule was neo-Bolshevist. Travkin continued to head the Democratic Party, but he failed to rally the support of democratic elements in Russia. In December 1991, Travkin was appointed chief administrator of his home Shakhovskiy region. In 1992 he was defeated as party chairman of the Democratic Party, which then joined the Civic Union. In September 1993, because of opposition to Aleksander Rutskoi, the partisans of the Democratic Party withdrew from the Civic Union. In October, Travkin supported President Boris Yeltsin's suppression of the legislature. He was elected to the Duma in December 1993 and was reelected in 1995 as a representative of the pro-Yeltsin Our Home is Russia party. From 1994–96 he served as minister without portfolio in the government of Prime Minister Viktor Chernomyrdin.

Bernard Cook

Trimble, David (1944–)

Ulster Unionist Party (UUP) leader (1995–); MP for Upper Bann (1990–); First Minister, Northern Ireland Assembly (1999–). David Trimble was born on October 15, 1944, in Belfast. He trained as a barrister and was a law lecturer at Queen's University, Belfast, from 1977 to 1990. He became deputy leader of the Vanguard Unionist Progressive Party (VUPP) in 1973, and when it was disbanded as a political party in 1978, he joined the Ulster Unionist Party (UUP). As a member of both the VUPP and the UUP, he argued for devolved government for Northern Ireland, which had been directly ruled by Britain since 1972. He became the surprise leader of the UUP in 1995, when he won the support of the party rank and file. His high-profile stance in support of the Orange Order marchers at Drumcree during the summer, when he supported their march down Garvaghy Road in Portadown despite the opposition of the Catholic residents, had impressed the party faithful. Once he became leader of the party, however, he disregarded the wishes of some of the party members by meeting with leaders in the Irish Republic. He was a participant in multiparty peace talks and a supporter of the 1998 Good Friday Agreement, which called for a Northern Ireland Assembly in which Catholics and Protestants would share power. The agreement, however, split his party, with more than half of the parliamentary members opposing it. Nevertheless, Trimble became the first minister in the new Northern Ireland Assembly, which was set up in late 1999. Trimble shared the Nobel Peace Prize with David Hume in 1998.

Ricki Schoen

Trotta, Margarethe von (1942–)

Internationally known auteur of New German Cinema. Margarethe von Trotta has directed fifteen films and collaborated on others. In addition to directing, producing, and screen writing, von Trotta has also acted on television, stage, and in film, most notably in Rainir Werner Fassbinder's *Beware of a Holy Whore* (1971) and *Gods of the Plague* (1970), and Wim Wender's *The American Soldier* (1970).

Von Trotta's films address social ills and confront political injustices of modern Germany. In 1970, von Trotta wrote her first screenplay and co-directed her first film with Volker Schlöndorff, *The Sudden Wealth of the Poor People of Kronbach.* She then assisted Schlöndorff in directing *A Free Woman* (Moral der Ruth Halbfass, 1972), in which the protagonist seeks emancipation from her confining routines as a bourgeois housewife but does not anticipate the sacrifice and difficulties her actions will cost her.

Stylistically, von Trotta's films ascribe to a realist tradition that reflects her theatrical training. Her brand of narrative realism offers an uncompromising look at women struggling in a hostile, unaccommodating world. Despite the very real obstacles, her protagonists actively define their lives and identities, often with immense sacrifice.

Many of von Trotta's films feature a close bond between women. Her second film, *Sisters, or the Balance of Happiness* (1979), for example, portrays the different choices two sisters make in a world of male power. The younger sister, a student studying philosophy, commits suicide because of her unrealized desires, while her older sister sacrifices any semblance of a personal life to succeed as an executive's assistant.

Sheer Madness (1982) also addresses the complex ties that draw women together. This complex character study explores the connection between a successful college professor, Olga, and a troubled artist, Ruth. Opposites attract; and the two talented women forge a friendship subsequently broken by Ruth's domineering husband Franz.

The adaptation of Heinrich Böll's novel of the political persecution of a woman in Cold War Germany, *The Lost Honor of Katharina Blum* (1975), co-directed with Schlöndorff, catapulted von Trotta to international recognition. Katharina Blum is the victim of ruthless political and media slander. Despite the merciless judgment of patriarchy, Blum refuses to succumb to her expected social position. Like von Trotta's later features *The German Sisters* (1980) and *Rosa Luxemburg* (1985), her solo directorial debut in *The Second Awakening of Christa Klages* (1977) depicts a powerful true story of a social worker who robs a bank to secure the financial future for a daycare center about to go bankrupt. In the process, the protagonist, Christa, experiences a voyage of self-discovery and empowerment.

Die bleierne Zeit (Marianne and Julianne, 1981), a beautifully directed film about female agency and political change, centers on an intense sororial bond; each character responds differently to the resurgent political conservatism of Germany in the seventies. Julianne works as an editor at reforming the system, while her sister Marianne, a loosely based biographical composite of Gudrin Meinhof, joins the terrorist organization, the Red Army Faction (RAF), and is subsequently incarcerated. When Marianne turns up dead in prison, Juliane becomes obsessed with uncovering the facts. The film portrays her struggle to refute the official story of a collective suicide and demonstrate that Marianne's death was a government-directed murder. The controversial circumstances around the prison deaths of the three incarcerated RAF members remains a sore spot for German democracy.

Similarly, *Rosa Luxemburg* (1985) dramatizes the personal and political struggles of Spartacist leader Rosa Luxemburg. Luxemburg's passionate pursuit of justice during the early part of twentieth century caused her to be repeatedly imprisoned and eventually murdered.

The Promise (1995) is a metaphor for a now reunified Germany. Two lovers are separated while trying to escape from East to West Berlin in 1961. The film chronicles their three decades lives, which coincide with the life span of the Berlin Wall. A melodramatic recreation of historical events in the service of a love story, it remains the only major depiction of the effects of German reunification on the micro level.

Most recently, von Trotta has made a television drama, *The Winter Child* (1997), a drama of an unjustly imprisoned young Russian and her efforts to reclaim her son. *The Blue of Heaven,* on which von Trotta was working at the end of the century, features her and other notable German woman directors, Jutta Brückner, Regine Kuhn, Helke Misselwitz, Ulrike Ottinger, Helga Reidemeister, Helke Sander, and Ula Stöckl.

BIBLIOGRAPHY

Elsaesser, Thomas. *New German Cinema: A History.* New Brunswick: Rutgers University Press, 1989.

Fischetti, Renate. *Das neue Kino.* Frankfurt/Main: Tende, 1992.

Jill Gillespie

SEE ALSO Schlöndorff, Volker

Truffaut, François (1932–84)

Highly regarded French film director. François Truffaut was one of the key figures in the French New Wave (*Nouvelle Vague*) cinema of the late 1950s and early 1960s, a major movement that sought to break the established rules of filmmaking and introduce personal and adult themes to films. Truffaut (with cohorts Jean-Luc Godard and Claude Chabrol) began as a critic for the influential journal *Cahiers du Cinéma* under the tutelage of cinema's most renowned critic, André Bazin.

Truffaut, despite his relatively short life, was a prolific filmmaker; the films mentioned here are only his most prominent. His first feature, *The 400 Blows (Les quatre cents coups)* (1959), took the prize at Cannes for best director. This autobiographical film tells the story of a Parisian boy who finds no hope in his school or home life and winds up in reform school. In one of the most famous endings in film history, the boy escapes from the institution, runs to the sea, and in a final freeze-frame looks out at the audience. Typically for Truffaut, the film is more positive than the plot summary suggests.

Shoot the Piano Player (Tirez sur le pianist) (1960) is the tale of a concert pianist who fails to prevent his wife's suicide, and then seeks to bury himself as a barroom piano player in a poor Paris neighborhood. But he cannot withdraw; he becomes attached to a waitress in the bar, but she is killed by two unlikely mobsters out to get his brothers. The film is a lyrical, existential tragicomedy that pays homage to American gangster films.

Jules and Jim (Jules et Jim) (1961) is the bittersweet story of a femme fatale (Jeanne Moreau) and the two men in her life, set in the years before and after World War I. The cinematography is New Wave at its most dazzling and liberating, and the film is usually considered Truffaut's finest achievement.

Antoine Doinel, the hero of *The 400 Blows,* reappears in *Love at Twenty (L'amour à vingt ans)* (1962) and again in *Bed and Board (Domicile conjugale)* (1970), a sort of ongoing quasi-autobiography.

In Day for Night (La nuit Americaine) (1973)—the title refers to the American filmmaking practice of shooting night shots in daylight using a filter—Truffaut himself plays a filmmaker in the middle of shooting a film melodrama. Art and life mingle and collide, and as director he is called upon to solve aesthetic, practical, and personal problems. Truffaut's poem to his art is exhilarating; it stands out as one of the best films about making films.

BIBLIOGRAPHY

Allen, Don. *Finally Truffaut.* New York: Beaufort, 1986.

Insdorf, Annette. *Francois Truffaut.* Boston: Twayne, 1978.

Petrie, Graham. *The Cinema of Francois Truffaut.* New York: A. S. Baranes, 1970.

Truffaut, François. *The Films in My Life.* New York: Da Capo, 1994.

William M. Hammel

Truman Doctrine

Articulated by U.S. president Harry S. Truman in an address before a joint session of Congress on March 12, 1947, the Truman Doctrine marked a defining moment in the foreign policy of the United States during the period of the Cold War. It launched the policy of containment, containing the expansion of the USSR, by providing economic and military aid to Greece and Turkey.

Early in his presidency, and after a few initially uncertain steps, Truman and his advisers hit upon a strategy that would set the tone for the foreign policy, not only of his administration, but of the administrations of succeeding presidents for virtually the next half century. That strategy, and the Truman Doctrine that embodied it, was popularly known as *containment.* Developed in the postwar atmosphere of increasing tension between the U.S. and the USSR, containment aimed at thwarting what the White House assumed to be the primary objective of the Soviet Union: expansion, the ultimate goal of which was world domination. This expansionism, the Truman administration believed, would not necessarily involve military aggression, especially because the U.S. held an atomic monopoly. Instead, the Soviets would use infiltration and subversion. Thus, by late 1946 the Truman White House had grown increasingly suspicious of its World War II ally and concerned about communist expansion.

The Grand Alliance had, in fact, begun to unravel sometime before 1946. Indeed, within two weeks of becoming president, Truman had made his displeasure with Soviet actions in eastern Europe clear. He had summoned Soviet Foreign Minister Vyacheslav Molotov to protest what Truman claimed were repeated violations by the Soviet Union of the Yalta accords. Molotov took exception to Truman's tone, complaining, "I have never been talked to like that in my life." Truman reportedly replied, "Carry out your agreements, and you won't get talked to like that." In February 1946, Premier Joseph Stalin did some finger-pointing of his own when he delivered a speech citing "monopoly capitalism" as a cause of World War II, adding that it must be replaced to prevent future wars. A week later, Canadian authorities announced they had arrested twenty-two people for trying to steal atomic secrets for the Soviet Union.

A week after that (on February 22, 1946), the famous Long Telegram of George F. Kennan, minister-counselor of the American embassy in Moscow, arrived in the State Department. It provided an explanation for Soviet behavior to which the White House, if not yet Congress or the American people, was particularly receptive. According to Kennan, the history of Russia, and now the Soviet Union, was one of "Oriental despotism" in which "extremism was the normal form of rule and foreigners were expected to be mortal enemies." The Kremlin believed that there could be no permanent peace with the United States, wrote Kennan, and that "it is desirable and necessary that the internal harmony of our [U.S.] society be destroyed, the international authority of our state be broken . . . if Soviet power is to be secure." Soviet communism was but the most recent expression of Russian nationalism and imperialism, Kennan cabled, and that, coupled with its "traditional and instinctive sense of insecurity," meant that accords and agreements with the Soviet Union were of little value. The Russians "have learned to seek security only in patient but deadly struggle for the total destruction of rival power, never in compacts and compromises with it." While the telegram was widely distributed throughout the White House and the State Department, the implications of Kennan's argument were not widely understood either within or outside those offices. Kennan would later elaborate on his views in an article published in *Foreign Affairs* (July 1947) under the name "Mr. X." He called for what he had only hinted at in his telegram—a policy of containment of the Soviet Union.

A year earlier, in March 1946, Winston Churchill had entered the dialogue when he delivered his "iron curtain" speech at Westminster College in Missouri. Observing a now-divided Europe and warning of a Soviet Union that understood, and respected, only strength, especially military strength, Churchill was cheered by the crowd. His advice—military preparedness and an American-British alliance—was not as well received. In fact, American policy and popular opinion had been just the reverse. The U.S. armed forces by the end of 1946 had been reduced from 10 million to just over 1.3 million, distributed mostly at home or at occupation bases in Europe or Japan. The Soviets at that time had over 260 divisions. In the United States, the newly elected Republican Congress wanted demobilization, less government, lower taxes, and a de-emphasis on foreign entanglements. There was no stomach, nor even a perceived need, for confrontation with the Soviet Union. Besides, the United States had rebuilt its stock of atomic bombs to about a dozen, producing, some would later argue, more bang for the buck. On the left, former vice president Henry Wallace called for conciliation with the Soviets. Congress, along with the majority of Americans, and the White House were moving in opposite directions in foreign policy.

Then, in early 1947, a situation arose that presented an opportunity to put the Congress and the White House in greater sync. In February the British told Undersecretary of State Dean Acheson that they would have to pull out of Greece and Turkey because they could no longer maintain political stability there. The British had tried to restore a monarchy in Greece in 1944 after the Nazis had withdrawn. Leftists, aided by Communists, resisted. Now, even though the United States was providing some help, the British could not afford to continue to support the Greek government. Acheson and Secretary of State George C. Marshall both feared communist expansion into those areas, and both favored U.S. involvement, including military aid, to replace the British. President Truman agreed; Congress was another story. The Republican Congress generally opposed any increase in U.S. commitments to Europe.

Truman called congressional leaders, including the influential head of the Senate Foreign Relations Committee, Arthur Vandenberg of Michigan, to a meeting to hear the argument for intervention. Marshall presented the administration's position, but it was Acheson who made the case. Describing the situation in Greece as "Armageddon," Acheson spoke of the chain of events that would follow a communist takeover of Greece and Turkey. "Like apples in a barrel infected by one rotten one, the corruption of Greece would infect Iran and all to the East. It would also carry infection to spread throughout Asia Minor and Egypt, and to Europe through Italy and France. . . . " Only the United States, Acheson warned, was in a position to stop this Soviet-spread infection—and it must. Shaken—and convinced—by Acheson's presentation of what would later be known as the "domino theory," Vandenberg remarked to Truman on his way out of the room: "Mr. President, if that's what you want, there's only one way to get it. That is to make a personal appearance before Congress and scare the hell out of the country." Truman, in a speech Acheson helped draft, did just that.

On March 12, 1947, President Truman appeared before Congress to ask for support for Greece and Turkey as countries on the front line in the global battle to stop the spread of communism. Greece, he said, was vulnerable after the war. The communists were exploiting this situation, exacerbating the desperate economic conditions in Greece in an effort to bring down its democratic government. The Greek government needed help, Truman said, and the United States, which was already providing some aid, should give more. "Greece's neighbor, Turkey," he added, "also deserves our attention." No less was at stake there, he asserted, than "the preservation of order in the Middle East."

Truman then gave a stark choice: "At the present moment in world history," he declared, "nearly every nation must choose between alternative ways of life." According to Truman, that choice was to be free or totalitarian. Then he stated the principle of what would come to be known as the Truman Doctrine: "I believe that it must be the policy of the United States to support free peoples who are resisting attempted subjugation by armed minorities or by outside pressures." There would be grave consequences, he warned, describing a domino effect of falling countries, if the United States did not provide support. "Should we fail to aid Greece and Turkey in this fateful hour, the effect will be far reaching to the West as well as to the East." So he asked that Congress provide $400 million in aid to Greece and Turkey, as well as the civilian and military personnel required to achieve "economic stability and orderly political processes." Truman concluded with a challenge to the Congress and the American people: "The free peoples of the world look to us for support in maintaining their freedoms. If we falter in our leadership, we may endanger the peace of the world—and we shall surely endanger the welfare of our own nation."

Though there was some opposition to Truman's speech, Congress voted overwhelmingly in favor of his request. Truman had succeeded in redefining the U.S. role in foreign policy and the world in which it would operate. The United States, he had charged, must accept its post-World War II responsibility of leadership and, as appropriate, act to contain the expansionist Soviet Union. It was a call that would be answered by future presidents as well. Writing in 1972, Senator J. William Fulbright provided some insight into the effectiveness of Truman's 1947 speech: "More by far than any other factor the anti-communism of the Truman Doctrine has been the guiding spirit of American foreign policy since World War II."

BIBLIOGRAPHY

Ambrose, Stephen. *Rise to Globalism: American Foreign Policy Since 1938* 5th rev. ed. New York: Penguin, 1988.

Carroll, John M., and George C. Herring, eds. *Modern American Diplomacy.* Wilmington, DE: Scholarly Resources, 1986.

Gaddis, John. *Strategies of Containment: A Critical Appraisal of Postwar American National Security Policy.* New York: Oxford University Press, 1982.

LaFeber, Walter. *The American Age: U.S. Foreign Policy at Home and Abroad,* 2d ed., vol. II. New York: Norton, 1994.

Patterson, James T. *Grand Expectations: The United States, 1945–1974.* New York: Oxford University Press, 1996.

David W. Moore

Tudjman, Franjo (1922–99)

First president of the Republic of Croatia. Franjo Tudjman was born on May 14, 1922, in Veliko Trgovisce in the Croatian region of Zagorie. His father, Stjepan, was a leading member of the Croatian Peasant Party. His brother, Stjepan, was killed while engaged in the antifascist movement in 1943. His father, though a founder of the antifascist resistance in Croatia and a member of the Anti-fascist Council of the People's Liberation of Croatia (ZAVNOH) and the Anti-fascist Council of the People's Liberation of Yugoslavia (AVNOJ), was executed in 1946 because of his criticism of Tito's new Communist regime.

Tudjman, who supported himself during secondary school in Zagreb from 1934 to 1941 by tutoring, joined a political opposition group and was arrested briefly in 1940. In 1941 he joined the partisan movement, and in 1945 he was sent as a Croatian representative to the headquarters of the National Liberation Army (NOV) in Belgrade. He subsequently worked in the personnel office of the Ministry of Defense, for the Joint Chiefs of Staff of the Yugoslav National Army, and then on the editorial board of the Yugoslav *Military Encyclopedia.* He studied at the Higher Military Academy from 1955 to 1957. He was promoted to the rank of general in 1960, but he left active service in 1961 to concentrate on research and teaching. He founded the Institute of the History of the Worker's Movement in Zagreb in 1961, serving as its director until 1967. In 1963 he was appointed professor of political science at the University of Zagreb, and received a doctorate from that university in 1965.

In his writings he asserted that every nation must have its own armed forces to assure the right of territorial defense. Tudjman argued against the assertion of Croatia's collective guilt for the Ustasha regime. He also attempted to prove that the number of deaths ascribed to the Croatians at the death camp of Jasenovac was an exaggeration.

For these positions Tudjman was accused of being an anti-Marxist Croatian nationalist. He was expelled from the Communist Party in 1967 and forced out of his institute and the university. During the repression of Croatian dissidents in 1972, he was accused of having ties to Croatian émigré groups and was jailed. Due to Tito's intervention, his sentence was limited to two years, of which Tudjman served only nine months; however, he was sentenced to three years' imprisonment in 1981 for giving interviews to foreign journalists in which he expressed support for pluralist democracy. He was released from prison in February 1983 for medical reasons. He was reincarcerated in May 1984, but was released in September, again for health reasons. After his passport was restored in 1987, he traveled abroad speaking to Croatian émigrés. Building on his increasing support, Tudjman founded the Croatian Democratic Union (Hrvatska Demokratska Zajednica, HDZ) in 1989 and became its president. After the victory of his party in the first multiparty Croatian elections since the advent of communism, Tudjman was elected president of the parliamentary presidency on May 30, 1990. In November 1992 he was elected president of the Republic of Croatia in a direct presidential election. Under his leadership, Croatia first declared its sovereignty, and then successfully asserted its full independence on June 21, 1991. It gained the recognition of the European Union on January 15, 1992. Under Tudjman, Croatia developed a credible military and was able to regain control of the Serbian secessionist regions of Western Slavonija and Krajina in 1995.

Tudjman died on December 11, 1999. Though he was the founder of independent Croatia, the country's independence came at a high cost. Over 8,000 Croatians died and approximately 200,000 Croatians were forced from their homes during Croatia's war for independence in 1991–92. In 1995 the Croatian army drove 150,000 ethnic Serbs from Croatia. The Organization for Security and Cooperation in Europe criticized Tudjman government for its treatment of the country's remaining Serbs, for suppressing media freedom, and for failure to cooperate with the International Criminal Tribunal for the Former Yugoslavia at the Hague.

After Tudjman's death, Croatian voters repudiated his Croatian Democratic Union. On January 27, 2000, following parliamentary elections, Ivica Racan of the Social Democratic Party of Croatia became prime minister and on February 7, Stipe Mesic, who had opposed Tudjman's nationalist policies, was elected president.

BIBLIOGRAPHY

Glenny, Misha. *The Fall of Yugoslavia: The Third Balkan War.* Second Edition. New York: Penguin, 1997.

Tanner, Marcus. *Croatia: A Nation Forged in War.* New Haven: Yale University Press, 1999.

Bernard Cook

SEE ALSO Croatia; Croatia: Independence and War

Tudor, Corneliu Vadim (1949–)

Extreme nationalist Romanian politician and newspaper editor. Corneliu Vadim Tudor first came to prominence in the 1980s as a court poet of the Romanian national communist dictator, Nicolae Ceausescu. He published anti-Semitic and ultranationalist diatribes, which grew even bolder after Romania embarked upon a halting transition to democracy in 1989.

Tudor has been prominent in promoting the cult of Ion Antonescu, Romania's wartime military dictator, and in seeking to rehabilitate Ceausescu. He has used his connections with unreconstructed elements of the state bureaucracy, especially the secret police, to smear former dissidents. His platform is the weekly newspaper *România mâre* (Greater Romania), which he launched in 1991. In 1992 his Greater Romania Party won just over 3 percent of the vote, which enabled him to be elected to Parliament with a phalanx of supporters. Because Tudor held the balance of power, he was able to extract numerous concessions from the government party, with which he concluded a formal pact in January 1995. As well as becoming very wealthy, he has been made vice president of the Romanian senate, and despite his verbal extremism, he appears regularly on Romanian television.

Tom Gallagher

SEE ALSO Romania

Turco, Livia (1955–)

Italian politician. Livia Turco was born in Cuneo on February 13, 1955. In her youth, even though her family was deeply Catholic, she joined the Communist Youth Federation (Federazione Giovanile Comunista, FGCI). When she was eighteen, she moved to Turin and studied philosophy at the University of Turin. In Turin she was actively involved in the women's movement. From 1978 to 1982, she was provincial secretary of the FGCI, and she became the leader of the women's section of the PCI in Turin. However, Turco always sought to maintain ties to the church and to Catholic organizations. For a number of years she was a member of the Catholic Association of Italian Workers (ACLI) in Turin. She was involved in efforts to reform family law, to prevent abortion, to provide aid to mothers, to combat sexual violence, and to gain for women the right to work. She was elected to the municipal council of Turin and to the regional council of Piedmont.

In 1986, Turco was asked by Alessandro Natta, the secretary general of PCI, to become a member of PCI's national secretariat and to serve as the party's national leader for women. Turco campaigned to increase the presence and power of women in the institutions of society. Of particular concern to her was the reorganization of working life to make it more flexible and to bring it into harmony with the needs of family life and with the stages of life and obligations of women in the context of family. She called for the recognition of the social and economic value of the labor of women in the home. She continued to advocate maternal benefits and the rights of children, and campaigned against sexual violence. Her efforts bore some important fruit. In 1987 the number of women in Parliament rose from 7 to 10 percent, thanks largely to the PCI, which elected seventy women. Turco was among the new PCI deputies. Among her accomplishments are her promotion of the law for equal opportunity in work, subsidies for mothers, the increase of support to one-income families, and the law against rape.

When the PCI was transformed into the Democratic Party of the Left, Turco retained her membership in the party secretariat. Following the April 1996 election, she became a member of the council of ministers presiding over the Ministry of Family and Solidarity.

Bernard Cook

Turkey

A country that straddles Europe and Asia. Turkey has pursued a secular path since 1924, but it is still not welcomed by the EU. Recently its social, economic, and political problems have fostered the growth of Islamic fundamentalism.

In January 1913, during the first Balkan War, Enver Bey and Mehmed Talât Pasha led a coup against Sultan Abdul Hamid. The leaders of this coup, known as the

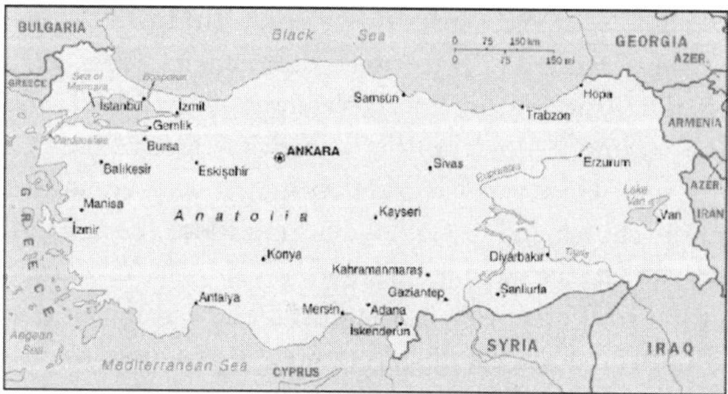

Turkey. *Illustration courtesy of Bernard Cook.*

Young Turks, wanted to modernize their country. Circumstances—including German hegemony at Constantinople, Britain's sequestration of two battleships ordered by Turkey that had been purchased by public subscription, and the arrival of two German warships, including the battle cruiser *Goeben*—all combined to bring Turkey into the First World War on the side of the Central Powers.

Turkey's defeat was the occasion for a revolution led by the military hero, Mustafa Kemal, the most important figure in modern Turkish history. Kemal led the nationalist movement against the partition of the defeated Ottoman Empire by the victorious Allies of World War I. He abolished the corrupt sultanate and rejected the Treaty of Sevres to which the sultan had agreed. Kemal waged a successful war against Greece, which was attempting to claim Turkish territory coast of A minor. On October 29, 1923, Turkey became a republic, with Kemal as its president. In 1934 he assumed the surname Atatürk ("father of the Turks").

Kemal's chief ambition was to make Turkey part of the West, and he did this through rapid and enforced Westernization. The basic tenet of Kemalism was the separation of religion and state. In 1924 the ruler's traditional position as Islamic religious leader was abolished, and religious instruction in the schools forbidden. Turkish replaced Arabic as the written language, and the traditional fez of Turkish males and the veil of women were banned. In addition, Islamic law was abolished in favor of a civil code modeled after that of Switzerland. Upon Atatürk's death in 1938, the leadership of the revolution and of the one political party, the People's Party, was inherited by his closest collaborator, the premier, Ismet Inönu, who was reelected president in 1943.

Perhaps in part because of its disastrous experience in the First World War, Turkey remained neutral during the Second World War. Its anxieties were divided between the advancing Germans and its old adversary, the Russians. The Turks were pro-Western and even nonbelligerent allies of the British; but, once the Germans controlled the Balkans, the Turks signed a treaty of friendship with them and agreed to economic concessions. After the tide of battle turned against the Axis, Turkey resumed its pro-Western position. The Turks were too concerned about the Russians, however, to join the war against the Germans.

The large Turkish army remained mobilized throughout the war and continued on a war footing for some time afterward, largely because of Russian pressures. Immediately after the war, Moscow tried to annex the two northeast Turkish provinces of Kars and Ardahan, which had long been in contention between the two states and had been Russian for a few decades before the First World War. The USSR also demanded a role in the defense of the Bosporus and Dardanelles. As a consequence, Turkey received the support of the United States and sizable economic and military aid, for the Truman Doctrine, although intended primarily for Greece, also covered Turkey.

In July 1952, Turkey joined the North Atlantic Treaty Organization (NATO). Largely to emphasize cooperation with the West, Turkey sent a 5,000-man brigade to fight in the Korean War. Nearly 15,000 Turks served in that war, and more than 900 of them died or were missing in action. Because of Turkey's strategic position, Turkish military cooperation and the establishment of American bases on its territory were regarded as vital to U.S. interests.

Internally, Turkey was the prototype of a developing nation struggling to achieve a Western economy and style of government. After the Second World War, Turkey embarked on the next logical step in its creation of a democratic parliamentary system when Inönu allowed the formation of a genuine second political party. The 1946 elections were held so abruptly, however, that the new Democratic Party, predecessor of the Justice Party, led by Celâl Bayar, lacked time to organize properly and was able to secure only 63 of 465 seats.

Four years later, in 1950, the Democratic Party was swept into power in a landslide victory, taking 408 seats to the 69 of the People's Party. Bayar became the president, and Adnan Menderes the premier, in the first transfer of power in Turkey since the founding of the republic in 1923. For the next decade the Democratic Party held power. It placed greater emphasis on private enterprise and civil liberties. This is ironic in view of what happened later.

Driven by the strong leadership of Menderes, the nation embarked on an overly ambitious economic development program. Agrarian reform had already been introduced by the previous regime, but the Menderes government continued to redistribute land by dividing up large estates, and government and ecclesiastical holdings. With the greater area cultivated and with modern methods of farming, production doubled over the next decade. Over 80 percent of the population was rural, and the benefits, including new roads, rural electrification, and tax breaks, gave the Democratic Party a powerful base in the countryside. Some state-owned industries were also privatized, and those remaining under state control were further developed. These included sugar refineries, cement plants, textile mills, and a large steel mill.

Development, however, produced deficits, debts, and inflation. Some $3 billion in U.S. aid and loans from Europe for massive construction projects drove up prices and the cost of living. This was particularly felt by the urban population. As its unpopularity increased in the cities, the Menderes government began to clamp down on political liberties. It won an easy election victory in 1954, but only repressive measures kept it in power thereafter. In 1957 all Turkish political parties combined to oppose the government. The government struck back by declaring this illegal and denying the opposition access to the media. At this point the Turkish army stepped in and, in May 1960, forcibly threw the cabinet out of office, a process it repeated in 1971 and in 1980. In all three cases, the Turkish army later voluntarily relinquished power.

In 1960 a national union committee, headed by General Cemal Gürsel and composed mostly of younger army officers, took power. The voters also approved a new constitution that set up a bicameral parliament and proportional representation. New elections gave the People's Party 173 of 450 seats in the new national assembly, and Ismet Inönu returned as premier to again try to put the country on an orderly path of political evolution. Unfortunately, proportional representation led to a proliferation of small parties in parliament and to a political stalemate. At first, the People's and Justice parties shared power in the Inönu government, but the chief concern of the Justice Party seemed to be securing amnesty for those in prison, and in 1962 a new Inönu ministry was formed of members of the People's Party and smaller political parties.

The government was plagued by the opposition of those who felt the revolution had lost momentum, including small landowners who favored the previous regime; by student riots; and by occasional coup attempts by junior military officers. Turkey also had chronic economic problems, including a large foreign debt of $1.2 billion, annual budget deficits, and lack of sources for new taxes. Appeals for foreign help brought some assistance, including a $100 million loan from a twelve-nation consortium. Turkey also gained some advantage from her 1963 admission as an associate member of the European Economic Community. Turkey's lack of internal development delayed full membership, however, and Turks resented this, as well as the feeling expressed rather openly by many Western Europeans that Turkey was an Asian and Moslem, rather than European, nation.

Complicating matters were deteriorating relations with Greece, especially over Cyprus. On occasion there was violence against Greeks still residing in Turkey as well as threats to expel all Greeks, including the patriarch of the

Greek Orthodox Church. The Turks also felt badly let down by the lack of support from their allies, especially the United States, after years of loyalty to NATO. By the mid-1960s, Turkey was distancing itself a bit from the United States and seeking improved ties with the Soviet Union.

Early in 1965 the Justice Party brought down the coalition government through a vote of no confidence, and for a second time Inönu, now in his eighties, stepped down peacefully in a transfer of power. Elections later that same year gave the Justice Party 240 seats, while the People's Party dropped to 134 seats in the 450-seat assembly. Suleyman Demirel became premier. The Justice Party continued the legacy of the former Democratic Party. It drew its support from the farmers, conservative Moslems, and part of the middle class. The People's Party, meanwhile, drew support from the majority of the urban middle class, intellectuals, and those sharing Atatürk's ideals.

In July 1974, Greeks on Cyprus, with the encouragement and aid of the Greek government, attempted to seize control of the island and carry out *enosis,* or union with Greece. Cyprus was about 80 percent Greek and only 20 percent Turk, but Ankara was determined to defend its compatriots there. In the crisis the Greek junta seriously miscalculated. In August the Turks invaded the island with a substantial contingent and easily defeated the Greek Cypriot national guard. They seized control of 30 percent of the island and expelled the Greeks who lived there. Since that time the Cyprus situation has remained frozen, with the island divided along a line that runs through the center of Nicosia. Turkey stationed some 25,000 troops on the island and proclaimed a Turkish Cypriot state, first called the Turkish Federated State of Cyprus, and after 1983, the Turkish Republic of Northern Cyprus. Athens took the position that it would never agree to partition. The temporary termination of military aid by the U.S. Congress angered the Turks but did not dislodge them from their positions on the island.

Turkey benefited, at least as far as foreign aid was concerned, from upheaval in Iran and from a Soviet destabilization campaign mounted through Bulgaria and Syria. In 1979 the United States increased its assistance from $300 million to $500 million a year. This substantially improved the climate for keeping the twenty-six U.S. military bases in the country.

For most of the 1970s the government was run by either the left-of-center Republican People's Party headed by Bülent Ecevit or, at the end of the decade, by Demirel's conservative Justice Party. Neither party had been able to win a majority in Parliament, and both were forced to form uneasy and ineffective alliances with splinter groups and independents. Parliament turned into a bazaar of wheeler-dealers, with little attention paid to the real problems facing the country.

In September 1980 the Turkish military seized power for a third time. The generals dissolved Parliament, suspended the constitution and some civil liberties, arrested Prime Minister Demirel and more than a hundred other politicians, and formed a military junta designed to preserve "national unity." The army also arrested thousands of suspected terrorists and executed a number of them. The coup was led by army chief of staff General Kenyan Evren. Again, these were moderate, pro-Western officers with a commitment to restoring democracy and continuing the country's role as a key player in NATO. The army's action had again been sparked by the politicians' bickering; their failure to address the country's staggering economic problems, with inflation running at nearly 100 percent; and both right- and left-wing terrorism that had resulted in the death of more than two thousand people in 1980 alone. The generals were particularly concerned with the rise of Islamic fundamentalists, who, in light of what had happened in neighboring Iran, were viewed as a serious threat to modern Turkey's adherence to Atatürk's secular principles.

In the short run, the military coup was a setback for Turkey's effort to join Europe. The country was banned from the Parliamentary Assembly of the Council of Europe, negotiations for closer association with the EEC were frozen, and Turkey was brought before the European Commission on Human Rights in Strasbourg. In the long run, the coup was good for Turkey. In 1982, General Evren became president for a seven-year term in a referendum that was simultaneously a vote for a new constitution. The referendum received a 92 percent favorable vote and was considered fair by foreign observers. The new constitution increased the powers of the presidency, and in the case of the Grand National Assembly, the Turkish Parliament, the constitution encouraged the emergence of a stable two-party system uncomplicated by the proliferation of small parties.

The return to democratization was steady. In the 1983 parliamentary elections, the party favored by the military, the Nationalist Democratic Party, came in third. The big winner was Turgut Özal's Motherland Party. It won an absolute majority in the Grand National Assembly, the first party to do so since the 1960s. Özal's economic policies, including promotion of a market economy, put the country back in financial order.

Özal was strongly pro-West in his policies, and Turkey was again accepted into the Western community. In 1985, Turkey was readmitted into the Council of Europe. In

1985, Turkey embarked on an ambitious ten-year, $10-billion, military modernization program. Five years later it had an army of 800,000 men, the second largest standing force in NATO, plus several hundred thousand in the reserves. Resentment toward the United States lingered, especially over the 10-7 rule imposed by Washington on military aid to Turkey and Greece after the Cyprus intervention, requiring that Greece receive $7 in U.S. military aid for every $10 going to Turkey.

In 1989 there was a crisis with neighboring Bulgaria when that country adopted policies that drove several hundred thousand of its Turkish minority into Turkey. Turkey did benefit, as far as its relations with the West were concerned, from the crisis with Iraq. Özal, who was elected to the newly created post of president in 1989, was quick to join his country to the anti–Saddam Hussein coalition, and he allowed U.S. aircraft based in Turkey to make sorties against Iraq. Turkey, however, suffered economically; by November 1990 its enforcement of the economic blockade had cost Turkey an estimated $3 billion, chiefly as a result of shutting down a pipeline that transported oil from Iraq to the Turkish coast. Economic problems, including inflation of 70 percent, brought defeat for Özal's Motherland Party in the November 1991 national elections. Süleyman Demirel returned to the prime minister's office for the seventh time.

Turks still resent the phobia and depreciation expressed by many Western Europeans and Americans toward its Muslim identity and their lack of sympathy with Turkey's efforts to stamp out demands for autonomy by Kurds in the southeast, who make up some 20 percent of the country's overall population. This was evident in March 1995, when in Operation Steel Curtain, Turkey sent 35,000 troops supported by aircraft into the Kurdish zone of northern Iraq in an effort to trap several thousand guerrillas and halt cross-border raids by the Marxist Kurdish Workers Party (PKK). The PKK had been fighting for more than a decade to establish a separate Kurdish state in southeastern Turkey. More than 15,000 people had been killed since 1984, and Turkey mounted the military campaign in an effort to wipe out the movement. The move carried substantial risk for Turkey's European aspirations. This action, reports of civilian casualties, and talk in Turkey of setting up a buffer zone all strained relations with Europe and the United States.

In June 1993, Tansu Çiller of the True Path Party became prime minister. She was the first woman to hold that office in Turkish history, and the first prime minister born on the European side of the Bosorus. Çiller, who had earned a doctorate in economics from the University of Connecticut, governed in a coalition with Erdal Inönu's Social Democratic Populist Party. But she was unable to bring down the inflation rate nor accelerate the sell-off of Turkey's vast, deficit-fostering state enterprises. These two problems were at the core of the country's economic difficulties.

In December 1995, Turkey was granted a customs accord with the European Union, but the nation of 63 million people remained plagued by budget deficits, a stumbling privatization plan, and an 80-percent annual inflation rate. Çiller called early elections after her party's coalition with the Social Democrats collapsed in September 1995. Economic problems in the cities had led to a rise in Muslim fundamentalism and bloodshed in Ankara. The pro-Islamic Welfare Party, led by Necmettin Erbakan, blamed Turkish problems on "world imperialism and Zionism" and pledged Turkish adherence to Islamic principles and to restore the country to its former greatness. In the December 1995 national elections, the Welfare Party threw Turkish politics into turmoil. In what was the closest election in Turkish history, the Muslim party garnered 21 percent of the vote and sent shock waves through the secular Turkish republic.

Çiller's Truth Path Party and Mesut Yilmaz's Motherland Party each won slightly more than 19 percent. Disgust over bickering between the leaders of these two parties with almost identical center-right programs was related to the Muslim victory; instead of presenting a united front, they had attacked each other. Other factors were the government's failure to resolve pressing economic and social problems, and disgust over endemic corruption and incompetence in the Turkish government. The Welfare Party was also aided by the failure of the Kurdish People's Democracy Party to win 10 percent of the nationwide vote needed to qualify for Parliament. Seats that would have gone to Kurdish nationalists in the southeast instead went to the Welfare Party.

President Süleyman Demirel was faced with a political crisis. The Welfare Party was unable to form a government, and neither of the right-center party leaders would step aside in favor of the other. Çiller remained as head of a caretaker government, and in late December she and Yilmaz agreed to work for a coalition supported by left-wing legislators to block the Welfare Party from power. The coalition between Çiller's True Path and Yilmaz's Motherland Party was formalized on March 3, 1996. With twenty votes short of a majority, the new center-right coalition was dependent upon the support of left-wing parties. The Welfare Party, however, had considerable strength across Turkey; its members were mayors in more than four hundred communities, including the two largest cities of Istanbul and Ankara. Muslim fundamentalism—even though 80 percent of Turkey's voters in December 1995 voted for secular parties—may yet prove the greatest threat to the secular Turkish state.

Relations with Greece also remained seriously strained. The two countries nearly went to war in 1987 over Aegean seabed mineral rights, and in January 1996 they again threatened war over the tiny uninhabited island of Kardak (Imia to the Greeks) in the eastern Aegean Sea, just four miles off the Turkish coast. This rising tension at a time of political uncertainty in both countries raised fears of miscalculation that could lead to war.

BIBLIOGRAPHY

Ahmad, Feroz. *The Making of Modern Turkey.* New York: Routledge, 1993.

Lewis, Bernard. *Emergence of Modern Turkey.* New York: Oxford University Press, 1969.

Mango, Andrew. *The Challenge of a New Role.* Westport, CN: Praeger, 1994.

———. *Turkey.* New York: Walker, 1968.

Shaw, S. J. *History of the Ottoman Empire and Modern Turkey.* 2 vols. Cambridge: Cambridge University Press, 1976–77.

Tapper. *Islam in Modern Turkey: Religion, Politics, and Literature in a Secular State.* New York: St. Martin's, 1994.

Walker, Walter F. *The Turkish Revolution, 1960–1961; Aspects of Military Politics.* Washington: Brookings Institution, 1963.

Zurcher, Erik J. *Turkey: A Modern History.* New York: St. Martin's, 1993.

Spencer C. Tucker

SEE ALSO Bulgaria; Cyprus

Turkey and European Union (EU)

Turkey, the unique pluralist secular democracy in the Muslim world, has always attached great importance to its relations with the West, especially with the countries of Europe. Since the foundation of the Turkish Republic in 1923, westernization as a state policy was followed with the reorganization of Turkish society according to Western standards. In fact, this trend started in the nineteenth century Ottoman Empire when Western educational, administrative, political, and legal systems were imitated. The founders of the Turkish republic wanted to elevate Turkey to the level of contemporary Western civilization through the transforming of Turkey into a European state. The main concern at stake in the relations between Turkey and the European Economic Community (1958–67), and its subsequent forms, the European Community (1967–93), and the European Union (1993–), has always been the extension of this Westernization project. However, Turkey-EU relations have fluctuated between cordiality and extreme tension.

In July 1959, shortly after the establishment of the European Economic Community (EEC) in 1958, Turkey applied to join the organization. This resulted in the signing of the Agreement Creating an Association between the Republic of Turkey and the European Economic Community, the Ankara Agreement, on September 12, 1963. The agreement entered into force on December 1, 1964. Turkey sought to fulfill requirements for full membership in the EEC through the establishment of a customs union and a resolution on financial cooperation with the EEC. The Additional Protocol of November 13, 1970, detailed the steps necessary for the establishment of a customs union and called for the harmonization of Turkish legislation with that of the European Community (EC) in economic matters. On January 24, 1980, Turkey shifted its economic policy from an autarchic import-substitution model to an export-oriented one and opened its economy to the operation of market forces. Although the military coup in Turkey on September 12, 1980, froze the relations between Turkey and the EC, there was a return to normality following multiparty elections in 1983.

In April 1987, Turkey applied for full membership on the basis of the EC treaty's article 237, which gave any European country the right to do so. The Opinion of the European Commission, the administrative body of the EC, was completed on December 18, 1989, and endorsed during the Dublin Summit of the European Community Council on February 5–6, 1990. Despite underlining Turkey's eligibility for membership, its application was deferred by the EC until the emergence of a more favorable environment. The EC stated that the need to complete its single market prevented the consideration of further enlargement. The Council, furthermore, has invited the Commission to make concrete proposals to improve co-operation within the framework of the Association Agreement. Meanwhile, on June 6, 1990 the EC Commission prepared a Co-operation Program, the Manutes Package, which covers proposals aiming at developing the Turkish-EC co-operation. A further cooperation program was signed in Ankara on January 21, 1992, with the EC Commission, gives priority to cooperation between Turkey and the Community.

On March 6, 1995, Turkey signed a Customs Union Agreement with the European Union (EU) in Brussels, and this was ratified by the European Parliament on December 13, 1995. With the entry into force of the Customs Union on January 1, 1996, Turkey abolished all duties and equivalent charges on imports of industrial goods from the EU and accelerated harmonizing its tariffs and equivalent charges on the importation of industrial goods from third countries with the EU's Common External Tariff. Turkey has progressively adapted itself to the EU's commercial policy and preferential trade arrangements with specific third countries. This process is to be completed in five years. Moreover, Turkey has progressively adopted many aspects of the Common Agricultural Policy. Turkish industry has also adapted itself very well to the new competitive environment. The Customs Union Agreement is regarded in Turkey as a very important step towards Turkey's full integration with the EU. It has also demonstrated that, despite predictions to the contrary, the Turkish economy was able to cope with the competitive challenges of free trade, competition, and EU intellectual property regulations.

At the Association Council of April 29, 1997, the EU reconfirmed Turkish eligibility for membership and asked the European Commission to prepare recommendations to deepen Turkey-EU relations, while claiming that the development of relations depended on a number of factors relating to Greece, Cyprus, the Kurdish problem, and human rights. On July 16, 1997, the Commission president, Jacques, Santer proposed Agenda 2000, which set the Commission's strategy to widen the Union, and suggested that accession negotiations begin with central and eastern European countries in 1998. This report stated that Turkey was far behind the EU standards in human rights. Moreover, Turkey was too large, too poor, too populous, with a high inflation and unemployment rate, an enduring rivalry with Greece, and a continuing Kurdish problem. He also stated that Turkey should accept the Hague International Court of Justice as the body where disputes between Turkey and the EU would be adjudicated. The Council, nevertheless, once again reconfirmed Turkey's eligibility and offered a Pre-Accession Strategy as well as an invitation to Turkey to the European Conference. The Commission, however, excluded Turkey from the enlargement process while conceding that the Customs Union is functioning satisfactorily. In the light of the EU's claims that all candidates would be judged according to the same objective criteria and that there would be no prejudice in their evaluation, Turkey found the Commission's approach unjust and discriminatory.

Although the decisions of the Luxembourg Summit on December 12–13, 1997, reflected by and large the contents of the Commission's Agenda 2000, the EU has decided to set up a strategy to prepare Turkey for accession and to create a special procedure to review the developments to be made. The Copenhagen criteria of the European Council and Agenda 2000 proposals of the Commission shape the Luxembourg decisions. During its Copenhagen summit in June 1993, the European Council decided on a set of criteria for EU membership: stable institutions such as democracy, rule of law, respect for human rights, and protection of minorities; existence of functioning market economy and the capacity to cope with competitive pressures and market forces within the Union and the capacity to adopt the obligations of membership, that is, the legal agreements of the Union as expressed in the Treaty, the secondary legislation, and the policies of the Union. Following the Summit, Turkey criticized the EU's attitude and did not participate in the inaugural meeting of the European Conference held in London on March 12, 1998.

Nevertheless, the European Council of Vienna of December 11–12, 1998, underlined the great importance it attached to the further development of relations between the EU and Turkey and the preparation of Turkey for membership. In addition to these positive developments, Turkey-EU relations have also been affected by the arrest and trial of Kurdish Labor Party (PKK) leader Abdullah Ocalan, as well as the death sentence pronounced by the Ankara State Security Court against him on June 29, 1999. As a response to that judgment, the EU presidency expressed "the hope that Turkey will follow what has invariably been the practice for the last fifteen years and not carry out the death sentence passed on Mr. Ocalan." In a resolution on July 22, 1999, the newly elected European Parliament also called on the Turkish authorities not to carry out the sentence. The death sentence against Ocalan has been appealed before the Turkish Supreme Court and would also have to be confirmed by Parliament before it could be carried out. If confirmed by the Supreme Court, the sentence could also be appealed to the European Court of Human Rights.

The catastrophic earthquake of Turkey on August 17, 1999, has also influenced the relations between Turkey and the EU, including positive developments in relations between Turkey and Greece. Ministers of foreign affairs from both countries agreed on exploring possibilities of promoting cooperation between the two countries in fields such as tourism, culture, environment, and combating organized crime including illegal immigration, drug trafficking, and terrorism. The Helsinki European Council Summit on December 10–11, 1999, made progress in preparing to accept new member states, among them Turkey, whose candidacy was the subject of a special decision that was not opposed by Greece. However, the

1999 Regular Report from the Commission on Turkey's Progress towards Accession stated that Turkey still had shortcomings in the areas of human rights and the protection of minority rights. It was also noted that, though torture is not systemic, it is still widespread, and, although there have been some improvements in terms of the independence of the judiciary, that the emergency courts system remains in place.

The future of Turkey's relationship with the EU is complicated. Throughout history Turks were never accepted as Europeans and the perception of them as the "other of Europe" is deeply embedded into European consciousness. Turkey's failure to uphold democracy, human rights, and an open free-market economy are convenient justifications for the EU's rejection of Turkey's membership, but they also conveniently mask the EU's general reservations about Turkey. Turgut Özal, prime minister from 1983–89 and president from 1989 until his death in 1993, said in 1987, following Turkey's application for membership, that "This path (of becoming a full member in the EU) is a long and difficult one." It appears that it will take a long time for Turkey to pass from the waiting room into the EU.

BIBLIOGRAPHY

Kinsky, Ferdinand. *The Future of the European Union: Deepening and Enlargement.* Nice, France: Presses d'Europe, 1999.

Müftüler-Bac, Meltem. *Turkey's Relations with a Changing Europe.* Manchester, U.K.: Manchester University Press, 1997.

Neuwahl, Nanette A., ed. *The European Union and Human Rights.* Hague, Netherlands: Martinus Nijhoff Publishers, 1995.

Murat Cemrek

Turkmenistan, Republic of (Turkmenia)

Independent successor state to the Turkmen Soviet Socialist Republic of the former USSR. The Republic of Turkmenistan consists of 186,400 square miles (488,100 sq km). It is surrounded by Uzbekistan, Kazakhstan, the Caspian Sea, Iran, and Afghanistan. Its population in 1996 was approximately 3,856,000. Its capital Ashgabat (Ashkhabad) had 407,000 inhabitants. Turkmen belongs to the Southwestern subgroup of the Turkic language. In 1929, Latin script replaced the traditional Arabic. The Cyrillic alphabet was imposed in 1940. In 1990, Turkmen became the official language, and in 1993 the Latin based Turkish script was introduced. The majority of the population, 68 percent of whom are Turkmen, are Sunni Muslims. Their Islam, however, is infused with Sufi mysticism and traditional shamanism.

Turkmenistan. *Illustration courtesy of Bernard Cook.*

In 1877, the Russians launched a campaign against the Turkmen. At the battle of Gök Tepe in 1881 as many as 20,000 Turkmen died. In an 1895 agreement the Russians and the British delineated a boundary between their respective Turkmen areas. Following the Bolshevik Revolution the Provisional Government of Transcaspia and the Turkmen Congress were set up in opposition to the Bolsheviks. But Soviet forces succeeded in imposing the Turkestan Autonomous Soviet Socialist Republic on April 30, 1918. In July, however, with British assistance the Bolsheviks were defeated and an independent government was set up in Ashgabad. As soon as the British withdrew, General Mikhail Frunze, who would succeed Leon Trofsky as commissar of war in 1925, and the Red Army restored Bolshevik control. The Turkmen Soviet Socialist Republic was proclaimed on October 27, 1924, and in May 1925 became a member republic of the USSR.

Resistance to Soviet rule continued in Turkmenistan under the Basmachi. With the imposition of collectivized agriculture the forced settlement of the nomadic Turkmen led to a guerrilla war that lasted until 1936. An anti-Islamic campaign launched in 1928 reduced the number of functioning mosques from five hundred in 1917 to four in 1979. The autonomist proclivities of the Turkmen intelligentsia brought persecution, which reached a crescendo during the Great Purge. Among those killed was the champion of Turkmen culture, the writer Abdulhekim Qulmuhammeoghli. Soviet rule did enhance literacy, which rose from 2.3 percent in 1926 to 99 percent in 1970. Many new members of the Turkmen cultural elite, however, chose to write and produce in Russian. In addition to literacy, the development of health care was also a progressive achievement.

Turkmenistan is a land of desert plains broken only by foothills and mountains in the south. The Kara Kum (Black Sand) Desert dominates 90 percent of the republic. There are oases along the Amu Dar'ya (Oxus) river and in the foothills of the mountains along the border with

Iran. Apart from these the land is arid. In the 1930s, agriculture was promoted through the development of irrigation, and in 1993 43.4 percent of Turkmenistan's workers were employed in agriculture. The largest Soviet irrigation project, the Kara Kum canal constructed in the 1950s from Kerki on the Amu Dar'ya river northwestward to Merv and Ashkabad, fostered the spread of cotton farming. The projects, however, had a devastating impact upon in the north and especially on the Aral Sea, as water from the Amu Dar'ya, one of its sources, was diverted. The irrigated soil became increasingly saline and the level of the Aral Sea dropped steadily.

The receding Aral Sea and the decreasing fertility of Turkmenistan's soil were very concrete indications that something was wrong. This ecological issue became coupled with dissatisfaction over Turkmenistan's position in the USSR as a provider of raw materials for more developed republics and the large role played by ethnic Russians in the area's administration. These three issues created the foundation for critical politicization in Turkmenistan. In 1958, Suhan Babayev, the leader of the Turkmen Communist Party (CPT), was dismissed when he proposed that only Turkmen should hold leading posts in Turkmenistan, even though Turkmen were still separated by tribe divisions and had no history of unity.

In 1987, with the permission of Mikhail Gorbachev, the Turkmen began to restructure their agriculture. With both economic and ecologically beneficial results, land was shifted from cotton to grains. Animal husbandry—especially the production of astrakhan and karakul wool—and the breeding of silkworms are important elements of the economy. The production of textiles from wool and silk, as well as cotton, constituted 36 percent of industrial production in 1990.

Babaev's successor, Juma Karaev died after two years and was succeeded by Balysh Ovezov. Ovezov was replaced by Mukhamednazar Gapurov in 1969, but with the arrival of Mikhail Gorbachev and his reform policy Gapurov was superseded by Saparmurad Niyazov (1940–). Niyazov was an electrical engineer who had become the first secretary of the Ashkhabad City Party Committee. In March 1985 he was appointed chairman of the Turkmen Council of ministers and in December the chairman of the TCP. By this time Turkmenistan had become dependent for its food upon imports from other areas of the USSR. The dismissal by Niyazov of all oblast first secretaries and the minister of agriculture struck a blow at corruption and placed the discussion of the agricultural future of Turkmenistan on the agenda. This opened the door to incipient politicization. However, the Turkmen were still divided and Niyazov was able to retain control of the situation. There were riots in May 1989 in Ashkhabad and Nebitdag triggered by the exasperation of the youth with poverty and unemployment.

In September 1989, Turkmen intellectuals formed Agzybirkil, an organization concerned with the status of the Turkmen language and culture, as well as the environment and the economy of the country. The Soviet regime was hostile toward Agzybirbil's political potential, and it was banned in January 1990, though it proceeded to hold a congress the next month. While the CPT and its collateral groups alone were allowed to place candidates before the electorate in the Turkmen Supreme Soviet (TSS) election, the TSS and Saparmurad Niyazov (1940–), the leader of the TCP and chairman of the TSS, made concessions. In May 1990, Turkmenistan became the last of the republics to elevate its majority or plurality language to the status of official language. On August 22, the TSS passed a declaration of sovereignty that asserted that Turkmenistan was to be nuclear free and was free to choose its sociopolitical system. On October 27, Niyazov, running unopposed, was elected executive president by 98.3 percent of those voting in a direct election. Though the TSS had asserted Turkmenistan's right to secede from the USSR, its underdevelopment and dependence upon subsidies from the central government made it anxious to remain attached to the USSR. In a March 1991 referendum, 95.7 percent of eligible voters elected to preserve the rule of the USSR.

Turkmenistan remained muted during the 1991 attempted coup in Moscow, but afterwards Niyazov, who retained power, announced that unlike elsewhere the CPT would remain the ruling party. In December, 1991, however, the CPT assumed a new name, the Democratic Party of Turkmenistan (DPT), and Niyazov became its chairman. Turkmenistan signed the October 18 economic community treaty and on December 21 the Alma-Ata accord ratifying the Commonwealth of Independent States (CIS). By this time, its electorate had also voted for independence, on October 26, and this had proclaimed the next day by the TSS.

During 1992, the DPT retained its dominance in the Council of Ministers and the TSS, and Niyazov his dominance over everything, including the DPT and the media. A May 18 constitution cemented his authority, making him head of government, with certain legislative prerogatives, as well as head of state. He was re-elected without opposition in June and claimed to have garnered 99.5 percent of the vote.

The new constitution also provided for a new fifty member legislature or Majlis, but until the expiration of its term in 1995 the old TSS, renamed the Majlis, would retain its legislative function. A new body, an advisory People's Council (Khalk Maslakhaty), presided over by the president, was established as the "supreme representative body of popular power."

An unabashed personality cult developed around Niyazov. He cultivated the title "Turkmenbashi," or "Leader of the Turkmen." Leading members of the DPT proposed that Niyazov be made president for life. In December 1993, the TSS/Majlis moved to extend Niyazov's term to 2002, stating that his leadership was indispensable for the realization of his ten year economic plan. On January 15, 1994, a purported 99.99 percent of the electorate gave its assent. The new Majlis was elected in December 1994 with only one of its fifty seats being contested by two candidates. Nevertheless, it appears that more opposition existed. In June 1995, two opposition leaders accused of plotting against Niyazov were sentenced to long terms in a labor camp. In July there were small demonstrations against the president and against economic difficulties.

Turkmenistan was one of the poorest republics of the former USSR, and after 1991 its industries were adversely impacted by the disruption of inter-republic trade. Consumer prices increased by 102.5 percent in 1991, 492.9 percent in 1992, and approximately 1,150 percent in 1993, and unemployment ran much higher than the official figure of 40,000 or 2.5 percent of the work force. Economic change was and still is slow. Niyazov expressed his support for the notion of private productive property, but privatization was not begun until December 1993. Since then it has effected mainly small enterprises, and Niyazov has expressed his preference for collective farms and rural cooperatives. In August 1995, Niyazov responded to the indications of discontent by dismissing a number of the country's local administrators for failing to fulfill grain quotas. In October 1995, he ousted several members of the Council of Ministers.

The new constitution raised concerns among the non-Turkmen population of the country. In addition to the Russians, who constituted 13 percent of the population, Uzbeks constituted nine, and Kazakhs three. The constitution stated that only ethnic Turkmen could be employed by state enterprises. Russian was no longer to be the language of interethnic communication. However, there was no ethnic violence, and Niyazov adhered to the notion of a secular state. In December 1993, Turkmenistan was the first Central Asian republic to sign an agreement with Russia to grant Turkmenistan's ethnic Russians dual citizenship.

Turkmenistan, despite its membership in the Commonwealth of Independent States (CIS), has opposed moves to establish closer economic and political relations between the CIS's members, though it signed an agreement of economic union in December 1993. It was courted by both Iran and Turkey to build a railroad to connect the countries, and the Turks proposed a trans-Iran and Turkey pipeline to transport Turkmenistan's most valuable resource, natural gas, to the West. The fourth largest producer of natural gas in the world, Turkmenistan was concerned that it would have to sell its natural gas to CIS members at a discount, which made it hesitant to agree to closer economic ties with the CIS. Turkmenistan also follows only Russia and Azerbaijan among the former Soviet republics in the production of oil. Its reserves of oil are estimated to be 6,300 metric tons. However, it had difficulty marketing its oil, since Armenia was its principal customer and its pipeline to Armenia was blocked by Azerbaijan due to fighting over Nagorno-Karabakh. Turkmenistan has two oil refineries and uses the natural gas, which it does not export, to fire power stations, which, in addition to domestic energy, produce much surplus power for export.

Turkmenistan is not actively involved in the CIS operation in Tajikistan, having declared its neutrality and non-aligned status, but it agreed to allow Russian troops to be deployed on its borders with Iran and Afghanistan.

BIBLIOGRAPHY

Batalden, Stephen K., and Sandra L. Batalden. *The Newly Independent States of Eurasia: Handbook of Former Soviet Republics.* Phoenix, AZ: Oryx, 1993.

Europa Handbook. 1996. "Turkmenistan." 3197–99.

Shoemaker, M. Wesley. *Russia, Eurasian States, and Eastern Europe 1995.* Harpers Ferry, WV: Stryker-Post, 1995.

Bernard Cook

Turks in Germany

Turks in Germany number about 2 million, the largest group of nonethnic Germans in the country. Five percent of all Turks live outside Turkey, and more than half of these migrants live and work in Germany; in the language of international labor migration scholarship, Turkey is a "sender" nation. Turkish citizens leave their homeland for better employment, hoping to return with sufficient wealth to buy a shop or farm, or simply to retire in relative ease. In past decades, Turks and other non-German workers were called *Gastarbeiter* (guest workers) or *Fremdarbeiter* (foreign workers), now-obsolete terms emphasizing their temporary position in the labor force. Today, Turkish Germans are as likely to be students as workers. About one-half of the Turkish population is under age 30. Moreover, two-thirds have been in Germany for over 15 years, and only 17 percent would like to return to Turkey. Clearly then, the conventional perception of Turkish Germans as a source of temporary labor is outmoded. Those residents of Germany who trace their ancestry to Turkey are now a permanent part of German society.

West Germany, like other western European nations, began to experience a labor shortage by the mid-1950s, as postwar reconstruction became an extended economic boom. Recruitment of workers from Mediterranean nations was one easy solution to this problem. In 1955 the West German government concluded the first bilateral agreement with Italy, whereby West Germany's Federal Labor Office (Bundesanstalt für Arbeit, or BfA), brought carefully vetted recruits to West Germany on one-year contracts with German firms. They were to stay in worker hostels, dormitories, or wood huts for the duration of their contracts, and then return home. Initially, this program was intended primarily to supply West Germany with farm workers, but industry, centered in urban areas, needed labor as well. In 1960, Spain and Greece joined Italy as official "sender nations."

In 1961 the construction of the Berlin Wall exacerbated West Germany's labor crisis by restricting the flow of immigrants from East Germany, and that same year Turkey's first recruitment agreement was signed. Morocco, Portugal, Tunisia, and Yugoslavia concluded agreements in the following years. Between 1962 and 1973, the number of foreign workers rose dramatically, increasing West Germany's population at a rate of 1.4 percent annually. The recession of 1967 temporarily halted worker recruitment, and when it resumed, the targeted employees had changed as the BfA granted most work visas to women. This was in part because labor shortages continued in low paying, low-status service jobs such as cleaning, and in part to further the goal of family reunification. Family reunification was a solution to the perceived social threat the foreign workers posed, single men living in worker hostels or dormitories, with extra money in their pockets. Many wives did join their husbands in Germany, but women also came hoping to bring their husbands and children to Germany in the future. Moreover, Turkish workers in Germany were able to save enough money to return home to marry and bring their brides back to Germany when the 1974 Unification of Families Law made this easier. By 1976, 27 percent of Turks in West Germany were women.

In 1973 the oil crisis put a serious damper on German economic growth for the first time since 1948. The worker recruitment scheme was halted and work permits almost disappeared. But the foreign worker population was already over 10 percent of the labor force, and of those 23 percent were Turkish (by 1998 this percentage had grown to 28 percent). Between 1967 and 1982, the high birth rate of Turkish families increased the Turkish population in West Germany from 172,400 to over 1.5 million. As the economic slump continued, resentment of native-born Germans against "guest workers" began to build. It was thought that foreign workers were taking jobs from Germans—a misperception since foreign workers generally took jobs that no German wanted, and many foreigners were not in the work force. In 1983, the federal government began offering "go-home premiums" to Turkish workers. The program advertised bonuses of up to 10,500 German marks, but usually the prize was much less once taxes and fees were subtracted, and in any case the money was not enough to attract many takers. Many Turks had been in Germany for two decades, and their children, born and raised there, had weak (or no) ties to Turkey.

By the 1980s, Turkish workers in Germany experienced double the unemployment rate of German workers, mostly because Turks had been employed in the building and construction trades or as unskilled labor, sectors hit hard by the economic slowdown. In the 1990s, however, the Turkish unemployment rate fell to 11 percent while the German rate remained at 16 percent. In part, the lower unemployment rate of Turks was due to their willingness to take unattractive jobs; an additional factor is the rise in Turkish entrepreneurship. By 1993, 213,000 Turks owned their own businesses, many of them small shops catering to Turkish consumers. The Turkish community in Germany has become an economic force in its own right.

With the fall of the Berlin Wall in 1989 and the reunification of Germany one year later, large numbers of ethnic Germans from Eastern Europe and the former Soviet Union flooded into Germany. While often possessing little knowledge of the language and culture of either western or eastern Germany, ethnic Germans were given citizenship and allowed full access to the social welfare system. In addition, large numbers of refugees and asylum seekers, especially those fleeing the war in Yugoslavia, found refuge in Germany. At the same time, Germany's economy continued to experience high unemployment and sluggish growth. The costs of unification turned out to be higher than expected, and adjustments were more painful. In some regions in the former East Germany, the unemployment rate neared 50 percent. In the early 1990s, increasing numbers of immigrants and the economic difficulties of the new Germany combined to fuel growing xenophobia and right-wing radicalism. Turkish residents became a favorite target for neo-Nazi attacks, most tragically in the Moelln arson attack on November 23, 1992, in which a woman and two children were killed, and the Solingen arson on May 29, 1993, which killed three girls and two women. Reports that bystanders cheered as flames destroyed the homes shocked the public, and thousands of Germans attended candlelight vigils in protest.

Racist rhetoric and violence directed against Turkish residents highlights widespread ignorance of the complexity of Turkish German society. Germans have tended to view Turks as a homogeneous ethnic bloc, but in fact the Turkish German population is diverse in religion, geographical origin, and ethnicity. Most Turks are Sunni Muslims, but from five to ten million of Turkey's population of fifty million are Alevi Muslims, a branch of Shi'ite. Of the 2 million Turks in Germany, approximately 300,000 are Alevi, while 1.4 million identify themselves as Sunni. A majority of Turks in Germany come from impoverished Central Anatolia, where traditional religious practice and social customs are a more central part of life than on the western coastal cities; on the other extreme are the 100,000 Turks who identify themselves as Germans and who hold German citizenship. Finally, about 350,000 of the "Turks" in Germany are actually Kurds from Eastern Anatolia, who have experienced repression in Turkey and feel little fellowship with Turks.

Political and cultural issues that divide society in Turkey often find their way into Turkish society in Germany. In the early 1990s, the Kurdish independence movement, the Kurdish Workers' Party (PKK), had strong support among Kurds in Germany, leading the Turkish government to demand a crackdown on the group by German security forces. Turks in Germany joined in the calls for suppression of the PKK, which they viewed as a terrorist group. The Alevi-Sunni religious division is another characteristic of Turkish German society. Since the mid-1980s, an increasing number of Turks in Germany have arrived as refugees or asylum seekers, and have brought other Turkish domestic political debates to the Turkish community in Germany.

Turkish politics and cultural issues have been a major factor in shaping Turkish German political behavior, but the experience of living in Germany shapes Turkish attitudes as well. Traditionally, Turks have been a relatively inert force in German politics, first, because the first generation of Turks saw their stay in Germany as temporary, second because few Turks have German citizenship, and third because the attention of many Turks focuses on Turkish rather than German politics. In recent years, however, there has been increasing political participation by Turkish Germans, even those who are not citizens. Because of its supportive stand on immigration and naturalization, most Turks favor the Social Democratic Party (SPD). In 1994 the SPD had 3,440 Turkish members, while the CDU, with a more restrictive policy toward citizenship, had a total of only 436 non-EU foreigners. The Christian Social Union (the Bavarian counterpart of the CDU) and parties further to the right do not accept noncitizens as members. Several Turkish Germans have become prominent in the Green Party. Cem Özdemir was elected to the Bundestag (parliament) in 1994 and 1998, and Ekin Deligöz in 1998. On the other hand, organizations created by the German government for Turks and other foreign residents have met with little success among Turkish Germans. The Ausländerbeiräte, or foreigner's councils, which advise policy makers at the communal and state levels, are seen as ineffective, while most Turks view the Wohlfahrtsverbände, or welfare federations, with distrust because of their assimilationist goals. Rather than join German political groups in which they fear they will have no voice, many Turkish Germans are active in local self-help and advocacy organizations.

Decades of exposure to life in Central Europe have left second and third generation Turks in a sort of cultural limbo. As natives of Germany, they know little about their ancestral land, tending to see it in idealized terms based on occasional holiday visits. At the same time, they are not entirely accepted as Germans, and therefore prefer to maintain cultural identity with the Turkish German minority. Sociological research on this group confirms the impression of the development of a third culture between Germany and Turkey. The role of women in Turkish German society provides an apt illustration: Turkish women in Germany are often chaperoned and protected to a degree distasteful to Germans, but they enjoy much more freedom of movement than women in Turkey. Turkish women in Germany have much higher rates of employment outside the home than do women in Turkey. Forty percent of Turkish women in Berlin hold jobs outside the home. Religious practice is another area where Turkish Germans have moved to a position between the two cultures. While most Turks in Germany continue to identify themselves as Muslim, their rates of religious observance are similar to those of the Christian German population: 18 percent of Muslims practice their religion, while 15 percent of Protestants and 10 percent of Catholics do. This corresponds with the increasingly secular nature of German society.

At the same time, Turkish Germans hold on to their language and culture through the traditional media, and, increasingly, the Internet. According to surveys, approximately 85 percent of German citizens of Turkish descent read Turkish language newspapers such as *Hürryiet* (nationalistic), *Sabah* (liberal), or the Kurdish-oriented *Özgür Politika;* the number of noncitizen readers is likely to be even higher. About 95 percent of Turks have satellite or cable television hookups and about 85 percent regularly watch TRT-INT, the official Turkish television station broadcast for Turks living abroad. Kurds, too, had a television station, MED-TV, broadcast from Great Britain until its suspension on April 23, 1999, due to allegations of PKK sympathy. Altogether there are eight different Turkish stations available through satellite, the most common type of pay television in Europe. Finally, there are growing numbers of Internet sites for Turks and Kurds in Germany. In 1993 a study by German journal *Der Spiegel* revealed that 15 percent of Turkish households owned a computer while only 11 percent of German households did.

It is clear, then, that many Turks who otherwise enjoy the relative freedom of German society are unwilling to give up all elements of their culture to conform to the norms German society. Germans, even those most sympathetic to the situation of Turks in Germany, tend to regard assimilation as the goal of Turkish German interaction and blame Turkish unwillingness to "become German" for continuing discrimination. Germany has a weak tradition of pluralism, and whether separatism results in discrimination or the reverse is a matter of contention. Turks are indeed more likely to be victims of prejudice than other traditional "guest worker" groups. In a 1995 survey, 33 percent of Turks reported an incident of discrimination in the previous year, compared to 25 percent of Yugoslavs, 20 percent of Italians, and 17 percent of Greeks. Moreover, young people, those most integrated into German society, are the most common victims of discrimination, and Turks born in Germany do not receive automatic citizenship although they may be third or even fourth-generation residents. In recent years, therefore, younger Turkish Germans have developed their own cultural identity using the forms of contemporary youth culture. In Berlin, especially, the "Kreuzberg" hip-hop culture provides young Turkish Germans a sense of belonging to Turkish German youth.

The continued existence of distinct Turkish-German cultures is one of the thorniest issues for those on all sides of the current citizenship debate. Germany has yet to define conclusively what "Germanness" means, and therefore is unable to come to a consensus on the permanent status of its Turkish residents. Are they permanent "guest workers?" Turkish citizens? Fellow Germans? Should there be cultural requirements of citizenship, and if so, what are they? In wrestling with these questions, Germany's Turkish population may well lead Germany to a greater understanding of contemporary pluralism.

Anni Baker

Ukraine

Successor state to the Ukrainian Soviet Socialist Republic. Ukraine consists of 232,046 square miles (601,000 sq km) of territory bordered by Belarus on the north, Russia on the north and east, the Black Sea, Moldova, Romania, and Hungary on the south, and Slovakia and Poland on the west. It has 52.2 million inhabitants, of whom in 1998 64.7 percent were Ukrainian, 32.8 percent Russian, and the remainder Hungarian, Tatar, Jewish, Romanian, and other. Its capital is Kiev, a city of 2.6 million inhabitants.

The immediate postwar years in Soviet Ukraine were marked by reconstruction and the reimposition of severe authoritarianism. A brief cultural thaw awakened Ukrainian nationalist sentiment in the late 1950s, a trend that continued in the 1960s under the leadership of Petro Shelest. The Brezhnev era (1964–82) brought further repression and economic stagnation. After 1985 General Secretary Mikhail Gorbachev's reforms propelled Ukraine and other Soviet republics toward independence, which it achieved in December 1991.

The Ukraine that emerged from World War II was very different from what it had been previously. Territorial expansion greatly extended Ukraine's western frontiers, which now included most of the former Polish regions of Galicia and Volhynia. Northern Bukovina (from Romania) and Transcarpathia (from Czechoslovakia) were added in 1944. After the war Soviet planners undertook a massive reconstruction effort to restore Ukraine's economy, which suffered much destruction in the war. In both material and human losses, Ukraine fared worse than any other European country during the war. In addition to the five to seven million Ukrainians who lost their lives, tens of thousands of villages, industrial enterprises, and collective farms were destroyed by the invading Germans. Postwar rebuilding under the Fourth Five-Year Plan (1946–50) stressed heavy industry, and by 1950 Ukraine's industrial output had surpassed prewar levels. Agriculture recovered more slowly, the result of low levels of investment, inefficient collectivization, and a catastrophic drought in 1946. A famine in 1947, the third visited upon Ukrainian peasants in as many decades of Soviet rule, claimed a million lives.

Ukraine. *Illustration courtesy of Bernard Cook.*

Throughout the Soviet Union, Stalin's last years were marked by an intensification of totalitarian controls and widespread repression. In Ukraine the chief agent of this crackdown was Nikita Khrushchev, head of the Communist Party of Ukraine (CPU) and later Stalin's successor as Soviet premier. Under Khrushchev's leadership, the secret police and party executed or imprisoned hundreds of thousands of Ukrainians alleged to have collaborated with the Germans during the war. All forms of Ukrainian nationalism, which the Soviets had permitted during the wartime mobilization, were now extinguished in the wake of a wide Russification campaign. In the newly annexed lands of western Ukraine, continued resistance to Soviet rule was brutally suppressed. Religious persecution also intensified. The few remaining Ukrainian Jewish communities were repressed by Soviet authorities, and in 1946 the Ukrainian Greek Catholic Church was forcibly merged with the Russian Orthodox Church.

Stalin's death in March 1953 and Khrushchev's ascendancy in Moscow marked a new era for Ukraine. Initiatives designed to decentralize economic management allowed the periphery to participate in planning. These reforms produced mixed results in Ukraine, where increases in heavy industrial output came at the expense of consumer goods and agriculture. Unlike Stalin, Khrushchev was favorably disposed to Ukrainians, and envisioned an alliance between Moscow and Kiev to govern the union, albeit with Moscow in the lead. Under Khrushchev a number of Ukrainians rapidly rose to prominence and occupied key party and government posts at the all-union level. In 1954 the new cooperation was feted during the three hundredth anniversary celebrations of the Pereiaslav Treaty, the agreement that unified Russia and Ukraine under Tsar Aleksey. As a gift to mark the occasion the Russian Republic ceded the Crimean peninsula to Ukraine, a gesture not entirely altruistic. Crimea was not only economically and politically troubled, but its population was 71 percent Russian. The transfer thus continued Ukraine's Russification.

Khrushchev's policy of de-Stalinization had far-reaching, if short-term, consequences for Ukraine. Stalinist tactics of mass arrest and terror ended, and repression became rarer and more discriminate. Amnesties for political prisoners initiated in 1953 allowed hundreds of thousands of inmates from the labor camp in the remote north and east of the USSR to return to Ukraine. Ukrainian arts and letters were promoted for the first time since the 1920s. Writers repressed during Stalin's reign were posthumously rehabilitated, formally banned works were republished, and a scholarly journal devoted to Ukrainian history appeared. But this experiment in tolerance lasted only several years. A 1959 education reform restricted instruction in the Ukrainian language. Toward the end of Khrushchev's rule Ukraine was increasingly Russified, and bold expressions of Ukrainian national culture were driven underground.

Khrushchev was replaced in 1964 by a collective leadership that gradually gave way to the authority of Leonid Brezhnev. While the new leaders ended Khrushchev's attempts to decentralize the administration and economy, the Soviet nationalities policy was liberalized, and the republics were again permitted limited cultural freedom. In Ukraine this renewed thaw led to the appearance of the "generation of the sixties," an alliance of writers, poets, artists, historians, film directors, and composers who embraced a renaissance of traditional Ukrainian arts and letters. In the most formidable display of this rediscovery of Ukrainian language and history, a seventeen-volume encyclopedia of Ukraine was completed in 1965.

Ukraine's cultural revival owed much to the leadership of Petro Shelest, Chairman of the Presidium of the Supreme Soviet of the Ukrainian Soviet Socialist Republic from 1963 to 1973, and from 1964 a full member of the Politburo of the Soviet Communist Party. The support of Shelest and other influential members of the party was essential for the success of the Ukrainization of the 1960s. Shelest also lobbied hard for Ukrainian economic reform, winning greater investment from Moscow and expanded local managerial control. Shelest's advocacy of economic and cultural self-determination greatly strengthened the party's popularity. During his tenure membership in the CPU grew at twice the USSR average rate to reach 2.5 million in 1971.

By 1970 the relative permissiveness of Shelest's Ukraine began drawing criticism from conservative members of the Soviet Communist Party. Plans to de-Russify higher education and other projects dedicated to strengthening Ukrainian culture were suddenly halted. Official propaganda criticized Shelest's policies as "anti-Soviet" and "bourgeois nationalist." As the window closed on Ukraine's cultural freedom, the dissident movement became more active. Writers began to circulate their work in typescript, or samizdat. Underground discussion groups formed and demonstrations were organized. The crackdown came in early 1972. In May of that year, after several hundred dissidents and protesters were arrested, Shelest was removed as CPU leader.

Shelest was succeeded by his long-time rival, Volodymyr Shcherbytsky, who would dominate Ukrainian politics until his resignation in 1989. Whereas Shelest was a fierce defender of Ukrainian national interests, Shcherbytsky was Moscow's obedient agent, enforcing Russification and dealing harshly with dissent. Shcherbystsky began his tenure by purging the CPU of thirty-seven thousand members, mostly loyal Shelest supporters. Arrests of national activists increased; thousands were interred in concentration camps or psychiatric institutions. The Helsinki Watch Group, a Ukrainian human rights organization founded in 1975, saw its entire membership imprisoned or exiled by the end of the decade. Shcherbytsky also silenced most overt manifestations of Ukrainian culture. Institutions that had flourished under Shelest, including Ukrainian-language presses and newspapers, scholarly and cultural organizations, and local societies of writers and artists, were now harshly repressed.

Under Shcherbytsky, Ukraine's economy continued to decline. Agriculture performed poorly, undermined as before by frequent droughts and inefficient planning. The lack of a transportation infrastructure prevented the timely delivery of foodstuffs, and harvests often rotted in the fields. Despite the continual investment imbalance that favored heavy industry, output in this sector declined steadily. In Ukraine the Eleventh Five-Year Plan (1981–85) yielded only 3.5 percent industrial growth, the lowest since the war. The republic's most important industries—coal mining and ferrous metallurgy—suffered precipitous drops in production. To respond to decreased coal production, as well as to the higher energy needs of an increasingly urbanized population, Soviet authorities launched an intensive nuclear power program. Between 1979 and 1984, four nuclear plants were constructed in Ukraine. The haste of the industry's expansion, and a conspicuous lack of quality and safety controls, led to the 1986 accident at the Chernobyl nuclear power station.

The appointment of Mikhail Gorbachev as general secretary of the Soviet Communist Party in 1985 had dramatic consequences for Ukraine. After decades of paralyzing economic and social stagnation, Gorbachev's policies of perestroika (restructuring) and glasnost (openness) initiated a Ukrainian national revival. Unlike the rapid and often violent transformation of the Baltic and Transcaucasion republics, Ukraine's response to Gorbachev's reforms was gradual and peaceful. Beginning in mid-1986, Ukrainian press and media sparked a public debate over areas of national concern. Widespread anger was voiced over the recent Chernobyl nuclear disaster and other ecological crimes perpetrated by Soviet economic planners. Russification was successfully rejected, and in 1989 Ukrainian became the republic's official language. The study of Ukrainian history experienced a revival, with previously proscribed subjects seeing the light for the first time. Details of the purges, the mass deportations, and the famine of the 1930s were published and widely read. A religious reawakening also swept Ukraine, with clergy and entire congregations emerging from underground. In 1989 the Ukrainian Greek Catholic Church was granted official recognition. As the national past was reclaimed, so were the nation's long-banned symbols: the blue-and-yellow Ukrainian national flag and the national anthem, which could again be heard at demonstrations and public events.

The tide of change in Ukraine soon became increasingly politicized. In March 1988 the Ukrainian Helsinki Union, formed by recently released political prisoners, issued calls for national sovereignty. In January 1989 an organization calling itself the Popular Movement of Ukraine for Perestroika, or Rukh, began advocating democratization, local rule, and human rights. These developments encountered fierce resistance from the CPU, but the wellspring of popular unrest soon made futile all official condemnations. Developments in Ukraine parallel the collapse of Communism in the Eastern European states and in the Baltic republics of the USSR. In September 1989 Shcherbytsky resigned as first secretary. In the parliamentary elections that followed on March 4, 1990, the Communist Party's monopoly on power finally ended. When the Ukrainian parliament met in May, only 239 of 450 delegates belonged to the CPU. On July 16 the parliament's communist majority and democratic opposition declared Ukraine's national sovereignty.

In response to the growing tide of nationalism now sweeping through most of the Soviet republics, Gorbachev proposed a new union treaty in fall 1990. In exchange for concessions of broad autonomy, the republics would permit central control of foreign policy, the military, and the financial system. In Ukraine the proposal triggered mass demonstrations and hunger strikes. Rukh, whose membership had continued to grow, began advocating total independence; only the CPU backed the Gorbachev plan. Within a year, however, events had overtaken Gorbachev and his supporters. A failed coup d'état by Communist hard-liners in August 1991 undermined the Soviet Union's remaining authority. Meeting in emergency session, the Ukrainian parliament declared full independence on August 24. A popular referendum ratified this decision on December 1. By the end of 1991, the USSR had ceased to exist.

As an independent state, Ukraine made rapid strides to enter the community of nations. Now the second-largest country in Europe, and one possessing enormous economic potential, Ukraine gained rapid international recognition. Even before the end of 1991 Ukrainian national armed forces were created out of Soviet military units remaining on Ukraine's soil. Presidential elections were called, and six candidates emerged, including two former political prisoners. On December 8, 1991, Ukraine joined Belarus and Russia to form the Commonwealth of Independent States (CIS), a loose association of former Soviet republics dedicated to military and economic cooperation. Despite this alliance, relations between Ukraine and Russia have remained strained over the disposition of the Black Sea Fleet. The question of the Crimean peninsula's sovereignty has also sparked debate and controversy. In 1995 Ukraine firmly asserted its authority over the Crimea by annulling the Crimean constitution and instituting direct rule from Kiev.

In recent years attempts at economic and bureaucratic reform have often been frustrated. In 1996 wage arrears in the state sector alone amounted to $200 million. The giant coal sector has experienced waves of strikes over both frozen wages and the accident rate, which is one of Europe's highest. Living standards have continued to remain low, and health care has not significantly improved over the course of the 1990s. Epidemics of hepatitis and diphtheria are common. Politically, however, Ukraine remains one of the most stable of the states created from the former Soviet Union, and the country has experienced virtually no ethnic or civil strife. This fact, along with the promise of increased foreign investment and NATO membership, suggests that Ukraine may soon be an active player on the European stage.

BIBLIOGRAPHY

Bilinsky, Yaroslav. *The Second Soviet Republic: The Ukraine after World War II.* New Brunswick, N.J.: Rutgers University Press, 1964.

Krawchenko, Bohdan. *Social Change and National Consciousness in Twentieth-Century Ukraine.* New York: Macmillan, 1985.

———. *Ukraine under Shelest.* Downsview, Ontario: Canadian Institute of Ukrainian Studies, University of Toronto Press, 1983.

Lewytzkyj, Boris. *Politics and Society in Soviet Ukraine, 1953–1980.* Downsview, Ontario: Canadian Institute of Ukrainian Studies, University of Toronto Press, 1984.

Magocsi, Paul Robert. *A History of Ukraine.* Seattle: University of Washington Press, 1996.

Shcherbitsky, V. V. *Soviet Ukraine.* Moscow: Progress, 1985.

Daniel Kowalsky

SEE ALSO Chernobyl; Crimea; Transcarpathia

Economy

The Ukrainian Soviet Socialist Republic was, after Russia, by far the most important economic unit of the USSR. Its famed black soil provided a fourth of the USSR's agricultural produce. Its heavy industry and mines provided machinery and raw materials for the other republics. Yet Ukraine has depended on the importation of natural gas and petroleum from Russia and Turkmenistan. Nuclear power from five nuclear power plants accounted for 44 percent of Ukraine's electricity in 1996. However, following the 1986 accident at the Chernobyl facility, the safety of its remaining plants has been in question.

With the collapse of the USSR the Ukrainian government removed many price controls and attempted to introduce the legal framework for privatization, but there was much resistance within the bureaucracy and the legislature. The process was thus stymied. Between 1992 and 1996 output fell to less than half the 1991 level. Ukraine's gross domestic product (GDP) is estimated to have declined by 6.6 percent annually between 1985 and 1995. Monetary indiscipline led to hyperinflation, which brought on widespread economic misery. Between 1985 and 1994 the average inflation rate was 160.9 percent. In 1992 inflation increased by 1,210 percent, and in 1993 it was 4,735 percent. Though only 380,400 people were officially listed as unemployed, it was estimated that three million were on unpaid leave.

After Leonid Kuchma was elected president in 1994, he promoted a comprehensive program of economic reform. He advocated monetary restraint and the removal of controls on prices and trade. In 1994 inflation decreased to 891 percent and in 1995 to 377 percent. A 1994 program initiated the privatization of state enterprises. However, there was still stubborn resistance from the bureaucracy and parliament. Inflation remained at 40 percent in 1996. State expenditures remained high, and the International Monetary Fund (IMF) suspended aid for a time. Though small-size enterprises were privatized, the privatization of medium and large-scale enterprises was halted until measures to prevent corruption in the transfer of assets from the state could be established. There was an extensive hidden (off the books) economy, which might have amounted to 60 percent of GDP. If the hidden economy were to be taken into account, both the employment rate and the GDP figure would be significantly improved.

In September 1996 a new currency, the hryvnya, was introduced but it has been severely weakened by inflation. The financial crisis in Russia in 1998, which led to a devaluation of the ruble, produced a sharp decline in exports from Ukraine to Russia. This undermined the possibility that Ukraine would have its first year of economic growth since independence. Despite increasing pressure from the IMF to accelerate reform, there was reluctance in 1999 to impose measures that in the short term would increase unemployment and boost prices.

BIBLIOGRAPHY

International Monetary Fund. *Ukraine.* Washington, D.C.: International Monetary Fund, 1992–.

Bernard Cook

SEE ALSO Chernobyl

Ulbricht, Walter (1893–1973)

Dominant political leader of the German Democratic Republic (GDR), or East Germany, from its founding in

1949 until his replacement as first secretary of the Socialist Unity (Communist) Party (SED) by Erich Honecker on May 3, 1971. A loyal Stalinist who frequently advocated more radical and intransigent policies than his Soviet patrons, Ulbricht presided over the imposition of Marxist-Leninist orthodoxy in the GDR, the suppression of a workers' revolt in 1953, and the erection of the Berlin Wall in 1961. In the 1960s he introduced economic reforms that enabled the GDR to become one of the ten leading industrial producers of the world. Growing differences with the leadership of the Soviet Union on how to respond to West German *Ostpolitik* led to Ulbricht's forced resignation in 1971.

Born into a working-class family and trained as a furniture maker, Ulbricht joined the Social Democratic Party in 1912, served in the Balkans during World War I (a war that he opposed), in 1918 joined the Spartakusbund, the revolutionary socialist group founded in 1916 by Karl Liebknecht and Rosa Luxemburg, which became the German Communist Party on December 30, 1918, and became a founding member of the Leipzig branch of the German Communist Party (KPD) in January 1919. A strong supporter of Lenin's model of a highly centralized party, Ulbricht went to Moscow in 1924 to be trained as a Comintern (the Soviet dominated international communist organization) official. He returned to Germany in 1926 as the newly appointed party chief Ernst Thälmann's close collaborator and was elected a member of the Reichstag (lower house of parliament) in 1928, where he exemplified Communist militancy by attacking Social Democrats (SPD) as "social fascists." As party leader in Berlin-Brandenburg from 1929 to 1933, he also organized Communist Party resistance to the Nazi Party. In October 1933, after the arrest of Thälmann and other party leaders, Ulbricht escaped to Paris, where he led the exiled KPD (nominally headed by Wilhelm Pieck) into reluctant conformity with the Comintern's new popular front strategy in 1935, renouncing revolutionary goals in favor of forming coalitions with bourgeois anti-fascist parties. Despite Soviet encouragement, collaboration between the KPD and the SPD remained minimal. Ulbricht actively enforced Stalinist policies in Spain during the Spanish Civil War from 1936 to 1938 against Trotskyites and other enemies of Stalin, who were fighting on the side of the Spanish Republic, which the Soviets were aiding and attempting to control. He spent the years of World War II in Moscow, where he prepared propaganda directed toward German prisoners of war in the USSR. The long exile in Moscow isolated Ulbricht and other party leaders from their social base in Germany and reinforced their subsequent total dependence on Soviet leaders. Germany's failure to resist fascism left in Ulbricht a lifelong distrust of the German people and of autonomous popular politics.

Ulbricht arrived at the outskirts of Berlin on April 29, 1945, as leader of one of the three "initiative groups" dispatched by the Soviets to organize the civilian administration in their occupation zone after the war. On June 11 the KPD was refounded with a gradualist program in keeping with the Soviet Union's goal of establishing a unified, demilitarized, and neutralized German state in which the KPD could exercise decisive influence. After the forced unification by the German Communists, with Soviet backing, of the SPD and KPD into the Socialist Unity Party (SED) in April 1946 under the cochairmanship of Wilhelm Pieck (KPD) and Otto Grotewohl (SPD), Ulbricht emerged as the new party's most important opponent of democratic gradualism and advocate of the centralization of power. After the founding of the COMINFORM in September 1947 to assure Stalin's control over the Communist Parties of Eastern Europe, and the hardening of Cold War divisions, Ulbricht received the green light from Stalin to convert the SED into a Leninist vanguard party with full authoritarian power, although Stalin continued to resist Ulbricht's demand for a separate socialist state in the Soviet zone until after the formal ratification of the West German constitution in May 1949. Ulbricht became deputy premier in the newly established German Democratic Republic (GDR) in October 1949 and general secretary (as of July 1953 first secretary) of the restructured SED in July 1950. His fear that the existence of the GDR could be sacrificed to the USSR's interest in a neutralized Germany and good relations with the West contributed to the urgency and intransigence of his policies for rapidly imposing socialism. Ulbricht's efforts to force the pace of state building in the GDR by arming the police, creating an army, and extending military training sometimes brought him into conflict with the Soviets, who, until 1955, fitfully pursued the chimera of gaining Western approval for a demilitarized, neutralized Germany (while at the same time continuing to exact heavy reparations from the GDR). Under Ulbricht's leadership SED control penetrated into every area of East German society in the 1950s. In February 1950 the Ministry of State Security (Staatssicherheitsdienst, STASI) was created on the Soviet model. A thoroughgoing purge led to the exclusion of some 150,000 members from the SED in 1950–51, most of them former Social Democrats. Wage levels were deliberately depressed to fund the expansion of the economy. Activist campaigns idealized workers and pressured them to overfulfill production goals, but the satisfaction of consumer needs received low priority. Forced by the unrealistic targets of its First Five-Year Plan to resort to authoritarian measures to increase production, the Ulbricht regime provoked a serious labor revolt in June 1953 that rapidly escalated into countrywide demands for democratic reforms and could be suppressed only through the declaration of martial law and the deployment of Soviet tanks. The crisis almost cost Ulbricht his leading role in the GDR as the Soviet post-Stalin leadership cast about for a ruler more popular with his own people and more sympathetic to the Soviet "new course." Ulbricht retained his position by skillfully exploiting the fact that former Soviet KGB chief Lavrenty Beria, arrested on June 26 and later executed had been his harshest critic. Ulbricht also benefited from the Cold War, as West German chancellor Konrad Adenauer's opposition to a neutralized united Germany and hostility toward communism left the Soviets little choice but to support the status quo in the East.

In 1956 Ulbricht tried to limit the impact of de-Stalinization in the GDR. The Hungarian Revolution of that year gave him the opportunity to purge moderates from positions of power in the party and state. Discipline, order, and moral rectitude were the guiding principles of Ulbricht's rule. Ulbricht amassed further power by becoming head of the National Defense Council in February 1960. After the death of President Wilhelm Pieck in September 1960, Ulbricht became head of state by assuming the chairmanship of the newly created Council of State, which replaced the office of president. In 1960 collectivization of agriculture was forcibly completed and further measures were taken to limit private retail and handicraft trades. All this contributed to the growing flood of refugees to the West, almost two hundred thousand in 1960 alone. By 1961 it became increasingly clear that the proclaimed goal of equaling West German per capita economic productivity by 1965 could be achieved only by sealing off West Berlin as an escape route for GDR citizens attracted by the much higher living standard in West Germany. After the failure of various Soviet attempts to pressure the West into changing the status of West Berlin so that it could no longer provide asylum to East German refugees, Ulbricht finally gained the approval of Soviet Premier Nikita Krushchev for the construction of the Berlin Wall on August 13, 1961.

The stabilizing effects of this "second founding" of the German Democratic Republic provided the precondition for pragmatic economic reforms, proclaimed by Ulbricht as the New Economic System of Planning and Managing the Economy in 1963. The New Economic System involved some decentralization of economic decision making; introduction of profitability as a measure of economic efficiency; greater scope for individual initiative and innovation; more emphasis on quality rather than mere quantity of production; greater reliance on economic, scientific, and technological expertise; and concentration on products best suited to East German resources and capacities. The reforms drew opposition from some party functionaries who resented their reduced role in economic decision making. The new command economy was more realistic and efficient than in the past, but still excluded all market mechanisms and still left the GDR economy dependent on raw materials, particularly oil, from the Soviet Union. In the 1960s the East German standard of living exceeded that of Eastern European states while still lagging well behind that of West Germany. The failure of the New Economic System to achieve its objective of economic parity with West Germany contributed to the weakening of Ulbricht's position in the early 1970s. But the crucial reason for his fall, in 1971, appears to have been Soviet mistrust of his independence and potential inflexibility in the face of West German chancellor Willy Brandt's *Ostpolitik*. Ulbricht was not averse to expanding contacts with the Federal Republic, as attested by the dramatic visit of Brandt to Erfurt in March 1970 and East German Premier Willi Stoph's return visit to Kassel in May 1970, but his commitment to gaining West German de jure recognition of the GDR and his adamant opposition to perpetuation of the status quo in Berlin made it unlikely that he would accept the kind of concessions necessary for the normalization of relations with the West sought by the Soviet leadership. Biographer Norbert Podewin's recent claim that Soviet leader Leonid Brezhnev feared Ulbricht's excessive readiness to negotiate with the West German SPD government appears doubtful. Rather, it was Ulbricht's control of these negotiations that Brezhnev feared. Soviet support and Ulbricht's declining health gave Erich Honecker the leverage to unseat Ulbricht as party chief in 1971. Ulbricht retained his formal title as chairman of the State Council, an office reduced to largely representational functions in 1972, until his death on August 1, 1973.

BIBLIOGRAPHY

Childs, David. *East Germany.* New York: Praeger, 1969.

Fulbrook, Mary. *Anatomy of a Dictatorship: Inside the GDR 1949–1989.* London: Oxford University Press, 1995.

Kaiser, Monika. *Machtwechsel von Ulbricht zu Honecker: Funktionsmechanismen der SED-Diktatur in Konfliktsituationen 1962 bis 1972.* Berlin: Akademie Verlag, 1997.

Podewin, Norbert. *Walter Ulbricht: Eine neue Biographie.* Berlin: Dietz Verlag, 1995.
Stern, Carola. *Ulbricht: A Political Biography.* New York: Praeger, 1965.
Ulbricht, Walter. *Whither Germany? Speeches and Essays on the National Question.* Dresden: Zeit im Bild, 1966.
Weitz, Eric D. *Creating German Communism, 1890–1990: From Popular Protests to Socialist State.* Princeton, N.J.: Princeton University Press, 1997.

Rod Stackelberg

SEE ALSO Berlin; Berlin Wall; German Democratic Republic: Grotewohl, Otto; Honecker, Erich; Pieck, Wilhelm

Ullsten, Ola (1931–)

Swedish prime minister (1978–79). Ola Ullsten was born in Umeå in the north of Sweden on June 23, 1931. After receiving his degree in social science from the Institute of Social Affairs in Stockholm, Ullsten worked in the temperance movement. Then he became a secretary to the parliamentary group of the Swedish Liberal, or People's Party (Folkspartiet, FP) from 1957 to 1961. In 1962 Ullsten became leader of the Liberals' youth organization and at the same time worked as a journalist for the *Dagens Nyheter,* the second largest newspaper in Sweden.

Ullsten was elected to parliament in 1965 and served there until 1984. In 1972 he became chair of the Liberal Party in the Stockholm area, and in March 1978 succeeded Per Ahlmark as chairman of the national Liberal Party. He held that post until the Social Democratic victory in 1983. Ullsten became a member of the government when the center-right coalition was formed under Thorbjörn Fälldin in 1976. Ullsten's first post was as minister of international development and cooperation (1976–78). He was deputy prime minister from March until October 1978. The Liberals and the Conservatives opposed Fälldin's efforts to halt the use of nuclear power in Sweden. When Fälldin resigned in October 1978, Ullsten headed a Liberal minority government. His government survived for nearly a year but lacked the ability to enact legislation in the problematic temporary areas of economics, welfare, and taxation. Ullsten achieved a temporary degree of popularity but was ultimately done in by the nuclear issue and Swedes' growing antipathy to nuclear power. After the September 1979 election Ullsten stepped down and Fälldin again headed a government composed of his Center Party, the Liberals, and the Conservatives. Ullsten served in it as minister of foreign affairs (1979–82) and also as deputy prime minister (1980–82). The Social Democrats regained control of the government in 1982. Ullsten was appointed Swedish ambassador to Canada in 1983, and transferred to Italy in 1989.

BIBLIOGRAPHY

Nordstrom, Byron J. "Ullsten, Ola." *Dictionary of Scandinavian History.* Westport, Conn.: Greenwood Press, 1986, 603–4.

Bernard Cook

Ulmanis, Guntis (1939–)

President of Latvia (1993–). Guntis Ulmanis was born in Riga on September 13, 1939. His great uncle, Karlis Ulmanis, was the last president of Latvia before its occupation by the Soviet Union in 1940. That year Ulmanis and his family were deported to Krasnoyarsk in Siberia, but were allowed to return to Soviet Latvia in 1946. In 1949 the Ulmanis family was deported again, but Ulmanis avoided the fate of his relatives because his mother had remarried and he temporarily was using a different surname. In secondary school he resumed using the name Ulmanis. He received a degree in economics from the Latvian State University in 1963. After military service he worked as an economist in the building sector and on the Riga Public Transportation Board. He was appointed deputy chairman of the Planning Board of the Riga Municipal Council but was fired because of his name and his family's past role. Nevertheless, in 1971 he was employed by the Riga Municipal Communal Services and eventually became its manager. He lectured on economics at the Riga Polytechnical Institute and the Latvian State University.

Ulmanis joined the Communist Party in 1965 but resigned his membership in 1989. He was appointed a member of the board of the Latvian Central Bank in 1992. He joined the Farmers' Union of Latvia in 1992 and became its honorary chairman in 1993. He was elected to parliament in June 1993 and was elected president in July. He was reelected president in June 1996. As president, Ulmanis stressed foreign policy and concluded the agreement on the withdrawal of Russian troops from Latvia. Under Ulmanis, Latvia was admitted to the Council of Europe and has applied for admission to the European Union.

BIBLIOGRAPHY

Dreifelds, Juris. *Latvia in Transition.* New York: Cambridge University Press, 1996.

Bernard Cook

Union of Soviet Socialist Republics

The Union of Soviet Socialist Republics (USSR), which was formed as a result of the Bolshevik Revolution of November 7, 1917, was, with 8,650,000 square miles (22,400,000 square kilometers), the largest state in terms of territory in the world. It had a population of 280 million in 1986 and its capital Moscow had approximately eight million residents. The Soviet Union was bordered by North Korea, China, Mongolia, Afghanistan, Iran, the Caspian Sea, Turkey, the Black Sea, Romania, Czechoslovakia, Poland, the Baltic Sea, Finland, Norway, the Barents Sea, the White Sea, the Kara Sea, the Laptev Sea, the East Siberian Sea, the Bering Sea, the Sea of Okhotsk, and the Sea of Japan.

The USSR was the successor state to the Russian Empire minus the territories that the new Communist regime was forced to relinquish as a result of the collapse of the empire, and the Treaties of Brest-Litovsk and Versailles and their aftermath. The USSR lost the former imperial territories of Finland, Estonia, Latvia, Lithuania, Poland, Northern Bukovina, and Bessarabia (Moldova). It gained, lost, and regained Karelia, Estonia, Latvia, Lithuania, Poland to the Curzon Line, and Bessarabia during World War II. During the war it also gained Tannu-Tuva, located between the Russian Soviet Federated Socialist Republic and Mongolia. Following World War II it gained the northern half of East Prussia (Kaliningrad Oblast); Petsamo (Petschenga) from Finland; and the lower half of Sakhalin Island and the Kuril Islands from Japan.

The history of the post-1945 USSR is rooted in the Russian Revolution, the Civil War (1918–20), Stalin's succession following the death of Lenin in January 1924, Stalin's consolidation of his power, the forced collectivization of the peasantry, the great purge of the 1930s, the horrendous destruction of World War II against Nazi Germany, and the move into the vacuum created in Eastern and central Europe by the collapse of the Third Reich.

Following the "Great Patriotic War," as the Soviets called World War II, any hope that Stalin might chart a more liberal course was rapidly dissipated. The Cold War followed immediately on the heels of World War II, and Stalin, acutely aware of the vulnerability of the war-weakened Soviet Union, eschewed liberality. In early 1946 he launched a campaign, headed by Andrey Zhdanov, member of the Politburo and the head of the party in Leningrad, at that time his heir apparent, to impose a terror-inspired conformity on the people of the USSR. Former POWs, regarded as untrustworthy and contaminated, were ushered from German concentration camps into the labor camps of the Soviet GULAG. Through the establishment of the Cominform, the Communist Information Bureau, in September 1947, Stalinist uniformity was imposed on the new Communist regimes of Eastern Europe. As Tito asserted his independence in Yugoslavia in 1948, Stalin carried out a brutal suppression of "national" Communists in the Soviet satellites. Real and imagined enemies of the state were rounded up and imprisoned or executed. Stalin apparently was planning a new purge when he died. After his death on March 5, 1953, the party leadership was determined to avoid the personal dictatorship exercised by Stalin. Collective leadership was to be the remedy. Georgy Malenkov, member of the Politburo and deputy chair of the Council of Ministers, who had positioned himself to succeed Stalin, was forced to choose between control of the state apparatus or of the party. He made the wrong choice, opting for the chairmanship of the Council of Ministers, or head of the state apparatus. Nikita Khrushchev, a member of the Politburo who was in charge of agriculture, was originally listed as one of three secretaries of the Communist Party, by September became general secretary, or head, of the party. From that strong point he eventually prevailed. As Malenkov and Khrushchev sparked for supremacy, they joined together to eliminate Lavrenty Beria, head of the secret police who was feared by all the party leadership. Beria was apparently attempting to position himself as a potentially liberalizing leader when the worker uprising in Berlin in June 1953 provided the others with the opportunity to move against him.

Khrushchev attacked Malenkov's emphasis on providing consumer goods and stressing agriculture at the expense of heavy industry. Once he had defeated Malenkov and replaced him as premier in 1955 with the second-rank Nikolay Bulganin, Khrushchev adopted Malenkov's economic program as well as his policy of peaceful co-existence with the West. In an effort to separate himself from the other leaders, Khrushchev launched his program of de-Stalinization at the Communist Party's Twentieth Congress in February 1956. When reverberations from his denunciations of Stalin led to unrest in Poland and outright rebellion in Hungary later that year, there was an attempt in June 1957 by other leaders in the party Presidium to remove Khrushchev. He countered the majority there by appealing to the party's Central Committee, which had supported his plan to decentralize the economy. In this he was supported by the army leadership, headed by Marshall Zhukov Georgy, the minister of defense. Supported by this broader representation of the party, he prevailed. Malenkov, Bulganin, Vyacheslav Molotov, the foreign minister who had long been a loyal supporter of Stalin and agent of his policies, and Lazar Kaganovich, another loyal Stalinist who had headed heavy industry, were all moved from the leadership and assigned low-level positions in the economy or state service. Khrushchev consolidated his power by assuming the office of premier as well as party leader. In October 1957 war hero Zhukov, who had helped to save Khrushchev but was now regarded by Khrushchev as his last personal rival, was removed as well. Zhukov was accused by Khrushchev of fostering a cult of personality and of attempting to make the army independent of the party.

The great technical achievement of the USSR, sending Sputnik I, the first artificial satellite into orbit on October 4, 1957, ironically played a part in Khrushchev's ouster. With the technology that enabled the USSR to orbit Sputnik, the country had capability of producing missiles that could reach the United States. The USSR had detonated an atomic bomb in 1949 and a hydrogen bomb in 1953, but the United States maintained strategic superiority in its ability to deliver bombs to targets in the USSR by aircraft and medium-range missiles stationed in Turkey. Soviet medium-range missiles could not reach U.S. targets in the contiguous forty-eight states. Khrushchev, however, decided to delay a massive construction of inter-continental ballistic missiles to concentrate limited Soviet economic resources on his Virgin Lands agricultural plan. In his opinion, the U.S. belief that the USSR could deliver atomic warheads was almost as good as having that capacity. Khrushchev's de-Stalinization campaign was a factor in increasingly strained relations with Chairman Mao Tse-tung, the head of state of Communist China. Mao taunted the USSR for not utilizing its missiles to provide an umbrella for the expansion of Communist in Asia.

Rather than using the supposed missiles for offensive purposes, Khrushchev sought to use them to achieve "peaceful coexistence" with the West. He traveled to the United States and met with President Dwight Eisenhower at the presidential retreat Camp David in Maryland in September 1959. Khrushchev was more interested in eliminating the ongoing problem of West Berlin, which as a capitalist island in the midst of the Communist German Democratic Republic was a visual indication of the material success of the western Federal Republic of Germany and an escape valve through which many talented and educated East Germans fled to the West, than dealing with Asia. He made a number of ultimatums but when the West did not give in, he gave his assent to the construction of the Berlin Wall in August 1961. By that time the West, with the use of American U-2 spy planes, knew that the USSR had not developed its ICBM capacity. Khrushchev, still dealing with severe economic problems at home opted to take advantage of the solution offered by Communist Cuba. He decided to install medium-range nuclear missiles there and ignited the Cuban Missile Crisis of 1962. Such a risk would be held against him by the same leadership that castigated him for his retreat under U.S. pressure. In addition to the Cuban fiasco Khrushchev was held responsible for the economic disaster of the Virgin Lands project and opposed by the army and the advocates of heavy industry for his decision to emphasize consumer goods. His decision to divide the leadership of the party into urban and rural sections and to establish a time limit for the holding of party posts threatened the privileged status of the party leadership. He was removed by the Presidium on October 15, 1964. Leonid I. Brezhnev became head of the party and Aleksey N. Kosygin became the chairman of the Council of Ministers, or premier.

Under Brezhnev the Soviet Union retreated from the mild liberalization allowed by Khrushchev. The regional administration established under Khrushchev was abandoned and central direction of the economy was reestablished. But, the new direction was not all-encompassing. Managers of local concerns were given authority over factory labor questions with the exception of the total figure to be expended on wages. They were also allowed to make minor investments from profits. Sales and profits also replaced gross output as the measures of productivity. Nevertheless, growth in the 1970s stagnated as a result of inefficiency, technological inadequacies, centrally determined allocation of resources and labor, and an increasing concentration on military production.

Brezhnev dramatically increased the resources dedicated to the military. His goal was parity with the United States so that the USSR would not be faced with the necessity of backing down again in the future. The direct relations of the two superpowers were to be governed by the policy of détente. However, Brezhnev wished to solidify the USSR's control of its sphere and to contest peripheral areas with the United States through proxy wars. When concerned with the stability of its sphere, the USSR intervened in Czechoslovakia in August 1968 to terminate the liberalization of the Prague Spring. The Brezhnev Doctrine was enunciated, declaring that the Soviet Union had the right to intervene in any socialist state threatened by external aggression or internal subversion, which endangered its socialist status.

The Soviet desire to freeze its control over its sphere was a compelling force behind the USSR's agreement to the 1975 Helsinki Accords, which set up the Organization for Security and Cooperation in Europe. The signers agreed to accept the frontiers established at the end of World War II. The price of Western recognition of these frontiers was the USSR's acceptance of a statement of basic human rights. This component of Helsinki came back to haunt the Soviet Union as Helsinki Watch groups were formed to protest Soviet abuses, including those committed by its fellow socialist states of human rights.

In 1979 the Soviet Union began a ten-year intervention in Afghanistan to prop up a Marxist regime that faced serious internal divisions and a growing anti-Marxist resistance. The struggle eventually proved difficult for the USSR to sustain. Its initial success against the rebels was followed by increasing failure as the rebels received weapons from the United States through Pakistan, especially shoulder-fired antiaircraft missiles, which neutralized Soviet control of the air. With the invasion of Afghanistan and the election of Ronald Reagan as U.S. president in 1980, détente gave way to a new period of tension.

In 1981 the Soviets responded to the threat posed by the Solidarity movement to the socialist system in Poland by pressing President Wojciech Jaruzelski to impose martial law or face the possibility of Soviet intervention. The USSR's deployment of its SS-20 intermediate-range missiles in Europe was countered by the introduction of new U.S. Pershing II and Cruse missiles. The proposal of the Reagan administration to develop an antimissile defense system, the Strategic Defense Initiative, presented the Soviet Union with a new threat. If the Americans were to develop such a system, which was clearly beyond the technical and economic capacity of the Soviet Union, this would neutralize the Soviet nuclear deterrent and make a successful U.S. first strike possible. The U.S. response to the Soviet deployment of its SS-20s and the "Star Wars" bluff, given the increasing feebleness of the Soviet system's command economy, made accommodation imperative.

Before accommodation became an obvious imperative the leadership made an effort to stem the economic decline that set in as Brezhnev dramatically increased Soviet military strength. The Soviet leadership had become increasingly elderly and hidebound, and corruption, nepotism, and inefficiency flourished. With the death of Brezhnev in November 1982, the Politburo chose Yuri Andropov, head of the KGB (secret police), as his successor. Andropov was know as a vigorous opponent of corruption and it was hoped that his leadership could improve lagging Soviet productivity by reducing alcoholism, absenteeism, loafing on the job, and corruption. However, Andropov's worsening health sidelined him for the second half of his brief tenure. He died in February 1984 with Soviet problems unresolved. The choice of the Andropov reform faction was seventy two-year-old sickly Konstantin Chernenko, Brezhnev's old friend and collaborator. He lasted little more than a year, dying in March 1985. The grave problems of the USSR had been put on hold for another year, but now Mikhail Gorbachev, was first secretary of the Communist Party. Gorbachev, who had been in charge of economic reform under Andropov, wanted to move away from the centralized decision making and bureaucratic inertia that had contributed to Soviet inefficiency. When his effort to introduce perestroika (restructuring) encountered bureaucratic opposition, he decided on a program of glasnost (openness) and democracy to pressure or bypass entrenched interests and fight corruption and inefficiency.

Gorbachev hoped to take pressure off the Soviet economy by coming to an arms accommodation with the West. He hoped to strengthen the Soviet Union internally by fighting corruption and inefficiency. He did not intend to be the grave digger of the Soviet system, but he unleashed the forces that did them in. While he called for openness and competition for office among multiple Communist candidates, he was not able to control what he unleashed. The greatest credit due Gorbachev is that he did not resort to force to try to preserve Soviet hegemony in Eastern Europe or to preserve the Soviet Union and communism at home. He gave his blessing to Jaruzelski's decision to relegalize the Solidarity movement in Poland and refused to give his backing to Erich Honecker's request for Soviet support for a repression of the East German protest movement in October 1989. Gorbachev also reluctantly agreed to the reunification of Germany in the Four plus Two Agreement in summer 1990.

Gorbachev was accused of moving too quickly and radically by conservatives and of insufficient commitment to reform by Boris Yeltsin and other proponents of rapid change. The conflict between Yeltsin and Gorbachev probably had more to do with ego and personal ambition than with substance. The two completely fell out in 1987 and Gorbachev removed Yeltsin from the Politburo and as first secretary of the Moscow party apparatus. But he did not exile Yeltsin from Moscow, and the latter was able to recoup his fortunes. The Central Committee of the Russian Congress of People's Deputies elected Yeltsin its chairman in May 1990, and he was elected president of the Russian Republic in a direct election. Though theoretically Gorbachev's post of executive president of the Soviet Union was superior, he had not acquired that position through a popular election.

In December 1990 Gorbachev's close adviser and foreign minister, Edvard Shevardnadze, resigned, darkly warning of a reactionary coup. The coup came on August 19, 1991, one day before a new Union Treaty reorganizing the Soviet Union was to have been signed. Though Gorbachev, who was on vacation in the Crimea, was placed under house arrest, the coup was miserably planned and executed. The conservative Communist leaders of the coup failed to arrest Yeltsin, who proceeded to the Russian parliament building (White House) and rallied popular opposition. The army and the KGB were not united behind the attempted coup, and what support existed for it soon cooled. Gorbachev was released and returned to Moscow, but he completely misread the situation. He appeared before the Russian Parliament and, without thanking Yeltsin for saving the day, announced that he had everything under control and that the Communist Party could be reformed. Yeltsin responded by banning the Communist Party of the Soviet Union (CPSU) in the Russian Republic. Two days later Gorbachev felt compelled to resign as general secretary of the CPSU. He called on the Central Committee to dissolve and issued a decree suspending the operation of the party and confiscating its property.

The Soviet Union crumbled around Gorbachev, who was by then powerless to prevent its demise. The Soviet republic of Estonia declared its independence on August 19, Latvia on August 20, Ukraine and Belarus on August 25, Uzbekistan on August 26, and Moldova on August 27. Though the Congress of People's Deputies of the Soviet Union, established by the new constitution approved in June 1988 as the body that would elect the Soviet president and a two chamber legislature, dissolved itself on September 5, Gorbachev and leaders of ten of the republics formed a new State Council to preserve some form of unity. Nevertheless, its first formal action was the recognition of the complete independence of Estonia, Latvia, and Lithuania. When approximately 90 percent of Ukrainian voters approved of Ukrainian independence in a December 1 referendum and 61.5 percent voted for Leonid Kravchuk, former head of the Ukrainian Communist Party, as the republic's new president, "a new political reality," in the words of Yeltsin, superseded any hope of a continuation of the union.

On December 8, 1991, Yeltsin, Kravchuk, and Stanislav Shushkevic, president of Belarus, meeting outside the Belarusan capital of Minsk, signed the official death notice of the USSR. They established a Commonwealth of Independent States to replace the old union. Bowing to the inevitable, Gorbachev, the last president of the Soviet Union, resigned on December 25, 1991.

BIBLIOGRAPHY

Åslund, Anders. *Gorbachev's Struggle for Economic Reform.* Ithaca, N.Y.: Cornell University Press, 1991.

Crummey, Robert O., ed. *Reform in Russia and the U.S.S.R.: Past and Prospects.* Urbana: University of Illinois Press, 1989.

Dunbabin, J. P. D. *The Cold War: The Great Powers and Their Allies.* London: Longman, 1994.

Eklof, Ben. *Soviet Briefing: Gorbachev and the Reform Period.* Boulder, Col.: Westview Press, 1989.

LaFeber, Walter. *America, Russia, and the Cold War, 1945–1996.* 8th ed. New York: McGraw-Hill, 1997.

Suny, Ronald Grigor. *The Soviet Experiment: Russia, the USSR, and the Successor States.* New York: Oxford University Press, 1998.

Tucker, Robert C. *Political Culture and Leadership in Soviet Russia: From Lenin to Gorbachev.* New York: Norton, 1987.

Bernard Cook

SEE ALSO Afghanistan War; Brezhnev Doctrine; Cuban Missile Crisis; Détente; Peaceful Coexistence; Strategic Defense Initiative

Soviet Union and Germany

For Stalin in 1945, Germany represented a defeated enemy that should be made to pay for the destruction it had inflicted on the USSR during World War II. Furthermore, Stalin wanted Germany reformed so that it would not again become a threat to the Soviet Union. Germany was also a country where the Soviet Union might gain lasting influence and enhance its economic and political power vis-à-vis the West. However, because of the outbreak of the Cold War, the Soviet dictator and his successors found it ever more difficult to further their objectives on the former enemy's territory. The Cold War and East-West disagreement over Germany were mutually reinforcing, and the Soviet Union itself bore much responsibility for the failure of its German policy. Not halfway into the first postwar decade, the Soviets came to pursue an essentially defensive German policy that on the one hand aimed to consolidate the Soviet-controlled east of the country and on the other tried to disrupt West Germany's integration into the West. By 1955 the new policy was succeeding on the first count but had failed completely on the second.

It appears that in 1945 Stalin did not have a detailed plan for Germany. Reportedly, he had little faith in the ability of the anti-Hitler coalition of the USSR, the United States, and Great Britain, to agree on administrative or economic issues in Germany but, probably in part because he believed there to be opportunities for the spreading of Soviet influence through the entire country, he was willing to try to work with the West. Meanwhile, the Soviet military established control over the Soviet zone of occupation, an endeavor for which it made heavy use of the services of German Communists, organized first in the German Communist Party (KPD), and as of April 1946, in the Socialist Unity Party of Germany (SED). The Soviet government also began to extract extensive reparations from the zone. The often harsh and ineffective Soviet/SED administrative and reparations policies contributed to the formation of a society in the Soviet zone that was pluralist only in name and with a population generally weary of Communist power.

By the end of 1947 attempts to create a single allied administration for Germany that would eventually hand power back to the Germans themselves had failed, mainly because East and West could not agree on economic policy. The inability to resolve the issue of reparations, particularly the question of whether the Soviet Union would share in reparations from the Western zones, had after 1945 worked steadily to split Germany into two parts. In response to this development the United States and Britain, later joined by France, continued steps that in 1949 would lead to a separate West German state. Stalin was left with few options other than to try to coerce the West back to the search for a common policy for a single Germany.

In this attempt—the Berlin blockade of June 1948 to May 1949—Stalin failed. When in spring and summer 1949 the Federal Republic of Germany (FRG) was created from the three Western occupation zones, the USSR followed suit on October 7 with the founding of the German Democratic Republic (GDR).

One of the Soviets' greater disappointments in these years may have been the lack of enthusiasm for its policies among the population of Germany, East and West. After 1945 and possibly as late as 1952, the Soviet leadership apparently believed that one of the ways in which it could gain influence in Germany and thwart Western policies there was for the SED to gain a certain measure of respect and popularity among the general population. After 1949 Stalin still believed that by making nationalistic appeals to all Germans, he could cause upheaval in West Germany, disrupt the Western integration of the Federal Republic, and thus leave the question of Germany's political future open. This kind of thinking produced the Stalin note of March 1952 to the U.S., Britain, and France. The note proposed a four-power conference to discuss the establishment of a unified, democratic, neutral, armed Germany. That scenario, however, failed to materialize, and left the USSR with its own poorly functioning German state.

When the West did not show any interest in the Soviet proposed four-power conference, and, more important, when West German public opinion also failed to support his proposal, Stalin quickly ordered what amounted to Sovietization of the GDR. This intensified socialization campaign and its insensitive, haphazard implementation by the SED, along with continued Soviet reparations demands on a country that was itself in great need of economic assistance, in large measure caused the nationwide, anti-Communist East German uprising of June 1953.

By this time Stalin had died (March 5). His successors debated the growing East German crisis intensively during spring 1953, eventually deciding to modify the harsh socialization campaign. One of the Soviet leaders, Lavrenty Beria, head of the secret police, argued for complete abandonment of the socialist aim for the GDR, as well as a renewed push for German reunification, but he was outvoted by his colleagues and executed shortly thereafter.

Beria's removal from office in May and the June uprising in the GDR ended virtually all talk in the USSR of abandoning the SED and prepared the way for a gradual policy shift away from emphasis on all-German issues and toward consolidation of the GDR and its regime. Two factors would cement this policy in place: the retreat in the ongoing Kremlin succession struggle of Georgy Malenkov, the last proponent of an accommodating policy toward the West, and the final resolution in the West, through West Germany's membership in NATO (May 1955), of the quest for German rearmament in a Western framework.

At the Geneva conference of July 1955, the first meeting between the leaders of East and West since the Potsdam Conference of 1945, no progress occurred on a resolution of the division of Germany. By this time the Soviet leadership led by Nikita Khrushchev had decided, and stated so openly, that no East-West agreement on Germany could be concluded at the expense of the interests of the GDR. The second Geneva conference of 1955 of the foreign ministers of Britain, France, the Soviet Union, and the United States confirmed that there would be two Germanies for much longer than many had been willing to accept in 1949.

BIBLIOGRAPHY

Naimark, Norman. *The Russians in Germany: A History of the Soviet Zone of Occupation, 1945–1949.* Cambridge, Mass.: Harvard University Press, 1995.

Richter, James. *Krushchev's Double Bind: International Pressures and Domestic Coalition Politics.* Baltimore: Johns Hopkins University Press, 1994.

Wettig, Gerhard. "All-German Unity and East German Separation in Soviet Policy, 1947–1949," in *Jahrbuch für Kommunismusforschung.* Berlin: Akademie Verlag, 1994.

———. "Die Deutschlandnote vom 10. März 1952 auf der Basis diplomatischer Akten des russischen Aussenministeriums: Die Hypothese des Wiedervereinigungsangebots." *Deutschland Archiv* 26, no. 7 (1993): 786–805.

Ruud van Dijk

Gorbachev's Political Program: Glasnost and Perestroika

Reform project of 1985–1991 that precipitated the collapse of the USSR. As the last general secretary of the Communist Party of the Soviet Union and the last Soviet president (head of state), Mikhail Gorbachev initiated a series of reforms designed to transform a stagnant and corrupt system. Known collectively as New Political Thinking, Gorbachev's reforms constituted a revolution from above designed to recast all aspects of Soviet society. The reforms not only failed but led to the disintegration of the Soviet Union and the transformation of the postwar order.

The Gorbachev reform program, though spanning only six years, evolved through three stages. From 1985 to 1986 Gorbachev consolidated his own power, attempted to invigorate the economy, launched an antialcohol campaign, and took the first steps toward the policy of glasnost (openness). During the period 1987–1988, Gorbachev promoted economic and political perestroika (restructuring), generous overtures of reconciliation toward the West, and greater toleration of nationalist aspirations in the Soviet republics and Eastern Europe. The final attempt at reform, from 1989 to 1991, was characterized by economic failures and wide-ranging demokratizatsiya (democratization).

Gorbachev came to power under extreme handicaps. As the leader of the largest nation in the world in terms of square miles, he presided over a highly corrupt and mismanaged bureaucracy that was impotent to solve the myriad economic and social problems plaguing Soviet society. Gorbachev's election as general secretary by the Communist Party's Politburo was on the slimmest of margins; only the absence of key opponents at the time of the vote permitted his ascension to the highest office in the party and hence to the most powerful and important post in the USSR. Gorbachev's first task was to consolidate his own power and eliminate potential opposition. With considerable skill and speed, he appointed like-minded reformers to high positions, including Edvard Shevardnadze as foreign minister, Aleksandr Yakovlev as head of party propaganda, and Nikolay Ryzhkov as chair of the Council of Ministers. Less than a year after taking office, Gorbachev's reform team was in place.

During his first two years as general secretary, Gorbachev's priority was economic reform. He believed that the planned economy was basically sound, but corruption among managers and the bad work habits of Soviet citizens had undermined the system. Using the catchword *uskorenie* (acceleration), Gorbachev introduced a series of policies designed to reinvigorate the economy, reward hard work, and crack down on laziness and corruption. His Five-Year Plan (1986–90) called for dramatically increased production targets and national income. To eliminate bureaucratic waste and inefficiency, he streamlined individual agricultural ministries into a coordinated superministry, Gosagroprom. Gorbachev also created Gospriemka, a quality-control organization whose inspectors monitored factory output. Shoddy goods were to be destroyed and the responsible managers reprimanded or fired and factory workers penalized. Finally, a temperance campaign was launched in May 1985 to curtail the rising economic and social costs of rampant alcoholism.

In both the short and long term, the acceleration reforms were conclusive failures. The overly ambitious production targets, the creation of new layers of bureaucracy, and the simplistic anticorruption drive revealed a poor understanding of the realities of the Soviet economy. The goals of the 1986–90 plan raised only expectations, while no real incentives were introduced to encourage success. The antialcohol campaign was a major miscalculation and cost the Soviet treasury billions of rubles in lost revenue. Alcoholism continued unabated as black market distilleries flourished, sugar stocks were depleted, and incidences of alcohol poisoning increased.

Mentioned first by Gorbachev in December 1984, the term "glasnost" was originally intended to encourage party members to discuss economic problems whose very existence had hitherto been denied. The spirit of glasnost soon led to a relaxation of state censorship over intellectual and cultural life. One of the first beneficiaries of the new policy was noted physicist and dissident Andrey Sakharov, who in 1986 was released from internal exile. The full potential of glasnost was revealed in November 1987 when Gorbachev delivered a startling speech in which he, like former Premier Nikita Khrushchev, condemned Stalin's crimes, and encouraged Soviet citizens to question their history. A flood of official revelations followed, including the state's admission of responsibility for the massacre in 1940 of thousands of Polish officers in the Katyn Forest, as well as details of the secret protocols of the Nazi-Soviet Pact, in which Germany and the USSR agreed to attack and divide Poland between them at the start of World War II. In the next several years thousands of Stalin's victims were posthumously rehabilitated, literary works long proscribed such as Aleksandr Solzhenitsyn's *Gulag Archipelago* were published, and journals and newspapers such as *Ogonyok* and *Argumenty i fakty* were permitted to address formerly taboo subjects. In contrast to the secrecy and denials surrounding the 1986 Chernobyl nuclear disaster in Soviet Ukraine, the 1988 earthquake in Soviet Armenia was openly discussed and honestly covered by the press. By 1989 glasnost had initiated a reassessment of the entire Soviet period, eventually extending to the very legitimacy of the Communist Party.

During the second wave of reform, from 1987 to 1988, acceleration gave way to perestroika, a radical restructuring of the economic system. Gorbachev now broke with the command economy and initiated limited market mechanisms. Hoping to infuse the Soviet economy with foreign capital, legislation passed in January 1987 allowed foreign firms to open joint ventures in the USSR. Later that year, new laws legalized the establishment of small private businesses and cooperatives and encouraged further private initiatives. On January 1, 1988, the State Enterprise Law decentralized some state decision making and allowed enterprise managers greater authority. The growth of private entrepreneurship, however, was stymied by exorbitant taxes and bureaucratic obstacles, while the state continued to control prices in key sectors of the economy. Gorbachev's reforms created not a capitalist economy but market socialism: private ownership of small shops, restaurants, and farms, and state ownership of large productive facilities. These new economic reforms did not appreciably alter the entrenched system, which permitted corruption to thrive and inefficient producers to maintain monopolies.

Closely allied with domestic reform was Gorbachev's reinvention of Soviet foreign policy. On taking office he began to downplay the hostility between the Soviet Union and the West. His 1985 arms control talks with President Ronald Reagan in Geneva paved the way for future meetings aimed at reducing both the risks of nuclear war and the high cost of maintaining the arms race. In 1989 Gorbachev withdrew the last Soviet troops from Afghanistan, ending a decade-long conflict that had cost the USSR millions of rubles and thousands of dead. In Eastern Europe Gorbachev adopted a hands-off policy and encouraged liberalization. On a state visit to East Germany in October 1989 he formally repealed the Brezhnev Doctrine, freeing the satellite regimes to pursue independence and political reform without the threat of Soviet intervention. Within a year all the Communist regimes of the Soviet bloc had fallen. For Gorbachev's role in ending the Cold War, he was awarded the Noble Peace Prize in 1990.

Foreign successes were not equaled at home, where the final stage of Gorbachev's reform effort was marked by swift moves towards *demokratizatsiya.* By 1989 it was clear that the economic policies of acceleration and perestroika had failed, and glasnost had only augmented and given voice to public discontent. In the Soviet republics, nationalist calls for self-determination and violent protests over Moscow's rule became more frequent. Gorbachev believed that only political reform would shore up public confidence in the system, prevent the union from splintering, and permit his economic policies to succeed. As early as January 1987 he had offered explicit support for competitive elections. At the Twenty-ninth Party Congress held during the summer of 1988, a new legislature was created—the Congress of People's Deputies of the USSR. The first all-union elections for it were held in March 1989, and on May 25 the Congress held its inaugural session. The delegates elected Gorbachev president. The following year, a constitutional amendment formally ended the leading role of the Communist Party in Soviet politics.

Although Gorbachev had not created a bona fide democracy, his policies introduced genuine pluralism to the Soviet Union for the first time. For Gorbachev's conservative and radical opponents, however, the political reforms were either too much or too little. In the second half of 1991, Gorbachev's reform agenda and position of prominence was seriously undermined, first by a hardliner coup and then by Boris Yeltsin's democratic reaction. As one Soviet republic after another declared its sovereignty, Gorbachev, general secretary of the CPSU and president of the USSR, found himself presiding over a meaningless political party and a union with dwindling membership. The Soviet era was drawing to a close.

When Gorbachev came to power in 1985, he hoped to modernize and strengthen the Soviet Union, not destroy it. Attempts by the general secretary to reform the country revealed the intractable problems created by an inefficient command economy, a bankrupt ideology, and a corrupt and oppressive political system. Like Khrushchev, Gorbachev's greatest successes came abroad, where he liberated Eastern Europe and diffused the Cold War climate of fear and hatred. By contrast, in the Soviet Union Gorbachev's New Political Thinking brought chaos, economic dislocation, and ethnic strife. Gorbachev himself was not to blame, for the failure of glasnost and perestroika demonstrated above all that the Soviet system could not be reformed.

BIBLIOGRAPHY

Brown, Archie. *The Gorbachev Factor.* Oxford: Oxford University Press, 1996.

Dallin, Alexander, and Gail Lapidus, eds. *The Soviet System in Crisis.* Boulder, Colo.: Westview Press, 1991.

Gorbachev, Mikhail. *Perestroika.* New York: Harper & Row, 1987.

Grachev, Andrei. *Final Days.* Boulder, Colo.: Westview Press, 1995.

Ligachev, Yegor. *Inside Gorbachev's Kremlin.* New York: Pantheon, 1992.

Miller, John. *Mikhail Gorbachev and the End of Soviet Power.* New York: Macmillan, 1993.

Walker, Rachel. *Six Years That Shook the World.* Manchester, England: Manchester University Press, 1993.

Daniel Kowalsky

Coup of August 19, 1991

Abortive attempt by hard-line apparachiks to halt the democratization and breakup of the Soviet Union. Poorly organized and widely opposed, the August coup collapsed in three days. Its failure accelerated Soviet disintegration, which was already well advanced. The Communist Party was discredited, the balance of power shifted irrevocably to the Soviet republics, and the demise of the Soviet Union was assured.

From 1985 to 1991 Soviet leader Mikhail Gorbachev's reform program of perestroika and glasnost unleashed two trends in Soviet society: A demand for the establishment of genuine democratic change and a call for self-determination in the union republics. By mid-1989 Gorbachev neither fully controlled nor consistently supported the pace of the Soviet Union's transformation. He sought at once to direct the reform agenda while attempting to preserve the continuity of the Stalinist power structure. Paralyzed by ambivalence, he alienated both democrats and hard-liners. In early 1991 Gorbachev allied himself with the forces of reaction. In January he called out the armed forces to crush an uprising in Vilnius, capital of Soviet Lithuania, and later purged Soviet central television. When this course failed to quell domestic turmoil, Gorbachev shifted to the radical and nationalist camp. Together with Boris Yeltsin, who had been elected president of Russia in June, Gorbachev drafted the Union Treaty, a treaty designed to reshape the structure of the Soviet Union, reducing the power of the central government and granting the fifteen soviet republics wide autonomy to control their own economies, legal affairs, internal politics, and taxation. On August 20, 1991, Gorbachev was to join the leaders of five republics to sign the Union Treaty.

For the conservatives, the new agreement marked the final stage of the unraveling of the Soviet empire. Already in July the Communist Party was dealt twin blows when Yeltsin issued a decree banning workplace activities of all political parties and Gorbachev submitted a highly radical party program to the party's Central Committee. Moreover, the rise of the republics and the decline of the Communist Party took place against a rapidly deteriorating economic situation, rising crime, impending food and fuel shortages, and the collapse of the command economy. After debating some kind of intervention for months, Gorbachev's conservative foes resolved to act.

The plotters took action when they realized that they were becoming increasingly irrelevant. However, they lacked a clear set of goals. The leading conspirators were Prime Minister Valentin Pavlov, Vice President Valentin Yanaev, Minister of State Security Vladimir Kryuchkov, and Minister of Defense Dmitry Yazov. To this core group were added Boris Pugo, the interior minister; Oleg Baklanov, first vice chairman of the Defense council; and two other men representing industry and agriculture, Aleksandr Tiziakov and Vasily Starodubtsev. None of the eight were Politburo or Secretariat members, but in terms of offices held, it was a powerful grouping. The final meeting of the conspirators, all of whom were Gorbachev appointees, took place August 16 at a KGB resort outside Moscow.

The coup began Sunday, August 18, 1991. Gorbachev was vacationing in the Crimea with his family. The plotters' first act was to send a delegation to Gorbachev, led by Valery Boldin, the president's chief of staff, along with Yury Plekhanov, chief of the security directorate of the KGB, to seek Gorbachev's own sanction of the transfer of power. Gorbachev refused and KGB agents from Sevastopol placed him and his family under house arrest. Gorbachev's private guards, however, erected a radio antenna so the president could follow the course of events through foreign broadcasts.

The putschists made three reckless gambles, none of which played out: Gorbachev would accept their initiative and provide the leadership for their emergency regime; they could retain the loyalty of the security forces (KGB, police, and armed forces); and they would face no popular opposition.

Troops were mobilized around Moscow and on Monday, August 19, tanks and armored personnel carriers moved toward the city. TV and radio broadcasts announced the formation of the State Emergency Committee (SEC). The broadcast stated that Gorbachev was unable to carry out his presidential duties "for health reasons" and that these functions would be performed by Vice President Valentin Yanaev. Martial law was declared in Moscow and Leningrad. In announcing the takeover, the "gang of eight" painted a dark portrait of Soviet society. They declared that reform had gotten out of control, the economy was in chaos, democracy was in fact anarchy, and crime and ethnic hatred was ripping the union apart.

Popular resistance grew slowly. The center of resistance became the seat of the Russian government, known as the White House (House of Soviets). Boris Yeltsin, the Russian president, was the galvanizing force in the resistance. Monday morning he issued a stirring statement and in the afternoon mounted a tank and appealed to the people to resist the coup. His patriotic defiance was captured by a CNN camera and beamed to Soviet viewers on an evening newscast. This most celebrated act of Russian defiance since Lenin arrived at the Finland station in 1917, the image turned the tide and assured Yeltsin his prominence in Russian politics through the 1990s.

The convoy of soldiers and tanks was halted by barricades and human chains. By 10:00 P.M. several tanks and armored scout vehicles had declared loyalty to the Russian government and turned to defend the White House. The next day, August 20, huge rallies were held in Leningrad and Moscow. The opposition spread to other republics, including the Baltics, Kyrhgyzia, Kazakhstan, Moldavia, and members of the Ukrainian government. Mass demonstrations also took place in Sverdlovsk in the Urals, Murmansk in the far north, and Kishinev, the Moldavian capital.

Yeltsin issued a call for citizens to defend the White House from attack. The attack was expected in the early hours of August 21, and indeed one had been ordered but was never carried out. The two KGB crack units assigned to lead the assault both mutinied. It seemed the KGB and the army were both infected with the same democratic spirit as the masses.

Early on August 21 tanks and armored personnel carriers began leaving the capital; at 9:25 A.M. Yazov resigned his post and the coup leadership quickly collapsed. Torn by indecision, unprepared for a bloodbath, and lacking coherent program, the SEC disintegrated. At noon on August 21, the plotters left Moscow for the Crimea, hoping to throw themselves on Gorbachev's mercy. The president refused to see them and was brought back to Moscow by a loyal security team. The plotters were arrested, except for Pugo, who committed suicide.

The following day was declared a Day of Freedom. Banned newspapers began publishing. Victory rallies followed. There was some spontaneous violence. A large crowd set upon the Lubyanka—headquarters of the KGB—and was not mollified until the imposing statue of Feliks Dzerzhinski, the first head of the Soviet secret police (CHEKA), that stood in front of the building had been dismantled.

Gorbachev in a press conference on August 22 made a major error by not disassociating himself from the Communist Party, which had been silent throughout the coup attempt. The tide had now turned against the party. On August 23, Yeltsin and Gorbachev came face to face in the chambers of the Russian parliament, or Congress of Peoples Deputies, in a defining moment for the fate of the Soviet Union. Gorbachev addressed the assembly and was heckled, interrupted, and generally subjected to disrespect. Yeltsin then forced him to read the names of the plotters, for they were all his own appointees. Yeltsin then issued numerous decrees punishing the CPSU for complicity in the coup. He also forced Gorbachev to accept the legality of a series of decrees the Russian government made during the coup, including the transfer of economic enterprises and resources on Russian soil to the jurisdiction of the Russian republic.

On August 24, a massive funeral was held for the three fatalities of the coup. Gorbachev and others spoke and made the victims heroes of the Soviet Union. Later that day he resigned as general secretary of the party and suspended all party activities.

The coup was defeated so rapidly and conclusively because of the ineptitude of the plotters, among whom there was no strong leader and because they failed to recognize that major changes had taken place in their country. The group failed to see that one could no longer announce that the leader was indisposed and expect people to blindly follow decrees from the center. Real power now resided in popular leaders like Yeltsin and other republic leaders and Leningrad Mayor Anatoly Sobchak. These elected leaders could muster the support of hundreds of thousands, as at the demonstrations at Palace Square in Leningrad and at the White House in Moscow. The plotters could command no such allegiance for the cause of the Communist Party or Soviet tradition.

BIBLIOGRAPHY

Billington, James. *Russia Transformed—Breakthrough to Hope: August 1991.* New York: Free Press, 1992.

Bonnell, Victoria, Ann Cooper, and Gregory Freidin, eds. *Russia at the Barricades: Eyewitness Accounts of the August 1991 Coup.* Armonk, N.Y.: M.E. Sharp, 1994.

Dunlop, John. *The Rise of Russia and the Fall of the Soviet Empire.* Princeton, N.J.: Princeton University Press, 1993.

Gorbachev, Mikhail. *The August Coup: The Truth and the Lessons.* New York: HarperCollins, 1991.

Grachev, Andrei. *Final Days.* Boulder, Colo.: Westview, 1995.

Remnick, David. *Lenin's Tomb: The Last Days of the Soviet Empire.* New York: Random House, 1993.

Daniel Kowalsky

Dissolution and Formation of the Commonwealth of Independent States

Political upheaval of December 1991 that saw the collapse of the Soviet Union and the founding of a successor confederation. The failure of the August coup precipitated tremendous upheaval in the Soviet Union. The Communist Party lost all authority, Mikhail Gorbachev fell from power, and the Soviet republics emerged as independent states. The dissolution of the USSR paved the way in December 1991 for the Confederation of Independent States (CIS), a weak, decentralized, and often ineffective union of former Soviet republics.

Following the aborted August 1991 coup, President Gorbachev returned to Moscow and attempted to broaden his policy of perestroika (restructuring) and institute new party reforms. But the coup, destroyed Gorbachev's political credibility, for all the plotters had been his own appointees. The president of the Russian republic, Boris Yeltsin, whose acts of defiance rallied resistance to the coup, now acted to end the party's authority. He demanded and received Gorbachev's resignation as general secretary on August 24; all party activities in the armed forces and the KGB (secret police) were immediately banned, and party property was nationalized. Gorbachev recommended that the party's Central Committee disband and the Secretariat concurred. Yeltsin ordered the party's headquarters in Leningrad and Moscow sealed, and its archives passed under the control of the Russian federation. On August 29 the Supreme Soviet formally suspended all Communist Party activities throughout the USSR. On September 5 the Soviet Congress of Deputies passed its last law, surrendering its powers to the sovereign republics of the former union.

The coup's failure demonstrated that power no longer resided in the center; it now lay in the republics. One after another they declared their independence: first the Ukraine on August 24; Belarus the next day; Moldava, Uzbekistan, and Kyrgyzstan soon after that; Tajikistan on September 9, and finally Kazakhstan in mid-December. The independence of the Baltic states—Latvia, Lithuania, and Estonia—was immediately recognized the world over, even by the Russians.

On October 1 in Alma-Ata, Kazakhstan's capital, the twelve republics (i.e., all but the three Baltic states) proposed the formation of an economic community. On October 18 eight republics signed on to the new Union Treaty (abstaining were Georgia, Azerbaijan, Moldova, and Ukraine). The document, which stripped Moscow of all central power, contained fifty-nine articles and made three fundamental points: The State Bank of the USSR, Gosbank, must share its prerogatives with the central banks of the member states; the federal budget depended entirely on the willingness of the republics to contribute; and no common governmental structures existed between Moscow and the republics

The new union was taken a step further on December 8 when Russia, Ukraine, and Belorussia declared that the Soviet Union no longer existed. The next day the three states founded the Commonwealth of Independent States (CIS). On December 21, again in Alma-Ata, eight other states—Armenia, Azerbaijan, Kazakhstan, Kyrgyzstan, Moldova, Tajikistan, Turkmenistan, and Uzbekistan—signed on formally to the CIS. (Georgia joined in 1993.) In the initial agreement, the CIS signatories agreed on joint control of nuclear arms and strategic forces, on the preservation of a single economic space, mutual respect for established borders, open frontiers between member states, and cooperation in foreign policy. The formation of the CIS marked the end of the Soviet era. Gorbachev resigned as Soviet president on December 25, passing nuclear weapons codes to Yeltsin. At midnight on December 31, all Soviet institutions ceased to function and exist.

From its inception, the CIS was beset by myriad problems, many of which threatened its effectiveness, if not its existence. First, the CIS was formed in great haste, with no consideration of the problems that would emerge nor any acknowledgment that the member states had conflicting intentions in joining. Second, no provisions were made for the transition to independence of the former Soviet republics. The disappearance of the central government left some states—such as Belarus (the former Belorussian SSR), Kazakhstan, and the other Central Asian republics—with no provisions for national armed forces, national currency, or demarcated frontiers. Third, the overwhelming size, population, and economic might of Russia prevented the CIS from functioning as a union of equals. Fourth, the republican leaders were wholly lacking in experience, most having experience only in the Communist Party bureaucracy, and were ill prepared to coordinate democratic or market reforms in undeveloped economies of states with no tradition of economic independence or political pluralism. Nonetheless, by the end of 1993 the CIS had acquired many of the institutions that would assure its viability for the longer term.

In the first several years of its existence, the meetings and summits of the CIS members were invariably the occasion for claims of success. The true picture was one of continued frustration and setbacks. Though the CIS leaders signed a great array of agreements, decisions, and protocols in their frequent meetings, these actions achieved little. Quite often agreements were not signed by all members, while others were not ratified by the members' parliaments. Signatories did not always see themselves bound by the agreements, yet the CIS had no recourse for noncompliance. On many of the most important issues no agreement could be reached. The CIS's agenda was further hampered by the divergence of allegiance to the principles of the agreement by its members. Of the twelve member states, Moldova, Ukraine, Azerbaijan and Turkmenistan have been reluctant participants. Moldova would countenance only economic agreements; Ukraine rejected all control mechanisms; Azerbaijani leader Abulfaz Elchibey, elected president in 1992, rejected the CIS entirely; Turkmenistan, economically independent because of its abundant natural resources, took far less interest in membership than the more troubled states.

With the narrowest central institutional base, the CIS was largely powerless to avert ethnic crises in several member states. In the Caucasus, CIS and Russian mediation efforts did not prevent armed struggle between Armenians and Azeris over Nagorno-Karabakh, the American inhabited enclave within Azerbaijan, in 1993–94. In Georgia the national armed forces engaged in violent conflicts with both Abkhaz and Ossetian minorities. In Moldova a dispute arose between the Russian population of the Dniester region and the forces of the new national government. Civil war in Tajikistan led to the overthrow of its president in 1992. Throughout the CIS, problems arose affecting the fates of some twenty-five million ethnic Russians who suddenly found themselves aliens in foreign states. Russia itself, the largest and most powerful of the CIS members, hardly provided a model for the transition. In October 1993 a dispute between the Russian executive and the legislature came to a head when President Yeltsin's dissolving of the Congress of Peoples Deputies led to a rebellion centered on the Russian White House. The Russian government was also forced to confront resistance in Russia's outer regions, most violently in Chechnya, to which Yeltsin sent the Russian army in 1994 to put down an independence movement. The more recent economic crises in Russia have demonstrated that the ruble will not emerge as a benchmark currency. Once seen as a doomed union that would degenerate into large-scale, Yugoslav-type ethnic conflict, the CIS now represents a potentially viable, if not fully developed, alternative to the Soviet Union, for at least some of the successor states to the USSR.

BIBLIOGRAPHY

Dawisha, Karen, and Bruce Parrot. *Russia and the New States of Eurasia: The Politics of Upheaval.* Cambridge: Cambridge University Press, 1994.

Dunlop, John. *The Rise of Russia and the Fall of the Soviet Empire.* Princeton, N.J.: Princeton University Press, 1993.

Grachev, Andrey. *Final Days.* Boulder, Colo.: Westview Press, 1995.

Tolz, Vera, and Ian Elliot, eds. *The Demise of the USSR: From Communism to Independence.* London: Macmillan, 1995.

White, Stephen. *After Gorbachev,* 4th ed. Cambridge: Cambridge University Press, 1993.

Daniel Kowalsky

Khrushchev's Reforms

Policy changes instituted by the Soviet Union's top leader from 1955 to 1964. At the international level, Nikita Khrushchev's reforms had far-reaching implications for the Soviet Union's relations with both enemies and allies. Domestically, Khrushchev broke the Stalinist mold, presiding over lasting alterations of Soviet politics, culture, and economic structuring.

Stalin died on March 5, 1953, without naming a successor, and none of his top associates had the power to claim supreme leadership. In the initial agreement to rule collectively, Georgy Malenkov headed the government, Lavrenty Beria the security forces, and Khrushchev was first secretary of the party. In July 1953, Beria's associates, fearing the inordinate power of the secret police, arrested and executed him. There followed a debate within the party leadership on economic policy. Malenkov advocated increased production of consumer goods and intensive agriculture, while Khrushchev stood for development of heavy industry and the opening of new lands to cultivation. By the end of 1954 Malenkov's proposals had yielded little and he resigned as prime minister in February 1955. The new prime minister, Nikolay Bulganin, was only a figurehead. Khrushchev, as party secretary, soon emerged as the most important and powerful figure in the Kremlin. His rule was marked by a series of reforms that transformed many aspects of Soviet society.

A major theme of Khrushchev's reforms was de-Stalinization. At the Twentieth Party Congress, held in February 1956, Khrushchev denounced Stalin's crimes in a secret speech. He attacked Stalin's cult of personality and catalogued many of the injustices and crimes perpetrated during the late dictator's reign. He revealed that Stalin had arbitrarily liquidated thousands of party members and military leaders and made serious military blunders during World War II. The revelations were sensational but highly selective. Khrushchev placed all the blame on certain negative aspects of Stalin's character; he made no mention of non-Communist victims of the purges, nor did he suggest that the Soviet system itself was flawed.

The secret speech had momentous consequences throughout the USSR and its Eastern European satellites. Almost immediately, the release of political prisoners was increased. Many who perished during Stalin's terror were posthumously rehabilitated. In 1961 in a highly symbolic act, Stalin's body was removed from the revered place next to Lenin in the mausoleum on Red Square. The breakthrough to openness, presaging Mikhail Gorbachev's policy of glasnost three decades later, sparked a wide movement of introspection and criticism within political and intellectual circles.

These developments were not universally welcomed. In June 1957 conservative party members rallied to oust Khrushchev, fearing that by disavowing Stalin the legitimacy of the entire Soviet system would be undermined. Failing to win sufficient support to eliminate Khrushchev, they were removed from the Communist Party's Presidium and Central Committee and their political careers came to an end. The "anti-party group," as they were called, were spared arrest and execution. Unlike Stalin, Khrushchev's vision of humane socialism extended even to his opponents.

The secret speech initiated a cultural thaw that transformed the Soviet Union's intellectual environment. Khrushchev permitted the publication of Vladimir Dudintsev's *Not by Bread Alone* (1957), an exposé of corrupt Soviet bureaucracy, and Aleksandr Solzhenitsyn's *One Day in the Life of Ivan Denisovitch* (1962), which depicted life in a Soviet labor camp. Yet Khrushchev's cultural reforms were uneven and at times contradictory. Poet Boris Pasternak's works, including his novel, *Doctor Zhivago* (1957), were repressed and published only abroad. Khrushchev also lashed out against modern influences in the arts, and he continued Stalin's practice of bulldozing churches and persecuting the faithful.

Domestically, Khrushchev attempted to carry out reform in a range of fields. In agriculture the state encouraged peasants to grow more on their private plots and increased payments for crops grown on the collective farms. In his ambitious virgin lands campaign of the mid-1950s, Khrushchev opened vast tracts of land to farming in previously barren parts of the central Asian steppe. The results were mixed: some years brought drought, others excellent harvests. Later attempts at agricultural reform were counterproductive. Khrushchev's plans for growing maize and increasing meat and dairy production failed, and an attempt to enlarge collective farms brought confusion in the countryside.

Many of Khrushchev's industrial and administrative reforms, while aiming to ameliorate living standards and improve the Soviet Union's economy and international standing, were overly optimistic. In 1957 Khrushchev did away with the industrial ministries in Moscow and established regional economic councils. He intended to orient the economy directly to local needs, but the decentralization of industry led to disruption and inefficiency. That same year, advances in rocket technology allowed the Soviets to launch both the first intercontinental ballistic missile and the first space satellite (*Sputnik*). Though a coup for Russian science, the ensuing arms race with the United States severely taxed the Soviet economy. A massive home-building program, carried on throughout Khrushchev's tenure, did much to alleviate the chronic Soviet housing shortage, but the quality of the new apartment blocks left much to be desired. Khrushchev's 1962 reorganization of party organs along economic, rather than administrative, lines alienated many in the party apparatus and increased his unpopularity. Finally, the abandonment in 1963 of the seven-year economic plan (1959–65), two years short of its completion, became a symptom of the country's economic difficulties.

Following Stalin's death in 1953, the reorientation of foreign policy became a major priority. In 1955 Khrushchev eased tensions between East and West by recognizing the neutrality of Austria. The same year he met U.S. President Dwight D. Eisenhower in Geneva and announced a new policy of "peaceful coexistence" with capitalism. In the developing world, however, Soviet diplomacy was more aggressive. Khrushchev courted nationalist leaders and challenged the West in Egypt, Syria, Afghanistan, Burma, and India. Cuba's entry into the socialist camp in 1961 won Khrushchev domestic support for his expansionist agenda.

Closer to home, Soviet diplomacy suffered setbacks. Reconciliation with Yugoslavia in 1955 sent a strong message to the Eastern European satellites that the USSR now approved of alternative roads to socialism. The whole of the Eastern bloc soon simmered with unrest. In Poland riots forced a change in Communist Party leadership, which the Soviet Union reluctantly recognized in October 1956. A popular uprising against Soviet control then broke out in Hungary, where local Communist leaders called for a multiparty political system and withdrawal from the Warsaw Pact. In the first week of November Khrushchev ordered Soviet tanks into Budapest. The revolt was crushed and several thousand Hungarians were left dead. Events in Hungary demonstrated that the Soviet Union had no intention of relinquishing control over its satellites in Eastern Europe.

Beyond the Soviet sphere of control, Chinese Communist Party chairman Mao Tse-tung began expressing dissatisfaction with Khrushchev's leadership following Khrushchev's denunciation of Stalin in 1956. Chinese discontent stemmed from low levels of Soviet aid to China and the Soviet rapprochement with the West, which Mao rejected as a betrayal of Marxism-Leninism. The dispute between militant China and Khrushchev's more moderate Soviet Union developed into a schism in the world Communist movement after 1960. Albania abandoned the Soviet camp to become an ally of China, while Romania distanced itself from the Soviet Union in international affairs. The world Communist movement was no longer Moscow's alone.

Soviet relations with the West seesawed between relaxation and crisis. Khrushchev professed to desire peaceful coexistence, not least to allow the Soviet Union to develop its economy. His meetings with U.S. presidents and his tour of the United States in 1959 demonstrated a sincere commitment to friendly relations. This emerging cooperation was dealt a blow in 1960 when an American U-2 spy plane was shot down over Soviet territory. Khrushchev demanded a personal apology from Eisenhower and canceled a summit meeting in Paris. The standoff over Berlin came the following year. Khrushchev insisted that the western sectors of the city be incorporated into East Germany. When his demands were not met, he authorized the erection of the Berlin Wall. Finally, during the Cuban Missile Crisis of October 1962, relations between the United States and the Soviet Union deteriorated to their worst point during the Cold War. In an attempt to improve the Soviet negotiating position, Khrushchev tried to install nuclear missiles around the island nation. A U.S. blockade and threats of war convinced Khrushchev to back down. Tensions eased in 1963 with the establishment of a "hot line" between Washington and Moscow. In the same year, the Soviet Union, Britain, and the United States signed the Partial Test Ban Treaty.

By 1964 Khrushchev's prestige at home was seriously eroded. The industrial and agricultural reforms that had promised so much yielded little. The Soviet Union's international stature suffered greatly in the wake of the split with China and the Berlin and Cuban crises. Khrushchev's efforts to improve relations with the West had antagonized many in the Soviet military establishment. In October 1964, while Khrushchev was vacationing in the Crimea, the party Presidium voted him out of office.

Khrushchev's reforms, though ambitious, were inconsistent and often unsuccessful. On balance, however, he was an agent of reform and progress. He sought to eliminate excessive bureaucracy and improve the living standards of Soviet citizens. He attempted to ease international tensions through rapprochement with the West. Most significantly, Khrushchev's repudiation of Stalinism began a process of democratization that laid the foundations for the reforms of Mikhail Gorbachev.

BIBLIOGRAPHY

Andrusz, Gregory. *Housing and Urban Development in the USSR.* London: Macmillan, 1984.

Filtzer, Donald. *The Khrushchev Era: De-Stalinization and the Limits of Reform in the USSR, 1953–1964.* London: Macmillan, 1993.

Khrushchev, Nikita. *Khrushchev Remembers,* 3 Vols. Boston: Little, Brown, 1970, 1974, and 1990.

McCauley, Martin. *Khrushchev and the Virgin Lands Programme,* 1953–1964. London: Macmillan, 1976.

———. *The Khrushchev Era, 1953–1964.* London: Longman, 1995.

Medvedev, Roy. *Khrushchev.* Tr. by Brian Pearce. Oxford: Blackwell, 1982.

Tompson, William. *Khrushchev: A Political Life.* New York: St. Martin's Press, 1995.

Daniel Kowalsky

SEE ALSO Cuban Missile Crisis; Détente

Nuclear Weapons

As of the early 1950s the Soviet nuclear arsenal grew from a few dozen atomic bombs to an estimated thirty thousand to forty thousand nuclear warheads. With the breakup of the USSR in 1991, the very real potential existed that some of those weapons, or enough weapons-grade material to create crude nuclear devices, would find their way via the black market to terrorist organizations or outlaw states. Concern over the accidental detonation of one or more of the remaining nuclear devices has also been expressed because of the lack of proper maintenance procedures.

Scholars have divided the Soviet nuclear weapons program into four phases. The early development of the program stretched from 1940 until the mid-1950s. The Uranium Commission was established in June 1940 with a broad research mandate that included exploration for uranium deposits. Research was temporarily disrupted with the German invasion of June 1941, but then continued with a new sense of urgency after Soviet spys uncovered the existence of other programs. With the U.S. detonation of atomic fission bombs over Hiroshima and Nagasaki in August 1945, Stalin gave the Soviet nuclear weapons program an even greater priority.

The first Soviet nuclear chain reaction took place on December 25, 1946. This was followed by the detonation of the first Soviet atomic bomb on July 29, 1949, and two further nuclear tests in fall 1951. These tests were followed by the detonation of a thermonuclear fusion bomb on August 12, 1953. The deployment of nuclear weapons by the Soviet armed forces began in late 1953 or early 1954. These devices were initially placed either on the older Tu-4 Bull or Il-28 Beagle bombers. In March 1954 custodial and transport duties for all nuclear devices were assigned to the Committee for State Security (KGB). In 1955 two intercontinental bombers, the Tu-95 Bear and Mya-4 Bison, were deployed along with the SS-3 medium-range ballistic missile (MRBM).

The second phase of Soviet nuclear weapons development took place between the mid-1950s and mid-1960s, centering on the expansion of the Soviet nuclear arsenal. The first submarine-launched ballistic missile (SLBM)—the SS-N-4 Sark—was test-fired from a retrofitted Zulu class attack submarine in 1955. By 1960 this SLBM reached operational status aboard Golf and Zulu class ballistic missile submarines. The first Soviet intercontinental ballistic missile (ICBM), the SS-6 Sapwood, was test-fired in 1957 and deployed in 1959. The deployment of nuclear torpedoes and sea-launched cruise missiles (SLCMs) had taken place a year earlier in 1958.

The fielding of growing numbers of other nonstrategic nuclear weapons such as artillery shells, rockets, and missiles also took place during this era. By 1959 this resulted in a consensus by the Soviet military that the use of nuclear weapons in future warfare was a certainty. Because of this shift in Soviet perspective, a new service was created, labeled the Strategic Rocket Forces (SRF). The SRF quickly became the premier Soviet armed service and the foundation of its military doctrine based on nuclear-war fighting. As an outcome, the land-based missile force became the dominant arm of the Soviet nuclear triad.

The third phase of this program spanned the late 1960s to the early 1980s; it represented the achievement of nuclear parity with the United States and an era of arms control talks that limited the growth of the superpowers' nuclear arsenals. These arms control talks, however, provided far more benefits to the Soviet nuclear weapons program than to that of the United States because of radically different premises regarding the basic intent behind such negotiations. The Soviets bargained primarily from a nuclear war–fighting perspective, while the United States did not. Hence, arms control supported the Soviet military doctrine based on nuclear weapons, civil defense, and antiballistic missile (ABM) programs that would prepare the USSR for nuclear war.

Increased accuracy, range, and reliability characterized the new generations of Soviet ICBMs and SLBMs deployed during this period. Multiple-independently-targeted-reentry vehicles (MIRVs) were deployed on SS-18 Satan and SS-19 Stiletto ICBMs in 1974, while the first MIRVed SLBM was deployed in 1978. The first mobile ICBM, the SS-25 Sickle, was in turn fielded in 1985. Coupled with these advances in ballistic missiles were those in long-range cruise missile technology with the deployment of the AS-Kent 15 on the Bear H bomber in 1984 and the SS-N-21 Sampson in the Northern Fleet in 1987.

The fourth phase of Soviet nuclear weapons development spans the ascendance of Mikhail Gorbachev in the mid-1980s, the implosion of the Soviet empire, the end of the Cold War, and the rise of the Russian Federation. It has been a dynamic period with a declaratory shift in Russian doctrine away from nuclear-war fighting toward deterrence and greater willingness to engage in more equitable arms control negotiations with the West.

While the future of the old Soviet nuclear weapons program is now uncertain, small numbers of qualitatively advanced forms of strategic weapons are being developed and deployed. If this trend continues and Russian society successfully rebuilds itself to exploit the technologies embodied in the current revolution in military affairs, a future Russian program will easily possess the capacity to outperform its Soviet predecessor. This potential coupled with recent Russian doctrinal viewpoints on future "technological war" (based on advanced military systems) in which strategic objectives can be achieved in an initial deep strike provide potent reasons for further efforts toward the control, limitation, and perhaps total banning of nuclear weapons.

BIBLIOGRAPHY

Cochran, Thomas B., et al. *Soviet Nuclear Weapons.* Nuclear Weapons Databook, Vol. 4. New York: Harper and Row, 1989.

Green, William C. *Soviet Nuclear Weapons Policy: A Research and Bibliographic Guide.* Westview Special Studies in National Security and Defense Policy. Boulder: Westview Press, 1987.

Miller, Mark E. *Soviet Strategic Power and Doctrine: The Quest for Superiority.* Washington, D.C.: Advanced International Studies Institute, 1982.

Robert J. Bunker

United Kingdom

The United Kingdom, officially the United Kingdom of Great Britain and Northern Ireland, is a constitutional monarchy located on the major islands of Britain and Ireland, and a number of minor islands. The island of Britain contains England in the south, Scotland in the north, and Wales in the west. Northern Ireland shares the island of Ireland with the Republic of Ireland. The island of Britain lies just across the English Channel from France and Belgium. The island of Ireland lies to the west of Britain and is separated from it by the Irish Sea. The minor islands or groups of islands, which are part of the United Kingdom, are the Isles of Scilly, southwest of Britain, the Isle of Wight to the south of Britain, the Orkney and Shetland islands, north of Scotland, the Hebrides, to the west of Scotland, and Anglesey, off the northwestern coast of Wales in the Irish Sea. The United Kingdom possesses 89,038 square miles (230,609 sq km) and has approximately 57 million inhabitants. London is the capital and largest city with approximately seven million residents.

United Kingdom. *Illustration courtesy of Bernard Cook.*

In 1945 the United Kingdom emerged from World War II as one of the victorious Big Three powers. Yet international conditions had changed for it since 1939. Similarly, ideas concerning the proper role of government in the economy and society had also undergone a transformation. The victory of the Labour Party in the July 1945 general election confirmed the acceptance of a package of interventionist policies that had been developed during the wartime years. The aim was to maintain high levels of employment, provide basic state welfare benefits, and to ensure smooth and constant economic growth. The government and the state were cast as key actors through the nationalization of essential industries, as providers of welfare benefits, and in the fine-tuning of the economy. This was the "postwar settlement" that formed the generally unquestioned basis of political, economic, and social life in the United Kingdom for more than two decades.

The Labour governments of 1945–50 and 1950–51 oversaw the process of recovery from six years of war, established the postwar settlement, and began to adjust the country to its new international position. The country's difficulties worsened in the immediate aftermath of war, a period of great austerity marked by extended rationing, unusually severe winters, and energy crises. Nonetheless, the government quickly carried through a limited program of nationalization of those industries, such as coal, railroads, and road transport, seen to occupy the commanding heights of the economy. In the social sphere, the National Health Service Act was passed in 1946, providing free treatment at the point of delivery for all British citizens. Education was reorganized and expanded, and other key welfare policies were introduced, such as the provision of child benefits. The ideas of "fair shares" and government planning that had figured so prominently in the country's wartime coalition government had borne peacetime fruit.

Although the Labour Party lost the 1951 general election, its opponents, the Conservative Party, had already accepted the basic welfare reforms of the Labour government. This bipartisan approach turned the postwar settlement into the postwar consensus. The 1950s were characterized by this similarity in approach, and although the Conservative Party won the general elections of 1951, 1955, and 1959, government intervention in the social democratic mold continued. The Conservatives oversaw the increased provision of affordable public housing, continued economic growth, and a rapid expansion in the availability of consumer goods. These were the halcyon days of the long postwar boom, and rising standards of living enabled Conservative Prime Minister Harold Macmillan famously to announce during the 1959 election campaign that the British had "never had it so good."

For many the 1950s marked a period of unprecedented optimism. Macmillan's confidence was reflected in the British political system. In contrast to other countries on the continent of Europe, such as France or Italy, the United Kingdom was characterized by the dominance of two main parties, Labour and Conservatives. In 1955, for example, the two parties between them gathered over 96 percent of the votes cast. This dominance was also reflected in the mass membership of the Labour and Conservative Parties, which were among the largest in the West. The two-party system was widely credited with providing the United Kingdom with effective and democratic government, reflecting, it was thought, the basic class makeup of the country.

The development of mass consumer society was also evidenced by changing social trends. The decade saw the discovery of a new phenomenon, "the teenager," and youth revolt was reflected in new forms of popular music, such as the blues, rock and roll, and even skiffle. More politically oriented activity took the form of antinuclear protest by the Campaign for Nuclear Disarmament (CND) and, later, the Committee of 100, while small groups of die-hard imperialists in the League of Empire Loyalists staged stunts objecting to decolonization. Commonwealth citizens began to arrive in larger numbers during the period, with immigration from the West Indies being a feature of the 1950s. The growth of the nonwhite population revealed limits to Britain's myth of toleration and fair play, and race riots in Notting Hill in London in the summer of 1958 were an unpleasant indicator of racism in the United Kingdom. Changes in the country's domestic circumstances were closely tied to changes in its position on the international stage. The country had emerged as a victorious power in 1945, with its empire intact and its global presence strengthened. Yet the reality was that the United Kingdom was a debtor nation in a world dominated by the economic power of the United States and the military strength of the USSR. The United Kingdom played a notable part with the United States in the establishment of a new world trading and financial order at the Bretton Woods conferences, but the implementation of that order revealed the extent of the United Kingdom's subordination to the United States. The U.S. government quickly brought about the effective end of the Sterling Area, thereby gaining access to new markets in the British Empire and Commonwealth, while weakening the United Kingdom's ties with its traditional trading partners. The United States was initially eager to see an end to the United Kingdom's worldwide military presence. But with the emergence of the Cold War, and particularly after the outbreak of the Korean War in 1950, Britain's global military presence became important to the U.S. policy of containment of communism. The United Kingdom's desire to maintain a "special relationship" with the United States, even after the debacle of the Anglo-French expedition to Suez in 1956, led to higher levels of defense spending than the country could afford. This diverted investment and resulted in long-term damage to the economy.

The first two postwar decades also saw a rapid retreat from empire. The abandonment of the Indian empire came in 1947, while African colonies gradually gained their independence as of the mid-1950s onward. This process was carried out comparatively easily, although a number of brief but vicious "emergencies" occurred before the independence of countries like Kenya and Aden. The Britain maintained close ties with many Commonwealth countries, particularly the "White Dominions" of Canada, Australia, and New Zealand. But as the country's global ties slowly weakened, it was forced to look elsewhere for its future. Yet the United Kingdom was initially reluctant to become too involved with continental Europe and was uninterested in joining the European Economic Community (EEC) at its foundation in 1957.

The 1960s marked a change in Britain's fortunes with the first clear signs of deep-seated economic problems appearing. The Conservative government faced numerous difficult choices as economic growth began to falter, and the Labour Party won its first general election in thirteen years in 1964. Labour leader Harold Wilson successfully portrayed himself as young and dynamic, promising a government-led technological revolution that would launch the country into a new decade of success and prosperity. Wilson's tactical skill was illustrated when he led his government to a resounding success at another general election in 1966, but that year was also a turning point for the British economy. Balance-of-payments problems, a devaluation crisis, the necessity for deflationary measures, and the failure to deliver a technological revolution all dogged the government. These problems were further compounded by labor unrest, particularly among dock workers, and the failure of the government's attempts at the reform of labor relations. The postwar consensus that had looked so successful in the 1950s now seemed to be under strain. The general instinct was to reinforce government intervention and extend the system of national collective bargaining and cooperation among organized capital, labor, and the government. This became known as the period of corporatism, or tripartism. But changes in the international economy, particularly those flowing from America's Southeast Asian–induced economic problems, and the reemergence of the German and Japanese economies, made Britain's position even more difficult.

Despite the economic and political difficulties of the 1960s, the period was seen as one of notable social change. The continuing impact of mass consumerism, the loosening of public morality, the extension of higher education, and the widespread availability of effective contraception all helped bring a sense of liberation to many people, particularly the young. These social developments were also reflected in legislation dealing with equal opportunities, racial discrimination, legalization of homosexual relations, and abortion. For a while, Britain, and especially London, became a center of modishness in fashion, music, and youth culture in general. Apparently more earnest youth revolt centered on anti–Vietnam War protest, the espousal of various ultra-left causes, and campus rebellions that reflected, to some extent, the more febrile atmosphere of the Events of May in Paris in 1968. The women's movement saw a rebirth of militancy, drawing primarily on American and French theories of women's liberation rather than native tradition. The U.S. civil rights campaign provided an example for the development of a civil rights movement in Northern Ireland, where the Protestant and unionist majority operated a devolved "Protestant Parliament for a Protestant People," which was a mirror of the Republic of Ireland's Catholic constitution. But issues of civil rights in Northern Ireland were quickly overtaken by more traditional nationalist and unionist antagonisms. The resultant violence involving republicans, loyalists, and the British state continued thirty years later to mar life in the province, and in other areas of the United Kingdom.

The disappointments of the Wilson government (1966–70) led to its defeat in the general election of 1970 and the return of the Conservatives, led by Edward Heath. But the 1970s was a decade of crisis that finally saw the death of the postwar consensus. Heath's government had only one real success, when he negotiated Britain's entry into the European Economic Community (EEC), which came into effect on January 1, 1973. This success came after two previous failures, in 1961 and 1967, when French President Charles de Gaulle vetoed Britain's applications. Membership in the EEC was a personal triumph for Heath, who had long been a convinced European. However, there was unease at this change in the historical outlook of the country, and its close links to Commonwealth countries such as Australia and New Zealand were put under great strain as the direction of British trade shifted to Europe.

Beyond membership in the EEC, Heath's government was a failure. He had intended to face the emergent economic problems of the country with a retreat from the basics of the postwar settlement aimed at improving Britain's international economic position. But widespread labor resistance to his industrial relations legislation, continuing balance-of-payments problems, and rising inflation forced a retreat. Instead, there was a return to traditional tools of economic policy, including the extension of nationalization, and the introduction of an incomes policy. With the sudden shock of international commodity price rises in the wake of the Arab-Israeli war of 1973, a miner's strike against incomes policy, and the introduction of a three-day working week because of a fuel shortage, an air of crisis pervaded. The government called an election in February 1974 hoping to gain a significant mandate to impose its will on the economy and the labor unions.

The outcome of the February 1974 election was a clear sign of the public's discontent with the two-party system. Although the result was a very narrow victory for the Labour Party, perhaps the more significant aspect of the election was the rise in third-party voting. The Liberals saw their share of the vote rise from 7.5 percent at the 1970 election to 19.3 percent in February 1974. In Scotland the Scottish National Party (SNP) mounted a strong challenge based on calls for an increased degree of self-government for Scotland, while the Welsh nationalists, Plaid Cymru, mounted a similar campaign in Wales. The two nationalists parties gained nine parliamentary seats, five fewer than the Liberals. Added to the fourteen members of parliament (MPs) from Northern Ireland, this gave third parties a significant presence in parliament. The two main parties had gathered only 74 percent of the votes cast, a substantial fall since the two-party system days of the 1950s.

The Labour government returned to the tripartite approach. It settled quickly with the striking miners and repealed the Conservatives' incomes and labor union policy. An attempt was made to move forward in Northern Ireland by introducing a power-sharing executive that would address the grievances of the minority Catholic and nationalist community. But this initiative came to nothing when Protestant and unionist workers organized the only successful general strike in British history, bringing the province to a standstill. Outrages continued as the various paramilitary groups sought to control events by terrorist murder, while the British authorities often reacted with brutality.

Prime Minister Wilson sought to strengthen his position in parliament by calling another general election in October of the same year. But the outcome was disappointing for Labour, which was returned to government with only a three-seat majority. Although the Conservatives lost ground, the Scots and Welsh nationalists maintained their challenge, returning fourteen MPs. More significantly for the future, the Conservatives removed Edward Heath from the leadership and replaced him with Margaret Thatcher, whose close adviser and confidante, Keith Joseph, was a disciple of the Chicago School of free-market economics.

The mid-1970s was a period of economic decline, rising inflation and unemployment, labor and social unrest, and growing concern that government could no longer deliver the sort of package that characterized the postwar consensus. The country's industrial base began to shrink as its international competitiveness declined and multinational industries abandoned production in the United Kingdom for the Far East. Traditional economic remedies no longer seemed appropriate as the country faced high and rising inflation and unemployment, a situation known as stagflation. Labor disputes appeared to be the chief characteristic of British industry, symbolized by the unofficial, wildcat strike, especially in motor manufacturing. The country's balance of trade continued to cause concern, and membership in the EEC, affirmed in a referendum in 1975, appeared to have bestowed few clear benefits. Evidence of wider discontent was reflected in the growth and activity of extremist, extraparliamentary parties. Ugly street violence characterized the clashes between these groups and seemed to throw further doubt on the postwar myth of British fairness and toleration.

The 1970s was confirmed as the decade of protest with the startling appearance of punk rock. Punks drew some inspiration from the anticulture ideology of the radical Paris-based anarchistic Situationists movement, but more from the perennial desire of the young to shock the old. This they achieved by denigrating the queen during her Silver Jubilee year of 1977, and by famously, though ineffectively, proclaiming "Anarchy in the UK." Punk quickly spread to other parts of the world and seemed to confirm the United Kingdom's talent for exporting youth culture, even if it was, as in the case of football hooligans or skinheads, not always welcome.

Economic difficulties forced the government to apply to the International Monetary Fund (IMF) for loans in 1976. This event, and the subsequent deflationary policies of the Labour government under James Callaghan (illness having forced Wilson's retirement), marked the real end of the politics and economics of the postwar consensus. Callaghan pursued policies of wage and price restraint, along with cutbacks in public spending designed to reduce inflation. He had some success in this respect, but the incomes policy came dramatically unstuck in the winter of 1978–79, when labor union leaders could no longer restrain their members. Widespread strikes, particularly in the public sector, led to the winter being termed "the winter of discontent." In parliament the government lost the support of the nationalists following the failure of the 1978 referenda on devolved government for Scotland and Wales, and Labour's pact with the Liberal Party was no longer sufficient to keep it in power. An election was therefore called for May 1979.

The 1979 election was a triumph for the Conservatives and their leader, Margaret Thatcher. She was in the fortunate position of having a forty-three-seat majority in the House of Commons, from which secure parliamentary base she began a program of reform. The new government continued the deflationary policies of the previous administration, but with new fervor. Control of inflation rather than unemployment became the first policy priority, along with the beginnings of a privatization program and an attack on the rights and privileges of the labor unions. The deflationary program did not immediately reduce the rate of inflation, but it did lead to a rapid rise in unemployment and continued deindustrialization of the economy. Opposition to Thatcher's policies was strong, even in her cabinet, and opinion polls indicated that she was the most unpopular prime minister since the war. But parliamentary opposition was in disarray as the Labour Party was involved in a damaging internal struggle between supporters of a more radical socialism and those who wished to advance a pragmatic social democratic approach. The result was a split in the party when a minority of notable Labour MPs left to form the Social Democratic Party (SDP). By-election success for the SDP and its allies, the Liberals, seemed to indicate that these center parties would do well, given the unpopularity of the Conservatives and the disarray of Labour.

Thatcher and the Conservatives were, however, saved by the Falklands War. British misreading of the situation between Argentina and the British Falkland Islands in the South Atlantic led the Argentine dictatorship to invade the barely defended islands in April 1982. U.S. attempts to broker a peace between the United Kingdom and Argentina were of no avail. The United Kingdom went ahead with the reconquest of the Falklands by June, no mean feat given the distance from the British Isles and the limited military assets available. Britain witnessed an extraordinary resurgence of patriotism as the brief war revived faded imperial glories. Thatcher rode the wave of victory and turned around her own fortunes. The general election of 1983 saw this remarkable reversal of fortunes confirmed when the Conservatives were returned to office with a stunning majority of 144 seats in the House of Commons. The election also saw the continued decline of the Labour Party under the benign, principled, but ineffective Michael Foot. Labour suffered its worst defeat ever, gaining only 27.6 percent of the vote. The Liberal/SDP alliance had, as expected, garnered a substantial portion of the center ground, with 25.4 percent, but its spread of votes gave it only 23 seats.

The landslide victory of the Conservatives in 1983 set a seal on the shape of the 1980s. Thatcher continued her policies, aiming to confirm the United Kingdom as "a property owning democracy," shifting the declared policy emphasis of government from society to the individual, from state provision to private, and from state intervention in the economy to the free market.

The cultural tenor of the 1980s seemed to reflect the new opportunities opened by the increasing freeing of the market and the final abandonment of full employment and welfarism. The "yuppie" seemed to symbolize the enthusiasm with which the market was embraced in many quarters. Despite the continued strains imposed by the restructuring of the economy, many people benefited from a new prosperity, low inflation, and falling unemployment. But there was resistance to the Conservative program. Bitter industrial disputes marked the accelerated process of deindustrialization under the Conservatives. The Iron and Steel Trades Confederation dispute had been the first such, but was overshadowed by the long and bitter miners' strike of 1984–85. But the economic and political balance had swung against organized labor, and the once powerful National Union of Mineworkers (NUN) split and was defeated. Following the defeat of the miners' strike the government's antilabor union campaign proceeded apace with new legislation aimed at marginalizing organized labor.

Other protests by opponents of the government focused on issues such as nuclear defense. With the heightening of international tension, the deployment of Soviet SS-20 missiles in eastern Europe, and U.S. cruise and Pershing missiles in the west, the Committee for Nuclear Disarmament (CND) and the peace movement as a whole experienced a revival. Other issues were intertwined with the peace protests, such as environmental and feminist concerns.

Thatcher gained a third successive victory at the polls in 1987 with a 102-seat majority that showed the Conservatives benefiting from the apparent revival of the economy following the long period of restructuring. The Labour Party under Neil Kinnock, who took over from Michael Foot in September 1983, was still undergoing a period of "modernization." The Liberal-SDP alliance held its own but, once again, failed to make the decisive breakthrough necessary to pick up large numbers of seats under the country's system of voting. It was clear that the 1980s had been the Conservative decade.

At the end of the 1980s new trends were clearly emerging in British society. Economic and employment pressures, coupled with changed social standards, meant that the institution of the family was coming under increasing strain, while single-parent families became more common. The structure of the workforce had also changed, and women were becoming increasingly important in wage-earning employment as manufacturing continued to decline and part-time and temporary work in the service sector became more common. The 1980s also saw a dramatic restructuring of the taxation system to the benefit of the better off as taxation increasingly fell disproportionately heavily on the poor. The gap between the richest and the poorest was, by the end of the decade, wider than at any time since 1886. A new class emerged in the United Kingdom's urban landscape, the "underclass," who, like the "undeserving poor" before them were often deemed by government to be the authors of their own misfortunes. Other strains had appeared in the 1980s with serious rioting by sections of the country's Afro-Caribbean community protesting against racism and a lack of opportunities in Britain.

Although Thatcher achieved much that she had set out to accomplish in 1979, her long period in power did not make her immune from tactical errors. She vigorously pursued a widely unpopular reform of local taxation, and the government was surprised at the strength of opposition to it. Widespread nonpayment of the "Poll Tax," and serious disturbances in London when the police indulged in a riot against anti–Poll Tax protesters, brought a retreat by the government. In retrospect this mistake seemed to indicate a loss of political sense by Thatcher. She further weakened her position within the Conservative Party itself by making too many enemies over the question of Britain's relations with its European partners. The prime minister entered the 1990s with high personal expectations but, in reality, her position was weaker than it had been. European problems continued to loom, and although she hoped to benefit from avid support for the United States in the Gulf Crisis, she faced a sudden and surprising election within the parliamentary Conservative Party that resulted in her resignation and replacement by John Major. Thatcher's resignation seemed to mark the real end of the 1980s.

The United Kingdom once again proved its commitment to the special relationship with the United States by providing more troops and equipment for the Gulf War (1990–91) than any other U.S. ally. Unlike the Falklands War, however, there was little real enthusiasm for the conflict, and John Major did not gain the same sort of benefit that Thatcher had in 1982. In domestic policy Major sought to continue the Thatcherite revolution, albeit in less strident tones. The Labour Party continued to "modernize" under Neil Kinnock, which effectively meant a slow rightward shift in the party's stance. Yet it was not enough for Labour to win the 1992 general election, which resulted in a narrow, and some thought surprising, victory for Major's Conservatives. The Conservatives were back in office for a record fourth time, although with a much reduced majority.

Problems soon arose for the new government as the economic recovery from the recession of the late 1980s failed to materialize. The 1990s appeared to be a less confident decade than the 1980s as Britain became subject to the increasingly strong pressures of the global economy. In Europe the collapse of communism in the late 1980s and the early 1990s seemed, for a moment, to bring new hope. However, the exit from communism turned sour in Yugoslavia. The United Kingdom, along with France, had substantial numbers of troops in the area dedicated to a humanitarian mission, but divisions among European Union (EU) countries prevented effective action being taken. Problems surrounding the future development of the EU began to dominate domestic politics too, especially in the Conservative Party, where a vociferous "Eurosceptic" wing took advantage of Major's small parliamentary majority. In other areas, however, there were bright spots. In 1994 the IRA announced a cease-fire in its long-running terrorist campaign. This was quickly followed by a similar declaration by loyalist terror groups. But initial hopes faded amid accusations and counteraccusations of bad faith, and the IRA returned again to their campaign of violence.

The 1990s have seen the continuation of social trends established during the previous decade, with widening divisions of income and wealth characterizing British society. It is common to talk of the United Kingdom as being divided into three parts, with a top portion of the population being very wealthy, the middle being comfortably off, while the bottom struggles to cope with poverty. Yet the extent of deprivation has not, proved politically significant enough to alter the continued rightward shift in British politics. The lack of traditional radicalism in the British political scene has confirmed the unpopularity of the political parties among the young. Youth protest has increasingly been channeled into environmental protest movements, animal liberation causes, and the phenomenon of the New Age Travelers, people who imitate the nomadic life of the traditional "Travelers" or British gypsies because it appeals to their counter-cultural outlook. Less radical young people continue to seek more hedonistic pleasures through raves, night long dances with psychedelic ambience often fueled by the drug ecstasy, and drug taking in general, which has become widespread among the young, marking a generational shift in attitudes. Continued problems for Major, both within his party and in the country, forced him to delay calling the general election until spring 1997. He hoped that the longest election campaign since the war would enable the Conservatives to win a record fifth term in office. However, the Conservatives were dogged by their reputation for arrogance and incompetence in office, matched by allegations of corruption among certain Conservative MPs. A serious split within the government over the future of the United Kingdom in Europe also damaged the Conservatives' campaign. Conversely, the main opposition parties—Labour under Tony Blair, and the Liberal Democrats under Paddy Ashdown—ran successful and largely trouble-free campaigns. The Labour Party promised constitutional reform and limited improvements in education and health. Blair's main aim was to convince previous Conservative supporters that his party could govern well on behalf of the majority of the United Kingdom. The election, on May 1, 1997, was an astonishing victory for Blair and the Labour Party. Labour gained 418 parliamentary seats, with an overall majority of 177 seats in the House of Commons, the biggest margin of victory by any party since 1945. The Liberal Democrats also benefited from widespread tactical voting, gaining 46 seats, and becoming the biggest third-party presence in the postwar period. The Conservatives saw their support collapse, losing many of their leading figures and seats in their heartland of the south of England, ending with only 165 MPs, mostly from rural areas. The 1997 general election result was greeted with widespread pleasure throughout the country, and the immediate feeling was that it marked a new turning point in the history of the British people.

BIBLIOGRAPHY

Butler, David, and Gareth Butler. *British Political Facts, 1900–1994,* 7th ed. Basingstoke: Macmillan, 1994.

Crafts, N. F. R., and Nicholas Woodward, eds. *The British Economy Since 1945.* Oxford: Oxford University Press, 1991.

Crewe, Ivor, Anthony Fox, and Heil Day. *The British Electorate, 1963–1992: A Compendium of Data from the British Election Studies.* Cambridge: Cambridge University Press, 1995.

Floud, Roderick, and Donald McCloskey, eds. *The Economic History of Britain since 1700, 1939–1992,* Vol. 3, 2d ed. Cambridge: Cambridge University Press, 1994.

Halsey, Albert. *Change in British Society, from 1900 to the Present Day,* 4th ed. Oxford: Oxford University Press, 1995.

Heath, Anthony, Roger Jowell, and John Curtice. *Understanding Political Change: the British Voter, 1964–1987.* Oxford: Pergamon, 1991.

Marwick, Arthur. *British Society Since 1945,* 2d ed. Harmondsworth: Allen Lane, 1990.

Morgan, Kenneth. *The People's Peace: British History, 1945–1990,* rev. ed. Oxford: Oxford University Press, 1992.

Stephen M. Cullen

Nationalization

When the Labour Party came to power in 1945, it began to effect its long-standing programmatic call for the nationalization of commanding sectors of the British economy. Nationalization was intended to bring about the reorganization and modernization of British industry and contribute to the social democratization of society. The Bank of England, telegraph, radio, and civilian aviation were nationalized in 1946. Coal mines, canals, docks, and road transportation followed in 1947, and electricity and gas in 1948. The nationalization of the Bank of England, public utilities, and public transportation were not controversial because the government had already assumed significant regulatory control over them. The nationalization of the coal industry, which the powerful Coal Miners' Federation had long advocated, was not seriously contested because the industry had long been in decline. The nationalization of iron and steel proved more difficult. This industry was rather efficient and profitable. It was in this case that the Conservatives chose to make their stand. Through the House of Lords, the Conservatives blocked its nationalization until 1950. The resistance of the House of Lords led to the enactment of an amendment to the Parliament Act of 1911. The power of the Lords to delay legislation was limited to only one session instead of three sessions during a period of at least two years. When the Conservatives returned to power in 1951 they denationalized the iron and steel industry and intracity trucking. Labour, once again in power, renationalized iron and steel in 1967.

The extent and character of nationalization was regarded as insufficient by the more radical wing of the Labour Party represented by Stafford Cripps and Aneurin Bevan. The Labour Party did not establish the kind of economic planning and direction adopted by Italy and France. Unlike those countries, it did not place the administration of the nationalized enterprises in the hands of government agencies but set up autonomous corporations. In the eyes of leftists, these public corporations seemed as impervious to the interests of the public and workers as private corporations. The prime objective of the nationalized enterprises, to the disdain of the Left, appeared to be profitability.

During Britain's economic doldrums of the 1970s, both Conservatives and Labour engaged in "lemon socialism," nationalizing a number of troubled industries to prevent their failure. After the election of Margaret Thatcher as prime minister in 1979, the whole process of nationalization was reversed. Thatcher's program of denationalization affected not only the industrial sector but utilities such as British Telecom.

BIBLIOGRAPHY

Welf-Cohen, Reuben. *British Nationalisation, 1945–1973.* New York: St. Martin's Press, 1973.

Bernard Cook

SEE ALSO Thatcher, Margaret

European Community

Great Britain has long been regarded as an ambivalent partner in the European Community (EC). This is partly the result of British domestic politics. When the European Coal and Steel Community began in 1951, Britain's Labour government declined to participate, at least partly because it had recently nationalized those industries and did not want them subject to foreign control. Opposition also came from those who supported preferential trade agreements with the Commonwealth nations. Britain at first participated in, and then backed out of, the negotiations for the Treaty of Rome, which created the European Economic Community in 1957. Again partly for domestic reasons, Britain argued for a free-trade agreement rather than a formal institution that would be committed to both economic and political unification of Europe.

At the same time, Great Britain's decision to join the EC in 1961 must be viewed in the context of its relations with France and the United States. In the wake of the 1956 Suez crisis, Britain hoped that EC membership would not only raise its standing in Europe but also revitalize its special relationship with the United States by giving the Americans a sympathetic voice in the EC. This prospect alarmed many French, especially President Charles de Gaulle, who ardently wished to limit American influence in the EC and in Europe generally. De Gaulle's fears were reinforced by the Nassau Agreement of December 1962, in which Britain accepted American Polaris missiles as its nuclear deterrent and at least partially agreed to integrate its nuclear forces into NATO. It was on this basis that de Gaulle in early 1963 unilaterally rejected Britain's application to join the EC. Britain reapplied in 1966, under Labour Prime Minister Harold Wilson, and was again rejected by France.

Conservative Prime Minister Edward Heath reopened negotiations to join the EC immediately after taking office in 1970. Heath had long been a vocal supporter of European integration, and his sincerity may have ensured the success of Britain's third application. However, three major, intertwined issues were left unresolved when Britain formally entered the EC in 1973: agricultural subsidies, the Commonwealth, and Britain's contribution to the EC budget. It would take at least fifteen more years of negotiations before real progress was made toward resolving these issues. A fourth issue, monetary policy, would prove the most vexing of all.

The EC's Common Agricultural Policy (CAP) was detrimental to Britain because it imposed high tariffs on non-EC food products, along with heavy price supports for domestic produce. Britain had not previously used price supports and did not impose tariffs on imported food. In 1970 a British government study argued that adhering to the CAP would raise food prices as much as 25 percent. At the same time, the CAP would force Britain to revoke its preferential tariffs on Commonwealth products, including West Indian cane sugar and New Zealand dairy goods. Moreover, the CAP had taken on a new importance in the EC in 1970, when it was decided that the EC budget would be drawn from Community-imposed tariffs, plus 1 percent of value-added tax (VAT) revenues from each country. Since Britain consistently imported more food than it exported, this policy meant that Britain would pay a disproportionate share of the EC's annual budget. This issue was addressed in the 1980s under Margaret Thatcher, who negotiated rebates from the EC budget, while also pushing for reforms in the CAP price support system.

Britain's ambivalence toward the EC is most evident in its rejection of the EC's long-standing goal of an economic and monetary union, including a common European currency. The goal of economic integration lacked diplomatic substance until 1979, when the European Monetary System (EMS) was formed, the key element of which was the Exchange Rate Mechanism (ERM) designed to bring stability to the member currencies. Britain joined the EMS but refused to follow the ERM, believing that the goal of stable currencies should be pursued by existing institutions, especially the International Monetary Fund (IMF). In the late 1980s, France and Germany called for expanding the EMS into a central bank with an all-Europe currency, but by the mid-1990s British officials steadfastly refused to consider the idea, making this perhaps the biggest ongoing source of tension between Britain and the European Union. When the European Monetary Union and its currency were launched on January 1, 1999, Britain, along with Denmark and Sweden declined to participate.

BIBLIOGRAPHY

Bulmer, Simon, Stephen George, and Andrew Scott, eds. *The United Kingdom and EC Membership Evaluated.* London: Pinter, 1992.

Camps, Miriam. *Britain and the European Community, 1955–1963.* Princeton, N.J.: Princeton University Press, 1964.

George, Stephen. *An Awkward Partner: Britain in the European Community.* Oxford: Oxford University Press, 1994.

Peter Botticelli

SEE ALSO European Union

Legal Liberalization

The British Parliament passed several laws between the mid-1950s and the mid-1970s that loosened the state's controls on personal morality and, more broadly, on people's bodies. Seen as "progressive" by their proponents, liberalization of the law drew support primarily from Labour Members of Parliament (MPs), but also from some Conservative MPs who challenged the authority of the state in people's lives. Opponents charged that it undermined values and reflected the loss of wartime discipline.

The process began when the Wolfenden Committee (1955–57) was formed to examine the law of public solicitation. The committee's report enunciated a basic principle that came to define the process. Although the state should regulate public behavior, it ought not interfere in private behavior between consenting adults. The committee therefore recommended the decriminalization of private, consensual sexual activity, both homosexual and heterosexual. Wolfenden resulted in passage of the 1959 Street Offences Act, which permitted private prostitution agencies but forbade public solicitation. A year later Parliament acknowledged the impossibility of suppressing behavior that enjoyed widespread support by passing the 1960 Betting and Gaming Act, which legalized betting shops.

Concurrently, in the late 1950s and early 1960s, a debate arose on the value of capital punishment as a deterrent to crime. This debate led to the suspension in 1965 and abolition in 1969 of hanging. Growing Commonwealth immigration after 1945 led to friction between whites and nonwhites. The Race Relations Acts of 1966 and 1968 attempted to eliminate discrimination in employment and housing by creating a conciliation board. Other groups benefited by legislation. Well-to-do women had been able to secure abortions in private clinics. The 1967 Abortion Act standardized the legal procedures, thereby allowing women of average or modest means to terminate their pregnancies without recourse to illicit providers. The 1967 National Health Service (Family Planing) Act permitted local health authorities to dispense artificial contraceptive devices and information. In the same year, the 1967 Sexual Offences Act decriminalized private homosexual relationships between consenting adults. The abolition of censorship in 1968 opened British theater to creative experimentation but also permitted nude reviews and, indirectly, pornographic magazines and books, to proliferate. The 1969 Divorce Reform Act established the legal right to termination of a marriage after the couple had lived apart. The 1970 Matrimonial Property Act valued the wife's contribution to the marriage as equal to that of the husband's, whether hers was unpaid home work or outside paid work. The 1970 Equal Pay Act introduced the principle that wages should be based on competence, not on the sex of the employee, and the 1975 Sex Discrimination Act created conciliation boards to enforce the principle that males and females had equal rights.

The consumption of drugs was the one area that did not see liberalization during the period. Although the legal age for purchase of alcohol followed the lowering of the age of adulthood to eighteen, British law continued to restrict access to other substances. The 1964 Drugs (Prevention of Misuse) Act penalized the possession of tranquilizers and amphetamines, and laws forbidding the possession of marijuana, hashish, and LSD were the most rigorous and rigorously enforced in Western Europe.

The debaters viewed the same issues from markedly different perspectives. Proponents believed that law was a means to the construction of a just society, which they defined in formal, legal terms as one that permitted "deviant" behavior within the adult, private sphere. Opponents thought that legal change subverted ancient and healthy social institutions. Hence, although proponents saw change chiefly as narrowly limited to the legal status of individuals, opponents feared the social dimensions of change, rightly seeing legal liberalization as indicating more profound shifts in the nature of postwar society.

The beneficiaries of legal liberalization remained unsatisfied, for their primary goal was social and economic equality, not mere toleration. Thus, although the legal liberalizers viewed legislation as the culmination of campaigns that addressed civil injustice, affected groups saw it as the first stage in campaigns to gain social and economic status equal to that of traditionally dominant groups.

In economic terms, the expansion of legal liberalization was made possible by the end of postwar austerity in the mid-1950s. The process was brought to a close by the serious economic problems that the economy faced in the mid-1970s.

BIBLIOGRAPHY

Jeffery-Poulter, Stephen. *Peers, Queers, and Commons: The Struggle for Gay Law Reform from 1950 to the Present.* London: Routledge, 1991.

Marwick, Arthur. *British Society since 1945,* 2d ed. Penguin Social History of Britain. London: Penguin Books, 1990.

Richards, Peter G. *Parliament and Conscience.* London: George Allen & Unwin, 1970.

Denis G. Paz

Profumo Scandal

British sex/spy scandal that contributed to the fall of Prime Minister Harold Macmillan's Conservative government. John Profumo (1915–), Macmillan's war minister from 1960 to 1963, had an extramarital sexual liaison in 1961 with Christine Keeler, an upscale call girl. Stephen Ward, a fashionable osteopath with both Conservative Party and underworld connections, had introduced Keeler to Profumo. Keeler was also having sex with Captain Yevegeny Ivanov, Soviet assistant naval attaché in London.

MI5, the British counterespionage service, believed that Ivanov might have used Keeler to extract defense information from Profumo or to blackmail him, but it was slow to warn the prime minister. When finally confronted with the charge in 1963, Profumo denied his affair with Keeler to Macmillan and the House of Commons. Profumo was later forced to resign when it was proven that he lied, Ward was arrested for pimping and subsequently killed himself, and the episode exploded into a major scandal in the press and media. It was also revealed that many other leading figures in the Conservative Party were involved in sexual improprieties.

An official investigation by a judge, Lord Denning, cleared Profumo of the alleged security leak. Nevertheless, the Macmillan government was badly compromised by its fumbling of the incident and discredited by the salacious disclosures about prominent Conservatives. The Profumo scandal followed closely on the more serious charge in 1963 that the British secret service had protected double agent Harold (Kim) Philby, a recent defector to the Soviet Union.

BIBLIOGRAPHY

Denning, Alfred T., Lord. *The Denning Report: The Profumo-Christine Keeler Affair.* London: Her Majesty's Stationery Office, 1963.

Irving, Clive, Ron Hall, and Jeremy Wallington. *Anatomy of a Scandal: A Study of the Profumo Affair.* New York: M.S. Mill, 1963.

Knightley, Philip, and Clive Kennedy. *An Affair of State: The Profumo Case and the Framing of Stephen Ward.* London: Jonathan Cape, 1987.

Don M. Cregier

SEE ALSO Macmillan, Harold

Election of 1997

Election resulting in the defeat of John Major and his ruling Conservative Party and the victory of the Labour Party, led by Anthony "Tony" Blair, with a majority of 179 seats. Held on May 1, 1997, it ended eighteen continuous years of Conservative government and proved that reforms launched by previous leaders Neil Kinnock and John Smith and continued by Blair had made Labour electable.

In 1992 the Conservatives won a 21-seat majority. By-election losses and defections decreased this margin until, in late 1996, the government lost its majority. Public opinion polls offered no hope. After Britain was forced out of the European Exchange Rate Mechanism on Black Wednesday, September 16, 1992, Labour's lead rarely dipped below 20 percent. The government was also tarnished by scandals and split over policy toward the European Monetary Union. Major sought to silence his critics by seeking reelection as party leader in June 1995. He won, but without the support of the party's right wing. The government hoped voters would give it credit for the improving economy, but the electorate, remembering Conservative tax increases and the recession of the early 1990s, refused to be swayed by current improvements. At the same time, in September 1993, Labour was modernizing by reducing its connections to the labor unions, electing Blair in July 1994, revising Clause Four of its constitution in April 1995, which had committed it to public ownership of the means of production, and shedding its image as the party of high taxes.

Major announced the election on March 17, hoping a long campaign would expose Labour's divisions and give the government time to emphasize the nation's economic recovery and the danger that Labour's plans for devolution posed to the United Kingdom. But Labour, aided by an effective media center directed by Peter Mandelson, turned the tables. The upbeat tone of New Labour contrasted with the continuing strife among the Conservatives, and Labour won the endorsement of tabloid newspapers that had opposed them in 1992. Labour's share of the vote, 44.4 percent, on a low turnout of 71.2 percent, was not crushing, but the electoral system, biased against the Conservatives, gave Labour a remarkable 419 of 659 MPs. Nevertheless, the Conservatives did poorly. They won only 31.4 percent of the vote, or 165 MPs, took no seats in Scotland and Wales, and were largely relegated to the suburbs and shires. Tactical voting helped the Liberal Democratic Party, led by Jeremy "Paddy" Ashdown, win 46 MPs, though their vote fell, while the nationalist parties in Scotland (Scottish National Party) and Wales (Plaid Cymru) increased their support but made no breakthroughs. The anti-European Referendum Party, led by Sir James Goldsmith, took few votes from the Conservatives, who were defeated by Labour's renewed appeal and by the widespread belief that it was time for a change.

BIBLIOGRAPHY

Butler, David, and Dennis Kavanagh. *The British General Election of 1997.* London: Macmillan, 1997.

Jones, Nicholas. *Campaign 1997: How the General Election Was Won and Lost.* London: Indigo, 1997.

Ted R. Bromund

SEE ALSO Blair, Anthony Charles Lynton (Tony)

Political Parties

Since World War II British politics has been dominated by the Conservative and Labour Parties. The two other parties of significance have been the Liberal and the Social Democratic Parties.

The Conservative Party has been the most successful party in Britain since 1945, holding office for a total of thirty-four years. It dominated the political scene during the peak of the long postwar boom, forming the government from 1951 until 1964, winning three general elections in 1951, 1955, and 1959. During that thirteen-year period the party was led by Winston Churchill, Sir Anthony Eden, Harold Macmillan, and Sir Alec Douglas-Home. It next held office, under Edward Heath, for four troubled years, from 1970 until the February 1974 election. Following a further defeat in the October 1974 election, Heath was replaced as Conservative Party leader by Margaret Thatcher, the first woman to lead a major British party. Thatcher subsequently became the first female British prime minister in May 1979, when the Conservatives were returned to office. The party won the next three general elections in 1983, 1987, and 1992, the latter under a new leader, John Major, but was spectacularly defeated in the 1997 general election.

Part of the reason for the Conservative Party's continued success was its flexibility in terms of ideas and policy. Following its defeat in the 1945 election, immediately after the war, the party accepted the basic idea of the welfare state as established by the Labour Party. In the 1950s Conservative governments continued to operate interventionist economic policies and supported the idea of social provision. Similarly, it oversaw the continued dismantling of the British Empire despite its traditional association with imperialism. These policies were pursued on pragmatic grounds, while the Conservatives continued to make their usual appeal as the party of strong government, the family, and law and order. As the postwar consensus began to unravel in the 1970s, the Heath government attempted to return to a more free-market approach to the economy but retreated in the face of opposition. The Conservatives were more successful in their attempts to revise policy under Thatcher, who led a gradual reversal of earlier policies in the 1980s. By the end of that decade the Conservative Party had established itself as the party of the free market in the economy and strong government in the areas of law and order, defense, and foreign policy.

The Conservative Party draws its core support from the middle and upper classes, although even during the 1940s and 1950s, it depended on a sizable vote from the working class. In regional terms, the party has tended to be more strongly represented in the south of England, and less so in the north of England, Scotland, and Wales. Women and older voters are more likely to vote Conservative, while Conservative support among more recently arrived ethnic minorities is small.

Less successful in electoral terms than the Conservatives, the Labour Party has been, nonetheless, a key part of British politics. Led by Clement Attlee, it formed Britain's first postwar government, winning the July 1945 election. During its period in office the Labour Party established the parameters of British politics for the next three decades. Attlee led Labour to a further, but narrow, victory in the 1950 election, but the party lost in 1951. This was the beginning of a long period out of office for Labour, which did not win another election until 1964. In that year, Labour, led by Harold Wilson, won by only five parliamentary seats, but Wilson took Labour to a more decisive victory in 1966. Economic difficulties and a sense of disappointment in Labour led to defeat in 1970. However, industrial unrest, short-time working, and economic problems led to a return of Labour and Harold Wilson to government, winning both of the 1974 elections. Wilson was replaced by Jim Callaghan in 1976, but the economic problems of the 1970s led to Labour's defeat in 1979. Not until 1997 did the party win another general election.

The Labour Party was originally conceived and delivered by Britain's strong labor union movement, and was long regarded as the political voice of organized labor. In addition, the party also counted on the support of socialist societies and some middle-class intellectuals. The 1945 government built on the wartime coalition's interventionist policies and the Labour Party's own history to introduce peacetime nationalization and the welfare state. Yet the Labour was never a dogmatic socialist or Marxist party in the European mold; rather, it was a labor party that sought to gain widespread support among the British people, and gain fairer shares of the national wealth for organized labor. In foreign affairs it claimed to be internationalist in outlook, but, in practice, it promoted British national interests. Factional stresses within the party came to the fore in the 1970s, and, more particularly, in the 1980s. In opposition for that decade, Labour was torn by internal dispute between those who wished to promote a more socialist program and pragmatists who argued that such an approach would leave the party permanently in opposition with shrinking support among the electorate. Following the party's disastrous 1983 election under Michael Foot, the next Labour leader, Neil Kinnock, began a process of "modernization." This program essentially meant that the party began to move rightward on the political spectrum, accepting what appeared to be fundamental shifts in British electoral behavior during the 1980s. This process was continued by subsequent party leaders, John Smith and Tony Blair. By the time of the 1997 general election, Blair successfully argued that "New" Labour was no longer the voice of any sectional group, and that it was a party of the center, not the left.

Support for the Labour Party has come traditionally from organized labor and old industrial regions of Britain: the north of England, south Wales, and the central belt of Scotland, along with inner-city areas. In the 1980s it appeared that the party was losing the support of some sections of the working class, or, at the least, deindustrialization was eroding this essential core of Labour's electoral support. But Labour's position in Scotland, Wales, and the north of England was strengthened, as the electoral map of Britain became more regionalized.

The Liberals' only involvement in national government since 1945 came with the loose Liberal-Labour governmental pact during the period of the Labour government from 1974 to 1979. Yet as Britain's most important minority party, the Liberals have, at times, had a notable impact on British politics.

During the 1950s it appeared for a while that the once powerful Liberal Party would disappear from national politics. In the 1951, 1955, and 1959 elections the Liberals held only six parliamentary seats, and fell to 2.5 percent of the vote in 1951. Yet the Liberals hung on, presenting themselves as the radical center party and providing an outlet for protest voting at by-elections. As the two-party system began to show signs of erosion in the late 1960s, and, more particularly, in the 1970s, so the Liberals grew in strength. In the February, 1974 election, for instance, they gathered nearly 20 percent of the vote, taking 14 parliamentary seats. During that decade the Liberals continued to build on their strategy of being very active in local politics, where they found success easier to come by. The turmoil within the Labour Party following its defeat in the 1979 election provided the Liberals with an unexpected boost. The growing strength of the socialist left in the Labour Party led to a group of Labour MPs leaving the party to form the Social Democratic Party. Their natural allies were the Liberals, and the two parties entered into an alliance in 1981. For a while it looked as if the alliance would create new ground for itself on the British political map. The combined vote of the two parties in the 1983 election was 25 percent, only 2 percent behind Labour. But the nationwide spread of the alliance's vote, and the system of voting, gave the alliance only 23 seats, compared with Labour's 209 and the Conservative's 397. In the 1987 election Labour began to regain ground, while the alliance's challenge faltered. In the wake of that election, Liberal leader David Steel mounted what some saw as a coup against the SDP, effectively absorbing that party into the Liberal Party, which was renamed the Social and Liberal Democratic Party in March 1988.

The party continues to provide a third-party input into national politics, under its leader, Paddy Ashdown, who led it to its greatest postwar success in the 1997 election, when it won 46 parliamentary seats. It appeals particularly to educated, middle-class voters, is traditionally strong in peripheral areas of Britain, and is more successful at local rather than national elections. Its policies continue to call for wide constitutional change in Britain, involving extended regional government, electoral reform, and the encoding of civil rights. It is also associated with environmental concerns and strong support for federalism in Europe.

Founded in March 1981, largely by a group of former Labour MPs under the leadership of David Owen, Shirley Williams, Roy Jenkins, and Bill Rodgers—the "Gang of Four"—the Social Democratic Party (SDP) had a short but dramatic life. The SDP felt that it was the guardian of pragmatic, center-left politics, and that, in the wake of the 1979 election, the Labour Party had moved dramatically leftward to rigidly ideological socialism. In partnership with the Liberal Party the SDP won a number of by-election victories and performed well in the 1983 general election. But the dominance of the Conservative Party, and the recovery of Labour, meant that the window of opportunity was quickly closed for the SDP. Following a disappointing 1987 election result, the Liberal Party leadership moved rapidly to absorb the majority of the SDP's members, while the rump of the SDP, under David Owen, struggled on until his retirement from politics in 1991. Apart from the brief excitement the SDP brought to British politics in the early 1980s, perhaps its only importance was its posthumous contribution to the Labour Party's shift to the right from 1983 onward.

BIBLIOGRAPHY

Blake, Robert. *The Conservative Party from Peel to Thatcher.* London: Fontana, 1985.

Crewe, Ivor, and Anthony King. *SDP: the Birth, Life and Death of the Social Democratic Party.* Oxford: Oxford University Press, 1993.

McKenzie, Robert. *British Political Parties.* London: Heineman, 1964.

Selden, Anthony, and Stuart Ball. *Conservative Century: The Conservative Party since 1900.* Oxford: Oxford University Press, 1994.

Shaw, Eric. *The Labour Party Since 1979: Crisis and Transformation.* London: Routledge, 1994.

Tivey, Leonard, and Anthony Wright, eds. *Party Ideology in Britain.* London, Routledge, 1989.
Vainwright, Hilary. *Labour: A Tale of Two Parties.* London: Hogarth Press, 1987.

Stephen M. Cullen

Economy

The direction of the British economy since 1945 has generally been dictated by memory. In the first half of the period, Britons remembered the difficulties of the depression years of the 1920s and 1930s. Government and industry dedicated their energies toward maintaining full employment and a strong currency—the pound—goals that increasingly proved incompatible. In the second half, Britons remembered the failures of these goals, which resulted in unemployment, high inflation, and strikes. Thus, the emphasis changed toward reducing inflation, curbing the power of labor unions, and emphasizing investment and entrepreneurship. These goals met with more success but came at the expense of the short-term cost of high unemployment and the long-term cost of tremendous inequalities in income.

During the worldwide depression of the 1920s and 1930s, Britain was plagued by high unemployment. The base industries of Britain's industrial revolution—coal, railroads, shipbuilding, textiles, iron and steel—were all in decline. When World War II ended, Keynesian economic principles were considered the new economic orthodoxy, dictating that the best way to solve these problems was for the government to intervene in the economy. Thus, certain economic goals were agreed on by industry, finance, government, workers, management, professionals, and other concerned parties. These goals were to maintain full employment in British industries, retain the pound's status in international markets, and assure London's position as a center of international finance.

The Labour government elected in 1945 set out to achieve these goals. A number of the old industrial revolution industries were nationalized, including coal, steel, and railroads, in an effort to provide them with government funding and direction to make them more efficient. Social welfare programs were adopted, like the National Health Service, national insurance, and a social security system. Added to already existing national pension and paid unemployment programs, these programs were designed to keep the average citizen free from medical and employment worries "from cradle to grave." These programs a feeling of community and prosperity among the British people in all sectors of the economy.

For the next three decades, government, industry, and unions were satisfied to maintain full employment and a secure social welfare system. But over time the large tax burden to pay for these programs became onerous. Also, the need to pay for continuing overseas commitments proved burdensome as well. This all meant that industries had little money for investment in research and technology, and a lack of improvements spelled a lack of competitiveness with foreign manufacturers.

Nevertheless, with the end of wartime austerity in the 1950s, economic growth allowed most Britons to achieve the highest standard of living in their nation's history. To the average citizen, the acquisition of a car and television, abundant food, and an unemployment rate below 2 percent meant that the British economy seemed basically sound. Like most other Western economies, Britain experienced a high economic growth rate; between 1950 and 1966, gross domestic product per capita rose by 40 percent. Britain imported numerous immigrants from former colonies to work unskilled jobs, and women entered the workforce as well, solidifying the sense of general prosperity. The British economy had never seemed more prosperous than it was in the first twenty years after the war.

However, owing to the continued dedication to full employment and high wages, both nationalized and private industries lagged behind the industries of other nations in the research, development, and acquisition of new technologies. British investors put their money into more profitable overseas investments, meaning that British industry had fewer resources to invest in technology. Thus, British goods remained high-priced overseas, and foreign competitors made strong inroads in the market at home. The trade deficit, coupled with the expense of continued defense commitments overseas, also created a balance-of-payments deficit so bad that the government twice had to devalue the pound, in 1949 and 1967. This was particularly a problem because, in accordance with the 1944 Bretton Woods Agreement, the pound was a reserve currency. Britain was obliged to maintain its strength on world currency markets to maintain the stability of weaker currencies measured against the pound. London's strength as an international financial center was jeopardized by these devaluations, but various governments saw this as preferable to laying off workers in nationalized industries to make them more efficient and cost-effective.

Conservative governments began a policy that came to be called "stop-go" economics to defend the needs of the pound against full employment. Using interest rates and, to a lesser extent, taxation policy, the Exchequer tried to make Britain's economic growth rate "stop" or "go" by providing incentives and disincentives for investors and consumers to create a demand for industrial goods. By lowering interest rates and taxes, the government could encourage people to buy and invest more, pumping up economic growth in a "go" cycle. However, the strength of foreign production, and shrinking markets for British goods and British investments in foreign industries meant that a "go" cycle led to a balance-of-payments deficit and increased inflation, and so threatened the pound's value. To stop a run on the pound, the government would then raise interest rates and taxes, encouraging people to save more, buy less, and thus put a "stop" on economic growth. A "stop" cycle meant that industries in Britain would lose profits and have to start laying off workers, which meant that the government would then try to lower taxes and interest rates again. Labour Prime Minister Harold Wilson coined the term "stop-go" to mock Conservative economic policy. In 1964 he created the Department of Economic Affairs (DEA) specifically to allow government, industry, and unions to come together to plan for sustained economic growth that would defer these economic cycles. However, DEA planning proved unsuccessful, and instead the government turned to wage and price controls. After the 1967 devaluation of the pound, Wilson's government ironically had to institute the most draconian "stop" to the economy up to that point. Meanwhile, inflation continued to be an apparently unstoppable problem, one that threatened the stability of Britain's working-class families by the late 1960s.

With full employment Britain's labor unions had high membership; with high inflation, they also made a continual demand to raise wages to meet rising prices. Despite the willingness of the Trades Union Congress to work with the government to meet its economic goals, individual unions and their workers refused to comply easily with requests to accept wage freezes, layoffs, and new technology. Wildcat strikes plagued production in the late 1960s. When the Wilson government tried to pass an Industrial Relations Bill in 1969 to curb the unions' radicalism, the storm of protest unleashed among the party's working-class constituency ensured that Labour would not be able to control the unions.

The rise of the Organization of Petroleum Exporting Countries (OPEC) that sought to increase the price of oil by limiting its production, and the explosion in international oil prices in 1973 hit the British economy hard, increasing worker demands even more. In 1974 coal miners' wage demands required Edward Heath's Conservative government to declare a three-day work week, and the nation bordered on a general strike. Unions tended to be slightly more conciliatory toward Labour governments, but by the mid-1970s rising inflation kept demand for increased wages more insatiable than ever. The 1974 Wilson government established a "social contract" with the unions by which they agreed to restrain their wage demands in return for expanded social welfare and an expanded nationalization program. This proved successful in curbing inflation, but it eventually backfired on the workers and the government. Unable to produce a competitive product, many private industries were forced to lay off workers. Over the course of the winter of 1978–79, a series of strikes over the government's refusal to allow a 5 percent pay raise paralyzed the British economy and, to many people, marked the low point of Britain's economic troubles.

With the accession of Margaret Thatcher's Conservative government in 1979, national economic policy changed dramatically. Thatcher was a student of the monetarist principles of Milton Friedman and Keith Joseph; she believed that the strength of the pound should be the government's top priority at the expense of employment. Her government then reversed previous policy: government, industry, and finance worked toward the goal of limiting inflation, to the detriment of Britain's unemployment rate.

Under Thatcher, businesses concentrated more on profit maximization over the welfare, jobs, and wages of their workers. Nationalized industries such as steel, British Telecom, British Airways, Jaguar, and others were made more efficient by laying off workers, and then were sold off to private investors. Workers were encouraged to buy shares in their own companies. Critically, anti-union legislation was passed, and in a dramatic incident, Britain's National Union of Mineworkers was defeated when it went on strike in 1984–85 in opposition to the closing of several mines. Because of these measures, manufacturing productivity rose even as massive layoffs brought Britain's unemployed population above three million before subsiding. Despite this improvement, the older industrial revolution businesses had to be abandoned as the British economy accelerated its long-term evolution toward becoming a service economy.

The profits from privatizing industries and newly discovered North Sea oil brought the government increased revenues in the 1980s. Thus, in a series of moves that created much resentment, taxes were lowered substantially for the wealthiest part of the British population to encourage investment. Entrepreneurship was greatly encouraged for the middle classes, and many new businesses started in the 1980s. Most successfully, housing purchases were encouraged, and council estate tenants were given the opportunity to buy their own apartments and buildings. The growth of home ownership also accelerated a long-term process and contributed greatly to the expansion of the economy. London's financial district (the City) solidified its status as one of the world's major financial centers, especially in gold and silver speculation and international currency markets. However, the huge drop in the New York stock market in 1987 caught many of Britain's new investors off guard and precipitated an early recession.

At first, the renewed focus on the inflation rate was a failure, as another OPEC oil increase in 1979 foiled the government's efforts. Monetarist practices proved a failure as they precluded the maintenance of welfare provisions. Much as the Thatcher government seemed to wish to do away with such provisions, the huge unemployment rate made this impossible. Nevertheless after the end of the 1982 recession, inflation dropped as a function of the general improvement in inflation rates around most of the Western world. In Britain it came at the expense of initially high unemployment and an overall adjustment in the mind-set of the average British citizen as to what an acceptable unemployment rate was. In the late 1990s Britain enjoyed the lowest unemployment rate in Europe, but at around 6 percent, it was at a much higher rate than what was acceptable in the 1950s and 1960s. Likewise, partially owing to the discovery of oil in the North Sea, Britain's balance of payments greatly improved, and the strength of the pound on international markets has been greatly enhanced. Yet all these improvements came at the expense of a higher poverty rate, a growing gap between rich and poor, and a general lack of certainty about the individual's economic future.

In recent years there has been some controversy attached to Britain's economic obligations in the European Union. Because of currency problems, Britain dropped out of the European Union's Exchange Rate Mechanism (ERM) in 1992. The ERM requires participatory nations to keep their currencies at a specific exchange rate with the German mark (deutsche mark) to strengthen all Europe's currencies against inflation. However, with the new strength of the pound, there has been much British opposition to reentering the ERM. Although Thatcher's monetarist policies had the pound shadowing the deutsche mark's value in the 1980s, she balked at the idea of a formal attachment in the ERM. This opposition continued in the 1990s, in effect splitting the Conservative Party. There is also some question as to whether the pound should be the central currency in the ERM, rather than the mark.

Regardless of the results, such speculation was evidence of the apparent strength of the British economy after a long period of instability. Yet the continued lack of investment in British industry, the lack of major British international corporate giants, and the buyout of companies like Rolls Royce and British Telecom by other international corporations had others speculating about the permanence of the economy's strength.

BIBLIOGRAPHY

Cox, Andrew, Simon Lee, and Joe Sanderson. *The Political Economy of Modern Britain.* Lyme, NH: E. Elgar 1997.

Crafts, N. F. R., and N. W. C. Woodward, eds. *The British Economy Since 1945.* New York: Oxford University Press, 1991.

Pollard, Sidney. *The Development of the British Economy 1914–1990,* 3d ed. New York: E. Arnold, 1992.

Peter Simonelli

SEE ALSO Thatcher, Margaret

Confederation of British Industry

Amalgamation of three older business employers' organizations—the Federation of British Industry, British Employers' Confederation, and National Association of British Manufacturers. The three organizations combined in 1965, with government encouragement, to become Britain's top service provider and pressure group representing the interests of industry.

The Confederation of British Industry (CBI) was formed to coordinate the lobbying activities of Britain's largest employers, who were previously organized in separate trade associations, chambers of commerce, and employment organizations. As a lobbying group the CBI concentrates on influencing the financial and tax policies of the Exchequer, the British department of treasury. As a service group, the CBI provides its member industries with research, surveys, and journals dedicated to the interests of employers. Though many efforts have been made over the years to include smaller businesses and financial concerns as members, the CBI's membership has remained mainly industrial, and thus both its lobbying and service activities have been directed toward the interests of Britain's large industries, both private and nationalized.

In 1960 the Federation of British Industry accepted the principle of government economic planning, and with the election of a Labour government in 1964, the FBI formed the alliance that created the Confederation of British Industry. The government created a working advisory group—the National Economic Development Council—which combined the resources and interests of the CBI, the Trades Union Congress (TUC), and the government's Ministry of Economic Affairs to help plan the future growth of the British economy. Together, the CBI, TUC, and the ministry worked to set prices and incomes policies, and the CBI put out quarterly forecasts of the economy's buoyancy. A later British government termed this economic policy "tripartism." Throughout the 1960s and 1970s, tripartism tended to work very poorly, as neither the CBI nor the TUC had enough control over their memberships to maintain price controls or wage controls. Likewise, the CBI's timetable to achieve economic results from reforms was far more long-term than that of the governments they served, because the governments needed to achieve political results in the short term to remain in power. As a result, during the Thatcher government of the 1980s, tripartism was abandoned, and many of the CBI's largest members began to negotiate with the government on their own rather than through the lobbying offices of the confederation. With the rise of a Labour government in 1997, however, the CBI has been consulted more often (though not heeded) by the government on union policies, the imposition of a minimum wage, and the measurement of economic growth projections against inflation.

The Confederation of British Industries has 2,500 members separated into thirteen regional groups. It is now a part of the European Union's Union of Industrial and Employers' Confederations of Europe. Its annual conference is held every November; its director general in 1998 was Adair Turner.

BIBLIOGRAPHY

Cairncross, Alec. *The British Economy since 1945.* Cambridge, Mass.: Blackwell, 1995.

Grant, Wyn, and David Marsh. *The Confederation of British Industry.* London: Hodder and Stoughton, 1977

David Simonelli

Taxation

Taxation has been a critical government instrument of national economic policy in Britain since 1945. British taxation principles have been generally dedicated toward a fair spread of the burden of taxation, equity from one individual to another within the same economic group, easy administration and collection, and simplicity in understanding. Despite the occasional conflict among these principles, they remained basically sound and unchanged until the 1980s, when British economic problems resulted in a major restructuring of the tax burden to rest more upon the poorer sector of the British taxpaying public. The results have been controversial both politically and economically.

British principles toward taxation have changed greatly over the course of the centuries, and the system of taxation has changed accordingly. In the nineteenth century liberal utilitarian economic principles dictated that money was best left in the pocket of the taxpayer, who was a better and more direct spender in the British economy than the government. In the early twentieth century a Liberal Party effort to attract the new British working-class voter and stave off class warfare resulted in a series of reforms, such as a health insurance system, unemployment compensation, and old age pensions, all of which required an increase in taxation. In 1945, however, with the election of a socialist Labour Party government, the taxation system was identified as the primary means to redistribute wealth in Britain from the rich to the poor. For the next three and a half decades this was the general principle behind British taxation.

British tax revenues come from many different sources. The income tax, first imposed in 1799 and renewed annually since 1860, supplies the bulk of British revenue. A surtax was first imposed on the highest incomes in 1909, and in 1943 the "Pay As You Earn" system was established to collect the income tax directly from the taxpayer's wage packet on a more gradual basis over the course of a year. The income tax is also graduated according to ability to pay and age, and relief is granted according to personal allowances (e.g., children, marriage, insurance, education, etc.).

Also introduced during the war was the indirect purchase tax, paid by producers as an excise duty and thus requiring producers to include the amount of the tax in their prices. Other indirect taxes include customs duties on imports; the most prominent and profitable imports are tobacco, alcohol, hydrocarbon oils, and television licenses. Customs have historically been imposed in particular to protect home industries, such as the production of automobiles, films, weaponry, and textile fibers. As a part of the General Agreement on Tariffs and Trade (GATT) and the European Union, many of these customs duties have been reduced or repealed over the last two decades.

At the local level, with a brief exception in the early 1990s, taxation has consisted mainly of a local property tax assessed differently in each of the different counties in the United Kingdom.

The history of taxation in Britain since 1945 has been marked by controversy and, in general, a failure of purpose. Immediately after World War II Clement Attlee's Labour government dedicated itself to redistribute wealth in Britain through the medium of taxation. Thus promises to lower the large taxation burden caused by the war were abandoned quickly, especially as new social programs like the National Health Service were established. However, the inability of the British economy to recover easily after the war meant that taxation also came to serve the purpose of directing monetary policy: strong measures of taxation were meant to curb inflation. Instead, owing to the continued slow growth of the British economy in the 1940s and 1950s, every raise in income or purchase taxes instead resulted in further inflation, as producers needed to be able to pay for higher taxes by imposing higher prices. Also, the desire to maintain full employment killed initiatives to use tax breaks as an incentive for companies to invest in research and development.

For the next thirty years taxes became the accepted method for the Conservatives, Labour, and the Treasury to influence the direction of the economy. Raising or lowering taxes were methods used to encourage investment and economic growth in an effort to micromanage the national economy. None of these efforts was successful, owing to a very unstable corporate tax policy that kept inflation high and because of continual reversals in economic policy between stimulating or cooling off the economy (known derisively as "stop-go" economics). New taxes were introduced to raise new revenues, such as a capital gains tax and a corporation tax in 1965, a raise in the surtax on high incomes, and the replacement of the purchase tax with a value-added tax in 1973. However, these new taxes did little to improve Britain's economic performance. By 1979 the British economy had reached crisis proportions owing to high inflation, strikes for higher wages, and an unstable pound on international markets.

Under Margaret Thatcher efforts to micromanage the economy through taxation policy were redirected, mainly by redistributing the taxation burden downward. Thatcher was the first British politician to sit in the prime minister's office since the war who was considered an expert on taxation policy. Drastic cuts were made in income tax rates for the very rich and middle incomes. At the same time, taxes on the poor increased. Corporate taxes were reduced by 20 percent, and the inheritance tax (capital transfer tax) was reduced to insignificance. The capital gains tax was indexed with inflation. All these tax cuts were made with the express purpose of improving the incentive for the rich and the middle classes to invest in the economy.

These efforts were moderately successful at curbing inflation until 1988, when a drop in the international stock market precipitated a recession in Britain. At about the same time Thatcher declared the government's intention to abolish the local property tax in favor of a "community charge," a flat head tax on all local voters. Thatcher was attempting to control local government spending by giving local voters a stake in how their own local tax revenues were spent. However, the tax was derisively labeled the "poll tax" for its attachment to local voter registration records, and nationwide protests expressed the anger of the electorate over a regressive tax that clearly placed the poor at a disadvantage. Polls indicated that 65 percent of the electorate opposed the tax, and its imposition eventually contributed heavily to Thatcher's resignation in December 1990. The poll tax was phased out in favor of a renewal property tax in 1993.

The British tax structure seems at the moment to have been relieved of its duties as the major director of government economic policy. Nevertheless, taxation remains the main producer of government revenues and thus will continue to have a strong impact on inflation and other economic indicators.

BIBLIOGRAPHY

Lawson, Nigel. *The View from No. 11, 1993: Britain's Longest-serving Cabinet Member Recalls the Triumphs and Disappointments of the Thatcher Era.* New York: Doubleday, 1993.

Steinmo, Sven. *Taxation and Democracy: Swedish, British, and American Approaches to Financing the Modern State.* New Haven, Conn.: Yale University Press, 1993.

David Simonelli

Trades Union Congress

Founded in 1868, The Trades Union Congress (TUC) is a national labor union organization representing most of Britain's craft and industrial labor unions. Between 1945 and 1979 the TUC was a central participant in the economic decision-making process in Great Britain. The important role of the TUC in post–World War II Britain has its origins in the wartime coalition government in which Ernest Bevin, the general secretary of the Transport and General Workers' Union, served as minister of labor and national service.

The British Labour Party was originally founded as the political wing of the TUC. Hence the victory of Labour in the 1945 British general election was also a victory for the TUC. At that time labor union density (the percentage of the workforce belonging to labor unions) was 38.9 percent. The Labour government continued the wartime tripartite relationship among government, employers, and TUC. That government also took measures to make the business environment more favorable to labor union organizers, most notably with the repeal in 1946 of the 1927 Trade Union and Trades Disputes Act. This act had placed severe legal restrictions on the activities of British labor unions. By 1951 labor union density had increased to 45.2 percent.

In 1951 the Conservative Party won power in the general election and was to remain in power until 1964. In principle the Conservatives accepted the greater part of the postwar social settlement, retaining the tripartite relationship. Indeed, in September 1951 they strengthened this relationship with the creation of the tripartite National Economic Development Council (NEDC). However, during the early 1960s, tension began to grow between the government and the TUC. For example, the TUC boycotted the National Incomes Commission, which had been established by the government to control wage inflation.

In October 1964 the Conservatives lost power to the Labour Party. A close relationship between the government and the TUC was expected, and between 1964 and 1970, labor union density rose from 43.2 to 47.7 percent. On the other hand, the macroeconomic problems experienced during this period meant that the government felt the need to control pay increases. In 1965 a statutory Prices and Incomes Board was established, but an attempt by the TUC to restrain pay increases on a voluntary basis was a complete failure. Hence, in 1966 the government introduced statutory controls including a six-month pay freeze. By 1968 the concept of a national incomes policy had become widely discredited within the TUC. This was reflected in an upsurge in industrial unrest between 1968 and 1970. The relationship between the TUC and the government was also affected by an attempt by the employment minister, Barbara Castle, to reform industrial relations with a White Paper, *In Place of Strife*. Pressure from the TUC forced the government to abandon the proposed reforms.

In June 1970 Labour was replaced by the Conservatives following the general election. The new government enacted an Industrial Relations Bill in 1971 intended to reform industrial relations. Although the act was relatively innocuous, the TUC saw it as a major threat to the interests of its members. At the same time, industrial unrest continued, a notable example being the coal miners' strike of 1972. Industrial unrest led to an attempt by the government to establish an industrial consensus with the TUC and the Confederation of British Industry (CBI), the employers' organization. However, the attempt failed. In 1973 the government introduced a statutory prices and incomes policy to control inflation without the consent of the TUC. Coal miners led the opposition to this policy with an overtime ban in the winter of 1973–74. As of January 1, 1974, the government introduced a three-day week to conserve declining stocks of coal at electric power stations. An attempt by the TUC to negotiate a resolution of the crisis with the government failed. In February coal miners voted for a national strike; the government called a general election to determine "who ruled Britain" and lost to the Labour Party.

During the period 1974–79 the Labour government also sought to suppress inflation by controlling the annual rate of increase in wages and salaries. Initially this policy was based on formal agreements, known as the Social Contract, between the government and the TUC. However, as of August 1977 growing discontent among rank-and-file labor union members led to the end of formal agreements. In January 1978 the government adopted a new policy of a "pay norm," whereby pay agreements were to be restricted to an increase of just 5 percent during the year as of August 1978. The policy resulted in a wave of strikes, abandonment of the "pay norm," and defeat of the Labour government in the general election of 1979.

In retrospect, 1979 marked a decisive turning point in the fortunes of the members of the TUC. The Conservative governments have followed a neoliberal economic agenda since 1979. Labor unions are seen as an impediment to a competitive labor market. The Conservatives abandoned the tripartite economic relationship among the government, the CBI, and the TUC. The last surviving remnant of this relationship, NEDC, was abolished in January 1993. The TUC has failed to prevent the enactment of eight pieces of industrial relations legislation that have effectively removed the hard-won legal security achieved by Britain's labor unions since the mid-1870s. Partly as a result of this, Britain's labor union density fell from 57 percent in 1979 to 30 percent in 1995.

BIBLIOGRAPHY

Dorey, Peter. *Trade Unions and Politics in Britain.* Hemel Hempstead: Harvester Wheatsheaf, 1994.

Taylor, Robert. *The Trade Union Question and British Politics: Government and Unions Since 1945.* Oxford: Blackwell, 1993.

Richard A. Hawkins

Education

The British educational system formerly differentiated the paths of its students at an early age. Performance on the "eleven-plus exam" determined whether a student would be tracked, on the one hand, into a trade or commercial school, or, on the other, into a state-supported grammar school or a private "public" school. The more prestigious of these "public schools" are Eton, Harrow, and Winchester. The path to the upper echelon of government and business generally ran through the private school to Oxford or Cambridge, or Oxbridge. Eighty percent of the Conservative candidates for parliament from 1950 to 1966 were graduates of either Oxford or Cambridge. In a 1992 study of Britain's elite, the *Economist* reported that 66 percent of Britain's "top 100" had attended public schools and nearly 50 percent had attended Oxford or Cambridge.

In 1976 Labour, in an attempt to break education-enforced class divisions, introduced the comprehensive school. Critics complained about the collapse of academic standards and some counties never introduced the comprehensive school. In 1995 a twelfth of British students still attended public schools and a majority of British children ended their education after reaching age sixteen. Critics blame the educational system for the fact that fewer than half of British workers can be classified as "skilled," in comparison with 85 percent in Germany, which has a vigorous program combining apprenticeship and academics.

In 1988 parliament enacted an educational act supported by Prime Minister Margaret Thatcher to give dissatisfied parents the right to remove local schools from local government control and have them reorganized as independent state-supported schools. In the late 1990s approximately 93 percent of students in the United Kingdom attended free state-supported schools. The remainder attended private schools where they paid tuition. Most state and private primary schools and most state secondary schools are coeducational.

Parents can exercise choice in determining the schools their children attend. They are permitted to examine the public examination results and truancy rates for the secondary schools in their particular area to aid them in choosing a secondary school for their children. Almost half of three and four year olds attend nursery schools or infants' classes in primary schools. Children usually complete primary school at the age of eleven (twelve in Scotland). Approximately 90 percent of secondary-school students attend the comprehensive schools that are open to pupils of varying abilities. Whenever possible children with learning, physical, or psychological disabilities attend regular schools. But for students with exceptional disabilities there are special schools.

There is a national curriculum that consists of a core of English, mathematics, and science. It also establishes norms in history, geography, technology, music, art, and physical science. In secondary schools a modern foreign language is required. All students must pass a national test at the ages of seven, eleven, fourteen, and sixteen. The test at sixteen is the main secondary examination. Further examinations, two years later, determine entry into higher education.

There are eighty-nine universities in the United Kingdom, which admit students according to a selective process. In 1971, 21.3 percent of the relevant age group attended British universities. By 1985–86 the percentage had grown to 30.5. The number of children of manual workers grew from 25 percent of students in 1960 to 30 percent in 1980. Working-class students predominantly attend the less prestigious universities, many of which were set up only after World War II. However, Oxford and Cambridge have accepted an increasing number of students from working-class backgrounds. There is also an Open University, which provides higher education access through distance learning via home-study materials, off-campus sites, and the world wide web. Full-time higher-education students receive awards to cover fees. Parents pay for maintenance according to their income. The quality of higher education in the United Kingdom attracted ninety-six thousand foreign students in 1991–92. Almost 33 percent of students engaged in postgraduate study were from abroad. Foreign students are supported by their own governments or pay the fees themselves.

BIBLIOGRAPHY

Thompson, Wayne C. *Western Europe 1995.* Harpers Ferry, W.V.: Stryker-Post, 1995.

Wegs, J. Robert. *Europe since 1945: A Concise History.* New York: St. Martin's Press, 1991.

Rosemary Cook

Press

The outlook appeared bleak for the British press immediately after World War II, owing to the advent of television and the rationing of newsprint that lasted until 1958. In addition the revelations by the Royal Commission on the Press from 1947 to 1949 of papers used as propaganda media for press barons, such as Lord Beaverbrook, tarnished the image of the press. The major developments for the press during the postwar period were consolidation, the growth of tabloids, and the "Wapping Revolution."

After 1945 British newspapers frequently changed owners, merged into another paper, often a rival, or disappeared altogether. The Liberal *News Chronicle* abruptly merged with the Conservative *Daily Mail* in 1961. In 1971 *Daily Sketch* disappeared into its sister paper, *Daily Mail.* The venerable *Manchester Guardian* changed its name to *The Guardian* in 1959 and permanently moved to London in 1961. In London the process of consolidation was the most evident: In 1945 there were six London dailies; in 2000 there was only one, *The Evening Standard.*

The first of the new style press barons, Cecil Harmsworth King, nephew of Alfred Charles Wilson Harmsworth Lord Northcliffe and Harold Sidney Harmsworth Lord Rothermere, sought to follow in his uncles' footsteps and build his own publishing empire. In 1951 he took over as chairman of the Mirror Group and helped set up the International Publishing Corporation (IPC), which controlled four national dailies plus newspaper, magazine, book publishing, and television holdings around the world. King also bought the Labour broadsheet *Daily Herald* in 1958 by persuading the Trades Union Congress to sell its interest in the paper. King relaunched the *Daily Herald* to appeal to a broader audience but it floundered; it was later sold to Rupert Murdoch, who converted the paper into a low-market tabloid. However, King's main interest was the *Daily Mirror.* He increased its readership by appealing to the working class and strongly endorsed and helped Labour win the 1964 election. King became increasingly disenchanted with the Labour government and began to use the *Mirror* to attack Prime Minister Harold Wilson. This annoyed the IPC board, and as King owned only 1 percent of its shares, it unceremoniously dismissed him.

Tabloids were nothing new in the British press, as a handful of them existed before the war. However, the "tabloidization" of the press in Britain began in earnest in 1969 when Murdoch bought the *News of the World* and *The Sun.* Murdoch, an Australian (now an American citizen), relaunched *The Sun* as an up-market tabloid and it became an instant success, vastly increasing readership. The *Daily Mail* followed suit in 1971. David Stevens (now Lord Stevens) relaunched the *Daily Express* as a tabloid in 1977 and created a new paper, the *Daily Star* (the first new national paper since 1945) as a tabloid in 1978. *The Mirror* became a tabloid as well when Robert Maxwell bought the Mirror Group in 1984. However, Maxwell died under mysterious circumstances in 1991, leaving behind a mountain of debt and fraud. Murdoch continued to consolidate, adding Times Newspapers, which prints *The Times* and the *Sunday Times* in 1981, to his growing media empire.

Murdoch further changed the British press with his "Wapping Revolution" in 1986. The press had not modernized since the war; the same prewar printing presses were still in use. The print unions virtually controlled Fleet Street, the seat of the newspaper industry in London before the shift to computer typesetting, as newspaper owners frequently resorted to blackmail payments to union leaders to ensure their papers were printed on time, if at all. Murdoch built a modern publishing plant in Wapping using the latest in modern technology, including computer typesetting. In January 1986 he moved his publishing empire overnight from Gray's Inn to the London Docklands. Nonprint union labor was bused in and "Fortress Wapping" became the scene of picketing, boycotts, physical attacks, and police confrontations. The print unions were further weakened by industrial relations legislation introduced by Margaret Thatcher's government. Other newspapers soon followed suit.

BIBLIOGRAPHY

Hartwell, William Michael Berry, Baron. *William Camrose: Giant of Fleet Street.* London: Weidenfeld and Nicolson, 1992.

Smith, Anthony. *The British Press since the War.* Totowa, N.J.: Rowman and Littlefield, 1974.

Snoddy, Raymond. *The Good, the Bad and the Unacceptable: The Hard News about the British Press.* London: Faber and Faber, 1993.

David Lilly

Social Services

In the United Kingdom social services consist of the National Health Service (NHS) and personal social services. The NHS came into being in 1948, its architect and sponsor a Labour government that saw it through its first three years of life. The immediate roots of the NHS lie in the Beveridge-inspired welfare state model (William Henry Beveridge, 1879–1963, and the 1942 Beveridge Report), which sought to conquer need and want by granting everybody an entitlement to basic social security and health and other social services. The original vision of the NHS was of a basic or minimum medical service, but by 1948 this had been broadened beyond a strict focus on need orientation to embrace the idea of comprehensive services for all. The original concept was radicalized in another fundamental way as well. Initially only those voluntary hospitals that chose to be part of the service were to be included, but by the time of its inception the service was truly nationalized, comprising all hospitals, municipal, voluntary, and poor law. Principles such as universality, equality, and comprehensiveness guided the very public approach to medical provision introduced in Britain after the war. The NHS was and is unique among capitalist welfare societies in being financed out of general taxation and free at the point of use. Britain is also relatively unusual internationally because its private medical sector is quite small, although it is growing.

One of the greatest challenges facing the architects of the new service was to devise an administrative structure that could effectively coordinate the three service providers, which were separate at the time: the medical profession, the hospitals, and the local authorities. During and immediately after the war there existed in Britain a relatively wide consensus on the need for a good health service that should be public and free. What generated controversy was not questions of principle but rather matters of organization. The medical profession, for example, feared that its independent status and clinical freedom might be jeopardized were members to become wholly dependent on the state for their income. The profession campaigned for the retention of contributory social insurance as the main mode of financing, and it wanted to restrict social insurance coverage to 90 percent of the population so that doctors would have some income from private practice. A second point of controversy concerned the institutional and administrative "home" of the new health service. Especially problematic was the division of authority between local and national bodies and the role of local government as distinct from local health authorities. When it came to finalizing the details of the service, the government of the day opted for general revenue financing, with a small contribution from the national insurance system, and administratively for a complex tripartite structure. The first arm of this structure in England pertained to hospitals, consisting of fourteen hospital boards, the members of which were appointed by the government. The second arm consisted of executive councils to coordinate services offered by the medical profession. Third, the local authorities, although deprived of all responsibility for hospitals, retained control over a miscellaneous group of services such as public health, ambulances, and vaccination. This fragmented and flawed structure, which prevailed until the 1970s, not only made coordinated planning difficult but to some extent institutionalized conflicts of interest. The medical profession especially was accorded considerable power from the outset.

The NHS grew rapidly in size. In fewer than twenty years it would employ almost a million people, or one-thirtieth of the country's working-age population. Its cost, although much decried domestically, was not exorbitant by international standards. Health-care expenditure in 1955, for example, consumed some 3.4 percent of the gross national product (GNP), compared with 4.1 percent in Sweden and 4.4 percent in the United States. By the mid-1970s the British system compared even more favorably, expending 5.5 percent of GNP compared with 8.5 percent in Sweden and 8.6 percent in the United States. But concern about costs and politicking over organizational and service issues were to dominate the development of the service in the decades to come.

While the NHS remains to this day, broadly speaking, a free, universal, and equal service, the reality departed very early on from the ideal. Within three years, charges were introduced for a few services, and the health contribution as part of social insurance was increased so that within ten years direct charges for services and insurance contributions were together providing almost 20 percent of the gross cost of the NHS.

The introduction of the welfare state in Britain also involved the provision of a network of social services to complement the health services. Services of a residential care, day care, domiciliary, and social work nature were provided for client groups such as children, mentally ill people, those with physical handicaps or learning disabilities, and the elderly. From the postwar period until 1970 the responsibility for these services and sectors of the population was shared by three local authority departments: the Children's Department, Welfare Department, and Medical Department. Over time, the organizational and other shortcomings of this cumbersome line of authority and service delivery led to significant pressure for change. Under a new act introduced in 1970, social services were upgraded and streamlined into the newly created Social Services Departments within the counties and metropolitan boroughs. Once reorganized, the social services expanded rapidly. By 1974, for example, expenditure on social services had risen fivefold to consume 1 percent of gross domestic product (GDP), a level of expenditure that has more or less retained ever since.

Apart from costs, a further, more general pressure for change lay in public questioning of the capacity of the existing providers to deliver an efficient and satisfactory service. While the NHS itself always remained dear to British hearts, the quality of the medical care received and of the administration and management of the health and social services was increasingly thrown into question by general advances in management, medicine, and technology. The Conservative governments that held power from 1979 to 1997 made great political capital out of the management and service shortcomings of the health and social services. Indeed, this was one of the major battlegrounds of these governments' war against state monopoly. Hence, the reforms planned for and implemented in health and other services must be seen as an integral part of Conservative efforts to restructure the British welfare state itself.

While the first three decades of the life of the NHS were certainly active ones in policy terms, they were as nothing compared with the 1980s. The changes in the 1980s were launched with a rhetoric of primary care, community services, and preventive medicine. But it was in administration, control structures, and service delivery that the reform efforts were at their most extensive. A relatively complex remodeling program may be summarized by saying that its essence involved on the one hand a greater degree of central direction and a concomitant reduction of power at local or regional level, and on the other the introduction of market principles and certain private-sector management practices into the public health system. Greater competition between providers within and across sectors was one objective. This was envisaged to improve not only the efficiency and effectiveness of the service but the degree of choice available to consumers as well. To realize competitiveness the structure of the system would have to be altered. In effect, a mixed economy of care, in which the market, the family, and the voluntary sector would exist as providers alongside the statutory sector, would replace the old state-monopoly model. This would occasion a change of role for the public health authorities: their funder and service provider functions were to be separated. In the future they would be funders and purchasers in the first instance and one of a number of service providers in the second. The changes also heralded new management structures. These introduced throughout the public service brought a greater emphasis on monitoring performance, accountability, transparency, and budgetary control. As part of the general marketization of health services in Britain, hospitals were allowed to opt out of NHS control and become self-governing. General practitioners (GPs) became purchasers of medical and other services on behalf of their patients, in the process acquiring a greater autonomy in the operation of their own practices.

A thrust toward privatization has also been part of the most recent policy agenda. Conservative governments introduced tax and other incentives for greater private medicine and greater use of private health insurance. These measures have had quite radical results. In 1979, for example, there were 149 private hospitals with 6,600 beds and 5 percent of the population had private health insurance, whereas ten years later in 1988 there were 203 hospitals with 10,370 private beds and the proportion of the population with private health insurance had doubled to 10 percent. The practice of charging for more and more services has also been expanded.

An aggressive policy of community care, deinstitutionalization in another guise, was pursued as well. Although as a policy objective community care in Britain dates largely from the 1970s and a general concern about the quality of institutional care for people with mental and physical difficulties, to the Conservative government the attraction of community care lay largely in its potential to cut costs and to mobilize a mixed economy of care. In large part these reformist governments defined community care as "nonstatutory residential care." Hence their policies in this regard aimed for a reduction in public provision of care as much as if not more than they sought a cut in the numbers of people in residential care overall. In the early 1980s the benefit system was changed to make it easier for low-income residents of private and voluntary nursing homes to have their fees paid by the social security system. This had a number of large-scale, perverse effects. First, it led to a significant expansion in residential care at a time when government policy, nominally at any rate, aimed to reduce it in favor of domiciliary services. Second, the public expenditure implications were enormous: public subsidies of private residential care rose from £10 million ($22.2 million) in 1979 to £1,872 million ($3.4 billion) in 1991. By the mid- to late-1980s it was clear even to the government that something had to change and that a set of comprehensive community care policies and services was badly needed. Finally, in 1990 legislation was introduced. This accorded the local authority social service departments the lead agency role, and it introduced more stringent procedures for evaluating whether people needed residential care as well as whether their fees and costs should be paid from the public purse. Mirroring the changes that had been made in the NHS, social service staff, too, experienced a change of role in the direction of enablers and purchasers rather than providers. At the level of the individual client, local authority personnel were to assume the role of care manager, which would involve the assessment of the individual's need for a service, the design of an appropriate service package to meet the specific need, and securing the delivery of this set of services for the ill or elderly person who was to be treated as a "consumer." At an aggregate level, social service departments were made responsible for producing annual community care plans that had to be based on an assessment of need within the entire community. Most of the funds involved in meeting the additional care responsibilities of the local authorities came from a transfer of money from the social security budget. Control over resource allocation remained with the government.

The long-term implications of the changes are not yet clear, but there is concern about the quality of the health and social services, growing inequality, and the consolidation of a two-track system of medical provision involving a private service for the better off and public medicine for those who cannot afford any better. However, at the end of the Conservative day, which involved eighteen years of a policy to roll back the frontiers of the state, the major responsibility for and provision of health care and social services continues to lie with the state. It is also clear, though, that private-sector agencies, whether in the market or the voluntary sector, now carry out work and offer services formerly the monopoly of the public sector. Although the community care reforms are still too new to evaluate conclusively, care in the community has tended to become care by the community. Scarce resources, heavy workloads, and new demands on the public authorities and concerted efforts to cut back costs have led to an increase in the volume of care provided informally, especially by the family. In this and other ways one could say that a mixed economy is in the process of transforming a health and social service model that was always strongly state-dominated.

Since the administrative structures vary among the four parts of the United Kingdom, those referred to here are in the main typical of practice in England. In Scotland and Wales responsibility for the service is under the respective secretaries of state. In Northern Ireland there are four health and social service boards with area responsibilities.

BIBLIOGRAPHY

Glennerster, Howard. *British Social Policy since 1945.* Oxford: Blackwell, 1995.

Gould, Arthur. *Capitalist Welfare Systems: A Comparison of Japan, Britain and Sweden.* London: Longman, 1993.

Hill, Michael. *Understanding Social Policy,* 4th ed. Oxford: Blackwell, 1993.

Lowe, Rodney. *The Welfare State in Britain since 1945.* Basingstoke: Macmillan, 1994.

Means, Robert, and Randall Smith. *Community Care Policy and Practice.* Basingstoke: Macmillan, 1994.

Mary Daly

Rock Music

The emergence of rock music in Great Britain can be traced to British youths' adoption of American popular music after World War II. Great Britain lacked a vibrant indigenous popular culture among its own youth, and the presence of American soldiers during and after the war allowed British young people to adsorb the strong images of American pop culture. British port cities were particularly affected. With these American images of popular culture came American music, spanning a spectrum from the new pop superstars like Elvis Presley, Jerry Lee Lewis, and Buddy Holly to rhythm and blues legends like Slim Harpo, Muddy Waters, and Willie Dixon. These musicians became icons for British youth starving for new heroes with which to identify. In essence, British youth absorbed this music, first copied and later reinterpreted it, and sent it right back to America in the form of the British Invasion. Though the initial process may have started with music borrowed from America, the British made this music their own and created a multiplicity of rock genres in Great Britain.

Popular music developed very differently in Great Britain from in the United States. In the United States specialized radio stations were an outlet for popular music to be played and commented on by the public. The demand for music was immediate. Those wanting to hear a certain song or musician let radio disk jockeys (DJs) know directly. England had a very centralized radio establishment with only two networks. These presented mainly classical music, reflecting the British focus on high culture, hardly competitive with the powerful images of American pop culture for working-class British youth. Great Britain's paucity of radio networks limited pop music to an underground network and live performances. When British bands were finally recorded, it was only after they had already gained a following while playing live.

The postwar baby boom also affected Great Britain, and the children of that boom were reaching adolescence in the late 1950s and early 1960s. Because of structural problems within the British economy at that time, many of these adolescents were unable to find jobs. These idle teens were especially willing to soak up the American pop culture they found around them. British youth divided into two main cliques—the Rockers and the Mods. The Rockers were also commonly referred to as Teddy Boys. Teddy Boys modeled themselves after iconic images of the American Rebel with slick hair, tight-fitting jeans, and leather jackets. The Mods usually had some menial employment. They were able to dress more fashionably and spend time socializing in clubs.

These two cliques had their own musical interests. The Rockers adopted the "skiffle" style. Skiffle was a mixture of Dixieland Jazz and country blues. Jazz musicians Tony Donnegan, Chris Barber, and Beryl Bryden formed the first skiffle group. They recorded the songs "Rock Island Line" and "John Henry" playing a guitar, bass, and washboard. Because of the simple musical instruments (which could literally be made at home) and the need for little musical training, skiffle groups began popping up all over Great Britain. One of these groups was the Quarrymen, later named Johnny and the Moondogs, the Silver Beatles, and, finally, the Beatles. Businessman Brian Epstein became manager for the Beatles in 1961. He changed their Rocker image, putting them in matching suits and worked with them on tightening their music and live performances. Because of the lack of popular music programs on British radio, British record companies were reluctant to record the new music coming from British youth. However, Epstein's persistence finally paid off, and on September 11, 1962, the Beatles recorded "Love Me Do." Epstein's persistence also provided recording opportunities for other English bands. Several bands emerged under the classification Mersey Sound. These bands came from the Liverpool and Manchester areas. They had a similar sound to the Beatles—a combination of blues, country, and rockabilly. Among these bands were Gerry and the Pacemakers, the Hollies, and Herman's Hermits.

Another significant contribution the Beatles made for British musicians was opening the doors to America. After their success in Great Britain, Epstein convinced Capitol Records to invest $50,000 in a publicity program to saturate the American popular music audience with the Beatles. Five million bumper stickers that proclaimed "The Beatles Are Coming" were distributed, and a promotional record was made and distributed to radio stations. This record was designed so that DJs could ask questions and play the record, making it seem that they were actually interviewing the band at the station. Radio stations gave the Beatles' records more airplay, and caused their songs to rise on the charts. All the major American magazines including *Time* and *Newsweek* featured articles about the band. The American market was so saturated by coverage of the Beatles that even those who were not familiar with the band were curious to see what all the fuss was about. To compound this massive publicity blitz, the time was perfect for the Beatles to conquer America. American pop and rock music was undergoing a slump. The great heroes of the 1950s were no longer in the forefront. Chuck Berry and Jerry Lee Lewis were experiencing legal difficulties, causing their popularity to dwindle. Also, Little Richard was focusing on a religious career, Elvis Presley was in the military, and Buddy Holly had died in a plane crash. America had also lost President John F. Kennedy, and America's youth were hungry for new idols.

The second British band to make a major impact on the world popular music scene was the Rolling Stones. American blues music had a much bigger influence on the Stones than the groups characterized by the Mersey Sound. Around 1960 the skiffle sound was evolving into a more sophisticated style, and blues music became more popular. In 1963 the Rolling Stones formed and began performing songs by Slim Harpo, Chuck Berry, Muddy Waters, Willie Dixon, and Bo Diddley. The Stones were the opposite of the Beatles. Adult reaction to the Stones was generally not favorable; the Stones were seen as crude, offensive, and raunchy, qualities that made them even more attractive to rebellious teenagers. Their first tour of the United States, in June 1964, was unpromising. However, when they toured the country a second time, in October 1964, and appeared on the Ed Sullivan Show, they were extremely successful. American and British youth alike could enjoy the Beatles, usually without upsetting their parents, but youth had the Rolling Stones as an added expression of their rebelliousness. Between the Beatles and the Stones, large segments of American youth became interested in British music.

A second wave of the British Invasion included groups that were modeled after the Mods in Great Britain. They had a wild image like the Rolling Stones and many of the same blues influences but wore the fashion of the Mods. These bands included the Who, the Kinks, the Animals, the Yardbirds, and a host of others. Their music was louder and heavier, but also more experimental.

In 1967 the British government shut down illegal radio stations that had been popping up as a result of the limited airplay of British pop on the BBC. The government then created Radio One, which had a popular music format and employed previous pirate radio station DJs. However, less of the music played on these stations had a heavy blues influence, and popular music can be seen as splitting into two basic categories. Pop was played on the radio, but rock was live music and had a tendency to be more experimental. However, the record industry in Great Britain was more independent than its counterpart in America. Though British radio may have been promoting a less energetic-sounding music, independent British production companies and record labels were producing music that did not necessarily conform to radio standards. As a result, British music remained highly diversified.

The next major form of rock music to come out of Great Britain was psychedelic rock, music influenced by a young counterculture that experimented heavily with hallucinogenic drugs and alternative lifestyles. Extraordinary technical advancements in the fields of musical instruments and recording methods furthered experimentation with music. Psychedelic rock was more than entertainment; it was "head" music, music to be listened to and contemplated. The success of previous British bands caused many British musicians to experiment, and even look to their own cultural past for inspiration. British psychedelic rock is full of baroque classical music characteristics and references to Celtic myth and fantasy fiction. Indian and Oriental influences are also apparent in psychedelic music. George Harrison of the Beatles and Brian Jones of the Rolling Stones used the sitar on albums, and following their lead many rock musicians either used Indian instruments or tried to imitate their sound.

In 1966 a new club named the UFO opened in London, and a new band called the Pink Floyd became its unofficial house band. The UFO became a showplace for the psychedelic sound in London. The early Pink Floyd, under the influence of guitar player Syd Barrett, experimented heavily with distortion and feedback in their live music shows. These experimental sounds influenced the future American psychedelic hero Jimi Hendrix. Though Hendrix was an American, he is more often associated with British psychedelic music than American. Chas Chandler of the Animals discovered Hendrix playing at a club in New York. Hendrix, an African American musician, was regarded mainly as a rhythm and blues guitarist, but he wanted to experiment with the psychedelic sound. Chandler paid for his passage to London and became Hendrix's manager. It was in London that Hendrix developed his style and formed his own band. Hendrix later returned to America with his band and they signed with Reprise records.

As psychedelic rock began to fragment, new genres of rock music began to emerge. The two best-known offshoots of psychedelic rock are hard rock and progressive rock. Hard rock was born out of the heavy blues guitar influence of bands like the Yardbirds. Three future guitar heroes came from the Yardbirds—Eric Clapton, Jeff Beck, and Jimmy Page. Page worked with the Yardbirds and as a session musician with many bands. After the Yardbirds disbanded in 1968, Page formed the New Yardbirds with sessions musicians John Paul Jones and John Bonham and blues singer Robert Plant. After a tour of Scandinavia, they renamed the band Led Zeppelin. Led Zeppelin was a heavy guitar blues band that eventually had the world's best-selling group of albums in the early 1970s. Led Zeppelin is thought by some to be the first heavy metal band. Their heavy guitar sound may have had an influence on heavy metal, but their soulful, blues stylings set them apart from heavy metal.

The first true heavy metal bands were Black Sabbath and Deep Purple. Black Sabbath was formed by four working-class youths in Birmingham. Black Sabbath added a demonic aspect to their music that became common for heavy metal groups. Deep Purple started out as a classically influenced band in 1969. However, after achieving little success, their guitarist, Richie Blackmore, steered them into a heavier sound, and they eventually recorded albums that would be considered classics and major influences on later heavy metal bands like Metallica.

The second highly successful genre of rock music to emerge from the psychedelic sound was British progressive rock. Many different influences came together to form this complex style of music. Edward Macan sees the 1967 Beatles' album *Sergeant Pepper's Lonely Hearts Club Band* as a major influence on progressive rock. On *Sergeant Pepper,* the Beatles experimented with different musical styles, including classical chamber music in the song "She's Leaving Home." *Sergeant Pepper* is also considered the first "concept album"—an album of individual songs unified by a common theme. Both these approaches were utilized by future progressive rock musicians. The Moody Blues also influenced progressive rock by adding elaborate orchestration to their music, first through the use of a mellotron, a keyboard instrument that imitates the sound of strings. The Moody Blues extended the orchestral sound in 1967 by recording with the London Festival Orchestra on their album *Days of Future Passed.* Pink Floyd and Procol Harum also added classical elements to their music. The second incarnation of Pink Floyd (after Syd Barrett entered a mental institution and David Gilmore became their guitarist and co-vocalist) utilized the structure of multimovement suites on their albums. In 1967 Procol Harum recorded their successful hit "Whiter Shade of Pale," a surreal poem backed by music adapted from the bass line movement in Bach's orchestral suite (BWV1068).

One of the leading experimental progressive rock bands of the 1970s was King Crimson. Formed in 1969 by classical guitarist Robert Fripp, King Crimson became a paradigm for the progressive style. They utilized the mellotron and fantastical lyrics to create an epic style of music. The guitar playing was also revolutionary in that its technique was mainly classical and departed from the earlier blues style. One of the guitarists in King Crimson, Greg Lake, left the band in 1970 to form Emerson, Lake and Palmer with classical pianist Keith Emerson and drummer Carl Palmer. ELP adapted the music of Bach as well as other classical composers. In 1971 the band Yes added guitarist Steve Howe and classical pianist Rick Wakeman to their lineup and created complex, classically influenced multimovement suites.

In the mid-1970s the British economy was faltering. Inflation was 24 percent and unemployment reached new highs. Again, British youth were out of work and many were wandering the streets. These youth could not identify with the classically influenced rock genre that had emerged in Great Britain. The result was British punk rock, which featured simple chord progressions and a raw, unpolished sound. The Sex Pistols were the quintessential punk band. They were known for wild live shows that included taunting their audience with insults and acts of self-mutilation on stage. Despite extreme criticism, radio bans, and legal difficulties, the Sex Pistols climbed British record charts. However, punk became a fad, and because of this, the desperation that inspired it was lost. Characteristics like extremely short hair, originally intended to avoid lice, and the use of safety pins to hold ragged clothing together became fashionable. Punk bands like the Clash started to experiment with other styles of music, like reggae, and the Sex Pistols disbanded. Though punk declined in popularity, its influence carried into the 1980s with bands like the Police, Billy Idol, and Adam Ant.

British rock was built on American foundations, but by the mid-1960s British musicians had successfully incorporated rockabilly and blues into a new, distinctly British type of music that they in turn introduced to America. In the late 1960s and early 1970s British rock evolved into richly complex and experimental music. With the arrival of punk however, the second generation of British rock musicians brought rock back to its rebellious roots and it became the music of the streets once again.

BIBLIOGRAPHY

Cooper, Laura E., and B. Lee Cooper. "The Pendulum of Cultural Imperialism: Popular Music Interchanges Between the United States and Britain, 1943–1967." *Journal of Popular Culture* 27 (1993): 61–78.

Gillett, Charlie. *The Sound of the City: The Rise of Rock and Roll.* New York: Pantheon, 1983.

Macan, Edward. *Rocking the Classics: English Progressive Rock and the Counterculture.* New York: Oxford University Press, 1997.

Rotondi, James. "Sunshine Supermen: Britain's Psychedelic Guitar Wizards." *Guitar Player* (February 1997: 86–102.

Szatmary, David. *A Time to Rock: A Social History of Rock'n'Roll.* New York: Schirmer, 1996.

Whitcomb, Ian, and Robert Love. "Confessions of a British Invader." *American Heritage* (December 1997): Infotrac Search Bank.

Heather Planke

U.S. Armed Forces in Europe

Component of NATO forces in Western Europe. U.S. forces fought with the Allies against Germany in World War II, then administered the U.S. Occupation Zone in southern Germany. In 1949 those forces were incorporated into the structure of NATO and remained in large numbers in Western Europe until the early 1990s, when the Cold War ended and most American personnel were withdrawn.

A tradition of U.S. foreign policy since the founding of the nation was isolation from the affairs of Europe, particularly military matters. In 1917 this policy changed with America's entry into World War I. Although after the war the United States reverted to a policy of isolation, the nation broke with tradition once again to become involved in World War II.

American forces began to arrive in Great Britain in November 1942, as Allied leaders prepared for a 1943 landing in France. That attack was delayed until 1944, so U.S. troops lived among the British for many months, impressing their hosts as wealthy and generous but at times arrogant and spoiled. American forces were well supplied with goods from the United States, and received as much as five times the pay of their British counterparts. Many lasting relationships were formed; authorities recorded over seventy thousand marriages between British women and American men between 1943 and 1945. By May 1944, one month before D-Day—the Allied invasion of France—1.5 million American military personnel were stationed in Great Britain.

American, British, and Canadian forces landed on the Normandy beaches of France on June 6, 1944. They fought their way across northern Europe, reaching the German border city of Aachen in October. In November the Germans attempted a counteroffensive in France's Ardennes Forest that temporarily halted Allied progress, but by February 1945 Allied lines were roughly parallel to the Rhine. On March 7 Allied armies crossed the river; British and Canadian forces moved to the north while the U.S. Sixth Army Group moved south. The Germans surrendered to U.S. General Dwight Eisenhower on May 7, and to Soviet Marshal Georgy Zhukov on May 8.

In May 1945 there were 3.1 million American troops in Europe. This included personnel remaining in the liberated nations of northwestern Europe and the Mediterranean, as well as occupation troops in Austria and Italy. The majority were in Germany, however, which had been divided into occupation zones administered by separate military governments of the United States, the United Kingdom, the USSR, and France. General Eisenhower was appointed the first military governor (MG) of the American zone, although he left most administrative tasks to his deputy, General Lucius D. Clay. Clay took Eisenhower's place as MG in 1947 and became the figure most closely associated with the Office of Military Government for the United States (OMGUS).

The responsibilities of the hastily planned military government included caring for millions of displaced persons and refugees from all over Europe, providing the rudiments of life—food, water, fuel, sanitation—to the civilian populace, and eliminating the remnants of Nazi German culture and punishing Nazi leaders. These were huge tasks, for which American military officers were not always prepared. Few spoke German with any fluency or had any knowledge of German traditions or culture.

Moreover, OMGUS was responsible for maintaining order among both European civilians and American military personnel. In the aftermath of the war, however, this task became more difficult as troop morale and discipline plummeted. Their mission accomplished, combat veterans impatiently waited to return home, and in poverty-stricken, bombed-out Germany they encountered ample opportunity for looting and exploitation. Perhaps the most famous example of corruption was the attempt by an American colonel and his Women's Army Corps (WAC) officer wife to steal the crown jewels of the German state of Hesse, worth between $1.5 and $3 million dollars. Most American crime did not involve objects of such value, but the black market for personal valuables was ubiquitous. The American cigarette quickly became the only accepted currency for military and civilian personnel alike; one pack of American cigarettes equaled the monthly wage of the average German worker. Americans were able to live in luxury, and some amassed wealth or collections of art or jewelry by trading cigarettes for valuable items. In a few areas, soldiers formed gangs, engaging in smuggling, extortion, and even violence. As increasing levels of crime and corruption began to threaten the reputation of American forces, General Clay created the U.S. Constabulary, a military police force that restored order and discipline among U.S. troops as well as local residents. In addition, by 1947 wives and children of servicemen were allowed to travel to Europe, which helped build morale among the troops.

As the military government in Germany and the liberation governments in other nations made strides in restoring order and civil authority, U.S. military authorities quickly demobilized the 3.1 million veterans in Europe at the war's end. By May 1946 the number of Americans in Europe had dropped to 391,000, and by 1950, only 79,500 remained.

During the late 1940s, however, tensions between the United States and the USSR worsened. After the Korean War began in 1950, U.S. President Harry S Truman increased the number of troops stationed in Europe. By 1952 there were 257,000, and by 1955 the number rose to 357,000. With the exception of personnel in Berlin, who retained the status of occupation forces, most other American military personnel in Europe were assigned to units associated with the North Atlantic Treaty Organization (NATO), which had been created in April 1949 as a defensive alliance against the USSR. U.S. troops were an important part of the NATO defense, and the commander of NATO forces (Supreme Allied Commander, Europe—SACEUR) was always a U.S. general, with headquarters in Casteau Mons, Belgium.

The American military presence in Europe included land, air, and sea forces, organized by three European commands: U.S. Army, Europe (USAEUR), headquartered in Heidelberg, Germany; US Air Force, Europe (USAFE), headquartered in Wiesbaden, later Ramstein, Germany; and U.S. Navy, Europe (USNAVEUR), headquartered in London. In 1952 the U.S. European Command (USEUCOM), headquartered in Stuttgart, Germany, was formed as an overall command of all American forces in the European theater, which encompassed an area from Norway to the Azores to parts of the Middle East and Africa. U.S. units in Europe had their places in the command structure of the American forces worldwide and parallel places within the structure of NATO. During a war USEUCOM would support NATO with its combat and supply forces, while retaining administrative control.

By the mid-1950s it appeared that American forces would remain in Europe indefinitely, and the defense budget increased to include financing for housing, education, shopping, and recreational facilities that became known as "Little Americas." As military-sponsored amenities became more common, personnel and their families no longer were forced to interact with their host communities. However, Cold War fears created close partnerships between American and European communities in most areas of Western Europe, and intercultural social clubs and activities were common. Perhaps the most notable example of this was in West Germany, where the Federation of German-American Clubs, established in 1948, included as many as seventy-five member clubs and thousands of individual members. Although in areas of greater cultural difference, such as Turkey and North Africa, contact was less frequent, American units often performed humanitarian missions, as in 1963, for example, when U.S. aircraft flew seven-hundred thousand pounds of supplies to flooded areas in Morocco and aided earthquake victims in Libya, Yugoslavia, and Iran.

Beginning in the mid-1960s, the U.S. forces in Europe experienced a series of challenges as the immediate threat from the USSR seemed to recede. In 1966 France announced that it was leaving the NATO command (but would nevertheless remain part of the NATO alliance);

all foreign troops had one year to vacate their installations in France. France's decision temporarily disrupted U.S. operations in Britain and West Germany, which absorbed most of the American personnel from France; the French action also called the future of NATO into question. The Vietnam War also began to take a toll on U.S. readiness in Europe, as experienced personnel were reassigned from Europe to Southeast Asia and the conflict absorbed an increasing percentage of the U.S. defense budget.

Other challenges came from the United States itself. In 1966 and 1967 Senate Majority Leader Mike Mansfield spearheaded an attempt to limit the number of troops in Europe. Although he was not able to implement wide-scale change, Congress did agree to withdraw thirty-five thousand U.S. troops. Mansfield believed that the nations of Western Europe should contribute more for the cost of their defense, while Europeans viewed the American presence in Europe as part of the defense of the United States and considered their role as the most likely battle site to be onerous. The Mansfield proposals, combined with America's increasing involvement in Vietnam, led many European leaders to doubt U.S. commitments to Europe's defense.

In addition, racial tensions and rising drug use among U.S. military personnel in the late 1960s and early 1970s led to increasingly severe discipline problems, as crime and unrest became more common on and off base. Moreover, the Vietnam War continued to drain the resources and labor power of U.S. forces, and antiwar agitation grew among military personnel. From 1970 to 1973 a large number of mostly short-lived underground GI newspapers criticized the war, military life, and conditions on American bases. Problems continued throughout the decade; beginning in 1973 military pay was less than comparable civilian pay, and by 1979 military pay was below the U.S. minimum wage. Discipline and morale problems eroded the earlier cordiality of relations between host communities and American installations. By the late 1970s American installations in Europe were plagued with poverty, crime, and drug abuse, low morale, rundown facilities, and isolation from European host communities.

President Jimmy Carter tried without success to improve conditions in the U.S. armed forces. His successor, Ronald Reagan, citing the continuing danger of the USSR, also pledged to increase military spending and restore the quality and status of U.S. forces, in Europe and throughout the world. Reagan had more success as Congress approved defense spending increases of 12 percent annually in the early 1980s. Military personnel received large pay raises, as large as 8 percent in 1982, and the amount of money spent on base maintenance and quality-of-life programs also increased. In the mid-1980s the dollar rose in value compared with European currencies, which gave military personnel in Europe extra spending power.

The Reagan administration increased spending on weapons systems, however, including nuclear weapons, even more substantially than spending on personnel and maintenance. Since the 1950s the U.S. arsenal in Europe included approximately six thousand tactical nuclear weapons, but in 1983 the Pershing II and ground-launched cruise missiles were added, giving the United States a first-strike ability. In response to the new nuclear capabilities of U.S. bases in Europe, peace and antinuclear groups burgeoned in the early and mid-1980s. In Britain, for example, women blockaded the U.S. base at Greenham Common, and in Portugal, Spain, Italy, and the Netherlands large antinuclear movements forced governments to reckon with widespread opposition. In West Germany the Green Party opposed NATO and U.S. bases, winning a considerable popular following, and in Greece the democratic government forced the removal of U.S. bases in 1988.

American personnel in Europe witnessed a sharp increase in anti-American incidents during the 1980s as a result of the renewed Cold War. While most Europeans distinguished between U.S. policy and individual Americans, numerous incidents of petty harassment occurred, ranging from graffiti to vandalism of American-owned automobiles. A more serious threat was terrorism from extreme left-wing groups, which began around 1970 but increased in the 1980s. The groups most dangerous to U.S. military personnel were the Red Army Faction (RAF) of West Germany and the Revolutionary Organization 17 November in Greece; both groups were anti-NATO and targeted high-ranking U.S. personnel and major U.S. installations for attacks. In 1985, for example, the RAF lured an American airman to his death and used his military identification card to access the Rhine-Main Air Base near Frankfurt, where members of the group set off a car bomb, killing two people. In 1987, 17 November detonated two bombs near military buses, injuring twenty-seven Americans and one Greek bus driver.

Another terrorist threat came from Libya, as tensions between Libyan leader Mu'ammar Gadhafi and the Reagan administration escalated. On April 5, 1986, terrorists, purportedly Libyan, detonated a bomb in the La Belle disco in Berlin, a popular meeting place for American military personnel. The bomb killed two Americans and one Turkish woman, and 230 people were injured. Nine days later President Reagan authorized an air strike against

Libya in retaliation for terrorism allegedly sponsored by Gadhafi. Although the air strike prompted fears of increased violence against American troops in Europe, Gadhafi was forced to cease his anti-American activities. The personnel and aircraft used in the attack against Libya flew from U.S. bases in Great Britain; other NATO nations refused to take part in the mission, and France did not allow U.S. aircraft to enter French airspace.

In 1989 the Cold War ended abruptly when the Communist governments of the USSR and the East bloc nations collapsed. Owing to the reduced threat, many American installations in Europe were closed and personnel sent home, in a large operation known as the "drawdown." The drawdown had serious economic and social repercussions for many towns in the vicinity of the bases. In 1990, for example, 213,000 Americans lived in Germany, but in 1995 only 65,000 remained. Many areas, particularly in the rural southwest of the country, continued to suffer from high unemployment because of base closures.

The U.S. role in NATO, as well as NATO's post–Cold War mission, continued to be debated. Ironically, NATO performed its first military mission in 1994, after the end of the Cold War, when it entered the conflict between the Bosnian Serbs and the Bosnian government after the disintegration of the former Yugoslavia. On February 28, after much high-level consideration, NATO warplanes shot down Bosnian Serb planes that had been bombing Bosnian towns. In April U.S. bombers attached to NATO attacked Serb ground targets to force the Serbs to withdraw from the Bosnian town of Gorazde. Following the November 1995 Dayton peace agreement, NATO forces, including large numbers of Americans, were stationed in Bosnia as peacekeeping forces.

American forces in Europe went from liberators and occupiers in the 1940s, to defenders in the 1950s and 1960s, to a discipline problem in the 1970s. Finally in the 1980s, those forces were seen as defenders to some and unwelcome intruders to others. With the end of the Cold War the numerical presence of U.S. troops in Europe diminished, but they remained an essential element of the first fifty years of postwar European history.

Anni Baker

SEE ALSO Clay, Lucius D.; North Atlantic Treaty Organization; Supreme Allied Commander Europe

Urbánek, Karel (1941–)

General secretary of the Czechoslovak Communist Party from November 24 to December 20, 1989. Karel Urbánek was born in Bojkovice, in the Nazi German protectorate of Moravia (Czechoslovakia), on March 20, 1941. He worked for the state railroad and became a station manager. He joined the Czechoslovak Communist Party in 1962 and eventually gained a reputation as a party functionary as a skilled operator. He was appointed a municipal administrator in the chief Moravian city of Brno in 1973. He studied at the party's college in Prague from 1976 to 1980. From 1973 to 1980 he also served as secretary for industry in Brno's Communist Party Municipal Committee. As of 1982 he headed the political and organizational department of the party. Urbánek was thus in charge of recruitment and promotion of cadres within the national Communist Party and, as such, was able to nurture an indebted following. In 1984 he was appointed chief administrator in Brno. In 1986 he was elected to the party's 150-member Central Committee, and in 1988 he became party leader in the Czech section of the country. In October 1988 Urbánek was elected to the thirteen-member Politburo, and became its second-youngest member.

Following the massive protests against Communist rule that erupted in November 1989, the Czechoslovak Communist Party on November 24, 1989, appointed a new Politburo, ousting the fourteen department heads who collectively constituted the party's Secretariat, and removed Miloš Jakeš as general secretary. The new nine-member Politburo, however, contained six members from the old body. In place of Jakeš, it appointed Urbánek, whose relative obscurity left him, the party hoped, untainted with responsibility for the shortcomings and repressiveness of the past leadership. As the new general secretary, Urbánek stated that the Communist Party had "ignored the people, the truth and everyday life" but "wants to start on a new path." He then announced that the Communist leadership was willing to "negotiate with everyone who is ready to contribute to the future of Czechoslovakia." This was a change of course not only for the party but for Urbánek as well. As recently as March he had written that the members of the opposition human rights group Charter 77 were "domestic enemies." At the beginning of Urbánek's brief tenure, the Prague municipal Communist Party Committee and the city's despised party boss, Miroslav Stepan, blamed for the police attack on student demonstrators at the start of the November protests, resigned. But Václav Havel, the playwright and dissident who became the president of Czechoslovakia on December 29, 1989, voiced the sentiments of the hundreds of thousands of Czechoslovaks who had taken to the streets when he stated that power still remained in the hands of hard-line Communists.

Havel's sentiments were echoed by the Communist rank and file. Regional Communist Party committees held emergency meetings. At a meeting in Prague one thousand local Communists expressed their support of an impending antiregime strike and demanded that the emergency party leadership meeting be reconvened to remove more hard-liners.

As communism crumbled around them due to the massive outpouring of public opposition, which is known as the Velvet Revolution, the party leadership scrambled to forestall disaster. A total of 1,530 delegates met in an emergency party congress on December 20. They ousted Urbánek as party leader and replaced him with Ladislav Adamec, who had resigned as prime minister on December 10. Adamec had shaken the old guard by meeting with the opposition in November. The congress also established a new post of first secretary to handle internal party administration. For that new position the delegates chose a thirty-seven-year-old youth organizer, Vasil Mohorita, who had conducted negotiations for the party with the insurgent Czech political movement Civic Forum.

BIBLIOGRAPHY

Fisher, Dan, and Tyler Marshall. "New Czech Leader Offers to Negotiate with Opposition." *Los Angeles Times,* November 26, 1989.

Greenhouse, Steve. "Clamor in the East." *New York Times,* November 25, 1989.

———. "Clamor in the East." *New York Times,* November 26, 1989.

Marshall, Tyler, and Charles T. Powers. "Protests Topple Czech Regime." *Los Angeles Times,* November 25, 1989.

Bernard Cook

USCINCEUR

The commander in chief, U.S. European Command (USCINCEUR), is the military commander of all U.S. forces stationed in Europe. The European Command (USEUCOM) is one of the Unified Commands of the U.S. military. A Unified Command is one that contains two or more of the military services. Established on August 1, 1952, USEUCOM is made up of the U.S. Army in Europe (USAREUR), the U.S. Air Force in Europe (USAFE), and the U.S. Naval Forces in Europe (USNAVEUR).

USEUCOM and all the other Unified Commands are commanded by a commander in chief (CINC), who is invested with unique Combatant Command (COCOM) authority. COCOM is a very specific term established under Title 10, U.S. Code Section 164, that gives a CINC full authority to organize and employ commands and forces as the CINC considers necessary to accomplish assigned missions. A CINC's chain of command runs through the chairman of the Joint Chiefs of Staff directly to the National Command Authorities (NCA), the secretary of defense, and the president.

By common consent among NATO members, the USCINCEUR is also the SACEUR, the commander of the Allied Command Europe (ACE). Although the USCINCEUR and the SACEUR are the same person, the two areas of responsibility do not overlap completely. The SACEUR is responsible to NATO for the defense of Europe and the Mediterranean. The USCINCEUR is responsible to the American NCA for all American military operations in Europe, portions of the Middle East, and most of Africa. The USCINCEUR's headquarters is in Stuttgart, Germany; the SACEUR's headquarters is located at Casteau, Belgium. As a result, most of the daily routine operations of USEUCOM are managed by the Deputy USCINCEUR.

BIBLIOGRAPHY

Kugler, Richard L. *The Future U.S. Military Presence in Europe: Forces and Requirements for the Post Cold War Era.* Santa Monica, Calif.: Rand, 1992.

David T. Zabecki

SEE ALSO North Atlantic Treaty Organization;

Uzbekistan

Independent successor state to the Uzbek Soviet Socialist Republic of the former USSR. The Republic of Uzbekistan consists of 186,400 square miles (447,400 sq km). It is surrounded by Kazakhstan in the west and north, Kyrgyzstan and Tajikistan in the east Afghanistan and

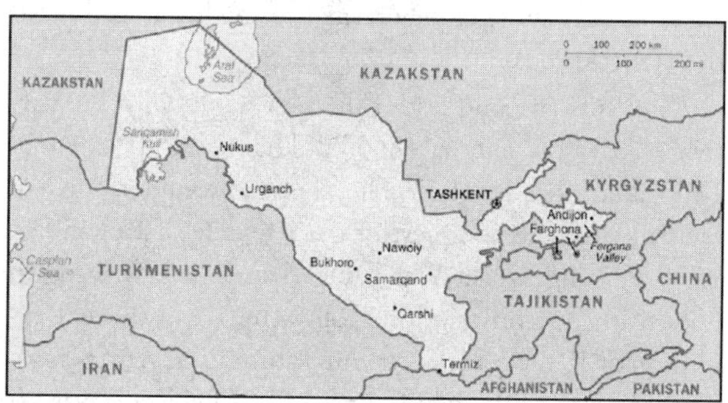

Uzbekistan. *Illustration courtesy of Bernard Cook.*

Turkmenistan in the south. Uzbekistan with approximately 21,301,000 inhabitants is the most populous of the Central Asian republics. Its capital, Tashkent, has 2,073,000 inhabitants. Russians constitute 11 percent of the population and Kazakhs 4 percent. There are 65,000 European Jews and 28,000 Central Asian Jews in the country. Uzbeks, who are the most numerous of the Turbic peoples of Central Asia, constitute about 69 percent of the population. The official language, Uzbek, is an eastern Turkic language. The Latin script is replacing the Cyrillic, which was imposed in 1940. The dominant religion is Sunni Islam of the Hanafi school, but there are also communities of conservative Wahhabis and Sufis. Tashkent under the Soviets was the spiritual center for Central Asian Islam. The chairman of the Tashkent-based Muslim Religious Board for Central Asia and Kazakhstan served as mufti (interpreter of Muslim law) and the official Soviet Islamic authority. Shamsutdinkan Babakhan, who long held the post, was ousted in February 1989 after a demonstration by adherents of the Islamicist political movement, "Islam and Democracy," who denounced him as a drinker and womanizer and who did not know the Koran but served the KGB (Soviet secret police). Tashkent is also home to the Naqshbandi, or tariqat-al-Khwajagan, school of the Sufi mystic sect of Islam. Another current of Uzbek Islam is a rebirth of the prerevolutionary tradition of the Jadid movement, which sought to integrate Islam with secular and democratic modernization.

Uzbekistan consists almost completely of desert and arid steppes broken by rivers flowing from the mountains to the south and southeast. It stretches from the constantly receding Aral Sea in the west to the Fergana (Farghona) valley in the east and contains part of the Amu Darya River valley. Since 1936 the Kara-Kalpakia Autonomous Republic along the Aral Sea's southern shore has been part of Uzbekistan. Its population of approximately 1.2 million contains almost equal numbers of Uzbeks, Kazakhs, and Kara-Kalpakians, who are also Turkic but are ethnically more closely related to the Kazakhs than to the Uzbecks.

The Russian conquest of the area began with the surrender of Tashkent in 1865. Bukhara was defeated in 1868 and Kiva in 1873 The area came under Russian control with the conquest of the Khanate of Kokand in 1876. During World War I there was a violent rising in opposition to conscription. Following the Russian Revolution of 1917, a Turkestan Autonomous Soviet Socialist Republic (TASSR), which included Uzbekistan, was set up. However, the anti-Soviet nationalist Basmachi (Qorbashi) in conjunction with a British expeditionary force drove the Soviets out temporarily. They returned in September 1919, but resistance continued into the early 1920s. Bukhara and Kiva were temporarily independent Soviet republics but were eventually absorbed into the TASSR. On October 27, 1924, the Uzbek Soviet Socialist Republic (UzSSR) was set up and included, until 1929, the Tajik ASSR. In May 1925 the UzSSR became a member republic of the USSR.

Uzbekistan had never been a nation-state. The people of Central Asia drew their identity from tribe, locale, or Islam rather than a "nation." Nor did Uzbekistan have a literary language. Only a few people could read Chatagai, the ancient Uzbek literary language. Only a small percentage could read and write modern Uzbek, which utilized a modified Arabic alphabet. In 1926 the Soviets introduced the Latin alphabet, and in 1940 Stalin introduced the Cyrillic script. The Soviets also promoted a new literary language. Their literacy campaign raised Uzbek literacy from 3.8 percent in 1926 to 52.5 percent in 1932. Along with the Soviet education campaign went a campaign against religion. Economic development in the 1930s was abetted by the transfer of industry to the area during World War II. Many of the workers, however, were Slavic imports. Most Uzbeks worked on the large collective farms that produced two-thirds of the USSR's cotton. In 1992, 43.2 percent of Uzbekistan's workers were employed in agriculture and forestry, producing 35.9 percent of its gross domestic product.

The first secretary of the Uzbek Communist Party (UCP) was always an Uzbek. Akmal Ikramov, an Islamic modernizer who had rallied to the Soviet cause, held the post from 1925 until 1938, when he was shot by the Soviet secret police for being a nationalist, as part of Stalin's purge. His successor, Usman Iusupov, a thorough Stalinist, was first secretary until 1950, when he received a promotion to Moscow. Sharaf Rashidov, first secretary from 1959 until his death in 1983, was subsequently denounced for corruption. In the Cotton Affair, he and his cronies provided Moscow with inflated figures for Uzbek cotton production and received a billion rubles for cotton that was never delivered. In 1986 Soviet Communist Party General Secretary Mikhail Gorbachev launched an anticorruption crackdown in Uzbekistan. Tens of thousands of members of the UCP were expelled and three-thousand police officers fired. Rashidov's successors, Inamzhon Usmankhojaev and Rafik Nishanov, campaigned against corruption, but they were regarded by many Uzbeks as lackeys of Moscow. When Nishanov was transferred to Moscow in 1989 his successor, Islam Karimov (1938–), strove to disassociate himself from Moscow.

There were few Uzbek intellectuals, and Gorbachev's policies of glasnost (openness) and perestroika (restructuring) did not alter the conservative political structure. A new degree of press freedom did bring questions of Uzbek history, the ecology, and the economy to the fore. Excessive irrigation of cotton had led to salinization of the land, while the diversion of excessive amounts of water from the Amu Darya and Syr Darya Rivers resulted in the progressive drying of the Aral Sea, which had a vital impact on the ecology of the whole area. Once the fourth-largest inland sea, its water level had dropped fifty feet and its total water volume had decreased by 60 percent since 1960. Farming on 10.75 million acres of Uzbekistan, principally along the lower Amu Darya, is made possible through irrigation. One result of the retreat of the Aral Sea was dust storms laden with salt from the dry lake bottom, which rendered agricultural land increasingly less productive. The water that reaches the sea is a sludge replete with insecticides and fertilizer, which in addition to polluting the dying sea is contaminating the area's groundwater. It has been estimated that 66 percent of the inhabitants of Karakalpakstan on the southern shore of the Aral Sea are suffering from hepatitis, cancer, and other serious illnesses.

Uzbekistan's first non-Communist political movement, Birlik (Unity, or Unity Movement for the Preservation of Uzbekistan's Natural, Material, and Spiritual Riches), organized in 1989, arose out of concern for the environment and the Uzbek language. It organized a massive demonstration in Tashkent in October 1989 attended by over fifty thousand. Although Birlik eventually became the principal challenge to the UCP, it was refused registration as a legal political party and was not allowed to run candidates in the 1989 election for the USSR's Congress of People's Deputies. It had the indirect impact of seeing its proposal that Uzbek become the official language adopted by the Uzbek Supreme Soviet (USS) in 1989, but Birlik was again denied the right to place candidates in an election, this time the February 1990 election for the USS. In March the UCP-dominated USS elected its leader, Karimov, to the new post of executive president. Shakurulla Mirsaidov was elected chairman of the Council of Ministers, but in November the Council of Ministers was replaced by a cabinet presided over by the president. Karimov did not speak out against the attempted hard-line coup against Gorbachev in Moscow on August 1991 until it was evident that it had failed. On August 31 the USS met in special session and declared an independent Republic of Uzbekistan. The UCP disassociated itself from the Communist Party of the Soviet Union and, still led by Karimov, changed its name in November to the People's Democratic Party of Uzbekistan (PDPU). On December 13 Uzbekistan agreed to join the Commonwealth of Independent States, the association for economic and security cooperation that replaced the bound Soviet Union, and this was ratified at Alma-Ata on December 21. On December 29 Karimov was elected president in a direct election with 86 percent of the vote. His only competitor, Muhammad Solikh, leader of the Erk (Freedom) Democratic Party, an offshoot of Birlik, won 12 percent. At the same time 98.2 of voters endorsed Uzbekistan's independence.

On December 8, 1992, a new constitution was adopted. It sought to establish democracy, a multiparty system, freedom of expression, and human rights. The next day however, the government outlawed Birlik as subversive. This followed a year of increasingly authoritarian and repressive government under Karimov. Pointing to the religion-fueled civil war in Tajikistan, he had banned all religious parties, and the new constitution had affirmed secularism.

During 1993 members of the opposition were kidnapped or attacked both within and outside Uzbekistan's borders, and debilitating restrictions were imposed on the media. Repression continued in 1994. Despite assurances from Karimov, when election for the new assembly, the Oly Majlis, established by the 1992 constitution, were held in December 1994 and January 1995, only the PDPU and its ally, Progress and Fatherland (PF), were allow to post candidates. No other party received the requisite government registration. However, 94 percent of registered voters did vote. Some nominal diversity within the Majlis was provided by the organization, with government approval, of the Adolat (Justice) Social Democratic Party of Uzbekistan in February, and Milli Tiklanish (National Revival) Democratic Party and the Khalk Birliki (People's Unity) Movement in May.

The developing collapse of the USSR helped to precipitate ethnic conflict in Uzbekistan. In 1989 there was violence between ethnic Uzbeks and the Meskhetian minority. Unemployment and the shortage of housing in the easternmost section of Uzbekistan, the Fergana valley region, provided the sparks. Uzbekistan's predominantly rural population more than doubled between 1959 and 1979. The population of the Fergana valley, Uzbekistan's most densely populated area, grew by 27 percent between 1979 and 1989, and by 1989 there were 280 people per square kilometer. In June one hundred people, most of them Meskhetians, were killed in riots. In the opinion of unemployed and impoverished Uzbeks, the Meskhetians—Islamicized Georgians forcibly relocated to the east by Stalin in 1944—lived better, as did the republic's Russians, Germans, Tatars, and Jews, than did Uzbeks. Clashes began around Kuvasai but spread to the regional capital Farghona, where young Uzbeks armed themselves and set fire to Meskhetian residences. Soviet Interior Ministry units were sent in to restore order. But ultimately the Uzbeks, whose slogan was "Uzbekistan for the Uzbeks," forced the relocation of eleven thousand of the area's sixty thousand Meshketians to the Russian Republic. In the middle of 1990 there was unrest as Uzbeks attempted to intervene in ethnic violence that had erupted in the Osh region of Kyrgyzstan, where Uzbeks constituted a majority. Karimov closed the border with Kyrgyzia and declared a state of emergency in the border region.

Uzbekistan has fostered close relations with its four Central Asian neighbors—Kazakhstan, Kyrgyzstan, Tajikistan, and Turkmenistan. In early 1994 an economic union was established with Kazakhstan and Kyrgyzstan, but plans for a joint currency were dropped. The five countries established a standing committee and joint fund to attempt to deal with the ecological disaster presented by the drying of the Aral Sea. All but Tajikistan committed 1 percent of their 1994 budget to the joint fund. Concerned about the spread of Islamic fundamentalism, Karimov sent Uzbek troops to participate in the CIS mission to Tajikistan.

Because of its self-sufficiency in energy and food, Uzbekistan was not hit as severely as many other republics by the collapse of the USSR. Uzbekistan was affected, however, by the general decline of the USSR and eventually by a shortage of primary products and the breakdown of interrepublic trade. Uzbekistan, with the second-highest birthrate of the Central Asian states, has a surplus rural population. Before the collapse of the USSR its unemployment rate ran above 10 percent. Gross domestic production declined steadily from 1985 to 1995. In 1995, however, the country recorded a trade surplus of $214 million. The annual inflation rate, which stood at 77 percent in 1995, dropped to only 12 percent in 1996. There has been practically no economic reform in the country, but in February 1994 Karimov delineated a program to promote a market economy.

Uzbekistan does have economic assets and potential. It possesses large reserves of natural gas, petroleum, coal, gold, silver, uranium, copper, lead, zinc, and tungsten. Gas is exported to Russia via a pipeline to the Urals, and Uzbekistan is the seventh-ranking producer of gold in the world. Its Murantau mine in the Kyzylkum desert is reputedly the largest open-cast gold mine in the world.

BIBLIOGRAPHY

Allworth, Edward A. *The Modern Uzbeks: From the Fourteenth Century to the Present, A Cultural History.* Stanford, Calif.: Hoover Institution, 1990.

Batalden, Stephen K., and Sandra L. Batalden. *The Newly Independent States of Eurasia: Handbook of Former Soviet Republics.* Phoenix, Ariz.: Oryx, 1993.

Critchlow, James. *Nationalism in Uzbekistan: A Soviet Republic's Road to Sovereignty.* Boulder, Colo.: Westview Press, 1991.

Shoemaker, M. Wesley. *Russia, Eurasian States, and Eastern Europe 1995.* Harpers Ferry, W.V.: Stryker-Post, 1995.

"Uzbekistan," *Europa World Year Book. 1996 edition.* London: Europa Publications, 1996.

Bernard Cook

Vacaroiu, Nicolae (1943–)

Romanian prime minister between November 1992 and November 1996. Nicolae Vacaroiu was born in Bolgrad, Bessarabia, but grew up in Bucharest. In 1969, he graduated magna cum laude from the department of finance at Bucharest's Academy for Economic Studies, where he later taught. He worked mainly on the State Planning Committee, which oversaw Romania's communist economy, rising within that body by 1989 to head the Directorate of Economic and Financial Synthesis. After Nicolae Ceausescu's demise in December 1989 he became a deputy minister in the Ministry of National Economy until the governmental reorganization that followed the May 1990 elections. Then he was appointed a secretary of state in the newly created Ministry of Economics and Finance, but was soon demoted to directing first the department of prices and then the department of taxation. One of his major projects was preparing a proposal for a value-added tax. He soon regained his rank as a secretary of state and was appointed president of the interministerial Committee for Foreign Trade Guarantees. Just before becoming prime minister, Vacaroiu was part of the Romanian delegation that sought credits from the World Bank and the International Monetary Fund.

When Iliescu was reelected president of Romania in November 1992, Vacaroiu was not his first choice for prime minister. But Ion Iliescu could not form a cabinet entirely from his party, the Democratic National Salvation Front, because it did not have a majority in the parliament. He could have fashioned a narrow majority by forming a coalition with extreme nationalist and socialist parties, but that would have isolated Romania internationally at a time when the country needed foreign economic assistance. To resolve these political problems Iliescu selected a government of technocrats whom the Romanian parliament would accept, and who possessed the skills required to lead Romania out of communism. As a technocrat without any apparent political ambitions or party affiliation since renouncing his membership in the Romanian Communist Party in December 1989, Vacaroiu met Iliescu's criteria for a minister. Furthermore, his credentials were remarkably similar to those of his immediate predecessor, Theodor Stolojan. During his tenure as prime minister, Vacaroiu was content to be the spokesman in the legislature for Iliescu's policies rather than to turn the prime minister's office into a powerful position as Romania's first post-communist prime minister, Petre Roman, had tried to do in 1990 and 1991. Besides their political compatibility, both Iliescu and Vacaroiu agreed that the social costs of Romanian privatization and implementation of a free market economy must be considered, even if it slowed down the process. However, Romania's market economy of a social type failed to improve the standard of living for the vast majority of Romanians, which was the main reason for the defeat of Vacaroiu's party in the October 1996 national elections.

Robert Forrest

SEE ALSO Iliescu, Ion

Vacek, Miroslav (1935–)

Czechoslovak minister of defense. Miroslav Vacek was deputy minister of defense and chief of staff of the army under the Czechoslovak Communist regime before it collapsed in late 1989. He joined in negotiations with Vaclav Havel, the leader of the Civic Forum, in November and early December 1989, which assured that the Czech army would not be used to shore up the collapsing regime. Vacek, a communist and career soldier, was appointed minister of defense by Ladislav Adamec in November

1989, but only assumed office on December 10, 1989, under the new government organized by Marián Calfa. General Vacek is credited with facilitating the formation of the first Czechoslovakian government since 1948 not dominated by the Communists.

His assurance that the Czech military would not interfere in political developments freed the opposition from the fear of armed suppression of their movement. Vacek's announcement was accompanied by the withdrawal of Communist political officials from the military and its ending of organized Communist groups within the military. After meeting with General Vacek, Havel informed a news conference that his meeting with the general had "confirmed my previous impression that the highest commanders of our army would not allow the use of the army's weapons against the citizens of the country."

On October 17, 1990, Vacek was dismissed as minister of defense and was replaced the next day by Lubos Dobrovsky, a co-founder with Havel of Charter 77, and the assistant foreign minister. Havel apparently was responding to protests against Communists and former Communists remaining in high governmental positions. Vaclav Klaus, the minister of finance and the recently elected new chairman of the Civic Forum, had just pledged to move the organization to the right. Though Havel had praised Vacek's loyalty and had promoted him to a four star general, Michael Zantovsky, the government spokesman, stated that a government committee had asserted that Vacek had been prepared to follow orders to employ the army against protesters during the beginning of the Velvet Revolution.

Vacek undoubtedly contributed to a smooth transition from communism to a democratic society. In an ultimate act of loyalty to the government, he publicly announced that he understood the necessity for his replacement. He stated that, "Objections voiced by some people against my person do not contribute to calm and an atmosphere necessary to carry out complex changes."

In May 1996, Vacek was elected to the Czech Chamber of Deputies as a representative of the Communist Party of Bohemia and Moravia. He became a member of the committee for defense and security.

BIBLIOGRAPHY

Kamm, Henry. "Evolution in Europe: New Prague Forum Chief Looks to the Right." *New York Times,* October 18, 1990.

———. "New Defense Chief Is Named in Prague." *New York Times,* October 19, 1990.

Tagliabue, John. "Prague Would Cut Defenses along West German Border." *New York Times,* December 16, 1989.

———. "Upheaval in the East; Czech Army Denies a Coup Plan; Opposition Leader Offers Support." *New York Times,* December 19, 1989.

———. "Upheaval in the East; Czech Premier Quits As Dissidents Press to Control Cabinet." *New York Times,* December 8, 1989.

Bernard Cook

Valle d'Aosta

The Valle d'Aosta is a traditionally francophone area of Italy that, until 1860, formed part of the Kingdom of Savoy. When, in the bargaining leading to the formation of the Italian state, Camillo di Cavour transferred the bulk of Savoy to France, Valle d'Aosta was retained by Piedmont and hence by Italy. Italian was progressively enforced as the language of administration and education. This tendency reached a peak under the fascist dictatorship that launched a serious effort to eradicate the French language entirely from Valle d'Aosta. The region's French character was further threatened by an extensive migration of Italian speakers into the area. After the collapse of fascism and an abortive attempt by France to occupy Valle d'Aosta, the Italian government was forced to concede limited autonomy to the area in 1945.

Valle d'Aosta is the smallest region of Italy with a population of around 120,000, of whom approximately 55 percent are francophones. The struggle against fascism and italianisation was led by Emile Chanoux, the leader of the Jeunesse Valdotaine movement founded by Abbe Joseph Treves. Chanoux's successors founded the Union Valdotaine (UV) in 1945 as the principal political voice of the francophone majority of the region. Severin Caveri led the UV until 1973. In its effort to implement the provisions of the Statute of Autonomy, the UV had to deal with internal divisions within the francophone community, complicated by the resolute hostility of the Catholic Church, and with the challenge from the region's large italophone community. The Catholic Church in Valle d'Aosta consistently opposed all political parties except the Christian Democrats and has attacked the UV for dividing the Catholic vote and for making political alliances with other parties including those of the Left. In 1993 the UV, supported by three small groups of autonomists, controlled the single seats that Valle d'Aosta has in the Italian upper and lower houses of Parliament. In addition, the UV was the largest single group in the thirty-five member regional assembly and dominated the local political administration. The prime concerns of the UV in 1993 were to make bilingualism, especially in education, a reality; to establish a separate voice for Valle d'Aosta at the European level; and to adjust to the new political opportunities in Italy occasioned by the crisis within the political system.

BIBLIOGRAPHY

Caveri, Severino. *Souvenirs et Révélations: Vallée d'Aosta 1927–1948.* Bonneville: Plancher, 1968.

Salvadori, Bruno. *Pourquoi être Autonomiste.* Aoste: Duc, 1978.

Mícheál Thompson

Varady, Tibor

Serbian political figure. Before entering politics, Tibor Varady, an ethnic Hungarian from the autonomous province of Vojvodina, was a professor of international civil law at the University of Novi Sad. He was a member of the Reform Party presided over by Ante Marković, the last premier of the former Yugoslavia. Varady was elected to the Serbian Parliament in 1990. He was minister of justice in the short-lived government of Milan Panic from July to December 1992. Varady was a cosmopolitan opposed to nationalism. After the failure of his effort to promote a liberalization of Serbia Varady returned to academia, heading the international law program at the Central European University in Budapest.

Catherine Lutard
(Tr. by B. Cook)

Vassiliou, George (1931–)

President of Cyprus, 1988–1993. George Vassiliou, the son of two founding members of the Cypriot Communist Party (AKEL), was born in 1932. He studied economics in Budapest and London. He established a very successful market research company that did research in the Middle East for multinational corporations. Vassiliou, a self-made millionaire, president of the Cypriot Chamber of Commerce, and a representative of the Greek Cypriot business elite, ran as an independent in the presidential race of 1988. The Communists, however, endorsed him and their support was of crucial importance. Despite the support of the Communists, however, Vassiliou was clear in establishing the fact that he was not a Communist. The Communists had broken with the incumbent president, Spyros Kyprianou, whom they had earlier supported, over his failure to advance a peace settlement. Doris Christofides, a member of AKEL's Central Committee, stated that, "It is not a question of right and left. We decided who would be best for all of the people. We are willing to let the economic questions on our program wait until later." In fact, Vassiliou's program differed little from that of his main rival, the right-wing Glafcos Clerides. Both candidates agreed that the Greek Cypriots had to demonstrate greater flexibility if the partition of the island into two opposing Turkish and Greek sectors were to be ended.

The incumbent president, Spyros Kyprianou, was excluded in the first round of voting. Before the second round Vassiliou made some rather intransigent statements to gain the support of the Socialists whose candidate, Vassos Lysarides, had won approximately 10 percent of the vote. He said that any solution had to include the withdrawal of Turkish troops and the removal of the 65,000 Turkish settlers brought in after 1974. He also said that 200,000 Greeks must be allowed to return to their homes in north Cyprus. In the second round on February 21, 1988, Vassiliou received 52 percent of the vote, and of that amount the communists provided about 60 percent.

After assuming the presidency, Vassiliou promised a peace offensive to end the standoff between the Turkish and Greek Cypriot communities. However, he had to contend with the divergent political agendas within the Greek Cypriot community and the interests and pressures of the two external players, Greece and Turkey. On March 2, 1989, Vassiliou expressed the willingness of the Greek Cypriots to make major concessions to the Turkish Cypriots to end the division of the island and bring about the withdrawal of the 29,000 Turkish soldiers stationed there. He said, "The Greek community is willing and ready to make extensive concessions in the field of power-sharing with the Turkish Cypriot community."

In the next presidential primary on February 8, 1993, Vassiliou, again supported by the Communists, won 44.15 percent of the vote. Because he did not receive 50 percent he was forced into a runoff with Clerides. In the first vote Clerides received 36.74 percent and Paschalis Pascalides, a businessman, an adamant opponent of a U.N. plan to reunite Cyprus, which was supported by Vassiliou, won 18.6 percent. The U.N. plan, advanced by secretary general Boutros Boutros-Ghali, called for the establishment of a bi-zonal, bi-communal federation.

On February 14, 1993, Vassiliou was defeated in the runoff by Clerides, who also opposed the U.N. proposal to reunify Cyprus. Clerides said that the plan would violate human rights by preventing Cypriots who had lived in what was now the Turkish zone from returning to their homes, and that it would preclude Cypriot membership in the EU. Clerides received 178,863 votes, 50.28 percent, to Vassiliou's 176,870, 49.72 percent.

BIBLIOGRAPHY

Cowell, Alan. "Greek Cypriot Chief's 'Peace Offensive' Fades." *New York Times,* March 30, 1988.

———. "Cypriot Leader Pledges Talks in Taking Office," *New York Times,* February 29, 1988.
———. "Greek Cypriots Seek Accord." *New York Times,* March 2, 1989.
Wallace, Charles P. "He Hopes to Unseat Kyprianou: Cypriot Capitalist Runs under Communist Aegis." *Los Angeles Times,* February 11, 1988.

Bernard Cook

Vatican Bank

The financial institution of the Holy See that administers the banking needs of the population and officials of the Vatican City State.

The Vatican Bank, one of the best known of the financial departments in the Vatican, is known officially as the Institute for Religious Works (Istituto per le Opera di Religione, IOR). Along with handling the daily banking needs of staff and others associated with the Vatican, the bank contributes to the investment strategy of the Holy See and authorizes funds for religious activities, including the numerous worldwide programs devoted to pastoral care. Pope's have historically condemned the taking of interest on loans (usury) under any circumstances, no matter how low the interest rate appeared. Centuries after peasant communities ceased, the church continued to condemn usury, and it has never officially lifted its ban.

Pope Leo XIII established the Vatican Bank in 1887 as the Administration for Religious Works to administer funds for church endeavors; it was a highly secret organization that answered only to the pope. The bank was hidden away in an office called *il buco nero* (the black hole) that had previously housed the headquarters of censorship of the Papal States. In 1942, Pope Pius XII replaced this office with the formally established IOR and changed its mission. It was charged with the oversight of all monies, as well as property, cash, and bonds, that were transferred or entrusted to the bank for works of religion. The Vatican Bank thus essentially functions as a massive trust fund set up to handle capital for religious orders, Catholic relief organizations, charitable enterprises, and Catholic schools. It has nothing to do with the operating budget of the Holy See. Anyone with an account in the Vatican Bank has many special privileges since it is not under the financial controls of the Italian government, a situation that has led to repeated charges in the Italian press that IOR was a conduit for sending vast sums of money out of Italy, thus circumventing currency regulations.

During World War II the IOR played a significant role in protecting the Church's finances, using its international associations to protect it against the threat of a Nazi seizure of the Vatican. Today the Vatican Bank is best known for the sensational scandals to which its name was attached in the late 1970s and early 1980s, involving the financial mismanagement of Vatican finances by Michele Sindona, as well as the involvement of American Archbishop Paul C. Marcinkus (head of the Vatican Bank) in the controversial $3.1 billion banking collapse of Italy's small but aristocratic and respected bank, Banco Ambrosiano. Revelations following the death of Banco Ambrosiano's president, Roberto Calvi, "God's banker," in June 1982, damaged confidence in the Vatican's ability to handle its finances. Charges were leveled against the Vatican Bank for its alleged role in these events, and 120 foreign banks demanded their money. But the Vatican eventually repaired the damage to the credibility and to the reputation of the IOR, culminating in a 1984 agreement with the foreign banks, to which the Vatican Bank paid nearly a quarter of a billion dollars in cash. In March 1990, Pope John Paul II, as part of his program of change to the papal finances and of the opening of some of the Holy See's financial affairs to public scrutiny, ordered reform of the bank.

BIBLIOGRAPHY

Briggs, Kenneth A. *Holy Siege: The Year That Shook Catholic America.* New York: HarperCollins, 1992.
Lernoux, Penny. *In Banks We Trust.* Garden City, NY: Anchor, 1984.
Packard, Jerrold M. *Peter's Kingdom: Inside the Papal City.* New York: Charles Scribner's Sons, 1985.
Wynn, Wilton. *Keepers of the Keys: John XXIII, Paul VI, and John Paul II, Three Who Changed the Church.* New York: Random House, 1988.

Martin J. Manning

SEE ALSO John Paul I; Sindona, Michele

Vatican City

The Lateran Treaty of 1929 recognized the sovereignty of the 108.7 acre (44 hectares) Vatican City, the seat of the Roman Catholic papacy, and compensated the papacy for its loss of income and territory at the time of Italian unification with approximately $37,500,000 (750,000,000 lire) in cash and $50,000,000 (one billion lire) in Italian state bonds. The treaty was incorporated into the Italian constitution of 1947. In 1984 the treaty was revised to end the status of Roman Catholicism as the state religion in Italy.

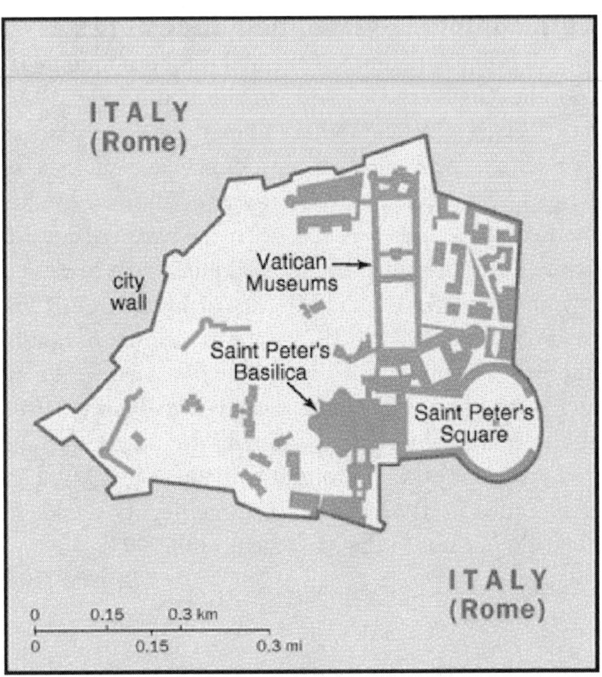

Vatican City. *Illustration courtesy of Bernard Cook.*

Fewer than one thousand persons, predominantly Vatican employees, live in Vatican City. But since it is the administrative center of the Catholic Church, over one hundred states find it useful or politically obligatory to have ambassadors at the Vatican. The U.S. established full diplomatic relations with Vatican City in 1984. The Vatican sends permanent delegates or nuncios abroad to represent the interests of the pope. The Vatican also has a permanent observer at the United Nations and was a party to the Helsinki Accords of the Conference on Security and Cooperation in Europe.

Vatican financial operations are handled by the Institute for Religious Works (Istituto per le Opere di Religione), popularly known as the Vatican Bank. In 1987, in conjunction with the Banco Ambrosiano scandal, an Italian court issued a warrant for the head of the Vatican Bank, Archbishop Paul Marcinkus, an American. He was charged with being an accessory to fraudulent bankruptcy. Marcinkus eluded Italian justice by remaining inside Vatican City, which has no extradition treaty with Italy. In a 1991 compromise, Italy's high court dismissed the warrant, and Marcinkus, who had resigned from the bank, returned to the diocese of Chicago. The Vatican subsequently placed the bank under the direction of an international board of lay Catholics and stated its desire to support its activities in the future through voluntary contributions rather than through investments.

The popes of the postwar era have been Pius XII (1939–58), John XXIII (1958–63), Paul VI (1963–78), John Paul I (1978), and John Paul II (1978–). The Second Vatican Council, a pivotal episode for the modern Catholic Church, was convened by John XXIII and held in St. Peter's Basilica in Vatican City from 1962 to 1965. John Paul I died less than five weeks after his election by the College of Cardinals. Accusations linking his death to his desire to end corruption at the Vatican Bank have been made. John Paul II, the first non-Italian pope since the Englishman Adrian VI (1459–1523), had an impact on political developments in his native Poland. Through his appointments and pronouncements, he has played a significant role in conservatizing and centralizing the leadership of the Catholic Church.

BIBLIOGRAPHY

Hebblethwaite, Peter. *In the Vatican.* Bethseda, MD: Adler & Adler, 1986.

Mayer, Fred, et al. *The Vatican: Portrait of a State and a Community.* New York: Vendome, 1980.

Walsh, Michael J. *Vatican City State.* Oxford: ABC-Clio, 1983.

Yallop, David A. *In God's Name: An Investigation into the Murder of Pope John Paul I.* Toronto and New York: Bantam, 1984.

Bernard Cook

SEE ALSO Vatican Council II

Vatican Council II

An ecumenical council of the Roman Catholic Church, convened in 1962. Pope John XXIII (1958–63) first thought of convening an ecumenical council less than three months after his election in January 1959. In his initial statements on this matter he expressed his hope that such a council would bring about, in his words, "a new Pentecost" and a time of renewal and updating, or *aggiornamento,* in the Catholic Church.

When the council opened in October 1962, 2,540 churchmen out of a total of 2,908 who were eligible attended the first public session. The major Christian churches and communities separated from Rome had also been invited to send delegates as observers. Of these, seventeen Orthodox and Protestant denominations accepted.

The first period of the council extended from October to December 1962; the second from September to December 1963; the third from September to November 1964; and the fourth and final session from September to December 1965. The first session was devoted to preparatory work, and its proposals were being discussed and implemented at the time of John XXIII's death in June 1963.

The new pope, Paul VI, in his first message after his election, promised to continue the council. The second session concentrated on the redefinition of the church's role in the world and on ecumenism. In the interval between the second and third period of the council the bishops and their advisors were directed by the pope to consider religious life, missionary activity, the education of future priests, and Catholic education in general. During the third counciliar period a broad ecumenical outreach was undertaken, with special attention to the Orthodox, and a document was prepared dealing with "Jews and non-Christians." Later, all derogatory liturgical references to the Jews and non-Christians would be purged from the liturgy.

The fourth and final period of the council opened in September 1965 and was devoted to the development of documents on the pastoral office of bishops and episcopal and papal cooperation and collegiality. A statement on religious freedom and one on the apostolate of the laity were prepared. On October 5, 1965, the pontiff returned from his visit to the United Nations in New York City and addressed the council's representatives assembled in St. Peter's on the subject of world peace. As the fourth period continued, the pontiff asked the bishops not to debate the law of celibacy while they were discussing the role of the priesthood, but he encouraged the role of episcopal conferences and synods. In December the Pope and the council members were joined by the non-Catholic observers in a ceremony for Christian unity held in St. Paul's Basilica, and in the same month Paul VI and the Ecumenical Patriarch Athenagoras I mutually removed the sentences of excommunication that had been administered by their churches against each other in 1054.

The formal declarations of the council upheld the principle of religious freedom and encouraged the spirit of ecumenism in the church's approach to others. As a result of Vatican II, the Catholic Church examined and adjusted its outlook and approach to the world, as well as its liturgical, religious, and community life and practices.

BIBLIOGRAPHY

Abbot, W. M., ed. *Documents of Vatican II.* New York: Guild Press, 1966.

Holmes, J. Derek. *The Papacy in the Modern World: 1914–1978.* New York: Crossroad, 1981.

William Roberts

SEE ALSO John XXIII; Paul VI

Veil, Simone (-Anne, née Jacob) (1927–)

French political figure. Simone Veil was born Simone Jacob, the daughter of a Jewish architect, at Nice in 1927. At 17, along with her mother and two sisters, she was sent first to the Nazi death camp Auschwitz and then to Bergen-Belsen. She survived her year of captivity, but her mother and a sister perished. After the war, Veil studied at the Paris Institut d'Études politiques. She became a lawyer and worked at the Ministry of Justice from 1957 to 1965. From 1974 to 1979 she was minister of health. She was a champion of the rights of women, children, and immigrants. Her name was given to France's 1974 abortion law, which she sponsored. She was elected the first president of the European Parliament in 1979. Her term ended in 1982 and she became deputy president. She held her seat in the parliament until 1993.

Bernard Cook

Veltroni, Walter (1955–)

Italian journalist and politician. Walter Veltroni was born in Rome on July 3, 1955. He studied at the Film Institute in Rome prior to his employment as assistant director to the Italian television serial *A Pistol in the Drawer.*

Veltroni joined the Federation of Young Communists (FGCI) in 1970 at the age of 15, and in 1973 became a member of its secretariat. He became the FGCI provincial secretary for Rome and a member of its national steering committee in 1975. He joined the Italian Communist Party (PCI) in 1976 and was elected to the municipal council of Rome the same year. In 1977 he was appointed the head publicist for the Rome PCI. In 1970 he became the national party's assistant director of press and publicity. Veltroni became a member of the PCI central steering committee in 1983, and head of its publicity and information commission in 1987. He was elected to the Chamber of Deputies in 1987 and was appointed to the parliamentary commission for culture, science, and education and to the bicameral supervisory commission for radio and television.

Veltroni has written a number of books. An admirer of Enrico Berlinguer and Robert Kennedy, in 1992 he published *Il sogno spezzato* (The Broken Dream) on Kennedy, and *La sfida interrotta* (The Interrupted Challenge) on Berlinguer.

In 1991 Veltroni supported the transformation of the PCI into the Democratic Party of the Left. He headed its mass media department. In 1992 he became editor of the party newspaper, *L'Unità.* He succeeded the party leader, Massimo D'Alema, as editor and rose to a position of prominence in the party second only to D'Alema.

In April 1996 he was elected to the Chamber of Deputies from the constituency of Lazio 1. In May he became minister of cultural heritage and sport and vice president of the council of ministers (deputy prime minister) in the government of Romano Prodi.

BIBLIOGRAPHY

Berlinguer, Enrico. *La sfida interrotta: le idee di Enrico Berlinguer.* Ed. by Walter Veltroni. Milan: Baldini & Castoldi, 1994.

Meli, Arturo. *Walter Veltroni.* Rome: Viviani, 1996.

Valentini, Carlo. *Veltroni al governo?: il "Kennedy della sinistra italiana" parla di se, della politica, dei politici e disegna il futuro del nostro Paese.* Bologna: Carmenta, 1995.

Veltroni, Walter. *La bella politica.* Milan: Rizzoli, 1995.

———. *Governare da sinistra.* Milan: Baldini & Castoldi, 1997.

Bernard Cook

Videnov, Zhan (1959–)

Former prime minister of the Republic of Bulgaria and leader of the Bulgarian Socialist Party (BSP). He resigned from the premiership and his party's leadership in December 1996. A graduate of the Moscow State Institute for International Relations, Zhan Videnov worked as a specialist in foreign economic relations for various Bulgarian companies before being elected as a BSP deputy of the National Assembly in June 1990, when he represented a constituency in the town where he was born, Plovdiv. A known conservative within the BSP, he was elected its leader in December 1991. A young politician untainted by the older BSP leadership, Videnov was initially popular in Bulgaria. Following new parliamentary elections in December 1994, when the BSP emerged as the largest party in the legislature, he formed a government, with himself as premier. A poor party manager who has often bereft of the complete support of the divided BSP in parliament, he barely survived a no-confidence motion introduced by the opposition Union of Democratic Forces (UDF) in December 1995. Supported by the president of Bulgaria, Zhelyu Zhelev, the UDF protested widespread corruption in BSP ranks and condemned Videnov's government for failing to tackle a local crime wave.

Worse was to follow in 1996, when Bulgaria experienced a serious socio-economic crisis exacerbated by the ineffective policies of the divided BSP government. Externally, Videnov was also charged with needlessly alienating the European Union (EU) that Bulgaria aspired to join by cultivating closer ties with Russia in the Balkans. In November 1996 new presidential elections resulted in the defeat of the BSP candidate, Ivan Mazarov, and the victory of the UDF's Petur Stoyanov. Against a wider background of economic collapse and social unrest, including large anti-government demonstrations in Sofia and other cities, Videnov's government was forced out of office in December 1996. Politically, this finished off the BSP as a credible political force in Bulgaria, where new parliamentary elections in April 1997 brought the UDF back to power after four years in opposition. Blamed for this political disaster, Videnov then lost the leadership of what remained of the disintegrating BSP. Looking back at his political career during the 1990s, it can be argued that Videnov was unable to transcend the corrupt and incompetent BSP nomenklatura that gave him birth as a politician. The result of this was a failure to formulate and implement a coherent and credible set of policies to deal with Bulgaria's post-communist political and economic crisis, a failure that has now condemned the BSP and people like Videnov to political oblivion in Bulgaria.

Marko Milivojevic

Villiers de Saintignon, Philippe le Jolis de (1949–)

French politician. Philippe le Jolis de Villiers de Saintignon, the son of the aristocrat Jacques le Jolis de Villiers de Saintignon, and Hedwig d'Arexy, was born in Boulogne on March 25, 1949. He graduated from the École Nationale d'Administration and worked in the Ministry of the Interior. He served as the private secretary to the prefect of La Rochelle in 1978, and in 1979 was made the deputy prefect of Vendôme. In 1981 he founded the regional radio station Alouette FM, and in 1984 the Foundation for the Arts and Sciences of Communication in Nantes. From 1986 to 1987 he served as the junior minister of culture and communications. He became a member of the General Council of the Vendée in 1987 and its president in 1988. In 1988 he became a national delegate of the Union for French Democracy (UDF) in charge of youth and liaison with cultural organizations. De Villiers was elected to the National Assembly as a UDF candidate from the Vendée in 1988. He held that seat until 1994. That year he was elected to the European parliament as a candidate of the "Majority for the Other Europe" (Majorité pour l'autre Europe).

He was the founder in 1994 and the president of the Movement for France (Mouvement pour France). He ran in the presidential race in 1995. If de Villiers had not been in the race, Jean Marie Le Pen's share of the vote probably would have been above 15 percent. De Villiers appealed to older, rural, and bourgeois voters, who were opposed to immigration, further European integration, free trade, corruption, and abortion. But he offered them a more restrained and respectable alternative to Le Pen.

BIBLIOGRAPHY

Thompson, Wayne C. *Western Europe 1996.* Harpers Ferry, WV: Stryker-Post, 1996.

Bernard Cook

Vllasi, Azem

Leader of the Communist Party in Yugoslavia's Autonomous Province of Kosovo, purged by Slobodan Milošević. A favorite of Tito, Azem Vllasi became the leader of the Communist youth organizations for all of Yugoslavia. After the strike of the miners at Tetovo Mitrovica in 1981, Vllasi was placed in charge of the Kosovo League of Communists. Slobodan Milošević was able to distort the situation of Kosovo minorities in order to fuel Serbian fears of the separation of territory elsewhere inhabited by Serbs from Yugoslavia or Serbia. Milošević undermined Vllasi's efforts to maintain order. After demonstrations in Prishtina, the capital of Kosovo, in November 1988 in opposition to new Serbian constitutional changes, Vllasi was expelled from the Central Committee of the Communist League. He was arrested in February 1989 and accused of counterrevolutionary activity. Although Vllasi was in prison at the time of a second miner's strike in March 1989, when twenty-four Albanians were killed, he and fourteen others were held responsible. A trial began in October but it aroused such international opprobrium that it was terminated and the charges were dropped. Vllasi was released from prison in April 1990.

Antonia Young

SEE ALSO Kosovo; Milošević, Slobodan

Vogel, Hans-Jochen (1926–)

Social Democratic (SPD) mayor of Munich from 1960 to 1972, member of the federal cabinet from 1972 to 1981, president of the SPD from 1987 to 1990. After completing the Abitur, the examination taken after completing the Gymnasium (university prepatory second school), in 1943 he was drafted and served as a noncommissioned officer. After the war he studied law at Munich and Marburg and received his doctorate in 1950. He had great success in the Bavarian state (*Land*) administration. From 1955 until the end of the SPD Bavarian administration in 1958 he served in the Legal Office of the State Chancellery. His subsequent entry into city politics was the springboard for a career as Federal minister. He was elected mayor of Munich in 1960. For the next twelve years he made his imprint upon his city through an extensive building program. In accord with the architectural philosophy of the 1960s, he established new residential quarters in green bands in order to relieve the great population pressure in the business and industrial agglomeration of Munich. At the same time he revolutionized the public transit system through an extensive construction of underground railway lines. He initiated an extensive building program to prepare Munich to serve as the site of the 1972 Olympics. Against abundant opposition he advanced the ingenious canvas roof of architect Günter Behnisch for the olympic stadium and sports hall.

In 1972 Vogel was named a "freeman" of the Bavarian capital. The same year he went to Bonn as the Federal minister of construction. In this position he was in charge of the housing construction program, and the construction of social housing reached its highest level in the history of the Federal Republic. In 1974 he became the Federal minister of justice. As a discreet reviewer of laws who had a passion for details he was an essential pillar of the Social-Liberal coalition. Chancellor Schmidt moved Vogel in 1981 from that post, so that as governing mayor of Berlin he could conduct what seemed to be a hopeless campaign against the designated candidate of the CDU, Richard von Weizsäcker. In 1983 Vogel was the SPD candidate for chancellor against Helmut Kohl and achieved the respectable result of 37.5 percent for his party. He succeeded Herbert Wehner as chairman of the SPD parliamentary *fraktion* and opposition leader in the Bundestag. As leader of the right wing of the party, he replaced Willy Brandt in 1987 as the chairman of the SPD.

Vogel's exceedingly correct debating style and his aversion to political tactics, as well as his attraction for excessive paperwork, became his trademarks. In 1990 the "gentleman of German politics" relinquished his position of leadership in order to make way for younger party leaders.

BIBLIOGRAPHY

Topitsch, Ernst, and Hans-Jochen Vogel. *Pluralismus und Toleranz. Alternative Ideen von Gesellschaft.* Cologne: Bachem, 1983.

Vogel, Hans-Jochen Vogel. *Die Amtskette. Meine 12 Munchner Jahre. Ein Erlebnisbericht.* Munich: Süddeutscher Verlag, 1972.

———. *Reale Reformen. Beiträge zu einer Gesellschaftspolitik der Neuen Mitte.* Munich: Piper, 1973.

Georg Wagner
(Tr. by B. Cook)

Vojvodina

Until 1989, an autonomous province of the Serbian Republic of the Socialist Federated Republic of Yugoslav. In 1989, the nationalist Serbian government of Slobodan Milošević asserted direct control over Vojvodina.

Vojvodina, to the north of Serbia proper, consists of the southeastern part of the Pannonian Plain, set off by the Fruska Gora mountains to the south and the Vrsac Mountains to the southeast. It is intersected by the Danube, the Tisa, and the Sava rivers. It consists of 8,304 square miles (21,506 sq km) and had 1,996,000 inhabitants in 1991. The provincial capital is Novi Sad, a city of three hundred thousand.

Before 1918 Hungarians were a majority in Vojvodina. In 1945 they still constituted 50 percent of the population. Before the migration occasioned by the collapse of the former Yugoslavia, the province had a richly diverse population belonging to more than twenty different nationalities. But 1989 Serbians were the largest group, constituting over half of the population, while there were 341,000 Hungarians, and 98,000 Croats. Since 1995, 150,000 Serbian refugees from Krajina and Bosnia have been settled in Vojvodina, and many intimidated Croatians and Hungarians have fled.

The province is a rich agricultural region. It produced approximately 80 percent of the cereal crops of the former Yugoslavia, and most of its cotton and oil seed. Its fodder crops sustained intensive beef and dairy production. Vojvodina also possessed food processing and metal working industries.

Vojvodina was settled by Serbs in the sixth century and became part of Hungary until the Ottoman Turks dominated the area in the sixteenth century. The Austrian Empire drove the Turks out in the eighteenth century. The Austrians gave special privileges to Serbs, who served as border guards in Vojvodina and Croatia. In fact the name Vojvodina stems from the leader, or *vojvod,* elected by the local Serbian border guards. The name came into use for sections of the Banat that were administered by the Austrians rather than the Hungarians. With the establishment of the Austro-Hungarian Empire in 1867, all of present day Vojvodina came under Hungarian administration. During World War I the Austro-Hungarians expelled prominent Serbians and destroyed some Serbian homes and cultural monuments. In 1918 Vojvodina became part of the Kingdom of the Serbs, Croats, and Slovenes, renamed Yugoslavia in 1929. In 1941, after the Nazi defeat of Yugoslavia, Vojvodina was partitioned between Croatia, which annexed Srem, Hungary, which annexed Backa, and the German occupation administration. Following the war many Germans, whose families had lived in the region for generations, were expelled. Since 1989 approximately fifty thousand Hungarians have left under Serbian pressure.

Bernard Cook

Vranitzky, Franz (1937–)

Austrian chancellor, 1986–97. Franz Vranitzky was born in Vienna on October 4, 1937. He studied economics at the University of Vienna and received his Ph.D. in 1969. His first employment was as an accountant at Siemans-Schukert. In 1961 he went to work in the Department of National Economics of the Austrian National Bank, where he eventually became first vice president. In 1970 Vranitzky left the bank to become the advisor to the Minister of Finance and Vice-Chancellor Hannes Androsch. The socialist Androsch became Vranitzky's political mentor. In 1976 Vranitzky became the deputy director-general of the Creditanstalt Bankverein, the largest bank in Austria. Due to his success in that position he was recruited as first executive officer of Österreichische Länderbank, Austria's second largest bank, which was practically bankrupt. He was able to restore the bank to sound footing within three years.

Franz Vranitzky, chancellor of Austria form 1986 until 1997. *Illustration courtesy of the Austrian Press and Information Service.*

His success at the Österreichische Länderbank led to Vranitzky's appointment in 1984 to succeed Herbert Salcher as finance minister. In that position he gained a reputation for economic acumen, with a pragmatic non-ideological approach to problems, and administrative capability. He took moves to reduce the national debt and lessen national borrowing, and has ended an unpopular tax on savings.

Following the June 8, 1986, defeat of Kurt Steyrer, the socialist candidate for president, by Kurt Waldheim, who was supported by the opposition People's Party (ÖVP), the Socialist chancellor Fred Sinowatz resigned. Vranitzky's popularity recommended him for the position, although some socialists objected to his conservatism. Vranitzky as chancellor (June 16, 1986–January 28, 1997) proposed addressing the losses incurred by state-run industries by selling shares in the industries. Though the People's Party welcomed this move, unionists feared that restructuring and privatization would cost jobs and endanger Austria's "social partnership."

Shortly after beginning his chancellorship Vranitzky felt compelled to dissolve his government. The Freedom Party, the Socialists' coalition partner, elected the right-wing nationalist Jörg Haider as its leader. If Haider had not been unacceptable by himself, his tendency to exonerate Nazis was compounded by the Waldheim Affair, the scandal surrounding Kurt Waldheim's presidential campaign and subsequent term of office (1986–92), when inquiry's into his World War II activities revealed the he had not fully disclosed his war-time record. Vranitzky and Alois Mock of the People's Party had similar programs and avoided rancor that might have prevented a post-election coalition. In the November 23, 1986, election the Socialist Party (SPÖ) dropped from 47 percent to 43 percent. They lost votes among the working class of Vienna and Upper Austria who disliked Vranitzky's reforms. Votes, however, were gained from the middle class, who were enamored with his measures. The People's Party slipped slightly to 41 percent, but Haider's Freedom Party doubled its vote, rising from 5 to 10 percent. President Waldheim commissioned Vranitzky to form a new government and Vranitzky crafted a grand coalition of the Socialist and People's parties. Mock was the vice-chancellor of the government formed on January 21, 1987, and the SPÖ and the ÖVP split the cabinet seats equally.

Bruno Kreisky, the former Socialist chancellor, expressed his opposition to the policy of Vranitzky by resigning as the president of the Socialist party on January 19, 1987. He accused Vranitzky of abandoning socialism in favor of the "banks and bourgeoisie." Vranitzky was unmoved. He asserted that, "It is possible that we have entered a phase in which political decisions cannot be explained only in terms of the red-black cliché." When Fred Sinowatz stepped down as chairman of the SPÖ, Vranitzky was elected chairman on May 11, 1988. In 1991, reflecting the changing perspective advanced by Vranitzky, the party changed its name to the Social Democratic Party of Austria.

The Waldheim Affair troubled Vranitzky's second chancellorship. He was compelled by international pressure to criticize Waldheim on February 14, 1988. Vranitzky stated that, "There is enough criticism at home and enough to be taken seriously. The president has not been very accurate with the truth in the course of all these events." However, he shied away from requesting Waldheim's resignation in order not to damage relations with his coalition partner, the ÖVP. The protagonist left center stage on May 24, 1992, when Thomas Klestil, a diplomat, the candidate of the ÖVP, was elected to succeed Waldheim. Klestil was re-elected with 63.5 percent of the vote on April 19, 1998.

The SPÖ, which won 42.8 percent of the vote in 1990, slipped to 34.9 percent in 1994. Though it rebounded somewhat to 38.1 percent in 1995, it performed disastrously in the election for the European parliament in October 1996, winning only 29.1 percent of the vote, while the Freedom Party garnered 27.6 percent. Though the performance of the ÖVP was even worse, and though public opinion polls indicated that the SPÖ's support had risen to the 40 percent level, Vranitzky decided to resign as chancellor and leader of the SPÖ. Vranitzky announced his decision on January 19, 1997. His successor in both posts was Viktor Klima, who served as finance minister in Vranitzky's last government. Klima maintained the grand coalition, which had been constructed by Vranitzky, and Wolfgang Schüssel of the ÖVP continued in the posts of vice-chancellor and foreign minister that he had held since Mock's resignation from those posts and the party's chairmanship in May 1995.

BIBLIOGRAPHY

Current Biography Yearbook 1989. "Vranitzky, Franz." 598–602.

Bernard Cook

SEE ALSO Waldheim Affair

Vyshinskii, Andrei Ianuarevich (1883–1954)

Chief prosecutor for Joseph Stalin during the show trials of the 1930s, later foreign minister of the Soviet Union and ambassador to the United Nations. Born in Odessa, Vyshinskii joined the Russian Social Democratic Workers Party in 1903, associating himself with the party's Menshevik faction. This group, archrival of Vladimir Lenin's Bolshevik faction, was less authoritarian in its approach to Marxism. Vyshinskii did not become a Bolshevik until 1920, when it became clear that Lenin's Bolsheviks would win the civil war that followed the Russian Revolution. This record as an opponent of the Bolsheviks made Vyshinskii fanatic in his efforts to demonstrate loyalty to his new masters.

Trained in law, Vyshinskii catapulted to prominence in 1928 when he served as presiding judge in the Shakhty trial of alleged saboteurs and foreign spies from the coal mines of the North Caucasus. Orchestrating the attack against the accused with great skill, despite the seemingly ridiculous nature of the charges against them, Vyshinskii later became prosecutor for the show trials in the "Industrial Party" and Metro-Vickers cases.

Vyshinskii was promoted to prosecutor-general of the USSR in 1935, and played a pivotal role in Stalin's great purges. A series of public trials on trumped up treason charges led to the conviction and execution of all the senior Bolsheviks who had opposed Stalin. For the trials of Lev Kamenev and Grigorii Zinoviev in 1936, Yurii Piatakov and Karl Radek in 1937, and Nikolai Bukharin in 1938, not to mention a host of lesser-known Bolsheviks, Vyshinskii received an Order of Lenin and became a member of the Central Committee.

In 1940 Vyshinskii moved from law to foreign policy, becoming First Deputy to People's Commissar (later Minister) of Foreign Affairs Viacheslav Molotov. After assisting in the imposition of Stalinism in Eastern Europe, Vyshinskii advanced to become minister of foreign affairs in March 1949. Molotov had fallen out of favor with Stalin and been removed from his post, creating a vacancy.

Vyshinskii put little personal imprint on Soviet foreign policy, and generally was content to carry out Stalin's directives. Upon Stalin's death in March 1953, Vyshinskii was demoted and Molotov returned as minister of foreign affairs. He died shortly thereafter on November 22, 1954, while serving as Soviet ambassador to the United Nations.

BIBLIOGRAPHY

Conquest, Robert. *The Great Terror.* New York: Macmillan, 1968.

Vaksberg, Arkady. *Stalin's Prosecutor: The Life of Andrei Vyshinsky.* New York: Grove Weidenfeld, 1990.

David Stone

Waigel, Theodor "Theo" (1939–)

German Christian Democratic politician. Theodor "Theo" Waigel was born on April 22, 1939, in the little village Oberrohr (Krumbach/Schwaben) where his Catholic parents were farm owners. After graduating from high school in Krumbach, Waigel studied law in Munich and Würzburg and received a Ph.D. He worked as a junior legal official at the office of the district attorney in the state council of Munich. Later he became the consultant to Anton Jaumann, who was secretary of state in the Ministry of Financial Affairs and minister of economy and traffic from 1970 to 1972. Finally Waigel attained the rank of senior executive officer.

Waigel's path to the political arena began in high school. He joined the Christian Democratic Junge Union in 1957 and eventually was elected its chairman; he became a member of the Christian Social Union (CSU) in 1960 and was elected to the Bundestag on the CSU slate in 1972. Since 1976 he has been voted into parliament directly by his constituents in New Ulm and has worked on several committees. In addition, he made a mark in debates about economic affairs.

Waigel has gradually improved his image: in 1982, the year in which Helmut Kohl came into power, he was elected chairman of the CSU state chapter in Bonn. As a result of the death of the Bavarian prime minister, Franz-Josef Strauß, who was later succeeded by Max Streibl, Waigel was elected chairman of the CSU at the party conference of the CSU in Munich on November 19, 1988, with 98.3 percent of the votes. In the course of the cabinet restructuring undertaken by Kohl in March 1989, Waigel was also appointed minister of finance, replacing Gerhard Stoltenberg, who was transferred to the Ministry of Defense. On the one hand, the CSU had increased its influence on federal policy, but on the other hand, Chancellor Kohl had made a strategic move by disposing, through political integration, of his rival Waigel, the chairman of the CSU, whom he called Kreuz des Südens (the southern cross, or the heavy cross from the South).

At the beginning of his term Waigel abolished the tax on interest (Steuer auf Zinserträge), but later introduced it again as the Zinsabschlag. At the meeting of the Silesian Association, in Hannover on July 2, 1989, he showed his support for the former refugees and exiles from East Europe. He also participated in meetings concerning German reunification and signed the monetary, economic, and social union between the two German states. Waigel has often been attacked for his promise on May 23, 1990, that "the taxpayers need not make sacrifices for the German Unity." His rival in parliament, Ingrid Matthäus-Maier of the Social Democrats, advocated "financing of the German Unity on credit."

In May 1993 another change took place in the position of the Bavarian prime minister. Streibl had to resign because of a political finance affair dubbed the Amigo-Affair. Waigel, the chairman of the CSU, applied for the position of his successor, as did the ambitious Edmund Stoiber, who was ultimately elected as the new prime minister. During the 1990s the attacks on the minister of finance have not ceased—rather they have been exacerbated by one of the worst recessions in postwar German history, coupled with high unemployment rates. For example, there were 4.7 million unemployed people in February 1997 alone. Waigel has often been viewed as a scapegoat, despite the fact that he had the longest term of any German minister of finance.

BIBLIOGRAPHY

Heinzmann, Erhard. "Die Erben von Franz Josef Strauß." Das Bayernland, April 1989, 10–11.

"Waigel, Theodor." *Munzinger-Archiv,* 44, 1995.

Annette Biener

Wajda, Andrzej (1926–)

Polish film and theater director, one of the founders of postwar Polish cinema. After serving as a member of the Polish Resistance in World War II, Andrzej Wajda studied at the Academy of Fine Arts in Cracow, and in the Film School in Lódz. He served as president of Polish Film Association (1978–83), and was elected a senator of the Republic of Poland (1989–91).

There is a vital link between Wajda's art productions and recent Polish history and culture. In several films, such as Man of Iron, he dealt with politics and influenced contemporary events in Poland. His most important successes have been in cinema, but he also works in television and the theater. His work with The Stary Theater in Cracow includes milestone adaptations of Dostoevsky. His influence may also be discerned in the work of the younger generation of Polish directors, such as Agnieszka Holland and Krzysztof Zanussi.

Among Wajda's major films are Generation (1955); Canal (1957); Silver Palm, Cannes 1957; Ashes and Diamonds (1958); Lotna (1959); Ashes (1965); Everything for Sale (1967); The Birch Wood (1970); Landscape After Battle (1970); The Wedding (1972); The Promised Land (1974); Man of Marble (1976); Without Anaesthetic (1978); The Maids of Wilko (1979); The Conductor (1980); Man of Iron (1981); Danton (1983); Love in Germany (1984); Chronicle of Love Affairs (1986); and Korczak (1990).

BIBLIOGRAPHY

Karpinski, Maciej. *Theatre of Andrzej Wajda.* Cambridge: Cambridge University Press, 1989.

Michalek, Boleslaw, and Frank Turaj. *The Modern Cinema of Poland.* Bloomington: Indiana University Press, 1988.

Wajda, Andrzej. *Double Vision: My Life in Film.* London: Faber and Faber, 1989.

———. *Wajda on Film: A Master's Notes.* Los Angeles: Acrobat Books, 1991.

Krzysztof Olechnicki

Waldheim, Kurt (1918–)

Austrian minister for foreign affairs (1968–70), U.N. Secretary-General (1971–81), and Austrian president (1986–92). Kurt Waldheim became both a political protagonist and a symbolic figure. Waldheim sought the Austrian presidency in 1971 but lost to the incumbent, Franz Jonas. When the Austrian People's Party (ÖVP) announced Kurt Waldheim's candidacy for the presidency in 1986, some members of the Socialist Party of Austria (SPÖ) sought to discredit him by bringing up his National Socialist past. In his memoirs, Waldheim had not mentioned his activity as a First Lieutenant in the German Wehrmacht, and he explicitly indicated that he had not witnessed any deportations of Jews from the Balkans.

An international commission of historians concluded that despite his low rank Waldheim, because of his education and knowledge, knew what was taking place during the German occupation of the Balkans. It also concluded that he had again and again participated in illegal procedures and thus facilitated their execution. Waldheim's own description of his military past was in many cases not in accord with the findings of the commission. Waldheim was eager to let his past fall into oblivion and, if this was no longer possible, to be minimized. According to the commission's opinion, Waldheim's forgetfulness was so sincere that it was impossible for him to provide helpful information.

Waldheim, who was elected on the second ballot with 53.9 percent of the vote, was not the first Austrian president with a Nationalist Socialist past. Rudolf Kirchschläger, president from 1974 to 1986, and others had participated in the Nazi regime. But it was not until the mid-eighties that the National Socialist past of political representatives was of serious political interest. Before March 1938 Waldheim was not a National Socialist, but after March 1938 he was certainly not an active opponent to the National Socialist regime. Waldheim was an average Austrian trying to survive the National Socialist regime. In the words of Anton Pelinka, during those years, "Waldheim closed his eyes—as did most of those who were in comparable positions."

BIBLIOGRAPHY

Born, Hanspeter. *Für die Richtigkeit: Kurt Waldheim.* Munich: Schneekluth, 1987.

Der Bericht der internationalen Historikerkommission. Vienna: Wirtschafts-trend-Zeitschriftenverlag, 15 February, 1988.

Khol, Andreas, Theodor Faulhaber, and Günther Ofner, eds. *Die Kampagne. Kurt Waldheim—Opfer oder Täter?* Munich: Herbig, 1987.

Pelinka, Anton. *Zur Österrelchischen Identität.* Vienna: Ueberreuter, 1990.

Waldheim, Kurt. *Im Glaspalast der Weltpolitik.* Düsseldorf-Vienna: Econ, 1985.

Reinhold Gärtner

SEE ALSO Waldheim Affair

Waldheim Affair

The events surrounding the election campaign and subsequent Austrian presidency of former U.N. Secretary-General Kurt Waldheim. In the course of the 1986 election campaign for the largely ceremonial Austrian presidency, inquiries into Waldheim's World War II activities revealed his failure to fully disclose his wartime record. The ensuing international cause célèbre was a highly illustrative example of Austria's long-standing refusal to openly address its Nazi past, and it became the country's most salient political event of the decade.

In March 1986, three months prior to Austria's presidential election, in which Waldheim was the runaway favorite, media reports suggesting his membership in various National Socialist organizations surfaced in Austria and the U.S. This came as a surprise in light of Waldheim's official biography, which had not indicated any such involvement. Over the next weeks the former U.N. secretary-general came under intense international scrutiny as various organizations, the World Jewish Congress most prominent among them, conducted investigations into Waldheim's past. These inquiries gradually revealed the extent of Waldheim's participation in the brutal war in the Balkans, where it was discovered that he had served, without command authority, as an interpreter and junior supply officer.

In the final analysis, the Waldheim affair was of particular relevance for post-war Austrian history in that, by hedging critical questions about his war-time activities, Waldheim had enacted, and therefore come to symbolize, the pervasive narrative of Austria's national history. This official trope, commonly referred to as the country's Lebenslüge (a combination of delusion and deliberate suppression), held that Austria was the first victim of Nazi Germany's aggression. In this framework Austria's incorporation into the Third Reich through the 1938 Anschluss was seen as an act of external aggression, the beginning of a seven-year period of foreign domination. What this version of Austrian history repressed, however, was the disproportionately high number of native Austrians serving in key positions of the Nazi machinery, as well as the steady support the regime enjoyed among the country's population, who for the most part regarded 1945 not as liberation but defeat. Along with the systematic persecution and annihilation of its Jewish population, these historical facts were at odds with the posture of victim that Austria had assumed following World War II.

For over forty years the allies and the international community at large vicariously supported the legitimacy of Austria's *Lebenslüge.* Spared the German fate of partition, ostracism, and the burden of paying proportionate reparations, Austria and its citizens were never adequately confronted with their role in the Third Reich. In turn, among the majority of the population, no particular feeling of responsibility in regard to the Third Reich or the Holocaust developed.

Set against this context, the Waldheim affair erupted at a moment when Waldheim's persistent reluctance to disclose his wartime past could be recognized as an embodiment of the pervasive pattern of Austria's unwillingness to deal with its Nazi past. This interpretation was further corroborated by the nature of Waldheim's election campaign itself. As more and more documentation on his wartime record was published, Waldheim and the Christian-conservative Austrian People's Party (ÖVP) backing his candidacy reacted defensively, accusing those who brought forth new evidence of slander and character assassination. This tactic not only enabled Waldheim to skirt the substantive issues raised, but it effectively shifted blame to his detractors, who were quickly demonized as a dishonorable lot. In light of the prominent position of the World Jewish Congress in the affair, allegations against Waldheim's critics ultimately tapped into a rich history of antisemitic prejudice. In this context, the affair was readily and strategically re-figured in terms of a Jewish conspiracy against Waldheim and Austria at large.

If Waldheim's handy victory in the runoff election of June 1986 documented the possibility of mobilizing political support on the basis of antisemitic prejudice, it was also met with stern reserve in the Western world, where many had begun to regard Waldheim's personal stance, and by implication Austria's official historical narrative, with great suspicion. Immediately upon the disclosure of documents suggesting Waldheim's proximity to Nazi atrocities in the Balkans, the World Jewish Congress had requested his placement on the United States Justice Department's "watch-list" of undesirable aliens; and, in 1987, Waldheim was indeed barred from entering the United States as a private individual. Shunned in consequence by all Western democracies, Waldheim was essentially cut off from the arena of world politics during his presidency, which lasted until 1992.

As invitations of Austria's highest representative to Western countries failed to materialize in the context of persistent criticism of Waldheim's and Austria's failure to address their Nazi past, intra-Austrian debates on these issues reached unprecedented dimensions. These discussions were fueled in large part by the findings of an independent commission of military historians, which had concluded in early 1988 that the available evidence did not establish Waldheim's personal involvement in war crimes, while at the same time criticizing Waldheim's failure to be candid about his activities during World War II.

In the course of 1988, the year marking the fiftieth anniversary of the Anschluss, the Austrian government reacted to the ongoing debates by re-evaluating Austria's official position regarding its role in the Third Reich. Rising political success of Austria's extreme right notwithstanding, these efforts culminated in July 1991, when, in the waning months of Waldheim's presidency, Chancellor Franz Vranitzky candidly acknowledged Austria's co-responsibility for the Third Reich in a speech at the national assembly. Coming in direct response to the Waldheim affair, it was the crucial signal that official Austria was ready to relinquish the false role of Nazi victim and face the country's past with all its consequences.

In his 1996 book, *Die Antwort*, Waldheim again denied committing war crimes "directly or indirectly." He wrote that "as a member of the German Army, I did what was necessary to survive the day, the system, the war—no more no less. I opposed it, but I was not a resistance fighter." He blamed his difficulties on a conspiracy involving Austrian political opponents, American Jews, and the World Jewish Congress.

BIBLIOGRAPHY

Herzstein, Robert Edwin. *Waldheim: The Missing Years.* New York: Arbor House/William Morrow, 1988.

Mitten, Richard. *The Politics of Antisemitic Prejudice: The Waldheim Phenomenon in Austria.* Boulder, Col.: Westview, 1992.

Rosenfeld, Eli, and William Hoffer. *Betrayal: The Untold Story of the Kurt Waldheim Investigation and Cover-up.* New York: St. Martin's Press, 1993.

Waldheim, Kurt. *Die Antwort.* Vienna: Amalthea Verlag, 1996.

Wistrich, Robert, ed. *Austrians and Jews in the Twentieth Century: From Franz Joseph to Waldheim.* New York: St. Martin's Press, 1992.

Matti Bunzl

SEE ALSO Waldheim, Kurt

Wałęsa, Lech (1943–)

Labor activist, co-founder and chairman of Solidarity (1980–90), president of Poland (1990–95), and Nobel Peace Prize winner (1983). Lech Wałęsa played a key role in political changes ("the Polish revolution") in Central and Eastern Europe and the fall of communism in 1989. As president he enjoyed prestige in the international arena and shaped Poland's road toward integration with Europe.

Leck Wałęsa, one of the founders of Solidarity and president of Poland from 1990 to 1995. *Illustration courtesy of the Polish Enbassy, Washington, D.C.*

Wałęsa, an electrician, gained some popularity during worker strikes in Gdańsk in December 1970. Then he led worker protests as one of the most active members of the Strike Committee in the Lenin Shipyard. Arrested, he returned to work in the shipyard after Władisław Gomułka's fall. In 1971, in democratic labor elections, he was elected to the new workers' council and on behalf of the union he acted as a voluntary work inspector. This gave him increased contacts with his fellow workers. Wałęsa gradually gained authority among workers and became their authentic representative. Active and tough, he tried to force his viewpoints. He criticized the Gierek led government.

Wałęsa participated in the Founding Committee of the Free Labor Unions because he was convinced that the existing labor unions did not represent workers but were an instrument of the Party apparatus to direct the workers. He was also a member of the editorial board of *Robotnik Wybrzeża,* an organ of the labor unions. He actively participated in various demonstrations and rallies. Wałęsa was frequently arrested by the security forces and in 1976 he was fired from his job in the shipyard. At that time he was not widely known in the country.

From the moment when on August 14, 1980, he jumped the fence of the Lenin Shipyard and the next day organized the Strike Committee, which under his direction was transformed into Interfactory Strike Committee, he became a legendary figure. On behalf of the Committee, Wałęsa conducted talks with government representatives and forced the communists to sign the August Agreement with the workers. The agreement consisted of twenty-one points, the most important of which was the legalization of the creation of independent labor unions.

As the result of the August strikes Wałęsa became an unquestionable leader of the workers. Simple language, directness, a sense of humor, intuition, political instinct, tactical and improvisation skill, self-assurance, and manifested religious feelings made him a charismatic people's tribune, accepted by a wide range of society. He also assumed great authority in the Independent Labor Union, Solidarity, created in September 1980. Under his leadership Solidarity, with about ten million members, soon became the biggest popular movement in the history of Poland, thus creating a serious threat for the communist establishment. Wałęsa toured the country, mediated in talks between workers and the government, represented workers on various levels in meetings with, among others, General Wojciech Jaruzelski and Cardinal Sefan Wyszyński. Wałęsa pursued a moderate policy directed towards achieving agreements with the authorities. For instance, after the Bydgoszcz provocation of March 1981, when the police raided the Bydgoszcz prefecture and beat a Solidarity delegation seeking to register a rural branch of the independent labor union, he did not, despite pressure from many labor activists, call for a general strike out of concern that there was danger of a civil war. His internal position was secured during the Solidarity Congress of September–October 1981, when he was elected chairman of the National Committee of Solidarity.

As leader of Solidarity he became well known all over the world and was invited abroad by many labor unions and foreign politicians. He became, next to Pope John Paul II, one of the most popular Poles of the twentieth century, a symbol of hope and social, moral, and political revival. In 1981 it was suggested he receive the Nobel Prize. In 1983 he received it, during the period of martial law in Poland.

Wałęsa's agreement with the communists in 1981 did not work. Both internal pressure—provocation from the Party conservatives—and external pressure—from Party and military leaders in the USSR—was exerted against the developing peaceful takeover by the Solidarity elites. Wałęsa was imprisoned from December 1981 until November 1982. After his release he was removed from political and public life and treated by the authorities as a private citizen.

The Noble Prize strengthened Wałęsa's position in the circles of underground Solidarity. In 1986 he founded the Solidarity Provisional Council, which acted as the union's provisional government. In mid-1988 Wałęsa again led a strike in the Lenin Shipyard and in the fall of that year began negotiations with the representatives of the Polish government. This led to the Round Table negotiations of February 1989 and the agreement between the communists and the democratic opposition. After the victorious elections on June 4, 1989, Wałęsa played a deciding role in creating the coalition that forced creation of the first non-communist government in post-war Poland, led by Tadeusz Mazowiecki.

In April 1990, during the Second Solidarity Congress, Wałęsa was again elected the union's leader. He also announced his readiness to compete in the presidential elections. He was elected Polish president in December 1990 and thus began a new chapter in his political career. Though he resigned from his position in Solidarity, he remained faithful to his ideals of human rights and worker welfare.

Wałęsa's presidency was rather uneven. Alongside his unquestionable achievements, there were also failures. Most significantly, Wałęsa espoused populist slogans, an easy and rapid attainment of prosperity, the liquidation of corruption and unemployment, and bringing the former communist elite to account, but he failed to develop his own vision and strategy for political and, even more crucially, economic transformation. His conception of creating strong presidential rule was only partly successful, which resulted in frequent conflicts with prime ministers and their governments, and with the parliament. The state was destabilized by his dissolution of parliament in 1993, his forcing the collapse of the governments of Jan Olszewski and of Hanna Suchocka, frequent changes in his presidential staff, and his chaotic style of presidency. Wałęsa introduced ideas that were never put into effect and he exhibited indecision with regard to coalitions, governments, and politicians. Wałęsa also failed to organize his own political camp. He skillfully isolated his opponents, including the Solidarity elites, and gathered around himself mediocre and compliant politicians, thus isolating himself from various social groups. As a result, Wałęsa lost the respect of Polish society. Despite all of this, and his defeat in the 1995 presidential election to the former communist Aleksander Kwasniewski, Wałęsa remains one of the most important political figures of the end of twentieth century.

BIBLIOGRAPHY

Andrews, Nicolas G. *Poland 1980–1981: Solidarity versus the Party.* Washington: National Defence University Press, 1985.

Ash, Garton Timothy. *The Polish Revolution: Solidarity.* New York: Vintage Books, 1985.

Boyes, Roger. *The Naked President: A Political Life of Lech Walesa.* London: Martin Secker and Warburg Ltd., 1994.

Fringer, Robert. *Strike From Freedom: The Story of Lech Walesa and Polish Solidarity.* New York: Dodd, Mead, 1982.

Walesa, Lech. *Un chemin d'espoir.* Paris: Fayard, 1987.

Weschler, Lawrence. *The Passion of Poland: From Solidarity Through the State of War.* New York: Pantheon Books, 1984.

de Weydenthal, Jan B., Bruce D. Porter, and Kevin Delvin. *The Polish Drama 1980–1982.* London: D.C. Heath, 1983.

Ryszard Sudzińksi

SEE ALSO Poland

War Crimes Trials for the Former Yugoslavia

In the 1946 U.N. Convention of the Prevention and Punishment of the Crime of Genocide, genocide, an act intended to destroy a national group in whole or in part, was declared a crime. On October 6, 1992, the U.N. Security Council voted unanimously to create a commission to punish crimes of genocide and the violations of the Geneva Human Rights Convention in Bosnia. On May 25, 1993, the U.N. Security Council, in resolution 827, established the International Criminal Tribunal for the Former Yugoslavia (ICTY) at the Hague. Prisoners are kept in the nearby Scheveningen prison. In the November 1995 Dayton Accords Bosnian president Alija Izetbegović, Serbian president Slobodan Milošević, and Croatian president Franjo Tudjman agreed to cooperate with the tribunal inquiries. Though they were not required to arrest indicted war criminals, they agreed to allow access to witnesses and to suspected sites of war crimes. Though Croatia at first dragged its feet, it did eventually cooperate to a degree, something which cannot be said for Serbia.

In November 1995 General Mile Mrksic, Lieutenant Colonel Veselin Sljivancanin, and Captain Miroślav Radic were indicted. They were the first officers from the Yugoslav army to be charged with war crimes. They were accused of crimes committed during the fighting around Vukovar, Croatia, in 1992. Arrest warrants were forwarded to Belgrade on November 9, but the Yugoslav government did not respond. The peace agreement signed at Paris on December 14, 1995, required the parties to cooperate with the International War Crimes Tribunal at the Hague and asserted that the tribunal had the right of access to pertinent individuals and sites. Noncompliance, including the refusal to hand over those indicted as war criminals, could be answered according to the agreement with a reimposition of sanctions. Nevertheless, NATO forces in Bosnia were long reluctant to apprehend indicted individuals. U.S. Secretary of Defense William Perry and NATO spokespersons said that NATO peacekeepers would arrest indicted persons if they were encountered, but would not seek them out. Javier Solana, the NATO secretary-general, stated that the arrest of accused war criminals was the responsibility of local police. A strategy of mutual avoidance prevailed until July 1997 when the British, in a raid in Prijedor, captured one suspect and killed another. In December, Dutch soldiers captured two more, and in January 1998 Americans apprehended another.

The presiding judge, Antonio Cassese, threatened to disband the panel in 1995 rather than participate in "an exercise of hypocrisy." He, however, was replaced by a former Texas federal judge, Gabrielle Kirk McDonald. On October 1, 1996, Louise Arbour, Ontario Court of Appeals Judge, was appointed chief prosecutor. She brought order to the proceedings and recommended dropping the charges against a number of lower level figures who did not participate in "exceptionally brutal of otherwise extremely serious offenses." The first sentence, five years imprisonment, was handed down to Drazen Erdemovic, a Bosnian Croat, without a trial after he confessed to taking part in the 1995 Serb massacre of Muslims in Srebrenica. The first trial, that of the Bosnian Serb Dusan Tadic, a prison camp guard, resulted in his conviction in 1997 for killing and torturing Muslims in 1993. He was sentenced to twenty years in prison, but his lawyers are appealing.

By April 1998 indicted detainees numbered twenty-six. They included twelve Bosnian Croats, nine Bosnian Serbs, three Bosnian Moslems, one Croat, and one Croatian Serb. They are all accused of one or more offenses from the categories of genocide, crimes against humanity, violation of the laws and customs of war, and violations of the Geneva convention. Another forty-eight have been publicly indicted but not apprehended, including the Bosnian Serb leader Radovan Karadžić and the Bosnian Serb military leader Ratko Mladic. In addition to those seventy-four individuals, two suspects died, and three others were released. There is also a list of indicted individuals whose names have been kept secret in order, hopefully, to facilitate their apprehension.

In view of the blatant atrocities that were carried out by the Serbian forces during the 1999 Kosovo conflict, the U.N. International War Crimes Tribunal for the Former Yugoslavia indicted Milošević and four other Serbian leaders for war crimes on May 27, 1999. The arrest warrant issued by the court's chief prosecutor, Louise Arbour, was issued for war crimes dating back to January. Milošević was accused of responsibility for atrocities carried out by Serb forces, including rape and murder, and for ordering the ethnic cleansing of the province. Indicted along with Milošević were Milan Milutinović, the Serbian president, Nikola Sainović, a deputy premier of Serbia and an advisor of Milošević, Vlajko Stojiljković, the Serbian minister of interior, and Dragoljub Ojdanic, head of the Yugoslav army.

BIBLIOGRAPHY

Honig, Jan Willem, and Norbert Both. *Srebrenica: Record of a War Crime.* New York: Penguin, 1996.

Perlez, Jane. "In Montenegro, an Indicted Soldier is Still a Hero." *New York Times,* January 5, 1996, A3.

———. "NATO Backs Off Helping Bosnia War Crimes Panel." *New York Times,* January 20, 1996, A5.

Trueheart, Charles. "War Crimes Tribunal Gathers Momentum." *Washington Post,* March 3, 1998.

"War Crimes Tribunal Detainees' List Now Stands at 26." *Agence France Presse,* April 9, 1998.

Bernard Cook

Warsaw Pact

The Eastern bloc "Agreement on Friendship, Coordination, and Mutual Assistance" signed in Warsaw, Poland, on May 14, 1955. The original members of the Warsaw Pact were the Soviet Union, Albania, Bulgaria, Czechoslovakia, the German Democratic Republic, Hungary, Poland, and Rumania. Although the formal signing of the treaty came as a reaction to the admission of the Federal Republic of Germany into NATO on May 5, 1955, the signatory states had announced their intention to form the Eastern bloc military alliance as early as the fall of 1954. The Warsaw Pact was a typical subordinate alliance system with all real power and authority firmly within the hands of the Soviet Union.

The Warsaw Pact had two main functions. On the one hand, it was a military alliance directed outside the Eastern bloc countries, and for thirty-five years its formidable specter haunted NATO and Western Europe. On the other hand, it was an internal security instrument, designed to help the Soviets maintain their hegemony over their Eastern European satellites. Throughout its history the military forces of the Warsaw Pact were operationally deployed only twice; both times in support of the latter function. In 1956 the Warsaw Pact crushed Hungary's attempt to secede from the alliance; and in 1968 it invaded Czechoslovakia to stem the tide of liberalism that was then sweeping the country. In reaction to the Czech invasion, Albania, whose membership had been "inactive" since February 1, 1962, formally withdrew from the Warsaw Pact on September 13, 1968.

The highest formal organ of the alliance was the Political Consultative Committee, composed of the various communist party first secretaries, premiers, and defense ministers. In 1969 the defense ministers were replaced by the foreign ministers. Although the Political Consultative Committee was supposed to have managerial authority over the entire Warsaw Pact on cultural, political, and economic issues, it in fact was little more than a figurehead organ. It had no say, for example, in the decision to invade Czechoslovakia.

The Political Consultative Committee had two principal working groups: the Permanent Commission, and the Combined Secretariat. The Permanent Commission was responsible for formulating foreign policy proposals. The Combined Secretariat, which exercised absolute authority over logistics, armaments, and armaments research, was the de facto executive organ of the Warsaw Pact. The general secretary was always a Soviet general or a senior Soviet Foreign Ministry official. The seat of both bodies was in Moscow.

The highest military organ was the Committee of Defense Ministers, which was formed in 1969 when the foreign ministers replaced the defense ministers on the Political Consultative Committee. Each defense minister served as the commander of his respective national military forces and also as a titular deputy commander-in-chief of the military forces of the Warsaw Pact. The chief of the Council of Defense Ministers was always the Soviet defense minister, and the seat of that committee too was located in Moscow.

The Supreme Command of the Combined Forces of the Warsaw Pact was established in 1956. The combined staff was located in Moscow until 1971, when it was relocated to the Ukrainian city of Lvov. In 1969 a Military Council consisting of all member states was established to advise the commander on matters of planning and operational control. The supreme commander was always a Soviet marshal, who also was a first deputy minister of defense of the Soviet Union. The chief of staff was also always a Soviet general, who held the position as well of a first deputy chief of the Soviet General Staff. The first supreme commander of the Warsaw Pact forces was Marshal Ivan S. Konev, who commanded the 2nd Ukrainian Front in World War II.

At its high water mark Warsaw Pact forces had a combined strength of over five million, with ready access to a reserve pool of ten million. In 1986 the bulk of these forces were deployed in two primary theaters of operations (Teatr Voennykh Deistvii, abbreviated TVDs). The Western TVD consisted of the national forces of East Germany, Poland, Czechoslovakia, the Soviet Northern Group of Forces in Poland, the Group of Soviet Forces in Germany, the Soviet Central Group of Forces in Czechoslovakia, and the Soviet forces stationed in the western military districts of the Soviet Union. The combined strength of these forces totaled 94 divisions, 29,260 tanks, 32,000 armored personnel carriers, 20,800 artillery pieces, and 3,920 tactical aircraft.

The Southwestern TVD consisted of the national forces of Hungary, Rumania, Bulgaria, the Soviet Southern Group of Forces in Hungary, and Soviet forces in the southwest Soviet Union. They had a combined strength of 51 divisions, 12,150 tanks, 10,800 armored personnel carriers, 9,750 artillery pieces, and 1,660 tactical aircraft.

Throughout the period of the Cold War, the issue of the reliability of the non-Soviet Warsaw Pact forces was a major question for Soviet and NATO military planners alike. Western intelligence agencies generally agreed that in any attack against NATO, the East Germans would be the most reliable. The Poles, on the other hand, were expected to be the least reliable, and might even turn on their erstwhile socialist allies if given the opportunity.

When communism collapsed in Eastern Europe and the Soviet Union, the Warsaw Pact went with it. On February 25, 1991, the members of the alliance agreed at a meeting in Budapest that the Warsaw Pact would be abolished on March 31, 1991. The original intention was to keep the political organs of the alliance alive, but that dimension of the Warsaw Pact also collapsed on July 1, 1991. Even by early 1990 a U.S. Defense Department publication had concluded, "The immediate threat of a Soviet/Warsaw Pact multipronged armored thrust that pushes NATO into the Atlantic is nearly gone."

BIBLIOGRAPHY

Lewis, William J. *The Warsaw Pact: Arms, Doctrine, and Strategy.* Cambridge, Mass.: Institute for Foreign Policy Analysis, 1983.

Michta, Andrew. *East Central Europe After the Warsaw Pact: Security Dilemmas in the 1990s.* New York: Greenwood, 1992.

Simon, Jeffrey. *Warsaw Pact Forces: Problems of Command and Control.* Boulder, Col.: Westview, 1985.

Wiener, Frederich. *The Armies of the Warsaw Pact Nations: Organization, Concept of War, Weapons, and Equipment.* Vienna: C. Veberreuter, 1981.

David T. Zabecki

Warsaw Pact (seen from Eastern Europe)

A pact crowning numerous bilateral agreements of friendship, mutual aid, and cooperation, signed after World War II between the USSR and its satellite states. Creation of the pact was officially justified by the need to enlarge the military potential of the central European states against the allegedly aggressive policy of the imperialist countries led by the U.S. The direct cause, according to the official propaganda, was admission of West Germany to NATO on May 5, 1955.

The founding conference in Warsaw (May 11–14, 1955) was called the "conference of European countries on securing peace and security in Europe." The member states committed themselves to the alliance for twenty years (in 1975 in was prolonged for another ten years, and in 1985 for another twenty). The pact imposed an obligation on the member states to consult concerning international issues of common interest, especially in the case of the "threat of military intervention against one or several member states" (article 3). If a member state was attacked, all other member states were to help, including the use of military power (article 4). All parties in the pact agreed not to participate in any coalitions or alliances that could potentially threaten other members (article 7).

The member states' troops were under the command of the Unified Command of Pact Armed Forces (article 5). Succeeding commanders-in-chief were Soviet marshals: Koniev, Grechko, Yakubovski, and Kulikov. All other key posts were staffed with Soviet military. In such a way, instead of Soviet "advisors" stationed with the satellite armies, a formal structure of control was established.

The Political Consultative Committee (PCC) was created to coordinate all activities, with the exception of purely military matters (article 6). It was staffed by first secretaries of communist parties, premiers, ministers of foreign affairs and ministers of defense. A commander-in-chief also participated in the Committee's sessions. The PCC was to assemble at least twice yearly. In reality, it assembled less frequently, but it became the main vehicle for unifying the foreign policy of the member states and for interfering in their internal affairs.

The functioning of the pact was "perfected" during the PCC's meeting in Budapest in March 1969. The Committee of Defense Ministers, to evaluate military readiness of the allied armies, and the Military Council, to coordinate training of the armies, were founded there.

According to article 11 of the treaty, if a common security system in Europe was created and NATO dissolved, the Warsaw Pact would cease to exist. In practice, the Soviets used the pact for their imperialistic aims and to strengthen their influence in the satellite countries. For instance, a December 1956 agreement between Poland and the USSR allowed for the continuing presence of the Soviet army in Poland. In the fall of 1956 the Red Army, having previously threatened Poland, brutally suppressed the Hungarian revolution and in August 1968 the Pact armies (except for Albania's and Romania's) took part in the invasion of Czechoslovakia. At that time Leonid Brezhnev formulated his doctrine of the limited sovereignty of socialist countries. The pact's military exercises conducted in 1980 and 1981 were one of the main ways of pressuring Polish authorities to dispose of Solidarity. Pact members in Moscow, on December 5, 1980, stated that "socialist Poland, the Polish United Workers' Party and Polish nation can rely on brotherly solidarity and support of the member states." This made intervention in Poland quite probable. However, when Wojciech Jaruzelski imposed martial law this became unnecessary.

The political and military importance of the pact, as well as its confrontational policy toward NATO, lessened in the early 1980s. It could not keep pace with Reagan's military build-up and "star wars." The peace offensive undertaken by Gorbachev in 1986 led to demilitarization agreements in 1987 and 1989, and in 1990. This was followed by a declaration of the end of hostility towards NATO. Perestroika in the USSR and opposition success in parliamentary elections, as well as the "Fall of the Nations" (1989) in Central Europe, the withdrawal of East Germany from the pact, and the withdrawal of Soviet troops from the region, fundamentally undermined the pact. When Soviet attempts to transfer the pact into a body for political consultation failed, the pact was dissolved on March 31, 1991.

BIBLIOGRAPHY

Grzybowski, Konstanty. *The Socialist Commonwealth: Organizations and Institutions.* New Haven, Conn.: Yale University, 1964.

Ross, Johnson A., Robert W. Dean, and Alexander Alexiev. *East European Military Establishments: The Warsaw Pact Northern Tier.* Santa Monica, Cal.: Rand Corporation, 1980.

Ryszard Sudziński

Wartime Conferences

The wartime meetings of leaders of the major powers set the territorial boundaries of postwar Europe. In many cases decisions designed to be tentative, pending postwar peace conferences, turned out to be long lasting, and as the war progressed options narrowed.

The first formulation of peace aims came in the Atlantic Charter of August 14, 1941, issued after talks between U.S. President Franklin Roosevelt and British Prime Minister Winston Churchill aboard ship off the coast of Newfoundland. Speaking for their two countries, the leaders eschewed any territorial aggrandizement and agreed to support the principle of self-determination of peoples. They also pledged to work for world economic prosperity and freedom from "fear and want," and to seek disarmament and international security. Churchill hoped for a statement about an international peacekeeping organization but Roosevelt, mindful of U.S. isolationist sentiment, balked. Moscow later announced its support for the Charter's principles.

Even this early in the war, however, there were differences between the Anglo-Saxon powers and the USSR. British Foreign Secretary Anthony Eden reported from Moscow that the Kremlin wanted the German Reich dismembered, to retain Finnish territory, and to incorporate the Baltic states and Bessarabia. Stalin also insisted on the Curzon Line, the boundary drawn by an Allied commission in 1920, as the western boundary for the Soviet Union. This would enable the USSR to incorporate its 1939 gains at the expense of Poland.

On December 7, 1941, the United States entered the war. Churchill arrived in Washington on the 21st and spent several weeks meeting with American leaders, in the course of which the two powers established an extraordinarily close working relationship, which included a Combined Chiefs of Staff Committee. The two leaders agreed that Germany was the more formidable military opponent and that it should receive priority over Japan.

On January 1, 1942, representatives of twenty-six nations signed the United Nations declaration by which they pledged to support the principles of the Atlantic Charter and not to sign a separate peace or armistice until the Axis powers were defeated.

In the winter of 1942–43 the tide of war turned. During January 14–24, 1943, following successful Allied landings in North Africa and the breakout of the Eighth Army at El Alamein, Roosevelt, Churchill, and the Combined Chiefs of Staff met at Casablanca, Morocco. Stalin was invited but declined to attend. The main topic of discussion was strategic military planning once North Africa had been cleared of Axis troops. The British, better prepared than the Americans, made a strong case for invasions of Sicily and then Italy, and the Americans reluctantly acceded.

But the Casablanca Conference is chiefly remembered for Roosevelt's surprise announcement that the Allies would insist on "unconditional surrender." Churchill, who had not been informed ahead of time that the announcement would be made, nonetheless immediately supported it. It is the view of some military historians that this decision needlessly prolonged the war by preventing negotiations with the German resistance to Hitler that might have led them to topple his regime. Certainly the declaration was a windfall for the German propaganda machine. In making the announcement Roosevelt wished to reassure Stalin, but he also had in mind World War I and the way the German Right had utilized the November 1918 armistice to spread the myth that Germany had not been defeated militarily.

Another aspect of the Casablanca Conference concerned relations with the French. General Charles de Gaulle, leader of the Free French, was not informed of the meeting beforehand; Churchill simply ordered him to Morocco, still a French protectorate. Roosevelt and Churchill pushed de Gaulle into a partnership with General Henri Giraud, who had been spirited out of Vichy France to Algeria by submarine. De Gaulle was eventually able to elbow the politically inept and equally stubborn Giraud into the shadows, but the whole affair affected de Gaulle's attitude toward the Anglo-Saxon powers. He was already upset by the British undermining of the French position in Syria and Lebanon.

In August 1943 Roosevelt, Churchill, and their military staffs met at Quebec. The principal topic of discussion there was planning for the cross-Channel invasion of France, now codenamed "Overlord" and projected for May 1, 1944. Churchill would continue to argue, almost up to the eve of Overlord, for concentration on the Balkans. But U.S. military chiefs were strongly opposed to this and reminded their ally that the invasions of Sicily and Italy had been carried out on the promise that the next objective would be the cross-Channel invasion.

Stalin notified the Western leaders that he was interested in further talks, and in October 1943 U.S. Secretary of State Cordell Hull and British Foreign Secretary Anthony Eden traveled to Moscow to meet with Foreign Minister Vyacheslav Molotov and Stalin. This meeting was intended to pave the way for a meeting of the three heads of state. Although this conference is usually overlooked, a number of important decisions were taken there, and it deserves to rank in importance with the Teheran, Yalta, and Potsdam conferences.

At Moscow the three foreign ministers decided that Austria was the first "victim of Hitlerite aggression." This allowed its restoration to full independence. They also called for the complete destruction of fascism in Italy and encouraged the Italians to set up a new government. And they set up the European Advisory Commission to meet in London and work out plans for the subsequent occupation of Germany and Austria. A similar group was set up for Italy. The Allies also issued a specific warning that "crimes against humanity" would be punished and that the guilty would be pursued "to the uttermost ends of the earth."

At Moscow the three governments also reiterated their pledge not to sign a separate peace, and they agreed to consult with one another on issues of peace and security until the establishment of an organization to handle these. With Nationalist Chinese leader Generalissimo Chiang Kai-shek threatening to sign a separate peace in order to extract more aid from the U.S., a representative of China was also induced to sign the document, which became known as the Declaration of Four Nations on General Security. Finally, Stalin assured Hull that the USSR would declare war on Japan after Germany had been defeated.

Also in November 1943 Roosevelt and Churchill, on their way to meet with Stalin at Teheran, stopped off in Cairo to see Chiang Kai-shek. Although Churchill had his doubts, Roosevelt hoped to see China as a fourth great power after the war. At Cairo all three leaders restated their determination to fight on until the war was won. They also decided that after the war Japan would be reduced to her home islands. China would regain Manchuria, the Pescadores Islands, and Formosa. Korea would also, "in due course," be restored to independence. The mandated Japanese islands would in all probability pass to U.S. control and it was implied that the USSR would regain South Sakhalin Island (lost in the Russo-Japanese War) and secure the Kuriles (which had never been Russian). Stalin also pressed for a warm water port for the Soviet Union, probably at Dairen.

From November 28 to December 1, 1943, one of the major wartime conferences took place at Teheran. It was the first time that Stalin and Roosevelt had met, and the American president, convinced that Stalin was "getatable," turned on all his formidable charm to try to win Stalin's confidence. Toward this end at Teheran and Yalta Roosevelt deliberately distanced himself from Churchill. The British prime minister could not believe that the democracies would take separate paths. Stalin did not have to travel far to attend the conference, but it was his first trip abroad since 1912.

At Teheran the Western leaders labored under disadvantages. The first was the strategic situation. British and U.S. troops were fighting the Germans on the ground only in Italy with fourteen divisions; the Soviet Union had 178 divisions in combat. If the Teheran Conference marked the beginning of the Soviet empire, it also reflected the reality of forces on the ground. There was also fear that the USSR and Germany might yet seek diplomatic accommodation, and Roosevelt wanted to secure Soviet assistance in the war against Japan.

At Teheran Stalin pressured the West on Overlord. The Soviet ambassador to the U.S., Ivan Maisky, had counseled Stalin to press for an immediate second front, which Stalin knew was impossible, in order to secure more Lend Lease assistance. Stalin insisted on learning the name of its commander as proof that the Western allies were indeed serious about Overlord, and shortly after the conference Roosevelt named General Dwight Eisenhower to the post.

At Teheran there was much discussion on Germany and its possible future division. Roosevelt suggested splitting Germany into five states and internationalizing the Ruhr and other areas. Churchill, worried about possible Soviet expansion into Europe, thought that Prussia might be detached from the rest of Germany. Discussions over Poland were more controversial. All three leaders agreed on the Oder River as the future boundary of Poland with Germany. There was, however, no agreement by the West for a tributary of the Oder, the Western Neisee River, as the southern demarcation line. Nor did the West sanction Poland securing the important port of Stettin on the west bank of the Oder. The three did agree that Poland would get most of East Prussia, although the Soviet Union claimed the Baltic port of Königsberg and land to the northeast. There was no major opposition by Western leaders to the Curzon Line as the eastern boundary of Poland. The British did object, however, to the Russian seizure of the predominantly Polish city of Lvov.

Churchill pointed out to Stalin that Britain had gone to war over Poland, but Stalin insisted that the Red Army needed security and that a primary goal of the war was Russian security against a future German attack. Obviously a Poland that would be compensated for the loss of eastern territory to the USSR by being given German territory in the west would necessarily have to look to the USSR for security. Churchill had the difficult task of trying to sell all these arrangements to the Polish government-in-exile in London. This exile government was adamantly opposed to moving its eastern frontier back to the Curzon Line. The Russians, however, had already broken diplomatic relations with the Polish government-in-exile when it requested an investigation of German revelations of a massacre of Polish officers by Russians in the Katyn forest and were preparing to recognize their own committee of Communist Poles as the new provisional government when the Germans were driven from the country.

Stalin also demanded that the USSR be allowed to keep its 1939–40 acquisitions of Bessarabia, the Karelian Isthmus, and the Baltic states. Although these were clear violations of the Atlantic Charter, the siege of Leningrad gave Stalin a strong argument for a security zone there. Stalin also demanded that Finland cede its arctic port of Petsamo, pay heavy reparations, and provide space for a base to protect sea approaches to Leningrad. In return he promised to respect Finnish independence, if that country conducted itself in accord with Russian interests. Stalin reassured Roosevelt that the USSR would enter the war against Japan after the defeat of Germany. The three leaders also agreed that after the war Iran, which was serving as a supply corridor to the USSR and occupied by Allied troops, would be restored to full territorial integrity and sovereignty and all troops would be withdrawn.

In September 1944 Roosevelt and Churchill met again at Quebec. Stalin was invited but declined on the basis of war responsibilities. The conference was primarily devoted to war plans against Japan. The one important development regarding Europe was the vengeful and ill-advised Morganthau Plan. Developed by U.S. Secretary of the Treasury Henry Morganthau, it envisioned turning Germany into an agricultural state. Wisely, the plan was ultimately scrapped.

In October 1944, as the Red Armies steadily pushed the Germans west, Churchill flew to Moscow to meet with Stalin. The high point in their talks was an agreement suggested by Churchill, and approved by Stalin without dissent, over spheres of influence in East Europe: Russia was assigned 90 percent influence in Romania and 75 percent influence in Bulgaria; Britain with the U.S., were assigned 90 percent influence in Greece; Yugoslavia and Hungary were to be split equally. Agreement was also reached on Austrian occupation zones. Churchill, fearful of a Russian dominated Eastern Europe, wished at least to keep Greece in the Western Camp in order to safeguard British lines of communication in the Mediterranean.

Poland proved more difficult. Stanislaw Mikolajczyk from the Polish government-in-exile came to Moscow to confer with Stalin. The Soviet dictator insisted that a majority of any Polish government come from the Russian-sponsored Union of Polish Patriots, the Lublin Committee. Mikolajczyk was prepared to compromise but his government in London was not. Unable to persuade his colleagues, Mikolajczyk resigned at the end of November. Demanding all or nothing, in the end the London Poles got nothing.

Meanwhile, the European Advisory Commission on Germany had begun meeting in London in January 1944. It decided that Germany's post-war government would be an Allied Control Council in Berlin composed of commanders of the occupying forces of the victorious powers. It still needed clarification from the Big Three on other matters. From August 21 to October 10, 1944, delegates at Dunbarton Oaks in Washington had also been at work drafting proposals for a United Nations international organization. They too needed resolution of a number of issues.

This second and last meeting of Churchill, Roosevelt, and Stalin took place from February 4–11, 1945, at Yalta in the Crimea. Yalta is the most controversial of all World War II conferences, but it certainly decided far less than what it is usually credited or blamed for. It should also be noted that at the time there was much satisfaction with its outcome. It was only with the Cold War and the realization that Russian help had not been necessary in the Pacific war that Yalta became such a fractious issue in U.S. politics, with Republicans charging a Democratic "give-away" to the Communists.

The bargaining position of the Western leaders had not appreciably improved since the Teheran Conference. Indeed, they had just suffered a humiliating rebuff by the Germans in the Battle of the Bulge. The Red Army, on the other hand, was just fifty miles from Berlin. Another factor at Yalta was Roosevelt's determination to draw Stalin "out of his shell" and bring the Soviet Union into postwar cooperation. As a result he went out of his way to accommodate the Soviet leader. It did not help the Western bargaining position for Roosevelt to announce that U.S. troops were unlikely to remain long in Europe. He also continued the practice of distancing himself from Churchill, most evident in colonial issues. Another factor at work was that Roosevelt and the Americans had waged the war to bring it to the speediest possible conclusion with the least expenditure of American lives.

In contrast, Stalin knew exactly what he wanted. After the First World War the Western Allies had sought to construct a cordon sanitaire against Bolshevism. Stalin's goal was the reverse. He wanted a belt of East European satellite states to keep the West out. This was to provide security against another German invasion but also to protect a severely wounded Soviet Union (over 20 million dead and terrible material losses) against the West and its influences.

Roosevelt secured Soviet agreement to the Declaration on Liberated Europe. The leaders pledged that the provisional governments of liberated areas would be "representative of all democratic elements" and that there would be "free elections . . . responsive to the will of the people." But such lofty phrases were subject to different interpretations.

In discussions regarding Germany, the Big Three agreed to government by an Allied Control Council. German occupation zones were also set and France was allowed a zone, although Stalin insisted it be carved from territory already assigned to Britain and the United States. The three leaders also agreed on steps to demilitarize Germany, dissolve the National Socialist party, and punish war criminals.

The Russians also insisted on heavy reparations. The Western Allies, remembering the trouble caused by reparations after World War I and fearful they would be subsidizing Soviet exactions, balked at setting a specific amount but they did agree to use a figure of $20 billion as basis for discussion. The Soviet Union was to receive half of any reparations.

Particularly important to Roosevelt was the establishment of a postwar United Nations organization. Well aware of this and not much interested in the proposed organization himself, Stalin used it to gain concessions elsewhere. The Big Three adopted recommendations from the Dunbarton Oaks conference that the U.N. have a General Assembly, Security Council, and Secretariat. It also set the composition of the Security Council. The Russians insisted on veto power for members of the Security Council. This became an issue later when the USSR exercised it so liberally, but the U.S. Senate would not have approved American participation without it.

Poland was a particularly vexing matter for the two Western leaders but Stalin held all the cards: the Red Army already occupied the country. Regarding boundaries, Stalin demanded and won the Curzon Line, with slight modifications, as Poland's eastern border. The Allies were more strenuous in objecting to the Oder-Neisse line as Poland's western boundary and there was no definitive agreement on this matter at Yalta. Regarding the Polish government, Moscow had, only a month before Yalta, recognized the Lublin Committee as the official government of Poland. Stalin agreed to broaden this puppet government on a "democratic basis," and he pledged to hold "free and unfettered elections as soon as possible on the basis of universal suffrage and secret ballot." The Western Allies secured the same concessions for Yugoslavia, Romania, and Bulgaria.

The most controversial actions taken at Yalta concerned the Far East. Stalin had already made it clear that the USSR would enter the war against Japan sometime after the defeat of Germany; this was in fact never in doubt. The problem was in the timing; here Stalin was in the same position enjoyed by the Allies before Overlord. Late Russian entry into the Pacific war might mean horrendous U.S. casualties and American military planners had in fact forecast a million U.S. casualties in an invasion of the Japanese home islands. No one knew whether the atomic bomb would work, and, even if it did, whether it would be decisive in bringing about Japan's defeat.

In return for a Soviet pledge to enter the war against Japan "two or three months" after the defeat of Germany, Russia was to receive south Sakhalin Island, concessions in the port of Dairen, the return of Port Arthur as a naval base, control over railroads leading to these ports, and the Kurile Islands (which had never been Russian). Outer Mongolia would continue to be independent of China, but China would regain sovereignty over Manchuria.

In effect these concessions sanctioned the replacement of Japanese imperialism with that of Russia, but the Western leaders thought they were necessary to secure a timely entry of the USSR into the Pacific War. What bothered Americans most about Yalta in future years was that these concessions need not have been made.

The final wartime conference was held from July 17 to August 2, 1945, at Potsdam, near Berlin. Its codename, "Terminal," signalled both the end of the war and the wartime alliance. Roosevelt had died in April 1945 and President Harry S. Truman represented the United States. He was assisted by Secretary of States James F. Byrnes. Results of British elections were announced in the midst of the conference and, in one of the most stunning upsets in British electoral history, the Conservatives were ousted. Churchill was replaced by Labor party leader Clement Attlee and Foreign Minister Ernest Bevin. No elections disturbed the Soviet delegation.

At Potsdam there were sharp disagreements over many issues. German reparations was one. Stalin held out for a firm figure whereas Truman would agree only to the USSR receiving a set percentage of a whole to be determined on the German capacity to pay. The American delegation also disagreed with the Russians over their very loose interpretation of "war booty," goods that could be confiscated without reference to reparations. Agreement was reached that the Russians would receive 25 percent of plants and industrial equipment removed from the Western zones. In return, the Soviets were to transfer the equivalent of 15 percent of the total 25 percent in food and raw materials from their zone. The Soviets also got permission to seize German assets in Bulgaria, Hungary, Finland, Romania, and their zone of Austria. No agreement on reparations was ever reached but it is estimated that the Russians probably took about $20 billion (the total sum discussed at Yalta) from their zone of Germany alone.

The Allies also reached agreement on the "three D's": democratization, denazification, and demilitarization; and German industrial production was set at a level no higher than the average for Europe as a whole. No peace treaty was signed between the Allies and Germany and so further "temporary" arrangements sanctioned by Potsdam became permanent. East Prussia was divided according to agreements at Teheran. Königsberg, Memel, and northern East Prussia were appropriated by the USSR, and the remainder of East Prussia went to Poland. The "orderly and humane" transfer of the German population from this region, agreed to at Potsdam, did not occur. Perhaps 2 million Germans lost their lives in the forced reparations and exodus that followed.

Agreement was reached at Potsdam over the surrender of Japanese forces in Korea. The Russians were to be responsible for their surrender north of the 38th parallel and the Americans south of that line. Never intended as a political boundary, it too became bound up in the Cold War.

Finally, the leaders at Potsdam set up a Council of Foreign Ministers to plan the preparation of peace treaties. Their discussions produced increasingly bitter exchanges that reflected the start of the Cold War.

BIBLIOGRAPHY

Byrnes, James F. *Speaking Frankly.* New York: Harper and Brothers, 1947.

Feis, Herbert. *Between War and Peace: the Potsdam Conference.* Princeton, N.J.: Princeton University Press, 1957.

———. *Churchill–Roosevelt–Stalin: the War They Waged and the Peace They Sought.* Princeton, N.J.: Princeton University Press, 1957.

Fischer, Louis. *The Road to Yalta, Soviet Relations, 1941–1945.* New York: Harper and Row, 1972.

Fontaine, Andre. *History of the Cold War, 1917–1966.* 2 vols. New York: Pantheon, 1968.

Mastny, Vojtech. *Russia's Road to the Cold War: Diplomacy, Warfare, and the Politics of Communism, 1941–1945.* New York: Columbia University Press, 1979.

Snell, John L. *Illusion and Necessity: The Diplomacy of Global War, 1939–1945.* Boston: Houghton Mifflin, 1963.

———. *The Meaning of Yalta: Big Three Diplomacy and the New Balance of Power.* Baton Rouge, La.: Louisiana State University Press, 1956.

Stettinius, Edward R., Jr. *Roosevelt and the Russians: The Yalta Conference.* Edited by Walter Johnson. New York: Harold Ober Associates, 1949.

Szaz, Zoltan Michael. *Germany's Eastern Frontiers. The Problem of the Oder-Neisse Line.* Chicago: Henry Regnery, 1960.

Thomas, Hugh. *Armed Truce. The Beginnings of the Cold War, 1945–1946.* New York: Atheneum, 1987.

Spencer C. Tucker

SEE ALSO Germany; Poland; Sikorski, Władysław E.

Wehner, Herbert (1906–90)

Influential Social Democratic member of the Bundestag of the Federal Republic of Germany, 1949–83. Herbert Wehner, the son of a cobbler and a seamstress, was born on July 11, 1906, in Dresden. He attended the Realschule in Dresden and intended to be a salesman, but instability in the Weimar Republic shifted Wehner's attention to politics.

Wehner joined the Young Christian Workers Association, and was a member until 1923. Three years later he became an active participant in the Radical Workers Syndicalist Federation. In 1927 he became a member of the German Communist Party (KPD), and was editor of the journal, *Fanal.* Wehner built a reputation as a skilled organizer and gifted public speaker. As a Communist, Wehner's work was directed against the German Social Democratic Party (SPD).

When the Nazis took power in 1933, the Communist International sent Wehner to Prague and then to Moscow. There he devoted himself to coordinating resistance in Germany. In 1941 he was sent to Stockholm, where he was instructed to establish a network of agents. A year later Wehner was arrested by the Swedish security police and sentenced to prison for espionage.

In 1945 Wehner returned to Germany and renounced Communism. Despite lingering suspicions about his former Communist connections, the SPD admitted him to membership. Wehner was elected to the Bundestag in 1949 and quickly became a member of the All-German Committee. In 1952 he was elected to the party executive where he formed an alliance with Willy Brandt and worked to bring the SPD to power over the rival Christian Democratic Union (CDU). During this period Wehner devoted his energies to forging a connection (with the goal of unification) between the Federal Republic of Germany and the German Democratic Republic. During the Grand Coalition, 1966–69, he served as Minister for All-German Questions.

After Brandt became Chancellor of West Germany in 1969, Wehner became the party leader in the Bundestag. In the May 1974 Günther Guillaume spy scandal, when a member of Brandt's staff was found to be an East German spy, Wehner advised Brandt to resign to save the party's credibility. In 1994 Greta Wehner, whom Wehner married in 1983, and Brigitte Seebacher-Brandt revived an old argument about the nature of Wehner's former communist connections with the possibility that he had participated in a plot to undermine Brandt. KGB documents, released in January 1994, showed that Wehner had been critical of Communist party members and contained no evidence that Wehner had conspired against Brandt.

Wehner retired from politics after the 1983 elections, which confirmed the CDU's hold on power. After the end of his political career, Wehner lived in seclusion in Oeland, Sweden. He died on January 19, 1990, at Bad Godesberg near Bonn.

BIBLIOGRAPHY

Scholz, Günther. *Herbert Wehner.* Düsseldorf, Germany: Econ, 1986.

Thompson, Wayne C. *The Political Odyssey of Herbert Wehner.* Boulder, Col.: Westview, 1993.

Wehner, Herbert. *Wandel und Bewährung. Ausgewählte Reden und Schriften, 1930–1967.* Berlin: Hannover, 1968.

Quinn Sebesta

Weiss, Peter

Slovak politician and leader of the Party of the Democratic Left (PDL), which was the successor in 1991 to the former Communist Party of Slovakia. A prominent member of the communist nomenklatura in the former Czechoslovakia, Peter Weiss was a founding member of the PDL and its first leader. Claiming to be a social democratic party, the PDL was the second most successful party in the Slovak parliamentary elections of June 1992, when the Movement for a Democratic Slovakia (MDS) led by Vladimir Mečiar emerged as the single largest party in the Slovak National Council (SNC). Appointed a deputy speaker of the SNC, Weiss was an important opposition leader, implacably opposed to Mečiar and supportive of President Michal Kováč in his long-running feud with the Slovak Premier. From March to December 1994, when Mečiar was out of power, Weiss and the PDL briefly participated in a short-lived coalition government led by Jozef Moravčik. With the return to power of Mečiar's MDS, Weiss remained the leader of the single largest opposition bloc in the SNC and hence the greatest potential threat to the ruling party in Slovakia.

Marko Milivojevic

Weizsäcker, Richard von (1920–)

President of the Federal Republic of Germany (1984–94). Richard von Weizsäcker was born at Stuttgart on April 15, 1920. His father, Baron Ernst von Weizsäcker, was a diplomat. Von Weizsäcker studied at the universities of Oxford and Grenoble. After service in the German army in World War II, he received his law degree from the University of Göttingen in 1954.

Von Weizsäcker, a deeply committed Christian, served as president of the Evangelical Church Convention from 1964 to 1970, and as a member of the Synod and Council of the German Evangelical Church from 1969 to 1984.

In 1954 he joined the Christian Democratic Union and in 1966 he was elected to its national executive council. He was a member of the Bundestag from 1969 to 1981. From 1973 to 1979 he was deputy chairman of the Christian Democratic Union/Christian Social Union Parliamentary Party, and from 1979 to 1981 Vice-President of the Bundestag. In 1981 he became governing mayor of Berlin, a post he held until he was elected President of the Federal Republic of Germany in July 1984. In 1989 he was re-elected for a second term.

Von Weizsäcker was not content to be a ceremonial figurehead. He utilized his position to speak out on contemporary problems and became a voice of conscience to Germany. He forthrightly addressed the problems associated with German reunification. "Freedom," he said, "is not a gift from which we can live cheaply. Freedom is an opportunity and a responsibility." He accordingly advocated that all Germans share the burdens connected with the economic integration of the east into the Federal Republic. He also unequivocally repudiated racism. He took part in the demonstration against racist terrorism at Solligen following the murder of three Turks by a firebomber in 1993.

Von Weizsäcker advocated European unity and called for the extension of European institutions to the east. He gave his complete support to the Maastricht agreement, but stated that economic and monetary union should be regarded as a step in the process of European integration rather than the completion of the process. He favored the integration of Europe's economic and social systems and eventual political union. He also hoped for the eventual extension of this political union to the east, so that a united Europe could then devote its effort toward the global challenges facing humanity.

BIBLIOGRAPHY

Weizsäcker, Richard von. *Die deutsche Geschichte geht weiter.* Berlin: Siedler, 1983.

———. *Die politische Kraft der Kultur.* Reinbeck bei Hamburg: Rowohlt, 1987.

———. *Von Deutschland aus.* Berlin: Seidler, 1985.

———. *Von Deutschland nach Europa.* Berlin: Seidler, 1991.

Bernard Cook

Welfare State in Europe

Europe is the home of the welfare state. One of the hallmarks of European societies is that they guarantee their citizens freedom from want. Many even go further, promising income security and a relatively constant standard of living over the course of life. The typical Western European nation state, either on its own or in association with organizations representing workers and employers, offers a comprehensive set of social security programs, as well as access to a network of social services. Over time, the nature and level of employment as well as the definition of what constitutes family and private social relations have come more and more to be influenced by welfare state and other public policies. It is no exaggeration to say, therefore, that in the late twentieth century what it means to be a woman or a man, married or single, young or old, in Europe is crucially influenced by the welfare state.

The most minimal undertaking of European welfare states is the prevention of poverty. To achieve this, safety net programs have long been a feature of the West European social model. Such programs usually provide an income floor below which no one is expected to fall. But the European citizen's guarantee extends considerably beyond the avoidance of poverty. Certain risks of income loss have been rendered social risks. Should people experience unemployment, illness, accidents at work, pregnancy, widowhood, old age, they have the security of knowing that they will continue to receive income from either the social insurance funds or the state.

Although financed differently, sometimes paid for through direct contributions, while in other cases financed through taxes, social solidarity is interpreted in relatively broad terms to embrace the well-being of the entire community. Hence, European states also tend to assume other public responsibilities apart from covering risks associated with loss of labor market income: financial assistance to families for the costs of children as well as in some cases payment to those who provide care for ill or elderly adults. Nation-states in Europe also assume responsibility for citizens' access to certain social and health services. While they may not always be the direct provider of these services, most states undertake to ensure that a satisfactory level of service provision exists to meet needs, and that these operate to a certain standard.

The development of the welfare state has been wide-ranging in Western Europe, and has accompanied, or indeed occasioned, the growth of a particular type of society. Welfare states coexist with, inter alia, particular power structures, labor markets, employment patterns, and family arrangements. This type of state is set apart not only by the degree to which the brute force of the market is tamed, but by the institutionalization of a set of social and economic policies that determine the distribution of power, income, and life chances. It embodies a contract between citizen and nation-state, a contract that is far more broad-ranging than that inscribed in earlier European social policies, whether those given life by poor law provision or the earlier versions of social insurance. According to Esping-Andersen in 1990, the nation-state makes a double and binding commitment through the welfare state: it grants citizens social rights and claims on government, and guarantees to uphold the welfare of the social community.

The welfare state is a post-World War II phenomenon. European welfare programs were, however, a relatively long time in the making. The beginning of the evolution of social policy tends to predate the full postwar flowering of the welfare state by at least half a century. Germany led the way in Europe by instituting, in the 1880s, social insurance as a means of dealing with the costs and consequences of industrialization. By the turn of the century, Germany already had sickness insurance, industrial accident insurance, and old age pensions. The spread of such institutions across Europe was rapid. By 1911 every country in Western Europe had some form of workers' compensation scheme, and by 1913 most had instituted sickness insurance. Austria, Belgium, Britain, Denmark, France and Germany had made provisions for pensions as well. The 1920s saw the growth of provisions for widows, and during this decade most European countries added unemployment to the list of risks also covered by social insurance. Typically the early forms of social insurance were organized either directly by the state or indirectly under public auspices. By the standards of the time, the introduction of social insurance can be considered radical.

In the immediate postwar period, European welfare states concentrated upon extending social insurance, introducing cash benefits to support families with children, and instituting a network of social services. Once the economic hardships of the postwar period had receded, energies were concentrated on making social insurance benefits more generous and on instituting a right to a minimum anti-poverty payment. During the 1960s and 1970s, the golden age of the welfare state, arrangements across Europe became more diversified. The Scandinavians moved increasingly in the direction of generous tax-financed benefits, whereas the continental European countries tended to favor a largely self-financing welfare state system, which acted to reproduce the status and other divisions created by the market and civil society.

Welfare states in Europe are historically very complex and vary considerably. One way of conceptualizing this complexity and variation is through the idea of welfare state types. It is a key insight of recent years that European welfare states can in fact be grouped into a number of base types or models. While the designation of both nations and types tends to be controversial, most analysts would agree that the differences and similarities among welfare states in Europe are such that one can speak of a Nordic model, a continental European model, and two other less easily definable models that include a liberal model along the lines of Great Britain and what we might call a Mediterranean model, which encapsulates arrangements in Italy, Spain, Portugal, and, to a lesser extent, Greece. The models are largely differentiated from each other by how they manage social security, the degree of state intervention, and, in turn, the effects of public policies.

In the Nordic countries the welfare state tends to have a wide reach, intervening not just in the labor market but also in the family. In these generally tax-financed systems, the idea of a basic benefit is well established, which means that people experiencing income difficulties have access to a relatively generous and wide-ranging set of social programs. In addition, full employment was, at least until recently a goal of government policy, so that women were almost as likely to be employed as men, while the state organized and provided a wide range of child care services.

The continental European model, which draws Austria, Germany, Belgium, Luxembourg, France and partly the Netherlands together, offers a stark contrast to the Nordic vision. Here, a social insurance model of income security prevails. This not only means that benefits have to be earned over a lifetime's employment—most people basically pay for their own benefits—but that the level of the income replacement depends on the level of the former wage or salary. In a sense, this model rewards the better-off, and instead of seeking to eliminate inequalities, as does the Nordic model, it reproduces them. This welfare state model tends to play a strong role in the economy, but it intervenes in the family only reluctantly. In other words, it relies on a traditional model of family relations, encouraging married women and mothers to care for their families. However, there are variations in the family- and gender-related components of these welfare states, with France especially encouraging employment on the part of mothers, so one should be careful about generalizing.

The third European welfare state model is of a liberal type and is to be found in Britain and to some extent Ireland. It may be, in the United States, the most familiar of the European policy models because it is generally agreed to have provided the template for the U.S. model. This kind of welfare state encourages labor market participation for all, by offering only minimal social security payments. The major goal of policy in this type of welfare state is to combat poverty, which means that everyone gets the same, low level benefits. In this it differs from the Nordic states, which are driven by the objective of eliminating inequality, and from the Continental European model, where the guarantee of income security over the life course is the motor of social policy. The liberal welfare state model is thus less interventionist, either in the labor market or in the family, as compared with the other two.

Among the Mediterranean countries of Spain, Portugal and Italy, welfare state institutions are still in the process of being developed. Social service provision is especially rudimentary and the social security system tends to be more fragmented and dualistic than elsewhere in Western Europe. They in general use a social insurance model, but the effects are not widespread, either in terms of the proportions of the population included or the risks covered. In addition, some of these countries have not even instituted a basic safety net income support program. Thus, since coverage is far from universal and has many gaps, private systems of support, especially the nuclear and extended family, are of high importance.

Theoretical developments in the field reflect the emergence of an increasingly broad-ranging conceptualization of the welfare state. Scholarship has moved from a focus on individual social policies to the welfare state as a complex institutional domain. In terms of its disciplinary roots, the welfare state was for a long time the province of a group of specialists, mostly drawn from the fields of social policy and social administration, whose concern was to enhance its functioning. Pride of place was held here by the British social administration camp, which in its purest form studied welfare within a pragmatic, empirical, and particularizing idiom. In the last two to three decades, welfare state scholarship has broadened as the field of study was colonized by students of social and political theory. This work has been the cradle of theory on the welfare state. To date, there have been four main theoretical approaches to the welfare state: the structural functionalist, the neo-Marxist, the social (democratic), and the state-centered interpretation. Taken together they proffer the following factors as explanation for the welfare state: the level of economic development, the differentiation process involved in modernization, the logic of and inherent contradictions in capitalism, the capture of politics by working class interests, the dynamics of the social or Christian democratic welfare states, class alliances, and the independent action of state resources and policy legacies.

Each approach has yielded its own insights. The structural functional approaches emphasize how economic growth makes possible the extension of structures for redistribution and they leave little doubt that economic development and industrialization are preconditions for welfare state development. In elaborating a more critical scenario on the welfare state, neo-marxists have produced a valuable analysis of the operation of social policy under conditions of capitalist social relations. They have, moreover, opened for debate the future of the welfare state and been foremost in exploring the different dimensions of the "crisis" that is seen to confront it. The social interpretation entails a unique focus on the processes and outcomes of working class power mobilization, as well as on the idea that welfare state development is closely associated with the progress of social democracy. Other recent work, such as the state-centered approach, has brought attention to how variation among welfare states requires approaches sensitive to history, to the nature of the state, and to the effects of other forces (such as class) within the national context.

In a feminist critique of conventional scholarship, work on the relationship between gender and the welfare state has flourished in the late 1980s and 1990s. This work has pinpointed an inferior position for women as an apparent welfare state regularity. It has demonstrated that the conventional understanding of the welfare state falters when confronted by the complexity of welfare provision in practice, and that in reality public systems of welfare tend to be secured by a combination of (largely female) paid and unpaid work.

Presently, welfare state scholarship is most interested in variation, and is dominated by efforts to typologize welfare states on the basis of both their programmatic distinctiveness and the nature of their insertion into national political and institutional structures. Comparison of policy regimes now looms large in a literature that models national policy logics by means of ideal types and conceives of the welfare state as a major motor of stratification, whether along class, gender, or other lines.

In the 1980s and 1990s a new period in the life of European welfare states seems to have emerged. They have more or less unanimously responded to general economic pressures by cutting social spending and hence cash benefits. As a result, European welfare states are getting more restrictive, and the lifelong guarantees to which the populace had become accustomed no longer seem so secure. People will have to work longer for lower pensions and fewer benefits. Add to this greater selectivity, conditionality, targeting of benefits, and increased privatization (not only in terms of contracting services to the private sector, but also through according greater responsibility to individuals to provide for their own protection against risks, or to family members to provide financially for each other) and one has the main measure of what is happening in European welfare states. However, it would be premature to speak of a transformation of the basic structure of the European welfare states themselves, or indeed of a withering away of the European social model. Only in the United Kingdom could a transformation be said to be underway, with the "privatization" of many benefits and services and the emergence of a productivist ideology in which the role of the state is increasingly to facilitate employment and self-sufficiency. To date, the general European pattern, to the extent that one can speak of such, is far more one of gradual reform with old principles holding fast, although starting to give way.

BIBLIOGRAPHY

Baldwin, Peter. *The Politics of Social Solidarity: Class Bases of the European Welfare States 1875–1975.* Cambridge: Cambridge University Press, 1990.

Daly, Mary. "Welfare states under pressure: Cash benefits in European welfare states over the last ten years." *Journal of European Social Policy* 7 (1997) 2: 129–46.

Esping-Andersen, Güsta. *The Three Worlds of Welfare Capitalism.* Cambridge: Polity Press, 1990.

———. "Welfare states and the economy," in Smelser, N. J., and R. Swedberg, eds. *The Handbook of Economic Sociology.* Princeton, N.J.: Princeton University Press, 1994.

Lewis, J. "Gender and the development of welfare regimes." *Journal of European Social Policy* 2 (1992) 3: 159–73.

Pierson, Christopher. *Beyond the Welfare State? The New Political Economy of Welfare.* Cambridge: Polity Press, 1991.

Mary Daly

Welsh Nationalism

Individuals from Wales have risen to prominence in British political life but the significance of Wales, their original base of support, was always subsumed into the United Kingdom. Politics in Wales was traditionally British politics as it expressed itself at the Welsh level.

Plaid Cymru (PC)—the Welsh Party—was the first attempt to articulate not only politics "in" Wales but politics "for" Wales. Plaid Cymru was founded in 1925 following a meeting in Pwllheli and was originally called Plaid Genedlaethol Cymru—the Welsh Nationalist Party. Among the initial founders was Saunders Lewis, who was party president until 1939 and who continued to exercise a dominant position in its policies until his death in 1985. From 1945 until 1981, the presidency was held by Gwynfor Evans. Although PC has run candidates in elections to the British parliament since the 1930s, its first success was in the Carmarthen constituency (electoral district), the largest Welsh county, a predominantly agricultural area in south Wales, which Evans won in 1966.

In 1979 the ruling Labour Party sought additional support in Wales by offering it a regional assembly with limited authority. The referendum on devolution failed by a vote of 956,000 to 243,000. While the rejection was a defeat for PC, it attributed the result not to a repudiation of self-government but to a dislike for this limited version of it. Despite this setback, in 1993 PC held four of the thirty-eight parliamentary seats in Wales, which was the largest number it had ever held. All of these were in predominantly Welsh-speaking areas. At the local level—county and district councils—the party also consistently increased its support.

PC has become more explicitly socialist and joined the European Free Alliance. It increasingly turns its focus toward Europe in the hope that the European Community will provide the framework for a Europe of self-governing regions. The major challenges facing the party are to increase its influence in an area where English speakers predominate and to gain a separate voice for Wales at the European level.

BIBLIOGRAPHY

Adamson, David C. *Class, Ideology, and the Nation: A Theory of Welsh Nationalism.* Cardiff: University of Wales, 1991.

Davies, D. Hywel. *The Welsh Nationalist Party 1925–1945: A Call to Nationhood.* Cardiff: University of Wales, 1983.

Míchéal Thompson

Wenders, Wim, (1945–)

German director. Of all late twentieth century German cinema directors, Wim Wenders is perhaps the most widely recognized in the United States. Wenders has made more than seventy films, mostly narratives that portray the alienation and aimlessness of modern life, primarily through a lone figure struggling with personal crisis. The theme of foreigners lost in strange countries permeates Wenders' films.

Wenders' first feature adapted Peter Handke's *The Goalie's Anxiety at the Penalty Kick* (1971), a story of modern alienation and self-discovery, in which a professional soccer goalie abandons his team and his profession and embarks on a personnel odyssey. Wenders use of washed-out color and his choice of blues music contribute to the sense of aloneness.

Wenders early favored the road-movie genre, as in *Kings of the Road* (1975) and *Wrong Move* (1974), and movies about life in big cities, such as *Alice in the Cities* (1973). *Alice in the Cities* features the unlikely pairing of a German born photojournalist in New York City and a young, abandoned German girl, who return to Germany together to locate the girl's relatives with only a photograph to help them on their quest. *Wrong Move* (1974) adapts Goethe's classic novel, *Wilhelm Meister's Apprenticeship.* The film, however, is set in postwar Germany and tracks a prospective writer's encounters with a trio of characters while traveling. The film culminates in a suicide, an unsuccessful murder, and a failed romance—a contemporary parable about the losses and legacies of the Nazi past. Like *Wrong Move,* his next film was also an adaptation, this time of Nathaniel Hawthrone's *Scarlet Letter.* In the last of his road movies, *Kings of the Road* (1975), one man joins a repairman and together they travel along the north coast of West Germany, fixing outdated cinema projection equipment in small towns. Their journey becomes a time of self-discovery, and in the process, the film articulates the literal dismantling and restoring of the German film industry.

After an extensive stint in television, Wenders cultivated a more international market appeal with his American-French-German production, *The American Friend* (1977), a filming of Patricia Highsmith's novel, *Ripley's Game.* Evocative of classic film noir and indebted to Alfred Hitchcock's *Strangers on a Train,* Wender depicts a world in which no person or situation can be taken at face value. This film delves into the mysterious undercurrents of the international art world and the interactions of Ripley, an art dealer who dabbles in forgeries, played by Dennis Hopper, and Jonathan, a German frame maker with a rare, terminal illness. The two begin an uneasy alliance speckled with betrayal, double-crossings, and murder, from which they barely escape alive. In the end of the film, Jonathan deserts Ripley only to die moments afterwards.

Despite Wenders' expressed desire to challenge the colonialization of consciousness by American culture, his ongoing fascination with the United States can be seen in his choice of topics. *Hammett* (1983), his first production in the United States, produced in Francis Ford Coppola's Zoetrope studio, proved a collaborative disaster; it was not released until 1986, after substantial refilming. However, *Paris, Texas* (1984), Wenders' next depiction of the United States, was a critical and international success. The film's open and seemingly endless Texas landscapes mirror the main character's inner emptiness. *Wings of Desire,* a rhapsodic take on historical collective memory in Berlin, followed *Paris, Texas.* Bruno, an angel who longs to experience human emotional and sensations, trades his eternity for the chance at being human. The film's shift from cold black and white scenes—to depict the angels' perceptions—to saturated color for portraying the human—underscores the vibrancy and immediacy of human experience. Its sequel *Far Away, So Close* appeared in 1993. In between sequels appeared *Until the End of the World* (1991), a futuristic look into a technological world in which even dreams can be the stuff that films are made of.

The recent Hollywood remake (*City of Angels,* 1998) of *Wings of Desire* rekindled his waning appeal after his last feature, *The End of Violence/Power* (1997), his first film based exclusively in the United States, received a lukewarm reception on both sides of the Atlantic. Two of his more interesting films—*Beyond the Clouds* (1995) written and directed with Italian auteur Michelangelo Antonioni and *Trick of the Light/Brothers Skladanowsky* (1995)—were scarcely shown in the United States. His recent project, the highly successful documentary *Buena Vista Social Club* (1998), traces the rediscovery and tour of the legendary Cuban musicians of the fifties. The film showcases an outstanding soundtrack by Ry Cooder and the members of the Buena Vista Social Club, Ibrahim

Ferrar among many others. Wender's *The Million Dollar Hotel* premiered in 2000.

BIBLIOGRAPHY

Elsaesser, Thomas. *New German Cinema: A History.* New Brunswick, N.J.: Rutgers University Press, 1989.

Corrigan, Timothy. *New German Cinema: The Displaced Image.* Bloomington: Indiana University Press, 1994.

Jill Gillespie

West, Harry (1917–)

Ulster Unionist Party (UUP) leader, 1974–79; Unionist MP for Enniskillen, 1954–72. Harry West was born in Enniskillen in 1917. He was opposed to any proposals that advocated power-sharing and so did not support the Sunningdale Agreement. He succeeded Brian Faulkner as leader of the Ulster Unionists in 1974, after the Ulster Unionist Council had rejected the Sunningdale Agreement. He and his party joined the United Ulster Unionist Council (UUUC), together with the Democratic Unionist Party (DUP) and the Vanguard (VUPP) in 1974. By 1977 his relations with Ian Paisley (DUP) and Ernest Baird (VUPP) had deteriorated, and after a failed strike in May, the UUUC broke up. He resigned as UUP leader in 1979 after having failed to win a seat in the European Parliament elections, and he was replaced by James Molyneaux. In 1981 he stood for the Fermanagh-South Tyrone seat and lost to Bobby Sands.

Ricki Schoen

SEE ALSO Faulkner, Brian

Western European Union

A defensive alliance established to facilitate the re-arming of Germany. The Brussels Treaty (Treaty on Economic, Social and Cultural Collaboration and Collective Self-Defense) of March 17, 1948, had produced the European Union (EU), a fifty year alliance between the U.K., France, and the Benelux countries to provide for Western European defense, promote European unity, and encourage its progressive integration. The signatories agreed to mutual support if any of them were attacked and to integrate their air defenses and command structures.

Encouraged by President Truman, the members of the EU agreed to participate in a larger North Atlantic alliance. The North Atlantic Treaty was signed on April 4, 1949, and in December 1950 the North Atlantic Treaty Organization (NATO) was set up to provide the necessary political and military structures to fulfill the objectives of that treaty. When General Eisenhower was appointed the first Supreme Allied Commander Europe (SACEUR), the members of the EU merged their military organization into NATO.

Though the EU had been superseded by NATO, it still existed. With the collapse of the proposed European Defense Community, Anthony Eden proposed that Italy and West Germany become members of the EU, and that its name be changed to the Western European Union (WEU). In 1954 both Italy and the Federal Republic of Germany became signatories of the Brussels Treaty, and the Western European Unity Treaty was signed on May 6, 1955. The WEU was also incorporated into NATO.

In joining the WEU, West Germany agreed that the size and armaments of its military would be determined by the WEU. This and the U.K. commitment to keep its forces in Germany indefinitely sufficiently soothed French concerns, and Germany joined NATO.

In addition to losing its military function to NATO, WEU's economic, social, and cultural roles were taken over by OEEC, the organization of Economic Cooperation and Development (which after the completion of its administration of the Marshall Plan continued to coordinate European economic cooperation), and the Council of Europe, and its political role was eventually assumed by the European Community (EC). However, it had played a role in the Saar settlement and as a liaison between the EC and the U.K. before Britain became an EC member in 1973.

At a conference in Rome on October 26 and 27, 1984, the WEU, which had been largely moribund, was resuscitated to serve as a framework for European security consultation. Two meetings were to be held yearly, to be attended by member states' foreign and defense ministers, to discuss the security implications of crises anywhere in the world. At a Hague conference in October 1987 the WEU members stressed the indivisibility of security issues from the question of further European integration, and the basis was laid for Portugal and Spain to join the WEU in 1990, and Greece in 1992.

When mines were laid in the Persian Gulf during the Iran-Iraq War in 1987–88, the members of the WEU dispatched minesweepers to deal with this threat to international commerce. During the Gulf War, the WEU states coordinated their actions to enforce U.N. Resolution 661, in conjunction with the U.S. After the conclusion of hostilities the WEU continued the coordination of minesweeping and aid to the Kurds in Northern Iraq.

In 1992 Iceland, Norway, and Turkey became associate members of the WEU, and Denmark, Ireland, and Finland became observers. In 1995 Austria and Sweden became observers. In 1994 the category of associate partner was created for countries of Central and Eastern Europe that had signed the Europe Agreement with the European Union. Bulgaria, Czech Republic, Estonia, Hungary, Latvia, Lithuania, Poland, Romania, and Slovakia became associate partners in 1994 and Slovenia in 1996.

BIBLIOGRAPHY

Cahen, Alfred. *The Western European Union and NATO: Building a European Defence Identity within the Context of Atlantic Solidarity.* London: Brassey's, 1989.

Rees, G. Wyn. *The Western European Union at the Crossroads: Between Trans-Atlantic Solidarity and European Integration.* Boulder, Col.: Westview, 1998.

Bernard Cook

SEE ALSO Council of Europe; European Defense Community; Pleven, René

Whitaker, Thomas Kenneth (1916–)

Secretary of the Irish Department of Finance (1956–69). Thomas Whitaker entered the Irish civil service in 1934. In 1938 he joined the Department of Finance, and was appointed secretary in 1956. His seminal *Economic Development,* based on Keynesian economic principles, became the basis for the 1959–63 first Programme for Economic Expansion implemented by Taoiseach Sean Lemass. The program was responsible for the major expansion of the Irish economy through the sixties and early seventies. The plan jump started the Irish economy out of the morass of the late 1950s, and its impact was to raise Irish standards of living by 50 percent and to help transform Ireland from a predominantly closed agricultural economy to a more free-trade-oriented industrial economy.

Whitaker was director of the central bank of Ireland from 1958 to 1969, and its governor from 1969 to 1976, when he retired. In 1976 he became Chancellor of the National University of Ireland.

BIBLIOGRAPHY

Fanning, Ronan. *The Irish Department of Finance.* Dublin: IPA, 1978.

McCarthy, John F. *Planning Ireland's Future: The Legacy of T.K. Whitaker.* Dublin: Glendale, 1990.

Michael J. Kennedy

SEE ALSO Lemass, Sean

Whitelaw, Lord William (1918–99)

First secretary of state for Northern Ireland, 1972–73. When he took office in Ireland in 1972, he faced animosity from the unionists because they had been forced to give up the Stormont assembly, and he faced an escalating campaign of violence from the republican paramilitaries. In an effort to reduce the violence, he arranged to meet with leaders of the republican movement in secret in London in 1972, after they had announced a cease-fire. But the British government found the demands made by the paramilitaries too sweeping and could not agree to them, and the cease-fire ended with no progress having been made.

While in office, Whitelaw agreed to give paramilitary prisoners special status category, a concession he later described as a mistake. He also tried to move the focus away from violence and to the political agenda, and in October 1972 he produced a position paper that became the basis for a new British government proposal for devolved government. This included a form of power-sharing at the expense of the majority government that ensured unionist opposition and Social Democratic Labor Party (SDLP) approval. In October 1973 Whitelaw met with the three party leaders at Stormont, Brian Faulkner (Ulster Unionist Party), Gerard Fitt (SDLP) and Sir Oliver Napier (Alliance), which produced a proposal for a power-sharing executive. However, the final details of the arrangement were postponed, to be sorted out at a meeting at Sunningdale in December. The Sunningdale Agreement was signed by the three leaders and a power-sharing executive was to be set up composed of the leaders of the Unionist Party, the SDLP and the Alliance Party. This attempt to resolve the conflict and restore order to Northern Ireland only lasted three months. Most of the Democratic Unionist Party, together with a sizable group within the Ulster Unionists, opposed it. It finally collapsed when the United Workers' Council loyalist strike was called in opposition to it and ground all of Northern Ireland to a halt in May 1974. Before the arrangement was finalized, Whitelaw took on a new position at the Department of Employment and was succeeded as secretary of state by Francis Pym. Whitelaw retired from government in 1988 and said at the time that the failure of the Sunningdale Agreement in 1974 had been a very sad event in his political life.

BIBLIOGRAPHY

Arthur, Paul. *Northern Ireland since 1968.* 2d. ed. Cambridge, Mass.: Blackwell Publishers, 1996.

Hadden, Tom. *The Anglo-Irish Agreement: Commentary, Text, and Official Review.* Dublin: E. Higel, 1989.

Owen, Arwel Ellis. *The Anglo-Irish Agreement: The First Three Years.* Cardiff: University of Wales Press, 1994.
Wichert, Sabine. *Northern Ireland since 1945.* New York: Longman, 1991.

Ricki Schoen

Willebrands, Johannes Gerardus Maria (1909–)

A leader of the Roman Catholic Church in the Netherlands and cardinal of the church. Johannes Willebrands was born in Bovenkarspel on September 4, 1909. He studied at the Warmond Seminary in the Netherlands and received a doctorate in philosophy from the Angelicum University in Rome. He was ordained in 1934. Willebrands began teaching philosophy at Warmond in 1940 and became the rector of the seminary in 1945. He organized the Catholic Conference on Ecumenical Questions in 1951, and because of his work in ecumenism was appointed secretary of the papal Secretariat for Promoting Christian Unity in 1960. Willebrands served as president of the Secretariat from 1969 until 1989. He played a leading role in attempting to create better understanding between the Catholic Church and the Jewish community. Willebrands was consecrated bishop in 1964, elevated to cardinal in 1969 by Pope Paul VI, and made bishop of Utrecht in 1975.

Bernard Cook

Williams, Betty (1943–)

Northern Irish co-founder of the Peace People in 1976, and, together with Mairead Corrigan, winner of the 1976 Nobel Peace Prize. Born in Belfast, Betty Williams launched the Peace People Movement, together with Mairead Corrigan and Ciaran McKeown, after having witnessed an incident that killed three children. In August 1974, a car went out of control after its Irish Republican Army driver was shot by British soldiers. It hit three children of Corrigan's sister, killing them. Williams traveled abroad and spoke about the movement, but eventually stepped down as an executive with the movement. In 1982 she married an American businessman and moved to the United States. Her relationship with her co-founders deteriorated after winning the Nobel Peace Prize, and when she returned to Northern Ireland in 1986, to mark the tenth anniversary of the Peace People movement, Corrigan and McKeown refused to meet with her.

Ricki Schoen

SEE ALSO Corrigan, Mairead; Ireland, Northern

Williams, Raymond (1921–88)

British literary critic and novelist. Raymond Williams was the most influential literary critic of the post–World War II period, influencing a whole generation of writers and teachers in what subsequently became known as "cultural studies." Williams's innovative and detailed studies of English literature were only part of his public career, however; he was also a novelist and a political activist. Indeed, he believed all of his critical, literary, and political activities shared certain common roots in working-class consciousness and socialist activism.

After serving in the British army in Europe during World War II, Williams became active in working-class adult education for Cambridge University, where he would eventually hold his major professorial posts. His pioneering study, *Culture and Society* (1958), established his reputation as a historical critic of key concepts that originated in the Industrial Revolution. He rescued the term "culture" not only from the anthropologists but from its reactionary status in both Matthew Arnold's Victorian *Culture and Anarchy* (1869) and T. S. Eliot's modernist *Notes towards a Definition of Culture* (1948), broadening its critical function to include working class and other oppositional cultures.

Three extremely influential books of cultural criticism followed. *The Long Revolution* (1961) moved beyond literary criticism into a neo-Marxist analysis of both the dominant culture and its emerging challenges. *The Country and the City* (1973) began as a critique of Marx's devaluation of the countryside ("rural idiocy" was his term) and developed as a recognition of the relationship of the written text to the actual social conditions of its production. *Keywords* (1976) was a work of historical philology that traced 120 important terms in British English, arguing that language is itself a "continuous social production."

His novels, such as *Border Country* (1960) and *Second Generation* (1964), dramatized aspects of his own life as well as the cultural history of the region in which he grew up, the Welsh "border country." As the grandson of an agricultural laborer and the son of a railway worker, he fused a working class viewpoint with the traditional realist novel, using class and political struggles to highlight the relationship between the personal and the political for his characters.

For much of his life, except during the Vietnam War, he supported the Labour Party. He was also a lifelong committed socialist, constantly redefining in his essays and activism what new forms of socialism were appropriate to the late twentieth century.

BIBLIOGRAPHY

Eagleton, Terry, ed. *Raymond Williams: Critical Perspectives.* Boston: Northeastern University Press, 1989.

O'Connor, Alan. *Raymond Williams: Writing, Culture, Politics.* Oxford: Basil Blackwell, 1989.

Williams, Raymond. *Politics and Letters: Interviews with New Left Review.* London: New Left Books, 1979.

Tom Zaniello

Williams, Shirley Vivien Theresa Brittain (1930–)

British politician, co-founder of the Social Democratic Party. Shirley Williams was born in London on July 27, 1930, the daughter of Sir George Catlin, a professor of politics and a Labour Party candidate in the 1930s, and Vera Brittain, a famous socialist feminist. She spent three years in Minneapolis during World War II. She was educated at both Oxford and Columbia University. In 1955, she married Bernard Arthur Williams, a philosophy professor. They had one daughter, but were divorced in 1974. She later married the Harvard political economist Richard Neustadt in 1987.

Williams was long a hard-working fixture of the British political scene, focusing her energy on domestic and economic affairs. She entered politics on the side of workers and those opposing the ruling elite, and she spent time as a waitress and factory worker to understand the life of the common laborer. She served in Parliament from Hitchin (1964–74) and later from Crosby (1981–83). Among her many important posts were minister of state for the Department of Education and Science from 1967 to 1969, and secretary of state for prices and consumer protection from 1974 to 1976.

Williams was firmly convinced that the United Kingdom had to integrate with the rest of Europe in the European Economic Community in order to survive in a rapidly changing global economy. In the 1970s she was directly involved in devising effective financial policies to check inflation and aid the working class. As a Catholic she was against liberalizing divorce and abortion laws. But her religion proved to be a handicap when she was head of the Home Office from October 1969 to June 1970, with responsibility for Northern Ireland. From 1970 to 1981, she was a member of the National Executive Committee of the Labour Party, where she argued for a smaller, more focused and accomplished platform, rather than one that tried to be all things to all people. Because of her national stature and wide-ranging governmental experience there was talk of her in 1976 as a potential leader of the Labour Party and possibly as the first woman prime minister to succeed the retiring Harold Wilson.

In 1981 she left the Labour Party, which she had joined at age sixteen, to co-found the Social Democratic Party, and was its president from 1982 to 1988. Since then she has been a member of the Social and Liberal Democratic Party. Williams has taught at several academic institutions, and since 1988 she has been a professor at the Kennedy School of Government at Harvard University.

BIBLIOGRAPHY

Williams, Shirley. *A Job to Live: The Impact of Tomorrow's Technology on Work and Society.* New York: Penguin Books, 1985.

———. "The New Authoritarianism." *The Political Quarterly* 60 (January 1989): 4–9.

———. *Politics Is for People.* Cambridge, Mass.: Harvard University Press, 1981.

———. "Sovereignty and Accountability in the European Community." *The Political Quarterly* 61 (July/September 1990): 299–317.

Williams, Shirley, and Elizabeth Holtzman. "Women in the Political World: Observations." *Daedalus* 116 (Fall 1987): 25–33.

Daniel K. Blewett

Willoch, Kåre Isaachsen (1928–)

Prime minister of Norway, 1981–86. Born October 3, 1928, in Oslo, Kåre Willoch, after graduating from the University of Oslo, served as secretary to the Federation of Norwegian Ship Owners from 1951 to 1953. He was counselor of the Federation of Norwegian Industries from 1954 to 1963. He was elected to parliament from the Conservative Party in 1958. In 1961 he was elected to the National Committee of the Conservative Party, and served as its secretary general from 1963 to 1965. Willoch served as minister of commerce and shipping in 1963 and from 1965 to 1970. From 1970 to 1974 he was leader (chair) of the Conservative Party and he headed its parliamentary group from 1970 to 1981.

After 1977 the Labor Party was increasingly weakened by foreign policy disputes and personal rivalries. Odvar Nordli resigned in February 1981. He was briefly replaced by Gro Harlem Brudtland until a new election brought the Conservatives, led by Kåre Willoch, to power. The Christian People's Party refused to join the Conservatives in a coalition because of the Conservatives' more flexible attitude on abortion, and Willoch was forced to form a minority government. After the 1986 election, Willoch's government had the barest of majorities, seventy-eight seats to the opposition's seventy-seven. Internal disputes destroyed this fragile majority and Labor returned to power under Brundtland in 1986.

Willoch gave up his parliamentary seat and his membership on the National Committee of the Conservative Party in 1989 when he was appointed co-governor of Oslo and Akershus.

BIBLIOGRAPHY

Strute, Karl, and Theodor Doelken, eds. *Who's Who in Scandinavia.* Essen, Germany: Sutter Druckerei, 1981.

Bruce Olav Solheim
Bernard Cook

Wilson, Harold (1916–95)

Prime minister of Great Britain (1964–70 and 1974–76). Harold Wilson was educated at Oxford, became a civil servant, was elected a Labour Member of Parliament in 1945, and from 1947 to 1951 was trade minister in Clement Attlee's government. He was leader of the Labour Party between 1963 and 1976. After retirement Wilson became a Knight of the Garter and in 1983 a life peer as Baron Wilson of Rievaulx.

Wilson's early leftist views and alleged Soviet sympathies attracted the unfavorable attention of the British and American security services, causing him considerable embarrassment during his terms as prime minister. He was prominent in the Labour Party's left wing as late as 1960, when he was its unsuccessful candidate for party leader against Hugh Gaitskell. During the early sixties, however, Wilson moved steadily rightward, enabling him to be elected party leader in 1963 following Gaitskell's death.

As prime minister Wilson aimed to give Britain and himself a high profile internationally. He was accused by Labour and opposition critics of having an idiosyncratic presidential style. Wilson was censured within his party for aligning himself too closely with the United States in world affairs, but also by the Americans for interfering annoyingly in their diplomacy. He was critical of American strategy in the Vietnam War, and refused to commit British troops. Nevertheless, Wilson's personal mediation with Soviet Premier Aleksei Kosygin in 1967 may have come near to ending the war. Although berated by many Labour party activists, Wilson remained pledged to Britain's independent nuclear deterrent and to the storage in Britain of nuclear-armed American missiles.

Wilson's first government was plagued by economic recession, monetary crises, and balance-of-payments deficits, necessitating a controversial devaluation of the pound in 1967. During the late 1960s, when the European economies were still booming, journalists began to speak of Britain as the "sick man of Europe." To save money the Labour government adopted a "west of Suez" policy of phasing out most of Britain's defense responsibilities outside of NATO, and of closing all British military, naval, and air bases in Asia and the Middle East. Although unenthusiastic about British entry into the European Economic Community (EEC), Wilson concluded in 1966 that joining was necessary to bolster the sagging British economy. His government in 1967 made the first formal application to join the Community since French President Charles de Gaulle's 1961 veto, but again de Gaulle rejected Britain.

Wilson in 1965 tried but failed to negotiate an end to the "unilateral declaration of independence" by Rhodesia's white minority. The Wilson government was criticized by the Labour left not only for waffling over Rhodesia, but for favoring a "genocidal" Nigerian government in 1967 during the Biafran secession and civil war. At home Wilson had to deal with tensions between Protestant and Catholic militants in Northern Ireland, beginning in 1968, as well as vocal nationalist devolution movements in Scotland and Wales.

In his domestic policies, Wilson tried between 1964 and 1970 to implement a moderate social democratic program featuring educational reforms, improved industrial relations, technological innovation, and increased productivity. A notable creation of the first Wilson administration in 1969 was the Open University, offering televised courses to mature, part-time students. Less successful was the government's institution of the comprehensive secondary school, which was unpopular with the middle classes and arguably lowered standards.

Wilson's rejection of socialist panaceas such as nationalization, heavy taxation, and monetary controls infuriated Labour Party leftists while gaining him few friends in the Conservative-oriented business community. To appease swing voters Wilson trimmed many of his reforms, notably his commitment to end racial discrimination. Although the Wilson government tried to reduce bias against black immigrants in education, housing, and jobs, in 1968 it made immigration into the U.K. from the Commonwealth more difficult.

The second Wilson government of 1974–76 was anticlimactic. Two back-to-back elections in 1974 failed to give Wilson an adequate majority to govern effectively. Returned to office largely because of the ineptitude of his Conservative predecessor, Edward Heath, Wilson offered himself to the public as a conciliator negotiating a social contract. Far from creating a national consensus, however, Wilson lacked the political clout to dominate competing interest groups. Excessive wage demands, galloping inflation, numerous bankruptcies, and an enormous trade deficit nearly wrecked the British economy. A left-wing revolt within the Labour Party in 1975 forced a referendum on the EEC, to which Britain had finally been admitted in 1973, though the "yes" forces championed by Wilson won by a two-to-one majority.

Wilson's premature resignation in 1976 was attributable to failing health, harassment by right-wing security agents, and loss of taste for office and power. The coming on line of Britain's valuable new North Sea oil deposits enabled Wilson to retire on a high note. Although not without accomplishment, Wilson's two governments failed to satisfy expectations. Wilson's character defects, including cynicism, deviousness, manipulativeness, and opportunism, unfortunately detracted from his undoubted enthusiasm, intelligence, and managerial skills.

BIBLIOGRAPHY

Crossman, Richard. *The Diaries of a Cabinet Minister, 1964–1970,* 3 vols. London: Hamish Hamilton and Cape, 1975–77.

Morgan, Austen. *Harold Wilson.* London: Pluto Press, 1992.

Pimlott, Ben. *Harold Wilson.* London: Harper Collins, 1993.

Wilson, Harold. *The Labour Government 1964–70.* London: Weidenfeld and Nicolson, 1971.

———. *Final Term: The Labour Government 1974–76.* London: Weidenfeld and Nicolson/Michael Joseph, 1979.

Ziegler, Philip. *Wilson: The Authorized Life.* London: Weidenfeld and Nicolson, 1994.

Don M. Cregier

SEE ALSO Callaghan, James; Heath, Edward; United Kingdom

Wolf, Christa (1929–)

One of the most important and lasting novelists and essayists of postwar German literature, Christa Wolf is exceptional in her popularity and respect among readers of both Germanies, before and after the *Wende* (the collapse of Communism in the German Democratic Republic [GDR]). Wolf grew up in the town of Landsberg an der Warthe (now Gorzów Wielkopolski, Poland) in a petit bourgeois milieu of shopkeepers and small-town, everyday Nazis, an experience meticulously documented in her best known novel, the 1976 *Kindheitsmuster* (*A Model Childhood*). During the war her family fled west and settled in Mecklenburg in the Soviet zone, where she finished school, joined the SED (Socialist Unity Party, or communists), and later began studies at the University of Leipzig under the important Germanist Hans Mayer. She began her literary career as an editor in Halle (1959–62) and began writing full time in 1962. From the 1960s through the fall of the Berlin Wall her works rarely conformed to the dogmatic demands of East German socialist realist standards, but her idealistic socialist convictions and prominence within East German literary circles earned her the privilege of travel and a place in the state literary bureaucracy. At the same time, her success in the West, her leading role in protesting the German Democratic Republic's (GDR) expulsion of the singer and songwriter Wolf Biermann in 1976, and the subtle yet powerful criticism of the state and society found in her novels always gave the East German cultural functionaries pause.

Her bold first novel about a young East German woman who chooses not join her lover in the West, her 1963 *Der geteilte Himmel* (*The Divided Heaven*), was an immediate success and catapulted Wolf to popularity in the GDR, despite its subtle invocation of suicide as a subject, something quite taboo for state-sanctioned GDR writing at the time. Even the simple fact that Wolf set the novel during the building of the Berlin Wall showed her courage. Her second novel, the 1968 *Nachdenken über Christa T.* (*The Quest for Christa T.*), treats the extremely non-socialist subject of death and subjective introspection through the careful chronicle of the passing of the narrator's good friend. Wolf's 1972 Lesen und Schreiben: *Aufsätze und Betrachtungen* (*Reader and The Writer: Essays, Sketches, Memories*), the first of many volumes of essays, went about explaining and justifying her own ideas about writing within the proscriptive framework of socialist realist doctrine. Key concepts from these and later essays are her notions of "subjective authenticity" and "female writing." Wolf's best known work, the autobiographical *Kindheitsmuster,* also moved against the stream of GDR doctrine to the extent that it showed Nazism to be a common German problem, not simply the legacy of capitalists and the problem of the West, as communist teachings would have it. The novel's complicated narrative framework brilliantly unifies the (socialist) narrator, who is very much like Wolf herself, and her (Nazi) childhood self, through flashbacks, pronominal shifts, and three different temporal levels, all of which converge into a unified, mature, and, to an extent, fallen subject at the conclusion.

Wolf helped reintroduce Romanticism and subjective romantic sensibilities to the GDR literary scene with her edition of Karoline von Günderode's forgotten works and a 1979 novel about Günderode and Heinrich von Kleist,

Kein Ort. Nirgends (*No Place on Earth*). She was the first East German writer to receive West Germany's most prestigious literary prize, the Georg Büchner Prize (1980). Devotion and attention to the place of women in society run through all of Wolf's works, and both the pair *Kassandra* (1983) and *Voraussetzungen einer Erzählung: Kassandra* (1983, published together in English as *Cassandra: A Novel & Four Essays*) and the most recent 1997 *Medea: Stimmen* (*Medea: A Modern Retelling*) question and problematize these mythic women and relationships between power and gender in general.

Wolf became the key figure in what became known as the *Deutsch-deutscher Literaturstreit* (the German-German literary dispute) of the *Wende,* through the combination of the publication of her 1989 story *Was bleibt* (*What Remains and Other Stories*), New York: Farrar, Straus, & Giroux, which describes the narrator's experiences as a victim of secret police observation, and the fall of the Wall: she was accused by the West German press of cowardice for not having published the tale earlier—it was written in 1979 and lay in a drawer for a decade—when it might have helped bring the fall of the Wall sooner. Haughty West German critics were further spurred on in 1993 by revelations that Wolf informed briefly (and trivially) for the GDR Stasi (secret police) herself from 1959 to 1963, though East German readers and many prominent West German authors (e.g., Günter Grass) stood by Wolf. She remains productive and one of the most honest, exacting, and profound literary voices of the postwar period in Germany.

BIBLIOGRAPHY

Arnold, Heinz Ludwig, ed. *Christa Wolf.* 4th ed. Munich: text + kritik, 1994.

Drescher, Angela, ed. *Christa Wolf: Ein Arbeitsbuch. Studien—Documente—Bibliographie.* Frankfurt am Main: Luchterhand Literaturverlag, 1990.

Fries, Marilyn Sibley, ed. *Responses to Christa Wolf: Critical Essays.* Detroit: Wayne State University Press, 1989.

Hahn, H. J. "'Es geht nicht um Literatur.' Some Observations on the 1990 'Literaturstreit' and Its Recent Anti-Intellectual Implications." *German Life and Letters* 50, Vol. 1 (January 1997): 65–81.

Resch, Margit. *Understanding Christa Wolf: Returning Home to a Foreign Land.* Columbia: University of South Carolina Press, 1997.

Wallace, Ian, ed. *Christa Wolf in Perspective.* Amsterdam: Rodopi, 1994.

Scott Denham

Wolf, Markus (1923–)

Director of the German Democratic Republic's (GDR) spy agency. Born and raised near Stuttgart, Markus Wolf fled Germany in 1923 with his German-Jewish father, the writer Friedrich Wolf. The family moved to Moscow in 1934, where Wolf changed his name to Mischa, joined the German Communist Party in 1942, and underwent a period of training at the Comintern school during 1942–43. A dedicated Communist, Wolf returned to Germany in May 1945 and joined the Socialist Unity Party in the following year. After a further spell in Moscow from 1949 to 1951, as a senior member of the GDR embassy, he carved out a career as the head of the GDR's foreign intelligence operations. From 1952 until his unexpected retirement in 1986 he was in charge of the Ministry of State Security's foreign intelligence organ, the Central Reconnaissance Agency, as well as deputy minister of state security between 1955 and 1986. Although a shadowy figure for much of this time, John le Carré used him as the model for his fictional spy master, Karla.

Wolf, an urbane intellectual, published an autobiographical novel, *Die Troika,* in 1989, in which he sought to distance himself from the dogmatic Erich Honecker and to express his sympathy for Gorbachev's reforms. During the transition period, or *Wende,* he portrayed himself as a reform communist, but his efforts to play an active role in the creation of a more liberal system in the GDR soon foundered on his *Stasi* (secret police) past. Since 1990 Federal German prosecutors have attempted to convict him of treason and espionage. However, while there is no doubt that his agents enjoyed much success in infiltrating the West German system, including Chancellor Willy Brandt's personal staff, Wolf has defended himself on the grounds that in serving his own state during the Cold War he was carrying out a task analogous to that performed by his West German counterparts.

BIBLIOGRAPHY

Colitt, Leslie. *Spymaster: The Real-Life Karla, His Moles, and the East German Secret Police.* Reading, Mass.: Addison-Wesley Publishing, 1995.

Reichenbach, Alexander. *Chef der Spione. Die Markus-Wolf Story.* Stuttgart: Deutsche Verlagsanstalt, 1992.

Villemarest, Pierre F. de. *Le coup d'Etat de Markus Wolf: la guerre secrète des deux Allemagnes, 1945–1991.* Paris: Stock, 1991.

Wolf, Markus. *Man without a Face: The Autobiography of Communism's greatest Spymaster.* Markus Wolf with Anne McElvoy. New York: Public Affairs, 1999.

Mike Dennis

Women's Movements

European women's movements have roots in the nineteenth century, but have flourished with great variety since 1945. In northern countries like Sweden, women's movements are less oppositional, partly because state feminism has addressed many gender inequalities. Eastern European states, including the Soviet Union, passed extensive but almost entirely ineffective legislation safeguarding women's rights in the 1940s and 1950s, while simultaneously crushing genuine women's movements. East European women's groups began reemerging in opposition to communism, mostly in the 1980s. In Central European countries most women join family and church related organizations, but a vocal if small feminist movement has existed since the 1960s. In other countries, like Ireland, there are many women's movements, on both the right and the left, due to national struggles and disagreement about the state's positions on abortion, divorce, and women's rights.

Northern Europe

The Scandinavian countries were the first to offer women legal equality and to foster broad cultural support for egalitarianism. Surveys show most Scandinavians today supporting principles of equality, yet, now that so many women work outside the home in addition to bearing children, many women still feel that the state and society are unable to address their burdens fully.

There are differences between the women's movements in Scandinavian countries, with Sweden and Finland having a much "quieter" feminism. In Sweden, the Frederika Bremer League, founded in 1894, and the socialist Group 8, which developed in the 1970s, continue, but feminism has been largely incorporated by the state and institutions. For instance, a women's university at Umea was established in 1982. But because the culture emphasizes family and community over the individual, consciousness-raising and separatist women's groups are unpopular in Sweden. In Finland, family oriented groups like Martta, founded in 1899, and community centered groups like the Feminist Union, founded in 1892, also survive. The radical Group 9, established in 1966, began working with the state in 1967 to implement women's rights. Thus, again, because of a very friendly form of state feminism, few grassroots, oppositional women's groups exist there.

In Norway, social and humanitarian women's groups from the 1880s and 1890s also survive, with the Norwegian Women's Public Health Organization, founded in 1896, currently claiming 240,000 members. But Norwegian women, more so than Swedish and Finnish women, developed a very active feminist movement in the 1960s, which has continued into the 1990s. The Marxist-Leninist Women's Front, organized in 1972, has fought for a shorter work day, while the work of anti-pornography groups in the 1980s led to 1986 legislation in that area. The state, universities, and political parties support numerous women's groups and centers. The Norwegian Research Council established the Secretariat for Women and Research in the Social Sciences in 1977, which remains active. In politics, Norwegian women are well represented, thanks to quotas in the Liberal, Socialist, and Labor parties, which were begun in 1973, 1974, and 1984 respectively.

Denmark's situation is similar, with both state and broad cultural support for equal rights. The umbrella National Council of Women in Denmark counts one million members—one-fifth of the population—belonging to diverse women's organizations.

Iceland's active feminist movement began with the Redstockings in 1968. Women's notable inequalities into the 1970s led to widespread feminist demonstrations in Iceland, including the 1975 Women's Strike in which 90 percent of Icelandic women participated. The movement also helped elect Vigdis Finnbogaddottir, the first female president in 1980.

The Netherlands supports numerous feminist and women's groups. In the postwar period associational groups, including the Dutch Federation of Country Women, have had a strong presence, while a powerful wave of feminist groups was begun in 1967. The umbrella Council of Women, organized in 1975, counts about one million members. The state consulted the Man-Woman-Society, set up in 1968, for advice on gender and sexuality. This led to extensive progressive legislation in the 1970s. Since the 1980s the government has funded women's studies programs and community activities promoting equality. The Netherlands, alongside Denmark and France, supports the broadest egalitarian attitudes and tolerance for sexual diversity in Europe. Despite such progress, both politicians and feminists are disappointed because Dutch women still have among the lowest representation in the European workforce, in higher education, in the professions, and in public office.

Great Britain (England, Wales, and Scotland) offered comparatively early support for women's basic rights to education, divorce, and the vote. Yet because British women have not achieved socioeconomic and professional parity with men, there has been a vigorous postwar women's movement. Women's liberation began in the 1960s both in working-class communities, where women protested labor conditions, and on campuses, where groups attacked discrimination, sexual violence, and restrictions on abortion. British feminists have been especially active in peace movements, perhaps most emblematically at Greenham Common military base in 1982, when twenty thousand women made a nine mile human chain to protest the arms race. Britain's ethnic diversity has created pluralism—though sometimes division—since the 1970s, and British feminists have striven to acknowledge difference. By the 1980s political parties began competing for women's votes, even establishing quotas. Although the Conservatives were the first to choose a female prime minister, Margaret Thatcher in 1979, the Labour Party eventually addressed gender issues with the establishment of a Ministry on Women in 1987.

The Center and South

Enjoying a tradition of cultural dissent and political change, France has witnessed waves of feminism since the eighteenth century and, since the 1960s, an adaptive state willing to address gender issues. France refused women even very basic rights until the 1946 constitution. Simone de Beauvoir's *The Second Sex* (1949) influentially and powerfully articulated women's second-class status. Other postwar female intellectuals wrote about gender discrimination, while the Movement for Family Planning, organized in 1956, campaigned against a 1920 law prohibiting contraception. Women began forming informal groups in the 1960s and more militant, public groups emerged in 1970. De Beauvoir's party, Choisir, organized in 1971, focused on the right to abortion and the criminalizing of rape. The party's efforts led to the legalization of abortion in 1974 and the state's creating a Secretary of State for the Condition of Women in 1974. Since then, governments have continued to fund gender-related programs. French feminism has been ideologically and institutionally divided, with scholarly work and institutes supported by the state, but it also has separatist and independent groups. English speakers may know best Julia Kristeva, Luce Irigiray, and other members of Politique et Psychoanalyse, organized in 1968 to reconstruct female identity by exploring the unconscious perhaps as exemplifying French feminism. In France, however, the group represents a small but wealthy faction, and is in fact considered antifeminist by most women's groups and institutions.

Italy's feminist movements have brought women together across classes and regions to challenge an extremely sexist culture. In the 1960s, the women's movement focused on sexual violence and nineteenth-century and fascist laws limiting women's personhood. Beginning in 1970, millions of women petitioned and demonstrated against fascist anti-abortion laws, which were overturned in 1978. Demonstrations against rape and violence led to a 1982 amendment finally making rape a punishable crime. Because of ongoing physical and sexual attacks from men opposed to women's rights, many feminists have trained in militant self-defense tactics. By the 1990s, at least one hundred women's research and crisis centers, and cultural and political women's groups had been established nationwide.

The Germanic countries have remained Europe's most conservative in regards to gender. Having inherited misogynistic nineteenth-century, as well as fascist, laws, the response to this tradition of legal conservatism was varied after 1949 as the East and West were divided. In the East, like other Soviet satellites, new laws made the sexes equal and offered limited access to abortion in 1950, with increased access after 1972. But, as in other communist countries, egalitarian policies were rarely realized in practice, nor were preexisting women's groups allowed to survive, since they were subsumed by the official Women's International Democratic Federation. By the 1980s, feminists were joining underground, independent movements that played a part in the fall of the Berlin Wall.

In postwar West Germany the state prohibited the right to abortion and structured a welfare and family support system that discouraged women from working. A women's movement began on campuses in 1968, and continued throughout the early 1970s. Feminists fought for access to abortion—legalized in 1974 and 1976—but the state's resistance to gender-related issues has discouraged feminists. Since the 1970s, many have focused on consciousness raising and the peace movement instead. Mostly an urban, elite movement, German feminism has few connections to Turkish and non-German women residents. Once Germany was reunified in 1990, western German feminists were revitalized by eastern German feminists who helped organize demonstrations to extend the east's more liberal abortion law to the west. The campaign, however, failed.

Austria and Switzerland have similarly resisted making the sexes equal. Austrian women have mostly belonged to traditional, family, community, and religious organizations, but a quiet women's movement, begun in 1972, has become more radicalized since the 1980s. The Austrian state conceded to revising family and civil law, but women otherwise have made little political progress. Swiss women have enjoyed very few rights. Women organized to work for enfranchisement in the 1950s, and a student feminist movement began in 1977. Women finally won the vote in most cantons by the 1970s, but have continued to fight for additional rights.

The Geographic Periphery

There exist broad differences between the feminisms in countries on the geographic periphery of Europe, yet Ireland, Turkey, Greece, Portugal, and Spain share striking features in regards to women's movements. Politically oppressive regimes have ruled in almost all these countries, often prohibiting feminism, yet women have been active in each country's nationalist movements, and, during political tumult, women's movements have emerged. These countries also have in common the presence of various powerful religious institutions, which have shaped state policies and public opinion, with women supporting fundamentalist policies as often as opposing them.

Although Northern Ireland politically belongs to the United Kingdom and therefore has mostly English laws, the region has been culturally divided for centuries, with many viewing the British as oppressive colonists. Women from both the north and the Republic have joined nationalist, anti-British groups, including the Irish Republican Army (IRA) and Sinn Fein, with IRA women first imprisoned for their militant activities in 1971. Many non-IRA women have also publicly protested conditions in Northern Ireland, beginning in the 1960s. More recent groups of the 1990s, such as Clár na mBan, have crafted a more overtly feminist form of republicanism. Reacting to the violence associated with the conflict with Britain, Irish feminists have also worked for cooperation, bringing together Protestants and Catholics in the Peace People's Movement, organized in 1976, which culminated in demonstrations and a Nobel Prize for its organizers.

While Northern Ireland is divided between Catholics and Protestants, the Republic of Ireland is 95 percent Catholic. Yet because of the Catholic Church's conservative positions, Irish women are sharply divided in their beliefs about abortion, birth control, divorce, homosexuality, and feminism. The Feminist movement began in Dublin in 1970. Because the Republic's very conservative 1937 constitution and other laws banned abortions, birth control, homosexuality, and divorce, liberal and radical women have fought to legalize information about these issues, and have traveled to Great Britain for contraception and abortions. Mary Robinson's election as president of the Republic of Ireland in 1990 led to the liberalization of some laws, but conservative women's family and pro-life groups have emerged and joined forces in protest.

Women's movements did not emerge in Portugal and Spain until the 1970s. Even though women's groups had existed earlier, Antonio de Oliveira Salazar in Portugal and Francisco Franco in Spain crushed them before World War II. Salazar took away all women's rights and political power in 1926, allowing women only to join family groups like the church's Mothers' Circles. In the dictatorship's last years, the underground Women's Democratic Movement, organized in 1968, began working to gain the vote; in 1973 women's issues gained public prominence when "three Marias", Maria Isabel Barreno, Maria Teresa Horta, and Maria Velho da Costa, were arrested for publishing a feminist anthology *The Three Marias* (1975). Portuguese women contributed to the 1974 Carnation Revolution, ending the Portuguese dictatorship. The reemergence of political parties led to a Women's Liberation Movement in 1975. Maria de Lourdes Pintasilgo established a Commission for Women's Condition in 1978 and was elected prime minister in 1979. The 1980s witnessed the formation of several professional and political women's groups, including the League of Women's Rights in 1986.

When Franco took over Spain he outlawed all women's left-leaning organizations and reinstalled nineteenth-century patriarchal laws. As early as 1963, the underground Women's Democratic Movement opposed fascism and worked for women's issues. Franco's death in 1975 led to the reemergence of political parties, such that feminists could publicly work towards legalizing divorce, contraception, abortion, and equal rights. Although the 1978 constitution and more recent laws are liberal, Spanish cultural attitudes still are not. Women's political participation spring the political spectrum, from the conservative Catholic Parent Federation to mainstream feminism to radical and separatist groups. The state has supported feminism, for instance establishing a Women's Subdirectorate in 1978, which has funded over four hundred studies, campaigns, and projects to encourage equality. In 1979 the Feminist Party was established, but women have not gained political power. The Basque Nationalists have the highest female membership, at 35 percent, and the Socialist Party has set gender-based quotas for political office. Overall, Spanish feminists struggle with both continuing cultural conservatism and ideological divisions among themselves.

Right-wing dictatorships stamped out women's official political participation in twentieth-century Greece. Ioannis Metaxas eradicated feminist groups in the 1930s, and although women's anti-fascist and feminist groups reemerged in 1945, they were again crushed during the civil war of 1946–49. When the military dictatorship ended in 1974, women's movements immediately blossomed as political parties reemerged. Margaret Papandreou, the prime minister's wife, campaigned to reform family laws. Her group, the Union of Greek Women, organized in 1976, has ten thousand members. Several women's groups began in 1974 to disseminate information on equal rights and contraception. The campaign has succeeded with the urban public and the state, which has since reformed traditional patriarchal laws. The Greek

Orthodox church has opposed liberalization and the state's support of women's rights.

Turkey's founding father, Mustafa Kemal Atatürk, supported women's enfranchisement as part of modernization. Although they gained many civil rights from the 1920s onward, Turkish women have not automatically gained social equality. Since 1945, both the secular right and left have generally supported legal equality and women's philanthropic, social, and professional participation, but feminism has enjoyed less consistent support, and women have won few political positions. Feminist organizations began developing in the 1970s and have since led campaigns against violence and sexism and established centers including a Women's Research Center at the University of Istanbul in 1989. Since the 1980s, Islamic fundamentalism has challenged both feminist and antifeminist women; the state and most feminist groups have opposed Muslim clerics' call for all women to be veiled in public and for the return to conservative moral traditions. Fundamentalists however, enjoy increasing support among both sexes.

Eastern Europe

Genuine women's movements have only recently emerged in the former Soviet Union and satellite countries. Although a nineteenth-century feminist movement flourished in Russia and Hungary, communist regimes outlawed feminism, branding it "bourgeois," and announced the end of women's problems by proclaiming equal rights in the Soviet Union and the satellites. Even traditional women's groups centered on family and church in Poland and elsewhere were banned. In attempts to indoctrinate women, the Communist Party in each country created monolithic women's branches that claimed to represent women's interests, including the Soviet Women's Committee, set up in 1956. Gender-based political quotas were also set, so that women achieved as many as 30 percent of seats in Albania and Latvia, and 20 percent in Poland. After the fall of communism, however, the number of women holding political office dramatically dropped throughout the former communist world.

Some communist countries in the 1950s and 1960s, including Poland and Russia, promoted more liberal policies towards gender, the family, and sexuality, even though these countries were culturally conservative. Communists legalized abortion and encouraged women in higher education and the professions. On the one hand, women achieved equal, if not greater representation, in the case of Estonia, Poland, and the Soviet Union, in medicine and academics. Communist states also slightly helped women manage their dual roles as mothers and workers by creating state run daycare and providing child allowances. On the other hand, Eastern European women were burdened by their multiple roles in the home, workplace, and party, plus their cultures' traditional expectations about gender and sexuality. In the East, women thus view women's rights cynically, since they were given under the terror of communist rule and led to heavy burdens as mothers, workers, and communists.

Other communist states, including Albania, Bulgaria in the 1970s, and Romania since the 1960s, adopted conservative policies towards family and women, even capping the number of women permitted in politics. Although women were forced to work, these regimes promoted pronatalist family policies. To increase its population, Romania promoted the most invasive policies against women in all of postwar Europe: it outlawed abortion and even contraception in 1966; the Romanian secret police spied on women and couples; the state placed gynecologists in workplaces, forcing women into monthly pregnancy examinations. With the fall of the Ceaucescus' totalitarian rule in 1989, the National Salvation Front's first proclamations included absolute freedom to abortion. Unlike the current situation in Poland, Hungary, and other former satellites, there is no movement yet opposed to abortion.

In virtually all former communist countries, women joined underground democratic movements. In Czechoslovakia women unofficially began raising gender issues in 1967 and 1968, but the Soviet invasion of 1968 crushed such dissent. By 1987 women again joined underground independent groups opposing the state. Although women in the 1980s and 1990s rarely participate in feminist movements, they do campaign for environmental and children's causes. Similarly in Lithuania, Albania, and Latvia, women were active in protesting communist rule in the 1980s, and have since focused on the environment, the community, and healthcare, rather than feminism. Small research centers for women's issues have been established in Lithuania in 1990 and Latvia in 1993.

In the Soviet Union in 1979, Maria, an independent Christian feminist group, spoke out for gender and health issues, as well as the end of the war in Afghanistan. In the 1980s and 1990s Russian women have focused on the environment, peace, and religion rather than gender issues. By 1991 only two official women's parties existed in Tomsk and St. Petersburg, but by the mid-1990s more independent feminist groups have begun, including the Independent Female Democratic Initiative (NEZHDI).

In Hungary and Poland, partly because of the Catholic Church's opposing communist totalitarian rule, the prodemocracy movements since the 1980s have lauded traditional gender and family roles and condemned pro-abortion policies. This has divided women in Hungary and Poland, with many supporting the pro-life movements, but many others opposed, especially in newly forming feminist groups. Whereas feminism is unpopular in Romania, Lithuania, and Albania—nations that have preserved abortion rights—feminism has grown dramatically in Hungary and Poland as access to abortion has been challenged. Women's groups span the political spectrum, and now include liberal and radical feminist groups. Feminist centers include the Women's Studies Center at Budapest University, set up in 1992, a Women's Studies Center at the University of Lodz, founded in 1992, and a Polish political party, the Women's Alliance Against the Difficulties of Life.

The former Yugoslavia has had a similar history of women's movements. Nineteenth-century movements and the Anti-Fascist Front of Women, organized in 1942, evolved into the Union of Women's Associations in 1953, but were outlawed in 1961 when the communists replaced them with the Conference for the Social Activities of Women. Postwar feminism emerged there much earlier than in other Eastern European countries, with the International Feminists' Meeting in Belgrade in 1978. The division of Yugoslavia that led to war between Serbia, Croatia, and Bosnia-Herzegovina has dislocated women and children. Torn apart by religious and political differences, families and communities have been severed, and many thousands of women have been tortured and raped in camps. Many women on all sides of the war in Serbia and Bosnia-Herzegovina, along with international groups, feminist and otherwise, have actively demonstrated and campaigned for peace, and developed modest programs to aid women and children.

BIBLIOGRAPHY

Funk, Nanette, and Magda Mueller, eds. *Gender Politics and Post-Communism.* New York: Routledge, 1993.

Morgan, Robin. *Sisterhood Is Global.* New York: Doubleday, 1984.

Nelson, Barbara J., and Najma Chowdhury, eds. *Women and Politics Worldwide.* New Haven: Yale University Press, 1994.

Winter, Bronwyn. "(Mis)Representations: What French Feminism *Isn't.*" *Women's Studies International Forum* 20 (1997), 211–24.

Women's Studies International Forum. Vols. 1–20. Oxford: Pergamon Press (1978–97).

Lisa Forman Cody

SEE ALSO de Beauvoir, Simone; Kristeva, Julia; Netherlands; Pintasilgo, Maria

Wörner, Manfred (1934–94)

German politician, chairman of the North Atlantic Cooperation Council (NACC) and secretary-general of NATO (1988–94). Manfred Wörner was born in Stuttgart on September 24, 1934. He studied at the Universities of Heidelberg, Paris, and Munich, at the location of which he received a doctorate in international law in 1958. He worked in the state (Land) administration in Baden-Württemberg, and in 1962 became Christian Democratic Union (CDU) parliamentary adviser in the Baden-Württemberg diet. Wörner was elected to the Bundestag in 1965 and served there until becoming secretary-general of NATO in 1988. He chaired the Working Group on Defense of the CDU parliamentary party until 1976, and was chairman of the Defense Committee of the Bundestag until 1980. He served as deputy chairman of the CDU parliamentary party with special responsibility for foreign policy, defense policy, development policy, and internal German relations. He was also a member of the Federal Executive of the CDU. He was outspoken in his defense of NATO's 1979 double track policy of deploying new U.S. nuclear missiles in response to the USSR's SS-20 deployment, while simultaneously negotiating with the USSR to obviate the deployment. With the formation of the CDU-led cabinet of Helmut Kohl in October 1982, Wörner was appointed minister of defense. Despite a scandal that threatened to end his political career, Wörner held that post until assuming his NATO office. (Some even suggest that the NATO appointment was a graceful exit from German politics.) Wörner, on the basis of intelligence reports on the alleged homosexuality of the deputy Supreme Allied Commander Europe, General Günter Kiessling, publicly accused the officer. When no proof could be produced Wörner offered to resign but Kohl refused to accept his resignation.

When Peter Carrington announced his retirement as NATO secretary-general, Wörner welcomed the opportunity to be rid of party politics. He began his tenure as secretary-general of NATO on July 1, 1988. He led NATO through a time of tremendous change. In 1990, leaders of the alliance at the London Summit extended "the hand of friendship" to the Soviet Union. In 1991, at the Rome Summit, they expressed a new strategic concept of flexibility and conflict management. NATO then invited the former Warsaw Pact states, including the republics of the former Soviet Union, to join NATO's NACC. Finally, at the Brussels Summit in 1994, NATO extended a broad invitation to all non-NATO states to join its "Partnership for Peace" program. In all of these developments Wörner used his office to push for closer ties with the new democratic states and to advocate a vigorous response to the Balkan War. Well before the Brussels Summit he had argued for a set timetable for the full inclusion in NATO of Poland, Hungary, and the Czech Republic in order to safeguard their internal transformation and to reassure them with regard to external security. He expressed his interventionist sentiments concerning the Balkans from July 1991. Wörner believed that a judicious use of force would restrain the Serbian dominated Yugoslav Peoples' Army. His insistence played a crucial role in NATO's July 1993 threat to use air power to defend the UN declared Muslim "safe areas." He pushed for the February 1994 ultimatum concerning the withdrawal of Serb heavy guns from the perimeter of Sarajevo. He was deeply frustrated by the caution of the NATO governments and their military advisors. He was bitterly distressed by the U.N.'s April refusal to sanction NATO strikes to stop the Serb shelling of Gorazde. As a German in a position of influence, he felt an ethical compulsion to actively combat "ethnic cleansing" and the associated atrocities of the Balkan War. His resolve was such that he often left his hospital bed, where he was being treated for terminal cancer, to plead forcefully for united and strong NATO action. He also feared for the credibility and relevance of the alliance. He said, "NATO will not survive a second Yugoslavia." When he died on August 13, 1994, his family asked that he not be remembered with flowers but with donations to the children of Bosnia-Herzegovina.

BIBLIOGRAPHY

Bertram, Christopher. "Manfred Wörner from Politician to Statesman," *NATO Review* 5, (October 1994) vol. 42, 31–5.

Wörner, Manfred. *Change and Continuity in the North Atlantic Alliance.* Brussels: NATO Office of Information and Press, 1990.

———. *Frieden in Freiheit: Beitrage zur Sicherheits- und Verteidigungspolitik, Strategie, Bundeswehr und zum Dienst des Soldaten.* Koblenz: Bernard & Graefe, 1987.

Bernard Cook

SEE ALSO Bosnian War; North Atlantic Treaty Organization

Wyszyński, Stefan (1901–81)

Cardinal and Roman Catholic primate of Poland. Born in Zuzela, in the Ostrów Mazowiecki district, Stefan Wyszyński became a priest in 1924, after graduation from the Wloclawek seminary, and later studied at the Catholic University of Lublin, where he received a Ph.D. During World War II he went into hiding, using the pseudonym Radwan III. During the Warsaw Uprising of 1944, he served as a chaplain to the Home Army and tended to the wounded. After the war, he became a professor and the rector at the Włocławek seminary. In 1946 he was ordained a bishop. In 1948 he became the bishop of the Lublin diocese and, shortly thereafter, the metropolitan archbishop for Gniezno and Warsaw.

In the 1940s, communists strengthened their attacks on the Catholic Church, the only remaining independent social structure. Wyszyński, instead of confrontation, pursued dialogue with the government. In 1950 he signed an agreement between the church and the government, the first such document signed between the church and a communist state. The government allowed the teaching of religion in public schools, the publishing of Catholic magazines, and the operation of seminaries. This agreement raised controversy in Poland and abroad but Wyszyński believed the dialogue to be a new model for the modus vivendi of the Church and the state. During his audience with pope Pius XII in 1951, Wyszyński described the situation of the church in Poland, the Pope expressed his full support for Wyszyński's activities, and in 1952 he was raised to the cardinalate.

In 1953 the episcopate issued a document, "Non possumus," in which it stated that, since the government had been breaking the agreement of 1950, the making of further concessions by the church was no longer possible. This statement and Wyszyński's sermon on Corpus Christi Day led to his house arrest. Released in October 1956, he returned to Warsaw and signed the Small Agreement with the government, which resulted in periodic meetings of joint committees of the episcopate and the government.

One of the issues Wyszyński undertook after his release from confinement was regulating the church situation in the western and northern part of Poland, areas taken from Germany at the end of World War II. His efforts resulted in legal normalization of the church affairs in the region, confirmed in 1972 by Pope Paul VI.

From 1961 Wyszyński actively participated in preparations for the Second Vatican Council. He was a member of several council committees. In 1965 he announced the millennial anniversary of the conversion of Poland and invited bishops from many countries to Poland. Among his letters to the episcopates of fifty six countries was a letter to German bishops. In this letter he wrote: "we extend our arms to you, forgive and ask for forgiveness." This letter was the first step in the reconciliation of the two states.

In 1978, during his pontificate, the Polish pope, John Paul II, told Wyszyński: "there would not be a Polish pope . . . if it were not for your faith, stronger than imprisonment and suffering." Wyszyński's greatest wish was for the church in Poland to acquire legal status. He pressed for this during John Paul II's first pilgrimage to Poland in 1979. Wyszyński's efforts did not, however, bring the desired results.

Wyszyński was a thriving force in sustaining the independence of the church in Poland threatened by the communists. He always demanded rights for the people and the nation. His moral authority played an important role in mediating social conflicts in Poland.

BIBLIOGRAPHY

Monticone, Ronald C. *The Catholic Church in Communist Poland, 1945–1985.* East European Monographs, 1986.

Grzegorz Wilczewski

SEE ALSO Poland

Xoxe, Koci (1917–49)

Albanian communist. Koci Xoxi, a tinsmith from Korca, was the only founding member of the Albanian Communist Party (ACP) who was not an intellectual. Until 1949, he was a member of the ACP Central Committee and Politburo. From 1944 to 1948 he was the assistant prime minister, interior minister in charge of the secret police and other security forces, and the chairman of the State Control Commission.

At the November 1944 Plenum of the Central Committee of the ACP, Colonel Velimir Stojnic, the representative of Tito's Yugoslav Partisans, backed by Xoxe, challenged Enver Hoxha, the party's leader, and attempted to have him removed. Hoxha survived. Nevertheless, until 1948 Albania was practically a satellite of Yugoslavia. Hoxha took advantage of the expulsion of Tito's Yugoslavia from Cominform, an organization founded by the Soviets in 1947 to gain control of the Communist movement, to assert the independence of Albania and to move against Xoxe, who had been supported by Tito. Xoxe was purged for "deviationism" (support of Tito) at the first congress of the Albanian Party of Labor, the renamed communist party, in November 1948 and was executed on June 11, 1949.

Bernard Cook

Yakovlev, Aleksander Nikolaevich (1933–)

Former Soviet political figure. Aleksander Nikolaevich Yakovlev was shunted off to the embassy in Canada in 1973 after he published an article criticizing Russian chauvinism and the existence of antisemitism among some of the party's leadership. He served as Soviet ambassador to Canada from 1973 to 1983. He was appointed to the Central Committee of the Communist Party by Mikhail Gorbachev in 1985, and in 1986 joined the secretariat of the Central Committee. In 1987 he was appointed to the Politburo where as head of the propaganda department he served as a guiding force in the processes of glasnost and perestroika. For his fervent promotion of reform he was attacked with increasing intensity by conservatives. Yakolev was ousted from the politburo and from the party itself two days before the attempted coup of August 19, 1991. Following the coup, though, he served as an advisor to Gorbachev, and allied himself with the democratic opposition.

Bernard Cook

Yanayev, Gennadi (1937–)

Vice-president of the Soviet Union (1990–91) and a leader of the August 19, 1991, attempted coup against Mikhail Gorbachev. Gennadi Yanayev was born in 1937. After studying law and agriculture he worked in the Communist Party controlled labor movement of the USSR and became the head of the Central Council of Trade Unions. In 1989 he was elected to the Congress of People's deputies. He was made a member of the Central Committee and the politburo of the Communist Party. In 1990 Gorbachev, to appease hard-liners, proposed Yanayev to the Congress of People's Deputies as his candidate for vice-president of the USSR. Yanayev was fearful that the new Union Treaty would lead to the collapse of the Soviet Union and undermine communism.

On August 19, 1991, Yanayev, Valentin Pavlov, the premier, Vladimir Kruchkov, head of the KGB, Boris Pugo, minister of the interior, Dimitri Yazov, the minister of defense, Anatoly Lukyanov, the leader of the Soviet parliament, Gen. Valentin Varennikov, the deputy defense minister and commander of Soviet ground forces, and Valery Boldin, the head of Gorbachev's administrative apparatus in the Communist Party, attempted a coup. They declared themselves the State Committee for the State of Emergency and announced that Yanayev was assuming the powers of the presidency "in connection with Mikhail Gorbachev's inability for reasons of health, to carry out his duties as president of the USSR." With the failure of the coup Yanayev was arrested. The trial of Yanayev and the others was postponed in May 1993 and, following the election of the communist and nationalist dominated Duma in December, Yanayev and the others were given amnesty.

Bernard Cook

SEE ALSO Union of Soviet Socialist Republics

Yandarbiyev, Zelimkhan Abdulmuslimovich (1952–)

Chechen political figure, poet, and writer. In 1989, Yandarbiyev became the chairman of Consent—an organization dedicated to the empowerment of the Chechens, which gave rise to the "Vaynakh" Democratic Party in May 1990. Yandarbiyev became chairman of this nationalist new party that advocated the withdrawal of Chechnya from the Russian Federation and the Soviet Union. It called upon Chechens to boycott all Russian elections, including the March 1991 referendum on the union, as well as the Russian presidential election in June. In 1991 Yandarbiyev became the deputy chairman of the National Congress of the Chechen People. This organization, led by Dzhokhar Dudayev, because of its support for Chechen independence, clashed with the Chechen-Ingush Supreme Soviet headed by Doku Zavgayev. Yandarbiyev served as vice-president of Chechnya after its sovereignty was proclaimed on November 1, 1991.

When Dudayev, then president of Chechnya, was killed by the Russians on the night of April 21, 1996, Yandarbiyev became the leader of Chechnya. Yandarbiyev then ran for president of Ichkeria (Chechnya) in the January 27, 1997, election, but he received only 10 percent of the vote and was defeated by Aslan Maskhadov, who commanded the Chechen military during the war with Russia and negotiated the peace settlement with Aleksandr Lebed. Many hoped that Maskhadov, more moderate than Yabdarbiyev, would more easily be able to reach a final agreement with Russia and gain financial assistance for the devastated area. Yandarbiyev was also blamed for rampant crime and corruption in Chechnya.

BIBLIOGRAPHY

Gall, Carlotta. *Chechnya: Calamity in the Caucasus.* New York: New York University Press, c1998.

Lieven, Anatol. *Chechnya: Tombstone of Russian Power.* New Haven, Conn.: Yale University Press, 1998.

Bernard Cook

Yavlinsky, Grigory Alexeyevich (1952–)

Russian liberal politician. Grigory Yavlinsky was born in Lvov in western Ukraine. His father, a former army officer, ran an orphanage and his mother taught in a forestry school. Yavlinsky left school after the ninth grade and finished his secondary education through evening school while working at a glassworks. After completing his secondary education he earned a Ph.D. in economics from the Plekhanov Institute of National Economy in Moscow. He successively held research and managerial posts at the Institute of Coal Industry Management, the Research Institute of Labor, and the USSR State Committee for Labor and Social Issues.

In July 1990, on the recommendation of Yavlinsky's mentor from the Plekhanov Institute, Leonid Abalkin, Boris Yeltsin appointed Yavlinsky deputy chairman of the Council of Ministers of the Russian Soviet Federated Socialist Republic. In that position Yavlinsky authored a reform plan, "Five Hundred Days," for the transformation to a market economy. His plan was transformed by Gorbachev and Nikolai Ryzhkov, the chairman of the USSR Council of Ministers, into "Main Trends of Development," and Yavlisky resigned on October 17.

While continuing to head the independent Center of Political and Economic Research, Yavlinsky served as an economic advisor to the Council of Ministers of the Russian Soviet Federated Socialist Republic and was a member of the Supreme Economic Council of Kazakhstan. During this time he authored with Graham Allison of Harvard University the "Grand Bargain," a program that proposed radical market reform.

After the failure of the August 1991 coup attempt, Yavlinsky became deputy chairman of the Committee for Operational Management of the Soviet Economy, but his support for the retention of a federation of the Soviet republics led to his eclipse after the dissolution of the USSR in December. Yavlinsky was not asked to serve on the new cabinet, headed by Yegor Gaidar.

In 1992 Yavlinsky became the economic advisor of the governor of Nizhni Novgorod province, Boris Nemtsov. The economic reform program devised by Yavlinsky and his team produced positive results and brought him national notice. In October 1993 Yavlinsky set up an electoral group, Yabloko, with a former Yeltsin aide, Yuri Boldyrev, and the former Soviet ambassador to the U.S., Vladimir Lukin. The bloc won eight percent of the vote in the December 12, 1993, Duma election. With its twenty-seven seats and ties to the Most Group and the Menatep Bank it became a thorn in the side of Yeltsin. Yavlinsky complained that Gaidar's reforms were a disservice to the Russian people. According to Yavlinsky, they created a "nomenklatura democracy" advancing only the interests of a narrow minority.

Yavlinsky without success attempted to mediate during the Chechnya crisis. He has advocated linking economic reform with a new federalism, in which Russia would be revitalized by reform in the individual republics and regions, all of which would be linked in an interdependent whole. In the December 1995 Duma election, Yabloko won 6.8 percent of the party list vote and emerged with forty-five Duma seats, 10 percent of the total seats. Yavlinsky was the Yabloko candidate for president in 1996. He attacked the self-serving corruption that had paraded as privatization in Russia and called for independence for Chechnya. He came in fourth in the presidential election, behind Alexander Lebed but ahead of Valdimir Zhirinovsky, with 7.3 percent of the vote.

BIBLIOGRAPHY

Suny, Ronald Grigor. *The Soviet Experiment: Russia, the USSR, and the Successor States.* New York: Oxford University Press, 1998.

Bernard Cook

Yeltsin, Boris Nikolaevich (1931–)

President of the Russian Federation from 1992 until 1999, president of the Russian Republic of the USSR (1990–1991), and an official of the Communist Party of the Soviet Union until 1990. Boris Yeltsin was a major force in both the movement to liberalize the former USSR and the drive to separate Russia from the USSR and develop Russia as an independent force in world affairs.

A man of humble origins, Yeltsin ascended to the top echelons of the Soviet leadership in the mid-1980s, was ousted from most of his positions by Soviet leader Mikhail Gorbachev, then staged an unprecedented comeback, becoming president of the Russian Republic in 1990 and later president of the independent Russian Federation.

Boris Yeltsin was born in the Sverdlovsk region of Siberia in 1931. Even in childhood his strongly independent streak manifested itself. As he was about to complete primary school, he publicly criticized an authoritarian teacher. As a consequence, he was not allowed to graduate. However, Yeltsin and his family pursued the case and the teacher was subsequently dismissed for her unethical use of students to do her housework and other errands: Yeltsin's first victory against dictatorial authority. Because of poor health during his last year, Yeltsin completed secondary school by independent study and had to fight to obtain his diploma because he had not attended school. His success in these personal struggles, which occurred during the repressive Stalin era, may have emboldened him to believe that one could successfully confront Soviet authority and emerge victorious.

Yeltsin studied to be a civil engineer and graduated from the Ural Polytechnical Institute. As a young adult, he was involved in sports and qualified for the Sverdlovsk volleyball team. He has retained an interest in sports and continues to participate in athletics well into middle age.

Unlike most Soviet political leaders, Yeltsin joined the Communist Party at the age of thirty, in 1961, much later than normal for an ambitious man of his era. He worked in the construction industry as an engineer and then as a manager. As his career progressed, he combined his work in construction with work in the Sverdlovsk party apparatus. He became prominent in Sverdlovsk political life, eventually rising to the position of first secretary of the Sverdlovsk Communist Party in 1976.

In 1985, when Mikhail Gorbachev came to power, Yeltsin was one of the regional officials invited to Moscow to help him reform the USSR. Because of Yeltsin's success in Sverdlovsk, he was appointed head of the Moscow Communist Party in late 1985. Initially Yeltsin was both successful and popular in the corruption-ridden Moscow party. He also defied custom by mingling with the masses and riding public transportation instead of the official limousines used by most officials.

Initially he was an important part of the reform team, but by mid-1987 he was frustrated by the slow pace of reforms. As a candidate member of the Politburo (the twenty members of which were designated as members or candidate, but nevertheless, were both voting members), he was part of the top leadership, but he felt that the Politburo was dragging its feet on reform. He became convinced that he was not suited to be part of the hierarchy and in August 1987 wrote Gorbachev a letter asking to be relieved of his responsibilities. Gorbachev initially did not acknowledge the letter or accept Yeltsin's offer to resign.

In the fall of 1987, at a plenum of the Central Committee of the Communist Party, Yeltsin criticized Gorbachev's leadership, and, it is believed, the excessive influence of Raisa Gorbachev on political life and policies. Gorbachev became furious and called for Yeltsin's dismissal. Yeltsin became ill during the confrontation and was hospitalized, but was summoned back to the meeting to be chastised and dismissed as first secretary of the Moscow Party. Later he was also removed from the Politburo.

Yeltsin remained in Moscow and was given the assignment of deputy minister of the construction industry. According to Yeltsin, the next two years were difficult for him, since he was regarded as a political outcast. But his popularity grew and he was increasingly viewed as an important opposition leader. In 1989 he was elected to the newly constituted Congress of People's Deputies and later to its standing body, the new Supreme Soviet. There he joined with noted reformers such as Andrei Sakharov in the Interregional Group of Deputies, a loose alliance of reformers organized prior to the legalization of opposition parties. By early 1990 thousands of marchers regularly conducted pro-Yeltsin demonstrations. In 1990 he was elected to the newly constituted Congress of People's Deputies of the Russian Republic and was successful in his bid to become chairman of the Supreme Soviet of the Russian Republic (president).

During 1990 and 1991, while Gorbachev tried unsuccessfully to balance liberal and conservative forces in the Communist Party, Yeltsin gained international recognition as a critic of Gorbachev's policies, and he became a rallying point for the opposition forces. In a master stroke of strategy he decided that the Russian president should be popularly elected, and he ran in a contested election for president of that republic in June 1991. Emerging victorious, he now had a psychological edge over Gorbachev, who was not popularly elected.

Yeltsin then played an unforgettable role during the attempted coup against Gorbachev, which occurred August 19–21, 1991. During the coup Yeltsin emerged as a symbol of reform and resistance, standing outside the White House (the Russian parliament building) in defiance of the conservative coup leaders. Resistance to the coup was successful and Gorbachev was rescued and returned to Moscow, though greatly shaken and politically wounded.

When Gorbachev returned it was clear that Yeltsin, although president of a constituent part of the USSR, was overshadowing him. In the next few months the USSR rapidly unraveled as republic after republic declared its independence from the authority of the central government. Yeltsin, for all practical purposes, led both the assault on the Communist Party and on the Soviet system. In December 1991 the presidents of Russia, Belarus, and Ukraine formed the nebulous Commonwealth of Independent States and declared that they would no longer recognize the USSR as of January 1, 1992. Seven of the remaining twelve republics followed their example and joined the CIS. The remaining five republics chose complete independence.

In 1990 and 1991 Yeltsin created a team of advisers who later served as his staff and advisers when Russia became independent. Initially no one knew exactly what Yeltsin's program would be, but it was understood that he stood for more rapid reform than Gorbachev. In late 1991 he endorsed a radical plan of rapid economic reform that combined the work of several Harvard advisers and Soviet economists and became known as "shock therapy." Introduced as the Yeltsin plan in 1992, "shock therapy" provided for a rapid transition to a market economy. Its introduction led to accelerated devaluation of the already rapidly falling Russian ruble and the decimation of people's savings as the value of their rubles plumeted. Progress toward a market economy accelerated, although many subsidized state enterprises continued to exist.

Yeltsin's program was repeatedly challenged by the Russian Parliament in 1992 and 1993. There were several showdowns between Yeltsin and the Parliament. In December 1992 Yegor Gaidar, the acting prime minister and chief economic adviser, was forced to resign, and Victor Chernomyrdin became prime minister. In 1993 the situation worsened. Yeltsin and his vice president, Alexander Rutskoi, became political enemies as the year progressed. The Parliament increasingly challenged Yeltsin on both political and constitutional issues. Yeltsin dismissed the Parliament in September, and the situation deteriorated into a military confrontation, when a significant number of the Parliamentarians refused to comply and barricaded themselves into the White House, the Parliament building. In early October, after the forces loyal to the Parliament made an effort to take over several key sites in Moscow, a battle ensued in which government troops stormed the White House. Yeltsin emerged victorious, but his image as a fighter for a more democratic Russia was tarnished. The White House, the symbol of resistance during the 1991 coup, became the battleground of 1993. Although the White House was repaired, it ceased to be the Parliament building.

In December 1993 elections were held for a new Parliament and to approve a new constitution. The newly elected Federal Assembly was no more friendly to Yeltsin's policies than its predecessor had been, and the struggle continued. As time passed it was clear that shock therapy had perhaps been too traumatic. Accusations were rampant between those who argued shock therapy had failed and those who argued that shock therapy had been compromised and had never really been implemented in Russia.

The political wars took their toll on Yeltsin's health. He aged markedly and there were rumors that he would sometimes drinking heavily. In 1995 Yeltsin was twice hospitalized with a heart condition, and rumors of a serious heart ailment persisted into 1996 as Yeltsin prepared to run for reelection. Yeltsin was victorious in a two stage election conducted in June and July 1996, narrowly defeating the Russian Communist Party's candidate, Gennady Zyuganov. Though Yeltsin rallied for the election, shortly thereafter his health became an obvious problem. He disappeared for periods when crucial issues confronted the government. Finally it was announced that he would undergo heart surgery at the end of September.

As Yeltsin entered his second term as President he did so amidst great controversy in the assessment of his leadership. Some have argued that Yeltsin has too dictatorial a style to be a consistent reformer or a democrat. Others have argued that Yeltsin's strength has always been as an opposition leader and critic rather than as the initiator of policies. Others may see him as a flawed, but well-meaning leader whose policies have failed because of the complexity of Russian society and a tendency to fall back on old Soviet ways of accomplishing change.

With not atypical dramatics, Yeltsin resigned the Russian presidency on New Year's Eve, 1999 and handed the office on an acting basis to his last prime minister, Vladimir Putin, who in turn promised Yeltsin immunity from prosecution and a generous retirement allowance.

BIBLIOGRAPHY

Adelman, Jonathan. *Torrents of Spring: Soviet and Post-Soviet Politics.* New York: McGraw-Hill, 1995.

Morrison, John. *Boris Yeltsin: From Bolshevik to Democrat.* New York: Dutton, 1991.
Steele, Jonathan. *Eternal Russia: Yeltsin, Gorbachev, and the Mirage of Democracy.* Cambridge: Harvard University Press, 1994.
Yeltsin, Boris N. *Against the Grain.* New York: Summit Books, 1990.
———. *The Struggle for Russia.* New York: Times Books, 1994.

Norma Noonan

SEE ALSO Russia; Union of Soviet Socialist Republics

Yevtushenko, Yevgeny Aleksandrovich (1933–)

Russian poet, born Yevgeny Gangnus at Zima, a lumber station one hundred fifty miles to the west of Irkutsk on the Trans-Siberian railway. His great-grandfather, Joseph Yevtushenko, had been exiled from the Ukraine to Siberia following the assassination of Alexander II in 1881. Yevtushenko, who took the last name of his mother, a geologist and singer, spent his childhood, apart from wartime evacuation back to Zima, in Moscow. Both of his grandfathers disappeared during the Great Purge. Accused of stealing records, he was expelled from school at age fifteen and went to Kazakhstan to join his father. Yevtushenko was regarded as the leading spokesperson for Russian intellectuals who came of age after the death of Stalin in 1953. That his calls for greater freedom of expression and his attacks on bureaucratism and dogmatism were tolerated was regarded as an indication of a degree of toleration under Khrushchev.

He published his first poem in a sports journal while training to become a professional soccer player. He subsequently turned fully to poetry, and his early work was so traditionally Stalinist that it won him entry into the Gorky Literary Institute and the Writers' Union. However, Yevtushenko did not do well at the institute and did not graduate. His second book, *Trety sneg* (Third Snow), published in 1955, was attacked by establishment critics but won him national popularity. Probably his best known poem, the 1961 "Babiy Yar," deals with a massacre of thirty-four thousand Ukrainian Jews by the Nazis and was an indictment of Soviet antisemitism.

When his *Precocious Autobiography* was published in Paris in 1963, Yevtushenko was summoned home in disfavor. His traveling privileges were restored, however, when he published *Bratsk Station* in 1966, in which he contrasted Soviet Siberia as a source of electric power and light with the dark symbolism of Russian Siberia's traditional prison. His first novel, *Wild Berries,* was published in Russian in 1982.

BIBLIOGRAPHY

Yevtushenko, Yevgeny Aleksandrovich. *Early Poems.* Edited and translated by George Reavey. New York: Marion Boyars, 1989.
———. *The Poetry of Yevgeny Yevtushenko, 1953 to 1965.* Translated with an introduction by George Reavey. Bilingual ed. London: Calder & Boyars, 1966.

Bernard Cook

Yugoslavia

The Socialist Federal Republic of Yugoslavia was a federated state in the Balkans bordered by Italy, Austria, Hungary, Romania, Bulgaria, Greece, Albania, and the Adriatic Sea. It had a population in 1991 of approximately 23 million and spanned 98,725 square miles (255,892 sq. km.). In 1991 and 1992 the country disintegrated, and what remained to be called "Yugoslavia" consisted only of Serbia, which had absorbed the old autonomous provinces of Vojvodina and Kosovo, and Montenegro, with 39,408 square miles (102,261 sq. km.) and 10,400,000 inhabitants. This new Yugoslav Federation was bordered by Bosnia-Herzegovina, Croatia, Hungary, Romania, Bulgaria, Macedonia, Albania, and the Adriatic Sea.

The original Yugoslavia was a formed at the end of World War I, was beset with national antagonism between the wars, and was reconstructed by Josip Broz (Tito) after World War II. Yugoslavia was long a powder keg, an artificial concoction although largely ethnically Slav, was fractured by religious and cultural animosities. Hatreds in the region reached back for centuries and were the result of geopolitical, cultural, and religious divisions and conflicts. The Balkan frontier between the Eastern Orthodox Serbs and the Catholic Croats was one of Europe's important dividing lines.

In 1918 at the end of World War I, both the Austro-Hungarian and Ottoman Empires were dissolved. One of the new countries created in war's after math, with Serbia, which had been on the winning side, as its nucleus, was the Kingdom of Serbs, Croats, and Slovenes. The new state incorporated nationalities that had not previously been united. It was renamed Yugoslavia, "land of the South Slavs," in 1929.

Serbs were the largest nationality and their ruler became king of the new state. Enmity between Serbs and Croats was especially bitter. Although they spoke the same language, the Serbs were Orthodox while the Croats were

Catholic; Serbs wrote in the Cyrillic alphabet while Croats used the Roman. Many non-Serb Yugoslavs complained of being second-class citizens. In 1934, a Croatian terrorist assassinated Yugoslav King Alexander while on a state visit to France.

In 1940–1941, Nazi Germany forced the Balkan states to join the Axis powers. Initially Yugoslavia agreed, but a coup in March 1941 repudiated the accord and young King Peter II assumed full powers. Hitler retaliated by ordering the invasion of Yugoslavia. The Luftwaffe (airforce) flattened Belgrade and within two weeks the Germans had smashed organized resistance.

When the Germans invaded, many Croats joined them. Croatian fascists set up a puppet government in Zagreb led by Ante Pavelić. It subjected the Serbs living in its territory to a policy of mass murder and forced conversion. In 1941 the Croatian fascist Ustaša killed at least 200,000 Serbs, Jews, and Gypsies at the Jasenovać concentration camp. A puppet general ruled a truncated Serbia. Montenegro was nominally independent under Italian protection. The rest of Yugoslavia was divided among Italy, Germany, Hungary, and Bulgaria.

Resistance did not end, however. Some Yugoslav military units took to the hills. Joined by other fighters, these men organized a guerrilla force under General Draža Mihajlović, who was named minister of war in King Peter's government-in-exile in London. These fighters called themselves Chetniks, a term originally used by Serbian rebels against the Turks.

But by the fall of 1941, there was a second rival underground in Yugoslavia. The Partisans were led by Josip Broz, known as Tito. He accused the Chetniks of unwillingness to fight the Germans, and it is true that they were far more reluctant than the Partisans to undertake actions that might expose the civilian population to German reprisals. Tito charged that Mihajlović was primarily husbanding resources to fight the Partisans after the war. The British, who provided military assistance to the Yugoslav resistance, were convinced of this, and in 1943 the Churchill government decided to send all its assistance to the Partisans.

For Yugoslavia the toll of World War II was especially heavy. An estimated 1.7 million Yugoslavs were killed as a result of combat and atrocities. When the Germans pulled out their troops, the Partisans, largely recruited from the peasantry, already held most of the countryside and the main lines of communication. In October 1944, Soviet forces moved into Belgrade.

At the end of the war Yugoslavia attempted to annex the southern provinces of Austria. Tito's Partisans moved into Carinthia and tried to take it by coup de main. The speedy advance of the British V Corps prevented this, but there was a tense standoff. The Yugoslavs were finally convinced by threat of force to quit Austria in mid-May 1945. Clearly Tito had hoped to seize any area where there was a blood tie to any ethnic group in Yugoslavia. This included Carinthia, Istria, and parts of Friuli-Venezia Giulia.

Tito did take vengeance on the Croats, many of whom, along with many Slovenes, had collaborated with the German occupiers. Perhaps one hundred thousand people who sided with the Germans were executed by the Partisans without trial within weeks of the war's end. In addition, the majority of German prisoners taken in the war perished in a long "march of hate" across Yugoslavia.

After the war Tito created a National Front. Superficially this appeared to be a coalition, but it was in fact dominated by the Partisans. In the November 11, 1945, elections for a constituent assembly opponents were either demoralized or refused to participate. The National Front won 96 percent of the vote. The assembly promptly deposed Peter II and proclaimed a republic. Yugoslavia's new constitution was modeled on that of the Soviet Union. It became a federal republic, a beneficial change for a country that had suffered severely from rivalries among its various ethnic groups. It consisted of six equal republics: Serbia, Croatia, Slovenia, Montenegro, Bosnia-Herzegovina, and Macedonia. In addition, two autonomous areas were set up: the largely Albanian-inhabited region of Kosovo-Metohija and the Vojvodina, in which half a million Hungarians lived.

General Mihajlović and some of the leading Chetniks were put on trial for collaboration with the Germans. Despite vigorous Western protests, they were executed in July 1946. Equally destructive of European goodwill was the sentencing of Archbishop Alojzije Stepinac of Zagrel to life imprisonment for his collaboration with the Fascist regime of Croatia during the war.

Because the Yugoslav resistance had fought well against the Germans and had liberated most of the country on their own, Tito was in a strong position to demand that the Red Army quit portions of Yugoslavia it occupied. Tito went to Moscow, met with Stalin, and secured the Soviet withdrawal. Tito was now ruler of Yugoslavia. Once in power, he muzzled dissent. Repression and fear of outside powers brought him loyalty. After June 1948, when Yugoslavia was suddenly expelled from the Cominform the Soviet dominated organization of Eastern European Communist parties, the chief threat was from the Soviet Union. Stalin apparently thought this step would topple Tito. The break with Moscow resulted from Tito's desire to form a Balkan confederation of Yugoslavia, Albania, and Bulgaria under his leadership, and there were differences with the Soviets over Communist support for the Greek civil war.

The break with Stalin and fears of a Soviet invasion led Tito to build up a large military establishment. In this he was assisted by the West, chiefly the United States. By the time of Tito's death in 1980, the Yugoslav standing army and reserves totaled two million men. To protect his freedom of maneuver Tito also linked Yugoslavia to the nonaligned movement, and in the 1960s he became a leader of this group, along with Gamal Abdel Nasser of Egypt and Jawaharlal Nehru of India.

Before the break, Tito was as doctrinaire as Stalin; after the schism he became more flexible. He allowed peasants to withdraw from collective farms and he halted the compulsory delivery of crops to the State. He decentralized industry by permitting the establishment of workers' councils to give workers a voice in the running of factories. He allowed citizens more rights in the courts and limited freedom of speech. He also opened cultural ties with the West and released Archbishop Stepinac, without, however, restoring him to authority. In 1949 Tito even wrote an article in the influential American journal *Foreign Affairs* entitled "Different Paths to Socialism." With this, "polycentralism" was born.

In 1954, however, Tito reacted sharply to the proposal of Milován Djilas, one of his advisors and one of the four vice-presidents of Yugoslavia, to establish a more liberal socialist movement that would in effect have turned Yugoslavia into a two-party state. Djilas's 1957 book *The New Class* charged that a new class of bureaucrats exploited the masses as much as or more than their predecessors. Djilas was condemned to prison. The reform movements stirring Poland and Hungary in 1956 found no response in Yugoslavia.

Despite rumblings of nationalism from the Croats, who, along with the Slovenes, resented subsidizing the underdeveloped republics in the south of Yugoslavia, Tito held Yugoslavia together. Before his death he set up a complicated collective leadership. The 1974 constitution provided for an association of equals that helped to minimize the power of Serbia and keep the lid on nationalism. There was even a multiethnic eight-man state presidency representing the six republics and two autonomous regions. Each of the six republics had virtual veto power over federal decision making.

Even after Tito's death in 1980, the multinational state seemed to work reasonably well until the death throes of communism and the Soviet Union became evident in the late 1980s. With the threat of Soviet invasion removed and the discrediting of communism, there was a political vacuum. Other political forces rushed to fill it and paramount among them was nationalism. It was played by all leaders of the Yugoslavian republics.

By March 1990 the Communist Party (League of Communists of Yugoslavia) had virtually ceased to function. Its component parts reorganized themselves as social democratic parties. They, along with other parties and ethnic constituencies, began demanding changes in the overall organization of the state. In July 1990 Serbia suspended the assembly and executive council of the autonomous region of Kosovo. It was made an integral part of Serbia, with Belgrade exercising direct rule over the region, which had only several hundred thousand Serbs but 1.8 million Albanian's who were predominantly Muslims. Serbia had already assumed power over the other autonomous region, Vojvodina.

In December 1990, the party in Serbia was formally transformed into the Serbian Socialist Party, led by Serbian President Slobodan Milošević. His hard-line policies and refusal to negotiate with the other republics to establish a looser federation helped push Yugoslavia to breakup. In May 1991, Serbia temporarily blocked the scheduled assent of Croatian Stipe Mesić to the collective Yugoslav presidency. On June 25, both Croatia and Slovenia declared their independence but subsequently agreed to delay its implementation for three months. On October 3, 1991, the Serbs seized control of the presidency. Mesic was absent and the Slovenes were boycotting the meeting. Brenko Kostic of Montenegro was elected. In addition to the Macedonian vote, he was supported by the Serbian vote and the Serbian-controlled votes, which normally should have been cast by Kosovo and Vojvodinia. With this Serbian engineered coup, Macedonia and Bosnia-Herzegovina withdrew their members from the collective presidency. The dissolution of the country followed rapidly. By 1992 Yugoslavia consisted of only two republics—Serbia and Montenegro—with less than 40 percent of its former territory and only 10.5 million of its nearly 24 million people.

In playing the nationalist card Milošević plunged the country deeper into debt, delayed the solution of problems, and cut it off from the world community. His policies also led, belatedly, to a U.N.-supported economic embargo from May 1992 to November 1995, which, though it leaked badly through Greece and Bulgaria and along the Danube, created misery in Serbia. All that Milošević had to offer during that time were the emotional issues of nationalism and xenophobia.

Milošević's encouragement of the Serbs of Croatia and Bosnia-Hercegovina to rebel led to disaster. The Serbs of Croatia were driven out of that country by the Croatian military in August 1995, and in November 1995 the Dayton Accords reduced the territory of Bosnia controlled by the Bosnian Serbs to 49 percent and forced them to participate in a single Bosnian state with a Muslim-Croat Federation. Milošević's anti-Albanian campaigns in Kosovo in 1998 and 1999 led to NATO intervention. Serbia, which suffered much destruction from air attacks, was forced to abandon Kosovo. Though NATO stated that the province was still part of Yugoslavia, its Serbian population fled and the Kosovar Albanians, for all practical purposes, asserted their control.

BIBLIOGRAPHY

Djilas, Milovan. *The New Class.* New York: Holt, Rinehart and Winston, 1957.

———. *The Unperfect Society.* New York: Harcourt, Brace & World, 1969.

———. *Tito.* New York: Harcourt Brace Jovanovich, 1980.

Ramet, Pedro, ed. *Yugoslavia in the 1980s.* Boulder, Colo.: Westview Press, 1985.

Rusinow, Dennison. *The Yugoslav Experiment, 1948–1974.* London: C. Hurst for the Royal Institute of International Affairs, 1977.

Wilson, Duncan. *Tito's Yugoslavia.* New York: Cambridge University Press, 1979.

Spencer C. Tucker

SEE ALSO Bosnia-Hercegovina; Croatia; Macedonia; Montenegro; Slovenia; Tito

Yugoslav People's Army

Second pillar of power in federal Yugoslavia after the Communist Party. The centralized command of the Yugoslav People's Army (JNA) was distributed among the different nationalities. In 1991 it consisted of 38 percent Croats, 33 percent Serbs and Montenegrins, 8.3 percent Slovenes, 8.3 percent Macedonians, and 4.1 percent Muslims. Dedicated to the maintenance of the federation, from 1986 it strongly condemned Serb nationalist aspirations, especially those of Slobodan Milošević. It placed on notice the leading politicians of separatist nationalist tendencies, whether Croat, Slovene, or Serb. Its mission being to defend the frontiers of the federation, the army intervened on June 27, 1991, to prevent the secession of Slovenia. However, the development of armed conflict in Croatia as of July 1991 fundamentally changed its national outlook. It became Serbian, as non-Serbs left the army, and, controlling all the heavy military armament, committed itself wholeheartedly to the Serbian cause.

BIBLIOGRAPHY

Milivojevic, Marko. *The Yugoslav People's Army: The Political Dimension.* Bradford, U.K.: Research Unit in Yugoslav Studies, University of Bradford, 1988.

Pejanovic, Dusan. *The Yugoslav People's Army in the Reconstruction and Development of the Country.* Belgrade: Vojnoizdavacki zabod, 1967.

Catherine Lutard
(Tr. by B. Cook)

Establishment of Communist Yugoslavia

In 1934, after his release from five and a half years in prison for his Communist activities as a trade union organizer in his native Croatia, Josip Broz (Tito) rose rapidly in the Yugoslav Communist Party. While working in Vienna for the party's Central Committee, he adopted the name Tito. In 1938, as Soviet leader Joseph Stalin's purges decimated even the ranks of the Communist leadership of Yugoslavia, Tito, who had spent twenty-one months as Balkan Secretariat of Comintern, the Soviet run international organization of Communist Parties, in Moscow, became general secretary of the Yugoslav party.

Despite the hindrance of the Nazi-Soviet Non-Aggression Pact of August 23, 1939 (in which Stalin pledged not to fight Hitler in return for territorial concessions in Poland and the Baltic States), Tito, whose independence had been stimulated by Stalin's purges and his personal experiences during two protracted stays in Moscow, began to prepare for resistance immediately after the German invasion of Yugoslavia on April 6, 1941. At the end of April, despite the recognition by the Soviet Union of German dominance in Yugoslavia, Tito issued instructions for Communists to prepare their cells for action by gathering intelligence and arms. Tito moved from Zagreb to Belgrade in May, and was prepared to issue his call to action when the Germans invaded the Soviet Union on June 22. On July 4 the Politburo of the Yugoslav Communist Party was rechristened the General Staff of the National Liberation Movement. The party, which had been illegal since November 29, 1920, had twelve thousand members and a seventeen thousand member youth organization. Underground regional organizations had been developed, and there was a clandestine radio station. Though Tito did not have many arms, he had the services of three hundred experienced veterans of the Spanish Civil War and, in addition to party members, many nonparty contacts and sympathizers were willing to join in a struggle against the Germans and Italians who had occupied the country and their Yugoslav collaborators. In particular the atrocities of Ante Pavelić's Croatian Ustaša won thousands of supporters in for Tito Croatia and Bosnia.

In July a Partisan-led revolt in Montenegro reduced Italian control there to a few garrison towns, and in August the Germans experienced a widespread rising in Serbia. By fall 1941, Partisan headquarters, including an arms factory and a printing press, had been established at Uzi̇će in Serbia. Draža Mihajlović, commander of the royalist resistance (Chetniks), had been directed by the Yugoslav government-in-exile to assume command over the Communist-led forces. But cooperation between Partisans and Chetniks soon collapsed because of conflicting objectives. The Partisans desired to use the struggle against the occupiers of Yugoslavia to revolutionize the country and ultimately transform it into a federated socialist state. The Chetniks, who wanted to reestablish the Serbian-dominated monarchy, saw the Partisans as long-term enemies. The Chetniks, despite appeals for action from the British, who provided them with supplies and gold, preferred to reach an accommodation with the Germans and preserve their forces for the ultimate conflict that would come after the Germans had been defeated by the Allies.

Although Stalin had instructed him to cooperate with the non-Communist forces, Tito refused to subordinate his Partisans to Mihajlović. In the midst of a German campaign to pacify Yugoslavia, the Chetniks attacked Uziće on November 1. They were beaten off, but from this time on, the Partisans were forced to contend with the armed hostility of the Chetniks as well as the occupation forces and the Ustaša. The Chetniks subsequently received arms from the Italians, who encouraged Mihajlović's anti-Communist campaign. The internecine struggle was a boon to the Germans, who were aware of the potential danger posed by the Partisan movement. They seized the opportunity to drive both Partisans and Chetniks from Serbia.

Hard pressed by the Germans and the Italians, the Partisans were forced to suspend operations and seek refuge in the mountains of Bosnia and Montenegro. Conditions were dismal and the Soviets, anxious not to offend their Western allies and faced with a perhaps insuperable logistical problem, did not respond to desperate pleas for aid. There were a number of defections but, owing to Tito's leadership and backed by veterans of the Spanish Civil War and former officers of the Yugoslav army, the Partisan movement survived and developed into a well-organized force of five brigades.

During summer 1942, Tito, pressed by the Germans, moved his main force in the Partisan's 115-day, 200-mile "long march" from Montenegro and eastern Bosnia to the mountainous region of northwestern Bosnia. There, without external recognition or support, he established control over a large area around Bihać. In November 1942 an assembly convened at Bihać and established the Anti-Fascist Council for the National Liberation of Yugoslavia (AVNOJ), which foreshadowed the Partisan claim to be the government of Yugoslavia. Under Tito, the AVNOJ functioned as the government of the areas controlled by the Partisans. It assumed civil administration, kept order, set prices, and instituted revolutionary social changes.

By 1943 Tito had almost 150,000 Partisan fighters organized into twenty-eight brigades. The very survival of this force was put in question by Operation Weiss, launched by the Germans on January 20. Fearing an Allied attack through the Balkans, Hitler ordered a merciless anti-Partisan campaign. The main Partisan force, which numbered about 20,000 was attacked by a combined force of Germans, Italians, Bulgarians, Chetniks, and Ustasha. Outnumbered six to one, the Partisans lost a fourth of their fighters and half their equipment. They staged a desperate withdrawal across the Neretva River, and, choosing the weakest point of their encircling foes, destroyed the Italian Murge Division on Mount Prenj. They then pursued the Chetniks into Montenegro and liquidated them as an effective fighting force.

German General Alexander von Löhr did not allow the Partisans time to recuperate. In conjunction with Italians and Bulgarians, he launched Operation Schwarz, or the Fifth Offensive. The Partisans again broke through the encircling force. Some 19,000 Partisans escaped their foes, who had amassed 117,000 men, by withdrawing through the narrow gorge of the Sutjeska River into the wilds of the Zelengora Mountains of Bosnia. Tito lost all his wounded, whom the Partisans always attempted to evacuate with their army, and a third of his fighters, but his movement survived.

The fortunes of the Partisans changed in fall 1943. When Italy surrendered to the Allies in September, large amounts of Italian arms and supplies fell into the hands of the Partisans. The Partisans took advantage of the Italian capitulation to move into the Italian satellite of Croatia and occupy the Dalmatian coast. At the same time the British decided to provide supplies and air cover for the Partisans. Though the British temporarily continued to provision Mihajlović as well, they eventually terminated their assistance because of his reticence to act against the Germans. In June 1944, the British withdrew their recognition of Mihajlović and the government-in-exile was forced to dismiss him as minister of war.

The upswing in Partisan fortunes produced a flood of new recruits, and the movement soon boasted 300,000 fighters. On November 29, 1943, at Jajce, Bosnia, the Council for the Liberation of Yugoslavia formally asserted its claim to be the provisional government of Yugoslavia, it imposed conscription on all males in liberated territory. Tito was proclaimed marshal of Yugoslavia and premier of the new government. After the Tehran Conference in December 1943, British aid was increased. The British supplied arms and evacuated wounded Partisans to hospitals in Italy. A Soviet military mission was finally sent to Tito's headquarters in February 1944, and some Soviet material support was received in the last stages of the war. The absence of earlier Soviet support intensified the independence of Tito and his national Communist movement. The greatest service provided by the Soviets to the Partisans was their advance on Belgrade.

The Partisans had been unable by themselves to dislodge the Germans from Serbia. In fact, in spring 1944 the Germans had invaded Bosnia and forced the evacuation of Jajce. In an airborne attack, code named Rösselsprung (Knight's Move), Tito's headquarters at Drvar was raided on May 25, his birthday, and he was almost captured. He subsequently established his headquarters on the Adriatic island of Vis, where British ground, air, and sea forces provided protection.

When Soviet and Partisan forces entered Belgrade on October 20, 1944, the Partisans had established their control over much of Yugoslavia and Stalin had agreed to recognize Tito as the commander of Yugoslav forces and to relegate the occupation of the country to him. Tito continued to clear Germans from his territory, but his prime concern was to occupy Istria and Trieste to bolster Yugoslav claims to these territories held by Italy before the war. On April 30, 1945, Tito's Fourth Army occupied Trieste two days before the arrival of Allied troops, but he was nonetheless forced to evacuate the city.

At the end of the war Tito had 800,000 men and women under arms. Their task now was not only to defend Yugoslavia against external enemies but to buttress Tito against internal opponents of his transformation of Yugoslavia into a united and socialist state. He single-mindedly pursued this goal though there were some tactical delays along the way. On June 16, 1944, Tito signed an agreement with Ivan Šubašić, the representative of King Peter, which provided for a Regency Council to represent the king. The three regents—a Serb, a Croat, and a Slovene—were not Communists, but Tito, who exercised the real authority in the country, approved of them. The AVNOJ, according to the agreement, was to serve as the legislature until the election of a constituent assembly. The agreement was approved at the Yalta Conference in February 1945 and imposed on the king.

In March, Tito formed a government that included Subasic as foreign minister and other representatives of the government-in-exile, but Tito was premier. Before elections were held, Subasic resigned in September over the disenfranchisement of "collaborators," a term the Communists interpreted broadly. Non-Communist parties boycotted the November election. According to Tito, his list won 96 percent of the vote, and the Constituent Assembly on November 29 formally announced the transformation of Yugoslavia into a People's Republic. In 1946 General Mihajlović was found guilty of collaborating with the Germans and shot.

BIBLIOGRAPHY

Auty, Phyllis. *Tito.* New York: Ballentine Books, 1972.

Dedijer, Vladimir. *The War Diaries of Vladimir Dedijer.* Ann Arbor: University of Michigan Press, 1990.

Deroc, Milan. *British Special Operations Explored: Yugoslavia in Turmoil 1941–1943 and the British Response.* New York: Columbia University Press, 1988.

Djilas, Milovan. *Wartime.* New York: Harcourt, Brace, Jovanovich, 1977.

Milazzo, Matteo J. *The Chetnik Movement and the Yugoslav Resistance.* Baltimore: Johns Hopkins University Press, 1975.

Roberts, Walter R. *Tito, Mihailovic and the Allies, 1941–1945.* New Brunswick, N.J.: Rugers University Press, 1973.

Bernard Cook

SEE ALSO Tito

Tito's Rupture with Stalin

Key event in post–World War II Yugoslavia with ramifications for Eastern Europe and the entire Communist world. In June 1948 Marshall Tito's increasing resistance to Soviet political and economic encroachment led to Yugoslavia's expulsion from the Soviet bloc. The split led Soviet dictator Joseph Stalin to unleash a blood purge against "Titoism" throughout the Soviet bloc, while the United States began to court Tito with economic assistance. The Tito-Stalin rupture marked the end of the Soviet Union's monolithic control of the world Communist movement.

Yugoslavia's break with the USSR owed much to the policies and character of Josip Broz, better known by his nom de guerre, Tito. After the war Tito became head of Yugoslavia's Communist-led government of national unity. For several years Tito was an ardent Stalinist and Soviet loyalist. At his invitation thousands of Soviet military and civilian advisers streamed into Yugoslavia after the war. Tito instituted Soviet-style central planning, nationalization of industry and banking, and collectivization of agriculture. The 1946 Yugoslav constitution was adapted nearly word for word from the 1936 Stalinist constitution of the USSR. Tito's secret police was modeled on the Soviet KGB; its victims numbered in the hundreds of thousands, including not only alleged German sympathizers but middle-class intellectuals, liberals, and democrats. Several show trials of former German collaborators also followed the Soviet script.

By the end of 1947 relations between the Soviets and Tito began to deteriorate. The Soviets sought to rigidly control the economic development of their satellites, often serving their own domestic needs. In drafting the first Yugoslav five-year plan, the USSR insisted that the Yugoslavs concentrate on heavy industry. Tito moved instead to increase production of consumer goods and diversify the economy. Tito became openly critical of other Soviet policies, first denouncing the behavior of the Red Army in Yugoslavia, then accusing the Soviets of recruiting agents at all levels of the Yugoslav Communist Party. Tito also undertook an aggressive foreign policy. In an attempt to expand his influence in the region, he made demands for territorial claims on Austria and Italy, and in late 1947 he sent two divisions into Albania. In addition, Tito concluded treaties of friendship with Bulgaria, Romania, and Hungary. Together with Bulgarian Communist leader Georgi Dimitrov, Tito hoped to unite all Slavs in the peninsula in a Balkan federation, the first stage of which was announced in January 1948.

Stalin reacted unambiguously to these developments, warning the Yugoslav and Bulgarian party leaderships that Communist states in the Soviet bloc were obliged to consult with him on all foreign policy issues. Dimitrov immediately recanted, but Tito stayed his course. Stalin underestimated Tito's political strength, remarking that he had only to "wag his little finger" to remove the Yugoslav maverick. In March 1948 Stalin withdrew all Soviet military and economic advisers from Yugoslavia, believing that loyal party members would unseat Tito. No coup was forthcoming. Tito attempted to assure Stalin of his loyalty, declaring that he was a Stalinist operating within his own jurisdiction.

Stalin was not mollified. Tito may have been a loyal Marxist-Leninist, but the Soviet dictator would not abide his refusal to submit to Soviet orders. On June 28, 1948, the Soviet led Cominform (Communist Information Bureau) accused Tito of "bourgeois nationalism" and expelled Yugoslavia from the Soviet bloc. Almost immediately, Stalin sought to isolate Yugoslavia. He instructed all countries in the bloc to break off diplomatic relations with Yugoslavia and tear up their friendship treaties. An economic blockade against Yugoslavia followed. Soviet troops maneuvered on Yugoslavia's eastern borders, but Stalin was reluctant to test the Yugoslavs' considerable skills in guerrilla warfare. Enraged at his inability to force Tito's submission, Stalin launched a purge of all Eastern European Communist parties. In the ensuing campaign to root out "Titoism," hundreds of thousands of party members throughout the bloc were executed or imprisoned.

Following its ostracism from the Soviet bloc, Yugoslavia's fate was uncertain. Tito's own position was never threatened, for he now appeared as a champion of Yugoslav independence in the face of foreign intimidation. The pro-Stalinist camp in Yugoslavia was easily extinguished in a purge of some fifty thousand party members. The issue of Yugoslavia's potential allies, however, had no easy solution. Anti-Western, avowedly Marxist, and yet now without ties to the USSR, Yugoslavia had no place in the Cold War alignment. Equally grave was the country's economic predicament. Denied its established trading partners and facing a drought in 1949, Yugoslavia was almost driven back into Stalin's arms by a potential famine.

Economic disaster in the first years after the split was averted only through U.S. aid, which was quite substantial from 1949 to 1952. Though wary of allying itself with an avowed Communist State, the United States seized the opportunity to undermine Stalin's hegemony in Eastern Europe. This economic assistance had no ideological strings attached, and Tito was free to gradually develop his own brand of socialism. Decentralization proceeded rapidly; local party officials were given increased authority, and worker councils were established to run factories. In the system that Tito dubbed a "socialist market economy," central planning gave way to capitalist laws of supply, demand, and profit. While the economy grew, foreign relations also improved. Within a decade Yugoslavia enjoyed peaceful coexistence with most Western countries and restored relations with the post-Stalinist Soviet Union.

Tito's defiance of Stalin ranks as one of the most bizarre events of the Cold War, and the decision to expel Yugoslavia from the Cominform was one of Stalin's worst strategic blunders. Instead of conceding limited autonomy to Yugoslavia, Stalin created what he feared the most: a rival Communist state in Europe. The Yugoslav example became the model for independent development throughout Eastern Europe, and was highly instructive for future rebels in China. The eventual unraveling of the Soviet empire in the late 1980s began with Tito's alternate road to socialism in 1948.

BIBLIOGRAPHY

Bass, Robert, and Elizabeth Marbury, eds. *The Soviet-Yugoslav Controversy, 1948–1958: A Documentary Record.* New York: East European Institute, Prospect Books, 1964.

Clissold, Stephen, ed. *Yugoslavia and the Soviet Union 1939–1973: A Documentary Survey.* London: Published for the Royal Institute of International Affairs by Oxford University Press, 1975.

Djilas, Milovan. *Rise and Fall.* San Diego, Calif.: Harcourt, Brace, Jovanovich, 1985.

Halperin, Ernest. *The Triumphant Heretic: Tito's Struggle Against Stalin.* London: Heinemann, 1958.

Rusinow, Dennison. *The Yugoslav Experiment, 1948–1974.* Berkeley: University of California Press, 1978.

Ulam, Adam. *Titoism and the COMINFORM.* Cambridge, Mass.: Harvard University Press, 1952.

Daniel Kowalsky

Collective Presidency

Executive power in Tito's Yugoslavia was exercised by the president of the republic elected for a year according to the principle of rotation in a collegial body. The president served as the commander in chief of the armed forces. He was chosen from among the eight members of the collective presidency, who represented each of Yugoslavia's six republics and two autonomous provinces for five years. They were elected by the assemblies of the republics or autonomous provinces. Actually, by virtue of his historic role, Tito was president for life. So the system, though embodied in the 1974 constitution, did not start to function until Tito, terminally ill, relinquished his duties as chief of state in 1980. The collective presidency set the political agenda for the country, promulgated legislative decisions and federal regulations, and proposed the members of the Federal Executive Council for the approval of parliament.

In the collective presidency each member represented a republic or autonomous region, and thus defined himself according to nationality. Thus an individual defining himself as Yugoslav could not accede to the presidency. In 1991 the last president was the Croat Stipe Mesić.

Catherine Lutard
(Tr. by B. Cook)

League of Communists of Yugoslav

The Communist Party of Yugoslavia, established in 1920, emerged from the Council of the Central Workers' Syndicate of Yugoslavia, a member of the Third International of Communist International established in 1919 to insure Soviet dominance over the world Communist movement. The new party, however, was outlawed in 1921. Faithful to Moscow, its struggle in World War II, led by Josip Broz (Tito), permitted it to take power in post-war Yugoslavia. As the sole legal political party, it directed the whole of political life with its decentralized cadres and controlled all the institutions of society, even if officially power belonged to the people. It changed its name at the Sixth Congress of the Communist Party of Yugoslavia in 1952 to the League of Communists of Yugoslavia. At the Fourteenth Congress in January 1990 the departure of the Slovene delegation, which was unwilling to submit to the policy of Serbian centralization pursued by Serbian president, Slobodan Milošević, confirmed the demise of the national party. In Serbia it continued as Milošević's Socialist Party of Serbia.

Catherine Lutard
(Tr. By B. Cook)

Agricultural Policy

Agrarian reform undertaken in Yugoslavia in 1945 and 1946 was minimal in order not to upset the peasantry, who constituted more than 75 percent of the population. Holdings larger than 111.2 acres (45 hectares) were nationalized and the land distributed to Partisans and poor peasants. Those who farmed the land became owners of the property. Those who did not personally farm it had the right to three to four hectares of arable land. State-controlled cooperative farms (SZR) were established in 1946, but joining them remained optional. But in January 1949, following Yugoslavia's rupture with the USSR, collectivization of land was accelerated to demonstrate to neighboring countries, and especially to Stalin, that Yugoslavia was not sliding toward capitalism. The SRZs, modeled on the Soviet collective farm (kolkhoz), grew in number, though the peasants were not always enthusiastic and also opposed the forced sale of the harvest to the state. Agricultural production declined significantly, creating a shortage in the food supply for the cities. A large number of peasants left the land for the industrial sector. Moreover, the First Five-Year Plan (1947–51) devoted only 7 percent of investments to the agricultural sector. The obligatory sale of agricultural products to the state was ended on June 7, 1952, and the new agricultural reform of 1953 suppressed the obligatory participation in cooperative farms while at the same time limiting private property to 37 acres (15 hectares) in mountainous regions and 25 acres (ten hectares) in other areas.

Catherine Lutard
(Tr. by B. Cook)

Cinema

Yugoslav cinema per se no longer exists since the dissolution of Tito's regime in the early 1990s. But the vibrant film industry called Yugoslav cinema developed from the emergence of Yugoslavia as a socialist state made up of various republics after World War II. Under the leadership of Marshal Tito, himself an avid moviegoer, Yugoslav cinema from the beginning had the freedom to experiment with themes and topics that other Communist states did not. As a country "in between" European, American, and Russian/Soviet influences as well as that of its own complicated Balkan history, Yugoslavia set up over twenty studios throughout all six republics and encouraged them to operate on a "mixed" self-management system of combining state art council funds with box office receipts and private investment, a system unique in the Soviet bloc, of which Yugoslavia ceased to be a member in 1948. The result was that Yugoslav cinema evolved through three distinct periods creating a disproportional number of excellent films and filmmakers from the 1960s through the 1980s, until war erupted in 1991–92.

The 1950s saw the development of the film industry in each republic with much excellent work being done in documentary film and animation, especially in Zagreb, capital of Croatia, which developed under such experts as Dušan Vukotić a "school" of "reduced line" animation—a technique that has become the standard fare of American Saturday morning children's shows. The major studios in the country mirrored the major republics: Serbia, Croatia, and Slovenia.

Feature films began with the still moving *Slavica* (1947, Vjekoslav Afrić), which traced the life of a young Partisan woman during the war, reflecting both Hollywood and Soviet influences. Films about the wartime Partisans quickly became a major genre for Yugoslav cinema of the 1950s and even into the 1970s, when the theme of the Good Partisans defeating the Bad Nazis became even more stereotypical than American Westerns. Yet the 1950s saw the appearance of many sensitive directors. Included in that generation of filmmakers would be France Stiglić from Slovenia (*Valley of Peace,* 1956), Branko Bauer from Croatia (*Blue Seagull,* 1953), and Vladimir Pogacić from Serbia with *Saturday Night* (1957) among others.

The 1960s led to a new generation influenced by both Marxism and the spirit of the 1960s everywhere that came to be called the Black Cinema group. Most memorable of the group was Dušan Makavejev, who created his own unique blend of "nonlinear narrative" cinematic satirical, provocative, and humorous collages of documentary footage mixed with dramatic scenes on film that, as in *W.R.: Mysteries of the Organism* (1971) mixed Nazi German war crime documentaries with Soviet films and footage shot in New York city in 1960s with hippies washed over with music as varying as Hawaiian, Russian folk ballads, and American pop.

Other major figures of the Black Cinema include Aleksandar Petrović, whose *I Even Met Happy Gypsies* (1967) took best film that year at the Cannes festival; its gritty examination and celebration of Yugoslav Gypsy (Rom) life came to be voted "Best Yugoslav film ever" before the 1991 war began. This generation earned the "Black" label for pushing as far as possible the limits of freedom of expression in Yugoslavia at that time.

The Soviet-led Warsaw Pact invasion of Czechoslovakia in 1968 resulted in a crackdown in Yugoslavia and thus Makavejev and others left the country while a new generation, ironically educated at the Film and TV Faculty of the Academy of Performing Arts (FAMU) in Prague, came of age in the late 1970s. The so-called Prague Group, including Goran Marković, Rajko Grlić, Srdjan Karanović, Goran Paskalović, and Lordan Zafranović, proved that the "impossible" could be done in a small country: they managed to make films that sold well at the box office and won many prizes at international film festivals around the world. Thus they built on the strengths of the Black Cinema but also learned to appeal to a wider audience. Karanovic's *Petria's Wreath* (1980), for instance, is an unsentimental but sensitive study of a village woman's life from the 1930s to the 1960s that mirrors all the changes that Yugoslavia itself went through.

Yugoslav filmmakers have always shown a special flair for comedy "with bite," or social significance, and this was nowhere better seen than in the first film of Slobodan Sijan, *Who Is Singing Over There?* (1980), which depicts a bus ride to Belgrade as the Germans invaded the country in 1941, a film that won many awards.

In the 1980s much of the center of creativity in cinema shifted to Sarajevo as a group of Bosnian directors, especially Emir Kusturica, came to the forefront. Kusturica won best film at Cannes in 1985 for his film about the anti-Stalinist purges of the early 1950s, *When Father Was Away on Business* (1985) and best director at cannes in 1989 for his Hollywood-financed Yugoslav Gypsy story, *Time of the Gypsies* (1990).

The wars of the breakup of Yugoslavia have destroyed what was a truly cooperative, multiethnic industry. It is one of history's ironies that even during the wars, filmmakers from the former Yugoslavia, many of whom moved to the United States or elsewhere in Europe, are still in close contact with one another, maintaining friendships that continue to be fruitful.

During more stable years the Yugoslav film industry produced upwards of thirty features a year and a wealth of shorts. Yugoslavia also boasted one of the most impressive film festivals, held in July each year in a Roman amphitheater in the seaside resort of Pula. Since the breakup of the country, however, most of the filming has been individual video work recording the horrors of war.

BIBLIOGRAPHY

Goulding, Daniel. *Liberated Cinema: The Yugoslav Experience.* Bloomington: Indiana University Press, 1985.

Horton, Andrew. "Satire and Sympathy: A New Wave of Yugoslavian Filmmakers." *Cineaste* 11, no. 2 (Spring 1982): 18–22.

———. "Yugoslavia: Multi-Faceted Cinema," in William Luhr, ed. *World Cinema since 1945.* New York: Fredrick Ungar, 1987.

Andy Horton

National Question under Tito

The Communist Party of Yugoslavia did not have a definitive answer to the problem of multiple nationalities with conflicting interests and historical grievances residing in the State of Yugoslavia. The party approached it, rather, in a pragmatic and opportunistic fashion, and, in a certain sense, encouraged nationalist sentiments.

People of some twenty nationalities and a multiplicity of languages lived in Yugoslavia. Of the languages, three were official—Serbo-Croatian (or Croato-Serbian), spoken by three-fourths of the population; Slovenian; and Macedonian. Politically Yugoslavia was a union of a number of nationalities and of six peoples formally recognized, for political-administrative purposes, as Croatians, Macedonians, Montenegrins, Serbs, Slovenes, and, since the late 1960s, Muslims. All peoples had equal rights regardless of nationality. The major religions, which were largely nationality specific, were Orthodox Christianity, Roman Catholicism, and Islam. The boundaries of the republics were not determined by the nationality of the inhabitants, and apart from Slovenia none were homogeneous.

The authoritarian regime of President Tito encouraged the different nationalities the better to divide and govern the country. Successive constitutions guaranteed the cultural rights of each, for example, education conducted in the national language and the availability of newspapers, radio, and television in the national language. Yet the various groups defended their rights on the basis of belonging to a nationality. The economic reforms of 1965, created a further gulf between rich and poor republics. The most prosperous republics Slovenia and Croatia, resented being forced to finance political projects in the poorer republics and the autonomous province of Kosovo. The nationalist bureaucrats of each republic, trying to reinforce their own privileges, played on conflicting economic interests. Nationality, the real bureaucratized political power, was allowed to develop into clientism. Nationalist pressures, like the Croat nationalist movement in 1971 (Maspokret, or Mass Movement) grew, undermining the experiment of a unitary collective Yugoslavia.

BIBLIOGRAPHY

Banac, Ivo. *The Nationality Question in Yugoslavia.* Ithaca, N.Y.: Cornell University Press, 1984.

Catherine Lutard
(Tr. by B. Cook)

Religion

The three principal religions of Yugoslavia, before its breakup in 1991 and 1992, were Orthodox Christianity, Roman Catholicism, and Islam. The Constitution of 1946 separated religion and the state and made religion a "private affair." The state, however, assumed the right to intervened in religious affairs. The teaching of religion was tolerated only in places of worship, proselytizing was strictly forbidden, and religious were forbidden to get involved in politics. A Commission of Cults was charged with regulating relations between the government and religious communities. The constitution of 1953 guaranteed liberty of conscience and the right to belong to a religious group. On the other hand, educational and social activities were forbidden to religious groups. The authorities relegated religion to the private sphere, and, unlike most other countries of materialistic and atheistic inspiration, restrained from openly persecuting believers. The Yugoslav state, though it promoted a secular attitude, even granted certain concessions, depending on the situation of the time, to certain religious communities.

BIBLIOGRAPHY

Mojzes, Paul. *Yugoslavian Inferno: Ethnoreligious Warfare in the Balkans.* New York: Continuum, 1994.

Raju, G. C. Thomas, and H. Richard Friman, eds. *The South Slav Conflict: History, Religion, Ethnicity, and Nationalism.* New York: Garland Publishers, 1996.

Samardzić, Radovan. *Religious Communities in Yugoslavia.* Belgrade: Jugoslovenska stvarnost, 1981.

Catherine Lutard
(Tr. by B. Cook)

SEE ALSO Stepinac, Alojzije

Z

Zanussi, Krzysztof (1939–)

Polish film director and screenwriter. The work of Krzysztof Zanussi includes feature films, short films, documentaries, and stage plays. He studied physics at the University of Warsaw, philosophy at the Jagiellonian University in Cracow, and cinema at the Film School in Lódz. In 1990 he was elected president of the European Federation of Film Directors (FERA). Zanussi has made films in Poland, the U.S., Italy, and the former West Germany. His highly intellectual art is concerned mainly with psychological, religious, and moral issues.

His major films are: *The Structure of Crystal* (1969); *Illumination* (1973); *Balance-Sheet* (1974); *Camouflage* (1977); *The Spiral* (1978); *The Constant Factor* (1980); *Imperative* (1982); *The Year of the Quiet Sun* (1984; Grand Prix Golden Lion, Venice, 1984); *The Power of Evil (1985); Wherever You Are* (1989), and *The Touch* (1992).

BIBLIOGRAPHY

Michalek, Boleslaw, and Frank Turaj. *The Modern Cinema of Poland.* Bloomington: Indiana University Press, 1988.

Zanussi, Krzysztof. *Scenariusze filmowe.* Warszawa: Iskry, 1978.

Krzysztof Olechnicki

Zápotocky, Antonín (1884–1957)

Czechoslovak Communist leader. Antonín Zápotocky, the son of a tailor who was a founder of the Czech Socialist Party, was born in Zákolany, near the mining town of Kladno, Austria-Hungary (Bohemia). After finishing public school Zápotocky worked as a stone mason, and, as his entree into trade unionism, founded the Association of Stone Sculptors in 1902. While still a teenager he joined the Social Democratic Party and in 1902 he became the head of the Propaganda Commission of the Social Democratic Youth in Prague, and in 1907 the political secretary of the General Trade Union of Kladno. In 1911 he was elected to the Kladno town council. He was imprisoned in 1920 for leading a general strike in Kladno. In 1921, Zápotocky was a co-founder of the Czechoslovak Communist Party and he became its general secretary in 1923. He was elected a Communist member of the Czechoslovak parliament in 1925 and worked as a party organizer and propagandist. He set up the party press in Czechoslovakia, and, as secretary general of the Communist Trade Unions from 1929 to 1939, he organized trade unions and cooperatives.

During the Nazi occupation of Czechoslovakia he was imprisoned at Sachsenhausen for six years. In 1945 Zápotocky became the head of the new United Revolutionary Trade Union Movement and served on the Provisional National Assembly. In 1946 he was elected to the Constituent National Assembly. He played a key role in the Communist coup in 1948 by organizing "action committees" among factory workers to support the coup. Following the coup he became deputy prime minister and was appointed premier when Klement Gottwald assumed the presidency vacated by Edvard Benes. When Klement Gottwald died in 1953, Zápotocky became president. Zápotocky and the new prime minister, Viliám Siroky, desired a slight relaxation from the repressiveness of Gottwald's Stalinism. However, riots precipitated in May 1953 by monetary reforms that wiped out the savings of many farmers and workers enabled Antonín Novotny, a Stalinist on the party is Politburo, to successfully oppose any liberalization. In September 1953 Novotny became first secretary of the Communist Party and Zápotocky was forced to accept collective leadership. In reality this meant that power was in the hands of Novotny.

Apart from the riots of May 1953, Czechoslovakia was stable during Západotocky's presidency. The population was relatively satisfied due to economic growth and an increase in the standard of living. Due to the Stalinist purges and the Slánsky Trial the leadership was monolithically conservative, and Khrushchev's denunciations of Stalin in 1956 had no substantial impact. After the death of Zápotocky on November 13, 1957, Novotny, while retaining the leadership of the party, also became president.

BIBLIOGRAPHY

Shoemaker, M. Wesley. *Russia, Eurasian States, and Eastern Europe 1994.* Harpers Ferry, WV: Stryker-Post, 1994.

Bernard Cook

SEE ALSO Novotný, Antonín; Slánsky Trial

Zehrer, Hans (1899–1966)

Journalist and chief editor of the German newspapers *Die Tat* (1929–33) and *Die Welt* (1953–66). Hans Zehrer profoundly influenced conservative thinking in Germany during the last third of the Weimar Republic and revived this intellectual tradition in West Germany after 1945.

A devout Protestant, Zehrer grew up in Berlin. During World War I, he joined the German army as a volunteer. After the war, he studied various subjects to ascertain what he called "the nature of man," but left the university in 1923 without a degree to start his journalistic career at the *Vossische Zeitung.* In 1929, Zehrer became chief editor of the monthly magazine *Die Tat,* whose readership he increased from one thousand to thirty thousand.

Influenced by his experience of war, Zehrer was convinced that life meant crisis. He believed in a German "nationally oriented socialism" to unite the diverging political forces. Zehrer told his readers that democratic dictatorship by a national elite was the only way to establish this unity and overcome the crisis, while liberalism, capitalism, and democracy were unfit for Germany. There are conflicting opinions on whether Zehrer helped Hitler come to power. While he did not personally back Hitler, he fought the democratic foundations of the Weimar Republic.

Between 1933 and 1945, Zehrer gave up journalism but stayed in Germany writing philosophical booklets. After World War II he launched his journalistic career once again, and in 1953 he became chief editor of the quality daily *Die Welt.* There, he took up his ideology of the 1930s. Again he underlined a general crisis of Germany, decried parliamentary democracy as unfit for the country and emphasized the good will of the Russians. But the influence of Zehrer on his editor, Axel Springer, waned when it became obvious that his dream of an early reunification of Germany with the help of the Russians would not come true.

Zehrer's journalism always aimed at revealing the deeper meaning of political events. He held firm to his basic values and helped to keep alive the German intellectual aversion to western political traditions after 1945.

BIBLIOGRAPHY

Demant, Ebbo. *Von Schleicher zu Springer. Hans Zehrer als politischer Publizist.* Mainz: v. Hase & Köhler Verlag, 1971.

Gudrun Kruip

Zenkl, Petr (1884–1975)

Czechoslovakian politician. Petr Zenkl spent six years in Buchenwald, the Nazi concentration camp. He was chairman of the Czechoslovakian National Socialist Party and mayor of Prague from 1945 to 1948, and deputy prime minister from 1946 to 1948. As the crisis deepened between the communists and the democrats in the Czechoslovakian government, Zenkl, and the other National Socialist ministers, Prokop Drtina, J. Stránsky, and H. Ripka, decided to force the issue. The precise point upon which they decided to focus their protest was the replacement of eight non-communist police commissioners by the communist Minister of Interior V. Nosek. On February 20, 1948, the four National Socialist ministers, joined by three Liberals and four Democrats, withdrew from the government. They hoped that thereby they would bring down Klement Gottwald's government and prevent the Communists from consolidating their power, but they failed. After the Communists consolidated their power, Zenkl went into exile in the U.S. and spent the last twenty-seven years of his life there.

BIBLIOGRAPHY

Bloomfield, Jon. *Passive Revolution: Politics and the Czechoslovakian Working Class, 1945–48.* New York: St. Martin's Press, 1979.

Bernard Cook

SEE ALSO Czechoslovakia; Fierlinger, Zdeněk; Gottwald, Klement

Zhdanov, Andrei Aleksandrovich (1896–1948)

Stalin's close associate and heir apparent. Though many aspects of his career remain shrouded in mystery, Andrei

Zhdanov's role as the party's chief ideologist after World War II made his name a watchword for stringent political orthodoxy in both domestic and international affairs.

Zhdanov was born in Ukraine to a moderately prosperous family. However, he joined the Bolshevik party in 1915 and served as a local party official in several regions after the October Revolution. He was a loyal supporter of Joseph Stalin in the factional struggles after Lenin's death.

After the assassination of Sergei Kirov in 1934, Zhdanov took over Kirov's powerful post as party boss of Leningrad. In that role, he helped organize the heroic defense of Leningrad during World War II. Once Finland, which had joined the Germans in their 1941 assault on the USSR, capitulated, Zhdanov coordinated the extraction of Finnish reparations as chair of the Allied Control Commission.

In the wake of World War II, Zhdanov engineered a campaign against all forms of ideological impurity to bolster his own authority as the Central Committee secretary responsible for ideology. Scholars continue to dispute whether Zhdanov's actions reflect his personal conviction or instead a political strategy aimed at maximizing his own authority. Whatever his motivation, Zhdanov grew in authority at the expense of Georgii Malenkov, who saw Zhdanov replace him as Stalin's heir apparent.

Zhdanov's ideological attacks expanded to include unorthodox approaches to literature and the arts. In August 1946 he condemned two Leningrad literary journals for insufficient ideological fervor. Two of the Soviet Union's greatest writers, the poet Anna Akhmatova and humorist Mikhail Zoshchenko, were savaged for neglecting the interests of the state and party in their work. This campaign, the *Zhdanovshchina,* would later expand to target ideological errors in the natural and social sciences.

In order to impose greater discipline on foreign communist parties, particularly the independent-minded Yugoslavs, Stalin turned to his chief ideologist. In August 1947 Zhdanov told a gathering of communist parties that the world was now divided into two hostile camps, and founded the Cominform to coordinate revolutionary activities and insure that they coincided with Soviet policy objectives.

Historians do not agree over whether Zhdanov's power was waning in the last months of his life. The consensus has generally been that Stalin held Zhdanov responsible for the Soviet-Yugoslav split, and as a result Zhdanov lost his position as Stalin's top deputy. More recently, other scholars have suggested that Zhdanov's declining health was to blame for his weakening influence.

Zhdanov died on August 31, 1948. While he had a history of heart disease, some circumstantial evidence suggests he may have been murdered at Stalin or Malenkov's hands. After Zhdanov's death, Malenkov engineered a vicious purge of Zhdanov's old supporters in the Leningrad party organization, and Stalin's anti-semitic "Doctors' Plot" blamed Jewish physicians for hastening Zhdanov's demise.

BIBLIOGRAPHY

Hahn, Werner G. *Postwar Soviet Politics: The Fall of Zhdanov and the Defeat of Moderation, 1946–53.* Ithaca, N.Y.: Cornell University Press, 1982.

Rieber, Alfred J. *Zhdanov in Finland.* Pittsburgh, Pa.: Carl Beck Papers, 1995.

Swayze, Harold. *Political Control of Literature in the USSR, 1946–1959.* Cambridge, Mass.: Harvard University Press.

Zubok, Vladislav, and Konstantin Pleshakov. *Inside the Kremlin's Cold War: From Stalin to Khrushchev.* Cambridge, Mass.: Harvard University Press, 1996.

David Stone

Zhelev, Zheliu Mitev (1935–)

President of the Republic of Bulgaria, 1990–97. Zheliu Mitev Zhelev was born in the village of Vesselinovo, in the Shoumen district of Bulgaria. He studied philosophy at Sofia University. In his dissertation Zhelev dared criticize Lenin's ideas about matter, and this resulted in long unemployment. Because of his ideas, Zhelev was not granted his first doctorate (the Bulgarian candidate of philosophical sciences) until 1975. He then became a researcher in the Institute for Culture, and from 1977 until 1982 he was then a chief of the section on Culture and Personality. In 1988 he received his second doctorate in philosophical sciences. Zhelev was elected to the 1990 national assembly. Due to his known capability and his resistance during the Communist period, he was elected president of the Republic of Bulgaria in 1990, and he held that post until 1997.

Among his books is Fascism (1982), which had a great impact in Bulgarian society. He contended that the communist society of Bulgaria shared characteristics of fascism. *Fascism* was published in more than ten languages, among them English, French, Russian, and Romanian.

Zhelev continues to participate in academic conferences in Bulgaria and abroad and participates as a consultant on many sociological studies of cultural problems.

BIBLIOGRAPHY

Zhelev, Zheliu. *Fashizmut sreshtu "Fashizmut."* Sofia: Univ. izd-vo "Sv. Kliment Okhridski", 1991.

Dimiter Minchev

Zhirinovsky, Vladimir Volfovich (1946–)

Radical right-wing Russian politician. Vladimir Volfovich Zhirinovsky was born in Alma-Ata and received a degree in oriental languages from Moscow State University. After performing his military service in Georgia, he studied law in night school at Moscow State University receiving a degree. He then worked in the international department of the Soviet Committee for Peace and the Soviet International Law Board where he was responsible for contacts with Germany. He served as pro-rector at the Higher School for the Trade Union Movement, and then as the chief of legal services at the *Mir* publishing house.

Zhirinovsky launched his political career as the Soviet Union began to unravel. He was a founder of the quite nationalistic and populist Liberal Democratic Party (LDP), which had its founding convention in March 1990. In 1991 he ran in the presidential campaign, winning six million votes or 7.8 percent, trailing Nikolai Ryzhkov. It was the success of the LDP in the December 1993 parliamentary election, in which it won 23 percent of the vote or 12.3 million votes, which catapulted Zhirinovsky into international notoriety. Although the LDP won only five directly contested seats, its total number of seats, sixty-four, made it the second largest faction after Yegor Gaidar's "Russia's Choice." The LDP won the largest number of votes in sixty-four of the eighty-seven regions where the vote took place (Chechnya did not participate and a boycott in Tartarstan deprived the vote of the necessary percentage of the electorate for validity). The strength of Zhirinovsky and his party was greatest in smaller cities and the countryside. Zhirinovsky's pointed denunciations of corrupt individuals in local administration and his calls for providing the public with ample supplies of cheap vodka resonated with the alienated. He offered his party as a "third path" alternative both to the Communists and to the liberal reformers. The economic uncertainty that followed the collapse of the Soviet Union and the implementation of Gaidar's "shock therapy" persuaded many to vote for the LDP. He also benefited from a general disgust with Yeltsin and the political parties following Yeltsin's assault on the rebellious Parliament in October 1993. Attacks on Zhirinovaky by politicians, and groups held in contempt by many, backfired.

In the 1995 Duma elections, despite Zhirinovaky's optimistic predictions, the LDP with 11.1 percent came in second to the Communists in the party vote and won only 11.3 percent of the seats, giving it a total number of seats inferior not only to the Communists but also to Viktor Chernomyrdin's "Our Home is Russia" party. The Communists led by Gennady Zuganov had become a more credible alternative to the economic liberals and a more restrained champion of restoring Russian prestige. Zhirinovsky's lack of verbal restraint deprived the LDP of some support. He had praised Hitler, denounced Israel and engaged in antiseminist rhetoric, advocated war against Russia's neighbors to the south and the reabsorption of the Baltic states, called for the regaining of Alaska, threatened the United States and Japan with nuclear war and threatened to dump radioactive waste on Germany. Needless to say, he has been an unrestrained adversary of NATO and expressed his support for Sadam Hussein and radical Serbian nationalists, in particular Vojislav Seselj's Serbian Radical Party. Zhirinovsky launched his presidential campaign in January 1996 with fulminations against the Chechen rebels, but in the first round in June he was knocked out of the race with only 5.7 percent of the vote. But despite the setbacks of 1995 and 1996 he has continued to be a visible factor in the Russian political scene, through his various pronouncements and antics on the floor of the Duma.

Andrey Alimov
Bernard Cook
Aleksandr Pidzhakov

Zhivkov, Todor (1911–98)

Communist leader of Bulgaria. Todor Zhivkov was born into a poor peasant family in Pravets, a village near Botevgrad, outside Sofia. He finished secondary school in Sofia at a school for drawing and engraving and became an apprentice printer. In the late 1920s he joined Komsomol, the youth league of the outlawed Communist Party, and became the secretary of the Komsomol local in the government printing plant where he worked. He entered the Bulgarian Communist Party (BCP) in 1932 and by 1934 had begun to rise in its ranks. In 1943 he was assigned the task of organizing partisan units. He became the political officer of the principal detachment, which was centered in the Sofia area.

He reputedly led the partisan detachments that converged on Sofia on September 8 and 9, 1944, and replaced the pro-Axis government with the Fatherland Front. Some, however, believe that this story was subsequently manufactured. Zhivkov, then a colonel, did head the People's Militia, which rounded up accused fascists. He served as the second secretary and then first secretary of the BCP Sofia district and was elected to the National Assembly in 1945.

He rose from a candidate to a full member of the Central Committee of the BCP in 1948. His career was furthered by his convincing espousal of Stalinism and his close ties to Prime Minister Vulko Chervenkov. In January 1951 Chervenkov appointed him to the secretariat of the BCP's Central Committee and named him a candidate member of the BCP Politburo. In 1951 he became a full member.

Following the death of Stalin, when the leadership of the Party and the government were separated in Bulgaria, Zhivkov became the youngest Party leader in the Eastern bloc, in 1954. Chervenkov, however, who retained the office of premier, was the real holder of power and Zhivkov was his subordinate. However, Zhivkov utilized the ascendancy of Khrushchev and his denunciation of Stalinism at the 20th Party Congress of the Soviet party as an opportunity to attack his erstwhile patron Chervenkov's "cult of personality." Chervenkov was then demoted and replaced as premier by Anton Yugov, and Zhivkov progressively drove his rivals from office. In October 1961 Chervenkov lost his post as deputy premier and was ousted from the Presidium. In 1962 Zhivkov replaced Yugov as premier.

In April 1965 Zhivkov survived an attempt within the party to oust him. The abortive coup staged by elements of the party and military was inspired by Zhivkov's subservience to the USSR. After crushing the insurgents, Zhivkov made some liberalizing moves, until he changed his tack when the Warsaw Pact, joined by Bulgaria, suppressed the Prague Spring of Alexander Dubcek in Czechoslovakia. Following a new constitutional arrangement in 1971, Zhivkov traded the premiership for the post of chairman of the Council of State and the degraded premiership went to Stanko Todorov.

The upheavals of 1989 spelled the end of Zhivkov's leadership. In November Zhivkov was forced to resign his party and state posts and in December he was expelled by the BCP, which was desperately attempting to transform its image. The campaign to oust Zhivkov was led by his foreign minister of nineteen years, Petar Mladenov, and the minister of defense, Dobri Dzhurov. They were appalled by Zhivkov's opposition to glasnost and perestroika, his repression of any divergent opinions, such as that voiced by the Club for the Support of Perestroika and Glasnost, and his nepotistic advancement of his son, Vladimir. Zhivkov was arrested in January 1990 and in 1992 sentenced to seven years in prison for embezzlement. Because of his poor health he was allowed to serve his sentence by house arrest. In 1998 his membership was restored in the Socialist Party, the successor to the BCP. Zhivkov died in Sofia on August 5, 1998.

BIBLIOGRAPHY

Brown, J. F. *Bulgaria under Communist Rule.* New York: Praeger, 1970.

Crampton, R. J. A. *A Concise History of Bulgaria.* Cambridge: Cambridge University Press, 1997.

Oren, Nissan. *Revolution Administered: Agrarianism and Communism in Bulgaria.* Baltimore, Md.: Johns Hopkins, 1973.

Shoemaker, M. Wesley. *Russia, Eurasian States, and Eastern Europe, 1994.* Harpers Ferry, W.V.: Stryker-Post, 1974.

Bernard Cook

Zhukov, Georgii Konstantinovich (1896–1974)

Marshal of the Soviet Union and minister of defense, 1955–57. Georgii Zhukov was the Soviet Union's best military commander in World War II. The son of a shoemaker, he was drafted into the tsar's army in 1915. In 1918 he joined the Red Army and participated in the Russian Civil War. Surviving Stalin's purges of the 1930s, Zhukov was sent to Outer Mongolia, where in 1939 he won a major battle at Khalkin Gol, in the undeclared war with Japan.

During World War II, Zhukov was a major figure in almost every significant Soviet victory against the Germans. He organized the defense of Moscow in the Winter of 1941–42; he coordinated the operations at Stalingrad and Kursk; he lifted the siege of Leningrad; and he led the 1st Belorussian Front (army group) into Berlin. Four times a Hero of the Soviet Union, Zhukov was the most popular Russian commander of the war, although some military analysts criticized his ruthless methods, such as clearing minefields by pushing his own infantry through them.

Stalin quickly became jealous of his marshal's wartime popularity. Soon after Zhukov became deputy minister of defense in 1946, Stalin had him exiled to the command of the Odessa Military District. Stalin then expelled Zhukov from the Communist Party Central Committee and further banished him to the out-of-the-way Urals Military District. His name no longer appeared in the press, and any mention of his wartime activities stressed that his successes were the result of his simply executing Stalin's brilliant orders. Throughout the period, however, Stalin refused to allow NKVD (Soviet Secret Police) chief Lavrentiy Beria to arrest the marshal. Zhukov's first rehabilitation started in March 1953. Within twenty-four hours of the announcement of Stalin's death, Zhukov was reappointed deputy minister of defense. In 1955 he became minister of defense, and in 1957 he became the first professional soldier elevated to full membership in the Communist Party's Presidium. That same year he was instrumental in helping Nikita Khrushchev defeat Vyacheslav Molotov, Georgii Malenkov, and Lazar Kaganovich in an internal power struggle.

Once Khrushchev consolidated his power base, he ruthlessly eliminated any other potential opponents, including Zhukov. In October 1957 Zhukov was dismissed for "Bonapartist tendencies" and relegated to the status of a non-person for the second time. For the next eight years Zhukov lived in relative obscurity in a Moscow apartment, enduring attacks against his military record by his jealous and ambitious former subordinates.

After Khrushchev himself was deposed, Zhukov entered into a second period of rehabilitation. On May 9, 1965, Zhukov re-appeared in public, in uniform, atop Lenin's tomb with the reviewing party for the twentieth anniversary V-E Day ceremonies. A few months later the Soviet government awarded him the Order of Lenin.

Zhukov spent many years working on his memoirs. Various versions appeared in the Soviet Union, in which the old marshal was severely critical of Stalin's role in World War II. In 1971 a toned-down and politically laundered edition of Zhukov's memoirs were published in the West under official Soviet auspices. In that version, Stalin once again emerged as the infallible wartime leader.

BIBLIOGRAPHY

Chaney, Otto Preston, Jr. *Zhukov.* Rev. ed. Norman, Okla.: University of Oklahoma Press, 1996.

Shukmaan, Harold, ed. *Stalin's Generals.* New York: Grove Press, 1993.

Spahr, William J. *Zhukov: The Rise and Fall of a Great Captain.* Novato, Calif.: Presidio Press, 1993.

Zhukov, Georgii. *The Memoirs of Marshal Zhukov.* London: Cape, 1971.

David T. Zabecki

SEE ALSO Khrushchev, Nikita

Zieleniec, Józef (1946–)

Foreign minister of the Czech republic. Józef Zieleniec was born in Moscow, studied industrial economics at the School of Nuclear Technology in Prague, and worked as an economic analyst at the Research Institute of Machinery Technology and Economics. In 1986 he received his doctorate from the Institute of the Czechoslovak Academy of Sciences. His dissertation in microeconomics offered support for a transition from a centrally planned economy to a market economy. He worked at the Academy of Sciences from 1986 to 1990. In 1990 Zieleniec founded the Center for Economic Research and Postgraduate Studies at the Charles University in Prague and served as its director. Since 1991 he has held the rank of assistant professor of economics at Charles University.

In 1991 Zieleniec became the vice-chairman of the Civic Democratic Party (ODS), which he had co-founded in 1990. In 1993 he was appointed minister of foreign affairs.

Bernard Cook

Zilliacus, Konni (1894–1967)

Left-wing British Labour Party opponent of the Cold War. Son of the Finnish Nationalist leader of the same name, Konni Zilliacus served as a League of Nations official from 1920 to 1938 and as architect of the British Labour Party's foreign policy in the mid-1930s. He was a member of Parliament for the British Labour Party from 1945 to 1949, and from 1955 to 1967, and he was a member for the Independent Labour Party in 1949–50. Zilliacus became the Labour left's leading back-bench opponent of Foreign Minister Ernest Bevin's anti-Soviet, pro-American Cold War policy. Although expelled from the party in 1949, Zilliacus's early advocacy of peaceful coexistence helped initiate the anti-nuclear campaign in the late 1950s and 1960s.

Representing Gateshead, Zilliacus entered Parliament in 1945 after having served the Labour Party for over twenty years as a foreign policy adviser while in Geneva. His "War and Peace" manifesto, adopted by Labour in 1934, vaulted him into the party's policy-making inner circle. In widely read books such as his *Inquest on Peace* (1935), *Between 2 Wars* (1939), *Mirror of the Past* (1944), *Mirror of the Present* (1947), and *I Choose Peace* (1949), Zilliacus postulated that World War II stemmed from the capitalist West's refusal, largely out of fear of an impending social revolution brought on by the Great Depression, to ally with the Soviet Union to halt fascist aggression.

As a newly elected Member of Parliament in 1945, Zilliacus hoped to convince his party that future peace depended on coexistence with the Soviet Union, which he thought entailed sharing atomic bomb secrets. Although never a communist, Zilliacus quickly felt the sting of redbaiting as he challenged his party's Foreign Secretary Ernest Bevin's pro-American and anti-Soviet policy. Other left-wing Labourites, especially those in the Keep

Left group, agreed with Zilliacus that Labour Britain was militarily too close to America, neglecting the United Nations and pursuing its foreign policy without democratic debate. The left's rejection of the Labour Party's foreign policy manifesto "Cards on the Table" antagonized Bevin and the Party's right-wing leadership, who moved from verbal threats through creation of dossiers to expulsion from the Party of non-recanting foreign policy critics. Gradually Zilliacus was alienated from other left Labourites by such factors as Keep Left's phobia about communism, their fear of Bevin's power, and Zilliacus's own refusal to criticize the Soviet-led coup in Czechoslovakia. This allowed Bevin to brand him in 1949 as a fellow traveler and crypto-communist.

Ironically, simultaneous with his expulsion from British Labour, the Soviet Union also denounced Zilliacus as a "pro-capitalist Titoist wrecker" for supporting Yugoslavia's break from the Eastern bloc. Zilliacus's personal friendship with Tito, his anti-Stalinism, and his support for independent communism led Stalinists to name him, in the infamous 1952 Rudolf Slánský show trial, as the chief Western capitalist Anglo-American intelligence agent and Slánsky's co-conspirator in seeking to overthrow communism in Czechoslovakia.

In 1952 Zilliacus was allowed to rejoin Labour, and in 1955 he was returned to Parliament. Soviet premier Nikolai Bulganin personally apologized to Zilliacus in 1956 for the Slánsky trial slanders. During his last twelve years as an MP Zilliacus continued to protest the Cold War, strongly supported the actions of the Campaign for Nuclear Disarmament (CND), and continued to criticize Labour's militarist anti-communist foreign policy. Until his death in 1967 Zilliacus remained firm in his conviction that capitalism bred war and that peace and socialism were intertwined.

BIBLIOGRAPHY

Birn, Donald. "Konni Zilliacus." *Peace Research* XVI, no. 3 (1984): 28–38.

Jenkins, Mark. *Bevanism: Labour's High Tide.* Nottingham: Spokesman, 1979.

Schneer, Jonathan. *Labour's Conscience.* Boston: Unwin, 1988.

Zilliacus, Konni. *Between Two Wars? The Lesson of the Last World War in Relation to the Preparations for the Next.* Harmondsworth, U.K.: Penguin Books, 1939.

———. *I Choose Peace.* Harmondsworth, U.K.: Penguin Books, 1949.

———. *Inquest on Peace: An Analysis of the National Government's Foreign Policy.* London: V. Gollancz ltd., 1935.

———. *The Mirror of the Past, Lest It Reflect the Future.* London: V. Gollancz ltd, 1944.

———. *Mirror of the Present: The Way the World Is Going.* London: Meridian Books, 1947.

Ken Millen-Penn

SEE ALSO Slánsky Trial

Zolotas, Xenophon (1904–)

A distinguished economist and director of the Bank of Greece during the years 1955–67 and 1974–81. Xenophon Zolotas is considered the leading contributor to the post-World War II reconstruction effort and the formulation of Greek economic policy.

Zolotas had an impressive academic education. He was accepted in the Athens School of Law in 1920 and continued his studies at the University of Leipzig, Germany, where he received a Ph.D. in Economics in 1926. In 1928, upon receiving his second doctoral degree from the University of Paris, he became assistant professor at the University of Athens, and a year later, professor at the University of Thessalonika. In 1931 he returned to Athens as full professor of political economy at the Legal School of the University of Athens. He resigned from that position in 1968 in protest against the military dictatorship instituted on April 21, 1967.

In addition to his academic distinctions, Zolotas participated in numerous committees for economic rehabilitation and monetary stabilization. He was a member of the Supreme Financial Council in 1932, the head of the Greek delegation to the Financial Council of Balkan Understanding from 1936 to 1939, and director of the Administrative Council of the Agricultural Bank of Greece from 1936 to 1939. He was codirector with Kyriakos Varvaressos of the Bank of Greece in 1944–45. He played an active role in the program initiated by the United Nations Relief and Rehabilitation Administration (UNRRA) for European reconstruction. In addition to being a member of the board of directors of UNRRA, Zolotas presided as director and representative of Greece for the International Monetary Fund in 1946 and 1947, and again from 1974 through 1981. He was a member of the Greek delegation at the UN between 1948 and 1953, as well as a representative of the Greek economic delegation in Europe. Between 1950 and 1954 he was a member of the Numismatic Committee while handling temporary responsibilities as minister of coordination in 1952, work he undertook again in 1974. He was a member of the International Committee of the "Four Wise Men" that was responsible for the coordination of the

Organization of Economic Cooperation and Development in 1960. He was also a member of the executive committee of the International Association of Economic Sciences, an institution of which he became honorary president in 1980. He became honorary director of the Bank of Greece in 1981, where he functioned as a consultant on monetary and economic matters.

Zolotas was unquestionably a guiding force in the evolution of Greece's economic and monetary evolution. He was the architect of the significant monetary reforms of 1944 and the devaluation of the drachma in 1953. As the designer of numerous specialized financial plans that were important in the rehabilitation of Greece after the war, Zolotas was responsible for the implementation of the "Zolotas Plan" in the early 1960s. In 1973 Zolotas, following the oil crisis and the American dollar disengagement from the gold standard, implemented a multicurrency system that replaced gold in international markets.

The reputation of Xenophon Zolotas is founded on his academic, administrative, and consulting expertise. He successfully put scientific theory and methodology into practice, a process that he elaborated on as early as 1926 in his dissertation *Griechenland auf dem Weg zur Industrialisierung* (Greece in the Stage of Industrialization), and he used his study to promote ways of developing the country. The ideological foundation of Zolotas's practice was based on a social-democratic principle. He believed that social justice and the just distribution of income cannot be achieved without an increase in production, which would contribute to the improvement of the living standard of the population. His efforts, principles, and philosophy have impacted the Greek economy and advanced the study of the science of economics.

Stelios Zachariou

Zuckerman, Solly (1904–93)

British scientist and government consultant. Sir Solly Zuckerman was chief scientific adviser to the minister of defense from 1960 to 1966 and to the prime minister from 1966 to 1971. He was knighted in 1956 and became a life peer in 1971 as Baron Zuckerman of Burnham Thorpe.

Born in South Africa, Zuckerman was trained as an anatomist. Moving to Great Britain in 1926, he was a researcher and lecturer in anatomy, physiology, and zoology at the University of London, Yale University in the United States, and Oxford University, specializing in primate behavior.

Zuckerman's *Social Life of Monkeys and Apes* (New York: Harcourt, Brace, 1932) was a standard text for years. His studies of animal and human reproductive systems contributed to the eventual development of the birth control pill. During World War II, Zuckerman's research into the effects of aerial bomb blasts significantly influenced military planning.

Following the war, Zuckerman was a professor at the University of Birmingham from 1945 to 1968, but was most influential as a government consultant on science and defense policy. His advice, not always taken, focused upon the impact of nuclear weapons. Deeply anxious about the risks of nuclear proliferation and the use of tactical nuclear weapons, Zuckerman was sometimes at odds with British and American policy makers.

After 1970, Zuckerman became passionate about preventing environmental pollution and served in many public and private bodies on the environment. He was a prolific writer of both academic and popular science works.

BIBLIOGRAPHY

Zuckerman, Sir Solly. *Scientists and War.* New York: Harper, 1966.

———. *From Apes to Warlords.* New York: Harper, 1978.

———. *Monkeys, Men, and Missiles: An Autobiography, 1946–88.* New York: Norton, 1989.

Don M. Cregier

Zyuganov, Gennady Andreyevich (1944–)

Leader of the Russian Communist Party. Gennady Andreyevich Zyuganov was born in Mymrino in the Orel region in 1944. He studied physics and mathematics at the Orel Education Institute and taught physics in high school. After earning a doctorate at the Academy of Political Science he taught mathematics and philosophy.

He joined the Communist Party of the Soviet Union (CPSU) in 1966. He was elected to the city committee of Orel and then to the Orel district committee. He became chair of the Propaganda and Political Agitation Department of the Orel region committee. In 1983 he became an instructor at the Department of Propaganda of the Central Committee of the CPSU and vice chair of the department in 1989. In 1990 Zyuganov helped found the Russian Soviet Federated Socialist Republic's Communist Party. He was elected to its Central Committee and became its secretary.

Zyuganov succeeded in reestablishing the Communist Party in Russia after Boris Yeltsin banned the CPSU in the wake of the coup attempt in August, 1991. In 1992,

Zyuganov became the first secretary of the Central Committee of the Communist Party of the Russian Federation (CPRF). In December 1995, the party won 22.3 percent of the party list vote in the Duma election, and with 34.9 percent of the Duma seats, 157 seats, it became largest party in the Russian parliament. The allies of the CPRF, the Agrarian Party, Nikolai Ryzhkov's Power to the People, and Women of Russia, provided it with an additional thirty-two seats.

In the Party's struggle against the leadership of Yeltsin, Zyuganov denounced the "reactionary-bureaucratic" approach of the Yeltsin-Victor Chernomyrdin executive, and advocated a "revolutionary-democratic" approach. His program espoused the stimulation of production and the "restoring of property rights to labor collectives." He has attacked the privatization process carried out by the Yeltsin government as a corrupt theft of the collective property of the Russian workers. Although stating that the free market was a natural human phenomenon, Zyuganov regards an unregulated market as unsuitable for Russia. He has stated his support for various forms of property, but regards forms of public property particularly in tune with the Russian character. For Zyuganov the optimum balance of public versus private property should be 61 percent to 31 percent. Zuganov advocates subjecting the executive branch to control by the legislature, and the restoration of an "independent international position and true sovereignty of Russia." He has denounced the Belovezhsk accord that terminated the USSR and has called for the voluntary re-unification of Russia with some of the former Soviet republics. In his view, Russia and its fellow republics should be the "last opponent of Western hegemonism" and the center of a Eurasian bloc, which would serve as a balance between the West and the East.

In 1996 Zyuganov was the Communist candidate for president. His candidacy was supported by twenty-five left-wing groups, and the Bloc of Popular Patriotic Forces, which included the Agrarian Party and Power to the People. Viktor Anpilov's Workers' Russia, the Russian Communist Workers' Party, and Sergei Baburin's Russian Popular Union refused to join the Bloc because its platform did not advocate the restoration of the Soviet Union. In the first round of the election, on June 16, Zyuganov received 32.0 percent of the vote, finishing a rather close second to Yeltsin, who received 35.3 percent. Alexander Lebed, who finished third with 14.5 percent, threw his support to Yeltsin in the July 3 second round. Zyuganov, who received 40.3 percent in the second round, was defeated by Yeltsin, who received 53.8 percent.

Despite his defeat in the presidential election, Zyuganov continued to lead the Communists in the state Duma, and remained one of the most formidable critics of Yeltsin and his government, until Yeltsin's resignation on December 31, 1999.

Bernard Cook

Index

B

E

G

L

M

O

P

Q

R

T